Content Management Bible, 2nd Edition

Bob Boiko

WILEY

Wiley Publishing, Inc.

Content Management Bible, 2nd Edition

Published by
Wiley Publishing, Inc.
10475 Crosspoint Boulevard
Indianapolis, IN 46256
www.wiley.com

Copyright © 2005 by Wiley Publishing, Inc., Indianapolis, Indiana

Published simultaneously in Canada

Library of Congress Control Number: 2004114477

ISBN: 0-7645-7371-3

Manufactured in the United States of America

10 9 8 7 6 5 4 3 2 1

2B/RQ/RR/QU/IN

 WILEY is a trademark of Wiley Publishing, Inc.

About the Author

Bob Boiko is a teacher, consultant, writer, programmer, and itinerant businessman. Bob is currently President of Metatorial Services, Inc. (www.metatorial.com) and Associate Chair of the Masters of Science in Information Management (MSIM) program in the iSchool at the University of Washington (www.ischool.washington.edu). Bob teaches information systems design, organizational management, and content management. He also conducts seminars and lectures around the world as part of his business. He has consulted on content management to a number of the world's top technology and publishing firms, including Microsoft, Boeing, Motorola, Honeywell, and Reed Elsevier. In addition to this book, Bob has written more white papers, articles, and reports than he cares to remember. Bob is helping to found and is serving as the first president of CM Professionals (www.cmprofessionals.org), a content management community of practice.

Bob began programming in 1977 and has practiced it since (it was always a great way to make money when he was broke). He entered the modern computer age, however, not as a programmer but as a writer. After earning undergraduate degrees in physics and oceanography and a Master's degree in human communication, Bob got his start in electronic information as a technical writer on contract at Microsoft. Among other projects, he wrote more than half of the MS DOS 5.0 User's Guide and one of Microsoft's first all-electronic User's Guides. From there, he began to develop electronic information systems on local networks, floppy disks, CD-ROMS, and when it was invented, the Web. In pursuit of electronic information and then of content management, he has created scores of applications and three businesses.

Bob lives in Seattle, Washington, U.S.A., with his wife Laura and sons Scotty and Corey.

Credits

Executive Editor
Chris Webb

Development Editor
Sara Shlaer

Production Editor
Angela Smith

Copy Editor
Mary Lagu

Editorial Manager
Mary Beth Wakefield

**Vice President & Executive
Group Publisher**
Richard Swadley

Vice President and Publisher
Joseph B. Wikert

Project Coordinator
Erin Smith

Graphics and Production Specialists
Beth Brooks
Andrea Dahl
Kelly Emkow
Carrie Foster
Lauren Goddard
Denny Hager
Joyce Haughey
Jennifer Heleine
Heather Pope
Heather Ryan
Mary Gillot Virgin

Quality Control Technicians
John Greenough
Joe Niesen
Carl W. Pierce

Proofreading and Indexing
Christine Sabooni, TECHBOOKS
Production Services

To Laura, Corey, and Scotty, for even more space

Foreword

Over the past three years I've encountered dozens of people around the world who purchased the first edition of the CMS Bible. Invariably, their copies are dog-eared and well-thumbed, because like any good reference, this book delves deeply into a complex subject that trails a surprisingly long history behind it.

Although many people associate "CMS" with the Web, the practice of content management goes back at least a couple of decades. For as long as we have had electronic documents, people have struggled with how best to manage the information those documents contained.

Early adherents of content management could be found especially among the technical documentation and scientific publishing communities. They had important reasons for wanting to reuse snippets of information at a very elemental level and, along the way, they redefined the entire notion of a document. But at the same time, these pioneers labored in relative obscurity, providing finished information products to enterprises that often had scant understanding of what went into assembling those publications.

Then the World Wide Web hit, and content management went mainstream — but this time for the specific purpose of automating the process of corporate Web site publishing. Content management became a front-office concern, drawing in marketing, design, and technology specialists, as well as line-of-business leaders.

Now the two communities — traditional information managers and Web content managers — are beginning to converge: core enterprise content increasingly gets exposed via the Web, whereas Web site managers seek to manage content further upstream in the organization. But convergence has not been easy and the process has brooked more than a little confusion among nearly all concerned. So the world needs a canonical written resource to explain, advise, and even exhort.

In short, we need a Content Management Bible.

I can't think of anyone better suited to the task of writing that bible than Bob Boiko. As a former technical documentation specialist, content management systems implementation leader, and now CMS strategy consultant, Bob brings a unique mix of practical experience to his explanations and advice.

The CMS Bible starts with an important discussion about content — what is it, how it differs from information and data, and why you should care about it. The book then delves into process. It then addresses technology. That is exactly the order in which you should undertake any CMS project.

Even if you already use a content management system (or more than one), some emerging trends in electronic information profusion should give you pause. According to recent studies, the amount of information generated worldwide doubles every three years and is likely continue to do so, with attendant compounding effects. Stop and think about that expansion for a moment in connection with your own enterprise. Surely, success in all your other initiatives — from knowledge management to enterprise search to Internet publishing to customer care to e-commerce — will be increasingly predicated on your ability to manage the growing flow electronic content into and out of your organization. Whether you are about to implement a content management system or not, the CMS Bible can serve as your guide to connecting all that content to real business objectives.

So take the time read the entire book through once, but then keep it close at hand. Like its namesake, the CMS Bible is really a collection of smaller books. Each passage will come in handy at some point as you work to manage content more effectively.

Tony Byrne
Founder, CMSWatch.com

Preface

I originally created this book because I had to. For more than 10 years, I'd been stuffing my head so full of the design, programming, management, and content of information systems that I had to let some out before I could learn any more. Seriously, from the first time I matched a printed user's guide against the capabilities of Windows 3.0 Help, to the last time I sat with a dot-com client and discussed the impact of massive content management on the architecture of an e-commerce site, I have been living the transition from print to the computer screen. I've seen a ton of technologies and a slew of systems. I've learned enough to know that there is a lot to discuss and figure out. When my thinking on what I had experienced reached some sort of embryonic maturity, it hatched as the first edition of this book. Now, three years later, the second edition seems to me like a toddler; not entirely steady on her feet but up and walking and talking up a storm! The discipline, as well, is just beginning to recognize itself as a distinct entity with common practices and a community of practitioners.

My big points are:

- ✦ As an organization, you have groups of people who consume the information and services you provide. To be an effective organization, you need to treat these groups as distinct audiences and make use of all the available channels of communication with them. To communicate effectively with a variety of audiences through a variety of channels, you need the organization and focus that a content management system provides.

- ✦ Content is the information and interactivity that organizations must harness in order to deliver value to their audiences.

- ✦ Content management systems (CMS) collect, manage, and publish this information and interactivity.

- ✦ A CMS is not a CD-ROM that you install, start, and forget about. Rather, it is an ongoing process of knowing your information and your audiences and how to match the two in a set of publications.

This book attempts to lay a comprehensive foundation under these concepts and create a solid methodology for the practice of content management. Content management is not an end in itself but rather a means to becoming the most effective organization you can be.

About the Second Edition

Since the first edition of this book was published I have:

- ✦ Given dozens of talks at conferences based on its content

- ✦ Given at least a dozen half- and full-day workshops based on its content

- ✦ Taught eight 10-week classes based on its content

- ✦ Spoken formally and informally with scores of people about the book.

These interactions have led me to the conclusion that the information in the book is still pertinent for the average consumer. I still spend almost all of my time explaining the simplest parts of the book. The information is still new to most people, and none have said that they "know all that already" and would like newer information. Thus, I am not motivated to update the book (generally) because the information is out of date. Clearly, as a rewrite happened, I found much to update and topics to articulate more fully. But the main thrust of the book still stands.

In general, the comments I have received about the first edition have been overwhelmingly positive. Here is a summary of what seemed to work:

+ **Book size**: While people love to kid me about the size of the book, it is clear that they regard this as a mark of comprehensiveness and definitiveness.

+ **The mix of upfront theory and later practical information**: People have been happy to have the background that I provide in the first part of the book. It still seems to provide the only conceptual background that is available on the subject.

+ **The style and readability**: Despite its size, I often hear that people really appreciate the open style and especially the sidebars and personal anecdotes in the book.

+ **The variety of audiences that are addressed**: The book seems to work well for managers, information architects, and technologists.

+ **The technology-neutral approach**: People like the fact that the information in the book stands regardless of the product or platform they use.

What I have heard on the negative side is that:

+ **The book is too exhaustive** (or exhausting): It is difficult to get through it all.

+ **The book details the largest of projects**: If you have a smaller project, where do you start and how do you use the book?

+ **Not enough specifics in the technology**: Although people do not seem to want product-specific information, they do want (in Part V) a more comprehensive approach to the technology that CM systems use.

+ **Vocabulary**. Some of the vocabulary I use (particularly the word *component*) is hard to understand and doesn't match well with what is becoming the accepted standard.

Given the positive and negative reactions above, I have crafted the new edition in the following way:

+ **Bringing it up to date**: I have reviewed the complete work to find any part that was out of date or where I have new material to add. As part of this, a **terminology review** has assured that the words I am using are the best for the discipline and the book.

+ **Quickstart chapters and sections**: In Parts III, IV, and V, I provide new introductory chapters that give you a summary and top-line methodology for these parts. This approach helps users who do not have the time or the project size to justify an in-depth reading of these sections. They also serve to focus users who are interested in a smaller, minimal CMS project on the barest essentials of what they must do (and can safely defer) in their project. In many of the chapters in Parts III and IV, I provide a "Jumpstart" section that overviews and highlights the methodology presented in the chapter.

✦ **Invited sidebars:** From industry experts and CM practitioners around the world, I have solicited real-world examples and short case studies that appear in the book. These commentaries serve to enrich and solidify the concepts of the book and provide an array of opinion on the topics of the book. Because each sidebar represents the views of its author, the opinions and perspectives of these invited commentators may differ from mine. (Sidebars that are unsigned are my own.)

✦ **Technology taxonomy:** I have completely rewritten the final part (Part V) of the book to be a more comprehensive view of the technology behind content management. This part is not a guide to CM products, but rather a hierarchy of all the systems and sub-systems that could be included in a CMS. The systems include overviews as well as lists of features that the systems could have.

I believe that these new additions (in the neighborhood of 250 new pages) bring this work up to date and keep it at the front of this emerging discipline.

Who Should Read This Book

This book presents a complete model of content management as well as a practical guide to doing content management. It brings together current trends in content management, with my own experience and thinking, into a unified framework. It will be of foremost use to people tasked with designing or implementing content systems (programmers, designers, writers, and managers). It will also be of use to decision makers within an organization who need to develop an electronic communication or content management strategy.

The people who have the most to gain from this book fall broadly into these categories:

✦ **Managers** in charge of a content project. These managers need to know how to get a project initiated and completed. The information in Part III, "Doing Content Management Projects," is most directly targeted to managers. In addition, senior level managers in charge of e-business, Web or communications strategy will benefit from this book. These people need to figure out how to do business in a wired world and, then, how to create an organization that can build and run an e-business system.

✦ **Practitioners** in areas such as content creation (writers and editors), content administration (database and information managers), and content publishers (site masters, designers, publishers, and Web designers). For these people there are relevant examples, methods, and overviews.

✦ **Programmers**, IT staff, and other technical professionals who need to understand how their skills fit into the broader framework of content management. The material in Part V, "Building a CMS," will be of particular interest to technical folks.

✦ **Information architects** who want to better understand the nature of a large, organization-wide content management initiative. For these people, Part IV, "Designing a CMS," may be particularly interesting.

✦ **Project staff**, who consist of the in-the-trenches creative, administrative, or publishing staff who want insight into their own jobs and to understand how their contribution fits into a larger framework.

+ **Students** of business, technology, or information who want to keep up with the latest trends in information management. For them, content management represents a viable future occupation.

+ **Business analysts and consultants**, who are called upon to help others figure out a content management strategy. With few standard sources to draw on in a rapidly changing field, those who help others will find help of their own in this book.

I also believe that there is value in this book for anyone else who wants to know what the new age of information management might look like. Even if you are not personally faced with creating a CMS, you may want to know what one is and how one is put together.

Why You Need This Book

To obtain maximum benefit from this book, you need to have felt the pain of too much content and not enough system to handle it. For those with a small site or only a little content to distribute, this work is overkill. For those who have tried and failed to, as we say, "tame the information beast," this book can help. It provides tools that you can use to win the battle next time. For those who are faced with helping to create a large Web site or other publication type for the first time, this book can help you approach the problem in a coherent and reasoned way.

Content management is important. It can underlie today's most significant digital technologies (including, among others, e-commerce, customer relationship management, personalization, advanced Web sites, and electronic communities). By understanding and properly implementing a CMS, organizations will have laid the groundwork on which the rest of these systems can stand. In so doing, they can save a tremendous amount of time and money and can unite these disparate systems with a single, enduring infrastructure.

This book matters for two additional reasons.

+ The field of content management is in its infancy. I believe that this book helps define it. In my work I daily experience the confusion and frustration of people who need to define or implement a content management system for their organization and do not know how to approach it. These people are being bombarded by product-centered white papers and superficial ad-speak that present an all-too-simple picture. In contrast, this book provides a thoroughgoing and impartial framework upon which to base an understanding of the problems and the solutions of content management. It is part of a small but significant library of works on content management that are available today.

+ There is a definite need for the kind of practical knowledge this book provides. The processes and practices that I, along with my colleagues, have developed can be of great use to people who need to implement and staff a content management system. From job descriptions to conversion code samples, you will find a good supply of methodologies, pointers, and insights. This practical knowledge, woven into an overall framework for implementing a content management system, should provide a powerful resource to anyone needing to understand or do content management.

When I began speaking on the subject of content management, my audiences consisted mostly of writers, marketing people, managers, editors, and librarians who were tasked with putting together a large Web site. Most had in-depth knowledge in their respective disciplines and some experience creating Web sites, but few had the resources for tackling the job they had taken on.

Today, my audiences consist of much the same people, but now they have job titles like Content Manager, Director of Web Strategy, and Chief Information Officer. In addition to creating an Internet presence, many are being tasked with developing an entire enterprise system for controlling the creation and dissemination of information. They have bigger titles and greater responsibility, but few extra tools to help them meet these new responsibilities. I hope that people in this position will find a useful methodology (or at least a kindred spirit) in this work.

How This Book Is Organized

This book consists of five parts.

Part I: What Is Content?

Content is information and functionality that has been harvested and organized toward some particular use. In this section, I dive into this definition and describe what is meant by organization and use. I use this definition to show why content is just information, but also more than information.

Part II: What Is Content Management?

Today, many people see content management as a way to create Web sites. As I present it, content management is a much broader process of collecting, managing, and publishing information to whatever medium you need. In this section, I present a full definition of content management and a complete model that you can use to understand and scope your own content management problems and solutions.

Part III: Doing Content Management Projects

This section describes content management from the manager's perspective. Given my model of content management, I turn to the practical problem of how you go about creating a CMS. Unfortunately, it is not simply a matter of buying a suitable product, installing it, and turning it on. No CMS you create or buy will tell you what content your organization should manage or why. Rather, doing content management is a process of getting your organization behind your project, designing all the details behind the system, selecting an appropriate system, and finally, implementing it.

Part IV: Designing a CMS

This section describes content management from the designer's perspective. Usually called information architect, the designer's job is to study and develop an interconnected system of collection, management, and publishing. The heart of this analysis is a metadata framework that ties all content together. In this section, I talk about this process in depth. I detail the exact sorts of information you have to amass to fully understand the system you want to create. I break the information to be collected down into a set of interrelated entities that rest on what I call the wheel of content management.

Part V: Building a CMS

This section describes content management from the perspective of the builder. Generally, CMS builders are content handlers, programmers, and information technology professionals. This section has information of interest to all three types of builders. For content handlers (who convert and tag content), it provides an under-the-hood picture of how content is constructed and how it can be processed. For programmers, it provides details on constructing publishing templates and programming content conversion systems. For IT professionals, it describes the software and hardware behind a CMS and how you might decide what is right for your organization.

Conventions Used in This Book

The book uses a variety of conventions to help you scan through it and quickly find information of interest. Most of the code samples in the book are either HTML or XML. In both of these sorts of code, I use uppercase letters for tag names and upper- and lowercase letters for tag attributes. In XML the capitalization of tag names really matters (it is a case-sensitive language). So, in a few cases, I break my all-uppercase convention where the sample code needs to be consistent with a system that uses a different convention.

Here are some of the other conventions you will see in the book:

Note This icon presents a quick aside to the general topic. You will find information of particular note or important caveats to the current discussion.

Tip This icon presents a short idea that you may want to implement as part of your own content management system design or implementation. There is advice, of course, throughout the book, but these paragraphs highlight "advice bytes" that you can immediately use.

Cross-Reference This icon introduces a link between the current discussion and another that is related to it. Cross-references also appear within sentences to more closely link them to the ideas to which they apply.

This Is a Sidebar

Sidebars present an extended aside. They contain stories and other devices that give you another perspective or angle on the discussion at hand. My sidebars are written by me or by invited experts, often in a lighter tone, and emphasize some of the quirkier aspects of content management.

Acknowledgments

Jim Larkin, president of Resources Online (www.ronline.com) is as responsible for this edition as I am. Despite a more than full time job and a new baby, Jim worked tirelessly to edit and oversee this edition. His fortitude and attitude made this edition happen. Thanks Jim. Along with Jim, Tom Richards helped shepherd the sidebars from vision to reality.

To everyone who wrote a sidebar for this edition, I would like to say thanks for continuing our great conversations in print and contributing to the larger conversation that is beginning to congeal into a community. And speaking of the community, I'd like to thank the people of CM Professionals (the original 23 and the thousands to come) for their contributions to and critiques of my thinking.

I'd also like to thank my many clients who over the years have seen the value in this approach and have supported it through its many twists and turns. I'd like to extend thanks, too, to Sara Shlaer and the production staff at Wiley for making my prose consistent, bringing to life my graphics, and putting up with my last-minute changes.

Finally, I'd like to thank Mike Eisenberg and the faculty and staff of the University of Washington iSchool for their confidence and advice, and their support of my work.

Contents at a Glance

Contents

Part III: Doing Content Management Projects   199

Part V: Building a CMS — 791

Chapter 34: Building a CMS Simply — 793

Chapter 35: What Are Content Markup Languages? — 805

Chapter 36: XML and Content Management — 821

Introduction

When I began working on content management, the term *content management* did not exist. As of five years ago, when my organization decided to strategically pursue content management as a focused practice, only a handful of software companies and industry analysts were using the term *content management*. The term *e-business* was all the rage, though. Today, you don't hear much about e-business, but content management is a fairly well-recognized product and industry category. Hundreds of products claim to do some form of content management, and all of the major analyst groups (Gartner, Forrester, and the like) continue to see content management as a major need and source of expenditure. I have no doubt that the term *content management*, like all others, will fall from favor as the next big thing comes into view. On the other hand, I have no doubt that the need for content management (under whatever guise it might assume) will only grow over the next few decades as we bring the entire universe of information online.

Interestingly, I believe that there is nothing new in content management and, at the same time, it is completely new. Most of the concepts that I build upon are from other fields. On the other hand, by bringing these ideas together, a new way of thinking about content and publishing emerges. For example, you need to know your audiences to do content management. This is not a new idea. Writers, marketers, and even computer programmers have been doing audience analysis in one form or another for a long time. On the other hand, by combining the way these three groups have looked at audiences and applying it to the very particular needs of personalization in a content management system, I can create an overall concept and practice of audiences that goes beyond what any of these disciplines has done. The results are not simply conceptual, they are a practical set of questions and data collection methods to make your audiences an integral part of your content management system implementation.

This book is my response to the questions I have been repeatedly asked. What I hear is, "This is so different I don't even know how to approach it," and "It's at a level of complexity far beyond what we have ever done before," and "This is so new that we can't find anyone with enough experience to pull it off." What I see most often is that people try to use their old methods and understanding to tackle a new problem, and it does not work. This book attempts to propose and detail a new approach that borrows heavily from older disciplines but forms a new discipline around the new needs of large-scale information creation, management, and publishing.

Three Good Reasons to Do Content Management

I see three major ways to enter into the ideas of content management. I present them here to help you understand why content management is so important. These on-ramps are the following:

✦ **Content management gives flesh and bones to today's notions of e-business.** If e-business is the process of reaching your constituents with the right information and transactions at the right time, then content management is the way to make an e-business real and workable.

✦ **Content management is an antidote to today's information frenzy.** Web sites are getting out of control; we are expected to harvest good information from wider and wider contributor bases; and we are expected to make information entirely reusable so that it can be distributed at anytime to anyone. Content management can help you organize and direct your information to keep it under control.

✦ **Content management addresses one of the key unanswered questions of the coming Information Age:** "How is it possible to give particular value and substance to a *piece* of information?" Content management systems create and manage pieces of information and tag them with all the information you might need to figure out what they are worth.

Content Management Underlies E-business

In an avant-garde business magazine, I once saw an advertisement proclaim: "Forget everything you know about business. It's all changed now." Has the basic fabric of business really changed? It has, according to a recent but widespread belief fed by the fantastic appeal of the new information technologies. Before the Web, there was just business. Although processes and technology changed, it was still possible to know and understand how to *do* business. Lately, as the capability to do business over the Web has become a reality, many organizations have lost their balance and have the uneasy feeling that the rules have changed somehow. They have been led to believe that the new capabilities of the Web alter the basic nature of business.

I don't believe this is true. Rather, I side with the client of mine who recently said, "Someday there will just be business again. We will just happen to do it electronically." I believe that the basic rules of business have not changed. Know your customer, project a good image, and provide real value are maxims as true today as they were in the markets and bazaars a thousand years ago. Electronic business is simply the latest way to put the basic rules into action.

 Tip

I've seen many strong businesspeople forget what they know as they wrestle with what they don't know. By remaining centered on the parts of business that do not change, you can retain a sharp ability to ask the right questions and appropriately judge the kaleidoscope of technologies that will pass in and out of focus in the coming years.

What is e-business?

In a nutshell, e-business is the process of delivering any part of your business to any audience wherever it is. E-business does not change the basis of business, but it does change the practice of doing business. Although the term e-business has lost a bit of its original shine, the concept remains an immensely important one. And although e-business does not change the fabric of business, it does bring a quantitative change in the following aspects of business:

✦ **Ubiquity:** Parts of your business can appear on any computer screen anywhere there is connectivity. Time and space are no longer barriers to conducting business.

✦ **Depth:** You can deliver as much detail and background as you can manage to create in a convenient and easy-to-consume fashion. Rather than racks full of catalogs and technical documentation, a simple URL is all that is needed to fully detail your organization's offerings.

✦ **Speed:** The slowness of your human processes is the only necessary delay between the creation of information and its general availability. Second-by-second changes to information are now possible and entirely practical.

✦ **Personalization:** Your ability to understand and serve your audiences is the only impediment to tailoring messages and offerings that are as individualized as you want them to be.

E-business is a more general term than e-commerce. E-business is about conducting all interactions electronically, whereas e-commerce refers specifically to buying and selling. If you think you are only concerned with e-commerce, I'd like you to take a hard look at this section and see if you don't see a wider goal on the horizon for your organization.

To explore e-business further, I'll drill through the definition one piece at a time.

The process of doing business

E-business is not a set of static outputs but rather a dynamic "best fit" of your practices to the environment inside and outside your organization. Because the technology is continually shifting, it is not possible to stand still. Because your organization, its audiences, information, and business practices are constantly shifting, you had better not stand still.

The technologies behind e-business are new and will change. Applications for customer relationship management, campaign management, self-service procurement, vendor relations, automated fulfillment, and a host of others are barely out of their first versions. In addition, the underlying infrastructure on Web servers is also in flux. Finally, new delivery platforms (such as Web-enabled phones) are appearing all the time. What you can do is changing so rapidly that you have no choice but to consider e-business a process that is never complete.

Note   With or without the new electronic medium, business is best done dynamically. Regardless of the way you conduct business, you are best served by continually reassessing your audiences, your products, and the ways you present your products to your audiences. As any one of the three changes, the other two must adjust to make use of new possibilities and jettison things that no longer work. In today's globalized and hypercompetitive world, business with no "e" is itself is a process that continually shifts.

To do e-business, you create a system for production, not a particular product. You focus more on how you will constantly readjust to the changing landscape of technology, your audiences, information, practices, and publications than on any particular configuration that you might happen to be in right now.

Tip   Recognizing that business is a process, the wise organization will create the right feedback channels so that your audiences can help you continually reexamine what information and functionality you are collecting and managing and what publications serve your goals and their goals most fully.

Delivering any part of your business

E-business is the process of electronically delivering the right parts of your business at the right time. Generally, you deliver your business through computer networks and onto someone's computer screen. The essence of e-business, however, is not in the particular way in which you deliver your business, but in the fact that the essential parts of your business are stored and managed digitally and can be delivered in whatever medium you desire. By digitizing the information and services your organization provides, you make it available for delivery over digital or nondigital channels. Your own Internet site is only one of these channels. Others include the following:

+ Your intranet site and any extranet sites you host to communicate with partners

+ The Web sites of other partner and promoter organizations

+ Kiosks and other offline digital publications

+ Print publications that include shared information and "paper functionality"

+ Screens for devices such as Web-enabled phones and personal digital assistants (PDAs)

+ Personalized broadcast e-mail messages

What are the parts of your business? Loosely, you can break these parts into information and interactions, as follows:

+ **Information** is the text, sound, image, and motion that communicate what you would like to convey to your constituents.

+ **Interactions** are the capabilities you would like to project, such as buying product, asking for help, contacting an individual in the organization, or participating in an organization-sponsored discussion. Interactions are pieces of functionality that your organization can digitize and treat just the same as information.

To do e-business, the wide and possibly unorganized information and interactions that are key to your organization must be identified, digitized, and segmented into useful chunks so that they can be delivered individually to those who need them—customers, members, staff, partners, or constituents.

Cross-Reference In Chapter 4, "Functionality Is Content, Too!" I focus on interaction. More aptly called functionality, interaction is the user interface and computer code that gives audiences the ability to communicate back to the organization in order to carry on their business with the organization. In Chapter 25, "Cataloging Audiences," I talk a lot more about audiences.

Reaching your audiences wherever they are

E-business means being present and ready to interact with someone—wherever she is when she wants to interact with you. Today, the overwhelming majority of organizations are focused on their Web site as the place through which to communicate with the outside world. They see the Web as *the* medium for communication, and they want their site to be a prime location on the net. The assumption is that if you build it and it is good, they will find you and come. With enough marketing or public relations, this might be true. But for the vast majority of organizations, getting people to find them and come is a tricky proposition. Undoubtedly, each organization needs a Web site that has its official and comprehensive information. The essence of e-business, however, is the capability to go to your audiences rather than wait for them to come to you.

As one example among many, consider a government organization that wants to communicate new regulations to its offices. It certainly wants to list the new regulations completely on its Web site. But are there other ways it could reach the intended audiences (staff members, say, in many locations)? Rather than expecting that staff will come to the Web site, the organization could send targeted e-mail messages to the staff, highlighting just the relevant sections of the new regulations. In addition, it could send automatic faxes to individuals that show the most important changes. Finally, it could produce small, printable color posters and send them via e-mail to the office managers, along with instructions to print them out and hang them in a prominent place. In this way, the information is targeted and delivered to the intended audience rather than passively listed somewhere.

Knowing where a person is when she needs to do business with you and being there with the right information and functionality is essential to e-business.

How do you do e-business?

E-business is the process of delivering any part of your business to any audience wherever they are. Even if this definition of e-business is clear, how to do it is not. In fact, how to make all of this happen is often not clear at all to organizations. If you follow my definition of e-business, however, the following dictates quickly surface:

✦ **Know your audiences.** As you will see, to know your audiences, you must study them to fully understand what they want and how they want it. You then segment them into groups based on traits you can discover and track. Finally, for each audience, you create a value proposition, including what the audience wants, what you want from them, and how you are going to give value equal to what you want from them.

✦ **Know your business.** To know your business, you first must study it to understand how your business can be segmented into small, useful information and functionality parts. You must name and organize the parts and understand how the parts are created, maintained, delivered, and destroyed.

✦ **Relate the business to the audience.** You need to decide which audience wants what information and functionality in which contexts (on which pages, on which sites, in what other publications, and so on). You must then create a set of rules so that staff can decide who gets what when.

Organizations have been doing this more or less formally forever. On the other hand, establishing technology and process to effectively divide the organization into parts and deliver them electronically is new and far from well understood.

I believe that you can do e-business the same way you do content management. That is, you can create a process to collect, manage, and publish information and functionality to a set of target audiences. Information and functionality are the content of e-business. To do e-business or content management, you must do the following:

✦ **Collect content.** Your organization must set up systems that efficiently capture the information and the functionality you want to deliver. To collect content, you need editorial and *metatorial* systems. Editorial systems ensure that the content has appropriate and consistent format and style. Metatorial systems ensure that the content is appropriately and consistently tagged to be part of the organization's content scheme. See the section "Metatorial Processing" in Chapter 24, "Working with Metadata," for more information on metatorial systems.

✦ **Manage content.** Your organization must set up a system to store and organize information and functionality outside of any particular delivery channel. Management systems are usually databases of one sort or another that store and categorize content, making that content easy to find and retrieve.

✦ **Publish content.** Your organization must set up a system to design and deliver the right information and functionality in the ways that your audiences expect and respond to favorably. The publishing system undoubtedly will manage a comprehensive Web site, but it could and should manage the other sorts of publications that your organization needs.

If your organization is wise, it will look past the hype and vague promises of e-business and focus instead on how to use the new technologies that become available to do what it has always needed to do. Rather than let yourself become overwhelmed by the immensity of e-business or even dismiss it as just another empty catchphrase, I would like to you consider how you can put it into its proper perspective. This book ought to help you to that perspective and, moreover, give you some specific tools to advance your adoption of e-business through the application of content management.

Content Management Cures Information Frenzy

It used to be that you could get away with creating new communications without worrying much about the old ones. Except for the occasional bibliography or citation, we could do most of our writing, recording, or filming in a vacuum. It was up to the reader, listener, or watcher to make connections between this new stuff and the rest of what might exist in the world. We also had the luxury of believing that our communications were single "things." We created memos, articles, books, songs, sitcoms, and movies. We could study and internalize the standards and techniques of our chosen genre, and then create an example of it. In our vacuum, we could assume that a book was just a book, and a movie just a movie. Although it is simple and comfortable, in the Information Age, life in a vacuum sucks.

Today, the comfortable vacuum of the single communication product has been replaced by the unfathomably complex, fully connected, multiply targeted content component! Starting with the Web and ending who-knows-where, your job as a communicator is now no longer to create a single item—not a book or a movie. You now create content. Content is meant to be connected, used, and reused with no great assumptions about how and when. The Web is the first (and only the first) big place where the premium is placed on how your communications are connected to others rather than on how complete they are in themselves. Books, songs, movies: They all have a beginning, an end, and a point—the good ones are nice little standalone packages of meaning.

The good Web sites are the ones that are entirely enmeshed in connections with other sites and resources on the Web. Far from standing alone, they integrate into the wider Web of communications around them. The old communications are designed to be taken as a whole. You're not supposed to watch half a movie or listen to half a song. The Web is the first (and only the first) big place where all of these bets are decidedly off. If I am lucky, bits and pieces of this book will be spread across the Web. This can happen only if I'm smart and make it so that these bits of book have value apart from the whole. If I am realistic, I will realize that to be digitally successful, my work can never be finished. Each time you come back, it will have to be more up to date, more connected, revised, and reinvented. In short, for this book to be a good electronic publication, it will have to be fully connected, highly divisible, and in continuous production and evolution.

This is no small order. There are no established models for how to create this sort of work, and there are no established rewards for doing it. Not only are there currently no good tools for connection, division, and continuous production, but also the concepts themselves are vague and ill defined. Add to this confusion the sheer volume of communication being created and disseminated, and you have a real mess. And that is how most people view the current situation—as a mess. Whether they are talking about their mailbox, office desk, company information, or the World Wide Web, most people suffer from the overload of disorganized, indigestible, always-in-your-face-but-never-there-when-you-need-it information.

So, we are stuck for a time in a tight dilemma. The force of history drives us toward faster and faster production of more communication. The force of the Web (which is the world's first global information repository) drives us to replace many of our time-honored notions of how to produce communication. Future generations might romanticize this era as the opening of the information frontier, but we mostly see it as a pain.

This book is my attempt to roll my experience and thinking into a complete picture of this new notion of communication and how it can address the dilemma of overload. By organizing content into wider and wider schemes of relationships, it becomes more accessible and memorable to the consumer, and more manageable to the creator. The same systems can help you organize and target information, so that rather than being overwhelmed by information, your audiences are exposed to just the right amount of information at the right times.

Content Management in the Information Age

People talk about the Information Age as a *fait accompli*. They suppose that because a worldwide communication network exists, we are fully connected. They assume that computer technologies already have turned the world into a constant digital information stream. The *coup-de-grace*, many contend, is the World Wide Web, which has combined the global network with the latest computer technology to create the first tangible information economy, complete with transactions and stock market value for information assets.

In fact, we are at only the very beginning of the Information Age. The global network connects only a small minority of the world's population at very low speed. Computer-based information is viable only as long as you reduce the enormous complexity of information to the absurd simplicity of data. The World Wide Web proves only that information *can* be valuable. It has helped frame the issues of an information economy, but it has not begun to really address them. The tentative steps we have made so far prove that there *will be* an Information Age, not that it is really here. We are no further into our new age than the first stone-age cave dweller was in hers when she felled her first wild boar with a stone-tipped spear.

Still, the signs are all around us that the Information Age is coming, and coming quickly. The volume of information that needs to be produced and somehow managed has grown to the level that, without serious planning and organization, the cycle of information creation and use bogs down or simply crashes. For many organizations, this is the key dilemma that drives them toward more sophisticated systems for information management.

What will finally push us into the heart of the Information Age, I believe, is the information itself. When it is as easy to put a value on a small chunk of information as it is to put a price on a manufactured good, the Information Age will really be here.

The quantity of information to be handled drives us forward, but what really heralds the new Information Age is qualitative, not quantitative. The most important signs are the more subtle, qualitative ways in which our notions of information are changing, as follows:

✦ **Information is gaining value.** Traditionally considered to be a necessary evil on the way to their true goals, organizations are slowly bestowing upon information the status of an asset, not a burden.

✦ **Individual works are being subsumed by wider information webs.** Information is beginning to coalesce across creators, organizations, disciplines, and industries. We are beginning to ask authors not to create a standalone work but rather to contribute to an existing content domain. Creators are beginning to contribute to overall repositories of reusable information, where their work is related to and cross-referenced with other contributions to produce a growing web of content.

✦ **Information publication is disengaging from creation.** The way information is consumed is beginning to be unlinked from the way it is created. How a particular piece of information is formatted, delivered, and connected to other pieces of information can now effectively be varied and changed, based on the needs of the consumers. Thus, an author may not know how or when her work will be delivered.

In the heart of the Information Age, the exact value of the information you create will be known. In addition, each piece of information will contribute specifically to some very large and very rapidly expanding schema of content. Finally, consumers will simply expect that the information they receive is delivered in the way that is most convenient and useful to them—and they will gladly pay for it.

The time between now and the heart of the Information Age is a period of transition. We will continue to move in fits and starts toward a world where information is more and more freed from the context of its creation but more and more constrained to fit within a known system of categories and relationships. This transition is spurred by the new technologies we have at our disposal to create, organize, and easily distribute information. It should be guided by the needs of the organizations that are using these technologies to interact more and more efficiently and intimately with their constituencies.

This book can help ease your transition from the information overload period we are now in to the information economy toward which we are headed. It tries to answer the following key questions:

✦ What does a system that handles massive amounts of information look like?

✦ How can a system be created that recognizes the value of each piece of information and guides contributors to most easily contribute to a growing knowledge scheme?

✦ How can a single system produce a very wide range of well-targeted custom publications from the same information base?

✦ How can all of this automation and systematization of information happen without endangering the very important relationship between the author and her readers, listeners, or viewers?

✦ What are the steps and processes you need to create such a system?

✦ How can this sort of system fit into and serve an organization's overall goals and initiatives?

So, I am promising you a lot in return for your commitment to content management. I am promising you that you will have a way to conceive of e-business and begin on your organization's journey into e-business. I am promising that you will have the tools you need to combat the onslaught of information that your organization is facing. Finally, I am promising that you will be closer than you were before to becoming part of the coming information economy.

You won't get this sort of return if you focus entirely on the products and problems of today. Instead, you must take a somewhat wider view of your organization, its constituents, and the content and functionality that your organization has to deliver to its constituents. Thus, I have really tried to discuss issues of the day without getting too stuck in today's muddle and confusion. I try, when possible, to stay clear of issues that have currency but no durability. Time will judge how well I accomplish this task.

My biggest hope is that this book raises the right questions and proposes answers that move you toward a successful system for matching content and consumers. I have no fantasy that this work is the last word on content management. I do believe, however, that it is one of the first.

What Is Content?

Defining Data, Information, and Content

You may be wondering why I begin this book with such a long and involved discussion of the idea of content. This is why: Most of the organizations I know come to the idea of content management very simply. They want a tool to help them deal with the onslaught of information that they want to use on the Web and beyond. They are understandably looking for answers, or at least "best practices," that will enable them to do content management so that they can get on with the real work of their organization. Unfortunately, instead of finding answers, most organizations find only a long string of questions. As they follow the string (usually in a series of meetings that get more and more frustrating), they begin to unwind more and more of the organization. The thread leads through every department and is entangled in every obscure editorial and publication process. This can be an awful process as the scope and cost exponentially increase and the motivation and excitement of the team plunge.

I believe that at the root of the problem in these organizations is a misunderstanding of the difference between data and content. People want content to be as simple and straightforward as data.

In this part of the book, I look in-depth at the concept of content. I try to give you a solid idea of why content is different from the data that computers have traditionally dealt with and why content is anything but simple and straightforward. I believe that with a firm concept of content you will be able to avoid (or maybe back out of) the morass where many organizations find themselves. Rather than becoming tangled and disorientated by unwinding the threads of content within your organization, you can start at the beginning of these threads. You will still find them tangled, but you will be prepared to cut through many of the knots and, most important, you will be able to remain oriented toward obtainable goals while you deal with the mess.

Of course, understanding the nature of content is just the start. Given an idea of what you are dealing with conceptually, you will need to craft a workable project from it, analyze your particular situation, and finally build a system to move the content your organization gathers to the people who need to consume it. These are the subjects covered in the latter parts of this book.

What Is Data?

Computers were built to process *data*. Data consists of small snippets of computer information—numbers, words, images, sounds—that have much of the human meaning squeezed out of them. Today, people call on computers to process content. Like data, *content* is also information, but it retains its human meaning and context.

In this chapter, I lay out one of the basic challenges of content management: Computers are designed to deal with *data* that's stripped of any context and independent meaning. Users want computers to deal with *content*, however, which is rich in context and meaning. How can you use the data technologies to manage and deliver very nondatalike content? This challenge isn't easy. If you err by making your information too much like data, it becomes mechanical, uninteresting, and hard for consumers to understand. If you make your information too rich, varied, and context-laden, you can't get a computer to automate its management.

The compromise, as you see in this book, is to wrap your information in a data container (known as *metadata*). The computer manages the data and the interesting, meaningful information goes along for the ride.

Computers were first conceived as a way to perform computations that were too time-consuming or complex for humans. The model was (and, to a large extent, still is) as follows: If you can reduce a problem to an algorithm, a series of simple mechanical operations on numbers and logical entities (entities that are either true or false), it is amenable to solution by a computer. As David Berlinski puts it in his great book, *The Advent of the Algorithm*:

an algorithm is

a finite procedure,

written in a fixed symbolic vocabulary,

governed by precise instructions,

moving in discrete steps, 1,2,3...,

whose execution requires no insight, cleverness, intuition, intelligence, or perspicuity,

and that sooner or later comes to an end.

In the early days, computer professionals were either programmers or data input clerks. Programmers reduced problems to a series of mechanical operations according to a simple maxim:

You input data; the computer processes it and then outputs it in a more useful form.

Clerks took care of inputting the data. They sat in long rows and columns, typing long rows and columns of numbers as well as small phrases, such as first name, last name, and street address. As time moved on, computer scientists invented databases (bases of data) to organize and hold vast quantities of these snippets.

As you may expect, some problems were better solved this way than others were. Thus, as computer technology developed, the use of computers moved naturally from science to manufacturing and finance, where managing large quantities of numbers was still the main event. Today, of course, computers are in everything—devices, tools, toys, processes, entertainment, and, of course, the workplace. But the part of everything that computers are in is the reducible part. The reducible part is the part where a finite set of very specific rules operating on numbers and logical entities can yield a useful result.

Content Is Not Data

The idea of computers as data-processing machines runs deep. Data processing continues to this day to be the main thing that computers do. On the other hand, everyone knows that most users want computers to do more than finely grind through mountains of snippets. Today, people want computers to sift through mountains of large, complete chunks (not snippets) of information and deliver the ones that they want most at that moment. In addition, people want computers to deliver information of the quality that they expect from more familiar sources of information, such as books, radio, TV, and film.

From manufacturing and finance, computers moved to the business desktop as the replacement for the typewriter and the paper-based spreadsheet. Then, three related developments occurred in the personal-computer industry. Together, the following breakthroughs set the stage for a major change in our expectations of what computers can and should do:

✦ Digital media creation (images, sounds and video) became possible.

✦ Digital media output (color displays, sound cards, and video accelerators) became available.

✦ Consumer-oriented mass removable storage (CD-ROMs, in other words) became available and cheap.

These developments led to the meteoric rise of the multimedia industry, and moreover, the use of multimedia in traditional industries. For the first time, you could create and cheaply deliver actual content and not just data. Soon, multimedia CD-ROMs proliferated, delivering everything from encyclopedias and catalogs to full-motion games. The computer began to emerge as a replacement for the more traditional information channels such as books, TV, and radio. What these traditional channels deliver is *content*, not data.

What the multimedia industry began, the Web is in the process of completing. Today, getting your content online isn't only possible, but it's often preferable to obtaining it in any other way. I now listen to more music and talk on my laptop computer and Personal Digital Assistant (PDA) than I do on my radio or stereo. Still, I'm usually frustrated whenever I go to the Web because I expect to quickly locate the content that I want and see it presented at least as well as in the traditional channels. Unfortunately, that's not always what happens.

Note   If you've worked with digital content for a while, you realize just how sticky a paradox this situation is. People expect access to prove easy and presentation to seem compelling. If they are, it's only because someone's put in an enormous amount of effort behind the scenes to make everything appear so easy and compelling. Making content natural is an unnaturally difficult endeavor.

Although users' needs and expectations changed, the guts of the computer didn't. Ten years ago, most people came to computers to input, process, and output data. Today, most people come to find and consume content. At the base of all computer technology, however, is still the idea that you can reduce any problem to a set of simple instructions working on discrete and structured snippets.

Data and content are different, certainly, but that difference doesn't mean that they don't interact. In fact, innumerable transitions from one to the other occur every day. Moreover, from the standpoint of the computer system, content doesn't exist — only data exists. Today, users have few tools for dealing with content as content. Instead, you must treat it as data so that the computer can store, retrieve, and display it.

Looking at the World through Information-Colored Glasses

It's really all about information. Information is central to every type of human endeavor—work, school, and even play. This is how information scientists view the world—information processes and systems acting on various kinds information to meet some type of need.

The information viewpoint applies at different levels: The building block of life, DNA, is an information system on a micro level; the New York Stock exchange is an information system on the macro level.

The foundation of the information perspective is something called *the information spectrum*— DATA - INFORMATION - KNOWLEDGE - ACTION. Data are the baseline representations of *stuff*—raw symbols, numbers, letters, for example, 30.41 - 45.99 APA 6-30. DATA take on meaning when they are assigned labels. For example: 52-week range, symbol, date. KNOWLEDGE involves gathering and combining lots of information, synthesizing, and reaching conclusions. For example: The price of Apache Corp went up over 50% in the last year; in May, APA gave stock dividends; it was upgraded on June 1 by First Albany analysts to a "buy," and so on. Finally, ACTION means doing something based on that information—buy or sell (or even just hold).

Of course, you may decide you haven't reached KNOWLEDGE and need to go back and gather DATA and INFORMATION in order to be better able to take ACTION.

The information spectrum represents a process that takes place in every human setting and situation, both professional and personal. Think about the information spectrum the next time you make a business decision, take a class, read a newspaper, or watch a baseball game.

It's all about information.

Michael B. Eisenberg, Dean, University of Washington Information School (www.ischool. washington.edu)

Consider, for example, a typical Web interaction where you go to a music site. You browse a page that features a music CD that you like; you add it to your shopping cart, and then you pay for it. What you experience is a series of composed Web pages with information about music as well as some buttons and other controls that you use to buy it. All in all, the experience feels like a content-rich interaction. What happens behind the scenes, however, is a set of data-oriented computer programs exchanging data with a database.

Some of the data behind the scenes is very content-like. A database stores, for example, the feature article with the artist's picture. The artist's name is in one field, and the text of the article is in another. A third field contains the picture of the artist. Some of the data is very datalike. It consists of numbers and other snippets that create an economic transaction between you and the record company. A database stores your credit card number, your order number, the quantity that you order, and the order price, for example, and uses them in calculations and other algorithms. Some of the data is between data and content. The song catalog contains song names, running time, price, and availability. These snippets of information can look a whole lot like data as the site's database stores them, but they appear more like content as the site displays them (as shown in Figure 1-1).

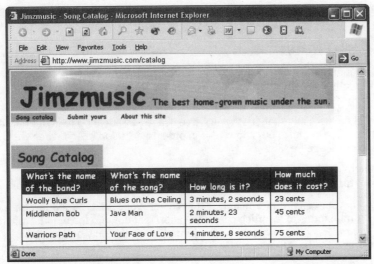

Figure 1-1: As a site stores content, it can look a lot like any other data. In displaying that content, however, it can't look like data if you want to hold your audience.

In the database, it's all just data. On the page, the transaction data still looks a little like data; whereas the feature-article data looks nothing like data, and the catalog data can retain or lose as much of its data appearance as you want. On a well-designed page, however, visitors perceive it all as content.

So, from the user's perspective, information is all content, whereas from the computer programmer's perspective, it's all data. The trick to content management, in an age when the technology is still data-driven, is to use the data technologies to store and display content.

Content Is Information Put to Use

People in the computer world more or less agree on the definition of *data*. Data are the small snippets of information that people collect, join together in data records, and store in databases. The word *information*, on the other hand, contains many meanings and no meaning at the same time. You can rightly call anything, including information, data.

The word *information* holds a lot of meanings. For the purpose of this book, I use a pretty mundane definition. I take *information* to mean all the common forms of recorded communication, including the following:

✦ Text, such as articles, books, and news

✦ Sound, such as music, conversations, and reading

✦ Images, such as photographs and illustrations

✦ Motion, such as video and animations

✦ Computer files, such as spreadsheets, slide shows, and other proprietary files that you may want to find and use

Information, Transformations, Information Products

My definition of information complements Bob's:

> Information is what human beings transform their knowledge into when they want to communicate it to other people. It is knowledge made visible or audible, in written or printed words or in speech.

From the point of view of the user, information is what we seek and pay attention to in our outside world when we need to add to or enrich our knowledge in order to act upon it. And when we find it, we transform it into knowledge.[1]

As Bob says, "you can rightly call anything information"—the thing that makes anything into information is its importance for the human beings who need to add it to their knowledge and use it.

The transformation of knowledge into information is the "lot of work" that someone else has done before "all the common forms of recorded communication" get out into the world. I call the end results *Information Products* (I don't much like the term, but it's the only one available and current at the moment), and I define them as:

> The visible (or audible) products, print on paper or electronic, through which information is presented for use. They embody the results of the transformation of knowledge into information and are an integral blend of content and container.

It's the meeting between a human mind and information embodied in information products that brings the results.

Liz Orna, Orna Information and Editorial Consultancy (lo@orna.co.uk)

---

[1] See Orna, E (2004) Information Strategy in Practice, Aldershot: Gower, p. 7.

Before you ever see a piece of information, someone else has done a lot of work. That someone else has formed a mental image of a concept to communicate and used creativity and intellect to craft words, sounds, or images to suit the concept (thus crystallizing the concept). The person has then recorded the information in some presentable way. The author of the information pours a lot of personality and context into the information before anyone else ever sees it. So, unlike data, information doesn't naturally come in distinct little buckets, all displaying the same structure and behaving the same way. Information tends to flow continuously, as a conversation does, with no standard start, end, or attributes. You disrupt this continuity at your own peril. If you break up information, you change it—and you run the risk of changing or losing the original intelligence and creativity that the author meant the information to express. If you break up information, you run the risk, too, of losing track of or disregarding the assumptions the author made about the audience and the purpose of the information.

The now-defunct ContentWatch organization (a group interested in content management theory and practice) came up with a useful definition of content:

> What is *content*? Raw information becomes content when it is given a usable form intended for one or more purposes. Increasingly, the value of content is based upon the combination of its primary usable form, along with its application, accessibility, usage, usefulness, brand recognition, and uniqueness.

Information that passes casually around in the world isn't content. It becomes content after someone grabs it and tries to make some use of it. You grab and make use of information by adding a layer of data around it. This data wrapper typically describes the information and provides a context for it; in doing so, it makes the information both usable by computers and useful for people. Here's a mundane example: the title of this chapter is a piece of *data*. If I gather all the chapter titles and headings together, I have a piece of *information* called a table of contents. When I include this information at the beginning of this book and you make use of it to navigate and find something of value to you, it's a piece of *content*.

The step of adding data may seem like a small step — from information to its use — but it's not. By refocusing from the nature of information to its practical application, you open up a world of possibilities for applying the data perspective to information. The crux of the data perspective is that, although you can't treat information itself as data, you can treat information *use* that way. As you begin to use information, you wrap it in a set of simplifying assumptions (metadata) that enable you to use computers to manage that use. Humans are mandatory in creating the information and figuring out the simplifying assumptions that wrap the information, but after that, the computer is fine by itself, doling out information in a way that usually makes sense. In my simple table of contents example, this might mean that I should make assumptions about my titles and headings — that they should serve to organize the information in the book, that they are informative, and so on — but I'll rely mostly on the computer to automatically gather them up, format them to be readable, make sure the page numbers are correct, and so on.

By wrapping information in data, a small action by a person can trigger a lot of work for the computer. Suppose, for example, that to simplify information management, you decide that you need to consider a piece of information as 1) new; 2) ready to publish; or 3) ready for deletion. By itself, no computer can decide which of these statuses to apply to a piece of information. By wrapping your information with a piece of metadata known as *status*, however, and by having a person set the status metadata, you can use a computer to perform a lot of work based on the status. The computer doesn't need to know anything about the information itself; it just needs to know what status a human is applying to the information, as the following list outlines:

✦ If you give a piece of content the status *new*, the computer sends a standard e-mail message to a designated reviewer.

✦ If you give a piece of content the status *ready-to-publish*, the computer outputs it to a designated Web page.

✦ If you give a piece of content the status *ready-for-deletion*, the computer removes it from the Web page and deletes it from the system.

In this way, the computer can accomplish a lot of work as the result of a small amount of work by people.

The Web version of the Merriam-Webster dictionary (www.m-w.com) defines content in part as follows:

1 a: something contained — usually used in plural [the jar's *contents*] [the drawer's *contents* b: the topics or matter treated in a written work [table of *contents*]...

This definition provides a nice angle on content — something that *something else* contains. By switching from information to content, you switch from a consideration of a thing to its container. You shift the focus from the information itself to the metadata that surrounds it. The container for information is a set of categories and metadata that . . . well . . . contain the information. This additional data corrals and confines that information and packages it for use, reuse, repurposing, and redistribution. To play off the container metaphor, if content were honey, metadata would be the jar that it comes in, with a label that describes the brand of the honey, its grade, quantity, and where it came from.

If content is information that you put to use, the first question to ask is, "What use?" What is the purpose behind marshaling all this information? Even though this is such a simple question, an astounding number of content management projects go forward without an answer to it. Or, to state the situation more precisely, all projects have some purpose, but the purpose may have little to do with the content that the project involves. A question such as "Why are we creating this Web site?" all too often receives one of the following answers:

✦ Because we need to.

✦ Because our competitors have one.

✦ Because our CEO thinks that we need one.

✦ Because everyone's clamoring for one.

These answers initiate a project, but they don't *define* it. To define the project, you need to answer the question, "What is the *purpose* of the content we're about to put together?" If you provide a solid and well-stated answer, it leads naturally to how you will organize the content to meet your goal. The key to a good purpose is that it's *specific* and *measurable*. Following are some examples of good purposes for an intranet:

✦ To provide a 24-hour turn-around in getting any new product data from the product groups to the field sales representatives.

✦ To provide a site with all articles from the identified sources that mention the identified competitive products.

✦ To show all the data on a pay-stub with a complete history for every employee.

Notice that these goals are pretty specific, so quite a few of them may prove necessary to motivate a large intranet. As you organize your goals, you organize the content behind them. Your process is complete after all your individual goals fit together into a coherent whole and you can ultimately summarize them under a simple, single statement such as "Full support for the field" or "Zero unanswered employee questions."

 Cross-Reference   In Chapter 16, "Securing a Project Mandate," in the section "The project mandate," I discuss the idea of a project mandate, which incorporates the organization's goals into a statement of purpose for the project.

Content and Containers

I like the Merriam-Webster dictionary definition of content, with its acknowledgment that content implies a container. I take a wider view than Bob, however, of what the container consists of. I see information products as an integral fusion of content and container. The inner layers of the container consist of the language (text, visual, musical, and so on) in which thoughts are expressed, the way the content is structured and presented, and everything that comes under the heading of information design—whatever is done to make the product appropriate for the content, the users, and the use they will make of it. Metadata, categories, index terms, and the like form the final, outside layer—the labels that identify the product and help users to find it when they need it.

Liz Orna, Orna Information and Editorial Consultancy (lo@orna.co.uk)

Content Is Information Plus Data

There is something human and intuitive about information that makes treating it simply as data quite impossible. With data, what you see is what you get. With information, much of what it conveys isn't actually in the information but, rather, in the mind of the person creating or consuming it. Information lives within a wider world of connotation, context, and interpretation — all of which make it fundamentally not amenable to the data-processing model. In fact, the concept of data was created specifically to remove these subjective qualities from information so that computers could manage it with strict, logical precision.

So, can computers ever really manage information? I believe that they can — albeit poorly by human standards. Until a new computer processing model appears, you can put methodologies, processes, and procedures in place to *handle* information by using data-age tools. Rather than reducing the information to mere data, you can capture whole, meaningful chunks of information and wrap it in descriptive data that computers can then read and act on.

Metadata is neatly described as data about data, but it's much more than this. Metadata makes the context and meaning of information explicit enough that a computer can handle it.

Adding data to information (metadata, that is) helps split the difference between keeping the information whole and enabling data techniques to effectively manage it. The data that you add to information is a way of making the context, connotation, and interpretation explicit. More important, metadata can make explicit the kind of mind that you expect to interpret the information. By adding a piece of metadata known as *audience type* to each chunk of information that you produce, for example, you can make explicit any implicit assumption about the target of the information: *expert users*, *dog owners*, or *subcontractors*, for example. Then, a computer can perform the simple task of finding information based on who's on the other side of the terminal. Of course, not all tasks are this simple, but the concept is always the same. You tag a large chunk of information with the data that the computer must access so that it can figure out what to do with that information. Metadata is a simplified version of the context and meaning of the information — simple enough for the computer to understand and work with.

Content, therefore, is *information that you tag with data so that a computer can organize and systematize its collection, management, and publishing*. Such a system, a *content management system*, is successful if it can apply the data methodologies without squashing the interest and meaning of the information along the way.

Until computers (or some newer technology) can handle content directly, you must figure out how to use the data technologies to collect and deliver content. Using data technologies to handle content is a central theme of this book.

From Data to Content and Back

From the perspective of this book, which attempts to reconcile the data and content perspectives, what is data and what is content depend mainly on how you create, manage, and bring each type of information onto a page, as the following list describes:

✦ **Transaction information** refers to datalike snippets that you typically use to track the processes of buying and selling goods. For transaction information and other very datalike sources, you don't generally use a content management system (CMS). Usually, they are managed as part of a traditional data-processing system. The templating system of a CMS, however, often does manage the displaying of such information on the publication page.

✦ **Article information** is the sort of information that is text-heavy and has some sort of editorial process behind it. You create and manage article information, and other very content-like information, most often using a CMS. In fact, without this sort of information, the CMS has little reason to exist. The CMS is also generally responsible for displaying this sort of information.

✦ **Catalog information,** which is information that might appear in a directory or product listing, can go either way. You sometimes create and manage it by using a CMS, and sometimes a separate data-processing application handles it. Obviously, if an organization already has a full-featured catalog system, tying your CMS to it is the easiest way to go. On the other hand, if you need rich media and lots of text, along with the part numbers and prices in your catalog, then including the catalog as part of the overall CMS may make the most sense.

The purpose of content management isn't to turn all data into content. The purpose of content management is to oversee the creation and management of rich, editorially intensive information and to manage the integration of this information with existing data systems. The CMS must, in all cases, carry the responsibility for the creation of the final publication. If this publication includes both data and content, the CMS is there to ensure that the right data and content appear in the right places and that the publication appears unified and coherent to the end consumer.

Summary

Data was invented because it was much easier to deal with than information. It's small, simple, and all its relationships are clearly known (or else ignored). Data makes writing computer programs possible. Information is large, complex, and rife with relationships that are important to its meaning, but impossible for a computer to decipher.

Here are some points to keep in mind as you hear and discuss the terms *data*, *information*, and *content*:

✦ Content (at least for the purposes of this book) is a compromise between the usefulness of data and the richness of information. Content is rich information that you wrap in simple data. The data that surround the information (metadata) is a simplified version of the context and meaning of the information.

✦ In a content management system, the computer manages information indirectly through data. The content compromise says, "I can't get the computer to understand and manage information, so I must simplify the problem. I must create a set of data that represents my best guess as to the important aspects of this information. Then, I can use the computer's data capabilities to manage my information via the simplified data."

✦ Someday, someone may invent computers that can deal directly with information. I'm not holding my breath, however, because to do so requires cracking some of computer science's hardest problems, such as artificial intelligence and natural language processing. In the meantime, everyone must make do with the current dumb but very strong beasts. (If someone does finally invent these new machines, the creators may need to change the name from *computers* to something less mechanical.)

In the following two chapters, I describe the two basic qualities of content that a CMS must account for: *format* and *structure*.

✦   ✦   ✦

Content Has Format

To communicate information, you must encode it — that is, provide a method for communicating it to a computer. This encoding is known as *format*. In the computer world, format covers two broad, but related, concepts: *storage format* (also known as *file format*) and *rendering format* (sometimes referred to as *display format*). For a CMS to function correctly, it must offer the capabilities to receive and create a variety of storage formats and to separate rendering format from the content it surrounds.

In this chapter, I focus on format and discuss why it's so important but often so difficult to deal with.

Storage Formats: Storing Information

For a computer to use information, it must convert the information to binary code. When you digitize a printed picture, for example, the scanner must convert the picture from tiny blobs of color on paper to a structured set of ones (1) and zeros (0). Over time, the various kinds of structures devised by programmers have been generally accepted. In images, formats such as JPEG and GIF are now the standards for Web publication, and formats such as EPS and TIFF are the standards in print publication. Computer files are the traditional way to store binary information, so binary format is also known as *file format*. Many binary file formats exist; data in a file is stored in whatever binary format the program that created it uses. Each binary format has its own way of representing the information that it encodes. Most image files, for example, feature code at the top of the file that specifies the kind of file and how big it is. In addition, the code provides a wealth of other format-specific data. Vector graphics are encoded as a set of equation values that, when calculated, create the shapes that you see in the image.

In text, the characters you type are generally encoded using *American Standard Code for Information Interchange (ASCII)* or its more modern equivalent, *Unicode. Format* is most fundamentally defined as the way information is encoded so that computer applications can use it.

In this book, I refer to these binary formats (along with nonbinary formats such as XML) generically and collectively as *storage formats*.

Binary format is important because you must often move between one binary format and another. You may receive images in EPS format, for example, and then must convert them to JPEG format for a Web publication. Or you may need to keep both versions because you must use the same images in print and on the Web. Although the various formats all represent the same sort of information, moving from one to the other isn't always easy.

Microsoft Word (DOC format) files, for example, have been notoriously hard to convert to Web files (HTML format). Although they're both text formats, DOC files are richer, more complex, and simply different; many of the conventions that exist in a DOC file simply don't exist in an HTML file. This means you get inconsistent, poor results if you try to convert from one format to the other without a lot of intelligent human oversight.

Note   If you open a binary file in a text-editing program so that you can view the code, you won't see a set of 1's and 0's. Why not? Because program code is usually stored in a higher-level, base-16 number format called hexidecimal, which is easier for programmers to manage and interpret than an endless string of 1s and 0s. The computer translates hexidecimal code to binary 1s and 0s for processing, but generically, any encoded base-16 format is referred to as binary.

Rendering Format: Presenting Information

In addition to being the way that you encode a file, format refers to the qualities that you use to visually render content. If I use the word *format* without qualifiers in this book, I mean this sort of rendering format. Typographic qualities (such as **bold**, *italic*, and underline, as well as layout qualities such as tables, right alignment, and margins) are all part of this definition of *format*. Although I dwell mostly on text formats in this work, the other media types (images, sound, and motion formats) all have unwritten equivalents of this notion of format. Rendering format is important. In order to make your content comprehensible to a reader, you must manage the format across all the content that you intend to handle in these two ways:

✦ **You must make format consistent** across content categories, as well as across all content, in a single publication. To ensure readability, for example, you want to make certain that all your news releases feature the title centered and boldfaced at the top of the page. You can also format a cross-reference link the same way, across all the content in your publications, to ensure that the user recognizes it as a link.

✦ **You must separate format from content** so that you can reuse the content in a variety of outputs. Although making your titles centered and boldfaced may be appropriate in your Web design, for example, you may prefer to make them left-justified and italicized in print. In this case, the title itself doesn't have any set format associated with it; rather the publishing system enables the title to adopt the title format that the specific publication uses.

For the content manager, rendering format is best thought of as separate from content. For the consumer of content, the two are inseparable. The typography and layout of the page tell you much of what you need to know about the page. Format is a kind of metadata. It's information above and around the language on the page that tells your brain what to do with the language on the page. It tells the reader things such as "This part is important," "Read this section first," or "This text is a link." It guides your eye and your emotions around the language, leading you, if it is done well, to a much faster and fuller understanding of the information on that page.

The Language of Formatting

Print editors and publishers have long understood the power of formatting and have developed strong formatting conventions to guide the user. Only a few such conventions exist today for the computer screen. Moreover, whenever the computer industry borrows too heavily from the print world, it fails because many conventions require specific qualities of the physical page. On the other hand, whenever the computer industry disregards convention and invents a new language of format, it also fails because people simply don't understand it. *Wired Magazine*, for example, features a great, innovative layout and design. But it defies so many conventions that, for some people, it's just plain hard to read.

My generation spent its youth learning the language of print formatting. It's familiar and subconscious. My children still learn the language of print, but now it has a counterpoint. My children also learn the language of the screen "on the street" as it were, as well as through games and on the Web. The language of the screen is a *pidgin* language. Like the pidgin English spoken on merchant marine vessels by natives of a hundred nations, it simplifies concepts, borrows from everywhere, messes with established meanings, and creates new ones at will. Like any pidgin language, the language of the screen is more fun, but far less agreed-upon and stable than its parent tongues.

In the end, we will have an unconscious and agreed-upon set of conventions for computer presentation—a real language of the screen. But, we will arrive at it in fits and starts as we find techniques that work. The language of the screen will likely be common, not just to one culture, but to the whole world. I can say from grueling experience that although we have a long way to go in creating conventions, we are certainly ahead of where we were 20 years ago when I started putting words on-screen.

Dealing with Formatting

Format is the part of content that's often the hardest to deal with. The reason is that authors don't apply formatting consistently. If formatting is inconsistent, however, automating the process of separating format from content is almost impossible. It requires a lot of manual labor to make content ready for your system.

To ensure consistent formatting, professional writers use a *style guide* that specifies very precisely how to format each element of the manuscript. Unlike the style guides you might buy in a bookstore, these documents go paragraph by paragraph through a model of the publication to be produced, telling you exactly how to do each kind of formatting the publication requires. Word processing programs help enforce consistency by providing a way to name and apply a style to a block of text. Even among professionals, however, you see a strong tendency to apply formatting directly rather than to go through the extra trouble of using word processing styles, often for the following reasons:

✦ Without a strict style guide, being consistent in the way that you apply formatting is really difficult. Creating good, complete style guidelines requires a lot of experience. Worse, adhering to style guidelines takes incredible patience and fastidiousness, at least until it becomes second nature to do so.

✦ Most word processors enable you to easily circumvent style constraints. The commands to apply formatting "correctly" (by consistently using style templates, for example) are generally harder to use than the ones that apply it "wrongly" (on an *ad hoc* basis) by clicking (the little bullets button in Microsoft Word, for example).

And even if applied diligently by a professional writer, styles for the most part don't serve top structure content.

For the person who must work with preformatted content, the problems compound. People who aggregate content (for example, publishers or front-line print and online production workers) are often very frustrated for the following reasons:

✦ Because the person creating the content often finds it hard to apply formatting consistently, content often arrives poorly formatted.

✦ In the absence of some institutional mandate (like "use styles or you're fired," or "we won't publish your book"), content creators frequently have little immediate incentive to apply styles consistently because the benefits of doing so don't accrue to them directly. Rather, the benefits appear downstream in the form of less work for production workers and a smoother publication process.

✦ Because style guidelines vary from group to group, if you aggregate content from many sources, it can become a tangle of conflicting formatting.

✦ Because the way in which rendering format is encoded as storage format varies widely from tool to tool, you often have no way to translate from one format to another. At best, you can translate only approximately and then massage the results. Each tool, for example, offers its own way to represent tables. You often find no way to represent the table attributes possible in one tool in the storage format that another tool uses.

The Inner Struggle of a Lazy Writer

I present the following brief inner dialog for the gratification of those of you who, like me, wish that they didn't know the "right" way to format text:

"Okay, I need to put in a bulleted list." My pointer moves effortlessly toward that little button at the top of the Microsoft Word window to make the bullets. Then I stop.

"No," I tell myself, "that's the coward's way to format a bulleted list. If I do it that way, it's sure to all turn out inconsistent, and who knows how it may translate to HTML. I need to use the style that I defined for bullets." So, I open the style drop-down list to find the right bullet style.

"Damn," I grumble. "Not there. I started a new document and didn't bring over the new styles." Finding my styles and bringing them into my document takes me ten minutes. I open the style list again.

Aaarrgg, which bullet style is it, again? I see "Bull," "Normal Bullet," "Bullet Indent," and "Body Bullet."

I can't, for the life of me, remember which one I'm supposed to use or even where some of these styles came from. I choose "Bull" (because it sounds like the kind of styles that I usually create) and hope for the best, even though it doesn't look quite right. I can change the definition of the "Bull" style to fit what I expect to see, but who knows what this change may do to the other lists that use "Bull."

"Forget it," I say to myself. "Let the editor deal with it."

For the content manager, who must ensure that the same content can appear in various publications, each with its own storage- and rendering-format conventions, the problems are also severe. Very few storage formats really enable you to separate formatting from content. XML and its parent SGML are among the few that do offer this type of separation. The manager faces the difficult choice of either converting all her content into a format (such as XML) or storing it in a storage format where rendering format and content are inseparable (such as HTML). If the manager chooses to convert to XML, she incurs a big up-front conversion cost. She also has an ongoing cost to reconvert it back to standard print and electronic storage formats for each publication. If she chooses to use a format such as HTML, producing Web publications is easy, but other formats may require extensive manual effort because of poor convertibility between text formats.

Categorizing Formatting

You can categorize formatting in three different ways: by emotional effect, by visual effect, and by scope of application.

Formatting for effect

An author may format text to achieve an emotional or psychological effect:

✦ **Emphasis or importance:** Size, position, and color all direct your eye. They tell your mind about the relative importance of the text to which they are applied. However, as everyone knows but few people seem to remember, *importance* is a relative term. If everything on a Web site screams at you, untangling exactly what is most important becomes impossible; each new item just ups the ante. Each competes for your attention in an ever-escalating battle of size, position, and (yes) blink rate.

✦ **Parsability:** You can take in only so much information in one eyeful. Well-used formatting breaks a mass of unparsable information into eye-sized chunks. White space (between paragraphs, tabs, spaces, margins, and so on) is the main type of formatting that you use to segment information, sometimes in combination with typographic elements, such as with an indented bulleted or numbered list. A well-formatted presentation moves your eye quickly and naturally from area to area.

✦ **Interest:** Authors often use formatting to break the boredom of a flat presentation. The eye and brain respond to variation. By breaking up the otherwise smooth flow of text with various styles, you entice the reader to continue. The savvy author knows when to break cadence and offer some interest.

✦ **Cultural norms:** Compare the formatting that you see in the *Wall Street Journal* and *USA Today*, two popular U.S. newspapers. The styling and layout of the *Wall Street Journal* reeks of formality, institutionalism, and stability. The styling and layout of *USA Today* exudes a casual, friendly, easily accessible air. In both cases, the formatting does far more than draw your eye or generate interest. It links the publication to a cultural context. Formatting is a major key to where the publication sits in the vast web of cultural relationships. This format-based social positioning is serious business — so serious, in fact, that most companies create strict usage guidelines that specify in detail the fonts, colors, and positioning that employees may use for the identity-creating elements of their publications.

Formatting by method

An author may employ a range of formatting methods that can be neatly grouped by the following types of visual effects:

✦ **Typographic effects:** These effects apply to the qualities and look of text. Font face, font size, kerning (the space between letters), text color, and effects such as underlining, bold, and italics are all examples of typographic effects. These qualities are the ones that most people think of when they discuss formatting.

✦ **Layout effects:** These effects apply to the positioning of content areas. Margins, columns, tables, wrapping, and indentation are all examples of layout effects. Layout formatting tends to be the hardest type of formatting to translate from one type of publication to another (especially from print to the Web).

✦ **Background effects:** These effects happen behind and around the content. Cell colors and images, background colors and images, watermarks, and reverse effects are all examples of background effects. The rule of backgrounds (familiar to print folk but still poorly understood on the Web) is this: "If you even notice the background formatting, it's too strong."

Formatting by scope

Typically, an author may apply formatting at a range of levels, from granular to gross, as follows:

✦ **Character formatting:** This type of formatting applies to one or more text characters. If changing between one character and the next in a particular sentence makes sense (such as making one or more words **bold**), you can count it as character formatting. Character formatting includes most of the typographic effects. The familiar bold, italic, and underline are character formats, as is your choice of font (or, more accurately, typeface). Although character formatting is the most familiar and easiest-to-understand type of formatting, it generally has little to do with structuring or managing content, and it often gets in the way of these important functions.

✦ **Paragraph formatting:** This formatting applies to blocks of text that paragraph breaks separate. Many of the layout effects such as indents and line spacing belong in this category. Unlike character formatting, paragraph formatting plays a major role in structuring and managing content. First, structural elements such as headings, summaries, and titles usually sit in their own paragraphs. Second, paragraph formatting is the most common application of the use of styles, where you roll a set of character and paragraph effects together under a single name and apply it to a set of text blocks. Style is not only a way to group formatting; it's also a way to give structural names to text blocks. Applying the style *title*, for example, to a paragraph doesn't just capture the fact that you want a big, bold, and centered paragraph. It can also serve as a marker to say that this paragraph contains the structural element, the part of the content that you call *title*. This structural use of formatting is commonly abandoned below the level of heads; *body text* or *bullet* styles, for example, are generic and don't tell much about the purpose of the text to which they're applied. Some styles tell us a bit more about their purpose (for example: *table head*) and we can infer a little more about their context, but they're still mostly devoid of information about how they fit into the structure of a chunk of content.

✦ **Page formatting:** This type of formatting unifies a set of text (and media) blocks into a coherent presentation. As the name implies, it applies to a single (printed or online) page. Effects such as margins, columns, and backgrounds are what you commonly apply at this page level in HTML. In print, page formatting is usually applied for an entire publication. In each medium, page formatting is applied at the smallest complete unit of presentation.

In print, you rarely take a single page away from its surrounding section (a chapter or maybe a subchapter). In HTML, viewing a single page apart from its neighbors is standard practice. Page formatting sets the layout and presentation of a standard block of a publication.

✦ **Subpublication formatting:** This formatting applies across pages to an entire section of a publication. As I mentioned earlier, you generally define layout effects at this level in print. On the Web, techniques such as the use of cascading style sheets and templates carry the burden of forming a single look across pages.

✦ **Publication formatting:** This type of formatting spans all characters, paragraphs, and pages in the publication. In most authoring environments, you can select an entire publication and make the text bold, but doing so is a truly vile thing to do from the standpoint of format or structure management. It means that someone will have to come along later and figure out how to interpret that global change and apply it in each separate element of the publication. Often, publication-level formatting is accomplished by extending subpublication formatting into the publication as a whole, usually by sharing style sheets and templates.

✦ **Suprapublication formatting:** This formatting applies across publications. Just as you share subpublication formatting to get publication-level formatting, you share publication-level formatting among publications to extend the same standards. Again, style sheets and templates are the vehicles that you use most often for defining and enforcing formatting across publications. Branding Guidelines, used by many companies, are examples of suprapublication formatting. Every publication that the company produces must follow these rules.

Summary

As people read, they tend to take formatting for granted. Words are boldfaced or centered, text lies in columns or tables, and readers barely take notice. For the content manager, however, format warrants great attention for the following reasons:

✦ The system that she works with must offer the capabilities to accept the storage formats that she submits and must create the storage formats of the publications that she must produce.

✦ If she applies rendering format inconsistently to the text that she receives, cleaning it up and separating the format from the content can require additional (and unnecessary) manual labor.

✦ She must recognize, analyze, and synthesize the wide variety of formatting that she receives into a single, coherent system. Whether it applies to a single character or to a whole family of publications, all formatting must fit into a single system of emphasis, interest, and structure.

✦ Formatting represents implicit or explicit understandings of visual meaning. An explicit style guide, for example, might say something like "Make all product names bold," and "Make all cross references italic and blue." So even *ad hoc* formatting reflects an underlying structure, even if imperfectly; and for the content manager the trick is getting this structure codified and put into practice.

Formatting is the first basic quality of content that you must account for. In the next chapter, I detail the second basic quality: structure.

✦   ✦   ✦

Content Has Structure

*S*tructure is the way that you put information together. It encompasses the parts and pieces of a *base of content* and their relationships to each other. The *title* of a Web site, for example, relates to each of its pages in the same way that the name of a movie relates to its scenes. Along with format, structure is one of the basic qualities of content that you must understand and control in order to manage content.

Structure, however, is much more important than format because format follows from structure. If you know and control the structure of a body of content, you can create whatever format suits your needs for a particular presentation. Format varies with the way that you present a body of content, but its structure remains the same.

In this chapter, I detail the structure of structure. As you'll see, structure is important, but determining the best structure for your content can be difficult. Your choices can create immense consequences downstream that can determine how difficult your system is for developers, authors, and users to work with.

Structure Is Important

If format is about presentation, structure is about management. Structure is the set of named relationships within, between, and beyond individual pieces of content. If a content base is well-structured, it has the following features, as illustrated in Figure 3-1:

✦ Its content divides into a set of well-defined categories (which I call *content types*).

✦ Within each content type, the content segments into manageable chunks (which I call *content components*).

✦ Each *content component* chunk divides further into a well-defined set of parts (which I call *elements*).

✦ Each element relates to other elements, from the same or another content component, by way of outlines, indexes, cross-references, and sequences.

For example, suppose an aircraft avionics company produces a number of publications promoting its products, among them a distinct sort of document — a *content type* — called a *white paper*.

```
Content type
    Content component
        Element
        Element
        Element
    Content component
        Element
        Element
Content type
    Content component
        Element
        Element
    Content component
        Element
        Element
```

Figure 3-1: Fundamental categories of structure in a content base

Each individual white paper that the company produces is a *component*—a complete chunk of content of the type white paper.

Each white paper has a standard structure, with *elements* such as title, abstract, product description, body, and so on.

The result of categorizing in this way is that you can manage white papers more easily, meaning that you can store them in some sort of electronic repository, and you can find them easily when you need them. Equally important, you can reuse a single white paper component in various publications and publication platforms (say, print and Web). In addition, because you know exactly what is in each white paper, you can pull elements out for reuse in other publications—for example, a publication that lists the titles and abstracts of all the white papers in the repository.

Finally, when all your publications are analyzed and modeled in this way, you'll see that many content types share elements. This helps you in (at least) two ways. First, if you standardize the naming of your elements, you can effectively and easily search across your entire content repository. For example, if all components include an element called *abstract* and you want to find content related to altimeters, you can simply search all your abstracts for *altimeter* and be sure that your search is comprehensive. Second, you can rationalize your content model, which means that you use a single instance of an element that may happen to be used in any number components.

In short, a well-structured content base is well-organized. Just as in a well-organized file cabinet, where every sheet of paper goes into a specific folder, every folder goes in a certain drawer, and every drawer has a particular location, a well-organized content base is one that you divide and completely catalog. If you look closely at the organization of the content, you can see that it is a set of structures laid in and around the content that you intend to collect, manage, and deliver.

 Cross-Reference Content types, components, and elements are a key set of concepts in CM that I discuss in detail in Chapter 27, "Designing Content Types."

Creating an overarching set of structures is *the* way to understand and control content. If you have well-defined categories, you can standardize the way that you create and evaluate them as well as use them. If you divide content into content components, you can track them individually. If each content component has the same set of named elements, you can count on a particular piece of information being available where you expect it to be when you need to lay out a page automatically. Finally, if each content component is stored within the same structures as all the others, you can create a fast and efficient storage and retrieval system that can automatically deliver targeted content into a variety of publications.

Traditionally, structure was solely the author's concern. She would compose, arrange, rearrange, and finally arrive at a structure that made most sense to her. From the beginning of composition to this day, authors have agonized (alone and with their editors) over the minute structure of what they were creating. Unfortunately, much of the intimate understanding an author achieves is lost to later users of her work. With the possible exception of academic and technical writers, few authors take the time to know how their work fits into any explicit and formalized wider framework. In academic writing, it is not only standard, it is mandatory to specifically cite the other works that relate to yours. Even academic writers, however, create their own worlds of structure, which may or may not relate well to any other content in the world outside. Although working in isolation enhances creativity by not imposing any outside restrictions, it makes relating one work to another extremely hard. And, of course, relating one work to another is what content management is all about.

Structure Provides Invaluable Information about Your Content

Structure is an extremely important component of content. In very early documents, sentences were written without spaces between words and with no periods. After all, when we speak we don't add spaces between words and often don't add "stops" until we need to take a breath. But the printed medium was different. Readers of these early materials often had to read them aloud to understand their meaning. Over time, the use of punctuation developed to enable readers to understand the content more easily. Similarly, printed-page structures have changed to include headers, footers, titles, and the like. Web pages, too, have evolved to provide space around content, clear divisions of content, and other visual indicators to help us understand and retrieve information.

Visual structure enables content users to quickly identify and retrieve the information. But the structure of content isn't just about the visual structure; it is also about the meaning of content. Content contains information with different meanings, such as conceptual, procedural, introductory, cautionary, explanatory, and so on. Good communicators know this and have been developing structures or templates and writing style guides for content to ensure that it is written consistently, clearly, and effectively.

As we at the Rockley Group have worked with our clients' materials, analyzing the content for effectiveness, usability, and opportunities for reuse, we have identified how the content can be more effectively structured. All content has structure. Some content, like cautionary information, contains a lot of structure (for example, an alert icon like Warning, a title, an alert body), while information like the body of a brochure may not have as much structure (instead it may just include descriptive paragraphs), but whatever the content it has clearly definable structure and lots of it. And the effective and consistent application of semantic structure (structure which uses meaningful tags) enables you to automatically format it for multiple media (multi-channel) delivery, retrieve it, and reuse it. Structure provides invaluable information about your content.

Ann Rockley, The Rockley Group (www.rockley.com)

Structure Is Like a Map

You can think of structures as maps that you lay over a set of content chunks to organize them and make them accessible to the people who need them. Just as many different kinds of geographic maps describe the same territory, many different kinds of structures describe the same content base.

A map of your neighborhood, for example, can show the area topographically, color-coded by household income, or by the distribution of electrical power. Each of these maps shows the same area, but organizes the information for a different purpose. Similarly, you can map your content base by content type, audience type, or by the date that you create each chunk of information. Again, each of these structures shows the same content, but each organizes the content for a different purpose. The content-type view shows authors how much of their type of contribution is in the system. The audience-type view shows end users the information that may be of most interest to them. The create-date view shows administrators how much new content is flowing into the system and how often.

Structure is always key to managing content. But the *kind* of structure needed depends on the management needs of a particular user. A content creator, for example, may want to see how her content relates to the other content that is in the system, so she wants to see her content chunk in the center of a set of relationships. An administrator wants to see all content organized by type or by source, so she wants a content outline categorized by content type and by author. An end user cares most that she can find just the right chunk of content to answer the question she has in her mind, so she wants to see outlines that divide the content based on the issues that she wants to resolve. All three of these people want structure, but each wants a different kind of structure. Thus, the same base of content needs a variety of structures to serve all constituents.

A good CMS enables you to design and apply a variety of overlapping structures on the same body of content.

Structure Can Be Difficult to Create

Structure is the way that the chunks of content (components) fit together into a unified framework. That sounds great, but it assumes the following:

✦ That such a unified framework exists.

✦ That you can figure out how to relate your components to your structure.

✦ That you can muster the effort to apply the structures over the base of content that you must deal with.

Consider a typical business intranet. It starts with a group of representatives from the various parts of the organization in a room. Everyone states what he wants on the intranet. The HR department wants all employee information to be there. The executives want to see business news and competitive analysis. Managers want policies and procedures. Each functional group wants its own set of specific documents and links. It all sounds fine. But as they start brainstorming, the farther they get, the less they know about what each of these categories of content actually consists of. Which business news? Exactly what competitive analysis?

Someone says, "Why not just start by putting up what we have now?" They all agree that this idea could solve the problem, and so they go away to collect key documents. The next day, they come back together, each with a large stack of papers. With all the stacks lying menacingly in front of them, they discuss how all this information fits together; but the enormity of the task starts to become apparent. Hours later, exhausted and disenchanted, someone sums up the meeting by saying, "I had no idea it was all this complex. How do we ever get anything done around here with this mess of information?" The fact is that an organization's content is rarely organized. It's a mess of loosely connected point-to-point communications, each with its own purpose, assumptions, and implicit structure. So it's not too hard to see what you need to do from the macro level; at the level of the whole intranet, you can easily see how it all fits together. But at the micro level, the level at which the content was first created, a given piece of content didn't need to fit with anything else. As long as the intended audience gets the idea, who cares whether anyone else does? When you are creating the intermediate level, however, where the micro meets the macro and where structure meets anarchy, the problems occur. This doesn't mean that you can't whip this rag-tag collection of information into content. It just requires a lot of thought and effort to do so.

So, the beleaguered group comes back with renewed purpose. "Yes it's hard," says the one. "But we can do it!" They agree, knowing that the alternative is to return defeated after just two meetings. One member, who was an editor on her college newspaper, rolls up her sleeves and leads the others in this new direction. They begin a major synthesis, painstakingly fitting each type of information into one big outline. They note any gaps in the material and how they need to classify and modify each kind of document to make them all fit together. In the end, they have a full-site outline and an idea of what it's going to take to make all these micro communications fit into the macro scheme that they came up with during their first hour together. They go home happy.

The final meeting is meant to clean up details and figure out how much budget to ask for to start the intranet. In the back of everyone's mind (except the Web Guy) is the idea that the Web Guy receives content from lots of contributors around the organization and just puts it together into a nice set of pages. So, they ask him how much time he needs to build the site. The Web Guy's jaw drops. "Me?" he stammers. "You think that I can do all this work alone? You all took hours just to figure out how one example of each of these documents fits in. I don't know about HR or product specs. How am I supposed to figure out how all your material fits together? And how many documents are we talking about? Sorry, but I have my hands full just keeping the servers running and designing pages for our Internet site." Now some other jaws drop as others start to realize that he's right. Few others in the organization besides the people at the meeting could successfully fit documents into the outline they created. And no way could any of them take on the extra task.

The woman from the organization's consulting group starts to smell a familiar situation — a scene that she's seen played out many times. It becomes clear to everyone that the task at hand far exceeds the available budget or staff. "It's a phased approach," she says calmly. "We start with just a few of the most important ones of each type. Then, as the concept proves itself, we can ask for more resources to grow the site." They all agree and leave the last meeting feeling as if they'd taken a course at the school of hard knocks.

The way the team approached this problem presents a number of problems, but who can blame the team? They had no idea of the magnitude of the task. Thinking it an easy problem, they approached it casually, looking for an easy solution. Structuring large quantities of information is similar to being hired to clean and maintain a large house where 16 children live. If you're lucky, it's merely a full-time job, because the house is basically organized but just a little messy. If you clean it every day and put things in their assigned places, you can maintain general order. You're more likely, however, to walk into a complete disaster on the first day. Before you even *start* cleaning, just figuring out the right place for everything will be a lot of work.

In summary, challenges you are likely to face when defining and applying structure include:

✦ **Understanding content in its entirety.** Creating structure requires an extensive understanding of the entire base of content. It simply isn't possible to do a quick overview of a limited sample and arrive at structures that can persevere.

✦ **Controlling all content.** To bring all content under control, you must subsume the structures already present in each type of content you receive. You must create a new structure that can encompass all existing content without changing it so drastically that it no longer meets the needs of the group that creates it. At the same time, the standards must make each group's content accessible and usable to other groups that need the same information for a different end goal.

✦ **Overcoming resistance to change.** Most groups that produce a lot of content arrive at some set of structure standards. The harder it is for the group to come to those standards and the more comprehensive the standards are, the harder that group is likely to fight to retain its standards (whether they serve the general good of the organization beyond the original group or not).

✦ **Providing a flexible solution.** Structuring is an iterative process. The structure that you originally define is very likely to change and deepen as you begin to fit the bulk of your content into it. Likewise, resource or time restrictions may require you to build your structure around a subset of the body of content you eventually want in your system, so the structure must evolve as your understanding of your content broadens and deepens.

✦ **Enforcing your standards.** Unless you give everyone specific direction, the structure that one author creates is unlikely to easily mesh with the structure that other authors create. Additionally, many authors often don't want to bother learning and obeying rules. Thus, you must make your standards enforceable, but at the same time, easy to understand and apply.

✦ **Understanding the mechanics of structure.** Generally, few individuals in the organization understand the mechanics of structure well enough to analyze and manage it. I coined a new term, *metator*, to describe this poorly understood job function. A *metator* is an information architect who edits a body of content from the standpoint of its metadata structures.

✦ **Finding the right balance.** No single structure can cover all your content for all its users. You must create an overlapping family of structures that all describe the same content base in different ways so that authors, administrators, and end consumers can all find the sorts of structures that they need to complete their respective tasks.

A CMS provides the structure and process you need to overcome these structure hurdles. Still, groups venturing into the world of content management should recognize it for the huge beast that it is, and start by upgrading the content creation skills of their staff and, in particular, by getting them to routinely add basic structures to their documents (for example, styles and metadata). Over time, by adhering to basic content creation practices, an organization will build a large enough body of well-structured content so that the task of implementing a CMS won't be so daunting.

How to Categorize Structure

If I scared you in the preceding section, that's good. Information is a beast. Taming it requires determination, strength, and cunning. Your best weapon against this many-headed monster is to understand how to analyze structure and apply it to information. So in this section, I look at the structure of structure (the metastructure, if you like). You can categorize structure based on the purpose for which you're creating it, the type of structure you're creating, and the scope of the structure you're creating.

Structure by purpose

You can categorize structure based on your *purpose* for creating that structure:

✦ **Structuring for a single publication:** Outside a CMS, most people have a particular publication in mind as they endeavor to create structure. Whether that publication is as small as a memo or as large as an intranet, the author has a single unified target in mind. She creates the structure that directly aids the presentation of that publication.

✦ **Structuring for a content base:** In a CMS, your purpose for creating structure is to make content easier to create, easier to manage, and easier to automatically build into a variety of publications. Although a simple outline may suffice for a particular publication (a Web site, say), you need a much more robust structure to organize the creation and storage of the entire body of information, as well as its output into more than one publication.

Structure by type

If your purpose is to structure a large body of content for a range of contributors and publications, then you need most, if not all, of the following types of structures:

✦ **Divisional structure** slices content up into useful chunks. Implicitly, at the lowest level, by ending a sentence with a period, you divide groups of words into sentences. At the highest level, by naming your Web site bologna.com, you separate the content there from the rest of what's on the Internet (at least you hope so). In a CMS, you focus mostly on the following two types of explicit divisional structure:

  • *Named segments (or types)* of content, such as product reviews, tech support articles, and press releases.

  • *Named elements* within the segments, such as title, abstract, body paragraph, emphasized text, footnote, and sidebar.

✦ **Access structure** presents the divisions that you and your audiences need to determine where (or if) a particular piece of content exists in your structure. This type of structure includes the one most people think of first as structure — the outline. It goes far past the outline, however, to include a range of other navigational structures, including the following:

  • *Hierarchies* (also known as *outlines*, *taxonomies*, and *tables of contents*), which show parent-child relationships between different segments of content.

  • *Indexes and concordances*, which provide a map between text phrases and the content segments that relate to them.

  • *Cross-references* (also known as *links*) from one content segment to another, either within the same work or to other works.

  • *Sequences* (also known as *browse sequences*) that specify which segment of content comes before or after the current one.

✦ **Management structure** specifies the attributes of a content component that enable you to track and manage it. Data such as author, creation date, version number, and review status are all forms of management structure. You can think of this sort of structure as an auxiliary map over the content, which gives the manager's cut on what's important.

✦ **Inclusional structure** specifies which components include others. If you create an image reference in an HTML page, for example, you're putting a little piece of inclusional structure in the HTML that says, "Go find this picture and include it here." Your structure may know little or nothing about the structure of the included content itself.

Cross-Reference   In Chapter 24, "Working with Metadata," I revisit each of these types of structure as metadata because that's how you actually code them into content. In Chapter 30, "Designing Content Access Structures," I talk in detail about the concepts of hierarchy, index, cross-reference, and sequences.

Structure by scope

Structure, like format, also has scope, as the following list describes:

✦ **Structure below the radar:** You can certainly say that a period is a bit of divisional structure, but so what? Every content system that you encounter includes a level below which it is both infeasible and unnecessary to deal with structure. The level of granularity that you deal with depends on the system. In a public library, for example, which is a content system, the librarians don't care about the structure of each individual book. They neither notice nor encode this structure. Rather, they code the structure among books, put it on little cards (digital cards or paper ones), and make it available to visitors. On the other hand, if you are managing a database of short landmark descriptions that are destined to be used in a variety of travel brochures and sites, you may very well need to know and manage the structure of your content at the sentence level. In any case, you should understand that there is a level of the structure below which you need not concern yourself.

✦ **Inner structure:** The structure that you find represented within a content component is the inner structure. In my library example, you can say that each book is a component. The table of contents and index within each book are the inner structures within these components. Librarians today generally don't care about the table of contents within the books that they manage. But this doesn't mean that people never care about internal structure at all. Imagine a day when a librarian decides to make a master table of contents for the entire library. The book is still the basic component in the system; now, however, the tables of contents, which are still inner structures, are of interest. The librarian must now access and combine them. The key point with inner structure is that it's part of a component, stored within it, and always travels with it — whether you notice it or not.

✦ **Outer structure:** This structure is what relates one component to another. In the library example, the card catalog is the outer structure that organizes the cards (and the books they represent) into a useful system. You always care about outer structure. Interestingly, you may store the outer structure inside or outside the component. In the library, in fact, you store it both within and outside the component: One paper card with the catalog number for the book, or its equivalent, is inside every book, and one record is in the catalog database. In electronic systems, you often store outer structure outside the components themselves. For example, you commonly create a hierarchy that shows how each component is related to its peers and parents.

Summary

Structure is the key to managing content. Control the structure and you control the content and its publication, which, of course, is easier said than done, as the following list attests:

✦ Structure is often buried in the formatting of source content. Even if the formatting is consistent, which it often isn't, extracting the structure and making it explicit in a set of tags or database fields may prove difficult. Although consistent, the structure based on formatting alone may be ambiguous, incomplete, unintended, or inaccurate.

✦ Organizations go to war over competing structures. "We should list jobs by department." "No, we should list them by type." Although a good CMS enables you to lay multiple simultaneous structures over the same content, reaching an agreement on exactly how to divide content may prove a more daunting task.

✦ The content architect (or metator) has her hands full dividing undifferentiated information into chunks and tagging it for access, management, and inclusion. In addition, she must create hierarchies, indexes, cross-reference structures, and sequences that tie each chunk into a wider system. Although you can ignore structure below a certain level, that level may be far lower than you might like it to be for your current workload.

In the next chapter, I extend the idea of managing information and describe how you can manage computer functionality as just another form of content.

✦   ✦   ✦

Functionality Is Content, Too!

Since the time computers first entered organizations as accounting and manufacturing automation systems, the industry's seen a steady movement toward computer-based business processes. Today, a worker in an organization commonly spends her entire day doing business in front of a computer terminal. Inside an organization, business is largely electronic. Until recently, however, the movement of information between one organization and every other organization or individual was slow. Organizations and their partners, vendors, end users (customers, members, media contacts, and industry watchers), and government were often on different internal systems and had different processes and standards that did not easily translate across company lines. The basic connectivity that would enable outside computers to communicate with the organization's computers was largely absent—until the advent of the Web.

With the Web and the open standards it engenders, the way is now clear for making the transition to computer-based business processes among organizations and their partners and end users. The Web provides both the basic connectivity for end users and a *lingua franca* that enables different computer systems to communicate. Today, business functionality can extend far beyond the office to reach anyone with a computer and an Internet connection.

The way is clear, but the road is still rough. But as you see in this chapter, you can go a long way toward making all your business electronic by applying a content model to computer functionality.

What Is Functionality?

In the software world, a computer-based process is known as *functionality*. The functionality that a computer application offers casts a human process into a series of human-computer interactions using a user interface. From the standpoint of the organization, you can say that functionality is the way that you do business by using a computer.

Simply put, functionality is the stuff that you *do* on the computer. Unlike text, sound, pictures, and motion, which you experience (by reading, hearing, or seeing), you *do* functionality (by requesting or responding to something). A user interface represents functionality as a set of buttons, menus, dialog boxes, and other controls that give you a particular capability. Microsoft Word, for example, provides table functionality. The functionality is available from the Table menu at the top of the Word window. If you choose the Insert Table command from the Table menu, Word displays a dialog box full of buttons and other controls that enable you to specify how you want the Insert Table functionality to perform. On the Web, functionality is programming code that lives in a Web page or on a Web server. It does useful things such as performing calculations, allowing you to submit data via a form, carrying out financial transactions, verifying your credit card information, and so on.

In the annals of computing, the implementation of functionality has taken the following two major steps:

✦ Implementation has moved away from monolithic programs, where all the functionality is built-in, toward mix-and-match programs, where the functionality exists in small chunks known as *objects*.

✦ Implementation has moved away from applications whose single purpose is presenting functionality toward Web sites in which functionality and content intermingle and become hard to distinguish.

Taken together, these two steps enable you to treat functionality as a form of content.

Monolithic versus Mix-and-Match Functionality

In the early days of computing, all the functionality of an application was built into the application. The application's programmers coded all their own functionality from scratch. Today, much of the functionality that an application provides comes from outside the application itself. It's created and packaged into functionality objects that programmers then glue together into an application. For example, the spell-checking program that comes with Microsoft Word is also used for other Microsoft products, such as Excel and PowerPoint. Microsoft develops the spell-checking tool once, and then developers plug it into various products.

Computers entered the organization one process at a time. First came accounting and manufacturing systems. Then came spreadsheet and writing applications. Today hundreds of different types of computer applications are used in organizations. Because of the way they entered organizations, however, these applications were often unable to communicate with other applications; they duplicated functionality and couldn't easily integrate with each other. Today, because of this incompatibility, much of an organization's functionality is locked in silos of distinct applications that don't cooperate easily with one another.

Most newer applications have taken solid steps to break down the borders dividing applications. Communication standards (such as XML) provide a method to produce standard accepted maps among the different vocabularies and methods of various applications. Open programming standards such as the Application Programming Interface (API), object-oriented programming, and Web Services ensure that interoperability is built directly into the core of modern applications.

This capability in newer application models makes it far less important for you to know or care which application hosts a particular functionality. You merely need to know how to connect to and use the functionality that you need. Conversely, building complex applications that combine the best functionality and data from a variety of sources is becoming easier and faster than ever.

Today, programmers pack pieces of functionality into programming objects. Objects serve as a standard way to package and transfer functionality. Every object programmer knows exactly how to access the functionality in an object and to include the object in her own programs. In fact, many programs (especially those on the Web) do nothing more than draw together a set of previously created objects into a customized look-and-feel.

My notion of content components shares a lot with the concept of programming objects. In fact, content components serve the same basic function as programming objects. They both allow and provide a degree of separation between the person who creates them and the person who uses them. If I create a content component or a programming object, for example, I give it a set of attributes that enable it to take on a life of its own. Later users of the component or object find it and use it based on these attributes (that is, the metadata for components and properties and the methods for objects). They know that the component or object serves their purposes, and they don't need to look inside the component or object to see what it contains or how it works.

Cross-Reference   In Chapter 27, "Designing Content Types," in the section "Components are like objects," I provide more information on content components and their relation to objects.

Functionality that you package in objects can have the following characteristics:

✦ **Segmented:** Just like information, functionality can come in chunks as small as you like. (*Small* in the computer world means not taking up many bytes, not requiring much of the computer's processing power to run, and not requiring a lot of supporting hardware or software to run.)

✦ **Shared:** Just like information, functionality should be easy to locate and use apart from the application for which it was originally intended.

✦ **Encapsulated:** Just like information, using the functionality in your application or Web page doesn't require you to know how the functionality works; you need only know how to invoke it and what sort of results it delivers to you.

These three attributes of modern computer functionality pave the way for treating functionality as content.

Functionality Interspersed with Information

Before the multimedia age, the state-of-the-art computer application used a graphical user interface (GUI) consisting of buttons, menus, and a small set of other program controls that gave the user the capability to interact with a given program. The application's aesthetic was efficiency of space and parsimony of language. Programmers prided themselves on their ability to use as few pixels as possible to convey the meaning of each action. Long explanations and anything else considered content was relegated to the system documentation.

Multimedia applications began to overturn this aesthetic, and the Web destroyed it. After users stopped working with data and started working with content, the assumptions about how to create an application shifted, too. Interspersing text, pictures, and sounds with application functionality became not only acceptable, but routine. And although the small set of standard program controls never disappeared, a whole host of other controls appeared to deal with the interesting new needs of content applications. The text hyperlink and the hyperpicture, for example, weren't part of the classic GUI, but were added later to deal with the need to link from one piece of information to another.

In the old world, the premium was on parsimony. Applications had terse menus, well-ordered and trim dialog boxes, and buttons with one word or less (such as Del instead of Delete) on them. On the Web, a new aesthetic has taken hold. If the old style was Spartan, then the new one is Attic. On the Web, the menus can come with a paragraph of text. Dialog boxes are interspersed with pictures, ads, text, and links to other sites and applications all across the Web. The "buttons," in the form of linked images, stretch all the way across the screen. The result is a tremendous amount of mixing of content and functionality, and a blurring of which is which.

Where Functionality Sounds Like Information

The challenge:

#1: Create a Web site that offers music from all over the world—music recorded over the past seventy years, stored in academic archives and rarely heard outside of the communities where it was collected.

#2: Design the site so that this music may not only be found by scholars but is also accessible to teachers, students and world music fans.

The solution:

Create functionality that informs as well as guides the users as they navigate the site.

To do this, the CMS must be constructed to enable each piece of music to be tagged with meaningful information—and in turn, the Web site designed to utilize this data.

If one was cataloging well-known western music, it might be adequate to describe the title, performer, and ensemble and perhaps where and when it was recorded. Because our music was new to Western ears, we also chose to capture:

✦ Language and culture group

✦ Instrument—including the "family of instruments," the western name of the instrument, and the name of the instrument as it is known in the region where it was recorded

✦ Ensemble type

✦ Musical genre

We then created a user interface that made use of all this abundant metadata, creating a navigation system that enabled the user to drill down by region, country, instrument, and then narrow it further by genre.

One might navigate to South Africa—wind instruments—trumpets—and dance tunes—and discover recordings that feature the "Imbungu," a horn made of bamboo played by the Natal Zulu people.

The user could also move in the reverse direction. A horn fan, by drilling on wind instrument and then trumpet, could quickly discover all the tracks featuring trumpet-like instruments throughout the world. She would discover songs featuring the *baha* played in the West Indies, the *didjeridu* used by the Aboriginal people of northern Australia, the *imbungu* from South Africa, and the *wak'rapuku* from Peru.

Susan Golden, Golden Information Group (www.goldeninformationgroup.com)

In the older software applications, the programming code that creates functionality was packed deep inside executable files (EXEs). On the Web, you can type computer code directly into HTML (today's basic language that you use to create Web pages), just as you can any other content. Although this mixing of content and functionality has caused untold thousands of all-nighters by frustrated programmers (who pine for the good old days of neatly encapsulated programs), it's also provided the capability to create an entirely new way of thinking about an application. In the past, an application was a single, defined thing. Applications changed interface or functionality only once every year or two, when the creators made another product release. On the Web, not only can you change interface and functionality, but you're fully expected to do so. A good site delivers personalized functionality based on what it can infer about the user. The same functionality may show up in different contexts, and a particular function may even be represented with different controls, depending on the situation.

On the Web, functionality and content are mixed and matched to whatever extent the site owners can manage. It's a management issue. To mix and match content and functionality, you must be well organized. You must have a lot of structure in place that enables you to efficiently store and deliver your functionality where and when you need it. In short, you need a CMS.

Functionality objects enable you to treat functionality more like content. The new aesthetic of content-rich applications that provide personalized functionality to the user demands the use of functionality as content objects. Not coincidentally, you can use the same tools and processes to manage functionality as you do to manage content.

Managing Functionality Like Information

Content management consists of collecting, managing, and publishing content. I define *content* as information that you enhance with data and put to a particular use. I can now extend the definition of *content* to include functionality that you've packaged for reuse in objects or in blocks of programming code.

Cross-Reference You can find more information about the definition of content management in Chapter 6, "Understanding Content Management." In Chapter 1, "Defining Data, Information, and Content," you can find more information about the definition of content.

To illustrate this notion, look at a piece of information and a piece of functionality that you must manage:

Suppose that Wingnuts, Inc., wants to make people aware of upcoming marketing events. *People*, in this case, means staff, partners, and customers. *Making aware* means listing the appropriate events on the company's intranet, on the Internet, and in e-mail messages.

The following *events* functionality is available to Wingnuts in a programming object:

✦ Listing event descriptions

✦ Showing the details of a single event

✦ Creating a new event

✦ Deleting an event

The information that the object can provide for an event is as follows:

✦ A name

✦ A location

✦ A date

✦ A description

✦ A picture

✦ An owner

✦ Target customer type

✦ Marketing purpose

You can imagine that, for the different combinations of person and outlet (which refers to audience and publication in CMS-speak), you must use the appropriate set of functionality and information, as follows:

✦ **Staff** should be able to list, show detail, and create events on the Internet or intranet. If any staffers are the event owners, then they should be able to delete events, too. Staff shouldn't be bothered by e-mail and should see all the information associated with an event.

✦ **Partners** see events only on the Internet site and in e-mail messages. On the Internet, they should be able only to list and show details of events. The information that they see on the Internet shouldn't include the marketing purpose of the event. In e-mail, they should see only a list of events, but each list item should contain a link to a page on the Internet site that shows the event detail.

✦ **Customers** (like partners) see events only on the Internet site and in e-mail messages and should have only two options on the Web, list events and show event detail functions.

How much difference exists between the way that you must manage functionality and the way that you manage the information? First, notice that you *do* need to manage both the information and the functionality. You need to publish both in the same three publications (the intranet site, the Internet site, and e-mail messages). You must store both in a way that enables you to access a subset of their parts. Finally, you need to subject both to the same rules that determine which parts are available to whom and in what publication. In other words, both the functionality and the information need to be managed.

Both functionality and information are kinds of content that you should create, store, and access in such a way that you can target and format them appropriately for publication. With functionality, as with information, you can tackle the problem of managing multiple publications by hand or by using a CMS.

Publishing functionality on the Web

Because you bring functionality onto a Web page via blocks of text, you can treat that functionality as just another type of content to publish.

If you look inside a Web page, you see that everything in it is text. In HTML, for example, the following text block causes a button to appear on the page. After someone clicks it, the button initiates a search:

```
<input type=submit value=Search>
```

Functionality as Information at the BBC

Here at the British Broadcasting Corporation, we have sites that are mostly made up of static HTML pages with a few interactive elements such as voting and quiz engines, "have your say" user feedback systems, and competition entry forms. These interactive elements are usually brought in via server-side includes and controlled by configuration files and URL parameters. And of course, anything that is driven by a configuration file is a prime candidate for modeling as a piece of content.

One of my favorite examples is our competition system. In our content management system, editors create a *competition form* object that includes a question and some possible answers, state which answer is the correct one, and enter the closing date for the competition. The system then publishes the entry form, including a radio button for each competition answer, name, address, and phone number fields (as specified by the editor) onto a flat HTML page, and our publishing process sends that to our Web servers.

When an end user submits the competition entry form, the user's contact details and their answer are sent into the system and collected in a hidden area. On the competition's closing date, the answers are collected and processed to select a winner based on the user's details—and, of course, whether they chose the correct answer! A workflow is then started, which sends a message to the editor that created the competition object, ready to give the winner the happy news.

Brendan Quinn, Technical Architect, New Media, British Broadcasting Corporation (brendan. quinn@bbc.co.uk)

If you want the same button on ten pages, you simply include the same text block on each page.

The next text block calls a Java applet onto the page. An *applet* is a *miniapplication* or, as I call it in this book, a *functionality object*. The following code passes the applet all the information that it needs to do its job:

```
<applet code="Events.class" width="468" height="234">
<param name="User Type" value="Staff">
<param name="Pub" value="Intranet">
</applet>
```

The <applet> tag tells you which Java applet you want on the page, and the <param> tags pass the applet all the information that it needs to perform its functions correctly. In this case, you can probably guess that this applet lists events and can behave differently based on the user type and publication. You really see no difference between storing the block of text that invokes this applet and storing a block of text that describes an event. Moreover, no extra process or software is necessary to embed this block of functionality in a container that tells a CMS the purpose of functionality, to whom it applies, its status, and on what pages to include it. The same process that you use to create a content component from a block of information can also be used to create a component from a block of functionality definition. Whether it's delivering functionality or information onto a page matters not at all to a CMS.

Of course, I don't discuss a lot of details here, such as how you package and deploy the events applet and exactly how you go about storing complete code blocks versus dynamically filling in the correct parameters. But that's not my task at the moment. The point here is that if you store a functionality-generating text block and call it into publications, you're making it into just another kind of content component.

Even at the highest level, the similarities are solid. Whether you're managing information or functionality, you make an agreement with the creator or owner that enables you to capture her valuable creation; you devise a way to store what you collect; and you devise a way to deliver the creation electronically to the people who need it.

As you see in more detail throughout this book, a CMS provides the following capabilities—and more—for effectively managing and delivering functionality:

✦ **The CMS repository** provides a place to store the code chunks that provide the functionality.

✦ **The CMS metadata** facilities provide a way to tag functionality so that you can effectively store, locate, and select it for use in a particular page.

✦ **The CMS workflow** system provides a way to wrap the functionality in a process for reviewing and approving it. Many CMS systems actually supplant the source code management systems that programming organizations traditionally use.

✦ **The CMS templating system** provides the capability to locate a particular chunk of functionality on a particular page based on the user, or any other criteria that you want to use to place information on a page. In addition, the templating system enables you to customize the user interface of the functionality based on rules that you design. You may present the beginner's interface or the advanced interface, for example, based on the perceived computer savvy of the user.

In Chapter 14, "Working within the Organization," in the section "Tracking Information Flow in the Organization," I talk more about the way you can go about collecting functionality. In Chapter 11, "The Branches of Content Management," you find a number of examples of how you can use a CMS to manage e-business functionality.

Where information and functionality diverge

Where information and functionality management diverge is in the details, as the following list illustrates:

✦ To collect content, you work with authors or bulk content sources. To collect functionality, you work with application developers. Instead of making an agreement with a person to deliver a certain type of information, you make an agreement with a programmer to supply software code segments that create the functionality. You also make an agreement with a system administrator, who assures that, when the code runs some day, the database or other system that the code works with will be available and ready to respond.

✦ To manage content, you send it through a variety of workflows that ensure its accuracy, connection to other content (metadata), and relevance. To manage functionality, you send it through a variety of workflows to ensure that it works as planned (that is, with no bugs), is the most current version available, and can connect to its data sources.

✦ To publish content, you create templates that draw in relevant content chunks and navigation. You ensure that the content always makes sense relative to the other content that surrounds it. To publish functionality, you create templates that draw in and integrate code chunks with the surrounding code in the template. You ensure that any supporting code registers on the Web server and is ready for the code that you draw into templates to call it. You also ensure that all connections to other servers or data sources are enabled on the server.

Grandfather's Wisdom

When I began to consider content management, I got to thinking once again about my grandfather. He lived nearby and was regularly in my life until my mid-twenties. He came from a small farming community named Doksicy in rural Byelorussia. He scrabbled hard to survive, raise a family, and instill decent values in his children and grandchildren. He was a practical man, having learned that the values he believed in and passed on didn't mean much unless they were directly applied in people's daily lives. Years of battle against immediate and personal injustice had ground that understanding deep into his flesh.

He was a quiet man, and mostly he taught by behavior and action rather than words and instructions. But on the day I graduated from law school, my grandfather, then age 87, gave me a rare and memorable piece of direct verbal advice.

The graduation ceremony was over, and he gently took me away from the crowd and the rest of our family. "I want to talk to you for a minute," he said in his quiet accented voice. "I need to say something to you. But first I want to ask you something." He asked me what I had learned about justice in my years of what he proudly called *college*, which to him meant my entire seven years of higher education — four as an undergraduate at Columbia and three in law school at Yale. And he asked me what I hoped to accomplish working in the legal system. I hadn't expected the questions, but I answered him as best I could, my grandfather nodding his head slowly up and down as he listened carefully. Finally he smiled, and then said, "I have only one thing to tell you." He paused, smiled again, and looked directly into my eyes, "You should always remember, you didn't go to college to learn how to become stupid."

A full understanding of his meaning didn't come to me for years, until I had added some age, gained more experience in the world and served as a judge. What my grandfather was telling me was never to lose my common sense; that the knowledge I had gained in my education should not corrupt practical judgment, but be used to enhance it. He was also talking to me about justice, telling me that unless it's down to earth, common, as basic as bread, it's a mirage. He was telling me what he knew very well — that theory doesn't put food on the table. He was telling me that justice is not an abstraction, that the concept has no meaning unless it has real effect in people's lives.

To exist, justice must have content relevant and immediate to people's lives. And the content of justice must be managed so that it is delivered regularly, understandably, and effectively to all. Justice can't exist separate from us; it must touch us, flow through our daily lives, help us to live with ourselves and with each other.

Everything I've written about justice from the perspective and experience of a life in the justice system applies equally to content management and the discipline of information and content development, management, and delivery. The necessity for the effective development, organization, management, and delivery of the substance and form of information so that it is immediate, relevant, understandable, and usable, so that it has practical and effective meaning and value for the recipients of the information is the same. It is a common sense approach that is the same whatever the subject area of the information.

We should repeat what my grandfather said, get it firmly into our heads — all of us: "We didn't go to college to learn how to become stupid."

Donald J. Horowitz, former Superior Court Judge, State of Washington; Chair, Access to Justice Technology Bill of Rights Committee, Washington Access to Justice Board

By and large, these details fall below the radar of a CMS. The biggest hurdle to overcome is the change in mindset that your developers and organization may need to undergo. They, too, must come to believe that functionality, like information, is a kind of content to collect, manage, and publish.

Tip People frequently ask when they should put functionality code into the CMS repository and when they should not. If programmers are accustomed to a different or more sophisticated version control system and the CMS that you choose or build doesn't offer that level of sophistication, you may not want to put code in the repository.

Summary

Functionality is the capability to interact with a computer to perform a particular task. You create functionality by programming it using computer code and by presenting it in a user interface. Here are some things to keep in mind about modern functionality and how it relates to content:

✦ In the past functionality was trapped within massive programs; today it's segmented into lightweight objects and code blocks that you can share and reuse in a variety of contexts.

✦ In the past functionality stood separate from information; today it so intermixes with text, pictures, and other types of information that it is often difficult to determine just where the information ends and the functionality begins.

✦ In construction and in presentation, functionality shares so many of the attributes of content that you have no reason not to treat it as just another type of content.

In the next chapter, I end the discussion of what content is by handling a few of the more philosophical aspects of the nature of content.

✦　　✦　　✦

But What Is Content Really?

I've spoken with any number of people who believe that the basic agenda for content management as I lay it out in this book is flawed. You can't, they often say, separate content from its context without destroying its meaning. Furthermore, they contend, you can't just create information in little chunks, move it all around, and still expect it to communicate in the way the author intends it to! In addition, they say, the job of the author is never to create neutral information that can serve anyone at any time. Authors need to know with whom they're communicating and why. Finally, they contend, each kind of publication is different, and each demands its very own, very different approach to content. How can you possibly create a content chunk that can work just as well in any publication?

To all these objections, I say, "You're absolutely right! Luckily, that's not what a content management system is trying to do." If you expect your CMS to enable you to ignore context, communicate to everyone regardless of different perspectives, or ignore the differences between publications, then you can stop reading now. If, however, you expect your CMS to help you to understand and manage the various contexts that you expect to create, to communicate with the range of people whose perspectives you understand, and to create the best fit between your content and the particular publications that you want to produce, then read on.

In this chapter, I deal with the relationship between content and context and discuss some of the other deeper issues behind my notion of content, such as naming and knowledge.

Content, Context, and Meaning

Content, context, and meaning are tightly intertwined. Still, you can separate content and context and then automatically mix and match them later. Content and its context so intertwine, however, that you could just as well call content management *context management*.

As you look at a Web page, your eyes continually travel between the core content of the page and the other information that surrounds it. The surrounding items consist of *stuff* such as banners, footers, navigation bars, and background colors. The point of good design is to create a unified experience. The content and its surroundings need to blend so cleanly that you never find a reason to differentiate between them. Moreover, the surroundings deepen the meaning of the core content by putting it in the context of the whole site. The banner tells you who's presenting the content. The navigation bar tells you how the content you're viewing fits into the entire site. The background color sets a tone for the content. Without the surroundings, the content is seriously less meaningful. On the other hand, the content isn't *meaningless* without the surroundings. Rather, the content should still carry some significant chunk of meaning to a particular type of person. One small news clip, for example, taken apart from the complex page in which it's embedded, can still convey some amount of meaning to the reader. A good page adds context, and thus meaning, to content. Good content can stand outside such context and still communicate.

On the page, you seldom discriminate between content and context, but behind the scenes, the story is different. The surroundings are likely stored apart from the core content. On a dynamically generated site, milliseconds before you see the page in your browser, a CMS brings the content and surroundings together to form the unified page. In fact, the surroundings themselves are often created dynamically. The banner and background color, for example, may result from plain old HTML in a page template; the navigation may have been created by a program (perhaps an applet) that retrieves and formats an outline; and the footer may be stored in a separate HTML file and included as the page is built. Furthermore, the same content may find its way into a completely different set of surroundings; and the same surroundings may host different content each time they appear on-screen.

Add to this scenario the need to create more than just one Web site and the need to gather content from a wide base of authors and existing content sources. Now, the capability to discriminate clearly between content and the context within which it appears becomes mandatory. I'm not saying, however, that you want to ignore the context. You don't ignore context; you simply differentiate it from the content that it surrounds.

The concepts of content and content management that I'm presenting don't require that you ignore context (and the meaning that it imbues to content) — far from it. To deal with content management well, you must intimately understand and account for context. Traditionally, authors account for context intuitively or through preimposed conventions. To produce the book version of this body of content, for example, I must follow the style guide and other production requirements that my publisher supplies to me. If I were creating only a book, I could take these guidelines for granted. I'd subconsciously assume that a reader is turning pages, and I'd simply follow the formatting and structure rules supplied to me. All in all, I'd not pay much conscious attention to context.

I'm not, however, creating only a book. As I must (given my subject matter), I'm actually creating a CMS that can publish all or parts of this same body of content as a book, on a Web site, as e-mail messages, training materials, white papers, and so on. To take this CMS approach, I can't afford to lapse into unconsciousness about the context of my various publications. Rather, I must remain very conscious of, and explicitly account for, the requirements of the various contexts in which my content may be used. As one example among many, consider the name of what you're reading right now. Are you reading this paragraph as part of a book named *The Content Management Bible*, a Web page, a white paper, or an e-mail? How am I to account for your context as I write? Here's how I do it: As I name the work, instead of typing one word or another (such as "…this book…" or "…this course…"), in my text I enter the following tag where the name of this work should be:

```
<Variable Name="TheWork"/>
```

This tag says, "The name of the work goes in this spot." Later, as I create the site, the chapter, or the course, the appropriate name is filled in programmatically by my CMS publishing templates. So, far from ignoring context, I must pay close attention to it and explicitly account for it.

Make no mistake, accounting for context is much harder than ignoring it. On the other hand, when you go beyond a certain volume of information and publications, recasting your content by hand is more work than setting up a CMS that ensures that your various contexts (publications) are all as well served as possible.

In Chapter 8, "Knowing When You Need a CMS," in the section "Estimating Complexity," I provide a way to make a ballpark estimate of when the trouble involved in using content management becomes worth the effort.

Creating Context Rules

To mix and match content automatically, you must somehow reduce the complex relationship of content and context to a simple set of rules. You can then turn the rules into a program that a computer can understand and run. In fact, programming rules about context is the easy part compared to the effort it takes to understand your contexts well enough to think up the rules.

The Future of Content: Is Your Net Working?

When I was a small boy, my parents would ask what I'd like for my birthday, and because I was at the center of my universe, I usually knew exactly what I wanted. When I was 5 I wanted a bicycle; when I was 10 I wanted a calculator; when I was 15 I wanted a computer. But as I got older and my parents asked me the same question, I would answer: It depends. Depends on what? It depended on what I already had and how I could augment my current stash of toys. It depended on where my father's next business trip would take him—maybe he could bring me something exotic from a faraway place. Like most young people, my world was constantly changing, interconnected, and interdependent; and what I wanted became more relevant to my current mindset, my hobbies, and my relationships at that point in time. The context of my life situation drove the content of my answers—and the variables seemed endless.

In the history of computing, digital content is really in its infancy. Much like the way human civilization emerged from isolated villages into a globally connected world, content is going through the same kind of evolution at an accelerated pace. Data was the first digital content we understood. It was serial and one-dimensional. Then we moved on to documents, which were a bit more complex and captured specific business or technical information. However, both data and documents can quickly lose the bulk of their true meaning when taken out of context, much like what one would find in a real world scenario: A lone tire on the side of the road is presumed discarded and useless, but when viewed on a snazzy new Porsche, it's a thing of beauty and style. For anything in life or business today there are major interdependencies—information may be power, but context is king.

Digitally placing content within the right context is at the heart of content's future. And there is no one, right way of connecting content and context. We know the human brain does not process knowledge in a fixed, one-dimensional manner either. It depends. We slice and dice information from many angles depending on our vantage point, past experiences, time, space, and audience, and so on. Context and networking are the key.

To network content with context dynamically, we need to introduce the third c—code. Computer programs are the perfect, flexible bridges to provide the right content to the right person in the right time with the right context. And don't think this concept is that far off. It is happening even now with new Web applications that power the likes of Amazon, eBay, Yahoo, and Google. Think about it—there are no obvious lines drawn between content, context, and code on a typical Amazon page. A book could be used as the core content for sale, or otherwise used as context to support other book choices, DVD promotions, together with reviews, and other collaborative filtering scenarios. Content that is presented as a multidimensional entity that provides information relevant to the user's preferences—content networked in context—is the key to success.

Jack Jia, Sr. VP & Chief Technology Officer, Interwoven, Inc. (www.interwoven.com)

One of the reasons creating context rules is hard is that no standard set of rules exists to relate contexts to content. I don't believe that anyone can create a set of rules that state how context and content interact *in general*. Fortunately, you don't normally write general rules. Typically, in a content management project, you must write rules governing the specific and limited relationships among the following:

✦ A small set of content elements.

✦ A small set of audience types.

✦ A small set of publications where the audiences consume the content.

This task is hard, but not impossible. And you don't need to get it right the first time. In the electronic channels, you can continually try rules and see how people respond.

The rules behind the naming of this work, for example, are fairly simple. Each publication type bears a different name. In the XSL programs that I wrote to transform the content into various publications, I inserted the appropriate rule for whether to include — or how to include — certain types of content based on the type of publication I'm creating.

A more complex set of rules may create changes in the layout and content on a Web page based on the user. For such rules, you begin by stating in plain English what you want to happen for each kind of user. A social-services Web site, for example, may follow these rules:

✦ For contributors, I want the pages to feel solid, professional, and contain a medium amount of content.

✦ For the staff, I want the pages to look fun and intriguing but contain the full content.

✦ For clients in need of service, the pages must look accessible and easy to use; they should contain a minimum of content.

Next, you may want to specify the elements of the pages that the rules affect, driving the rules down a level of specificity, as follows:

✦ For contributors, use banner 1, navigation scheme 1, background 1, CSS style sheet 1, and the content elements 1, 2, 3, and 4.

✦ For staff, use banner 2, navigation scheme 2, background 2, CSS style sheet 2, and all content elements.

✦ For clients, use banner 3, navigation scheme 3, background 3, CSS style sheet 3, and the content elements 1 and 2 only.

Finally, you specify the programming-level rules that implement the intention of the plain English and the element level rules, as follows:

✦ Detect the referring domain and login status to determine the user type (1, 2, or 3).

✦ Redirect to the appropriate template (Tpl-1 for user type 1, Tpl-2 for type 2, and so on).

✦ In the templates, include banners, navigation areas, backgrounds, and style sheets by user type as specified in the CMS repository. Select content elements as specified in the user configuration database.

Although intentionally simple, this example indicates that you must first understand the contexts that you want to create for your content. You can then begin to reduce that understanding to a set of rules that programmers can implement to produce the appropriate context for your content and audiences.

Context Is Necessary Complexity

Because content is what needs to be managed, it seems obvious—tautological even—that in content management you should separate content from its various presentation formats. The idea, simply stated, is that because presentation (read: context) can change, it ought to be removed from consideration altogether; otherwise, managing content gets unnecessarily complex.

Complex, maybe. But unnecessarily so? No. Context is *necessary* complexity. Just because you *can* remove content from context doesn't mean you *should*. And you shouldn't. The disbelieving stare that a content architect will cast your way at the mere mention of disregarding presentation might suggest that this belief is strongly held indeed.

Maybe the reason that content architects rail against the idea that content can be completely removed from presentation is that so many people try to do just that. Just the other day, I was talking to a man who wanted to create a system that completely divorced content creation from presentation. He reasoned that because the presentation of, say, a resume could change, the best thing to do would be to build an online form in which people can type in resume-like information. He would *not*, however, let them see how the resume will be rendered on the Web or print page.

Suppose, however, unbeknownst to the resume writer, that the unseen presentation system were to include a summary review mode, which displayed just the first ten words following each head in each section of the resume. Knowing this, a writer would do well to make sure the first few words adequately summarize each section, and she might decide to chunk the sections differently as well. But if she doesn't know about the summary presentation context, both she and the employer may suffer—the applicant because she doesn't put her best foot forward, and the company because it might overlook a qualified applicant (or at least spend more effort than necessary figuring out who fits the bill). So you can't manage content effectively without knowledge of the context in which it will be used. Instead, the context as well as the content is what you need to manage. Rather than building a form that ignores how a resume will be presented, why not build a form that allows the user to cycle through all the presentations that the resumes may have? Then, rather than ignoring the context, which may very well result in one—or all—of the presentations looking pretty bad, the user can adjust her writing to the context she sees so that all are as well served as possible.

I said earlier in this chapter that you could just as well think of *content management* as *context management*. By now it should be evident that, to be successful, a CMS must manage the surrounding context of the content as well as manage the content itself. The context must always support and enhance the content that it surrounds. The trick to content management is to really know your content, its contexts (or publications), and its users (or audiences). If you know these three very well, the rules for how they relate follow naturally. If you prepare yourself to try, evaluate, and try again, your rules will continue to get better.

Content Organization Starts with Purpose

To turn information into content, you organize it around a *purpose*. That purpose leads to the schemes and categories into which you can fit the information. The purpose is the start of the organization process. The process is complete after you construct a full system of names and categories into which the content can fit.

To make it useful, you first must get your system organized. Every large city has a day-labor corner where people stand around at dawn looking for a day or two of work. Suppose that you go down to the day-labor corner with a bus and pick up 50 workers. As they ride together, they begin discussing what you may have in mind for them. Rumors and opinions fly through the uncoordinated mass of workers, but no one really knows. After you finally arrive at a cleared-off piece of land, you gather them together and give them a purpose: "We're going to build a house!" The unconnected mass of workers is now connected—they all know what their purpose is. But this knowledge is the beginning, not the end of the story. If you were to stop there, you wouldn't end up with much of a house.

Next, you bring out a plan that shows each person what to do and how. Some of the workers are plan readers, some are nailers, some are cutters, and some are measurers. All receive detailed instructions about how to carry out a given job. In addition to the overall purpose, each worker now has a specific purpose that feeds naturally into the overall purpose. Finally, you instruct the workers on how to interact. You give them instructions on exactly how to build each part of the house as a combination of lumber, saws, nails, plan readers, measurers, cutters, and nailers. Now, you can build a house!

You can think of the lumber in this story as information. Although a lot of effort has already gone into its creation (felling, milling, and so on), if lumber is just lying in a pile on the ground, it's of no use. Similarly, you must put a lot of effort into information just for it to exist. But information in a pile on someone's hard drive is of no use. To put it to use, you start with a purpose for it. That purpose begins to transform the way that you see the information. It's no longer just stuff. It's a means to the end that you intend. You can measure each piece of information against that purpose. But that's just the beginning. You can compare the construction workers to information workers who measure, cut, and nail the information into a set of content components that they all target toward your purpose. Without that purpose, your workers have no target; and without an organized approach, they can never reach the target.

Organizing your information into content involves the following activities, each of which can be a major undertaking:

✦ **Deciding on the right types of information** for your particular purpose. Just as the type of building influences the types of lumber that you choose, the purpose of your content system influences the kinds of information that you need.

✦ **Deciding on the right sorts of people** you need to process the information. Just as the types of workers vary by building, the type of staff that you need varies with the kinds of content you manage.

✦ **Understanding the information** you have, can buy, or can create. You don't build a house only from the lumber that you have lying around. Similarly, simply taking what information you already have and putting it into a system isn't enough. You also need to ask, "What information do I need that I don't have yet?"

✦ **Finding ways to standardize your information.** Standardization ensures that any two items of the same class are of the same basic structure. Just as a lumber mill cuts wood into standard shapes and sizes, so, too, do you need to mill information to standard types.

✦ **Finding ways to track and easily assemble your information.** Building a house involves plans and materials lists that specify what goes where and when. A CMS needs metadata and templates to help you manage information. You may, for example, need to add a status field to a video review to indicate when it's ready for display. A template reads the status field to decide whether to put the video review on a page.

Much of this book concerns the details of creating an organizational scheme for your content. Not the actual scheme to use—only you can figure that one out—but the principles and elements of schemes that you must pay attention to.

Content Is Named Information

Names provide simple, memorable, useful containers in which to collect and unify otherwise disparate pieces of information. You can look at content management as the art of adding names to information.

Content is information that you organize around a specific purpose for a specific use. The key to the organization and use of content is *naming*. I had this concept pounded into my head again a while back. It was me, my team, and our clients (a major dot-com company). We were preparing for the first big presentation to the executive staff on "What We've Been Doing." Lots of good ideas and bits of presentation were floating around, and as the presentation approached, we began to feel pretty good that we'd actually been doing something. Still, we had no unity to our approach. Different subgroups had simply merged their slides into a single PowerPoint file. After the last run-through, a half-hour before the big event, someone finally nailed it. "We need a name for this thing!" she said. A dawn-breaking eyebrow-raise spread through the room. Within minutes, we settled on Grace, one of the characters in our user scenarios, as the name of our presentation. Except that it wasn't just Grace. It was GRACE for *Great Relationships And Customer E*-tailing. The entire process crystallized, and we all suddenly knew how our individual parts related to the whole project. The name stuck instantly, and we went into that presentation not as a collection of separate projects stuck together by PowerPoint, but rather as a team all working together on GRACE. We got lucky in coming up with a concept for all the content bits we'd been working on after we already created them and just before presenting them to the end user, our client; a less risky strategy would have been to figure out our concept first so everyone could tailor his or her work to that concept. In either case, however, without that concept our presentation might have seemed like just a semi-organized collection of stuff rather than a coherent story.

Names provide simple, memorable, *useful* containers in which to collect and unify otherwise disparate pieces of information. That's why I say that content and content management are no more than discovering and successfully applying names to information.

Names have always had a strange and powerful hold on us. To this day, many people refuse to speak the name of a disease lest they contract it. In the Jewish tradition, the name of God may not be spoken. In Native American cultures, a person's true name is crafted to speak a deep truth about him. This true name is never used lightly. In modern consumer culture, the power of the name runs through the phenomenon of brand identity, where a well-recognized name is valued above all else in a company's portfolio of assets. Finally, the mystique and power of law, medicine, and many other professions derive from the set of names (in the form of professional jargon) that each uses and that no one else understands.

Why are names so powerful in human life? It is because names capture and contain a potentially vast amount of information in a simple-to-use form. Those who *know* the name hold a lot of understanding that others lack. Why are names so important to the study of content? For the very same reason: Names help you capture and contain a vast amount of information and make it simpler to use.

In effect, names *datatize* information; that is, they provide a small snippet that can stand in for the larger and less manageable whole chunk of information.

Playing the Name Game

I can't overemphasize the importance of coming up with commonly understood names on your content management project. Just about everything you deal with needs a name — publications, content types, elements, groups, processes, database fields — you name it! It's particularly challenging when different groups use different names for the same thing. Coming up with a standard name that everyone understands can be challenging.

If you do decide to change a name that is widely used, beware. If the old name is too entrenched, the new one just plain won't stick. I've experienced this "name-change resistance effect" first-hand in my personal life. Having recently married, I started using my husband's last name_that is, until I realized what it would take to really make the change. There were literally *dozens* of places I would need to change it: Social Security, driver's license, credit cards, insurance, investment and mortgage accounts, subscriptions, memberships, not to mention e-mail names, online accounts, and business contacts. It was simply easier to keep my old name rather than trying to update all the people and systems.

So, when you're playing the name game, be open to keeping the most widely adopted name-- even if it's not your favorite. As long as the majority of people know what it means, you'll save yourself a lot of change management headaches.

Rita Warren (a.k.a. Rita Michaels), ZiaContent, Inc. (www.ziacontent.com)

After you gather a standard set of names for your information, you can start to create simple rules and procedures for selecting and displaying content. These rules are just the simple sort that a data-loving computer can handle.

Naming, in fact, lies behind all the major topics that I discuss in this work, as the following list summarizes:

✦ I discuss the notion of breaking information into discrete content types and then *components*. The way that you do so is to invent names for the various types of content that you plan to manage and then create a set of individually named content components of that type. You can find more on components in Chapter 27, "Designing Content Types."

✦ I discuss *metadata*, which is no more than a set of names that you associate with components to help find, relate, and use them. You can find more on metadata in Chapter 24, "Working with Metadata."

✦ I discuss a *content domain*, which is simply a name for the unorganized universe of information that you're trying to control. You can find more on the subject of the content domain in Chapter 30, "Designing Content Access Structures."

✦ I discuss the *hierarchy*, which is no more than an outline of names on which to hang each of your components. You can find more on hierarchies in Chapter 30, "Designing Content Access Structures."

✦ I discuss *indexes*, which extract the significant names from your content and put them all in a well-organized list. You can find more on indexes in Chapter 30, "Designing Content Access Structures."

✦ I discuss *markup*, which is a standardized system of naming that you can apply to content to make it usable to anyone who knows the markup's naming system. You can find more on markup in Chapter 35, "What Are Content Markup Languages?"

✦ I discuss the *metatorial framework*, where you invent the system of names that you use throughout your system. You can find more on the metatorial framework in Chapter 24, "Working with Metadata."

✦ I discuss *content collection*, which is the process by which you assign names to previously unnamed information. You can find more on content collection throughout this book especially in Chapter 38, "Building Collection Systems."

✦ I discuss *repositories*, in which you pool the names and make them accessible in a database or other management structure. You can find more on repositories in Chapter 39, "Building Management Systems."

✦ I discuss *publications*, which are named subsets of the content that you control. You can find more on publications throughout this book especially in Chapter 26, "Designing Publications."

✦ I discuss *workflow*, which is a set of named processes for the flow of named content components between named preparation and delivery stages and named staff positions. You can find more on workflow in Chapter 33, "Designing Workflow and Staffing Models."

From Data to Wisdom

The contrast between data and information is what you really need to know to manage content. You take the methodologies of data processing and wrap them around human-created information to create information methodologies. Still, to put content in the context of the wider world of communication and meaning, I'd like to reach beyond the basics, moving from data, the most concrete communication, to wisdom, the most abstract.

Data is raw and discrete

Data is unprocessed and uninterpreted. Data is the starting place. All the interpretation and most of the meaning are yet to come. Think of the data behind a payroll system for a small company: 100 employee names, 1,000 deduction entries, 10,000 time entries, and 1,000,000 calculations before 1,000 numbers can go on 100 checks. The data here is a very large number of small, uncooked ingredients. You don't need to know or understand much about any particular datum. Only after they're cooked together into a savory stew (read: *processed*) do they yield a consequence: money transferred to an employee in the form of a paycheck. Now, in the payroll system as a whole, you find plenty of processing and interpretation, but it's all in the software and accounting staff, not in the data.

Data comes in *snippets*. Each snippet is complete unto itself and doesn't rely on its neighbors for its meaning. Each datum stands alone as one whole integer, string, bit, date, or what have you. Because they're discrete, you can disassociate each datum from the others, use it interchangeably with any other of the same type, and create any sort of complex processing routine that works on the data. Table 5-1 describes the more common types of data that you find in Microsoft's version 2000 of its SQL Server database.

Table 5-1: Common Data Types in the Microsoft SQL Server Database

Data type	Description
Binary	Fixed length binary data (8,000 bytes max)
Bit	Either 0 or 1 (minimum 1 byte)
Char	Fixed length, non-unicode data (8,000 bytes max)
Datetime	Date and time data with an accuracy of 3.33 ms. (8 bytes)
Decimal	Fixed precision data with a range of -10^{38} to 10^{38} -1 (5-17 bytes depending on the precision)
Float	Approximate precision data with a range of -1.79E+308 to 1.79E+308 (4-8 bytes)
Int	Integer data with a range of -2^{31} to 2^{31} - 1 (4 bytes)
Real	Approximate precision data with a range of -3.4E+38 to 3.4E+38 (4 bytes)
Smalldatetime	Date and time data with an accuracy of 1 minute (4 bytes)
Smallint	Integer data with a range of -2^{15} to 2^{15} - 1 (2 bytes)
SmallMoney	Currency value with a fixed scale of four (4 bytes)
Text	Variable length, non-unicode data (2^{31} - 1 bytes max)
Timestamp	A value unique to the database and updated whenever a column changes (8 bytes)
Varbinary	Variable length binary data (8,000 bytes max)
Varchar	Variable length, non-unicode data (8,000 bytes max)

You don't need to be a programmer to see that the form for each data type is strictly defined—so strictly, in fact, that if you try to disobey and call a *Char* a *Bit* or a *Real* an *Int*, your program can go down in flames. These discrete info snippets that I call data are collected into named buckets called *database fields*, or *columns*. The assumption that programmers must make to ensure that their programs work is that any operation that you can perform on one snippet you can perform on any other in the same bucket—or, in any other bucket of the same type, for that matter.

On the other hand, look at the *Text* data type. It's not nearly as restrictive as the others are. It can contain anything up to about a couple billion text characters. The data type *Binary* is even less restrictive; if you have bits and fewer than 8,000 bytes, you can put it in that bucket. So just about anything that you can make into bits, including stories, sound, pictures, and motion, you can put in a bucket and treat as data. Well, then, isn't everything that you communicate just data?

The answer to this question is *yes and no*. Yes, everything that you communicate is data, but no, it's not *just* data. If everything you communicate were *just* data, you'd have no need for this book, because the methods that are currently in use would prove adequate to deal with the richness of human communication. The difference is that, although you can represent any communication as data (a series of ones and zeros stored in a database), if that data is information, you can't assume that any operation you perform on one data snippet can also be performed on any other data snippet.

So although you can represent all communication as data, it isn't all *just* data. It's often much, much more. You can't expect to simply turn text or sound or images into data (by digitizing it) and then be done. Instead, you have to carefully dissect and then reconstruct the context of the information you have digitized so that its meaning remains.

Data is nondiscursive and out of context

By design, data is too raw and fragmented to ever form the basis of a conversation. In fact, the whole point of data is to make information so raw and discrete that no conversation is necessary. What this situation means is that a datum has no life of its own. It's always an object, never a subject. The same qualities that make the datum easy to work with preclude it from ever being interesting in itself.

A short list of data types can explain most of what a programmer needs to know to work successfully with data. Contrast this list with what you need to know to work with the following sentence: "Pick me up at eight and don't be late." You don't have a little table that you can look at to see what this sentence means. You could diagram the semantic definition of the sentence, but you still wouldn't know the context that says what the sentence is actually communicating (such as: *You were late last time and you're in big trouble if you're late again!*). In fact, without a certain set of life experiences (and perhaps a love of the Big Bopper — the younger among you, read on for an explanation), you'd stand little chance of making use of the sentence. The difference is that data is stripped of any connotations or context. It is content reduced to so simple a form that a dumb program can safely and expediently handle it. The sentence, on the other hand, is a rat's nest of connotation and context. The way to use a datum is closely prescribed and easily determined, if you simply know the type of the data. The way to *use* a sentence is nowhere prescribed, and, at best, you can only guess at it.

Content Management and Data Management

Content management: Is it really that much different than data management? Is structured data that different than structured content? You do realize that you need to tag the content and then wrap it in rules? Oh yes, you do!

At any rate, both systems require extensive resources to build and maintain (if you really want a high-quality capability), require analysis of the *"stuff"* (content or data), and finally, both require an application infrastructure that allows for management of the stuff. Before you can build either type of system, you have to know a lot about the "stuff" to be captured and managed. Think about it: To build a data system you have to spend time learning what data is important, how it is created, how it is used, who owns it, and who is allowed to use it. Then, given this information you can design the data tables, records, fields, rules, and so on. Well, to build a content management system you have to do a very similar kind of analysis that concludes in a similar type of design.

And, when the analysis is complete and the basic capability specified, you then need to determine how to manage the stuff, that is, design and implement the application infrastructure. For a data system, you allow for data creation, modification, deletion, version control, security, and on and on. Guess what — the same applies to content management. So think about it: Is the approach to building and managing your content management system that different than what you do to build your data management system? The bottom line is that there is no magic. To have a successful content system requires high-quality upfront work and continued backend maintenance and operations.

Rex C. "Trav" Stratton, Pacific Northwest Laboratories

The long and the short of data is that it's easy to work with, but it carries very little interpretation or meaning. Data reminds me of the story about the guy who loses his wallet on the north side of the street. As I come across him, it's already night, and he's looking carefully for his wallet — but on the south side of the street.

"Why are you looking over here?" I asked. "Didn't you lose your wallet on the other side?"

"I did," he replied. "But the light is better over here."

Information is processed and continuous

Data, at least, has a natural meaning somewhere in the region where I've defined it — a definition on which most people can more or less agree. The word *information*, on the other hand, has many meanings and no meaning at the same time. You can rightly call anything information, including data. Still, I'd like to try to nail this concept to a particular kind of communication. As I said in Chapter 1, I take information to mean all the common forms of recorded communication that you find around you: writing, recorded sound, images, video, and animations. You can see right away that information is fundamentally more messy than data.

Can a Computer Ever Interpret the Way a Human Does?

Content management is an attempt to model *knowledge* as it exists in a human brain, as opposed to *data* on a hard drive. Using tools like rules and structure, we attempt to make explicit our internal human interpretation of data, and we use computers to automatically process and present this interpretation.

But can a computer ever interpret the way that humans do? To get some idea of an answer, contrast the brain and modern computers. First, consider basic design. Computer hardware is designed to run through a sequence of simple instructions, each one chained to the next. Something known as the *central processing unit* (*CPU*) is the means through which a set of instructions runs to create a particular result. Computers are just entering the age of parallel processing, where a small set of processing units divide the labor to speed things up. Generally, however, all instructions flow through a small number (usually one) of processors.

The brain, on the other hand, is so massively parallel that it's in a wholly different league. By parallel, I mean that there are a large number of processors simultaneously working on the same "computation." Each neuronal processing unit (and the brain has billions of them) performs a very simple function — it sums the activation that its input neurons provide, and if they add up to enough activation, it fires some activation off to its output neurons. What supplies the complexities in this simple system are the enormous number of input and output connections that each neuron makes and the effect of chemicals in the brain that subtly, but decidedly, change the way that the activation cycle proceeds. So, in the brain, a huge number of very simple processors intensely interact to achieve a result. In most computers, just one or at most a few processors perform a set of instructions in a computer's CPU.

Enough of a difference exists between how computers work and how the brain works that many good thinkers conclude that computers can never hope to do what a brain can do. Maybe so, but I'd say that *what* computers do is more important than *how* they do it. To probe further, let's consider software.

At first, monolithic software programs ran from start to finish in a fairly predictable way. Today, an event-driven model, where some user action invokes a large set of interacting modules, replaces this original approach. A button click, for example, triggers a module, which triggers other modules, which trigger still other modules in a complex hierarchy of delegation of responsibility. Each module performs some tasks, changes some data, and then passes results up to the module that calls it. This process, in the most rudimentary way, mirrors what the brain does. Regions of the brain specialize in particular processes, and an entire interpretive cycle involves the collaboration of a variety of regions. Activation in one region triggers activation in allied regions, which trigger still other regions.

But here is where the comparison ends. Computers are missing a number of fundamentally important characteristics that define interpretation in the brain.

In computers, modules form a hierarchy, with the parent modules calling and controlling child modules. In the brain, no such simple hierarchy exists. Instead, a very tangled and recursive relationship exists between regions. You do find parent-child, and caller-called relationships, but that is just the beginning of the story. In the brain, activation spreads from one processing region to another. It's sometimes amplified, sometimes squelched, but it is never just on or off, as calling is in a computer program. Processing regions can feed back to the regions that called them and influence them in a way that would be considered backward in computers. In addition, in the brain, chemicals wash over all regions and change the way they work. There is no analog to the endocrine system in computer software. Finally, like the hardware they run on, computer programs are digital. They can represent only a set number of discrete states. Neurons, on the other hand are analog, meaning that they can represent an infinite number of states that are not discrete but rather grade naturally from one to the other. Regions of the brain do specialize like the objects in a large program, but no one can yet predict which regions participate in which events and, more to the point, no one knows whether anyone will ever be able to predict that participation. So much interconnection goes on that almost any region could end up recruited in the processing of any event, based on relationships between that event and existing interpretive structures. These differences certainly don't mean that the brain is unstructured or haphazard, although it is likely that serendipity and random connection do play a role. It does mean, however, that the structure of the brain and of the interpretation that the brain performs is fundamentally different from what computers are currently capable of doing.

Computers take a starting input and figure out a result by breaking the input into pieces, interpreting each, and then reassembling the piece-wise interpretation under the control of a guiding module. Brains leave the input to spread by itself based on the strength of its existing associations. The associations trigger regions to interact and create a coordinated state, which represents an interpretation. This process, I believe, is the basis for the human nature of interpretation. Of course, although you can conceive of two computers set up exactly the same way producing exactly the same output, this will never be true of brains.

Computers can't reproduce this sort of interpretation now, but could they ever? In theory, I think that they could. As experiments in neural networks show, even with their incompatible hardware, computer software can model (crudely) the sort of massive interconnection and mutual activation of the brain. Are computers the best system for modeling this process? I think not. I suspect that some other physical or biological machine is sure to come along that will be much better at modeling the kind of interpretation that people do.

To find a solid center for the concept of information, I use the same distinctions that I laid out for data.

Before you ever see a piece of information, someone's done a lot of work. Someone's formed a mental image of a concept to communicate. The person uses creativity and intellect to craft words, sounds, or images to suit the concept (thus crystallizing the concept). The person then records the information in some presentable format and finally publishes it in some way (even if only to leave it lying by the printer).

Information doesn't naturally come in distinct little buckets, all displaying the same structure, and all behaving the same way. You can still put methodologies, processes, and procedures in place to handle information. As you see throughout the rest of this book, however, we are all just beginning to learn how. Information tends to be continuous—similar to a conversation—with no standard start, end, or attributes. You disrupt this continuity at your own peril. If you break up information, you always run the risk of changing or losing the original intelligence and creativity that the information is meant to express.

Information is discursive and full of context

A piece of data is the end of a conversation, but a piece of information is the beginning. Douglas Adams understood this concept perfectly in his *Hitchhiker's Guide to the Galaxy*, where the universe's biggest computer finally ended the conversation on the meaning of life, the universe, and everything, with the response "42." The computer did respond to the question, but in typical computer fashion, whether or not the answer was correct, the answer itself was irrelevant to a human.

To possess a piece of data, you simply must remember it. To possess a piece of information, you must interpret it in the light of your current beliefs and knowledge. The information starts a conversation within your head that seeks to surmise what it is, what it means, and what effect it should have on you.

The fact that information is continuous and discursive doesn't imply that it's unstructured. In fact, as the rest of this book reveals, information can be quite well organized. It's just not the kind of straightforward organization that we are prepared for in our data technologies.

What do you need to know to work with the sentence, "Pick me up at eight and don't be late?" You certainly need to know what "work with" means. Are you supposed to translate it? Obey it? Put it to music? You may need to know who "me" is and to whom he or she is talking. You certainly need to know any number of other details that you find nowhere in the actual information. In fact, what you need to know to work with this information is nowhere near the actual information. If it exists, which it certainly may not, it lies embedded deep within your psyche in some dark recess. Miraculously, it's also instantly accessible. Suppose that I stand by the printer and say to each person who arrives, "Pick me up at eight and don't be late!" Most will probably say "Huh?" or "For what?" or even, "Oh, sorry, I must have forgotten. What did we have planned?" Now, suppose that I say the same thing but with a booming bass voice. The younger ones probably just scrunch their eyes and think, "One of those Bob-isms" (which is one of those things that yours truly is known for among friends). The older ones smile and the bolder of them may actually do the work intended by Jiles Perry Richardson, otherwise known as The Big Bopper, in his song "Chantilly Lace" and respond, "Oooo, Baby, you *know* what I like!"

So, information requires a Web of unstated relationships — a context — to use. Data has these relationships stripped out. Some say that the United States is a low-context culture — that is, in the United States, people use a lot of words and make relatively few assumptions about what the other person knows or understands before talking. Japan, on the other hand, is considered a high-context culture, where most people assume, in no uncertain terms, that you're fully steeped in a deep understanding. The smallest gesture ought to invoke from within you a world of associations and appropriate behaviors. But even in the United States, people spend a lifetime learning to hear what isn't said.

Although data is a lot easier to pin down and discuss, information is the normal mode of life. Data is the newcomer. The quintessential Western idea that you can quantify and categorize meaning isn't normal even for the most scientifically minded, northern European, white, middle-aged male. You must learn it. Computer applications that work with data are commonplace. But as anyone who's worked much with computers can tell you, you must change your mindset to match the computer's total ignorance of what you intend and the context in which you're performing an action (not to mention the computer's lack of basic politeness). Why? The computer's lack of context is simply leaking through to the user interface. Computers are the ultimate low-context culture. Computers force you to shed your entire context and leave nothing unsaid.

Computers, perhaps, were invented to work with data, but they're now fully pointed at information. Why? Because users have collectively gotten to the point where they can begin to see the possibility of computers moving toward human mindsets rather than people always going to theirs. Users want computers capable of working with information and not just data.

The information technology (IT) departments of the world, whose names by rights should be data technology departments, are staffed with people who know exceedingly well how to create and run data systems. As the specter of information rises before them in all of its dirty complexity, human interference, and esthetic considerations, however, they shrink back. They respond by either mistreating information as data (thus denying or ignoring the problem) or by throwing their hands up in disgust and declaring the project impossible. And, from their perspective, it is. These people know how to reduce information to a strictly defined set of small, discrete buckets. To succeed in an information project, however, IT professionals need to change perspective and understand how computers can facilitate the creation and handling of continuous, context-rich, intensely human information. Having learned the data craft myself, I'm the last to condemn it. The reductionist methodology created all of science. In particular, it was responsible for the vast power of computers. Only now are people beginning to use that power to grasp and harness information (and not just data) by using computers.

Computers deal with facts very well because facts fit the basic way that computers work — put the world into discrete little buckets and work on these buckets by using long chains of very simple instructions. I suspect that a basic overhaul in this model is in the offing. (People seem to be culturally and technologically ready.) In fact, the very concerns that I discuss in this book may drive the overhaul. Until then, you can expect that whatever people make computers do, the computers are sure to do it with the same lack of subtlety that they now exhibit. The best we can do today is to try to make the best fit between the constraints of information and the capabilities of computers.

In summary, information is fundamentally messier than data. It contains enough human qualities to make it hard to parse, obscure in its interpretation, and complex to handle and use. Successfully working with it requires a different mentality and skill set. But when has that sort of thing ever stopped us before?

The Wisdom Web

Wisdom is a funny thing. It's the highest human achievement in learning and interpretation. At the same time, it's so rarefied and abstract that it transcends the complexity of language and knowledge systems. Wisdom contains a distilled and simplified logic that's been codified over the ages in a variety of easy-to-learn and use systems. Take a look at two of these codified wisdom systems, for example: tarot and astrology. You find two schools of thought regarding these types of systems. The first says that they're baseless pseudo sciences that have no part in a modern skeptic's life. The second says that they're mystical understandings, somehow tied to universal forces beyond human apprehension. I like a third alternative: These systems represent true wisdom concerning the human condition that's been distilled and systematized over the ages and is now wrapped in an easily remembered, presented, and consumed form.

Look first at astrology. No mysterious connection need exist between the stars and your birthday for astrology to be called a wisdom system. Further, even if your birthday has nothing to do with your personality (I happen to believe it does not), there is wisdom in astrology. The wisdom in astrology concerns human personality. You find in astrology elements of all the types that you meet in life. The basic personality traits combine in natural clusters. These clusters, which can make very subtle psychological distinctions in their combination, form a very comprehensive and precise profile of a person. A vast amount of interpretation is also captured and simply presented in the advice that astrology offers about the mixing of personality types in relationships. The cosmological nomenclature need not be literally true for the system to work. It need only serve as a platform to organize, systematize, and access a set of personality profiles. The profiles need not be "true" characterizations of a person to be of value. Rather, their value comes from their capability to provide recognizable personality types that people can relate to and use to understand themselves and others. The heavens do not have to be the determinants of personality to provide a subtle metaphor for understanding it. The only real relationship that needs to inhere between the heavens and your personality is that the two systems have about the same degree of subtlety and interrelation. Mapping from the heavens, then, to your personality (or even your fate), is possible because the two have comparable complexity. It is interesting in as much as the connections in one system bring up useful connections in the other.

Now take tarot. There does not need to be anything mystical about it to call it a wisdom system. Even if the particular cards you draw are random (I happen to believe they are), there is wisdom here. The wisdom in tarot concerns the human condition in general. The cards of a tarot deck represent the archetypal sorts of situations, characters, and turns of events that one confronts in life. The user arranges a set of these cards in response to a question. The cards entreat you to compare life's archetypes against the situation you present. The cards that you draw and their relative positions are a heuristic (an aid to learning, discovery, or problem-solving), dredging up fears, possibilities, and deeper interpretations of a situation than you may arrive at alone. Tarot, viewed this way, isn't fortune telling; rather it's a simple way to help you to a fuller analysis of the possibilities in any unknown situation. The cards that you draw are not the answer; they're the cues that lead you to your own answer.

If you extract the knowledge of the human condition that is embedded in either of these two systems (and many others, to be sure) from the mystical claims, you have some very workable content. It is a matter of debate whether many wisdom systems are "true." That's a debate I don't even need to touch. Whether a particular wisdom system is true or not, it might still have a set of well-organized concepts that it can deliver in a way that provokes thought and change in a person's life.

Philosophy aside, I would like to make another kind of point. How do these statements about wisdom systems involve the Web? The distilled and simple logic of many wisdom systems make them easy targets for a Web site. And indeed, most already have sites that you can visit to use them. But what if you combined a number of these systems in a single site that could lead you through the right part of each system to guide you to a comprehensive examination of your issue? The secret to doing so is to create a metawisdom system that codifies how to incorporate and weight the various systems toward the solution to the issue that you present.

Say, for example, you're having a row with your spouse and want to know the cause and solution, so you visit www.whycantwegetalong.com. After taking you through the requisite caveat page telling you that this process is a heuristic and not a predictive one, the site may help you characterize your issue as to how it concerns two conflicting personalities put together in a tough life situation. You further define the personalities and the life situation, and the site then accesses the astrological wisdom base (to provide personality insights) and deals out a few random cards from the tarot deck along with a suggested interpretation for the cards and their positions. The site tracks the tarot reading and the personality profiles you've generated, asks you to provide your own interpretation, and leads you through the process of sorting all this out to arrive at a set of possible solutions to your problem.

A curious paradox is that you can unlink wisdom, in this form, from human interpretation and treat it in a way that you normally treat data. Just as in data-processing applications, this wisdom application chunks wisdom into little buckets and automates their processing and presentation. Just as in data systems, the interpretation is completely in the hands of the operator, not the computer.

Knowledge and wisdom can be information

Data are material facts; information is matter-of-fact; knowledge is a matter of dispute; and wisdom is nonmaterial. Although both data and information have a face value, you must synthesize and extract knowledge and wisdom from a wealth of communication and direct experience.

"*Knowledge*," according to Merriam-Webster OnLine (www.m-w.com) is as follows: "(1): the fact or condition of knowing something with familiarity gained through experience or association . . .."

Knowledge, by this definition, is inside a person. It is a mental state, not a communication. So, although today's computers can conceivably store information, they can't store knowledge. But why can't computers store knowledge if books can? Books can't have a mental state any more than computers can, but aren't books where people currently store the world's knowledge?

Both books and computers store information. If information that the book presents to a person inspires a state of knowledge, then great — the storage and communication were successful. The communication from the book or computer screen doesn't cause the knowledge to happen; rather, the person in conversation with the communication causes knowledge to happen.

If you don't buy this argument, I've proven my point. I'm trying my hardest to give you some knowledge that I have (or think I do). Despite my best efforts, however, I can't do it. To my mind, codified knowledge (that is, knowledge that's written or otherwise recorded) is simply information—and that's a good thing, because it means that codified knowledge is manageable using the same techniques as you use for information. The act of knowledge, on the other hand, is an interpretive act and is, at least for the moment, reserved for humans and maybe a few animals.

Knowledge happens within a *domain*. I might know about cars, information, human nature, or God. Wisdom, on the other hand, is knowledge that transcends domains.

Again, according to Merriam-Webster OnLine (www.m-w.com), wisdom is defined as follows:

> a: accumulated philosophic or scientific learning : KNOWLEDGE b: ability to discern inner qualities and relationships : INSIGHT c: good sense : JUDGMENT d: generally accepted belief...

Wisdom encompasses discerning inner qualities, exceptional insight, and good sense. Wisdom is a highly synthetic process that's beyond simple knowledge. Consider any of the following pieces of folk wisdom:

✦ A stitch in time saves nine.

✦ Necessity is the mother of invention.

✦ Every cloud has a silver lining.

What's interesting about these wise sayings is that, although their literal meanings may be true, their bigger truths transcend the bounds of their subject matter and provide insight into the universe at large.

Wisdom isn't just a statement of fact, as is data. It's not a matter-of-fact statement, as is information. It's not a mental state of understanding, as knowledge is. Rather, it's an ultimately synthetic act where one expresses deep understanding, simply and universally. Consider these other wise statements:

✦ The opposite of a correct statement is a false statement. But the opposite of a profound truth may well be another profound truth. (*Niels Bohr*)

✦ When we try to pick out anything by itself, we find it hitched to everything else in the universe. (*John Muir*)

✦ I do not know whether I was then a man dreaming I was a butterfly, or whether I am now a butterfly dreaming I am a man. (*Chang-tzu*)

Each distills and synthesizes vast realms of knowledge into simple statements. Often using contradiction to capture and coalesce worlds, they pack as much as is humanly possible into a few words.

Like codified knowledge, you can treat codified wisdom as information. After you record it, wisdom functions the same as any other information (even if it's pretty tinny if you compare it to live communication with a wise person). The works of Lao Tzu, Socrates, or (in my personal opinion) Akira Kurasawa (the Japanese filmmaker) are wise indeed, but you can still collect, store, and distribute them as if they were just information.

Why Does Text Get All of the Attention?

Did you ever notice that when people (including me) talk about the promise and future of computers they include sound, video, animation, and other fun stuff, but how they only actually go into detail about text? Although tremendous growth has occurred in the amount and sophistication of electronic sound and images, our understanding of how to categorize and find them remains piddling at best. Why is that? Why is it that it is so much easier to talk about text as content — useful, organized information — and so much harder to talk about other sorts of media in the same way?

I'll never forget the time my wife and I visited the studio of a friend's husband. He had worked his way up through the ranks in Los Angeles and was now the main sound guy on a TV series, which I had never heard of, about a car that could do just about anything. He showed us a bevy of late model, very expensive software and hardware for getting just about anything you might want out of a sound. He could decompose a sound into its constituent wave forms, pull it apart, mix it precisely with other sound components and create the exact sound of fist against flesh from noises that came from nothing remotely human.

He showed us the way he took the director's vague instructions for backgrounds and effects and turned them into an audio tapestry that was behind as well as in support of every movement in the show. It seemed that he had the art of sound down so well that nothing was beyond his reach.

Then, being who I am, I naturally asked him, "So how do you catalog and find the sounds that you start with?" His answer stood in the starkest contrast to the advanced technology he had been previously demonstrating. "Oh, I just know." He said. "I have a few collections of sounds that I know pretty well, and I just work from there." I was surprised. "No indexes, no searching for just the right effect through enormous catalogs. *No table of contents*?" I returned. "Not really," he said. "There are a few things like that, but most of us work from feel. We know sound and know where to look for it. There is no master directory of sound that you can just look in. Besides," he said, "it's an art, not something you can just pick up from a book or something!"

Sound is possibly the most organized (in my sense of the word) of the media arts. Audio technicians have vast libraries of sound (both effects and music) that can be categorized, stored, and retrieved. They have developed vocabularies for precisely describing sounds and their characteristics. Video, by comparison, can also be highly categorical (including aspects like framing, focal length, focus, lighting, and movement), but the content of a particular video scene (no matter how formulaic a car chase may seem) is always unique. You can't drop a sequence from one movie seamlessly into another, but you may be able to re-use an audio clip of screeching tires in many different movies.

Yet despite the specialized techniques and vocabulary of the audio and video production worlds, ultimately a director is trying to achieve an emotional effect that may be difficult to put into words, let alone name and categorize it. This mirrors the way most people, either as producers or consumers, have approached media to date — from the intuitive, nonlinguistic side. When it is right, it just feels right. Artists go only so far in explaining or categorizing their work. After that, it either works or it doesn't. Fortunately for some, and unfortunately for others, that is changing, and will continue to change. As more and more people are using computers to turn art into content, artists will have to face that ways to name and categorize art will continue to advance against intuition.

Is this bad? I wouldn't be so bold as to say no. What I would contend, however, is that the two modes of being, the rational/linguistic and the intuitive/nonlinguistic are parts of a wider human unity that do not have to be pitted against each other. Just as the notes on a musical score (a naming and categorization system) help the musician achieve intuition into the art of music, other naming and categorization systems can help other artists achieve the same. And, of course, the reverse is true. As any good taxonomist will tell you, when you have gotten to just the right set of categories, it just feels right!

So, why then do most people focus on naming and categorizing text to the exclusion of other media?

✦ **Text is codified language.** Language is our main medium for organizing and communicating experience. We use language to name and categorize. No wonder it lends itself to this sort of analysis.

✦ **The light is better on the text side of the street.** With 1,500 years of experience, text categorizers are a bit ahead of the other communication disciplines.

Let me dive deeper into these arguments.

Text is codified language

In his fascinating book *Breaking the Maya Code,* Michael Coe explains in detail how written language has been characterized in a variety of ways, but now agreed to be simply codified language:

> Writing is speech put in visible form, in such a way that any user instructed in its conventions can reconstruct the vocal message. All linguists are agreed on this, and have been for a long time, but it hasn't always been this way.

Of course, codifying language is not as simple as just writing down what you say. I was rudely reminded of this in writing this book. I had delivered much of this material as lectures. I figured that if I had the lectures transcribed, I would have a fair start on the writing. I was sadly mistaken. Rather than having a composition whose content was the same as the lecture, I had a jumble of half sentences that only vaguely resembled the composition I had envisioned. I ended up starting the composition from scratch. The spoken word and the written word are two distinct media.

Transcription problems aside, it is clear that text has the jump on other media types when it comes to naming and categorization. What are names and categories if they are not text? This is not to say that it is easy to categorize text, just that it takes no big conceptual stretch to do it. A fair amount of evidence, in fact, supports the claim that the brain process behind the sort of naming and categorizing that we are aiming for is linguistically based.

To index a book, you scan it for important words and concepts (read *names* and *categories*). The words and concepts are usually explicit in the text — they are words and phrases that you can pull out and attach page numbers to. Of course, good indexers can pull out words and phrases that are implicit in the text, but even these terms are never far from the surface of the words. Now consider indexing a set of pictures. You would most likely invent a set of descriptive names and categories first, and then apply them to the pictures. None of the words would be explicit in the pictures; abstraction and interpretation would always be needed on your part to associate a picture with a word. Furthermore, your audience would have to have a basic understanding of keywording—or you would have to educate them about how the words you chose relate to picture qualities. Stock photography companies like Getty Images (www.gettyimages.com) and Corbis (www.corbis.com) have tackled just this task; try entering abstract search concepts such as *intellectual property* or *escape* on their sites to appreciate the complexity of applying even the most basic organizational methods to nontext information.

Text has the lead

Pictures and sound have existed a lot longer than text. They are embedded much more deeply into the fabric of humanity than is text. On the other hand, reason (another word for the process of naming and categorizing the universe) developed hand in hand with text. It's hard to know exactly how organized we were before writing because little record has been left. We do get a glimpse from the Greeks. When they first learned to write, they spent a lot of time writing about what they did when they could not write. We know from their early writings that, for the Greeks at least, reason was verbal before it was written. It was natural for the Greeks to extend their reasoning skills from verbal to written form. In these western roots, as well as from other traditions, writing has been used to name and categorize the world. Confucius did nothing if he did not divide the known universe of social interactions into a rigorous set of categories that his followers could easily digest and understand.

It is no surprise, then, that text has a well-established tradition of being named and categorized that the other media types do not share. Consider again the indexing of a book. Some professional indexers do nothing but name and categorize text all day long. Millions of librarians and archivists spend all of their time making catalogs of written works. Published writing has rigorous, time-honed methodologies in place for naming and categorizing within and between works.

Now look again at the issue of indexing a set of pictures. It's more difficult to know where to start. Do you index them by the colors used? By the subject matter? By the objects shown in the pictures? No entrenched standards exist, and in practice, stock photo agencies use a variety of categorization schemes—by photographer or company, subject, concept, location, photographic effect, color depth, and licensing to name a few. But these systems are invented by each company or organization, and then only by those large enough to undertake this huge effort. There is no accepted way and few rules available to help make creating a photo index a universal undertaking.

As time goes on our ability to index and retrieve media will increase. A number of efforts are under way, for example, to analyze and index video based on scene transitions and to try and discern what the central elements are in each frame. In these studies, the researchers learn as much about how we construct meaning from images as they do about how to extract meaning from them in order to index them. Natural speech-recognition tools that recognize and index the spoken word, albeit imperfect, are also commercially available. But for the time being, indexing the meaningful elements in text is way in the lead. So, I am hoping you will forgive me if I claim that content is all media, but I focus mainly on text.

Summary

Computers have no problem with data. I can add little to the codified knowledge or wisdom about how computers can better deal with these bucketized facts. On the other hand, I *do* try to add to our codified knowledge (not quite wisdom, I fear) about how computers can work with information. Keep these ideas in mind as you make your way through the less philosophical aspects of content management:

✦ Although the act of creation and interpretation must remain for the present in the hands of humans, you can, after you create it, use the computer's considerable power to manage the information as well as its codified context and interpretation.

✦ Your job as a content manager is to organize the mass of information and functionality with which you're presented into a cohesive body of well-structured content.

✦ You are ahead in your daunting task if you understand that you're in the business of choosing and applying names. These names reduce the complexities of context, interpretation, and meaning to the kind of data (in this case, *metadata*) that a computer can handle.

No one's asking you to make your computer become creative (well, hardly anyone). Everyone's asking you to get your computer to deal with vast quantities of information—to make that information accessible and to interweave it with other related information. In the next chapter, I leave the subject of content and focus on the main event of this book: content management.

What Is Content Management?

Understanding Content Management

I assume that most people come to this book because they want to know how to make large and well-managed Web sites. You can learn that here. In the process, I hope that you also find that content management isn't about Web sites, although that's where it's mostly practiced today.

Content management is about gaining control over the creation and distribution of information and functionality. It's about knowing what value you have to offer, who wants what parts of that value, and how they want you to deliver it. Knowing that, you can build a CMS machine to help you get the right stuff to the right people in the right way.

In this chapter, I put some definition around the phrase *content management*, relate it to the major streams of thought about what CM is, relate it to the very young industry with the same name, and link it to some of the Web technologies that you may now be using to deal with sites that have gotten out of control.

Defining Content Management

Like most things that have complexity, Content Management means different things to different people. Where you sit may determine where you stand — that is, your job probably influences what you think content management is, does, and should do.

The ways that people think of content management breaks down into several streams that I'll describe here and that you'll see recur throughout this book. Reasonable minds may disagree with how I break this down, but my theory has (at least!) one undeniable nugget of truth: More than anything else, CM is a process of getting organized about creating your publications. From hard experience, I can say that if you don't put some thinking behind any system for creating publications of moderate or greater complexity, you're in for some long, painful days with possibly little to show for it.

You organize around content management in any successful CM project, whether organically or explicitly, as part of a well-defined planning process. Imagine that you're part of a cross-company team that's been tasked with coming up with a strategy for getting content to customers. How would the team get started? First someone might ask, "What do we want this initiative to do for us?" That's the idea that content management delivers *business value*. Someone else might state, "We need to figure out what hardware and software it will take to pull this off." That's the idea of the CM *infrastructure and technology*. A third person says, "We have to get a rag-tag bunch of authors to create information that is good enough to produce a Web site and a print catalog." That's the idea of the CM *process*. All these perspectives are correct and all will eventually have to be taken into account. In doing so, you can either hope that these key concepts eventually come to the surface, or you can build a process that is sure to include them. Each of these angles on CM is all about getting organized. You need CM when the job of delivering information is too big and too important to do without structure.

If you've previously heard about content management, it's most likely because you have connections to a large Web-development project. Today, that's where most of the interest and activity lies. As the Web moved past small, informally designed sites and into large, rapidly changing sites, the need for strong management tools became pressing. Product companies moved in to address this need and called their offerings *content management systems* (CMSs). If your only problem is to create and maintain a large Web site, you have reason enough to want the strict structure and formal procedures of a CMS. CMS helps you get and stay organized so that your site can grow and change quickly while maintaining high quality. The Web, however, is simply one of many outlets for information that must be organized. And as the amount of information sharing between these outlets grows, the desire for an organized approach becomes an absolute need.

I've been giving talks, running seminars, and teaching classes on content management for the last five years. I often ask my audiences what publications they're responsible for. In the past, the large majority of the responses were "Web site only." Perhaps half the respondents today, however, say, "Multiple Web sites, print publications, and anything else that we can create from the same information."

This broadening of the role of content management in the organization is significant. Although content management may have come to the fore as a way to manage large Web sites, to my mind that is just a byproduct of what content management can do for an organization. The important perspectives on what content management does for an organization serve as definitions of what content management is. Specifically:

✦ From a business goals perspective, CM distributes business value.

✦ From an analysis perspective, CM balances organizational forces.

✦ From a professional perspective, CM combines content-related disciplines.

✦ From a process perspective, CM collects, manages, and publishes information.

✦ From a technical perspective, CM is a technical infrastructure.

Content management is and does all these things. The trick is making sure that whatever system you create is organized enough to bring them all together.

In this chapter I discuss each of these perspectives, in turn. And, because content management means different things to different people, you'll also find a number of sidebars in this chapter where content management professionals share their perspectives as well.

What Is Content Management?

One of the most confusing things I have to deal with is the question of what is content management. Many people think of content management as the technology (tools) — and it is — but it is much more than just the technology. Content management also has a lot to do with people. People use the technology and make content management happen. A successful content management initiative is about more than selecting and implementing effective technology; it is about changing the way people work, helping people to overcome resistance to the changes, and ensuring that you support the authors in the way they work. Failing to focus on the people may diminish the success of your initiative.

Many people think of content management as Web content management — and it is about Web content management — but Web content may be only one of the types of information you need to manage. Most organizations need to manage both paper and Web, and they often also manage common content between the mediums. Sometimes this is known as enterprise content management.

Often content management is only perceived as the management of the content, but effective content management begins with authoring and finishes with delivery. You need to author your content effectively for effective storage, retrieval, and reuse. If you don't take the time to effectively structure your content before you store it, you will not realize the full benefit of a content management system and methodology. Ensuring that you can also deliver the content in the form that is most appropriate to the user is also important.

So what is content management? Effective content management is a repeatable method of identifying all content requirements up front, creating consistently structured content for reuse, managing that content in a definitive source, and assembling content on demand to meet your customers' needs.

Ann Rockley, The Rockley Group (www.rockley.com)

CM Is Distributing Business Value

At the highest level, content management is the process behind matching what *you* have to what *they* want. You're an organization with information and functionality of value. They're a set of definable audiences who want that value. Content management consists of the processes and tools behind the distribution of that value.

Distributing information of value means that you first must figure out what information you have that is valuable. This statement may seem obvious, but it reaches to the core of the organization's aims, which determine what information of value it wants to deliver. For example, if your organization aims to promote a political agenda, then arguments to constituents in the form of text, video, sound, and image are very valuable. If you work for a pharmaceutical firm, information you provide to regulators to facilitate approval of your new drug is valuable. For a school it might be curricula for teachers; for a manufacturer it might be up-to-date product specifications for engineers and subcontractors; for an HR department if could be benefits information for employees. In every case, what is important depends on what your organization is trying to accomplish. This is true at all levels of organization, from enterprise to department in a local subsidiary.

It's useful to think of a singular set of information goals for an organization. But in reality organizations often have multiple sets of organizational goals for delivering information value, some of which may overlap with others, and some of which have little apparent overlap except to make the organization run smoothly and efficiently. For example, a pharmaceutical firm might need to deliver information to government regulators, but it might also want to deliver some of the same information to a very different but important audience: investors. It may also provide valuable product information to potential customers, such as doctors and medical insurers; and it probably also has an HR department that distributes benefits information that is valuable to employees. All this information is valuable; the information provided to one audience may be somewhat similar to information provided to another (government regulators and investors) or completely dissimilar (HR information and customer information). Managing any or all these kinds of information may be an important goal within a single organization. Doing so in a comprehensive way may or may not be, however.

If you can figure out what you want as an organization at any level (which I have found is not always easy), you can then figure out what information you can deliver to which audience in order to get closer to the goals you have defined. After you have this concept of who needs what, a CMS can help you create a solid system for actually doing so.

However, content management is important for a deeper reason. It's not just the common forms of information that I call content that you must collect, manage, and deliver. It's all business. As organizations begin conducting their business electronically, they open the same Pandora's box as they did when they began delivering information electronically — namely, one that invokes the following questions:

✦ How do I break my business down into electronically deliverable parts?

✦ How do I make sure that I know what parts I have and that these parts are the right ones for my staff, partners, and customers?

✦ How do I ensure that the right part reaches the right person at the right time?

If content management is the process of collecting, managing, and publishing content, e-business is the process of collecting, managing, and publishing parts of your business. Of course, much of that business entails publishing information. For example, if your business sells electronic components, you may need to publish content such as product offerings, specifications, manuals, and the like — all the stuff that literally or figuratively accompanies the new component out the door. But suppose your customers use your components in their own products and, to improve their own planning, they want you to provide information about processes, quality testing results, inventory, production rates, country of origin, and your fair business practices — in other words, they want (or require) you to publish parts of your business as a condition of doing business.

So, with no stretch at all, you can see how content management may underlie some e-business. But organizations conduct business by providing for actions as well as for information. Actions, in an electronic world, take the form of computer functionality. Functionality, in turn, takes the form of objects and blocks of computer programming code, which you distribute in exactly the same way as you do run-of-the-mill content. To extend the preceding example, if your system allows customers not only to view your production rates and inventory, but to reserve parts of your inventory and increase your production run to meet their needs, the functionality that enables them to do this is computer code. You provide this code to them in the same way that you provide a user manual.

It's the People, Stupid!

For more than 100 Web years, we've tried to come up with the answer to controlling, or at least harnessing, this escalating information frenzy with one-word panaceas. In the earlier Web days, pundits at Internet conferences were proclaiming, "It's the content, stupid!" As if to say, it's so obvious that if you focus on the subject matter and not the technology, everything will fall into place. Duh! To be fair, that was a good start to shifting focus from the technology alone. As always, just because the technology lets us do something, doesn't mean we *should* do it. However, the new emphasis on content still didn't solve the "silo" problem. We still found ourselves unwilling patients in the information asylum. Then we found a new answer: "It's the context, stupid!" OK, now we had it: If we could understand how our information/content/communications fit into the grand scheme of things, we were sure to keep our heads above the information ocean. The challenge here is that understanding the context means that we have to understand the content environment. Because today's environment is the World Wide Web, that means understanding the world.

Although I understand where the author is coming from when he says in the introduction of this book (in the section "Content Management Cures Information Frenzy") that, "There are no established models ...and... rewards," I disagree. Just because today's information context is unfathomably bigger and more complex than ever before, we need to remember that we can apply tried-and-true business tools and processes to this new environment. Organizations and individuals can be successful in this information age by using their core competencies of careful visioning, planning, and executing content projects. Who are you trying to reach? What are your key messages? What information channels will best reach your audience? How will you know when you are successful? I'm not saying that it's easy. I'm just saying that we have established tools that can be applied to the information frenzy. It's (always has been and always will be) the people! We're not stupid, we're just overwhelmed. If we stay calm and remember what we want to accomplish as businesses or individuals, we can use the tried-and-true business tools to get the results we want in this information age.

Marcia Olmsted, Senior Product Manager, Microsoft Corporation

Cross-Reference   In the Introduction to this book, you find more information about e-business. If you're unsure about functionality, check out Chapter 4, "Functionality Is Content, Too!"

CM Is a Balance of Organizational Forces

Another way to look at content management is based on the interests within your organization that must be represented in a CMS.

As you'll see throughout this book, to create a CMS, you must account for a cast of players (which I call the *content management entities*) and ensure that you design the system in accordance with their needs. These players represent both requirements for your system and constraints upon it, because they're interrelated. In other words, meeting the requirements of one entity may affect your ability to meet the requirements of another entity, and so your CMS must take both into account and try to find some balance.

The organizational interests group together into eight entities:

✦ Goals and requirements

✦ Audiences

✦ Publications

✦ Content types

✦ Authors

✦ Acquisition sources

✦ Workflow and staffing

✦ Access structures

Cross-Reference   In Chapter 23, "The Wheel of Content Management," I discuss each of the entities in detail, as well as the similarity between organizational entities and database entities.

I won't go into detail here about what each of these entities is; what's important to understand is that these players must be accounted for in a CMS, individually and collectively. In the process of addressing, negotiating, and balancing these interests, you come up with a definition of CM: CM is getting a set of authors and sources to create a set of content components that fill a set of publications, all in a way that satisfies the requirements of the organization's entities individually and collectively.

CM Is the Combination of Content-Related Disciplines

Content management is the dynamic combination of information architecture, business management, software and network engineering, content creation, and publications development.

✦ Business managers put together the teams and initiatives that bring together the rest of the crew. They also get the organization to attempt CM in the first place.

✦ Information architects put the structures and methods in place to assure that the content you produce can be found and used.

✦ Engineers build the machines that make CM possible on the scale that the whole organization needs.

✦ Content creators originate information in such a way that it can be delivered in a variety of forms.

✦ Publication developers create the venues in which content will be consumed.

Cross-Reference   In Chapter 16, "Securing a Project Mandate," I discuss how business managers line up institutional support within the organization.

Each of the jobs can be complex in its own right but all are necessary and integral to a successful CMS. More broadly, all the people and departments that create, structure, or deliver content can (or ideally should be) part of a CMS.

Actually achieving this level of participation is something of a double-edged sword. On one hand, assimilating all these content roles at a company level represents an incredible opportunity to integrate the sometimes divergent perspectives of all these interests into a coherent strategy for getting the most value out of your staff. On the other hand, because CM forces you integrate these often very separate functions, you may find it difficult to get everyone agreeing and moving in the same direction — you can end up in a big mess of argument, deadlock, and political morass.

If you can manage to bring all these people together and get them to agree what they want to do and how they will do it, you have the beginnings of not only a great CMS, but a great organization with a model for how to function effectively in the new electronic world.

Of course, you need to actually staff a CMS project, which provides its own challenges. For one thing, your organization may not have workers with the skills needed to fill out a CMS project. Some jobs within a CMS project are best accomplished with a variety of specialized, but diverse skills. And the number of staff members will fluctuate — a large staff at the outset as you build the system and tools and migrate your initial content base into it — and then a smaller staff as you manage and maintain the system. For any organization, implementing a CMS is a big undertaking, and one that is not likely to fit into the already-full schedules of current staff members.

Cross-Reference In Chapter 13, "Staffing a CMS," I categorize the jobs involved in creating and running a CMS. In Chapter 33, "Designing Workflow and Staffing Models," I discuss how to estimate staffing needs for a CMS.

We All Know What Content Management Is

Content management isn't difficult to understand, really. I always say this to people who have their first-time experience with the concept — especially when they have just met vendors, or even worse, consultants, who have confronted them with "the concept of content management."

It seems that there's always someone in every group who was involved in a school paper in his or her youth. Remember? Back then, you got copy from all kinds of people. And they almost never submitted their work on time. And they would send you newer versions, and you would lose control of the versions. And you were also expected to publish the scores of the football team. And you had to put some illustrations in it. And although you were the editor, some articles would have to be checked by a teacher. Sound familiar? That is content management!

If you keep the concept this plain and simple, we all have a similar starting point. From there, we can define what content management is within our specific organizations.

Good luck!

Erik Hartman, Hartman Communicatie BV (www.hartman-communicatie.nl)

CM Is Collection, Management, and Publishing

From a process point of view, CM is a process for collecting, managing, and publishing content.

✦ **Collection:** You either create or acquire information from an existing source. Depending on the source, you may or may not need to convert the information to a master format (such as XML). Finally, you aggregate the information into your system by editing it, segmenting it into chunks (or components), and adding appropriate metadata.

✦ **Management:** You create a repository that consists of database records and/or files containing content components and administrative data (data on the system's users, for example).

✦ **Publishing:** You make the content available by extracting components out of the repository and constructing targeted publications such as Web sites, printable documents, and e-mail newsletters. The publications consist of appropriately arranged components, functionality, standard surrounding information, and navigation.

If these definitions seem familiar, they should be. At some level, anyone who has been involved in the creation of a content-driven Web site has done collection, management, and publishing. As I'll show in this section, familiar Web-page editing tools incorporate these fundamental CMS features, albeit at a much more basic level. Basic, but the processes are recognizable because they are fundamentally of the same nature.

Like an archeologist, you can trace the evolution of content management systems by looking at the range of content tools starting with basic Web page editors for basic Web sites; dynamic tools designed for sites that provide frequent updates and consistency across pages and sites; tools for creating managed sites as the content creation process syncs up with the publishing process; and finally, full-blown content management systems that provide component-level management and publishing to multiple sources.

Digging down into the earliest strata, as people started creating Web sites, they did so by typing HTML into plain text editors (such as Microsoft Notepad). As time moved on, the need for better tools grew (fueled by enterprising product companies, less technically adept users, more ambitious Web sites, and the need to automate tedious tasks). At first, these new HTML authoring tools did little more than help you remember the arcane syntax of HTML. Later, they began to be true WYSIWYG (what you see is what you get) environments for creating Web pages. Today, some of these tools add just enough management to serve as a nominal Web CMS for organizations with small sites and no additional publications. They share, however, the fundamental functions of a CMS (collection, management, and publishing). So understanding how these familiar tools work takes you a long way toward understanding the most sophisticated CMS.

For example, tools such as Macromedia Dreamweaver and Microsoft FrontPage intend to serve as the single tool from which you not only create pages but also share resources between pages and manage the layout and organization of your site. The main functionality that they offer for these management tasks includes:

✦ **Collection:** Web tools typically provide a somewhat structured authoring environment, with basic authoring templates, styles, guidance, and features that help you create a basic Web site quickly, even if you have little understanding of HTML. They also provide acquisition features through automatic conversion editing, although flexibility and power is limited. These tools help authors create consistent and well-formed content.

✦ **Management:** Web tools provide basic workflow features through status tracking and commenting. The basic repository is a file system, with some level of user administration, site outlines or diagrams, and link managers.

✦ **Publishing:** Web tools provide page templates, which enable you to create standard page layouts and apply them across pages. You can share resources such as images and standard text blocks, and auto-generate basic navigation based on the pages in a site. Deployment managers enable you to upload the site you create locally to the Web server where it's publicly available.

Today's Web-authoring tools (including certainly many more than just Dreamweaver and FrontPage) are making their first halting steps into the realm of content management. I have no doubt that, as time moves on, these tools will be expanded to cover more and more of the territory. Still, to really enter the world of content management, some of the fundamental assumptions inherent in these tools must be changed to alleviate the following limitations:

✦ **The existing tools are small-scale by design.** They assume a small and loosely organized team producing pages one at a time. A CMS assumes a large, very well organized team producing content that will be moved onto pages in bulk.

✦ **The tools are page oriented.** As I discuss elsewhere (see Chapter 27, "Designing Content Types," for more information), in a CMS, pages aren't the things that you manage; content chunks (or components) are. Managing pages is convenient at a small site. But after your site grows to a larger size—and especially if you must create more than just a single site—you need to move beyond managing pages to managing content components.

✦ **These tools assume that you're creating one Web site.** (Or, if you're creating multiple Web sites, they assume the sites are completely independent of each other.) They offer no capability to share the same content between pages of the same site, let alone between pages of two different sites. They don't create any publication that's not in HTML or, at most, simple XML.

✦ **Authoring templates provide little or no detail about content.** Beyond a few descriptive styles (*Head1*, *Head2*), authoring templates provide no guidance about the nature or structure of the content they're designed to contain. Most styles are generic and not structural (*body text* and *bullet list*) and tell you nothing about the content that's supposed to be authored and how it relates to other content.

✦ **The tools provide little support for metadata below the page level.** Although you can add metadata about pages, you can't add metadata about content components. Therefore, content created by a Web tool is hard to disaggregate and reuse without a lot of intermediate human work.

All in all, today's Web-editing tools provide a fine environment for creating small single sites. When your site becomes large, its base of contributors expands, or it turns into multiple sites and other publications all sharing the same content, a larger-scale solution is called for. That larger-scale solution is a CMS. Of course, a CMS is not necessarily incompatible with a Web-authoring tool. In fact, many CMS products integrate directly with Web-authoring tools. In this case, rather than being the entire system, the editing tool becomes just another device that authors use to originate content (and that is what these tools do best). The CMS takes care of the rest of the tasks involved in collecting, managing, and publishing content.

How Telemedicine Influenced CMS

Some of my strongest beliefs about CMS I learned in telemedicine.

At a company I worked at in the mid-1990s, we created what we thought was a perfect technology solution to a real-world healthcare problem. We enabled physicians to collaborate via the Internet to review medical images and assist on diagnoses.

The technology, rooted in videoconferencing, was emerging as a solution to enable physicians to engage in long-distance collaboration to review medical images and make diagnoses. If it worked for CEOs, why not for orthopedists reviewing X-rays?

When our technology hit the market we quickly learned what we didn't know about physicians — and about barriers to technology adoption. Doctors resisted altering their existing routines and processes to accommodate other doctors' schedules. They were beholden to their schedules — they didn't have time or patience to sync up with other doctors in real-time. The effectiveness of our solution was never fully realized.

I left that company in the late 1990s and started building a content management software company with these core beliefs, informed by my telemedicine experience: In order to be widely adopted and effective, a Web CMS must introduce efficiency, not complexity. It must complement existing processes and users' roles. It must make lives easier, save time, and save money.

Like the practice of medicine, the practice of content management is fundamentally a human activity, bound by human behavior. I learned the hard way that it's a challenge to drastically change human behavior. It is easier, instead, to build a CMS that inherits their behaviors and supports human processes — authoring, workflow, administration.

Like medicine, content management is a human effort *enabled* by technology, not replaced by technology.

Bill Rogers, Founder and CEO of Ektron Inc. (www.ektron.com)

Cross-Reference   In Chapter 7, "Introducing the Major Parts of a CMS," I fully develop the definitions of *collect*, *manage*, and *publish*.

CM Is a Computer Infrastructure

For most IT professionals, a CMS is the combination of hardware and software that comprises a CMS. Unfortunately, some think that this is all a CMS is. It should be apparent by now that if the other perspectives I've discussed in this chapter are correct, content management is a lot more than the computer infrastructure it runs on. Still, without an infrastructure, the best-laid CMS plans cannot be implemented. Put in its proper perspective, the computer infrastructure comes last. That is, after you have decided how a CMS delivers business value, how it balances organizational forces, and what sort of collection, management and publishing process you need, it is time to figure out the infrastructure to make it all happen. In this section, I'll build sequentially toward a definition of CM from the perspective of the hardware and software that comprise it.

The static Web site

A static Web site is a set of HTML pages and related file resources (such as images), all of which are stored as individual files on a Web server. Static pages are pre-built — by definition, they're not created on the fly or personalized in any way, beyond the logic contained within the script for each static page. You update content changes on a static Web site by replacing the pages on the site with new ones. See Figure 6-1.

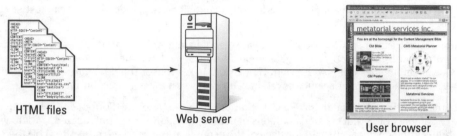

HTML files   Web server   User browser

Figure 6-1: A static Web site delivers pages that are already built.

Static Web sites are the simplest kind of site, suitable for small sites that don't change much and don't require personalization. An additional advantage of a static Web site is speed — static pages are served up by a Web server very quickly, because no is processing required. A limitation of a static Web site is lack of flexibility and scalability — beyond a few hundred pages or so, managing a static Web site can be tedious because content must be updated on each and every page.

The dynamic Web site

A dynamic Web site, sometimes known as a database-driven site, is a system for producing Web pages on the fly as users request them.

A data source (a relational database, or possibly an XML structure) on the Web server receives a query in response to a user clicking a link. The link activates a template page. The template page contains regular HTML as well as programming scripts, objects, and other programs that interpret the request, connect to the data source, retrieve the appropriate content, and do whatever processing is necessary to form an HTML page. After the template creates the appropriate HTML page, the Web server sends it back to the user's browser (see Figure 6-2).

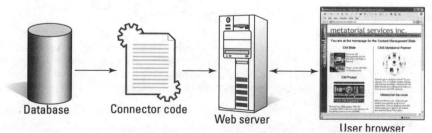

Database   Connector code   Web server   User browser

Figure 6-2: A dynamic Web site creates pages programmatically, sending them back to the inquiring browser.

In a purely dynamic site, no HTML files exist — only the capability to build them whenever someone wants them. Contrast this fluidity with a static site, where all the pages are pre-built and stored on a Web server as HTML files (see Figure 6-1).

Given this definition of dynamic sites, you can easily see why people often confuse them with content management systems. For one thing, you can say that content management systems do essentially the same thing. They, too, maintain databases or XML structures, retrieve appropriate content, and return built pages. On the other hand, you have compelling reasons to distinguish between the two. Why? Because you can have a dynamic site that really isn't doing content management at all. In addition, a content management system can just as easily build a static site.

Suppose, for example, that you maintain a large, dynamic Web site that uses advanced scripts to put a user interface on your organization's financial system. The system responds to user requests and dishes out just the right HTML page in response. You'd be hard-pressed to call this setup a content management system — it's really just a Web-based application.

You can, on the other hand, have a CMS that produces a static site. Suppose that I set up a very complex CMS that contains millions of components, offers a sophisticated workflow, and produces 100 distinct publications. One of those publications is a Web site. After I hit the right button, out flows a static Web site of one million HTML files. I put those files on a Web server and I'm done. If I want to change the site, I hit the button again, and out flows a new static Web site that replaces the first one. In this case, I have a robust CMS producing a static Web site (see Figure 6-3).

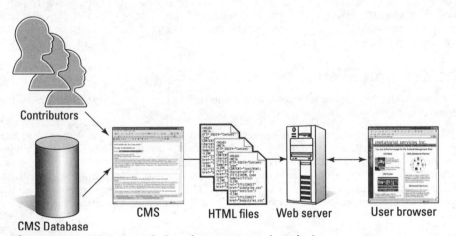

Figure 6-3: A CMS can, and often does, create static Web sites.

So, dynamic Web sites and content management systems aren't the same, and you don't need to produce a dynamic Web site from a CMS. In fact, if you can get away with producing only static Web sites from your CMS, you're better off. A static site is faster and much less prone to crashing than a dynamic one. But you rarely can get away with static sites, or at least not entirely static ones.

You need a dynamic site if you don't know beforehand some or even all of what may appear on a page you deliver to a user. A lot of the content on a dynamic site actually might as well be static — for example, what I call the surrounds (the navigation, title bar, and so on) might well be the same for all users, as could standard chunks of content that you show all users — such as the latest news. However, if you must assess user input or some other factors to figure out at least some of what belongs on a Web page, you need a dynamic system. For any realistic degree of personalization, for interaction with data systems (transactions, catalogs, and so on), or for live updates (such as changing news stories or stock quotes), you need the processing power on the Web server that a dynamic system gives you.

Although dynamic sites aren't content management systems, they illustrate a number of the qualities of a CMS, as follows:

✦ **The template pages** on a dynamic site are very similar in approach to the templates in a CMS. Unlike the template systems in some of today's Web-authoring tools, which cannot be modified and which offer a limited set of features, dynamic sites use generalized Web programming technologies such as Java Server Pages (JSP) and Active Server Pages (ASP). These programming languages are virtually unlimited in scope and can create any sort of page layout and logic that you want. The templating system in many commercial CMS products is no more than an enhanced version of the kinds of template files that dynamic sites use.

✦ **The types of data sources** on a dynamic site are similar to and sometimes even the same as those you use in a CMS. In either a dynamic site or a CMS, you're likely to use the same database or XML products, employ the same programming techniques, and write the same sorts of content selection, layout, and navigation-building code. A good CMS, however, provides you with enhancements that make these tasks much easier. CMS data sources also tend to store more management information (metadata) than the data sources for dynamic sites.

What's typically missing from a dynamic site system is the capability to create more than just a Web site, along with the collection system that a CMS includes. Of course, nothing is stopping the enterprising programmer from extending Web-site code to perform these functions, but then she's not creating a dynamic Web site; she's creating a CMS!

The Web CMS

Sites don't need to be 100 percent static or 100 percent dynamic. In fact, the vast majority of large Web sites are a little of both. Parts of your site can consist of HTML files, and you can dynamically dish up other parts out of a database. In addition, a variety of databases may provide different parts of your site (see Figure 6-4).

In a full Web CMS, you can have any or all the following:

✦ **A CMS application:** Sitting safely behind the Web server, this application takes care of collecting content from contributors and managing your content's workflow and administration. The actual architecture varies by product. In some CMS products, you have software on the organization's local area network (LAN) — inside the firewall — for collecting and testing your content, and software outside the organization's LAN on the live Web server for dynamically serving up pages.

✦ **A repository:** Also behind the Web server is a relational or XML data source. The repository holds all your content, administrative data, and any of the resources that you need to build the site (such as graphics and style sheets).

✦ **A set of flat HTML files:** The CMS manages and deploys files to the static part of the site.

✦ **A live data source (the CMS-generated database):** This is located on the Web Server for the dynamic parts of the site. The CMS can deploy data and content from its repository to the CMS-generated database. In this way, even dynamic content can be managed behind the firewall and kept off the server if it is not ready to be seen publicly. In addition, the template pages that access the CMS-generated database can be pages that are created by the CMS.

✦ **Other data sources:** You can connect other sources of data to the Web site that you don't connect to the CMS. A transaction database for conducting sales on the site, for example, you may connect to the Web site but not to the CMS. The other data sources can run completely independently of the CMS (or the template pages) that accesses the sources.

✦ **Templates:** A set of publication templates moves data from any source to the state it needs to be in for the site. In some cases, the data must be put into finished static HTML pages. In other cases, it is put into databases that will live on the Web server.

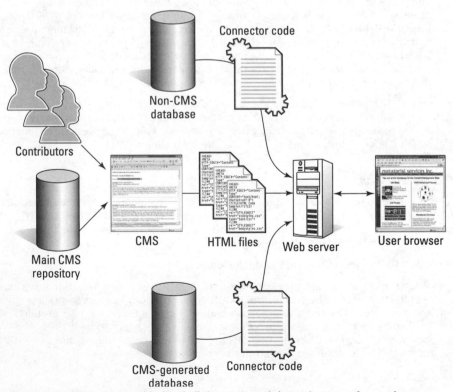

Figure 6-4: CMS can stand behind all the static and dynamic parts of your site.

As you can see, you can quickly get a Web site that is pretty complex. It is complex in two ways. First, it has a lot of software and hardware parts that must be coordinated. Second, it has complex information structures that must be stored and correctly delivered. You can manage the complexity of the information with a CMS. If you consider the various chunks of code in the template pages as chunks of functionality (which they are), you can treat them as just another kind of content to collect, manage, and publish onto the right pages.

Tip　In general, your best bet is to drive as much of your site as is feasible toward static pages. Even if content changes once a day, you're probably better off producing it as HTML files and posting the ones that change to your server daily. Flat pages are tremendously faster and more reliable than dynamic pages. You need compelling reasons to dynamically generate pages—for example, the content is changing minute by minute or you need to personalize the content for each user or user type.

The full CMS

Most discussions of content management today center around creating a large Web site. Although large Web sites are the primary use of content management systems at the moment, the potential for a CMS to help an organization goes far beyond the Web.

Clearly, a CMS can do a lot more than produce a Web site. It can encompass whatever part of your content creation and organization system you want it to. It can provide a content repository where you can review and work on information independently of any page it may land on. Most important, a CMS can produce Web sites and any other publication that you want to create from the stored content.

For example, fewer and fewer organizations are willing to accept that their print publications are entirely separate from their Web publications. They are unwilling to accept the separation for the following reasons:

✦ It is expensive to duplicate effort between a print team and a Web team.

✦ It is costly in customer satisfaction (and can cause other ramifications—even providing a cause for legal action) when there is a lack of synchronization between the two sources of information that they produce.

✦ It is no longer acceptable to let one publication (the Web site) wait for content until the other goes to press. Formerly, the Web site always waited. Now, however, it is the print publication that must wait for Web content.

When there is a reluctance to combine these two publication processes, it is often because of the entrenchment of print-based teams in their traditional tools and methodologies. For some print team members, the CMS attitude (veering away from a specific publication and toward creating good content that can serve multiple purposes) is a godsend that enables them to reach new heights. For others, it only means learning a lot of new programs and unlearning a lot of old habits.

Not surprisingly, I've seen much more desire to think globally from those who must share content between Web sites or between the Web and other digital devices (PDAs and wireless phones, for example). These teams already embrace the new authoring tools, content formats, database technologies, and templating models that dynamic Web sites have taught them. Going the final steps to a CMS is no longer such a big stretch. See Figure 6-5.

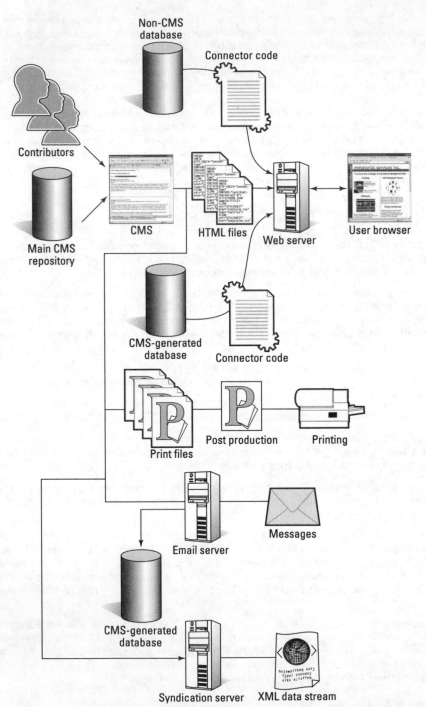

Figure 6-5: A full CMS encompasses your site, plus the other publication channels. This CMS includes a print, e-mail, and syndication system.

Note Interestingly, although the attitudes of team members may be closer, the content divide between publications on handheld digital devices and the Web is much wider than the divide between print publications and the Web. Handheld appliances can show only a couple of sentences of text at a time and only very, very small pictures. They require a major rethinking when you want to deliver anything you're normally used to seeing either in print or on the Web.

In this book, I talk most about full content management. Although the Web still figures most prominently, nothing's exclusive about the Web's demand for well-managed content. If your sole concern is the Web, it likely won't stay that way for long.

The hardware and software infrastructure behind a full CMS can, however, be fairly elaborate. On the other hand, IT professionals are used to creating lots of connections between inter-communicating computers. That aspect of CM, although complex, is well within the reach of most IT departments to accomplish.

Cross-Reference Part 5 of this book, and in particular Chapters 38, 39, and 40, elaborate the functional design of each of the major components of a CMS.

The enterprise CMS

If you look at your content collection, management, and publishing needs from the perspective of the whole organization, you quickly see that the potential for content management goes way beyond the Web. In fact, it's not hard to imagine a situation where all the information resources of an enterprise flow into a single giant repository and are at the disposal of anyone in the organization who wants to create any kind of publication. This kind of system is generally called an enterprise CMS. Although the idea is great in theory, in practice it is usually neither possible nor desirable. It is not possible because the amount of effort and money it entails are way beyond the means of most organizations. It is not desirable because, in many cases, it unduly complicates information creation and dissemination and actually hampers the organization's capability to deliver information.

You can over-organize. Take your e-mail inbox as an example. On the one hand, you can do nothing to organize the stream of the messages you receive. If you get only a few messages a day, this is a wise move. Why waste effort on organizing? It will never pay you back. On the other hand, you can create and maintain an elaborate system of folders, titles, flags, and colors that fully categorize and organize each message and make it instantly findable. This "dream inbox," seems (in theory) to be a great idea. Perhaps you have even tried to create one. If you did, I suspect that you found it impossible and undesirable. It is impossible because you can't figure out the amazing scheme that makes messages immediately findable and don't have the time to process all the messages you receive. It is undesirable because you rarely need to get back to most messages. Only a few are important enough to warrant the effort of organizing them. Somewhere between no organization and total organization lies the amount of inbox organization that is right for you. You usually find that happy medium by trial and error. Usually, you conclude that important-enough messages need to be organized enough so you can find them most of the time.

As goes your inbox, so goes your CMS. Somewhere between the current chaos and the dream of a single place where all information is organized and immediately accessible lies the happy medium of the most important information, well-organized enough so that it can be found and reused in most of the situations where you need it. In your organization you can come to the right amount of organization by trial and error, or you can step back and analyze. You can find out what information is most valuable, needs to be discovered and then reused. Your CMS can (and should) make sure that that information is taken care of first. If you focus on only the most important information, your CMS can become quite possible and overwhelmingly desirable.

A full CMS, as I have defined it, creates more than just a Web site. An enterprise CMS, as I would like to define it, creates more than just a Web site and serves the entire organization. Unfortunately the idea of an enterprise CMS has gotten somewhat clouded by the idea that it has to serve *all* the information of the entire organization. If you can rid yourself of the idea that it serves all the information, you can begin to understand and build the system that delivers the right amount of structure to give your whole organization a clear return on its efforts to manage information.

From a somewhat different angle, as the purveyor of CM in your organization, it is not in your interest to preach *total* organization (as much as you might like to). If you were to somehow convince the organization to do as you ask, you would quickly find that you were spending a lot of money and time organizing useless information that does little or nothing for your organization. It is in your interest to preach *optimal* organization, and then to know how to figure out how to attain the optimum.

In all the organizations I know, reaching the optimum is a hard enough task to occupy you for many years.

The Content Management Industry

At the beginning of the year 2004, the industry of content management is no longer new. It is still, however very much a work in progress. No standards are universally accepted for what content management systems are or do. Companies still argue over even the most basic aspects of content management. Compounding the problem, CM has become a buzz word. When I wrote the first edition of this book, the term CM was known but was by no means popular. At the writing of the second edition, it has become quite commonly used. The result is that all sorts of companies that do all sorts of dissimilar things are trying to get a piece of the pie by calling their products content management systems. A noticeable dip in the economic fortunes of many high-tech companies has also led to a trend toward consolidation that results in one company with one perspective consuming another that may have had a very different approach to CM. This results in product suites that are in conflict with themselves. So, far from coalescing since the first edition of this book, the CM industry has continued to expand and meander. Let's hope that by the third edition, I will be able to report that a set of stable common concepts and functions have emerged and are agreed upon by the industry as a whole.

Do all these caveats mean that you should avoid buying a commercial product? That depends. With a little help and customization, the products available today are certainly up to the task of managing a large Web effort. In addition, the CMS products aren't the only ones that are immature and growing. That's the case with the entire digital-information industry. So if you can afford to wait for the entire "online information" phenomenon to settle down, you're sure to have an easier time getting a CMS going. But be willing to wait quite a while. If, like most of the organizations that I know, you've already waited far too long and the weight of your own information is crushing you, you may as well buy a product and start now. Simply understand that you're signing up for more than a single purchase. You are signing up for participation in the ongoing definition of digital publication technologies.

The majority of content management systems in use today were created by programmers and Webmasters who were simply trying to keep up with their explosive sites. In the last few years, most organizations have had to face the fact that they are not software development shops and have decided to transition to one of the many commercial or open-source CM systems that are on the market.

In this book, I don't describe particular content management products. If I did, the information that I'd present would be out of date before I could finish writing it (and the book would be even larger than it already is!). In addition, other sources exist for up-to-date product information (see www.cmswatch.com and www.cmsreview.com, for example). My purpose (and I must say my desire) is rather to work through the concepts and frameworks of the discipline of content management. I firmly believe that your first task in confronting CM is to decide what you need. Then you can evaluate the products that are available with an independent and thorough assessment of what they need to accomplish for you.

See Chapters 38, 39, and 40 for more guidance on for choosing collection, management, and publishing technologies. These chapters will help you make your way through the large range of possible features you may want your CMS to have.

Today, you can't find a commercial system that does everything that I present in this book. Most major CMS products offer some capabilities in the three areas of collection, management, and publishing, but they concentrate most of their strengths in only one of these areas. In addition, because there is no agreed-upon center to the discipline of content management, any company offering a CMS product is free to define the term *content management* as it sees fit to best appeal to its customers. As time goes on, this situation is certain to change. What isn't likely to change, however, is your responsibility to understand what you're trying to accomplish with a CMS, and how to organize your content enough to benefit from one. That's what I hope that this book teaches you. In addition to providing solid concepts and advice to people working with content management "in the trenches," I also hope that this book helps move the content management discipline and industry toward a unified set of concepts and a clear target for the range and depth of functionality that it must provide to truly serve the needs of its clientele.

Despite my downplaying of CM products, in Chapter 19, "Selecting Hardware and Software," I detail a process that you can use to select the right hardware and software for your particular needs.

Summary

Content management systems have a simple purpose — to enable you to get content with the least hassle so that you know what content you have, and so that you can get it out to a variety of places automatically. The details are less simple, as the following list illustrates:

✦ The content management industry is just beginning with only immature products currently available.

✦ Most content management systems in place today cover only the Web.

✦ Web-authoring tools are great for small sites, but they lack the functionality or scalability to serve as real systems.

✦ Today's most sophisticated, dynamically generated Web sites go a long way toward content management but are still much too narrowly focused to do the whole job.

While the technology matures, you're best off spending your time and energy taking what steps you can to move toward a content management approach. This strategy entails figuring out in detail what you want to happen and then seeing how far you can get with today's tools.

In the next chapter, I go into detail about the structure of a full content management system.

✦   ✦   ✦

Introducing the Major Parts of a CMS

✦ ✦ ✦ ✦

In This Chapter

A high-level view of CMS features

Collecting content

Managing content

Publishing content using templates

✦ ✦ ✦ ✦

Some years ago, it dawned on me that I had been creating and recreating the same sort of system over and over in my information projects. Not too surprisingly, I came to think of my work as creating *information systems*. As silly as this may sound, before I named what I was creating, they just seemed like a series of projects. After I came up with the *information systems* tag, the notion and my understanding grew. Each new project was an opportunity to sharpen my ideas about what an information system was and to begin to build standard vocabulary and processes around them. As I developed these ideas in my head, the company I had created to do all these information projects began to grow. I found myself describing over and over again to clients, staff, and colleagues what I thought was similar in all these systems.

In my office I used to have a big, low, tear-shaped desk that was covered with white-board material. We used the desk for impromptu design sessions. The same diagram kept coming up on my board, but each time with a bit more detail. The diagram had a place for the authors for whom we had to design a user interface, a place for the database that stored the information that the authors created, and a place for the custom browser we would create to display the information from the database. Later I generalized these three areas to become the *collection*, *management*, and *publishing* areas of a CMS. (One result of these deliberations was a poster, which is still in use today, which you can view at www.metatorial.com.)

In this chapter, I present a perspective that describes CMS as a system that collects, manages, and publishes information and functionality. I present a top-level view of content management that's partly hardware and software, partly process, and partly an organizational vehicle.

These concepts serve to organize the field and allow us to talk about content management as a coherent and complex *system* rather than a convoluted set of events and relationships. Following the overview, I identify the elements that comprise each of the major parts of the CMS: the collection system, the management system, and the publishing system. Keep in mind that collection, management, and publishing are concepts; you won't necessarily find distinct features called or organized by these names in a commercial CMS, but you can certainly use the concepts to understand any CMS you come across or devise.

A CMS Overview

At the broadest level, a content management system (CMS) is responsible for the collection, management, and publishing of chunks of information known as *content components*. Schematically, you can envision the process as shown in Figure 7-1.

> **Note**   The illustrations in this section are based on the CMS Possibilities poster my colleagues and I created at Chase Bobko, Inc. For more information, go to www.metatorial.com.

Flowing from left to right, the illustration shows how raw information runs through a *collection system* and turns into content components. A *management system*, which is a sort of database, stores these components. The *publication system* draws components out of the management system and turns them into publications. This illustration is the highest-level view of the content management process model that I use throughout this book.

Notice that, although logically separate, the three parts of the system can involve large physical overlaps, as the following list describes:

✦ **The management system can serve as part of the collection system.** You very often deposit content in the content repository of the management system before it is fully processed (making it part of the collection system).

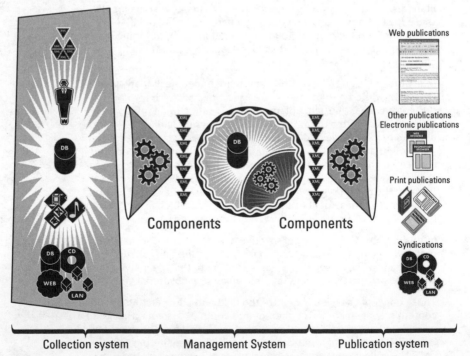

Figure 7-1: A schematic overview of a content management system

✦ **The management system can serve as part of the publication system.** The repository, for example, often sits on the Web site it creates, and you can't easily distinguish it from the system that publishes the site.

✦ **The publication system can serve as part of the collection system.** In a Web-forms collection system, the author types content into a Web form. That content is stored in the repository. Behind the scenes, the publication system may create the Web forms that the collection system uses.

The following sections move down a level and put a bit of sinew on the CMS skeleton that I'm describing by addressing the collection, management, and publications systems, in turn.

The Collection System

A CMS collection system is responsible for all the processes that happen before a piece of content is ready for publication. It turns raw information into a well-organized set of content components. Figure 7-2 presents an overview of the collection process, showing authoring, acquiring, converting, and aggregating as well as the collection services that a CMS provides.

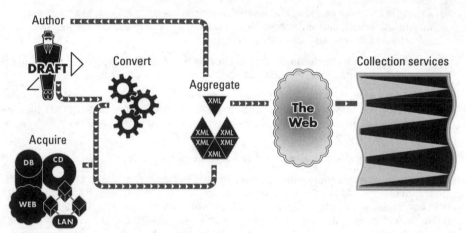

Figure 7-2: An overview of the collection process

These processes include the following:

✦ **Authoring:** create the content from scratch.

✦ **Acquisition:** gather the content from some existing source.

✦ **Conversion:** strip unnecessary information from the content and change its markup language.

✦ **Aggregation:** edit the content, divide it into components, and augment it to fit within your desired metadata system.

✦ **Collection services:** CMS programs and functions that aid the collection process. For example, the collection services might produce the Web forms into which you enter the content for components.

I discuss each of these processes in more detail in the following subsections.

Note For clarity, Figure 7-2 implies that these processes happen serially and in a particular order. In reality, they may not happen in the order that the figure implies. In addition, the entire process is shown apart from the management system for simplicity only. In fact, much of the collection process can and usually does happen after content enters the repository.

Authoring

Authoring refers to the process of creating content from scratch (see Figure 7-3).

I define an *author* as someone you specifically commission to create content for you. If the content creator isn't under your jurisdiction or creates the content for any purpose other than for your CMS, I define her content as acquired, not authored.

A CMS can help the author work efficiently and effectively by doing the following:

✦ **Providing an authoring environment** (either a full application or extensions to the author's native environment).

✦ **Providing a clear purpose and audience** for the author's efforts. In a CMS, you direct authors to create particular content components that already are defined in terms of their basic purpose and audiences.

✦ **Providing aids** for including standard information. The CMS can easily fill in the create-date and author's name, for example, to save the author effort.

✦ **Providing templates** that break down the content the author creates into its constituent elements. You may provide authors with a Microsoft Word template (a DOT file), for example, that already includes places to type a title, summary, and body for the component's author to create.

✦ **Providing workflow, status, and version control** for content that's in process.

Regardless of how many tools and processes the CMS provides, authoring is essentially a manual process. No CMS can tell an author what to say or, more important, how to say it to best communicate an idea or goal. Because authoring is manual, it's slow and expensive. Creative people can create only so quickly. Creative people with the knowledge and skill to create good content are a limited resource and thus come at a high price. On the other hand, you can count on the quality and applicability of authored content. By definition, authors are under your direction, so you can control the quality of their output.

All these features of a CMS can help you maintain this control by governing how authors do their work. The tools are as much about making authors do what is required as they are about helping authors work efficiently.

Cross-Reference In Chapter 38, "Building Collection Systems," the section "Authoring Applications," I describe in detail the kinds of tools a CMS provides for authors.

The authoring process itself is one of creation and revision, where the author (possibly in conjunction with others) drafts and revises her work until she is satisfied that it's ready for use. The author may keep her work outside the CMS until it's complete, or she may load her early drafts into the CMS to take advantage of its management functions (workflow, status tracking, version control, and so on).

Figure 7-3: The authoring process is an essentially human process of creation and revision.

Acquiring

Acquiring is the process of gathering information that wasn't originally created for your CMS (see Figure 7-4). This process might be partly manual or fully automated.

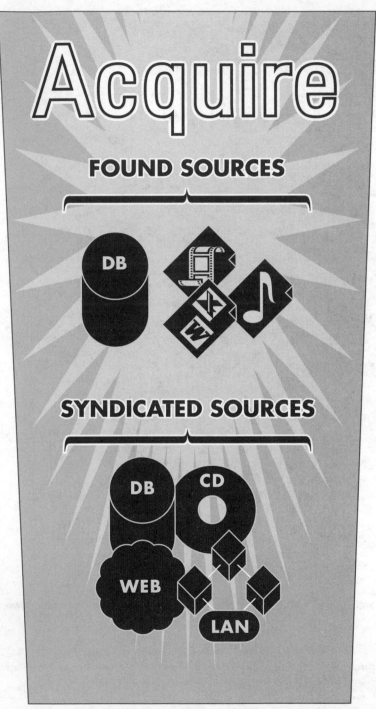

Figure 7-4: Acquiring is the process of gathering information that was created for some other purpose.

Unless you're extremely lucky (or have lax quality standards), you're going to have some work to do to get this information ready for the CMS. Acquired information comes from the following types of sources:

✦ **Syndications:** Syndications are sources that are designed for reuse. *Designed for reuse* means two things. First, it means that the information is delivered in a generally useful format (XML, for example). Second, it means that the information is already segmented and has metadata attached. Syndicated news, for example, generally comes in story segments that are tagged with at least a headline, byline, date, and story. Today a small, but quickly growing commercial industry sells reusable information. Commercial syndicators can package and deliver a wide range of high-quality information (for the right price, of course). Not all syndications, however, are commercial. You can use your CMS to package and distribute your components in a reusable form to others in your organization, for example; and if you're lucky, others can do the same for you.

✦ **Found Sources:** These are files you have come across or are given to you and that must be processed and added to your CMS. They can be any sort of pre-existing information, including nonelectronic sources such as paper photographs, analog video, and printed text that, after you digitize them, all end up in files as well. Source files generally aren't designed for reuse. They're often not in an easily reused binary format, are unsegmented, and have no metadata attachments. Except for databases, which can be (but certainly aren't always) well structured, source files require work on your part to transform them into a usable form.

Note

Many acquired sources require legal permission for reuse, either instead of or in addition to payment. In your organization, this may involve anything from getting a signed permission letter from a contributor to managing distribution and payment of royalties using a Digital Asset Management system. I describe how this is done in Chapter 11, "The Branches of Content Management," in the section "Digital asset management (DAM)." Managing these permissions and rights may be one of the things your CMS does; I describe digital asset management as part of a CMS in Chapter 38, "Building Collection Systems," in the section "Rights and usage."

Authored information is generally low volume but high quality. Acquired information is generally high volume but low quality. You may have photographs of all your products available as JPEG images, for example, but they may need hand processing to crop them and adjust their contrast.

You may get lucky and find syndicated sources that are high quality (meaning that you have little to do to process them), but don't count on it. Most information that people create is for a limited use. If you bring it into a system for unlimited use, you can reasonably expect to do additional work to make it usable.

Receiving acquired information may prove as simple as saving attachments sent to you by e-mail or as complex as setting up a sophisticated server that receives information feeds at regular intervals and automatically processes them. As often as not, it's a simple process of receiving files from a network location or on CD-ROM.

Cross-Reference

In Chapter 38, "Building Collection Systems," in the section "Acquisition System" I describe acquisition tools.

Tip

Make sure that, after you receive acquired content, you move it into your own storage area. Doing so prevents the contributor from inadvertently deleting or modifying the files after you start processing them.

Converting

If the information that you create or acquire isn't in the format or structure that your system requires, you must convert it to match the accepted standards of the content system (see Figure 7-5). Note that when I talk about converting content, I'm referring to converting from an editorially finished form — not, in other words, converting raw data, but rather analyzed information, just as you don't import shapes and colors but rather a finished drawing.

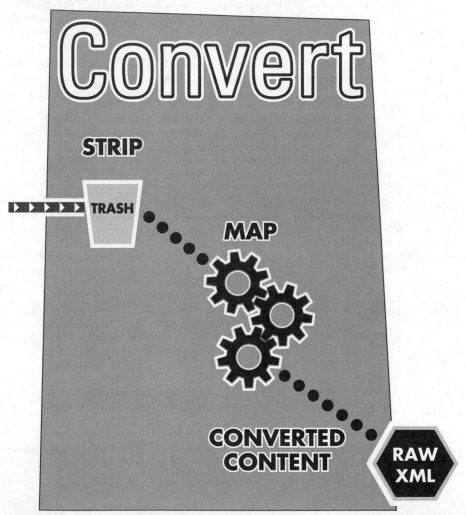

Figure 7-5: Conversion is the process of digitizing and then changing the binary format and/or remapping the structure of information.

The conversion process consists of the following three logical steps (these steps usually mix in an actual conversion process):

✦ **Stripping:** removing and discarding unneeded surrounding information such as page headers and footers, unnecessary content, and unwanted navigation.

✦ **Format mapping:** changing the information's binary format to a standard one that the CMS supports, as well as separating its rendering format from its structure.

✦ **Structure mapping:** making the information's structure explicit or changing it as necessary.

Information that you acquire from nonelectronic sources, such as printed text and analog sound, you must first digitize — that is, you must give it a binary format before you can change that format.

I define *format* as the storage file structure and rendering characteristics of a piece of content. In Chapter 2, "Content Has Format," you find more information about this definition. I define *structure* as the set of named relationships within, between, and beyond individual pieces of content. See Chapter 3, "Content Has Structure," for more information about structure.

Obviously, you need to convert information only if what you receive isn't what you need. Thus conversion is usually associated with acquired information because you don't control its format and structure. But just because you receive HTML (for example) and you need HTML doesn't mean that you need not convert that information. If the target HTML (what you want) has a different structure or format from the source (what you have), you must still convert its structure.

The result of a conversion process is information that conforms as nearly as possible to the standards you develop for format and structural tagging. I sometimes use XML as shorthand for these qualities. If you convert your information to XML, you're (most probably) standardizing its tagging. On the other hand, you don't need to convert information to XML to get the same effect. Any format that can represent structure works.

In Chapter 37, "Processing Content," I discuss in depth the mechanics of conversion.

Aggregating

In addition to authoring or acquiring your information — and converting it, if necessary — you must aggregate it (see Figure 7-6).

I define *aggregation* as the process of bringing disparate information sources into one overall structure through:

✦ **Editorial processing:** performing the familiar functions of styling, consistency, and usage.

✦ **Segmentation processing:** breaking the information into chunks that I call *content components*.

✦ **Metatorial processing:** performing the less familiar function of fitting new content into the prescribed metadata system. The metadata that you apply to the content enables the system to effectively store and retrieve it. This system consists of the rules that you create for how to supply metadata values for each new piece of content that you bring into the system.

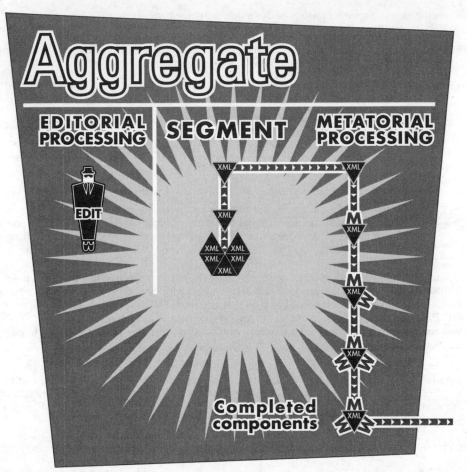

Figure 7-6: Aggregation refers to bringing information into a CMS through editorial processing, segmentation, and metatorial processing.

Note   Aggregation is often a part of the conversion process. As information goes through stripping, formatting, and structure mapping, you can accomplish much of the segmentation, editorial processing, and metatorial processing. I break the two apart because some information may not need converting, but you must still aggregate it.

Metators, who are the editors of metadata, tag the segmented information with metadata to enable you to automatically store, find, and later combine that information into publications. Just as editors edit, metators *medit*. A metator uses a metatorial guide that describes accepted metadata values and how to tag each kind of content.

Cross-Reference In Chapter 24, "Working with Metadata," in the section "What does metatorial mean?" I discuss the idea of a metator in more detail.

Editors, segmentors, and metators aren't necessarily different people. In fact, in a small system, the same person (who may have other tasks as well) probably performs these three tasks. But as the size of the system grows, these three tasks present the natural way to divide the workload.

Additionally, you don't usually need to apply the same amount of effort to all information. Content that someone with good editorial and metatorial skills authors directly into the CMS as a component, for example, may need no work because the author aggregates as he authors it. On the other hand, information that you acquire from a source with little metadata, a divergent editorial framework, and no correct segmentation may need a lot of work to aggregate.

These editorial, segmentation, and metatorial processes of aggregating are described in the following subsections.

Editorial processing

All professional publishing groups use an editorial framework to guide their work. This framework consists of the following types of rules:

✦ **Correctness rules:** These rules ensure that you prepare content in accordance with generally accepted standards. Rules on punctuation, word usage, and grammar are all within this realm.

✦ **Communication rules:** These rules ensure that the content projects a specific image and targets a specific audience. Rules concerning the voice of the content (active, passive, first person, third person, and so on) as well as other stylistic rules are within this realm, as are rules concerning the correct way to communicate with the intended audience (such as the right vocabulary to use).

✦ **Consistency rules:** These rules ensure that you apply all the other rules evenly across the entire content base and that, after you define it, you always use a term the same way.

Without such a framework, publications can lack unity and seem disorganized and unprofessional. For static publications (such as books and magazines), which people manually produce and handcraft, the editorial framework is all that you need to ensure unity.

I don't suppose that I need to say too much more about this subject. Much is written elsewhere, and I'm a pretty lousy editor myself. I don't catch errors very easily, and unless I'm under the iron thumb of a schema (a set of rules used to enforce consistency in documents coded in XML), I tend to disobey the rules as often as I follow them.

What I can say about editing is that it's a very human effort. Tone, style, usage, and the like are certain to prove the last of the pillars of language to dissolve before the advancing tide of digitization.

Note Although editing is a human effort, you can still create good tools to help the editor in her very labor-intensive task. To work, however, the tools need to be very local in scope, and under the direct and immediate control of the editor. They're on the quick-return side of the automation ROI spectrum. You can learn more about these tools in Chapter 37, "Processing Content," in the section "Focusing on the long-term benefits."

One of the few additions that content management offers to the art of the editor is the idea of loosening the constraints on the content so that you can use it in the widest variety of contexts. In the content management realm, the editor must constantly ask the following questions:

✦ What if I remove this piece of content from the text and media that I now see around it? I can't assume, for example, that what I see as I write this paragraph precedes or follows the words that you're reading now. Maybe you're receiving them in an e-mail message quite apart from the surroundings that I see. Maybe they're stripped of all imagery for display on a tiny screen. Maybe they're combined with sections widely dispersed in this work to form a custom white paper.

✦ What constraints does the content put on the frame that may surround it? Are the colors in the graphics, for example, likely to clash with the branding and advertisements that may surround them on a Web page? Can the line lengths cause a horizontal scroll bar to appear on-screen?

✦ Do links make sense in all media? Do the terms *earlier* and *later* or *above* and *below*, for example, make sense in every publication in which the content is to appear? How can you refer to external information in a way that makes sense regardless of the publication platform?

All in all, content that you compose for componentization and multiple use must be far more open and forgiving than single-use continuous stream content. Finding just the right language devices that work well enough in every medium isn't easy. Of course, you can always fall back to writing multiple versions for multiple outlets, but the return isn't high on such a labor-intensive effort. In the long run, it is better for everyone if you create certain language devices that can easily become second nature for those attempting to represent content in a high-value but output-neutral way.

Segmentation

Segmentation is the process of dividing content into convenient and useful chunks. In other words, segmentation is the process of putting content in components. Obviously, before you begin segmenting content into components, you must know what kinds of components you're trying to create.

 In Chapter 27, "Designing Content Types," I discuss the nature and composition of components. Here, I want to focus on the processes involved in creating them.

The process that you use to create components depends on the source of the components, as the following list indicates:

✦ **Components that you author one at a time** you can create as you author them.

✦ **Components that you acquire** you can segment after or as part of the conversion process.

How you segment content depends on the nature of its source. In all cases, however, what's most important is how well marked each component is in its source. Components are generally marked in source files in the following ways:

✦ **By a file boundary:** You may receive 50 files, for example, each containing one office location fact sheet. If each file is to become one Office Fact Sheet component, the segmentation is already complete. If you receive two fact sheets per file, then you have some segmentation work to do.

✦ **By a database record boundary:** Suppose, for example, that you receive a database full of employee data, and you want to turn it into a set of Employee Profile components. You process the database records one at a time. Each time that you load a new employee record from the database, you create a new component in your system.

✦ **By explicit markup:** Suppose, for example, that you're receiving international restaurant menus from a good XML syndication source. Each menu yields a Menu component. You're unlikely to receive one file per menu. Rather, you're apt to receive one file with many menus. Each menu is *explicitly* marked (by, say, a <Menu> tag) to show where it begins.

✦ **By implicit markup:** Suppose, for example, that you receive a file that contains a printed product catalog from which you want to create a set of Product components. Each new product is marked in the catalog by a hard page break. As you process through the catalog, you look for this *implicit* markup to begin a new component.

✦ **Not marked:** Suppose that the print-product catalog that you receive formats each new product name with the font Times New Roman, 12-point, Bold. But Times New Roman, 12-point, Bold, isn't a reliable marker because it's also used in other ways throughout the catalog.

Cross-Reference

As I discuss in Chapter 37, "Processing Content," in the sections "No correspondence," and "No or poor markup," if you have a "Not Marked" situation, you need a trained eye and not a computer to ensure that you can find the component boundaries in the file.

Most segmentation of acquired content occurs as part of the conversion process. I categorize segmentation, however, as part of the aggregation process. Although mechanically it may consist of stripping and mapping, conceptually you can describe it much as a process of bringing outside content into your CMS.

Metatorial processing

Metatorial processing is designed to ensure that the metadata you apply to incoming content is complete and consistent. But how does this process actually happen? To explore this further, this section follows a fictitious metator, Argun, through his day at an organization that collects and publishes product information and reviews from a variety of sources.

At 8 a.m., Argun arrives at work. After fixing his tea, he sits down to his e-mail. He's set up a rule in his e-mail system that routes any e-mail message displaying the prefix *CMS-Related* into a particular folder. (The CMS administrators previously set up the system so that any e-mail message it auto-generates carries the prefix *CMS-Related*.) His CMS-Related folder contains about 40 new e-mail messages since the last time that he checked. Twelve of these messages are asking him questions about how to tag something. The rest are notifications of newly submitted content that he must review by the end of the day.

By 9:30, Argun dispenses with the questions by pasting the same 10 or 12 sections from the metatorial guide into his e-mail responses. In one case (the only one he enjoyed dealing with), the contributor found a nice hole in the rules. Argun sets himself a task to update the guide to cover the new situation. In each e-mail message that requests a review is a link Argun can click to go directly into the CMS Web-based administration system and see the component to review. He opens the first new component and begins to review it. The message is what he expects, given the author. She's entered the required management metadata and made some pretty good guesses about which access metadata wasn't required. She knows her audiences well and always nails the targeting metadata. With a few short corrections, Argun sends this component on to its next phase, editorial review.

Cross-Reference   In Chapter 24, "Working with Metadata," in the section "Understanding the Types of Metadata" I discuss the types of metadata.

Within the next hour, he dispenses with the majority of the new content. He's cheated, however, by opening the ones from the "good" authors. Argun takes a morning break and decides to switch from tea to coffee before returning to the "bad" authors and the sources.

This time, Argun goes for the worst first. He opens the e-mail message that announces the arrival of the latest catalog conversion. It involves updates to 35 of the 123 entries in the catalog. The attached conversion log tells the whole sad truth. Only 45 of the entries were reliably converted into Product components. The failed entries are attached in a pseudo-XML file that needs hand-working. Argun sighs to himself, "With one or two more people on the conversion staff (or just one good programmer), my job would be cut in half. Yeah right," he quickly adds. "I'm cheaper."

Argun loads the pseudo file into Microsoft Word (the only editor he really feels comfortable working in). Using the tool that he kludged together with the help of a programmer friend, he begins his work. It's not particularly hard—just tedious. He highlights a section of the document and then chooses the appropriate custom toolbar button. The button performs the appropriate tagging for the section he has selected by hand. He moves steadily through the file, marking the Product components first. As he clicks the component button, the right XML elements automatically surround each block of text. Next, he makes a pass for the elements within the components that are never converted quite correctly—the price and the customer quotes. Finally, he clicks the button that blasts through the file and stores all his marked components in the CMS database. Argun has no idea how the conversion process actually works—only that it doesn't always work the first time, and when it doesn't work he has to fix it.

After a late lunch, thanks to the catalog team, Argun returns to work on the stuff from the good sources and bad authors. The good source turns out to be better than he expected. It's a syndicated source of industry news items. After he's repeatedly asked for it, they finally sent him the one with keywords in it. Now, instead of taking him 30 minutes to add the right keywords to the stories, reviewing and verifying them takes him only 10. The hard part of this source—but the part that Argun likes best—is finding the places in the existing content that he can link to the new stories. This task represents one of the few times during his day that Argun feels that he's functioning at the peak of his abilities.

With the news finished, Argun moves directly to the bad authors. Mostly managers with a lot of other stuff going on, these misbehaving contributors do as little as possible and never think before typing. They put stuff in the wrong fields on the Web forms, never consider to whom they're writing, and *never* fill in anything that they can get away with leaving blank. After Argun set up the forms so that they couldn't submit stuff without filling in all the required metadata fields, he got nothing (except excuses) from this lot. Brow furrowed, he plods through the bad authors' work. The only saving grace is that he can anticipate by author the kinds of mistakes to expect. He makes a little game out of seeing how many of the mistakes he can name before opening the component.

Four o'clock comes, and it's Argun's appointed hour to head off future problems. He long ago vowed to himself (and unfortunately to his boss) that he'd avoid getting plowed under the load by spending at least one hour a day heading off problems upstream. He sends his weekly e-mail reminder to the catalog team, asking again for a meeting to discuss ways that they can work more consistently. He begins work on a mapping file that he intends to use that can, eventually, automatically convert the keywords that the news agency uses to the ones that his company uses internally. He wishes that he'd had the agency's list when he started so that he could just use its terms. To change over now, he laments, would require days of retagging.

On his way out of the building, Argun casually drops by the office of one of the bad authors. He tells the manager that he has a question about something she wrote and asks whether she'd please open it on-screen. She hesitates because she doesn't know how to open it on-screen. Argun knew full well that she didn't know how to do so and counted on using that fact as an excuse to provide a little guerilla training.

At home that night, Argun makes a revision to the metatorial guide based on the one original question he received that morning. He dozes off in his big recliner reading *Women, Fire, and Dangerous Things: What Categories Reveal About the Mind* by George Lakoff.

Collection services

CMS collection services aid the collection process. The main service that they provide is to help get content into the repository. This service, in turn, breaks down into the following tasks:

✦ Authoring components directly into the CMS repository.

✦ Loading previously created components into the repository one at a time or in bulk.

The most common way that someone authors components directly into the repository is through Web-based forms. In these forms, an author types blocks of text, enters metadata, and uploads images and other media. Most CMS products include some tools that enable you to design a form where you can collect all the information that you need to create a particular component. To contribute to the system, an author goes to a Web page, chooses what sort of content to contribute (that is, which content type), and then begins typing. After the author clicks the Submit button, the system creates a database record or XML element in the repository to store the content component. Fancier systems can even read a schema or relational database structure and automatically create a Web form with all the right input controls and validations.

People can also author components outside the system and load them in after they're complete. The most common tool for authoring text-based components outside the system is Microsoft Word. The usual convention is that one Word file yields one component. Although Web-based forms give you tight control and validation, open tools such as Word give you flexibility. Creating a form that spurs creativity in your authors is difficult. On the other hand, creating a word-processor–based system that can constrain the creativity of your authors is also difficult. The usual method of control in a word processor is to create a template that authors must follow. The template contains spaces where the author types text, enters metadata, and specifies images and other media. In Word, these templates can be as simple as an example file that you load, modify, and then save, or as complex as template (DOT) files with fill-in fields, validation macros, and data connections to metadata lists and the CMS repository.

Finally, you can move content into the repository in bulk. In some systems, collection services connect to non-CMS databases and automatically upload and componentize database records. Other systems incorporate sophisticated services that scan the Web for targeted content and automatically download and componentize it.

Just getting content into your CMS can require a fairly complex — but well-designed — set of processes and good old-fashioned work. A good collection system (and in that I include the processes you use to collect content) is the foundation of effective management of the content.

The Management System

The management system in a CMS is responsible for the long-term storage of content components and a range of other resources. The management system contains the repository, workflow, and administration facilities. At the highest level, it enables you to know what you have collected and what its disposition is. Your management system, for example, should be capable of telling you the following:

✦ Details about your content, including what kinds of components you have and where in its life cycle each is now

✦ How well utilized your staff is and what bottlenecks are coming up

✦ How you're using components in publications and which content is unused or ready for removal

✦ Who has access to what content and who has contributed the most

In short, whatever reasonable questions you have about your content, publications, or collection system, you should find the answers available from your management system.

To provide this capability, a management system includes:

✦ **Repository:** a place to store the content.

✦ **Administration:** an administration system for setting up and configuring the CMS.

✦ **Workflow:** defined sets of steps for doing the work necessary on the content to get it ready to be published.

✦ **Connections:** a set of connections (hardware and software) to other systems within the organization, ranging from networks and servers to data repositories.

I discuss each of these elements in detail in the following subsections.

The repository

The *repository* is the main piece of the management system (see Figure 7-7).

The repository is the set of databases, file directories, and other system structures (for example, custom settings for the CMS) that store the content of the system as well as any other data associated with the CMS. Components and other CMS resources come into the repository via the collection services, and the publishing services extract them. The repository can contain the following components:

✦ Content databases and files

✦ Control and configuration files

Content databases and files

Content databases and *files* hold the system's content components. Content databases can consist of standard relational databases, XML object databases, or some hybrid of the two.

Relational databases use standard tables, rows, and columns to represent components. In the simplest case, you have one table per content type, one row per content component, and one column per component element.

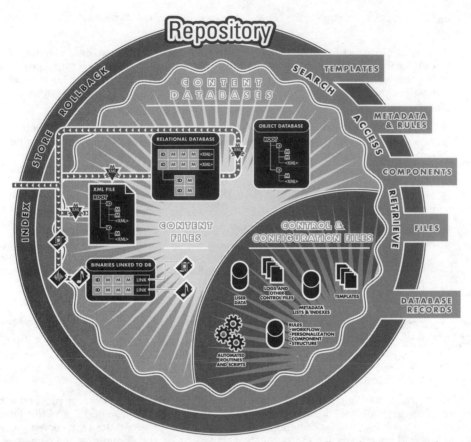

Figure 7-7: The repository contains the CMS databases as well as other storage and retrieval mechanisms.

Content databases can also consist of object databases, where components are fully represented as XML and are stored in a large hierarchy. In this case, content types, content components, and elements all have their own tags, which a DTD brings together into a complete system.

These two technologies aren't mutually exclusive. You can store an XML fragment in a relational database field, for example, to give you control of the content at a level more granular than a database column. In addition, a new round of hybrid object/relational databases are now available that blur the distinctions between the two.

Cross-Reference See Chapter 39, "Building Management Systems," in the section "The Repository" for the complete story about storing components in relational or object databases. In addition, check out Chapter 27, "Designing Content Types," for much more information about content types, content components, and elements.

Content files simply hold content outside of any database.

In the following circumstances, the repository can store content as files as well as database entities:

✦ You can store media files in a database, but you more often store them as binary files outside the database and link them to database records. In some ways, this procedure is a throwback to the days when databases were incapable of handling binary data very well. In other ways, having media files directly accessible through the file system is quite convenient.

✦ Files such as word-processing files and spreadsheets, as well as other files such as Adobe Acrobat (PDF) files, which are intended for use by the CMS in their existing format, can be stored and distributed as files. In this case, the CMS is functioning more as a document management system than a content management system. See Chapter 10, "The Roots of Content Management," in the section "The Principles of Document Management," for more information on the distinction between document and content management.

✦ Rather than using a database at all, the main content storage facility may consist of one or more XML files that the CMS services manage. The structure of the XML file is similar to that of the object database (content types, content components, and elements all having unique XML tags), but standard and custom XML programming techniques replace the accessing and indexing of an object database.

The Management System in a CMS

You may wonder why I use the term *management system* to describe one of the three parts of a content *management* system. Here's why:

I use the term *content management* to capture all the processes involved with the procurement and use of content. You may, however, hear a popular and more constrained use of this term. Rather than using it to stand for the end-to-end process, many interpret the term *content management* refer to only the part of the system that actually holds and administers the content. As one CMS product company puts it, "Our system focuses on managing the content. We let other companies focus on creating it and distributing it." I can certainly understand this usage. On the other hand, the processes for creating and distributing content seem to me so tied up in its management that trying to separate them too far is useless. Given this argument, I originally shied away entirely from the more limited meaning for content management. I used the term *repository system* to stand for that part of the system that stores and administers content. But no one really understood that term. After much discussion, they'd eventually say, "Oh, you mean management." Thus I decided that the best course was to trade some collision between the two meanings of content management for the fact that it's the right term in both its general sense and its constrained sense.

Still, after you're past the surface of the management system, you're likely to see that its core is a repository that holds and makes accessible the content and supporting files that you need to manage. So I use the term *management system* to refer to the part of the CMS that contains the repository, the workflow system, and the administration system. I use the term *CMS* to refer to the entire system that includes these management functions, as well as all the other processes and functions necessary to collect and publish content.

Control and configuration files

Control and configuration files are the noncontent files that you manage within the CMS repository.

Control and configuration files include the following types:

✦ **Input and publishing templates:** You retrieve and use these templates for content input or publication output, respectively.

✦ **Staff and end-user data files and databases:** These elements hold information that you use for access and personalization.

✦ **Rules files and databases:** These elements hold the definitions of component types, workflows, and personalization routines.

✦ **Meta information lists, content index files, and databases:** These data sources augment the metadata that you store directly in the content files and databases.

✦ **Log and other control files and structures** (such as system catalogs and registries): You use these files for analysis as well as to store the parameters that control CMS routines and functions.

✦ **Scripts and automated maintenance routines:** These elements are programs that the CMS uses to help manage content.

The administration system

The *administration system* is responsible for setting the parameters and structure of the CMS (see Figure 7-8).

The administration system affects all the parts of your CMS in the following ways:

✦ **In the collection system:** Administration includes staff configuration, where roles and access rights are set; metatorial configuration, where the system of metadata fields and lists is maintained; and system configuration, where the structure and workflows of the content management system are maintained.

✦ **In the management system:** Administrators perform many of the usual database administration tasks such as user maintenance and permissions, backup, and archiving. In addition, management-system administrators perform content-specific tasks such as creating content types, performing metadata reviews, and creating workflows.

✦ **In the publishing system:** Administrators ensure that all the hardware and software for displaying content is working according to plan. For Web publications, the job is much like that of a site administrator who ensures that the Web server, application server, content management application objects, databases, and other associated programs are always running and never overtaxed. For other publications, the administrator watches over the publication creation process. If the publication is one that requires work by outside agencies, the administrator may deliver publication files to them via removable media such as floppy disk or CD-ROM. The administrator will oversee the production process to ensure that the right publication files are created and delivered to the vendor that does the final production.

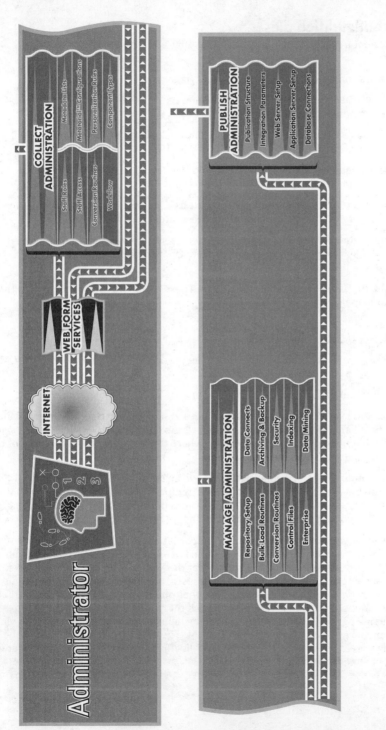

Figure 7-8: The administration system affects all three parts of a CMS.

The workflow system

The *workflow system* is responsible for coordinating, scheduling, and enforcing schedules and staff tasks. The workflow system affects all three parts of the CMS as follows:

✦ **In the collection system:** Here you find workflows for content collection, creation, and aggregation tasks. In most cases, the workflow follows a particular kind of content from creation until it's ready for publication. You may, for example, create a workflow that involves creation, review, and approval tasks for policy statements that you list on an intranet. After all steps of the process are complete, a policy statement is ready for display. In some cases, you design a workflow that crosses content types. A content-conversion workflow, for example, may include steps for logging in all content that arrives, distributing it to the people who are to process it, and then passing it to the appropriate editors after conversion.

✦ **In the management system:** Here you find workflows for standard administrative tasks such as backup and archiving. Additionally, you find workflows for reviewing, changing, and verifying the usefulness of content. Other workflows schedule data-mining and synthesis tasks. Finally, workflows also manage the connection between the management system and other non-CMS systems that provide data to the CMS.

✦ **In the publishing system:** Here publication cycles and their associated workflows ensure that each time you create a publication, it's as good as is possible. Suppose, for example, that your Web site operates on a daily publishing cycle, during which you update news and special announcements. You may create a workflow that includes steps to review all pending content, perform test builds of all affected pages, test personalization rules against new content, and change status to publish.

Connections

You likely need to connect the management system to various infrastructure and data systems, including the following:

✦ **The organization's LAN and WAN environments:** You connect the management system to these environments so that you can receive and deploy content anywhere in the organization.

✦ **The organization's user-management system:** You need to connect to this system so that, instead of retyping user data, you can simply reference the company's directory of users. If, for example, authors of a particular sort are all in one department and have a particular job title, you can reference the entries for these folks in the organization's user-administration system. Security clearances, e-mail addresses, and biographical information become accessible through enhanced administrative or HR systems.

✦ **Company metadata systems:** If the company has a global product catalog system that's not part of the CMS, for example, you need it to supply the list of product names for the CMS to use. A direct connection to the outside system with frequent updates ensures that the metadata that you use in the CMS stays current. You may also want a two-way connection so that content that you create or modify in the CMS can be posted back to the outside source.

✦ **Enterprise data systems:** If, for example, your CMS holds a copy of employee information records (with the master remaining in your organization's enterprise resource planning [ERP] system), you need a connection to the ERP system. The connection is a physical one that employs the LAN as well as a logical one that maps entities and relationships in the enterprise system with those you need in the CMS. You may, for example, want to combine the multiple address fields in the ERP system into a single Contact Info element in the Staff component type in the CMS.

Cross-Reference   For a complete discussion of the connection features a CMS may need, see Chapter 39, "Building Management Systems," in the section "External Connections."

The collection and management subsystems in a CMS help you gather and process your content. Next, you need to create a system to deliver the content to its consumers. That system is the publishing system.

The Publishing System

The *publishing system* is responsible for pulling content components and other resources out of the repository and automatically creating publications out of them (see Figure 7-9).

A publishing system includes:

✦ **Publishing templates:** programs that build publications automatically.

✦ **Publishing services:** a set of tools for controlling what is published and how it is published.

✦ **Connections:** tools and methods used to include data from other (non-CMS) systems in finished publications.

✦ **Web publications:** the most common output for most CM systems.

✦ **Other publications:** other non-Web publications, including electronic, print, and syndications.

I discuss each of these aspects of a publishing system in the following subsections.

Publishing templates

At the heart of the publishing system are *templates*, which bridge the gap between the neutral content in the repository and the needs of a particular publication (see Figure 7-10).

Publication templates are files that guide the creation of a publication from the content stored in the repository. Unlike more common word-processing templates, CMS templates are programs that use either a proprietary or an open programming language to specify publication-building logic. Templates include the following components:

✦ **Static elements:** These elements are text, media, and scripts that pass directly through to the publication without further processing.

✦ **Calls to publication services:** These calls retrieve and format components and metadata from the repository and perform other necessary functions such as running personalization rules, converting content, and building navigation.

✦ **Calls to services outside the CMS:** These elements integrate publications into a wider organizational infrastructure by calling in enterprise data and functionality and other Web services.

Cross-Reference   In Chapter 26, "Designing Publications," you'll find much more information on publishing templates.

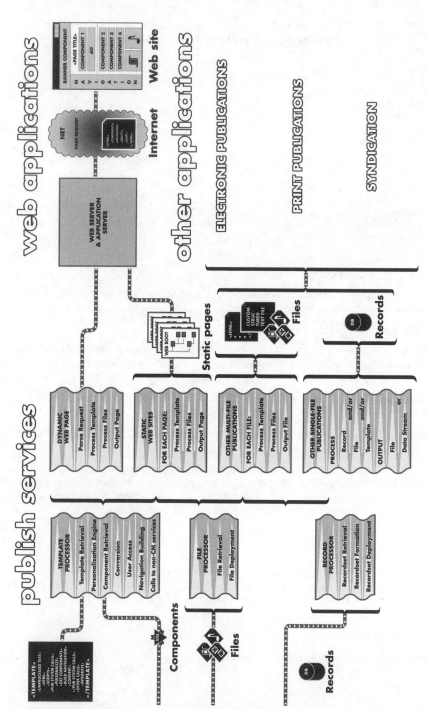

Figure 7-9: A publishing system uses templates and publishing services to produce Web sites as well as other kinds of publications.

```
[Template]
    [Static elements]
        [HTML]
        [Scripts]
        [Media references]
    [Pub service calls]
        [Personalized]
        [Get components]
        [Build navigation]
        [Other template logic]
        [Convert]
    [External calls]
        [Enterprise data]
        [Web services]
        [Commerce]
```

Figure 7-10: The publication template is a program that builds publications from the content in the repository.

Publishing services

Publishing services are the application logic and business services provided by a CMS that aid in the creation of publications from the content and metadata in the repository.

The publication services provide the following functions:

✦ **Load and execute templates:** These services process the personalization, conversion, content extraction, and navigation-building calls that the templates make to create a publication.

✦ **Provide publication-specific services:** These services include output to PDF for print publications or incremental updates to a Web site.

✦ **Provide a bridge to non-CMS services:** These are services that you call to provide data that you can include in publications.

In the case of a dynamic publication (such as a live Web site), you invoke the publishing services via a request from a browser and produce a single page. In static publications (static Web sites as well as other publications), a staff member or a prescheduled automation routine triggers the publication services that then produce a complete publication.

You may create part of a publication by using services that aren't part of the CMS by having the publishing services call them as independent software objects. Non-CMS services generally provide e-commerce transactions and access to enterprise data and other resources not under the control of the CMS. They may also augment interactivity in a Web publication by providing collaboration or other software-intensive features. These services often provide functionality that appears within a user interface that the CMS publishes onto Web pages.

Connections

The publishing system often maintains connections to other (non-CMS) enterprise data systems, such as those mentioned in the previous section. Enterprise data is the organization's data that you want to use but don't want to store in the CMS repository. Examples include ERP application data, user data, and other files and databases that you maintain outside the realm of the CMS. Data from these systems can be read live from the source at the time that you create a publication (which on the Web may be constantly), and you lay it out appropriately on the publication page at that time as well.

Note   You can also load enterprise data periodically from the source to the CMS repository. In this case, you consider the enterprise data source as acquired content.

The CMS isn't responsible for the management of enterprise data, but it can handle publishing enterprise data and publishing the functionality that enables users to interact with enterprise data systems.

Cross-Reference   In Chapter 11, "The Branches of Content Management," you can find a number of examples of a CMS handling the publication of non-CMS data.

Web publications

The most common use for a CMS today is to create Web publications (see Figure 7-11).

Web publications are Internet, intranet, and extranet sites that a CMS produces. If they're dynamic, the CMS produces these sites one page at a time in response to user clicks. In this case, the user's click passes a page request to the Web server that triggers the CMS publishing services to do the following:

✦ Load a template

✦ Pass it any parameters that came along with the user's page request

✦ Execute the code in the template to produce a finished page

✦ Pass the finished page back to the Web server for display in the user's browser

If they're static sites, the CMS produces them all at once and serves them as HTML files. The CMS administrator triggers a build of the static site using some user interface in the CMS. The CMS then calls the appropriate publishing services and templates to produce all the pages of the site.

Cross-Reference   In Chapter 6, "Understanding Content Management" in the section "CM Is a Computer Infrastructure," I describe static and dynamic Web sites.

The pages are a combination of content elements drawn from the repository by templates. The pages can also include functionality drawn from non-CMS services called in by templates and integrated into the content and navigation that the CMS provides.

Especially in dynamically built sites, the CMS publishing services are embedded within a Web server and an application server. The Web server is software that takes care of the basic function of receiving requests from the Web user and returning the results to her. The application server is software that provides caching, database connection pooling, and other services that help the CMS scale and increase its performance.

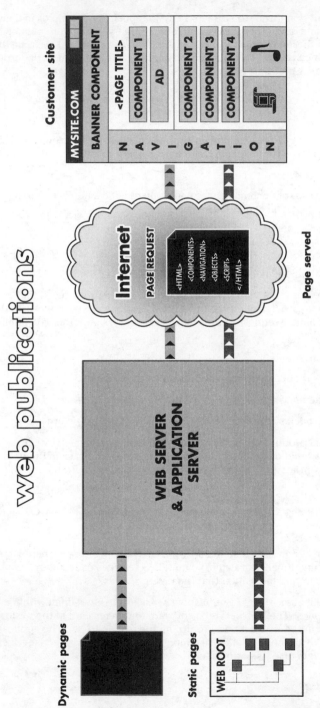

Figure 7-11: The Web-publishing system can produce a fully dynamic site.

Other publications

A CMS isn't limited to producing Web-based publications. In fact, the same processes that you use to create Web pages can also be used to create any other form of publication, such as electronic publications, print publications, and syndications.

You can potentially use the same templating engine that produces Web publications to create other publication formats. Unfortunately, most of the commercial systems in production today offer limited support for formats other than HTML. Still, with a little extra effort, you can create text-based publications of any format. With significant extra effort, you can even make many publications that aren't text-based — for example, a publication comprised of standard graphic elements that produces a building diagram. Of course, many of the publications that you may want to produce are HTML or variations on XML.

Note

If at all possible, you should seek to avoid manual post processing. *Manual post processing* requires you to change by hand the publication files that the CMS produces. You may, for example, need to manually number the figures in a print publication. As soon as the CMS and supporting automated routines can't automatically produce the publication file, you have two content branches. One branch is the master content that you store in the repository. The other branch is the content that's in the publication file, which is able to contain the changes that you make. If one branch changes, you need more manual effort to update the other branch — not a happy situation.

Publications that aren't destined for the Web include the following:

✦ **Print publications:** For print publications, the appropriate components and metadata are drawn out of the repository and converted to the format that the print system expects. Templates and conversion routines, for example, can create a FrameMaker (MIF) file that goes to a printer for publication. Other print formats such as QuarkXPress and Adobe Acrobat (PDF) files require that you use specialized tools, such as macros or scripts (some of which you may need to create yourself), to fully automate the process.

✦ **Electronic publications:** These publications are static Web sites that you distribute on CD-ROM or any other type of CD-ROM- or network-based multimedia system. The CMS uses templates and services that can produce the sort of text and media format and navigational structure that the electronic publication requires. Microsoft Help files, e-mail files, and the variety of formats now under development for wireless phones and Personal Digital Assistants (PDAs) are examples of non-HTML electronic publications

✦ **Syndications:** Syndications are sets of content components that you publish for distribution and reuse in publications outside your CMS. (As discussed in the section "The Collection System" earlier in this chapter, syndications may also be a source of the content you aggregate with the collection system.) The most useful format for syndication is XML, but the most common format is ASCII with a header that contains metadata for each syndicated component.

Summary

A large scale CMS is a complex system of many interacting parts. To help divide and conquer this complexity, I break the CMS into the following three interacting parts:

✦ The *collection system* shepherds content from an author or an existing source through the process of conversion and aggregation. *Conversion* maps the format and structure of the information to the one that you want. *Aggregation* brings the information into the component, editorial, and metatorial frameworks you establish.

✦ The *management system* provides an administrative infrastructure. This infrastructure includes a repository for storing content and necessary system files, an administration module for setting up and maintaining the CMS, and a workflow module for defining the tasks and processes that you expect to occur.

✦ The *publishing system* uses templates to extract appropriate content from the repository and fashion it into a publication. Although Web sites are the main event for today's CMSs, with a bit of extra effort, you can create almost any other kind of publication that you want.

In the next chapter, I outline the reasons why an organization would go through all the effort that a large CMS requires.

✦　　✦　　✦

Knowing When You Need a CMS

Any organization that creates publications practices some form of content management. Even the sole proprietor organizes files on her hard drive and tries to keep track of her content and share it across publications. The sole proprietor, however, has little need for the formality and tight structure that I present here. But if the sole proprietor grows to a small organization and then to a large organization, file-system directories and informal content sharing begin to cost too much and take too long. A content management system (CMS) may then become necessary to help organize and automate the process.

You need a CMS if your collection, management, and publishing processes are too complex to manage informally.

You can gauge complexity by the following guidelines:

✦ **The amount of content that you have.** This amount includes not only the number of items, but also the number of kinds of items that you're trying to manage.

✦ **The amount of contribution.** Take into account not only the number of contributors, but also their relationship to you, as well as the complexity of the existing content that you receive.

✦ **The amount of change that you expect in your content.** Change can occur in the amount of content you add or remove from the system or in the number of design changes that you intend to support.

✦ **The number of publications that you intend to create.** Complexity in publication depends on the number of different publications that you intend to create, as well as on the degree of personalization that you intend to implement.

Figure 8-1 illustrates what you need to look for to determine whether you need a CMS.

Too much content	Too many contributors
• Content items • Content types	• Diverse authors • Complex sources
Too much change	Too many publications
• Content throughput • Design revision	• Content channels • Personalization

Figure 8-1: I break the complexity of a content problem into four areas of concern.

Gauging the Amount of Content

You need a CMS if you have too much content to process by hand. Although the concept of content management can help you with even small projects, until you have a big system, you can't realize enough cost savings to justify the effort that constructing a solid CMS involves.

What is a *big* system? A big system is one that's too big to fit in one person's head. Say, for example, that, in the past, you counted on your Webmaster to know what content is on your site and where it all goes. Maybe you recently started to notice that she can no longer keep up with the influx of information and quickly assess and place new information on your site. You may now need a system to help the Webmaster. In particular, a big system has the following characteristics:

✦ **A lot of content:** Based on my experience, by the time that a Web site reaches 1,000 pages, it's clearly too big for anyone to manage informally. This number, however, is far from standard. You must view the sheer size of the content base in the context of all the other factors that I list here to decide finally whether your situation warrants a CMS. And although pages make up the usual unit of site size, the number of content components on your site is a better measure of the size of the content base than is the number of pages.

✦ **A lot of content types:** A content base of 1,000 components, all of the same type, is obviously easier to manage than a base of 1,000 components of five different types. For each component type, you must invent, implement, and oversee a corresponding collection, management, and publishing process. The more types that you have, the harder this task becomes to accomplish without help.

 Cross-Reference In Chapter 27, "Designing Content Types," in the section "Components versus pages," I go into detail about the contrast between components and pages.

You manage 1,000 items of content the way that you manage 1,000 items of anything: by arranging them into groups and storing them in a place where you can find them by type or by other key qualities (color, size, and the like). Content management systems provide the tools to divide content into like chunks (or components), arrange them into groups (in outlines and indexes), and store them in a place where you can get to them (in databases and XML files). By using a CMS to break 1,000 components into five types, you reduce the number of things that you need to know from 1,000 to five. Rather than needing to know what's in each of the 1,000 components, you need to know only what's in each of the five types. Reducing the complexity of a body of content so that you can again understand and master it is what content management is all about.

As you're measuring the amount of content you have, don't forget to include multiple languages or localities. If you have 100 items of content, for example, but you must deliver them in 10 languages, you really have 1,000 items of content to deliver.

Managing the Size of the Contribution Base

If one person creates all the content that you provide, you can usually count on her to create her own rules and follow them. As soon as you involve two people in the creation process, however, they need to agree on these rules and not change them without prior notice. If the system expands to dozens or hundreds of contributors, a much more complex system of automatically enforceable rules becomes necessary.

Suppose, for example, that you have 30 people throughout the organization whose task is to create Frequently Asked Question items (FAQs). Without further instruction, they all go their merry ways, creating FAQs in any way that they choose. The result is 30 different types of FAQs that you must reconcile. If, on the other hand, you're using a CMS, you can define a FAQ content type as follows:

✦ FAQs have the following required elements: question, answer, date, submitter, and subject area.

✦ Questions may run no longer than 256 characters and may contain no formatting. They must start with a question word (who, what, where, when, why, or how).

✦ Answers can run no longer than 3,000 characters with an optional link to more information. They can contain only bold, italic, and underline as formatting.

✦ Dates must appear in the correct format (MM/DD/YYYY).

✦ Submitter name must match exactly one of the names on the list of submitters.

✦ Subject areas must come from your accepted list. A FAQ must appear in at least one subject area, but it can appear in others as well.

You can probably see that simply writing and publishing these rules goes a long way toward standardizing FAQs. With a CMS at your disposal, however, you can turn these rules into part of the fabric of submission, as the following steps describe:

1. First, you can specify in the CMS that you have a content type that you call FAQ. As an author submits a piece of content, that author must specify whether it's a FAQ or something else. No space is available for submitting content that's not of some recognized type.

2. Second, you specify in the CMS that the FAQ type displays certain elements. If an author submits a FAQ, no discussion about what a FAQ consists of is possible. Either it displays the elements that the CMS knows about or it's not a FAQ.

3. Third, you specify in the CMS what values you allow for each of the elements of a FAQ so that the CMS can validate the content that an author submits. If an author types a date for a FAQ, the CMS can validate it and decide whether it's an acceptable value for the date element. If it's not an appropriate value, you can ask the author to correct it before submitting the item. For textual content, you have somewhat less control. Authors can, if they choose, type nonsense and you have virtually no way to validate whether the content has any meaning. You can, however, set limits as to the length of content in a text field.

4. Finally, the CMS can give you a convenient and easy-to-use way to present and facilitate the submission process. You can, for example, create a Web-based form for FAQs that neatly lists all the elements and requirements (see Figure 8-2).

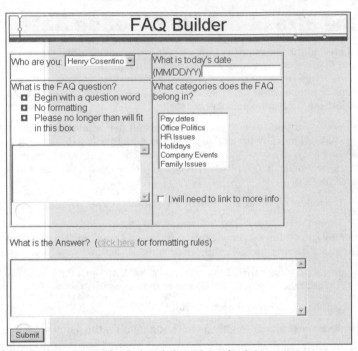

Figure 8-2: A hypothetical Web form for submitting FAQs

Where limitations exist, the form can state them. Where choices are constrained (for example, to lists and checkmarks), the form can make them simple to specify. Many commercial CMS products provide strong support for Web-based forms. This support seriously reduces the time necessary to create and maintain them.

The point, again, is that you will need the authoring rigor that a CMS provides when the diversity of authors exceeds your ability to manage their submissions casually.

Cross-Reference See Chapter 28, "Accounting for Authors," for more information about figuring out how to collect material from authors.

In addition to authoring, most organizations acquire information as well. Acquired content is originally created for some other purpose. To bend acquired content to your own purpose requires work. The amount of work depends on how different the content source is from what you want, as the following list describes:

✦ If you must convert the source from a format that's different from the one that you need for your system, that process requires work. Such conversion can prove to be cumbersome and sometimes quite difficult if, for example, your source is Quark Express format, and you must convert it to XML.

✦ If one unit of the source yields multiple content components, acquisition will require more work. If, for example, you must split one source document into three articles, two reviews, and five editorials, someone must decide exactly where to split it and then do the work to split it.

✦ If the information that you want to find and extract in the source is poorly marked or isn't present, finding and extracting that information requires work. If you need to find an author for each article in a source, for example, but the source doesn't always cite authors in the same way, someone must do extra work to find and extract authors' names.

Cross-Reference　In Chapter 29, "Accounting for Acquisition Sources," you find a lot more information about figuring out how to analyze your acquisition sources.

A CMS can't tell you what rules you need to keep authors consistent. Neither can it tell you how to convert, divide, or extract information from acquired sources. After *you* decide these rules, however, a CMS can help you keep the rules organized and can really help you promulgate and enforce them.

In any case, the more complex that your acquisition sources are and the bigger and more diverse your author base, the bigger is your content management problem and the greater your need for a CMS.

Anticipating the Amount of Change

Most people focus on the volume of content they have. In fact, after the system is up and running, the amount of change, not the volume, is what determines the complexity of a system. A 1,000-component system is simple if it never changes. The following two sorts of changes most directly affect complexity:

✦ **Component throughput:** This type of change refers to the number of content components that you modify in some way per unit of time. If, for example, you intend to create 100 new components per week and believe that about 50 per week are sure to become outdated — requiring deleting or archiving — and that about 50 more need editing in the same period, your total throughput is actually 200 components per week.

✦ **Frequency of design change:** This type of change refers to the rate at which you plan to do major layout, look, or navigational redesigns on your publications. In the Web world, for some level of redesign to occur monthly isn't unusual. The more frequently that you change the design of your publications, the more you need a content management system that can separate the design of your publications from their content so that, as the design changes, you don't need to modify each page of the publication by hand.

The act of updating or deleting a content component can be done quickly, but the process of finding the components to change or delete can prove to be slow if you don't have an effective CMS. Suppose, for example, that I have 1,000 FAQ components and want to review any that were submitted more than a year ago. I must either update them or delete them if they're no longer relevant. If these FAQs are on HTML pages, I may get stuck going through each page to decide which ones to work on. If the editor is even remotely like me, at the end of the process, she probably wonders whether she inadvertently messed something up on any (or all) of the 1,000 pages she touched.

If you store the FAQs as components in a CMS, however, you can simply search for FAQ components with a date more than a year old and review only the ones of interest. As you save each changed component, the system validates it so that you can be confident that it's still constructed correctly. Even better, you can use your CMS workflow module to send you an e-mail reminder message after a FAQ ages past a year. The message can even include the FAQ and a link to it in the CMS. If it's okay, you just delete the message. If the FAQ needs changes, you click the link in the e-mail message and go directly to the CMS Web form for that FAQ, where you can do your work.

Outside a CMS, making design changes can become a nightmare. Simply moving a button from one position to another may require a Web editor to open and make the same change on all the pages of the site. In a CMS, design changes become quite easy. Suppose, for example, that you want to change the layout of your FAQ page, in which answers are now shown below questions, so that answers display to the right of questions in a table. If your FAQs are in an HTML file, you must perform an extensive edit of the page, undoubtedly messing something up as you do it. If, on the other hand, you store your FAQs in components in a CMS, the CMS builds the HTML FAQ page automatically from a page template (see Figure 8-3).

```
[Template]                          [Template]
 [Get FAQs]                          [Get FAQs]
 [For Each FAQ]                      [For Each FAQ]
  <p>                                 <tr>
  [Insert FAQ Question]                <td>
  <br>                                  [Insert FAQ Question]
  [Insert FAQ Answer]                  </td>
 [Next FAQ]                            <td>
[Template]                             [Insert FAQ Answer]
                                      </td>
                                     <tr>
                                    [Next FAQ]
                                   [Template]
```

Figure 8-3: This illustration shows two templates for the same content. A small change in a template can make a global change in design.

The prototypical templates that I provide in Figure 8-3 show the small bit of code that inserts each question and answer. For each FAQ, the template on the left inserts an HTML paragraph break (<p>), following it with the question, an HTML line break (<br>), and an answer. The template on the right goes through every FAQ, too. Instead of separating the questions and answers with a line break, however, it embeds them in an HTML table.

In a minute or two of edits to the template on the left, you can change it to the template on the right, thus changing the layout for any number of pages. You don't touch any FAQs, so you can't possibly mess up any of them. In addition, you can try different table layouts and styles very quickly simply by changing a few lines in the template. Of course, not all templates are this simple, and even the ones that I show here aren't actual code, but just short descriptions that stand in for code (sometimes called *pseudocode*). Still, you can see that, with the help of templates, design changes needn't prove hard or scary.

Knowing the Number of Publications

Even a small system can become complex if you use it to create a number of distinct publications. Compare, for example, two businesses that both sell the same 100 vacation packages. One company provides a single printed brochure for each package. The second business provides brochures, a Web site that lists all the packages, a printed magazine that features some of the packages, and a set of one-page, black-and-white, electronically faxable fact sheets. All other factors being equal, the second company clearly faces a much more complex task. In gauging how many publications you have, consider the following two factors:

✦ **How many publication types you have.** In the preceding paragraph, the first company offers one type of publication (a brochure) and the second offers four.

✦ **How highly personalized your publications are.** A Web site that looks exactly the same regardless of who views it, for example, is obviously less complex than one that presents very different pages depending on the user. The same principle holds for nonelectronic publications. Complexity certainly rises for the company creating only brochures if they decide that they want to publish five variations of the vacation package descriptions, depending on the income level of the recipient.

If you want to create a number of publications from the same content without using a CMS, your only realistic option is to produce them in series and then make independent updates to each. The vacation company with four publications, for example, is likely to first create a set of brochures with all the right facts and pictures, as well as all the formatting and layout necessary, on a glossy brochure. It then passes the source files for the brochures on to three teams (or, just as likely, to one person wearing three hats). The Web team strips away all the formatting and layout and rearranges the brochures into Web pages (or relies on a layout program to do this — imperfectly — for them). The magazine team reintroduces all the extra text that the brochure creator needed to delete for lack of space and also dismantles and reassembles the brochure. Finally, the fax team does a similar reconstruction of the brochures, simplifying the layout and deleting most of the graphics that don't transmit well via fax. If all goes well, four publications may prove only twice the work of one. But all rarely goes well. Prices change, times change, and resorts send in better photos. Each publication must deal with these changes independently. You have no way to avoid each change becoming four times the effort. Across a large number of vacation packages, this extra effort can represent a huge cost (not to mention the cost of customer service and angry customers because of inevitably inconsistent information).

Using a CMS streamlines this process enormously. The CMS can contain a set of Vacation Package components. Each component contains enough elements to cover the needs of any of the publications. A Vacation Package component can, for example, contain both a Short Text and a Long Text element. Short Text is what you need for the fax version, whereas Long Text is for the Web site (see Figure 8-4).

```
[Template]                          [Template]
 [Get Vacations]                     [Get Vacations]
 [For Each Vacation]                 [For Each Vacation]
  <p>                                 <p>
  [Insert Vacation Title]             [Insert Vacation Title]
  <br>                                <br>
  [Insert Short Text]                 [Insert Long Text]
 [Next Vacation]                     [Next Vacation]
[Template]                          [Template]
```

Figure 8-4: Small differences in templates can make very different publications.

To create the two publications, the CMS simply uses two different templates. The one on the left in Figure 8-4 inserts the Short Text, and so you can use it to create the faxes (given that your system can fax HTML). The one on the right inserts the Long Text. You can use it to create Web pages from the same Vacation Package components. Of course, templates generally involve much more than I show here, but the idea is the same. The same content produces two very different publications depending on which template you use.

You do incur an up-front cost for developing these templates, but much of it's the same cost that you incur designing these publications in the first place. So the cost of developing the four publications in a CMS is more than the cost of developing them separately — but not necessarily *that* much more. (Your mileage may vary.)

The real advantages to a CMS approach come after you start to produce publications. As content changes occur, they are made only once in the component in the CMS repository. Then you simply click the button to rebuild your publications. Or, for dynamic publications, after each updated component is approved, it automatically appears for any Web visitor who requests that page. Any time that you create a new publication, it's guaranteed to contain the most up-to-date information. Your staff is less stressed, and your customers are more satisfied.

Note You might have to wait a few years for a CMS that can update magazines and brochures that are already printed. It's hard to make ink on a page rearrange itself (although research on digital ink technology continues).

Cross-Reference In Chapter 26, "Designing Publications," you find more information about multiple publications and the use of templates.

Personalization adds an entirely new dimension to publications. On the Web, you're not surprised anymore that a site knows your name and offers you content different from that for other users. Even in the print world, the custom printing of magazines or catalogs (offering a look and content specific to unique customer segments or even individual customers) has become more common for many publishers.

Cross-Reference

In Chapter 11, "The Branches of Content Management," in the section "Personalization," I fully detail the relationship between personalization and content management. Here I simply want to make the point that, the more personalization you require, the more a CMS can help.

The whole point of personalization is to locate and deliver content that's well-targeted to a particular audience. If you've ever tried to target an audience without the tagging, storage, and retrieval functions of a CMS, you have no doubt found that you must create the equivalent of a CMS yourself. By using a CMS, especially one offering strong personalization tools, the job becomes much easier.

The degree of personalization that you want to achieve matters. If you simply want to put someone's name at the top of a Web page, you don't need a CMS. If, however, you want to restructure the look-and-feel of a page and lay out targeted content depending on who's visiting, you need a CMS.

Cross-Reference

In Chapter 26, "Designing Publications," in the section "Analyzing Publications," I cover how you can accomplish personalization in a CMS.

Estimating Complexity

Content management isn't an exact science. It has no governing equations and laws. In the end, you will not judge your need for a CMS based on a disinterested calculation of complexity but on the careful but subjective balancing of the content factors I mentioned earlier (content, contributors, change, and publications), with the political and technical constraints in your organization. Still, it is useful to have some way to account for the content factors. It's worth some effort to be able to see:

✦ To what extent your content compels you to pursue a CM strategy

✦ Which factors are really driving your need

✦ Whether your situation is likely to get better or worse

Communicating the degree of complexity to a client or other stakeholders can itself be complex—there are so many factors to consider that often the answer to the question is "it depends." To help stakeholders get a handle on complexity using meaningful measures that are understandable, I've developed and refined a formula over the past five years that can serve as a kind of complexity index. Practice has shown that, although imperfect, this complexity index does do a fair job of representing the complexity of the task at hand and, therefore, the need for a CM strategy. The formula gives you a way to clearly account for and compare the various content factors that might predict your need for a CMS:

```
(Authors) X (Sources) X (Components) X (Types) X (Throughput) X
(Publications) X (Personalization) X (Redesigns)
```

This formula will yield a rough guide to the complexity of your situation, which, in turn, spurs your need for a CMS.

Table 8-1 explains the various factors and values of this formula.

Table 8-1: The Factors of a Content System

Factor	Description	Value
Authors	The number of authors you intend to include.	For fewer than 20 authors the value is 1. For more than 20 authors, the value is the number of authors divided by 20.
Sources	The number of complex sources.	For one or zero complex sources, the value is 1. For two or more complex sources, the value is the number of sources divided by 2.
Components	The number of components (or pages if you can't count components) in the system at its inception.	For 1 to 500 components, the value is 0.5. For 501 to 1,000 components, the value is 1. For more than 1,000 components, the value is the number of components divided by 1,000.
Types	The number of component types in the system, calculated as in the Value column.	For one to three types, the value is 0.5. For four and five types, the value is 1. For more than five types, the value is the number of types divided by 5.
Throughput	The number of components created or modified per week plus the number of components archived or deleted per week.	For zero to 25 components, the value is 0.5. For 26 to 50 components, the value is 1. For more than 50 components, the value is the number of components divided by 50.
Publications	The total number of different publications the system must create.	The number of publications.
Personalization	The degree of personalization that you intend for your publications.	A value of 1 indicates no personalization; 2 indicates that you personalize for a small number of large user segments; 3 indicates that you personalize for a large number of small user segments; 4 indicates that you personalize for each user. In all cases, the personalization needs to be more than simply putting someone's name at the top of a page.
Redesigns	The number of major layout, look, or navigational redesigns that you plan to perform per year.	For one to two redesigns, the value is 1. For more than two redesigns per year, the value is the number of redesigns divided by 2.

The equation works by multiplying all the factors that influence complexity, as I explain them here:

✦ All the factors have some method for arriving at a quantity (components per week, redesigns per year, and so on).

✦ Some factors also have a scaling value so that you can compare their quantities on a par with the rest. The number of components, for example, you divide by 1,000. (If you don't divide by 1,000, the effect of one new component on the overall complexity of the system is the same as the effect of one new publication. From another angle, you can say that the effect of adding a single component to the system is one one-thousandth as great as the effect of adding a publication.) I created these scaling values based on intuition and experience.

✦ I've imposed values on the components, types, and throughput if they're below threshold values. I add these thresholds so that some factors don't gain undue influence over the others because of small values. For example, for a system with 50 components, the components value is 0.5 because of the threshold I imposed. Without the threshold, the value would be 0.05, which would unduly bring down the overall value of the equation.

As you gain experience with your own system, you can tweak the scaling factors to best reflect the relative importance of the factors that you see. You can also add factors that you determine affect complexity in your situation.

I designed the equation so that a result of 1 is the break point for recommending a content management system. At this value and higher, a content management system is likely to prove a valuable asset in managing the complexity that you face. For results of less than 1, the value of a content management system is questionable, and as the result increases from one, the necessity of a system increases.

Note   I did not impose caps on the values of the factors. Therefore, the overall value of the equation can get very high very quickly. So far, the record for highest value is held by a government organization I have worked with whose equation yielded a value of over 10 million!

In the following sections, I run through a few scenarios that illustrate the use of this formula.

Vacation company "A"

Let's start by following the example of the brochure-only vacation company. In addition to the single brochure that it already has, assume that the company also wants to do the following:

✦ Produce or change two new brochures per week.

✦ Redesign the brochures two times per year.

✦ Have only one person do all the authoring.

Their data arrays as follows:

Factor	Complexity Variable	Complexity Value
Authors	1	1
Sources	0	1
Components	100	0.5
Types	1	0.5
Throughput	2	0.5
Publications	1	1
Personalization	1	1
Redesigns	2	1

The calculation is as follows:

```
[1] x [1] x [.5] x [.5] x [.5] x [1] x [1] x [1] = .0125
```

At a complexity value of .0125 (1/8), this company's need for a CMS is small. It may benefit from getting more organized, but unless its employees plan to change what they're doing, I see no reason for this company to invest the time or money necessary to put a CMS in place.

Vacation company "B"

Now look at a second vacation company. Say that this company acts as a broker for many vacation-package companies, performing the following tasks:

✦ It handles 600 vacation packages of four basic types.

✦ Each week, 30–40 of these packages change in some way.

✦ The company's only publication is a Web site, which it wants to redesign two times per year.

✦ The company has two authors and one complex source (say, a set of printed materials) to digitize and tag.

The data on this company arrays as follows:

Factor	Complexity Variable	Complexity Value
Authors	2	1
Sources	1	1
Components	600	1
Types	4	1
Throughput	35	1
Publications	1	1
Personalization	1	1
Redesigns	2	1

The calculation is as follows:

```
[1] x [1] x [1] x [1] x [1] x [1] x [1] x [1] = 1
```

At a complexity value of 1 (which I rigged, of course), this company could consider creating a CMS. A value of 1, however, doesn't indicate that the company's need is overwhelming. It would definitely benefit from the sort of thinking that a CMS requires, but as likely as not, it can still get by with mostly manual processes.

The key question for this company is "Which way are we going?" If the numbers are steady, a CMS is overkill. If the numbers are rising, the company may want to start planning before the system starts to overwhelm its personnel.

Vacation company "C"

Third, consider a vacation company with a big need. Say that it wants to grow to dominate the vacation package industry by performing the following tasks:

✦ It plans to handle 1,600 vacation packages of 10 types.

✦ Each week, 100 of these packages change in some way.

✦ In addition to its Web site, which it wants to redesign two times per year, the company plans to produce a printed catalog and a set of data sheets that it can send out via fax.

✦ The company wants to personalize at least to the level of broad user segments by promoting the packages and extras that it predicts each of four audiences will be interested in.

✦ It has five authors and four complex sources of information (and, as luck has it, each vacation-package supplier has its own hard-to-convert format).

This company's data arrays as follows:

Factor	Complexity Variable	Complexity Value
Authors	5	1
Sources	4	2 (4/2)
Components	1600	1.6 (1600/1000)
Types	10	2
Throughput	100	2 (100/50)
Publications	3	3
Personalization	2	2
Redesigns	2	1

The calculation is as follows:

```
[1] x [2] x [1.6] x  [2] x [2] x [3] x [2] x [1] = 76.8
```

At a complexity value of 76.8, this company should definitely consider creating a CMS. I suspect that the five authors are straining to keep up with the workload, the redesigns are late, two of the three publications are out of date, and unless its employees are very organized, the company's lack of a system shows in the quality of its publications.

If it's like most of the aspiring companies I've seen, this situation is only the start. Management wants to see more publications, faster redesigns, and a higher throughput of information. If so, the managers are in just the right frame of mind to pay for a CMS.

Vacation company "D"

Finally, I arrive at the 800-pound gorilla of vacation companies. This company works exclusively online, acting as a kind of online vacation-package clearinghouse. It originates its own packages, and it also resells packages from other specialized companies on a large scale. It wants to rule the vacation package industry by performing the following tasks:

✦ It plans to handle 3,000 vacation packages of 15 types.

✦ Each week, 200 of these packages change in some way.

✦ The company publishes only to its Web site — no printed catalog or faxed data sheets. It redesigns its Web site about once a year.

✦ The company also wants to personalize at least to the level of broad user segments by promoting the packages and extras that it predicts each of four audiences will be interested in.

✦ It has at least 40 authors and 100 complex sources of information (with most sources in their own hard-to-convert formats, of course), and it adds or changes about 25% of its complex sources per year.

So this company is somewhat bigger in terms of number of packages than vacation company "C." Company "D" publishes only one kind of content — its Web site — but it has a lot more authors and outside complex sources.

This company's data arrays as follows:

Factor	Complexity Variable	Complexity Value
Authors	40	2
Sources	100	50 (100/2)
Components	3000	3 (3000/1000)
Types	15	3
Throughput	200	4 (200/50)
Publications	1	1
Personalization	2	2
Redesigns	1	1

The calculation is as follows:

```
[2] x [50] x [3] x  [3] x [4] x [1] x [2] x [1] = 7200
```

At a complexity value of 7200, this company simply can't operate without a CMS of some kind. A tidal wave of content arrives every day, dozens of part-time authors are clamoring for help with questions, and requested updates to the Web site are getting farther and farther behind. Unless it does something fast, this company will collapse under its own weight.

For this company, the question of a CMS is not *if*, but *which one*.

Notice that the solution to this company's pain would be different than that for company "C," even though it deals with a not too-dissimilar number of packages. For one thing, company "D" doesn't care so much about publishing flexibility as long as whatever system it adopts can publish to the Web. What it does care a lot about, however, is content collection—both for authoring done in-house, as well as for the changing multitude of complex sources that must be massaged into shape. Clearly, a system that gives this company great authoring tools and powerful conversion tools will address its biggest problem.

So Tell Me, Are You Willing to Give Up Your Cartoon Time?

Have you ever bought software thinking it will solve all your problems? I was so taken by the promise of having my home accounting all neatly managed that I picked up a copy of Quicken last year. It was an impulse buy in an office supply store. Standing there in front of the Quicken display, I could almost see the reports rolling out of my home printer: "See here, Honey?" I was going to say to my wife, "This month we spent 2.5% more on crackers and 10% less on turnips." I was in my own obsessive-compulsive reverie, and I could see it all: financial transactions would be imported, metadata magically added, and everything would be at my disposal at the click of a button.

That was a year ago. Today, Quicken is still sitting on my hard disk; installed and ready to go. Every weekend I make plans to start importing transactions and setting up accounts. But I never do it. All the potential remains locked up in my hollow and content-starved Quicken database.

What gives?

Well, at the end of the day, I have a perfectly good Excel worksheet that I built many years ago, and it tracks everything I need. It helps ensure I pay all my bills on time each month, save for things I want, and plan my expenses. It's not perfect; but it does the trick. I guess my pain just isn't great enough, and the benefits aren't grand enough for me to change my ways.

That's the way it is with all content management systems. They may look good on the shelf, sitting there in the magazine ad, or on display at your local office supply store. But most of the work is in making sure you can "power up" the software with people and processes. This invariably requires planning, coordination and, more often than not, some cultural changes in your group.

When I work with groups interested in content management systems, I've always found that the skills of the team, their habits, and their needs dictate whether they need a full-blown, workflow-managed, feature-rich, auto-tagging, open-API, fully-integrated content and knowledge management combo-system, or simply a database with generic input screens.

If I had thought through what I would need to invest to print off those itemized grocery reports for my wife, I would have realized it would cut into precious Saturday morning cartoon time with my 7-year-old daughter. And that would have stopped me cold.

So before you make the decision to buy a content management system or grow your own, ask yourself if you're ready to give up those cartoons and change the way things are done in your organization today.

Rahul Joshi, Fred Hutchinson Cancer Research Center (rjoshi@fhcrc.org)

Evaluating your own need

Table 8-2 provides a general framework for evaluating your own situation.

Table 8-2: Evaluating Your Need for a CMS

Complexity	Your Need for a Content Management System
Below 0.25	Little need for a system.
0.25 to .05	Could begin thinking about a system if you believe that your need may grow.
0.5 to .075	Should begin thinking about a system if you believe that your need is likely to grow.
0.75 to 1.0	This range is the beginning of the gray zone between no need and need. In this range, go with your intuition about what you need. Take into account whether your complexity may grow. If yes, this point is a good time to begin a content management analysis in preparation. If your need isn't likely to grow, a system may well prove more effort than it's worth.
1.0 to 10	This range is still in the gray zone. A system, however, is more likely a need than not in this region. Even if you don't expect your complexity to grow, a small system may save more than it costs.
10.0 to 100	A system is recommended. You can perhaps start slowly or cover the factors that have the highest values, but eventually you want to implement a system.
Above 100	A system is necessary. You're likely experiencing content management problems now. If your complexity is much more than 100 and is still growing, you may need to act quickly to either control complexity growth or implement the parts of a system that relieve the highest pressures. As your complexity becomes much greater than 100 (say 1000 or even more) your need may become acute.

I want to emphasize again that I've designed this method to help you estimate, not pin down, your need. At its core is the assertion that a set of factors affect complexity and, therefore, the need for a CMS. You can decide whether the factors that I present are the complete set for your situation and whether the scaling that I provide adequately reflects the relative importance of these factors in your organization and content base.

In addition to giving you a ballpark estimate of your need for content management, this formula also helps you focus on the capabilities that you need to find in whatever system you choose. If your need for level 4 personalization is what's driving your complexity number so high, for example, you can immediately assume that your solution must be very apt at personalization. And you can begin to apply whatever sort of near-term solution that you can find to personalization to buy you time while you implement a full system. Of course, this calculation is rough, and gives you little more than a starting place to decide what kind of system to construct. To clarify what kind of system to construct, you need to perform a logical design.

Cross-Reference   For more information on logical design, see Chapter 19, "Selecting Hardware and Software," as well as all of Part IV.

Summary

If you ask most people why they may need a system to manage their content, they're likely to say, "Because we have too much." That "too much" is just a start toward getting your arms around the idea of whether you need a CMS.

More specifically, the general "too much" can mean:

✦ You have too many items or too many types of items.

✦ You have too many contributors or too much hard-to-process information.

✦ You have a high rate of change in content or publication design.

✦ You have many different publications or a high need for personalization in your publications.

Using the rough calculation that I provide in this chapter, you can begin to assess your own need for a CMS and decide whether — or when — you need to make the leap, and what kinds of capabilities to look for in the CMS you adopt.

In the next chapter, I trace some of the industries and disciplines that contribute to the concepts and practices of content management.

✦   ✦   ✦

Component Management versus Composition Management

✦   ✦   ✦   ✦

In This Chapter

CM systems can be modular or linear, or some of both

Component, composition, and schema-driven systems compared

Which system is right for you?

✦   ✦   ✦   ✦

It may come as no surprise that how you organize and manage information in a CMS depends greatly on how your content fits together.

On one end of the range is a system that contains completely modular, componentized chunks of content, or a *component management* system. On the other end of the range is a set of content chunks that must go together in a particular order, or a *composition management* system. And as you might expect, between the two extremes are systems that have attributes of both component and composition management systems.

Component and composition management systems (and all the systems in between) all share the characteristic of being organized and unified, but the kind of the unification is different, and how you manage it is also different. In this chapter, I explore what it means to unify information and how your content itself may lead you to manage it in different ways.

CM Systems Can Be Modular or Linear

Most CM systems are similar to data management (DM) systems in that they treat items of content as discrete entities, connected only through metadata. For example, a typical Web CMS may manage a couple of dozen distinct types of content, each with its own internal structure. Each chunk of content (a content *component*) is tied only weakly to other chunks. Even though many chunks may come together to form a unified publication, each chunk is really designed to stand alone. Each may even have been created from a separate original document. This sort of CMS is quite similar to a library; each content chunk is its own domain (book) but is still linked to other chunks by metadata (card catalog). I call these types of modular systems *component systems* to indicate that the primary emphasis is on collecting, managing, and publishing discrete chunks of information.

In contrast, some CM systems contain content that is more tightly tied together, more like a single book. In many books (including this one), each piece of content fits into an overall outline of parts. Some sort of narrative runs through most of or all the content. It is meant to be read in a particular order. Where the data management-like component systems bring together separate standalone chunks and organize them into wider publications, book-like composition systems start with a fully-integrated content base and use it to produce a variety of targeted publications. I call these types of linear systems *composition systems* to indicate that the emphasis is on collecting, managing, and publishing a single tightly integrated composition.

Table 9-1 summarizes the differences between these two types of systems in terms of the essential functions of a CMS: collection, management, and publishing.

Table 9-1: Component and Composition System Comparison

	Component Systems	Composition Systems
Collection	Authoring can be done by any number of people who do not know one another or know much about content other than that which they're authoring. Pre-existing content may be easily aggregated from outside sources. Content fits into stand-alone buckets that aren't organized in a linear fashion.	Authoring is done by those who have an intimate understanding of how the content that they're authoring relates to all the other content in the system. Pre-existing content may be difficult to integrate into the content system. Content fits into a (usually linear) structure from which it derives part of its meaning.
Management	Content hangs together loosely and vertically. That is, the links between branches of the content tree are weak; primary links are vertical to the top-level categories in the system.	Content hangs together both vertically and horizontally. Links between one branch of content and the other are strong; meaning is reflected in the structure of the content. Links are to other content categories at all levels.
Publishing	Publishing consists of choosing and assembling the desired chunks of content. The challenge of publishing is to get the result not to resemble a collection of independent information chunks.	Publishing consists of extracting relevant sections from the larger whole. The challenge of publishing is to get the result to not resemble just an excerpt from a larger narrative.

The kinds of processes you need to work with modular components differ from those needed for linear composition content. For example, for component content you might need tools that help you locate what kinds of information you have and then assemble them in a structure that makes sense for your Web site. With composition content, you already have a pretty good idea of the structure and content you have, so you might need tools that help you extract a subset of your content to publish on your Web site. In one case, you are building content up; in the other, you are pulling it out.

Somewhere between these two models lies a *schema-driven CMS*, which contains attributes of both models. Like the book system, in the schema-driven system there is a single overarching outline into which all the content fits. However, like the DM system, the schema system does not have a single story line that runs through the repository, and it is not meant to be read in a particular sequence. For example, the information that goes into the release of a new product can be in a well-defined structure and sequence, yet individual pieces of information (product strategy and product descriptions, for example) are only loosely linked and aren't meant to be read in a particular sequence.

To get a better idea of what might best suit your content and need, take a closer look at all three kinds of systems.

Component CM Systems

A component CMS is the typical type used for managing an organization's Web content. The CMS contains a variety of content types that—although they are organized around the content a particular organization creates, manages, and publishes—are weakly related to one another. The components of each type might be related only by being in the same site hierarchy. If the system has stronger relations, it might also relate components with a single set of keywords applied across all of them and by having a set of cross-references between them. Still, each chunk of content is relatively standalone.

Table 9-2 shows the content types that a typical product company might use a CMS to manage. By defining a system for collecting, managing and publishing a Web site full of these types of components, the organization hopes to save itself a lot of effort and create a better Web site.

Table 9-2: Typical Content Types in a Component System

Content Type	Description
Locations	This class stores information about the places where the organization does business.
Product	This class groups product and service components and wraps them in introductory information that shows how the combination of products and services solves a customer need.
Annual Reports	Web-delivered versions of the company's annual report.
Events	This class stores information about the events that the organization is planning or has staged. Best practice for organizations with lots of events is to buy a separate event management system and simply link to the CMS through page templates.
Press Releases	This class stores the press releases that the organization has issued.
Outside News	This class stores information about news stories produced outside the organization.
Outside Links	This class stores information about Web links that audiences might be interested in.
Articles	This class is a general-purpose place to store any component that behaves like an essay.
FAQs	This class stores question and answer pairs. Grouping the pairs into FAQ lists is accomplished by the way they are indexed and cross-referenced.
Customers	This class stores information about customers and the company's interactions with them.
Jobs	This class holds information about jobs available at the organization. Best practice is to have this information stored in a separate HR system and have it accessed but not owned by the CMS.
Downloads	This class stores information about the binary files the organization wants to offer as downloads.

Cross-Reference This set of content types is more fully described in Chapter 27, "Designing Content Types," in the section "A Sample Set of Content Types."

It's pretty easy to see how all the types fit together; each type neatly parallels the major areas you'd find on a fairly typical company Web site. But each of the content types is simultaneously a world unto itself. No one type really depends upon the others to be meaningful from the standpoint of collection, management, or publishing. Content in the Annual Reports class doesn't need to know much about content in the FAQ class; Events doesn't need to know much about Jobs, and so on. Each can be created on a separate form or in its own application by authors who do not know each other.

Figure 9-1 gives a high-level view of how a component-driven document system works.

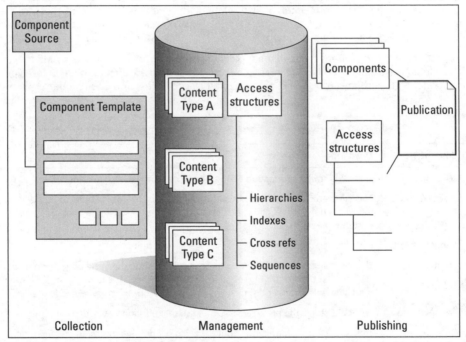

Figure 9-1: In a component-driven system, content components are created independently of one another and are later related in the repository by the metadata they are tagged with.

A component-based CM system deals with these chunks of content throughout the collection, management, and publishing life cycle, as follows:

✦ **Collection:** In the system shown in Figure 9-1, individual components have very little to do with one another at the point of creation. Each distinguishable class of original content forms a content type. Processes are devised to create each type following its own schema.

✦ **Management:** When a component of content of any type is added to the repository, it is tagged with metadata that allows it to be accessed later and related to other components of the same or different types. This type of metadata constitutes the access structures of the CMS. For example, if an article and a FAQ are about the same subject, both might include a subject keyword element (an index access structure) with the same keyword in it ("Transport" for example). The access structures are separate from the content components they relate.

✦ **Publishing:** In this type of system, publishing consists of pulling the right components and access structures out of the repository and using them to create a publication.

Cross-Reference

I discuss access structures in detail in Chapter 30, "Designing Content Access Structures."

So, in this kind of system (which is, by the way, the kind I discuss throughout most of this book), content chunks are basically atomic. The elements that tie the content chunks and allow the organization to make a unified Web site (or other publication) out of them are the various types of metadata that are attached to each and the relationships that are specified for each type of content.

Composition Systems

In contrast to standard CM systems that focus on the assembly of components of content from different sources, book-like composition systems focus on authoring, managing, and publishing content that must hang together in an overall outline and narrative.

Taking a page from my own book (so to speak), the system I constructed to manage the creation of the first edition of this book (which I call the *CM Domain System*) is a good example of a composition system. It produces a book, a Web site, training materials, weekly e-mails, and other publications. The system has all the major aspects of content collection, management, and publishing. On the other hand, its content types are quite different from those of a component system, as Table 9-3 shows:

Table 9-3: Typical Content Types in a Composition System

Content Type	Description
Section	Sections are named blocks of text that cover one topic. The strange thing about sections from the standpoint of content management is that one section component can be embedded within another. A large part of the content repository consists of sections within sections.
Concepts	Concepts are two to three paragraphs of text and media that express a single idea. The strange thing about concepts is that they are all embedded within Section components.
Media	Media are images or slide decks with multiple image files and captions. Media elements exist in the repository inside concepts and sections.
Seminar	Seminars have titles, learning objectives, and exercises. In addition, they have references to the section and media components that present the substance of the seminar.

All in all, the composition system is like a book that has been divided into content components but not split apart. Many components risk losing much of their meaning and significance if torn out of the higher-level component within which they're embedded. For example, a biographer of Sigmund Freud could pull out chapters of her book to deliver as a lecture series or publish them separately based on subject matter—Freud's time in Berlin, his relationship with associates, his major theories. But she'd have to be careful to avoid sundering the necessary context that the book as a whole provides, such as information about Freud's childhood, education, and family.

A quick comparison between this list of content types and the one for a standard component system outlines one of the major differences between the two types of systems. The component system includes more types, and they are all created based on what sort of information is in them (product information versus location information, for example). In the composition system, fewer kinds of content types exist, and they reflect the structure and interrelationships of the content, as shown in Figure 9-2.

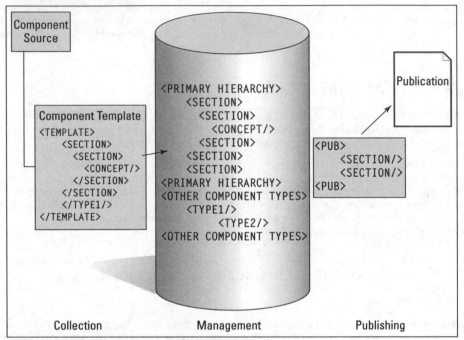

Figure 9-2: In a composition system, content is authored directly into a master schema where each component is embedded or referenced within other components. Care should be used when publishing portions of the content to avoid losing narrative context.

Collection in a composition system

The collection process in a book-like system is not that different from collection in a standard component system. For example, the CM Domain system I used to create the first edition of this book includes:

✦ **Authoring:** The system enables the direct authoring of Concept components through an XML-based authoring interface. This interface is designed for technical authors who are close to the CMS team. It also includes Web-based forms for authoring some components one at a time by people who are less technical and farther from the core team.

✦ **Acquisition and conversion:** The system enables acquisition of content from Microsoft Word, converting it and placing it in the proper place in the repository.

✦ **Aggregation:** The system metator is responsible for ensuring that all components are filled in completely and are included in the system's access structures.

Cross-Reference For an explanation of access structures, see the section "Understanding Access Structures" in Chapter 30, "Designing Content Access Structures."

The major difference in collection between the two systems is that in a component system, authoring templates reflect only the structure of the internal parts of the content type you are authoring. In the composition system, on the other hand, each author needs to be much more concerned with how her content fits in with the rest of the content already in the repository. As such, the templates in a composition system reflect the structure of the component but also represent how that component is embedded within the rest of the content.

Management in a composition system

Management in a book-like system is significantly different from that in a standard component system. First of all, the repository is structured in a very different way.

The following segment of XML, for example, shows how the various components of the CM Domain system developed for this book are embedded within and reference each other within the repository:

```
<CMDOMAIN>
    <PRIMARYHIERARCHY>
        <SECTION><TITLE>Building A CMS</TITLE>
            <SECTION><TITLE>Building Collection Systems</TITLE>
                <SECTION><TITLE>An Example Collection System</TITLE>
                    <CONCEPT>
                        <SUMMARY>
                            An XML environment should offer enforcement
and visibility.
                        </SUMMARY>
                            <BODY>Some text <MEDIAREF/> Some more text
</BODY>
                    </CONCEPT>
                </SECTION>
            </SECTION>
        </SECTION>
    </PRIMARYHIERARCHY>
    <MEDIACOMPONENTS>
        <MEDIA>
            <TITLE>Illustration of a CMS</TITLE>
            <TYPE>Image</TYPE>
            <FILE>CMS.JPG</FILE>
        </MEDIA>
    </MEDIACOMPONENTS>
    <SEMINARS>
        <SEMINAR>
            <TITLE>Doing CM</TITLE>
            <OBJECTIVE>
                <TITLE>Learn CM</TITLE>
                    <SECTIONREF>
                    <SECTIONREF>
            </OBJECTIVE>
        </SEMINAR>
    </SEMINARS>
</CMDOMAIN>
```

This sample shows the gross structure of the CM Domain repository (disregarding a lot of intervening XML elements and attributes). Although you may not be familiar with the syntax subtleties, it should suggest how tightly integrated the various content types are and how the overall repository reads like a book. Notice that:

✦ The PRIMARYHIERARCHY tag holds all the section components.

✦ The MEDIACOMPONENTS and SEMINARS hold Media and Seminar components respectively.

✦ Section components are embedded in other Section components.

✦ Concept components are embedded within Section components.

✦ Media components are referenced within Section or Concept components.

✦ Seminar components reference Section components.

All in all, the structure of the repository in a composition system is an intertwined mass of highly interrelated components. This is as it should be, because the composition you are managing is a single unified mass of content. In essence, most if not all the access structures that are separate in a component system are embedded within the content or actually encompass the content (as is the case with the primary hierarchy) in a composition system.

In addition to the very different sort of repository structure in the composition system, the workflow and user administration have very different requirements. In the standard component system, each content type has a workflow of creation, review, and publication. Individuals own some number of components of a particular class. They do their work and then pass ownership to the next person. In other words, they can work fairly independently. In the composition system, because components are so interrelated, such simple workflow and ownership will not work. For example, Nien-Tzu might own a Section component within which is a Section component that I am working on. Does that mean she owns my Section component, or do I own it? In fact, we both have a stake in the section component I am working on, and so we had better keep in touch. The workflow and ownership model that we create must allow us to stay as tightly connected as our content is.

Cross-Reference For information about how to analyze and design an appropriate workflow model, see Chapter 33, "Designing Workflow and Staffing Models."

Publication in a composition system

The hallmark of a composition CMS is that all the chunks of content fit together neatly into a single grand organizational scheme. Unlike the data-management sort of component system, each chunk (each section) is a tightly integrated part of the whole.

If that were the end of the story, you would not have a CMS, you would have a book. But you don't have just a book. What differentiates a CMS from, say, a three-inch stack of handwritten pages (or a long Word document) is the system—what it requires of you and what you can do with it. Because you author the tightly integrated content in a structured way, and store and manage it in a repository, you can easily build a wide range of publications in a wide range of formats as often as you like. That is what differentiates a composition CMS from a book.

In a composition system, publications combine components just as in any other CM system. On the other hand, in the standard component system, each component comes without strong attachments to other components. However, in the composition system, special care has to be taken when you pull components out of the ones within which they are embedded.

Cross-Reference You can find specific advice for dealing with problems related to pulling embedded content out of its context in Chapter 26, "Designing Publications," in the section "Publication gotchas."

Even though you need to take care when reusing components from a composition system, it does not mean that you shouldn't do it. Quite the contrary, in fact; you created a composition CMS rather than a book precisely so that you *could* reuse components in numerous types of publications. The CM Domain system produces the following sorts of publications:

✦ **Printed book:** The files that produced the first edition of the *Content Management Bible* printed book were themselves produced from the content in the CM Domain repository. Each chapter is produced by a section template. Each section template calls in component and navigation templates as needed to create the finished publication.

✦ **CM Domain Web site:** The HTML files that create the CM Domain Web site are published from the CM Domain repository. Various page, component, and navigation templates are used to create the site that houses the same primary hierarchy and Concept components as the printed book, plus other components. For more information on the CM Domain Web site, go to www.metatorial.com.

✦ **Seminar materials:** The Microsoft Word files that contain CM Domain training materials are published from the CM Domain repository. A section template creates the materials for any of a number of training modules by pulling in Concept components from the primary hierarchy into a set of training objectives. For more information on seminars, go to www.metatorial.com.

✦ **Marketing materials:** Web and print data sheets and other materials that are published from the CM Domain repository.

✦ **White papers:** Excerpts from the CM Domain that span any part of the primary hierarchy can be published as print or HTML white papers. White papers (mine and others) are available on www.metatorial.com.

✦ **E-mail messages:** Individual Concept components that can be published as flat text and sent inside e-mail messages to subscribers. (See the www.metatorial.com for subscription details.)

A schematic of the system that creates all these publications is shown in Figure 9-3.

The publication system has the following parts:

✦ **XML repository:** Content for all publications is drawn from the CM Domain XML file by the Publication processor. (See the third bullet in this list.)

✦ **XSLT templates:** For each publication, the system has a set of XSLT style sheet files (templates). These templates, if applied to the XML file, create the pages or sections of any publication.

✦ **Publication processor:** This application provides a user interface to the various kinds of publication builds you might want to do. It loads XML and XSLT, directly manipulates the XML as may be needed, and then transforms it by using the appropriate XSLT template for the publication you chose.

✦ **Web files:** The XSLT system produces the HTML pages of the CM Domain Web site as well as a variety of other HTML pages. These files can be staged for testing and then deployed to a production server.

✦ **Print files:** The XSLT system produces files that are destined to be print publications. This is a multistage process. In the first stage, XML content is rendered into a plain-text format that can be opened easily in the target print platform (Microsoft Word).

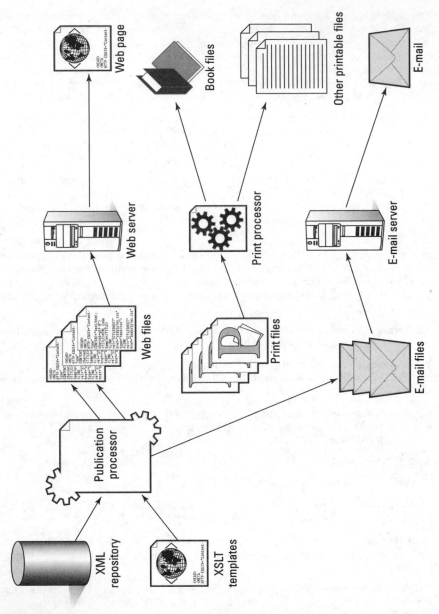

Figure 9-3: The CM Domain publication system

✦ **Print processor:** In the second stage of the print process, the print publication is formatted. The print processor program applies the appropriate Word formatting for the content, based on the codes that are included in the plaintext print files. It transforms the flat text of those files into standard Word files that are ready to be printed.

✦ **Book files:** The book files in Microsoft Word format leave the CM Domain system to be part of a standard print publication process. They will be manipulated considerably but not structurally altered on their way to becoming a printed book.

✦ **Other printable files:** Other print format materials (seminars, white papers, and so on) can be printed directly from the Word files the system creates. The print templates contain all the front matter, headers and footers, and navigation that publications need to be complete and well-presented.

It should be clear that a composition CMS is the right fit for a large base of information that is all about a single subject, and if you have a variety of audiences and many needs that the same information must meet. A book is a useful and common product of a system like this, but it's just one possible output among many—and in fact, a system like this need not result in a printed book at all. In my teaching, for example, I create all my course materials in a composition CMS. I author, edit, and update content as part of large corpus of highly interrelated course information. I publish course Web sites and printed materials as needed from the corpus.

Schema-Driven Systems

Between the modularity and flexibility of traditional CMS systems and tightly interwoven book-like systems is a third type of system that shares aspects of both. This kind of system provides the flexibility of multiple content types as does a component system, and it also provides a high level of integration just as a composition system does. What enables this hybrid of capabilities is the XML or database schema that underlies the content structure, which is why I call this a *schema-driven system*.

Like a component- or composition-driven system, a schema-driven system can easily produce a wide range of publications. Just as in the other systems, content types unite content thematically, regardless of how it will be published. And just as in the other systems, publications are produced by combining bits and pieces of various components at the time you want to publish them.

In a typical scenario, an organization pursues this sort of CMS because it wants to take control of a body of information that is now being created as standalone documents. For example, a marketing department might produce 100 semi-related documents as part of a product launch. Rather than trust that those 100 documents are going to share information, cover all the information needed to be produced, and jointly support the product launch, the group might decide to implement a CMS to make sure they get the sharing, comprehensive coverage, and support they need. In addition, a CMS will offer them a chance to do the following things that are not possible without one, including:

✦ **Really figure out what kind of information is needed** to support a product launch

✦ **Make sure the right person is assigned** to create each piece of information

✦ **Ensure that only one definitive version of each piece of information is created,** rather than as many versions as there are authors and documents

✦ **See and review content** as it is being created

✦ **Distribute content** in wide and evolving formats and structures

Figure 9-4 shows how a schema-driven system works at a high level.

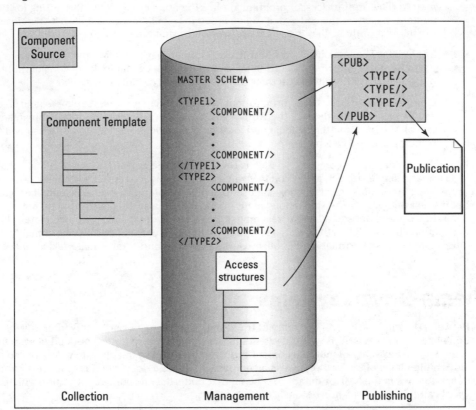

Figure 9-4: A schema-driven system has aspects of the component and composition systems.

Following the process in Figure 9-4 from the left, you see that instead of replicating document-like components, the system is based on a total picture of the content needed for a whole set of outputs. In practice, this schema might be based on an analysis of existing documents, which results in the synthesis of a schema based on key content types. Notice that this system has aspects of both the component and composition systems:

✦ **Like the composition system**, the authoring templates are schema-like and reflect not only the structure of the content type being authored, but also how it fits with other content. Similarly, the repository is guided by a master schema that embeds much, but not all the access structures used to tie the content together.

✦ **Like the component system**, the schema system is based on content types that are distinct from each other and are pulled out of the repository independently to form publications.

The schema system sits somewhere between the total integration of the composition system and the minimum integration of the component system. It shows that you can decide for yourself how much integration you need in your own CMS.

A schema-driven system for creating marketing content, for example, might contain the content types listed in Table 9-4.

Table 9-4: Typical Content Types in a Schema System

Content Type	Description
Overview	This content type describes the overall aims of this marketing initiative.
Market	This content type describes the market, including information about its size, composition, and segmentation.
Value proposition	This content type describes the value proposition of the product offering.
Vertical mapping	This content type describes how the product fits into the vertical markets that are described in part in the Market content type.
Partner strategy	This content type describes the target types of partners desired for the marketing initiative, as well as the nature of the partner relationship.
Marketing strategy	This content type describes the approach to marketing the product that the company will take.
Positioning	This content type describes the positioning message for the product as related to its competitors.
Sales strategy	This content type contains information about the sales force, structure, and approach that the company will use to sell the product.
Competitors	This content type contains information about the number and size of the competing companies in this market sector, as well as their market share and prospects.

Collection in a schema-driven system

Collection in a schema-driven system is not all that different from collection in standard component and composition systems. For example:

✦ **Authoring:** Like component and composition systems, schema-driven systems can include direct authoring of content types through an XML-based authoring interface. The authoring environment may include a kind of contextual wrapper to tell the author how the content is related to other content in the schema.

✦ **Acquisition and conversion:** The system requires breaking up content from outside sources either by means of templates that require authors to apply XML tags in other environments like XmetaL or Word; or by way of transforming content based on known characteristics such as content-based style tags. However, acquiring content that was not prepared specifically with the content schema in mind usually requires the extensive work of identifying and tagging content by hand.

✦ **Aggregation:** The system can produce reports of missing content. These reports can be as simple as generating output documents with *This content missing* placeholders for any content not yet in the system.

Management in a schema-driven system

Management has similarities to both composition and component systems.

Like a composition system, components in a schema-driven system may be embedded within other components and may reference one another within the repository. Unlike a composition system, however, the overall repository doesn't read like a book. Instead, content is organized thematically; unlike either a composition or component system, content is not based on either a single narrative or the smaller narratives that comprise individual documents. Instead, the thematic nature of the organization scheme means that all the content of a particular type — all market segment definitions for a wide range of products, for example — are gathered into one place in the repository hierarchy.

When it comes to workflow, schema-driven systems are more similar to component systems. Each content type has a workflow of creation and review. Individuals own some number of components of a particular class. They do their work and then pass ownership to the next person. In other words, they can work fairly independently.

Publishing in a schema-driven system

A schema-driven system shares more with a component than a composition system when it comes to publishing. As in a component system, publishing content from a schema-driven system consists of selecting and assembling content from the repository.

Somewhat more similar to content in a composition system, however, content in a schema-driven system is likely to require integration into a larger whole to be meaningful, and it is more tightly integrated than in a component system. But where a component in a composition system must be integrated with other particular pieces of content (that is, in the narrative), components in a schema system can be integrated with any of a number of other pieces of content.

Seen from the standpoint of a composition system, the classes in a composition system (for example, *annual reports*) might be just a list of schema components that must be assembled to create a given piece of finished content. Because the components are modular, they readily fit together into finished documents of various types. A given piece of content may be reused in multiple types of finished documents. Content from a component called *product features*, for example, might be used in a marketing white paper, a catalog, a brochure, and a product description on a Web site. In each case, the product feature component is combined with a changing cast of other components used in the document.

Figure 9-5 shows how a schema system would assemble combinations of components (or parts of them) into documents at publishing time.

Building the schema forces you to plan the shape of the content and each element's relationship to the others. Having the schema means that you can then dump content of a particular type into the buckets you've created without worrying too much about how it fits with the rest of the content in the repository.

In practice, adopting a schema-driven system can be a tricky, because authors who are accustomed to writing documents may need to adjust to this brave new world of authoring content without necessarily knowing how it will be assembled with other content into documents. However, the benefits of doing so may be considerable if your content is reused frequently in different document types.

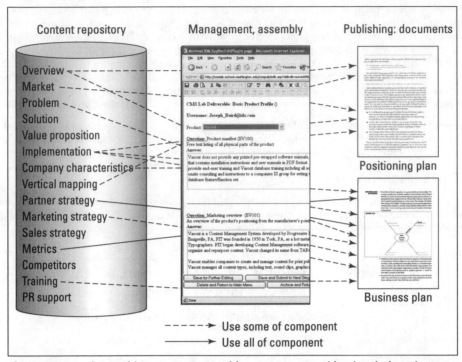

Figure 9-5: A schema-driven system assembles components, either in whole or in part, into output documents.

Which System Is Right for You?

The type of system you should use depends on the extent to which your content needs to be interconnected. Standard component-type systems are, by far, the most common systems in use. They are suitable for content types that are only loosely related, which is where most organizations today find themselves. Component-driven systems are easier to maneuver within than are composition- or schema-driven systems; it's relatively easy to add or modify content types because dependencies across content types are low. For example, a *technology summary* element within a *white paper* content type might be authored and stored separately from the same kind of element in a *technology overview* content type, even if the content itself is identical. Although this design provides the maximum flexibility to customize content for each content type, the tradeoff is that it does not govern consistency across content types, and requires the same content to be authored redundantly (and possibly inconsistently).

Composition systems are really effective when you are ready to take an entirely integrated approach to creation and know exactly what you want. The advantage of such a system is that a lot of the organizational work is done by the system. The tradeoff is the relative inflexibility of the content structure compared to a component system, and the resultant care you have to take in reusing content in publications. Still, when you are ready to treat your content base as a fully integrated set of highly interconnected components (which means you really know and can control your information), the composition system is the best approach to take.

Schema-driven systems are suitable for content that is all part of single integrated whole, but not quite to the point of being fully integrated. Schema CM systems provide strong governance over the content your organization produces without having components become too intertwined. However the cost of this governance is flexibility—designing such a system in essence requires treating a collection of content types as if they are just instances of a larger integrated work—because, to the system, they are. Although not as tightly integrated as a book-like system, schema-driven systems require you to have a more detailed grasp of your content as a whole than do component systems, and they are harder to change after you've created them.

Possibly the largest advantage of component-driven systems is that you can buy one and implement it in fairly short order. CM venders have recognized that most organizations are not ready to fully integrate all their content, and that organizations are largely much better off treating content as distinct components rather than trying to integrate it even to the level of a schema-driven system.

In the end, the three systems represent the tradeoff between control and flexibility. The most flexible (a component CMS) also gives you the least control. Table 9-5 summarizes the main tradeoffs characteristics among these types of systems.

Table 9-5: Tradeoffs among Component, Schema, and Composition Systems

	Standard (Component)	Schema-Driven	Composition
Control of the content	Medium	High	High
Narrative	None	Weak	Strong
Extensibility	Easy	Medium	Hard
Integration	Medium	High	Very High
Sequencing	None	Low to medium	High

Summary

Three types of CM approaches show the tradeoffs between flexibility and control:

✦ Component systems offer the most flexibility but the least overall control.

✦ Composition systems offer the least flexibility but the most control.

✦ Schema systems lie between the two extremes.

Component systems are the most common type of system in use, and are suitable for most Web site management tasks. Composition systems are great when you know exactly what you want and your content is tightly related thematically. Schema-driven systems combine aspects of the other two by providing governance, rationalization, and reuse of the content, while remaining reasonably flexible. Which type of system you need depends on the kind of content you want to manage.

✦   ✦   ✦

The Roots of Content Management

Content management began when the first scribe needed to keep track of and reuse the scrolls he'd amassed. Since then, any number of disciplines have arisen that have some wisdom or practice to offer the new discipline of content management. In this chapter, I detail some of the contributions of the following fields:

- **The publishing industry** provides much of the knowledge behind content collection. It must now, however, adopt a multiple-publication paradigm.

- **Document management systems** contain a lot of what you want in a CMS (such as metadata and workflow) but they fall short of completely meeting your needs because of their reliance on files rather than on content components. The computer's file system is an inadequate way to organize content, and a file isn't the best container for content components.

- **The information management discipline** provides a good source of infrastructure and can usually implement much of a CMS, but it's not designed to handle most of the collection and publication tasks in a CMS.

- **The multimedia industry**, although short-lived, provided much of what I build my work on. In its focus on types of media other than text and because of its adherence to managing units of content separately from their final published form, the multimedia industry anticipated many of the problems and solutions now in use by content management systems to create Web sites.

- **Computer and corporate technical communication systems** provided the first real tests of the capability to manage large-scale content bases and produce multiple publications from them.

- **Communication theory** reminds us that the ultimate purpose of CM is communication.

- **Library and information-science professionals** provide a firm footing on which to base the content management concepts of metadata, storage, categories, and information retrieval.

✦ **The software development industry**, obviously, provides all the software that you need for content management. It pioneered the distribution of electronic functionality that all electronic publications now use.

✦ **The marketing and communications disciplines** provide much of what I base my concepts of audience and personalization on.

In this chapter, I discuss these older disciplines and concepts and tie them into the framework that I've constructed around content management in earlier chapters of this book. My purpose is to demonstrate that content management didn't just drop out of the sky, like the soda bottle in the film *The Gods Must Be Crazy*. Rather, almost every aspect of CM has a previous incarnation within a professional discipline or system. Describing the CM aspects of these older disciplines helps me explain the historical needs that CM tries to address, and also points to where CM might go in the future.

I apologize in advance for the disciplines I've left out and for any misrepresentations that someone more fully versed in these fields may detect.

The Knowledge Base of the Publishing Industry

The point of content management is to create good publications. The definition of a good publication comes directly from the publishing industry, which has known for a very long time what is necessary to *deliver content in a compelling way to a particular audience*. In addition, the publishing industry has laid the groundwork for much of the collection process that I describe. On the other hand, the publishing industry is mostly concerned with handcrafted single publications. This focus gives the industry the luxury of collecting content with a very particular output in mind. Because of the direct connection between collection and publication, the publishing industry hasn't traditionally dealt with the abstractions of metadata, content components, and repositories. As traditional publishers have made more of their content available online, they've had to graft these concepts onto their existing publishing concepts and practices.

The publication

Publishing—which I define in the section "What Is a Publication?" in Chapter 26, "Designing Publications," as making public content that was previously private—has been around as long as humans have communicated. And from the first orators to the latest e-zines, the requirements for success haven't changed. A successful publication knows why it exists, speaks to a particular kind of person, is structured so that its content is easily assessed and accessed, and is laid out in a way that is compelling. A professional publisher knows these standards intuitively. Unfortunately, in the electronic publications world, you find few professional publishers and, thus, a dearth of publications that follow these standards or even know their importance.

Web sites in particular have blossomed, not as an outgrowth of established publication organizations, but as a groundswell of individuals and small groups with a penchant for the technology and some content that they feel is important to share. Today, with user-friendly tools, little technical skill is required to get some content onto the Web. Unsurprisingly, most self-publishers have not followed the field's established wisdom in their pursuits. I'm certainly not saying, however, that the Web should have developed directly out of the publishing industry. The way that the Web developed was just right. The massive parallel development of Web sites was just what this new medium needed to reach critical mass. Now that the Web is at critical mass and the dust is beginning to settle, it's time to acknowledge that the standards for publications can be applied to Web sites.

Publishing Is about What You Don't Publish

A while back I had a conversation with a book publisher. He told me that for every book he publishes, he gets 300 manuscripts. They say there's a book inside everybody. Well, the Web let the book out. We publish on the Web vast quantities of low-quality content—just because we can; just because the technology makes it very easy for us to do so.

For every book that is published traditionally, the equivalent of 30,000 "books" are published on the Web. Content management needs to become more than processes to cheaply shift around vast quantities of low-quality content. We need to become publishers, and that means learning to say no a lot more often.

Gerry McGovern is a content management author and consultant

Content collection

Nothing causes an organization to get efficient about its processes quite like a deadline. Moreover, nothing else equals a continuing string of deadlines to really hone an organization's processes. The periodicals publishing industry has just such deadlines. Consider a newspaper organization that produces a large book's worth of content each day. Streamlining every part of its process, from content creation through final publication, is absolutely essential for a newspaper. I was involved in the launching of one of the first online news organizations—MSNBC. I was quite impressed to see how, with practice, it (and we) got better and better at putting out the day's news on time. In the end, we developed a hybrid between standard news processes and new electronic processes that enabled us to move a piece of content through a sophisticated series of tasks quickly and reliably.

Although publishers who publish trade books, catalogs, and phone directories, for example, may not face the same daily deadlines, they all share a similar interest in honing the process. Specifically, they have a similar need to manage collection of their content in a timely and efficient way.

Out of this environment of continual deadlines and large team efforts comes much of what I describe as part of the *collection process*, including the concepts of workflow, aggregation, and acquisition. I'm lifting my entire concept of syndication intact from the publishing world.

Abstracting the process

Although some publishers deal with separate content components that are simultaneously going into a variety of publications, most don't. Instead, the usual publishing process is a direct connection between collection and publication. It proceeds loosely as follows:

1. The publisher decides what sort of publication to create (daily journal, book, leaflet, magazine, and so on).

2. The publisher finds authors who are experts in the chosen medium (journalists, book writers, marketing writers, and so on).

3. The publisher creates a style guide that constrains the way authors create content by tone, word usage, length, and audience.

4. The authors create content that they target to fill a particular spot in a particular version of the publication.

5. Editors, formatters, and/or layout staff merge the authors' content into the publication one piece at a time until the publication is complete.

6. Post-production staffers do the final formatting and conversion to enable mass production of the publication.

The assumption behind this process is that you're creating a single target publication. The assumption behind a content management system (CMS), on the other hand, is that you're creating a number of simultaneous publications that you must fill with the same content. You might also be working with one publication that changes so frequently (for example, every time that someone accesses it) that a direct connection between collection and publication isn't feasible. Moreover, the promise of a CMS is that it can harvest and organize the information and functionality not only for the publications that you create now, but also for any of a range of publications that you will create in the future. The general CMS-based process proceeds loosely as follows:

1. Those running the organization decide what value they have in information and functionality. This information and functionality makes up the content that the organization must manage.

2. They decide the audiences for this content and what parts of the content to target to which audience.

3. They decide what sorts of publications can best reach these people.

4. They install systems to produce, store, and manage the content effectively and to retrieve the content and automatically form it into the right publications at the right frequencies.

5. Over time, they collect feedback on the effectiveness of their publications and adjust the system as necessary.

6. Over time, they add new kinds of content and audiences to the system, which affects the types and composition of the publications.

The first publishing process I describe in this section is direct and manual. The second publishing process is indirect and automated. The first process begins with the publication. The second begins with the audiences and content. The first process is particular to the publishing industry and small groups within organizations. The second process borrows from the publishing industry and is useful to any organization. The first process describes how publications have already been produced. The second process describes how they're going to be produced in the future.

In summary, the publishing industry exemplifies the following strengths and weaknesses for CM:

✦ It's good at targeting its audience.

✦ It's good at collecting content.

✦ It's not good at separating content from a particular publication.

The Principles of Document Management

Before there was content management, there was document management. People who wanted to keep track of and use lots of information (as opposed to data) used DM (document management) systems. Many of the technology and processes that are now used in CM systems were first developed in DM systems. However, document management systems remove themselves from content because the file, not the component, is the basic unit of management. That is, DM systems are designed to manage what for a CMS is merely the finished product — a completed document. DM systems don't generally deal with any of the upstream issues of collection. DM systems also ignore how important it is for an information management system to publish successfully.

The idea of a file is at the core of both traditional and modern (specifically, computer file) ways of thinking about managing content. According to Merriam-Webster Online (at www.m-w.com/home.htm) computer files are defined as a "complete collection of data (as text or a program) treated by a computer as a unit especially for purposes of input and output."

Document Is an Empty Word

The word *document* is not a very precisely defined term. According to Merriam-Webster OnLine (www.m-w.com/dictionary.htm), the prevalent meaning of *document* is "an original or official paper relied on as the basis, proof, or support of something." If you search back through your old movie memories, you find any number of scenes in which the border guards say to the heroes trying to escape, "Show me your documents!" Clearly, however, if you're talking about electronic information, this definition is of no use. Computer documents are rarely original or official, and they're never paper.

Most computer references I checked don't even list the term *document*. The Microsoft Computer Dictionary defines a document in the following way:

Any self-contained piece of work created with an application and, if saved on disk, given a unique filename by which it can be retrieved. Documents are generally thought of as word-processed materials only. To a computer, however, data is nothing more than a collection of characters, so a spreadsheet or a graphic is as much a document as is a letter or report.

The definition boils documents down to word processing files and other common file formats (despite the fact that spreadsheets and graphics don't consist of characters). On the other hand, the definition clearly states that a document is any file, which of course breaks the metaphor from the paper world, where a file is a different thing than a document.

In the traditional (paper) world, a *file* is a collection of related documents (which is stored in a *folder*). In the computer world, *document* and *file* have been munged into *file*. I think that's why *document* is an empty term in the computer world — its meaning has been hijacked by *file*. Interesting (to me, anyway) is that in the older sense of the word, *document* is more like *component* as I use it — the idea being that a paper document is a chunk of content, and paper files are collections of such related chunks.

So why use the term *document* at all? For files, you can say exactly how they behave and what they contain; for documents, you can't. As widespread as this word is, I believe that it has little place as any sort of official term. I intend to stick to the word *file* instead.

Files, of course, were sets of related papers systematically organized into folders within file cabinets long before computers were a gleam in Alan Turing's eye. The metaphor carries nicely into the computer world. Computer files are sets of related records that are full of bits of data on a file system. Anyone who's ever used a real file cabinet knows the following:

✦ Determining to which file a particular piece of information belongs is often a very arbitrary decision.

✦ The folders serve simply as a system for getting to the particular information inside them.

In the computer world, as in the "real" world, files are convenient objects of manipulation. In fact, much of what a computer operating system does is manipulate files. The operating system enables the user to create, open, edit, and delete files.

Note   As foundational as files are to the operation of a modern computer, nothing about them is necessary. A file is just an arbitrary wrapper around a set of bits that enables the operating system to treat these bits as a unit. We could just as easily (or *more* easily, as some computer architects believe) get along with a giant database on each computer that stores bits of data in a more detailed and accessible way than do files. Still, in computers today, everything comes from files and to files it all must return if you expect to see it after the next crash.

Given this definition of files, how do they relate to the concepts of content and content management?

Files contain content

Most fundamentally, in the computer world files are containers for information. Just as content components do, files house information in a useful way. Just as content components do, files wrap information in a set of metadata that you can use to store and retrieve them. Although people often use files as content components, in general, they're inadequate for that purpose for the following reasons:

✦ **The metadata that the files contain is too general** and is the same regardless of the information that you store in the file. You understand this concept if you've ever tried to really organize your computer's file system. You can get only so far trying to organize files based on name, edit date, file size, and file format. Soon you realize that that you also want to use other kinds of metadata to organize your files and that different kinds of files need different types of metadata for effective management.

✦ **The file's metadata applies to the entire file.** Thus, files can contain only one component. If you try to put two components in the same file, you lose the capability to use the file's metadata to identify individual components. But if you break up components into individual files, keeping track of the content becomes nightmarish.

These two concerns are not new to content. Computer scientists realized long ago that the basic function of the file is to provide a standard way to store any data. They also realized that applications, not the operating system, should access the data. Thus, they invented *file formats*. File formats are structures inside the standard file wrapper that enable you to add whatever metadata and other structure you want. So, although you *can* treat files as components, the better course is to let files serve as the gateway to a file format that can more effectively represent the variety of components that you create.

Cross-Reference Look in Chapter 2, "Content Has Format," in the section "Storage Formats: Storing Information," for a further discussion of file or *storage* formats.

Databases enable you to apply different metadata to each information type. In addition, they can store vast numbers of components in a single file (or a small cluster of files). Databases are simply a specific file format that enables a database application to store and retrieve information. Similarly, an XML file is a file that enables you to store and retrieve numerous components from within a single file.

Files are the only choice for storing information on a computer. However, they are in no way the smallest unit of useful information. Rather, the information units within files are often much more significant than the file as a whole. To be useful, however, the information must be easily discoverable, which means it must be organized. For example, suppose you're applying for a job at XYZ Corporation. You get to the corporate campus to find a set of large identical buildings. Within each building are a hundred identical offices. You know that the Information Technology building is Number 6, Human Resources is on the 4th floor, and the Personnel office is room 407. With the help of this metadata you have no problem getting to the interview on time. If no signs are posted on the buildings or the offices, however, it doesn't help you much to know that Personnel is in there... somewhere.

Files store BLOBs

In the DM world, databases have relatively recently been given the capability to store large amounts of data in a single field. With the digitization of pictures, sound, and motion, you can now assume that a single field in a database can contain many megabytes. The term *Binary Large Object (BLOB)* was invented to describe the collection of binary data that you can store in these large fields. Databases, however, are far from optimum for storing this sort of data. Thus, standard procedure today is still to store BLOBs in files. Instead of putting an image directly in a database, for example, the preferred method is to put metadata *about* the image (such as its name, size, and the location of the file) in the database and keep the image in a separate file. Programmers have solved many of their problems by storing BLOBs in databases, but the penchant for storing media in files remains. Going hand and hand with the tradition of using files (which dies hard) is the fact that accessing media through the file system is often easier than doing so through a database interface.

In the CM world, XML was invented with BLOBs in mind, so XML files have little problem storing large binary data sets. Still, because most software for authoring and editing BLOBs (image, sound, and video editors) expects to work with files, storing BLOBs in separate files is still the most convenient way to work, with just the link and other metadata about the file stored in XML.

Publications are files

The end purpose of a CMS is to create publications. All publications are some sort of file. A Web site is a set of HTML files; a print publication is one or more files in a desktop-publishing format; and a syndicated publication may exist in the form of an XML file, in a database, or some other structured data stream. So the end purpose of a CMS is to create files of various formats.

In a way, this system is incredibly paradoxical. You do a lot of work creating your CMS, bringing information out of restrictive proprietary formats and into an open workable repository, only to push that information back into a set of restrictive proprietary formats.

Computer scientists invented the file as a generalized container for any sort of data format that *you* care to invent. The result is that programmers have invented different formats for each software product. Their formats perform well under the restricted environments of their particular programs, but today these restrictive environments are butting up against each other as organizations need to coalesce what were previously many efforts into one.

A CMS can help bridge the gap between today, when content creation and publishing occurs in a wide variety of formats, similar in nature to a cyber Tower of Babel, and the (maybe distant) future, when a single master file format can serve for all your content-creation and publishing needs.

Document management systems versus content management systems

Despite the vagueness of the word *document*, the document-management industry is quite well defined and has enjoyed considerable success. Document management systems seek to organize and make files accessible. You can think of them as the file system that you wish your computer had. The better document management systems offer the following:

✦ **File storage:** The system knows the physical location of each file that it tracks but doesn't require the end user to know that location.

✦ **File categorization:** You can assign file types and groups based on the criteria that you choose.

✦ **Metadata services:** You can attach any kind of extra data to a file (such as owner, status, create date, and so on) based on its type.

✦ **Collaboration services:** You can check files in and out of the system and jointly edit them.

✦ **Workflow services:** You can route files from worker to worker in an organized and standard way.

✦ **Versioning services:** You save a historical series of files and retrieve them as you need them.

✦ **Access services:** End users can find files through tables of contents, indexes, and full-text searches.

The first thing to notice is that document management systems have little to do with even the vaguest definition of *document*. Although you may often target systems toward word-processing and other office files, they have no restrictions at all about the types of files that you put in them. Thus, they're much more accurately called *file management systems*.

The next thing to notice is that document management systems share a lot with the concept of a CMS that I'm developing. Both systems seek to categorize information, apply metadata to it, organize its creation through workflow and collaboration, and give end users complete access to it. On the other hand, the two systems differ in the following significant ways:

✦ **DM manages files; CM manages components**. Document management systems deal with files, whereas content management systems deal with content components. You may recall that, in the preceding section on files, I say that files don't make good containers for content. They're an extra container that's unnecessary for the storage of content components. In addition, they can hold only one component per file if their metadata is to prove at all useful for finding individual components.

✦ **DM controls sharing; CM controls creation**. Document management systems were invented to manage files that other applications create. These systems make no attempt to open any of the files under their control and work with what's inside. Content management systems, on the other hand, are directly concerned with creating content as well as managing it. In both systems, you control the creation of metadata for storage and access, but only in the CMS do you control the creation of the content as well.

✦ **DM is about access; CM is about publishing.** Document-management systems provide access to the files under their control. The purpose of a CMS is to create publications that are a combination of the components under its control. To create publications, content management systems need all the access power of document management systems plus an extra capability to automatically construct a publication out of the components that it finds. Although some document management systems can create *compound documents*, which combine separate files into one, their capabilities fall far short of those necessary to create a solid and varied set of publications.

In a way, you can say that document-management systems are content management systems in which each content component is a file and publications typically contain only a single component. For this reason, I fully expected the document-management industry to easily capture the content management market; it did not, however. Instead, the industry as a whole had a hard time making the transition. A new industry with new companies has grown into the content management space and given DM companies real competition for dominance. Given the document-management industry's depth of experience in metadata and workflow and its primary position in many of the world's largest organizations, adding the capabilities that I mention in this section should have proven relatively easy. Perhaps the document-management industry's success created enough inertia to prevent it from taking even these relatively small steps into the future.

Whether the document-management industry comes to dominate the content management industry in the future, much of what's central to content management comes directly from document management.

In summary, document management brings the following to CM:

✦ DM shares important concepts with CM, including metadata and workflow.

✦ DM works at the level of files as an organizing component, which is too general for CM.

✦ Both DM and CM are well suited for dealing with media content.

✦ DM and CM share many functional attributes.

The Limits of Information Technology Groups

Every organization of any size has a department that takes care of its computers. This department might be known as the *Information Technology* (*IT*), *Information Systems* (*IS*), *Management Information Systems* (*MIS*) or *Information and Communications Technologies* (*ICT*) department. As the old motto of Microsoft's IT group goes, they "keep the train running." Until recently, every computer decision, from the official word processor to the obscure transport protocol of the company's network, flowed from this group. Before the Web, if you wanted to know anything about computers or how to use them in your organization, you'd ask someone from this department. Typically, an organization's IT group installs and maintains the organization's data systems, runs the network, and supports desktop applications. Some IT groups also develop software around the organization's data systems.

Many (if not most) of the groups I have worked with avoid their IT groups like the plague if the group has questions involving the Web and electronic publication systems. Why? I offer the following two separate but related answers:

✦ IT departments have avoided the Web.

✦ The Web begins where IT groups leave off.

The following sections elaborate on these answers.

IT departments have avoided the Web

IT departments have avoided the Web because it's been an unstable and out-of-control technology. A client of mine is a major software company with one of the world's biggest Web presences (measured in pages and throughput). Although (or maybe because) this company invented much of the software that runs the Internet, its IT group approaches the task of keeping the Internet running with extreme caution. The IT group often views the Internet effort as more of a train wreck than a train ride. I certainly can't blame them for this attitude. Especially in the early days, the company's site was growing by an order of magnitude each quarter. The staff's ability to create wild and wacky new Web stuff far exceeded this IT group's ability to certify that the next cool thing didn't bring the whole bubble-gum and rubber-band system to its knees. To get even a semblance of control over this explosion, the IT group created a set of super-strict guidelines for what people could and couldn't post to the Internet. Of course, these guidelines upset those who were champing at the bit to release all the great stuff that they'd created.

Note

In the past few years, many IT groups have awakened to the realization that if they're not Internet savvy, they are shooting themselves in the foot. IT execs are increasingly being measured, at least partially, based on their company's success on the Web.

Look at this problem from another angle: By what measure does an organization evaluate its IT group? On its vision and far-reaching strategy? No, that's for marketing and R&D. You evaluate IT on its ability to stay within the budget that management gives the department and to keep corporate information systems up and running. Innovation is not predictable, and cost overruns and downtime are death. No wonder IT departments avoid the flaky technology and costly downtime of the Internet.

Content begins where IT groups leave off

A friend of mine tells a wonderful story of the company CEO who sees his daughter playing on the Internet at home. He comes to work the next morning and tells his IT department head, "We need one of those things, too." The IT head says, "I'll get right on it, sir." He walks down the hall and calls on his top manager. "The CEO wants a Web site," he says. "Can you do it?" "Sure," says the manager. "I'll get right on it."

The manager forms a rapid response team from his top systems people. For a month, the team scours the world for the top Internet products. They spend three million dollars in product and services. The manager reports to the IT head, "We've created a world-class system." The head reports to the CEO, "Sir, for only three million, we've created a world-class system," and he scribbles the URL (that the company needed to purchase from a domain name "investor" who was expecting the call) on a piece of paper. The CEO comes proudly home and shows the paper to his daughter, who's busy surfing the Web. "Here," he says. "We have a Web site, too."

His daughter pulls herself out of her immersive multiplayer Web game. She types the recently bought URL into her browser's Address text box. Up comes the great new site. It consists of a blank page with the following words in the upper-left-hand corner:

```
Text Goes Here
```

Most IT groups just don't have the mindset or skill set to deal with content. Yet, as my story shows, their companies are calling on them to do just that. Dumb organizations expect that IT can just figure it out and produce electronic publishing technologies. Smart organizations build alternative groups that pick up where the IT group leaves off. The smartest organizations recognize that the very nature of IT is changing and are building a new awareness and skill set in their IT groups. Fortunately, such a new department doesn't need to change its name. It only needs to fully embrace its current name. For a long time, computers were called on to deal only with data, and you could blithely imagine that data was information. Information Technology groups grew up in this environment. Today, as any CEO's daughter knows, information is a whole lot more than data but no less important to the organization.

I believe that, to survive, IT groups must take their part of the responsibility for Web sites and content management systems that create sites and other publications. What's their part of the responsibility? It certainly includes installing and maintaining the data systems behind the CMS and its electronic publications. If, in addition, IT groups can rise to the challenge of dealing with information and not just with data, they could be the right place to put overall ownership of a CM effort. After all, why shouldn't IT groups be as much about information as they are about technology? Interestingly, the groups that are called ICT (Information and Communication Technology) have an even more significant name to live up to.

In summary, IT brings the following to CM:

- ✦ The IT perspective emphasizes that systems must be stable and supportable.

- ✦ IT is familiar with the issues and process of deploying new computer systems into an existing technical infrastructure.

- ✦ Their familiarity with data management positions IT groups to extend that perspective to information management as well.

The Legacy of the Multimedia Industry

Before the Internet came the multimedia industry. This short-lived industry (which was at its height in the early 1990s) was where some of the key issues of electronic publication first were explored and confronted. Basically, early multimedia groups and companies were interested in collecting interesting information and making it available on CD-ROM, mostly in the form of catalogs, games, and electronic books. Thus, people often refer to this industry as the CD-ROM industry, but CD-ROMs were merely the first medium with enough memory to distribute the content.

The essential aspect of the multimedia industry is right in its name. When I was young, I remember going to multimedia presentations. They consisted of slide shows with music playing and a person speaking. My sister Linda introduced me to multimedia art, where the artist uses acrylic- and oil-based paint and maybe embeds some objects in that paint. In both of these more archaic uses of multimedia, the concept is the same — bringing more than one medium of communication together to create a fuller communication experience.

Merriam-Webster OnLine defines media, in part, as "a channel or system of communication." Text, pictures, sound, and motion are all channels of communication. The multimedia industry brought the media of text, pictures, sound, and motion (video and animation) together with computing functionality to create the first electronic publications with real popular appeal. In the few, short (unprofitable) years that the multimedia industry was in vogue, it managed to formulate much of what the Web became and is still becoming. In particular, the multimedia industry fostered the following breakthroughs:

✦ The multimedia industry pioneered the electronic publication.

✦ Multimedia developers were among the first (maybe just behind game developers) to feel the pinch of trying to simultaneously display text, pictures, and sound. In addition, multimedia teams needed to face the task of a massive collection and cataloging effort to prepare content for display. In response, they created some of the first end-to-end content management systems.

Clerical Workers and CM

When I'm not writing and managing content for a Web site, I like to sing Gregorian chant. Though this might seem about as far away as possible from the CM world, there might just be a connection. After all, medieval musicians needed their own strategies for information storage and retrieval.

Throughout the Middle Ages, singers and priests and deacons performed an elaborate annual cycle of liturgies for several hours per day, with many nuanced changes based on the solar and lunar calendars, the balance between central papal control and local traditions, and the steady development of more and more complex forms of ritual practice over the centuries. In the first few centuries of the church's life, the chants, prayers, and other ritual formulas were committed to memory. As the material grew more voluminous and sophisticated, written notation developed: first texts only, followed by mnemonic devices for recalling melodic patterns. It was only after centuries of use that teachers and practitioners developed a full-fledged and fully decipherable musical notation. Even then, a system of conventions and abbreviations (think TLAs) made the notation challenging to interpret.

Adding to the difficulty was the way chant books were organized. There was one set of books for priests, another for soloists, and another for choir members. Different books might be used at different times of year, or for different portions of the ritual day. Singers sometimes used revolving music stands, with ledges on each of their four sides, on which the many requisite books could be propped. The stand would be rotated during a service to make the component parts available at the appropriate times.

As the Middle Ages progressed, this traditional information delivery system supported more and more complexity. People wanted more saints, more feasts, more opportunities for blessing and salvation. The burden of carrying this complexity rested on the shoulders of the information experts: the choirs and soloists and liturgists who performed the rituals. And despite the inefficiency of the content management system they had to work with, they were equal to the task. These services were sung year in and year out (with the help of revolving music stands and other logistical tricks) all over Europe.

Among the religious, social, and cultural resonances of medieval Gregorian chant practice, an important content management principle emerges. The absence of efficient, integrated, and user-friendly information delivery mechanisms does not mean that the information can't be effectively deployed—if the information is of high enough value. Medieval "users" (both clergy and laypeople) viewed their content (the chants and prayers of the liturgical year) as almost infinitely valuable. So the remarkably clumsy mechanisms for storing and accessing liturgical content persisted, and were fully adequate, for many centuries.

Today's clerical workers (pun intended) often develop their own revolving music stands. They comfortably scan through eight or ten or twelve disparate knowledge systems, assembling the choicest bits of information to enact the rituals of their business. As long as the information being integrated in these awkward ways is of sufficient value, their processes and practices can persist unchanged for far longer than one might expect.

Consultants and knowledge managers—true heirs of John Calvin and other radical Protestant reformers—are often eager to sweep away the inefficiency and excessive complexity of organizations' traditional knowledge systems.

It may be true that some business environments really do demand a tidy white-washed chapel instead of an elaborate and drafty Gothic cathedral. But it might be worth stepping back, smelling the incense, and taking in the reverberant sound of the chant before you pick up that axe. Like a medieval choir, the organization may have found an effective—even if inefficient— way to make beautiful music together.

Joe Anderson, Editor, Content Manager, and Gregorian Chanter, The Center for Sacred Art (www.centerforsacredart.org)

Electronic publications

Not that long ago, you'd have been hard-pressed to find anything that you could call an electronic publication. Computer display technology has only recently become sophisticated enough to represent the color and pixel density that consumers require before using a publication. In addition, electronic publication tools are in their infancy, and people are only now really beginning to debate the standards of *online* publications. Electronic publications began in earnest only with the advent of the graphical user interface (GUI). While some software engineers labored to create the visual standards to guide all future programs, others began to use the enhanced capabilities of the GUI operating systems more creatively to present text in multiple fonts and to incorporate images, sound, and motion.

The multimedia industry, which arose to take advantage of the vast new possibilities of electronic publications, produced everything from history to science fiction on CD-ROM. Along the way, it initiated much of what became standard in electronic publication. Many basic digital-design principles (the icon, VCR controls, and button bars, for example) first appeared on a computer screen in one of the thousands of custom user interfaces that late-night designers and programmers hacked together. Artists, creative writers, and media experts of every variety were co-opted and merged into the world of software development. Although the Web put a wet blanket on the multimedia industry and its CD-ROMs, it only fanned the flames of digital publication. Early developers of multimedia, if they are still in the field, are certainly doing digital publication today, bringing their wealth of relevant experience with them.

End-to-end content management

The multimedia industry swept hundreds of thousands of content creators online. They brought with them what they knew of publications content. Despite the chaos of the multimedia-development process, these creative types crafted their own systems for moving content from place to place and ensuring that it arrived where it belonged on the CD-ROM. Having built a number of these systems myself, I can say with assurance that the process wasn't pretty. Our systems did, however, make an impossible process merely difficult.

Authoring systems, as they were known, provided creation, tagging-conversion, and compilation tools. Storage was generally in a proprietary binary format. Few used commercial databases to store content. Specialized proprietary browsers (not that the term *browser* actually existed at the time) were created that could lay out and display content. Over time, many of the companies that produced high-content, multiple-version CD-ROMs (such as those containing encyclopedias, periodicals, and corporate directories) developed systems that included most of the features of a full CMS.

Somewhere about midway through the multimedia epoch, the term *asset* crept into the vernacular. To my mind, this word did more than any other to popularize the component way of thinking about content. Merriam-Webster OnLine says that an *asset* is "an item of value owned." The two key words here are *item* and *value*. Rather than a continuous stream of information defining a publication, the multimedia world came to define its systems in terms of the individual items they managed. Each item has its own value (sometimes literally, as in the case of photographs that you may purchase), and you track and manage each item separately. These items, which you store as separate components, are brought together in the creation of a particular multimedia CD-ROM, and you can mix and match them as necessary on the published page.

Those multimedia teams that forged decent content management systems had little trouble moving to another publication type—the Web—after it swept away CD-ROMs and the multimedia industry.

In summary, the multimedia industry brings the following to CM:

✦ Multimedia brings together different media types and delivers them as integrated content.

✦ Multimedia producers were early adopters of highly managed content assets.

The Challenges of Technical Communication

At about the same time as multimedia was working its way to the top of the public mind, software manufacturers and large industrial companies were confronting problems that were just as important to the nascent field of content management. In software companies, the need to create online Help to supplement existing print documentation gave a boost to the notions of multiple publications from the same content base. In large industrial companies, the sheer volume of documentation about their products, as well as their enormous parts catalogs, spurred the creation of the first real, structured text-management systems. Technical communicators (writers, editors, and project managers who produce documentation) in the academic and practitioner communities rose to the challenge of the new systems and transformed their discipline.

Huge information bases

Because I live in Seattle and am in the electronic publication business, about once a year I hear the story of how the documentation for a Boeing 747 requires a 747 to transport it from place to place. As the story goes, Boeing reduced the load to the cost of an airmail stamp (or two) by putting all that documentation on CD-ROM. What Boeing and many others like it did to create these CD-ROMs has a lot of bearing on the current world of content management.

XML Is the Beginning and Not the End

Once I sat with a client who wanted something quite simple and reasonable. He was unhappy with the way that his organization continually needed to work around the peculiarities of the electronic and print publication systems that they'd purchased. He wanted to put his entire print and electronic publication process into XML and be done with all this restrictive proprietary software. As we worked through his options, we arrived at the following two conclusions:

✦ In the near future of computing, you're unlikely to see the print and electronic worlds converge enough that you can use something such as XML for a simple, coherent solution.

✦ Even if all publication systems can magically agree on and implement a standard such as XML, each publication system has very different needs. The divergent needs of each publication type require very different systems. So even under the best of circumstances, you can't create a single, simple system.

So is there no hope for creating a single system that encompasses the print and online worlds? I would not go that far. What I would say is that you can't expect to get such a system simply by adopting standards like XML. Rather, these standards are the beginning of the process your organization must work through so it can create information in ways that can be published most easily in whatever format your audiences need.

The main problem that these industrial giants needed to tackle was organizing the enormous amount of information they'd created. Older print publication systems had no capability to know what the information was *about*—only how to format it on the printed page. To get organized, what Boeing and others needed was a way to capture and store information—not by how it looked but by what it meant. The answer they found was the *Standard Generalized Markup Language* (SGML).

 In Chapter 35, "What Are Content Markup Languages?," I talk a lot more about SGML. For now, simply understand that SGML brings database-like rigor to the creation and tracking of content.

Some companies developed their own tools for implementing SGML, but a number of software companies provided tools and management systems as well. This set of vendors and customers together pioneered the use of strictly structured, text-based management systems to author, manage, and publish huge volumes of rapidly changing information.

Many of the vendors who were most popular with the industrialists have since made the leap to XML and are now serving the wider content management industry. Unlike those companies in the document-management industry, they've branched out as their potential client base broadened. As is true of those still in the document-management industry, however, their original client base may prove to be their worst enemy. The closed, arcane world of SGML and its back-room clientele has weighed down these companies and made them move much more slowly than their newer competition toward the future uses of structured text in electronic publishing.

Simultaneous publications

With the advent of Windows 3.0, the Microsoft side of the personal computer world turned many corners. In addition to the main events of its graphical user interface (GUI) and API-based programming, Windows included Windows Help. In the previous DOS world, Help meant a load of unformatted text that scrolled along the bottom of the screen and was all but unreadable. By using a tool that became known as WinHelp, the Help author could create well-formatted, well-indexed hypertext systems that he could tie directly to the application functions they described. The system worked well enough to contain large amounts of documentation. WinHelp was not the first hypertext document system by any means, but it was one of the big new standards of Windows programming. In other words, to be a good Windows application, a program had to come with documentation created in WinHelp.

A few software companies used the new system as a pretense to do away with the most expensive part in their shrink-wrapped box — the book. Most simply added a requirement for Help to the list of the deliverables they expected from their User Education departments. This new requirement fundamentally changed the way these departments worked. It mandated that a group of people who had, in the past, defined themselves simply as book writers now become proficient in electronic publication. To most, this new requirement meant that they needed to translate their books into Help systems. To others, it caused a fundamental rethinking of what publishing means and what content is in the absence of a particular publication to which it's targeted. The result of this rethinking was a spate of single-source publishing systems. These systems took a single base of content and alternatively produced either a Windows Help system or a print publication.

My very first content management systems were of this variety. They used Microsoft Word for Windows 1.0 and its macro language to create a simple repository for content that contained enough information to produce either a book or a Help system. The systems contained a rudimentary authoring system (which aided in tagging new content), a publication-neutral storage format, and routines for producing either of the two publications.

Producing two publications of very different format and structure necessitated the use of many of the concepts of content management to keep the creation and later publication organized and efficient. The content must, for example, remain separate from the final format. Structural metadata had to be added to the content so that it could be automatically chunked into named Help topics or book sections.

Unfortunately, the efforts of many documentation teams are directed only toward documentation and aren't always applied to the wider questions of electronic publishing. The success of Windows Help also led to a group of people who consider themselves Help authors and not, more generally, electronic publishers. Thus, much of the talent and innovation of these documentation groups waits to be tapped in the wider enterprise. Still, people with a background in electronic documentation are a great source of talent, especially for the collection process in a CMS.

As the tide of enterprise content management rises, however, the knowledge of the documentation groups is now spilling out into the wider organization.

In summary, technical communication brings the following to CM:

✦ Technical communication has a lot of content that must be authored, managed, produced, updated, and retrieved frequently. The field adopted early technologies such as SGML to help do all these things.

✦ Technical communication pioneered multiple publications from a single content base.

Communication Theory

What is electronic information? From a communication perspective, it is a conversation that has been automated, unmoored, and made ubiquitous. The old forms of information were entirely tied to the people who created them. They were direct and personal. Electronic information is characterized by its distance from its creator. Its creation is removed from its use by technologies that automatically route and deliver it in forms and configurations that its author may never have envisioned. It is unmoored in that it is free to move from format to format and be copied *ad infinitum*. It is ubiquitous in that it is available anywhere. (As I type this, I am sitting in an airport in Taipei, Taiwan, wirelessly connected to the Internet and all my local networks.)

But as radically free and unattached as electronic information may be, it is still a conversation. To forget this basic fact about information is to risk losing the communication link between the creator and the receiver, between the author and the audience of the information. (You can see just how literally I intend you to take this statement in the "What Is a Publication?" section in Chapter 26, "Designing Publications.")

Communication theory explains that people use these conversations to negotiate and coordinate their understanding of the world. These common understandings are shared meaning, and communication is how people develop these shared meanings.

Likewise, information is a kind of conversation that helps people develop shared understanding and meaning. In this view, electronic information, and more specifically, content management systems are a means to effectively manage a complex set of interconnected conversations. The aim is to create a sphere of shared meaning between an organization and the people it cares about.

Your information is your organization's most powerful tool for creating a community of people who understand the world in the same (or at least a similar) way. So, at the very tips of the roots of content management I would place the theories and concepts of communication. These concepts may not build your system, but they will tell you why you are building a system and what it is really capable of doing.

In summary, the communication theory brings to CM the perspective that CM is ultimately all about communication and developing shared understanding.

It's All About Communication

I was recently explaining to a client what I hoped to accomplish for him. I had tried unsuccessfully to convey the idea that I coordinate audiences, publications, and content. Then I tried this. I said, "What I will do is help you craft a coordinated communication strategy." I told him that, in essence, what he was trying to do was to communicate with a variety of people. He had information, and other people had need of that information. What a content management system would do for him, I said, was to organize what had become for him an overly burdensome process of getting people the information they needed. The light bulb went on and, in a flash, we stopped talking about his Web site and started talking about what information he had, who needed it, and how best to get it to them. Of course, the Web still figured prominently in our discussions, but it was no longer *about* the Web; it was about communication.

That discussion clicked for me as well. It brought me back to the point of all the methodologies and technologies I had created. It's all about communication.

The Traditions of Library and Information Science

Librarians have felt the pinch of organizing information bases for as long as libraries have existed. Librarians organize and provide access to large volumes of information. Whether they oversee books, periodicals, images, sounds, or moving pictures, librarians create and maintain collections, catalogs, and content. The parallels to the concepts of content management should be obvious. Just as a library does, a CMS must catalog a collection of content.

Information science, which grew out of cognitive science and computing and now is effectively merged with library science, has brought depth and substance to our understanding of how people find and consume information. Information scientists study and create the theory of electronic information categorization, retrieval, and use. They created the theory on which I base much of my model of content management.

Information behavior

A considerable segment of information scientists study how people look for information. They try to find the paths people take between the time they identify some need for information and the time that need has been satisfied. Interestingly, but not surprisingly, the most consistent finding in these studies is that when people have a need for information they first ask someone. Once again, conversation shows itself at the root of information. The importance of these sorts of studies to CM is pretty hard to miss. To do CM well, you must learn:

✦ What information your audiences need

✦ How they express those needs

✦ What they already know about how to meet those needs

✦ How you expect them to navigate from what they already know to what they need to know

The iSchool

As I wrote the first edition of this book, I was suspended between my previous life as a CM architect and businessman and my future life as a CM expert and academic. With the bursting of my own little Internet bubble, my old life was finished; but I did get the time I needed to write this book. As I wrote, I knew that in a few months I would be starting a full-time faculty position at the Information School (iSchool) at the University of Washington. From the exposure I had had to the iSchool, I knew it was the right place for me to be, but I did not know much more. I struggled to write this section, knowing how little I knew about the field of Library and Information Science. Now, three years later, I know a lot more about the field and am struggling even more to capture the myriad contributions that it makes to CM. Information schools are a very recent addition to academia. Some are part of a computer science department, and some are part of communications departments. Ours stands alone. It is its own school, reflecting the university's view that information is a subject unto itself. The iSchool takes as its mission to integrate the more established disciplines of library science and information science with the newer realities of electronic information. Just as organizations struggle to reconcile their long-standing publication methods with the newer ones, our department struggles to wrap a definition around information that can encompass all its forms.

As organizations get more and more serious about doing CM, they inevitably turn to the methodologies of the information behavior researchers.

Note A good place to begin exploring the ideas of information behavior is at IBEC (Information Behavior in Everyday Contexts), at `http://ibec.ischool.washington.edu`.

User services

How does a librarian know where to look to get you the information you need? How does the same librarian even know what it is you are talking about? A trained reference librarian is somehow able to pull from you a usable definition of what you want, and can then figure out the best way to find it. The process of finding out what you want is generally called a reference interview. It consists of a set of questions that narrow your possibly vague initial request into a set of phrases that can be used to search a specific set of information sources. Again, the connection to CM is clear, but it is often missed entirely by the people who create CM systems. Many designers assume that if you just show users how all the information is organized, they will find what they need. In fact, a conversation is necessary to move the user from the words she can think of and the areas she might think to look to the words your system uses and the sources of information it provides.

Cross-Reference In the "Indexes" section in Chapter 30, "Designing Content Access Structures," I discuss indexes as the structures that let you map a user's current vocabulary to the vocabulary of the CMS.

If you have done your information behavior homework well, you will know how your audiences express their needs and will prepare an appropriate set of publications that are organized in such a way to as to move users to the appropriate information. If you take a lesson from the reference librarian, you will not assume that users either know the words to use or know where to look for the information you may know they need. You may even discover that hiring a reference librarian to help people navigate the trickier parts of your publications is the best way to ensure that people find what they need.

Knowledge representation

Knowledge representation is the fancy term for how you go about structuring a body of information. It maps quite well to the concept of access structures I present here. In fact, librarians invented and commonly use the hierarchies, indexes, and cross references that comprise much of an access structure.

Cross-Reference See Chapter 30, "Designing Content Access Structures," for more information about these terms.

Access structures are the tools of the trade of librarians. Each library's collection is organized into a taxonomy that's no more than a hierarchy. Librarians use all kinds of indexes to map the keywords of a collection to each other and to the content in the collection. Cross-reference strategies lead the visitor from one category of book to the next. In addition, the reference librarian is expert at turning a vague question into a firm strategy for access.

Structuring Information for Retrieval

Information scientists and librarians have worked for years to structure and organize information in such a way that it is easier for individuals and groups within organizations to find sources that are accurate and relevant.

In organizations that are information-intensive and that require a significant degree of critical thinking, research librarians have been the "gold standard" for sending and receiving information in context. It's been said that everyone would like to have his own personal researcher. Of course, that is usually not an option given the extensive reach of information through the intranet, extranet, and Internet, as well as the cost to an organization of having a cadre of such highly skilled professionals. With the advent of content management as a discipline — and with a broader investment by technology companies in software development that supports it — the work of information scientists and librarians can scale to support an organization.

Mary Lee Kennedy, The Kennedy Group (www.maryleekennedy.com)

In both their conceptual categorization of information and very practical strategies for finding the right content, librarians hold the keys to much of what the metator needs to effectively catalog content in a CMS. Although many of the world's finest librarians remain sequestered in stacks, many others are joining the ranks of the *digerati* and applying their incredibly valuable skills to digital information. Print librarians are always going to be needed, but the future holds a much greater need for the same skills in a broader (and more highly valued) context.

Information retrieval

Information scientists have spent decades working on the issues involved in amassing and searching through huge bodies of information. All the major Web search engines (Yahoo, Google, and the others), not to mention all the bibliographic systems (LexisNexis and Dialog for example) are based on the work of information retrieval experts. In particular, these researchers study:

✦ **How can you retrieve information?** What are the best ways to store information so that you can most easily find it again? How do you learn from the kinds of searches that people have previously conducted? What are the fastest and most efficient indexing processes so that you can most effectively retrieve information?

✦ **What is relevance?** How do you measure the value of information? How can you rank by importance the information that you find in response to a user question? How do you resolve ambiguities in people's questions?

✦ **How can you pull structure out of information automatically?** How can a computer recognize the significant words, sentences, and even concepts in a body of information? Can you get a computer to answer a question in plain English (or another language)? What sorts of structures require a person (rather than a computer) to decipher them? Can you integrate the automatic discovery of a program with the more intelligent discovery of a person?

Information science overlaps considerably with cognitive science, which seeks to answer questions such as "What is context?" and "How do people perceive and understand?" As content management moves from art to science, these are the questions that you need to address.

Information science also overlaps with linguistics and artificial intelligence. Information scientists are in a unique position to apply the concepts of human language processing and computer language processing to the content management issues of automatic tagging and advanced personalization, based on intelligent rules.

Note If anyone eventually creates some future generation of content computers that can transcend the limitation of data computers, as I describe in Chapter 1, "What Is Content?," in the section "Content Is Information Plus Data," the idea may well start in the mind of an information scientist.

Unfortunately, the skills and tools that information scientists possess all too often fail to make their way out of the university setting. People possessing these skills, however, are prime candidates for structuring an organization's information and deciding how best to make it accessible.

For years, I've been fond of saying that librarians are the gurus of the future. When I said so in the late 1980s, I got nothing but blank stares. At the turn of the century, I still get some confused looks, but the insight is slowly dawning that those who can make information accessible — and especially those who can find the content needle in the haystacks of electronic content — are destined eventually to reign among the most valued professionals in our society.

In summary, library and information science brings the following to CM:

✦ Librarians and other information sciences professionals have extensive experience in making complex repositories useful to mere mortals.

✦ Librarians invented most of the principle components of access structures — hierarchies, indexes, and cross-references.

✦ Librarians deal with fundamental issues common to CM, such as storage methodologies, relevance, and information structure.

How are Content Management and Information Architecture Related?

Sorry to over-anthropomorphize here, but I see information architecture gleefully holding a squirming content management's feet to the fire, ensuring that CM, in its zeal to support those users known as content owners, doesn't forget those other users, namely end users.

I remember attending my first CM conference a few years ago and being dumbstruck at how surprised many attendees were when they were reminded that their work impacts end users. What's the point of doing CM if end users are left out of the equation? IA provides tools, techniques, and expertise to help content management benefit from metadata and integrate well with search and navigation systems, thereby delivering value to end users and content owners alike.

You might also say that IA provides a model for how CM might develop as a profession. IA is technology-agnostic. Until content managers start thinking this way, and focus on users and the processes that serve them, CM will continue to be dominated by CMS vendors to the detriment of all.

Ann Rockley, The Rockley Group (www.rockley.com)

The Technology of Software Development

The software industry powers all content management and provides the most basic principles of electronic publication. Physically, a CMS is a collection of computer hardware and software, so it is no surprise that the work of a software developer lies behind every CMS. In particular, the software development industry created all the technologies currently in use to collect, manage, and publish content. In addition, software developers (and architects) were the first to confront the issue of the computer-human interface. Their work led to all our standards for representing functionality in electronic publications.

Collection technologies

Long before the age of electronic publications, programmers grew tired of typing. To help themselves, they invented powerful text-manipulation programs. Tools with names such as grep (the UNIX tool to Globally search for Regular Expressions), sed (the Stream Editor), AWK (created by Alfred Aho, Peter Weinberger, and Brian Kernighan), and the Perl scripting language were created to enable programmers to reprocess code, efficiently produce reports from organizational data programs, and convert data from one system to another. Perl, as you may know, became the basis for most of the early automation systems behind Web sites. Perl and many other tools have also served as the basis for the kind of text manipulation that you need in a CMS collection system. Creative programmers have also used the text-manipulation capabilities that are native to most programming languages (C, Java, BASIC, and so on) over and over to make effective content-processing systems. These custom systems include features such as text parsing, automatic tagging, form-based input, content preview, and custom workflow management.

Much of this early work is still in place, moving content around. New custom development work continues as well, but it's now becoming more focused on filling the gaps in the commercially available CMS collection systems rather than on creating new systems from scratch.

Management technologies

Databases are at the center of both the programming and the CMS worlds. Database software and database programmers are as much a part of a CMS implementation as they are for any other major application. In addition, the administrative functions of a CMS are mostly the same as they are in any enterprise database system. In any application that serves multiple users (for example, the tasks of defining and changing user records and giving them access permission) the data administration tasks are basically the same. As the capability of databases to store, index, and retrieve increases, CMS software is sure to change as well to take advantage of the new possibilities.

Most CMS products work with one or more of the major commercial database products. From a software developer's perspective, a content management system is nothing more than a complex user interface to a standard database and file system.

Publishing technologies

Programmers created (and continue to create) all the electronic delivery systems that a CMS uses.

Today, the major publishing technology is the *template*. Templates are programs. These programs decide what content you need on the page, make queries to the repository to retrieve content, and format the content for correct placement and display in the publication. The first Web-publication templating system that I ever saw was Microsoft's IDC/HDX system, which shipped with an early version of Internet Information Server (IIS). This system, which Microsoft's Active Server Pages (ASP) system quickly superceded, was invented by programmers to plug the newly discovered gap between Web pages and databases. The system was little more than a set of database queries embedded in an HTML page. From that sort of humble beginning, programmers evolved a world of technologies that go way beyond queries to now provide any sort of data retrieval and formatting that you may want. The latest templating tools that I've seen feature a graphical user interface and enable you to drag and drop elements onto a Web page. Some elements are simply static text and graphics, but others are complex programming objects that perform a tremendous amount of content access and processing.

Templates perform content layout and formatting using many of the same text manipulation programs that collection systems use. They also employ specialized routines for layout, personalization, and building navigation.

Needless to say, programmers created the Web browser, which is *the* vehicle today for electronic publications.

The functionality in electronic publications

Web sites have developed a language of their own. Standard display elements such as the link, the banner, and the icon didn't come from software developers but from designers. But without creative programmers to make them work, these new Web controls would have never come about. In addition, wherever you find functionality on the Web, you also find the same small set of standard controls that appear in any application. Buttons, lists, check boxes, and menus are as common on the Web as in any standard application. And in any publication that includes functionality, a programmer is lurking somewhere in the background, writing code to hook the buttons and other controls to databases and other back-end programs.

Software developers were the first to confront the issue of how to represent functionality. In response, they borrowed from the mechanical age of functionality (the button, for one example) and invented some new methods (the drop-down menu, for another example). Over time, they created and perfected a small but very versatile set of controls that successfully direct attention and convey meaning in the impoverished environment of the computer screen.

You may never have stopped to think about it, but the following small set of widgets (creatively combined and artfully extended) provides the interface for almost all computer functionality:

✦ **Text box:** This control enables you to type small snippets of text. Three variations of the text box are shown in Figure 10-1: the Password Field control, which masks your input; the File Field control, which accepts only valid paths and filenames; and the Text Area control, which is simply a large text box that accepts any text.

✦ **Check box:** This control enables you to specify true or false to the computer.

✦ **Radio Button:** The name of this control comes from that of the little push buttons on a car radio that you use to select preset radio stations. This control enables you to answer multiple-choice questions for the computer where the responses are always mutually exclusive.

✦ **List box:** This control enables you to display lists of choices from which you can select an item. Two variations appear in Figure 10-1: the Dropdown, which opens up after you click it, and the plain List box, which is always open.

✦ **Button:** You click this control to make something specific happen. (The Submit and Reset buttons, as shown in Figure 10-1, are just buttons to which HTML browsers assign particular functions.)

✦ **Menu:** The menu is a standard control that doesn't appear in the illustration. Menus provide a hierarchy of commands. They are, in effect, buttons in an outline.

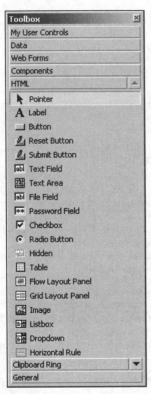

Figure 10-1: The Toolbox window from Microsoft's Visual Studio shows the basic controls available on a Web page.

These few controls have had amazing durability. When these controls first arrived on the consumer's screen, I'd never have thought that they'd remain so many years later as the basis of all functionality in both electronic publications and standard applications. The success of the standard controls came, in part, because they were promoted so well by the major software firms. I believe that their continued success, however, is based as well on the forethought and hard labor of the programmers who invented them.

A measure of the success of these controls is how often they now appear in print and television advertisements that seek a high-tech appeal. These controls have literally become the icons of the electronic age.

In summary, the software industry brings the following to CM:

✦ Software provides *collection* tools, which have moved from custom tools to commercial tools, although some custom development is still done.

✦ Software provides *management* technologies, starting with database software and technologies.

✦ Software provides all *publishing* tools, as well as the principal functional metaphors for a user interface.

The Premises of Marketing

The central premise of content management is to collect and deliver value to a set of known audiences. This premise is familiar to anyone involved in marketing, corporate communications, or public relations. They're intimately involved in defining value in the organization, understanding the organization's audiences, and ensuring that the right audience gets the right value. Manipulation notwithstanding, marketing people know how to define and deliver value. From this realm, I've drawn the following concepts:

✦ **Goal setting:** My concepts of project definition and goal setting derive from standard business planning as well as from the marketing realm. To become successful, any organization must begin by knowing exactly what they're trying to accomplish.

✦ **Value determination:** As any good marketer knows, you begin by understanding what you have that's of value to others. My notion of value propositions and value-based content chunking follow this same reasoning.

✦ **Messaging:** My ideas of creating the messages that a publication must deliver derive directly from the message-setting exercises used to develop marketing communications.

✦ **Audience analysis:** The kinds of information that you need to gather about an audience, the conclusions that you can draw from this information, and the techniques of audience segmentation come directly from marketing.

In the high-tech world, among the liberal masses anyway, the word *marketing* is often followed by some less-than-laudatory moniker. The derision isn't wholly undeserved. One lesson that the marketing family can teach the rest of its high-tech cousins, however, is how to know your audiences quantitatively. Moreover, unlike many other disciplines that give mostly lip service to *user-centered* design, marketers know that success comes only if the audience is the central concern of your entire system.

Marketers know that a carefully crafted message delivered in the right way to the right set of people has the power to move the world. CM practitioners need to know that carefully crafted content delivered through the right channels to the right set of audiences has the power to move your organization toward its goals.

In summary, marketing brings the following to CM:

✦ Marketing focuses on the audience rather than the features of a system.

✦ Marketing understands the value of content.

Summary

I didn't invent the concepts of content and content management. Rather, I've tried to synthesize the best of the concepts that I've found in various fields into a coherent framework that you can apply to the information problems that you confront.

The central point is worth reiterating: much of content management is designed to address a need that's been around for a while and that older disciplines have dealt with in their own ways. Some of the older disciplines, and library science in particular, have a lot of well-formed knowledge to offer CM, and the expertise of these professions will only become more valuable in the future.

In the next chapter, I go from the roots to the branches of content management. I describe the places where content management has proven of use to organizations.

✦   ✦   ✦

The Branches of Content Management

One of today's content management companies is fond of saying that content management is the operating system for e-business. Hyperbole aside, this statement does contain some truth. An operating system is the infrastructure that lies below applications. It provides a common set of services that applications draw on. Similarly, content management can underlie many of the Web technologies and applications that constitute e-business. In this chapter, I discuss how content management can underlie the following key business applications:

✦ **Personalization:** To effectively deliver personalized content requires a content management system (CMS) behind it to make the content accessible and targetable.

✦ **Advanced Web sites:** Most of the technology to create and maintain large and complex Web sites is based on content management.

✦ **Multiple publications:** To effectively share an information base across multiple publications, you need the infrastructure and publication systems that a CMS provides.

✦ **E-commerce:** You can use content management systems to directly manage the catalogs behind commerce sites. In addition, a CMS can fully manage the presentation and personalization of e-commerce functionality.

✦ **Knowledge management:** If knowledge management is the collection, management, and distribution of what an organization "knows," a CMS can prove the best platform behind a knowledge-management system.

✦ **Online communities:** Like geographic communities, online communities are based on affiliation and common knowledge. A CMS can provide the infrastructure behind the community.

✦ **Other kinds of management:** A wide variety of other sorts of managements are related to CM in one way or another.

Every segment of the computer industry tends to put itself at the center of the universe and see the other segments as revolving around it. I don't see content management this way. It's not at the center of the computer universe but at the bottom of it. Just as an operating system provides basic services that any number of applications can draw on, a CMS also provides the basic system of information capture and distribution that any other system can draw on to meet its particular needs.

Just as you learn about an operating system that underlies all applications on a computer, you need a basic understanding of how the system (OS or CMS) works and what it requires to be productive. A CMS requires you to get a solid understanding of your information sources, your audiences, and your information outlets. This exact knowledge can help you succeed whether you're creating Web sites, e-commerce ventures, community sites, or any of a range of other systems. In the end, all these systems have the same goal — get the right information and functionality to the right people at the right time through the right channel. Each of the disciplines I mention in this chapter is a branch of the larger tree of content management.

Personalization

If you personalize a publication, you tailor its content and presentation to the particular individual who's viewing it. Although personalization has taken on an almost mystical air in the current Web era (an era lasting about six months), the basic concept is quite simple: Match content to audiences. In this sense, personalization is one branch of CM.

What is personalization?

Personalization is delivering the most appropriate content to a person from within a standard framework. Although personalization is a Web buzzword, the concept applies to any delivery channel (as the personalized address labels that I keep receiving in the mail clearly show). More specifically, personalization proceeds as follows:

✦ You collect data about the user.

✦ You match that data to content.

✦ You deliver that content within a standard context (for example, a Web page with standard branding imagery, banners, navigation, and so on).

Suppose, for example, that you want to produce a personalized automobile Web site. On the home page, you may ask what kind of car the user owns (*collecting user data*). Then you use the car that the user enters to select content for the next page (*matching content*). Some parts of the second page, such as your logo and company name, are always present and in the same positions (*delivering within a standard context*).

To personalize, you create a dynamic dance between the data that you collect on users and the structuring of the content in the system. On the one hand, you want to structure your content according to the level of the data that you will collect. (What's the point of finding out the age of the user if you're not going to tag the content in a way that enables you to deliver age-specific content?) On the other hand, if you can identify obvious discerning parts of your content, collecting the data that enables you to personalize based on that content structure makes sense. If a summary level and detail level are already distinguished in the structure of your content, for example, why not collect the data that you need to decide which level the users want?

Personalization

Does personalization work? Is it worth doing? Certainly in the dotcom golden days personalization was very much in favor, and some content management vendors repositioned themselves as providing "personalization platforms" or "one-to-one marketing platforms" to capture that demand. Not long after the crash, however, personalization became almost a dirty word, dismissed as something that just couldn't deliver as promised.

There are, of course, different forms of personalization. At its heart, personalization is about dynamically matching content to users' interests. You can do this by inferring the users' interests — for example, by looking at their browsers or their purchase histories and serving content accordingly — or the users can make their interests known explicitly.

We have experimented with both of these approaches and have certainly found the latter to be very powerful. If you can get your users to explicitly state their interests and preferences, you can build strong relationships with them by giving them what they want, when they want it. At its simplest, this might just be e-mail alerts when new content, products, or services become available and match your users' stated interest areas.

What does this all mean for content management? The challenge with personalization is one of return on investment (ROI) — how much time and money can you spend on personalizing your users' experience and still get a return for yourself? If you have to put in too many resources to make personalization work, your ROI may well go negative. The trick is to make your content "*smart*." *Smart content* is content that can be easily — and cost-effectively — packaged, sliced and diced, repackaged, and reassembled to be delivered to the right person at the right time through the right channel. You need smart content to make personalization pay.

The real trick to creating smart content that will make personalization pay is in your metadata and content taxonomy. You need to think very carefully about the ways in which your users, as opposed to your organization, might want to have your content filtered and organized in order for it to be personalized for their own benefit. This customer insight then needs to be translated into metadata and content structures. For example, you might want to tag your content not just by the type of content it is, but the customer segments it would be relevant for. Your content might be most valuable to your users personalized by industry sector, by lifestage, by geographic relevancy...

Ashley Friedlein, CEO, E-consultancy

This section provides a conceptual overview of personalization; for information about the mechanics of personalization, see Chapter 32, "Designing Personalization."

You can use either of the following basic types of personalization:

✦ **Profile-based personalization:** If you can identify traits in the audience of your publications and group those traits into profiles, you can deliver information based on a user's profile. On the content side, you must identify the components that are of most interest to members of that segment. You can use this method to target entire segments of your users or to create a one-to-one publication, where each user sees a publication personalized to her particular profile.

✦ **Behavior-based personalization:** You can potentially infer a great deal about what someone wants to see, based on what she previously chose to see. If you can identify visited components, associate them with desires, and then link them to other components that meet the assumed desires, you can build behavior-based personalization into your dynamic publications. For static Web sites and other publications, behavior-based personalization isn't possible because you have no way to change the pages delivered based on the user's behavior.

✦ **Campaign-based personalization:** A campaign is a planned content *push* to users who meet certain criteria. For example, you might plan to push information about an upcoming lunar eclipse to users that you have identified as being interested in astronomy. Campaigns have defined start and finish dates and a defined audience.

Content management underlies personalization

I believe that personalization is so much a part of content management that it serves little purpose to tease the two very far apart. In this work, I consider personalization as simply the last piece of management that happens to content before you lay it into a publication. Every other process prior to that last act also serves to target content to audiences. In fact, the entire purpose of a CMS is to deliver the right content to the right audience. So you may say that the entire CMS is a personalization system. On the other hand, a specific, generally agreed-to part of the process is known as personalization: the rules and software that select particular content and navigate it into a publication, based on some data that the system obtains about the person viewing it.

 You can find more information about personalization in Chapter 32, "Designing Personalization."

In the following sections, I discuss how a CMS underlies the three steps in personalization.

Collecting data about the user

The structured delivery that a CMS provides enables you to very accurately associate the user information that you collect to its context. Instead of asking what kind of car a person owns, for example, your system can observe that the person went to the page for a Toyota. From that choice, you can assume that she's interested in Toyotas. That's a fine design, but for a CMS behind the scenes delivering structured content types to standardized pages, it creates a more difficult task. First, if you did not systematically produce the pages, you have little chance of knowing exactly what's on any particular page. Second, the user data that you collect is itself content for some system to manage.

Matching data to content

Suppose that you want to personalize your home electronics site — that is, you want to provide information that's most relevant to the people visiting your site. Your marketing research uncovers the following four basic visitor types:

✦ **Generation M** (for millennium), ages 6 to 20, whose interests lie in electronic games.

✦ **Generation X**, ages 21 to 35, whose interests lie in handheld audio devices, such as MP3 players.

✦ **Baby Boomers**, ages 36 to 55, whose interests lie in home stereo systems.

✦ **Empty nesters**, ages 56 and older, whose interests lie in videophones.

You want to deliver information about these product types to these demographic groups. In addition to figuring out what group a particular visitor belongs to, you also must locate the right type of electronics for that visitor's group. To do this personalization, you need many of the main features of a CMS, including the following:

✦ **Content components:** To deliver product information, you must differentiate it from other types of information. You can then find and deliver the product content components. (You can find more information about content components in Chapter 27, "Designing Content Types.")

✦ **A repository:** To effectively organize and find your product components, you must store them in a database or other repository system that can deliver them to your personalization program quickly. (You can find more information about repositories in Chapter 39, "Building Management Systems.")

✦ **Metadata:** To find the right product components, you must mark each product component with additional information that identifies which demographic it applies to. Then, after you identify a visitor as a member of one of your target audiences, you can query your repository, basing your query on this audience metadata, and return the appropriate information. (You can find more information about metadata in Chapter 24, "Working with Metadata.")

Delivering personal content in a standard context

Regardless of the particular information that interests a user, certain publication elements needn't change. The name of your organization very likely remains the same regardless of the audience you're serving. Your brand and the general layout of your publication also probably don't vary. These elements remain the same — not because they can't change, but rather because they usually don't need to and probably shouldn't. To stay cost effective as well as present a unified identity to all your audiences, you need to create a standard frame around personalized content.

 Note   I mean *frame* in a general sense, although on a Web site, you may actually use frame sets to create the standard frame.

In a CMS, publishing templates provide this sort of framework. They house the standard elements that don't change from page to page. They also host the computer code that decides who the user is and what particular content to include on the page inside the context that the standard elements create.

Personalization, as I discuss it throughout this book, is the last crucial mile in the journey of content to an individual user. How important it is depends on the goals for the CMS, but it should always be a consideration.

Advanced Web Sites

As I originally wrote this section, I was en route to yet another client whose Web site was getting a bit out of control. To quote one of the documents that I received from this client:

> Most of the attendees agreed that establishing a consistent publishing process is important to ensure both the quality and accuracy of Web content. Some said that if their department had an established editorial process, they either didn't know what it was or it wasn't being followed. Although the content management system must allow for the different needs of all departments, establishing a consistent process was viewed to be important to a collaborative publishing effort.

Some of those in attendance cited a 'startup mentality' as a problem. Without an established publishing flow model, content creators are often forced to act as writer, editor, producer, and reviewer. They mentioned some consequences of this situation including a lack of accuracy, substandard quality, and a feeling of isolation among editors and writers within different departments of the company.

As in so many other organizations, these folks started with a few energetic technologists and writers who were enthralled by the new challenge of the Web. They attacked this exciting new venture with the entrepreneurial spirit that the phrase *startup mentality* captures. In a startup venture, the premium is on getting something together and releasing it as quickly as possible. This situation usually involves heroic efforts by a few very dedicated individuals who are willing to do whatever's necessary to keep the venture afloat. This startup mentality has driven the Web to its current heights at its current velocity, but it can last only so long. Eventually, staff members become burned out and unable to continue the pace. In addition, after innumerable crises that they could easily have averted with a modicum of planning, they become cynical and stop picking up the slack. Finally, and most important, after the effort is really running, the entrepreneurs leave for the next exciting venture; the managers, whose job it is to go from a startup to a running system are required to replace them.

Content management, as the name implies, is a manager-type activity. It is, in fact, antithetical to the startup mentality that's permeated Web activities so far. A CMS is a well-oiled machine; its purpose is to create a smooth and manageable process around the publication of a Web site (and other publications). Interestingly, the introduction of a CMS often accompanies an exodus of the types of individuals who thrive on the chaos of a startup technology.

Tip If you're smart, you anticipate this situation and find other cutting-edge activities for these valuable adrenaline junkies to lead before they leave your organization entirely for more stressful activities.

The reason that this company and most other organizations with large Web sites are pursuing content management is that the startup mentality that launched their sites is too expensive and too inefficient to keep their sites going and growing.

In particular, their sites now display the following characteristics:

✦ A lot of content and types of content

✦ A lot of change in their content and their designs

✦ A wide and distributed contribution base

✦ A lot of content sharing among pages

A CMS provides an appropriate infrastructure for handling the challenges of an advanced site. In fact, most commercially available CMS products currently make this type of infrastructure their main goal.

A CMS is designed specifically to deal with content in bulk. The idea of content types is to categorize and organize your content so that you can manage it as classes and not as independent parts. Although you manage the content as classes, you can still deliver it as individual chunks. In a CMS, templates enable you to separate content from the design of particular publications. As publication design changes, therefore, you needn't modify content. Generally, you can accomplish a design change very quickly after a CMS is in place, because only a small number of templates are affected.

Most CMS products offer the capability to present easy-to-use forms that give remote and non-technical authors a quick way to submit content. The forms guide the authors through the process of entering content in the manner that the CMS expects them to structure it and provide a foolproof way of ensuring that they add the appropriate metadata to the content as necessary.

Finally, because you store content in a CMS as independent components and later form them into pages by using templates, sharing content between pages is simply a matter of calling the same component into both pages. Of course, you must create components and decide which pages get them, but at least you don't need to retype the same content in two different places — nor do you need to keep two different versions in sync if the content changes.

Multiple Publications

Today, the content management industry emphasizes the Web. In fact, many CMS products only create Web sites. Some companies that now offer CMS products previously saw print as their main target and have all but abandoned this older medium, pointing their products only at the Web. This situation is unlikely to last. As many of my clients tell me, they experience an enormous duplication of effort in their organizations for each different publication format. My typical publishing client, for example, produces a final book or magazine and then passes print files on to its Web team. That team pulls the final files apart and puts them back together as Web pages.

Clearly, a CMS, correctly implemented, can save a tremendous amount of effort and enable companies to create their print and electronic publications simultaneously. Of course, print publications aren't the only issue. Most organizations create an Internet site as well as an intranet site. They may also create extranet sites aimed at their partner organizations or their customers. In addition to the variety of Web sites that such companies can produce from the same content base, they may address everything from Wireless Application Protocol (WAP) telephones to Personal Digital Assistants (PDAs), to television set-top computers. Organizations have a large and growing need to feed information into a wide variety of delivery channels. No organization can possibly create a separate staff, system, and support structure for each channel. Fortunately, with a CMS in place, it doesn't need to.

As an example of the sort of system that's still most common, consider a magazine publishing company that wants to put its great magazine content on the Web as well as in print. Figure 11-1 shows the process such a company might use. Notice that the print publication is complete before the Web publication can begin. Notice, too, that the company must discard much of the good work of the authors because it's of no use to the print process.

The editorial board of the magazine creates a publishing schedule for the year. For each issue, the board members identify the articles that they want to publish. The next level of editor assigns articles to writers, giving them a subject, angle, and a word count. The writer begins researching the article. She collects a tremendous amount of background information, performs extensive interviews, and writes an article that may run two or three times the word count that the editor assigns her. She puts all her research in a box, cuts out half the words from her article, and passes the result to the editor. The editor expects a certain number of words from the author, so he either adds to or, more commonly, takes out text to reach a word count. Production staff then lays out the article and any associated artwork in a desktop publishing tool to see how it fits in the magazine. They assign the article to space in the front on the magazine and decide where the continuation jumps to in the back of the magazine. Production may also call in the editor to copy fit (make further edits to make the article fit the space allotted). Other editors and production staff do the same until all the articles fit. The production staff then builds the table of contents for the magazine, and editors make their final checks and release the magazine files to the printer.

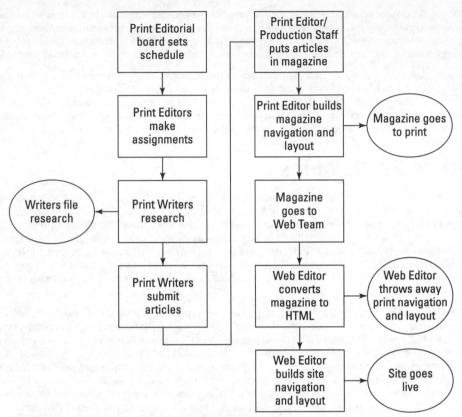

Figure 11-1: A typical pre-CMS publishing process

Only then does the Web process begin. The Web editors start by stripping out all the print layout and navigation. They convert the print files to a Web format. Finally, they rebuild the navigation and indexing in HTML. All in all, a lot of time and redundant effort goes into bringing the same content to both print and the Web.

Note   This process that I describe is a generalized version, and I don't intend it to represent the definitive word on what publishers do.

To simultaneously create multiple publications that share significant amounts of content, you must perform the following tasks:

✦ Segment the information that you want to publish into content chunks that are independent of any of the particular publication's needs but that you can make serve the purpose of any of them.

✦ Separate the publication design from the content so that each publication can have its own separate format and structure but still accommodate the content.

✦ Create rules for how to select the right content chunks for each publication, how to format them correctly, and how to lay them into the overall publication structure.

Clearly, this process is a job for a CMS. Using content chunking, workflow, publication templates, and publication rules not only makes multiple publications possible, but also makes them inevitable. The CMS provides the infrastructure to turn the old serial process of creating multiple publications into a much more efficient parallel process. You can, for example, streamline the publication process that I outline earlier in this section considerably by using the tools that are available in a CMS. Print and Web publications can occur simultaneously and can, therefore, take advantage of different parts of the authors' work, as shown in Figure 11-2.

To publish to multiple publications, the publisher doesn't change the editorial board and assignments, which is where the organization creates value. Instead of altering the basic information-creation process, organizations generalize the process so that it can feed the entire range of target publications. For the publisher, this generalization means that the writer submits all the content and not just finished articles. Although the print publication contains only the tip of the research iceberg, the site can contain all the content that the writer produces, including background information, links, interview transcripts, media, and anything else that the writer can turn up.

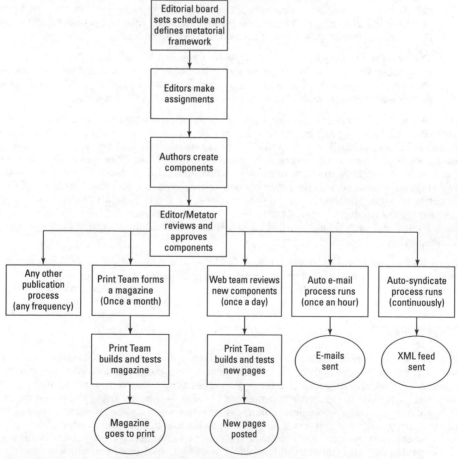

Figure 11-2: The publication process if a CMS is present

In the old model, Web production happens after print production is complete. In the new model, the print and Web production happen in parallel processes. You can approve each chunk of content separately and move it into its range of publications independently. You can, therefore, update the site continuously, even if the magazine comes out only once a month. Even before a full article receives approval, you can approve its abstract or headline and push it to the Web or other electronic channels, such as e-mail, to build excitement for the coming full release.

Producing multiple simultaneous publications isn't without its problems. In fact, to create such a system, your organization must overcome a number of serious hurdles, including the following:

✦ **The attitude of content contributors** who normally think of only one target as they create.

✦ **The need to share content** across output formats, which mandates that you store the content in an output-neutral format such as XML.

✦ **The need to store and organize more information** than is necessary for any one publication. In the magazine example that I describe earlier in this section, the writers must organize and upload their research as well as the small article it produces. In the past, they could safely archive or even discard this extra information.

✦ **The need to create publication designs** that you can fill automatically. This situation is a problem especially for sophisticated print publications, where designers normally handcraft every page. If handcrafting is to occur in the context of a CMS, it must happen as a post-process, after you draw content out of the CMS repository.

A CMS is the clear choice for an organization that needs to create multiple simultaneous publications. Even so, using a CMS for this purpose doesn't mean that the process is necessarily an easy one. Automatically creating simultaneous publications that are as *good* as those that you create through separate, targeted processes is a difficult task. (*Good*, in this context, means of the same quality as if you were to prepare each part of the publication by hand with the utmost care and finesse.) On the other hand, a CMS approach offers the possibility of creating better publications than a manual process does. (*Better*, in the CMS context, means fuller, more timely information, targeted more directly to the consumer, delivered in whatever format the consumer needs, and more efficiently than if you had hand-crafted each part of the publication.)

For writers, editors, and production people, a CMS doesn't radically change their jobs, but it does require them to increase the breadth of their publication intelligence — their ability to produce a body of content with several publications in mind simultaneously.

E-commerce

Some years ago, Web technology matured enough to deal securely with monetary transactions. After it did so, the rush to e-commerce began. Every organization with even the most rudimentary Web site began to plan for how to accept credit cards. Certainly, large organizations had been making electronic transactions for years — but not using the young Web technologies. In the rush to e-commerce, many organizations lost sight of the wider uses of the Web and other electronic channels. E-business, as I define it, became reduced to e-commerce. As the furor over transactions died down, the core of e-commerce emerged in the form of an online catalog that site visitors can browse through and buy from. In addition to offering the basic catalog, e-commerce encompasses a range of supporting functionality, such as exchanging money across the Web; hooking into legacy systems for inventory, pricing, and fulfillment; and other commerce mechanics such as the use of a shopping cart, which enables customers to add items and see how much they're spending.

You can find more information about e-business in the Introduction.

Catalogs and content management

The demands of a full-featured, usable, accessible catalog are content management demands. In particular, the catalog system must do the following:

✦ **Collect information:** The workflow and editorial process behind getting a product into the catalog mirrors that of any CMS. You must, for example, figure out what information to collect for each product. (That is, you must define the product component.) In addition, you establish the steps that take each product's information through review and approval. (That is, you must establish a workflow process.)

✦ **Manage information:** A catalog is a repository. Management and administration of the catalog follows all the familiar trails of a content repository. You delete or archive old products, for example, and you also periodically review and update certain pieces of information (for example, price and availability).

✦ **Publish information:** To be useful on the Web, the catalog system must show product information on an HTML page. It may contribute to a print catalog as well. Thus, the catalog system may require the same sort of query and template capability that a CMS offers.

The content in the catalog has many of the same needs as any content in any CMS. This does not mean, however, that the catalog is always integral to the CMS. The catalog data may be stored within the CMS repository, or it may be better to store the catalog in a separate database. If, for example, the catalog is already in a separate database whose collection and management procedures are established, there may be little point to moving the catalog content into another system. Also, a product catalog often has built-in relationships to other enterprise systems, such as inventory and manufacturing systems that would be hard to migrate or duplicate in the CMS. Thus, it is not obvious where the content of the product catalog is best kept. It depends on the situation.

Regardless of where you store the catalog, however, using the CMS to publish the product content is usually the best way to go. Catalog databases rarely have robust templating capabilities. And to standardize look-and-feel across all publications, your best bet is to use a single system. If you intend to store the catalog outside the CMS repository, you must make sure that the CMS can get product information out of the catalog system and format it for presentation on publication pages (as most can).

In some cases, your best route is to store the basic product data in a separate catalog system and the supporting information in the CMS. If the existing system stores only pricing, part numbers, and a short description, for example, you can store a picture, a long description, and reviews of the product in the CMS. Then, after you build the product page, the CMS can take some information from the catalog system and some from the CMS repository to create the complete presentation.

E-commerce functionality and content management

Next to the presentation of a catalog, e-commerce most involves the functionality to support and conduct transactions.

Cross-Reference

I detail the relationship between functionality and content management in Chapter 4, "Functionality Is Content, Too!" You see this relationship in each of the functionality areas that I cover in the following sections.

Exchanging money across the Web

Consumer e-commerce sites that accept payment on the Web generally communicate with the payee's bank behind the scenes to complete the transaction. Business sites reference an existing purchase order or, in some other way, validate that the transaction can go through. In either case, exchanging money across the Web isn't about information as much as it's about functionality. So although a CMS doesn't create the capability to exchange money on the Web, it can be responsible for putting the capability to exchange money on the Web on a particular page at a particular time. The CMS can treat the functionality that enables money exchange as a piece of *content* that it needs to manage and present.

Legacy systems and content management

Companies found out pretty quickly that e-commerce systems needed to talk to a lot of other corporate systems to support any significant amount of sales. In fact, they needed to fully integrate these systems into a vast range of existing (or legacy) data systems. Many software products help connect Web pages to older systems. The best of these products today use XML as a translation layer between the legacy system and the software that runs directly on a Web server. Exactly as in the case of exchanging money across the Web, these connections are functionality and not information. Thus, a CMS doesn't create the capability to connect to these other systems; instead, it gives you the capability to put the code that enables connections on the right page at the right time.

Take the example of a chunk of computer code (the functionality) that passes order information to a legacy inventory system and returns a *yes* if the item is in stock or a *no* if the item isn't in stock. The inventory system manufacturer or some third party that specializes in integration likely created this functionality outside the realm of the CMS. After its creation, however, the chunk of code (or the chunk of code that invokes the chunk of code) can enter the CMS repository, where the CMS tags it appropriately and delivers it to the pages that need it, just as it does with any other piece of information. In this way, the CMS manages the delivery of the functionality without needing to know anything about what the functionality actually does.

Tip

Alternatively, you can type the code directly into the CMS templates that produce the pages that need the functionality.

Shopping mechanics

The shopping baskets, order status screens, and order histories that are common on e-commerce sites generally consist of functionality that interacts with Web databases and legacy systems. As such, these types of functionality follow the same path through the CMS as transaction functionality and legacy integration functionality — that is, the CMS manages the presence of the code on the page but doesn't play a significant role in creating the functionality or exchanging data with the background databases with which the functionality communicates.

Knowledge Management

The term *knowledge management* has significant currency in today's computer vernacular. In fact, it may have more currency than the less glamorous concept of content management. Furthermore, in many a conversation, I find that people who are uncomfortable using the term *content management* freely use the term *knowledge management* to describe the process that I define here as content management. The vagueness of both terms notwithstanding, the knowledge-management industry addresses a related but different concern from the content-management industry. Although knowledge is a kind of content that you can manage, the core of knowledge management is discovery and synthesis, whereas the core of content management is collection and distribution. Still, knowledge that you discover or synthesize you must also collect and distribute. To my mind, the appropriate relationship between the two disciplines is that *content management is the infrastructure to amass and distribute the knowledge* that your organization identifies by using knowledge-management tools.

What is knowledge management?

The knowledge-management industry serves organizations with vast but balkanized repositories of data and terabytes of word processing and other binary files. These organizations pose what seems at first blush a modest question: What do we know? With all this information at our disposal, surely we know a lot, but how do we get to it? A number of answers come back from product companies and academics, each of which addresses a different part of the knowledge management issue, as the following list describes:

✦ **Synthesis and auto-discovery:** Through advanced data mining, analysis, and synthesis, many products seek to find the needles of knowledge in an organization's data haystack. Using the latest search technologies, they index and pattern-match their way through the terabytes of text and data to isolate just the right snippets of knowledge. This approach attempts to electronically winnow down vast information stores to squeeze out the knowledge.

✦ **Categorization:** Many products attempt to categorize and index work products as you create them. By being embedded in every application that your staff uses to create work products, the systems attempt to proactively capture and route significant information to those who need it.

✦ **Knowledge portals:** Many products take the approach of organizing and personalizing an organization's knowledge into a single easy-to-use interface. They seek to connect all the diverse sources of information and put them all at your fingertips in a one-stop shop on your computer screen.

If you put all three of these approaches together, you get a more complete answer to the question of how an organization knows what it knows. Your organization must obtain tools for synthesizing and collecting knowledge from the vast data and file stores that you now possess. Furthermore, you must obtain tools for correctly cataloging new information as you create it. Finally, you must deliver the knowledge that you collect in an integrated and personalized way that takes into account what each staff member needs to know, given that person's current tasks and concerns.

The Human Side of Knowledge Management

Another part of knowledge management is less talked about but, to me, is possibly more important than the harvesting and delivering of information. Given that organizations live or die based on the knowledge that they are able to acquire and put to use, how can an organization manage the process of knowledge acquisition and use? The answer, I believe, lies partly in the realm of information dissemination (the realm of this book) and partly in the realm of purely human interaction. People surely acquire knowledge by consuming information, but just as surely they acquire knowledge in interaction with other people.

This more human side of knowledge management is easy to overlook. There are no products to buy, no systems to install, and no visible repositories of knowledge created. Rather, there is a climate to create, relationships to foster, and conversations to start. The concept of communities of practice bears on this notion of the human side of knowledge management, but more important, I believe, are the far less tangible aspects of the atmosphere in an organization. Is honest debate rewarded in the organization? Are people isolated in their offices or do they meet by chance throughout the day? Is it social suicide to talk about work issues at lunch? Are *ad-hoc* groups of peers getting together to mull over the serious intellectual issues of the organization? If a person has a great idea is he more likely to hide it or share it?

If an organization is serious about managing its knowledge, then installing systems is the easier half of what it must do. The other half is to foster a culture of knowledge that ensures that the systems it installs have something worth managing in them.

Knowledge is content to manage

Each of the three approaches to knowledge management (synthesis and auto-discovery, categorization, and knowledge portals) that I describe in the preceding section relates to the concept of content management that I develop in this work.

The same synthesis and auto-discovery tools that you may use to ferret out knowledge in the organization, you can also use to help discover and tag content for a CMS. Unfortunately, these tools do little more today than prescreen and tag easily discerned metadata.

The categorization tools that live within a content creator's native environment play a larger role in a CMS. Many CMS products include categorization interfaces that show up as new buttons or menus inside authoring applications such as Microsoft Word and Macromedia Dreamweaver. These interfaces enable non-technical users to store and retrieve content in a CMS repository without knowing anything particular about the CMS or its repository.

The area of knowledge portals is where knowledge-management systems and content management systems have the most in common. In fact, the creation of personalized pages of information that you draw from a variety of sources is much more a content management than a knowledge management task. The templating and personalization systems within a CMS are portal-creation tools. As one colleague recently commented, you can create a CMS without a portal, but you can't create a portal without a CMS.

Knowledge management most concerns discovery and synthesis of information, whereas content management most concerns collection and distribution of information. Clearly, a CMS can help collect and distribute the kind of information that enables us to know what we know.

Siloed Branches Can Be Problematic

The many branches of content management can be problematic. Organizations have lots of different types of content to manage. Different departments will have different requirements. For example, the Web design team needs a Web content management system, the engineering development team needs a product development system, the technical publications department needs a publications content management system, and the training group needs a learning content management system. Each of these different types of content management systems is specifically designed to address a unique set of needs, and most do it very well.

The problem with multiple content management solutions in an organization is that they are "*siloed,*" meaning that content cannot easily be shared among the different content management systems, and there is a lot of information that would be more effective if it could be shared rather than re-created and re-managed over and over again. For example, Marketing creates product and service descriptions that could be reused in training and documentation; Marketing, Training, Documentation, and Product Support all create content that could be used by Customer Support. When multiple content management solutions are implemented, departments tend to focus on their requirements and do not think about the larger organizational content requirements.

So what should an organization do? In recent years, content management vendors have moved towards enterprise content management. Enterprise content management systems are billed as technology that can manage your entire enterprise needs. Some can, some can't. Each system has a different set of capabilities; it's up to you to determine if they truly address your enterprise needs. Alternatively, you could consider a federated content management system that makes it possible to access content from any content management system in your organization by mapping the metadata from one system to another. If you have the opportunity, plan to share content by developing common structures for your content and common enterprise metadata taxonomies.

Work towards a single content management strategy if possible, or at minimum design your content and metadata to make it possible to share content across content management systems.

Ann Rockley, The Rockley Group Inc.

Online Communities

In society, *communities* are groups of people that share some common purpose or kinship ties. The situation is no different online. Although many people talk about creating online communities, few do so from this sort of understanding. The most popular concept of community I have heard is to become *the place* to go for some sort of information. If you add a chat room or a threaded discussion and collect user data, it is called a community. Many community sites hope to *own* the attention of their users and sell it to advertisers or direct it toward other organizational goals.

Without real community, however, which offers a core of common purpose or kinship (in the widest sense of sharing some important aspect of life), these sites can never really be communities. To be a real community, an online community needs to fulfill its members' needs for affiliation and knowledge. Affiliation is the members' desire to belong to something. Knowledge is the members' desire to know something. More to my current interest, a Web-based community needs a system behind it to support both affiliation and knowledge.

What is a community?

An *audience* is a group of people who share common traits and to whom you communicate in the same way. To become part of an audience (for example, women in their childbearing years), individuals needn't know about each other or care to communicate with other members. An audience is like a neighborhood where each family keeps to itself. Each family is likely to display similar traits (income level, interests, hometown, and so on), but they don't consider themselves really *part* of the group of people who live near them.

In contrast, *communities* are like neighborhoods where everyone knows each other. These neighbors share experiences and knowledge, have a lot of cross-communication, and most important, feel that they're part of the neighborhood. The neighborhood undoubtedly contains meeting places (schools, parks, the grocery store, and so on) where members congregate and share information and advice and feel a part of a larger group.

Online, the same analysis holds. A community site provides a meeting place where members can congregate and share information and advice and feel a part of a larger group. Although all sites should communicate to one or more audiences, community sites go further by fostering communication among audience members.

How are online communities constructed?

Figure 11-3 shows the major components of an online community system.

The common interest domain

The *common interest domain* is the boundary around the community. It's the realm of content and interaction. It's the basis of a community. For all the members, it offers a reason why they come together. Specifically, the *domain* is a statement of purpose for the community. The statement can be as general as "We love Barbie dolls" or as specific as "We're all female C++ developers working at atomic-accelerator laboratories on software designed to track the trails of subnuclear particles." Whether specific or general, the statement must clearly define the entrance requirement of the community. It's absolutely the first thing that you must determine about the community, and the rest of the structuring of the system springs naturally from it. The common interest domain defines what members affiliate with and on what subject they want knowledge.

Note   The common-interest domain shares a lot with the concept of the *content domain*. As I describe fully in Chapter 30, "Designing Content Access Structures," in the section "The content domain," the content domain is also a boundary and a statement. The content domain defines the boundary between the content that's relevant to manage and the content that isn't. It's a statement of the range of coverage of the CMS, such as "All content pertaining to the history of Barbie dolls."

The members

Members join the community for affiliation and knowledge. After they fully immerse themselves in the community, they may contribute as much of these goods as they receive. The purpose of a community Web site and its underlying system is to facilitate the exchange of affiliation and knowledge among the members. Much more tangibly, members come to the site for the following reasons:

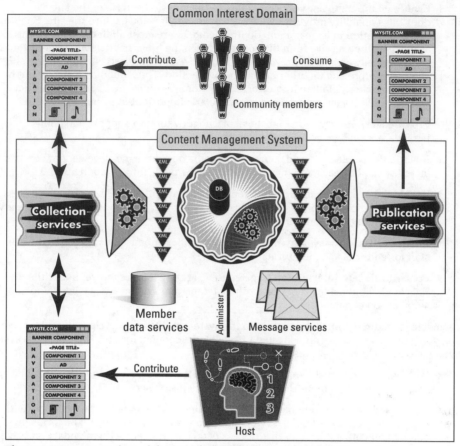

Figure 11-3: An overview of the CMS behind a community Web site

✦ To find new content of interest or contribute content.

✦ To find members or have other members find them.

✦ To participate in a communication forum such as an online meeting or presentation.

All these activities consist of uploading and downloading messages, files, content, and data. The goal of the system that runs the site is to facilitate contribution as well as consumption by the members and to position these mundane upload and download actions in such a way that they create a sense of place and belonging in the members.

The CMS behind the community

If the community site is to draw a wide member base, it must provide enough relevant and accessible content to warrant attention. If the site is to hold the attention of its member base, the content must continually grow and deepen. To accomplish this level of content management, a system is necessary. As is true of any CMS, the site must collect, manage, and publish content. Specifically, in the context of a community site, the CMS must perform the following tasks:

✦ **Enable members to actively contribute** to the knowledge base of the site. Not only does this capability provide a wide base of knowledge flowing into the site, but it also brings affiliation to its maximum depth. Members are most affiliated if they contribute as much as they receive from the community. On the other hand, member contributions are useful only as long as they're pertinent and well-structured enough for the site to effectively store and its other members to later find. Thus, building a strong but not overly complex metadata framework that naturally guides members to contribute relevant, well-tagged information is particularly important in a community site.

✦ **Provide a repository** with a fine level of categorization to support maximum personalization.

✦ **Include the semistructured sources** that come out of the message center. For example, include e-mail threads and messages that can be made into components.

✦ **Enable the repository to grow** in a constrained way with content expiring as necessary, missing or ambiguous information clearly identifiable, and new content areas ready for publication to the community members.

✦ **Include a workflow system** that can route member submissions through community staff for editorial and metatorial processing.

✦ **Present relevant information** targeted to what the system "knows" about the member. This kind of publishing requires a robust templating system and well-developed personalization capabilities.

To enable structured content to come into the system and targeted, relevant content to come out, you must have a fairly sophisticated CMS behind a community site. The collection system must have the following features:

✦ **Web-based forms** that lead members through the process of submitting small pieces of original content (content that they type into fields on-screen).

✦ **Web-based forms** that enable members to submit files with larger pieces of pre-authored content (word-processing files, video files, sound files, and so on). The forms must guide the members through the process of tagging the files with metadata and give them the opportunity to upload the files from their computers to the repository.

✦ **Batch-content processors** that can harvest the information from community bulletin boards and chat sessions and catalog it along with the other submissions.

✦ **E-mail acceptors** so that members can e-mail content directly to the community CMS.

✦ **Syndicated-content processors** that can accept and process information feeds from commercial providers. The site may, for example, include daily targeted news that an outside service provides, delivering stories electronically throughout the day.

To provide relevant information to members, the community CMS must collect user data and use it to subselect content to present to each user. In addition to using member data to target content, you can use member data on a community site to target certain members to other members. Such a member match-up service provides for a much greater sense of affiliation. Members, in the end, want to affiliate with other members—not with a Web site.

To match members to members or to match content to members, the system must collect categorization data on each member. In fact, it must categorize them in a way quite similar to the way that it categorizes content. In this way, affiliation groups can form around subject matter of common interest. In the successful system, the categorization of members and the categorization of content happen hand-in-hand, where one continually deepens the other. Of course, making friends involves more than answering questions the same way. So, the successful member-matching system needs to go beyond mere matching to enable members to experience each other's virtual company and decide for themselves with whom to affiliate.

On the more mundane side of matching members to content, as in any personalization system, the site must have mechanisms for the following tasks:

✦ Gathering member data.

✦ Tagging content.

✦ Mapping the type of data gathered to the appropriate tags in the content.

✦ Dynamically rendering the selected content within a standardized page. *Dynamic rendering* is the function of CMS templates. They contain the software code necessary to determine who the user is, access her member data, and match her with the content that is most relevant to her.

 For more information about templates, see Chapter 31, "Designing Templates."

The message and user services

The message services provide the communication hub for the site. They include any or all of the following technologies:

✦ Basic e-mail

✦ Chat and hosted forums

✦ Threaded message boards

✦ Online meetings

✦ Online presentations

✦ Member location services

✦ Member classified ads and goods or services exchanges

The exact number and types of technologies in use depend on the common interest domain, the computer savvy of the members, and their degree of affiliation. Generally, the more affiliation your community can muster, the more members put the time and energy into these communication channels. The surest sign of a low-affiliation community is one where all the bulletin boards are empty.

The CMS behind the community must obviously support these communication vehicles. In particular, although the CMS doesn't control the communication services themselves, it's responsible for rendering the interface for these services on the Web pages that the members access. In the same way that the CMS can target content to members, it can target particular communication services to users. It may, for example, put a registration form for an online meeting on the home page for all members who express an interest in the subject matter of the meeting. In addition, the CMS must harvest information from the communication services and successfully transition their semistructured, real-time output (like meeting notes and sound clips) into more enduring content that you can deliver by using the same targeting techniques as you do for any other community content.

 For more information about using a CMS to manage functionality such as that mentioned in the preceding text, see Chapter 4, "Functionality Is Content, Too!"

Member data is essential to the system behind the community. In addition to serving as the basis for personalization, the system needs this data for a variety of other purposes, such as the following:

✦ Member bulletins and global e-mails

✦ Member rights to particular content

✦ Member rights to the communication services

✦ Member rights to submit and modify content

✦ Administration of member fees or other initiation rites

For all these purposes, the site needs a strong and extendable user data-management system. That system is the same as the one a CMS uses to do personalization.

The host

A community host is the organization that is in charge of the site's infrastructure and maintenance. This organization must implement a CMS, communication services, and member-administration services. It must also input enough content to get the site off the ground. You find the following two typical types of hosts online:

✦ **Commercial hosts:** A *commercial host* is one that targets the community members as a market for goods or services. This host is willing to trade the cost of maintaining the site in return for exposure to the members. In a typical scenario, the host has the original idea for the community, creates an initial implementation of the site's system, fills the system with enough content to make it viable, and then launches the site and opens it to members. The host continues to feed content in, administer user data, and create communication events. The major issue to resolve in this circumstance is what right the host has to market to the members or sell member data to outsiders. Members can leave if they feel exploited. On the other hand, the host may stop if it sees a lot of cost and little return from the community.

✦ **Member hosts:** A *member host* is one or more potential members who decide to create a Web presence. Typically, some existing trade or interest organization with a current membership organizes and funds the initial system. As in the case of the commercial host, the member host creates an initial implementation of the site's system, fills the system with enough content to make it viable, and then launches the site and opens it to members. The key issues here are continued funding of the site from often cash-strapped organizations and whether sufficient attention is paid to the site maintenance by what are often volunteer-run organizations. Of course, selling member data is also an issue for member-hosted communities.

For both the commercial host and the member host, the primary issue is to make the site truly belong to the members. As time goes on, members should become the major contributors to the site, with the host needing to supply less and less content. In a high-affiliation community, members even plan and execute the communication events (chats, online meetings, and so on). If the community is successful, its success comes from the host's creation of a system that promotes affiliation and targeted knowledge-gathering among a group of people who naturally gravitate to a clearly stated and well-founded common interest.

In any case, for the community to become successful, it must have a full-featured and robust CMS behind it. Without a CMS, the site can serve neither its members nor its host. At best, it becomes an enhanced bulletin board or, at worst, an unenhanced one.

Online Communities

The single biggest question we hear about online communities is whether you get a return on investment from them. Resources are required not just in terms of technology, but also moderators, editors (and in some cases, lawyers) to manage and run an online community. It is not a thing to be undertaken lightly. So how do you ensure that your community brings you value?

From talking to numerous other online community managers and drawing on our own experience as well, we think the way to make online communities pay their way is to ensure that your community content all ties into, and interrelates with, your own content, products, or services and vice versa. (*Community content* is user-generated contributions, opinions, and comments.) So if you are a publisher, make sure that your community can comment on your content and that your content links in to your community's comments on it. If you are selling products, make sure that your community can comment on them and that any community content also links in to related products. This keeps things relevant and useful for your users, but also ensures they find their way to areas of your site that deliver direct value to you. Amazon and eBay, for example, do this very successfully.

There are clear content management implications to achieving this successfully. If your community software is not linked to your e-commerce catalogue or your content management system, it is much more difficult to dynamically and cost-effectively inter-link them. We believe that it is best if your CMS is also the platform that runs your community; or at the very least, you need to make sure that the categories and metadata that you use to manage your community match those that you use to manage your products, services, or other content. In this way it is vastly easier to ensure tight and efficient integration between your community and those areas of value that you need to promote to drive your business.

Ashley Friedlein, CEO, E-consultancy

Other Kinds of Management

The number of different kinds of *information thingies* organizations think they are managing is a good indicator of how early it is in the evolution of information management systems. I use the term *information thingy* to convey the vagueness and confusion that many organizations have concerning the information objects they want to manage. Lest you think I use this term in jest, let me assure you that I have often heard it in use! In content management, the information thingy is really called a component. In a document management system, the thingy is really a document (or to my mind a file). In this section, I discuss some of the other information thingies that are current and how they might relate to my concept of content management.

I have already discussed the relationship between content, document, catalog, and knowledge management. I haven't touched on a variety of other kinds of management, such as the following:

✦ **Digital asset management** is where the information thingy is a media file or file set (usually digital images, videos, or sound files).

✦ **Learning object management** is where the information thingy is a learning module or some other unit of instructional information.

✦ **Source management** is where the information thingies are programming code segments and other files associated with an application (images of buttons, icons, and so on).

✦ **Digital records management** is where the information thingy is a file or file set that is important enough to archive and make available for later retrieval.

✦ **Digital rights management** is where the information thingy is a file or file set that has usage restrictions on it that must be observed.

Note

I apologize if I failed to mention one of the managements that you might use. More appear every day. My hope is that the ones I chose represent most of the possibilities for interaction with a CMS.

I believe that the number of types of information thingies will continue to increase (possibly quite dramatically), whereas the number of types of systems to manage them will decrease. There is no limit to the number of different kinds of information that you may want to exert control over (that is, manage). However, a clear limit exists to the number of ways in which you exert control.

Each type of information is differentiated from all others because of its nature, intended audiences, or use, and a single information thingy may mean different things to different people at different times. For example, the nature of some images is that they are application icons, so they are managed as source and not digital assets. Or, as another example, a digital record is a *record* and not something else because of how it is used. That is, the content of the record originally may have been a digital asset (say, an image) or a learning object (say, a course assignment), but it is a record (and not an asset or a learning object) when you use it as an archived history of what the organization produced.

Similarly, a video might be a learning object when its audience is a student and a digital asset when its audience is a buyer of course materials. I think it makes little sense to try to pigeonhole an information thingy into one type or to try to stem the onslaught of new categories for the things you create. Rather, as you find useful distinctions for information, you ought to be free to draw those distinctions if it helps you do the job of managing that information. Information thingies, if you have not already guessed, seem to me to be quite a bit like what I have previously called content types. They are both classes of information that share a common nature, audience, structure, and/or use.

You should be allowed to devise new information thingies the same way you create content types: as you need them. On the other hand, it seems silly to create an entirely different management infrastructure for each kind of information thingy. First, too many information thingies exist now, and organizations are overwhelmed and confused by the current array of systems. More systems will only make the situation worse. More important, even though an unlimited number of information thingies exist, you will want to perform only a limited number of management activities on information thingies. As you might suspect, I would break the management activities into these categories:

✦ **Collection**, where you want to create, gather, and process the information thingies.

✦ **Management**, where you want to store and retrieve the information thingies.

✦ **Publishing**, where you want to make the information thingies available to some audience, perhaps in combination with other things of the same or different types.

I'm not trying to reduce all of these other sorts of management to content management. In fact, I'd be just as happy to enlarge the tent of content management to include the needs of a variety of other management types. However, I am arguing for the consolidation of management systems so that a single system can handle the core management functions of the whole range of information thingies. I contend that whatever type of information thingies you have, you will still need to collect, manage, and publish them. In addition, the more types of information thingies your organization needs to manage, the greater your need for standardizing their management, and more important, the more possibilities you will have for creating publications that include multiple types. Why shouldn't it be easy to include a learning object with rights-managed digital assets in it within a Web site that is later automatically archived?

Digital asset management (DAM)

Digital asset management systems arose from of the need to manage the creation and use of media assets such as images and sound files. They are exceedingly good at the tagging, storage, and reuse of media. There is no reason why these features could not be standard equipment on a CMS. I don't mean to say that DAM should go away and be replaced by CM systems that do the same job. That would be like saying that because cars can do the same thing as motorcycles, we don't need motorcycles. Where the organization needs only DAM, it should not be burdened by the bulk and inflexibility of a CMS. But where the organization needs both CM and DAM, and moreover, where the organization needs the digital assets to be used in the publications that the CMS creates, it should not be required to buy and integrate two systems.

What DAM has to teach CM is that media files have their own world of authoring, editing, workflow, and presentation. Few CM systems today do more with media files than store them and move them to the Web when they are called for in a Web page. Most systems behave as if text were the only real form of content. Everything else is just a file to be moved around.

Learning object management (LOM)

When I started teaching, I immediately felt the pain of constructing learning materials — it's hard work to create all the lectures, activities, and other resources it takes to mount a good class. So, I immediately tried to start automating away the pain. The possibilities for reuse of materials within a course and between courses were just too obvious and compelling to ignore. Three years later I am just coming to fully realize how hard it is to automate the construction and reuse of learning materials. Of course, many smarter minds than mine have been working on this problem as well, and they have created any number of systems that instructional designers can use to construct learning materials so that they can be shared and reused.

Many of these systems take a decidedly CM approach to the task (in fact, many such systems are called *Learning CMSs*). They create learning objects that are just like content types. They store the learning objects in repositories with workflow, versioning, and metadata services. They publish the objects into course materials targeted toward a variety of audiences. Once again, I have no desire to see learning object systems be subsumed by CM systems. What I would like to see is the capability to add learning management to a CMS when the organization needs to integrate learning content types with other types. It also seems clear to me that LCMSs could buy rather than build a core set of collection, management, and publishing services. Then the developers of these systems could spend more of their time of cracking the very hard problems of learning and less on the common problems of authoring, tagging, storing, and generalized publishing.

Source management

For as long as there have been programming projects, systems for sharing programming code have been used among the various people on the project. These systems allow programmers to check out files, manage the edits they make to the files, and create file versions that can be backed up, archived, and re-stored as needed. (Some CMS products began as fancy Web source systems.) Many CM systems have the same type of versioning and check-out as source systems. All CM systems could benefit from the rigor of the backup, rollback, and recovery that source management systems have.

Even though significant overlap exists between the features of a source and content management system, my feelings about source management are different from those for the other managements I have discussed. There is overlap in features, but not in audience, nature, structure, or use between the two systems. Source systems are solely for programmers; the content type—computer code—is like no other; its structure is both unique and very important to manage. Its use is extremely tied to the particulars of the software development process and to the tools that programmers actually use to write code. In short, I can't see programmers using a CMS. Although CM systems can learn from the source management tools (and vice versa, no doubt) I see little reason to propose that the two become one.

Cross-Reference   I discuss what I see as the way to have code interact with a CMS in "Managing Functionality Like Information" in Chapter 4, "Functionality Is Content, Too!"

Digital records management

For as long as there has been paper there has been a need to keep the old but important documents safe somewhere. Traditionally, that has meant large warehouses filled with stacks of labeled boxes filled with folders filled with paper. Today it may still mean warehouses, but smaller ones, augmented by very large hard drives and tapes that save the old but very important digital directories filled with computer files. In either case, a database is involved that catalogs where the files have come from, what they are about, where they are stored, how long they need to be retained, and how to dispose of them when they are no longer needed.

What does this have to do with CM? Well, wouldn't it be nice if:

✦ The content to be archived were put into a set of files that is most convenient for management and for later retrieval, or disposal?

✦ The database containing information about the archived documents could be filled automatically?

✦ The electronic files themselves were automatically moved to the hard drive where they would be archived?

✦ The files to be archived were named appropriately and if they contained information within them that let them be identified even if they were somehow separated from the rest of the collection?

You can probably guess that a CMS would allow you to do all this with its publishing system. The archival form of the content can be treated as just another type of publication. So, at the very least, a CMS can feed a records management system with the information it needs. It is conceivable that the CMS could *be* the records management system, but that is not usually feasible. If all records were electronic (which they are not) and if all content that needs to be retained were part of the content in your CMS (which it isn't—lots of information such as financial records and receipts have no business in a CMS), a CMS could do everything you need to archive, retrieve, and finally dispose of your important records. In fact, most organizations are and will remain a long way from this state of affairs. However, any organization with important information in a CMS will have a leg up on archiving that information. Any organization with unimportant information in a CMS should pull the plug!

Digital rights management (DRM)

If I own information you want to use, you had better convince me that it is to my advantage to let you use it and that you will protect it as I would. If you use information from a number of sources, each having its own rules of use, you had better get organized about managing its use. Digital rights management systems help you get organized.

In essence, once you have figured out what the rules are for a type of content, you encode those rules in the delivery software for the content. You also mark each piece of content of the type with the restrictions it holds. For example, suppose you have a Web site with photos that can be reproduced in thumbnails for free, but a user must pay to them reproduced at full size (say from $1 to $5 per view). You would use your digital rights system to tag each photo with its price and to ensure (through some sort of code) that your site shows only thumbnail views until the user has paid.

It is not hard to see how a CMS would be a help to the DRM or even how it could replace the DRM. In CMS terms, the preceding example could be carried out as follows. You create a content type called Pay Pictures. One element of the Pay Pictures content type is price, another is the full-sized picture, and a third is the thumbnail picture. The authoring system requires that you upload both versions of the picture and that you give it a price between $1 and $5. The publishing system templates use the thumbnail images in the site pages and link them to the payment page.

If you are already using a CMS and have modest DRM needs, you can probably get your existing system to do the trick. If you have more sophisticated needs, you can buy software (that should integrates with your CMS) that allows you to create complex rules of use, encryption, and digital signing of files, and aids the template logic that decides what to show and allow on a particular publication page.

Content Management Helps Make Ideas Visible

At a recent industry meeting, 22 heads of knowledge management from a variety of industries agreed that "world-class organizations exploit their inherent knowledge potential by ensuring their expertise, information, and ideas are visible, shared, and applied." Content management is a key process in making expertise, information, and ideas visible, and in creating ways to share them.

Particularly when I think of how portals have evolved from simple access points, to publishing platforms, to collaboration spaces, to communities and meeting places — and now more often than not to "my relevant stuff" workspaces — the *"knowledge portal"* would not be possible without the underpinnings of information architecture and content management. What would the personal portal experience be without the ability to tailor it based on audience or the ability to manage Web parts and the content within them? What would a collaboration space be without a clear understanding of the context behind each contribution? Who would know whom to contact for the best source of information and experience on a given topic without metadata to flag or sort results in meaningful ways?

Mary Lee Kennedy, The Kennedy Group (www.maryleekennedy.com)

Except for source management, all the kinds of management I have discussed (including knowledge and catalog) are all part of the growing need to take control of digital information. Each has its own information thingy and unique features that distinguish it from the general ideas of content management. Each, however, shares the basic collection, management and publishing needs that all content shares. In addition, each information thingy is also a content type that might need to be mixed with other content types and used within a broader CM framework. In the future, it would be nice if all the managements got together and decided not to reinvent the common stuff, but rather to focus on their uniqueness and leave the collection, management, and publishing to a common shared platform for content management.

Summary

Although each of the electronic technologies that I describe in this chapter has its own segment of the computer industry focusing on it, I hope that you can see clearly that, like branches of the same tree, they all share the need to collect, manage, and publish content. To this extent, any of these technologies can benefit from the concepts of content management. Moreover, a well-constructed CMS can serve the needs of any of or all the following technologies:

✦ Personalization systems need the content tagging, selection, and targeted delivery of a CMS.

✦ Advanced Web sites buckle under their own weight without the organization and efficiency of a CMS.

✦ Without a CMS, producing multiple publications from the same content base is, at best, a very long process and, at worst, impossible.

✦ E-commerce systems benefit greatly from the delivery system in a CMS.

✦ Knowledge-management systems needn't reinvent the collection and publishing software already present in a CMS.

✦ Online communities can position a CMS at their core to help match members to content and to each other.

✦ Other kinds of management include a wide assortment of information thingies that organizations must manage using methodologies similar to content management.

In the next chapter, I move on to content management projects. I explain how you may go about getting your organization behind a well-thought-out and well-presented design and how you can get through CMS implementation with the least hardship.

✦   ✦   ✦

Doing Content Management Projects

Doing CM Projects Simply

If you've read the chapters up to this point or poked around in other sections of this book, I wouldn't be surprised if you're a little daunted by the prospect of doing a CM project. In fact, I'd be surprised if you weren't; there's no getting around the fact that CM projects are complex. The chapters that follow this one in this part of the book focus on the complete package — the maximal, ideal approach that includes all the things that you can do — without regard to what constraints you may be working within. It's useful to study the maximal approach because it is what you need for really large CM projects.

But to make that maximal, no-holds-barred approach a bit more accessible, in this chapter I summarize the major issues you have to deal with in doing a CM project. I concentrate on just the essence of a project, both to provide a guide for what's to come in this section, and to clarify what tasks are necessary in even the most minimal CMS project. By reading this chapter, you can get a jump on what's to come, or get an overview of how the details found in various chapters fit together at a high level.

I refer throughout this chapter (and in the other chapters devoted to doing CM simply — Chapters 22 and 34) to the "minimal CMS." I do this to remind you that this chapter is a guide to what is crucial and what is merely relevant in a simple CMS project. Before undertaking even a "minimal" CMS project, however, I hope you will take the time to go beyond this chapter; it provides only a skeleton that you can flesh out with the rest of this section as well as the rest of the book.

Why Create a Minimal CMS?

If you're interested in finding out about the minimal CMS, it's a good bet you're facing major constraints, yet you must create some sort of CM project within those constraints. Your constraints may have several sources:

+ Maybe your department or company is not well-funded.

+ Maybe you need to prove something this time so that you can tackle the bigger problems next time.

+ Maybe you are in a small organization that has a big information problem.

+ Maybe you've been launched into the middle of a project and do not have the luxury of starting from the beginning.

The Long View

We had a roundabout approach to the whole problem of content management.

Being in a large research university, I know decentralization is key to maintaining the level of chaotic activity that we thrive on. Imagine thousands of authors happily creating millions of pages on hundreds of servers. Most departments don't have the problem of the IT bottleneck—the problem, where there is one, is more of coordination. So the idea of managing content didn't seem like a natural fit, especially for our IT department, which is just as decentralized as the rest of the place.

One day, though, another unit bought a CMS and told us that we could use it too. As it happened, it wasn't something that would work well for our department, so a group of us decided to come up with an alternative plan.

We all bought, borrowed, and stole copies of the *Content Management Bible* and started a series of meetings.

Many things went wrong along the way. We always had people who were interested but too busy to help, and we were sadly short on people who had time to do things. The budget was strained. We didn't really know what we were doing and didn't have answers for all the questions.

But over time things came together, and just as we were hoping to solidify the mandate, we were told to pick a system quickly. Not the right order, we pointed out, but it didn't matter. The need for content management was becoming painfully clear, and the fear was that the department would splinter into many tools that didn't work together.

So at this moment, we're doing research on systems (open source), interviewing authors, collecting user research, creating the logical design, and building a feature spec. But I'm not worried. If we don't get it all right this time, we'll have an opportunity to try again.

Content management is a process as much as a technology set. Once you climb on, you're in for a great time.

Melody Winkle, University of Washington Computing and Communication

Whatever the reason, I assume that you still want to do CM right, meaning that you want to be sure that you really solve the information problem that your organization is experiencing. Of course, doing the right thing also puts you in the best position to get the maximum support that the organization can realistically offer and, possibly, to expand the project from its current underpowered state.

First and foremost, my advice in this sort of situation is not to simply ignore tasks because you can't afford to do them. Instead, understand all the tasks you should do so that you can make knowledgeable decisions. Just because you know you can't hire a staff of 20 specialists to do your CM project, you're still better off considering all the jobs that ideally should be done and coming up with a strategy to deal with them, for several reasons:

✦ **You'll know how to expand the project** when the time comes.

✦ **You'll have the basis for making the hard decisions** about what you can do without.

✦ **You won't set yourself up for failure.** As you read this book, you should have no illusions about how easy it is for a CMS to fall short, particularly if your project overreaches your resources. Instead, you'll figure out exactly what is essential for success, so that you know what your bottom line is in negotiating the demands of a project within the organization. Ultimately, you need to make a cool and reasonable decision about whether the tasks you need to do can be accomplished given the resources available. In my experience, a well-reasoned argument can carry the day. In other words, you won't promise too much, you won't fail to include something that's crucial for success, and you won't agree to do a project that is destined to fail simply because you've ignored unpleasant realities.

✦ **You'll identify what to do in the next phases of the project**, assuming the current one is successful.

✦ **You'll have answers** when stakeholders ask about what you are or are not doing in the current phase.

So even if you don't or can't hire someone to do a particular job, you should at least consider the job as a task that you must address — even if it's to decide not to do something.

The maximal CM project approach is comprehensive, and covers all considerations. This rest of this chapter balances this ideal approach with the minimal approach — the essence of CM and what you can do to just get by. Your project should fit somewhere between these extremes.

Staffing on a Shoestring

The biggest constraint on a project is usually money, and the biggest cost is all the hungry mouths that need to be fed. It's natural to look here first to get within constraints. But as we've seen, you need the staff members to accomplish certain key tasks. All the jobs have to be accomplished, somehow. Your strategy here should be to identify the key players and limit their participation to the core things that each needs to accomplish. Avoid having them suck in additional people to work for them. In addition, in the minimal CM project, the people on the team must each wear a number of different hats, and these hats will change during a project — most particularly, when the system shifts from the startup to run phase. At certain phases, all hands may be required to pitch in, whether the task is editing and marking up source content, testing the system, or reviewing publications.

This section boils down the essential jobs and tasks of the people you need for even a minimal CMS project. Looking at the tasks that these core people are responsible for can help you crystallize what you most need people to accomplish in any CM project, including a minimal one. This section also serves to introduce you to the full set of jobs that are covered in Chapter 13, "Staffing a CMS."

The business person

You need someone to make the project thrive in your organization: the *business person*. The business person is the person responsible for making sure the CMS fits into your business (business is used here in the wide sense of what your organization is trying to accomplish). The business person is the ultimate authority for your project — the link between the organization and its goals and your project and its goals. The business person provides the justification and enables the activities that you will do. She is the one who has the authority to answer the fundamental questions "Why are we doing this?" and "How much will we spend to do this?" The answers to these questions underlie everything that comes after and, in particular, are the foundation for your mandate.

Because these questions come up at the outset of a project, you need the business person's involvement early, as part of the startup planning process. After the project is ready to be implemented, for the most part, the business person's work is done—although in a small organization, the business person may have other involvements, such as ongoing business management responsibilities. After the CMS is firmly established in the organization, the business person becomes responsible for overseeing major changes to the system and ensuring that the CMS continues to get the resources it needs from the organization.

In the minimal CM project, the business person:

✦ Is responsible for establishing the organizational goals for the project.

✦ Is responsible for the business side of organizing resources for the project.

✦ Works mostly during the startup phases and, for the most part, goes away after the system is up and running.

Overall the business person covers all the roles I mention in Chapter 13, "Staffing a CMS," in the sections "Managers" and "Business Analysts." Thus, the business person not only analyzes the CMS situation and gets it accepted in the organization, she may run the project itself. As you form a minimal team, the business person is the one most likely to have the management talents you need to keep the project team running well.

The content person

You need someone who can really know and stand up for the content of the system. The content person is responsible for the core work of understanding the content and collecting it. This person will handle much of the collection work, as well as the construction of the content model itself. In the minimal CM project, the responsibilities of the content person are as follows:

✦ She is responsible for all collection planning and activities. This includes any authoring, conversion, and tagging needed.

✦ She is responsible for creating the content model for the system. On the most basic level, she defines what is in the system and how it is structured.

✦ She is responsible for administering the CM system during deployment and while it's up and running. She works closely with the technology person in this responsibility.

✦ At runtime, she becomes the metator on an ongoing basis and is responsible for creating and maintaining the tagging taxonomy for content already in the system, as well for as new content that comes into it.

Throughout Chapter 13, "Staffing a CMS," I fully describe the various content roles in a CMS project. If you look at those descriptions, it may strike you that I'm rolling up a large number of distinct jobs into this content person's job, including the roles of content analyst, content processor, and content creation staff. In the minimal CMS, the content person (like the others) must have a lot of blades in her Swiss Army knife and must also have a good grasp of content from start to finish.

The publications person

You need someone to really know and stand up for the publications that you will produce. The publications person is the counterpart to the content person in the publishing arena. She must cover all design tasks for all the publications and work closely with the technology person to create output templates.

In the minimal CM project, responsibilities of the publications person are as follows:

✦ She does all output design. She may work with the content person (or others within the organization) to determine what the publications should consist of. She designs the required publications based on the content in the repository, does (or assigns) graphic design and layout tasks and, in general, establishes the publication standards and schedules.

✦ With the technology person, she builds the output templates. The publications person provides output document specifications that that the technology person executes. She tests the work of the technology person to identify problems and bugs.

✦ The publications person is the chief editor of all the publications at runtime. She's responsible for making sure the system is publishing the correct content on an ongoing basis and identifying problems that may originate in any stage of the collection, management, or publishing processes.

In Chapter 13, "Staffing a CMS," in the section "Publications Staff" I fully describe the publications jobs that are rolled up in the publications person's job in a minimal CMS project.

The technology person

The technology person may wear the most hats of all in the minimal system. She's responsible for determining technical requirements, acquiring the CMS, programming, connecting, and supporting the content and publications person.

In the minimal CM project, the responsibilities of the technology person are as follows:

✦ She is responsible for all necessary infrastructure, including acquiring and configuring hardware and software. In particular, the technology person selects, installs, and configures the CMS.

✦ She is responsible for all programming, including any programming needed for content processing, implementing the content model, creating functionality not provided by the CMS and templates.

✦ She is responsible for all connectivity, meaning that she must ensure that the CMS is able to get content from other systems within the organization and outside of it.

✦ She assists in administering the CMS after rollout, essentially handling any technical issues that are beyond the expertise of the content person or the publications person.

In Chapter 13, "Staffing a CMS," in the sections "Infrastructure Staff" and "Software Developers," I fully describe the jobs that are part of the technology person's job in a minimal CMS project.

Getting Ready for the Project

In a small organization, the early stages of a CM project can (and sometimes should) happen in stealth mode. It can be dispiriting to make a splashy announcement: "We're going to do a content management project!" followed by...nothing. Competing demands on time (you probably have other job responsibilities), as well the degree to which you may underestimate how much time you need to get started add up (in the eyes of others) to not a lot happening.

On the other hand, if you start doing your homework quietly, you may be able to get something done without all eyes upon you. This way, the early work can happen as slowly (or quickly) as you want. Because a lot of the early work involves just talking to people, listening to what they say, and organizing existing information, you don't need to expose others to the larger plans unless they can help you do this early work.

This is not to say you won't need approvals, or that you should be secretive. But you might consider characterizing your initial efforts as a side project rather than staking your reputation on delivering something that is larger than you can know or control. By taking a low-key approach, you put yourself in the position of hatching the project when it is well-formed, at a time of your choosing. Your credibility gets a boost, which (aside from making you feel good) is a very useful tool to help move project forward. Finally, if things do go sideways and you have to shelve the CM project for whatever reason, the only cost you've incurred is your time—not your reputation.

The sections that follow detail the tasks that you can accomplish without a lot of time and effort during the preplanning stage.

Exploring the organization

Your first task is to get a sense of what the organization does, has done, knows, and wants to do. If you don't know about some aspects the organization, this is the time to find out what everyone does. As you gather information, it's also a good time to start educating by raising awareness. No need to proselytize, at least at this point—you can raise awareness as effectively by asking questions.

At this stage, your activities include:

✦ Performing an **informal readiness assessment.** In Chapter 15, "Getting Ready for a CMS," the section "The readiness assessment" describes the readiness assessment in the context of a large project. However, the same questions required for a large organization scale down to a small one as well. Namely, you need to assess:

- **What mandate** exists in the organization for the project now?

- **What audiences** does the organization expect to serve and how well developed is the organization's approach to these people?

- **What publications** does the organization expect to create and how suitable are they to a CMS approach?

- **What content** does the organization want to deliver, and how well known are its quantity, structure, and use?

- **What system** does the organization expect to be under the CMS? Are there well-formed requirements or a variety of opinions?

✦ **Making contacts.** Find out who the key players are in your organization—not just those in power, but those who have the power of knowledge. In particular, you need to determine who your potential sponsors are, as well as those within the organization who must pitch in to make the CM project successful.

✦ **Acquiring documents.** In Chapter 15, "Getting Ready for a CMS," the section "Document inventory and analysis" details the types of documents in a large organization. All you really need to know in a smaller setting is: What are the key documents your organization produces? Organize them in a spreadsheet by source, filename, and date, a brief description of their contents, and the readiness questions that each addresses.

✦ **Learning about the history of content at your organization.** In particular, you want to understand what systems are currently in place; what projects are already under way; what projects have been completed and which were shelved (and why); the successes and failures; and barriers and constraints on content projects.

✦ **Educating others in your organization.** Starting with the key contacts you identify, your project can be well-served if, when you unveil it, others in your organization already have some understanding of the need for content management. Your education at this stage might be about the business problem your organization faces, rather than about specific products and solutions.

Finding the right project

Although, in exploring the organization, you gathered documents of all kinds, at a fairly early stage you should start considering where your point of access should be. Your CM project is unlikely to address all the content issues that your organization faces, and it shouldn't. Instead, you ambition should be to set the agenda for a clearly focused small project, at least until you have some success under your belt. The biggest danger here is to be too ambitious — the right project is not one that reproduces your organization's Web site or creates a brand new intranet. The right project is one that delivers tangible value quickly.

So where should you start? Here's a general approach that at each step will winnow down the candidates:

1. Based on your research, figure out what is the most important information in the organization — the stuff that people (or the organization as a whole) can't live without.

2. Find the people who can't live without it. You could even rank them, roughly, by how important they are to the organization.

3. Figure out how getting these important people the important information does something that is really needed by the organization.

These triples (a goal tied to a kind of person and a kind of content) are the basis of any CMS. In the minimal project, you simply focus on fewer of them. You should end up with a list of one or more opportunities to create a system that improves how an important person gets important information and, thereby, makes a noticeable impact on the organization. These are your potential projects.

Finding the right sponsors

Your sponsors are senior people in the organization who have — or should have — a strong interest in doing content management. When the going gets tough, your sponsor is the one who keeps you from twisting in the wind — the sponsor has the standing and authority to keep the rest of the organization focused around the CM project. In a small organization, you may be the primary sponsor, but even if so, it may be helpful to identify a secondary sponsor to serve as an ally.

You may be able to come up with the right sponsor with just a little thought. However, you should already have a good idea of what project you would like to do, as you identified in the previous section, "Finding the right project." It may be difficult to pick the right sponsor until you know what your project is.

The following steps can help you focus on what you need from the sponsorship:

✦ Find out who in the organization cares about your information and about your audience. You should be able to identify your audience(s) if you've gone through the exercise of identifying the right project.

✦ Make sure the potential sponsor cares about the organizational goals you have set your sights on.

✦ Start talking with your sponsor about the organizational need and your approach to addressing it, giving her insight into your proposed process. Educate her, and in so doing, recruit her support. Let her know that her support is crucial.

✦ Make sure that the information and audience you want to serve is completely your sponsor's province. If it isn't, you may need additional sponsors.

Getting a mandate

A mandate in content management is a lot like the electoral mandate that winning politicians sometimes claim to have, only your mandate will be in a more black-and-white form. The mandate is what you are charged to do in the CM project. It represents the actions that you will take to address the needs and goals you've identified. Most importantly, the mandate is a document that the organization as a whole has reviewed, negotiated, and signed off on.

In a large organization, the mandate results from multiple rounds of meetings, negotiations, and reviews. In the minimal project, you still need the mandate, but you can cut down on the number of meetings and negotiations. Instead, work out what the mandate should be verbally with your sponsor and, with your sponsor's assistance, enlist the key players in the organization. Then memorialize the verbal agreements in a document that they all sign.

The idea behind the formality of a document and signature is that you will be held to delivering on the promises of the mandate — but so will the rest of the organization. The mandate is the document that empowers you to keep the organization focused.

The mandate document itself can be simple — maybe deceptively simple given all it represents. However, make sure it contains:

✦ **The organizational goals** that the CMS is supposed to achieve.

✦ **A project statement** that states precisely what you are trying to accomplish with the CMS including the audiences and content you have decided to focus on.

✦ **A small set of goals** that the CMS will be expected to accomplish, along with a way to measure the system's progress against each of the goals.

In the last point, the word *small* should be underscored — don't promise large. And the measurements against goals should be specific — for example, instead of "We will be more efficient," use statements like "We will reduce the number of person-hours required to publish our newsletter by 20% within six months of the system going live."

 Cross-Reference   Chapter 16, "Securing a Project Mandate," discusses the full-blown mandate process. It may be useful background reading for what a mandate is supposed to achieve, but in the minimal project, you don't sign up for the extended negotiations discussed in that chapter.

Key planning deliverables

In the minimal system, some of your deliverables flow directly from the research activities that you've undertaken already. Even in a minimal system, you should take the time to prepare the deliverables described in the following list, because they will force you to consider all the key aspects of your system that you must confront sooner (before you start building) or later (after budgets are committed and work has begun).

✦ A **simplified readiness assessment**, which you prepared as described in the section "Exploring the organization," earlier in this chapter.

✦ A **written mandate with project statement and success measures**, which you prepared as described in the previous section, "Getting a mandate."

✦ A **project plan.** Chapter 20, "Implementing the System," may be useful background reading for understanding the maximal project plan components. Your minimal project plan should include the major phases of the project as well as what tasks must be done, what staff is required, and what schedules have been set.

✦ A **risk assessment** that lists risks, when they may occur, the consequences if they occur, and how you anticipate adjusting your plan to deal with them.

Doing Design

Design is where you start stitching together what your CM system will do. Although in the minimal CM system you're trying to do as little as you can get away with, you shouldn't scrimp on the essential design tasks discussed in this section. A stitch in design saves nine in implementation and deployment.

Getting minimum requirements

In designing a minimal CMS, you're going to get used to saying no a lot. One way to minimize this is to get a sense of the absolute minimum your stakeholders can accept as the final result of your CM project, and then holding them to that. That way, when you keep saying no, you can point to the minimal requirements as the reference point. You do, however, need those requirements, however minimal. Here are suggestions for gathering them:

✦ **Get a minimum of stakeholders involved in the requirements process.** Requirements seem to expand exponentially as you give more people a say, and sorting them out takes time.

✦ **Ask for minimum and absolute musts from your stakeholders.** For each requirement your stakeholders present, a good question to ask them might be: Would this system be a failure if it could not satisfy this requirement?

✦ **Start saying no early** and often. Remind stakeholders that the minimal system must succeed, and each additional requirement introduces risks and increases the possibility that the whole initiative will fail.

✦ **Stick strictly to the mandate.** Point to the mandate as the set of agreed-upon organizational goals, audiences, and content, and ask how each requirement furthers those specifics.

✦ **Cross-reference and synthesize requirements among the stakeholders as you collect them**. That way, you'll have a finished requirements document at the end of this process.

Logical design essentials

The point of the logical design process is to decide what publications your system should create to deliver the most important information to the most important people in the best way. (You identified the most important information and people when you identified potential projects, as described in the section "Finding the right project," earlier in this chapter.)

Chapter 18, "Doing Logical Design," presents logical design for the maximal project in detail and may be useful background information. However, Chapter 22, "Designing a CMS Simply," describes a process that is probably closer to the level of effort you need to put into logical design. Refer to that chapter for the basics, but filter it through these points:

✦ You can simplify the logical design process further by scaling back the extent to which you drill down into detail. You must still get the essential information, however.

✦ Consider tradeoffs you can make that, although they deliver less functionality or personalization, are still acceptable. For example, can you drive all audiences to the same site rather than personalize for particular audiences that you identify?

✦ Can you lower the number of audiences, publications, content types, and authors? Doing any of these will simplify your project.

Key design deliverables

The key design deliverables you need for the minimal CMS include:

✦ **Lists of the entities.** Entities are the players that interact to form your CM system. Chapter 22, "Designing a CMS Simply," in the section "The Entities at a Glance" explains entities briefly. Chapter 23, "The Wheel of Content Management," in the section "The Content Management Entities" describes entities in detail.

✦ **A business case report.** This report is brief, an executive summary that presents the business case for the system. It argues that the system you're proposing addresses the business goals you've identified within the mandate you've been given. The report should include:

• Mandate and major goals

• Requirements summary

• Audience description

• Publications list

• Personnel required

✦ **A design description of the collection system** at whatever level of detail you can muster. It should include the sources of the content you will gather (authors and acquisition sources), the types of processing you need, the tools you'll use, and the workflow process you expect to implement.

✦ **The content model for your content.** At this point, you should be able to model the content for your system at least to the level of content types and, if possible, down to the level of content components. (Chapter 27, "Designing Content Types" in the section "What Are Components?" explains what content types and content components are.)

✦ **Basic publication definitions,** as well as mockups, if possible. (Chapter 26, "Designing Publications" in the section "What Is a Publication?," describes the sorts of information that you should be sure to collect.)

Implementation

Implementation is, of course, where the rubber hits the proverbial road. All the planning you've done pays off, or lack of planning starts making you pay. For the minimal CM project, the question is: How little can you get away with doing and still reach your goals? A parallel question is: How much can you do with your existing tools, technologies, and people? This section contains some strategies you can try to minimize the costliest part of a CM project — implementation.

How low-tech can you go?

Begin by asking yourself, if you had no CMS, what you could do to deliver the content you arrived at to the audiences you selected. What parts of the manual process would be hardest? What is the minimum assistance you could give to the people using these manual processes to accomplish their work? This exercise will give you a feeling for how little you can really get away with doing. It also shows you very clearly what CMS features you really need. For example, do you really need an advanced workflow system, or could you get away with well-documented procedures and a few nagging e-mails delivered when needed?

Focus in on the parts of the process that give a quick and reliable payoff from the money or time you put into them. Rather than assuming that you need a CMS product, assume that you just need a few job aids and see where it leads you. At the very least, you will know what parts of a CMS to stand firm on in your selection process. At the most, you may find that your problems are very specific and could be solved in a more straightforward way than by acquiring a software package.

If you do go low-tech on your first time around the CMS project cycle, I guarantee that you will be a very savvy buyer on your second time around.

On the low tech side, you can get a lot of mileage out of tools that you may already be using or that may be easy to acquire.

✦ **Use Web design tools to design and build your system**. If you're already using some kind of Web tools to maintain your current Web site, see if you can extend them to cover the new requirements of your system. With every release these tools are coming closer to a CM approach. Can yours come close enough to create the system you need? At any rate, you should be able to continue using the tools you're already familiar with to build some of the deliverables you'll need, such as mockups and templates.

✦ **Desktop applications.** How much of a CMS can you construct from the desktop tools you have in your organization today? I have seen amazing (if kludged) work done by novices using Microsoft Access to manage and deploy content. Can you draw your word processors, spreadsheets, and desktop databases together into a loose system? Check out what your e-mail server is capable of. It is not unlikely that it has some form of workflow support built- in. I would not say that desktop tools are a replacement for a real CMS, but they can certainly help hold the line for you as you work toward a real CMS. Of course, spreadsheets are the Swiss Army Knife of project management. You can use basic databases in a similar way — to keep track of all the stuff you need to manage. Which you choose depends on your expertise — if you're a spreadsheet expert and a database dilettante, by all means do your work using a spreadsheet. For that matter, using dedicated project management tools is a viable option, but only if you already are highly skilled in their use — otherwise, you'll spend valuable resources learning a new tool to replace a familiar one that is perfectly usable. You may also be limited by how well you can learn to wield this new tool.

✦ **Open source tools.** For a low cost CMS, consider open source tools. Solid programmers have created an amazing amount of really good CM functionality and are willing to share it. The tradeoff, however, may be in support—open source tools may not be as well-supported, and you have to pay for any support you do receive. On the other hand, you may find a community of users who can answer questions via discussion groups dedicated to the tools or class of tools you're using. If you need outside talent to help with your project, you may find it or, at least, you may get a referral in a discussion group. In general, be prepared to sort through the many options available if you go this route. You can find links to open source tools at a number of Web sites dedicated to open source solutions, including www.cmsreview.com, or just Google "content management open source."

✦ **A simple Web application**. Are you looking for a CMS or just a dynamic Web site? If one Web site is your only publication and you just need to get it under control, maybe you can simply move your content into a database. Then you can find a server scripting environment that will let you create Web pages from the database. Add a few administrative pages and you may be able to hit your first mark with a minimum of trouble.

✦ **Networking to find existing code and process.** Although new to you, it's pretty likely that someone has trod the path you're on before. If so, you may be able to find and make use of the tools and experiences others are willing to share. (This book is a good start for the process.) The links at http://lists.cms-forum.org/mailman/listinfo (as of this writing) provide a number of lists of CMS professionals. And, whether you're using a commercial or open source CMS, you may find newsgroups and resources on the CMS publisher's site. I have found that the CM community, although not well centralized (yet), consists of a friendly bunch who don't mind sharing.

A somewhat similar perspective to going low-tech is to identify and take advantage of opportunities to get an immediate benefit from a quick fix, the "Kamikaze automation" approach. For details on this approach, see Chapter 37, "Processing Content," the section "Focusing on the short-term benefits."

Process versus product

Although it is perhaps the mother of all clichés, trying to work smarter and not harder is always worth a shot. Even modestly smart innovations can save you a lot of work (or rework) in content management. It should be obvious that any routine, repeated process that you can get down to a set of steps is a candidate for automation, whether by acquiring a tool or creating scripts that help with processing source documents (which is, typically, where a lot of repetitive hand-work may occur). However, until you get your fancy automation tools together, you can save a lot of time by figuring out and instituting manual procedures. Doing CM manually is not without its benefits. Just like the man who has used hand tools all his life, when you are finally introduced to power, you have a healthy contempt for it. You have the personal experience to tell a real time saver from a fancy gadget that takes more time to set up and maintain than it saves you.

In addition to these obvious tools and scripts for smartening up process, here are a few less obvious questions to ask yourself:

✦ **Can you push authoring upstream?** A huge part of the startup work in a CMS is getting the initial body of content into shape for inclusion into the repository. This may include some editing and probably includes metatorial work. Can you push this work off to the groups and individuals who originate the content? If you provide them with the proper templates and training for applying the tags you need, they can certainly use these tools going forward. If you're lucky, they'll volunteer to sweep through existing content as well. Your strategy may be to appeal to their sense of ownership and their familiarity with the content.

✦ **Can you outsource processing?** It makes sense to ship some tasks out to another company that specializes in the work (unless you have a bunch of really cheap interns). In general, this is the work that, although it requires special skills, does not require much or any content knowledge. For example, if you have a large number of documents in paper that need to be scanned and OCR'd, hire a local scanning/OCR company that does this kind of work in volume. You'll get better results and achieve a more efficient use of resources.

✦ **Can you fix skill gaps with training, good documentation, and incentives?** For key skills that you want people (including yourself) in your organization to acquire, can you provide (or get) the training and support they need, and provide a positive incentive for them to want to acquire the skill? For example, can the new work replace some lower-skill responsibilities that some will appreciate not having? Can you demonstrate that learning new skills will make jobs easier or more satisfying? Some workers will appreciate simply having an opportunity to acquire a new professional skill.

✦ **Can you just figure out, write down, and then enforce processes?** Can you reduce some skilled tasks to practice to the extent that they can be well-documented? If so, you can reduce the skill level required of the person who will be doing the work, as long as you can enforce adherence to the instructions that you document. This is the essence of the fast-food–franchise model — identify all the tasks that a person doing a given job is supposed to do, document the exact steps they must follow for each task, and then make sure everyone who does the job does it in exactly the same way. (There's still room for individual initiative, insofar as you can encourage people to suggest improvements to the process.) Process changes should be rolled out to everyone at the same time, and then only if the changes will improve efficiency.

To interface or not to interface?

Creating a friendly user interface (UI) to your system is a significant project in itself. In addition to the customizing the CMS UI, you may want to integrate all the other components you use into a nice, unified whole. Doing so, however, may be a big chunk of work — including design, programming, testing, and support. If you can avoid having to build a UI — or if you build only a minimal UI — you can save a time and money and incur lower risk. Here are some questions to consider:

✦ **Can your team work in native file formats (such as HTML and XML text formats)?** If so, you need not provide or integrate WYSIWYG editors, or only minimal ones designed for users familiar with these formats.

✦ **Can your team open CMS configuration files and edit them directly?** If so, you need not build configuration wizards that walk users through configuration tasks. (Documenting configuration settings and procedures is always a good idea, however.)

✦ **Can your team use the UI that ships with your CMS or database?** It may not be pretty, but if it does what you need and costs nothing, it's functionally beautiful.

✦ **Can your team use command lines or pages that trigger native APIs?** If so, you need not build programs that do this for them. Again, documentation will be key, but documentation for native APIs should already exist.

Slimming down product selection

A lot of CMS products are out there, and independently evaluating them could be a career in itself. In fact, it is a career for a number of people, and so it need not be for you. For the minimal CMS project, the critical part of picking a CMS product is making the choice as quickly and efficiently as you can. You have to accept that your product knowledge will not be universal, perfect, and all-seeing. Here are some methods for getting to yes:

✦ **Do more research and less meeting to discuss products.** Visit sites such as www. cmswatch.com. Try a Google search such as "content+management+software+ review+OR+reviews." Post to newsgroups to find people who have used products you're considering.

✦ **Cut down the size of the selection team.** Limit the cooks and, if necessary, have each one designated to represent the perspectives of a number of other groups or individuals. In a sense, you want the selection team to have a mandate.

✦ **Don't scrimp on design diagrams.** Hand-simulating your process against candidate systems can quickly tell you whether a given system will do what you want easily or at all.

✦ **Do logical design first and come to the table with a small set of defining requirements.** This is your short list of must-haves. Any product that doesn't fulfill all these requirements well is out of the running.

✦ **Cut down lengthy RFPs** (Requests for Proposal). If you issue an RFP, do your research and pre-qualify those vendors you include in the request. Provide your defining requirements as a guide, and see how well they respond. Request that the vendors limit the length of their proposals and be prepared to refine the proposal with the selected vendor.

✦ **Talk to the potential vendors.** Be persistent, even to the point of bugging them, to see how responsive they are and how comfortable you are with them. You are about to form what could be a long marriage, so don't be afraid to ask what may seem like basic questions. (One of the mistakes that some of our potential clients make is to be too guarded about what they want and need, fearing that we'll somehow use this information against them. On the contrary, this is just the information we need.)

✦ **Set a date and really, really, really stick to it.** For budget, credibility, success — you must say how long something will take and then meet that deadline. Your assessment of risks should give you contingencies for dealing with most unforeseen events — ways to scale back, reassign resources, but to nonetheless reach a milestone. (You'll get a lot of mileage out of your reputation for delivering as promised — and when promised.). The number one factor that affects the cost of your selection (or any other) process is how long it takes.

Saying no

The absolute worst situation you can get yourself into (and I've seen it happen more times than I would care to recount) is to have the CM project be funded at a minimal level, but have the organization treat it as if it were funded at a maximal level. Requests for changes, although individually innocuous, cumulatively can sink your project or, at least, distract it from the core goals. Death by a thousand small cuts, in other words. How do you manage saying no to reasonable, useful requests? Ultimately, you may lose a few of these arguments, but you can at, least, try the following:

✦ **Refer to the project mandate and goals.** In the planning and design stages, anything you agree to incorporate into the plan must directly and explicitly further the goals. In the minimal system, if it is to *be* a truly minimal system, everything you agree to do must be critical to the success of the project. Or, in other words, if the project can be successful without a feature or functionality, that feature or functionality should probably be dispensed with.

✦ **Discuss budget.** The only way to assure you can stay within your budget is to do only the things that you set out to do. In response to an added-feature request, explain that the project mandate has been approved and that changes endanger your ability to deliver on the goals. If the requester is a sponsor or other important person in your organization, field requests in the context of the budget: Ask what the new request replaces in the current budget and plan, or how the work will be budgeted for.

✦ **Discuss schedule.** Again, the only way to ensure you can stay within your schedule is to do only the things that you set out to do. Adding or changing features, no matter how simple, ripples through the project. Use the same approach you do when discussing budget — to accommodate a change, what else can you sacrifice? If you've included only the essential features in your project plan, a change request must result in increased resources, time, or both; but in any case, it raises the project risk.

✦ **Reframe the request as a start for a larger project** — the next project, not the current one.

✦ **Reframe the request as a potential side project** — but not part of the current one.

Note that saying no to additional features does not mean that you should say no to any changes in the project plan. It's possible that the success of the project depends on making some critical changes because certain things weren't known at the time you started the implementation phase. Say, for example, a CMS company releases a new tool that could replace one you're developing in-house for a lot less money — that would be a smart change. Depend on your sharp eye to distinguish this sort of change from the more mundane kind.

In the end, all the great features and content that you say no to may be your ticket to a project with the support you really want to have.

Key implementation processes

When it comes time to roll out the system, several strategies can keep your focus on the prize if you can anticipate the challenges you might face. The points that follow really apply to any implementation process; but when you are building the minimal system, they are particularly important.

✦ **Cut back viciously.** Use cuts you make now as a justification for other projects or for later expansion of this project. Recently, a group I worked with did a project that, because of changing client requirements, was cut down from over 20 publication deliverables to a single one, with no reduction in budget. Yet the client considered the project a success because the organization took delivery of a well-thought out, tested system that could someday be rolled out to include those other publications.

✦ **Start content conversion early and slowly.** Before you've coded a line or acquired a CMS, you can already be working with the content. If you make assumptions or believe assurances that the content is well-formed and easy to convert, or you may be disappointed. Determine the quality of the content well in advance of any production process.

✦ **Test content and code early and often.** You don't want surprises when the whole thing is supposed to be coming together. Your development and testing strategy should concentrate on functional components that come online as you go through the project, so that testing can concentrate on individual modules. This spreads the workflow for the testing effort, and it's a lot easier for testers to isolate bugs in the larger system when they've already hammered on the various components.

✦ **Understand what you must prove out after launch and what you can prove out before.** With a first generation system, you have to accept that you won't anticipate all the issues around the system. Also, beyond a certain point, it doesn't make sense to. In the minimal system, you give it your best effort, build it, and get it out. For example, don't argue about navigation forever. Instead, launch the system with a decent set of navigation features and then be ready to refine the navigation when you get some real-world feedback.

✦ **Scrimp on integration.** If you need to cut back on specified functionality to make your date, look at integration with other systems as a candidate. First, decide if the level of integration that you've specified is really necessary. Could the same thing be accomplished using other methods, down to and including sneaker net (that is, carrying the data in your hand from place to place)? If you can cut back on integration, you're still delivering core functionality, and you're also setting up some clear next steps to improve the system in the near term, which your users will like.

Key implementation deliverables

The implementation deliverables that you're staked to are important enough to do, even for the minimal CM project. Doing a cursory job on these deliverables is a waste of time and may give you a false sense of having a more thought-through system than you actually do.

✦ **Don't scrimp on preparing the project plan** and then later wield it as if it were knowledge received from on high. Review it and excise any tasks that don't directly contribute to the minimal system. (In Chapter 20, "Implementing the System," in the section "Taking Stock of the Deliverables," I discuss project plans and other implementation deliverables in detail.) Consider including the following in your full project plan:

   • Implementation specifications for your collection, management, and publishing systems. These include all the tools you use to author, acquire, manage, and publish content, as well as the processes (such as conversion, workflow, metatagging) by which you move content through your system.

   • A full description of the CMS product you've chosen and how it will be configured.

   • A discussion of how you will set up your relational, object, or XML content repository. Integration with other data systems should be described, as well as your publication system — including templates, the Web, or other infrastructure you'll use to deliver content. List the publishing software and processes you'll use. Finally, describe the personalization system you implement, if any, and any other outside resources with which your content should integrate.

   • Enumeration of additional tools that need to be programmed or acquired.

   • Enumeration of integrations with other systems that that will be necessary.

- A testing plan (which should include systematic testing, not just ad hoc testing).

- A basic staffing plan that includes the jobs to be done, the skills needed, the tasks associated with each, and the amount of effort expected during startup and at runtime.

✦ **Don't scrimp on the Risk Assessment.** Think through the possible risks to your project, and make sure that none of the foreseeable risks happen. You may have your hands full with the unforeseeable or unforeseen kind.

✦ **Critique how deliverables will be accomplished.** Are the tasks that are planned all really necessary, or is a shortcut to the same end available?

✦ **Specify only really key features** for the initial system. Again, your criteria should be: If we drop this feature, would this system fail to deliver on the goals we've identified? If not, then drop the feature. For more information about the kinds of features that a CMS might contain, the final three chapters in this book (Chapter 38, "Building Collection Systems;" Chapter 39, "Building Management Systems;" and Chapter 40, "Building Publishing Systems") describe these features comprehensively and in detail.

Deployment

After you've finished implementing your system, you can't just throw it over the wall and forget about it. Like a child, you've created something that you're going to have to live with for a long time. It may be tempting to cut costs during the deployment stage, but you should be careful if you do so, because any CMS is only as good as it becomes during deployment. What I mean is that, after the system is launched, how well it's supported and how quickly you address any bugs or other issues affect the perceived value of the system to its users and, as a result, to the organization. Realistically, you should expect to make many changes that improve the system after it goes live.

In fact, a good process might be to launch your system early to a select group of users, and use the issues these brave pioneers encounter to hone your deployment approach. There is nothing like being live to make things happen fast and effectively!

Key deployment processes

When you roll out the thing of beauty that is your new CMS, keep in mind that not everyone in the organization has been living with it daily (and dreaming about it at night) as you have. You shouldn't scrimp on documentation and training, but rather consider them as investments that pay you back in the need for less UI, metatation, and quality control. Consider documentation and hands-on training efforts as high-yield investments, particularly if more users will gradually start using the system—and you don't need to reinvent the training wheel. Ideally, some users will become expert in the system and can support new users in the future. By providing documentation and training, you're making your users smarter so your system doesn't have to be.

Tip A simple, narrated screen recording demonstration can be a great tool to help new users quickly understand the overall system and how to get around in it. If you record such a demo, write a script first to make sure that you cover everything you intend.

You can, however, scrimp on powering up the system. Just go for it and learn quickly from your mistakes. But be prepared for the system to crash horribly when it first comes up, and be prepared to eliminate missteps with backups and clean installs.

Key deployment deliverables

In addition to the actual system you've built, at deployment time you should make sure the deployment plan and the technical specification are all up to date. By up to date, I mean that you should use the deployment plan and technical specifications to log deployment-related issues that occur to the development team during the development cycle — the kind of issue for which you say, "We'll have to remember that when we roll this out... ." Now is when you need to remember all those stray issues. They can focus your work plan, as well as help you avoid deployment risks.

The training deliverable is a great thing to do during deployment, because you have an actual system doing actual work for your users to play with. Prepare people in advance when your system gets close to deployment. Odds are that if you train them before going live, they'll have forgotten much of the training, which is another way of saying you've wasted their time. One effective training method is to walk them through an actual contribution, stepping through all the main features of your system until they can see the final results published on a site.

Summary

Even the minimal CMS is a lot of work, but it's work that's within reach of small to medium-sized organizations. At each stage of a CM project, you have to make decisions; these choices should always be guided by the goals you've established for the system. In the truly minimal system, you do nothing that does not directly address those goals, and everything that you do is done as simply as possible.

If you're deciding whether you can do a minimal CMS, the questions are all about doing the least possible:

✦ What are the minimal organizational goals, requirements, and audiences?

✦ What is the minimum that the CMS must do to meet the requirements, serve the goals, and provide value to the audiences?

✦ Aside from cutting back on the scope from a maximal CMS, what alternatives should you consider that may address your goals at the least cost?

The nice thing about a minimal system is that, if it does what you've promised, selling your organization on doing the next version is a lot easier than selling it on the first. The benefits of the Phase 1 system are evident, but its limitations are obvious as well, if not glaring. If anything, you may have to deal with a bunch of others in your organization jumping on your successful CM bandwagon.

In the rest of the chapters in this section, I return to the perspective of the maximal CMS, discussing all the organizational tasks and processes that it requires.

✦　　✦　　✦

Staffing a CMS

By looking at the kinds of jobs a CMS requires, you get a lot of insight into what it takes to make one happen. You can classify the jobs involved in a CMS in the following ways:

✦ Each phase of the CMS process (collection, management, and publishing) has its own jobs and responsibilities. In a well-planned CMS, the people in these three areas can do their jobs without becoming overly entangled in the jobs of people in the other areas.

✦ CMS jobs generally break down into analysis, implementation, and management. Analyzers figure out what to do, implementers do it, and managers keep them all on the straight and narrow path to success.

✦ Some jobs are part of the CMS design and start up, and others are involved in running the completed CMS. Often it takes a large team to start up a CMS but a small team to run it. A common method is to outsource all or parts of the CMS design and implementation effort to an outside vendor, while you are simultaneously putting together the longer-term team that will run the system.

✦ CMS jobs can be categorized by discipline, including managers, information architects, infrastructure staff, and software developers.

In this chapter, I categorize the jobs in a CMS by discipline because this approach is comprehensive, yet usefully breaks down the implementation of a CMS by the disciplines needed to actually staff a project.

About CMS Jobs

Your CMS may affect the jobs of numerous people in diverse areas throughout your organization. Few of the tasks to start up or run a CMS require full-time, long-term staff. Rather, you start up your system with a large short-term staff and run it with a small full-time staff and a larger casual and part-time staff.

Content management is a difficult task—not only does it bring together a large number of people from quite diverse backgrounds, but it also requires individuals who split their skills and attitudes between different, often conflicting disciplines. You will find that many jobs in this chapter call for at least two widely different skills.

The array of jobs I present assumes a very large organization with a big team. I do this to show the most complete picture of the jobs to be

accomplished. Obviously, in smaller organizations, or in large projects in earlier stages, one person will do many of these jobs. Understand, however, that each job does need to get done in its entirety, even if there is only one person to do them all.

Note   I apologize in advance if I leave out your current job title; you may recognize parts of your job description under other titles.

In addition, my intention is not to write job descriptions that you can cut and paste and send to your HR department to be filled. Rather, I group the necessary tasks involved in the startup and running of a CMS into logical clusters around personality and task types. You must look carefully at your particular situation. Depending on whom you have already at your disposal, your own skills and talents, how many people you can feasibly bring onto the team, and how long you have to accomplish the project, the cutting and pasting you are most likely to do will involve the few, from the many positions I have outlined here, that you can afford or desire.

Cross-Reference   In Chapter 12, "Doing CM Projects Simply," in the section "Staffing on a Shoestring" I discuss the bare bones of staffing you need for a minimal CMS.

Finally, my goal is to be complete, but not exhaustive. You will find the most detail about the jobs that are particular or most pivotal to a CMS and little or no detail about those that are the same with or without a CMS.

Table 13-1 shows how the various positions I detail in this chapter might be distributed between the startup phase of your CMS, where you plan and implement the system, and the run phase of the CMS after it is live. The positions I do not list in a particular column may still be needed but are not the core jobs in that phase of a CMS.

Table 13-1: CMS Jobs at a Glance

Staff Position Type	CMS Startup Positions	CMS Run Positions
Managers	Content manager, Project manager	Content manager, Production manager
Business analysts	High level of participation	Periodic participation
Information architects	Content analyst	Metator
Infrastructure staff	Deployment analyst, Trainer and documentation specialist	CMS administrator
Software developers	Software analyst, Template and CMS developer, Custom application developer, Software integrator, Test analyst and test engineer	Template and CMS developer, Test engineer
Publications staff	Publication analyst, Publication designer, Page developer, User interface specialist	Publication designer, Page developer
Content processing staff	Conversion analyst, Tool developer, Content processor, Content QA specialist	Content processor, Content QA specialist
Content creation staff	Writers and other content creators, Editor	Acquisitions manager, Traffic cop, Writers and other content creators, Editor

Managers

As in all group efforts, someone must be in charge. Clearly, an enterprise CMS is too big not to have its share of chiefs. In addition, as you can see from the number and range of positions in this chapter, it is not reasonable to expect that your management staff themselves will have the skills to do all the work behind a CMS.

Content manager

More and more, organizations are realizing that content management exists, and that someone ought to be responsible for it. That job has loosely come be called *content manager* (or Director/VP/Chief of Content Management). Although this job sometimes falls to someone with a loftier title, such as VP of Electronic Media, the idea is the same. Conversely, the title content manager might be given to someone who functions more like an acquisitions specialist, or in a smaller organization, even like a Web page creator. Variations in usage notwithstanding, a content manager's responsibilities should include the following:

✦ **Fully understanding the discipline** of content management. (For example, she might be required to actually understand everything in this book!)

✦ **Leading the planning and execution** of the organization's CM initiatives. She might be the lead of the CM project team and the person with ultimate responsibility for a successful CMS implementation.

✦ **Representing the needs of the CMS** to departments throughout the organization. This person must teach, negotiate, and pester groups throughout the organization to get them to help with or, at least, not stand in the way of the CMS.

✦ **Representing the needs of the CMS** to the outside world. The content manager is likely to be the person to preside over the selection of CMS hardware and software and to be the official interface between the CMS system and third-party products with which the CMS interoperates.

All in all, the content manager is the head of the CM endeavor in the organization. Formalized education in content management is just in its beginnings, so no degrees in content management are given yet, and little exists in the way of recognized curricula that offer credentials for this position. In addition, few people can say they have much experience being in such a position. Still, you can look for a core set of skills in a content manager. The person must be capable of understanding the multiple disciplines involved in CM including the following subjects:

✦ **Publication technologies,** including server and client software and the construction of Web sites and Web applications. She does not need to be a Web developer, but a good content manager understands the Web. She also has a working understanding of print technologies and the processes behind any other kind of publication platform you will use.

✦ **Editorial processes,** including the writing and review process. She does not need to be a writer or artist, but a good content manager must recognize well-constructed content when she sees it.

✦ **Cataloging and information organization.** A content manager does not need to be an information architect, but she does need to be good at finding structure and making sure it is enforced.

✦ **Information technology infrastructure,** including database and network administration. Because the system has to integrate with the enterprise communication infrastructure and because the collection, management, and publishing systems of a CMS are all network and database applications, decent knowledge in this area is a must.

✦ **Analysis and abstraction.** This may be the most important but least measurable skill of a content manager. If you haven't noticed, content management requires you to think very abstractly about information. If you get too stuck in the concrete details of how one page or another looks, you will lose sight of the main goal of CM, which is to break information away from its presentation and focus on its structure and how that structure can be used to make any of a range of pages. If this light bulb has not appeared over your content manager's head, you will never have a robust system.

The CIO

From the title "Chief Information Officer (CIO)," one would think that organizations already have just the right person to understand, champion, and initiate large-scale content management strategy and implementation. Typically, however, this is far from the case. Instead, most CIOs would be better called CDOs (Chief Data Officers) or CNOs (Chief Network Officers) or possibly the more standard CTOs (Chief Technology Officers). If you accept the definition of information that I have been working from—that information is the texts, images, sound, and motion that you want to consume—then you can clearly see that information officers don't much deal with information. Most commonly, these people deal with the infrastructure that lies beneath information and not the information itself. Just like the Information Technology (IT) groups that CIOs usually preside over, if the computers are not crashing and are all well connected, they feel that their jobs are done.

Instead, suppose that a CIO really fit her title. What else would she do? For starters, she would understand what information is and could be for her organization. She would have a high-level but comprehensive knowledge of how information is created and flows within the organization. She would know what types of information are most valuable and how that value is maximized. She would know at any moment how far the organization is from the targets she has set for efficient and effective creation, storage, and delivery of the organization's most critical information.

With her vast knowledge of information in the organization, she would craft the information strategy for the organization. Just as a CMO (Chief Marketing Officer) sets marketing strategy and a CFO (Chief Financial Officer) sets finance strategy, the CIO would be in charge of deciding what information could do for the organization and how to make it do that. A CIO in her proper role would have a plan for maximizing the benefit of information to the organization's widest goals (as set by her boss, the CEO).

Finally, the CIO, in the role her title implies, would work in conjunction with her C-level peers to ensure that the information strategy succeeds. She would work with the operations officer (COO) to ensure that the most important information is created in a consistent and usable way. Moreover, she would work to ensure that information creation and its capture are respected and integral parts of each person's job. She would work with marketing to assure that the information resources of the organization both aid and influence how the organization presents itself to the world. She would work with finance to build information asset models that quantify the value of information to justify investments in and returns from information.

In short, a CIO would be in charge of information.

Project manager

All project managers attend to the scope, schedule, and budget of their projects. It is really no different in a CM project. Project managers usually appear most in the start-up phase of a CMS. After the CMS is running, the other sorts of managers tend to step in and take charge.

Project managers do the following:

✦ **Manage project staff,** apprising them of their deliverables and schedules. Perhaps the most difficult thing in managing a CMS project is the potentially long list of characters whose input is needed. Especially during the requirements-gathering phase for the CMS, a lot of meetings, phone calls, e-mail messages, and small documents have to be scheduled, accomplished, and accounted for.

✦ **Manage budgets,** ensuring that the money allotted for the project lasts as long as the project does. Conversely, a good project manager will see an overrun a mile away and let the world know that some sort of change is needed long before the money actually runs out.

✦ **Create and enforce the project plan.** It might well be beyond the ability of a project manger to create the plan for a large CMS, but it should be fully within her ability to make sure it is updated and adhered to.

The kind of project manager that you want is the kind that can keep a lot of balls in the air and make sure a thousand little things get accomplished and no one is left out. Project managers with strong technical skills but little ability to negotiate competing constraints need not apply.

A good CM project manager will have strong negotiation skills and a streak of insistence. The successful CM project is a careful balance of stopping the unending conversation about what content and functionality will be included, and assuring that all relevant and necessary content and features are fleshed out and used. Finally, although your project manager need not be an expert in any of the CM skill areas, she should have somewhat the same ability as the content manager to understand the staff's subject matter enough to know a big problem from a little one.

Production manager

A production manager ensures that content flows into the system at an established rate and quality. I have seen production managers most often in the context of acquisition source conversion, where large bulks of source content have to be processed under tight deadlines. Production managers are called for, however, wherever a steady, high volume of content must be produced. If, for example, you need 100 images drawn, checked, converted, and deployed each week, you might want to put a production manager in place to assure that the volume and quality you expect is consistently accomplished. Production managers work both in the start-up phase of a CMS, to convert the backlog of information, and during the run phase of a CMS, to ensure the required throughput of content.

Production managers do the following:

✦ **Manage production staff.** They hire, fire, promote, and motivate. You may think that in a production environment, the staff is expected to act like cogs in the machine. On the contrary, a strong production team is one where people's individual skills are recognized and used. Staff can move from entry-level jobs that require little initiative and skill but high focus to more advanced jobs managing the newcomers, handling the special cases that arise, and designing more effective processes.

✦ **Design production processes** that make the most efficient use of people and the most effective use of automation. A good production manager knows when something is worth programmer time to automate. She can tell when a problem is due to inattention, rather than bad input or faulty procedures.

✦ **Create and enforce production schedules,** ensuring that content creation proceeds like a well-oiled machine. She will also have methods at her disposal to even out, as much as possible, the inevitable lows and highs in content flow through her system.

✦ **Create and enforce quality** and speed metrics. In a production environment, you must create a set of gauges that tell you at any moment how the process is going. After creating such gauges, a good production manager will pay close periodic attention to her gauges to catch problems before they snowball.

A good production manager is a cross between an editor, a programmer, and a factory manager — not the easiest person to find. The editor in her understands the way information is constructed, and she can design processes that editorial staff can and want to use. The programmer is always looking for a way to do it more quickly and knows the hallmarks of a process that can be automated. The factory manager understands the dynamics of the *floor*, where emotions as well as tools determine how much gets done in a day.

 Cross-Reference Much more information about production processes is contained in Chapter 37, "Processing Content."

Business Analysts

Someone must recognize or create the wider business strategy into which the CMS must fit. I call that person the CMS business analyst. Without someone to do this job, a CMS project team can quickly become unmoored in the organization and may find itself in the position of asking for a lot of money for a project that does not seem to do much more than save your group some time. The business analyst is most active in the very early stages of a CMS implementation project, when the business case and mandate for the project are being crafted.

The business analyst does the following:

✦ **Figures out how the content management project fits** into the overall strategy of the organization. Part of the job is finding justifications for the plans you may already have, but the more important part is finding out how to change your plans so that the project fits cleanly into the organization's most important goals (see Chapter 15, "Getting Ready for a CMS," for more information).

✦ **Finds out what has been accomplished to date** in the organization. The analyst must be able to track down and document the existing efforts that might contribute to the CMS.

✦ **Creates a strategy for cooperation and support** in the organization. This job includes determining the appropriate sponsors for the initiative, as well as what groups need to be represented and by whom at planning and strategy meetings (see Chapter 16, "Securing a Project Mandate," for more information).

✦ **Presides over the mandate process.** Although the analyst might not actually facilitate the mandate meetings, she is responsible for ensuring that they reach a successful conclusion. At the end of the process, it is the business analyst's responsibility that there be widespread consensus and support for the CM initiative.

✦ **Creates and promulgates the project mandate.** The analyst is likely to draft the project's mandate statement, solicit feedback, and distribute the final version. She can serve as the point person for any discussion in the organization about what the project is or how it will be done.

✦ **Devises a strategy,** in consultation with others in the organization, for how the workload and budget of the startup and running of the CMS will be shared in the organization. In addition, she will have to ensure that the governing body created to preside over the effort coalesces into an ongoing working group (see Chapter 14, "Working within the Organization," for more information).

✦ **Works with the project team** to ensure that the project mandate is fully embraced and specifically acted on.

A lot of responsibility comes with this position, and a lone ranger who works in isolation is not ideal. In fact, what the business analyst really must do is ensure that these tasks are accomplished — not do them herself. Most of these tasks require other people to come together and agree. The best person for this job, then, will be someone who has the following qualities:

✦ **Knows the business.** Obviously, to accomplish the tasks I laid out, this analyst must be able to move nimbly throughout the organization. It really helps if this person knows a lot of people (or at least makes friends quickly).

✦ **Knows how to negotiate.** All the analyst's tasks require consensus-building. It is essential that the analyst be considered neutral. It is a great help if she is already well respected in the organization.

✦ **Understands the concepts and execution of a CMS.** The analyst must have a solid understanding of what a workable mandate looks like if she is to facilitate its creation. Without such an understanding, all the negotiation talent in the world might still result in an agreement that will not work or be too expensive.

✦ **Can synthesize and motivate.** The analyst will be faced with a lot of opinion and fact. She will have to quickly distinguish one from the other, sort them, relate them, and suggest ways to combine them into a best approach. Unfortunately, she will not always have time to think first. Therefore, it is important that she have an ability to think on the move and the good judgment to know when to postpone a decision on issues that require more thought. It also essential that she has the stature to make herself heard when she speaks.

The obvious place to look for business analysts is among the MBA/consultant types who have considerable business, communication, and Web skills. These people are likely to have the requisite interpersonal and technical skills. But remember, they also need the respect of your organization and an understanding of what you are trying to accomplish with content management.

Information Architects

Information architects (IA) create and implement strategies for structuring, accessing, and displaying information. They know how to harness the mechanics of information to create methods and models for structuring the content within the CMS and within each publication that the CMS will produce.

Like content management itself, information architecture is a new and evolving discipline. Most IAs today practice on the Web, creating layout and access schemes for important sites. Thus, many IAs have worked previously in graphic design, editorial services, or Web development. A few universities are beginning to take IA seriously enough to start to formulate and teach its principles. The Asilomar Institute for Information Architecture (AIfIA) (www.aifia.org) is the best place I know of to learn about this new discipline. How can IAs participate in a CMS? An IA with good experience on a large (10,000-plus page) Web site ought to have the right experience to work on a major CMS project.

Note   The same caveat that applies to IAs applies to content managers. Content management requires you to think very abstractly about information. If you get too stuck in the concrete details of how one page or another looks, you will lose sight of the main goal of CM, which is to break information away from its presentation and instead focus on its structure and how it can be used to make any of a range of pages.

For the kinds of work that you need done in a CMS, I differentiate IAs into content analysts and metators.

Content analyst

The content analyst oversees the middle phases of a CMS implementation project, including:

✦ **Gathering content requirements** and organizing them into a unified system (see Chapter 17, "Doing Requirements Gathering," section "What Are Requirements?" for more information).

✦ **Conceptualizing the logical design** for the content aspects of the system (see Chapter 18, "Doing Logical Design," for more information).

✦ **Translating the logical design** into a physical design in the implementation specifications (see Chapter 18, "Doing Logical Design," for more information).

✦ **Creating staffing estimates** and plans for the collection effort.

✦ **Planning the architecture** and the organization behind localization.

Logical design is the center of the content analyst position and it results in what I call the metatorial guide. But the content analyst can participate throughout the project, helping from the first readiness assessment to the final training during deployment. Wherever the content analyst is, she is ensuring that the content you manage can be and is divided and tagged for maximum access and flexibility. The IA analysts will be central in gathering and processing the content requirements and turning them into a solid content model.

Cross-Reference   Chapter 21, "Rolling Out the System," has more information on the metatorial guide.

To do the job I have laid out, content analysts need these sorts of skills:

✦ **Business process design.** The collection system of a CMS is a business process for interacting with content authors and sources. To account for this in her metatorial framework, the content analyst must understand the people and processes that can or should be used.

✦ **Cataloging, storage, and retrieval.** Clearly, this is the heart of the content analyst's world. Without a solid focus and passion for cataloging schemes, the analyst will not succeed. It is not enough, however, to know how to divide and categorize information;

the analyst must also understand the technology you intend to use to store and deliver that information. Thus, a strong focus on database or XML technologies is a must.

✦ **Publication systems.** In the end, the content analyst is there to ensure that the right content can be rendered in the right way in each publication. To do so, the analyst must understand the mechanics of each publication to be produced. For Web sites, this means a very good knowledge of Web applications and, in particular, the concepts and mechanics of Web templates. For print, this means a strong understanding of the particular print publication application that the organization uses. An understanding of the end user is a start, but to be successful, the analysts must also understand publication from the standpoint of one who wants to automate its layout and content structure.

The best content analyst is a librarian, editorial type, or indexer who has a demonstrated ability to understand and apply technology. The content segments and metadata that the analyst proposes must be collected, stored, and published using programming and networking technology. To succeed, therefore, the analyst must not only know how information should be structured in general, but how it needs to be structured for the particular collection, management, and publishing systems the organization will use.

Metator

A content analyst creates a metatorial framework, and a metator applies it. Metators are quite analogous to editors (as you might have guessed by now). An editor reviews an author's work for style, usage, grammar, and so on, and makes changes to bring the work into compliance with the organization's standards. A metator does the same thing, but for metadata rather than for editorial qualities.

Cross-Reference For an illustration of a metator's job, see Chapter 7, "Introducing the Major Parts of a CMS," under the section "Metatorial processing."

A metator might be expected to do the following:

✦ **Review an author's submission** of a component to ensure that its metadata fields are filled in correctly.

✦ **Review the output of content conversion** processes to ensure that they correctly identify, divide, and tag components.

✦ **Fill in metadata fields** that authors don't understand how to complete or that conversion processes can't locate.

✦ **Train and guide others** on what metadata is, how it is used by the CMS, and how to choose the right values for particular components.

✦ **Distribute and update the metatorial guide.** Metators are in the best position to see what is working and what is not in the system created by the content analyst. They are also closest to those who must use the guide in their daily work. More on the metatorial guide is located in Chapter 21, "Rolling Out the System," in the section "Creating documentation."

A good metator is a content analyst in training. She has the same basic skills as the analyst, but less experience or talent in designing metatorial systems than in implementing them. Of course, the analyst often must be the metator as well. Metators can serve as CMS front-line support to the content contributors, so it is a good idea to choose metators who have the skill eventually to be considered power-users of the CMS.

Information Architects

Classification has consequences. Nowhere is this more evident than in the passionate debates that surround the labeling and definition of jobs and roles. Should you be called an information architect, an interaction designer, a usability engineer, or a content manager? Who owns user testing? Who is responsible for metadata? Who should shape the overall strategy for the Web site?

Of course, there are no right or wrong answers to these questions. In reality, we live in the borderlands, the soft edges between one category and another. Information architects, in particular, must be adept at bridge building. At its best, information architecture is about making connections, not just between users and content, but also between people from different departments, functions, disciplines, and cultures.

For example, information architects are often categorized as "*user experience professionals.*" And indeed, we do have a lot in common with designers and usability experts who focus on user interface design and testing. And yet, information architects must also inhabit the world of content management, linking an empathy for the end-user with a rich understanding of content structure, metadata schema, business processes, and publication systems.

Just as content management systems enable us to present multiple views of and paths to the same information, we should embrace the multifaceted nature of our jobs and the complementary strengths of our colleagues.

Peter Morville, President, Semantic Studios; Coauthor,
Information Architecture for the World Wide Web

Tip　A content analyst can gain good insight into how well her system works by doing the job of the metator every so often.

You can treat the job of metator as an entry-level position — that is, because she is applying already-created guidelines, she need not know as much about the CMS or its technology. This is not to say that she needs no relevant experience. Rather, the perfect person for the job of metator is someone who has had ample experience as:

✦ A technical writer who has had to focus on highly structured material

✦ An indexer who has had experience with electronic publications

✦ An editor (of course)

✦ A librarian or archivist who has a knack for technology

Infrastructure Staff

The infrastructure staff defines and builds the system on which the CMS will run. They are in charge of deploying the completed CMS and its related software and hardware and of administering the system once it is running.

CMS administrator

The CMS administrator must set up and run the CMS.

Note

I might have chosen to list this position under information architecture, even though most often it is thought of as an IT position. Here is why: The basic purpose of the CMS is to organize information and make it as available and flexible as possible. Thus, the person who runs the CMS should have this perspective above all else. Just as it is preferable to have a person with a background in finance running your enterprise accounting system, so it is preferable to have someone with a background in content running your CMS. This is not to say that CMS administrators do not need to be quite technical — of course they do. Rather, it is to say that they need to be able to confront content problems as well as infrastructure problems.

The administrator is responsible for all the end-user tasks required to set up and run the system. Like all administrators, the CMS administrator is neither a programmer nor a network professional (although experience in these areas is a help). Rather, CMS administrators are responsible for tasks such as the following:

✦ **Configuring the chosen CMS.** The administrator enters or imports all the component definitions, user profiles, publication definitions, and other data that the CMS needs to begin working.

✦ **Inputting content.** Where content comes into the system in bulk (for example, as the result of a conversion process), the administrator oversees the process and takes action when anything fails. Where content comes in one component at a time (for example, when authors fill in Web forms), she is responsible for ensuring that the proper methods are up and working. This may entail creating new Web input forms, distributing appropriate end-user software, or simply receiving e-mail attachments and importing them into the system.

✦ **Fully understanding the chosen CMS software.** The administrator ought to be able to make the CMS do anything it can do without additional programming. In many commercial systems, there is quite a bit that does not require programming. A CMS, however, requires you to understand content management concepts and to be able to find the right combination of options (which are often buried in text files and the system registry).

✦ **Maintaining users and workflows.** The administrator is responsible for ensuring that all staff with access to the system are accounted for by the system. Staff may need to be profiled and added to groups in order to get access to the resources they need. In addition, the administrator needs to set up and maintain the system workflows. This may be as simple as dragging and dropping icons onto a page, or as complex as modifying a massive XML structure in a text editor.

✦ **Triaging bugs and finding fixes.** After the system is running, the administrator will be the first line of defense against problems that arise. From rebooting after a crash to spending days tracking down why one user can't seem to log in, the administrator must ensure that the train keeps running. Of course, many problems must be escalated past the administrator, but like the triage nurse in an emergency department, she sees them all first.

✦ **Ensuring data hygiene.** The administrator ensures that the content stored in the repository is in the best state possible. This responsibility includes making sure that required data is supplied, that content is archived or deleted on the specified schedule, and that periodic reviews and updates to content and system configurations happen as scheduled.

So, what sort of person can do all this? Well, I see two basic ways to go: Start technical and train on content, or start content-oriented and train technical. Either way could work, given the right person. One woman I know, who graduated with a degree in library science, craved technology so much that she all but gave up on cataloging to pursue a career in programming. I know of a man who began as a network professional but gave it up to write. Either of these two people would make a great CMS administrator. If you can't find a hybrid soul like the ones I described, look for the following qualities:

✦ **Someone who is a super power-user** of every application she uses. The power-user is always looking for a way to make the application do something more, different, or more easily and will stop at nothing until it all works. That is the attitude the administrator needs in order to deal with the powerful but vaguely documented and obscurely located functionality that many CMS products provide.

✦ **Someone who is not afraid to get technical** but knows where to stop. A good administrator will open up a programming script to see where it is crashing. A bad administrator will try to fix the script instead of turning it over to the programmer who created it.

✦ **Someone who is not afraid of people and process.** At least half of the problems an administrator will encounter concern people, not machines. A good administrator will not always reply with a technology fix, but may change process or simply diffuse emotions to solve a problem.

✦ **Someone who is meticulous.** The administrator is running a highly tuned, very complex machine. She must be careful that at all times the machine is well oiled, all the parts are moving as they should, and no dirt (bad content or data) can foul up the gears.

Deployment analyst

A CMS can, but usually does not, stand alone in the organization. As likely as not, it will be connected to many of the organization's main computer systems, such as the staff information systems (network user directories), security protocols, network and database systems, and any of a number of enterprise applications for financial or employee transactions. Someone has to figure out all these connections. I call that person the deployment analyst. This person's responsibilities include the following:

✦ **Determining what supporting hardware and software** the CMS will need and how to procure it.

✦ **Determining what platform and configuration requirements** the organization has for the CMS (supported databases, required operating systems, and the like).

✦ **Figuring out the integration of the organization's other computer systems** with the CMS. The analyst will need to work closely with the owners of the other systems to forge an agreement and alliance.

✦ **Determining how to deploy the collection system** of the CMS across as much of the organization as necessary.

✦ **Determining how to deploy the publishing and Web-server system** of the CMS across as much of the world as necessary.

✦ **Planning and overseeing the rollout** of the system in the organization.

✦ **Determining the appropriate training and technical support** infrastructure for the CMS.

✦ **Creating estimates and plans for staffing** the management system of the CMS.

Many of these tasks are common to any deployment of enterprise software. And unlike many of the other CMS jobs plenty of people out there have done this sort of thing before. Although the level of integration and the depth of penetration of a CMS can be larger than other enterprise systems, the skills required to perform the integration are the same. Thus, people with a strong IT and enterprise deployment background (with a focus on the Internet) are the ones to find.

Trainer and documentation specialist

By the time a large CMS is deployed, a tremendous amount of effort has been directed toward organizing information and creating processes to collect, manage, and publish it. Someone needs to write all this down so that users can learn it. Moreover, someone must develop and deliver training to the variety of people who need to interact with the system.

Not unlike other enterprise implementations, CMS documentation and training will likely be a combination of the materials supplied by commercial product companies and the custom processes you have developed. The person (or people) in this position has the challenge of offering the appropriate education to everyone from the most novice content contributor to the most expert developer who needs to know how a sophisticated integration was performed.

Software Developers

Some day, it may be that you can buy a CMS that does not require you to do large amounts of programming. Until that day (and most likely beyond), you need a development staff. This staff creates the custom software behind a CMS. They create the templates that a CMS product needs. In addition, they create the code to implement custom features, integrations with non-CMS systems, and custom authoring and conversion programs and routines.

Software analyst

Like the other analysts I have described, the software analyst strategizes and plans. The software analyst plans how best to accomplish all the programming that must be accomplished to start and run the CMS.

In particular, the software analyst is responsible for the following:

✦ **Choosing the development environment** (or environments) that will be used. You have quite a few competing environments from which to choose. The right one is the one (or ones) that requires the least retraining of the programmers you intend to use, fits most cleanly into the required system architecture supplied by the deployment analyst, and of course, provides the tools you need to create the needed functionality.

✦ **Creating a development framework.** In a CMS, code is everywhere. From the programming macros in a Microsoft Word document template to the stored procedures in an enterprise resource planning (ERP) database, more programming sites exist than anyone in her right mind would call a single system. It is the job of the software analyst to get all these different parts of the system corralled into a single programming framework. The framework organizes the creation of code, its versioning and testing, its deployment, and the sharing of code modules and objects between applications. This is no small task in an enterprise CMS.

✦ **Deciding which features of the CMS should be custom-coded** and which should be done using commercially available tools. For example, should the organization use the database connectivity code supplied by the CMS manufacturer or should it extend the code it has now, which works well with its ERP system?

✦ **Writing the specifications** and development plans for the programming tasks that require them (see Chapter 20, "Implementing the System," for more on specifications).

✦ **Creating estimates and plans for the staffing** needed to accomplish all the programming to start and run the CMS.

As with the deployment analyst, some people in the world have done this sort of thing before. Still, someone who is a good general analyst but also has significant experience programming content-manipulation applications would serve you best. This is not a rare skill set, but it is not the most common. People of this ilk can be found in the back rooms of Web sites that use Perl or PHP extensively, or in the documentation groups of large companies that have had to use Structured Generalized Markup Language (SGML) to structure and manipulate massive document databases. In any case, stay away from the people who think that content can be treated just like data. They will underestimate the complexity of their tasks every time.

In addition, this person, like the other analysts, cannot be a back-roomer. She must be able to negotiate among the competing development interests (which are often more vehement than the business interests) and come to a workable compromise between competing platforms.

Finally, be careful not to choose someone who is more interested in writing code than getting other programmers organized. Note that the software analyst's job description does not say "writes a lot of programs." Even if you are in a position to have only one person who is both analyst and developer, because the code will live in so many different places, it is essential that this person really be interested in staying organized, creating standards, and adhering to them rather than simply writing code.

Template and CMS developer

You will need entry- to mid-level programmers who have learned the templating language and associated programming tasks of a particular CMS. These people are responsible for the following:

✦ **Implementing publication templates,** given the specifications the software analyst and publication analyst have created. To do the implementation, the programmers use standard programming environments (such as JSP and ASP), the syntax of the CMS's templating language, and any custom objects that have been created by custom application developers.

✦ **Implementing input templates,** given the specifications the content analyst has created for content components and metadata. Most input templates are standard Web forms that are enhanced with custom objects supplied by the CMS product you use.

✦ **Doing the smaller programming-like tasks** associated with a CMS that are too technical for the CMS administrator, such as creating workflow scripts using an XML editor or writing event triggers that fire when a new file is added to the system.

Custom application developer

You will need mid- to high-level programmers to create any custom functionality that you want added to a CMS. These programmers are generally responsible for the following sorts of tasks:

✦ **Programming to enhance collection,** including extensions to word processors, special tagging tools, and complete custom authoring environments when a standard tool will not suffice. In addition, programmers may be called upon to create other collection tools, such as automated acquisition routines and collaboration applications for authors to jointly work on content (see Chapter 38, "Building Collection Systems," for more information).

✦ **Programming for management,** including enhancements, extensions, and (unfortunately) replacements to the CMS's standard database environment, programs for automated review and archiving of content, and special indexing and retrieval routines.

✦ **Programming for publishing,** including enhancements, extensions, and replacements to the CMS's standard templating system, custom server objects that provide extra functionality for particular publications, and custom browser objects (for example, Java applets) to deliver functionality locally in a Web page.

The most successful custom extensions do not fully supersede the CMS; rather they integrate closely into the CMS's core architecture. To be good at custom extensions, therefore, a programmer must be familiar enough with the chosen CMS to use its application programming interface (API) and be able to tie the new programs into the user interface (UI) of the CMS as needed. The kind of programmer you want in this position will not be afraid to go way beyond what the CMS can do out of the box, but will always try first to make the CMS do as much as possible without custom code. She will also be very reluctant to write extensions that circumvent the CMS's API, knowing that when the next version of the CMS ships, all her back doors into the system might be closed.

Software integrator

You will need mid- to high-level programmers to write the code that glues the CMS to other systems. Like the custom application developers, these programmers must be versed in the API and other workings of the CMS. In addition, they will have to fully understand the other system and have skills in the appropriate language for connecting the two. Software integrators may be called upon to do the following:

✦ **Connect the CMS repository** and collection systems to other enterprise resources, such as the organization's user registry and ERP systems.

✦ **Connect the CMS's publications** to enterprise or outside resources. To create a full transaction system on the Web, for example, they may have to do a massive amount of integration between the CMS, inventory and fulfillment systems, financial and banking systems (inside and outside the organization), and product catalog systems.

✦ **Connect Web publications to the Web server.** The CMS may or may not come with the Web application server and Web database system that you intend to use. If it does not, then a programmer (with assistance from networking professionals) will have to make the connections either through configuration or through custom code.

Without a doubt, the main skill to look for here is proven expertise in the system or systems with which you want to integrate the CMS. If your integration is mainly on the Web, then experience with the target system *on the Web* is best.

Test analyst and test engineer

Quality assurance (QA) ensures that all parts of the CMS system work properly and that the publications that the CMS produces have a minimum of bugs. This is not an easy job. (If you have read through all these job descriptions, you are no doubt tired of hearing those words.)

A test analyst is the one who sets up your test plans and coordinates the effort, and a test engineer executes the plans. Test analysts and test engineers must do the following:

✦ **Develop and execute test plans** against a collection and management system that is constantly changing as the CMS grows and evolves.

✦ **Work with each user's individual configuration** and set of access rights to the system to be sure that the CMS works under all configurations.

✦ **Be able to test a collection of loosely coupled,** independently operating components (the CMS, that is).

✦ **Be able to ensure the quality of publications** that are created on the fly or are constantly being updated. They must figure out how you can test publications when you can never see them completely.

Clearly, this is no task for a beginner. The kind of testers you need are comfortable in an ambiguous situation where the test plan is never complete and you can never test all possible cases. Of course, many organizations hardly test their CMS at all and leave the publication testing to the publication team (in other words, the person who develops the page or the template, clicks around a bit, and calls it a day). If you choose this path, you get what you get.

If you choose instead to get as organized about testing as you would about collection, management, and publishing, then you'll find someone who knows how to test code and its potential to create output, rather than someone who must click though every page of a Web site each time it is produced to ensure that it is all right.

Publications Staff

The publication staff ensures that each publication is high quality, published on schedule, and makes the best use of the content in the CMS repository. Given the wide differences today between print publications groups and Web publications groups (and, for that matter, between the Internet and the intranet groups) in a large organization, you may very well start with a different group for each major publication. I imagine that as time goes on and the idea of content management takes hold, the various groups will coalesce into a single publications group (but don't hold your breath).

Publication analyst

The publication analyst is a graphic designer or other design professional who is responsible for designing the CMS publication system so that it can automatically create compelling publications.

The publication analyst is responsible for these general areas:

✦ **Choosing the design tools and environment for the publications.** Like the software analyst, the publication analyst is likely to come into a situation where groups already have chosen tools and are not interested in switching. The analyst must weigh these considerations against the advantages of standardizing tools and using tools that are most amenable to automation by the CMS. Especially in the print publication world, the efforts required to automate various tools can differ tremendously.

✦ **Choosing which publications to include in the CMS and when.** The analyst must balance between the two extremes toward which people will want to draw her. On one side, some people will say, "This can all be produced automatically if we dumb it down a little." On the other side, other people will say, "Our publication is too complex and our readers expect too much crafting for this to ever be produced automatically." It is the unenviable job of the publication analyst to find the compromise that allows as much as is technically feasible, esthetically advisable, and economically viable to be produced by the CMS.

✦ **Creating the general publication specifications** that detail how a publication will be created by the CMS.

✦ **Creating estimates and plans for the staffing** required to accomplish all the design needed to start and run the CMS.

✦ **Creating the overall plan for how content will be targeted** and scheduled for publication. Given that a particular content component may find its way into any number of publications, all on different publication schedules, this can be a difficult task.

The publication analyst is the prime example of the schizophrenia that many CMS staffers must embrace and overcome. The analyst must be firmly in favor of beautiful, compelling, well-crafted publications. The analyst must also understand and believe in the philosophy of automated publication. This publication analyst is the key negotiator between the specific needs and requirements of a particular publication and the generalized and neutralized content that is in the CMS repository. To be successful, this person must know how to work with the creative staff, who will want handcrafted pages, and the technical staff, who will want fully automated pages. The result must be a design that can be configured and automated, but that still meets the qualitative design goals of the publication. Ideally, this person is someone who really can't decide if she likes art or science better but has practiced both. Finding such a person may not be easy. Here are some of the attributes to look for:

✦ **Someone with a strong background in at least two media.** Look for someone who has worked on the Web and in print, for example, or someone who has worked in film and on magazines. This ensures that the person is not stuck in one way of looking at the publication process.

✦ **Someone who is process-oriented.** A highly creative and energetic designer who depends more upon the drop of inspiration than the downpour of perspiration is the wrong choice. The inspiration must be there, but the job mostly concerns getting the publication process organized and systematized.

✦ **Someone who is not afraid of technology.** The best publication analyst is excited about the possibilities that new technologies can offer, but has a healthy cynicism about how soon or how much the technology will help.

✦ **Someone, like the software analyst, who knows how to negotiate** within design, within technology, and between the two. This person must be respected and be able to deal with others, whether the room is full of creative people, technologists, or is split between the two.

Publication designer

A publication analyst creates a publication framework, and a publication designer applies it. This relationship is the same as between the content analyst and the metator. In both cases, the analysts' grand plans succeed or fail based on the day-to-day work done by their less lofty associates. In both cases, the analyst is a more experienced and organizationally savvy (and more respected) version of their associate. The distinction between the two can be fine; in some organizations, these two jobs are done by the same person.

The publication designer is responsible for these tasks:

✦ **Creating the publication specifications** for how each particular publication will be produced by the CMS. These specifications include wire frame drawings, template designs, standard page and section elements, and the plain language version of the logic needed to decide what goes where on the published page.

✦ **Working with the page developer** and CMS template programmer to ensure that the pages she designed can be coded.

✦ **Working with the content analyst** to ensure that the content that must get onto a page is segmented and tagged in such a way that it can be found and appropriately formatted.

The publication designer is a negotiator in the world of the template programmer, IA analyst, and page developer. She must find a fit between the best page design, the one that can be produced in the publication medium (Web page, magazine page, and so on), and the one that can be programmed in a publication template. Many of the global issues will have been worked out by the analyst before the designer is involved. But the devil is in the details, and like the metator, the publication designer is in much closer contact with reality than the analyst.

You can find publication designers in the ranks of analyst *wannabes* and page developers at the top of their talents. Analyst wannabes are people who would like the job of analyst, but don't have quite the experience and maturity yet to fulfill the role. If you find yourself saying "She looks right for an analyst, but she's not quite there," you have found a good designer. You can find out more about the requirements for publication analysts in the preceding section.

Page developers at the top of their talents are people who are ready to move on to more challenging and abstract work than creating pages, but may never be cut out for a job like analyst. They are likely to be extremely skilled in a particular medium (a QuarkXPress guru, for example, or an HTML junkie) but have little interest in moving beyond that medium. They may be very smart and able to negotiate with their current peers, but not ready in the foreseeable future to play at the level of the wider organization. These people are doing superior work in their medium and could easily take on the added responsibility of entire publications. For more information on the job of page developers, read the next section.

Page developer

Someone has to take the design specification for a publication and turn it into actual template pages. I call this person the *page developer*. I choose the word *developer* here with a bit of trepidation. The page developer acts as a pseudo programmer. She doesn't actually write code, but she knows enough about it to recognize particular code modules, move them into and around on pages, and slightly modify them so they will work in a new context (changing their parameters, for example). True to CMS form, however, page developers also have an opposing skill: They are pseudo designers. They don't actually design the page, but they know enough about it to pay attention to a pixel's worth of detail, move design elements into and around on a page, and make slight modifications to them so they will work in a new context (widening a table, for example, to fit a larger title). Page developers have the following responsibilities:

✦ **Turning the publication designer's specifications into files** that are usable by the CMS. A developer, for example, might take a drawing created by a designer in Macromedia FreeHand, illustrating layout and design elements, and turn it into an HTML file. Or she might create an Adobe InDesign file that includes all the publication conventions that a particular publication requires.

✦ **Working the design to completion.** For example, a publication specification might call for a particular page to have ten variations. The developer actually creates those variations and ensures that they will all work. In this process, a fair amount of interaction occurs between her and the publication designer.

✦ **Working with the CMS template developer to merge design with code.** At some point, the page developer and template developer must merge efforts and produce one file that has both design and programming in it. Anyone who has had to share the same file with a competing interest knows that this is always a pain. Nevertheless, the two developers must work hand-in-hand to bring a page to completion.

Page developers are less difficult to find than many of the other CMS staffers. In each major publication medium, a large numbers of people are qualified for this position. They congregate in interest groups and in the publication groups of large organizations. The ones to focus on are the ones who can span technology and design and like to play intermediary between the two.

User interface specialist

This person knows user interface design for a particular publication type. In the print world, this job falls on the publication designer. In the Web world, the publication designer may or may not have the skills to complete the following necessary tasks:

✦ **Web form layout,** including the naming of controls and their layout on the page.

✦ **Web application design,** including the logic and presentation of the functionality of the application in a Web page.

✦ **Usability and page parsibility,** including designing and running user tests to see how understandable and navigable a page is.

✦ **Resolving issues associated with the integration of text,** media, graphic design, and branding with the application interface.

You may be able to cross-train a publication designer to meet these needs. If your content analyst or metator has worked as an IA on a large or complex Web site, she too may have these skills. On the other hand, you may have to hire or contract out this position. In any case, understand that this is a real need and find some way to staff for it.

Content Processing Staff

Your content processing (or content conversion) staff designs and implements a content processing system for dealing with acquired content. Information destined for the CMS that needs to be cut into components, have its format converted, or have its structure altered flows through this group. The content processing staff analyzes the tasks needed to turn acquired information into content; she also designs tools to aid in the process and trains and manages staffs of processors.

Conversion analyst

Someone must be responsible for the overall design and creation of the system you will use to change the raw information you acquire into finished content. I call that person the conversion analyst. Her responsibilities include the following:

✦ **Selecting or designing the tool set that the team will need.** Given the set of information inputs and content component outputs that the content analyst has specified, the conversion analyst must figure out what tools to buy or create to make the transformation as efficient as possible.

✦ **Creating the specifications for the programs** that tool developers will follow. For more information on these specifications, see Chapter 37, "Processing Content."

✦ **Designing the methods the team will use.** Given the inputs, outputs, and selected tool set, the analyst must determine the right set of methodologies to move information quickly through the system.

✦ **Designing the facilities and needed infrastructure** if the team is going to be large. For example, you might need to create a large work area where dozens of people can sit and easily interact.

✦ **Planning and estimating the staffing levels and skills** required to process the expected throughput of information. It can be difficult to accomplish this task if (as often happens) wide swings occur in the amount of information that will be received per week.

This job is the analyst companion to the production manager job I described earlier. Whereas the manager is responsible for the day-to-day operations of the processing group, the analyst is responsible for understanding the situation and getting the system set up. A good candidate for this position deeply understands text formats such as HTML, XML, PDF, and SGML. She must be very analytical and meticulous by nature. Because this person must write content processing specifications, she must be familiar with, if not well-versed in programming. Because she has to create procedures, she also must be familiar with, if not very experienced, in process management and the techniques used by data processing facilities.

Data processing facilities are one good place to look for people with this skill. Wherever teams of people have been brought together to make their way through masses of semistructured or unstructured information, you may find people who have the analytical skills and experience to be a conversion analyst. In my experience, I have seen such people in the back rooms of CD-ROM companies that publish huge catalogs, as well as in large law firms that must process grand mounds of court documents.

Tool developer

A tool developer creates the programs that automate the conversion process. These people use whatever text formats and programming tools necessary to make processes faster, cheaper, or higher quality. Tool developers create the following:

✦ **Programs that convert information** from one binary format to another.

✦ **Programs that create components** by crunching through files and directories, automatically separating and storing individual chunks.

✦ **Programs that create elements** within components by scanning the component content and inserting tags that separate one element from another.

✦ **Programs that infer the appropriate metadata** to add to content and automatically insert it.

✦ **Programs that present choices** to content processors and automatically carry out the result. These programs save the staff hours by doing all the manual labor and presenting them with only simple choices (simple by human standards, but obviously too hard for the program to make).

Tool developers are strong programmers. But the kind of programmer you want for this position takes a sort of guerrilla attitude toward her work. In other words, she enjoys diving into a problem, applying a rapid response at just the right place to make a big impact, and then retreating to watch the effect. This attitude allows the tool developer to materially affect production processes when the problem occurs, rather than spending a lot of time automating things that are not worth the effort, or stopping ongoing production for too long a time while she hangs back and considers the best approach.

Content processor

I use the title content processor for the people who come in every day to move information through the processes designed by the analyst. Content processors do the following:

✦ **Check the results of automated processes** to ensure that they worked as expected.

✦ **Perform manual processes** where automation cannot be applied or where it has not yet been employed.

✦ **Add metadata to masses** of content following prescribed rules.

You might be tempted to describe the work of a content processor as repetitive and rote—like a line worker at a factory. This is true in the sense that they work on parts moving through a larger process and perform the same function over and over. In a more telling sense, it is not true. For if the procedure a content processor is doing is repetitive and rote, you should be able to get the tool developer to write a program to do it. In fact, the hallmark of a good processor is someone who has the patience to apply good judgment in a consistent way without losing focus or ceasing to care (qualities that forever bar me from the ranks of the processing elite).

On the other hand, these jobs do not require a lot of experience and only rarely require any subject matter expertise. That's good, because you can't afford to pay too much for these positions, especially if you need a lot of staff quickly. It's also bad, because the person best suited to this position is not your run-of-the-mill temporary placement staffer. You need to find people who are both conscientious and underskilled, wise and underpaid—yet another example of the contrary qualities of CMS staff.

Content QA specialist

Quality assurance is a mandatory part of content processing. You need people whose main (or at least, most important) job is to go over the work of automation routines or other people and assess how close it is to the quality targets you have set. Generally, these people can be drawn from the upper ranks of the content processing staff. You can usually spot the high-accuracy people pretty quickly and give them the task of checking the work of others.

To find good QA people, look for graduates from the ranks of the content processors.

 Cross-Reference For more about what a QA specialist does, see Chapter 37, "Processing Content," the section "Drafting the processing specification."

Content Creation Staff

Content creation is the process of inventing new text, pictures, sound, or other media. I won't attempt to catalog all the jobs that might be involved in creating content. Rather, here are brief descriptions of some of the creation jobs that are most central to a CMS.

Acquisitions manager

An acquisitions manager handles your relationship with all content acquisition sources. This person does the following:

✦ **Negotiates and forms an agreement** with the source. The agreement includes quantity and schedule terms and may also include payment if the source is not free.

✦ **Keeps abreast of the deliveries** from the source and is the point of contact for any discussions of delay or changes to the quantity or quality of the source.

This manager should be skilled at project management and negotiations. She should know enough about electronic content formats and publishing processes to be able to understand the agreements she is forming.

Traffic cop

A dizzying number of separate pieces of content can fly around when a CMS is in full swing. You may very well need a person to coordinate and keep all this information straight. I call this person the traffic cop. Her main responsibilities are as follows:

✦ **Overseeing the delivery** of content from authors and acquisition sources.

✦ **Keeping abreast of the CMS workflows** and ensuring that everyone is on schedule.

✦ **Resolving any bottlenecks** that may be affecting the flow of information.

✦ **Resolving any disputes** about who is responsible for what.

A good cop has experience in large-scale task management. She is not afraid to pressure people to meet commitments, but she knows how to do so in a way that does not alienate contributors.

Writers and other content creators

Writers, illustrators, sound artists, videographers, animators, and the like (artists, for lack of a better word) create content for you from scratch. Aside from knowing their own trade well enough to ensure that you are getting the best product from them, they must also be able to understand and embrace the abstractness of the CMS process. For professionals, this ought to present little problem. Most have had experience being hired to create something whose form they never see until it is finished. For some, especially nonprofessional artists, it takes some cajoling to get them to pull away from the final product and just create content.

Artists with whom you are likely to have the least problems have the following characteristics:

✦ **They are used to creating for a purpose.** Writers who have written for a particular marketing purpose or graphic artists who have done illustration for magazine articles are examples.

✦ **They are used to creating for multiple audiences.** If a candidate does not ask you about audiences in the first few minutes, beware. If they wrinkle their noses at the list of your audiences, stay away.

✦ **They have created for more than one medium.** For example, people who have only done graphics for the Web may not understand the different constraints of print. People who have only written for print may not grasp the right style for the Web.

✦ **They don't mind working on a team.** Artists who want to hold on to their work for as long as possible and be its shepherd through every stage of the process will be trouble in a distributed and multistage process.

Editor

Most of the same caveats that I gave you for writers apply equally well to editors. The problem of the editor, relative to content creators, reminds me of the following quip:

> "If you think Fred Astaire was good, consider Ginger Rogers. She was doing all the same stuff backward!"

A good editor knows how to keep in sync with the creator and gently push her in the right direction. This challenge is compounded by the fact that a single editor may be responsible for many creators and many types of content (text, pictures, sound, and motion). Professional editors are no strangers to this situation and are, generally, able to deal with it. Still, in the context of a CMS — where the content in not only does not look like what comes out, but must come out in a variety of forms, juxtaposed with who knows what other content — the editor must be able to think extra-abstractly about the content she reviews.

In addition, editors who are tied to particular methods (for example, being able to make changes to the text in the final publication rather than in the copy that is stored in the repository) will have to change their ways even if the new ways are not as foolproof as the older ways. Clearly, an editor who is comfortable only with pencil marks on a piece of paper would be a poor choice for your CMS staff.

Summary

There are a lot of potential positions in a CMS project. You may not need one person (or more) in each position, but you will need someone to cover each of the major roles in a CMS:

✦ CMS types tend to have multiple, sometimes conflicting, skills.

✦ Content managers and other types of managers direct and oversee the construction and maintenance of the system.

✦ Business analysts figure out how to fit the CMS into the organization.

✦ Information architects figure out the structure of the content you will manage and help out, tagging content as it comes into the system.

✦ Software developers write the programming code behind CMS templates and integrations.

✦ The publications staff designs and creates the publications that the CMS will produce.

✦ The content processing staff creates and runs conversion processes.

✦ The content creation staff writes the text and creates the media that the CMS manages.

In the chapters that follow, I discuss how you can use all these wonderful people to design and build a CMS.

✦   ✦   ✦

Working within the Organization

Each department in an organization has something to add to the design or implementation of a CMS, but none of the traditional groups has the inherent right to own the system. Because the job of a CMS is so closely aligned with the job of the organization, a CMS must be integrated fully into an organization in order to succeed.

In this chapter, I discuss how a CMS fits into a stereotypical large organization.

Content Management and the Organization

The purpose of any organization is to create and offer something of value to the world. Commercial organizations produce valuable goods or services to sell. Government organizations produce laws and regulations for distribution. Nonprofit organizations produce goods and information that promote a particular social concern.

The purpose of a CMS is to help organizations create and offer valuable content and functionality. For commercial organizations, the content and functionality aid in the sale of goods or may even be in production of the goods that are sold; for government organizations, the content and functionality aid in the running of a jurisdiction and promulgation of regulations; and for nonprofit organizations, the content and functionality support a social concern. In each case, content supports the goals of the organization.

Before you read on, ask yourself this very important question: "In what way does information support the wider goals of my organization?" If the answer comes quickly to mind, in a form that is very specific, understandable, and compelling to anyone, then you are already on the right track. If, like most people, you have never seriously considered the question before and do not have a strong, detailed, and compelling answer, you are at a disadvantage as you begin this CM initiative. You can use what I offer here, along with your own intelligence and experience, to understand exactly what content has to do with the success of your organization. Then you can use that understanding to guide everything else you do.

As I said before, because its task is so closely aligned with the job of the organization, a CMS must be fully integrated into an organization in order to do its job well. Many organizations, however, are diverse and have a variety of types of value to create and offer. In these cases, the CMS may be designed to serve a unit within the larger organization. Regardless of the size or scope of the group that the CMS serves, its purpose is so intertwined with the purpose of the organization that the more integrated it becomes, the more able it is to serve the goals of the organization.

A CMS becomes integrated into the organization in the following ways:

✦ It organizes many departments and job types into an overall system.

✦ It harvests information from throughout the organization.

✦ It unifies the organization's communications to itself (an intranet site, for example) and the outside world (an Internet site, for example).

✦ It ties into the organization's existing information management infrastructure.

Before you read on, ask yourself this question: "Are we ready to have any system integrate our various departments or are the barriers just too high at the moment?" If you decide that the barriers are too high, you must either lower the barriers or scale back your initiative to a size that is more feasible. You might rephrase the question again as: "What parts of the organization are we ready to integrate?" Today, the answer most organizations give is "the whole enterprise," if only because they want to create a unified Web site. In reality, the whole enterprise may really not be ready. In the sections that follow, I'll assume that you are interested in integrating the entire enterprise, but the principles I discuss apply equally well to smaller slices of your organization.

Quite often, the need for a CMS is felt most acutely by one part of the organization. The group that feels the pain organizes a team to confront the problem. In my travels, I have seen these originating groups:

✦ **A business unit** (or department) that needs a much fuller Web site than it now has. The business unit has diverse content and core functionality that it needs to bring to its audiences.

✦ **The organization's corporate communications** or editorial group that finds it cannot keep up with the explosive growth of content that must be created and delivered.

✦ **The organization's IT group** that needs to unify all the divergent requests it receives for Web pages into a single, manageable system.

✦ **The organization's marketing department** that wants to both unify the organization's appearance to the world and better target market segments.

If all goes well, the originating group brings in all other groups and they coalesce into a tight team that serves all the groups' needs. More often than not, however, this does not happen. Rather, the originating group avoids the hassle of dealing with other groups' budgets and politics and decides to go it alone. The result is, at best, inefficiency and redundant efforts. At worst, the result is massive infighting and paralysis while the organization decides who owns the effort. I'll discuss this later in this chapter in the section "Understanding Organizational Roles."

I have seen organizations waste a tremendous amount of time and effort sorting out ownership of the new function of content management. The problem is that each group has a fair claim to ownership based on the part of the problem that they own. The business unit owns the content, the editorial group owns the management process, the marketing group owns the recipients of the content and the messages they receive, and the IT group owns the computer infrastructure that makes it all happen. Any group on its own can only duplicate the expertise already in another group. If a member group does not have the experience or skill to participate, the group ought to be built up, not avoided.

The deadly forces of bad interpersonal dynamics and poor communication notwithstanding, the solution is obvious. Each group needs to understand the contribution of the others and make the best use of it. If the CMS effort is to remain in a single group, that group must reach out to the others to be sure they are included. If the effort is to lie outside of any group (a solution I favor), then the purpose of the outside group is to marshal the resources of the other groups toward the goal of easily collected, well-managed, and fully deployed content.

For good or ill then, in order to do its job, a CMS must integrate and unify the organization (see Figure 14-1).

To serve the whole enterprise, the CMS must accept a wide variety of information from a cross-section of the organization. To crunch all this disparate information into a single system requires that you develop a single editorial approach to the organization's information (preferably with a unified editorial staff). If you are lucky, the organization will embrace this approach and will eventually create information in a unified way. If you are unlucky, you will be converting and reworking content for the indefinite future.

To allow information to flow into the CMS from throughout the organization and then from the CMS out to a variety of delivery platforms requires a unified infrastructure. CMS systems generally assume you will have a unified Web infrastructure for collecting and distributing information. Whatever infrastructure you create may be one of the few that spans the whole organization. If you are lucky, the infrastructure will be embraced and maintained by your existing IT group. If you are unlucky, the CMS infrastructure will exist as a separate network apart from the "standard" one.

To allow diverse information sources to coexist in the same publications requires that you create a single brand (or small family of related brands) for your organization. Broadly speaking, a CMS must integrate and unify multiple marketing approaches into a single approach with many channels. If you are lucky, your organization will be firmly behind this effort and will see it as a great step forward. If you are unlucky, you will be stuck trying to unify groups that would rather go it alone.

The challenge of a CMS is to be able to unify the organization enough that it is possible to have a single system collect, manage, and publish its information. Even if you can't get all the way there in the current phase of your system, it is important to keep this ultimate goal in play as you move forward.

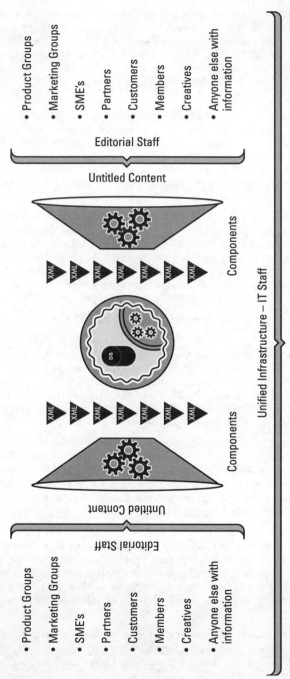

Figure 14-1: To do its job, a CMS must integrate many of the parts of an organization.

Content Management versus Other Systems

All organizations have systems that capture, store, and give access to data. A CMS rarely replaces these data systems. Rather, it brings the same degree of management to content that the organization is accustomed to applying to data. This is not to say that no interaction exists between the two sorts of systems. Especially in the publication system, significant interaction may occur.

Consider a typical staff management data system. Such a system has data about each employee or member of the organization, including name, ID, address, compensation package, position, and so on. The human resources and administration departments are likely to access the system via a specialized application. You are not likely to want to replace this system with a CMS. You may, however, want to connect the CMS to the system. For example, you might want to create a printed and Web-based company directory. You can base such a directory on the data system as follows: Once a week, software that is part of the CMS repository contacts the employee data system and retrieves data records for new or changed employees. It also retrieves the IDs of any employees that have left the organization. For each new employee, the CMS software adds a work item. The work item tells a CMS collection staff member to get a picture and a memorable quote from each new person and to add these items to the data that has already been retrieved. When employees leave the company, the software automatically deletes their information from the CMS repository. To create the Web-based and printed directories, the CMS publication staff creates templates that draw the employee information out of the repository and format it as a set of Web pages and as a book.

In addition to being integrated with other data systems, the CMS itself is an organizational system that requires the same sort of administration and maintenance as other organizational systems. Like any data system, the CMS is one in an overall set of systems that run the organization.

Tracking Information Flow in the Organization

All organizations create content. To create a successful CMS, you must be able to separate the content with a value that goes beyond the context in which it was created from the content that serves one specific purpose and does not need to be managed and shared. Put another way, not all information is important enough to be managed. Your job is to find the kinds of information that are important enough and begin there.

It is not uncommon for valuable content never to make it out of local distribution within a small segment of the organization. In order to do its best, the CMS must reach into each area where valuable information exists and tap into it. To reach in and tap, the CMS must be designed to target the right information sources, creators, and accumulators. The system must be easy to use, even for employees with little or no background in the CMS.

In a typical organization, valuable information and functionality is created at all organizational levels, as shown in Figure 14-2.

After it's created, information can flow within the organization in a number of ways.

Some information is created by an individual, who then passes it on to others higher up in the organization in the form of reports, analyses, presentations, and recommendations. The creator of this sort of information usually thinks of it as creating a particular deliverable for a particular person. Often, the creator does not consider his information to be valuable beyond its original purpose (whether or not this is true).

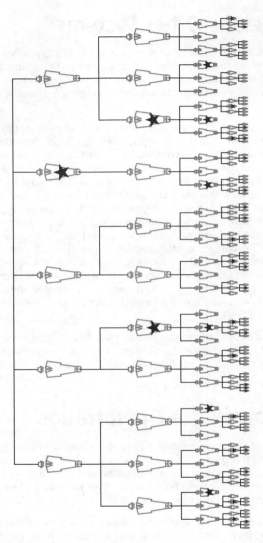

Figure 14-2: Valuable information and functionality (represented by the stars) is created throughout the organization.

Other times, a manager creates information and distributes it to her team. Information such as plans, policies, new initiatives, and background is developed to give context to employees but, often, this information is not considered to be generally useful by its creator (whether or not this is true).

Finally, some information is created by an individual who then distributes it to peers. Information (such as discipline-specific analyses, tips and tricks, and training resources) is developed and distributed to help certain people do their jobs more effectively. Once again, this information, often, is not considered generally useful but certainly may be.

If you begin to notice and then actually chart the creation and flow of information in your organization, you are mapping out the sources and reservoirs of valuable content in your organization as the first step toward actually harvesting it.

Understanding your information

People will not naturally seek out the CMS and contribute to it. Rather, the CMS team must seek out contributors and go to them. To begin, you must define what makes information valuable to your organization. If you don't know what is valuable you will not know where to find it and will end up putting a lot of effort into information that is not important. (See Chapter 18, "Doing Logical Design," in the section "From business to system" for a look at one process to decide what the most important information is.) Some of this valuable information comes from outside the organization (industry news, for example) and some comes from within the organization (case studies, for example). For the information originating inside the organization, you must discover the following:

✦ Where in the organization is it created?

✦ What particular people or job descriptions create the information?

✦ What is its initial purpose?

✦ To whom is it distributed?

✦ Are there places (individual computers, network directory locations, or file cabinets) where the information naturally collects?

✦ Are there particular people or job descriptions that collect and save this information out of interest or as a job function?

✦ In what formats is it produced?

The main obstacles to harvesting information from the organization are finding it, understanding how to remove it from its original context, and overcoming any adverse attitudes in its creators. However, if you can answer the questions in this list, you at least understand what information lives inside the organization.

Note   If you are having trouble discovering what information exists in your organization and what value it might have to your organization and audiences, you might try conducting an information audit. A great place to start learning about this subject is Elizabeth Orna's book *Information Strategy in Practice*.

Understanding your functionality

All organizations create and distribute functionality (even if only internally and on paper). Just as the CMS must reach into the organization to tap into the valuable content that exists in the organization, so the CMS must reach into the organization to tap into the valuable functionality (like the functionality that enables someone update her own HR records, or the functionality that allows customers to see their past transactions). And just as with content, you first should learn about your functionality and then plan for its harvest. The main obstacles to harvesting functionality are making it suitable for electronic distribution, tying into existing programming processes, and overcoming any adverse attitudes in your programmers and administrators.

Functionality, like content, might exist throughout the organization. To understand the functionality in your organization, you might start with these questions:

✦ Where in the organization is it created and maintained?

✦ Is it suitable for being segmented and delivered electronically on a Web site? If not, what would need to be added or changed?

✦ Who is responsible for programming the functionality? Was it developed in-house or is it part of a commercial package?

✦ Who is responsible for managing the data behind the functionality?

✦ Can it be accessed by code executed on a Web server?

✦ Who is the current audience for this functionality?

✦ What knowledge or experience is required for someone to use the functionality?

✦ Is there other functionality to which the functionality is related or on which it depends?

So, before you begin to work on your organization to prepare it for CM, first find the parts of the organization that produce the functionality that you will manage. Chart the current creation and flow of functionality so that you can decide and influence how it should flow.

The Enterprise CMS and One Source of the Truth

Deploying a content management system is not strictly a technology decision; it's also a business decision. While choosing and deploying an effective enterprise content management system involves many hours of input and work from an organization's IT staff, it also requires a commensurate amount of commitment from business users. Enterprise content management systems ultimately solve business problems, not technology problems. It is crucial that the business users, the owners of the processes and information, have bought into and, ideally, initiated the process of deploying an enterprise content management system.

Vignette technology powers many of the most highly trafficked Web sites in the world. One of the biggest benefits organizations identify after deploying an enterprise content management system from Vignette is the ability to have "One source of the truth" through the virtual repository model they've deployed. What this means is that a company has a single version of a document that is re-purposed throughout the entire enterprise. There is no need for duplicating, copying, and saving the information to local drives, with the accompanying revision and maintenance headaches and risks that go with multiple copies of a document maintained in multiple locations. By having one source of the truth, organizations can easily update content once and have it reflected on every Web point, alleviating contradictory and incorrect information.

Some enterprise content management systems replicate or duplicate information, or batch the delivery of information to a separate content repository. The implications of such a design should be carefully considered. Inherent in this model is the possibility that different documents can exist for days or weeks, presenting customers, partners and suppliers with potentially inaccurate or outdated information. Business users are forced to rely on IT administrators for revision management.

There are many benefits to deploying an enterprise content management system, such as a lessened dependence on IT and providing a consistent brand look and feel on all Web properties. Some of the most compelling benefits manifest themselves only once the system has been installed, including the efficiency and power of a single source of the truth.

Leif Pedersen, Vice president of worldwide marketing and market strategy,
Vignette Corporation△ (www.vignette.com)

Understanding Organizational Roles

Each of the major groups in your organization has something different to add to a CMS initiative, as the following list indicates:

✦ **Business units** create the valuable content and functionality that the organization must deliver. These groups are, or should be, designed to produce important information effectively.

✦ **Editorial teams** aim to create unified content across the organization.

✦ **Marketing teams** create a definitive audience analysis and unified messaging in all publications.

✦ **The IT group** implements and maintains the CMS infrastructure and, possibly, is responsible for functionality.

Business units generate value

The valuable information and functionality that the organization delivers comes from business units. Don't be confused by my use of the term *business* here. The member services group within a non-profit organization and the printing office within a government organization are as much business units as the engineering group in a commercial manufacturer. Business units are, or should be, designed to produce important information effectively. In addition, business functionality (ordering, getting support, making deals, and so on) originates and terminates in a business group. Business units should rightly be expected to create the value that the organization needs to deliver.

On the other hand, business units should not necessarily be expected to know how to gather, target, or deliver this value. Often, the valuable information the unit produces remains lodged on some individual's computer and never sees wide distribution. In addition, much of the valuable information is produced for an internal audience. Product specifications, for example, are extremely valuable information that is often inaccessible to the outside world because of its style or format.

Editorial teams unify content

All organizations create some sort of written communication. Organizations employ technical writers to create product documentation, marketing writers to create brochures and press releases, and subject matter experts to create white papers and other background documents. In addition to these writers (and other content producers, such as graphic artists) is a group of editors who ensure that the output of the various writers is aligned and consistent. Consistency is the currency of content management. Without a strictly consistent approach to content structuring and tagging, the CMS cannot manage or publish content effectively. If your organization has editors, they should mediate between the business units and the central repository. Editors within the business units forge consistency within the content of the units. Editors outside any business unit forge consistency in the organization's content. When you implement a CMS, these two types of editors should form a common understanding and a common set of rules to make the editorial processes flow smoothly between the business units and the larger CMS effort. Many organizations recognize the need for editorial consistency across the organization in the form of a corporate communications style guide — often adopted from another organization or from a standard editorial style reference such as the *Chicago Manual of Style*.

On the other hand, editorial organizations are rarely called upon to perform the very granular metadata tagging needed by a CMS. Thus, editorial skills in the organization must be augmented by the metatorial skills needed to develop and apply the level of metadata consistency required by a CMS.

Marketing teams direct and unify publications

An organization's marketing group is responsible for understanding and controlling the way the organization presents itself to the outside world. Two of the main ways that marketers present the organization is through branding and messaging. The brand is the identity of the organization. It is a set of traits and associations that encompass how the organization wants to be seen by the world. Messaging consists of the small set of clear messages that the organization wants to deliver to the world (for example, "We are the place for information on the third world," or "Buy our cars and you will have lots of admirers"). Because of this responsibility, the marketing group is often in control of all the organization's communication, including its Web site and other publications. What the marketing group brings to these publications is clear, directed communication about who the organization is and what the organization most wants the world to know about it. In terms of content management, the marketing group plays an even more central role—it knows the audiences. The marketing group knows what kind of people the organization is trying to serve and what these people want. This is the key knowledge that enables the organization to identify and target valuable content and functionality.

On the other hand, the marketing group often knows little about the technology and process behind designing and building a CMS. The analysis and development skills needed to create a CMS are often beyond the desire and ability of a marketing group.

Why Organizational Roles Are Important

So often the lack of content quality is one of the critical competitive weaknesses and costly challenges within organizations. Content management can bring about accuracy, relevancy, and consistency... but not just by implementing a technology solution and communicating a change in processes.

Other than establishing the vision of success, getting clarity about roles and responsibilities is the single most important starting place for any project. If you're in a position to influence the direction of content management within your organization, you have several choices in bringing about clear roles and responsibilities: establishing a governance framework, leading by example, setting the standard by "owning" the content repository (or repositories), developing and deploying standard templates, delivering "deployment" tools, running quality checks (for example, link checkers), delivering user analysis, documenting and facilitating "proven good practices," and even establishing training for content managers. How you achieve these will depend on the culture you work in: Is it competency-based, collaborative, control-based or cultivation-based? How are decisions made—as a group via consensus, or, at the other extreme, by an individual on their own? Take culture into consideration and establish clear roles and responsibilities.

Successful organizations know that the cost to their customers, partners, and employees is high without clear roles and responsibilities within the organization.

Mary Lee Kennedy, The Kennedy Group (www.maryleekennedy.com)

IT groups build and maintain infrastructure

An organization's IT group keeps the computer hardware and software running and performing. Because a CMS is a set of interlocking software and hardware components, the role of the IT group is clear — to install and administer the system. In addition, the IT group has the knowledge and experience (or should have) to integrate the CMS into the array of other organizational systems (catalog and staff data systems, for example) that the CMS needs in order to provide content and, especially, functionality. In one sense, the CMS is just another enterprise information system and can be maintained by the same group and in the same way that other systems are.

On the other hand, just as you would not ask an IT professional to enter invoices into the organization's accounts receivable system, so you would not ask her to create content or publications. The natural place for the IT group is not creating the content but in supporting the system behind the content.

None of the groups I have discussed are candidates for sole and exclusive ownership of the CMS. They *are*, however, integral players in the overall success of the CMS effort, and each has a different contribution.

What Can Be Shared?

It would be silly to think that, right off the bat, your organization can share all aspects of the CM products and processes it will need. Even if that is your ultimate goal, in the near term it may be more useful and realistic for you to share the parts of the system that give you the most advantage for the least effort. Certain elements may make better candidates for an early sharing effort, namely *product*, *code*, *content*, and *publications*.

Product

Most people think that collaborating on CM means buying one product for everyone to use. In fact, sharing a product can be a good way to collaborate, but it is certainly not the only way. In addition, exactly how you share a CM product can vary from minimal to maximal as the following list shows:

✦ You can simply buy an enterprise license for the CMS and then have everyone who might make use of it install it separately. Here you are simply sharing costs.

✦ You can provide support and training for common uses. Through a support and training effort, you can foster the development of common skills in your staff members and also provide shared administrative resources.

✦ You can share technical and administrative staff. Even if you are not using the same installation of the product, you can possibly still leverage staff and technical expertise.

✦ You can share the repository. If you don't share the same repository or methodologies, you don't have to confront the issue of standardization across the enterprise — at least not yet. However, when it's for real, *sharing* means sharing the same repository.

Installing separate versions of the product may be the easiest to do, but you glean more benefits from using it as a point of collaboration across the organization, and you can do so in stages. For example, your organization may be able to distribute the CMS and provide integrated training and support in the short term while your CMS team figures out how to create a repository that all groups can share in the longer term.

Code

Sharing code development can similarly provide a range of benefits, depending on the level of sharing your organization wants to (or is able to) achieve. From lowest (least integrated) to highest (most integrated):

✦ You can standardize on a development platform across the organization, possibly through site licenses, to save money and provide the basis for further sharing.

✦ You can share techniques, tools, and training costs across the organization.

✦ You can share modules that are developed in-house. For example, a form to provide users with a single sign-on might be developed for one group and used by all.

✦ You can syndicate the development of functionality. For example, if one group writes a search UI, you can ask them to do it in such a way that other groups can also make use of their work with some modification to fit their own purposes.

✦ You can actually use the same code across the organization—that is, develop whole systems that everyone in the organization can use.

Once again, the first is easiest and the last is most integrated and unified. As you might guess, developing the integrated solution may or may not present more technical challenges than a less-integrated system, but it definitely will require more work in understanding and addressing all your audiences' needs and requirements.

Content

Content and functionality are more alike than different in the CM world, as I discuss in Chapter 4, "Functionality Is Content, Too!" Consequently, sharing content parallels sharing code:

✦ You can share discrete pieces of content in whatever form. For example, you may post files on a common network location or intranet site and let everyone know they're there. You may create Adobe Acrobat versions of your files, enabling anyone to view your content without regard to tools and file formats.

✦ You can try to syndicate to each other using standard interchange file formats that you agree upon. This could be as simple, for example, as splitting up the tasks of collection among several groups, and agreeing that the product of each can be adapted by all for their own needs.

✦ You can share parts of the content model so that everyone creates content in exactly the same way. A typical example would be a set of templates and editorial guides so that all press releases are standardized, with the same elements filled in the same way.

✦ You can share the whole content model. Depending on the type of system and content model you have (component-driven or schema-driven), this might require a moderate or a high level of integration.

Again, sharing small bits of content is easiest, but integrating your content sharing yields the most value. In practice, you may find that your organization shares content at several or all these levels.

Publications

Sharing in the creation of publications can range from the superficial to the thorough:

✦ You can share look-and-feel across publications of a similar type and across the organization. For example, your organizations might create standard branding elements and style sheets that everyone is required to use. Often, the publications specialists are the ones who enforce this uniformity at the publishing stage.

✦ You can share page templates across the organization so that, for example, the actual page-building mechanisms and processes are common across all content of the same type. (Page templates are distinct from the templates the authors use to create the content, but might depend on the consistency that authoring templates enforce when it comes time to build the pages.)

✦ You can share publication functionality. For example, a good navigation system that you develop for one group may be useful across other groups as well.

✦ You can share the whole publication system. Everyone is aware of and using the system in a highly integrated way to publish most of or all the content that the organization publishes.

Just sharing look-and-feel is easiest, and many organizations are still striving to achieve just this level of sharing. As you move down the list, the value of integration is greater, as is the effort required to achieve it.

How do you decide?

You have a number of considerations to guide you in deciding how much your organization can and should share. For starters, look for existing overlaps that signal opportunities, such as:

✦ **What overlap in goals and audiences do we have?** If there is overlap, this represents an opportunity to integrate publication sharing more thoroughly.

✦ **What overlap in content do we have?** Look for redundant or at least similar kinds of content across the organization — the more similarities you see, the higher the potential benefits from sharing content.

✦ **What overlap in technology do we have?** Different products that do the same thing or different groups that have independently developed different solutions to the same problem are signals that sharing products and code would benefit all.

That said, sharing does not always make sense. Don't be afraid to stand up for not sharing when sharing is not warranted. If the extent to which sharing makes sense is not clear because of the enormity of the organization and its content, consider starting with a set of smaller groups based on the sharing needs you can identify.

As you address the overlaps, your level of sharing may be a staged plan. As these lists suggest, you may be able to get immediate benefit from doing intermediate levels of sharing (picking the proverbial low-hanging fruit) while you plan for and implement a more integrated strategy. Implementing interim measures can also help build institutional support as sponsors and others see the near-term benefits. Small local steps in the right direction might converge later.

Finally, it's quite possible that within an organization there really are distinct content domains that would not benefit from sharing. Beware, however, of those who attempt to convince you of this at the outset!

Cross-Reference   I talk more about the content domain in Chapter 30, "Designing Content Access Structures," in the section "The content domain."

Exploring Organizational Models

For simplicity, I present content management systems as single systems. Although it is surely most efficient to have a single system throughout the organization, it is by no means mandatory. If a single, monolithic CMS represents too much of a hurdle too soon for your organization, you can create a more or less loosely coupled system of relatively independent but interacting systems.

It's never a good idea to force a CMS on the organization. You are too much in need of the organization's active and creative participation ever to risk that sort of alienation. Rather, you need to figure out how the CMS can bring value to the groups it will encompass. You need to be clearly convinced that the CMS brings value to a group greater than the cost they will bear. Then you can present your case to the group and hope for the best. Be prepared for groups not to be convinced immediately. They may have a lot of personal and financial investment in the way they do things now. Think as objectively as possible: Is the problem that they just don't want to change? Is it that you have not presented your case well? Or do you just not have a compelling case?

A Good Idea Well-Presented

One of the first things I ask new clients is, "Can a good idea that is well presented and well defended be adopted in your organization?" I've received many strange looks when I've asked this question and more than a few non-responses from people who would rather not openly discuss the issue. But overall, this question has led to some of the best organizational-dynamics conversations I have ever had.

The point of the question is to understand the mechanism by which the organization adopts a new idea. In the ideal world, the governors of the organization would forthrightly discuss the merits of the idea, weighing every pro and con, and would adopt it or deny it based on its merits alone. Conversely, in the most cynical world, the merit of the idea would not count for anything. Adoption or denial would be granted solely on the basis of how the idea would help or hinder the personal agendas of the individual governors. If it would help enough powerful people, the idea would be adopted. Those whom it would ignore or even subvert would oppose the idea to whatever extent they could.

The real world is somewhere between those two extremes. Just because a CMS is a good idea, it does not mean that it will be adopted. On the other hand, just because the CEO favors a CMS, it does not mean that it *should* be adopted. You need to be sure that you have a good idea, that it is well presented, and that you can defend it against all reasoned attacks. In addition, you need to have an idea that has political support and can be defended against interpersonal attacks.

If, in the end, good ideas win out in your organization, you are pretty safe. Content management is a good idea.

For any of these reasons, you may need to fall back to a looser connection between the CMS and a particular group. You have a number of ways to loosen the connection.

Collection variations

On the collection side, the "normal" way to proceed is by having contributors submit content directly to the central CMS repository (see Figure 14-3).

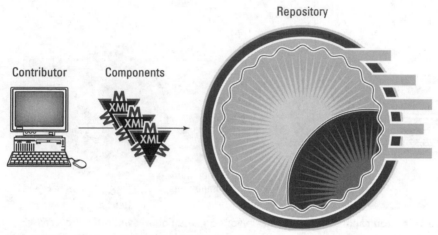

Figure 14-3: The usual collection mode

It is not always possible, however, to immediately encompass every group's collection process. Suppose that a group is already creating a set of print publications that you can't duplicate with your CMS in the near future. Still, you need the content in those print publications for the Web site that the CMS will produce. Rather than taking on a task you know you can't do, or worse, forcing a group to "dumb-down" their publications so you can create them, you can get the group to behave like a syndication source, as shown in Figure 14-4.

Your main task in this scenario is to get the other group to begin to think of its own system as a CMS. If they can figure out how to separate their own content from its publications, they can figure out how to give clean input to your CMS. Even if they never fully automate their process, you still will have accomplished two major tasks:

✦ The group will be on the road to becoming a full part of the CMS. As they get better at separating their content from their own publications, they will make their own compromises in their publications and learn the art of CM along the way.

✦ You will get a good content source without having to participate in its creation. Given that you can get the group to give you good stuff (valid XML, for example), you will have all you need to easily incorporate their content in your repository.

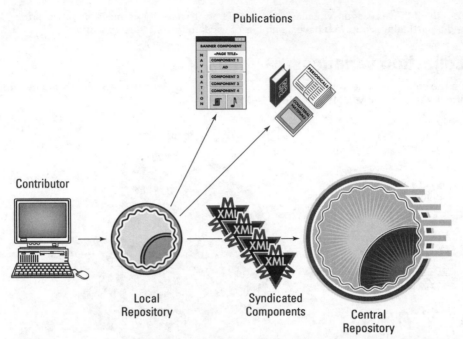

Figure 14-4: You can treat other groups in your organization as syndication sources.

What you lose in this approach is time and control of the master source. You probably will not receive content from this group until it has already been released in their publications. In addition, can you be sure that they will not make significant changes to the content after they deliver it to you? However, if a realistic assessment of the group indicates that you will not be able to completely integrate, you should go for the next best thing, syndication. If syndication does not work, you may be left pulling apart and converting completed publications.

Publishing variations

On the publishing side, the usual way to proceed is to have the CMS create all the publications, as illustrated in Figure 14-5.

But it is not always practical or advisable to have the CMS control all publications (at least, not right away). Suppose that you have a group that has already set up a dynamic Web presence with a set of content databases and a complete Web infrastructure. Rather than migrating all this to the CMS publication system and Web platform, you can simply fill their databases full of content from your repository (see Figure 14-6).

Using this method, you can embrace all the collection and management of content destined for the site without disrupting the site itself. In effect, you are syndicating content to the Web database. Although this may require some programming on your part, it will probably be a lot less work than re-creating the entire site from your CMS.

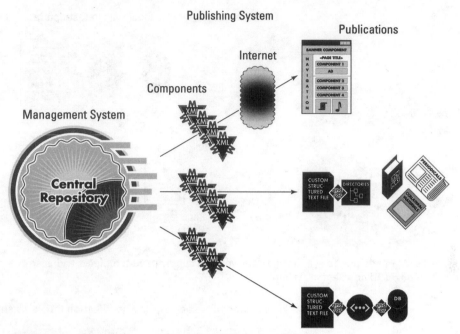

Figure 14-5: The usual case, where the CMS creates all publications

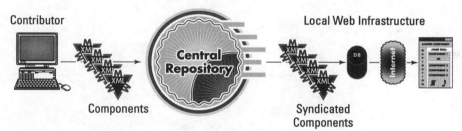

Figure 14-6: Using the tools you have for syndication, you can fill a Web database with content.

Of course, you may want to re-create some of the site. For example, maybe the site design is out of line with the other publications you are creating, or maybe the site really should include other content that it is not currently set up to handle. In this case, you may want to consider having the CMS produce not only data for the site, but also some of its page templates and even some of its pages (see Figure 14-7).

This scenario is a bit tricky. To produce page templates for an existing Web site, you have to know a lot about the code and conventions of that site. In effect, your CMS would be managing much of the publishing of the external site. To produce pages, you have to make sure that they fit into the site. Both the look-and-feel as well as the navigation must match the way the site is constructed. Of course, if you are producing templates for the site, both of these variables are already in your control.

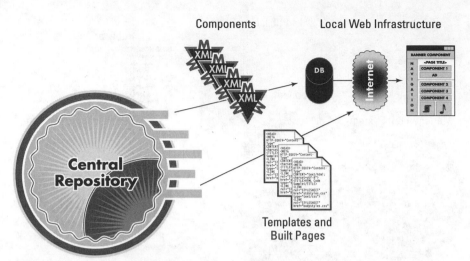

Figure 14-7: In addition to syndicating data, you can supply page templates and even complete pages to an external system.

Finally, you can simply treat any system external to the CMS as a syndication target, as shown in Figure 14-8.

The external system controls its own publications and may have other content that you do not control.

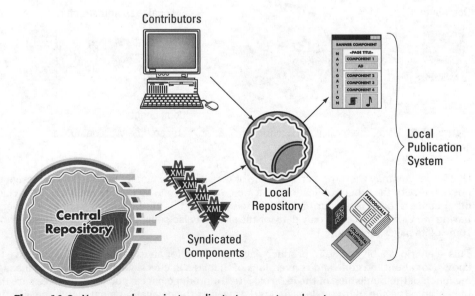

Figure 14-8: You can always just syndicate to an external system.

The long and short of this story is that if you can't (or don't want to) encompass the needs of a group, then you should aim for making the intersection of two groups as organized and clean as possible. In essence, this means your two groups must coordinate your content structure and workflow processes.

Management variations

In all the collection and publishing variations I mentioned, the only thing that was absolutely under the control of the CMS was the central repository. Even if the external collection system is syndicating to the CMS, the central repository contains the definitive content to be shared by the organization. If you back off and allow the definitive content to be shared in two or more places, you are asking for trouble.

It is not so much that you shouldn't have more than one database, but that you shouldn't have more than one content structure and access methodology (if you can help it). Regardless of how many physical databases you have, if you have a single organizational structure for your content and unified access methods, you have a single repository. On the other hand, if you do not have a single organizational structure and unified access, even if you have all your content in a single database, you do not have a single repository.

That said, if you can manage to have a single database for all your content, you will spare yourself the unenviable task of distributed data management. At the very least, you must have a single place where you can tell people to go to get the blessed version of a particular kind of content.

Optimally, you want to create a central repository that really unifies your content and content access (see Figure 14-9).

Figure 14-9: A central repository unites content structure and access.

Communication in Organizational Models

Communication is also a huge part of an organizational model, especially in a distributed organization, where all team members may not be physically located together. For example, recently a project team had the apparent luxury of starting from scratch to design a CMS for their content. However, the entire editorial team was on the West Coast and the entire technical team on the East Coast. The editorial team knew what they were looking for in a CMS, and tried valiantly to communicate those needs to the technical team, but had little success until an outside party was brought in to broker the conversation. Even then, progress was often slow, and required constant course corrections with prototypes and mockups to make sure both parts of the team were on the same page.

This disconnection in mental models of what a CMS is can be helped by clear requirements definition and strategic objectives that all the team generates together and can agree upon. Using these as a constant reminder of what the CMS is being built for helps keep expectations at a reasonable level, and helps prioritize the actual deliverables for everyone. The editorial team is under pressure to get content out, and often will be far ahead of the technical team in their expectations, so it's important to have a means to synchronize the two through continuous updates and standard reports.

It's a lot more fun to build the system and create the content than it is to keep everybody on the same page, but without that extra effort, frustration and problems will end up taking the pleasure out of the whole project.

Michael Crandall, Chair, Masters of Science in Information Management Program, University of Washington Information School

To function as a central repository, your system must extend the following qualities over all your content:

✦ **Unified content structure.** The way content is chunked and tagged (your components and their elements) must be standardized across all data sources.

✦ **Unified organization.** The hierarchies and other organizational schemes you use to categorize and get to your content must extend to any place where the content is stored.

✦ **Unified access.** The way you query and make use of the content you retrieve must be the same across all data sources.

My best advice concerning management variations is to try not to vary too much. The headaches you will have—trying to keep track of what content is in what structure, organization, and access system—will be unending. You will also inevitably find yourself in a position of not being able to get to the content you need in a publication or particular page. On the other hand, sometimes you have no choice but to have different kinds of content in different places and structures. If you find yourself in this situation, your job will be to manage the mapping from one system to another and to make sure you always know which source has the master version of which content components. This could be a big job for the systems administrator or content manager who is tasked with it.

Using Functional Collection and Publishing

By far, your best bet is to have a single central repository and management system that extends across all the content you will manage. That's not the case with collection and publication systems. As long as all contributors and publishers use the same small set of interfaces to the management system, you are free to allow them to do their own thing—within limits.

In fact, for a system with real enterprise reach, you release control of specific collection and publication activities and focus instead on serving general collection and publication needs. At first, you are most likely to create the specific collection systems that gather the content you have identified. Likewise, you create specific publications. As time goes on, however, other content and publications may come to the fore that you also want to include. Rather than continually trying to do the collection and publication for the organization, you can start providing the tools for groups to do it for themselves.

Note   You may rightly be saying at this point that it will be hard enough to do this in your own team, let alone teach everyone else. This will be true for the first few versions of the CMS, but eventually you will be ready.

Organizing collection systems and publications by type

A good architecture for taking a distributed approach to collection and publication activities is to focus on types of inputs and publications (see Figure 14-10).

After you have developed a process for bringing in Microsoft Word files, for example, you need not develop another process just because another group also has Word files. Instead, you can take the process you developed for group A and extend it so that group A *and* group B can both use it. In the end, your process should be general enough that group Z can train on it and adopt it without much intervention on your part at all. As you might expect, the learning curves will be steepest for the early adopters (and for you) as you sort out the basic process during the first iteration.

Likewise, for publications, you can begin to class your publications by type and extend your publication methods so that they can be used by others with the same types of needs.

When you have reached the state where you can route most new content and publications through standard collection and publishing interfaces, you have a CMS with a very compelling value proposition for your organization. Your proposition might run something like the following:

> You can do your own thing and continue to face all the problems that we have had (and resolved) over the last two years, or you can sign up with us (the CMS team). With a short training session and an agreement to adhere to some standards, you can be up and running very quickly. Your contributors will have well-tested and full-featured tools for creating your content, and your publications will have all the bells and whistles of the best publications our organization now offers.

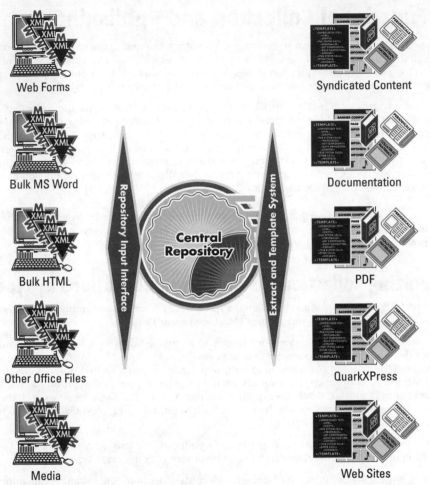

Web Forms

Bulk MS Word

Bulk HTML

Other Office Files

Media

Central Repository

Repository Input Interface

Extract and Template System

Syndicated Content

Documentation

PDF

QuarkXPress

Web Sites

Figure 14-10: In the long run, you can focus on types of input and output, not on particular components and publications.

Creating functional teams

In addition to organizing your CMS functionally, by type of input and output, you can organize your team functionally by dividing it into central teams and a variable number of independent collection and publishing teams. Dividing your team in this way offers a number of advantages:

✦ **You can distribute the cost** of the system, and especially new additions to it, across the organization. Each group that wants to join the CMS initiative can field and pay for its own team.

✦ **You can give a fair measure of independence** to participating groups. As long as they stay within the CMS guidelines, they should be free to organize their effort as they see fit.

✦ **You make your initiative more scalable** by creating a small central group that maintains standards and starts other teams and any number of independently operating peripheral groups. As the effort grows, the central group will grow only very slowly. The peripheral groups provide most of the new staff required to collect or publish more content.

✦ **You make a place for the people who know the content** best to be in control of its creation and for the people who know the audiences best to prepare publications for them.

The set of groups I show in Figure 14-11 represents one way to organize your CMS modularly so that you can adapt as your CMS matures.

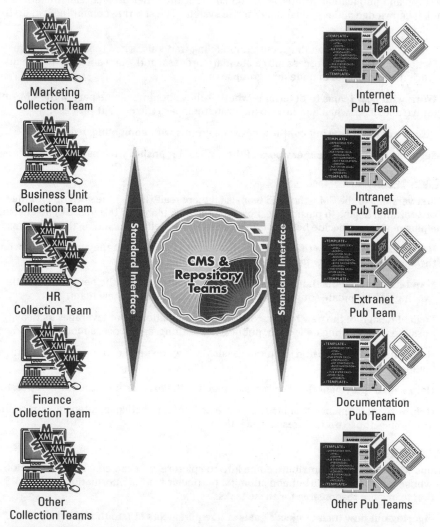

Figure 14-11: The functional teams of a mature CMS

The functional teams of a CMS fall into several categories. Beginning with the core groups that establish the mandate and assemble around the initial CMS effort, additional functional teams organize around the collection, management, and publishing domains of the CMS.

The CMS steering committee

The steering committee is the ongoing remnant of the mandate and requirements processes. (For more about this crucial step in a CMS project, see Chapter 16, "Securing a Project Mandate.") They are the people in the organization who have a continuing interest in the system and enough authority, expertise, or both, to determine the direction of the CMS. The steering committee can have representatives from the CMS project sponsors, members of significant contribution and publication groups, and CMS analysts and other project team members with continuing knowledge and responsibility for the system. The steering committee can do the following:

✦ **Set CMS standards,** including content modeling tradeoffs, when to make a custom collection or publishing process into a standard process, and when and how to extend current standards to include new groups.

✦ **Work with new teams** to determine whether they should become part of the CMS initiative and, if so, when and how to integrate them into the current process.

✦ **Resolve content-sharing conflicts** between groups with competing needs.

✦ **Serve as the ultimate supervisors** of the CMS and repository teams.

The CMS team

In the first versions of the CMS, the CMS team is all there really is. As time goes on and the rest of the organization begins to participate, however, the CMS team can take more of an advisory role, helping new teams decide how best tie into the existing effort, including the following:

✦ **Readiness assessments** that help the new team to decide what they have so far, what they still need, and how they will fit into the existing standards.

✦ **Mandate assessments** that help create team mandates and fit the new team into the existing CMS mandate (or modify the CMS mandate to fit the new team).

✦ **Logical design** of the new team's content and publications that leverages as heavily as possible from existing collection, publication, staffing, and process models.

✦ **Help with implementation,** including assistance with specifications, development, and testing.

✦ **Help with deployment** that leverages as much of the existing infrastructure as possible.

✦ **Help with maintenance** that fits the new team into the existing maintenance procedures or modifies those procedures as needed.

Collection teams

As groups with content to contribute come into the picture, you can constitute collection teams whose purpose is to gather and submit a particular kind of information to the CMS. Collection teams are responsible for these tasks:

✦ **Figuring out how their project's goals** and requirements fit into those of the wider CMS.

✦ **Performing a logical analysis of their collection needs,** including defining audiences, authors, sources, components, staff, and workflow.

✦ **Designing any additional conversion processes** needed for information from acquisition sources.

✦ **Implementing, deploying, and maintaining** any additional software and hardware that is particular to their systems.

The repository team

The repository team members are the keepers of the system and its standards. Team members may well overlap with those in the CMS team, which got the CMS up and running. The repository team is responsible for the following:

✦ **The CMS system,** including any ongoing installation, maintenance, or enterprise integration issues.

✦ **Ongoing training** on, and updates to, the CMS content schemas, including new and updated content types and elements.

✦ **Standard collection interfaces,** including any Web-based form interfaces and batch upload systems.

✦ **Standard publication interfaces,** including the templating, personalization, and integration systems.

Publishing teams

As more groups arrive with needs for publications, you can create publication teams that design and maintain the new publications. If you are making the best reuse of the content in your organization, you have far more publication teams than collection teams (although a single publication team may handle a range of similar publications). Only so many sources of information exist in the organization, but it has an unlimited number of ways to use that information. Publication teams are responsible for the following tasks:

✦ **Figuring out how their project's goals** and requirements fit into those of the wider CMS.

✦ **Performing a logical analysis of the publication** needs, including defining audiences, components, templates, personalization, staff, and workflow.

✦ **Doing publication design,** including page layout and content, look-and-feel, editorial and graphic style guidelines, and user interface.

✦ **Implementing, deploying, and maintaining** any additional software and hardware that is peculiar to their systems.

Identifying Your CMS Hurdles

As much as an organization may need the services of a CMS, it might not be easy for members to agree on and implement a CMS. As a colleague likes to say, "When you pour milk on oatmeal, all the lumps come to the top." Likewise, when you install a system that touches as much of the organization as a CMS does, all the disorganization and local tensions come to the fore. In addition, the CMS requires a level of coordination and effort that many organizations are hard-pressed to muster. Following are some of the hurdles an organization may need to overcome to be successful when implementing a CMS:

✦ **Who owns the system?** The organization's departments must be able to work together to plan and implement the CMS, regardless of which group initiates or leads the effort. It will require contribution from a wide range of groups. Organizations that are mired in intergroup rivalries risk failure in implementing a CMS.

✦ **What is our content model?** The major part of a successful CMS is a single, comprehensive scheme that says what all your content is, what each part consists of, and how each type relates to the others. Without such a scheme, you have little chance of successfully sharing content across groups and publications. The key to creating a content scheme is constructive debate and compromise. No one person or group can dictate the whole scheme; rather, it is agreed to and shared across the organization. The organization's departments must be able to work together to create this scheme. In addition, the content must be untangled and organized into a tight system. If the departments can't cooperate or if the content itself is too scattered and disorganized, the CMS project is at risk.

✦ **How do we create general content?** Most content creators are accustomed to writing with a very particular publication in mind. For the CMS to succeed, authors have to think more widely about a set of target audiences and publications. If authors cannot break through to a less-narrow definition of their job, they will not effectively serve the CMS.

✦ **How do we create automatic publications?** Most publication specialists (print producers, Webmasters, and so on) are accustomed to creating publications directly. They lay out a publication and populate it with content by hand. They can change and tweak the layout and content until it satisfies them. In a CMS, publication teams do not create publications. Rather, they create the templates that create the publication. This level of abstraction is sometimes misunderstood or even resisted by publication specialists who prefer to create products, not systems.

✦ **Will the CMS stifle creativity in our authors and publications?** Many authors and publication specialists think that by putting together a CMS, they will no longer be able to express their creativity and will instead become cogs in a system, endlessly producing the same product over and over. Although a CMS does require that content be standardized and publications be created automatically, it does not require that creative efforts cease. Quite the contrary, a CMS requires an enormous amount of creativity to figure out how a base of content can be modeled and then successfully delivered to a potentially diverse set of audiences. The creativity in a CMS is simply at a different level. Rather than being creative at the level of individual content components and publication pages, you must be creative at the level of the types of components, the relationships between components, and the ways that they can be delivered in publications. Far from being a static system, where the same activities happen over and over, the CMS requires constant feedback and refinement to get better at meeting the organization's goals. If authors and publication teams cannot rise to this new level of creativity, the CMS will not succeed.

✦ **Don't we already have a mandate?** Your project team may want to believe that it already has a clear mandate and that no further probing is needed. If this is so, it ought to be easy for members to list the appropriate sponsors to write a complete mandate statement (like the one detailed in Chapter 16, "Securing a Project Mandate," in the section "The project mandate") and have the sponsors sign off on it. It is also possible that they are leery of losing control by bringing in others who might outrank them, are afraid of the controversies they know exist, don't believe that the sponsors have anything to add to the project, or just don't want to be bothered initiating a big process. In any case, proof of a mandate ought to be required before you skip this step.

✦ **How can we do this project when our project team has no power?** This is a real problem, if it is true. True or not, many project teams think this way and silently agree either to proceed covertly or just to give up trying to accomplish anything. Either the team really is disempowered and needs new leadership or a new sponsor, or it just feels that way and needs a renewed sense of itself. One sure way to find out is to get started with a readiness assessment (as outlined in Chapter 15, "Getting Ready for a CMS," in the section "The readiness assessment"). Either your team will start to feel its oats, or it will find exactly where the brick walls are.

In addition to these existential questions, you might encounter a number of simpler problems, such as the following:

✦ **The project has no team.** You will not need a team to start, but before long, you will not be getting much sleep without one.

✦ **There is a division between the team and sponsor.** This can be a killer if left untreated. I've seen more than one project drop dead because of an unresolved but underground conflict between the team and its sponsor.

✦ **The team wants to do it alone.** It is undoubtedly more trouble at the start to solicit a lot of input, but you will pay in the end if you do not.

✦ **The team is not interdisciplinary.** You can start from one department, but you will eventually need an entire range of skills represented on your team. All CMS jobs and skills are listed in Chapter 13, "Staffing a CMS."

✦ **The sponsor is not available.** If you can't get her attention, ask yourself if she is the right sponsor. Then decide exactly what you need from her and ask her very specifically. If you still get no response, find another sponsor.

✦ The **sponsor does not understand or accept her responsibility.** A lack of understanding is easy to deal with — educate her. Not accepting the sponsor role is a bit more difficult. Does she not want the role, not have the time, or not know how to fulfill the role? Keep in the back of your mind that whatever department you and she happen to be in now, this will eventually be an enterprise endeavor. Keep your eye out for potential sponsors who get that idea, have a sincere interest in the issue, and have the wherewithal to help make it happen. If you are lucky enough to find such a person, gravitate toward her, and maybe she will adopt you and your crazy ideas.

✦ **The organization underestimates the magnitude of the problem.** I hope that after reading this far, you are not underestimating the size of your project — but others might. Maybe your organization is not ready for a large-scale solution if it is unaware of a large-scale problem. Maybe you just haven't found enough pain in the organization yet (as described in Chapter 15, "Getting Ready for a CMS," in the section "Look for pain in the organization").

✦ **There is a rush to buy something.** I've seen this one a lot. The organization feels that by making a product purchase, they have done something tangible. Having bought other enterprise software packages, they might also have more of an idea how to accomplish this than how to spec-out a CMS. On the one hand, after you have bought a product, your life simplifies to just how to make a piece of software function. On the other hand, if you don't take the time upfront to figure out what you want, the system might never be able to do what you end up wanting it to do, or you might never actually even figure out what you want to do in your rush to make something happen.

✦ **The team wants to move forward** even though they have no consensus and still have lots of issues to resolve. Direct that frustration toward getting closure on the key issues. If you must move forward, work in the areas that bring the issues into highest focus. If you are being stonewalled by a group that will not send you content samples, for example, make some quick prototypes of their pages and tell them that you will hold them to the component structure you came up with unless you are otherwise notified.

I hope that by giving you this long list of problems (which I ended long before I could have), I have inoculated you against them. Just like a vaccine, maybe if I give you a little bit of the disease now, you will not catch it later.

Structure Is Not the Antithesis of Creativity

"If I have to follow a prescribed structure when I write, it will stifle my creativity." So we hear from staff members asked to work with standardized structure, encoded into XML or SGML by a schema or a document type definition. But just by looking briefly at the ubiquitous nature of structured writing, we learn that following prescribed structures ordinarily frees writers to focus their message and their audience.

Shakespeare wrote sonnets, a remarkably rigid poetic form. Yet his creativity flowered within the form, leading to some of the most beautiful sonnets ever written. Business communications are often heavily structured, from legal documents, policies and procedures, and financial reports to laboratory records and correspondence. Structure engenders predictability both for the information author and for the audience. Authors know what they're supposed to write; readers know what they can expect to read.

Following a prescribed structure for business and technical documents frees authors to be more and not less creative. Reinforcing that structure by developing semantic markup in XML or SGML provides benefits beyond the typical formatting structures we are used to working with in desktop publishing applications. Not only can we ensure that standard structures are maintained by validating them with schemas or DTDs (document type definitions), but we can ensure that content rather than style is emphasized.

Structured writing provides many opportunities for creativity–opportunities that benefit both authors and readers. Plain old text becomes malleable, ready to be repurposed in new ways.

JoAnn Hackos, PhD, Director, The Center for Information-Development Management

Summary

Your organization can be your biggest asset or an albatross around your neck. If you can figure out how to fit the CMS naturally into the organization, and if the organization will let you do so, it can become a part of the fabric of the enterprise.

✦ Content management systems directly serve the organization's need to produce and distribute value.

✦ Information now flows in the organization through well-worn channels. Learn where these channels are and how to tap into them.

✦ Each group has a part to play in the overall system and none has the right to own the system to the exclusion of others.

✦ If you organize functionally and do not force every contributing group into the same collection or publishing model, you will have a better chance of acceptance and scalability.

✦ Any number of factors can slow you down or stop you. If you are aware of those factors from the start, you might be able to head them off before they present a problem.

In the next chapter, I describe some techniques and deliverables you can use to prepare yourself and the organization for a CMS.

✦   ✦   ✦

Getting Ready for a CMS

Before planning the entirely new process that CMS represents, you are well advised to study you current process. Your organization creates and distributes content today. Before designing your new system, you should understand the ways your organization currently creates and publishes information and functionality and what constraints they will put on the system you want to create. Your goal here is to work outward from your CMS project team, to the sponsors of the project within your organization, to the audiences you hope to reach, and to the contributing groups in your organization in an effort to find their needs, constraints, assumptions, and blind spots. The work you put into understanding the organization, its players, and its systems today will be invaluable to planning your new system.

In this chapter, I'll provide an overview of the CMS project process and discuss how you might go about getting yourself and your organization ready for a CMS.

Readiness Jumpstart

At the beginning of this and many of the other chapters in Parts III and IV of this book, you'll find a section called "Jumpstart." Jumpstarts give you a quick summary of the steps that are explained in the chapter that follows. Use jumpstarts as a summary without the weight of detail, or as a quick review if you've already read the chapter and want a checklist of what you need to accomplish to get ready for a CMS.

This Jumpstart summarizes the steps you should take to figure out how ready your organization is for CM before pushing forward into a CM initiative. I describe the complete process for assessing your organization's readiness in the rest of this chapter.

To assess your organization's CMS readiness, follow these steps:

1. Meet with your project team to determine:

   a. What skills the team has now and what skills you will need to complete the process. Discuss what prospects you have for filling the gaps.

   b. Which people and projects are relevant to your current initiative. If the team does not know, decide which people and projects you must learn more about.

2. Send your team out into the organization to determine:

   a. What information management problems people are having.

   b. What successes and failures have occurred in the past and the reasons for these successes or failures.

   c. The key people from whom you must get support and why their support is significant.

   d. Who knows the most about content creation and publishing in the organization and how can you engage them.

3. Form as clear an idea as possible about what you are being asked to do as a team and by whom (your current mandate). Compare this to what you and your team think you should be doing and use it to begin planning a process for making your mandate official.

4. From the people you have identified as important or in the know, discover what they think your content, audiences, and publications should be. Also find out what assumptions they have about the kind of system you will need to collect, manage, or publish content.

5. Gather up as many documents as you can that describe past and current organizational policy toward information. Read these policy documents and make sure your team is aware of all their implications.

6. From all the information you have collected, put together the following deliverables:

   a. A concise, honest, and complete appraisal of how ready your organization is to do the CM project it is proposing.

   b. An inventory and analysis of all the documents you have uncovered that can serve as a reference source for the rest of the project.

   c. A State of the Content System report that makes your findings about the current and proposed systems public and understandable.

   d. An education plan that outlines the gaps in people's understanding of CM and describes how to span them.

   e. A very preliminary project plan and risk analysis that you can use to check the validity and viability of the initiative.

When you have completed this process, you will know where you, your team, and your project stand in the organization.

Understanding the CMS Project Process

Any large software development/integration project has these broad phases:

1. Business justification

2. Requirements gathering

3. Design

4. Implementation

5. Deployment

6. Maintenance

The process I propose for doing a CMS project is quite a bit like this general process, as shown in Figure 15-1.

Even though I use some different names, the ideas are generally the same, as I show here:

1. **Business justification:** This step is taken care of in my readiness assessment and mandate processes. In these two processes, you decide what the organization has accomplished so far and then build consensus around a plan of attack. The readiness assessment is discussed later in this chapter. The mandate process is discussed in Chapter 16, "Securing a Project Mandate."

2. **Requirements gathering:** This is a specific step in my CMS process, but it is not as extensive as the standard process. I favor a short requirements-gathering phase, followed directly by what I call *logical design*. During logical design, you continue to gather requirements of a sort, but your real task is to fashion those requirements into a clear idea of what your system must accomplish. I cover requirements gathering in Chapter 17, "Doing Requirements Gathering," and logical analysis and design in Chapter 18, "Doing Logical Design."

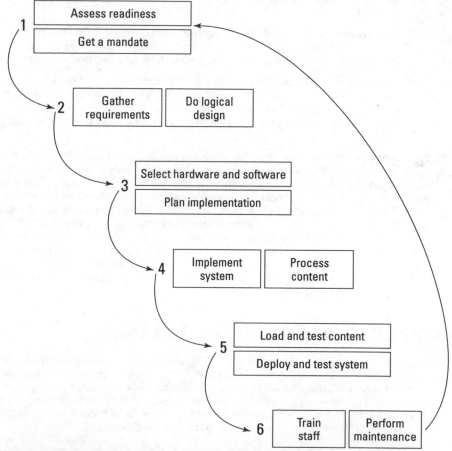

Figure 15-1: The CMS project process follows the same general process as any other large development project.

3. **Design:** In my process, this step begins with logical design, but cannot conclude until you have selected a particular CMS system. In system selection, you use the requirements you have completed and part of the design to create an evaluation process for selecting a CMS product (or, possibly, concluding that you want to build your own). Before you select a system, you have to do enough requirements gathering and design to know what you want. But because the capabilities and features of the CMS product you select (whether bought or built) will affect the design of the system, you have to know what product you will be using to before you can complete and implement the design. Between design and implementation, then, is a system selection stage that overlaps them both. You can find more on system selection in Chapter 19, "Selecting Hardware and Software."

4. **Implementation:** In my model, this step includes the last part of what is often categorized as design — specifications. I call specifications the physical design of the system and include it as the first part of implementation. Following physical design, CMS implementation proceeds as usual — with a lot of programming. In addition to programming, however, in a CMS project, a lot of content processing might be required. So that you accomplish this by the time the system is ready, you must start the preparation work as soon as possible. See Chapter 20, "Implementing the System," for more on implementation.

5. **Deployment:** As with other systems, during this step you install the system in its production environment and test it there. In a CMS project, however, loading and testing the content and publications that the CMS produces is also part of deployment.

6. **Maintenance:** In my model, as in other enterprise systems, a CMS project never ends — it just goes into maintenance mode. This is doubly true of a CMS, where you will be adding content continually and also want to restructure the repository and publications on a regular basis. Deployment and maintenance are covered in Chapter 21, "Rolling Out the System."

The major difference between the CMS process I use and the standard software development cycle is that in the CMS process, you do enough design to fully understand what you want to happen and to be able to select a product (or choose to build your own). Then you select a system that can achieve the design you have made. Next, you complete the design by developing the specifications for your system. After that, you are back on the usual implementation, deployment, and maintenance track. One other significant feature of a CMS project, over and above the usual software development project, is the potential size of the content processing portion of implementation. In the standard development project, moving data into the system is not nearly the task that it can be in a CMS. Of course, a CMS project is a large-scale systems integration project, so it shares a lot with other projects where software must be purchased and integrated into the organization.

Techniques for Getting the Job Done

To get ready for a CMS, you can start within whatever project team you happen to have. Working outward, you can survey the organization for signs of pain related to poor or nonexistent information processes and catalog them for later use. It is most important to try to uncover and document whatever CMS mandate might exist in your organization, to see just what kind of project is currently expected and by whom. Your biggest task is to catalog the current assumptions in the organization on the following important issues:

✦ Audiences

✦ Publications

✦ Content

✦ Infrastructure systems

Having assessed all these, you will have enough background to begin to understand how content can be used to help your organization meet its goals. Then you will be ready to move from the content-oriented systems that currently exist in the organization to the systems that the organization needs to meet its goals.

Start with the project team

Some individual or group must have been given the task of figuring this all out. I state it so vaguely because that is about how precisely most organizations have defined the problem at the start. Generally, a loose consensus confirms that something must be done, but when you ask, "Done about what?" the answers vary. The problems most often cited are the ones I have listed elsewhere. In most minds, they boil down to this statement: "It is too expensive and ineffective to handle our Web presence in the *ad hoc* way we have handled it so far." Somewhat more enlightened minds see the duplication between the Web and other publications as an unnecessary evil. Very few can succinctly define the problem as one of delivering value through information or frame a comprehensive solution.

Even in the fog, everyone seems to have a gut sense that there must be a better way to handle the large and growing body of content that the organization is amassing. Few know to apply the words *content management* to the problem or solution.

In sum, a person or small group is directed by someone to figure it all out. Let's call this group the *project team*. Unfortunately, the person who directs the team to figure it out (the *project initiator*) is often not someone who has the perspective to see the forest for the trees. As often as not, the project initiator has a particular problem to solve (like "I can't get my changed pages on the site fast enough"). In addition, the initiator might or might not have the authority, skill, or desire to pursue the kind of grand solution that this book addresses.

But at least he or she had the foresight to get the process started. What the team will soon need is a solid set of sponsors that do have the perspective to see the entire problem, the foresight to envision a whole solution, the authority to mandate a solution, the skill to negotiate throughout the organization, and the desire to transcend organizational politics and do something new and risky but replete with reward.

One way or another, then, a team is created to figure out how to more effectively create a Web site and maybe other publications as well. Job one for this team is to get their bearings in the organization and chart a course toward a solution that will stick. If they are a savvy team, they will not rush toward a quick-fix solution. Rather, they will hang back a bit (despite the pressure to produce) and try to define the problem, realistically assess the progress the organization has made, build consensus around an appropriate solution, and then begin to build a system. Admittedly, the savviest team in the world might not be able to resist the pressure of nearsighted goals and deadlines, but the savvier they are, the more the team will realize that, in the end, their own success will be judged not on how quickly they acted, but on how well their solution worked.

Still, an enormous amount of finesse and fortitude is called for if you are being asked to do X and you believe that you need to do 100 times X. Of course, I am painting the darkest picture here, a picture of sponsors not up to the job and teams with myopic mandates. I have seen too many of these sorts of situations not to acknowledge them and provide some moral support to those who face them. However, I have also seen sponsors who are up to the task and teams whose mandate is broad indeed.

At any rate, I'll assume that the team has management that is enlightened enough to expect and respect a fair amount of up-front due diligence. This due diligence amounts to understanding what the organization has accomplished already; gaining general agreement on the goals and success metrics of the project; compiling the requirements for audiences, publications, content and infrastructure; and educating the organization to ensure a shared vocabulary and concept set that you can communicate and agree on.

The core tasks of the project team show what skills the team needs to have in order to succeed. The following list addresses the skills that at least one member of your team must possess:

✦ **Analyze and assess your organization.** For this task, you need a *business analyst*. This person is responsible for answering questions like: What groups need to be involved? Whom do I contact to get permission to...? Who are the key supporters we need to have on our side? Who needs what education? How do we maneuver through the organization's bureaucracy? How will we build consensus around a mandate? How do we align and extend organizational goals? How do we measure success? Someone from management is a logical choice for this job, but it must be someone who can manage up and not down. It must also be someone who is quite analytic and strategic in her approach.

✦ **Understand your audiences.** You need an *audience analyst*. This person is responsible for figuring out who the appropriate audiences are, what they want, what you want from them, how finely to divide them, what good analyses exist in the organization, how to align your system to current marketing approaches, what data you need to collect on audience members, and how to collect it. Someone from marketing or public relations is a logical choice for this job, but it must be someone who is less focused on campaigns and more focused on analysis. Someone from an editorial background is also a possibility, but in that case, you need to be sure the person is comfortable being quite quantitative in her approach to audience analysis.

✦ **Understand the publications** that your organization will be creating from the system. Thus, you need a *publication analyst*. Even if your first plan is only to create a Web site, you should still have your eyes open for the ways in which the Web site needs to share content with other publication efforts. This person is responsible for finding out what publications exist now, how they share information, how they are produced, how often they are produced, what their audiences are, how they are distributed, and how they can be deconstructed into pieces that a CMS can produce and coalesce. Someone from the current Web effort or another major publication group is a logical choice for this job, but that person must be able to climb out of the publication she has been creating and look beyond the particulars of any one publication to how publications, in general, can be created.

✦ **Understand the content** that the system will manage. This task requires a *content analyst*. This person is responsible for finding out what kinds of content you have, what you need, how it serves audiences and publications, how it can be divided into content classes, how each class can be reduced to a set of content elements, and how those elements can be fashioned into a metadata framework for tagging content. She is responsible for understanding how information is produced in the organization and where it can be found. She will assess the amount of work required to write or acquire content and how much will be needed to start and run the system. Someone from an editorial background is a logical choice for this job, but it must be someone who is less focused on creative writing and more on mechanics. Someone with a library background is another good choice, but the librarian must be able to understand the creation process as well as the cataloging process.

✦ **Understand the computer infrastructure** upon which the system will run. You, therefore, need a *technology analyst*. This person is responsible for understanding all the systems in the organization that will interact with the CMS. She is also responsible for understanding any constraints or technical requirements the organization might have. Later, she will be central in the selection of any new hardware or software you will need to build the system. She must be able to understand and piece together every piece of technology used, from the first authoring application to the final piece of JavaScript in an end user's browser. Someone from a development or IT systems background is a logical choice for this job, but she must have a head for content as well as data. A technologist who is comfortable ignoring the human parts of the system will not do.

You will need to bring all the diverse perspectives together and unite them around a clear vision of how they all fit together. Thus, you will need a *project leader* who can form and articulate a clear plan of attack that takes advantage of all the skills in the team. This person needs to have a little bit of the skills of each team member but also a wider perspective of the entire system and process. Because she will often be improvising (for lack of any established process), she needs to be a strong communicator and a forceful director. Finally, she needs to embody an information perspective. Rather than focusing too much on any of the team member skills, she brings them to bear on the central problem of the entire project — what is the right system for us to best collect, manage, and publish the information and functionality that our audiences want and from which our organization can benefit.

 Cross-Reference I present a more comprehensive look at the jobs and skills required for a CMS in Chapter 13, "Staffing a CMS."

After the system is in development, of course, you will need other skills. But the skills you need later are just a deeper and more technical version of the skills just discussed.

Look for pain in the organization

A good way to begin any conversations when examining your organization's CMS needs is to ask what information problems the staff is facing. If you ask (and even if you don't), you probably will hear a plethora of issues, dilemmas, worries, and horror stories that surround the core issues of content management. If you do not hear a lot of woe, you should question the need for a CMS! Be sensitive not only to the types of problems, but also to the actual stories that people tell. These stories will come in very handy when educating the organization. They bring a measure of "ground truth" to the abstract discussions you will find yourself in and keep your team on track toward solving the problems that are most pressing. As you hear these stories, try to do the following:

✦ **Record and categorize them.** Distribute them freely to let everyone know where the problems are.

✦ **Try to find the common themes.** These are the major issues for your organization to resolve.

Try to rate the severity of the problems. See if you can apply some numbers to the comments you hear, especially the problems that concern a glut of information, slowness of the system, and employee and customer complaints.

Assess the current mandate

If you are extremely lucky, you have a one-page, crystal-clear description of what the organization expects to accomplish with a CMS. The page has a paragraph that anyone can understand that says why this system is necessary and what it will do. It then goes on to list the major goals of the system. Finally, it has a short list of the criteria by which the system's success will be measured.

More likely, you have had a set of discussions with the project initiator in which you learned her goals and requirements. You might have an e-mail message or a memo that reiterates the discussions. Maybe that is all there is, but maybe not: Where did the initiator get the idea? Were others involved? Is there some wider initiative of which this is a part? If you dig around a bit (gently, of course), you might find that a number of overlapping movements have led to your project and that it serves a number of organizational goals. If others are unaware of the connections, you have material for an education plan. Most likely, a loose agreement (and some disagreement) exists on the issues surrounding a CMS. Where exactly is the agreement and who agrees? Where is the disagreement, and what are the divergent opinions?

In addition to the text of a mandate (or lack of one), you should explore its scope. Given your current understanding of how far-reaching your system will need to be, are the right people involved? Are other initiatives out there that are not connected to this one that, perhaps, should be?

Assess the organization's assumptions

For each of the kinds of analyses you must later do, there is a set of relevant documents and people in the organization that you have to find, understand, and present back.

Audience assumptions

You would be exceedingly lucky to have a good audience analysis in your hands at the start of your assessment. On the other hand, you would be in a very strange organization indeed if you didn't have a tremendous amount of raw material that you could use to begin a good audience analysis. Any marketing or public relations group worth its budget will have a lot of information about the organization's customers, constituents, members, or whatever else audiences may be called. If some of or all your audiences are internal staff, then the human resources department is the place to go for the divisions and groupings that matter.

I'll stress again that this is raw material, but at this point, raw material is all you need. Your purpose is not to complete an audience analysis, but to see what the organization has to offer when you do one later. Editorial groups are also storehouses of audience analysis. Although the amount of written material might be sparse, you will find many people who have thought about audiences and have a very clear idea of whom they address in their work. Finally, the people in your organization who are in closest contact with audiences will have a lot of good, practical input for you to put in the hopper (along with the more abstract definitions you get from people who think about but do not actually talk to audience members). As you work to uncover information about audiences, keep an eye out for key members of audience groups. Does someone out there typify a particular audience? Would that person be willing to talk to you, or even consult with the project team concerning what is best for her peer group?

Publication assumptions

All organizations create some set of publications (even if it is only internal information). To implement a CMS successfully, you must decide which publications ought to be part of the system and then how to subsume them into a CMS, and where they can share content, functionality, and design.

To begin this process, you can simply catalog the publications your organization produces that might be part of the system. It is quite possible that each major publication your organization creates comes from a different publication group. Each group is focused on a particular author group, content set, and publication format. One group, for example, might produce case studies and industry intelligence for sales support. Another group might produce documentation for post-sales training. A third group might produce an internal newsletter that highlights recent advances and best practices. Talk to the people in each of these groups to find out what content is in their publication, how often it is produced, who receives it, and how it is delivered.

Just as important as understanding the structure of current publications is understanding the structure and attitudes of publication groups. Find out how the groups are staffed, who does the writing and other content creation, and who does the layout and other production tasks. How do these groups feel about the idea of a CMS? Do they understand it? Do they support it? How do they think it will impact their jobs? This sort of information will be crucial to you later as you develop an approach to the system.

Content assumptions

In the end, you will have to be very specific about the information you include in your CMS. To start, however, you can cast a much wider net and find out what kinds of information are out there in the organization and what sorts of information people are assuming will be included. As with audience information, it is unlikely that anyone has created the definitive guide (eventually, you will), but an enormous amount of raw material exists in the organization. Rather than trying to amass the whole bulk of information that might be included, focus on collecting representative samples and any catalogs that might exist. Catalogs can be anything from official content inventories, to the TOCs and indexes of existing publications, to a listing of the files in a directory.

Tip   It is almost lost wisdom that, at the DOS prompt (that funny blinking cursor that used to be the entire user interface for an IBM-style computer and is still available in Windows under the Command Prompt command on the Start menu), you can navigate to a directory and use the command `dir /s > filelist.txt` to save into that directory a file called `filelist.txt`. The saved text file lists names and details about all files and subdirectories in that directory. (Or, to get just a list of filenames with paths, you can add the switch `/b`.)

Without a CMS, content and publications are pretty much the same thing. That is, the publications contain the content that you will collect and manage. A group creating industry analyses now, for example, will be creating the content and simultaneously publishing it (as, say, printed white papers).

Just as important as creating a general content inventory is discovering the structure and attitudes of the content groups. What staff and workflow do they use now? Do they use any automation systems, templates, or style sheets? What kind of standards do they adhere to? Is there an editorial guide? What are their assumptions about their audiences? How do these groups feel about the idea of a CMS? Do they understand it? Do they support it? How do they think it will affect their jobs? This sort of information will be just as crucial as the publication assumptions when you develop an approach to the system.

System assumptions

Eventually, you need a thoroughgoing analysis and specification for the technological structure of the CMS and for how it will interact with other organizational systems. To start, however, a simple description of the requirements people have in mind and a listing of existing systems will do.

Especially in a large organization, the technical staff may want to set a variety of conflicting requirements for the CMS. Some groups might have already begun working with a particular CMS and will want the entire organization simply to adopt their plan; other groups might have a strong preference for one development environment over another. Still others will have requirements based on a particular sort of content or publication that they want to create. People concerned with the organization's infrastructure (the IT group, for example) will want any new systems to tie into the existing network and Web systems.

Avoid adding to the debate at this point and simply record and categorize what you hear. Later, you can take the time to reconcile these various opinions into the best fit for the entire effort. From the very start, your best position is not as a combatant in the war of requirements, but as a mediator and neutral provider of unbiased information.

For each system that you come across that might have to interact with the CMS, find out how it communicates with other applications. For example, is it able to exchange data using XML? How does one connect to it? Is it accessible from a Web server outside the firewall?

The Web infrastructure your organization uses is of particular interest. On what platform does your Web presence run? What databases and application server software (if any) are in use? What methods are there for moving information to the Web server (or servers)? How is content replicated and distributed worldwide (if it is)?

Similarly, study the distribution of information in non-Web publications. How must print files be delivered to the printer? How are mass e-mail messages and faxes distributed today? How are publications that come in file form distributed internally?

The CMS's CMS

There's a lot of "content" that goes into designing your CMS, and the tasks of acquiring, managing, and publishing that content are not unlike the tasks your CMS is being designed to address. It's surprisingly easy to overlook this similarity and get right to work designing your CMS without the appropriate tools for the job.

The design process is an iterative one, and the design documents undergo constant change. While it might initially take more time to capture this information in a database or XML than it would to simply write narratives in a word processing document, that investment yields dividends throughout the process. Record your requirements and logical design with a word processor, and you've got a bunch of discrete documents—often with overlapping information, and all requiring separate maintenance. Record this same information in a database or XML, on the other hand, and you've got a collection of components that can be reused in many different design documents. Update one of your content components (for example, a description of one of your audiences) and the design documents that reference that component are also updated. It's like a CMS that helps you design your CMS.

Todd Koym, Edgerton Foundation

Finally, gather what information you can on collection tools and processes now in use. What authoring tools do groups use? Have they created any productivity tools? What development skills do they possess and how have these skills been applied?

Taking Stock of the Deliverables

As you prepare your organization to begin a CMS project, you can create the following tangible outputs to document your progress and provide a starting place for the rest of the CM project process:

✦ A **readiness assessment** gauges the organization's progress toward a CMS in a number of key dimensions.

✦ A **document inventory** catalogs all the plans, memos, decisions, and other artifacts that you can uncover about past and current CMS-related initiatives.

✦ A **state-of-the-system report** summarizes your findings in a form that is easily understood and consumed.

✦ An **education plan** identifies the people in the organization who need to know more about content management and how and what you will attempt to teach them.

✦ A **preliminary project plan** charts out the major phases of the coming project and broadly estimates the amount of effort you expect each one to take.

The readiness assessment

The best way to start a CMS project is by getting a firm feel for what the organization has accomplished so far. Such an assessment gives the project team an immediate, action-oriented task. Go through the whole organization and find out what has been done and what the current assumptions are.

In the process of assessing the current situation, the team will become acquainted with all the players and significant documents. The people with whom you interact get the chance to assess you informally and see that you are ready and interested in what they have to offer. Conversely, you can assess the various organizational contributors and decide what offers are worth following up on. If you do this first job well, you build an enormous amount of brand equity for your CMS project team within the organization and initiate just the relationships needed to continue and complete the project. Of course, the main reason for this task is to uncover a lot of great information to be used in the coming project. I call this process a *readiness assessment*.

Note   Both before you begin, and then again when your readiness assessment is complete, you may want to apply the complexity equation that I presented in Chapter 8, "Knowing When You Need a CMS," to assure yourself and the organization that a CMS is indeed warranted.

The following parts of the readiness assessment should be no surprise to you if you read the first part of this chapter:

✦ **What mandate exists** in the organization for the project now?

✦ **What audiences** does the organization expect to serve and how well-developed is the organization's approach to these people?

✦ **What publications** does the organization expect to create and how suitable are they to a CMS approach?

✦ **What content** does the organization think it needs to deliver, and how well known are its quantity, structure, and use?

✦ **What system** does the organization need or expect to be under the CMS? Are there well-formed requirements or a variety of opinions?

If you do no more than ask yourself these questions, you are ahead of most teams. If you go out to the organization and collect and organize opinions and documents on all these subjects, you have the start of a great project. That, in fact, is a good method for doing the assessment. Start with the project team. What do you know and believe about these subjects? Who knows what you do not? What documents have you seen that mention any of these things? Who would know if there are other documents? Who in the organization cares about any of these subjects? What kind of people would care about them? Begin with what you know and then follow the trail until you uncover the people and policies that bear on your subject matter. Then try to get beyond what the project team assumes or has seen. In so doing, you will gain valuable experience about how to engage the wider organization in the system you later need them to support and to which they must contribute.

You can also look at readiness from more of a project-completion standpoint. You focus on how far the organization has gotten in defining the mandate, drawing up project requirements, determining publications, and taking steps toward constructing a system, as shown in Figure 15-2.

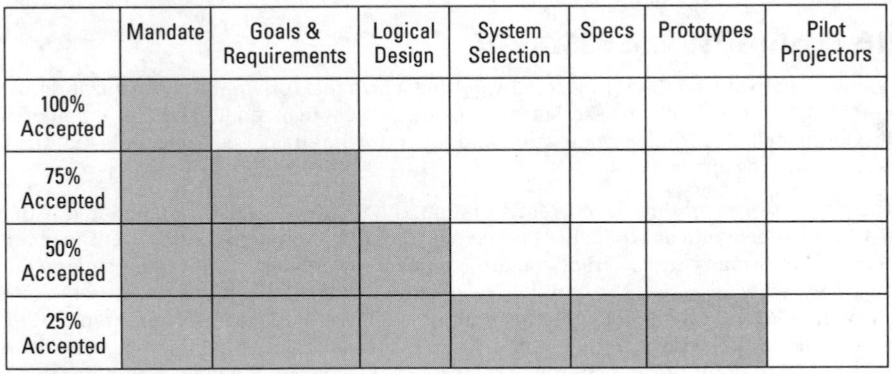

	Mandate	Goals & Requirements	Logical Design	System Selection	Specs	Prototypes	Pilot Projectors
100% Accepted	▓						
75% Accepted	▓	▓					
50% Accepted	▓	▓	▓				
25% Accepted	▓	▓	▓	▓	▓	▓	

Figure 15-2: This chart shows at a glance how far the organization has gotten toward a CMS.

This chart combines general project milestones with general levels of completeness. The project milestones are organized more or less in sequence so that early milestones are toward the left. At the start of the project, you hope for a profile somewhat like the one shown. The most work has been accomplished on the early milestones and the later ones have not been started.

Unfortunately, as often as not, the profile is much less regular. It is common, for example, for the organization to have gotten quite far in system selection before even beginning on a mandate. A chart like this can help you get an early snapshot of the areas that are overdeveloped and those where the most early effort is needed.

Document inventory and analysis

Some organizations have a tremendous amount of documentation hanging around from previous electronic publication efforts. Other organizations have very little. In either case, it is worth your while to become the central repository for all such documents, to become very familiar with their contents, and to know how they relate to the current effort. As you make your way through the organization, look for these sorts of documents:

✦ Requirements documents

✦ Specifications

✦ Lists of content in spreadsheets and documents

✦ Site maps

✦ Policy statements and other memos that show the intent of the organization

✦ Presentations and demonstrations of concepts

✦ Vendor evaluations

✦ Proof-of-concept projects and their documentation

✦ Audience analyses in their various forms (market studies, focus group reports, and so on)

✦ Strategic direction reports

✦ Competitive analyses

✦ Publication process documentation from the various groups that might participate in the CMS

✦ Publication design documents and illustrations

✦ Marketing strategy documents

✦ Usability studies and user interface documentation

✦ Lists of organizational resources, products, assets, or any other documentation that might help you create metadata lists later on (typically, at least some sorts of product or service taxonomies exist)

✦ Tables of contents and indexes from any potential publications or content sources

✦ Any other artifact that looks like it might bear on the CMS

I'd be very surprised if you did not come up with a wealth of information if you really look. A thorough document inventory provides you with an enormous resource. First, it familiarizes you with where the organization has been, who proposed what, and what the outcome was. In your continuing efforts, you will have a tremendous advantage over most people you encounter, who will have vague, secondhand knowledge of what has been tried but nonetheless will be willing to base strong opinions on it. The more obvious benefits are that you can leverage a lot of this information toward your effort, meet all the right people in your search for these documents, and avoid repeating the mistakes of others.

The effort of a document inventory also pays for itself in the security you feel because you know what went wrong and what went right in the past and can, therefore, better design the future.

I suggest that you *ultimately* organize your inventory based on the part of the CMS that each document relates to, but that you start much more simply. For example, you might start simply by gathering and perusing each document. Classify them in a spreadsheet by source, file-name, and date. Add a *Note* column for contents.

As you make your way through the mounds of information that you collect, you can begin to categorize them by the readiness categories: mandate, audiences, content, publications, or system infrastructure. Alternatively, you can use the project completion categories I outlined in the preceding section. I don't think it is worth the effort to go much further in categorizing these documents. For one thing, it is enough of a struggle getting them to fit into the few categories that I mentioned. For another thing, one document will often totally cross boundaries. If you can spare the effort, you can pivot your spreadsheet, list the major CMS categories, and then cite the parts of each document that bear on each issue.

Your team ought to become pretty familiar with the key documents that you unearth. You might be surprised at how handy it is to be able to refer, off the top of your head, to the right official document when you want to underscore a point.

The state-of-the-content system report

After a week or two of research, you ought to be able to say something definitive about the current state of content management in your organization. You can make your research public in a state-of-the-content system report. The point of the report is not to show solutions, but rather to do the following:

✦ **Educate.** Simply by laying out the organization's knowledge using the categories and terms of your analysis, you can do a lot of education. Understand that this report is, for many people, their introduction to a content-management approach. Be sure the report frames the issues from a content-management perspective and shows why these categories are helpful in starting to frame a solution.

✦ **Provide the first stage of consensus.** Send the report first to the people with whom you worked to gather information. Do they agree with the way you represented them? Did you miss anything? What did they think of the stuff others provided that is similar to or different from their opinions and information? By doing this, you can gauge the intensity of the coming process. If people are so polarized that they cannot even agree on what the situation is now, you have a long way to go to get them to agree about what it should be! On the other hand, if no profound disagreement appears in the report or if those in disagreement see some validity in each other's positions, you are set to drive to consensus on a solution.

✦ **Position the CMS project team as the central point of contact and expertise** on the system. It is not unlikely that, even while you conduct your research, other groups and individuals are questioning your authority to be leading this effort. Or, more benignly, they are simply wondering what you are up to and how much they should support you. If your first report is authoritative, well-constructed, complete, and compelling, you have, at least, seized the initiative and, at most, secured it.

✦ **Provide a platform on which to build the rest of the project.** The information you gathered ought to provide a bounty of ideas and discussions for how to move forward. You ought to have discovered the low-hanging fruit as well as the key stumbling blocks to moving forward. You should have ample input for the next stage of the project: building a project mandate.

✦ **Relate the project to the existing efforts.** You can include enough of your document inventory in the report to show that you have done your homework and that the assessment you have made relates directly to the organization's key policy and design documents.

You can choose your own format for the report. You will be well served, however, if the document contains some explanation of the process and its goals, as well as a section for each of the parts of the analysis.

The education plan

Your State-of-the-Content System report can help educate people concerning the current situation in your organization. Given the analysis you have performed, you can also take a more direct approach to educating your organization on the ideas and methods of content management. Your analysis ought to have shown you who the concerned parties are and what they know. If you can identify the gaps in knowledge in your organization, you can put together a formal or informal plan to fill them.

This may seem like an optional move, but I don't believe it is. In an area as new as content management, the lack of knowledge often presents itself as a lack of agreement. I've seen many hour-long arguments end with "we are just using different words for the same thing." More important, without a shared vocabulary and understanding of concepts, you cannot create consensus. It is not that everyone needs to become a content-management expert, but rather that they must have the same basic idea of what content management is and what, for example, a publication is.

The analysis you performed ought to give you all you need to design an education plan. The following are some suggestions for how to go about it:

✦ **Include in your plan those people who understand what you are trying to do.** It's really helpful to have these people assist you in some way to educate their peers. This need not be a big-time commitment. Rather, what you want is their moral support to help explain, uphold, and proliferate the set of common words and concepts.

✦ **Find as many ways to educate as possible.** Anything from one-on-one meetings to mass e-mail messages can help get the organization wrapped around the new concepts. In general, face-to-face meetings are better for education, but do not hesitate to create short white papers, memos, and reports to spread the word quickly and effectively.

✦ **Don't imagine that you have all the right words and answers.** Content management is not a done deal. Even this book is just my bid to help define the content-management playing field. It is much more important to reach consensus on some set of words than to have them be the words you prefer. If you should insist on anything, it is that the words your organization adopts to describe the problem and its solution do more to clarify than to muddy the waters.

✦ **Find the right message for the right person.** For each significant player in your organization, decide exactly what she does not understand and the right approach to teaching her.

✦ **Do not confuse education with propaganda.** If your organization perceives that you are using an education banner to slyly convince them to follow your agenda, they will neither learn nor be convinced. Instead, create a separate forum, where the merits of particular approaches can be debated. It is a big enough task simply to get the parts of the organization to agree to a definition of the problem without adding the mistrust involved by pushing for a particular solution.

Start with a Common Language

No matter what the subject matter of the content to be applied to the CMS, there comes a time early in the requirements phase where all members of the team must come together and define terms. This is especially true when the team must adapt content that has been presented in a traditional structure for a CMS that will publish it to a new structure or metaphor.

In 2001, a team comprised of one cataloger and one librarian/information architect, two engineers, and three ethnomusicologists/archivists came together to create the CMS for a new world music Web site. The mandate for the CMS was to merge existing CDs and individual pieces of recorded music from world music archives. The CDs typically were collections of 12 to 15 tracks, with a common theme and accompanied by liner notes. The music coming from the archives were individual tracks recorded at festivals and sacred ceremonies by ethnomusicologists over the past 70 years, in remote regions of India, Africa, Central Asia, or Indonesia.

The purpose of this Web site was to enable listeners to choose from the individual selections of music and create their own collections. (This concept, made common by the introduction of iTunes, was unique at the time.)

The engineers on the team, who had previously worked on a traditional rock music Web site, found it difficult to embrace the track-centric metaphor. Before they could fully understand and implement the requirements, it was essential that they broaden their way of thinking and not concentrate their interpretation on the "CD" model.

The team ultimately reached an agreement to use the term "container" in place of "CD" or "collection." Collection was a problem because the tracks of music on a CD were obviously a collection, but the archives themselves were also considered to be collections. We agreed upon the term "intellectual container" for the archival music that we grouped together, purely for ease of cataloging. This phrase was also applied to groups of "favorites" tracks, selected by guest curators.

Susan Golden, Golden Information Group (www.goldeninformationgroup.com)

A preliminary project plan

Regardless of how much pressure you are feeling, in this early in your project you are not in a good position to put together a project plan. Still, you *are* in a position to put together the form of the plan, note any of the expectations people have for cost or schedule, and get the project plan process rolling.

Cross-Reference

You can and should revisit the project plan many times. Each time you visit, you can add a lot of reality to it. See Chapter 18, "Doing Logical Design," in the section "A revised project plan," for details.

If you follow the process I lay out, your project will go through the stages I laid out earlier in this chapter (refer to Figure 15-1).

To actually create the plan, you might want to engage a project manager and use an official project-planning tool, or you might want to be a bit more informal. In either case, consider including the following information in your plan for each stage of the project:

✦ **Degree of completion.** Include any assumptions you have found for how complete people think that the stage is, plus your own estimate of the same.

✦ **Cost and time.** Include any assumptions you have found for the cost and schedule that are expected for this stage. Include your own estimates or your reasons for believing that it is too early to say. If it is too early, indicate what you must know to better fix the price or timeframe.

✦ **Deliverables.** Again, include others' assumptions and your own ideas. I have listed deliverables for all stages in other chapters. Use these or create your own.

✦ **Staffing.** Include whatever anyone has suggested about how to staff the effort. In addition, don't forget to include your guesses as well. (My guesses are detailed in Chapter 13, "Staffing a CMS.")

Tip

If you do use a formal approach to project planning, be sure you clearly communicate that this is a preliminary plan. As any graphic designer will tell you, "If your preliminary effort looks too professional and clean, people will mistake it for what you really intend to do!"

A risk assessment

At this point in the project, you have proceeded far enough to start assessing potential risks. Admittedly, these risks will mostly be those that bad organizational processes introduce, but they are project risks nonetheless.

Tip

You may not want to call *people* risks, even though they often are. Try phrasing your risk in a general enough way that it can't be assigned to a particular person. If you don't have your own favorite format for risks, a simple table like this one will probably do:

Risk	Impact	Probability	Score	Mitigation

where

✦ **The risk column** names the risk.

✦ **The impact column** rates how bad the consequences will be if the risk actually occurs. You can choose whatever scale gives you enough of a range to differentiate the various risks.

✦ **The probability column** rates how likely the risk is to occur, using a scale of 0 to 100 percent.

✦ **The score column** multiplies the impact by the probability to come up with an overall score for the weight of this risk.

✦ **The mitigation column** explains what you are doing to make sure the risk does not occur and what you will do to recover if it does occur.

Cross-Reference   I suspect that you can discover any number of risks for yourself, but if you need a start, you can look in Chapter 14, "Working within the Organization," in the section "Identifying Your CMS Hurdles," to get some ideas.

Taking Stock of Your Staffing Needs

At this point in your project you may very well be working alone. If not, you may have just a few people who have limited time to offer. This is not as bad a situation as it might seem for, at least, a couple of reasons. First, you don't know yet exactly who you need on your team. Second, the work at this stage of the project is not so extensive that you need a real team. Still, the work here does require specific skills, so if you don't have a team you must be versatile. The skills you need include sleuthing, writing, coalition-building, and of course, information organization.

Summary

The effort you put in up front to understand where your organization has been, who the players have been, and what they have accomplished so far will be handsomely rewarded throughout the rest of your project. In fact, whether there *is* a project might depend largely on how well you perform these preliminary efforts. Even if you do so more casually than I describe, don't neglect to do the following:

✦ Assess the knowledge of your project team (if you have one).

✦ Find the major pain spots in the organization.

✦ Discover what sort of mandate exists for your effort.

✦ Assess the assumptions that the organization has now for the CMS audiences, publications, content, and systems.

✦ Develop a knowledge base of relevant documents, be able to say how far the organization has gotten in any previous CMS-like efforts, know who needs more education and how you will help them get it, and be able to roughly estimate the project before you.

If you do all this, then only a few reasons would prevent you from starting the project. These might include a dysfunctional organization or the fact that your organization simply doesn't need a CMS yet.

In the next chapter, I talk a lot more about dysfunction and function in the organization as you seek to build consensus around a workable mandate for a CMS project.

✦   ✦   ✦

Securing a Project Mandate

✦   ✦   ✦   ✦

In This Chapter

What it means to have consensus on a CMS project

How to recognize and understand project sponsors

The project statement and other mandate process deliverables

✦   ✦   ✦   ✦

A typical content management project begins with wide agreement that there is a problem—too much information to manage informally. There is tacit approval from organizational decision makers that some solution must be found, and there are the beginnings of a content management project team. On the other hand, the project begins with little or no understanding (let alone agreement) about what the solution will be, what parts of the organization will be affected, how long the project will take, or how much it will cost. Without compelling answers to these and many other questions, the project will flounder from the start.

In this chapter, I discuss how you might work outward from your team to both your organizational sponsors and to your audiences to drive toward consensus and a workable project.

Mandate Jumpstart

This Jumpstart summarizes what you need to do to line up crucial organizational support for your CMS initiative. I describe how you can identify sponsors within the organization and secure from them the organizational imprimatur necessary to make your project successful—or even possible.

Use this jumpstart as a summary without the weight of detail, or as a quick review if you've already read the chapter and want a checklist of what you need to do to get a mandate for your CMS initiative.

To secure a mandate for your CMS project, follow these steps:

1. Do a readiness assessment to be sure you have the background and authority to approach sponsors (as I discussed in Chapter 15, "Getting Ready for a CMS," in the section "The readiness assessment").

2. Determine who your sponsors are (or could be) in the organization.

3. Learn about the sponsors to best know how to approach them, how they relate to your CMS initiative, and how it will serve their aims.

4. Create a mandate process, where you bring the project sponsors together in a series of meetings and other interaction so they can form a consensus on:

- What organizational goals a CMS can support

- A project statement that you can use to guide the rest of the endeavor

- What audience, content, technology, and publication assumptions you should start from

- How the success of your initiative will be measured

If you complete these steps, you will have the firmest foundation possible on which to build your project. Without a mandate, be prepared to be buffeted by the winds of favor and narrow interest in your organization.

What to Agree on

The place to start a CMS project (or any other major organizational initiative) is by building consensus around some fundamental issues. You build consensus among the three *major* stakeholders in the project: the organizational sponsors, the project team, and the final judges of the system (your audiences). The internal stakeholders (sponsors and the project team) must agree on the following issues:

✦ **What exactly is our information management problem?** Where do we feel pain, and what are the most significant changes that need to be made? How big is the problem?

✦ **What are the organizational goals we think a CMS can address?** From the range of objectives that the organization might want to accomplish, which can be addressed by delivering a specific sort of information to a specific set of people via a specific set of publications?

✦ **Where are we now** in our efforts to address these problems? What steps already have been taken, and what documentation of current approaches and analysis has there been?

✦ **What group of people will be responsible** for creating a solution? Who will lead the group, and what will the responsibility of each person be?

✦ **What is the project's mandate** and upon what criteria will success be judged?

✦ **Who are the intended audiences** for the publications that the system produces?

✦ **Are there organizational standards** for development or deployment that must be used?

All three sponsor groups must agree on these issues:

✦ **What sorts of information and functionality** are most important to capture and distribute?

✦ **What sorts of publications** will be needed to distribute content most efficiently and effectively?

Maybe you are lucky and during your readiness assessment you uncovered the perfect mandate for your initiative. More likely, you uncovered areas of both agreement and disagreement from which you must build an overall consensus for your project. To build consensus, you must find and coordinate a set of sponsors.

Techniques for Getting the Job Done

Negotiating your way to a happily agreeing organization may be tough. It will take skills beyond technical expertise or any knowledge of content management processes. To my mind, the best way to approach the task is to learn about the people who will make or break your initiative — your sponsors. If you go into the consensus-building phase of the project armed with all the knowledge you gained in the readiness assessment, fortified with a thorough understanding of the people you must get to agree, and reinforced with a fair but strict consensus process, you might just make it out of this phase with your pride and project intact.

Recognize sponsors

A *sponsor* is someone whose support you need to make the project successful. The ultimate test of a sponsor is to ask, "Without this person's support, will the project be seriously compromised?" Conversely, you can ask, "With this person's support, will the project be seriously enhanced?" Either kind of person is a sponsor. Sponsors can come from a number of areas, as follows:

✦ **Organizational executives.** These are the classical sponsor types. They are people who have sway in the organization, promote ideas they believe in, and can get budget allotted to projects that they, well, sponsor.

✦ **Key influencers.** These are people whose opinion is often sought to test whether an idea is worth pursuing. They might or might not have budget authority, but they do have respect and credibility in the organization.

✦ **Key outsiders.** These people usually are from important audience segments, such as customers, partners, members, or other pivotal constituencies. More than just being part of the audience segment, to be truly a sponsor, they must speak for the audience or have some specific influence.

✦ **The person who initiated the project.** Undoubtedly, this person feels like a sponsor but might or might not, in fact, be someone who can make or break the project.

Most sponsors are from within the organization, but some might not be. In fact, the presence of an outsider in the sponsor group can help enormously to create a mood of solidarity and agreement. Most sponsors are decision makers, but some might not be. They might have influence, but no direct power. The presence of influencers in the sponsor group helps to deepen the discussion, especially if the influencers are known experts in some aspect of the system.

If You Do Nothing Else...

I am often hired by companies to help them develop the business case for implementing a content management system. I was once in a meeting with an executive who was one of several key decision makers for a proposed content management initiative. After pitching the business case to him, the first question he asked was "What is the #1 reason why content management projects fail?"

My response: "Lack of executive support."

He nodded knowingly, had no more questions, and shortly thereafter became a key sponsor for the project.

Rita Warren, ZiaContent, Inc.

Regardless of where a sponsor comes from, she must be someone who can truly offer support. This means that sponsors are both in a position to offer support and want to do so. I have often seen groups make the mistake of seeking weak support from a more powerful sponsor rather than strong support from a less powerful sponsor. The road to completion of a CMS is long and can be quite rocky. Without strong personal interest and commitment from your sponsor, you might not make it. As you seek sponsors, then, try to assess the degree to which the person can commit for the long term to your goals. (And if you are lucky, over time your highly committed but lower-powered sponsor may work to raise the level of commitment among the higher-ups.)

It is useful to think about a sponsor as someone who will help you get beyond your organization. That is, a good sponsor will help you avoid the red tape that might be involved in getting an initiative off the ground. Without such support, your project can get mired in a morass of meetings that never manage to merge the multitude of opinions and make measurable progress toward real milestones.

Every sponsor comes with her own set of attitudes and interests. Some will want to exert direct control, whereas others will want only quarterly reports. Some will have a lot of background in what you are doing, whereas others will have no clue. Regardless of background, however, a good sponsor will understand what is your responsibility and what is hers. Possibly the best statement I have heard from a sponsor went something like this:

> I don't understand what you are doing nearly as well as you do. On the other hand, I know our business and I know a good decision when I see one. I'll question you mercilessly until I understand the significant facts and figures. I'll let you know where we agree and disagree. Where we agree, I'll support you wherever I can. Where we disagree, we have some more work to do until we agree.

Techniques for Getting the Job Done

One of the most effective ways to engage sponsors in your project is to acknowledge their role explicitly through a steering committee or advisory board. It's one more organization you have to juggle in your daily rounds, but can prove to be the most important of all since they are ultimately the ones who will approve and fund your project. By containing them in a specific role, you also make the rest of your job easier, since you can have the high-level discussions with them, and the working discussions with their appointed representatives who are involved in the hands-on development work.

The best way to structure this arrangement is to explicitly diagram the relationships between your sponsor group, your implementation group, and your users, and define roles and responsibilities for each so everyone is clear on their part. By making these clear to everyone, you make it easier for the players to understand both their importance and their boundaries, and minimize confusion and misplaced expectations. The sponsors know what they're expected to provide, and where they shouldn't be interfering, and you can always point back to your organizational chart if issues arise that are outside their scope of responsibility, and remind them that they've already appointed someone in their group to take that role as part of the implementation team and they're doing a fine job, thank you; now let's get back to the issues we need to deal with.

Michael Crandall, Chair, Masters of Science in Information Management Program, University of Washington Information School

You and the sponsor must agree that your job is to know what to do and hers is to know how to get it done in the organization or with an important audience group. If you can get to this accommodation with your sponsors (and they with each other), you will have cleared the first major hurdle on the way to success.

Learn about your sponsors

A good sponsor will help your project because she believes in its goals and in your ability to achieve them. Still, if you recognize the needs and motivations of your sponsors, you will be more likely to craft a project that helps them achieve their own goals. In addition, if you are not lucky enough to handpick your own sponsors, you will do well to try to understand the perspective of the project sponsors so that you can best navigate among their dispositions and desires. Following are some of the questions you might want to answer about your sponsors (whether you choose to write down the answers is a different question):

✦ **Why is she a sponsor?** If this is simply part of her overall job, is it a part she particularly cares about? If she does not seem to care a lot, will this mean that she will default to accept or not accept what you propose to her?

✦ **What will make her successful?** How does a CMS relate to the criteria by which she is judged in her job? What risks to her success does your project represent? In many organizations, the way each person is judged is public. If you can get this information about your sponsors, you can use it to craft your approach to your project and to them.

✦ **What will compete for the attention and support of your sponsor?** Is this the smallest, largest, or one of many initiatives in which the sponsor is involved? If this is a big initiative, expect it to receive a lot more scrutiny and attention, and remember that it will be much more important to plan your communication with this sponsor.

✦ **What alignments does your sponsor have?** Are there particular groups in the organization to which she is particularly close? Are there individuals whose opinion she particularly respects or disrespects? How are these groups or people disposed toward your project?

✦ **What stake does she have in your success?** How noticeable will it be to her peers and supervisors if you succeed or fail? Similarly, who is watching the sponsor and what does she want or need from the project?

✦ **How well does the sponsor understand the organization's problems?** Are her assumptions about what is wrong with the status quo the same as what you have discovered? What education might she (or you) need before you see things the same way? How will you deliver education to this sponsor? Are e-mail messages and memos enough, or will you need something more?

✦ **How well does the sponsor understand content management?** Does she know enough to understand the words and concepts you use? Does she understand it in a way that you don't? Can you help her understand how to apply her implicit understanding of what goes on in the organization to your set of words and processes?

✦ **What specific reviews and approvals does she require?** What sorts of communications and project policy statements does she think she should a) not see, b) review, c) approve, or d) write? How formal should each review be?

✦ **How does she relate to your audiences?** Some of the worst sponsors I have seen erroneously have believed that they could speak directly for an audience. They used this position to squeeze the project team from both sides (using their purported knowledge of the audience to back up any statement of opinion that they made). Not that sponsors can't understand audience needs — quite the contrary. Many have had a lot of experience with audiences and can add to the discussion. It is the specific responsibility of sponsors, however, to speak for the organization; it is only an added benefit if they can speak for an audience. Conversely, if the sponsors do not understand the needs of an audience, they must certainly be made aware of them. A recognized but unmet need of an audience is an argument that a sponsor will have difficulty ignoring.

Taking Stock of the Deliverables

Your mandate-building process will consist of a lot of talk and very little action. Your job is to keep the talk productive and leading toward an agreed-upon set of goals and success measurements. You can produce the following tangible deliverables to help the process along:

✦ **Sponsor profiles** that list exactly what each sponsor wants and needs

✦ **An issues hierarchy** that fits all the contending needs of all the sponsors into a single framework

✦ **Notes and minutes** that mark progress and help you stay on track

✦ **A mandate process** that encourages debate, then progresses toward consensus, and ends in acknowledged closure

✦ **A project mandate** that captures the agreement you reached and presents it to the organization

Sponsor profiles

To really study your sponsors, you can create written profiles that answer all the learning questions I listed earlier in this chapter. Now, if you are truly a consensus builder, you immediately will be questioning the wisdom of this endeavor. Taking notes on people and creating files on them is not the way to gain their confidence and trust. So, if this seems just too risky or Machiavellian, skip it and content yourself with thinking about the questions and discussing the answers you find with the sponsor and your team.

On the other hand, if you can get past the feeling that you are acting like the next J. Edgar Hoover, this approach can be of immense value. If you act covertly and sequester the information you collect, you will indeed be doing espionage. If you are open about your motives and up-front about your techniques, however, you are just being conscientious. Moreover, if you have the sponsors participate in filling out their own profiles and openly discuss the profiles in group meetings, the profiling process can be a great way to have open and constructive dialog on the competing interests that you have to reconcile.

The point of profiling is to be explicit about how you will approach each sponsor. The more open you can be with this information, the better for everyone. In fact, the degree to which you can be open with your profiles indicates the degree of general openness in the organization. If you can manage to create a climate in which it is all right to share your approach to sponsors openly, you will be creating just the right climate for honest debate and real agreement.

Still, you can only be an idealist for so long. To my mind, it is always best to lead with complete openness and retreat as required to retain your personal comfort and your job.

One way or another, you should have in mind a profile for each sponsor so you can think explicitly about how to get each one to agree.

A hierarchy of issues

As you leap or crawl toward consensus, you will hear a blizzard of seemingly unrelated opinions, recommendations, and dictates. These will become a tangled web that will confuse and then derail the group, unless you control them. The best way I know of to control blizzards of information is to organize them (no surprise there). And, of course, Western culture's greatest organizational tool is the outline—or the hierarchy.

Note   If you want to be really anal about it, you can produce indexes of the issues and cross-reference them as well.

By getting all the statements detailing what you should do in one outline, you have done all you need to keep them from getting the better of the group. Your outline can do the following:

✦ **Assure the group** that all issues are captured and available. People then do not have to keep in their heads everything they have heard, and it should forestall their feeling that "there are big issues out there that we are forgetting about."

✦ **Contain the issues** by putting them in the wider project context. By organizing the issues into an outline, you cause contrasting opinions to come together, similar issues to merge, and sub-issues to be clearly seen as part of wider concerns. Hierarchies are syntheses of the items they contain. That is just what you want to accomplish.

✦ **Center yourself** as the one who is keeping track of the issues and bringing back potential resolutions to the group. The outline can be your main tool for showing progress, or lack of it, to the group. It also provides you with the perfect platform for offering options and potential solutions.

✦ **Provide an ongoing working draft** of the final project goals. If you drive your outline toward a small number of top headings, you can be simultaneously driving your group toward a small number of top-line goals.

Take care that you don't get too far ahead of the group. The work you do on the goals hierarchy should be logical and reasonable extensions of what the group has said or meant, not of your own opinions and ideas. You must maintain a careful balance between synthesizing the ideas of others and inserting ideas of your own. If you are too far on the side of your own ideas, you may lose credibility as a facilitator of the process, and you might be seen as trying to drive rather than direct.

If you maintain balance and keep driving the outline toward a final resolution to which everyone can agree, you will have a great tool for keeping the process under control and progressing. You will also know when you are finished.

Notes and minutes

Any group of highly placed individuals can have an exceedingly short group memory. Group effectiveness can suffer over time because of competing demands for the group's attention or as a result of the dynamic environment of the organization. The group may repeatedly revisit decisions they've already made, avoid making decisions that should be made, and contradict earlier decisions without remembering that they used to think differently or why. In addition to this, during the mandate process, a lot of facts must be recorded and organized. To help the group be effective over time and to stay on top of the issues, you are well advised to take good notes.

It is probably not a good idea to have the same person who facilitates group meetings also take the notes. The facilitator needs to be actively listening, responding, and directing. The note taker needs to be faithfully recording. In taking notes, be sure to listen for and record the following things:

- ✦ **Whether an issue raised is an opinion,** fact, recommendation, or directive. Later, it will be important to know how strongly stated the issue was and in what context any solution was offered.

- ✦ **Disagreements.** Note the disagreeing parties and the exact point of contention. Sometimes merely writing these down these problems miraculously cures them.

- ✦ **Agreements.** Note the issue as well as the agreement that was reached.

I think you can figure out how to take notes at least as well as I can (someone who never takes notes). My main point is just to make sure that you capture an ongoing record of what was suggested, what agreements were reached, and what still needs work. This record will help you construct an issues hierarchy and will ensure you have something to go back to when people forget.

The mandate process

Assuming that you have done all your readiness assessment homework, you will have a good idea of what the organization's main information problems are. If you have managed to get around in the organization to talk with all concerned parties, you will have a good idea of whose opinion counts. From this beginning, your next task is to formulate a solid mandate for the system that you will create.

I've never seen an organization that has no established rules for how to get something done. Whether these rules are explicit or in the collective consciousness of the staff, rules of engagement exist. Thus, I cannot presume to provide you with some process that you can use as such. Instead, I'll propose general considerations that you must take into account regardless of the process your organization uses.

A lot of people will want to be heard on the issues, but only the small group of sponsors will get to decide. You might consider providing a voice for the larger group by soliciting their input and cataloging it for presentation to the sponsor group. I have created simple Web-based forms for this purpose. The forms ask questions such as "Rate these audiences in order of importance to the organization," or "Which of these publications is most critical for us to deliver electronically?"

You probably already will have talked to many of these people and will have asked them some of these same questions. You haven't asked them to officially register their opinion on specific issues, however. By doing so, you are officially including them in the process. This is not only a goodwill gesture. As your sponsor process unfolds, it is really helpful to be able to canvass a wide range of opinion on a matter of dispute. There is nothing like getting hard facts back when you hear a lot of what seems to be second-guessing the needs of the organization.

It is helpful to categorize your opinion-givers by the kinds of opinions they are most qualified to give. You might guess that audience, publication, content, and system are the categories I would use. These categories will help you keep the number of questions you ask any one person to a minimum and will ensure that you get back the highest-quality responses.

You need to establish some procedure for sponsors to process a possibly large amount of information, provide input, review the input of others, and come to agreement. I have used a variety of methods to accomplish this, all of which shared these common qualities:

✦ **Setting the rules of the process before you begin.** Some rules I have found useful are a commitment to attend meetings and answer all e-mail messages, and a commitment to end with a single agreed-upon statement.

✦ **The process ought to offer a degree of anonymity to those who offer input.** That is, you should offer ways for people to offer opinions without a name attached. This ensures that not only the dominant or highest-ranking people get to decide. I have often used tools, for example, that enable anonymous ranking and commenting on alternatives (MeetingWorks, `http://www.meetingworks.com`, is a good example).

✦ **The process ought to include bottom-up and top-down decision-making.** For example, you can ask, "What are our goals?" and keep merging them up to a single project statement (bottom-up). Then you can ask, "What is our project statement?" and, from that, begin to derive goals (top-down). I have found that whichever way you start, it is a good idea to validate your results by going the other direction.

✦ **Present the facts.** Make sure that any facts you have found (things such as how many we have, how long it takes, and who is currently responsible) are presented and agreed upon by the sponsors before a discussion begins. Then be sure to refer to these agreements concerning the facts as people begin to get creative in the heat of debate.

✦ **Present the opinions you have collected *as* opinions.** Be especially sure to outline contrasting opinions. Put the sponsors in the position of reconciling approaches and opinions, as opposed to presenting and defending them.

✦ **Make sure you cover all angles.** Dominant players will tend to drive the discussions toward their areas of interest. Remember that in the end, you must have covered all four topic areas (audience, publications, content, and systems).

✦ **Make sure you play angles off each other.** It is not enough to dive into each of the four topic areas separately. Ask questions like "Which content is most important to each audience?" and "To which publications does this content naturally lend itself?"

✦ **Be prepared to break and educate.** Note when the discussion would be helped by a quick discussion of vocabulary or concepts. Be aware of when disagreements are based on dissimilar terms. You are not only building consensus on the solution but also on the definition of the problems. Sometimes a quick presentation to kick off a discussion can make a big difference in the quality and focus of the discussion.

✦ **Stay out of the fray.** It rarely serves you to jump into the debate and offer opinions. For one thing, it puts you on a winning or losing side. More important, while you are in the fray, there might be no one watching the process to ensure that all voices are heard and a single group opinion emerges. If you think that you must contribute, make sure someone else is there to facilitate the meeting. Consider using a professional facilitator if you think that the group will be particularly contentious or if you think that you want to be part of the discussion. If you do intend to participate, remember that later you will want the support of the people with whom you are debating.

✦ **Be prepared to break for more facts or wider opinions.** As a tactic to break up contentious discussions, as well as a way to quietly deflate unfounded opinions and facts, create a method for tabling an issue in order to canvass opinions for others not currently in the discussion. If you have previously created a method to get quick turnaround on questions from the wider group of concerned parties, this would be the time to use it.

✦ **Reward conflict and consensus.** In this process, you need to walk a fine line between too much and too little contention. Often, groups will deadlock with conflicting opinions. But just as often, they will seem to have agreed when, in fact, those who did not agree were not paying attention, did not understand what they were agreeing to, or did not want to speak up. Pay attention to both situations and test a weak consensus by restating it plainly and getting each person specifically to agree.

✦ **If you can't solve the problem,** solve the problem of how to solve the problem. Don't let a deadlock go for long without backing up one step. Divert the discussion from the problem to the process for resolving the problem. Go back as far as necessary in order to find agreement. Then start working back toward the deadlock one step at a time, trying to build on the agreement you reached.

✦ **Note the dynamics.** Use every clue at your disposal to understand how people are disposed to the process and each other. Note body language, attitudes of boredom, frustration, apathy, or anything other than honest interest and engagement. It is up to you to decide what to do about dynamics (good or bad); but even if you don't know what to do, be sure to pay attention.

✦ **Use a variety of venues.** When working with sponsors, it is useful to have a bag of discussion tricks up your sleeve to deal with their chronic lack of time and focus. Big group meetings have the advantage of everyone meeting face-to-face to work through issues. (We have found that the statement "We will not leave this room until we have agreed about X" is particularly helpful if you find that the group meanders and fails to decide.) Your process can drag on for weeks or months, however, as you try to find a time that works for everyone. Consider smaller group meetings, gathering opinions via e-mail, one-on-one meetings between warring parties, and any other gatherings that will help you hammer out consensus. I have found that bringing the entire sponsor group together at significant times (the start, major decisions, and the end) is very helpful in building group identity and ensuring that every sponsor gets the same message at the same time.

✦ **Discourage ad hoc discussion on process.** The best way to suck the energy out of a group and leave it in turmoil is to let the discussion turn to the process itself. When people start debating the process you have laid out, the frustration in the room rises and it begins to feel like you are making no progress or, worse, that the validity of the entire process is in question. At these times I recommend a break, skipping on to another subject where the process is not in question, or at the very least tabling the process discussion until a later time. That said, one of the most difficult things to do during a meeting is to know when the process you so cleverly devised is no longer working and to fix it before the rest of the room begins to fix it for you.

However you design your mandate process, the result ought to be a strong consensus. Specifically, the consensus should not be on the details of the system but on the concept, goals, and success metrics of the system. You are finished when all the sponsors exit the mandate process with the same idea of what you are doing, what organizational purpose it serves, and how they will measure your success.

Of course, some groups run out of time or sponsor patience before they reach this nirvana. If you find yourself in this position, pull back toward an acceptable mandate. The worst outcome from a mandate process is a public stalemate. If the process ends and it is clear to everyone that major rifts prevented a unified statement, you are in a poor position to move forward. If you choose to move forward anyway, beware. However you choose to proceed, your action will be in opposition to someone. More important, the organization will know that you failed in your first major test.

It is not enough for a room full of sponsors to agree on the solution; the rest of the concerned parties must agree as well. Given that you have strong sponsors, a strong statement, and have solicited input at all significant junctions, it will be difficult for others to find fault. Still, unless you publicize the results of the process, how will the others know what mandate emerged? Moreover, your mandate is your calling card to any group that you call upon for assistance. It should be right out in front of your group as you make your next moves. Finally, your mandate is your contract with the organization about what you are going to do. It behooves you to make sure that anyone involved in the project understands the ground rules that the mandate represents. Don't be afraid to ask questions of your team, such as "Which goal does that help us meet?" or "How does that support our mandate?"

In short, your mandate is the rule of law behind your project. It ought to keep the organization from changing the rules, and it ought to keep your project team from changing the rules. This does not mean that you are locked in to any specific course of action. Quite the contrary, a well-crafted mandate specifies outcomes, not actions. It leaves open your options on how to achieve the outcomes. Rather than restricting action, then, the mandate motivates it. It serves as the context in which your decisions must live. When someone comes to you with a proposal for an approach or a technology, the mandate does not say yes or no. It does say, however, "Whatever you do, make sure it results in X."

The project mandate

When politicians win an election by a large majority, the first thing they do is claim a mandate. They mean to say that the people are united behind them and in overwhelming support of their initiatives. It is less important, in the present context, whether a politician actually has a mandate, but it is very important that he claim to have one. A mandate is a powerful tool to keep skeptics and critics at bay and forge ahead, especially when times get rough.

In politics, a mandate is often a vague and vacuous statement, such as "People believe in my positions." Many content management projects are begun with a similarly vague statement, such as "Everyone agrees that we need a CMS to better deal with our information." If you expect your mandate to stick or provide any measure of support, you must be much more precise and clear. I can point to the following three specific elements that a mandate must have to stand up over time:

- ✦ **A set of organizational goals** that outlines what the CMS is supposed to achieve.

- ✦ **A project statement** that precisely and clearly defines what you are trying to accomplish with the CMS.

- ✦ **A small set of goals** that the system will be expected to accomplish, along with a way to measure the system's progress against each of the goals.

Organizational goals

Your final issues hierarchy (see the section "A hierarchy of issues" earlier in this chapter) ought to yield an outline of all the agreements your sponsor group has reached. You can take this outline and reshape it slightly as an outline of the business goals that a CM might address. For example, it may turn out (as it often does) that one of the major issues addressed in your mandate process is the cost of training. You may have further decided that the cost of training sales staff is chief among your concerns. This concern naturally leads to the business goal of reducing training costs. This is not just any goal; it is a goal that you can clearly address with content.

Whether they all fall out naturally from your issues hierarchy or not, be sure to capture and present the outline of all the goals and sub-goals that the CMS is meant to address. This outline, culminating in the overall goal of the system, will be your chief method for deciding what can and cannot be a part of the final system.

The project statement

To function as a mandate, a statement must be short and simple enough to be learned and recalled, but powerful enough to continue to exert influence over the project. Over the course of a project, staff and sponsors must be able to restate the mandate over and over to different concerned people in order to explain and justify the project. If it is not crisp and convincing, it will not last through the first telling. On the other hand, if it is clear and compelling, it will require little extra effort to show anyone interested the scope or importance of the CMS. A good project statement has the following attributes:

✦ Is no more than a few sentences.

✦ Is phrased in plain language that anyone can understand.

✦ Captures the essence of what you are trying to accomplish.

✦ Can be used as a yardstick for the remainder of the project to determine whether something or someone fits into the project.

The project statement is a proposed solution to the pain you found in the organization, as well as a way to coalesce the audience, publication, content, and system assumptions that you uncovered in your readiness assessment into a simple paragraph to which everyone can agree.

Suppose that you decide that the main problem in your organization is the inability to get product information to sales people who need it in a timely way. The organization experiences this as a high training cost for sales staff (because it takes a long time for them to learn where the information is and how to get to it). Your project statement might read as follows:

> We will reduce training costs by building a complete Web-based information base of our product line — SBase. SBase has all our product information stored logically and presented in a way that the sales team can access quickly and understand easily.

Anyone who hears this (inside or outside the organization) would understand what you are doing and why. In a few words, it gives all the most salient facts: reduce training costs, Web-based, all product information, understandable and accessible to sales staff. The paragraph does one additional thing: It names the system. This may seem like a small move, or even an unnecessary one, but it is very important. If you can create a name for your system that is memorable and descriptive, you will go a long way toward creating first, consciousness, then understanding, and finally, acceptance of the system.

To keep the example simple, I purposely made this statement limited in scope. This system has only one major content type, one publication, and one audience. Not a particularly sophisticated project. Nevertheless, it is a start. It might very well represent the project that all sponsors agreed was important enough to fund. It might be the point of most pain and what the organization felt needed its limited resources most. It might represent the core information that later will be leveraged from sales staff to customers. The point here is that the statement must reflect what the organization can really accomplish.

You can pretty easily imagine how the statement might be extended for a wider mandate—a broader content base, more audiences, more publications. The real trick is to keep the statement short and sharp, given a wide mandate.

System goals and measurement

The organizational goals state what the organization feels it should get out of the CMS. The project statement includes a top-level view of the organizational goals for the system. It answers the question, "Why are we doing this?" This goal level is good for getting people to understand the project but is not concrete enough to use as a measure of the project's success.

To get more concrete, you can create a list of specific system goals—the concrete outcomes you expect from your project and how you intend to measure those outcomes. The goals of using SBase, for example, might be to help the sales group as follows:

✦ **Reduce training costs.** We note that today it requires an average of eight weeks before a newly hired sales representative is ready to take an incoming call. Our system will be successful if this time drops to seven weeks after the system has been in place for six months.

✦ **Reduce sales closing time.** We note that today our average time to close a sale is 17 days. We will consider the system a success if we note any drop in this closing time after the system has been in place for six months.

✦ **Create a single source for all product information.** Our analysis found a total of nine different directories, Web sites, and individuals that are used today by salespeople to get product information. Our system will be a success if a similar analysis six months after the launch of the system shows that the nine information locations are no longer used.

✦ **Create a logical organization for all product information.** Our analysis shows that the organization has four major competing schemes for organizing product information. Our system will be a success if we are able to create a single product information outline, index, and cross-reference structure that is deemed better by users than the other four schemes. In addition, we will consider the system successful if it takes no longer than two minutes on average for a contributor to correctly categorize a new piece of product information.

✦ **Provide quick access to product information.** We will consider the system a success if it takes no longer than five minutes on average for a salesperson to find product information or discover that what she is looking for is not on the site.

Note that each goal has a statement, a benchmark of today's metric (if there is one), and a quantitative measure of success. The statements try to squeeze all the vagueness out of the goal in order to provide an objective and very tangible standard by which you can be judged. Many project teams would cringe at being held to such tangible standards. There is no room to fudge on success. I'll assume that your attitude is not to hide behind vagueness, but to have a bright-line test for success to which you can hold the organization as you make your way toward success.

This method of goal setting does require a bit of extra effort to track the success metrics that you are using to judge your project. But it is effort well spent. In the preceding example, the training time and the sale closing time ought to be measured regardless of the CMS. The alternative product-information sources will be good to know anyway, because they are your competition. If you do not get agreement on your organizational scheme, or if it takes too long to categorize new information, not only is your system not succeeding, but it will fail. Finally, the average time to find information is, for this kind of site, the key metric you need to know to gauge how well the site is performing.

Good metrics are far from extraneous; they are the key gauges on your management console. That said, in many cases, it will be difficult to prove definitively what direct impact the CMS has had on a goal. For example, if the time to close a sale decreases, it may be the CMS that caused the decrease — but other, completely unrelated factors may also have contributed. However, by formulating goals meaningfully and specifically, it's more likely that you can account for extraneous factors that affect your goals in one way or another.

Taking Stock of Your Staffing Needs

At this stage of a CMS project, your project team can still be pretty lean. In addition to the core team, a few additional skilled people (or at least multiple skills in the same person) can help you through this process.

✦ **A facilitator** can help sponsors move towards agreement, avoid pitfalls, and keep discussion on-track and productive. The neutrality of a facilitator can also help reduce the heat of what may be contentious disagreements among the project team and sponsors.

✦ **A note taker** can perform the essential task of memorializing arguments, points of view, goals, and discussions, all the while saving others from the distraction of taking and collating notes.

✦ **A scheduler** can save you from a lot of back and forth as you round up the myriad sponsors and others whom you have to get in the same room at the same time, as well as set up the many one-on-one meetings you'll need to have.

✦ **A sponsor of record** is the person to whom you deliver the results of the mandate process. This is where your choice of sponsors (if you have one) can make the difference in how effectively your mandate is promoted throughout the organization.

Summary

If you go forward into a CMS project without securing a project mandate, you might get very lucky and feel no effect. On the other hand, your entire project might fall apart because of forces you never even knew were active. On the positive side, a mandate causes the entire organization to side with your effort. Even if you don't absolutely need support, don't you want it? The process of securing a mandate does the following:

✦ Requires you to recognize and understand the potential sponsors for the CMS project.

✦ Consists of a guided process for garnering support and agreement by your sponsors.

✦ Is aided by creating sponsor profiles, designing an issues hierarchy, and taking careful notes.

✦ Results in a project statement, a set of project goals, and an agreed-upon way to measure progress toward those goals.

In the next chapter, I describe requirements gathering, in which you use your mandate to figure out what stakeholders want from a CMS.

✦   ✦   ✦

Doing Requirements Gathering

◆   ◆   ◆   ◆

In This Chapter

A simpler sort of requirements-gathering process than you might be used to

Techniques for doing requirements

The types of deliver-ables that result from requirements

The people you may want to include in your requirements gathering

◆   ◆   ◆   ◆

After you have secured a project mandate, you can begin to collect the information you need to design the system with your sponsors and other stakeholders in mind. You begin by gathering your organization's requirements for content, publications, and CMS infrastructure.

In this chapter, I'll lay out some project techniques and deliverables you can use to collect and organize requirements.

Requirements Jumpstart

This Jumpstart summarizes how you gather requirements for your CMS. I describe the types of requirements to gather, how to ask the right questions, and how to deal with roadblocks within the organization.

Use this jumpstart as a summary without the weight of detail, or as a quick review if you've already read the chapter and want a checklist of what you need to accomplish to gather requirements for a CMS.

To gather requirements, follow these steps:

1. Meet with your team to decide:

   - How widely your requirements-gathering effort must extend. Who will you ask, and what questions? How quickly will you need responses?

   - Whether you are staffed appropriately for the effort to come.

   - When and how you will get review and consent for the requirements document you will produce.

2. Plan for dealing with roadblocks. Establish a deadline for responding, and expect that some groups and individuals may be less helpful than others. Have a plan for escalating organizational issues to your sponsor. If all else fails, incorporate gaps in information into your requirements document.

3. From your discussion, prepare a *requirements plan of attack* document, which describes with whom you'll talk to gather your requirements.

4. Organize your efforts into three types of requirements:

   - Gather *content* requirements first, if you can. Keep your questioning simple: What information to deliver and how it is created or acquired.

   - Gather *system* requirements. The list of questions for this phase is more extensive, but many are specific to your particular technology environment.

   - Gather *publication* requirements. These requirements are centered on identifying and serving your top three audiences.

5. From all the information you have collected, put together the *requirements document*, which describes the requirements for the CMS project.

6. Get a review of and official consent for the requirements document to inoculate your project against additional requirements proposed later in the planning and implementation phase.

When you have completed the requirements process and document, you are ready to move on to the logical design phase.

What Are Requirements?

Requirements are the specific qualities, features, and objects that the system will ultimately include. In a CMS project, three sorts of requirements are collected:

✦ **Content requirements,** which specify the kinds of content to be managed and how it must be gathered and organized.

✦ **CMS requirements,** which specify how the CMS hardware and software should operate.

✦ **Publication requirements,** which specify the kinds and structure of the output you want the CMS to produce, including how to target content to your chosen audiences.

It is likely that you already have a lot of this sort of information hanging around. For example, during your readiness assessment you collected the assumptions that people made regarding just these subjects. Now, however, it is not opinions that you are after, it is requirements. By the end of this stage of your project, you must cull the range of opinion down to a solid set of must-haves that will drive the rest of your project.

I think the word *requirements* says it all. You will be required by your organization to follow these guidelines in designing and constructing your system. If you take this seriously, it can work very well for you. In particular, be very careful about what you call a requirement. Be sure that 1) the proposed statement is of enough importance to be called a requirement, and 2) you are happy to be held to it. In addition, as you collect and organize requirements, you can get the organization to help you by underscoring the importance and durability of requirements.

Techniques for Getting the Job Done

The techniques in the following sections help you understand what I mean by requirements and how you might go about gathering them, including how to approach your organization most effectively to obtain the requirements you need.

The requirements process I lay out here is quite a bit simpler than the one most software developers use. Rather than asking an exhaustive set of questions that will lead directly to a design, I recommend that you ask simple questions to provide an overall direction. From that point, you can dig further to come to the more fundamental questions and answers that you put together during logical design, as discussed in Chapter 18, "Doing Logical Design."

The process I present is predicated on the assumption that the people you approach for requirements have neither the time nor the insight to give you real answers. They do, however, have the ability and the authority to determine the broad outlines of the system. This assumption has been borne out in every project I have been a part of. People just do not know enough about CM systems to give you real requirements in an explicit and comprehensive way. But they possess information and knowledge you can gather and analyze to form the requirements that you need. After you have found out what people want, you are in the best position possible to give it to them or tell them why it is not possible.

The requirements process

Your requirements process must result in an agreement on content, publication, and system requirements. The point here is to get the people in the organization to tell you what they really need. You are not trying to get them to learn all the terminology and processes that you must use to turn requirements into action. Nor are you trying to get them to work any harder than absolutely necessary. So, your best approach, I believe, is to ask simple yet comprehensive questions that require only short answers.

Before diving into the more precise set of questions to ask, let me propose an overall process for gathering requirements: canvass widely, catalog everything, and get consent.

Canvass widely

Cast a net as wide as is feasible to get input from a wide base of contributors. With any luck, through your previous work in assessing readiness and building a mandate, you have already isolated the list of potential contributors. The list ought to be narrower than the one you used originally to find out what was going on in the organization. It should include only those people who are in a position to require something of the system. On the other hand, the list should be wider than the people who participated in the mandate process. They are probably not the only ones with the knowledge and authority to state what the CMS must accomplish.

Tip You can certainly get the process off to a good start by providing a list of the potential requirements that you already have amassed from your initial communication. In addition, it also helps to ask different people for different types of requirements, based on what they are qualified to comment on.

Catalog everything

Your position in the requirements process is scribe and librarian. The most help you can offer is to keep the list of potential requirements from getting out of control and becoming confusing. The work you do to synthesize people's input into an easy-to-read and easy-to-understand document is crucial. When someone does not see her words in the document you produce, you should make it clear that her requirements are being superseded by larger and more central concerns rather than ignored. There is a subtle art to combining requirements in a way that no one feels slighted, but that still ensures inferior input is weighted less than superior input.

A technique I have found useful here is not to wait until I am finished to get feedback. Rather, I go back and forth with a number of contributors, passing small pieces of the requirements between us as I work on the final draft. This technique has the effect of giving work to people in bite-sized chunks (that is, the size of chunk that can get done in an e-mail exchange) and building consensus before the draft is even circulated.

Get consent

Formal approval of the requirements is a must. When someone comes along weeks (or even months) later with a must-have requirement, you just point to the formally approved requirements. This may not stop you from having to include the rogue requirement, but at least it will make the "rogue requiree" think twice. In addition, the formality of official consent helps people take their parts seriously. By now people may be tired from all the work that they have put into getting this project started. You can assure them that this is the last big push they will be involved in, and smile inwardly that you have exhausted them into giving you the space you need to do the tasks ahead.

In addition to approval of the list of requirements, you should push for consent on their priorities. Your list of requirements is likely to be longer than you are comfortable accomplishing in the limited time you have for the project. In addition, it is likely that the list includes items that are there because you stopped arguing or simply because someone was willing to stand up for them. By having priorities, you can let the organization decide the relative importance of the requirements and prepare the organization for not getting all required items on the first go-round.

Tip You can get your contributors to take the first cut at prioritization by asking them to mark requirements as "must have," "should have," or "could have."

In gathering requirements, your goal is to get people to think out of the box about what is really needed, not just what they already have or are already doing. You want people to give you the constraints without which the CMS will not work, rather than tell you about their favorite white papers, Web sites, and development platforms. A fine and not-so-visible line exists between a desire and a constraint (especially if the "desiree" is a person with sway!). If there are disputes in the organization, especially in the platform questions, they will show up in your requirements. If you are lucky, the support and consensus that you forged in the mandate process can carry you through any difficulties here — but don't count on it.

Note I have seen more than one content management initiative stall as all the organization's disputes were visited on the content management requirements-gathering process.

The requirements

Because of the broad range of requirements it is possible to gather, you must first organize your efforts by figuring out what sorts of requirements you need to gather. Note that, although your requirements needs don't necessarily break down along job descriptions, some requirements questions are best targeted to particular people in your organization. Broadly speaking, the three kinds to gather include the following:

✦ **Content requirements** deal with the types of content your organization must deliver and how it gets created. Business planners, information architects, and publications people will provide a lot of this sort of information.

✦ **System requirements** deal with the physics of the CMS you need—the hardware and software as well as performance characteristics and criteria. Your IT people will be primary sources of information for these requirements.

✦ **Publication requirements** focus on identifying the kinds and characteristics of the audiences you need to serve. Your publications, marketing, and business planning people are among the principal sources of information for publications.

I discuss each of these kinds of requirements in detail in the following sections.

Content requirements

Content requirements are a good place for you to start if your organization has its business goals solidified. If not, you may get stuck by starting with something else (such as system or publication requirements). Without a solid marketing plan, you may not know who your customers or other audiences are or which of them are most important, making it extremely difficult to define and prioritize content. Without clear business goals, the simple question, "What content should we deliver?" may open a can of worms. The result may be a CMS effort that either forces those plans to be solidified, protracting the process, or an effort that pushes on without clear goals and ends up with a half-baked system.

If you find that you are not making much headway with content, try starting with the questions about publications and working back to content.

Describing Content Management Requirements

I've often explained to organizations that before they invest resources in developing a content management capability, they must understand their requirements for the system. But when I ask "What are your content management requirements?" there is a resounding silence, not because the organization doesn't have content management needs, but because they don't know how to express their needs.

One technique for discovering these needs is to use a kind of *"use case analysis"* to develop and document content management requirements. Your organization has defined processes by which it operates and does business. Each process both generates and consumes content. If you analyze all the organization's processes and specify how the activities in and between the processes intersect, you will have a pretty good understanding of your content management requirements. To do this:

1. List the organization's processes. Identify event-driven processes and calendar-driven processes.

2. Pick a process or set of interacting processes.

3. Determine and document the process steps and their precursor for execution (event or calendar).

4. Determine the content "chunks" in each. For each chunk, identify the content creator (owner), consumer (user), and modifier (co-owner).

Now you have a first-order understanding of content management needs as they pertain to the process you analyzed. Repeat this analysis for the remaining processes (or what you consider a core set of processes).

Rex C (Trav) Stratton, Pacific Northwest National Laboratory

The questions behind the content requirements are quite simple:

✦ What information do we need to deliver?

✦ For each type of information, who in the organization creates this information or how will we otherwise acquire it?

From these humble beginnings, you can begin to construct the entire collection system. The answers to the second question serve as much to make the respondent think as they do to provide you with information. If the respondent has a clear idea of how you will come by the information she suggests, great. If she does not, maybe question two will cause her to think a bit more before suggesting that you collect such information. You can also use the answers to question two as an aid to prioritization. If no one knows how to get a hold of a certain kind of information, maybe the cost of collecting it is higher than the value that the content provides.

System requirements

System requirements are the set of technological constraints that the organization imposes on the CMS.

You must ask a few more questions to gather system requirements, and they are more specific than the content and publication questions. The following are such types of questions:

✦ **System integration.** With what existing systems will the CMS have to integrate? Existing systems include those connected to the management system, as well as those that provide information to the publishing system. In Chapter 7, "Introducing the Major Parts of a CMS," you can find more information on management and publishing system connections.

✦ **Hardware and software.** What company standards for hardware and software apply to the CMS? If, for example, all your graphic artists use Macintosh computers, you need to know that so you can make sure your collection software works on their computers.

✦ **Development environments.** What requirement or preference does the organization have for software development environments? The question is not "What platform do you prefer?" but "Has the organization or any department mandated the use of a particular platform?" This phrasing helps avoid getting back a lot of personal preferences (which, for some strange reason, you do not need a lengthy process to uncover).

✦ **Deployment platforms.** What requirement or preference does the organization have for publication deployment platforms? The obvious answers are about Web servers, Web application servers, databases, firewalls, and server farms. You may find this sort of information easiest to collect. Either the organization has all its platforms set up and prefers to continue using them, or the organization does not and wants this choice to be part of your job. Less obvious are the deployment platforms for non-Web publications. For example, what infrastructure exists or is preferred for print publications? Is there a group that really has this nailed down? What e-mail platforms are in use that can do bulk mailings (if that is part of your publication set)?

✦ **Performance.** What requirements exist for scaling and performance in the management or publication systems? What you are most likely to get are the current statistics for your organization's Web initiatives. What you might probe a bit deeper for, however, is how long the current systems can go on before they begin to degrade. It is quite likely that your systems will be pushed much harder with a CMS behind them than they are being pushed now.

✦ **Deployment.** Are there standard rollout procedures? If you are in a large organization that has existed for more than a year or two, you have undoubtedly rolled out an enterprise system before. If this rollout was done well, you have a written legacy of good procedures and guidelines. If you can find this legacy, you will save a tremendous amount of time and effort.

✦ **Maintenance.** Are there system maintenance standards? Your organization probably maintains enterprise systems now. What standards are used to measure the quality of maintenance agreements and support procedures? As with rollout standards, you can save a lot of time if you can find an existing process with which you can connect the CMS.

✦ **Localization.** Are there localization standards? If your organization is in more than one culture, you have no doubt already come across the issues associated with multiple languages and localization of content (localization includes, for example, making sure half-naked bodies do not show up on screens in cultures where they offend). I have seen few organizations that have dealt with this problem in a comprehensive and well-documented way. If your organization has done so, in addition to having a great career opportunity in localization, you will have a great start on this difficult issue.

Publication requirements

The questions to ask about publications are a bit more complex, but ought not to cause any huge workload for the respondents. They are the following:

✦ Who are the top three audiences we are trying to serve with our information?

✦ What categories do the top three audiences fall into?

✦ What other audiences would it be nice to serve?

✦ How do we provide information to the top three audiences now?

✦ How would these audiences prefer to have information provided?

By starting with the audiences, you put the respondent in the right frame of mind. Rather than telling you directly what publications they think the organization needs to create, they tell you how audiences prefer to get information. The questions nudge the respondent to begin to prioritize publications by the audiences they serve. All respondents choose three audiences (an arbitrarily low number that you might want to change). That means that they will all have to choose the most important ones. In addition, by asking them to choose three audiences, you force the respondents to give you audiences that are at the same level. One can't (or, at least, has no excuse to) say, "sales engineers, sales reps, and inside sales," while another says, "staff, partners, and customers."

Notice, in the questions I provide in the previous paragraph, you ask your interviewees about what your organization does now, but purposely *no* questions about what they think you should be doing. Rather, the questions are about what the audiences would like. In your questioning process, you need to keep people away from offering prescriptions; too often, people try to fit the audiences into their preconceived notions (or, more to the point, their preexisting outputs) of the right set of publications. This questioning is a not-so-subtle attempt to get people to break those molds.

As with the content requirements, these questions are designed to make the respondents think, as well as simply provide information.

The Requirements Process

User requirements are defined in terms of business need and the business process. The goal is certainly always to improve the current state. Requirements often come to life in the form of personas or characteristics that define the audience behavior in terms of role, function, geography, technology preferences, information requirements, and so on. With the advent of content components and mix-and-match functionality, user expectations are much higher than in the past. They expect to be able to accomplish more at once, with easy access or even immediate access to the information relevant in the context in which they find themselves. This is evident in the increased adoption of personal portals, embedded Web parts in line of business applications, and the use of alerts and notifications.

A well-orchestrated CMS is the foundation for a successful user experience — especially in terms of delivering a contextual workspace that is meaningful to the user at the time he or she needs it. While standards are critical, actual management of content in terms of functionality is essential. Imagine the difference between your own 3-D adventure that adapts to your situation — maybe even before you realize adapting is required — versus watching a 2-D movie with 200 people in a big dark room where you're working hard to follow the story line. It's the difference between being relevant and wondering if it is relevant.

Mary Lee Kennedy, The Kennedy Group (www.maryleekennedy.com)

Approaching the organization

Sometimes the organization itself can stand in the way of completing your requirements gathering in the following ways:

✦ **It's difficult to establish ownership of many of the requirements.** Who is the right person to say which database you must use? Who can decide whether a particular type of content is a "must have" or a "nice to have"?

✦ **People don't have time to answer your queries.** This is especially true for questions that require real effort such as, "Can you sample those 1,000 files and tell me how consistently formatted they are?"

✦ **People will speak with authority when they have none.** When you ask a question, you may get an answer whether or not the respondent has the knowledge or position to properly answer.

✦ **People cannot (or will not) deal with your collection methods.** My teams have tried everything from Web-based forms and e-mail messages, to Microsoft Word templates and personal phone calls, and still people cannot understand how to respond in the appropriate way. The good angel on my right shoulder says, "It's not easy enough." The bad angel on my left shoulder says, "Lazy #$%#!"

✦ **People don't know how to answer your questions,** so they will stall or try to divert you by heaping information on you (such as those people who say, "I don't know what is important so I'll just give you all of it and let you decide").

✦ **CMS requirements tend to cross department lines,** so you end up chasing facts around all of the loops and down all of the blind alleys that your organization might have in its structure (for example, being bounced around from person to person until you are back at the person where you started). You may find that, notwithstanding the weight of your mandate, big differences exist from one department to another regarding how helpful people can or want to be. In particular, your work will be easiest the closer you are to the departments containing your sponsors, and may be more difficult in departments that don't include your sponsors.

So, what do you do? First, a small amount of common sense and organizational savvy can go a long way. Note when you are getting heaped on or put off, and then stop wasting effort. Use your mandate and the support of your sponsors to cut red tape and hold people to the responsibilities of their job descriptions. Note whose interests are being served by holding you back or stalling the process, and act on that rather than on the frustration you feel toward a particular person.

More generally, you can create a plan of attack that identifies organizational contacts and their responsibilities (the plan of attack deliverable is detailed later in this chapter).

Above all, realize that people are unlikely to understand what you are doing and why you are asking questions. With patience, an attitude of respect, a desire to teach them as well as learn from them, and a good sense of humor, you can build alliances while you collect requirements that will last you through the rest of the project.

If you have built your readiness assessment as I outlined, you have no doubt already interacted with many of the people to whom you are turning now. If you performed a mandate process anything like the one I outlined, you will have all the organizational support and muscle you need to get back good, timely information.

Finally, use your mandate as a tool to set the context of the discussion. Rather than saying, "What content should we include?" say, "What content best fits the mandate we received?" Keep referring back to the mandate until your respondent (and you, for that matter) cannot help but take it seriously into account.

Through this all, try to keep perspective—the barriers you encounter are not just roadblocks, they're information that you must take into account to be successful. In fact, you can recognize these barriers in your analysis, and propose requirements around them. For example, if a particular department simply can't or won't come up with implementation documentation for a legacy system, a requirement might be to document the legacy system to the extent needed for planning its integration with the new CMS. This type of requirement highlights gaps in the requirement-gathering process. In my experience, shining a bright light on a dark place can help make the needed information materialize if it does indeed exist somewhere.

If all of this good advice fails you and you are still left on Thursday night with not enough information for the Friday deadline, take heart. I have been there, everyone I know has been there, and now you are there too! Welcome to the Frustrated Analysts Club!

Taking Stock of the Deliverables

You can use the following deliverables to form the basis of your requirements process:

✦ **The requirements plan of attack** charts how you can reach all the people you must talk to in your organization.

✦ **The requirements document** solidifies and makes official the requirements for the CMS project.

The requirements plan of attack

If you prepare a little, your foray into the organization to collect requirements is much easier. In addition, in the heat of collection, you will be able to refer back to your plan and not have to remember what to do next.

One way to approach this plan is to focus, not on the requirements, but on the people in the organization from whom you collect them. My assumption here is that, given the questions I have laid out, you already know enough about what requirements to capture. On the other hand, I assume that you want to know more about how to collect them from your colleagues. To work this through, you can create a spreadsheet that lists your requirements contacts. Before you send out any questions, get together with each contact and define the following:

✦ **Which questions will you ask?** You might want to number your questions to make it easy to refer to them.

✦ **What kind of turnaround time** will you expect on answers?

✦ **What kind of review** of your synthesis will she require?

✦ **Whom can you contact** if she is not comfortable answering certain questions? (Should you seek a higher authority?)

✦ **Who are the other people who should answer the same questions**? You can compare her answers to this question to the list of people you have targeted to be sure that you have not missed anyone and that she is aware of the other people you have chosen for each question. It is better not to surprise her later.

With this task complete, you can create a second spreadsheet that focuses on the requirement questions I laid out earlier. For each requirement, you can enter the following information:

✦ The names of the respondents

✦ The overall turnaround times for responses

✦ The review process you will use for the requirement

✦ The arbitration process for conflicting answers

The second spreadsheet is a plan of attack for gathering requirements.

Note   The length of this process is another reason I boil requirements down to so few questions. You could not practically do this sort of process with dozens of questions.

The requirements document

Prepare an official result of the requirements process to hang next to your project mandate. When the arbitration is finished on the last question, I suggest that you gather the final results into a document and get specific sign-offs from the following people:

✦ The respondents to the requirements questions

✦ Your sponsors or their assigned point persons

✦ Your project team

I believe that it is worth making this much fuss over the requirements document because it is the last input you expect the organization to provide to you for a while. As such, you want to make sure it gets full closure and that the signatories know that their chance for major input is now done. In addition, these requirements are your true marching orders. If the mandate is the goal of the war, the requirements are your orders. What is left, of course, is a battle plan.

Be sure to include in your requirements document clear references to the mandate. You want to be sure yourself first, and then communicate to others, that the requirements derive clearly from the mandate. For your own sake, as well as for the effect it will have on others, be sure that this is actually true. Later, it may be too late to reconcile those nagging little inconsistencies between the overall goals and means you have chosen to achieve them.

As you might have guessed, my major organizing principle for all content management materials is collect, manage, and publish. To the extent that you can organize your requirements document with these three categories, it will clearly tie into the later deliverables as I describe them. However, you needn't go too far with this. The requirements document is the pivot point between the world of the organization and that of the CMS. The categories content, system, and publications that I presented earlier map very loosely to collect, manage, and publish, but they are about halfway between the language of the organization and that of the CMS. They may be a bit clearer to the audience of the requirements document than collect, manage, and publish.

Taking Stock of Your Staffing Needs

Staffing for the requirements process is organized around tasks at hand. The team can be small at this stage but, if necessary, some of the legwork can be handed out to additional personnel. The principal tasks and staffing are as follows:

✦ **The requirements plan of attack** effort is led either by the content manager or a business analyst. (If not leading the effort, the business analyst, at least, supervises this activity.) Other analysts may be added to the project as needed, depending on the time frame in which the requirements must be gathered.

✦ **The requirements document effort** is led by the business analyst, again with the likely participation of the content manager and supplemented by additional analysts as necessary.

Chapter 13, "Staffing a CMS," includes full descriptions of these job titles.

Summary

Requirements and, as you'll see in the next chapter, "Doing Logical Design," are the introduction to the meat of a CMS project. My version of requirements has you ask the organization for the most general, but also the most important content, infrastructure, and publication needs.

✦ In doing requirements gathering, use common sense and organizational savvy.

✦ Prepare a plan of attack for requirements before starting out on them.

✦ Get formal approval of the requirements document you produce.

After you've completed your requirements document, you're ready for the logical design process, addressed in the next chapter.

✦   ✦   ✦

Doing Logical Design

◆ ◆ ◆ ◆

In This Chapter

The concept of logical design

Techniques for doing logical design

The types of deliverables that result from logical design

The people you may want to include in your logical design process

◆ ◆ ◆ ◆

After you have collected all your requirements, you can begin to create a product-independent (or logical) design for your CMS that defines exactly how you intend to collect, manage, and publish information. In this chapter, I'll lay out some project techniques and deliverables you can use to construct a logical design.

Note   This chapter covers the project process behind requirements and design. The actual requirements and design considerations are covered in the chapters in Part IV, "Designing a CMS."

Logical Design Jumpstart

This Jumpstart summarizes what is needed to do logical design for your CMS. I describe logical design and why you need it, techniques for doing it in all its complexity, and how to communicate the results to others in the organization.

Use this jumpstart as a summary or as a quick review if you've already read the chapter and want a checklist of what you need to create a logical design for a CMS.

To create logical design, follow these steps:

1. Meet with your team to get yourself organized for the effort to come.

   - Discuss the documents you will produce as part of the design process. Decide exactly what belongs in each document and how you will manage the details that go into it. Specify whatever tools, spreadsheets, XML schemas, or databases you'll use to manage the content you gather.

   - Decide the process you'll use to create each design document. In particular, decide how much iteration you'll need to complete each design document and what you will accomplish in each iteration. Decide how you will determine constraints, and in particular, the extent to which you will triangulate to identify design constraints.

2. Document the results of your discussion with your team in a Design Plan of Attack document, which details your approach, tools, and processes.

3. Determine whether you're adequately staffed for the effort to come. If necessary, identify and secure additional staff for carrying out the design effort.

4. Following the plan you have created, collect information, analyze it, and create the design documents. The documents you create should include:

   - Collection design, which specifies the logical design of the collection system and processes, including authors, acquisition sources, creation or conversion of components, and staff required.

   - Management design, which specifies the logical design of the management system and processes, including the content schema, the access structures, and content life cycle processes.

   - Publication design documents, of which there should be several, including a strategy document, page design files, personalization plan, and administration.

   - Audience analysis, which informs everyone in the organization who you are trying to reach with the system you're designing.

   - A localization plan, which describes the extent to which content will be localized, as well as the processes and systems required to produce the level of localization you specify.

   - A risk assessment, which identifies issues, situations, and contingencies that might require modifying the logical design or implementation plan, schedule, or budget.

5. Revise the project plan based on the resources, deliverables, and constraint needs you've identified in the design documents.

6. Produce an executive summary that briefly encapsulates the design documents in as few pages as possible.

7. Get approval of (or revise as necessary) the design document. In particular, scale back mandate items to reach the budget and time restraints the organization requires.

When you're done, you'll be ready to start making implementation decisions, starting with hardware and software.

What Is Logical Design?

At the end of requirements gathering, you will have a head (and a hard drive) full of other people's dictates to you about how the CMS should be designed and why it is being created. Next, it is your turn to respond. In logical design, you decide how the CMS can meet all the goals and requirements that have been set out for it.

I use the term logical design to contrast this process with the later process of physical design. In physical design, you put together the specifications and plans that say how the CMS will actually be constructed from hardware and software. In logical design, you put together the system outside the constraints of a particular platform. Another term for logical design might be platform-independent design. Why would you do such a thing? Here are a few good reasons:

✦ CMS involves much more than hardware and software. Content, for example, is neither hardware nor software.

✦ You should understand what you *want* to happen before you decide *how* you will make it happen. There is nothing more time-consuming and potentially career-adverse than creating a system, only to find out later that it can't do what you never took the time to figure out you wanted it to do.

✦ You need information to help you decide what sort of hardware and software you need to build your CMS. The best tool you have for deciding what sort of platform you need is to know what you want it to do. Even if you already have a CMS in place, before you start pushing a bunch of buttons, you should have a clear idea of the results you intend.

Your Logical Design

Logical design specifies what you want to have happen in a system. Physical design refers to the particular parts you bring together to make the system happen. A number of other situations involve the same relationship between physical and logical design, as the following examples illustrate:

✦ A computer itself has a physical design, with chips, disk drives, and a lot of wire. It also has a logical design. In response to a given set of inputs (ones and zeros that are presented to the computer's central processing unit), the computer is designed to perform a particular action and produce a certain output. The computer's physical design can run software with its own organization and internal logic.

✦ A supermarket has a physical design, with shelves, floors, ceilings, and lots of products. It also has a logical design. It is a system for moving products from loading dock to shopping basket. The physical design of the supermarket can *run* promotions that move your body and eyes to the products that the *supermarketeers* most want you to buy.

✦ Your brain has a physical design, with neurons, hormones, and a lot of connections. It also has a logical design. Groups of neurons form functional areas that take care of particular functions. Groups of functional areas gang together to perform more complex functions. At an even higher level, the physical design of the brain can *run* consciousness and thought processes that have their own organization and logic.

In all cases, the physical design allows but does not determine the logical design. The logical design works within the broad constraints of the physical design. It can't do something outside the bounds of the physical design. On the other hand, it can do things that are beyond the physical design. My word processor, for example, enables me to write. Writing is not something that is part of the physical design of the computer. In a CMS, the hardware and software that make up the system allow (but do not determine) the kinds of content and publications you will create.

There is not a single physical and a single logical design. Each shelving unit in a supermarket and each neuron also have a physical and a logical design. In fact, in interesting systems such as computers and brains, myriad levels of designs exist. In a CMS, the physical design itself is composed of software and hardware with their own internal logical and physical designs.

The logical design is the real reason for the system. The physical design of the computer, supermarket, or (arguably) the brain is there so that the logical design has a place to exist. The same is true for a CMS. You want the logical design of contributors, components, and publications. You need the physical design of computers and networks that enable it to happen.

Logical design is like a big puzzle. The pieces are bits of information you collect or derive from the requirements related to authors, sources, components, publications, and so on. You have to fit them all together so that they make a complete and sensible picture of the collection, management, and publishing process you intend to create. If a piece does not fit, you must rearrange the others until it does — or get rid of the outlier.

Logical design results in process, relationship, and structure, as follows:

✦ **You design the processes** by which you intend to collect, manage, and publish content. For example, you must figure out how a particular kind of content can be collected at the right rate to meet the publication cycles of all the publications in which it will appear.

✦ **You work through the relationships** between the significant players in the system until they all support and enhance each other. For example, you must figure out how you can get your authors to create content types in such a way that they can be targeted to your various audiences, using publication templates.

✦ **You design a content structure** that fully represents the information you need to distribute and also adds enough metadata to the information to enable you to automate its management. For example, you create a set of content types that organize the information you want to deliver and also augment it with management data you can use to automate its delivery.

By the end of the process, you might long for the days when everyone was telling you what to do. Or, if you're like me, this might be your favorite part — figuring, finessing, and finding a way to make very human factors fit into a logical and very effective framework.

Techniques for Getting the Job Done

The techniques in the following sections help you learn and practice some techniques for logical design, including how to go from business goals to a system, how to iterate a number of times through the process, how to triangulate on the various aspects of design, and how to manage the enormous amount of detail you collect.

Logical design is the design of the CMS outside of the particular hardware and software you use to implement the CMS. This is not to say that it cannot help you choose the right system or that it will not be used by the system you end up installing. It surely can. A logical design specifies what is to be done, and a particular CMS dictates how it is to be done.

Here are the aspects of logical design that you must take into account:

✦ **Audience analysis:** This details the kinds of people you will serve. In Chapter 25, "Cataloging Audiences," you will find the full description of audience analysis.

✦ **Publication design:** Here you define what content and navigation each publication will include and exactly how they will be built and personalized automatically by the CMS. In Chapter 26, "Designing Publications," you will find the full description of publication design.

✦ **Content type design:** Here you determine the complete set of content types you will manage and exactly how each one will be constructed. In Chapter 27, "Designing Content Types," you will find the full description of content design.

✦ **Author analysis:** Here you decide which content authors you need and how you will serve them. In Chapter 28, "Accounting for Authors," you will find the full description of author analysis.

✦ **Source analysis:** Here you decide where you will acquire information and how you will process it to make it ready for the CMS. In Chapter 29, "Accounting for Acquisition Sources," you will find the full description of source analysis.

✦ **Access structure design:** Here you define the hierarchies and other access structures you will need to keep your content organized in its repository and to produce the navigation you required for publications. In Chapter 30, "Designing Content Access Structures," you will find the full description of access structure analysis.

✦ **Workflow and staffing design:** These designs specify the kinds and numbers of jobs and tasks that are required to start up and run the CMS. In Chapter 33, "Designing Workflow and Staffing Models," you will find the full description of workflow and staffing analysis.

These various analyses and designs do not stand alone. Rather, they overlap and inform each other in many ways.

Cross-Reference
In Chapter 23, "The Wheel of Content Management," you will find an overview of all these analyses and a discussion of how they interact.

Why do logical design?

Most people underestimate the amount of information they must accumulate to fully define a CMS. In fact, many organizations skip the stage of defining their requirements for the CMS entirely and simply begin using whatever software they have purchased, trying to make it produce pages like the ones they have now.

Contrary to what you might expect me to say, I don't believe that this is a bad approach. Given that you have a long time to play with a system, experiment with what it can do, and determine what it requires of your organization, this method can give you a very good start. It can teach you all the basics of content management and give you practical experience with a real tool.

On the other hand, there is a big leap from a system that can produce some pages like the ones you have now to one that can organize your entire production and distribution process. You can't expect the latter process to happen just by turning on and using even the best CMS. The experience that you get by using a CMS, however, will help you do the logical design that you must still eventually do.

Other organizations rush to buy a tool and then begin an analysis. Again, this can work. By immediately imposing the constraints of a particular product on the project process, you get to use a lot of the methods and tools that the CMS product company might provide. In addition, you can show immediate results and hit a big milestone quickly. On the other hand, if you buy before you study, you risk the very real possibility of having purchased a (possibly, very expensive) system, only to find after using it for a while that it was the wrong one for your needs. Finally, by choosing a tool before you really know what you want to do, you may end up not doing something simply because it is off the tool's radar screen (regardless of how much value that *something* can have for your organization).

If you have followed the steps I have laid out so far, you already have spent a lot of time working through the issues. You should also have a lot of detail about what people want and require of the system. You might think that what you collected during the readiness assessment and mandate process ought to be enough to define the system. Maybe it is, but probably it is not. What you have collected so far certainly establishes what people want, but does it define what your organization needs? At the very least, you will have to organize and augment these wants and get the organization's departments to agree that they are complete. More likely, you have a good start and a lot of general statements but nothing specific enough to be the basis for a system design.

If you take the trouble to do a complete logical design, it will help you significantly in the following ways:

✦ **System selection:** In logical design, you say exactly what you want your CMS to do. If you already have a CMS package in mind, your planning team can use the design to decide the degree of fit between the selected system and the design. If you have not yet selected a system, the design will give you a clear picture of the system you want. You can compare your picture to the one presented to you by the product companies you review. You will also be able to ask intelligent questions of the CMS product vendors and not be overly swayed by slick presentations. Finally, if you choose to develop a custom system, the logical design provides great input for your software requirements specification.

✦ **System implementation:** To implement a CMS, you create a set of specifications. The specifications combine what you want to do with how you will do it. The logical design is what you want to do. The features and functions of the CMS you will build or buy are how you will do it. If you do not get a clear idea of what you want to do, the features and functions of the CMS you use will decide for you. A logical design puts reality into your specifications by making sure that the features and functions it defines are seen in light of the exact content and publications you want the system to manage.

✦ **System rollout and maintenance:** The logical design should provide just the right starting point for many of your system deployment deliverables. For example, the logical design describes in detail the staff that will contribute to the CMS. These are the same people to whom the system must be deployed. In addition, much of the documentation you need to train users and maintain the system can come directly from the logical design deliverables.

From business to system

I'll assume that you are starting this phase of your project with a hierarchy of business goals, a mandate statement, and a set of requirements (see Chapter 16, "Securing a Project Mandate," in the section "Taking Stock of the Deliverables," for more information on coming up with these items). You can use these goals and requirements to make your way into a design. Figure 18-1 illustrates the hierarchy of business goals — a mandate statement is at the tip of an organized set of business goals; a content domain statement is at the same tip of an organized set of publications and content types.

Your mandate can be rephrased as a content domain statement if you ask the question, "What information and functionality do we need to deliver to meet this aim?" Then, from the single domain statement, you should be able to start constructing an outline of the kinds of content that belong in the domain (the content hierarchy). In this way, you can pivot naturally from the knowledge of the business you have gained in the mandate process to knowledge of the content you must provide.

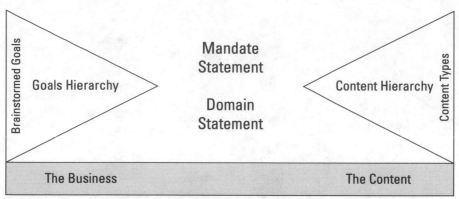

Figure 18-1: The hierarchy of business goals can lead directly to a hierarchy of content, which in turn can lead to a set of content types.

Cross-Reference

In Chapter 30, "Designing Content Access Structures," in the section "The content domain," you can find out more about the content domain statement.

Tip

When you construct a content hierarchy, try not to be overly influenced by what you already know about the content that people plan to deliver. If you can work strictly from the mandate statement and then the domain statement, you will have an independent means of evaluating what belongs in the system. Inconsistencies between your outline and what people have asked for in their requirements are a good thing. Use them to rework your content hierarchy, your domain statement, and even your mandate statement (if you dare). Otherwise, you can state with confidence why the proposed requirement does not belong.

With a good content hierarchy in hand, you can begin to decide what sort of content types you need. This is only a beginning, however, because you will work and rework your list of types throughout the design process. (See Chapter 27, "Designing Content Types," for much more information on content types.) Loosely, each terminal node (one with no children) of the hierarchy is a potential content type.

With the preliminary list of content types, you are ready to begin the real work. From the content you know you have to deliver and the requirements you have gathered, you can work through the design of the system you will use to collect, manage, and publish content (see Figure 18-2).

Your independently created content hierarchy and the requirements you have gathered are the starting place for design. After you have reconciled these two, you can begin to perform the in-depth logical design of your system. Logical design answers the myriad questions about what you want the CMS to do. In your design, you can organize the answers you find into the usual three categories: collect, manage, and publish.

As you can see, a lot is going on here. You can go from business goals to a preliminary list of content types, all on a piece of paper in a coffee shop. To go from the preliminary content types to the final classes and the system you need for them, however, is another story. You must know much more about your audiences, publications, information sources, staffing, workflow, and the access structures used to manage components before you can begin to implement the system.

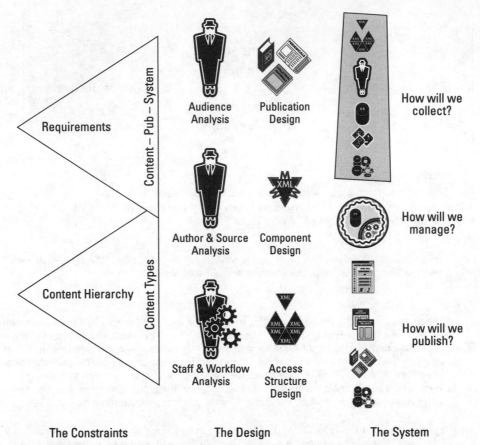

Figure 18-2: Your requirements and the content hierarchy are the starting place for your design.

I'm sure you are not surprised to know that there is a lot of work to do. I hope that this overview shows you, however, that the work is neither insurmountable nor unknown. Keep these diagrams in mind (or at hand) as you dive into the details of design.

Iterating through your design

No clear dividing line exists between the amount of categorization you need and the amount you can do. (For example, should you break your audiences into 3 categories, 9 categories, or 27 categories?) Frankly, you can go on forever, collecting and refining your approach to your CMS and never begin to feel that you have completed the task. In Part IV, "Designing a CMS," I present a comprehensive list of all the design criteria you should eventually uncover. If you simply dive in and try to capture all these constraints at once, you may get bogged down and confused and then run out of time with an incomplete analysis.

The solution is to pass through the same set of constraints many times, each time going deeper than the last and each time coming to a feeling of completeness at some level. When you run out of time, you may not have all the constraints worked out, but you will have an even and complete amount of detail in all areas. In other words, approach constraints in a series of deepening iterations. Here is an example of a five-pass process that you can use as a starting place to design your own set of iterations:

✦ **Pass 1 — Preload:** Review all the documents and notes you have collected so far and use them to create a general statement for each category of design (audiences, authors, publications, and so on). For example, your analysis so far might lead you to say, "We will have about 30 authors, all of whom will be inside the organization." Use your best judgment to create these statements and note any gaps in your knowledge that cause you to have to guess.

✦ **Pass 2 — First cut:** From the large number of questions that I provide in Part IV, "Designing a CMS," decide on no more than three or four questions that you need to be answered in each category to feel that you understand the major issues in full but at a high level. For example, you might divide the 30 authors you came up with in Pass 1 by their savvy and their closeness to your team. Take no more than a few days to get good answers to those questions, and then create a short but comprehensive design report. Get immediate feedback on the report to ensure that you are in sync with the project stakeholders.

✦ **Pass 3 — Design detail:** Begin to fill in the detailed design constraints in each category presented in Part IV. Prioritize the questions that are most important to get answered most quickly and then act on the highest-priority questions first. In this way, your details will come together in waves from most to least important. You can break this pass into smaller increments, each with its own tight deadline, to further organize your approach. This pass ends when you are at the point of diminishing returns (that is, it is too much effort to drill down any further at this point). You undoubtedly will have important unanswered questions, but you must resolve to push on while you await responses.

✦ **Pass 4 — Triangulation:** One design constraint does not live in isolation from all others. More often than not, you will discover conflicting constraints or ones that force you to reconsider and perhaps deepen your analysis. This is a good thing. It means that you can play one constraint off others to make them all stronger and more consistent. In this pass, you can focus solely on how the different classes of design constraints affect each other. See the following section for more information on triangulation.

✦ **Pass 5 — Finalization:** In this pass, you go through the entire set of constraints (which might be quite large by now) to finalize them for approval. It is likely, however, that while you are doing this, the project can begin to move forward into design and specification.

Triangulating on constraints

To find the exact location of a point in the landscape, a surveyor triangulates. First, he measures the compass bearing to the point from one location, and then he measures the compass bearing to the point from a different location. After measuring the distance between the two locations, he can draw a triangle that tells him the exact location of the point in question. If he wants to be more precise, or check himself, he can use more than two locations. The more locations from which he takes measurements, the surer he is that he knows the location of his target.

To find the exact types of content you must create and manage, you too can look at them from different perspectives, as shown in Figure 18-3. For example:

1. **You can look at your components from the perspective of the collection requirements:** What kinds of components are your authors able to create? What kinds can you acquire?

2. **You can look at your components through the lens of management requirements:** How will you determine when it is time to archive or delete a component? What indexes and storage requirements will they have?

3. **You can survey your components from the vantage point of your publications:** What kinds of content belong on each page? What sorts do our audiences expect? What will we need to know to personalize?

By addressing the same target entity from a number of perspectives, you can be sure that you have accounted for all its parts. Of course, the same notion works for any other part of the system. For example, I could have triangulated on publications by looking at them from the perspective of the components, the audiences, and the sources. Any combination will work.

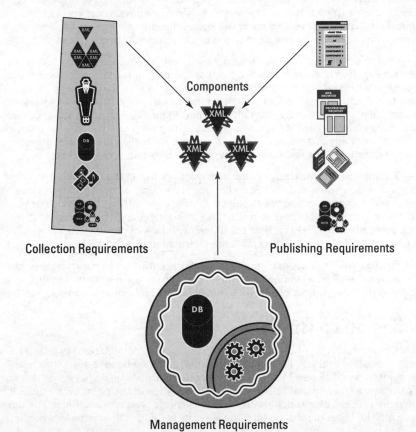

Figure 18-3: The more ways you use to define content types, the more sure you can be that they'll meet all the necessary requirements.

Triangulation, or cross-correlation as it is more properly called, is more than just an interesting exercise; it is the way to get at and solidify the requirements and design of your system.

Cross-Reference

In Chapter 23, "The Wheel of Content Management," I provide a more complete picture of the various aspects, which I call *entities*, which must be cross-correlated in a CMS.

Managing the details

Don't be surprised if you end up with hundreds of pages of data when you have fully fleshed out your design. For each content type (and you may have dozens), you might need three or four pages to detail its elements, element values, source information, target, audiences, the publishing templates where it shows up, and the personalizations that access it. For 25 content types, that's already 100 pages!

The volume of information is increased by the fact that you can cut the same information many ways. When you are detailing a content type, for example, you should mention the audiences it serves; but when you are detailing an audience, you need to mention the content types that are targeted to it. The combinations are numerous. To keep all the information straight, I have employed a variety of word processing systems, spreadsheets, and databases, but nothing has worked as well as XML. In my current version, I have all the design constraints I can think of nicely organized into an XML schema. The relationships between the classes of constraints (between components and audiences, for example) are specified in relationships between XML entities. The system enables me to:

✦ Have one central place where all my constraints are typed

✦ Account for the relationships between constraints as well as the constraints themselves

✦ Find and sort constraints

✦ Slice through a set of constraints and their relationships in any way I desire without needing to continually cut and paste

✦ Produce well-formatted reports

My approach may be overkill for you, especially at the beginning of your project, but keep in mind that you will eventually have all the same needs that I listed. So, whatever system you use to type in and keep track of constraints, it needs to be robust.

Taking Stock of the Deliverables

You can use the following deliverables to form the basis of your logical design project:

✦ **The design plan of attack** charts how you will move through the logical design process.

✦ **The collection, management, and publishing design documents** summarize the results of your extensive logical design process.

✦ **The audience analysis** presents your selected set of audiences for comment and acceptance by the organization.

✦ **The localization plan** shows what you consider the most practical approach to localization for your organization to understand and approve.

✦ **The risk assessment and project plans** that you developed earlier can be updated and deepened considerably based on your requirements gathering and logical design processes.

✦ **An executive summary** can help you inform and continue to receive support from your organization.

The following sections address each of these deliverables in turn.

The design plan of attack

A lot is required to fully develop and document a logical design. (It is for good reason that I devote so many chapters to it.) In planning for requirements, you could get away with a couple of spreadsheets. In planning for design, you had better trot out the best project management tools you have. Up until the end of requirements, the project is relatively small. Starting with design, it can begin to explode. It is the number of details and the number of relationships between details that cause such a large expansion of the project workload during logical design.

It behooves you to get organized early in the logical design phase—*and stay that way*. Lack of organization can drag out this phase of the project and result in a lot of missed details and relationships that may surface later in the project to haunt you.

The main things to account for in your design plan of attack are the following:

✦ **How you will collect and manage** the detailed information you will gather. As I mentioned earlier in this chapter, if you can manage to get a database or XML system together, it will repay your efforts.

✦ **Who will help gather** and process the information. Obviously, the same people who provided requirements can be of assistance. Be careful, however, not to count on people with a lot of other responsibility to do substantial work for you. If you don't already have a staff of your own, this may be the time to get one.

✦ **How you will time the data collection** and processing. As one example in many, it is just as valid to work backward from publications to components as it is to work forward from components to publications. In either case, how will you ensure that, in the end, components and publications are completely tied together? I mentioned the techniques of triangulation and iteration earlier to help you find ways to figure this out. In your plan, it is not enough to say that you will iterate, you must say how long each cycle will be and what exactly it will accomplish.

✦ **What you will deliver.** I'll provide a general framework for the design deliverables, but it is up to you to turn it into a solid plan.

✦ **How you will deal with overload.** Be prepared at the start for the amount of detail to overwhelm you. As you move forward, how will you reset expectations on required content and publications if you can't do them all? Don't wait until you have run out of time to confront this issue.

I prefer to use a project Gantt chart to show all the milestones to be accomplished in the design process (see Figure 18-4).

Based on what is most convenient for your team and organization, you can create one big logical design document or a number of smaller ones that fit together as a set. As you might expect, I organize the information to be presented in three parts: collection design, management design, and publishing design.

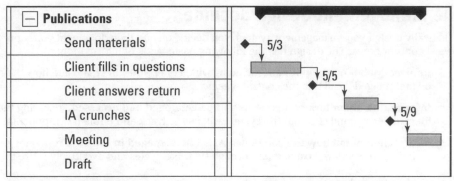

Publications	
Send materials	5/3
Client fills in questions	5/5
Client answers return	
IA crunches	5/9
Meeting	
Draft	

Figure 18-4: A Gantt chart can help you stay organized and on target during design.

The collection design document

To logically design your collection system, you decide and then document how content will move from outside the CMS to the point where it is ready to be used in publications. Following my discussion of what occurs in a collection system, the collection design document should cover these topics:

✦ **Who are the authors** and how will they be tied into the CMS? (More information on this is in Chapter 28, "Accounting for Authors.")

✦ **What are the acquisition sources** and how will they be tied into the CMS? (More information on this is in Chapter 29, "Accounting for Acquisition Sources.")

✦ **What components will be created** by which authors and sources and at what rates? (More information is on this in Chapter 27, "Designing Content Types," in the section "Plan.")

✦ **What conversion processes is needed** to transform the format and structure of the information? (More information on this is in Chapter 27, "Designing Content Types," in the section "Plan.")

✦ **What staff will be needed** to collect content and what will their tasks and processes be? (More information on this is in Chapter 33, "Designing Workflow and Staffing Models.")

You can use the information provided in the referenced chapters to decide what you need to say about these topics. As far as how to construct the document, consider its audiences. First, the staff it mentions will want to read this document. The document should, therefore, have well-marked sections that divide responsibilities by position name. Next, specification writers will want to read it to understand how to set up the collection systems. Thus, you should make sure that it divides the information by functional units (for example, authoring tools, conversion systems, acquisition procedures, and so on). Finally, it will be used as input to the system selection process, so it should call out any information to be included in the selection process.

If you are starting to think that you need a CMS just to produce the various cuts on the design of your CMS, you are on the right track.

The management design document

To logically design your management system, you decide on and then document your approach toward content types. The design has the following basic kinds of information:

✦ **Information about components,** including which ones you will create and how they will be metatagged. I call this the *content schema*.

✦ **Information about how components will be cataloged and accessed,** including the hierarchies and indexes that the system will use to track and publish components.

✦ **Information about how the components will be managed in the CMS repository,** including how you will track them through their life cycles and eventually retire them.

The content schema

A content schema divides content into types and types into elements. The schema specifies the following:

✦ **The set of types** to be managed.

✦ **The set of elements** for each type that includes both content and management elements.

✦ **The allowed values** for each element.

✦ **The subset of the elements that are shared** among a number of components to keep consistent naming. For example, you might have an element called Illustration that is used in any of the components that require a demonstration image.

✦ **The subset of elements that are universal;** that is, shared among all (or almost all) components that will be used for accessing and managing them. For example, you might decide that every component will have a Status element so that you can track its life cycle.

To construct a content schema, you divide and organize your information until every part is accounted for and you can confidently say that you have a workable system of content, management elements, and the types of which they are a part.

For more information on the content schema, refer to Chapter 27, "Designing Content Types," in the section, "Analyzing Content Types."

To deliver the schema, you document the components, elements, and values. A spreadsheet or word processing document may suffice. If you use these methods, your problem will be how to cut the same information in different ways. For ease of use later in the process, you want to deliver the information sorted by component as well as by element. This is cumbersome but possible in a spreadsheet application. It is, however, a real pain in a word processor. For that reason, I tend to use a database or XML application where I can switch easily between component and element views of the information.

Just as content types are the center of the content management process, so the content schema is the center of the logical design process. This means that it depends a lot on the other parts of the design. Therefore, don't expect the schema to come out quickly and stay the same. Rather, it will come out slowly and evolve throughout the logical design process. It will continue to evolve (though much more slowly) throughout the implementation process. Even after your system is running, you should expect the schema to change as you respond to the changing needs of your information marketplace. At that point, of course, you are performing maintenance, not design.

The content schema is the starting place for both the schema that you use to implement your system and the metatorial guide that you produce for system deployment.

Note   If you know that you will be using a relational database for your repository, you can deliver the schema to the implementers of the system as a database design. If you will be using an XML system, you can deliver it as an XML DTD or schema.

Component access

A big part of the logical design of the CMS is to figure out exactly how to catalog components so that you can find them and automatically generate the navigation of your publications.

Cross-Reference   The concepts and practice of access design are detailed in Chapter 30, "Designing Content Access Structures."

The feature that you cannot do without in this section of your management design document is the component hierarchy. The hierarchy is an outline that categorizes all the components you manage. By creating this hierarchy, you are sure that all your components fit together in a single access system. It is equally important to show how this overall component hierarchy can map to the hierarchies of each of your publications. If your system must produce components in multiple languages, you can show the relationship between the versions in this hierarchy.

You can also include the following sections in your management design document:

✦ **Indexing terms:** It is less important that you actually come up with an exhaustive set of terms than that you come up with the first list and also decide how the master list of terms will be generated (when and by whom). You must also decide how to translate the master list into the indexes that you include with any publication that uses an index.

✦ **Cross-reference strategy:** Here the point is not to create any cross-references, but rather to decide on general policies for when cross-references are needed, how they will be created, and how they will be represented in each publication.

✦ **Sequencing strategy:** Again, you are not in a position to actually create any component sequences; instead, you create the policy for how sequences will be represented.

Component administration

In addition to putting together a component schema during logical design, you decide on and document the staff, processes, and tasks that components will have assigned while they are in the repository. These processes include the following:

✦ Periodic editorial reviews

✦ Periodic metatorial reviews

✦ Archiving procedures

✦ Versioning procedures

✦ Deletion procedures

Cross-Reference   You can find more information about these reviews and procedures in Chapter 33, "Designing Workflow and Staffing Models," in the section "Clustering skills and tasks into jobs."

The form this deliverable takes is up to you, but it should match the way you document staffing and workflow in the other parts of the logical design.

The publication design documents

Publication design is somewhat more involved than collection or management design. Because each publication has its own interface (even books have a paper interface) and visual design qualities, you may have quite a bit to do to fully design even one publication, let alone the variety of publications that a CMS may be called upon to create.

Note   It's beyond my expertise to offer process or advice on the aspects of publication design that are outside of the content management arena (graphic design, branding, styling, look-and-feel, and the like). Instead, I'll focus on parts of publication design that are directly created by the CMS (for example, how branding elements created outside the CMS will be laid out on a publication page by the CMS).

In publication design, you define and prototype the pages of the publications that the CMS will be called upon to produce. The goal of publication design is to create the most compelling publications possible that can still be efficiently produced from the CMS. Ideally, publication design should begin at the same time, or even before you begin collection and management design. Collection and management design ensure that a viable system can be created behind the publications, and publication design ensures that the system produces compelling output.

The deliverables from the publication design process can be a large number of files rather than the few files that result from a collection or management design process. These deliverables include the following:

✦ **A publication strategy document,** which specifies how you will deal with your publications in general.

✦ **Page design files,** which define, at increasing levels of detail, how the pages will look and be built.

✦ **Personalization strategy documents** that show how you intend to target and deliver personalized content.

✦ **A publication administration document** that details who will be needed to create publications on a start-up and run basis, what tasks they will have to accomplish, and how frequently they will have to accomplish them.

Publication strategy

Although each publication is its own world with its own constraints and design, the set of publications you will create need to hang together as well. To figure out how individual publications fit into the whole, you can create these deliverables:

✦ **A component-to-publication analysis:** This document tracks each component from its neutral state in the CMS repository to its display in various publications. It ensures that you know how each component will be used in the final publications and that no conflicts exist. The core of this document is a large table (word processing, spreadsheet, or, preferably, a database report) that summarizes all the relationships between publications, pages, and components.

✦ **A template design document:** This document describes the overall approach to take to your publication templates. It includes a discussion of any sharing or commonality between publications, as well as sections for the templates for each separate publication.

In the publication-specific sections, the names of the page templates to be used are listed, as are the static text, component, and navigation templates to be included in each page template. Finally, it gives some definition of the logic that the template mentioned in the document must include in order to access and assemble content properly. (For more information on template design, see Chapter 31, "Designing Templates," in the section "Analyzing Templates.")

Page design

Page design concerns the look, layout, and building of publication pages. The deliverables for this process that have the most bearing on a CMS are as follows:

✦ **Page wire frames,** which are schematic drawings of pages with boxes where the content will go. The wire frames name the various areas of the page and show their overall layout and size. Because of their simplicity and lack of detail, it is often a good idea to do a set of wire frames as a first step in your publication design to get an overall view of the pages you intend to create (see Figure 18-5).

✦ **Page mock-ups,** which are illustrations of completed pages, give people an early view of what a final page might look like. Sometimes called comps, these illustrations enable you to see an average example of the pages in your publication without going though the effort of actually producing them. Be certain, however, that your page mock-ups adequately reflect the diversity of content that may appear on a page of a single type.

✦ **Page prototypes** are page mock-ups done in the actual publication medium. For example, an HTML prototype would look the same as the corresponding page mock-up. The page mock-up, however, is only an image, whereas the HTML prototype will actually run in a browser, just as the final site will. You can use page prototypes to prove that your designs will work and also to test the variability of content that may find its way onto a page. For example, if you have decided that you can have from 1 to 10 components on a page of a particular type, you can quickly add components to and subtract components from the prototype page to make sure the final page will always look all right. Prototype pages, created as part of the logical design process, do not generally include any logic or other CMS programming code. They are simply there to make sure that pages can be rendered in the target environment as desired.

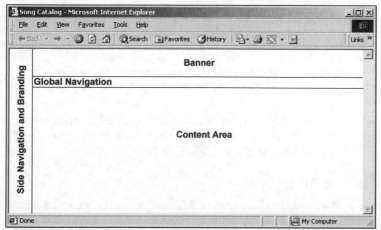

Figure 18-5: A very simple page wire-frame diagram that shows the locations and sizes of the areas of a Web page in the context of a browser

Look in Chapter 31, "Designing Templates," in the section "Publications and Templates," for a lot more examples and information on page design.

Personalization strategy

Even if you will have only a couple of audiences for starters and a static Web site as your only publication, it is worth your while to study and document an approach to personalization. This approach can include the following deliverables:

✦ **A messaging strategy:** This document combines audiences, publications, and components together at a high level. It defines what each audience is supposed to get from each publication and which components and publication design features will be used to communicate with them. It is a high-level precursor to personalization analysis. Particularly for publications targeting external audiences, it provides a marketing context within which to do personalization. For internal publications, your messaging strategy clearly identifies which types of information are appropriate for each audience. (You can find more information on messaging analysis in Chapter 26, "Designing Publications," in the section "Messages.")

✦ **A personalization strategy:** This document goes into detail about exactly how you intend to do personalization in each publication. It specifies a personalization rule for each combination of publication, page, audience, and component. The core of this document is the set of personalization rules. The rules state how to fetch components from the CMS repository based on what you know about the user, plus the values of the component's management elements. The rules also say which elements to display and how to lay out the components on the publication page. (See Chapter 32, "Designing Personalization," in the section "Analyzing Personalization," for a more detailed discussion.)

Publication administration

If you have more than one publication depending on the same base of content, it is important that you work through all the scheduling and dependencies to ensure that each publication can get the content and staff attention that it needs. In addition, as part of the logical design of the CMS, you must decide on and document the staffing and workflows you might need. Following are the documents you will produce when working on this aspect of your CMS:

✦ **A master publication schedule** shows the proposed release dates of each publication, as well as the components on which the publication relies. Using this schedule, you can make sure that the component collection and management workflows you create conclude at the right times for each publication to be released. It must also ensure that two publications do not put conflicting constraints on component completion schedules. (More information on this subject is in Chapter 33, "Designing Workflow and Staffing Models.")

✦ **A publication staffing and workflow plan** outlines the jobs, tasks, and workflows you expect the publication process to require. (More information on this subject is in Chapter 33, "Designing Workflow and Staffing Models.")

An audience analysis

The audience analysis itself is a natural part of logical design (fully covered in Chapter 25, "Cataloging Audiences"). In addition to the data you gather on audiences and how it plays into your other analyses, I think it is a good idea to produce a specific deliverable on audiences for the following reasons:

✦ **Perspective:** The conclusions you reached on audiences ought to be out in front of the project, giving the rest of the organization the same perspective it gives you. You want the members of your organization to think first about the people served by the CMS and only then about their own perspectives.

✦ **Purpose:** For many organizations, it is valuable simply to state what the core audiences are. If there are disagreements and different audience sets in use throughout the organization, your report makes these explicit and may serve as the one point of officially sanctioned segments. Others can adopt it, or at least orient to it, as they work though their own audience analyses.

✦ **Use:** In addition to the list itself, others in your organization are bound to find the information you have collected about audiences at least interesting, if not incredibly useful. If you do a good job, you will save the organization from the recurring expense of doing the same research over and over again.

✦ **Feedback:** Of course, the information flows both ways. By publishing and publicizing your audience analysis (under a more enticing name, please), you will elicit feedback from competing initiatives as well as from closet experts who know more than you could ever hope to about some aspect of some audience.

In most organizations, the work you do to analyze audiences will be ahead of the pack. Other analyses are likely to be either less broadly focused or not as thorough. Your analysis needs to be both broad and thorough to fully power a content management initiative. On the other hand, because your success depends so much on the audience analysis you have done, you need to protect it from frivolous attacks by competing schemes. If your analysis is well known and supported, other schemes will have to prove merit, not just support, to challenge it.

In the end, you don't want to be the one to define the organization's market segmentation, nor do you want to be constrained by audience definitions that are inconsistent with your other plans. You want the CMS initiative to be a player in the ongoing determination and refinement of your organization's constituencies. It would be less work for you if someone could simply hand you a good analysis already done. On the other hand, the CMS perspective can deepen and make more tangible the analyses that others have done.

A localization plan

Localization is the process of making content as understandable as possible in the variety of cultures in which people view it. Localization is a core requirement for the logical design of your CMS because you need to design an authoring, management, and publishing process that makes your content understandable in the languages, regions, and affiliation groups that you care to serve.

Content and publication localization is difficult. It can add orders of magnitude to the budgets of systems that do not handle it well. Even for the most efficient system, localization can expand schedules and budgets enormously. Expectations for localization tend to be unrealistic, either way too high or way too low. If you plan to localize, it is crucial that you define and set reasonable expectations for what will occur and when.

Cross-Reference You can find a full account of localization in Chapter 25, "Cataloging Audiences," in the section "Audiences and Localization."

Logical analysis is the right time to create and publish a localization plan. It is late enough in the project that you will have good information to base it on and early enough that you can debate and then finalize a plan in time to implement it.

It's also an ideal time to make a localization plan because localization requirements can have a significant impact on overall system design. The ideal CM system would require you to do as little as possible to get the highest level of localization you want. In other words, your goal with localization is to make sure that the CM system you design is flexible enough to make it as easy as possible to localize your content. The extent to which localization requirements drive system design depends in large part on how important localization is to the organization — both in terms of complexity and depth, as well as metrics such as the amount of content and number of languages.

The core of your localization plan is the set of localities that you plan to support and how you intend to support them. Because localization cuts across all parts of logical design and implementation, be sure you cover each locality from all significant angles, as follows:

✦ **Audiences:** Will you create audience types for each locality or will you create local segments within each audience type? (See Chapter 25, "Cataloging Audiences," in the section "Audiences and Localization," for more information.)

✦ **Publications:** How will navigation differ from locality to locality? Will you replicate templates or will you branch within them? What modifications are needed to your personalization approach to have it work across localities? (See Chapter 26, "Designing Publications," for more information.)

✦ **Components:** How will translated content be stored? Will you need any extra component elements to account for locality differences? (See Chapter 27, "Designing Content Types," in the section "Locality in components," for more information.)

✦ **Authors:** Do local authors constitute a different author group or can they be grouped with other authors? (See Chapter 28, "Accounting for Authors," in the section "Local authors," for more information.)

✦ **Acquisition sources:** What source material originates outside the core region? How will that information be processed and merged with content from the core region? (See Chapter 29, "Accounting for Acquisition Sources," in the section "Local sources," for more information.)

✦ **Workflow and staffing:** What are the specific tasks involved in localization? How long will they take and how many and what kinds of people will be involved? (See Chapter 33, "Designing Workflow and Staffing Models," in the section "Fitting Localization into Your Workflow," for more information.)

✦ **Access structures:** Will structures be simply translated or will they be localized as well? (See Chapter 30, "Designing Content Access Structures," the section "Plan," for more information.)

✦ **Deployment:** How is locally originated content distributed throughout the system? How will local and global content be merged and deployed to the appropriate servers throughout the world? (See Chapter 19, "Selecting Hardware and Software," in the section "Deployment," for more information.)

✦ **Support:** What support for translation and localization do you expect from the CMS that you choose? (See Chapter 19, "Selecting Hardware and Software," in the section "Localization," for more information.)

A fair accounting on all the preceding issues ought to give you the information to gauge the magnitude of the localization effort before you. One perspective to keep in mind is that if the CM system doesn't accommodate localization well or if the localization requirements themselves are very extensive, at some point, the parts of the CM system may diverge enough that they become really two systems. One of these systems provides content to the other that must be processed and converted. Your goal is to prevent this by finding the right level of flexibility required so that the system can accommodate localization.

Be sure that this analysis makes it out of the depths of logical design and into the hands of your sponsors or other decision makers so that they can either fund localization at the level it deserves or scale back the organization's expectation about how much localization will occur.

A risk assessment plan

As you proceed through logical design, you will make any number of assumptions that might turn out to be untrue. If a bad assumption could cost you significant time or money, it is a risk. In addition, you are bound to want to suggest strategies that might not work. Instead of suggesting them anyway—or worse, not suggesting anything that you think might fail—suggest your idea and assign it a risk probability. If the risk is too great, you can drop the idea. If, as is often the case, the risk is close to the reward or can be mitigated with a little extra effort, it might be worth a try.

At any rate, before you finish logical design, revisit the risk assessment that you created as part of your readiness assessment (which is covered in Chapter 15, "Getting Ready for a CMS," in the section "A risk assessment").

Here is a starter list of risks from requirements and logical design to get you thinking:

✦ **System requirements:** Do requirements conflict? Were you unable to get them down to a comfortable level?

✦ **Audiences:** Was there agreement? Are there too many audiences? Too few? Will you be able to get the data on each?

✦ **Publications:** Are there too many? Are they too complex? Will you be able to make all the integrations required?

✦ **Content types:** Are there too many types? Are there more types to come that you have not yet categorized? Will you be able to gather the metadata you propose to include with each type?

✦ **Authors:** Do you trust the information you have gathered? Are there too many different types of authors? Are they skilled enough to do their jobs? Are they close enough to you to follow the rules you create?

✦ **Acquisition sources:** Are there sources out there you could not analyze? Will some take too much effort to convert? Are you dubious about the quality or consistency of some? Are there too many?

✦ **Access structures:** Can you muster the effort to create the ones you suggested? Are they adequate to make content accessible? Will people really be able to assign components to the right categories? Can publication navigation be built from the access structures you plan to put in the CMS repository?

✦ **Workflow and staffing:** Will the system take more effort than you can muster? Are your task time estimates accurate enough for you to make predictions from them? Can you find skilled people or train them? Are there bottlenecks in your workflows?

A revised project plan

At the end of logical design, you know everything you need to know about what the CMS is trying to accomplish. Although this is not all you need to know to lay out a final project plan, it is enough for a next hard look at the plan. If you followed the process I laid out for getting ready for a CMS (in Chapter 15, "Getting Ready for a CMS," in the section "A preliminary project plan"), you have already produced a preliminary project plan. You can choose to revise your project plan either after requirements and logical design, or just once after logical design.

After logical design, you should be in a position to revise that plan as follows, based on what you learned:

✦ **Staffing:** You should have a very good idea of the people and tasks required to start and run your CMS. This new information should help you infuse reality into your plan.

✦ **Quantities:** You now know exactly how much content you have to process and how many publication pages per month you have to produce. This ought to help you refine the schedules and budgets for these activities.

✦ **Level of development effort:** You should have a good idea, from both the functionality components you designed and the system requirements you gathered, of how much software development will be involved in your CMS project. You should be able to do some basic calculations at this point on the amount of time, staff, and budget you will need for programming and other technical services. Of course, not until you have created implementation specifications for all the software development tasks can you know precisely what it takes, but at this point you should have a good first approximation.

✦ **Estimated schedule:** One of the big and recurring questions sponsors will ask—and be asked—is "when?" How long will it take, and when will it be done? Extrapolating from the level of development effort involved, you can provide some preliminary estimates of how long the development effort may take. Much may change, and make sure everyone knows that these estimates are speculative at this point, but at least you can start to set expectations within an order of magnitude.

✦ **Level of infrastructure:** From both the system requirements you gathered and the logical design you did, you should now be able to estimate the kinds and amounts of hardware and software you will need. Of course, until you select a CMS product and complete your implementation specifications, you will not know for sure, but there ought to be enough information available at this point to make reasonable guesses.

At this stage of the project, you should be able to revise a project plan so that it is clearly doable within the time frames and budgets that you have. As likely as not, when you first revise your project plan, you will find that you now have exceeded even your most liberal time and budget estimates. This is a sign that you have done a complete analysis. In this case, you can either ask for more time and money or you can cut back.

If you need to cut back, the appropriate thing to do is to start at the mandate. What can you cut from your mandate that, in turn, negates certain requirements, which, in turn, negate content types and publications? If you start, as most will, cutting components and publications first, you will have done the following:

✦ Ruined the coherence and unity of the mandate-requirements logical design relationship that you worked hard to create.

✦ Lost a great opportunity to argue for more resources based on what the organization loses under the present budget. It is easy for the organization to let you cut content and publications and still hold you to the original goals (which is, after all, what they really care about). It is difficult for them to let go of the goals they themselves crafted. In my experience, the first response from an organization is likely to be: "Yes, we want to reach all the goals in the mandate, but for less money." If you agree to this, you have only yourself to blame for the future misery you are bringing on yourself.

Inevitably, you will have to cut back your design. You can be upset about the cutbacks, or you can take it as a sign that you have been smart and have designed ahead of implementation. It is good to make your current design incorporate more than you can accomplish in your next implementation. A bigger design helps you be sure that the implementation is meeting current needs and preparing you for the future.

Tip
Don't look at cutbacks as a defeat. They very well might be a good thing for both the project and the organization. If you cut the parts of the system that were the biggest stretch, you will be buying more time to really understand them before you actually have to do them. In addition, the success of the system that you go forward with will build compelling institutional support for adding back the stuff you cut in future versions. History is on the side of content management. Eventually, you will do all that you have designed and more. You needn't be in a rush to do it all at once, especially if you are not quite sure how you could do it, even if you had all the time in the world.

An executive summary

Sponsors and anyone outside the project team are unlikely to want to wade through the mountains of information you generate from the logical design. For these folks, it is best to create an executive summary that is fewer than 10 pages long. The summary should present the business case for the system. In essence, your business case states that by delivering the stated content to the stated audiences via the stated publications, you will help the organization make significant progress toward achieving the stated goals.

Here's a list of the sections you might consider including:

✦ A reiteration of the mandate and major goals of the project

✦ A summary of the requirements you gathered

✦ An overview of authors and sources

✦ A shortened, annotated version of the component hierarchy

✦ The messaging and personalization strategy

✦ A few choice page mock-ups to show what the final publications will look like

✦ An overview of the major staff positions and workflows you worked out

Note
If you don't recognize some of the items in the preceding list, read on. They are all covered in the chapters that follow.

In addition, you might consider including the updated project plan (or some shortened version of it) as an appendix to the report.

Taking Stock of Your Staffing Needs

Table 18-1 lists the sorts of people you might want to include in your logical design process (see Chapter 13, "Staffing a CMS," for the full descriptions of these job titles).

Table 18-1: Staffing Needs

Task	Leader	Participants	Notes
Design plan of attack	Analyst or Business Analyst	All other analysts as needed.	Content manager will probably supervise this activity.
Executive summary	Content Manager or Business Analyst	All other analysts as needed.	Content manager might be best suited to create and present this document.
Audience analysis	Business Analyst	Publications analyst, outside marketing staff, and all other analysts as needed.	The business analyst is in the best position to lead this effort, but will need to rely heavily on the other people in the organization who specialize in marketing or in serving a particular audience.
Collection design document	Content Analyst and Software Analyst	Strong input from the conversion analyst and input from all other analysts are needed. Leader will bring in content contributors and others from the organization as required.	If practical, the two analysts should collaborate because it touches each of their disciplines separately. If this is impractical, one should own the document and the other contribute a lot to it.
Management design document	Content Analyst and Deployment Analyst	All other analysts as needed.	If practical, the two analysts should collaborate because it touches each of their disciplines separately. If this is impractical, then one should own the document and the other contribute a lot to it.
Publication strategy documents	Publications Analyst	There should be strong input from the Content Analyst and other analysts as needed.	The Software Analyst might need to participate in the templating section.
Page design	Publications Analyst	Content Analyst, Publication Designer, Page Developer, and UI Specialist.	The Publications Analyst should direct the effort, but the other staff members are the ones to create the deliverables. The Content Analyst should consult heavily on the parts of the analysis that concern the content type. The Publication Analyst or Publication Designer will need to bring others in for specific input.

Task	Leader	Participants	Notes
Personalization strategy	Publication Analyst	Content Analyst and Software Analyst.	The Publication Analyst should lead the effort, because the personalizations affect the structure of the publications. However, the Content Analyst will need to consult heavily on the access and retrieval of the content, and the Software Analyst might have to consult on the personalization rules and their implementation. Input from marketing groups also might be needed for the messaging analysis.
Publication administration	Publication Analyst	Deployment Analyst and other analysts as needed.	The Deployment Analyst can aid in understanding the role of infrastructure staff in the publishing workflows and tasks.
Revised project plan	Content Manager	All other analysts as well as a Project Manager as needed.	The analysts might be responsible for each part of the plan, but the Content Manager is in the best position to own the plan, make the tough compromises, and get continuing support for the plan.

Summary

Logical design means that you are in up to your hips in your CMS project. My version of logical design has you work from the general requirements that you created (see Chapter 17, "Doing Requirements Gathering") to a very specific design for what you want the system to accomplish:

✦ In creating a logical design, be sure to iterate a number of times through the process and find a way to manage the tremendous amount of detail you will amass.

✦ Prepare a plan of attack for logical design before starting out on it.

✦ Prepare analysis documents for collection, management, and publishing (or along any other outline that covers all the logical-design bases).

✦ Give the organization's leaders an audience analysis and a localization plan that they can debate and, ultimately, accept.

✦ Give the organization's leaders an executive summary that they can easily read and, thereby, get a feel for what you are doing.

✦ Finally, revise your project plan and risk assessment at the end of logical design so that it reflects your most current thinking.

In the next chapter, I deal with one of the most contentious and stressful parts of a CMS project: hardware and software selection.

Selecting Hardware and Software

In years past, there were no CMS products on the market. In the future, you'll no more think of creating your own CMS than you'd think of creating your own ERP system. Today, it's likely that you can get most of what you need from one of the commercially available CMS products. Still, it's likely that you will have to do a fair amount of custom programming to get the results that you desire.

In this chapter, I provide an overview of the build, buy, or rent decision, giving you some basis on which to decide how to proceed. Assuming that most organizations prefer to buy or rent a commercial product, I spend the bulk of the chapter discussing the process for selecting the product most suitable to your needs.

System Selection Jumpstart

This Jumpstart summarizes what you need to do in the hardware and software selection phase of a CMS project.

Use this jumpstart as a summary without the weight of detail, or as a quick review if you've already read the chapter and want a checklist of what you need to implement your CM system.

To implement the CM system you've planned, you can follow these steps:

1. Decide whether to build, buy or rent your CMS. (The remainder of this chapter is for you if you are buying or renting your CMS.)

2. Create a high-level overview of the CMS project that you can distribute to vendors as well as to your selection committee. It should include information from the project mandate, requirements, and logical analysis.

3. Canvass the market for the products that seem to fit. Casting broadly, you may end with tens of companies in this initial round.

4. Make the first cut from the list of candidates, selecting those that seem worth really pursuing.

   • Use additional information you can collect easily, such as from each company's marketing package and Web site, to cut down the list.

- Invite the companies that make the cut to make a sales presentation — their standard one, which does not require much investment in time from them or you. Aim to get an understanding of their product offering.

5. Send a Request for Proposal (RFP) to those who make the first cut.

   - Create a spreadsheet containing a scoring system (and determine scoring weights before beginning to score responses) to evaluate responses to the questions in the RFP.

   - Allow vendors ample time to respond, particularly if your RFP contains many detailed questions.

6. Select a small number of finalists by scoring the RFP responses and any follow-up questions that you ask.

   - Follow up with meetings within your group to determine scoring.

   - Use multiple quick passes over answers to quickly determine which questions vendors answered well or poorly.

7. Have technical drill-down meetings and check references from each of the finalists.

   - Get vendors to involve members of their technical team who can contribute.

   - Diagram the resulting system as described in each meeting.

8. Have a presentation from the remaining candidates.

   - Resolve any big issues before the final presentation.

   - Involve your executives.

   - Make sure your team has done its homework about the candidates — having to bring people up to speed with basic product demos is a waste of time at this point.

   - Get a cost estimate and discuss terms.

9. Evaluate the remaining candidates.

   - Rescore their RFPs in light of subsequent presentations.

   - For each remaining candidate, create a modified version of the project plans based on the assumption that you choose their project.

10. Check references.

    - Try to get references outside of those the company supplies.

    - Look for references that have used the company's product for projects as similar as possible to yours.

11. Make a final decision by combining the scores for the references and presentations with those for the RFP.

    - Use all the materials you have gathered to drive to consensus.

    - If consensus doesn't happen, create an objective scoring system to determine the winner.

    - If a scoring system isn't feasible, escalate the decision to an executive who can make the decision.

The Product Paradox

Between the time that it became possible to deliver information electronically and the time that it became necessary to do so, an impressive array of content mills were invented to fill the gap for organizations that had no choice but to create their own CMSs. In the 1980s and 1990s, I invented any number of authoring and publication systems that were tailored to a particular group of people with a particular content set. About the time that I started taking a more general approach to the problem of content management (as did others), and the content management industry was born.

In the mid 1990s, I did most of my work for Microsoft. At that point, the company's Web site (at www.microsoft.com) was already getting out of control. One of the main contributors, the Microsoft Office group, had thousands of pages that needed to be tracked and posted each month. I was given the assignment to create some sort of management system for this process. "What's to be on the pages?" I asked Howard, the project manager. "We don't know," came his response. "Okay," I said. "What kinds of pages are you creating?" "We're changing that all around, so we can't really tell you," replied Howard. "Hmm," said I. "What sort of metadata do you need to track for these pages?" Howard smiled. "Any kind," he told me. "We're going to want it to be open, so make it that way." This wasn't going to be an easy project. "Wow, okay, umm, I'll see what I can do," I said. "When can I get the final page designs?" Howard smiled even wider. "You can't," he chuckled. "We'll be redesigning right up until launch. Make it so that whatever design we come up with, the tool can handle it." I picked my jaw up off the floor and we started designing. Before too many hours, Howard and I had a plan that *ought* to work.

Working feverishly with Daniel, a very young (but quite brilliant) recent immigrant from the former Soviet Union, I conceived and birthed WebPub. WebPub was open. It made no assumptions about the kinds of pages that the company would produce. We could set it up for any navigation structure, page types, and page design. We invented the following:

✦ **An administrative interface** for setting up the components and elements of the system (although we didn't call them that).

✦ **A contributor interface** that presented forms where the user could enter the content of a component (although we didn't use Web-based forms).

✦ **A templating system** that enabled you to type special syntax into an HTML file to add content and navigation to the design of the page (although the syntax was proprietary and limited).

WebPub was a success. It became one of the first Web site content management systems used at Microsoft. The system helped the Office group cut the redesign cycle on their large site from three months to three weeks and was used for more than two years (a real accomplishment at Microsoft).

I spin this tale not to get you to buy WebPub, but to discuss the lessons that it taught me.

Because WebPub was such a success, other groups inside and beyond Microsoft also wanted to use it. We hastily produced version 2.0 with documentation and tutorials and called it a product. *Ha!* After a few months, we realized that WebPub was the idea for a product, not the product itself. To turn this idea into a reality, we'd need to remake our entire company. In addition to a great idea, a product company needs the following:

✦ **Continual development:** Before version 2.0 was even released, we saw how much more flexibility we really needed. Potential clients constantly asked for more than our immature application could deliver. Daniel and Bob needed to be replaced by a complete development group.

✦ **Support:** Few people trust a software product (for good reason), and they all have a lot of questions. Daniel and Bob needed to be replaced by an entire support staff.

✦ **Sales and marketing:** As a service organization, we were accustomed to personal relationships with a small number of clients. Selling product is a numbers game. You need to hit as many people as possible and move a lot of units.

✦ **Finance:** A product organization spends a lot of money up front and reaps profit through high sales down the road. As a service organization, we were set up to be paid for every hour that we worked. There was no pot of money up front waiting to be spent.

After much debate and controversy, we decided not to pursue WebPub. We decided that the change to our company was too great and that we really preferred to be a service rather than a product company.

Note   Other CMS product companies are on the road not taken by WebPub. They had a good idea that worked in a particular context and the vision to sell it to the world. They've tried, more or less successfully, to remake their companies into product development, marketing, and sales organizations. The good ones are those that have a strong and continually developing technology base as well as an organizational structure that supports the continual revolution that's needed to keep the product moving forward. The bad ones think that having done it once for one client, they now have a product and a product company.

Doing and then not doing WebPub taught me a lot about the contradictions and paradoxes that motivate the content management industry. Being involved in CMS vendor-selection processes since then has helped me see from the customer's side the following contradictions that CMS companies must live with:

✦ **Innovation versus legacy:** In any fast-moving industry, product companies have a constant struggle between continuing to support their old versions and releasing new versions that transcend the old rules. This conflict, I believe, is what kept the document management industry from dominating the content management industry. The drag of its existing client base kept it from seizing the new opportunities of the Web. (See Chapter 10, "The Roots of Content Management," in the section "The Principles of Document Management," for more information on this topic.)

✦ **Sales versus technical staff:** To build a strong product, you need a great technical staff. To sell that product, you need people who know how to make and close deals. The people who want to buy a CMS usually prefer to talk to the technical staff. The people who sell a CMS want you to talk to the sales staff. The sales staff has more time to talk to you, is usually much better at talking, and knows how to get you to buy. The technical staff is usually too busy, not good at talking, and may even tell you not to buy the product. The position of *sales engineer* was created to deal with this dilemma. If they're good, sales engineers can talk as well to programmers as they can to business people and bridge that gap. If they're bad, they're too poor at interpersonal communications to make it in sales and not technical enough to answer even the least-probing questions.

✦ **The "next version" issue:** The functionality that you really want is always going to be in the next version. The reason is simple: The released product necessarily lags behind the market need, which, in content management, grows and evolves really quickly. In your search for the right product, you naturally take for granted the basic functionality that most products have and focus most on the stuff that's particular to your initiative and infrastructure. So that's what you ask for. To survive, the product companies must be responsive to customer needs and so, if enough people ask for it, they must plan to include functionality to meet the new need in the next version. Of course, by the time the next version ships, the new functionality is taken for granted and there's a new set of needs to meet. You should expect the next version issue. In fact, if you don't hear "next version" in response to many of your questions, you should be suspicious that the company isn't keeping up with the market. On the other hand, you should require solid evidence that there's more than vapor behind the next version.

✦ **Vision versus reality:** Every good company has a vision of the future (such as the paperless office, a computer on every desktop, and so on). On the other hand, just like the next version, the future is always brighter than the present. The present is marred by the sad facts of reality. (The supporting technologies aren't yet ready; bandwidth isn't high enough, and so on.) The company needs to sell you fully on the future, so you put up with the present. You should listen to this vision of the future and make sure that you like it and then get back to the present and make sure that you can really live with all those sad facts.

✦ **Biggest versus newest:** As all big software companies have learned, you can be market leader or you can be market innovator, but you can't be both. The bigger the share of the market that you own, the more legacy customers you must support and the more new customers you need to attract to hold your position. Market leaders need to play it safe and play to the masses to remain market leaders. Innovators, on the other hand, are up-and-coming players: They seek to undercut the leaders with their speed of development, revolutions in technology, and their ability to remake themselves as the market changes. Neither position is bad or should necessarily reflect poorly on a particular company. But you should question any company that claims to be both, and you should recognize that, in an industry as immature as content management, long-term industry leadership is far from decided.

✦ **Me, too! and Not me!:** Especially in these early days, the content management industry is extremely competitive. Companies are constantly monitoring each other's messages and coming up with responses. If one has a good idea, for example, the others quickly latch onto it and say, "Me, too!" Conversely, if one product is seen to have a flaw, the others are quick to claim, "Not me! I do it right!" From the company's perspective, this attitude is necessary for survival. It's a hostile world out there. Customers judge you based on a single random fact that they pick up in an article or by hearsay. You must get past the first uninformed hurdles to get to the real value that your product can offer. If you don't have quick and decisive answers to the *me, too* and *not me* comments, you're sunk. From the customers' perspective, pat answers that always manage to be just what they want to hear can be a real turnoff.

✦ **Alliances:** No CMS product can do the job by itself. Too much is involved for one product to cover everything. On the other hand, customers naturally expect that the CMS can handle any issue remotely related to their information. Some CMS companies respond by continually widening their offerings to try to cover the entire process. Even these companies, however, can't cover everything. And even if they did cover everything, they'd be accused of being proprietary and not allowing you to integrate "best of breed" third-party products. It's a bind — companies lose if they're perceived to cover too little or too much. The answer most product companies have found is alliances. They tell you, "Rather than do all this ourselves, we partner with X, who's a known leader in the field of Y." But what does it mean to *partner*? In the computer industry, it can mean anything from agreeing to put your partner's logo on your Web site to having an ownership stake in your partner's company. The alliance that the customer wants to see is one where the two companies have tested and documented integration methods and have agreed in writing to ensure that their future releases stay compatible. Such solid agreements, however, aren't easy to find. They bind the two companies to a lot of work and to each other for the highly competitive and unknown future.

✦ **Defining the terms of the discussion:** Successful product companies are proactive. They craft messages that they think will resonate with an audience, and then they design campaigns to deliver these messages in as many ways as possible to that audience. (Some even use their own systems to do it.) Companies want to lay out the issues and frame a solution using their products. Then they can train sales staffs to deliver the set messages, and they can ensure progress from problem to solution to purchase in an effective way. Finally, by using set messages, they can quickly qualify sales opportunities. If you're too far from the message, you aren't a viable prospect. A set message can be propagated widely and used to quickly find the portion of the target audience that's ready for the message. Customers, on the other hand, want to get comfortable with the messaging and then move into how this product meets their specific needs, not a general need. In a field as immature as content management, your needs are likely to vary from the norm (or at least you're likely to think so). A set message works well for the product companies, but may be seen as shallow or too marketing-oriented by customers.

✦ **Simple versus complete:** A product can either be simple to use or complete in its coverage. This is a basic fact of application development. The more stuff that the application can do, the more difficult it is to make it all simple to understand and use. Customers, however, want both. The answer that people want to hear is, "We can do that, and it's really easy." In reality, the best applications make the easy things easy and the difficult things difficult. Beginners mostly want to do the easy things and need a simple user interface. Advanced users eschew simple interfaces and want all the power of the application in front of them in one hugely complex screen, where they can see everything and do everything. The best products layer functionality so that the beginner's tasks are in front of the more advanced functionality. So, rather than expecting that all features be easy, you should ensure that the difficulty of a feature is proportional to the ability of the intended user.

✦ **Why you shouldn't just wait:** From the product company's perspective, of course, you should never wait. You should buy now before your problems get the better of you. Also, while you wait for the right price or functionality, new needs may arise and you may end up waiting forever, your needs always ahead of the released product. From the customer's perspective, waiting may or may not be good. If there's money that needs to be spent, waiting is bad. If there's indecision or lack of budget in the organization, waiting is good. Decide for yourself how long you ought to wait for the right product to come along.

✦ **Stock versus custom functionality:** From a product company's perspective, the best approach is to build an application infrastructure that provides a robust set of basic services that can be mixed and matched to meet any of a range of needs (as I discuss in Chapter 4, "Functionality is Content, Too!," in the section "Monolithic versus Mix-and-Match Functionality"). They can then build a user interface on top of the basic services that can be easily modified to meet a range of needs (with some extra programming, of course). From the customer's perspective, customization is a nasty word. Customers want to flip the switch and have everything that they want already there and working. If that can't happen, they at least want to know that people are available (internally or on contract) who can do the customization and that it's not going to cost too much.

✦ **Single support versus realistic support:** Customers want a single solution and a single place to go for support (or, as one client put it, "a single throat to strangle"). No matter what or where the problem, customers want a single number to call and an immediate response. This very reasonable requirement makes most product companies cringe. Just think what it takes to provide such support. First, the CMS is so intertwined with organizational infrastructure that to even figure out where a problem originated, let alone fix it, is tantamount to supporting the organization's entire infrastructure. Second, it takes a lot of skill to diagnose and fix problems in a CMS. It isn't cheap to have this kind of talent sitting around waiting for problems to arise. Finally, with organizations that stretch across the entire world, the support must be in multiple languages and across all time zones. Can you blame companies for cringing?

✦ **Planning versus action:** The more planning that you do, the longer it takes you to buy and the harder are the questions that you must ask of a CMS vendor. In addition, the more planning that you do, the less likely you are to want to let the product company set the terms of the discussion. Given this, you'd think that product companies would work against planning. This is rarely the case. With the exception of some companies that try to minimize the entire content management problem, most are in complete agreement that you need to plan before doing a content management project. The reason is simple: If you don't plan, the project is likely to fail, and you're likely to blame the product company. (Some have even been sued by unhappy customers.) To resolve the dilemma between planning and purchase, most product companies try to get you to buy first and plan later. They have professional services to help you do much of what I outline in this book. Many do a good job. The only problem is that the entire planning process starts with the assumption that the product in question is the right one for the task. There's no opportunity (as you'd expect) to define the problem and then choose the product.

✦ **What customers want versus what they need:** Product sales staffs see a lot of projects go by. If staff members are good, they can pick up a lot of practical understanding about what you, the customer, should do. On the other hand, it's not in the interest of a sales engineer to tell you things that lead you away from her product. It's also not in her interest to slow down the process by showing you how your simple understanding needs to be revisited and deepened. The customer, of course, wants the sales staff to be consultants, directing her toward the right solution and offering practical advice where needed. It serves the sales staff to become trusted consultants and offer advice, as long as it doesn't hamper the sale. Be aware of this dilemma and thank a salesperson who slows the sales process for you or offers advice that's adverse to her real goal of getting you to buy something.

It's difficult being a vendor. There are contradictions at every turn that keep honest and straightforward sales staffs up at night. There can be either an overly dependent or an overly adversarial relationship between vendors and potential clients, neither of which is good.

The long and the short of it is that customers expect too much, and companies give too little. I don't even bother to discuss companies or customers with ill intent. The best of intentions still aren't enough to resolve the conflicts inherent in the software development process, the sales process, and the content management industry. I've seen many shades of gray, but never a vendor or a customer I'd call dishonest. Mostly, I've seen vendors who want a product they believe in to succeed and customers who don't want to be taken advantage of and are afraid that they don't know all that they need to know to make the right decision.

I've seen a lot of blame thrown around — customers accusing vendors of lying, cheating, and stealing, and vendors accusing customers of trying to soak them for knowledge with no intention to buy. Both sides would do better simply to understand the constraints of the other and the contradictions of the system in which both sides are embedded.

As a customer, if you don't expect vendors to be objective or to act in your interest if interests diverge, you can still trust and believe what you hear. As a vendor, if you don't expect that customers are ready or able to make a decision or that they'll easily give trust, you can still gain that trust and make a sale. After all, most customers are willing to buy something and most products have something worth buying. The process turns out best for both sides if the customer knows what to ask and the vendor knows how to quickly answer the questions that determine whether the product fits the need.

Build, Buy, or Rent?

It wasn't so long ago that there were no commercially available content management systems. In those days, the decision was easy: Do all management by hand, build your own system, or stay out of the game. With the exception of the old SGML systems doing documentation (as discussed in Chapter 10, "The Roots of Content Management," in the section "Huge information bases") and some text-manipulation tools for programmers, you could buy nothing that advertised any sort of management functions at all. This was less a problem than you may imagine, looking at today's world. Few organizations had made any kind of move to electronic publishing, the Internet was a government experiment, and any companies putting information on CD-ROM were expected to be software development houses.

Today, everyone in this business is at or near a crossroads. I can't tell you categorically to build your own CMS, and I can't tell you that you should clearly buy or rent a system. In some circumstances, you may not have an option, because nothing like what you need exists. More and more commonly, however, something does exist. Then the question becomes whether it's cheaper and faster to start from the existing system and augment it or start from scratch. It's still rare, but getting less so, to find a system you can either buy or rent that does all that you want with little or no additional customization.

Building a CMS

The build-or-buy decision, then, is a matter of degree. If a commercial CMS is cheap enough to buy or rent and does enough of what you want it to, it's no longer worthwhile to build your own. What I *can* say categorically is that you shouldn't take on a CMS building project unless you have the following:

✦ **A strong leader:** You need someone with the vision to conceive and then direct the development of the effort. This person needs to have a firm foundation in content management as well as in the tools and platforms that you intend to use.

✦ **A strong development staff:** You're going to do some hard-core database and Web development. You need a seasoned and sizable team to handle this task. You want developers who not only know their languages and databases, but also have a feeling for and comfort in editorial and publishing systems.

✦ **A desire for an ongoing effort:** It's not enough to create a CMS; you must continue to develop it to keep up with the pace of change in your organization and in the content management industry. You can perhaps compete with product companies today in delivering the features your organization requests, but can you still compete in the future?

✦ **A strong support organization:** You must be willing to support the CMS as well as build it. All the support headaches that I mentioned in the preceding section, "The Product Paradox," are yours, not some other company's.

Indeed, all the contradictions that I mentioned for a product company in the content management industry apply to you if you take on the task of building a CMS. The organization looks to you as the "vendor" and traps you in all the same snares into which product companies fall. In short, you should be prepared to create a little product company inside your organization to build and maintain a CMS.

Buying a CMS

Given all the challenges you would take on by building your own CMS, you may be saying, "That's pretty conclusive. I wouldn't bite off that task!" If so, wait while I balance the scales a little in the following points:

✦ **You still may have a lot of development to do**, even if you buy a CMS. You can outsource this development, but you still must manage it and ensure that it fits into the architecture of the CMS that you buy. In fact, the jobs that I discuss in Chapter 13, "Staffing a CMS," don't change whether you're building or buying a CMS. Of course, the number of positions and the job duration of the staff do change.

✦ **You still have a lot of support to do**, even if you buy a CMS. Many CMS companies simply can't provide the kind of support that a large enterprise needs. If you use one of these products, you're still faced with building a robust support infrastructure.

✦ **You may end up replacing most of the CMS** anyway. I've seen more than one project where the custom code ended up dwarfing the contribution of the CMS product. At first, it seemed that the CMS would take care of large chunks of functionality. As these projects wore on, the CMS just seemed to get in the way of what could just as easily have been programmed. (At least, it was presented that way by the programmers.)

✦ **You must pay a pretty penny** — a CMS is expensive. For the cost of many of the major packages, you can buy an awful lot of programmer and analyst time.

Buying a CMS is clearly no panacea.

Renting a CMS

To try to split the difference between these two options, some CMS companies have taken the road of becoming CMS Application Service Providers (ASP). The basic idea here is that the CMS company owns a set of servers that run its CMS. It rents you space on its servers to host and publish your Web sites with its CMS. Whether this solution is the best or worst of the build and buy worlds depends on your needs. It is the best of the two worlds if:

✦ You want a solid solution and don't want to incur large up-front purchase and customization costs.

✦ You have no need or desire to publish anything but a Web site with your system.

✦ You are willing to fit into the production and publication processes that the product assumes with little or no customization. That said, some CMS companies offer customization as a service or as a task you can undertake on your own, much as you might with a CMS that you buy.

✦ You need to implement the CMS quickly. Because a rented CM solution is already up and running, you eliminate nearly all the infrastructure that you'd otherwise plan for, acquire, and deploy, as well as the CMS itself.

✦ You have few of the IT resources needed to host your own CMS.

✦ You have few user-support capabilities in-house, which the CMS company may provide along with training.

It may very well be the worst of the two worlds if the converse is true:

✦ You want a variety of publication types to come from your CMS.

✦ You want your own special production processes.

✦ You fear your content being captured by the CMS company, making it difficult to migrate to a new and different system in the future.

✦ You have all the skills you need in-house.

✦ You have an IT staff that will rankle at not having control over your CMS.

Are We Really So Different?

Consider how absurd this statement is: "Our company handles financial information so differently that there is no way we could buy a standard accounting package. We have no choice but to build our own." Any CFO worth the paper she pushes would laugh. Except in the rarest of cases, accounting practice is so standardized that you would be a fool to write your own system. In the (possibly distant) future, I believe the same argument will hold for content management systems. Agreed-to practices for the collection, management, and publication of content will be better to obey than to recreate.

Even today, it is worth asking "How different are we from the others? Would we be better off just going with the systems that others have found useful? When a system does not do what we think we need to do, is it the system or is it, perhaps, we who have the wrong idea. If we change our attitude to fit the mindset of the application rather than changing the mindset of the application to fit us, will we get the results that we want with a whole lot less effort?" In short, the key question to ask your CMS team is "What makes you think you know more about what we need to do than the companies that have been doing this for years?"

At first glance, this approach might seem at odds with my repeated claim that you must go to market knowing what you want to do rather than expecting the market to tell you what to do. It says that your problems are not unique, whereas I claim that your problems are unique.

But *which* problems? I don't believe that your collection, management, and publishing problems are unique. If I believed that, how could I write a book hoping to provide useful advice on how to solve them? However, I do claim that the combination of your content, audiences, goals, authors, and so on is unique. A common comprehensive CM infrastructure is possible; what you do with that infrastructure is unique. Just as a good word processor has all you need to create a print document with any conceivable goals, audience, and content, so a good CMS would allow you to produce any type of publication, given any goals, audiences, and content.

So, the question to ask is "Given our unique context, how much can we leverage standardized practices for CM?" Thus, you go to market fully understanding your unique context so that you can see what standardized practices you might be able to use.

With modest needs, modest means, and the capability to just fit into someone else's ideas of how to do CM, an ASP-style relationship could be perfect for your organization. On the other hand, if you don't fit this profile, a rented CMS could be a like a rented home: You have to eat, sleep and die in it, but it's not quite your own.

If you're thinking in general about building, buying, or renting a CMS, I hope that I've put you right on the fence (because that's where I am). On the other hand, I hope you see that, if you weigh the issues of your specific situation, the balance ought to tip in one direction or the other.

Finally, take heart in the fact that whatever decision that you make today undoubtedly needs to be reviewed in the next two years and very likely gets overturned by another decision (or, at least, undergoes a thorough reworking) within five years. This industry is moving too quickly for any decision to last for long.

If you're at all in doubt, it's worth your time to go through a product-selection process. You don't need to buy at the end of it if you decide its better to build, and you just may find a product out there that gets you enough of the way toward your goal (even if only in the next version) to be worth the price.

In the remainder of this chapter, I assume that you're selecting from among the commercially available CMS products. If you're set on building your own CMS, you can use the information in Part V, "Building a CMS," to start thinking about how to proceed.

Techniques to Get the Job Done

Whether you buy or rent your CMS, the CMS vendor selection process isn't so different from any other vendor selection process. Thus, most of what I suggest is common sense to people who've done a lot of product procurement. In the sections that follow, I infuse this common-sense approach with a content management focus to give you some advice and guidelines to follow.

How to select decision makers

I've seen more politics wrapped around the product decision than involved in any other part of a CMS project. More than once, I've seen a CMS project stall and die because of the following:

✦ The lack of consensus that you previously could choose to ignore comes out and fouls up the entire process.

✦ Some groups have their favorites and inside players, others have the tools that they're already using, and yet others have one tool that they've heard of and just want.

✦ Some people see this as the most significant decision of the project and one where they can have a say.

✦ Some people see this as a way to influence how large budgets are spent.

✦ Some people think that, if you make a bad call on the product, the project's doomed; so they put too much emphasis on the process and drag it down.

✦ Some people just think that they're good at system or vendor selection and plug in because they have experience.

All these reasons have some validity and some invalidity. My overall feeling is that selection gets so much attention because it's so tangible and easy to understand. Money is spent and a product is chosen. The other parts of the project are more difficult to get your hands around and are not so straightforward.

For whatever reason, system selection can be a real hassle if you don't put serious effort into reining in all the people who want to decide, as follows:

✦ **Depend on the consensus that you built** during the mandate process. If the process didn't yield a list of who gets to decide, you at least should have gotten a group of people with enough authority to help you choose a small, but evenly distributed group with no members who've decided before the process starts.

✦ **Ratify a group process before you begin.** Don't create a process on the spot as you need it. This leads to a lack of respect for the process and rigging by people who can figure out how to manipulate the criteria and scoring. Make sure that everyone agrees to it and agrees that the winner wins. Too often, I've seen a clear winner emerge in this process, only to be shot down by people who don't like it "for some reason." If they can articulate a reason, it can be added to the list and scored with the rest of the criteria that you use. If they can't articulate why they like or don't like a product, their opinion shouldn't count for much.

✦ **Decide on a fair and impartial scoring mechanism** for each scoring step that you include in your process. Agree to the range for each scale and agree to what constitutes each value in the range. Then each person can make a judgment in the strict context of the scale and scoring criteria that you established.

The more numbers that you have in a scoring scale, the more room you have to differentiate between products—and the more work that you must do to define what each number means. I prefer scales that have 3 values for subjective measures (bad, okay, and good) and no more than 10 for more objective measures. (Zero is no functionality, and 10 is far more than you'd ever need.) Make your scales as small as possible although they should still retain enough room to differentiate products.

✦ **Agree to stick to what your process decides.** It helps no one to add up all the scores and then ignore them because they don't come out right.

If you find yourself stymied by the continual subversion of your objective process, you may try giving up. Maybe an executive decision just needs to be made about the product to use. Maybe your offer (to give up) gives new incentive to those who need to respect the process (or, at least, gives incentive to their supervisors). In the end, it's more important that some product be used than that it be the absolute best choice.

As far as who should be in the reviewers group, I can think of two types of people: those who represent a significant organizational interest, and those who have the expertise or perspective to judge vendors. Obviously, you should shoot for people who have both qualities. I'd resist people who represent a constituency but have no basis to judge between vendors. As much as someone like this may want to serve as a reviewer, she can slow down the process and cause a general lack of respect for the rest of the reviewers from the vendor and the organization.

You find more suggestions for how to staff a product selection process later in this chapter, in the section "Taking Stock of Your Staffing Needs."

How to select a product

I've seen all manner of processes used to decide on the best system to buy. In many cases, you can't call them processes at all: You call around, see what other people are using, and go with that. In most cases, however, the process centers on a list of requirements, vendor presentations, and some sort of selection committee. The process that I present is comprehensive and exhaustive. If you're planning to spend a lot of money on your CMS, it's worth the extra effort. On the other hand, you should balance the full treatment that I give you with the timing and depth that you think you need. In the full process that I describe, there can be a lot of questions to ask and answers to process. To reiterate the "Jumpstart" section earlier in this chapter, the process runs as follows:

✦ Create a high-level overview of the CMS project that you can pass around.

✦ Canvass the market for the products that seem to fit.

✦ Make the first cut from the list of candidates, selecting those that seem worth really pursuing.

✦ Send a Request for Proposal (RFP) to those who make the first cut.

✦ Select a small number of finalists by scoring the RFP responses and any follow-up questions that you ask.

✦ Have technical drill-down meetings and check references from each of the finalists.

✦ Have a presentation from the remaining candidates.

✦ Make a final decision by combining the scores for the references and presentations with those for the RFP.

The following sections give more detail to the process.

A high-level overview

To start the selection process, it's useful to create a short project overview that you can include in early correspondence with the vendors. The overview also should orient your selection committee to the major points toward which you're aiming.

To create the overview, take the high points from your project mandate, requirements, and logical analysis. Here's a sample overview:

> Our company is seeking to implement an enterprise-level content management system that aids in the creation, management, and publishing of personalized content to the Web and beyond. At the highest level, the system is successful if it does the following:
>
> • Provides a solid framework behind the staff and processes involved in creating and tagging content.
>
> • Supports our wide and diverse contributor base with tools and processes appropriate to skill level and commitment (see our collection analysis report for details).
>
> • Provides a full-featured repository where content components and file-based resources can be stored, tracked, updated, targeted, combined, and archived (see our content model for details).

- Provides strong, easy-to-use workflow tools that can guide the entire creation, storage, and publishing process and integrates with our existing internal systems and current Web infrastructure (see our management analysis for details).

- Provides a flexible, template-driven publishing capability that can format and output any combination of content and file resources to standard databases and file formats (including XML, HTML, flat text for e-mail messages, and QuarkXPress for print output) (see our publications analysis for details).

- Supports a robust publishing, testing, and deployment environment. Provides a full-featured but extendable personalization capability for targeting and custom publishing of content (see our publications analysis for details).

The product or products selected are successful if they do the following:

- Have out-of-the-box functionality capable of covering a wide range of the preceding requirements with minimal customization.

- Have standards-based customization and extension capabilities that enable full integration with existing systems and rapid development of additional functionality.

Use this sort of statement to orient all parties involved to the key selection criteria and also to provide them with an on-ramp to the fuller analyses you have created.

Canvassing the market

You can begin your search for the appropriate software by performing a broad overview of the CMS market, looking for products that address your general needs. Colleagues and the Web are good places to start.

Here are a few tips for conducting your search:

✦ **Get recommendations.** Try sending your overview via e-mail to anyone you can think of who may have an opinion. The recommendations give you a place to start and a set of products to which you can compare the ones that you find yourself. Interestingly, this technique may also turn up biases and inside favorites from the people in your organization whose opinion you ask.

✦ **Keep your analysis close at hand.** Nearby, you should have your requirements, logical design, and the selection criteria that you think are most important; look at them often as you do your search. This helps you avoid the disorientation that you're bound to feel as you follow endless links and get lost in the rhetoric and marketing spin of the Web sites that you visit.

✦ **Develop a short set of questions that you ask at each Web site that you visit.** This helps you stay on task and give an even, standard treatment to each product. As you may suspect, I like these three: What collection processes do they cover; what management functions do they cover; and what publishing functions do they include? Use these or create your own, but don't let the site control how you find information or what information you look for.

✦ **Consider core products versus peripherals.** I'd estimate that, in mid-2004, roughly 100 or 150 products do enough to really be considered content management systems. (A few years back there were fewer than half that many.) On the other hand, hundreds of products advertise some connection to content management. Develop a quick eye for the products that don't have enough core content management functionality to qualify for your search.

✦ **Keep a side list of your special needs.** This list should go beyond standard content management concerns (special marketing needs, unusual publications, particular integrations, and so on). You may come across products that don't address all your needs but do hit one or two. You may find these products helpful later on, either as add-ons to the system that you purchase or as good examples of how a particular need can be met.

✦ **Document your search.** If you stay on a site for more than a minute or two, there's something of interest there. Paste its URL into a file so that you can track your way back to it later as you say, "I know I saw that somewhere..."

✦ **Don't spend too much time on this process.** You can easily get lost for days and days. Continue keeping up with the subject on the Web, but don't hold up the rest of the process for more than a day while you choose your initial list of candidates. If in doubt, include a company on your list. You can easily remove it later.

✦ **Start a file.** In fact, start both a physical and a computer file on each interesting company. You eventually accumulate a lot of material on the ones that make it to the end of the process.

The preceding points address Web sites of CMS product companies. My informal estimate is that far more than 90 percent of your Web search results come from such companies. The rest are from service organizations that do content management projects and from articles, publications, and conference presentations on the subject. Although I've not been overly impressed with the depth or breadth of coverage in the pages I've seen in this category, they're certainly worth perusing for general information and, especially, for comrades who may have faced problems similar to your own. I've always had good luck contacting and getting help (and even friendship) from people I've heard of on the Web.

No need to be stingy in this process: Include any product that looks seriously interesting. If you end up with a list of more than 10 and as many as 40 products, you're on the right track.

Making the first cut

With a little effort, you can winnow down the large number of product companies that have something to do with content management to the handful that seem to address your particular needs.

If you have enough lead time, you can send an e-mail message to or call each company on the list and request a complete marketing package. In addition, go back to each site and collect as much relevant information as you can about each candidate.

Tip

If you request marketing packets, make sure that you ask them to include all white papers, case studies, demo programs, sample documentation, industry analyses, and pricing sheets that they have. These tell you much more than the glossy sheets that are standard fare for marketing folders.

Don't be afraid to summarily dismiss some candidates as you collect information and find out that they really don't fit. If you have time, you can also search the Web for each product name. This finds you reviews and other commentary on the product (as well as any flames or accolades that the product's received publicly).

Note the names of people who've commented on a product. You may need to talk to them later about their experiences.

The core of the first cut is a preliminary set of evaluation criteria (usually a spreadsheet). Start by synthesizing your requirements and logical analysis with the questions listed in this chapter, as well as any others you came up with, to create a high-level cut on your selection criteria. Go back over your notes and links from your market survey and narrow the list to no more than 10 to 20 criteria to apply to each of your initial candidates. Use simple criteria and simple scoring rules (short scoring ranges). Have all your reviewers apply these criteria and, as quickly as possible, score each candidate product, using all the resources that you provide as well as any others that they may uncover and share with the group.

In this process, I prefer a small set of quick passes through the list to find products that easily drop out. People shouldn't expect to do complete and exhaustive analyses. They don't have time for a complete analysis and may become very frustrated. Rather, ease them into the process by doing a number of quick passes. With luck, the one or two passes drop out half or more of your initial list of products. This may be all that you need to make the first cut.

The first cut should yield between five and 10 candidates. With five, you risk having too few to make it to the end of the process; with 10, you risk having to spend too much time collecting information. You decide what's appropriate for your organization and schedule.

The sales presentation

After the first cut, it's time to get serious. Your group should have enough practice reviewing and scoring to be comfortable with going deeper, and you should have a group of good candidates.

At this point, some groups choose to have a preliminary demo from each of the candidates. This is a nice idea to become familiar with the products and the organizations behind them.

If you choose to have demos, I recommend the following:

✦ **Don't require preparation of your team or the vendor.** Ask for the standard presentation. This serves a number of purposes. It gets the process going quickly, the company can send its usual talent, and your people can either attend or not, depending on their schedules. It gets the standard presentation over and done with so that, at the next meeting, you can get down to details quickly. It gives the vendor's representatives the opportunity to present their best face and walk you through the stuff that they're most proud of. In the next meeting, you talk much more about the parts that the vendor's not so proud of.

✦ **Aim to understand the product, not question it.** Save your probing questions for later and become as immersed in the product as you can. Be positive, to draw the presenter out and to have her give you the fullest demo possible. Each product has lots of interesting and good features that you should try to understand and appreciate.

✦ **Freely discuss your requirements and needs.** The vendor's presenter is trying to qualify you as a prospect as much as you're trying to qualify her company. Try to answer her questions as openly as possible so that she can get a solid feeling for what you've accomplished (which, by now, ought to be quite a lot) and what you want to accomplish in the end.

✦ **Learn the names of the people inside the product organization** that you can contact directly for specific information. If you're lucky or persistent, you can build a good list of expertise for future reference whenever you're having trouble getting an answer.

The RFP (or Tender)

Your main job here is to create the complete selection criteria list and form it into an official Request for Proposal (RFP) or Tender. You may call it an RFP, or you may prefer to be less formal, but the idea is the same. You create a complete scoring system (most likely a spreadsheet that extends the simple one that you use to make your first cut) that lists all the questions that you need answered in order to arrive at a list of finalists, along with a place to score each finalist.

Note Vendor sales representatives may like to do more of a consultative sell, sitting down and talking at length with you about your issues before trying to propose how the solution would work. You can use the first demonstration meeting to accomplish this or schedule separate meetings. But make sure that it doesn't end up slanting your process toward the company that sells the hardest at this early stage.

Usually, my preference is to ask a lot and expect a lot of my questions to go unanswered. Others choose to ask only the most essential questions and insist on complete responses. I like the former approach because it provides a lot of discussion and input to the next stage of the project, and you can learn something about the responsiveness of the vendor by the way he tracks down responses to unanswered questions. Besides, even if you ask only essential questions, you're not guaranteed to get complete responses without a lot of probing and pushing.

Tip Just because you get a bad answer doesn't mean that the product isn't worth your time. Assess the credibility of the answerer and, if you want, give the company a break by digging deeper until you find an answer that you can trust. Similarly, answers of "yes" or "we do that," count for little unless you dig deeper.

If you choose to send a complete set of questions, warn the vendors that you're giving them a big job and make sure that you give them ample time to respond. Of course, no matter how much time you give them, most wait until the last minute and then panic if they can't complete the document.

Cross-Reference The section "Sorting through the CMS Selection Criteria," later in this chapter, has a large number of questions that you can include in your RFP.

Selecting finalists

I've learned not to expect too much from RFP responses. They often fall far short of what I'd prefer to see. I believe that the problem usually is that I expect too much detail and the respondents have too little time and training to respond adequately. You may think that, after a while, companies would build up a pool of stock responses to respond in full to almost any question that you may have. So far, this has not been my experience. Still, because this very young field is growing so quickly, it's understandable that vendors can't spare the time or talent to respond in-depth at the first request.

That's why I believe that it's a good idea to plan to have follow-up meetings with the candidates that make the RFP cut. Before you schedule these meetings, see whether you eliminate any candidates due to lack of response or unacceptably poor performance on the RFP. For those that make a reasonable effort and have answers that are on the target, if not on the bull's-eye, more discussion is warranted. By this time, you've undoubtedly been noticed by the companies, and if you're a big enough fish, you have their eager attention.

Again, in these meetings, I favor multiple quick passes through the questions over a single, in-depth pass. On the first pass, focus on the issues that the candidates did particularly well or poorly on in their RFP responses. If they did poorly, was it because of a lack of responsiveness to the question or because they can't do what you want? Make a list of all the weak points. Do these points amount to a disqualification from the process, or with some additional time, can they be resolved favorably? If more time is warranted, divide your list into topics. (The criteria categories that I propose in the section "Sorting Through the CMS Selection Criteria," later in this chapter, may help here.) Rather than asking the same person to answer the same questions again, see whether you can find the right person inside the product company for each type of question. Provide your questions in writing and let your sales contact know that continued participation hangs on deeper responses from a qualified expert in order to bring in the right people.

You can use e-mail, phone calls, one-on-one meetings, or group discussions to move each question to a final score. You may find it helpful to divide your team by expertise or interest to ensure the most efficient coverage of the questions.

Tip   Don't divide your team by product if you know that there are favorites. Instead, divide them by question type so that each person sees all products.

At some point after your first pass through the RFPs and before your follow-up is complete, you should officially score the responses. A spreadsheet with the tallying built-in is helpful. Make sure that each reviewer is fully aware of and in agreement with the process. An answer of "I don't know" or "I need more discussion" ought to be allowed. The reviewer herself can decide whether her reservations are enough to postpone the final scores. I've generally had several team members score each product based on their ability to judge the products and vendors. Then I've used the spreadsheet to average the scores to come up with the final score for each criterion.

You want to prioritize each question that you score by giving it a weight. A question with a weight of 10, for example, is counted 10 times as heavily as a question with a weight of 1. Make sure that you establish these weights *before* you begin scoring.

Note   How much of your process to reveal to the vendors is always an issue. I'm of two minds. On the one hand, I think that the more they know about the criteria, how they're scored, and what you're questioning, the better they can respond. And most use the information that you provide to try to serve you better. On the other hand, the more that they know, the more some of them may try to interfere and bias the process toward their product. You decide.

Your schedule and allotted effort should decide how many finalists you can choose. Two is low, and five is high. The process to select from among the finalists requires much more effort on both sides.

I emphasize again the points that I made earlier about who gets to decide. If you want a clean, decisive process, decide beforehand what your process is and stick to it. If you continually change your criteria or decision process, you frustrate your team and the vendors and you end up with no result or a result that's questioned and subverted.

Technical drilldowns

With a small pool of finalists, the time is right to get down to the real details. Do a more thorough job of analyzing the RFP and follow-up questions from the finalists, and schedule one or more meetings where your technical experts and theirs gather to envision what the relationship between the groups will be. Experts can be of a variety of stripes, as follows:

✦ **Business experts** can gather to discuss terms of the contract that you may sign.

✦ **Editorial experts and information architects** can come together to discuss the collection system and metadata modeling facilities.

✦ **Programmers** can meet to understand how the system may be developed.

✦ **IT folks** can envision the architecture and deployment of the system.

✦ **Publications staff** can deliberate on the system's capability to produce the appropriate output.

As part of this set of meetings, you may want to schedule additional demos of the product or other background sessions to get your team fully up to speed on the capabilities of the products.

These discussions should result in a clear idea in the minds of your team of how you'd complete your tasks with the different systems. At this point, you should feel comfortable sharing your full requirements and logical design with the vendors to give them as much as possible to go on and to test the strength of their understanding and desire to work with your team.

The vendors should understand that they need to move beyond the sales staff to bring in people from their development groups or from their professional services groups who can really contribute. It helps to bring in these people only if you're clear, during these meetings, that you're testing the relationship that you hope to have with the company that you finally choose to work with. You should push as much as possible for the people who attend these meetings to be the actual staff that the vender will assign to your project.

I favor having each meeting result in a diagram that each side believes represents what the system may look like or do, given your needs and their product. Although the content of the diagrams changes based on whom you're meeting with, the concept should be the same across all the meetings that you hold. If you do this, you will thank yourself later. You can hang all the pictures next to each other to help you choose from among a, possibly, confusing array of competing approaches.

Envisioning the project

In the technical drill-down meetings, you've worked through most of the issues that were troubling. If you have, you're now ready to figure out just how the project would progress with each potential product.

You can start by adding detail to the RFP responses that you receive and rescoring them based on the information that you receive through follow-up meetings. If you can get past the bad feeling that the vendors could have told you in the first place all the stuff that you found out later, you can capture and organize a lot of the detail that you discover and still have a single place to grade the company (in your scoring matrix). Make sure that you mark the revisions that you make to the RFPs so that you can tell what you added and what they originally said.

Compare the first scores that you came up with to the revised ones, as follows:

✦ The second set of scores is more reflective of what the product and the vendor are really capable of doing.

✦ If the second score is higher than the first, you had a bad sales rep.

✦ If the second score is lower than the first, the difference is the amount of spin added to the original RFP response.

Your biggest task is to create modified project plans for each prospective product. Work through your existing project plan with representatives from the product company. Work through the complete plan, but pay particular attention to the parts of the project that the product can't do out of the box, as follows:

✦ **For the major tasks that require custom development**, add an extension to the project plan that has enough information in it to be used as a basis for cost and schedule estimates. Try to get as good an approximation as you can of the amount of customization that you need to do to augment the stock functionality of each product. You can, perhaps get the vendor to separately estimate the cost of doing the custom development.

✦ **For the major integrations**, try to get as specific an explanation as possible of how the integration would occur. Get whatever time and cost estimates that you can and try to plan the integration in the same way that you planned the major customizations. You can also, possibly, get an estimate from the vendor for integration services.

You can update your risk assessment, once per potential product, noting any new, heightened, or reduced risks that using that particular product entails.

Note   If you think that this is a lot of work, you're right. The only consolation is that one of the project plans that you create now is the one that you can actually go forward with later.

The vendors can be very helpful to you in this endeavor. They have a lot of great experience doing CMS projects and can bring a great level of detail to your plan. If they're not helpful or know less than you do about your plan, that's good information to know as well.

References

Rightly or wrongly (rightly, I believe), most companies don't give you references until they're sure that you're a highly qualified prospect. The reason that they wait is that they have precious few clients willing to put out the effort that a reference requires, and they want to reserve them for the highest value. Some companies don't have many references because they're not well liked — but that's not something that they're likely to tell you. With any luck, you have weeded out these vendors in your first cuts.

If you've followed anything like the process that I've laid out, you have more than enough proof at this point that you're serious. References are just about the last step that you take on the path to your decision.

You want these references to be people who are using the product to do the things that you want to do. You need to be very lucky to get such a perfect match. More likely, you find people who speak kindly of the product (the same as you'd do if you agreed to be a reference) and are in a different industry or have only some of the same issues that you face.

One mistake that people make with references is to leave the choice entirely up to the vendor. What can you do to come up with two or three people who are similar to you and are using the same products that you're reviewing? Following are some things that you can do to reach that goal:

✦ **Check the Web.** In your initial search, did you find any people who had opinions on the product? If so, ask them to talk to you. If you didn't fully search the Web for the products that are finalists, do it now.

✦ **Check the logos on the vendor's site.** Product companies proudly display the names of their major clients. Who in these organizations can you talk to?

✦ **Check conferences and journals.** Although content management is still a bit obscure, most technology magazines have done at least one story on it. In addition, look for content management conferences where people do case studies on the use of one product or another. Maybe you can find just the person that you need to talk to in one of these venues.

The point is that you need comparable installations to help you decide which product is best for you. Whether you get those from the company or by yourself is irrelevant. Besides, if you tell the companies that you're doing your own search, they may be a bit more helpful in the references that they provide.

After you have the references, schedule a conversation. If you can go to them, you will get a lot more time and effort from them. Plus you can sometimes see the system running and talk to all sorts of people. If you can't manage to make it to the reference's site, a phone call may still be enough.

The biggest issue is how much time and effort you can get from the references. You should need no more than an hour or two if the person is sufficiently briefed on her own system. Prioritize your questions to make sure that, if you're suddenly cut off by a higher priority issue, you've at least gotten the main points out.

To me, the best approach is to recognize that these references are your peers. Even if you choose a different product, here's a person who's in the same boat as you. What do you have to offer her? At the very least, you should have a little sympathy for her problems. More likely, you have some ideas or information that she can use as well. If you can establish a relationship rather than being a single inconvenience that the reference must endure, you get more and better information. More important, you may get a friend that you can collaborate with over the course of your career in content management.

What should you ask the reference? The same questions that you've been asking yourself and the vendor. Use the reference in conjunction with the technical drill-downs to solidify your feeling about how it would be to use this product. Of course, general questions such as the following are always a good start:

✦ Did the vendor deliver what she said that she would?

✦ Did the product do what you expected it to do?

✦ Have you gotten the support that you needed?

✦ Was the training any good?

✦ How close are your requirements to ours?

✦ What problems did you have with the installation?

✦ With what systems and applications are you integrating?

Some of the most telling answers come from asking questions such as the following:

✦ What was the most surprising or least anticipated part of the implementation?

✦ If you had to suggest one improvement to the product, what would it be?

These may be good icebreakers, but make sure that you get quickly to the key issues to make the best use of the limited time that you probably have.

Vendor presentations

By now, you're very close to a decision; in fact, you may have a clear leader or you may even have decided who you want to work with. But there's no contract yet, only a lot of discussion. You also likely have a list of issues that have never been successfully resolved for each vendor. Finally, you may have people with the authority to sign the purchase order who'd like a chance to meet these people before giving them a lot of money.

You can combine all these needs into a final vendor presentation that has the following purposes:

✦ **Final resolution of any outstanding issues.** Getting to the final presentation means that you should resolve any big issues first. You should aim to settle any outstanding issues that would be embarrassing to talk about at such a weighty meeting.

✦ **A full discussion of the terms of the agreement** that you may sign with the company. Prior to the meeting, you should get sample contracts and pricing and service schedules that you can review and comment on.

✦ **An executive review of the company.** This gives your sponsors (or whoever else wants to attend) the chance to meet with whatever executives the product company can send. Having the big guns there on both sides can have an amazing effect on the issues that seemed unsolvable before. In addition, you have the right people present to discuss any strategic aspects of the relationship that you may form. Can the two companies help each other in more than just content management?

✦ **A cost estimate.** You should work to have a final price tag for the product available at the meeting. Alternatively, you can set this meeting as the point at which the price is set. You may have a lot of hoops to jump through to arrive at a price. In my experience, CMS companies aren't forthcoming with cost estimates. That's another good reason to set this meeting as a deadline. You also may want to have all the customization and integration estimates that you prepared ready at this meeting to verify them with the company's official representatives.

This is decidedly not a meeting to demo the product or have the sales people present their slide shows. It's a down-to-earth, do-we-want-to-work-together meeting. The time has passed for features. It's time to make a final determination of the company itself.

Tip   Make sure that you brief your sponsors on the need to avoid wasting meeting time on demos. Find out whether they'd like a demo and then schedule a separate time before this meeting, or invite your sponsors to one of the earlier meetings where they can ask functionality questions.

Centering the discussion on the contract has the effect of putting a seriousness and reality on the discussion that no other context can yield. There's nothing like saying, "So can we insert a sentence here that binds you to the conditions that you just agreed to?" to make the point hit home and finally be decided.

The result of your final vendor meetings should be that your sponsor group (and the people who sign checks, if they're not the same) should form an opinion about the companies that you're reviewing. If their opinions match yours, your work is finished. If the two don't match, you have a bit more work to do.

There's Always Speed Enough

Professor Wolfgang Coy of Berlin's Humboldt University once explained that the ratio of speed between computers and humans is similar to the one between humans and trees. Seen from the computer's perspective, waiting for the next keystroke is like waiting for a growing branch of a tree to reach out and touch you.

We've proven that. Given enough time to optimize a solution, there seems to be no limit to the reduction in the use of resources one can achieve. Most tasks are implicitly routine, and so if one can avoid doing them manually, the effective speed of the system rises. Automating your tasks effectively will have a much greater effect on your overall productivity than the speed of your hardware. In our case, we are down to using a 700 MHz computer with 768M of RAM (which is still massive if you remember the "no-one-needs-more-then-640K-of-RAM" legend). This machine is hosting storage, a (meta-) database, GUI, and rendering functionality all together. The key for our productivity is the control we have over the system—we use libraries optimized for our particular problem, and that we can modify as necessary. (Another lesson here is: Don't trust a solution with unidentifiable components, such as locked libraries.)

Think of what you really need. Then think again.

Peter M. Buhr, DIE ZEIT, Zeit_online GmbH

Making the final call

If you've followed the process to this point, you have enough information to make a selection, as follows:

✦ You have large files on each product.

✦ You have RFP responses that are augmented and scored.

✦ You have diagrams showing each possible approach.

✦ You have prospective project plans for each product.

✦ You have risk assessments for each product.

✦ You have references from peers using each product.

✦ You have cost estimates.

✦ You have agreement in principle on a contract for each product.

You have the information that you need, but you also need the organizational will and process to decide and move on. Your selection process should have produced a numerical winner in the RFP scores, as well as project costs. In addition, you have one or more subjective assessments from your team and sponsors on each of the other deliverables from the process.

If you're really lucky, all these align and point toward a single winner. Otherwise, you have the following options (in order of my preference):

✦ **Drive for consensus** by hashing through the disagreements in open debate until all opinions converge enough for a decision. You can expect a lot of debate but a solidly supported decision.

✦ **Create an objective scoring** method for the subjective factors. You can create a scale for each factor and a weight for each subjective factor relative to the weight of the RFP score and the product cost. Then create a calculation that sums the scores for each reviewer and product and calls a winner.

✦ **Escalate the decision** to someone who can make and enforce it. Provide the decision maker with all the information that you've collected and let her decide.

Clearly, the process that you choose has more to do with the nature of your team than the information at hand. A well-coordinated team with mutual respect and a strong unified vision of the project can easily reach consensus. A team that feels bound by the process more than by respect for each other is likely to accept an objective scoring. Even for a well-functioning team, the objective scoring method may be fastest and easiest. If the team isn't functioning well, the only good course may be to punt the decision to someone higher in the organization. That, at least, ensures that the decision is made and everyone abides by it.

Of course, the worst time to decide how to decide is at the end, when emotions may be high. At the beginning of the selection process, you should assess your team's inclinations and decide how to decide.

Taking Stock of the Deliverables

I've spent ample time on the selection deliverables in the course of describing the process, so I just provide a few additional comments in the following sections.

Product files

It's a good idea to have the files that you created for products in a central place where the whole team can access them. I also favor having them jointly owned by all team members, who can add to them as they find good material. Don't forget to attach a URL or other identifier to all materials so that you can track their sources as needed. You undoubtedly need a directory as well as a physical file for each product. I've had luck with a big binder, where all materials were three-hole punched and the directory location for computer files was written on the cover.

You can include the notes that you compiled from content management Web sites in a separate file. If you're way more organized than any group I've ever worked with, you can continue to add to the links file and periodically publish it as a resource for people in your organization to learn about content management.

The selection criteria and RFP

I'd suggest starting with a spreadsheet that catalogs all your criteria and their weightings. You can continue to develop the spreadsheet until it's time to send out the RFPs. At that point, you can send a spreadsheet to each vendor, but it's more friendly to convert the spreadsheet into an electronic document (Microsoft Word is an accepted standard) and send it that way. The conversion takes a little extra effort, but it makes the RFP easier to work with (at least, for the CMS product vendors). In addition, you can add a cover page and company background that's difficult to do well in a spreadsheet.

I've found it particularly useful not only to provide a long list of questions in an RFP, but also to include a short description of what you're trying to accomplish at the start of each section. You can draw from your logical design to create these introductions. By doing this, you not only provide needed context to the person answering the questions, but you also give yourself a way to make sure that you've covered all the most important questions that your logical design may have raised. As you put in the introductions, ask yourself, "Do the questions that I ask here cover the implementation of what I just said that we want to do?"

You may also consider including parts of your project mandate and the high-level overview that you wrote at the beginning of the selection process (which I present in the section "A high-level overview," earlier in this chapter). Finally, consider augmenting your lists of fill-in questions with scenarios. Suppose that you have some authors who seem particularly problematic. (Maybe they use strange tools or are remote.) In addition to (or, in some cases, instead of) asking your authoring questions, you can explain your concerns about your authors and ask the vendor to propose a solution. You may get mixed results, as scenarios require more thought and effort by the respondent than do short answers, but it may be worth a try to see who has the most creative solutions.

The score card

You can build your RFP scorecard directly into the spreadsheet that you devise for selection criteria. If each reviewer gets a copy of the spreadsheet file, each has her scores immediately tallied for her. To combine the scores of all reviewers, you can create a master spreadsheet that looks inside each reviewer's copy and tallies the full results, or you can just copy and paste the individual scores into a new sheet.

Tip　Make sure that you have a way to link questions in your RFP to your scoring matrix. I prefer to number the sections in the RFP so that I can refer to them exactly in the scoring matrix.

If you decide to score subjective factors, you can simply add them to the RFP spreadsheet file and sum them with the rest of the RFP questions.

The design diagrams

In design, a picture is worth more than 1K words. By making a diagram deliverable from each technical drill-down meeting, you accomplish the following:

✦ Ensure that the meetings focus on design rather than become unfocused discussions of what's possible.

✦ Ensure that some solution is reached. Meeting notes can meander and never conclude. A picture can be more or less precise, but it always tells a complete story.

✦ Make it easy to compare one product easily to the others. Each diagram is a possible solution to the same problem.

✦ Provide good input to the implementation process that comes next.

Convinced? If so, here are some guidelines to help you make the most out of these diagrams:

✦ **Title them.** Preferably, the titles should be the names of the systems that they describe (such as "FrameMaker Publication System" or "Repository Structure"). You also may include a short description of the problem that each diagram addresses.

✦ **Label all major shapes and lines.** It's amazing how quickly people forget what all those parts are and do.

✦ **Include inventories in the margins.** Lists such as staff, CPUs needed, and connections all help you later develop plans from the diagrams.

✦ **Use a standard iconography.** If everyone agrees on the picture for a database, LAN connection, Web server, and the rest of your symbols, your diagrams are easily read by anyone on the team and more easily compared to each other.

The decision report

At the end of the selection process, you've reached a major milestone in the project. You're finished with the last big decision. From now on, the decisions are all about *how*, not *what*. To mark the milestone and also to inform the organization, you should prepare a short decision report.

Include the following in the report:

✦ The high-level overview that you wrote at the beginning of the process.

✦ An overview of the process that you followed.

✦ Major factors that led to the decision.

✦ An overview of the product selected.

✦ Information about the company selected.

This report should be distributed, at least, to all the people who participated in the project so far, and, ideally, to anyone who may participate in the CMS in the future.

If there's enough interest, you may want to schedule an open session with representatives of the product selected so that anyone can come and see a demo and ask questions.

 Tip

After all the hard work that you do on product selection, don't forget to reward yourself and your team. This decision is a clear cause for celebration. Don't forget the people at the product company. If you used this process, they worked as hard as you did and deserve a party, too!

Risk assessment update

At the beginning of system selection, your risk analysis has mostly high-level organizational issues and stuff about how you possibly can't do what everyone wants to do. As a result of the selection process, you can add a set of more concrete risks and mitigations to your assessment. Table 19-1 provides an example of a simple product risk assessment to get you started. (Effect and probability are on a scale of 1 to 5, where 1 = low and 5 = high.)

Table 19-1: Product Risk Assessment Example

Area/Risk	Effect	Probability	Score
Design/Planning			
Technical training and implementation, support not timely	3	1	3
Development			
Major development effort required	3	3	9
Inadequate developer documentation	2	3	6

Area/Risk	Effect	Probability	Score
Integration			
Major technical issues related to integration	3	2	6
Integration results in poor site performance	3	2	6
Personalization inappropriate or inadequate	1	3	3
Rollout			
Usability/training issues	2	2	4
Ongoing Support			
High level of end-user support required	2	2	4
Inadequate end-user documentation	1	3	3
Incapable or unresponsive help-desk staff	2	2	4
Scalability issues, significant hardware requirements	2	4	8
Futures			
Vendor's technology becomes obsolete	2	2	4
Vendor becomes financially unstable	2	3	6
Vendor experiences high level of change/turnover	2	4	8
Vendor's technology direction becomes misaligned with ours	2	2	4
Vendor's market direction becomes misaligned with ours	2	0	0
		Overall Score	78

Project plan update

If you did your homework in the selection process, you need little extra work at the end to update your project plan. Make sure that you go through it again, however, and fill in all the spaces that you left blank because you ran out of time.

If you've added people to your team from the product company, make sure that you add these new staff members to your plan. They probably have their own project plan, so you must work together to integrate the two. In any case, you should maintain a master plan where the all staff and schedules come together to complete the rest of the project.

Taking Stock of Your Staffing Needs

The CMS product selection process begins with the build, buy, or rent decision. This is a big decision with lots of political and technical overtones. I believe that the decision should be presided over by as high-placed a person as you have on the core team. In my taxonomy, that's the content manager. The content manager should at least supervise this activity and pass the recommendation by the sponsors before making a final decision. The content manager or her equivalent probably also should be the one to write and circulate the high-level overview.

I favor having a single person head up the vendor-selection process and others participate as reviewers or outside observers. My preference is also to have the person running the process refrain from being a reviewer as well. There's just too much conflict of interest between coming up with the evaluations and doing them. Also, the leader may have her hands full managing the opinions of the reviewers and may not need the extra hassle of offering opinions as well. Finally, as main contact to the vendors, it's useful for the leader to be able to say, "It's not my decision!" Whether she participates in the selection or not, the leader should take responsibility for the following:

✦ **Doing or supervising the market canvass** that begins vendor selection. It may be easier for one person to do this, but it may be faster and more politic for a group to do it.

✦ **Overseeing the first cut.** Although the reviewer group should make the cut, it may need a lot of help keeping to the process and closing on a decision.

✦ **Creating the final set of selection criteria.** With ample input from the reviewers, the leader can still be responsible for forming the final selection matrix.

✦ **Creating the RFP.** The mechanics and styling of the RFP document should come from a single source.

✦ **Overseeing the process of creating scoring metrics.** Again, help and prodding may be needed to get a final agreement.

✦ **Overseeing the selection of finalists.** Here, the impartiality of the leader really comes in handy.

✦ **Deciding which technical drill-downs need to happen** and receiving the design diagrams that result. Diagrams result only from constant but amicable pressure. Of course, input to the decision should come from all quarters.

✦ **Overseeing the vendor presentations.** You need an officiator of these events who understands both the vendors and the organization well enough to negotiate between them.

✦ **Overseeing the final call.** You hope here is that facilitating this process doesn't go beyond process and prodding.

✦ **Producing the decision report.** The selection leader is in the best position to create this report, but the content manager, or her equivalent, ought to be the one who circulates it and gets feedback from it.

Here are some of the other roles that you may need to fill in the selection process:

✦ **Reviewer group.** Earlier in this chapter, I discussed staffing the reviewers group, so I'm not repeating that here. I add only that you should aim for between 4 and 10 reviewers for optimum team performance.

✦ **Scheduling** is a big part of selection. I suggest enlisting administrative help to make sure that all the vendors and reviewers are where they're supposed to be and know what's required of them at all points in the process.

✦ **Technical drilldowns** require an appropriate analyst to lead them and participation from other analysts and subject-matter experts (implementers) who can drill as deeply as needed into a topic and help construct the diagrams.

Try Before You Buy

Would you buy a car before test-driving it? Probably not. We all want to get behind the wheel and check: Does the car feel safe? Does it accelerate well enough? How tacky are the breaks? Is the turning ratio as tight as advertised? Does the interior feel too big or too small? After all, a car is a complex system, and you'll be in it perhaps every day, maybe several times a day. Sure, the written specifications — like gas mileage — are important to your selection, but unlikely to be decisive in the absence of a real test run. After all, cars are complex systems, different people want different features, and automakers — like smart companies everywhere — usually have a particular prototype buyer in mind for each particular model. Are you that person?

You should buy a content management system the exact same way. Do your homework, figure out what your stakeholders need, and then insist on a test drive with at least two final contenders. The things you need to prepare for an adequate software test drive are just the pieces you need to put out a solid RFP anyway: representative content, important usage scenarios, and expected outcomes.

So insist that any vendor put together a proof of concept using some of your content. Then have your key users try it out. Explain to your team that not all the options will be there — "no sunroof yet" — because it's impractical for a vendor to build everything you need in a short timeframe. But after the end of your test drive, the people most impacted by the CMS will get a good "feel" for how it works. I say "feel" because some of the more subtle vendor design approaches can have a big impact on how their tools work. Does the system push content to pages, or pull content from templates? Same outcome, perhaps, but big differences for the way authors work.

More importantly, a test drive can give you a good "feel" for the vendor itself. Companies have personalities, and software vendors have strong ones. A test drive will ideally enable your team to work with various vendor staff members beyond their sales and marketing force. Do you click with them? If not, don't buy. In the long run, your relationship with vendor staff may well have a greater impact on how well you manage content than picking the right software.

Tony Byrne, Founder, CMSWatch (www.cmswatch.com)

Sorting Through the CMS Selection Criteria

You may have a vast number of questions for a vendor in order to decide if you want to buy her product. In the sections that follow, I outline a number of them. As you read through these questions, I'm sure that you can think of some of your own, as well as ways to reword the ones that I supply so that they will fit into your selection process. Recognize that not all these questions are relevant to your needs, so choose accordingly. Make sure, however, that you take into consideration future needs and ask the questions that may not apply today but that could conceivably apply a year from now.

These questions are the same ones that you must answer later to implement your system. In this chapter, I call these questions *selection criteria*. After you've selected a CMS product, however, they serve as *physical design constraints*. You can use them to specify how your system is to be created from hardware, CMS functionality, third-party software, and customizations that you develop.

This section covers how to create CMS selection criteria for a CMS that you buy or rent. The chapters in Part V, "Building a CMS," cover building your own CMS in detail.

The selection criteria in the sections that follow ask about how certain functions are accomplished in a particular CMS. Use the logical design that you created previously to augment these questions. In addition to the following questions, use your logical design to explain what you're trying to accomplish and to ask vendors questions about what you want to do and why.

For each of your criteria, decide in advance what the ideal responses to each of your questions would be. Doing this makes it much easier for your reviewers to score by comparing the vendor's response to the ideal response. I include some suggested "right" answers to the criteria that I propose.

Business criteria

In addition to meeting the technical and process requirements you may have for your CMS, you want to make sure that the CMS product company that you decide to work with meets your business criteria for a successful relationship. After you have its product installed as part of your e-business initiatives, you're quite tied to the fortunes of this company. You don't want to find out that it isn't the company that you understood it to be.

Here are some of the business criteria by which you may want to judge CMS product companies:

✦ **History:** You can ask vendors for short descriptions of the history of their companies. Understand where they came from. Did they morph from a different industry (document management, for example)? Did they "ride a WebPub" from concept to product, bootstrapping from a service to a product company? Did they raise a lot of capital and burst onto the scene as a startup? It's less important which paths they took than that you understand their history and how it may affect their culture and future.

✦ **Business profile:** You can ask for general business data, including the number of years they've been in business and have been producing the proposed products. What's the ownership of their companies? What are their capitalization strategies? What have their earnings been in the past and what kind of growth have they seen? You may be surprised at how small even some of the major players are. If you're dealing with public companies, you can certainly check their growth and analysts' guesses as to their viability in the future.

✦ **Customer profiles:** One of the best questions you can ask of vendors is how well they know their audience. If they can send you the profiles of the accounts that they see as key to their success, you can decide whether you're one of them. If, on the other hand, you're nothing like their target customer, are you looking at the right product? Ask for the number of completed and ongoing installations they've done that are similar to yours. Which use their current versions and which use earlier releases?

✦ **Next versions:** Given that next versions are going to be needed (a near certainty), you should ask vendors about their upgrade policy, including how new releases, upcoming features, hot fixes, betas, and patches are communicated to customers and released. Ask how often to expect updates or upgrades and how much they cost.

✦ **Binding agreements:** If you raise issues that aren't resolved in the current version but are promised to be in future versions, what sorts of binding agreements or penalties are these vendors willing to take on? These binding agreements are one way to ensure that vendors are serious about what's in their next versions. But don't be surprised if they refuse. Such agreements would make their lawyers cringe.

✦ **References:** Ask for references at the sites of the projects that are like yours. If possible, the references should include a business as well as a technical contact.

It's a lot to ask of vendors that they supply this much information (especially on top of the technical requirements, which are even more voluminous). As you negotiate the delivery (or lack of delivery) of these items, notice as much what the process is like as what's delivered. Is the vendor accommodating? Is the information available, or does she make it up? Do any vendors stall on items that they don't give you, hoping that you stop asking, or are they up front about why they can't deliver? Finally, do they just say what you want to hear, or do you detect a measure of sincerity and genuine desire to work with you? The impression that you get up front is likely to carry through the rest of the relationship.

Overall criteria

The selection criteria in this section apply to the CMS as a whole. You find selection criteria sorted by collection, management, and publishing later in this chapter.

Project process and staff

The goal of asking the questions listed in Table 19-2 is to assess not only the process that the company recommends, but also how well the company knows its own product implementation cycle. If it can provide you with this information in an organized and well-considered form, you can assume that it has the project process down.

Cross-Reference   You can compare the process that the product company uses to the one that I overview in Chapter 15, "Getting Ready for a CMS," in the section "Understanding the CMS Project Process," to see whether it's (or I've) missed anything.

Table 19-2: Project- and Staff-Related Questions

Question	Notes
Describe the general steps involved in an implementation of your product.	Does it seem overly simplified and does it diverge widely from the steps that I outline in Chapter 15, "Getting Ready for a CMS"?
What factors are necessary to ensure a successful deployment?	Does the vendor offer any particular wisdom that shows that the company has seen and surmounted a lot of problems?
What's the typical time frame for a deployment and what can be done to minimize the time and effort required?	Does the vendor's time frame include the full customization that probably needs to be programmed in or just general installation and some basic template setup?
Provide an example of project plans and deliverables from projects that are close in scope to ours.	The response tells you whether the vendor has completed projects like yours, how organized the project process is, and how strong the deliverables are.
Describe the various project roles (both those of your own staff and of your customers) and the numbers of people involved in each role. Describe what roles people had before the implementation and how their roles changed after implementation.	How complete and realistic are these lists? Do they miss any categories?
What professional services does your company provide?	Many CMS product companies can provide full service, from design to maintenance. Each, however, has its own particular way of doing so.
For a project such as ours, what sort of professional services do you recommend?	You'll likely get a description of the standard services packages that the company offers. Try to get past this to the particular project composition that it sees for your project.
Can you provide a list of your service staff positions and their billing rates?	You can compare this list to the staffing list that I provide (in Chapter 13, "Staffing a CMS") and your own staffing plans to decide what you need.

Development environment

The questions in Table 19-3 should give you a fair appraisal of the kinds of development tools that are allowed and preferred in working with their product. Keep in mind that some of these criteria are fairly technical in nature, so if you're not too familiar with software development, make sure that you have a technical resource review this section.

Table 19-3: Development-Related Questions

Question	Notes
What development languages and tools were used to create your product?	It's good if the company used the more common Web-ready tools, such as Java and C++.
Please provide an overview of the ways programmers can customize or extend your product, including the languages and tools needed.	Here you're looking for a clear description as well as the tools that you want to use. Nonproprietary development languages and tools are preferred if you don't have ones that you particularly want to use.
What APIs are provided as standard with your product?	An extensive, well-documented API is preferred. Best is that the company builds its own user interface from the same API so that you can make sure that it's well tested and provides complete coverage of the product's functions.
What skills and tools are needed to create and modify basic templates for authoring, submitting, and publishing content?	Basic templates shouldn't require programming skills. Ideally, the tools are those that a person who can use a graphical HTML editor can easily learn and use.
What skills and tools are needed to extend and integrate templates beyond basic content inclusion and layout?	Nonproprietary development languages and tools are preferred if you don't have ones that you particularly want to use. You may prefer layout tools that are targeted at the kind of skills that a graphic designer may have. If a programmer is required to create page layouts, you may have trouble.
What languages and tools does your system support for automating administrative functions?	You want to hear that you can call all the administrative functions of the product independently, including workflow, user administration, database management, and reporting, using Web technologies that you want to use (.NET, ASP, JSP, CORBA, COM, J2EE, and the like).
What languages and tools does your system support for automating content authoring and acquisition?	At the very least, you should be able to modify collection Web-based forms and embed them in your own Web applications. It's better if the product offers out-of-the-box integrations with the authoring tools that you like. (Microsoft Word is usually the most important, but integration with HTML editors and graphic design applications is becoming increasingly common.) You should be able to extend and modify these tools, using the programming languages that you like.

Localization

Localization is a complex issue, often barely recognized by CMS products. If you have localization needs, first understand exactly what they are. Don't expect a product company to tell you how to localize. Given your plan, however, it should be able to tell you how its tools can help. Table 19-4 lists a series of localization-related questions.

Cross-Reference There's more on localization in Chapter 25, "Cataloging Audiences," in the section "Audiences and Localization," and in Chapter 39, "Building Management Systems," in the section "Localization System."

Table 19-4: Localization-Related Questions

Question	Notes
Please provide an overview of how your product supports publication localization. What specific tools and processes do you provide?	The overview ought to tell you how well the company understands localization and the depth of its support for it.
How is translated content produced and synchronized with the source content?	Ideally, the system maintains linkages between translated components to manage updates. It may be capable of handling content in different languages, including support for double-byte character sets or Unicode, international date formats, and global currencies. The screens that the content maintainers use must be easily translatable into different languages.
Are there any facilities in your product for multiple selection images or other media?	You may need various versions of graphics and other media that are localized for your various regions.
Please give a full example, with references and URLs, of a customer that has successfully used your system to create a localization and translation solution of the magnitude of ours.	A successful implementation by a customer who agrees to be a reference is a strong point in the company's favor.
Do you have any translation aids in your product, or do you integrate with any?	Translation aids help you put the master and translated versions of content side by side for comparison and difference checking.
Can you version and track changes at the element level?	It's really helpful to be able to send some component elements for localization separately from others that don't need to be localized.
Is there template functionality for sniffing the origin nation and redirecting?	The CMS may be capable of reading HTTP headers and helping you decide the region of origin of Web visitors.
Do you provide a multilingual UI for content contributors and producers?	Your international contributors may need, and are certain to appreciate, anything that you can do to localize their CMS interface.

Training

The questions in Table 19-5 assess how complete, convenient, and affordable training on this product is.

Table 19-5: Training-Related Questions

Question	Notes
Please provide an overview of the training that you provide.	You're looking to see a well thought-out response that shows that the company has put effort and resources into training and that the training is professionally delivered.
What's the availability and cost of training, and how frequently is it offered?	You want to make sure that the training schedule doesn't affect your implementation timing.
Is training held at your site or ours?	Some may offer on-site training for large enough groups. Otherwise, travel costs need to be included in budget considerations.
What CMS staff positions do you train for?	There's almost always end-user and administrator training, but is there training for developers, managers, information architects, IT staff, or designers?

Technical support

Bad technical support can make you very sorry that you chose a product. The questions listed in Table 19-6 should help you assess what sort of support to expect. Remember to be reasonable in your expectations of the support that you receive. It's not reasonable to expect the company to provide one-hour turnaround on all requests, anywhere, anytime. Recognize also that the better the support that you require, the more expensive it is. The correct response from the vendor to unreasonable support expectations is, "We can provide whatever level of support that you're willing to pay for."

Table 19-6: Technical Support-Related Questions

Question	Notes
Please provide an overview of the technical support that you provide.	As with training, you want to see a well thought-out response that shows that the company has put effort and resources into support and that it's professionally delivered.
Do you provide support, or do you work with any partners?	If the company's small, it's better if it's partnered with a larger support organization that can bring its support up to enterprise levels. On the other hand, you want to see that the company can provide the specific expertise to the partner to augment the partner's ability to address problems.
What's the geographic coverage of support, and at what hours is it available?	Obviously, the company should cover the same territory as your organization does.
In what languages is support available?	This may be an important consideration for you if you're embarking on a global deployment.

Continued

Table 19-6 (continued)

Question	Notes
What's the guaranteed response time for a support request?	How willing is the company to guarantee anything having to do with support?
Is there a single point of contact for support, or do people need to know whom to call for what?	A single point of contact with fast triage and routing to the appropriate contact is preferred.
What kinds of self-help facilities do you provide?	FAQs, known bugs and workarounds, and tutorials for beginners can save a lot of money for the support organization.
What guaranteed expertise is available on the first call, and what are the escalation procedures? How high in the technical organization can an issue be escalated?	The optimum cost-effective solution is to have enough skill on the first call to correctly route the problem. You want to see that, from the first call, there's problem tracking and a logical and reasonable set of criteria for escalating to each new level of expertise.
Describe your support licensing plans and associated costs. Do you offer a pay-as-you-go plan as well as contracts?	You may prefer a cost-per-use model that you can charge back to contributing groups rather than a fixed fee.
What comes as part of the purchase price and what are the costs associated with ongoing support after the initial purchase and installation?	The extent of services for setup and the cost of ongoing support can vary. You need to take into consideration the "total cost of ownership," not just the initial purchase price.
Are there any provisions for downtime or loss of revenue from systems impaired by a CMS bug?	Depending on how mission-critical your system is, this sort of discussion may be necessary. A willingness to enter into this sort of agreement shows that the company has extreme confidence in its system (or isn't smart enough to know that these sorts of agreements put it at grave financial risk).
How wide is the support? What software and hardware is covered?	How are problems that may be outside the CMS software supported? Are extensions using the standard API supported? Are template bugs supported? Are issues involving platform, operating system, Web application server, and database and network connectivity supported? For issues that aren't supported, how is it determined where the problem lies and how does the staff then tie into the appropriate alternate support organization?

Deployment

The questions in Table 19-7 help you understand how the product can be rolled out in your environment.

Table 19-7: Deployment-Related Questions

Question	Notes
What operating systems does your product run on?	The right answer includes the operating system that you use!
What operating systems are required on the client machines for the database client and authoring tools? Describe any client-side software needed to use the system.	All basic functionality should be available through a Web interface so that the client needs only a Web browser. Client software might be available, but not required, as a supplement to a browser interface to enable a richer and more responsive UI.
Which Web browsers are supported for authoring, management, and administrative functions?	You hope that it's the ones that you use.
Describe the skills and size of the team needed to successfully deploy and maintain your product.	This is an open-ended question that you can use to assess the company's process and savvy on this issue.
What models do you employ for distributing the management and publishing environments across business units that aren't in the same facility?	If your people contribute from around the world and publish locally, you want to assess how the CMS can help you keep this distributed environment organized and minimize redundancy.
Is your system best deployed inside or outside a firewall? Describe the difference in requirements or performance if your system is deployed inside or outside a firewall.	This question helps get at the distinctions of using this system for an intranet versus an Internet site. It also uncovers any problems that you may experience with remote contributors accessing the CMS.
Describe the process that you'd use to deploy your system across an organization with a structure such as ours.	This is another open-ended question to see how well the company can understand and provide for your specific environment. You want to add a list of the significant factors that are present in your organization.

Collection criteria

The criteria in this section can help you assess the collection technologies and processes that come with the product or can be integrated with the product.

Authoring criteria

CMS products vary widely in their support for authoring. The questions in Table 19-8 should give you a way to compare each of the products that you review.

 Cross-Reference

For more on authoring criteria, see Chapter 38, "Building Collection Systems," in the section "Authoring System."

Table 19-8: Authoring-Related Questions

Question	Notes
Do you ship with any specific authoring tools? If so, which one(s)?	Only a few CMS products ship with authoring tools (word processors, image-creation tools, HTML editors, and so on). Although it's helpful to know whether the product includes these tools, it's probably more important to find out whether the product supports the tools in use by your organization.
With what third-party authoring tools do you directly integrate?	Direct integration means that some aspect of the CMS appears within the authoring tool. Some CMS products create a menu within a particular authoring tool, for example, so that you can save content to and retrieve content from the CMS repository.
What file formats can your CMS repository store?	Many CMS products can manage files that are authored in any tool. Of course, they generally don't manage the content *within* these files. In other words, the CMS serves as a document management system for files that it can't interpret.
What file formats can your product recognize and convert to XML or database records?	In this case, you're interested in the product's capability to open foreign file formats and parse them. The result is, generally, either XML that can be stored in an XML repository or relational database records with the full content of the source file in them. Some products, for example, take the text that you write in Microsoft Word and convert it automatically into HTML or XML for storage in the product's repository.
Please describe how a novice content contributor could author the textual content for a Web page and include graphics or other types of media to go along with the text.	You want the system to be simple enough to enable your beginners and casual authors to create simple pages with little or no help.
Please give an overview of your Web-based form system for content input.	Almost all products now have a Web interface for content entry. Some may have a non-Web system, as well, that has fuller functionality than the Web-based forms.
Do you enable rich HTML or XML editing within the fields on your Web-based forms?	Some products include a little editing environment right in a Web-based form so that authors can format information as they type it.
Can Web-based forms show different sets of elements based on the user's permissions?	In other words, can you personalize input forms so that different people see different parts of the same content component, based on what you want them to enter?
What support do your forms offer for linking and uploading images and other media?	If this is a common need within your organization, you want to ensure that it's easy to add media and associate it with textual content.
Can your forms be automatically created from a DTD or database schema?	Some products auto-generate Web-based forms from the structures that you've previously defined, saving you a lot of work.

Question	Notes
Can your Web-based forms be extended or modified by additional HTML or other programming?	This is an important factor, because it's likely that you want to customize forms and need additional features. Ideally, the forms can be customized by using a nonproprietary programming language.
Can your forms represent hierarchical relationships?	All products enable you to put a set of fields on a Web-based form. A few also enable you to nest some fields within others. This is really handy for entering the titles and text in sections and subsections.
Can authors create content while they're not connected and then submit it later?	In other words, can you use the CMS authoring tools offline, a handy feature for authors who don't work on-site or for contributors who travel frequently?
Can authors preview content (as it may appear in publications) before they finally submit it?	A preview function is extremely helpful and streamlines content creation and quality assurance workflows considerably.
Can authors view a revision and workflow history for their work?	An audit trail of workflow for each component is helpful for accountability as well as for content troubleshooting.
Can authors perform a spelling check on their work?	A spelling check feature isn't standard in all CMS products. If you have worked without one, you will know how important it is.
Describe the training expectations required for new content contributors.	The system should require minimal training for novice or casual contributors. You can expect some training requirements for more advanced authors.

Acquisition criteria

The questions in Table 19-9 can help you decide how well a product meets your needs to gather and process existing information.

Cross-Reference

For more on acquisition criteria, see Chapter 38, "Building Collection Systems," in the section "Acquisition System."

Table 19-9: Acquisition-Related Questions

Question	Notes
With what acquisition tools does your product ship?	Some products include advanced tools for scanning content sources and automatically capturing content. Some have syndication tools that enable you automatically to accept incoming syndication feeds.
With what third-party acquisition tools do you integrate?	Most of the larger companies have strategic relationships with other companies (often, content syndicators) to augment their capabilities to acquire content automatically.

Continued

Table 19-9 *(continued)*

Question	Notes
How would we migrate our existing Web sites and other publications into your system?	Is there an automated process to import an existing Web site, or does it require an in-depth content analysis and restructuring into predefined content structures? Are there any tools for migrating publication types other than Web-based ones?
Can your product help manage the scheduling, usage rights, attribution, and payment for acquired content?	There's probably not much beyond the standard workflow system that the company can offer, but the question may get its people thinking.
Can your product automatically retrieve records from a database available locally and turn them into content components in your repository? Can these downloads be scheduled to happen periodically, with no human intervention?	The company may depend on standard programming to accomplish this, but it should demonstrate that its people understand the issue and have worked through it. You may have a product catalog database, for example, and want to create new components after new products are added to the database.

Conversion criteria

It may be that a product comes with few advanced conversion tools. The CMS product company, however, should be able to answer all the questions in Table 19-10 if the company is aware of and well versed in conversion issues.

Cross-Reference   For more on conversion criteria, see Chapter 38, "Building Collection Systems," in the section "Conversion System."

Table 19-10: Conversion-Related Questions

Question	Notes
Does your product ship with any conversion tools? If so, please describe their capabilities.	Products really vary on this count. Some have no converters at all. Others have a wide range of built-in tools for text and media conversion.
With what third-party conversion tools do you integrate?	The answer ought to give you a feeling for how well the company understands conversion. Does it have any partners in this area? Does it have an idea of how conversion fits into the process?
How does your product support on-the-fly conversion of text and media on a Web site?	As pages are requested, can the product retrieve content and convert it to the appropriate format? If so, you can store your media in one format and have it converted only if it's requested in another format. This isn't typical functionality, but some products can do it.
What can your product do to help us organize and manage our conversion scripts and teams?	The system is not likely to have any direct support for managing the process of conversion, but maybe the vendor knows of other teams you can talk to who have developed their own.

Aggregation criteria

When I first proposed a list of metadata management tools like the following one, very few product companies even recognized that it was an issue. Today, they're beginning to see the point of managing the metadata system. Over time, if you don't manage it, the system becomes unwieldy with conflicting lists and values, and it finally stops working as a way to unite all your content. Although the questions in Table 19-11 are still difficult for many product companies to answer even today, I suspect that, over time, most or all these metadata capture and management features will become standard equipment in enterprise CMS products as they are beginning to be included in third-party metadata tools.

Cross-Reference   For more on aggregation criteria, see Chapter 38, "Building Collection Systems," in the section "Aggregation System."

Table 19-11: Aggregation-Related Questions

Question	Notes
Does your product include or integrate with any metadata management tools?	Some products include auto-discovery and taxonomy creation tools that help you design metadata lists and automatically find metadata in the files that you process.
Can you automatically apply metadata values to content based on its type or location?	Some products enable you to choose a directory or other branch and batch-apply a metadata value to it. In addition, some can supply default values for metadata fields, based on the type of content being tagged.
Does your product have any tools for helping the administrator combine or split metadata fields that currently exist in the system?	As you move forward, you inevitably need to combine two similar metadata fields into one (for example, you may decide to merge an author field and a contributor field into one field) or split one field into two. (A single status field may need to be split into a publishing status field and an archive status field, to give you more control.)
Can you define mandatory and optional metatags?	This may be done in the Web-based form interface, but it may also be possible to do it globally for all uses of a particular metadata field.
Can you pull metadata lists from other sources, such as a database or a flat file?	You want to see, for example, if the product enables you to draw your list of products automatically out of a database and present them in a Web-based form.
Can you write metadata lists to other external files and databases?	You want to see whether the product enables you, for example, to add to the list of products and then periodically export the updated list to the database in which it originated.
Can you automatically bring up metadata lists or values for periodic expiration or review?	As part of managing your metadata system, you need to periodically review the validity of lists or values and either update or delete them. If you do, it's nice to have a tool that helps you update all the content that's affected by the change that you're making.

Continued

Table 19-11 *(continued)*

Question	Notes
Does your product tie into any accepted standards for metadata?	The Dublin Core Metadata Initiative and a host of other industry-specific metadata systems are being created and revised. At some point, you want to use one or more of them. Can the CMS help you do it, or does it stand in your way?
Does your product support all metadata types in the repository and metadata fields in your collection forms?	See the section "Categorizing Metadata Fields," in Chapter 24, "Working with Metadata," for more information on types of metadata.

Management criteria

The questions in this section can help you understand how the product stores and administers content and how it creates the infrastructure of a CMS.

Storage

The questions in Table 19-12 address the basic repository structure of the CMS.

Cross-Reference   For more on management criteria, see Chapter 39, "Building Management Systems," in the section "The Repository."

Table 19-12: Storage-Related Questions

Question	Notes
How do you store content? In a relational database? An object database? A file system? A hybrid of the preceding types?	You want to know how the company structures its content storage to know whether it's compatible with your infrastructure requirements and whether it can handle the sorts of content that you intend to manage.
Describe how your system stores the following content relationships: multiple hierarchies, multiple indexes, cross-references between components and between publication pages, and sequences.	These are all the access structures that you store and manage. All decent CMS products enable you to build a hierarchy. See how well the products that you survey do at building more than one hierarchy for the same set of components. You may need this facility if you intend to build multiple publications, each with its own TOC.
Does your content repository support extended character sets (double-byte) as well as international date and currency formats?	This is a must if you intend to localize in Asian or other double-byte languages.
If your repository system supports XML DTDs or schemas, can you create one DTD for the entire repository? Can you create multiple DTDs that are enforced for part of the overall structure of the repository?	There's more information on the issue of multiple schemas in Chapter 39, "Building Management Systems," in the section "Storing the content model in XML."

Question	Notes
Does your product have the capability to check the validity of links and media references that appear within text fields in the repository?	In many systems, the hyperlinks and media references (such as an `<IMG>` tag in HTML) that are embedded in the middle of a block of text go unnoticed and can be broken without any clue. Some systems enable you to track these links and references even inside paragraphs of text.
What indexing and searching does your repository support? Does searching respect security?	A good answer includes rich indexing and querying, metadata (keyword) searching, full-text searching, proximity searching, and relevance ranking of search results, as well as the capability to exclude results that a user doesn't have rights to see.

Administration

Any CMS that you buy should do most of what I point out in Table 19-13. The differences are in how well it performs these tasks and how convenient it is.

Cross-Reference

For more on administration criteria, see Chapter 39, "Building Management Systems," in the section "CMS Administration System."

Table 19-13: Administration-Related Questions

Question	Notes
In what ways can your system enable nontechnical business users to manage their own content?	This is an open-ended question designed to give the company a chance to address ease-of-use issues and how well it caters to novice or casual users.
Please describe the utilities provided for system administration and operations personnel to effectively manage and support the system. Please identify any administrative functions, such as configuring workflows or publishing schedules and so on, that can't be accomplished through Web-based tools.	Ideally, all administration should use Web-based tools. If some administrative functions require other software, you should know about them and make sure that they work in your context.
Can you do a global search and replace throughout the repository?	Though most do not, the CMS should support search-and-replace functions through free text and metatags, assuming that appropriate permissions and security rights are observed.
Can you automatically verify and manage broken internal and external links?	This is a very nice feature to have.

Continued

Table 19-13 *(continued)*

Question	Notes
What user roles and rights model do you use, and what tools do you provide for managing and manipulating them?	There are many variations on how user roles and rights are configured, including those that tie into your own network directory services and ones that support "inheriting" permissions based on a hierarchy of user roles.
What's your approach to data synchronization and replication across multiple databases? At what level is synchronization managed and communicated?	It's unlikely that it does a lot of this automatically. Instead, you're most likely to get replication tools that you must control to ensure synchronization.

Workflow

CMS products vary from no workflow support to integration with third-party tools to strong native workflow modules. The questions in Table 19-14 can help you correctly place the products that you survey on the spectrum.

Cross-Reference For more on workflow criteria, see Chapter 39, "Building Management Systems," in the section "Workflow System."

Table 19-14: Workflow-Related Questions

Question	Notes
What workflow tools does your product include?	You're looking for the vendor's description of its workflow tools. You may end up with a paragraph or two of marketing information or a good overview here.
With what workflow tools does your product integrate? What support do you provide for the integration?	Even if a product has internal built-in tools, and especially if it doesn't, it's important to know whether it enables you to use strong third-party workflow systems. If you're thinking of integrating in a workflow system, make sure that you get the company to answer all the questions in this table from a support perspective, as opposed to an implementation perspective. You want to make sure that events and content status transitions in the CMS can correctly trigger events in the external workflow system.
Please describe the internal or external inputs that can be used to trigger workflow steps.	Look for the capability to trigger workflow steps by an external process, such as an e-mail message arriving or a file being added to a directory.

Question	Notes
Please describe how your system handles the configuration of user roles for workflows.	You want to see that the product has a strong user interface that gives administrators complete and easy access to the functions that the product offers. Users in the workflow system ought to be the same as users in the CMS user-administration module.
Do you support parallel as well as sequential workflows?	In a parallel workflow, two people work on an item at the same time. In a sequential workflow, one person finishes before the other begins.
Please describe the range of system activities (such as content submission or deletion) that can be supported by workflows.	You want to find out whether the system can handle requests for a range of activities such as content submission, content addition, deletion, edits for existing content and content bundles, content reviews, content approvals, content migration, migration approval, and so on.
Please describe the content or system attributes that can be used to drive the rules for automated workflow routing.	In other words, what can the system look at in deciding what to do next with a piece of content? (Submitter, content type, and status are some of the usual attributes.) The best answer is that the workflow module can use any piece of metadata that you create.
Please explain or demonstrate the process for creating or modifying a workflow process.	You want to make sure that creation of workflows doesn't require programming skills. The slickest systems have a visual workflow designer with drag-and-drop manipulation of processes. Make sure that the interface is either very complete or that it's extendable.
What types of content collection, content management, content publishing, and administrative activities can be handled by an automated workflow process?	You want to know whether the workflow module can handle all authoring and publishing requests, including content submission, content addition, deletions and edits, content review/edits, content approvals, content migration, publishing, and testing. It is likely that it can handle collection activities, but can it extend to management and publishing?
Do you have the capability to include an external service provider (HTML provider, graphics, or translation services) in the workflow?	If it's an issue for you, make sure that the workflow tools can manage people with a slow Internet connection to your CMS, no access to your LAN through your firewall, or only an e-mail connection to you.
Can you view all content that's in a particular state for a particular user?	The best systems have rich queues that show each user what task she must accomplish.
Can you add comments at the end of each workflow stage?	This is a handy feature to have. (If not built-in, you probably want to customize the system to include a comments field.)
Do you maintain an audit trail for all workflow processes?	It would be super if you could roll back a piece of content to any step by selecting that step in the audit trail.

Continued

Table 19-14 *(continued)*

Question	Notes
Using your product, can you integrate e-mail into the workflow processes?	Some systems can run the entire workflow process through e-mail. Users receive notifications in their inboxes and then click links in their messages to complete tasks in the CMS.
Is there an administrative override to automated workflow processes?	This feature is a must if you need to stop or redirect workflows in process.
At what content level can you create workflows?	Most systems can attach a workflow to a file. The better ones can attach a workflow to a component (or whatever name is given to a component in the product). The best ones can attach a workflow to a particular element of a component. The body element, for example, can have a localization workflow attached to it to make sure that it gets translated. The rest of the component may not need to participate in that workflow.

Management integrations

In all questions about integration, don't settle for the typical answers, such as "We have a partnership with X," or "I think someone has done that." Rather, ask for the documentation describing how the integration was done. If that fails, ask for the name of a person who's done the integration and talk to her about how it went. At the very least, get specific information about the system on which the integration was done to make sure that it's similar to your own.

Here are some of the external systems with which you may want to integrate:

- ✦ Document management systems.
- ✦ Media and asset management systems.
- ✦ Operating system user registries (such as Microsoft Windows 2000 Active Directory).
- ✦ Enterprise resource planning (ERP) systems.
- ✦ Custom databases that your organization uses for catalogs and other content storage.
- ✦ Asset management systems.
- ✦ Records management systems.
- ✦ Source control systems.
- ✦ Backup and recovery systems.

For each type of system with which you expect to integrate, tell the vendor the name of the product that you're using and what platform it's running on. Ask the vendor to tell you specifically how her product interoperates with yours.

Table 19-15 lists some other integration questions that you can ask.

Cross-Reference For more on management integrations criteria, see Chapter 39, "Building Management Systems," in the section "External Connections."

Table 19-15: Integration-Related Questions

Question	Notes
What capabilities does your system have out of the box and with additional programming to connect to and share data with other databases?	The best case is a nontechnical interface for connecting to simple databases that can be used by administrators, plus the capability for the connection to be extended by programmers using a standard language.
Can you launch other applications from within your system? If so, how? What outside applications are supported?	Many products integrate with Microsoft Office products and Adobe Acrobat. The CMS product also may be capable of launching any viewing and editing tool that the system recognizes based on a file extension.
Do you follow any open standards for data access and data sharing?	Some products follow the XML schema or other open standards such as ODBC for data exchange.

Version control

Not all CMS products have a version control module. For those that do, the questions in Table 19-16 can help you decide whether it can work for you.

Cross-Reference   For more on version control criteria, see Chapter 39, "Building Management Systems," in the section "Versioning System."

Table 19-16: Version Control-Related Questions

Question	Notes
Can users check content into and out of your repository?	This is the most basic form of version control.
Does your product save earlier versions of content that can be restored later if necessary?	Make sure that it's reasonably easy for a user with permissions to restore the previous version without the need of a database administrator.
What level of granularity is supported for checking content in and out?	File level is most common; component level is the most useful; and element level check-in and check-out is necessary for more complex tasks, such as localization and collaborative authoring.
How is locking handled if content is checked out?	In the best case, you have the option to lock the component being checked out and, if you want, also its siblings or parents in the repository hierarchy.
Describe the different levels of granularity at which content can be rolled back to an earlier version. How do you support rollback of a complete site, an individual page, or a single content component?	You may need any of or all these kinds of rollback functions.
Can you perform differencing between two versions of the same content?	The best system enables you to put two versions side by side and compare each change.

Reporting

You may want your CMS to provide any number of reports. Table 19-17 has some of the questions that you can ask to find out what sort of reporting a product supports.

 Cross-Reference For more on reporting criteria, see Chapter 39, "Building Management Systems," in the section "CMS Administration System."

Table 19-17: Reporting-Related Questions

Question	Notes
Describe the logging capabilities of your system. What types of activities can be monitored, for both content producers and consumers? How would you track usage by user, group, or geographic area?	In the best case, you can track and log users, their time of access, and actions performed (such as downloading a particular version of a file or checking out/editing a file). You can also track system usage by user, group, geographic area, and so on. Logging and analysis usually can be performed on a Web server by third-party tracking products. You can use these programs for tracking the use of your Web publications. In addition, you should know what kind of logging the CMS provides for staff activities.
Describe how you integrate with Web server logs or other logs that are external to the CMS.	If you produce a Web site, you will want to be able use data from its page access log. In all likelihood, this feature will be outside your CMS's province.
Describe the workflow tracking reports that your system can generate.	Workflow reports that are most commonly used show each component or document and its workflow status, along with other supporting information. Or you may want reports that show all components that are at a particular workflow stage.
Can your product track usage and fees associated with copyrighted media elements?	If you buy media, you probably need to track and report on where it was used and how many times it was accessed or downloaded. This is rarely part of the product, but it ought to be possible to integrate into the product.
Can your product generate a complete site map of the Web sites that it produces, including page names and statistics (size, components, and so on)?	These sorts of reports are very useful to publication teams.

Disaster recovery

If you ever have a catastrophic failure of your system, you're going to be glad that you asked the questions in Table 19-18.

For more on disaster recovery criteria, see Chapter 39, "Building Management Systems," in the section "Robustness."

Table 19-18: Disaster Recovery-Related Questions

Question	Notes
What features does your system support for content backup and disaster recovery?	Features to look for are versioning, rollback, and automated backups. These features may be part of the database software that the CMS uses but could be controlled from the CMS administrative interface.
Can you provide any statistics on the failure rate of your product, such as average time between failures or the average percentage of system availability?	Some can provide this information and others can't. It's a good question to ask when you get around to checking references.
Describe any functional and architectural features of your product that are optimized to maximize the reliability of your system.	This is an open-ended question to give the company a chance to brief you on its reliability. Some companies can provide technical white papers that describe their system architecture and reliability features.

Security

The questions in Table 19-19 can help you assess the user and access features of the CMS.

For more on security criteria, see Chapter 39, "Building Management Systems," in the section "CMS Administration System."

Table 19-19: Security-Related Questions

Question	Notes
Describe how your system can leverage existing operating-system or directory-services security profiles to avoid the need to re-create definitions and duplicate security maintenance. With what servers and services can you integrate?	In the best case, whatever permissions or user groupings are already available in your operating system also are available and extendable in the CMS.
Do you support a hierarchical security model?	Especially if the system doesn't tie into existing security systems, you need the capability to group users and have them inherit permissions from parent groups.
Can your product help us enforce intellectual property rights and security permissions by controlling the capability to publish media?	If you work with content that has restrictions because it's copyrighted or because it's secret, the CMS may enable you to create and enforce a policy.

Performance

The questions in Table 19-20 help you assess how well the product can scale to the size that you need it to be.

Cross-Reference For more on performance criteria, see Chapter 39, "Building Management Systems," in the section "External Connections."

Table 19-20: Performance-Related Questions

Question	Notes
Describe the minimum and recommended hardware, software, and network requirements of your product at the level of usage that we expect.	The trick here is to specify your level of usage. Usage has two parts: the usage of your Web publications and the usage of the CMS by your staff. Check both.
Please provide examples and references that demonstrate your system's capability to scale to an enterprise-wide, global implementation. These examples should illustrate your capability to scale to multiple instances on multiple servers, to scale beyond a single Web farm, and to fully support load balancing.	If this is an important criterion for you, asking this question provides an opportunity for the company to present you with its scalability story. Check the story that it provides for architectural validity and applicability to your situation.
Describe any data size or performance limitations of the content repository. Include any known limitations, such as maximum number of rules, number of unique components that can be stored, number of concurrent content contributors that can be supported, or number of concurrent content consumers that can be supported.	Make sure that you check these capacity limits for staff as well as for concurrent audience users of your major Web publications.
Describe your mechanism for content replication to regional sites.	Replication usually consists of a master version and copies that are distributed regionally to improve performance.

Publishing criteria

The questions in this section help you assess how many of your publishing needs the product can cover out of the box or with customization.

Templating criteria

The questions in Table 19-21 canvass the product's templating capabilities.

Cross-Reference For more on templating criteria, see Chapter 40, "Building Publishing Systems," in the section "Templating System."

Table 19-21: Template-Related Questions

Question	Notes
Describe your overall approach to publication templating?	This is your chance to get an overview.
What programming languages can be used to develop Web templates?	The right answer is the languages that you use. Barring that, open languages that have a wide skill base in the programmer world are the best choices.
Do you support developing templates for non-HTML publications?	Sadly, most don't. One day, CMS products will support templates in word processing and graphical layout program formats as well. So when you ask this question, you may want to phrase it as: "How hard would it be for us to use your system to create our own non-Web templates?"
Can your system process templates in a batch mode, producing complete static sites?	In other words, can the CMS render static, Web-based publications as well as serve dynamic sites?
Can your system process templates on demand, producing dynamic sites?	Not all products can do this.
Can your system mix batch and on-demand processing to produce sites that are partly static and partly dynamic?	This is the ideal. You want to produce as much of a publication as possible statically for performance and robustness, but still produce other parts dynamically for the flexibility that it offers.
Describe the methods that you support for dynamically creating site navigation components. How are searches, links, a table of contents, or other navigational aids built by logic in the templating system?	You want to see some tools for this. Moreover, you want the system to be open enough that it can be extended to whatever navigation you want to produce.
Does your system support the concept of component and navigation templates? If so, how?	Refer to Chapter 31, "Designing Templates," in the section "Publications and Templates," for more information.
Do your templates support integration with outside systems? If so, how?	Some tools may be provided, but you really want to make sure that the CMS doesn't get in your way as you do this yourself.
How is personalization accomplished in your templates?	This is a very open-ended question that ought to yield a general discussion of the product's personalization tools and integrations.

Content deployment

CMS products have a variety of capabilities for distributing content from the central repository behind the organization's firewall to servers inside and beyond the firewall. The content deployment questions in Table 19-22 are weighted heavily toward the Web because that's where most deployment happens today.

Cross-Reference   For more on content deployment criteria, see Chapter 40, "Building Publishing Systems," in the section "Deployment System."

Table 19-22: Content Deployment-Related Questions

Question	Notes
How can your system be used to deploy content files to remote Web servers?	This is the basic deployment functionality. Surprisingly, many products expect you to do this with third-party products.
How can your product be used to deploy database records to remote databases?	In addition to files, you may need the CMS to send data to databases outside the CMS repository.
Describe or demonstrate a scenario illustrating how content is deployed from a staging server to a production server.	A staging server enables you to test a Web site before it goes live. Find out whether the CMS can support staging. (Also notice that many products' licensing models require that you purchase separate licenses for each server. The staging server counts as one of those.)
How can your system deploy appropriate content to various destinations, based on properties of the content?	You may, for example, want to key on various values within content components (language, for example) to determine which server to deploy the content to. Can the CMS help you here, or do you need to write your own routines?
Does your product enable you to assign default values for file directories based on content type?	It's useful to have all pages of a particular type deploy automatically to a particular output directory.
Can your product automatically deploy files referenced in a field?	If a file (an image, say) is referenced inside text that's being published, it's a good idea to have the CMS deploy the file to avoid a broken reference.
Can you set the publish and expiration dates of content to be published?	It's useful if you can have the CMS automatically release and remove content based on the rules that you establish.
Can you publish on a set schedule without manual intervention?	This is what you want for small, frequently published material (weekly e-mail broadcasts and syndications to other systems, for example).

Publication platforms

With the questions in Table 19-23, it helps to ask for specific examples of users who are doing the kinds of publications that you want. Don't stop with the answer, "Sure, we can do that."

Cross-Reference   A number of sections in Chapter 40, "Building Publishing Systems," cover publication platforms, including "Web System," "Print System," "E-mail System," "Syndication System," and "Other Publication Systems."

Table 19-23: Platform-Related Questions

Question	Notes
Can your system produce broadcast e-mail?	The system should be capable of integrating to your e-mail system and pushing content to it. Alternatively, it may integrate to a third-party bulk e-mail system.
Can your system create individualized e-mail messages?	As opposed to bulk e-mail, in which the same message is sent to a lot of people, individualized e-mail is where a lot of different messages are sent to one or a few people each. This capability ties the personalization functionality to the e-mail creation functionality.
How can your system be used to produce print publications?	You want to focus this question more on the specific kinds of print publications that you produce.
Can your system create publications based on WAP and other XML-based formats?	Again, have a good idea of the exact publications that you want the system to create.
Can your system syndicate content?	Syndication capabilities include creating format-neutral (generally, XML) content chunks and deploying them to FTP sites, remote servers, or to mass storage devices (hard drives, CD-ROMs, DVDs, and the like).
Can your system create content for proprietary electronic formats, such as Microsoft Help, Macromedia Director, or other CD-ROM platforms?	You should query specifically for any non-HTML electronic platforms that you may need.
Can your system create downloadable documents in Portable Document Format (PDF) or other proprietary formats?	PDF is good for downloads that can't be modified by the user. Query for any others that you may need.

Personalization

The questions in Table 19-24 helps you figure out the types of personalization that you can expect to get from a product.

Cross-Reference For more on personalization criteria, see Chapter 40, "Building Publishing Systems," in the section "Personalization System."

Table 19-24: Personalization-Related Questions

Question	Notes
Does your product ship with any personalization tools?	Some don't, although most don't easily admit it. Others have extensive offerings.
Does your product integrate with any third-party personalization tools?	Most, at least, have marketing alliances with personalization companies. Look for documented integrations.

Continued

Table 19-24 (continued)

Question	Notes
What kind of user interface do you provide for creating and modifying personalization rules?	Some products have very well-developed point-and-click interfaces for rule building. Others require a programmer to code the personalization rules—not a good long-term solution.
Describe or demonstrate the process for defining personalized experiences. What skills and training are needed to work with your personalization engine?	See whether you can get a concise description of the overall approach to personalization that includes a discussion of how it's actually accomplished.
How does your system facilitate the collection and storage of user-profile data?	Some products have functions for monitoring the user's actions and their responses to questions and then storing the results in an accessible profile—but don't count on it.
Can your product receive syndicated data from third-party suppliers of customer profiles?	You may want to supplement the information that you collect about your users with data from commercial suppliers. Can the CMS help this happen?
What forms of data are accessible to your personalization engine?	Good answers include user-session data, HTTP header information, page history, all content metadata, user profiles inside or outside the CMS repository, user groupings, and personalization rules.
What facilities do you have for producing individualized print publications or other non-Web personalizations?	Most of the action today is in dynamic HTML page building. The same tools could be used to make any other kind of personalized publication, provided that there's template support for the publication format that you need.
Do searches, links, a table of contents, or other navigational aids reflect the personalized content that's available to a specific user? If so, how does it work?	For relatively sophisticated personalizations, the system should be able to modify these access structures automatically, based on the personalization rules.
What sort of personalization rule-building process and user interface do you employ?	Some products have well-developed user interfaces for point-and-click personalization rule building.
Can your system perform collaborative filtering?	Collaborative filtering is the process in which the system recommends content based on requests of similar users (an approach popularized by Amazon.com).
Please outline the kinds of personalizations that are possible based on user profiles.	This is an open question that gets the company to talk about how personalization interacts with profiles. The product may enable you to define profiles, for example, and then target content to them.
Please outline the kinds of personalizations that are possible based on a user's actions on a Web site.	This is also called behavior-based personalization. Some systems track a user's behavior and modify the subsequent pages accordingly.
Can your system facilitate the creation or running of push campaigns?	In a push campaign, the system actively presents certain content on a Web page or in another form to a group of selected users for a specified period of time.

Publication integrations

You may want to tie your Web publications to a number of systems. As with the management integrations, make sure that you get as much detail about the ones that you care about as the company can provide. The following list features some of the systems to which you may want to connect. It may be that the CMS does some of these functions as well, so phrase your question so that the CMS product companies tell you how much of the function their products do, as well as what third-party products they integrate with if you want to integrate with one or more of the following systems:

✦ Ad management and server products

✦ Brand management tools

✦ Campaign management and promotions systems

✦ Merchandising systems, including up-selling and cross-selling tools

✦ Customer relationship management systems

✦ Lead generation products

✦ Surveys and questionnaires

✦ Web access and security tools

✦ Data logging and mining tools

✦ Product configurator systems

✦ Decision tree tools

✦ Download packaging tools (which automatically bundle together and compress electronic content for efficient download)

✦ Chat products

✦ Bulletin board and threaded discussion systems

✦ E-mail acceptor and automated response systems

✦ Event planning and registration tools

✦ Webcasts and streaming technologies

✦ E-commerce and financial transactions systems

✦ Credit card transaction systems

✦ Any of the enterprise systems that I mention in the management integration section, earlier in this chapter, that also need to be accessed dynamically from the Web

✦ Conversion systems for on-the-fly conversion of content (for example, from XML to HTML)

✦ Custom database applications and custom programming objects that you may have created or may use on your Web site

✦ Web servers and Web application servers

Web UI

The Web is guaranteed to be one of your publication platforms, and Table 19-25 lists questions that can help you assess how much help you can expect from the CMS product in building Web sites.

Cross-Reference   For more on Web UI criteria, see Chapter 40, "Building Publishing Systems," in the section "Web System."

Table 19-25: Web UI-Related Questions

Question	Notes
What types of searching and indexing capabilities can be made available to an end user viewing a Web site produced by your system?	Searching isn't necessarily performed by the CMS. For static sites, a standard third-party search engine may be fine. For dynamic sites that are produced by the CMS on the fly, you need integration between third-party search engines and the CMS search functions.
What particular support do you have for producing browser-independent Web pages?	Some products include browser sniffers and supporting code to make serving browser-specific pages easier.

Web architecture

If you have the CMS active on a Web site, ask the questions in Table 19-26 to see how the product integrates into your Web infrastructure.

Cross-Reference   For more on Web architecture criteria, Chapter 40, "Building Publishing Systems," in the section "Web Platform Support."

Table 19-26: Web Architecture-Related Questions

Question	Notes
Which Web servers are supported by your product?	Yours, you hope.
Does your product include a proprietary Web application server?	Some products still have their own application servers. You want to make sure that the product doesn't lock you into its own application server but enables you to integrate to one of the better commercial application servers.
With what Web application servers does your product integrate?	For any product that you expect to use for more than the next year, the company needs to have plans for how it intends to integrate it with industry-standard application servers.
What databases can your system use?	The right answer includes the databases with which your technical team is familiar.

Question	Notes
How does your system facilitate or perform content caching?	Caching can happen at many levels. Make sure that you understand the difference between the caching models used by the various contenders. Make sure, too, that the company can demonstrate Web-server performance commensurate with the amount of traffic that you expect.
How does your system facilitate or perform database connection pooling?	This may be handled completely outside the CMS. Know which parts are performed within the CMS and which parts depend on a third-party application server.
How does your system facilitate or perform server load balancing?	You'd like at least some support from the CMS for this.
Does your product support user-session management, including cookies or database caching of user profiles?	Does the system rely on cookies, or does it provide other methods of tracking user sessions?
Can your system leverage user-profile information stored in directory services? Is any custom development needed to implement this functionality?	Probably there's some integration effort needed.
List the LDAP servers with which your system can integrate.	This is a concern if you're using LDAP services in your environment.

Summary

If it's done well, system selection can galvanize the entire organization behind a platform and approach to your CMS. If done poorly, it can create wide rifts between groups and result in a system that was nobody's favorite. To keep the selection process on the good side, do the following:

✦ Understand the position of product companies. Trust the people who are trustworthy, but understand the constraints and goals that guide their behavior.

✦ Develop a process before you need it. If you're in the heat of decision, there may be too little energy and good will to yield a fair and binding selection process.

✦ Develop a set of selection criteria that ask the key questions that you need answered to compare and choose products.

✦ Be diligent. Rather than jumping ahead, start as wide as possible and continually narrow the field until only one choice remains.

✦ Be official. Include the people from outside the process who must understand and support the process as well as those inside the process who decide. Herald your final decision and your great process.

✦ Update your ongoing project deliverables, such as your project plan and your risk assessment.

In the next chapter, I stop talking about planning and start talking about doing a CMS.

✦　　✦　　✦

Implementing the System

In This Chapter

Taking stock of the process and project so far

Looking at the specifications and plans of a CMS implementation project

Providing an approach to staffing and implementing the project

After you've designed your publications, content, and system and you've chosen an appropriate CMS platform, you're ready to implement your project. To begin, you must turn your requirements and designs into a set of specifications.

Following specification, work can begin to put the system together. You may divide the work by the three phases of content management (collect, manage, publish) or by functional tasks (programming, authoring, publication creation, editing, and so on.). Either way, you're best served by adhering closely to your specs and project plan.

In this chapter, I present an overview of the processes that you may use and the deliverables that you might create to implement a CMS. Please note the following:

+ I can present only a general model for implementation. Without knowing the particulars of the system you're creating, it's difficult to provide specific advice.

+ I assume that you're working with a commercial CMS product and that your job is to implement it rather than create a CMS from scratch. If you're creating your own system, you can still use this information, but you may find the information in Part V, "Building a CMS," more helpful.

+ If you work with a product's professional services group to do implementation, that group no doubt has its own methods and deliverables. If so, you can use this information for comparison and general guidance.

Implementing the System Jumpstart

This Jumpstart summarizes what you need to do in the implementation phases of a CMS project. Of necessity, this chapter ties together many of the threads developed in earlier chapters.

Use this jumpstart as a summary without the weight of detail, or as a quick review if you've already read the chapter and want a checklist of what you need to implement your CM system.

To implement the CM system you've planned, you can follow these steps:

1. With your team, assess where you are in the project planning process. Look at the major planning products you've created, such as gathered and codified organizational mandates, collection plan, a content model, publication design, and the choice of a CMS product.

   • Decide what can be cut from your requirements to meet your budget and schedule constraints.

   • Decide how to split up the work effort into smaller projects.

2. Decide what you need to deliver for your implementation and then create a detailed implementation specification for each of your collection, management, and publishing systems. Use your logical design to determine the deliverables that are required; or use CMS selection criteria to frame your deliverables.

3. Install and configure the CMS system you've chosen (over and over), and test it. Play with it.

4. Create a content processing plan and implement it.

   • Create the plan to maximize workflow.

   • Test the plan on a subset of content

5. Start the template coding effort for input templates (such as Web forms) and publication templates.

   • Modularize code as much as possible to make collaborative work and updates easier.

   • Figure out a workflow that works for all the people who have to touch the files.

6. Get started on any custom application development required — and treat this as a separate project.

7. Create and test the code that integrates parts of the CMS system with components that you've created outside it, such as templates and external data sources. Assess and make any changes needed in external systems to integrate them with the CMS.

8. Create a test plan for your system that's based on more than simple ad hoc testing.

   • Stress-test the system by simulating high traffic volumes, live publishing, and live authoring of content.

   • Plan for usability and beta test cycles.

9. Using the other plans and specifications you've created, update your project plan. Continue to update it and expect it to change throughout your project.

10. Update your risk assessment plan to anticipate risks, the conditions under which the risks may occur, the effects, and mitigations.

11. Assess the leadership and communication structure of your project staff. Optimally, you'll need a leader with content expertise, an overall project manager, as well as individual project and technical leads.

When you're done, you'll be ready to roll out your system to the organization.

Looking at the Process So Far

Maybe you think that I want you to put a whole lot of processes in place before you get to the real stuff. You may feel that you go through a lot of talking and planning but no doing until late in my process. You're right, sort of. Contrary to some, I believe that the technology to do content management is much less a problem than the attitudes and processes of the people who do content management. The technology is immature, indeed. It requires a lot of added customization and can't do all that you want it to do. Still, it can do most of what you want, if you know what you want to do.

In many other computer applications, it's much easier to know what you want. In a financial application, for example, you want to put a user interface and storage mechanism around all the finance operations that accountants, bookkeepers, and financial officers have been doing for years. In scientific applications, you want to create an algorithm that collects data and then processes it according to the equations you've devised. Even in a standard Web application, you know what you want to do. You want to store information of a known structure in a database and then access it for use on an HTML page.

The simple explanation for what you want to accomplish with a CMS is as follows:

> You want to create a system that harvests valuable information and functionality from the organization and its allies and delivers it to a known set of audiences wherever, whenever, and however they want it.

This simple definition immediately forces you to confront a number of questions that have nothing to do with technology. And until you've gotten past these questions, no amount of technology in the world can help you.

Now, to my grand language here, you may reply, "The simple explanation for what I want to do is to make my Web site easier to create by putting it in a database!" I wouldn't question this attitude. Maybe that's all you need to do. I'd just ask you to consider the following two points:

✦ You've described a Web application, not a CMS. Maybe you're biting off too big a solution to a smaller problem by considering a CMS.

✦ If you think that you need a CMS for what it offers beyond laying out stored content on a Web page, you very well may be backing yourself into the same nontechnical issues that I suggest you consider. If you need a CMS to organize authoring as well as to produce Web pages, for example, you must take at least some of the prior mandate and logical design steps that I propose, simply to figure out who your authors are and how you can work with them.

It's still early in the electronic Information Age. The idea of orienting your organization around the collection and distribution of content (both information and functionality) is new enough that it requires a lot of education and time to get the process started and still more energy to keep it going. Over time, perhaps, as the ideas sink in and become part of the fabric of organizations, much of the groundwork that you lay today will become a given in most organizations. The life of a pioneer is spent breaking ground that later settlers don't even notice.

Looking at the Project So Far

I assume that, happily or grudgingly, you've done most of what I've proposed prior to beginning implementation. Or, if you're working up a project somewhat smaller in scope, you've at least considered what I've proposed and then cut your plan down to size, as I discuss in

Chapter 12 "Doing CM Projects Simply." In either case, if you have, you've accomplished a lot. You've done all that you can do to ensure that the organization is ready for a CMS and can make use of it. You've worked completely through what you want it to do and now simply must make it do that. In particular, you've done the following:

✦ **Built a strong consensus in the organization** for what the system should accomplish. More to the point for implementation, you have a fixed set of goals that are measurable. You can gauge and direct your implementation based on these goals to make sure that you hit and then surpass them.

✦ **Organized a collection effort** that ensures that the CMS has a steady supply of high-quality input. More to the point for implementation, you know exactly what must be done to the existing content to get it ready for the system. You also know what sorts of tools and processes can help your authors and acquirers move content efficiently into your system.

✦ **Produced a content model** that unites all your content in a single, overarching structure. More to the point for implementation, you've produced just the input you can now use to create a relational database or XML schema that will structure much of your repository.

✦ **Designed a set of publications** that deliver the right content through the right channels. More to the point, you've defined the output of the system in such a way that it can be programmed into a set of templates that can produce those publications automatically.

✦ **Chosen a CMS product** that meets as many of your needs as possible. More to the point, you've created an alliance with an organization that can help you make this system work. You've also produced the project plans and architectural diagrams that feed directly into your implementation specs.

If you've followed the process to this point, you've done a lot of work; and all of it can help you better and more quickly implement your CMS.

Techniques for Getting the Job Done

Implementation is largely a process of making your plans come true. It's equally a process, however, of making your plans consistent with the reality of what happens as you try to make them come true. It's just as important to know when to change plans as it is to know how to stick to them.

Cutting back

At the point that you begin implementation, reality sets in. You become all too aware of the magnitude of the collection effort, the system setup, and system integration, plus the complexity of the publications that you want to produce. As this happens, be prepared.

You inevitably plan a bigger project than you can really do. If you know that this stage is coming, you needn't panic and run from the entire endeavor, and you needn't stiffen your upper lip and agree to do it all.

The attitude that, I believe, serves you best is this: The requirements and design stages defined the foreseeable goals for the organization and that the implementation and roll-out stages define what's immediately doable for the organization. Interestingly, this attitude both closes down and opens up the project, as follows:

✦ Just because something isn't immediately doable doesn't mean that it can't be done. The only question is when. The parts of the design that can't be done in the first version of your CMS are the starting points for the second version.

✦ Just because something wasn't foreseen in the design doesn't mean that the organization doesn't want to do it. The design process itself needs to continue. As you move into implementation, and especially as you begin to use the system, new content, system features, and publications become apparent. You can decide to implement these new features and make room for them in your plans or defer them to the next version of the system.

Cutting back, then, is not some necessary evil; it's just a part of the ongoing design process.

Cutbacks may be natural, but they're not easy. Someone's desire may be thwarted in this version, and she won't be pleased. In addition, you must go back and redo some amount of the planning process to account for the change in project scope.

You have a few tools for coping with unhappy campers. First, you have the prioritized requirements that you originally collected and had approved. Your cuts should start at the low-priority content and publications in order to be fair to all and to avoid conflict. Second, you have your sponsor group, which is in place to help with just these sorts of events. Make your case for cuts to your sponsors, not to the people whose requirements you must deny. Finally, you can console hurt feelings with the assurance that a high-priority implementation in version 2 can produce a much better result in the long run than a low-priority implementation in version 1.

Tip Resist the temptation to keep all content classes and publications and just do less volume. In a CMS, most of the work consists of setting up the component classes and publication infrastructure. So cutting volume rather than types of publications, content, and system features gives you less bang for your cut.

You also must decide at what stage in the planning to make the cut, as follows:

✦ **Do you simply need to scale back the logical design?** If so, you can get by with some markup on your design documents, showing which parts must be postponed. In addition, you must make whatever changes are needed to your project plan.

✦ **Do you need to drop requirements?** If so, you need to get the requirements reworked and approved again. Then you can mark up the design documents and project plan.

✦ **Do you need to change the goals?** If so, you need to reconvene the mandate group to make the change. Then you can make the corresponding changes to the requirements and get them approved again. Finally, you can change the design documents and project plan.

Obviously, the further back you go in the process, the more work it is. On the other hand, the further back you go, the bigger the change you can make. Personally, I think you derive collateral benefits from reengaging your mandate or requirements group. Doing so gives members a chance to stay active as a part of the process and to reassert their support. You want this to remain everyone's project.

Do you have one project or many projects?

Up until now, I've referred to *the project* as the entire CMS initiative. And it behaved as that. You had one team, whose members were all working together to create consensus and design the CMS. In the implementation phase of a CMS project, however, it may suit you better to think of a number of simultaneously running projects, each with its own project plan and team. This approach has a number of advantages that I believe outweigh the extra effort it entails — namely, the following:

✦ **It helps you manage the complexity** of the project at this stage, where a lot of different teams are working individually rather than with other teams. Rather than managing tasks, you can manage entire efforts and enable the team project managers manage to the tasks.

✦ **It enables you more easily to scale** to a larger project team from the smaller team that you've needed so far.

✦ **It helps you incorporate external resources**, such as the product company's professional services group and other third-party development and processing companies.

✦ **It isolates problems and setbacks.** If one team is having problems, it needn't bog down the rest of the effort.

✦ **It makes for more effective meetings.** Most meetings need only be within a particular team.

✦ **It prepares you for later**, when you may want to move to a functional project organization. (See Chapter 14, "Working within the Organization," in the section "Creating functional teams," for more information.)

 Note   Even if you share staff extensively across projects, it's still worth the effort to differentiate the projects for the organizational advantage that it gives you.

If you use this method of project management, you must be very careful to understand and closely manage the dependencies between groups. As one example, you must make sure that, at the time an integration team is ready to test a connection, the CMS team has the system running.

The key to this approach is to keep a master plan and schedule that has each team as a black box except for where its effort connects to that of other groups.

The following are some of the projects that you may want to create:

✦ **The CMS infrastructure project**, which is responsible for installing and configuring the CMS product. This team has mostly IT people on it and may be led by the future CMS administrator. (See Chapter 13, "Staffing a CMS," in the section "CMS administrator," for more information on the role of an administrator.)

✦ **The template project**, which is responsible for template design and programming.

✦ **Custom development projects** that create auxiliary applications for features that the CMS itself can't provide.

✦ **Integration projects**, which are responsible for connecting and establishing communication between the CMS and other existing systems.

✦ **Content-processing projects**, which are responsible for content preparation.

✦ **The test project**, which ensures that all the pieces work together and are as bug-free as possible.

✦ **The documentation and training project.** Although I class these activities as rollout and not implementation, it's not too early to start them. Most of the information needed for training and documentation is created during the implementation phase.

Detailing the implementation process

In the sections that follow, I lay out the major parts of a CMS implementation project. If you've done either a custom software development process or an enterprise integration process in the past, part of this process probably seems quite familiar. I've drawn from both software and integration to create these materials. However, I skew the process in the direction of collection, management, and publishing to make it solidly a CMS implementation process.

Preparing specifications

As in any development and integration project, the core of the CMS implementation is a set of specifications that tells the doers (programmers, IT specialists, data processors, and so on) what to do and how to do it. In a CMS system implementation, the specs merge the logical design that you created previously with the functions and procedures of the product that you chose.

The physical design of CMS includes the software, configuration, and hardware that you need to turn the logical design into reality. If you're lucky, the majority of the software doesn't need to be created from scratch; the majority of the configuration can be done in a good user interface; and the majority of the hardware is stuff that you already own — but don't count on it.

To prepare specs, you can start from your logical design. For each part, you can ask, "What must we do to make this happen given the system that we chose?" Write the answer down in the most explicit terms possible. The logical design is what you want to do, and the system (plus any additional programming or processing resources you have) is the tool set that you use to do it.

> **Note** Many people, who don't have the benefit of having done a logical design, turn this process around. They ask, "For each thing that the system I bought can do, what do I want it to do?" This process gets you to a system, but it's unlikely to be a system that addresses any more than your most crucial needs. But, hey — it's a start!

Following the logical design, your specs can detail the following parts of your implementation:

✦ **Your collection system**, including all the tools that you use to author or acquire content, all the CMS interfaces (such as Web-based forms) that you use to load content, all the conversion processes that you use to transform content to your master format, and all the metatorial processes that you use to completely tag each kind of content.

✦ **Your management system**, including the way that you install the CMS product; the way that you set up your relational, object, or XML repository; the way that you configure all the options of your CMS (to create component classes, users, workflows, version control, and so on); and the way that you connect and integrate the management system with other data sources.

✦ **Your publication system**, including the templates that you program to create the publications; the Web infrastructure that you create to deliver Web publications; the other software and process that you need to create other publication types, the personalization system setup, and the rules; and, finally, the way that you call or otherwise integrate with the range of non-CMS data sources and functionality components that your publications require.

You've probably seen enough of these terms by now to know what they all mean (another reason to do a lot of homework before launching into implementation).

I've seen any number of styles and layouts for specifications, most of which seem fine (although people always seem to find a favorite to argue for). The only things that I feel any motivation to agitate for are the following:

✦ **A numbered section heading style** (where, for example, 1.2.3 is the third subsubsection under the second subsection under section 1), which makes it so much easier to refer to sections and makes the hierarchy of the specification show through quite easily.

✦ **Enough concept** to keep the reason why you're creating a particular function from getting lost. You should always begin a section by stating why the function described is important and what goal it relates to. Then, as readers work through the specification, they can make their inevitable tradeoffs and enhancements based on a solid knowledge of the real goal of the function.

✦ **Enough detail** that the person doing the implementation knows exactly which part of the CMS or third-party application is being used for a function and what part she's expected to custom code. You can never put too much detail into a specification. You almost always run out of time and energy long before anyone would say that it's too specific.

✦ **Don't overspecify.** Although you want a lot of detail in your spec, the detail should be about what you want, not about exactly how to do it. Make sure that you leave room for the creativity and initiative of the implementer to have an effect on the product. This makes for happier implementers and results in a better system.

Tip   The vast majority of specifications I've seen are created as print documents. If you're smart, you create yours in HTML (or better, XML, if you can manage it). This gives you a lot better chance of repurposing your specs later into documentation and training. A little push now to make your authors learn and use an electronic authoring environment (or even a CMS) to create their specs saves you a lot of time later when you really need it.

Installing the system

Even if I knew which system you chose, I wouldn't know much about how to install it. IT infrastructure (system setup) isn't my greatest strength. What I can help with is the attitude that you should take toward installation. Keep the following points in mind:

✦ **Be prepared for it to be difficult.** A CMS has its tentacles into a lot of systems, including databases, Web servers, operating system services, user and other system registries, LAN connections, and the host of other systems with which you expect the CMS to integrate. Your installation may go without a hitch, but just as likely, even with the expert help of the product company, it may take a long time and might not work correctly the first time.

✦ **Document the installation.** Especially if the documentation from the product company is lacking, keep your own log of the options that you need to choose in the operating system. You're sure to thank yourself later (as will others) if you must reinstall the whole system.

✦ **Don't be afraid to play.** If you treat the system like a fragile china dish that you're afraid to break, you quickly develop a can't-do attitude that prevents you from trying half the things that you must do over the life of the system. Instead, break it on purpose a few times to see how it responds (and to learn how to fix it). Become accustomed to seeing the system crash or stop connecting after certain parts are changed.

The more that you play before the system is live, the better able you are to understand a problem and fix it quickly after the system is live.

✦ **Start early.** Don't begin to set up the system a week before you must start filling it. Install it a bunch of times, months before it goes live. Using your diligent documentation and your reckless disregard for crashing and trashing the system, you should spend as much time as possible mucking around to get comfortable with the system.

✦ **Make a test bed.** Create a hardware and software set that you can use to test installation and configuration options in safety.

✦ **Get comfortable with flakiness.** CMS systems aren't mature software applications. In addition, especially on Web servers, you have so much interconnection and dependency that something is always broken or limping. Rather than complaining about it, get used to it and enjoy the challenge of keeping all the parts in place. Like a high-strung racehorse, a CMS needs special care and attention, but they're both beautiful when they run well.

You can't change how difficult it is to install a CMS, and you can't make it much less flaky. But you can come to terms with the difficulties and not let them hold you back.

Configuring the system

After you have a blank CMS system installed, you need to configure it. Configuration is the process of setting the options and parameters that structure the CMS to prepare it for your purposes.

If you're lucky, your configuration can be done through a convenient user interface. To create a workflow, for example, maybe you can just click the workflow button and begin to drag tasks onto the screen. If you're less lucky, you must do your configuration by using one or more of the following options:

✦ **Text files**, which require that you type parameters and options by using anything from a simple to a very arcane syntax.

✦ **System registries**, which require that you enter configuration information into the interface (provided by the operating system) for specifying options.

✦ **Third-party tools**, which require that you use the interface (or lack of interface) provided by add-on products to type your parameters. Some systems, for example, require you to do a lot of database configuration in the database system itself.

✦ **XML files**, which require that you enter parameters into a set XML structure.

✦ **The software that you create.** If you write a batch-upload program, for example, you must figure out how the user configures it to post files to the appropriate directory. You can put in a nice user interface or use one of the more difficult techniques. After creating a few configuration interfaces yourself, you may understand better why so much configuration doesn't have a better interface to go with it.

Of course, I can offer no specific advice on configuring a particular system, but here are some tips to help you adopt a good perspective on configuration:

✦ **Configuration is behind many problems.** A configuration is a specific piece of information that the system uses to accomplish a task. If the system isn't doing what you want it to do, ask yourself, "What information is needed to complete this task and where is it likely to be hiding?" Directory names, user names, on/off choices, and display parameters are typical examples of the many bits of information in a system configuration.

✦ **You can take it back.** In the vast majority of cases, if you mess up a configuration param-eter, all you must do is change it back for the system to work again. Some systems let you restore defaults. This automatically restores the configuration to an out-of-the-box state. Don't be afraid to play around with configuration parameters (after you've writ-ten down what they were before you started). They're a low-risk way to get to know how your CMS works.

✦ **You must look for them.** Many CMS systems are notoriously bad at telling you where the configuration you're looking for is hidden. If you know something should be config-urable, make sure that you check all the sources that I mentioned earlier (text files, the system registry, and so on) before giving up. Do yourself and everyone else a favor by documenting any parameters that you find in out-of-the-way places. If you needed it, someone else will, too.

Doing content processing

Content processing can take a lot of time and effort to do well. It can also spiral out of control quickly if it's not well organized.

All of Chapter 37, "Processing Content," is dedicated to content preparation, so I don't dwell on the details of the process here.

Aside from the process itself, the main thing to understand about content processing is that it's a project unto itself and should be treated with the same respect and planning as any of your custom development or integration projects. In fact, depending on how much content that you need to prepare to launch and run your system, it may be your largest project. It may require more people and programming than any other single deliverable. Why?

If you have 1,000 items to prepare (not a particularly high number) and each takes 1 hour to process, that's a 1,000-hour project. If you can spend 100 hours of programmer time and 50 hours of manager time to cut the time down to 15 minutes per item, you can save yourself a lot of money. As the number of items to process gets higher, the economics become even more convincing and you can't debate the wisdom of processing content like a professional.

From a project perspective, here are some of the key tips to keep the content processing pro-ject running smoothly:

✦ **Plan first.** You learn just how expensive content processing can be if you start chang-ing the processing plan after production has begun.

✦ **Start early.** After you know the exact format and tagging you're aiming for with a partic-ular content source (somewhere between the end of logical design and the end of sys-tem selection), you can initiate the project to convert that content.

✦ **Don't depend on casual resources.** Anyone who volunteers to process a mound of con-tent for you has probably never done it before. Can she produce decent-quality work? Can she guarantee that she will finish all that she promised? Can she follow your rules? If you're sure, go for it. If you're not sure, you may be better off paying for a resource.

✦ **Keep the flow.** Ensure that, after your processing team is in place, you can keep a steady flow of information going to the team. It's cheaper and better for morale and quality to wait longer but work at a higher flow rate than to start and stop. So make sure that you can ensure a steady flow of raw information before you get the team started.

✦ **Check the output.** Don't assume that the output from your process is exactly right. Instead, do the process in advance on a small sample and test it to make sure that you can move it without problem into the next stage of its life (metatorial processing or right into the CMS repository). Not only does the sample content help you gain confidence in the conversion process, but it also provides good sample content for the people setting up the CMS.

Template coding

Templates are a cross between programs and design prototypes. In fact, most templates are created by using a page prototype in which the dummy text and other placeholders (standing in for dynamically generated content and navigation) are progressively replaced with their programming equivalents.

Cross-Reference This section covers the project process behind template coding. You find more information from the analysis side in Chapter 31, "Designing Templates," in the section "Analyzing Templates," and more from the technology side in Chapter 40, "Building Publishing Systems," in the section "Templating System."

The following are two different types of templates you can implement:

✦ **Input templates** such as Web-based forms that structure the content creation process. They generally use the same code base and technologies as publication templates but move information in the opposite direction (into the repository, as opposed to out of the repository).

✦ **Publication templates** produce output pages. They're the kind that I discuss most often under the heading of *templates*.

The two kinds of templates are quite similar and depend on the same sorts of processes and skills. I suggest that in your project, however, you separate input and publication template coding. Even if the same people are doing the work, the input templates are part of the collection system and should be developed with the needs of content contributors in mind. The publication templates are part of the publication system and should be developed with the needs of audiences in mind.

Although each CMS has its own templating techniques and languages, the general process of template development remains the same.

The Slime Line

I'll never forget working one summer at the salmon canneries on the Aleutian Islands of Alaska with my friend Tim. I learned more there about content processing than from any other job I've had. My job was *gutter* on the Slime Line. Salmon with a long incision on their abdomens would come my way on a conveyor belt. My job was to make sure that no guts were left by the time they passed me.

Like all factories, the cannery ran on a very tight schedule and margin. The biggest lesson the cannery taught me was this: Do your organizing and planning before the fish arrive. After the fish start flowing, the whole process had better go like clockwork; or you end up with a lot of dead fish on the floor, a lot of not-busy workers, and one very broke fish company.

Based on whatever you may have heard about how easy it is to create templates in your system, you may be tempted to give the task to a CMS administrator or even to your design staff. Be careful. If you scratch the surface of even the most user-friendly templating system, you find real programming needs underneath. And although template programming doesn't tend to be the hardest programming task, its scripting and programming-like tasks can get beyond a nonprogrammer quickly. Some systems, for example, use XML syntax to specify content inclusion in templates. These commands don't strictly require a programmer, but they end up providing all the major programming constructs (looping, variable creation, conditional statements), and if you want to do anything nontrivial in your templates, you need all the commands that are provided (and probably more).

From a project perspective, the main issue with templates is mediating between all the people who have some part in creating the final page. By definition, a template mixes design and programming code. You also have editorial content in a template (at least to the level of deciding what content placeholders belong in a given template) and user interface design. Sometimes the work becomes mixed to such an extent that any one person's contribution is indistinguishable from the others.

Suppose that the design calls for cross-references to be placed in a table, with a small identifier on the left telling what kind of link it is. The page designer creates a page mockup that shows the spacing, fonts, and general properties of the cross-reference table, as shown in Figure 20-1.

Links	
More detail	Programming Templates
More detail	Analyzing Templates
Background	What Are Templates?
Beginners	The Parts of a CMS
Experts	Template Integrations

Figure 20-1: The design element on the left identifies the link type, and the text on the right names the link.

Next, a page developer comes along and turns the design into an HTML page prototype that shows the exact code used to produce the design, as follows:

```
<H3>Links</H3>
<TABLE border="1">
  <TR>
    <TD>
        <DIV class="LinkType"><A href="http://link1">More
        detail</A></DIV></TD>
    <TD>Programming Templates</TD>
  </TR>
  <TR>
```

```
        <TD>
            <DIV class="LinkType"><A href="http://link2">More
            detail</A></DIV> </TD>
        <TD>Analyzing Templates</TD>
    </TR>
    <TR>
        <TD>
            <DIV class="LinkType"><A
            href="http://link3">Background</A></DIV>
        </TD>
        <TD>What Are Templates?</TD>
    </TR>
    <TR>
        <TD>
            <DIV class="LinkType"><A
            href="http://link4">Beginners</A></DIV>
        </TD>
        <TD>The Parts of a CMS</TD>
    </TR>
    <TR>
        <TD>
          <DIV class="LinkType"><A
          href="http://link5">Experts</A></DIV>
        </TD>
        <TD>Template Integrations</TD>
    </TR>
</TABLE>
```

Finally, the template programmer comes through to turn the HTML sample into a piece of working code, as shown here:

```
<H3>Links</H3>
<TABLE border="1">
[FOR EACH LINK]
    <TR>
        <TD>
          <DIV class="LinkType">
            <A href="[INSERT URL]">[INSERT LINK TYPE]</A>
          </DIV>
        </TD>
        <TD>
          [INSERT LINK TITLE]
        </TD>
    </TR>
[NEXT LINK]
</TABLE>
```

For the purpose of illustration, I've used a simplified pseudo-programming language in the preceding example. The lines that are all capital letters and enclosed in square brackets ([ ]) stand for programming commands. The point here isn't to dwell on the mechanics of template coding, but to illustrate how tied together design and programming can become.

What happens, for example, if the page designer changes her mind about the look of the links table? Or what happens if the page developer decides that she needs to change the system names used? Their work product has been totally subsumed by the work of the programmer. They may not even recognize where the table is anymore, let alone know how to modify it. But suppose that they do understand enough to change the programming code. What's to keep them from changing the code, only to have the programmer change it back later by pasting new code over the change?

The often-sad fact of template programming is that a number of people of very different stripes must play nicely together in the same files and even on the same lines of the same files. If you don't want continual blunders and territory wars over your template files, you'd better come up with some workable processes for ownership and changes to templates. Here are some rules to get you started:

✦ **Modularize code.** The more distinct and chunked that you can make your code, the more you can separate it from the template file. You may, for example, create a function that builds the cross-reference table and moves it out of the template file entirely, leaving behind only a function call (such as [BUILD LINKS]). This not only minimizes the need to share the same files, but also helps produce reusable code segments.

✦ **One owner at a time.** This maxim seems simple, so why is it so often ignored? If you have a version control system in your CMS, use it to manage work on your templates. If you don't have version control in your CMS, get a source management product. It pays for itself in the rework that you don't need to do.

✦ **Strict touch and no-touch zones.** Mark each template section. (HTML comments are usually what people use.) Then be clear and consistent about who gets to change what sections and when. A simple spreadsheet with the section names along one axis and job titles along the other axis can do the trick.

✦ **Close communication.** Of course, you can find no substitute for a close working relationship among all the people who must live together in the same file. If the page developer actually talks to the template programmer periodically, they avoid the majority of potential collisions.

Template programming is a real project and should be treated that way. You may have dozens or scores of templates to create and other parts of the implementation depending on their completion.

Custom application coding

In a large CMS project, you're bound to create at least a few standalone applications to augment the stock functions built into your CMS. By *standalone,* I don't mean completely independent, but rather separate enough that you use a language outside the CMS tool set to create and test the application. The following are a few examples of custom applications:

✦ **A Java applet** that sits inside a CMS input template (a Web-based form). The applet connects to your organization's product catalog database and enables you to select one or more product IDs to attach as metadata to a content component. From the contributor's perspective, the applet looks like just another control on the CMS form. The programmer knows, however, that the applet is a standalone program that is able to query the product catalog and pack the user's choices into the data that's passed back by the form to the CMS.

✦ **A C++ program** that scans the CMS database once a day and automatically archives components whose archive date has arrived. Maybe after trying to get the CMS to do this, the team decided it was much easier to write a small program that's triggered by the operating system scheduler.

✦ **A Perl script** that turns the HTML stored in the CMS repository into Maker Interchange Format (MIF) for use with the organization's Adobe FrameMaker print publication system.

As you can see from these examples, far from being independent of the CMS, the custom applications tie directly into it. For this reason, it's useful from a project standpoint to pay close attention to the dependencies between the custom applications and the stock CMS functions, as follows:

✦ **Make sure that the CMS can't perform a function** and that you really need this function before custom coding it. I've seen programmers overly anxious to take on functions that the CMS already has. You don't need the added burden of scheduling and supporting programs that offer limited return over what the CMS can do natively.

✦ **Make sure that you use the front-end CMS interface if possible.** If the CMS supplies an API or other standard automation interface, prefer it to faster and more direct methods. In later releases of the CMS, the front-end interface is likely to remain compatible with your custom code, whereas the sneakier methods you may discover are likely to break. You may want to check with the CMS vendor about any back doors that, you suspect, may disappear in the next version.

✦ **Treat custom development as a separate project.** Even as you pay close attention to the part the CMS plays in a custom application, understand that you're creating a separate application because the CMS isn't capable of doing everything. Keep the custom application teams small and separate. This enables you to keep them effective and also enables you to engage and disengage them as your budget and schedule allow.

Integration coding

Integration code connects your CMS to other systems. The connection may be input (getting HR data, for example) or output (passing transaction data from a Web site to an e-commerce system, for example). It may consist of a custom application, template programming, or both.

Suppose that you plan to integrate with an inventory system from a Web site that your CMS produces (see Figure 20-2).

Initially, the template draws from the CMS whatever content and navigation it may include. In addition, the CMS recognizes a call within the template to an external object (called the *Connection Object* in Figure 20-2). The object connects to the inventory system (over the Internet, in this case) and retrieves data. The object also puts data into the inventory system if, for example, the user orders something and the inventory must be decreased. Finally, the object returns data to the template, which formats it to appear on a page that's sent to the end user's browser.

Note　For simplicity, I've excluded other integrations to transaction and fulfillment systems that you'd probably need in an e-commerce application.

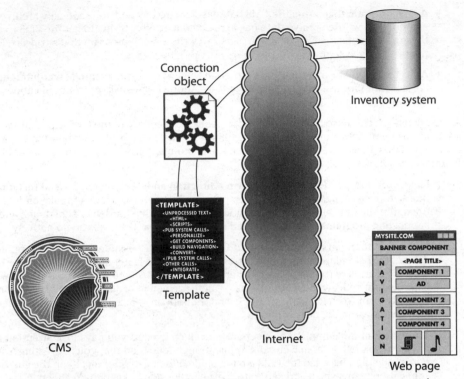

Figure 20-2: Integrating a Web site with a CMS and an inventory system may require programming in a number of different areas.

In this situation, programming may be required in three situations:

✦ **The custom object must be created.** On one hand, the object needs to know how to establish a connection with the inventory system, how to access the inventory data, and how to correctly store data in the inventory system. On the other hand, it needs to know how to package the data that it retrieves from the inventory system for use by the template. In any case, the code that creates the object has to be written and tested.

✦ **Template code must be created.** The template needs to be programmed to include the calls to the custom object and routines for formatting the results. In addition, a user interface may be added to the template to give the end user the capability to make choices (such as the choice to buy the items displayed from the inventory system).

✦ **The inventory system must be changed.** You may have to make some changes to the way the inventory system itself is set up to enable access and data exchange with the custom object. The changes may simply require reconfiguration of the system or some amount of new programming code.

Integration projects, therefore, result in a variety of programming tasks in a variety of places. From a project perspective, then, it's important to closely manage integration projects, as follows:

1. You must clearly determine the programming areas for integration.

2. You must gain access to the systems to be integrated in the templates (not always the easiest task). You might create a separate custom application development project, and you definitely must figure out the dependencies between the template coding project and the integration project.

3. You can task the template programmers with hooking up the integrations in their own templates, or you can add the integration programmers as another group of people who share the template files. Both approaches have the following benefits and drawbacks:

   • If you task template programmers with integration tasks, you have fewer problems sharing template files, but you also have two different people working on the same integration. Also, template programmers may have less expertise in working through the integration issues.

   • If you task integration programmers with template tasks, you may get higher-quality integration but more trouble working through the sharing issues.

Of course, this isn't as black and white as I may be presenting it. Again, the compromise position comes with good communication and trust among the team members who must share responsibility as well as files.

Tip   Have the implementation team members keep track of all the key problems that they encounter and the solutions they've found. You can use these lists later as the basis for troubleshooting tips aimed for the people who administer the CMS.

Testing the system

I assume that you're likely to be familiar with Web site testing, software-application testing, or, perhaps, no testing at all. If you have no familiarity with computer testing at all, your effort to read up on it or take a short course will definitely be repaid. I don't spend any time at all going through standard testing methods.

Cross-Reference   I talk more about quality control in Chapter 37, "Processing Content," in the section "Defining testing methods."

If you come from a software testing perspective, your best information is found under the heading of enterprise integration. Assuming that you do all the standard testing on the CMS's custom applications and template code, your main concern is the innumerable dependencies between the CMS and other systems. The most critical of these are on the Web server. Web servers aren't the most robust systems to begin with, and if you add the complexity of dynamic, high-volume sites to them, they can and do fail frequently. Stress tests on the server are thus critical to your peace of mind and future ability to sleep. You should consider testing for, at least, these following sorts of loads:

✦ **High browser transaction volumes** on your most dynamic pages. In your logical design, you've estimated transaction volumes. I suggest doubling these values in testing. Or, better yet, increase the volume of page requests until the system fails.

✦ **The effect of live publishing.** Try pushing a lot of new pages and database records to your site while it has an average-to-high transaction load on it. This simulates a publishing cycle. You want to make sure that no bad things happen if you do large updates later.

✦ **Simultaneous authoring.** If your live databases have data added to them at the same time they're accessed by end users, make sure that the process doesn't destabilize your system. If you collect and publish news stories on your live site, for example, ensure that the news-story page continues to publish correctly even as you plow in as many news stories as your staff can add simultaneously. Of course, it's rare that you wouldn't impose a workflow step or two between the news-story creation and its publication; but still, make sure that nothing strange happens.

In planning for system tests, the best approach that I've seen is to create a large dependency spreadsheet that lists all the parts of the CMS and supporting systems (Web servers, enterprise data systems, and so on) on both the row and column headers. In the cells of the spreadsheet, type what can go wrong for the row and column that intersect there. Then use this as your first test plan. As you (or your test crew) test each intersection, don't forget to enter the new scenarios that come up.

Tip   In addition to being a great way to test the system, this is a great way to learn the system and how all its parts interact. Make sure that you pass this spreadsheet on to the people who must document the system and do training.

Publication tests

If you've come from a Web-testing background, the training that helps you the least is the standard click-through tests. Many Web sites are tested simply by having someone click every link to see what happens. The whole point of a CMS is to create publications that change constantly. To keep up with the productive capacity of a running CMS requires that you have an army of clickers constantly trying every new page.

You must take a much smarter approach to testing the publications that your CMS produces. You find an analogous issue in software testing. In applications that can produce an unlimited set of output screens, instead of trying to use the application's user interface to test that all screens come out all right, testers back up to the code itself. They test the screen-producing functions to make sure that, for all scenarios they can think of, the functions produce reasonable screens.

The same methodology can work for testing CMS publications. Suppose that you want to test the employee information page shown in Figure 20-3.

Name	Job Title	Email	Phone	Hobbies
Frank Kocher	EVP Sales	fx@here.com	x3456	Swimming and trainspotting.
Eleanor Kocher	EVP Marketing	ee@here.com	x7890	Lifeguarding while Frank is swimming, antiquing.
Sylvia Lucia	EVP Networking	syl@here.com	x6633	Startups and reality shows.
Catherine Westel	EVP R&D	cjw@here.com	x7285	Thinking, running, testing cell phone reception.

Figure 20-3: To test this page, don't just look at the output.

By looking at the output, you can see only so much. You're better off looking behind the page to see what's likely to go wrong, as follows:

✦ **Rather than clicking the links** associated with names and e-mail addresses, check how they're built. What happens, for example, if an e-mail address is missing? Does the template logic catch this and not add a broken link? Back up one more step. Does the input form or conversion process ensure that an e-mail address is present? If it does, you have no need to worry. If it doesn't, where's the bug? Is it in the input method or in the page code?

✦ **Rather than checking the actual text on the page**, look behind the page to how the table is built. Are the column widths set? If not, can you think of a way to make the table become too wide for the page? Are text lengths limited for any of the columns, either in the page logic or in the input methods? If not, how might this table build poorly?

✦ **Rather than assuming that the same components are always there** or are in the same order, imagine many more components or their order changing. Note, for example, that Eleanor related her hobbies to Frank's (in the table in Figure20-3). That's fine if they're right next to each other as they are now, but what if many more employees are added and the two components become widely separated? This is a subtle bug (if it's a bug at all), but the concept is quite important. Not only must the tester test for the mechanics of the publication, but she also must test for sense. Does a page make sense in any of the varieties in which it may appear? The page designers must be the first to ask this question, but it's the tester who's in the best position to judge whether they got it right.

As you see in the few examples I gave, to test a page you must know and test the whole system. As clear as the problem appears on the completed page, sometimes it's not at all clear where the problem originated and where it should be corrected. The result of a testing bug report may be a change of algorithm in a conversion routine; a change of rules in an authoring process; or a change of template design, template implementation, or template programming.

Usability tests

Usability tests determine how understandable and useful your user interface is. Publication designers often perform professional usability tests on prototypes of publication pages to make sure that audience members can navigate through them and find what they're looking for. Professional usability studies use advanced observation techniques such as eye-movement detectors, click recorders, videotaped use sessions, and directed tasks. You should also try to do some form of usability tests on the custom application interfaces, Web forms, and other interfaces that you create for staff members. You needn't go overboard with these tests. They can be as simple as watching a typical staff member try to do a series of common tasks using your interface. If she gets stuck, you know that you need more work on the interface.

Beta tests

In a beta test, you test an entire system with a small number of real users shortly before releasing the system to the world at large. The usual assumption is that the system is finished except for the bugs that you find during the test. This assumption is almost always violated by people who count on the beta test time to fix all the known deficiencies that they couldn't get to during the normal course of implementation. For that reason alone, it's good to plan at least one round of beta testing. It puts a nice cushion between the project completion and release. But the benefits go way beyond the extra time you get. A beta test cycle does the following for you:

✦ **Gives you an inside user group.** You have the chance to build an unusually loyal set of audience members who are on your side not only in finding problems, but also in suggesting new directions.

✦ **Gives you a dry run** before you release for real. Any big problems that are going to come up in your system ought to appear in your test. Of course, a lot of the biggest problems have to do with performance when you have large volumes of users, and these don't show up during a beta test unless you simulate them by using stress-testing tools.

✦ **Gives you a deadline that's serious** but not deadly. People work hard toward a beta release with much less anxiety than they do toward a looming release date.

If you can afford the extra time for a beta test that includes both internal users and external audiences, it's worth your while.

Cross-Reference   You can find more information on the beta system in Chapter 21, "Rolling Out the System," in the section "The beta system."

Taking Stock of the Deliverables

For consistency and simplicity, I break the implementation deliverables into collection, management, and publishing system specifications. You can choose these three major divisions or break your deliverables into a larger set of specifications. Rather than give you a blow-by-blow account of creating implementation deliverables, I offer the following two broad angles of attack on your implementation deliverables:

✦ **You can use your logical design** to decide what the system must accomplish and to provide all the parameters and lists of particulars required to specify the system. Logical design is described from an analysis perspective in Part IV, "Designing a CMS."

✦ **You can use the selection criteria categories** to define the main areas of implementation that must occur. The selection criteria categories are described in Chapter 19, "Selecting Hardware and Software," in the section "Sorting through the CMS Selection Criteria."

Consider, for example, this sample overview and the accompanying table shown in Figure 20-4 from the content-deployment section of a publishing specification:

Our logical design calls for our publishing system to deploy content to our Web servers in North America, South America, and Europe. The same base content must be replicated at each site. In addition, locale-specific content must be deployed only to the sites for which it's marked. All components have a Locale element, with values of NA, SA, EU, or ALL. Components are also all tagged with Type and Audience elements. The [following] table ... shows the values for those elements and how they're used to calculate a destination directory for each component file that's deployed.

The table from the sample document shows the major functions of deployment, what software supplies those functions, and where in the document they're fully specified. Notice the following aspects of this sample:

✦ **It combines the logical design with the physical design.** The logical design is cited in the introduction and is elaborated in other parts of the document (section 2.4.3, in this example). The physical design criteria for deployment are listed in the table. Called *functions* here, they're simply rephrasings of the deployment system selection questions that I pose in Chapter 19, "Selecting Hardware and Software," in the section "Deployment."

✦ **It points to CMS functionality.** If the CMS is capable of performing a function entirely, it cites the function and states where that function is documented.

✦ **It points to custom functionality.** If the CMS functionality must be augmented by custom programming, it points that out and states where the CMS functionality is documented, as well as where the custom functionality is specified.

✦ **It points to other software.** You can assume that the OS Scheduler, for example, is neither part of the CMS nor a function that you code yourself.

Whether you use a method similar to this one or make one up of your own is less important than that you make full use of your logical and physical analyses and decide what functions are stock, custom, and third-party.

Of course, it's not enough simply to state what you must do. Somewhere, you must write down exactly how you plan to do it. You must provide enough detail that someone who's not studied the logical analysis or system selection can know just what to do to implement the system.

Deployment Functions

Function	Source	More Information
Deploying content files	CMS Distribute function accessed through the admin interface	CMS Admin Guide p. 96 and in section 3.4.5 below.
Deploying database records	CMS Distribute function augmented with custom connection object	CMS Admin Guide p. 112 and in section 3.4.6 below.
Deploying appropriate content to each locale	OS Scheduler set to run deployment script periodically for each locale. Passes appropriate Filter and Destination parameters to the CMS Distribute function	OS Reference Guide Vol. 1 p 352, CMS Admin Guide p. 115, and in section 3.4.8 below
Deploying to a staging server for testing	Destination parameter in the CMS Distribute function	CMS Admin Guide p. 101 and in section 3.4.4 below
Directory targeting by content type	Destination parameter in the CMS Distribute function. Use CMS event script to access component elements Type and Audience	CMS Admin Guide p. 101 and in section 3.4.3 below
Deploying files referenced in a component element	Custom script that scans files as they're deployed.	Section 3.4.7 below
Expiration dates	Passed as part of the Filter parameter of the CMS Distribute function	CMS Admin Guide p. 115 and in section 3.4.8 below
Scheduled automatic deployment	OS Scheduler set to fire periodically for each locale	OS Reference Guide Vol. 1 p 352 and in section 3.4.8 below

Figure 20-4: A sample from the deployment section of a content publishing specification

Collection specifications

You can create a collection specification that does the following:

✦ **Fully details your assumptions for component sources** (authoring or acquiring) and how each component loads into the CMS repository.

✦ **Details ownership and workflow steps** for each component to be created and how the jobs and workflows are created in the CMS.

✦ **Lists standard collection tools** and how they should be configured.

✦ **Fully specifies any custom tool** or process development that must be done.

✦ **Includes any content conversion specifications** that are required. (See Chapter 37, "Processing Content," in the section "Managing the Processing Project," for more information.)

✦ **Details the parameters of any integration** that you use to connect the collection system to the enterprise.

The collection specification can draw directly from your logical analyses. Your author and acquisition source analyses, of course, figure most prominently in a collection specification. Use the following list to begin to transform your logical design into collection specifications.

✦ **Author analysis:** Most of the information that you collect on authors goes into the specification of the authoring system and the tools that you provide each group. I favor creating sections for each author group that include information about the group and how you can set up the group's tools and processes. Among the major points that you want to cover is the configuration of input templates. Depending on how much metadata you think each author group can enter, you can show more or fewer elements on the input form. You also want to describe the primary tools of each group and how they're configured to interface most cleanly with the CMS. Finally, make sure that you include everything from the description of any custom authoring tools to their complete specification.

✦ **Acquisition analysis:** The information that you collect in an acquisition analysis contributes mightily to any content processing specs that you create. The source model data that you collect is the starting point for a conversion, and the component and element analyses show the target of the process. The quantities show the processing marks to hit. The only thing left to specify is how you can use your limited resources to do all the work that you've so aptly specified! The source analysis can either be brought into the collection specification or just referenced. It's probably best to recapitulate the source model analysis, for example, but only reference the source agreements.

✦ **Workflow analysis:** Your workflow modeling should be all the input that you need to decide what tasks, triggers, and steps to set up in your chosen CMS. Of course, if your chosen CMS can't do the sorts of tasks, triggers, and steps that you propose, you must specify how you intend to augment the CMS (or cut back on your workflow needs).

✦ **Component analysis:** Finally, your content model analysis ought to give you an additional set of constraints to put on the collection system. How is each component tagged to fit into the structures that you define? You have plenty of room here for innovation and labor-saving aids. You can provide lists and other controls on any input form, for example, to put a point-and-click interface on the selection of keywords, cross references, and with a little work, hierarchies. You also can write code that makes educated guesses about expected values for these controls.

Among the categories of selection criteria (described in Chapter 19, "Selecting Hardware and Software," in the section "Sorting through the CMS Selection Criteria") and collection criteria, of course, are the ones applicable to the collection system. You can use these criteria as a starting point to decide how each major collection function can be accomplished. As you may suspect, I favor organizing the collection specification overall under the collection headings of authoring, acquiring, converting, and aggregating (as I lay them out in Chapter 7, "Introducing the Major Parts of a CMS," in the section "The Collection System") But you may find a different organization better, given the way that your chosen CMS is organized and presents its user interface.

In addition to the collection criteria, pay attention to the following criteria categories as well:

✦ **Management administration:** Make sure that you include a specification of how you can use the CMS and other tools to configure and manage the collection system over time.

✦ **Workflow:** The criteria here ought to help you gauge the workflow possibilities of a system and choose the ones that are best for the workflows that you laid out in logical design.

✦ **Version control:** The criteria here guide you through what sort of version control is possible and what level you need for your authoring processes.

✦ **Reporting:** Decide what sorts of reporting your collection system requires and how to accomplish it.

✦ **Security:** If access to controlled areas of content is an issue, you want to devise a security policy for authors and other staff who can access the content in the CMS repository.

✦ **Personalization:** Personalization happens in the publishing system, but it's made possible by the tagging that's done in the collection system. For the personalization that you intend to do, specify how each of the tags that support it is determined and entered in the collection system.

Management specifications

A *management specification* can detail the way that the chosen system must be set up and configured. It can also include the complete content model, fully describe each workflow that you create, and include any integration specifications that you need to connect the management system to other systems.

On the logical analysis side, the core of the management specification is the content model. Somewhere in the CMS, you enter your content types, elements, and element values. In some products, you can do this completely within a user interface. In others, it's accomplished, in part, by using database management tools. In either case, you convert whatever general modeling you did in logical analysis to a specific set of actions in the CMS and its repository software. In addition, because the management system is (quite literally) central to the CMS, every other part of the logical design plays some part in your management specification, as the following points indicate:

✦ **Your audience analysis** yields audience profiles that must be entered somewhere in the system. Either in the repository or in a separate database, you might establish a user profile table, in which you can collect and track data on your audience members.

✦ **Your template analysis** yields a set of template files that must be managed. Either by using your CMS version control or other software, you must figure out who shares these templates and how you can facilitate the sharing.

✦ **Authors and other staff members** must be created as user groups in the CMS system. You already know what each group does. Knowing the capabilities of your chosen CMS and the extensions that you plan to create, you can specify exactly how groups are to be set up and what access each can have.

✦ **Acquisition sources** often have a batch interface to the CMS repository. Maybe you configure your CMS to scan for new material on a partner Web site once a day, for example, and load it as a batch into components of a particular variety. You're likely to have a lot of configuration and custom programming behind these types of sources.

✦ **Management workflows** must be configured and added to the CMS workflow system.

✦ **Content access structures** must be implemented in the CMS repository. The structures you want may be easy to set up through the CMS user interface, or you may have a lot of custom coding to do to get your structures (especially multiple hierarchies) to work and integrate with the rest of the CMS.

It should come as no surprise that the management selection criteria (as described in Chapter 19, "Selecting Hardware and Software," in the section "Sorting through the CMS Selection Criteria") have the most influence on the management specifications. And again, because of the centrality of the management system, all other categories of criteria play some role in the management specs. A few, however, deserve special mention, as follows:

✦ **The collection criteria**, as a whole, impose requirements on the metadata creation and administration facilities of the management system. Make sure that you specify which functions of the CMS can and can't be used to create and update the metadata that your collection system tells you to store in the CMS repository.

✦ **The deployment criteria** are as accurately cast as management constraints as they are as publication constraints. After all, it's the management system that contains the functionality for deployment.

✦ **The Web architecture criteria** are management constraints to the extent that the CMS runs on a Web server. Many systems are located on the same server that's used for serving the Web publications. In fact, you can rightly say that the CMS interface is just another Web publication produced by the CMS!

Publication specifications

Publication specifications state exactly how each page or section of each publication is constructed. They augment the concepts and drawings done during logical design with detailed specifications of the graphic, style, and layout elements to use. In addition, a publication specification spells out the logic and coding behind the templating model for each publication. The publication specification details the queries, content manipulation, and personalization processing needed to structure and format each publication. Finally, the specification details any integration that must be done to connect to other systems.

In general, I recommend a separate specification for each publication. This specification gathers all the information for that publication in one place. Sections that are common to more than one publication (a style guide that applies to a whole range of publications, for example) can be broken into a separate global publishing resources specification.

Your publication logical design has three parts (publication, template, and personalization analysis) that contribute in related ways to the publication specifications, as follows:

✦ **Publication design:** Very little of the publication analysis (audience, author, purpose, and the rest) shows up directly as system customization or configuration. It mostly results in publication guidelines and specifications. Indirectly, however, the analysis is reflected in the audience, author, and personalization specifications and in the customizations and configurations to which they lead.

✦ **Templating design:** How much of the templating process happens as configuration rather than as programming varies from product to product. Usually, not much of the templating process is done through a user interface. One exception exists for products that have a visual template designer that enables you to drag content components and navigation elements onto a screen. Regardless of how the templating is accomplished in the chosen system, the templating analysis gives you everything you need to determine what templates are needed and how they should be constructed.

The only thing that the templating analysis is missing is the technical detail explaining how the logic is implemented. Given that you now know the templating language that you're going to use, you can state the number and kinds of routines and other programming code that implement the template logic you describe in the logical design.

Tip Make sure that the specification contains a solid plan for code sharing between templates. The worst thing that you can do is use the same code in a variety of templates that change independently of one another. Instead, try to modularize template code, move it out of specific templates, and then call it back from some central location. You can even include template code as a kind of component that's automatically added to a template as it's published.

✦ **Personalization design:** Personalization systems in commercial CMS products range from no system at all to very extensive ones. Assuming that you augment any deficits in your product with third-party personalization systems, you have a lot of configuration to do. You must somehow provide the audience profile information to the personalization system. The system probably automatically accesses the component configuration that you create. Additionally, you may configure it to look at other data sources. Finally, and most important, somewhere you must enter your personalization rules. If you're lucky, a slick point-and-click interface makes rule building easy. More likely, however, you must enter rules in text or XML configuration files, and you must augment the system that you use with custom code to get the personalization results that you want.

Many of the other parts of logical design also inform the publication specs, as the following points indicate:

✦ **Audience analysis** is, of course, a part of the personalization process.

✦ **Component analysis** enables you to plan how each component can find its way onto the correct publication page in the appropriate format. For each component/publication combination, you can state on which pages the component appears. For each page where the component appears, you can specify which elements are used for accessing the component (and what values they must have), the elements that are displayed, and the number of other components of that type that also may appear on the page.

✦ **Author analysis** provides the right data for deciding how to attribute and reference authors in your publications.

✦ **Publication workflows** must be incorporated into the CMS workflow module or implemented by using third-party tools and customizations.

✦ **The content access structures** you've devised must be transformed. Your publication specs should describe how the general access structures in the repository can be turned into the very specific content-access structures that you have in your publications.

As before, the selection criteria that you used to decide upon a CMS product can also be used to guide your publication specifications. Pay particular attention to the criteria in the following categories:

✦ **Management administration:** To whatever extent the management administrative interface can help you set up and lay out publications (usually not a lot), you should include a discussion of it in your publication specs. If it can't help you very much, make sure that you describe what else you must do to configure your publications.

✦ **Management integrations:** Some of these integrations happen in a Web publication as well as in the management system itself. You may, for example, connect to a live product catalog in your Web publication. Make sure that you state how these integrations occur.

✦ **Version control:** Do you version and keep track of finished publications? If so, include the versioning system of the CMS or alternative tools in your publication specs.

✦ **Security:** The CMS security system may or may not extend out to the Web publications that you create. If it does, how does it do so? If it doesn't, and you need security on the Web publication, what else can you do?

✦ **Performance:** To the extent that the CMS serves dynamic pages for you on a Web site, you must include information about its performance metrics in your publication specifications.

The project plan

After you've created the specifications for the CMS, you're finally in a position to create a definitive project plan. Your hope is that the changes that the specs introduce to the plan are in the details, not in the major headings. You may, for example, have a line that reads, "Template coding . . . 3 weeks." After creating a publication specification, the single line may turn into 100 lines for the tasks associated with each template and the templating system as a whole. As you expand the project plans, make sure that you work with the entire team. This gives you the best set of tasks and task estimates and also helps you get the full team's commitment to work according to the plan. I've seen mixed results if the team itself is responsible for creating the plan detail. Sometimes you get unreasonably long estimates from people who don't know and so guess very high, and sometimes you get unreasonably low estimates from people who have optimistic attitudes. The best method that I've seen is to have a scheduler work together with the staff. That way, staff estimates can be leveled out by the scheduler, and the scheduler can negotiate the support of the staff for the plan.

 Note I've often seen scaling factors applied to the time estimates made by staff. If a person characteristically underestimates by half the amount of time it takes to accomplish a task, for example, you can simply multiply all her estimates by 2. The multiplication is easy; knowing the factor by which to multiply is difficult. It requires that you really know and understand the personalities on your team. Of course, by the end of implementation, you should have your scaling factors very well estimated.

The remainder of implementation is a time for doing, not thinking up project plans. It's also the time when some projects abandon their project plans because they're too difficult to maintain in the face of a rapidly evolving project. Abandoned project plans are a sign of the following:

✦ **A changing mandate:** If outside forces continue to change the agenda for the project during implementation, no amount of project planning can save you. If you have the sort of mandate that I've suggested, this ought not to be a problem. If you don't have such a mandate, or if you still get pressure to change plans while in implementation, your project plan can be your best ally. The plan is where the effect of any change can be quantified and debated. If you have a strong project plan, use it to assess and communicate the results of the changes that are being suggested. Become accustomed to trading scope changes for schedule and budget changes.

✦ **Poor planning:** Abandoned project plans are often the ones that weren't very good to begin with. If you didn't quite figure out the project before beginning, the project begins to take its own direction as you get into implementation. Its direction may be quite different from the one sketched out in the project plan. If, on the other hand, the project was completely thought out, it may change, but each change is an increment from the existing plan. And each increment can be tracked and merged into the plan to keep it relevant and definitive.

✦ **Poor training or no time:** Project plans are a lot of work to maintain. Every task and person is interrelated in the plan in a giant web. If you change one part, it's likely to have a wide effect throughout the rest of the plan. If the person who's in charge of the plan isn't really comfortable with the project management tool that you're using, or if she doesn't have enough time to keep up with the changes, the plan is bound to get out of sync in the heat of the project. If the same person's been in charge of the plan from the start, she should have had ample time to really learn it by now. If time is the issue, you need to shift responsibilities to make sure that you have room to continually mend the net that holds the project together.

If you put effort into a well-maintained project plan, here are some ideas for how to make it pay you back:

✦ **Inertia:** The project plan is a big, bulky, complicated mass that's difficult to change. It's just the sort of thing that you need to keep a big project on course. Given the amount of time and energy that you've put into the planning of the system and the fact that you're no longer planning, it should be very difficult to make changes to the plan. The project plan is like the massive keel of a sailboat. It's below the waterline, keeping the boat on a straight course and making sure that it doesn't tip over.

✦ **Effects:** Use the project plan to gauge the effect of a change on the implementation. If a change is suggested, work it out in the plan first and prepare an assessment of what it took to fit it in. If it takes you all day just to adjust a copy of the plan to accommodate the change, you know that this change may be major. The difference between the original plan and the changed plan tells you exactly what the change means.

✦ **Scale-backs:** Given that even the most liberal estimates of time often aren't enough, the project plan gives you a way to manage the continual growth of the project before it explodes. A 10 percent schedule overrun in the first week may compound to a 15 percent overrun in the second week, 20 percent in the third week, and so on. As you see overruns occur in your plan, run them forward, trying to judge how they may compound. Make the first cut in the tasks that have the most ripples throughout the rest of the project.

A project plan is a model of how the project ought to behave. If you put enough time and intelligence into planning, it's a reasonable model. But it's not an accurate model. After a lot of people start working, too many contingencies arise for you ever to account for them all ahead of time. Instead, you must be willing to continually test and revise your model using what really happens. If you accept this responsibility, your plan can be your biggest aid. Your plan is a place to record the effect of what you didn't account for in the past and to predict its effect on the future of the project. Only the parts of your plan that are in the past are 100 percent accurate. The parts that are to come, however, ought to be more and more accurate as you continually revise them with the lessons that you're learning.

In addition to being your project model, a plan is also a project contract. You can use it to form agreements with the staff about what happens and how long it takes. Your plan is a grand negotiation of all the factors that make and break the project. The biggest part of that negotiation is with the staff of the project. And it truly must be a negotiation for it to work. If you hand out schedules at the beginning of each week and say, "This is what you must do for me by Friday," on Friday, you get back all the reasons why you were wrong in your estimates. If, instead, you say, "Here's the plan; tell me how to make it work," you get active participation and a deeper commitment to make it work. On Friday, you still may get excuses, but at least they're phrased in terms of tangible changes to the plan rather than in terms of all the reasons that you, not they, are responsible.

The key to staying in the general vicinity of your plan is the commitment and a shared sense of responsibility that everyone on the project feels for the plan.

The risk assessment plan

Implementation is the time when most of the risks that you've predicted either come true or go away. You can use your risk assessment to plan contingencies in advance of beginning the risky activity. If you predicted that the CMS may not be capable of communicating with your catalog system, for example, be prepared for it not to work. Assess your options and start the planning enough in advance to be able to change directions quickly. In advance, get pricing and training costs on different catalog systems, for example, and estimates from custom development groups. Then, if the communication risk comes true, you can change directions quickly.

Of course, just because you're in implementation doesn't mean that no new risks occur. Quite the contrary. Every day you hear of new risks from your staff. You hear that you may need twice the number of templates or that an integration may take twice the time that you'd anticipated.

Your risk assessment and project plan can help you defuse the tension and panic that often surrounds the gloomy feelings of a staff person who's had a bad day. To mitigate the risk, and the feelings that surround the risk, you can do the following:

✦ **State it:** Have the staff member clearly articulate the risk. What exactly are you afraid may happen?

✦ **Find the contingencies:** Have the staff member state clearly the conditions under which the risk may become a problem. Have her be as precise as possible and lead her through a thorough examination of the situation.

✦ **Find the probability:** Looking at all the contingencies, how likely is it that the risk may become a problem?

✦ **Find the effect:** If it does become a problem, how big a problem is it for the project?

✦ **Find the mitigations:** With the project plan in front of you, work through a variety of scenarios with the staff member. Go wide at first, to get at all the possible ways to handle the risk, and then work through the most promising ones in the plan.

My experience is that, with the vast majority of risks, you never need to go through this complete process. Each step filters out problems that are less project risk and more staff anxiety. The first step, especially, is the best way to sort anxiety from fact. Simply stating the problem as clearly as possible is often all that's necessary for the staff person herself to solve it immediately.

Taking Stock of Your Staffing Needs

The whole range of CMS job types could be involved in a CMS implementation. Rather than going through the process person-by-person (a subject that is well covered in Chapter 13, "Staffing a CMS"), I focus here on the leadership and communication structure only.

The main concerns that I have about CMS implementation are keeping the process focused, keeping the scope steady or shrinking (not growing), and ensuring that all the dependencies between processes and teams are resolved to the timely completion of the implementation project as a whole.

With this in mind, I'd design the staffing as follows:

✦ **A single overall leader** taken from the ranks of the leading analyst or content manager. This person is in place for final escalation of project issues and to keep the various teams cooperating nicely.

✦ **An overall project manager** to manage the scope, schedule, and budget of the overall project. Because so many contingencies and dependencies are possible between CMS teams and between the CMS effort and other groups in the organization, this is a very important job.

✦ **Individual project managers** for each part of the implementation that you designate as a separate project. These managers control the scope, schedule, and budget of a part of the project *in the context of the entire project*. Their goal is to make sure that their project is at the milestone where it needs to be to interact with other projects and that, at all other times, the project needs no attention other than that provided by their own project team.

✦ **Technical leads** to make the projects happen. They should be free to create an informal communication network for discussing project issues and for looking actively for appropriate responses. If this group functions as well as it can, it detects problems long before they cause slowdowns or bottlenecks. The trick is to give enough rope to the technical leads (who may be involved in any kind of implementation) so that they can freely communicate and explore, but not enough that they can constitute a separate management or decision-making structure.

Summary

Most people think of the implementation of a software system as the part with the most action. As I've laid it out, a CMS implementation ought to be as uneventful as possible. All the major technical and organizational hot points should be worked out (or, at least, anticipated and planned for) before the first line of code or setup program runs. During implementation, you do the following:

✦ Decide how to segment your project into multiple parallel projects that can interact within a larger project framework.

✦ Create a set of specifications that guide the actions of implementation staff.

✦ Install, configure, and code the CMS.

✦ Test the CMS, its publications, and its integrations.

✦ Decide how far to scale back, given the contingencies that arise.

✦ Deal with new risks and changes to the project plan as they arise.

In the next chapter, I discuss the final stage of a CMS project: rolling it out to the organization.

✦　　✦　　✦

Rolling Out the System

◆ ◆ ◆ ◆

In This Chapter

A definition and over-view of deployment

Techniques for deploy-ment, including how to power up your system

Deployment deliver-ables, including docu-mentation, training, and maintenance plans

◆ ◆ ◆ ◆

A CMS can become a very large development project. The work that you do to plan and organize the system is the only thing keeping the CMS from becoming an even larger administration and maintenance project. To keep the deployment process on track, you can create a set of guides and plans that state exactly what's to occur and when.

In this chapter, I provide an overview of those guides and plans to give you a feeling for the kinds of issues that you're likely to confront in rolling out your CMS and how you might handle them.

As in the case of implementation, I can't (and really shouldn't) give you much specific advice about deployment without knowing your particular situation, so I intend to stick to those points that apply regardless of the particular CMS that you're using.

Rolling Out the System Jumpstart

This Jumpstart summarizes what you need to do to get ready to roll out your CMS to your organization.

Use this jumpstart as a summary without the weight of detail, or as a quick review if you've already read the chapter and want a checklist of what you need to implement your CM system.

To roll out the CM system, follow these steps:

1. Create documentation for your CMS. You may need to figure out processes for gathering and creating the documentation, which should include: an overview; a set of the company's doc-umentation for the CMS; and authoring, acquisition, metatorial, editorial, administrator, and template guides.

2. Decide who needs training. Depending on your situation, your staff may need relatively little training (for example, if the same people who build the system stay on to run it) or they may need more. All may benefit from general content management training; specific jobs may require training, including authors, processors, administrators, page developers, template devel-opers, localizers, and deployment people.

3. Decide how the training will be organized. Your choices include: documentation; self-paced learning guides; product-company training; apprenticeships; boot camps; and long-term training.

4. Power up the system in stages.

   - Bring up the basic CMS product in a standalone environment.

   - Run the basic CMS in your production environment.

   - Add content and publications to both the standalone and production environments.

   - Add third-party software and integrations to the production environment.

   - Release a beta version of the final system.

   - Release the final system.

5. Make adjustments to your content strategy, if necessary, to accommodate the CMS as it now exists.

   - Revise your content processing plan and assumptions about processing rates.

   - Adjust the processing team to match the new environment after you clear the initial backlog of content.

6. Make adjustments to the system. Decide either to make incremental changes to the system on an ongoing basis (a *rolling release*) or to defer changes to a more formal version 2 of the system.

7. Create a system maintenance plan, which should include information about backups, content retirement, revisions, technical support, routine maintenance, bug fixes, and performance logging.

What Is Deployment?

System deployment is making the CMS that you develop run well in the context of your organization, your existing infrastructure, and any new CMS infrastructure that you create. After you roll out the system, you finalize the CMS integration with enterprise systems and begin to integrate the system with the people in your organization.

At the risk of taking this analogy of programming too far, you can think of your staff as having an existing set of methods (skills) and functions (job duties). To make the CMS run, you must tie into these methods and functions as well as possible and extend them as necessary. People aren't enterprise systems, however, so if you want to make the integration a success, you must account not only for the intellectual effect the new system has, but for its emotional effect as well.

Integrating the CMS with the organization involves the following activities:

✦ **Fully planning** the deployment before performing it.

✦ **Creating documentation** for the system.

✦ **Initial and continuing training** of CMS staff and contributors.

✦ **Powering up the system and testing it** in a realistic setting before turning off the existing collection and publication systems.

✦ **Ongoing content preparation** to move new content into the system.

✦ **Bug fixes** for the software that you create and updates to software that you purchase (or build).

✦ **Revising the CMS configuration** to meet new or changed needs.

✦ **Revising the publishing templates** to meet new or changed needs.

✦ **Adding new content types and elements** to meet new or changed needs.

✦ **Adding new author types or new acquisition sources** and the work on the content types and elements that these types and sources require.

Techniques to Get the Job Done

In addition to the myriad techniques that you devise for your particular CMS, I offer a few that can help you, regardless of the system that you use.

Creating documentation

Most people's least favorite task, creating documentation, is also one of the most important things that you can do to ensure that your organization uses your system correctly and that it's as easy to support as possible. If you've followed the project process that I've proposed in this book at all, you have more than enough source material to create exactly the right type of documentation to keep your system running smoothly.

To my mind, the primary purpose of the documentation is to specify precisely the contract between you and the people who interact with the CMS. The "how-to" aspect of documentation is important, but people get that information from a variety of sources and can figure it out if necessary. As a contract, your documentation must outline the assumptions on which you build the system and the specific rules that people should follow to keep content flowing from creation to publication to eventual retirement. In return, the documentation must clearly spell out the benefits that accrue to the individual and the organization if they do things in the way that you prescribe. Just because it's a contract doesn't mean that the documentation is dry or overly formal. The essence is that it codifies an agreement between the system and its users.

The key items that I see as part of the CMS documentation set are the following:

✦ A CMS overview for all staff to read

✦ A full set of the product company's documentation for the CMS that you buy (or the equivalent, if you build one yourself)

✦ A set of authoring guides

✦ A set of acquisition guides

✦ A metatorial guide

✦ An editorial guide

✦ An administrator guide

✦ A template guide

You may also want other written information available, including all the documents that you produce during the project; organizational and departmental policy regarding content creation and publication; content management background information (perhaps even this book); Web links; and any sort of glossary that you may produce.

Tip Producing a miniature CMS implementation to keep track of and publish all your documentation is a great training exercise for your staff.

Move all the information that you want to continue on after the release of the CMS from the project documents that you create to the documentation set. The CMS project team should probably own the task of putting the documentation together, but it should quickly transition the review and maintenance of the documents to those who are to continue to maintain the CMS.

The CMS documentation set requires updating over the life of the first version of the system. For this reason, make sure that people can suggest revisions as easily as possible. If you can manage to include messaging functionality (for example, e-mail links) right in the electronic form of your CMS documentation, it really helps you capture and process comments.

The CMS documentation serves as a starting point for work on the next version of the system. In this process, new information moves back from the documentation to the CMS specifications, where you augment it with new functionality. Again, you can facilitate this process immensely by adding messaging functionality to the electronic version of the documentation. If, in addition to revision suggestions, people can submit extension or new functionality comments right into the documentation at the appropriate place, you get a great leg-up on the next version. In any case, using a numbered section style so that people can accurately refer to the section that they believe needs changing may prove well worth your while.

The CMS overview

It's a very good idea to produce a short overview of the system that each staff member can read to understand what you've created and what that person's part is in it is. The point of the document is to provide a single official perspective on what the CMS is and does.

Tip In addition, you can use the document to help "brainwash" new recruits into the CMS way of thinking. I'm only half kidding: The CMS mindset is different enough for some to require a bit of education and, possibly, convincing to instill the idea in people who are new to it that it's a good thing to do.

Consider including the following information in your overview:

✦ **The final project statement:** That statement comes from the mandate process. (See Chapter 16, "Securing a Project Mandate," for more information.) This statement establishes the same context for everyone who joins the project as well as for those you've carried forward from the start.

✦ **The final requirements:** These are the requirements that are ratified prior to logical design, along with any changes that you've made over the course of the project. (See Chapter 17, "Doing Requirements Gathering," and Chapter 18, "Doing Logical Design," for more information.) You set up the CMS staff to succeed, but they alone ultimately fulfill or fail to meet these requirements.

✦ **A high-level diagram of the CMS:** Produce a diagram with enough detail that any staff member can see his or her place in the team. Stop before the diagram no longer fits on a page or when no one can understand it after 5 or 10 minutes of trying. This diagram is what you want each staff member to visualize whenever she thinks of the CMS.

✦ **A high-level chart of team structure and responsibilities:** This chart answers the question, "Who is everybody and what does everyone do?" To make the chart a bit more durable, you may avoid people's names and instead list job titles. On the other hand, including and maintaining names is a good reason for people to return to this document over and over again.

✦ **An overview of components:** Add just enough detail that the staff can answer the question, "What kind of content are we managing?"

✦ **An overview of the publications:** Make sure that you make the case of why, without the CMS, this set of publications isn't possible to produce as well or as efficiently. (If this statement isn't true, you've done a lot of work for nothing.)

This document serves not only to orient staff members, but also as the general overview that you send out whenever anyone asks what you're doing.

Product documentation

You'd think that a CMS company would offer automatically produced, totally personalizable, and perfectly componentized documentation that you can publish in any form. In fact, you may think that it would just load all the documentation into the repository that it ships so that you can publish it as you see fit. Unfortunately, most don't. Instead, most of the product documentation that I see is sparse, incomplete, unchunked, and in one format only. (For some reason, CMS product companies, by and large, follow a software-development model of documentation rather than a content management model of value creation and distribution.)

Therefore, it's up to you to gather product documentation and disseminate it as best you can. At the very least, you need it all in one place and you need to task someone with keeping track of it and making sure that the latest versions are available.

Product documentation is necessarily generic. You're likely to find the parts that apply to your system packed away deep inside a lot of irrelevant information. If possible, you can produce an index to the product documentation, listing the sections that apply to your system and describing how they apply. This approach may not prove as much work as you think if you've already produced a specification such as the one that I suggest in Chapter 20, "Implementing the System." In any case, cross-referencing product documentation in the documents that you produce is worthwhile.

Authoring guides

Each type of author that you define should receive a short, task-oriented guide to the sort of authoring that he's to do. The point of the guide is to educate authors of a particular type on the assumptions that you make about them, the rules they're to follow, and what results you expect.

Tip You may find that, as you write the guides, your assumptions about your authors sharpen and the groups that you create for them change. Don't fight it. Reorganize your approach now or fight against reality for the life of the system.

The guide should draw heavily from your logical and physical design and include the following items:

✦ **The author profile:** This profile comes from your logical design (as I discuss in Chapter 28, "Accounting for Authors"), which defines the assumptions about system savvy, closeness to the CMS group, and any other information from that analysis to help authors of this type understand how they fit within the context of CMS. Include information as specific as possible about the production rates and target audiences for these authors.

✦ **Attribution guidelines:** These guidelines describe how you intend to cite authors in the finished publications.

✦ **A tools guide:** This guide describes the tools that you expect the authors to use and how to them set up. Ideally, the guide would be linked directly to a setup and configuration program for the tools. Such a guide not only makes distributing tools more convenient, but it also makes the documentation a must-have for authors who are just starting out.

✦ **Workflow descriptions:** You need such descriptions for any workflows in which these authors are to participate. Make sure that you fully describe the conditions that authors must meet for their work to move to the next stage and what they can expect to happen before they see their work come back to them again.

✦ **Editorial and metatorial guidelines:** If you can manage the personalization issues, you can directly include the parts of the editorial and metatorial guides that apply to this author group. If you can't, provide the authors, at least, with links or an index to the parts of those documents that apply to them.

✦ **A guide to the use of their work:** Describe and illustrate what happens to authors' work after they finish it. Include the stages of additional processing and tagging; later reviews, where you display their work in each publication (the pages, other content that appears with it, and the surrounding navigational and branding elements); and how you finally retire it. Emphasize that you may add new processes and publications. Your goal with this information is to provide enough context that the authors feel oriented to the later use of their work, but not so much that the authors expect the context always to remain the same.

Acquisition guides

Acquisition guides provide instructions for processing and tagging information from each major acquisition source. The audience for the guide is all members (and managers) of a processing team who turn to it to learn or review the requirements of the source transformation, as well as their tasks related to the acquisition.

All the information for these guides can come from your logical analysis and processing specifications. These guides can include the following items:

✦ **The source agreement**, which specifies how much of the source to expect, what form to expect, how to expect delivery, and whom to contact if any problems arise with the source.

✦ **Workflows** that include this source.

✦ **Processing instructions** that state the exact transformations that must occur and step-by-step instructions for performing them.

✦ **Processing tools**, which can be referenced or linked to in the documentation. You can also provide links to the setup programs of individual tools.

✦ **Metatorial requirements** that include, link to, or reference (in order of my preference) the parts of the metatorial guide that apply to this source.

✦ **Editorial requirements** that include, link to, or reference the parts of the editorial guide that apply to this source.

✦ **Samples of the input and output** of the transformation that serve as the official standards to which to compare all other input and output.

✦ **Processing team structure**, including job descriptions, reporting structure, and escalation procedures.

✦ **Expected quality and throughput metrics**, which, if you make this document *the* place for your assumptions about quality and quantity, ensures its centrality to the processing team.

After you write (or maybe even just conceive of) these guides, turn them over to an owner on the processing team for updates and redistribution as necessary.

The metatorial guide

A *metatorial guide* details the ongoing content creation and retirement process. It answers questions such as the following:

✦ What type is each element (free text, pattern text, open list, closed list, and so on)?

✦ For each element, what are the allowable values (or maximum character lengths for text fields)?

✦ What are the rules for changing the allowable values of each element?

✦ Which elements are authors responsible to fill in? Which do other staffers fill in? Which are filled in automatically?

✦ What are the review and quality-control processes for the metadata elements of each content type?

✦ How many of each content type do you expect to add each week?

✦ Can some content types have an indefinite number of components, and which ones may reach a maximum limit?

✦ What tells you that a component is ready for expiration, archiving, or deletion?

 Cross-Reference You can find more information about the metatorial guide in Chapter 24, "Working with Metadata," in the section "The metatorial guide."

If you've completed your design, you already have answers to most of these questions and can simply organize and publish them in an easy-to-use format, such as a Web page or printed guide.

The audience for the metatorial guide is the metator or metators of your CMS. You distribute appropriate pieces of the guide, however, to anyone who touches metadata. Therefore, you need to write it in a generally understandable manner. I suggest organizing the guide as a reference, listing all elements alphabetically. Include indexes that organize elements by content type and component type.

The fundamental question that each section on an element must answer is, "How do I fill in this element?" Your metator or metatorial team leader should create and maintain the guide.

Tip   Don't forget to account for localization in your metatorial guide. Ask not only how to fill in each element, but also how to fill in each element for each localized version you intend to produce.

The editorial guide

An *editorial guide* is substantially the same in a CMS context as it is in any publication's production environment with some exceptions. Following are some of the differences that may warrant changes to the way that you may, otherwise, produce an editorial guide:

✦ **Organize it the same as you do the metatorial guide.** Consider organizing your editorial guide by element, component, and content type. You can then organize your comments into three layers:

• Any style or usage comments that are global to an element can go in the section on the element.

• Any comments that apply to the usage of an element in the context of a particular component can go in the component.

• Any comments that apply to the entire system can go into overview sections that you create.

If this organizational scheme seems too complex for you (and you can't find a database programmer to help), I think you're still best off if you organize by element. That way, people creating content can most easily locate the specific guidelines for that element within the particular components with which they're working.

✦ **Account for variation in the usage or style per publication and audience.** Creating a single style that works for all audiences and publications is obviously easiest, but doing so isn't always possible or advisable given that different audiences and publications have very different needs. In these cases, listing style variations in families of related elements and explaining them separately may prove your best option. Suppose, for example, that you decide to create a novice summary and an expert summary of a white paper. You can create two overview elements that you fill in separately, basing them on two sets of style guidelines. The system can select which overview to use for which audience and publication, and the author knows exactly how to write each of the two summaries.

✦ **Distribute it on the spot.** If at all possible, make your editorial (and metatorial) guide information available in the application that authors use to create content. If you use Web-based forms, for example, include a link next to each control on the form to access the metatorial and editorial guidelines behind that control. (As you probably know, each control is the interface to a single element.) You can see why organizing by element is helpful.

✦ **Account for any localization.** If you plan to localize, include specific guidelines in your editorial guide. Quite possibly, your localization group knows better how your guidelines need modification for other languages and regions, so make sure that you consult with it. In any case, include localization style and usage guidelines per element and region.

The administrator guide

The CMS administrator and her assignees need comprehensive documentation on how you put together and configured the system. In a way, an *administrator guide* is the sum total of all the system configuration and setup that you do. Thus, even if you do no more than gather this information from the specs and other sources that you may have and then put it all in one place for the administrator to access, you're doing enough. Don't expect authors and processing teams to plow through raw information to learn what they need. You can, on the other hand, expect that a CMS administrator is familiar enough with the source documents and the system itself to find the needle that she needs in the haystack of files. As you gather the administrator's stack, don't forget to include the following:

✦ Any system diagrams created to show the relationships between parts of the CMS.

✦ The documentation from all third-party software that you include.

✦ All support agreements that you sign.

✦ The full documentation set that you prepare for other staff. (The administrator, by the way, is a good point of distribution for this stuff.)

You should also include in the administrator guide the list of responsibilities, the reporting procedure, and the escalation path for the administrator to follow. You can draw most of this material from the staffing plan that you create.

The template guide

The *template guide* is the living form of the template specification that you create for implementation. Undoubtedly, since you did the template implementation, things changed and didn't find their way back into the specification, so you may need to do some rewriting. The audience for the template guide consists of the following people:

✦ **The publication staff member** who wants to know how something was done (usually to know how difficult it is to change it). These people try to match a visual element in the final publication to some sort of definition in the guide.

✦ **The programmer** who wants to learn the templating system before trying to fix it or change it.

For the publication staff, make sure that you can find your way around the guide by publication, page, and design element. For the programmer, make sure that you feature the code-sharing and version-control system prominently in the documentation so that she doesn't think to subvert it.

For more experienced staffers, the templates speak for themselves, so don't put too much effort into a template guide for them. You can expect the users of this guide to be fairly expert and not need much hand-holding. Still, you want to publish and enforce the programming and design standards by which you expect publication staff and programmers to live.

Doing training

The kind and amount of training that you may need to prepare depends quite a bit on the particulars of your situation. If the team that creates the CMS stays on to run it, for example, your staff needs little training. If you create a strong user interface for authors, you need little author training. For the purposes of discussion, however, I assume that you need to train everyone to some extent. If you do, the following list describes the sorts of training that you may provide during the deployment of your system:

✦ **Content management training:** You may want to create a general training course on what content management is, how your system fits together, and what each person is responsible for. This training follows the CMS overview document and serves to reinforce its main points.

✦ **Author training:** Especially for novice authors, you may want to offer a short training session on how to use the Web-based forms, workflow interface, and other tools they have. While you have the ear of the author, delivering editorial and metatorial training is a good idea as well.

✦ **Processor training:** Content-processing teams tend to be task-orientated, low in skills, and high in turnover. For processes that require more than a few minutes of training, you're well served by creating some form of training course. These training methods, of course, focus on the particular tasks that a certain kind of processor does and on the tools that he uses.

✦ **Administrator training:** If you have only one administrator, you hardly need to develop training. If you have multiple sites where content originates or is deployed, however, you have parts of the CMS in locations that are possibly quite far apart. If so, you may want to make sure that each site has some sort of administrator and that each administrator has the same sort of training.

✦ **Page developer training:** If you have turnover in the page-developer group, you may want to standardize the training that new workers receive. This training follows the template guide and focuses on the overall structure of the template system, the names and positions of all the design elements, and the HTML and other page code behind the templates. (See Chapter 13, "Staffing a CMS," in the section "Page developer," for more information on the job of page developer.)

✦ **Template developer training:** Like page developers, template developers may come and go. If they do, training is a good idea. This training overlaps with the page-developer training at the level of the page code (HTML or other) and goes on to teach the programming methods that the system uses, the code-sharing system, and the version-control techniques that you're employing. (See Chapter 13, "Staffing a CMS," in the section "Template and CMS developer," for more information on the job of template developer.)

✦ **Localization training:** Translators and other localizers of content need to know enough about the CMS to interact with it. You best hope is that you can extend the CMS to your localizers so that they can work directly with content. If so, their training resembles the author training in the use of CMS Web-based forms, workflow interface, and other input tools. Even if you must export content to the localization group, you still want to train them on how not to mess up the exported text so that you can import it again. Localizing your CMS documentation may even prove worthwhile, although perhaps you can localize just the most basic training material. In most countries, technical people expect to read documentation in English. (You find more information about localization in Chapter 25, "Cataloging Audiences," in the section "Localization.")

✦ **Deployment training:** If you must deploy your system over time in a variety of locations, you may want to create a training regime for the people who must install and support the system in other locations. This training follows the deployment specification and provides information on system installation, configuration, and integration.

Just because you're training people, you don't need to make it seem like school. The only essential thing about training is that it results in usable knowledge. Assuming that, late in the project, time and money are at a low point, you can scale back your training to the least-effort activity that still gets the result that you want. Following are the kinds of training that I usually see:

✦ **Read the documentation:** If you do a good job on your documentation, it often suffices for people who already have experience in content management tasks or whose job doesn't require anything more in-depth. A template programmer who's already done a number of template systems using your chosen CMS, for example, usually needs no more than your documentation to get going.

✦ **Self service:** If you do a good job on your electronic documentation (chunking it into components and making them accessible independently of what surrounds them), creating tutorials or other self-paced learning guides is usually pretty easy. Of course, the more effort that you put into this type of training, the better a learning tool it is; but the minimum is simply to arrange the most important parts of the documentation in a sequence, with comments and supplementary material in between. This approach may prove an appropriate way to train new content processors or authors whom you can move through the process that you expect them to do one step at a time and at their own speeds.

✦ **Product-company training:** Most CMS product companies employ some sort of product training. For the most part, this training is more suitable for your project team before it starts an implementation than it is for your ongoing staff. Still, product-company training provides a convenient alternative to creating or delivering training yourself. Usually, you can get one- to three-day sessions on authoring, configuration, and basic programming techniques. Of course, this training is generic and doesn't target your particular system, so you still may want to augment it (or pay the company to augment it) to deal with your customizations and particular configuration.

✦ **Apprenticeship:** You may get good results from attaching a new person to someone who's already doing a job. If you pursue this path, make sure that you brief both the existing staff member and the trainee on your learning goals and hold them to these goals. That way, everyone takes the apprenticeship seriously and makes it result in a well-trained person. Apprenticeships are particularly useful if a lot of informal information is necessary to do a job. CMS administrators and production managers, for example, possess a lot of process knowledge and useful tips in their heads that are not on paper. For these positions, an apprentice can learn a lot. If you're smart, you instruct the apprentice to document any information that she gets orally so that as little as possible remains informal.

✦ **Boot camp:** The boot camp idea involves creating a fast, intense experience where the student works exceedingly hard and comes out with workable knowledge right away. Boot camps are mostly an immersion and not a learning experience. In other words, they produce an attitude more than a set of skills. A person can retain only so much from the masses of information that you present in the one or two days of boot camp. You can, however, present a person all the material that she needs to go back and really learn later on. And, more important, the experience can give the person a mindset that she can take on and use over the course of her job. (Picture the army recruit that a drill instructor strips down and rebuilds in boot camp.) Because CMS jobs often require an attitude as much as they require particular skills, a boot-camp approach can prove useful. You may want to consider creating a boot camp for all full-time staff prior to final launch. You can cover the CMS overview material in more depth than you can in the overview document, introduce all the other key documents to which you expect people to refer, and run exercises that foster teamwork and appropriate divisions of responsibility between collection, management, and publishing staff.

✦ **Long-term training:** This type of training is the traditional idea of a class, with assignments, texts, and tests. To the extent that you have the time or resources to mount such classes, they're a great way to really teach skills. I haven't seen many CMS organizations that are large enough to warrant creating and running classes. Sometimes, however, you can support staff members who want to attend classes in colleges and universities that provide overlap with the skills that you need.

Powering up the system

As part of deploying the CMS, you may want to power it up slowly. You can begin powering up the CMS at the beginning of implementation. Throughout implementation, you can bring more and more of the system into operation until, during deployment, you have all the CMS systems running.

Note   Your CMS product vendor or IT staffers may have different ideas about how to best power up the system. Listen to them, but see how much of what I present here you can work into their plan. The most essential thing to preserve is the capability to retreat at any point back to a system that works.

Following are the steps that you may want to follow to bring the CMS to full power:

✦ Get the basic CMS package running in a simple, standalone environment.

✦ Get the basic package running in your production environment (that is, the full environment in which the CMS eventually must operate).

✦ Progressively add content and publications to the standalone environment and then add them to the real environment.

✦ Progressively add third-party software and integrations to the production environment.

✦ Release a beta system that can do everything that the final system can do.

✦ Release a final system that you can trust.

I explain each of these steps further in the following sections.

The generic installation

Starting with a generic installation that has as few external complexities to it as possible is always your best course. This type of startup gives you proof that the CMS in its native state can work without difficulty.

Native state, by the way, means the following:

✦ **Using one or two computers:** The product company may recommend that you use one computer for the CMS server and another one for the database server.

✦ **Outfitted to the product company's exact system requirements:** These requirements include operating system service packs, patches, and so on.

✦ **Using whatever sample database structure and content the product company provides:** The samples that come with the system provide a good baseline that you can always return to if the system gets messed up later.

✦ **Not connected to any external systems except your LAN:** Keep the connectivity as minimal as possible at first to avoid complicating factors. You have plenty of time to complicate the system later.

✦ **All the features of the CMS installed:** You want to install all features, even if you don't immediately need them, so that you expose as many CMS internal dependencies as possible.

The preceding configuration is your CMS reference platform. Later, if you can't get something to work on your production installation, you can try it on the generic installation to see whether it works if you remove the rest of your infrastructure. The generic installation also gives you practice and confidence installing and configuring the CMS.

Finally, this platform serves as the testing ground for content and publications as you move through implementation. Before moving on, back up this reference configuration using a disk copy or other system backup process. Later, you may want to reinstall it on the same or a different computer. You want to avoid the trouble of reinstalling the system if something goes awry.

Cross-Reference

You can find more information about the generic installation in Chapter 20, "Implementing the System," in the section "Installing the system."

The production installation

Soon after you get the generic installation running, you want to start to build your real infrastructure. Your real infrastructure includes the following items:

✦ The Web, file, and database server hardware and software that you intend to use. Preferably this hardware and software isn't what you currently use for Web sites, but rather a different set of computers that you want to use for your sites and CMS.

✦ At least one typical end-user machine running the authoring tools.

✦ An administrator's machine running the full CMS interface suite.

✦ End-user machines running the operating systems and browsers that you expect your audience members to run.

✦ The Web server and application server that you intend to use.

✦ Your determined LAN and Internet connectivity.

✦ Any firewall and security software that you plan to run.

✦ Whatever database connectivity you plan to employ.

✦ The replication and deployment systems that you intend to use to move and synchronize content at your various locations.

The production installation is also a reference installation. It shows that the selected CMS can run inside your chosen infrastructure before adding the complexity of content, publications, third-party software, and integrations. Make sure that you fully document the installation and configuration of this system. If possible, make disk images of each of the machines that you set up so that you can restore them later if they get really messed up.

Over the course of implementation, you continually add third-party software, system integrations, content, and publications to this system. Make sure that, as you do, you can always back up to the last working configuration.

Content and publications

The generic installation is the one to use for initially loading content and accessing publications. The production installation is much less stable and may go down often during implementation. In addition, you can put the generic installation on a computer in someone's office or in a common workspace where you can reboot and even totally reconfigure it, as necessary, to keep you going.

As you finalize content structure and begin to collect components, load them into the generic installation of the CMS. As you develop and finalize your database or XML structures, this machine contains the master copy of the content structure that you're creating. At each convenient milestone, you can upload the content set from the generic installation to the production installation to give it more content for testing.

Tip   If possible, keep a copy of content outside the CMS. Make good backups of the content that you process *before* loading it into the CMS database. For content that you load directly into the CMS through Web-based forms, back up the database records frequently. If the database becomes corrupted or otherwise unusable, you'll be glad that you did the backup.

Build your collection of Web-based forms and batch upload tools to access the generic installation at first. Doing so isolates them from any infrastructure complications as you're first creating them. Begin to test them on the production installation as soon as it's ready, but continue to develop them against the generic installation for as long as feasible to keep your collection effort out of the way of the infrastructure effort.

Build and test your publications on the generic installation first. It's easier to manipulate and more robust than the production installation. Of course, you can go only so far on the generic installation. You install none of your publication system integrations or third-party add-ons on the generic machine. Still, you can work through the majority of content access, navigation, and layout issues in this easy environment before moving on to the real world.

Third-party software and integrations

While working through collection and publication on the generic installation, you can work through connection and integration on the production system. Add the third-party products that you intend to use and the integrations that you expect to need to the infrastructure system in whatever order seems to cause the fewest problems (for the schedule as well as for the system). Bring in only as much content and publication stuff from the generic installation as you need to test the integrations you're doing.

Test as generic a connection as possible to each system first. Then, after you're sure that the generic connection works, complicate the system by bringing in the particular connection that the CMS requires. If you need to connect a publication to an enterprise data system, for example, make sure first that you can get any data in and out of that enterprise system. Then go for the specific data that you need to exchange. Finally, access the data that you need by using the template that accesses it in the final system.

As the system nears full connectivity in the management and publishing system, you're ready to consider switching over fully from the generic to the production installation.

The beta system

After your production installation has a full complement of connections to other products and systems and you test all collection and publication interconnections, you're ready to create a beta CMS.

Cross-Reference   For more information on beta tests, refer to Chapter 20, "Implementing the System," in the section "Beta tests."

The beta system is a full working version of the system that you think you're finally going to use. All content is flowing into it, and all publications, fully formed, are flowing out of it. In other words, it's a major cause for celebration!

From the standpoint of deployment, the major issue with the beta system is when to flip the switch on any systems that the CMS is replacing. You probably haven't stopped creating your Web sites and other publications the old way until now. Now, however, is the time to flip the switch and start treating the CMS as your only source and destination for content. This move is often scary (especially if you're not quite as organized and fastidious as I recommend). If you're unsure, you can always publish in parallel while you work through the final kinks. If you do publish in parallel, realize the following:

✦ **Expect to take significant extra efforts** to collect content and form it into publication pages in two different ways.

✦ **Plan on having a difficult time** making sure that the changes that you make in one system end up in the other.

Regardless of the extra effort, supporting two efforts for a while — instead of abruptly shutting the old one down, only to find that the new one can't yet make its deadlines — may prove well worth your while.

Another way to approach the change from the old to the new system is to specify a *freeze period*, a (short, you hope) period of time when you stop updating content the old way so that the content processors can have a fixed set of content to migrate. Finally, if neither a freeze nor parallel publishing works, you can get a *cut* of the content on a certain date and then track every single change to the content after that so that the change can get into the new system in the final hours before it goes live.

The full staff may or may not use the beta system, and it may or may not create publications that all audience members see. To power up more slowly, you can release the beta system to one contributor group or one publication at a time. You can use it to create only some of the pages on your Web site, or you can use it to create a separate site to which you route only a smaller percentage of users.

Tip   A simple Web script can route a percentage of your site visitors to a different URL. You can install a script that selects randomly or by any other user-profile data that you can ascertain (audience type is best, if you can detect it) and then redirects the browsers of chosen visitors to your test pages.

However slowly you begin, by the end of the test, you should have the complete system in place, accepting all content and creating all publications. Another possibility is that the test fails and you're back a step or two — but I'm assuming that won't be the case.

The final system

The way that I lay out the deployment process, the final system is no more than the last small step. This approach minimizes surprises and makes sure that the final launch of the CMS is as uneventful as possible.

Besides its benefits for testing and deployment purposes, the incremental process that I propose in this chapter is a good idea for another reason. Nothing is particularly final about the final system. The whole point of a CMS is to give you the capability to change and create content and publications without some arbitrary versioning or release cycle for your publications. Of course, you still may choose to create big launches and release dates for certain publications, but you don't need to do so. And as the world gets more and more accustomed to the continuous-update model of the Web, you're called on less and less often to create distinct publication versions and releases.

More than an end, the final system is the beginning of a new process. You're no longer building — you're maintaining. You're out of the startup phase and into the run phase of your CMS. You're now beyond the CMS project and into the CMS as an integral part of the organization.

From now on, your work results in innumerable small improvements to the processes that you initiate rather than in overhauls and complete revolutions. Don't just sigh and move on, however; take a break to pop a cork or two and sing the praises of your team, which has done an amazing amount of work, and your organization, which let them get away with changing everything!

Preparing content

After the release parties all end, you may find that you already have a backlog of content to get into the system. Did you hold off on new content near the end to make sure that your first set of publications was just right? You can get away with this approach at your first release but not in the longer run. Rather, you must set up the process so that content flows in independently of how it flows out. In fact, if you're smart, you simply queued up new content in a workflow stage rather than stopping its production entirely.

As part of your logical design, in your specs, and finally in your authoring and acquisition guides, you worked through and presented everything that could be said about moving content into the system. Now the trick is to make it work the way that you planned it. First, prepare to change. Make sure that your guides have owners who commits to keeping them up to date with the real production rates and processes that the systems uses. As you move from the project phase (where everyone expects extraordinary effort) to the run phase (where you can expect only ordinary effort), you're certain to need to readjust your expectations and find a point of stability where you can really count on the flow of new information. For the long-term viability of your CMS, finding a sustainable production rate is much more important than getting all information into the system as soon as possible. During the CMS project, you want the hare's agility and speed. During the running of the CMS, you want the tortoise's slow but always-steady plod.

Tip   As you move from starting up to running a CMS, expect some of your top talent to leave. The hare that prefers the adrenaline of a fast-paced project may not want to become the tortoise that you can count on for years to come.

Second, adjust your processing team structure to the new environment. You're likely to need only the top talent from your processing teams to handle the smaller quantities of information that you have after you make your way past the backlog. You can use the same processes, but make sure that you review them. You designed them to move information at a high rate. After you slow the rate and create a smaller team, you probably need to rethink some of your processes and job descriptions. You may also want to go from a model of one project team per source to one department of content processing that handles all sources.

Revising the system

As much as you may want it to happen, in the run phase of a CMS, none of the project activities stop; they just slow down.

Of course, you face the inevitable bugs, which may call for a burst of activity that reminds everyone of the bad old project days, but unless you missed a lot in testing, these bugs are normally just short squalls on an otherwise calm sea. I'd advise you to put a good plan in place for quickly discovering the source of any bug and bringing as much power as necessary to bear to quickly address any potential problem.

If your system is a success, you know immediately, because the following things occur:

✦ **Content appears out of the woodwork:** People you couldn't ever pin down and people you've never even heard of (despite your great search) turn up and want you to "hook up" their content.

✦ **Publication ideas flourish:** In addition to publication teams approaching you to include their stuff, you find that everyone has a great idea for a new page or publication that you can produce.

✦ **Personalization moves to the forefront:** As people see the new possibilities of the system, you get more and more requests to slice content in a particular way for a particular person or group.

These signs of success may seem more the harbingers of your imminent demise if you don't have a way to handle them. The worst thing that you can do is open the floodgates, embrace them all, and get to work. A better move is to establish a clear process for evaluating requests and preparing a measured response.

Chapter 14, "Working within the Organization," in the section "Using Functional Collection and Publishing," provides a detailed discussion of how you structure your organization to handle requests and changes.

As you entertain revisions to the system, I believe that the most important thing to do is to preserve the integrity of the logical design. If you add a new information source, for example, it may introduce changes to your component and element models, author or source assumptions, and publication-template models and personalization routines. If you don't consider the changes carefully and work them through for each change, you eventually end up in a bind, where the new stuff breaks the old stuff. Maybe the new source that you're adding overlaps with the information in one of the existing components, for example, and somehow appears on the same page and looks redundant.

Chapter 23, "The Wheel of Content Management," addresses the connections between parts of the logical design. You can use it to create a process for assessing the effects of changes on your CMS.

A question that you eventually must address is, "When's version 2 coming out?" You can handle this issue in either of the following two ways:

✦ **No version 2 is necessary:** Following the idea that the running CMS evolves rather than revolutionizes, you can say that you make changes as they're suggested and ratified and that the system, therefore, never actually needs a new version.

✦ **Hold back for a major pass:** Given the realities of budgeting and staffing, you may decide to make only small changes in the normal course of running the CMS, holding back major changes for a defined next CMS project cycle.

The first method makes the most of the CMS and enables it to evolve as necessary. The second approach is more realistic for organizations that can't muster the ongoing budget or staffing necessary to continually review and develop new functionality. (It also may make particular sense if you deferred including some requirements in the initial system, and the next version is already a cloud on the horizon.) You may want to start out on a defined revision cycle and move into continuous revision as the system proves its value. If you do choose revision cycles, you must determine the difference between a small and large change. The only natural break that I can think of that works for any situation is as follows: Changes to existing components and publications are small changes, whereas creation of new components and publications qualifies as a large change.

Of course, continuous change doesn't mean no schedules. It simply means that a particular change happens on its own schedule, which is often independent of any other change.

Taking Stock of the Deliverables

Aside from delivering the CMS itself, during deployment you can prepare a set of plans and specifications that ease the transition into the new world of the CMS. Although I list these deliverables in the deployment stage, you may very well need to begin to create them during implementation to have them ready at deployment time.

The deployment specification

The *deployment specification*, which I describe in this section, you actually want to develop along with the other specifications during implementation. It details the process that you undertake to roll out your system. The deployment specification includes the following parts:

✦ **The power-up schedule:** This schedule details the plan that you devise for powering up the system. Especially during the earlier stages of development, it's critical so that each team knows when you expect its deliverables to continue building the production system.

✦ **The CMS system architecture:** This architecture includes all the parts that I mention in the section, "The production installation," earlier in this chapter. The system architecture should include system diagrams as well as hardware and software requirements for the generic and production installations.

✦ **Integration plans:** These plans include schedules and techniques to connect the CMS to all third-party products and enterprise systems.

✦ **Staff rollout plans:** These plans detail how and when you deploy the collection system to different contribution groups (author groups and acquisition groups).

✦ **Publication rollout plans:** These plans describe the order and timing in which CMS-produced publications replace the current publications. This plan shows exactly when the old ones stop and the new ones begin. If you're planning a period during which the old and new publication productions overlap, the plan shows how you're handling staffing and synchronization.

✦ **The beta plan:** This plan describes the timing and participation that you expect in a beta release. If you're including certain audience groups, the plan needs to state how you plan to ask for or notify them of their participation.

✦ **Expected and allowed volumes:** The deployment plan sets the expected range and the maximum values for the page views and other transactions that occur in the CMS at release. It should include contingency plans for how to bring more hardware or bandwidth to bear if the actual volumes (of page requests, database queries, or other publication pages, for example) exceed the maximum.

✦ **The distributed system plan:** If the CMS system or databases is spread over various locations, the specification should provide a schedule and staffing plan for how the deployment spreads through the set of locations.

✦ **A deployment staffing plan:** This plan shows how many and what types of people you need to power up and roll out the system.

✦ **Setup and configuration data:** You need this data for all the end-user tools that you must deploy to contributors and other CMS staff.

The deployment specification dovetails with the implementation specs. Whereas each implementation specification shows how to build a particular part of the CMS, the deployment specification shows how all the parts come together as you build them to form the production system and how you intend to progressively release that production system to staff and audiences.

The staffing plan

The *staffing plan* that you produce for deployment shows the kinds and numbers of people that you need to run your system. All the input for the plan comes from the workflow and staffing analysis that you do during logical design.

 Chapter 33, "Designing Workflow and Staffing Models," details the logical design of staffing.

The plan should include the following:

✦ **An assessment of your current content management staffing:** Include all the contributors that formally or informally contribute content now and all the project staff that you've mustered.

✦ **Job descriptions:** Gather descriptions for all the people that you need to run the system.

✦ **The gap in staff:** What's the gap between those people you have now and those you still need to run the system?

✦ **The gap in skills or training:** What skills or training are necessary for the people who are to run the system?

This plan is the culmination of the process that you expect to use to secure CMS staffing and not the beginning of it. If you suspect that you can't turn the project team into the running teams, start as early as possible to secure funding and support for finding your ongoing CMS team.

The training plan

I discuss the training possibilities themselves in the section "Doing training," earlier in this chapter. In addition, you need to plan how you're going to develop and deliver the training materials. In the training plans, make sure that you include the following:

✦ **Who will create the training?** You can sometimes use an instructional designer from the product company's professional services division or an outside contractor. Failing that, the people creating the documentation may prove a good choice. My last choice is the project team members, who probably are busy with other tasks and are unlikely to have any particular skills in creating training.

✦ **When can you complete it?** Obviously, having the training plans ready to go well in advance of the beta release of the system is your best course. Doing so gives you the most time to train staff before they ever need to do real work. This timing is pretty ambitious, however, given the rest of what must happen before the beta release. The next fallback is to make training ready at the beta release. Then you can train as people ramp into using the beta release. If you simply can't ready the training by the beta release, make other plans for how to train the initial staff.

✦ **Who will take the training and when?** Schedule the delivery of the training around the power-up plan, making sure that you train people in advance of calling on them to use the system. In any case, don't get too far ahead of the actual power-up—if there's a long gap between training and actual use of the system, your users may need a refresher, at the least. Better would be to schedule—and reschedule, if power up slips—training to keep it close to when people will get their hands on the system. Pay attention, too, to the amount of training that each individual needs. More experienced staff can often get ready just by reading the documentation.

You don't need to overplan training. A simple spreadsheet is all that you really need to chart out the creation and delivery of training. The difficult part of the training plan is ensuring that training is ready in time to prove useful at the release of the system. If you can't find a way to train people before they begin work, the value of the training severely decreases and you must re-evaluate your plan. Less training, delivered earlier, may provide a higher overall value to you.

The documentation plan

In the section "Creating documentation," earlier in this chapter, I discuss the documentation that you may want to create. In addition, plan how to create all the different documents in the specified time with the resources that you have. In your documentation plan, make sure that you include the following:

✦ **What document to create?** Plot out the migration of information from the specs and other project documents that you've created so far to the documentation set. This exercise tells you how much extra work is necessary to complete the documentation, given the existing information. It also helps you figure out who should contribute to each document.

✦ **Who creates documents?** My first choices for the document writers are the authors of your specifications, augmenting them with a professional writer who can take the raw materials that the authors supply and turn them into readable, accessible publications. This method gives you the most leverage of the limited time that analysts and other authors may have near the end of the project.

✦ **A publication plan:** This plan needs to include the formats in which the documentation is delivered. I suggest that you focus first on HTML versions, because they give you the most flexibility (in repurposing) for the least effort. As much as you can manage, make this plan a microcosm of the wider CMS—that is, make sure that it covers how to segment the content and how to template and build the documentation.

✦ **A release plan:** This plan needs to show when each document is ready. As is the case with training, getting documentation ready well before your beta release is preferable. At beta is fine as well. If you can't manage to get the documentation ready at beta, you want to decide how to plug the information gap with selected parts of the specs. Make sure that you prioritize the creation and release of the documentation to correspond to the major information needs that you expect to have at and after the beta stage.

If you treat your CMS information as content to collect, manage, and publish, you have no problem creating targeted, well-delivered documentation. If you went as far as using a CMS to create the specs, you're already in a position to take complete control of publication. If you didn't use a CMS (or other Web-authoring environment) to create specs, it's not too late to start doing so. Organize the creation and publication of your documentation now to ensure that you can update and repurpose it back into specifications for your next round of changes to the CMS. The generic installation of the CMS is often the perfect server for the ongoing collection and distribution of CMS-related content.

The maintenance plan

A *maintenance plan* details how to administer the system over time. It's the marching orders for the CMS administrator and support staff. Include the following types of information in your maintenance plan:

✦ **Backups:** How often do you back up the CMS repository and how does this backup occur?

✦ **Content retirement:** How do you archive or delete content from the repository and what are the procedures for doing so?

✦ **Revisions:** What are the rules for modifying CMS components, configuration, or publishing routines? Who must agree to a change, who makes the change, and who tests it? Include here, too, the expected and maximum number of changes that your administrators must do. What are your contingency plans if the number of changes surpasses the maximum for which you've planned?

✦ **Turnaround times:** For each type of request for a change to the system, what's the expected and maximum amount of time until the change is complete?

✦ **Technical support plan:** This plan can entail an entire document of its own if you're going to create and run your own technical-support group. If so, use the technical-support criteria that I describe in Chapter 19, "Selecting Hardware and Software," in the section "Technical support," to get a start on what you design and build. At the very least, your technical support plan must catalog expected problem types. For each type of problem, it provide an initial contact, an escalation procedure, an expected time for resolution, and expectations for logging and reporting on the problem. In addition, the plan overviews the kinds, numbers, and distribution of technical support staffing that you expect to engage.

✦ **Connections:** The maintenance plan should include a section on each connection that the CMS makes to outside systems (enterprise data, Web transaction, and other systems). For each connection, the plan states any periodic tasks that must occur, any troubleshooting tips that the implementation teams come up with, and any diagrams or definitions of the way that you make connections to the system.

✦ **Logs and reports:** The maintenance plan specifies logging and reporting requirements such as the following: which logs you must maintain and what data they include, what sorts of reports you generate from logs and databases, how often you produce reports, how often to clear or archive logs, who gets which reports, and what are the expected minimum and maximum allowed values for each key report data field. If a report data field goes below the allowed minimum or above the allowed maximum, the plan must state what the required action is. If, for example, you access a component fewer than two times per month, you may want to trigger a workflow to review its accessibility and desirability.

✦ **Maintenance:** The plan should contain schedules for routine maintenance tasks, such as clearing out old pages from Web sites, reviewing metadata lists, reviewing personalization rules, and purging bad data from the user profile tables.

✦ **Maintenance contracts and contacts:** For the parts of CMS maintenance that outside agencies (technical support groups, contract programmers, publication facilities, and so on) do, the plan needs to include or reference the agreement that you have with them and list the contact people for those organizations.

The maintenance plan tries to anticipate any issue that may arise during the running of the CMS. Of course, you're sure to miss a lot, so prepare yourself (or your system administrator) ahead of time to update and maintain the plan.

Summary

Rolling out your CMS is a matter of making it part of the daily life of your organization. In other words, expect a transition between the time before the CMS and the time after which the CMS no longer seems strange or cumbersome. You can ease that transition by doing the following:

✦ Preparing a complete and easily accessible documentation set.

✦ Bringing the system into its final production environment in a series of steps.

✦ Preparing for the ongoing processing of content and publications from the system.

✦ Figuring out in advance how to support and fix the system after its release.

✦ Preparing in advance for an inevitable series of enhancements and versions that come quickly on the heels of your first release.

That's it for the project process. In the following part of the book, I take you back into logical design.

✦   ✦   ✦

Designing a CMS

Designing a CMS Simply

◆ ◆ ◆ ◆

In This Chapter

Why you need
logical design

Understanding the CM
entities at a glance

Logical design
made simple

◆ ◆ ◆ ◆

In Chapter 18, "Doing Logical Design," I introduce the concept of logical design and discuss how you might plan and then do a logical design project. Chapter 18 is directed toward the project manager who has to fit logical design into an overall CMS implementation. Although a project manager plans a project, a content analyst actually does the logical design work in a project (see Chapter 13, "Staffing a CMS," for more on these roles). Part IV of the book is directed toward content analysts. It fully describes each part of a logical design analysis and how the parts relate. This chapter introduces the major parts of a logical design and helps the analyst scale her logical design to the amount of effort she can afford to spend on the task.

Logical Design Essentials

A CMS logical design is a plan for your system that is hardware and software neutral. It states the organizational problem you have and how a CMS will solve it. Content management systems deliver information and functionality to audiences in publications. So, the most basic statement concerning the purpose of your CMS ought to take the same form: It should describe what information and functionality your CMS will deliver to audiences. For example:

> By delivering a particular kind of content (information and functionality) to a particular set of audiences via a particular set of publications, we will help the organization make a set amount of progress toward a particular set of goals.

The trick, of course, is to work through the particulars until you are satisfied that the system will work. Notice that this statement says nothing about the technology you will use to create your system. Any infrastructure that delivers the right content to the right people in the right way ought to give you the progress you desire. Of course, the technology matters in other ways. It can make your system affordable, efficient, scalable, and even possible. However, it is the balance of goals, audiences, publications, and content that really defines what the system must do.

So, if you do no more than turn the word *particular* in the preceding goal statement into a series of short lists, you will have made progress toward designing a system that will do what you really want it to. On the other hand, just quickly listing these entities will not give you much insight into the details of your system. By going further with each entity (goals, audiences, and so on) you can get as much detail as you care to manage and a correspondingly deep understanding of what your systems needs to do. You can then use whatever depth of understanding you may have arrived at to guide the technical implementation of your system.

The Entities at a Glance

The traditional way to create and update publications is to establish a direct connection between an author and a publication. In a CMS, you create an indirect connection between author and publication through a collection, management, and publishing system. This system enables the work of authors to combine with other source materials to create a variety of publications. You can understand a CMS as a set of significant players or entities that all interact to create a living system.

I discuss the content management entities in one form or another all through this book. Now is the time to define them directly, describing what they are, what they contain, and how they interact. In this chapter I encapsulate as simply as possible the idea of the CM entities and the design implications they yield. In the rest of Part IV, I go into much greater depth to describe all the ways you can study and interrelate the entities to create a detailed CMS design.

The chapters in this section describe the logical design in terms of the CM entities, which are described more fully in Chapter 23, "The Wheel of Content Management." The major considerations in a CMS are what I refer to as the *CM entities*. Briefly, the entities are as follows:

✦ **Goals and requirements.** *Goals* are the business concerns that drive the need for and the major uses of a CMS. You determine these goals in conjunction with your project sponsors—the key players in the organization who support and enable the CMS project. A goal is something that an organization wants to accomplish. A *requirement* is something that your system needs to do, be, or have to meet your goals.

✦ **Audiences.** An *audience* is a group of people with common traits that you decide to serve. Your CMS logical design must consider audiences from a number of perspectives, including marketing, software development, and writing. For a complete discussion of audiences and audience analysis, see Chapter 25, "Cataloging Audiences."

✦ **Publications.** In the end, the point of a CMS is to create *publications* that audiences want. Although most systems in the past were used to create only a single Web site, today most are being turned toward multiple Web sites, print materials, and a growing number of other publication types, such as syndications and personal digital assistant (PDA) screens

✦ **Content Types.** At the heart of any content management system are chunks of information that are reused in your various publications. Each of these chunks, which I call *content components,* belongs to a group which I call a *content type*. Dividing your information into types is the first and largest step toward being able to manage the creation and distribution of your information.

✦ **Authors.** *Authors* are the people who create content for you. In the past, authors were professionals. Today, in the world of electronic information, anyone can be an author. And your job as a CMS architect is to provide each group of authors with the appropriate training and interface to allow them to contribute content most easily.

✦ **Acquisition sources.** Whereas authors create content, *acquisition sources* supply content that already exists in some form. You might acquire content that's too expensive or inconvenient to author. You may also acquire content because someone's already creating it on an ongoing basis. (No need to reinvent the wheel.)

✦ **Content access structures.** *Access structures* are the ways that you organize and link content so that people can more easily find it. In your CMS repository, access structures are how you organize components. In a publication, access structures are the navigation methods that you provide for users to move through the publications pages or sections.

✦ **Workflow and staffing.** *Workflow* is the process of creating flows of sequential and parallel tasks that must be accomplished in your CMS. I group this subject together with considerations of staffing because the two are best figured out at the same time. If you know what and how much you need to accomplish, you can figure out who you need to do it. On the other hand, if you know whom you have and whom you can get, you can build processes to suit them.

Logical Design: An Example

In this section, I introduce a real organization that I use as an example throughout the following chapters to illustrate concepts and give tangible examples of the issues that I raise. In the example here, I use the organization to build a very simple logical design.

PLAN International — an example organization

PLAN International is a wonderful organization that helps children worldwide. PLAN, similar to any organization, has information and functionality that it wants to publish. Here is some information about PLAN that I got from its Web site (at www.plan-international.org/) to give you a flavor for the organization:

✦ **PLAN's identity:** PLAN is an international, humanitarian, child-focused development organization without religious, political, or governmental affiliation. Child sponsorship is the basic foundation of the organization.

✦ **PLAN's vision:** PLAN's vision is of a world in which all children realize their full potential in societies that respect people's rights and dignity.

I use PLAN as an example, but not as a literal one. Rather, I base my examples on a combination of what you can see on its Web site, what I can guess or make up about what it wants to accomplish, and what I need to stipulate to make a good example. Please don't believe that what I say has any relation to what PLAN believes or intends to do.

A very simple logical design

In this section I outline a very simple, prototypical logical design process. My idea here is to illustrate how you can account for the most important considerations in your logical design while making intelligent compromises to scale the effort to your current capabilities. To illustrate a simple logical design, I use my fictionalized account of PLAN International.

Let's suppose that you, as the content project manager for PLAN, already have some sort of organizational mandate and have created a set of requirements that's based on input from people in the organization. Your mandate must clearly establish the goals of your CM project. These goals might include:

✦ **Increasing awareness in members and donors**. PLAN wants to ensure that current and future members (those who contribute monthly to support children in need) know all they should about the organization and the communities it serves.

✦ **Affecting public awareness of PLAN**. PLAN wants to increase awareness in the general press about its mission and methods.

✦ **Providing tools for staff**. PLAN wants to provide job-related information to staff both at the main and regional offices.

Merely stating these goals in a simple and direct way clearly puts the designers of this system on the right path to success. Contrast the guidance provided by these statements with the guidance provided by the more typical motivating statement "We need a CMS because our Web site is out of control."

PLAN might have the time and energy to complete a full logical design for a CMS to meet these goals. On the other hand, it might have only enough available resources to complete a very general design. Most likely, it has enough resources to complete an analysis somewhere between the minimal one I will now present and the maximal one that is outlined in the remaining chapters of Part IV. Even if your organization has resources sufficient to complete an in-depth analysis, you might still want to begin with a simple one.

To perform a minimal logical design, follow these steps:

1. Make an outline (in a word processor or spreadsheet) in which you list the entity types that you will include in your simplified logical design:

   - **Audiences**. Following the goals it has laid out, PLAN might see its audiences as members, in-country staff, donors, and the press.

   - **Publications**. Plan, for example, might want to produce a Web site for members and donors, a different Web site for staff, and automatic e-mails, printed brochures for donors, and a syndication feed for the press.

   - **Content**. PLAN might see its content as news, press releases, funding success stories, events, and organizational information.

   - **Authors**. The PLAN authors might be field managers, paid staff, and volunteers.

   - **Sources**. It may expect to receive batches of information from news syndicators, the PLAN Public Relations group, and government-report originators.

   In a simple analysis like this one you can probably skip an analysis of templates, personalizations, workflow and staffing, and access structures. For one thing, you need more than this simple analysis to be able to work out these entities, and for another, you can always come back to the analysis later to take it deeper and wider.

2. Fill out your outline with all the information you can manage to gather (from your requirements or other sources) about each entity. As you do:

   - Refer to the chapters in Part IV for lots of advice on the sorts of information to collect.

   - Put aside technical requirements for the time being.

   - Note requirements that don't seem to fit anywhere in the entity outline.

   - Draw simple conclusions from your requirements to get them to fit. For example, the PLAN site may want to implicitly (but not explicitly) address an audience consisting of potential corporate funding sources; or use a content type (such as donor information) that is currently expressed only as a publication (say, a list of donors).

   - Choose the names for your requirements carefully. Make them descriptive and memorable because you'll be referring back to them.

   - Try to find any obvious gaps, such as categories of requirements that apply to one audience but aren't addressed for others. For example, is degree of literacy in English addressed for one audience, but not for another? Try to fill in the gaps, inferring if necessary.

3. When you have all the information organized under each entity and believe it is complete (if not deep), ask all the questions time allows to interrelate the entities in your lists. In particular:

   - How do these audiences help us meet these goals? Make a chart of goals and audiences, and describe for each goal how each audience relates to that goal and vice versa. Note any obvious gaps. (For example, if educating donors is a goal, are corporate giving officers represented among the audiences?)

   - Do these audiences want these publications? Chart publications and audiences to determine which audiences want each publication. If possible, rank their interest (High, Moderate, Low). For example, potential donors and funders may not be likely to go to a Web site, but they may respond favorably to a printed brochure.

4. Review the list of content types you expect to publish. (See Chapter 27, "Designing Content Types," if you don't yet know what a content type is.) When you believe the list is complete, use it to chart against several other entities in turn: your audiences, your publications, your authors, and acquisition sources. Then ask yourself:

   - Is the content we charted sufficient to fill the publications? What is missing? What is not needed? (For example, if one publication is a report to potential funders and donors, do we have content about program accomplishments that they'd be interested in?)

   - Is it content that the audiences want? Which audience wants which content?

   - Are the authors and sources sufficient to create this content? Are there sources or author groups we don't actually need? Is there some content we don't actually need (which would be nice)? Are there overlaps? If so, where?

   - Can the authors and sources we have speak to these audiences? Which authors and sources speak to which audience?

5. Make diagrams that relate entities. (For examples of these sorts of diagrams, refer to the various diagrams in Chapter 23, "The Wheel of Content Management," in the section "The Content Management Entities.")

6. Make a report that summarizes your findings in layman's terms and circulate it for approval.

7. Cap the process with a statement of the problem, and a case for why the particular system you have designed meets the challenge. PLAN would include in its problem statement a summary of its goals and an explanation of why these goals are not being reached now (for example, PLAN might briefly describe the low level of awareness about leave policies among in-country staff and how the system you outline will resolve the goals).

8. Make sure you clearly understand the boundaries of your content domain by asking, "What divides all the content we want from what we don't want? How will we organize our content so we can manage it and others can discover it?"

9. Use this simple logical design to decide if requirements people bring you fit, as the beginning of a more detailed logical design, and as a way to galvanize the whole team around the purpose and basic function of the system.

At the end of the process (which could happen in a day if you have your team and research in place), you should be able to make specific statements about your system. You should also be able to evaluate, at a high level, what sort of technological system will meet the requirements of your logical design. For example, it is clear that the CMS that PLAN uses needs to create Web, print, and e-mail publications.

Tip   It's important to establish a common vocabulary among your team, and this is a good time to do it. Get used to calling sources "sources," for example, and begin to call each source by the descriptive and memorable name you chose for it. It may seem a little artificial at first, but you'll warm to the idea as you see your team adopt the common terminology and use it to avoid ambiguity.

Getting Beyond the Simple Logical Design

After completing a simple logical design, you may choose to move on to other aspects of the project. The constraints of the project may be too pressing to do more than the minimum logical design. If you do move on quickly, please realize that it's likely that you will regret this decision later, but that's how it goes.

On the other hand, the process of creating a simple logical design may have sparked your appetite for going further. If you are in this camp, you can say that your simple design was just the first iteration through the entities to prepare you for the next, deeper pass. (I discuss this iterative approach to logical design in Chapter 18, "Doing Logical Design," in the section "Iterating through your design.")

If you choose to iterate through your logical design, here are a few ways to do it:

✦ You can expand the outline on your own, adding, below its name, the essential facts you need to know about each entity.

✦ You can move your analysis to a database or XML system, where you can expand it and begin to formalize the connections between entities. (For a complete discussion of the entity attributes and relations to track, see Chapter 23, "The Wheel of Content Management.")

✦ Even after you move on into other aspects of your CM project, you can continue to do logical design as you feel the need to better understand what your system must accomplish. The new decisions you make can either be brought into the current project or saved up for the next version of the project.

Summary

It's difficult to keep the logical design process a simple one, because doing so means that you are cutting out the level of detailed design that your system will benefit from. At the least, you should read the chapters in this section of the book so that if you do need to make the tough decisions of what not to do, you'll make them in an educated way.

✦   ✦   ✦

The Wheel of Content Management

✦ ✦ ✦ ✦

In This Chapter

An introduction to the content management entities

The information that you collect on all the entities

The relationships that you need to forge among the entities

How to start collecting information in a logical analysis

✦ ✦ ✦ ✦

In Chapter 22, I introduced you to the set of forces or entities within your organization that lead you to a particular CMS design. In this chapter, I present a more in-depth overview of these entities and discuss their major relationships. In the chapters that follow, I describe each entity individually and discuss, at length, how you may analyze it and use it to construct the logical design of your CMS.

Just as you can use the previous chapter to do a very simple logical design, you can use this chapter to understand enough about the entities to do a comprehensive, but still high-level logical design. If you are ready to tackle a full-blown logical design, you can treat this chapter as an introduction and use the more detailed information in the chapters that follow to build your design analysis.

The Content Management Entities

Regardless of any CMS products that you may currently use or how you structure your CMS project, you must face a certain set of issues in order to make the most of your system. These issues group together into the following categories that, by now, probably seem quite familiar to you:

- ✦ Goals and requirements
- ✦ Audiences
- ✦ Publications
- ✦ Content types
- ✦ Authors
- ✦ Acquisition sources
- ✦ Access structures
- ✦ Workflow and staffing

I call these categories the *content management entities* because they're the basic players in a content management system. These are the categories that I've found are important enough to be included in any complete logical design process. You may add entities if your level of analysis requires it, or remove entities if your project limitations require it. (Chapter 22, "Designing a CMS Simply," discusses creating the minimal, bare-bones logical design using primarily just three entities: goals and requirements, audiences, and publications.) To create a CMS, you must account for each entity and ensure that you design the system in accordance with it. The entities each have unique needs that your system must address, but each is directly or indirectly related to all the others. Thus the entities are constraints as well as players. They put limits on each other and decide for you what's possible and what isn't. The system you end up with is the result of many-sided negotiations that you conduct between the entities during the design phases of your CMS. You may, for example, want to serve 10 different audiences until you find out what that means for the complexity of your publications. You may want to acquire content from a certain source but find that transforming it into content types is too much effort. You may change your whole approach based on the number of authors you can realistically recruit.

Entities broaden as well as constrain the system. The set of content types that you choose to create can, for example, give you ideas for new publications that didn't seem feasible at the start of your design. Your audiences can suggest access structures that make personalization more natural. Your sources can suggest a set of content types.

The word *entity* has another connotation as well. In relational database design, an *entity* is a table or other significant data structure that you build your design around. In an inventory database, for example, you may use a product entity as well as entities for locations and users. You associate a set of data with each entity. A product gets an ID, a name, a description, a price, and so on. A location gets an ID, an address, a phone number, a size, and so on. A user gets an ID, a name, an e-mail address, a job title, and so on.

Each entity has relationships with others. You warehouse a product, for example, at a location. A location needs a manager, and a particular user of the system is in charge of a product. Figure 23-1 provides an example of how to depict entities and relationships in database diagrams.

Each entity has a table that holds its data set. If its relationship with another entity is one-to-many—one user is in charge of many products, for example—you can include the ID of one entity in the data set of the other. If the relationship is many-to-many—for example, some products may reside in many locations and each location may contain many products—you need an intermediate table to hold the matched sets of IDs (such as the LocationProd table in Figure 23-1). The intermediate table can also hold additional data about the relationship (although this is not evident the preceding figure). You can, for example, specify whether a certain location is the primary distribution point for a product.

Whenever I talk about content management entities, I use the term in the database sense as well as in the logical design sense. Entities are both categories of information for your logical design, and they are players in a data model of the constraints on your CMS. And as you can see throughout this chapter, the logical design of a CMS entails defining each entity and determining its relationships to the other entities.

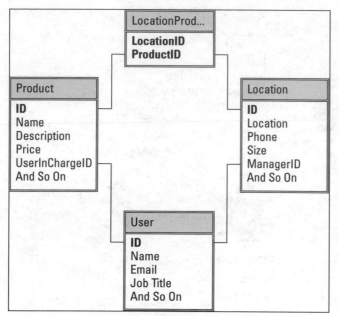

Figure 23-1: Entities and relationships in a simple database

Introducing the CMS wheel

You may recall (or, by now, you may be tired of hearing) that I define a CMS as a system that collects, manages, and publishes information and functionality. I want now to offer another definition — just as valid — that I believe can deepen your understanding of what really goes on in a CMS: A *content management system* is a *balanced interaction* between the forces of the significant entities that define it. Metadata maintains the balance.

If the entities are in balance, they form a stable and effective system for content creation and use. I envision that system as a wheel, as shown in Figure 23-2.

Note   I compress publications, templates, and personalizations together because they are all part of creating publications. However, there is a lot to know about each of these three entities, so each can stand alone as well.

At the hub of the wheel is the set of content types that you create. More than any other entity, the content types lie at the center of the system. They're the place where all the other entities come together. They're the result of all the knowledge you've gained about the other entities, and they are the resources from which you draw to provide all the system's value.

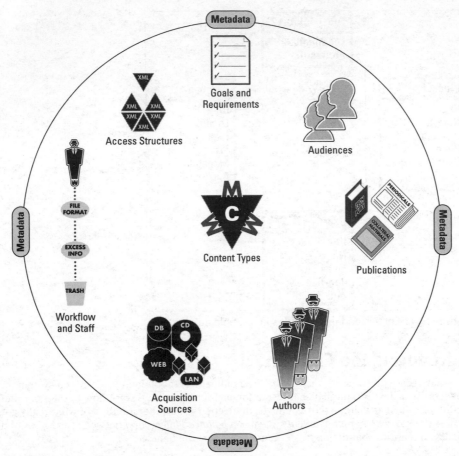

Figure 23-2: The wheel of content management

The rim of the wheel is metadata. Metadata holds the system together and gives it shape. Any decision that you make ultimately results in some change to the metadata system that you construct. Metadata and content types relate closely to one another. (I discuss metadata in detail in Chapter 24, "Working with Metadata.") The majority of your metadata is stored in the elements of the content types that you define. Content types are information or functionality chunks that you wrap in metadata. So although I place content types in the center of the wheel for simplicity, you can just as easily imagine them spanning out from the center to the rim of the wheel.

The spokes of the wheel are the major entities. Like the spokes of a wheel, these entities keep the system from collapsing or flying apart. Each spoke puts constraints on the system that tend to make it smaller and more well-defined. Each spoke also offers possibilities and additional resources to the system that tend to expand it and keep it growing. As with a wheel, if the centrifugal (outward) and centripetal (inward) forces are in balance, the system is in good shape.

From this vantage, content management is independent of the particular hardware and software from which you choose to construct the system. Instead, it's an organizational process to bring a set of competing yet collaborating forces into alignment to amass and deliver valuable content.

Lest you think that I've gone off the philosophical deep end, I can assure you that, abstruse as it may seem, the idea of content management entities, in practice, just represents a lot of good old-fashioned hard work. They're a convenient set of categories that you can use as you collect the information that you need to understand and construct your CMS.

Entities add a layer of abstraction

The traditional way to handle publications is to create a direct connection between an author and a publication. In a CMS, on the other hand, an *indirect* connection exists between author and publication. Authors create content types, and publications consume content types. Traditional publication systems don't ignore the content management entities. Rather, in traditional systems, the entities are considered implicitly; they're just part of the author's and publisher's mindsets. They are also coded directly into the process. In a traditional publication system, for example, authors know their audiences very well and write directly to them. They know how to address the audience and do so very well. In addition, the publication designers keep the audience in mind at every step as they develop publication styles and layouts.

In a CMS, the same process occurs, but it's quite explicit. Rather than residing in the minds of the authors or publication analysts, their understanding is shown in metadata values and publication templates. In other words, they make the way that they serve an audience so explicit that even a dumb computer can figure out how to serve that audience. The native knowledge that authors and publishers have is captured and expressed as metadata. *Metadata* is the language they use, however imperfectly, to say what they know about things in a way that both humans and computers can understand.

A CMS adds a layer of abstraction between the author and the audience. The author speaks indirectly to the audience through a set of well-crafted content types that he's sure can find their way "somehow" to the right person in the right form. The publication designer similarly designs indirectly. She creates publication structures that "somehow" are filled with appropriate and well-designed content.

The pros and cons here are simple. A direct connection is, well, more direct. It enables an author to see particularly and in detail what he's communicating and how. On the other hand, it's not very efficient and requires an inordinate amount of effort to create multiple or rapidly changing publications from the same content.

The compromise is also simple. Create a system where you can pour your best thinking about your audiences in all at once and then leave it to the system to accomplish the task of sorting through the details of targeting content and formatting publications. And that's exactly what the logical design of a CMS is all about — putting your best thinking in a form that's complete and simple enough for a dumb computer to begin to simulate a very intelligent process.

Goals and requirements

Goals are the business concerns that drive the need for and the major uses of a CMS. You determine these goals in conjunction with your project sponsors—the key players in the organization who support and enable the CMS project. A *goal* is something that an organization wants to accomplish. A *requirement* is something that your system must do, be, or have to meet your goals. You make goals explicit and document them in your project mandate. In my process, you gather requirements as the first step toward logical design by asking people what they think you should include in the CMS. Those people may or may not derive the requirements that they give you from the goals that you provide to them, so you may need to reconcile goals and requirements before doing a logical design.

From one standpoint, you can say that goals and requirements stand outside the CMS and provide an overall set of rules within which the CMS must live. But what if a dispute arises between a goal or requirement and one of the other entities? Which should prevail? If the answer is that the goal should always prevail, goals are indeed outside the logical design of your system. They remain constant throughout the design process. If the answer is that it depends on the dispute, goals aren't outside your design, and you must include them in your design. As part of the process, goals might vary as your design process progresses. Suppose, for example, that you discover that creating a partner Web site (a new publication) is easy given the amount of work that you already must do to create an intranet site. Your goals, however, are to serve only staff. Should you drop the idea of a partner site or widen your goals? Suppose that you're required to produce product specifications. None of the audiences that you've identified, however, is technical enough to read a product specification. Should you change the requirement or the audience divisions?

If your answer is, "It depends," or even "The goal or requirement should change," clearly you shouldn't take goals and requirements as a given but rather include them in your logical design as simply another kind of entity. To create the best CMS, you must balance goals and requirements with the other entities (audiences, authors, publications, and so on) and make tradeoffs and among them.

Tip   I have found it possible to skip gathering requirements altogether and move directly into logical design. Because your logical design uncovers more information than the usual requirements process, it can often replace that process. Especially if you have a small group of people who are not overly opinionated, skipping a formal requirements process, or rather using logical design as the requirements process, can save you a lot of trouble.

Goals and requirements differ from other entities. In order to modify goals and requirements, you must go back to your sponsors or requirements group for permission. (In contrast, it's likely that you can adjust the other entities without such permission.) But the prospect of opening up goals for discussion again after (possibly) an exhausting mandate process may not be appealing to you. Moreover, goals and requirements tie into other organizational initiatives. Changing them may have an effect beyond the CMS.

So, although goals and requirements form and change beyond the logical design process, you don't need to exclude them from the process.

Cross-Reference   You find more information about sponsors and the project mandate in Chapter 16, "Securing a Project Mandate," in the section "Techniques for Getting the Job Done."

What data do you need to capture about each goal entity? As shown in Figure 23-3, you have a distinct few pieces of information to gather.

Data elements for the goal entity are as follows:

✦ **A goal ID** that you can use so you always know what goal you're referring to, even if its name changes.

✦ **A goal name** that captures the essence of the goal in a few words.

✦ **A description** that fully elaborates the goal.

✦ **A way to measure** whether you've reached the goal.

✦ **A target value** that you want to reach for this goal (for example, number of page views, number of content types, growth of registered users, and so on).

✦ **A set of relations** to the other entities that directly affect goals: requirements, publications, audiences, and content. (The other entities also affect goals, but do so indirectly.)

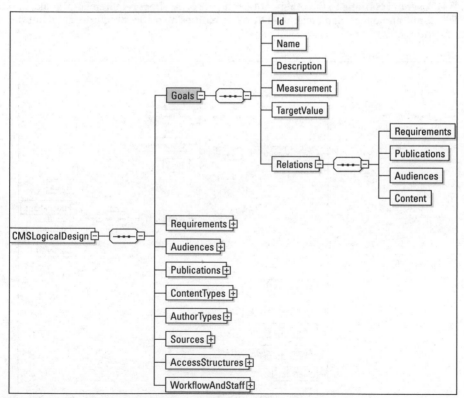

Figure 23-3: Data elements of the goal entity

CMS *requirements* are the tangible statements of what you expect to have in the CMS and what you intend to do to create the CMS. Requirements set the overall scope of your CMS.

Cross-Reference   You can find more information about requirements in Chapter 17, "Doing Requirements Gathering" "in the section "The requirements process."

Requirements can include data similar to that associated with goals, as shown in Figure 23-4.

Data elements for the requirements entity are as follows:

✦ **A requirement ID** that you can use to identify what requirement you're referring to, even if its name changes.

✦ **A requirement name** that captures the essence of the requirement in a few words.

✦ **A description** that fully elaborates the requirement.

✦ **A type** that you can use to categorize the requirements into content, publication, and system (or whatever other scheme you feel is more appropriate).

✦ **A set of relations** to the other entities that directly affect requirements: goals, publications, audiences, and content. (The other entities also affect requirements, but do so indirectly.)

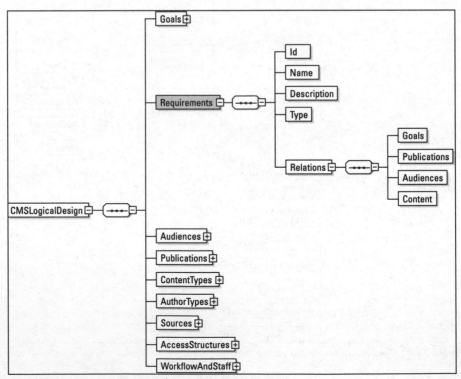

Figure 23-4: Data elements of the requirements entity

I'll Know What I Want When I See It

If you have a pet or a small child, you can probably relate to this. My pet is a bird, a cockatoo named Mr. Hellolo. He's about a foot tall, snow white, and pretty darned smart, with a fairly strong vocabulary — 10 or 15 words or so. The problem with my bird is that, while he's very vocal, he's not very articulate about expressing his needs.

Often, the best way for me to figure out what he wants is to put different things in front of him. Want a grape? No. Some corn? No. A nut — Yes!

Your business stakeholders are also pretty darned smart. But some of them are probably not used to articulating their needs in the form of system "requirements." Ask them to describe what they want in their CMS, and you're likely get blank stares. But show them what it could look like and you'll have them eating out of your hand.

Rita Warren, Zia Content (www.ziacontent.com)

I spend ample space describing the nature of both goals and requirements in other parts of the book. Here I want to describe a *goal entity* and how you may relate it to the other entities. You gather all the data that you need during your mandate and requirements-gathering processes. To make that data really work for you, however, you need to relate your goals to your requirements and other significant entities, as shown in Figure 23-5.

Be sure to cover the relationships among the audiences, content types, and publications. For each of these relationships, answer the following few questions to be sure that your system is in balance:

✦ **Which goal does it serve?** Each requirement, audience, content type, and publication ought to directly serve at least one goal of the system. Naturally, give preference to those entities that serve more than one goal. On the other hand, be very suspicious of any that serve no goal or for which you must stretch to determine a goal.

✦ **Are inconsistencies present?** Do any of the entities directly conflict with a goal? Are any in conflict with each other, given a particular goal? If your goal is to cut down support costs, for example, does a Wireless Application Protocol (WAP) version of your Web site drive costs up? If so, which is more important?

✦ **How can you track and measure your goals?** Extend your goal-measurement criteria to the other entities to give more substance and detail to the measurements. If you need to drive up the conversion rate (the percentage of those interested who ultimately buy) from 10 to 15 percent, for example, you determine from which audiences the increase must come. Which content types are key? Through which publications does the increase occur?

In addition to correlating entity by entity, look at the entire system. Do the most important goals get the most coverage in the other entities? Do the goals suggest entities that you never thought to include before? Do the entities compel you to revisit and perhaps modify your goals or, especially, your success metrics? Overall, does serving these audiences, this content, or these publication channels seem to ensure that your organization is going to see the benefits that you promise in the goals?

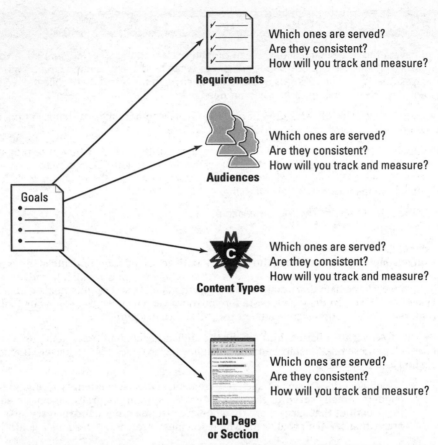

Requirements

Which ones are served?
Are they consistent?
How will you track and measure?

Audiences

Which ones are served?
Are they consistent?
How will you track and measure?

Content Types

Which ones are served?
Are they consistent?
How will you track and measure?

Goals

Pub Page
or Section

Which ones are served?
Are they consistent?
How will you track and measure?

Figure 23-5: Goals relate most directly to requirements, audiences, content types, and publications.

Tip

You can carry out a similar analysis of your sponsors to determine how much *effective* sponsor support you actually have. Doing this analysis early in a project can help you make sure your boosters are literally on the same page or, conversely, whether the sponsors are a little too hazy on the implications of their sponsorship to effectively help the project. To do this analysis, bring your sponsors into the picture as an entity and then cross-analyze them with project goals, requirements, publications, and content types. The questions to ask are how well the sponsors understand and support each of these other entities.

Audiences

Audience entities contain information on the constituencies to which the CMS provides content. The basic information to collect on your audiences is shown in Figure 23-6.

✦ **Identification,** including an ID and name for each audience group.

✦ **A description** that fully elaborates the audience.

✦ **Demographics,** which describe the personal data and habits of the audience.

✦ **Attitudes,** which tell you what responses to expect from the audience.

✦ **A value proposition,** which states why you believe that you are delivering value to the audience equal to what your organization wants from them.

✦ **Uses**, which describe for what purposes and how often you expect this audience to use your publications.

✦ **A set of relations** to the other entities that directly affect this entity: goals, requirements, publications, authors, content, and sources. (The other entities also affect this entity, but do so indirectly.)

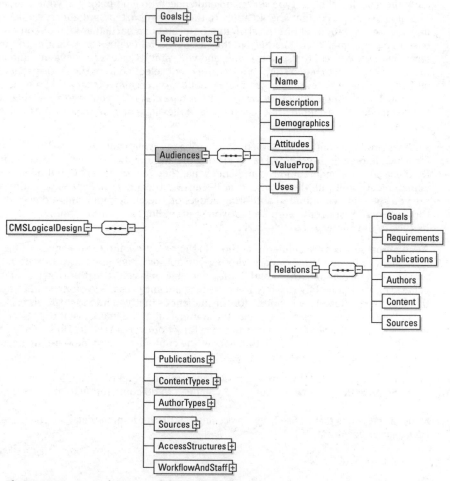

Figure 23-6: Data elements of the audiences entity

As you may expect, audiences relate in some way to all CM entities. Their most important relationships, however, can be mapped to the following CM entities, as shown in Figure 23-7

✦ **Goals** and **requirements** relate to audiences as I describe in the section "Goals and Requirements," earlier in this chapter.

✦ **Publications** have an obvious relation to audiences. You must decide what the audience is for each publication. Then you need to determine what structure and "format your audiences expect in a publication such as yours and what other publications they're likely to compare yours to. In addition, you must work hard to determine exactly how to personalize a publication for the various audiences that it's to serve.

✦ **Content types** relate to audiences in that you can target your content types to particular audiences. If a content type serves no audience, it doesn't belong in your system. The most (or best) content should apply to the most important audiences. Audiences may have expectations about the structure or format of a particular kind of content based on past experience. In addition, they assign certain values or priorities to the different kinds of content that you provide, and you want to assess these values and priorities beforehand to understand how to order and select content types for particular audiences. Finally, determine how to represent the different audiences that a content type must serve in the structure of the content type class. Do you need special content type elements, for example, that recast some of the element's content for particular audiences?

✦ **Authors** produce content for audiences. Figuring out which authors are going to write for which audiences is essential (as is making the authors aware of what you decide). Do these authors understand the audiences that they're writing for? Can the authors communicate well with their audiences? Because authoring is an expensive endeavor, are you spending your limited authoring budget on the most important audiences? Do the audiences respect the authors that you're providing? Do your authors have credibility with the audiences they're writing for?

✦ **Acquisition sources** are similar to authors in their relationship to audiences. In fact, an audience may not know or care whether you author or acquire the information that you show them. On the other hand, if they perceive that you're just borrowing a lot of generic information, they're likely to value it significantly less. So you must determine the perceived value of each source for the audiences that you intend it to serve. Does an audience respond better if you cite the source name or if you leave it out? How close is the original audience for a source to those for whom you intend it? Do you need to change (reword, add, delete) anything about the content to accommodate the needs and characteristics of your audiences?

Overall, always ask yourself, "How are my audiences likely to perceive this information?" If you ever come up with the answer, "Not well," you need to do some rethinking.

Cross-Reference   Many of the issues that I raise in the preceding list, I cover in more detail in Chapter 25, "Cataloging Audiences."

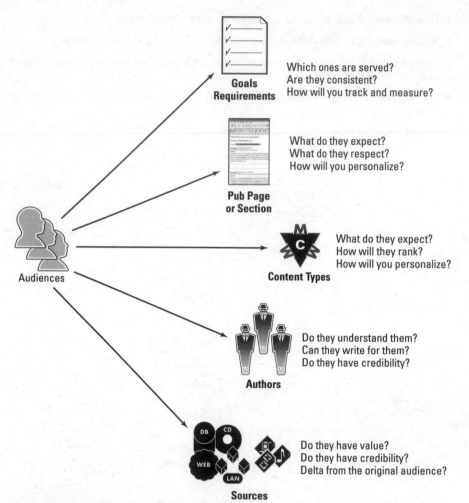

Which ones are served?
Are they consistent?
How will you track and measure?

Goals Requirements

What do they expect?
What do they respect?
How will you personalize?

Pub Page or Section

What do they expect?
How will they rank?
How will you personalize?

Content Types

Do they understand them?
Can they write for them?
Do they have credibility?

Authors

Do they have value?
Do they have credibility?
Delta from the original audience?

Sources

Audiences

Figure 23-7: Audiences relate in a big way to most of the major content management entities.

Publications

Publication entities contain information about the publications that you want to create, how you plan to personalize them, and how you're going to create them from the CMS by using templates, as shown in Figure 23-8.

The basic information that you must capture about publications is as follows:

✦ **Identification**, including an ID and name for each audience group.

✦ **A description** that fully defines the intended audience for the publication.

✦ **Purpose,** which is the basic reason why the publication is important to your organization and to its audiences.

✦ **Format**, the medium in which the publication will be delivered, and its basic layout and design.

✦ **Templates**, which specify how the publication is built.

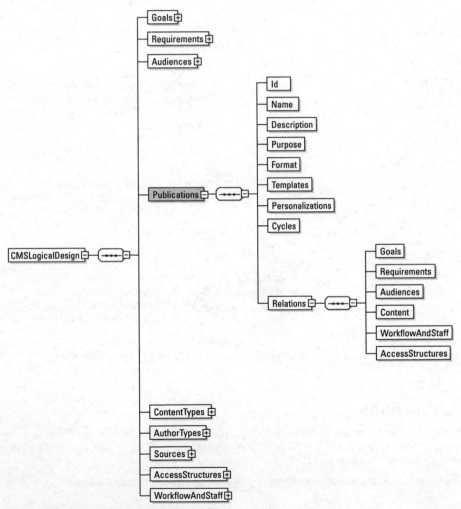

Figure 23-8: Data elements of the publications entity

✦ **Personalizations**, which match content types and audiences together in the context of a particular publication.

✦ **Cycles**, the schedules with which the publication will be released or updated.

✦ **A set of relations** to the other entities that directly affect this entity: goals, requirements, audiences, content, workflow and staff, and access structures. (The other entities also affect this entity, but do so indirectly.)

Note   It may seem strange to you that I don't cite a relationship between authors and publications. Don't authors create publications? In addition, a relationship is missing between acquisition sources and publications. In a CMS, I prefer to think of these relationships as indirect. Authors and sources produce content of various types, and that content is later laid into your publications. In addition, publications are related to authors through audiences. Authors write for audiences, and publications are directed at audiences. All of this is not to say that authors and sources are not related to publications, but rather that their relationship is covered by the mutual relationships they have with other entities.

In addition to collecting all this information about publications, you must relate the publication entities that you create to the other entities that make up your system, as the following list describes (see Figure 23-9):

✦ **Goals** and **requirements** relate to publications as I describe in the section "Goals and Requirements," earlier in this chapter. To summarize, specific publications must meet requirements and help fulfill certain goals.

✦ **Audiences** relate to publications as I describe in the section "Audiences," earlier in this chapter. Obviously, every publication has an audience or set of audiences to which you direct it.

✦ **Content types** must find their way into publications via content type templates, which you embed within publication templates. Part of working through the templates of your system is to chart precisely how to format and include each content type on each page where it's to appear. In particular, for each publication page, you must figure out which content types to include, how to format these content types, and which content type elements to display.

✦ **Workflow and staff** are entities that you must determine for each publication that you create. You may need any number of workflows. In particular, each distinct cycle you discovered must have a workflow. In addition, you must figure out what sorts of people and how much time you need to complete the tasks involved in creating and distributing each publication.

✦ **Access structures** are another entity that you must determine for each publication. You must map between the general access structures that you store in the CMS repository and the navigation that you produce to move users through the publication. In particular, after you create a publication, you need to decide how to transform the hierarchy, indexes, cross-references, and sequences that apply to content type in the repository into page or section navigation.

Cross-Reference   The full story on publications is in Chapter 26, "Designing Publications."

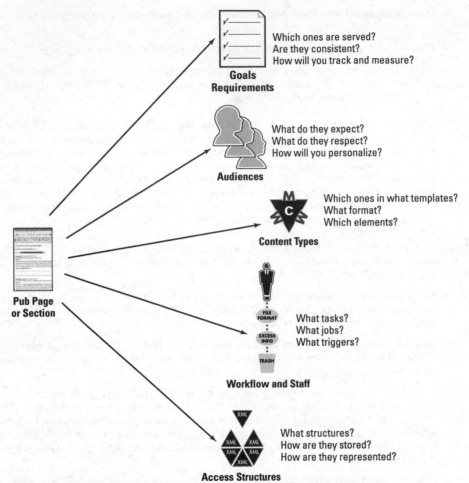

Figure 23-9: Publications relate directly to most of the other entities.

Content types

Content type entities contain information about all the content that you collect and manage. The main areas of information that content type entities contain are shown in Figure 23-10.

The basic information that you must capture about content types includes the following:

✦ **Identification,** including the names, IDs, and overall priorities of the types in your system.

✦ **A description** that defines the content type.

✦ **Quantities**, specifically how many of each type of content type you intend to gather initially and over time.

✦ **Elements**, including the way to divide the information inside content types and what metadata to add to each type.

✦ **A set of relations** to the other entities that directly affect this entity, specifically, all of them.

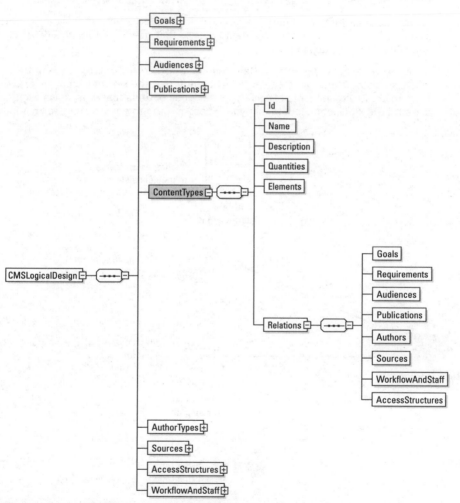

Figure 23-10: Data elements of the content types entity

As you may suspect, content types relate in a major way to all the other entities. Figure 23-11 shows the relationships that content types have with the following CM entities:

✦ **Goals and requirements** relate to content types as I describe in the section "Goals and Requirements," earlier in this chapter. In essence, the content types must contain required information that helps you reach your goals.

✦ **Audiences** relate to content types as I describe in the section "Audiences," earlier in this chapter. You must target content types to particular audiences.

✦ **Publications** relate to content types as I describe in the section "Publications," earlier in this chapter. You must create content types so that they're automatically selected and laid into your publications.

✦ **Authors** create components of certain content types. To relate these two entities, you assess which authors create which content types, the rate at which you expect them to create components of each type, the kinds of tools that you expect them to use, and the kinds of metadata that you expect authors to enter as they're creating.

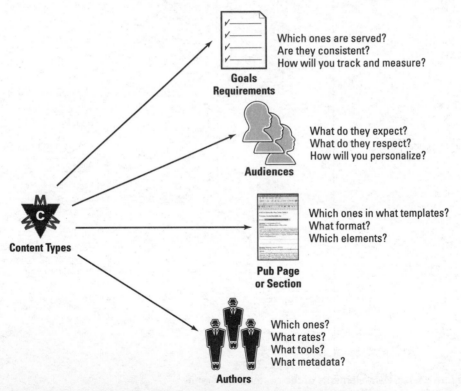

Figure 23-11: The relationships between content types and four CM entities

Figure 23-12 shows the relationships that content types have with the other CM entities:

✦ **Acquisition sources** also create components of particular content types. So, for authors, you must figure out which sources create which content types and at what rate. In addition, you assess how well marked the content is in each source (that is, can you get a program to pull out content automatically?). Finally, you must assess and account for any editorial or metatorial changes to be made to each source to yield its target content types.

✦ **Workflow and staffing** are entities that you must determine for the creation and subsequent life cycle of each content type. You must arrive at a set of tasks, jobs, and triggers that you can use to manage the creation, maintenance, publishing, and eventual retirement of each content type.

✦ **Access structures** relate to content types in a deceptively simple way. Access structures often become metadata elements and values in a content type. Your content types may have an element that you call *keywords*, for example, which includes the set of index terms under which you index that content type. Assigning a keywords element to a content type is the easy part. Filling in the keywords for thousands of components of that type is the hard part. In addition, you must figure out how to store your various access structures in the CMS repository and display them in its interface.

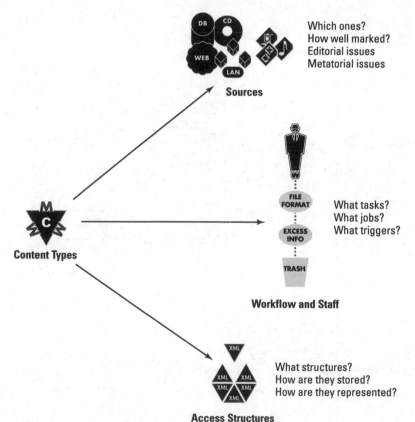

Figure 23-12: The relationships between content types and the other three CM entities

Cross-Reference   I describe content types more completely in Chapter 27, "Designing Content Types."

Authors

An *author entity* describes one or more people who share enough in common (namely, everyone in it creates the same kind of content, uses the same tools, or has the same relation to the core CMS group) that you can treat such people as a group — or, as I refer to it, as an *author type*. An author type may share more than one of these traits (or, at least, you hope so). The point of creating author entities is so that you can work in the same way with a group of people rather than with individuals.

Figure 23-13 shows the kinds of information you need to find out about your author entities.

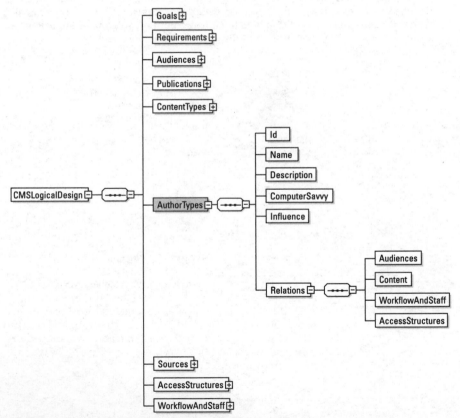

Figure 23-13: Data elements of the author types entity

The basic information that you must capture about authors is as follows:

✦ **Identification**, including a unique ID and a name for each group.

✦ **Description** of the author type.

✦ **Level of computer savvy,** which determines what sorts of tools they are willing and able to use to author content.

✦ **Your influence** over them. To work effectively with a group of authors, you should understand how the group relates to your team and its goals. You may hire authors to create content; they may simply contribute out of kindness; or you may have any other relationship with them. Their savvy and your influence combine to suggest a plausible way to approach each author type.

✦ **A set of relations** to the other entities that directly affect this entity: audiences, content, workflow and staff, and access structures. (The other entities also affect this entity, but do so indirectly.)

Cross-Reference You find much more information about authors in Chapter 28, "Accounting for Authors."

Although authors relate indirectly to all the other entities, they have a major and direct relationship to only a few entities, as shown in Figure 23-14.

The lack of direct relationships is, as you may expect, because a CMS adds a layer of abstraction between creation and publishing. Authors put their energy into creating content types with a given structure that become of value to an audience. The system takes care of the rest. Authors relate to the entities shown in Figure 23-14 as follows:

✦ **Audiences** relate to authors as I describe in the section "Audiences," earlier in this chapter. Authors create with one or more audiences firmly in mind.

✦ **Content types** relate to authors as I describe in the section "Content types," earlier in this chapter. Authors create content as components of a particular type rather than as standalone documents.

✦ **Workflow** relates to authors as you may expect. Authors create within the constraints put on them by your workflows. The relationship between authors and workflow is the only one that most people discuss as workflow. Author workflows are also the ones most well thought through in CMS products. Authors, of course, must follow a set staging of their content from creation through review and into production. But workflows can associate with every entity. Publication workflows, for example, guide the creation and deployment of Web sites. Content type workflows determine when you need to archive and review components of particular content types.

✦ **Access structures** relate to authors in that authors may need to apply an access structure to content as they create it. For example, an author may need to apply keywords or add components to a hierarchy as they create them.

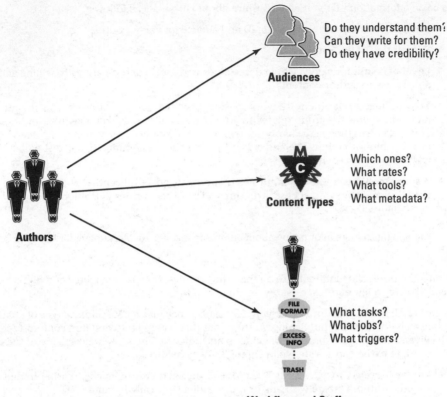

Do they understand them?
Can they write for them?
Do they have credibility?

Audiences

Which ones?
What rates?
What tools?
What metadata?

Content Types

What tasks?
What jobs?
What triggers?

Workflow and Staff

Authors

Figure 23-14: Authors relate directly to only three of the other entities.

Acquisition sources

Acquisition source entities describe a single kind of preexisting content that feeds into the system. You may tap the source once at startup or consistently over time as the CMS runs. You need to collect the information about your acquisition source entities shown in Figure 23-15.

The basic information that you must capture about sources is as follows:

✦ **Identification,** including a unique ID and name for each source.

✦ **Description** of the source

✦ **Quantities,** including the number of components the source will yield at the startup of your system and over time.

✦ **Source owner information,** including the person in charge of the acquisition source, the agreement you reach with her, and the way that you get information from her.

✦ **Connection to the source,** including how source files will be delivered or how you will retrieve them from a remote source.

✦ **A set of relations** to the other entities that directly affect this entity: audiences, content, workflow and staff, and access structures. (The other entities also affect this entity, but do so indirectly.)

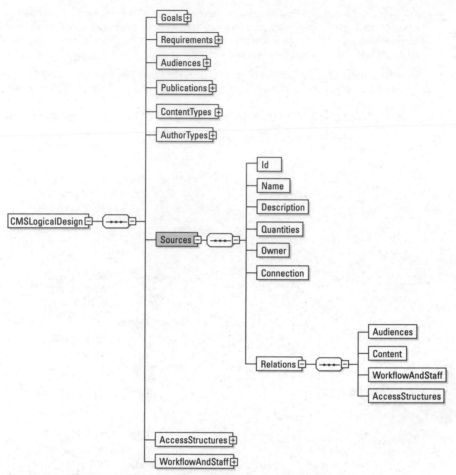

Figure 23-15: Data elements of the acquisition sources entity

Like authors, acquisition sources have major relationships only to a few entities, as shown in Figure 23-16.

Content types insulate acquisition sources (as they do authors) from most of the other entities. After the source transforms into content types with a complete set of well-produced elements, its job is done. The content types then enter into relationships with the structures and publications of the wider CMS, as follows:

✦ **Audiences** relate to acquisition sources as I describe in the section "Audiences," earlier in this chapter. You must make sure that the source is appropriate to your audiences or that you can change it to make it so.

✦ **Content types** relate to acquisition sources as I describe in the section "Content types," earlier in this chapter. You must figure out how to chop each source into components of various types and how to recognize the individual elements that you have designed for each type that the source will give rise to.

✦ **Workflow** can be applied to acquisition sources prior to the creation of the CMS. A conversion team, for example, may perform an extensive set of staged tasks on the source before anyone logs any content into the CMS repository. I don't mean here that the CMS workflow tools can't extend into the conversion process—just that they probably don't.

✦ **Access structures** may be derived from a source. For example, you might build an author index structure from the names of all the authors that you pull out of a source file.

Cross-Reference Chapter 29, "Accounting for Acquisition Sources," contains the full story on acquisition sources.

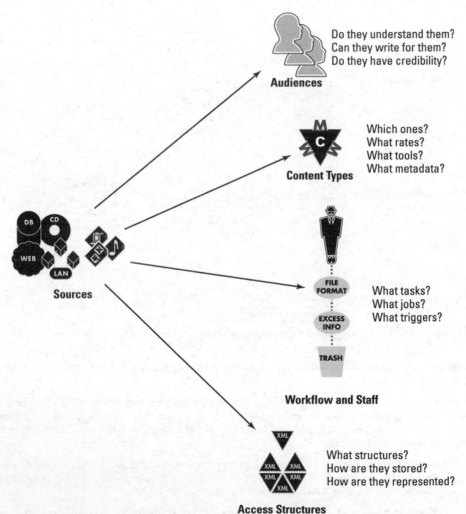

Audiences

Do they understand them?
Can they write for them?
Do they have credibility?

Content Types

Which ones?
What rates?
What tools?
What metadata?

Sources

File Format
Excess Info
Trash

What tasks?
What jobs?
What triggers?

Workflow and Staff

Access Structures

What structures?
How are they stored?
How are they represented?

Figure 23-16: Sources relate most directly to audiences, content types, workflows, and access structures.

Access structures

An *access structure* relates content types or publication pages to each other or to an external set of concepts that can be used to get to a particular content type.

The types of access structures are as follows:

✦ Hierarchies (outlines)

✦ Indexes (keywords)

✦ Cross-references (links)

✦ Sequences (next and previous)

An *access structure entity* is a set of data about the structure and how you intend to create it. The entity includes the kind of data shown in Figure 23-17.

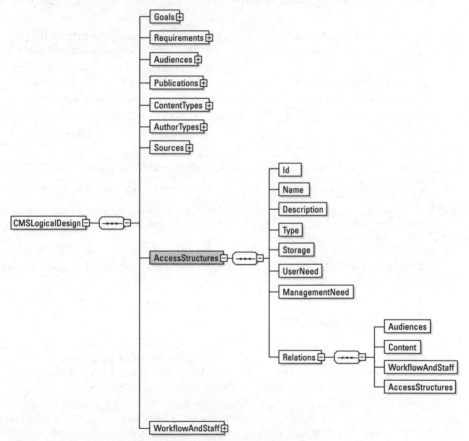

Figure 23-17: Data elements of the access structures entity

The basic information that you must capture about access structures is as follows:

✦ **Identification,** which is the name, type, and a unique ID for the structure.

✦ **Description** of the access structure.

✦ **Type,** which is one of the four types in the preceding list.

✦ **Storage,** which describes how and where the structure is contained (in a database table, as a content type element, in a text file, and so on).

✦ **User need,** which describes the ways in which this access structure will help audiences find content.

✦ **Management need,** which describes the ways in which this access structure will help manage content.

✦ **A set of relations** to the other entities that directly affect this entity: audiences, content, workflow and staff, and access structures. (The other entities also affect this entity, but do so indirectly.)

Access structures apply to content types in the CMS repository and publications that the CMS produces as well as to the authors and sources that may populate them, as shown in Figure 23-18.

✦ **Content types** relate to access structures as I describe in the section "Content types," earlier in this chapter. In the case of content types, access structures become metadata.

✦ **Publications** relate to access structures as I describe in the section "Audiences," earlier in this chapter. In the case of publications, access structures become navigation for finding and moving to the content that you want to view.

✦ **Authors,** as noted in the section, "Authors," earlier in the chapter.

✦ **Sources,** as noted in the section "Acquisition Sources," earlier in the chapter.

In either case, you must decide what structures to support, how you intend to store them in the CMS repository (or perhaps in publication templates), and how to represent them to the user so that he can best access content.

Cross-Reference   Chapter 30, "Designing Content Access Structures," provides the complete scoop on access structures.

Workflow and staffing

A *workflow*, as I present it in this book, is a sequence of steps, each having a task that an actor (a staff member or automated process) performs on some object (a component or other part of the CMS). Workflow is triggered by some event. A *workflow entity* is a collection of data that specifies the steps, actors, objects, and triggers for a particular workflow.

As Figure 23-19 shows, the information model behind a workflow or staff entity is a bit more complex than the others. Workflows involve steps that, in turn, require you to collect certain kinds of information. Similarly, staff entities involve tasks which themselves have information to be collected:

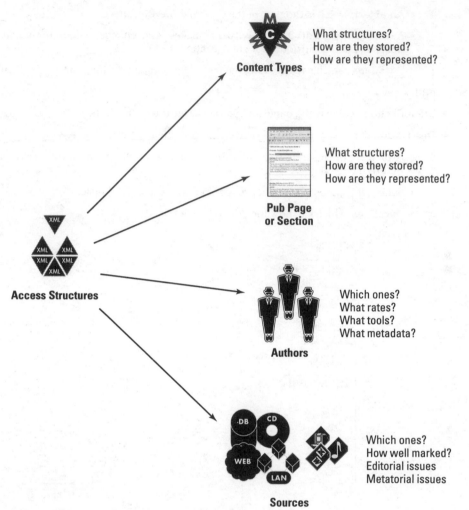

Figure 23-18: Content types, publications, authors, and sources relate to access structures.

Workflows have:

✦ **Identification,** which is the name and unique ID for the workflow.

✦ **Description** of the workflow.

✦ **Steps,** which are the sequenced stages of the workflow. Steps in turn have:

• **An actor,** which is a staff member who performs the tasks as part of her job, or an automated process (for example a conversion script) that handles the task.

• **A trigger,** which is an event that signals that the step is to begin.

- **An object,** which is the part of the CMS that the step affects.

- **A task,** which is a discrete activity that makes some change to content, publications, or the CMS structure or configuration.

- **Durations,** which say how long the task will take and how long the step will take.

Staff entities have:

✦ **Identification,** which is the name and unique ID for the staff member.

✦ **Description** of the staff member — usually his job title and basic duties.

✦ **Tasks,** which are the discrete parts of a staff member's job that he performs repeatedly. Tasks in turn have:

- **Skills,** which are talents that are required to complete the task.

- **Durations,** which say how long the task will take.

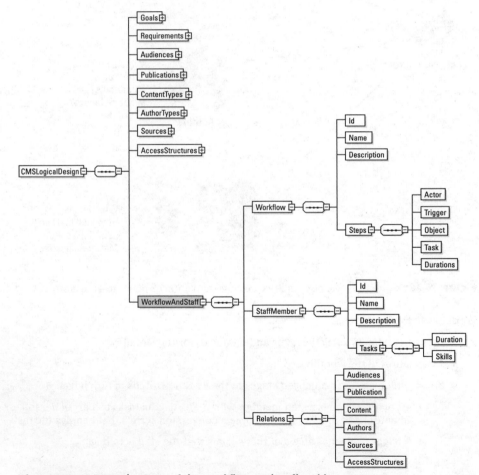

Figure 23-19: Data elements of the workflow and staff entities

Both workflows and staff entities have:

✦ **A set of relations** to the other entities that directly affect this entity: audiences, publications, content, authors, sources, and access structures.

From this vantage, you can see why I group both workflow and staff into the same general entity—they both are derived from tasks. Workflows are tasks strung out into processes that may involve one or more staff people. Staff members perform one or more tasks based on their skills. I could have just as easily created a task entity, but workflow and staffing are really what you must determine for your CMS, so I broke the basic task entity into these two related entities.

Cross-Reference I present the complete model for workflow in Chapter 33, "Designing Workflow and Staffing Models."

Workflows relate to all the other entities that can serve as objects, as shown in Figure 23-20.

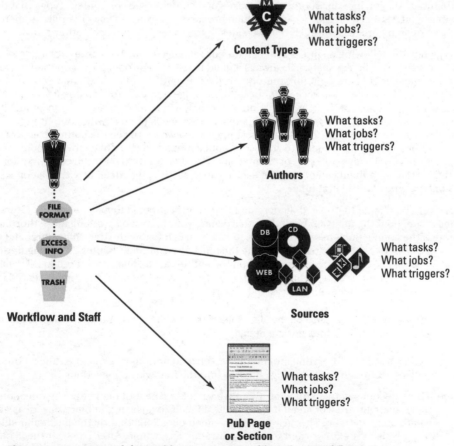

Figure 23-20: Many of the entities can serve as objects in a workflow.

The relationship between a workflow entity and any other entity is always the same. The other entity serves as the object that a workflow step changes in some way. For each step and object, you must also arrive at a task, a trigger, and an actor who is to complete the task.

I discuss the particulars of the relationship between workflow and the other entities in the sections earlier in this chapter that discuss each entity (authors, content types, and so on).

Think, Plan, Integrate

In this chapter, I give you an overview of the entities that I consider most central to the design of a CMS. In addition, I hope you can see that the relationships among these entities are as important as the entities themselves in designing a system. The chapters that follow go into greater detail about each entity.

As you can probably already guess, logical design involves a sort of "chicken and egg" problem. Which comes first? Publications or the content types that create them? Do you design your access structures around your content types or your content types around your access structures? Do you look for sources that make good content types or content types that the sources you want can create? As with all such processes, no single answer is right — there is only an ongoing process in which the two sides of the issue push on each other.

I sequence the following chapters as much for convenience as for their true order. I do believe that an audience analysis is always a good first step. For one thing, you then have a set of audiences that are right for your organization, regardless of the CMS that you create. For another thing, the audiences are your ultimate judges, so you need to do all your planning with a good idea of them in your mind. After that, where to start and how to sequence your analyses are really up to you. My personal preference is to start with content types. As the center of the system, they're the best place from which to see the entire structure. Most other people I know prefer to start with publications and work back toward content types. Publications give you a lot of tangible and visual material to start the conversation with; starting with them can prove a lot easier, especially if you're dealing with the concept of content types for the first time.

However you decide to proceed, understand that your best bet is to make a series of iterations throughout the analysis, each time sharpening your focus and working more thoroughly through the connections between entities. In fact, you can follow the iterative approach I've used in this book. The first iteration can be the one I presented in Chapter 22, "Designing a CMS Simply." The next iteration can focus on the entities at the level presented in this chapter. The final iteration can account for all the facets and relationships that are presented for the entities in the remaining chapters in this part.

Cross-Reference   I go into much more detail on the idea of iterations in Chapter 18, "Doing Logical Design," in the section "Iterating through your design."

To give you a head start iterating around the wheel of content management entities, I break each analysis section in the following chapters into the following subsections:

✦ **Think** sections get you thinking about a particular aspect of planning. The questions in these sections are working if they're really difficult to answer and blur your ideas about what you need to do. They ask you open-ended questions that tie the particular subject of analysis to the others and to the organization as a whole. After you beat these questions to death, you're ready to start planning.

✦ **Plan** sections detail the specific data that you must collect. The questions in these sections are the deliverable analysis that you need to do. I elaborate extensively on the lists which spell out the content of each entity in these Plan sections.

✦ **Integrate** sections help you to relate one area of analysis to the others. The questions in these sections are working if they force you to rethink assumptions and come to better answers in Plan sections. Many of the relationships that I present in this chapter I cover again in more detail in the Integrate sections.

Summary

You can think of a CMS as a set of software programs running on a set of computers, or you can think of a CMS as a dynamic balance of influential entities in an organization. If you're smart, you think of a CMS in both ways. As a set of interacting entities, a CMS balances the following elements:

✦ The goals of the system against the realistic means by which you can accomplish those goals.

✦ The original sources of content (authors and acquisition sources) against the content types that they must create.

✦ The publications that you want to create against the content types that you have available to create them and the audiences that have an interest in them.

✦ The staff and processes (workflows) that you can manage to put together against the labor and processing needs of other entities.

✦ The access structures that you can manage to create and maintain against the navigation that your publications need and the accessibility that you want in your CMS repository.

In the next chapter, I deal directly with the thing that holds this balance together — metadata.

✦   ✦   ✦

Working with Metadata

*M*etadata are the small snippets of information (or data) that you attach to content so that you can more easily catalog, store, and retrieve it. A coherent system of metadata draws diverse kinds of content into a coherent scheme in which content components relate to each other as well as to the collection, management, and publishing systems that you devise.

In this chapter, I dive into the concept of metadata, discussing its meaning, types, and uses.

What Is Metadata?

More than anything else, the metadata system behind a CMS is what defines the system. The set of names and relationships that a metatorial framework contains are the skeleton on which you hang the content. Without this structure, the content is as formless and flaccid as a body without bones.

What does meta mean?

The word *meta* itself has no meaning except (according to the *Oxford English Dictionary*) as a column that marks the boundary of a circus. In more general usage, *meta* is a *prefix*. It modifies the meaning of the words that it precedes.

Merriam-Webster OnLine (at www.m-w.com) states that, as a prefix, *meta* means the following:

✦ Occurring later than or in succession to.

✦ Situated behind or beyond.

✦ Change or transformation.

✦ Later or more highly organized or specialized form of.

✦ More comprehensive or transcending.

All these definitions give depth to the idea of meta that I have in mind in this book. Meta-things come after the things themselves to add context and organization to them. They go beyond the things themselves to a higher level of abstraction, where you see the things in a different light.

I first became enamored by the concept of meta while reading Douglas Hofstadter's book, *Godel, Escher, Bach: An Eternal Golden Braid*. This wonderful work uses meta as one of its most central and subtle threads.

In the following dialog, Achilles (a character Hofstadter borrowed from the Greek philosopher Zeno) meets GOD, who turns out to be a never-ending hierarchy of genies:

Achilles: Tell me, Mr. Genie — what is a meta-wish?

Genie: It's simply a wish about wishes. I am not allowed to grant meta-wishes. It's only in my purview to grant plain ordinary wishes, such as wishing for ten bottles of beer, to have Helen of Troy on a blanket, or to have an all-expense-paid weekend for two at the Copacabana. You know — simple things like that. But meta-wishes I cannot grant, GOD won't permit me to.

You must read the book to find out exactly who GOD is and get Hofstadter's deep and wide view of metaphenomena. For the present, I need take only one word out of his work — *about*.

To my mind, the best way to understand the prefix *meta* is to substitute the word *about*. The word *metadialog*, for example, is a dialog about a dialog. A *metatorial* (not my usage of this word, but another one) is an editorial opinion about editorial opinions. *Metadata* is data about data.

The word *about* captures the large majority of the dictionary definitions of meta. If you're talking about a thing, you must be coming after the thing, and you must be speaking at a transcending or higher level of organization than that of the thing itself. Most important, by talking about the thing, you're changing its meaning. My recent favorite, which I use on every new kid I meet, is a statement that is its own metastatement: "Everything that I say is a lie!"

Note   You may be familiar with the word *meta* from HTML where you have a <META> tag. This tag is now a catch-all for any information that people want to put in it, but its intended use is quite consistent with its name. You're supposed to use the <META> tag to list information *about* the HTML file.

What does metadata mean?

Just saying that *metadata* is *data about data* isn't much of a description. The term is in wide enough usage these days to have a fuller definition.

You can get a fair feeling for how people use the word by looking at the following few sentences from the home page of the Metadata Coalition at www.mdcinfo.com/:

> The Coalition allies software vendors and users with a common purpose of driving forward the definition, implementation, and ongoing evolution of a metadata interchange format standard and its support mechanisms. The need for such standards arises as metadata, or the information about the enterprise data emerges as a critical element in effective data management. Different tools, including data warehousing, distributed client/server computing, databases (relational, OLAP, OLTP...), integrated enterprise-wide applications, etc... must be able to cooperate and make use of metadata generated by each other.

This excerpt, one among many that you can find on the Web, shows the main characteristics of metadata as people most commonly use the term. The following list describes those characteristics:

✦ **Sharing:** Metadata provides the capability to share data across applications. By employing data that describes the use and meaning of the data that it surrounds, one system can interpret and translate the data that it receives from another. In a content management context, metadata enables publications that each require a somewhat different form of the same data to draw from a common repository.

✦ **Standards:** Metadata is a set of standards that groups agree to for information definitions. Standards, which are the basis of any kind of data sharing, bring the possibility of large-scale efficiencies in information interchange among groups that don't even know one another. In the content management context, the standards may be mostly internal, but they serve the same purpose. Standards ensure that others can automatically reuse the efforts of one person or group if they all follow the same standards.

✦ **A focus on databases:** The main reason for the interest in metadata, today, is the sharing and standards behind standard database applications. Data warehousing and interapplication data transfer are huge concerns for organizations with an enormous amount of data (trapped in databases and other files) that no one can interpret except by using whatever application created the data.

✦ **An awareness of the wider world:** Today, metadata is mostly used in data systems. A vague but growing understanding exists, however, that metadata isn't just for data. The previous quote from the Metadata Coalition mentions "integrated enterprise-wide applications." A CMS is an integrated enterprise-wide application. Metadata is critical, not only to allow the CMS to integrate with other enterprise data sources, but also to enable the CMS to unify and make the best automated use of the information and functionality that it manages.

Note   By the way, Metadata, apparently, is a registered trademark of the Metadata Company, headquartered in Long Beach, California (and at www.metadata.com on the Web).

Merging this information with the definition of the prefix *meta* can give you a deeper understanding of what metadata is.

First, metadata is what you need other than the data itself to understand and use that data. Metadata acts as the instructions that come with the data. In addition, metadata is what isn't there if you look at the data itself. Metadata exists in addition to or after the data. It adds context and a wider interpretation to the data. Consider, for example, the following piece of content that has no metadata:

```
Cinder Riley is the anti-Cinderella. She wants nothing to do
with fame and riches and longs to run away with a pauper...
```

Without any other information surrounding this content, it is hard to know what to make of it or what you would use it for. By adding some metadata, however, its meaning and use become clear, as the following table shows.

Metadata Element	Value
Author	Claire Taylor
Publication date	January 1968
Source	Plays Magazine
Reviewer	Bernard Lewis
Audience	Children, primary school teachers, and librarians
Title	The Adventures of Cinder Riley
Review	Cinder Riley is the anti-Cinderella. She wants nothing to do with fame and riches and longs to run away with a pauper.

Now you can tell that the content is a review of a play called "The Adventures of Cinder Riley." All that extra information isn't the content; it surrounds the content and tells you *about* it. As I said, the chunk of text alone is hard to make use of. But add metadata and the chunk becomes part of a wider system of shared attributes that help to store, locate, and present it in the context of the other content that you have.

The metadata isn't the content. I make this claim because it exists apart from the content. Contrast the preceding table with the following representation of the same basic information:

In January 1968, Claire Taylor published "The Adventures of Cinder Riley" in *Plays Magazine*. Bernard Lewis provided this review of the play, which is of most interest to children, primary school teachers, and librarians. Cinder Riley is the anti-Cinderella. She wants nothing to do with fame and riches and longs to run away with a pauper...

In the table form, *Claire Taylor* is a piece of metadata. In the paragraph form, it's not. What makes *Claire Taylor* metadata is not only the fact that it's descriptive of some other content, but also that it's separate from that content. As a content manager, you choose what information to separate from content and make into metadata and what remains part of the content. This depends, of course, on how you need to use each chunk of information. This distinction is a practical one, not a philosophical one. If you use the words *Claire Taylor* as metadata because you want to be able to tag content as being authored by Claire Taylor, you must somehow name and separate the expression so that a computer can find it and use it to categorize the content that it surrounds.

As a final point, notice that putting metadata in a table is not the only way to extract it from the content that it surrounds. The following paragraph, for example, uses XML tags to distinguish metadata from the content it's embedded in:

In < PublicationDate>January 1968</ PublicationDate>, <Author>Claire Taylor</Author> published <Title>The Adventures of Cinder Riley</Title> in <Source>Plays Magazine </Source>. <Reviewer>Bernard Lewis</Reviewer> provided this review of the play, which is of most interest to <Audience>children, primary school teachers, and librarians</Audience>. <Review>Cinder Riley is the anti-Cinderella. She wants nothing to do with fame and riches and longs to run away with a pauper...</Review>

So, metadata describes content for you. No intrinsic difference exists between metadata and content. You make the distinction by somehow tagging some piece of information as metadata. Often when you make a piece of information into metadata, you remove it from the content it was originally part of (for example, by putting it in a database). However, as the preceding example indicates, you do not have to remove the information to make it metadata. The tag can sit right within the content. Although it can be confusing, this situation is not unusual. Combine your desire to describe content (that is, to create metadata) with your desire to avoid typing things twice and you end up with metadata that is embedded in its content and that serves both as metadata and as content. Consider it job security that one of the most important concepts of content management is so difficult for the average person to understand.

What does metatorial mean?

Over the years during which I've been building electronic publication systems, I've hit again and again on the problem of metadata. At first, I didn't think of metadata as a problem unto itself. Rather, I confronted related issues such as, "How do I know what content is ready for an audience to see?" or, more widely, "How do I pack a bunch of data in with the content, knowing that this data isn't going to appear but that I need it to manage the production and display of the content?" Over time, I began to standardize the ways that I dealt with this "bunch of data" so that it became easier and easier to find, parse, and manipulate. For some time, I used a *dot* system, which means each line of the file that I was processing began with a period and the name of the data field. (See Chapter 29, "Accounting for Acquisition Sources," in the section "Syndicated content," for an example of a *dot* system.) This system of standardized tagging made it easy to isolate metadata from the information it surrounded and to use it for my purposes (usually that meant loading it into database fields). At about the same time (I would guess about 1996), the term *metadata* became fashionable in the electronic publications arena as a way to describe "data about data."

As is apt to happen, over time I began to notice some patterns, as the following list describes:

✦ **Metadata consistently fell into a few distinct categories.** These categories include *navigational* (TOC, index, cross reference, and browse), *management* (author, create date, last edit, and so on), *content type*, *internal structure* (title, abstract, body, and so on), and *inclusion* (add media here, add a banner here, add standard text here, and so on).

✦ **Without a rigorous consistency and careful attention, metadata becomes useless.** What good is sometimes including a chunk of pre-authored text and sometimes typing it in from scratch? How useful is a TOC if every submitter has a different notion of how to organize content and where it belongs? (You can guarantee that every submitter's own content always comes out on top!) Someone or, better, some system is necessary to ensure that people handle metadata thoroughly and consistently.

✦ **A different set of skills is necessary to deal with this metadata.** Authors, who are generally subject-matter experts and not experts at the system for managing their expertise, are often unable to add this extra data. One very fundamental piece of metadata, for example, specifies where, in the overall outline of content, a particular piece of information belongs. In larger systems, authors who have no problem creating content often don't know enough to decide where to put it. The problem is worse for cross-references. Authors rarely have the wherewithal to discover what content others are submitting and exactly how to relate that material to what they submit. Overall, you need the type of person who's a cross between an editor, a librarian, and a database administrator to do a good job creating and maintaining metadata.

✦ **To do metadata well requires a lot of human energy.** Simply writing some scripts and pulling out what's easy to find isn't sufficient. A perfect example of this statement is keywording. I've seen many systems fail miserably at indexing because people thought that all they needed to do was create a program to find and mark every example of a small set of words and phrases.

With all these patterns in my head and with clients becoming ever more numerous and more demanding about the quality of their publications, I became creative. What's needed, I reasoned, is something like a standard editorial framework for metadata. This framework required the right kind of leader (such as an editor), a set of rigorous metadata guidelines (such as an editorial guide), and a metadata process that everyone must follow (such as an editorial process). Thus the *metator*, the *metatorial guide*, and *metatorial processing* were born.

As much as I like coining words, I recognize that it isn't the particular names I chose that matter. What's important is that I gave names to these entities. The most significant thing for me in selecting these names was that doing so gave me a reason and a way to begin thinking about metadata systems as separate entities. Metadata became, for me, not just a part of gathering and tagging content but a subject of concern and importance on its own, apart from any particular content management process. For me, this was a turning point that represented a critical change from creating content management systems to *understanding* them.

The narrow view of metadata

The definitions of meta and metadata that I describe in the preceding section clearly point to a wide-ranging and deep notion of metadata. A more narrow view of metadata is, nonetheless, the most well-understood and accepted version that I've encountered. As best I can tell, this notion arose from file- and document-management and now informs most of the uses of metadata in content management products and literature. The following is my (admittedly) ill-informed interpretation of how the term evolved to its current usage.

First came file properties that the operating system exposed and surrounded with a user interface. File name, size, creation date, and file type were some of the first kinds of metadata available. Although these file properties weren't called metadata, they clearly were metadata. They weren't the files themselves but rather data about the files.

After the document-management industry came along, one of the things that product companies did was to extend these file properties to include all manner of other data with which you could tag a file to describe it. Over time, people began to apply the term *metadata* to the set of properties that they could assign to a file. Document-management systems used these properties to help store, manage, and retrieve files.

Today, people still most commonly use the term *metadata* to describe a set of management data that you can use to categorize and manage complete chunks of content. In a CMS, the chunks may not be files, but the concept is the same. Metadata is administrative data about content that enables you to manage its use.

The wide view of metadata

The narrow view of metadata corresponds best to my notion of the management component elements. *Management elements* are the administrative data (such as author, create date, and status) that you attach to a component to help you keep track of it, find it, and know what to do next with it.

Cross-Reference   You can find more information about component elements in Chapter 27, "Designing Content Types," in the section "Content Types Have Elements."

But aren't the body elements of a component metadata? And how about the tags within an element that tell you what a piece of text is or does? Why wouldn't you call that metadata? In addition, why can't you call your access structures metadata? Don't hierarchies and cross-references offer data about the content in your system?

In fact, my view of metadata goes far beyond administrative attributes to include anything in a CMS that's data about the content you're storing. To some extent, the difference between the narrow and wide views of metadata is a consequence of a general principle of metas: *What is the thing itself and what is the meta-thing depends on your level of awareness and concern.*

For someone concerned with entire files, who never cracks those files to see what's inside, the thing itself is a file. The meta-thing is data about the file. In a CMS, you're concerned with smaller content chunks (which I call elements), and you're concerned with the parts that make up the chunk (the formatting and structural tagging that lie within an element). So a wider view of metadata assumes that you mark entities smaller than an entire file with metadata.

A wider view also assumes that you manage metadata at a level larger than a file. Someone whose last task is to retrieve a file generally has no need to capture metadata on anything larger than a file. In a CMS, you need to name and track a number of things larger than files. These things are, for example, publications and access structures that include components.

I'm not saying that the narrow view is wrong and the wide view is right, but I want you to take the view that gives you the most advantage for the task that you're trying to accomplish. In a CMS, you need to take a view of metadata that's wide enough to encompass all the levels of content that you must manage.

Metadata and content management

If content management is the art of naming information (as I claim in Chapter 5, "But What is Content Really?"), metadata is the set of names. In other words, content management is all about metadata. Recall the diagram that I present first in Chapter 23, "The Wheel of Content Management." I reproduce it here for your convenience (see Figure 24-1).

Metadata forms the rim of the wheel. It holds together the entire system and ensures that it neither collapses in on itself nor expands out of control. Control is the essence of metadata in a CMS. If you name and account for everything, you're organized enough to exert complete control over your content. All the entities around the circle contribute to the system by supplying types and values for its metadata.

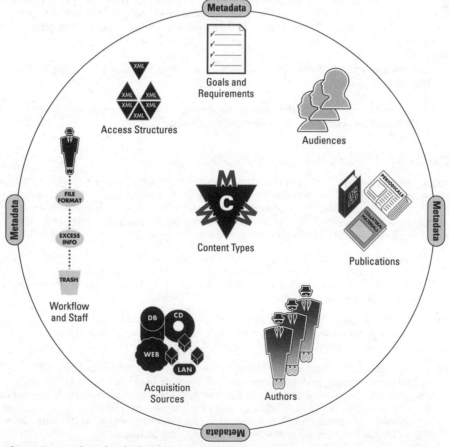

Figure 24-1: The wheel of content management

Understanding the Types of Metadata

In the spirit of casting a broad metadata net, I offer the following list of the types of metadata you're likely to encounter in your travels through the domain of content management:

✦ **Structure metadata:** The ruling monarch of metadata. It precedes most other kinds of metadata by creating structural divisions in your content.

✦ **Format metadata:** Applies to any level of structure that you define and marks how you intend to render that structure.

✦ **Access metadata:** Organizes the structures that you create into hierarchies and other access structures.

✦ **Management metadata:** The data that you attach to structures to administer and track it. Management metadata is the narrow view of metadata.

✦ **Inclusion metadata:** Stands in for external content. It marks the place where the external content is to go.

One of the best ways that I can think of to get quickly immersed in the wide view of metadata is to look at some good markup. Markup languages (such as XML) are the major way that you apply metadata to content. The other major way that you apply metadata is in database rows and columns.

 Cross-Reference You find much more information about markup languages in Chapter 35, "What Are Content Markup Languages?"

In the sections that follow, I discuss each of these types of metadata in more detail and give markup examples showing how to apply them to content.

Structure metadata

Structure metadata says, "You call this stuff..." It's the most basic of the kinds of metadata in the sense that, before you can say anything more about something, you must name that something. Structure metadata creates things by delineating them from their surroundings. In a CMS, structure metadata divides text all the way from defining character boundaries to dividing large collections of publications, as the following list details:

✦ **Characters:** The smallest structural unit that you're likely to need to notice, although you often ignore this smallest unit. Because each character is stored separately (you can't type half a character), you don't need a specific marker to show where one character begins and the other ends.

✦ **Words:** Collections of characters that you intend a reader to take as a unit. Spaces or punctuation set off words. You can say, although doing so stretches the definition a bit, that the spaces and punctuation are the metadata that tells you that a word is a word.

✦ **Paragraphs:** Collections of words that you mean for a reader to take as a unit. You mark paragraphs by using specific metadata to show their boundaries. (In HTML, for example, you use the <P> tag, whereas in flat text, you use a carriage return.) Paragraphs are important to notice because you can apply format metadata at the level of a paragraph. Although a paragraph can be considered a structural unit of text, in the current list it is a part within the smallest named structural unit, the element.

✦ **Elements:** Collections of characters, words, or paragraphs that you intend the reader to take as a structural unit (such as a title). Elements overlap with paragraphs and words in their range. You can have a paragraph composed of multiple elements, for example, as well as an element composed of multiple paragraphs. What distinguishes an element is that it's the smallest structure that you intend to access separately in your system. You mark elements by using specific metadata to show their boundaries (for example, database columns in relational databases and element tags in XML).

✦ **Components:** Collections of elements that you intend the user to take as a whole (such as a white paper). In a CMS, components are the structures that you intend to manage. Thus they're the structures to which you apply management and access metadata. You mark component boundaries by using specific metadata (for example, rows in relational databases and element tags in XML).

✦ **Nodes:** Collections of components that, after publication, you intend the reader to take as a unit. On Web sites, nodes are pages. In print materials, nodes are sections (headings, chapters, parts, and so on). Nodes put a standard set of surroundings around the components that they contain. In this sense, the node itself is metadata to the components. Nodes say, in effect, "You are to understand these components in the context of the surroundings in which you see them." On Web sites, file boundaries surround the node. (Each node is an HTML file.) In print, you're most likely to mark the node boundaries by using format metadata (heading styles and the like).

✦ **Publications:** Collections of nodes that you intend readers to take as a unit (a single department's intranet site, for example). On the Web, you set off publications from each other mostly by using graphic conventions and the internal navigation conventions of the site. (A site may have one or more publications on it.) In print, you most often delineate publications by using a file boundary. The publication is metadata to the nodes as the nodes are metadata to the components that they contain. The publication says, "Take these nodes in the context of the wider publication."

✦ **Publication groups:** Collections of publications that you intend the reader to take as a unit (the volumes in an encyclopedia, for example). Publication groups are set off on both the Web and in print by the formatting conventions and navigational structures that you provide for moving between publications in the group. Again, the group is metadata to the particular publications providing a wider context in which to interpret the meaning of the constituent publications.

 Chapter 3, "Content Has Structure," offers a somewhat different slant on this same basic information. There you find descriptions of the structures without reference to metadata.

The common thread among all these structural divisions is that each defines a unified whole that you can separate from its surroundings; each puts a wider context and another level of meaning around its content; and you must somehow mark each division (even if only with formatting metadata or graphical conventions).

Following is a simplified example of some XML that demonstrates many of the types of structure that I describe previously:

```
<COLLECTION>
  <PUB>
    <SECTION>
      <NODE>
        <HEADER>...</HEADER>
        <COMPONENTS>
          <COMPONENT>
            <ELEMENT>
              <PARA>
```

```
      <COMPONENT>...</COMPONENT>
       <PARA>
      </ELEMENT>
     </COMPONENT>
    </COMPONENTS>
    <FOOTER>...</FOOTER>
   </NODE>
  </SECTION>
 </PUB>
</COLLECTION>
```

Even such a simple example, however, shows a lot about structure metadata. First, notice that no data appears in this example — only metadata. The description is there, but I leave out the thing that it describes (for simplicity). Next, notice the nesting. Each wider set of metadata literally contains the ones within it. The interpretation of a component deepens as you reach the node, the section, the publication, and even the collection level. Thus all the higher levels are metadata of the component (or meta-metadata, meta-meta-metadata, and so on).

Finally, notice the overlap between components, elements, and paragraphs. In this example, an element contains a paragraph that contains another component. This situation isn't only okay; it's common. Consider the following more realistic XML example:

```
<ELEMENT>
  <PARA>
    This is my body text, and in it I'm embedding an image.
    <MEDIA ID="m1" URL="dabw.jpg">
      <SIZE>100,300</Size>
      <CAPTION>This is a separate component</CAPTION>
    </MEDIA>
  </PARA>
  Normal things seem strange if you really think about them!
</ELEMENT>
```

The <MEDIA> component (in this case, an image) I embed within the paragraph, which I embed within the element, which I embed within a component. If I render the <MEDIA> component in HTML, it turns into content and a piece of inclusion metadata, as follows:

```
<IMG SRC="dabw.jpg" WIDTH="100" HEIGHT="300">
<H6>This is a separate component<H6>
```

Once again, the preceding example shows how complicated metadata can be. Not only can information be metadata as well as content, but metadata can be at various levels and intertwined. So, although components are at a higher level than elements, there is no reason you cannot have a component within an element. In the end, you must do what makes your content most manageable, worrying less about strange loops and tangled hierarchies you might create and more about reducing redundancy and increasing access.

Format metadata

Format metadata says, "Here's how to render the stuff that I surround."

Cross-Reference   Chapter 2, "Content Has Format," provides a complete taxonomy of format types and purposes.

Format metadata can apply to any level of structure in your system. In many cases, the structural tags themselves are what you interpret and turn into platform-specific formatting metadata. Take, for example, the following structural XML metadata:

```
<SECTION LEVEL="1">Some Section</SECTION>
```

The Section tag says, "What I surround is a section and it has a level of 1." You can turn this example into format metadata for presentation on a Web page, as follows:

```
<H1>Some Section</H1>
```

Quite often, formatting metadata is "under the radar" of the CMS by residing inside an element. You may, for example, permit authors to include HTML codes for bold, italics, and underline in the Web forms that they use to input a component. The codes sit, unparsed in a database field, and make it onto a Web page without anyone ever noticing them. Of course, if the component's destiny is that of any other format besides HTML, you need a more robust approach.

Following is the XML structure example, enhanced to show a variety of formatting metadata:

```
<COLLECTION>
  <PUB DISPLAY="child">
    <SECTION>
      <NODE>
        <HEADER>...</HEADER>
        <COMPONENTS LAYOUT="table">
          <COMPONENT>
            <ELEMENT TYPEFACE="Arial">
              <PARA STYLE="body">
              Some <FORMATTAG>text</FORMATTAG>
                <COMPONENT>...</COMPONENT>
              <PARA>
            </ELEMENT>
          </COMPONENT>
        </COMPONENTS>
        <FOOTER>...</FOOTER>
      </NODE>
    </SECTION>
  </PUB>
</COLLECTION>
```

Although I've cheated a bit by putting some formatting in the content that normally goes in templates, the example still holds.

Here are some of the formatting concepts that the preceding XML illustrates:

✦ **The** <PUB> **tag** has the attribute DISPLAY as an addition. This attribute controls the display of the publication within the collection. It says, "Display the publication in a child frame of the collection." The display metadata value thus controls the rendering of the publication. This metadata is usually in a template and not a content structure.

✦ **The** <COMPONENT> **tag** has the attribute LAYOUT. This attribute controls the display of the components within the site. In this example, it says, "Display the components in a table." The layout metadata value thus controls the rendering of the components. This metadata is also usually in a template and not a content structure.

✦ **The** `<PARA>` **tag** has the attribute `STYLE`. If you render the paragraph, the formatting associated with the style *body* surrounds the entire contents of the `PARA` element. For each type of publication that you produce, you can associate different formatting codes with the same style name.

✦ **The word** *text* has the metadata `<FORMATTAG>` surrounding it. If you render the word, the formatting associated with the tag surrounds the word. For each type of publication that you produce, you can associate different formatting codes with the same tag.

✦ **Any tag** can have formatting associated with it even if it isn't specifically designated as format metadata. You may decide, for example, that headers on the Web are 12-point bold text. To do so, you treat the `<HEADER>` tag just as you do the `<FORMATTAG>` tag. If you render the header, you make sure that the software surrounds it with 10-point bold formatting codes.

Note   You may ask, in a tag such as `<PUB DISPLAY="child">` is `PUB` the metadata, is `DISPLAY` the metadata, or is `"child"` the metadata? `PUB` and `DISPLAY` are the names of metadata. `PUB` is a Boolean metadata element (either on or off). `DISPLAY` is a list type of metadata element. And `"child"` is one of the allowable values in that list.

Access metadata

Access metadata says, "Here is how this structure fits in with the rest." I call it *access metadata* because you most often use it to gain access to the content. You can, however, just as easily categorize it as structural metadata because it describes the logical structure of the content. Actually, calling it *structure meta-metadata* is more correct, because it describes the structure of the structures. Still, I prefer to differentiate it from structure metadata because different techniques are used to store and manage it. You can store access metadata within a component or outside it in a separate place. The types of access metadata correspond to the types of access structures: hierarchy, index, associations, and sequences.

Following is the XML structure example, this time enhanced to include some access metadata:

```
<COLLECTION>
  <PUB>
    <SECTION>
      <NODE KEYWORDS="rollup">
        <HEADER>...</HEADER>
        <COMPONENTS>
          <COMPONENT INDEX="term1,term2,term3">
            <ELEMENT>
              <PARA>
              <COMPONENT>...</COMPONENT>
                <LINK TARGET="C123">For more information, see</LINK>
              <PARA>
            </ELEMENT>
          </COMPONENT>
        </COMPONENTS>
        <FOOTER>...</FOOTER>
      </NODE>
    </SECTION>
  </PUB>
</COLLECTION>
```

To show a hierarchy and sequence, you need nothing other than what I show here. By its nature, XML provides a default hierarchy (tags are nested within tags) and a default sequence (tags follow tags). To show indexing, I add the following two new attributes:

✦ **The** `<COMPONENT>` **element** has an `INDEX` attribute where it lists the index terms for the component.

✦ **The** `<NODE>` **element** has a `KEYWORDS` attribute that specifies how the node is to treat index terms. In this case, the attribute says, "Roll up all the index terms from all the components that are on the node." On an HTML page, this command may result in the creation of a `<META>` tag at the top of the HTML file that lists all the index terms for search engines to find.

To show associations, I add a `<LINK>` tag. The tag includes a `TARGET` attribute that names the structure that it links to and some text that it uses in rendering the link. In a Web page, the result may look as follows:

```
For more information, <A HREF="C123.htm">click here</A>
```

In print, the link may look as follows after rendering:

```
For more information, see "Links" in Chapter 5.
```

Access metadata is as often outside the content structure as it is inside. The way I that show index terms, for example, isn't the best way to do so. Instead of typing the terms into the component, you want to type the component into the terms as shown in the following example:

```
<INDEX>
  <TERM>
    <NAME>NOAA</NAME>
    <COMPONENTS>C123,C456,C789</COMPONENTS>
  </TERM>
</INDEX>
```

This approach is a better way to manage a large index. More to the present point, it places index metadata outside the content structure and instead references the structure.

Management metadata

My notion of management metadata is quite close to the common definition for metadata itself (what I have termed the narrow view). Management metadata helps you keep track of and administer content. Following are some of the more common management metadata types:

✦ ID

✦ Title

✦ Author

✦ Create data

✦ Modify date

✦ Status

✦ Size

✦ Owner

✦ Publish date

✦ Expire date

Notice that management metadata isn't always only for management. Any of the types that I list here can just as easily be considered to embed as content to publish as well as data to help manage the content to publish. That's fine. Notwithstanding the limitations of some CMS systems, whether or not you show the values of these metadata elements to your audience, their use to you is the same—to help you keep track of and administer your content.

Following is the XML structure example enhanced to show some management metadata:

```
<COLLECTION>
 <PUB ID="p1">
   <SECTION ID="s1">
     <NODE ID="n1">
       <HEADER>...</HEADER>
       <COMPONENTS>
         <COMPONENT ID="C123">
           <TITLE></TITLE>
           <ADMIN>
             <OWNER>0234</OWNER>
             <CREATE>9/23/01</CREATE>
             <MODIFY>9/30/01</MODIFY>
             <STATUS>Status1</STATUS>
           </ADMIN>
           <ELEMENT NAME="intro">
             <PARA ID="p1">...</PARA>
           </ELEMENT>
         </COMPONENT>
       </COMPONENTS>
       <FOOTER...</FOOTER>
     </NODE>
   </SECTION>
 </PUB>
</COLLECTION>
```

The management metadata in this example is fairly self-explanatory. First, every significant entity gets a unique identifier so that you can always precisely locate it. Components get a set of new elements that specify the management metadata that you want the component to contain. For clarity, I make these new elements all XML tags. In real life, many would be XML attributes instead.

Inclusion metadata

Inclusion metadata says, "Put the following external entity here." It enables you to reference content that isn't physically in the content structure.

Recall the example that I present in the section "Structure metadata," earlier in this chapter, that demonstrated how to embed one component in another:

```
<ELEMENT>
 <PARA>
   This is my body text, and in it I'm embedding an image.
   <MEDIA ID="m1" URL="dabw.jpg">
```

```
        <SIZE>100,300</SIZE>
        <CAPTION>This is a separate component</CAPTION>
    </MEDIA>
  </PARA>
  Normal things seem strange if you really think about them!
</ELEMENT>
```

If you really intend to make the `<MEDIA>` element a separate component, you're better off not directly embedding it in another component by pointing to its URL. Instead you reference it based on its ID, as follows:

```
<ELEMENT>
  <PARA>
    This is my body text, and in it I'm embedding an image.
    <INCLUDE REFID="m1">
    Normal things seem strange if you really think about them!
  </PARA>
</ELEMENT>
```

The `<INCLUDE>` tag, on evaluation by the code that renders the page in HTML, finds component "m1" and puts it at that spot. In the meantime, component "m1" isn't stuck embedded in a particular place in the content structure; it's stored with the other "m" components so you can more easily find, manage, and include it in any part of the content structure.

A common use for inclusion metadata is in publications to reference media, as I show in the section "Structure metadata," earlier in this chapter. Here, for example, is how to reference an image in HTML:

```
<IMG SRC="dabw.jpg" WIDTH="100" HEIGHT="300">
<H6>This is a separate component<H6>
```

You may be tempted to cut out the middleman and just put media tags right in your content as follows:

```
<ELEMENT>
  <PARA>
    This is my body text, and in it I'm embedding an image.
    <IMG SRC="dabw.jpg" WIDTH="100" HEIGHT="300">
    <H6>This is a separate component<H6>
    Normal things seem strange if you really think about them!
  </PARA>
</ELEMENT>
```

Before you do, however, pause and consider the following issues:

✦ **This is HTML.** Are you sure that you can translate this publication-specific formatting metadata into whatever other type of formatting metadata you may need?

✦ **The image and its caption are locked in this location.** Do you need this image elsewhere? If so, you're stuck making multiple copies of the exact same lengthy version of the tags and text. By referencing an image component rather than literally typing it, you avoid the redundancy. In addition, if you use a reference, when you change the component in one place, you change all instances of the component.

✦ **The reference may break.** Like HTML embedded within a component element, this image may fall under the radar of your CMS. If "dabw.jpg" changes its name or moves to a different place, most CMS products don't tell you that the reference is no longer valid. In addition, you must somehow remember that this image file is referenced in this element and make sure that it's published anywhere that the element it's part of is published. This task could prove a tall order.

✦ **You have no place to put other info that you may need.** Suppose that you wisely decide that your images need to carry a status that tells you how ready they are for viewing. If you represent them as components, the change is easy. Simply add a status element to the component. But if you represent your images as HTML references, where do you put the extra information?

Although just typing media references into your text may seem convenient, hidden costs could outweigh the time that you save up front.

Finally, consider the HTML notion of the INCLUDE file. This one uses Microsoft ASP syntax, as follows:

```
<!--#INCLUDE FILE="Reusable.txt"-->
```

HTML INCLUDEs are the poor man's way of simulating components and templates. INCLUDEs are essential in dynamic Web applications, where they enable you to "type once and include many." In a CMS, the "type once and include many" processes, which are inherent mostly in components and templates, replace the concept of the INCLUDE file.

Note　I'm a bit ambivalent about the inclusion metadata category, because it isn't as clearly metadata as the rest. You can surely say that the INCLUDEs are data about the content. But on the other hand, you can say that inclusion metadata is just a way to reference content that you don't want to type (or otherwise include) over and over again. I'm leaving the debate unresolved for now to enable me to cover the subject of inclusion in the most logical location for it.

Categorizing Metadata Fields

So far in this chapter, I've looked at metadata from an XML perspective. In XML, all metadata boils down to elements and attributes. I now turn toward a more database-centric approach to metadata as I discuss how to categorize metadata not by the meaning it conveys, but by its allowed values.

Before discussing allowed values, I'm going to pause to mention briefly how the structure of a relational database itself represents metadata. Consider the simple database table shown in Figure 24-2.

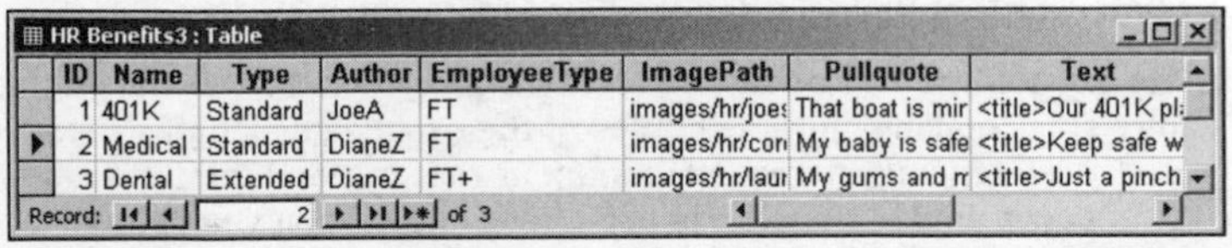

ID	Name	Type	Author	EmployeeType	ImagePath	Pullquote	Text
1	401K	Standard	JoeA	FT	images/hr/joes	That boat is mir	\<title>Our 401K pl:
2	Medical	Standard	DianeZ	FT	images/hr/con	My baby is safe	\<title>Keep safe w
3	Dental	Extended	DianeZ	FT+	images/hr/laur	My gums and m	\<title>Just a pinch

HR Benefits3 : Table

Record: 2 of 3

Figure 24-2: Rows are component boundaries and columns are element boundaries.

The content is in the little boxes of the grid. The rest is metadata, as the following list describes:

✦ **The column names** are structural metadata that delineate element boundaries.

✦ **The rows** are structural metadata that delineate component boundaries.

✦ **Management metadata** is in the ID, Name, Type, Author, and EmployeeType columns.

✦ **Inclusion metadata** is in the ImagePath column.

The structure of the database itself, as well as the ways that you assign values to database columns, yields a lot of well-structured and strictly consistent metadata.

Cross-Reference

In Chapter 39, "Building Management Systems," in the section "Relational database systems," you find much more information about how you can represent metadata in relational databases.

Continuing to look at metadata from a database perspective, you can say that metadata falls into a set of categories based on the values that the metadata element can have. The value of the metadata element Author, for example, may be "Karl Weyrauch." The value of the Create Date element may be "3 January, 2005." To make the transition from XML to databases complete, instead of metadata elements, I refer to them here *as metadata fields*.

Note

Those familiar with programming probably notice that I mix database and user-interface vocabulary with other words that come from neither discipline. I do so with full knowledge that I'm mixing metaphors to create a content management-centric view of metadata.

The metadata fields frequently used in a CMS fall into the following categories:

✦ **Free text**, in which the value of the field can be any text string. Titles, for example, are of this variety because every title is different.

✦ **Constrained text**, in which the value of the field is text, but the text must follow certain rules. A "BodyText" metadata field, for example, may allow any ASCII characters as well as the HTML codes for bold, italics, and underline. Or the field may put constraints on length, limiting the number of characters that can go in that field.

✦ **Pattern text**, in which each value of the field must follow particular formation rules. Dates and times are of this variety because you can form them only in a set number of ways, based on patterns such as *yyyy-dd-mm*.

✦ **BLOB** (Binary Large Objects), in which the value of the field is any binary data that's interpretable by some application. Image and other media fields are examples of BLOB fields.

✦ **Boolean**, in which the value of the field is either true or false. You may, for example, create a field that you call "Public." If its value is true, people can view the component on the public Web site.

✦ **Closed lists**, in which the user can choose the value only from a predefined list. You may, for example, create a field that you call "Review Status," in which the review status can be one of only 10 possible values.

✦ **Open lists**, in which the user can choose the value from a list or can add new entries to the list and then choose them. You may, for example, create a field that you call "Keywords," where the user can either select one of the keywords in the existing list or add a new one. If you use open lists, make sure that you trust users to add new items responsibly.

✦ **Unique ID**, in which the value must differ from that of any other field. All components should have an ID field so that you can easily locate them in any database.

✦ **References**, in which the value is a reference (an ID) to another component. You may, for example, create a field that you call "Link." Inside this field is the Unique ID of the component to which you want to link. As a very different example, you may create a field that you call "Image Path." Inside this field you place the directory and filename of an image that you want to associate with the component. In both these examples, the content of the field *refers to* a separate entity. References are how you create inclusion metadata.

✦ **Outline lists**, in which users choose the values from a hierarchical list. You may create a field that you call "Product," for example, where the user can select a product from an outline of product categories and products.

✦ **Compound fields** that combine one or more of the preceding types. You may, for example, create a "Link" field as a combination of an outline list and a reference field. To fill in the field, the user chooses from an outline of all the available components. What gets stored in the field is a reference to a component.

Notice that these categories span two realms: how you enter information into the field and what gets stored in the field. The compound field illustrates this concept well: One field type specifies the user interface (outline, for example), and one provides the storage. In this sense it's a very CMS-centric view of field value types. It focuses on what's important to the management system and its users. A more general (and, to you, less useful) approach is to take a data-centric view and focus on the data type of the field. (Is it text, integer, real number, BLOB, and so on?) Although the programmer who sets up your CMS database uses its standard data types, some additional coding may be necessary to combine and uniquely present options in the user interface that serve the needs of the users and the database programmer.

Metatorial Processing

Editorial processing ensures that your content obeys the rules that you construct for correctness, communication, and consistency (see Chapter 7, "Introducing the Major Parts of a CMS," in the section "Editorial processing"). Similarly, metatorial processing ensures that metadata is complete and consistent.

Metatorial processing accomplishes the following tasks:

✦ Ensuring the completeness of metadata.

✦ Enforcing the consistency of metadata.

✦ Ensuring that you can manage the content.

✦ Ensuring that you can access the content.

✦ Ensuring that you can appropriately target the content.

Developing Searchable Content with Metadata

Publishing for the Web or for systems with large content repositories such as corporate intranets requires a well-planned system for tagging content with metadata. The sheer volume of data in such systems can render documents useless if they cannot be queried by the people who need them. Thus, the goal of a metatagging system should be to connect users with the information they need. This requires that content authors are aware of the content elements that are employed in search algorithms.

One difficulty of metadata creation is the fact that content authors are often the most qualified people to create metadata for their content, yet they have no metatagging expertise. Authors understand the material they are producing and presumably the audience they are producing it for, far better than anyone else. On the other hand, content authors do not generally possess the expertise necessary for metadata creation, nor the time to keep up with it. In this case *metators* can help authors by creating search algorithm-aware standards for content authoring. Thus, *metators* can play a role by educating content teams on metadata creation and by imposing content creation requirements.

The metadata of relevance to search engines is what is termed structural metadata. It is important to note that this data can be both standard content and metadata. The distinction is based on whether the information is being catalogued by a search engine or consumed by a human being. For Web-based content management applications this data must ultimately translate into elements such as HTML page titles, headers, image alternate text, meta keywords, and meta description attributes. *Metators* who are familiar with search algorithms should identify these important elements and include them in content creation standards. HTML form validation can help impose these standards within content authoring templates by requiring that specific metadata is included before content is published. This can be required at the time of content authoring, but it is also possible to assign this task to a *metator* or editor as part of a content publication workflow.

Peter Emonds-Banfield, University of Washington

Although authors and a conversion system can do much of the tagging, they can't do it all. Authors may not possess the ability or willingness to do all the tagging that you need, and an acquisition source may simply not have all the information that you expect in the target markup. Thus you may need additional aggregation processes that ensure that the tagging is complete for each content component that enters the system. Missing metadata is quite easy to find (a blank space appears where some value goes), so the problem isn't to find the blanks, but to correctly fill them. Of course, with a well-written metatorial guide in hand, this task usually isn't too difficult, even if it is time-consuming.

Your system must ensure that metadata is consistent among all the content that flows into the system. You need to apply similar content types to similar metadata so that your use of metadata is consistent across your content model. You must apply a particular metadata element (status, say) with an even hand across all components that it's a part of. In a sizable system with numerous contributors you can almost guarantee that you will find wide variation in the ways that people interpret and apply even the most precisely stated tagging rules.

Complete and consistent metadata is a means to the real end of metatorial processing—to make content manageable, accessible, and targetable.

Whenever most people speak about metadata they usually do so in the context of management: data such as the author, create date, last edit, status, and so on that you attach to content. It is not attached for publication purposes, but rather to provide "handles" for accessing and using the content before you publish it (as well as to help you decide when to stop publishing it). Obviously, for the content to remain manageable, management metadata must be complete and consistent.

In addition to management metadata, other metadata makes the content accessible. This accessibility goes in two directions. Individual elements must be accessible within components. If you want to show summaries of each of your feature articles, for example, each Feature Article component must include a tagged summary. In the entire CMS, individual components must remain accessible by the metadata that positions them in hierarchies, indexes, cross references, and sequences. Needless to say, if you don't correctly tag components as separate entities (that is, you don't segment them correctly), you won't be able to find them at all. So metatorial processing must result in complete and consistent access tagging.

Finally, metatorial processing must ensure that the tagging that you direct at targeting content for personalization is complete and consistent. Suppose, for example, that your logical design says that you target families differently than you do single adults. The simplest way to do so (simple conceptually, if not practically) is to tag each component with a piece of metadata that you call *audience type*. You can imagine that the end system can't function well if some components are missing these tags (completeness) or if various contributors make divergent decisions about how types of content are tagged (inconsistency). In reality, targeting content is usually much more complex than this example, but the idea is the same. Whatever tagging you add to content to enable you to target it must be applied consistently and completely.

Cross-Reference   See Chapter 11, "The Branches of Content Management," in the section "Personalization," for more information about personalization.

The metator

I expect that either your authors and your conversion system handle much (maybe even most) content tagging. If an author fills in a create date on a Web form, for example, she's tagging her content with a piece of metadata. Similarly, if a conversion program finds and converts an author name, it tags that author name for use by the CMS. Expecting your authors or converters to do all the tagging is a nice luxury, but realistically, it's pretty unreasonable.

Authors don't always have the wherewithal to know how to tag their content. Yes, you can usually count on them to tag their names and other ready-to-hand information. But can (or, more important, should) you count on authors to know where in your overall outline of content to list their contributions? Depending on the size and complexity of your system and degree of involvement of your authors, you can't always count on them having much knowledge beyond the boundaries of their particular creations. As a general rule, authors should always be responsible for the internal structure and format tagging of their work. They should be responsible for relating their content to the rest of the system (the external structure of their work) only to the degree that they're experienced and knowledgeable about your metatorial guide. Moreover, it's dangerous to assume that just because someone is a good author, she can or wants to become involved in concerns that go beyond the boundaries of her contribution. All in all, in a system of any size, you're better off planning for the likelihood that authors can't fully tag their own work. You must, consequently, find a metator.

Acquired sources simply may not contain all the metadata that you need to capture. Or the information may be present in the source, but so poorly marked that it requires a person to review and tag it by hand. In either case, it's the responsibility of the metator to ensure that acquired content is fully tagged.

Cross-Reference

In Chapter 37, "Processing Content," in the section "Understanding the principles of mapping content," I fully describe the idea of marked content.

Most basically, a *metator* is a person who does the metatorial processing that authors and conversion systems can't do. She may do so directly by adding XML or other tags to the content; or she may do so indirectly, by choosing from lists and typing into input areas that later result in the tagging or other organizing of the content (for example, putting it into the correct database table).

In a small system, you can get away without appointing someone as an official metator. But in a system with scores of authors and sources and a large variety of content types, the job of metator becomes mandatory to keep the metadata system complete and consistent. What a metator does, in this regard, isn't dissimilar to what an editor does in her realm. She reviews, adds, and modifies not content but metadata.

In addition to filling in missing metadata, the metator must ensure that the metadata that's already present is consistent with the metatorial guide. Authors and conversion systems are apt to make poor choices if they face any ambiguity at all about how to use a tag. This statement isn't a pejorative. Laziness notwithstanding, squeezing all the vagueness out of any set of rules is impossible. (That's why lawyers exist.) Maintaining a central point of decision about a rules system becomes mandatory after the system reaches moderate complexity and has more than just a few people are using it.

Whether or not the job title is metator, the task of looking after the metadata health of a CMS is crucial if you want to be confident that the content in the system will show up when you expect it to.

Cross-Reference

You find more information about the job of metator in Chapter 13, "Staffing a CMS," in the section "Metator." I provide an illustration of a metator's job in Chapter 7, "Introducing the Major Parts of a CMS," in the section "Metatorial processing."

The metatorial guide

You can think of a metatorial guide as the master catalog of your content. For every kind of content you manage, this guide fully describes the structure and construction. From another angle, you can say that a metatorial guide is all your system's meta-metadata. It isn't the metadata itself; it's everything *about* the metadata. From yet another, more practical angle, you can say that the metatorial guide is the place to go to find out what a component consists of and how to fill in all its elements. However you choose to describe it, a metatorial guide, more than any other document, is at the center of your CMS. Metadata is the one place where all the parts of a CMS meet, and the metatorial guide is where you describe the metadata.

Tip

The metatorial guide must remain accessible. If you can maintain it in only one form, make it a set of Web pages with one page per element. That's the most flexible form for including it as online Help in your content collection forms, as well as for making it a standalone publication.

The metatorial guide may seem similar to the content model and, in fact, it is built on top of the content model. In developing a CMS you create the content model for your content. The content model determines the structure of the metadata, access structures, and content in your system. The content model leads directly to the database or XML schema that you use to store and access content. The metatorial guide then tells contributors and metators how to "do" the content model. It documents the content model so that contributors and metators can add content that is consistent with the content model.

Cross-Reference   I describe the metatorial guide from a project perspective in Chapter 21, "Rolling Out the System," in the section "The metatorial guide." In Chapter 30, "Designing Content Access Structures," in the section "The content model," I describe the content model from the standpoint of a comprehensive analysis of the access structures a system requires.

Meta-metadata rules

Meta-metadata rules tell you how to formulate and change metadata. They're not the rules for filling in metadata; they're the rules for changing *how* you fill in metadata.

You need to consider and document the rules, because as soon as you begin using the system, it's certain you will need to change it. If this change happens in an orderly way, the metadata system has the best chance of staying ordered. If it happens ad hoc, you can bet that the tight system you constructed is sure to begin to unravel.

Tip   Of course, as you begin to change, you must reconsider the rules of change. That mean you also need to construct the rules for the rules of change. But of course, those rules change, too, so you must also consider the rules for the rules for the rules of change. But those rules change, too, so... It's not a true meta if it can't go on forever!

In all seriousness, taking the time to figure out the following issues ahead of time is well worth the effort:

✦ **Control:** Who's in charge of deciding when you need to change a metadata element and when you need to add a new one? Elsewhere, I suggest a CMS steering committee. (See Chapter 14, "Working within the Organization," in the section "The CMS steering committee.") Is that what's right for you?

✦ **Lumping and splitting:** How do you decide when to combine two metadata elements into one (*lumping*) or when to create two elements from one (*splitting*). What methods do you use for these procedures? The effort behind splitting, especially, may prove enormous, so planning ahead is worth your while.

✦ **Top down or bottom up:** In general, do you want what you find in the content to generate metadata (*bottom up*), or do you want your team to generate metadata and impose it on the content that arrives (*top down*)? In other words, do you prefer a metadata system that expands on its own and risks disorganization (bottom up) or one that remains very organized but doesn't discriminate well between similar sorts of content (top down)?

✦ **Entry:** In general, what sorts of elements do you expect authors to fill in and what sorts require a metator?

✦ **Freeform or constrained:** How do you decide which metadata to keep open-ended (where you can add whatever you want) and which to close down (where you restrict what anyone can add)?

✦ **Optional or mandatory:** When do you make metadata optional and when do you make it mandatory?

The answers to these questions aren't yes or no, either one or the other. The right answers are more or less all "Yes." In addition, you need to think hard about a policy so that you can maintain an organized metatorial framework but stay prepared to examine each metadata element individually to craft the best approach for it.

Note   To say "meta-metadata rules" is a bit redundant. Rules are, by their nature, metadata. To become a metadata rule, a statement must talk *about* the metadata that it seeks to control. I use the phrase anyway, just to underscore the point.

Metadata and collection

A metatorial guide is an invaluable resource for keeping content collection on track, efficient, and pain free. You have a winner if your guide can provide quick answers to any question such as, "What do I type here?" More specifically, the guide should use the results of your logical design to address the following concerns:

✦ **Content types:** What content types exist? What is the name of each one and what's its source (or sources)?

✦ **Elements:** What elements does each content type consist of? What are their names and where do they originate?

✦ **Element types:** What kind of field is each element (free text, pattern text, open list, closed list, and so on)?

✦ **Element values:** For each element, what are the allowed values?

✦ **Usage rules:** How do you know what value to choose or type for each field?

✦ **Responsibilities:** Which elements are contributors responsible to fill in? Which do other staffers fill in? Which are automatically filled in?

✦ **Change rules:** For each content type or element, which of the meta-metadata rules that I cite in the preceding section are relevant and need describing to the contributing public?

Notice the switch here from the term *metadata element* to *component element*. You shouldn't expect contributors to know what metadata is. They should, however, know what a component is if they're going to create them. In all likelihood, the word that contributors respond to best is *field*. What they are likely to see isn't a component element nor a metadata element, but a field on a Web-based form that they must fill in.

Metadata and management

The members of your collection staff use the metatorial guide daily. Management staff use it less frequently, but it should still prove a valuable resource if it addresses the following issues:

✦ **Review:** What are the review and quality-control processes for the elements of each content type?

✦ **Retirement:** What tells you that a component is ready for expiration, archiving, or deletion?

✦ **Creation rates:** How many components of each content type do you expect to add each week?

✦ **Growth:** Which content types continue to grow indefinitely and which have a maximum number of components?

You can code much of this information directly into the configuration of the CMS. A component may display both a Retirement Type and a Retirement Date element, for example, that specify what to do with it. You can set up the CMS so that, as the retirement date arrives, a workflow trigger fires and sends an e-mail message to the administrator telling her what to do with the component (as the Retirement Type element specifies). Thus the administrator doesn't need to consult the metatorial guide to decide what to do. On the other hand, you probably have no place in the system to see all the management rules and metadata laid out and organized. If an administrator wants to see the big picture, the metatorial guide is the place to go.

Metadata and publishing

Publishers look at a metatorial guide even less frequently than administrators do. Still, as buried as metadata rules may be in the management system, they're even more buried in the publishing system and templates. To help provide publishers with a clear picture of how the publishing system is using metadata, the metatorial guide can address the following concerns:

✦ **Content types:** What content types does each publication use? Which types are used by more than one publication?

✦ **Templates:** For each publication template, which content types are used?

✦ **Selection:** What elements do you use to select components into each template? (Do you select components because their Date element, for example, displays a date that's less than three weeks old?)

✦ **Personalization elements:** What elements and what user profile elements do you use in the personalization process in each template?

You code all these rules directly into publication templates. The elements that you use to select components for a template, for example, are typed into the queries of the template. This approach is just fine if the system is working as planned, but when you want to find and fix a bug or make a change to the templating system, you need something more easily navigated than the code in each template. At these times, the overall picture that the metatorial guide provides can really help you. It can help you see inconsistencies (such as why a component appears fine in one template and not in others) and opportunities (for example, the requirements of two templates are so similar that they can just share code) that you may never see, let alone notice, if your metadata system is implicit in the publication system and templates.

Localizing Metadata

You need to localize metadata values that you publish to the world beyond your team, just as you do any other content. If you intend to publish a create date for article components, for example, you must adopt the local date formatting conventions as you display it.

For management metadata that the end user never sees and for the names of the metadata elements themselves, avoid the duplication of effort and the system complexity that localization involves. You're better off without it. If you do decide to avoid localizing metadata, make sure that the following conditions are true:

✦ **The elements that you skip are pure management.** Make sure that no one down the line is likely to decide to start showing the end user any elements that you're not localizing.

✦ **You choose unambiguous words.** You must make the meaning totally clear in the metadata element names and metadata lists that you create. To save yourself work, understand that, if you use colloquial words, you're making things harder for the people who aren't native speakers of the language you're using. It is best if you use standard words (no jargon) and full words (no abbreviations) when you name metadata elements and list values. If you don't do this as a favor to your international staff, do it to save yourself the extra effort of correcting their tagging mistakes.

✦ **You take extra care in your metatorial guide to explain the names and metadata values.** Consider localizing portions of the guide if you can't localize the entire system.

If you choose to localize element names and management metadata values, you may run into significant difficulties. Few systems make changing element names easy. Even providing an alternative list of values by region can prove a big task and can require extensive customization.

Cross-Reference

You can find a complete overview of localization and content management in Chapter 25, "Cataloging Audiences," in the section "Audiences and Localization."

Summary

Metadata is data about data. More specifically, metadata has the following characteristics:

✦ You can divide metadata into structure, format, access, management, and inclusion categories.

✦ In a CMS, metadata can have a variety of formats that vary from free text to references to components. You use a correspondingly wide range of user interface elements for metadata entry.

✦ To provide the organization and structure to turn the metadata that you manage into a working system, you can construct a metatorial guide.

✦ Just as an editorial system is codified in an editorial guide, your metadata system results in a metatorial guide. The metatorial guide establishes the guidelines that staff members use to divide and tag all the content that crosses their desks. Metators and others use the metatorial guide to do metatorial processing on the content that they manage.

✦ You may or may not choose to localize management metadata, but you must localize any of the rest of the metadata that you capture to display to your local audiences.

In the chapters that follow, I dive into each of the content management entities, in turn, to describe all the information that you may want to collect on them to perform a complete logical analysis of your proposed CMS.

✦   ✦   ✦

Cataloging Audiences

An *audience* is a group of people that is defined by both a common set of traits shared by its members, and by your decision to deliver value to that group in the form of content or functionality. In this section, I discuss the idea of audiences from the perspectives of marketing, software development, and writing. I discuss how you may go about segmenting users into audiences, and then I detail the information that you need to capture about each of your audiences so that you can deliver the best content to them.

It never ceases to amaze me how much lip service people pay to understanding their audiences and how little real effort they put into doing so. I've never run into someone who disagrees with the statement "You must understand who you're serving if you're to serve them well." On the other hand, I know of precious few who do anything more than a cursory analysis of those they intend to serve.

Cataloging Audiences Jumpstart

This Jumpstart summarizes what you need to do to include localization in your CM process and system.

Use this jumpstart as a summary without the weight of detail, or as a quick review if you've already read the chapter and want a checklist of what you need to do localization.

To analyze your audiences you can follow these steps:

1. Define your potential audiences. If your organization doesn't already have a well-defined audience document, expect to spend several iterations refining your audience definition with key stakeholders.

2. Refine your list of audiences. Determine how the CMS can help you serve each audience better and also reach your goals.

3. For each audience on your final list:

   - Identify them by giving each audience a name and charting the characteristics that describe it.

   - Describe their demographics using a narrative that explains the audience and how they benefit from your organization. Also include descriptive characteristics such as their jobs, technical savvy, and traditional demographics, as well as the size of this audience.

- Determine their attitudes, including their beliefs and opinions about the subjects of your content. Describe how you will establish credibility with the audience, what arguments will resonate with them, how to approach them effectively, and how much personal data you can gather from them.

- Understand how they will compare your offerings to competitive publications. Determine what publications (yours and others) the audience most commonly reads.

- Determine what you offer of value to them. Outline what benefits you offer and what costs you extract. Describe how you communicate this value equation to them and monitor it over time.

- Decide how they will use your information. Start by identifying their goals for each of the publications you target to them; next, develop use case reviews, test usability, and describe how you expect the audience to use each publication.

- Figure out what sort of profile to create for them. A profile is a collection of traits and trait values. Decide which traits you can use to categorize individuals and place them in the correct audience.

- Determine the localities that your audience encompasses. Localities take into account the local culture as well as the capability of your organization to provide content tailored to that locale. Include primary, constituent, and key localities in your description.

- Determine the tasks that you must do on an ongoing basis to accommodate the audiences that you identify. These tasks can range from periodic review of audience definitions to monitoring their activities via site logs. You might also review competing publications and do periodic usability and use case reviews.

4. Relate your audiences to the other entities in your analysis. Be sure, above all, that by serving them with the information they want you are able to advance your goals

After you've identified and described your audiences, you can use the traits to serve as the user profiles on which you can build your personalization module.

Serving versus Exploiting an Audience

At the same time as you want to serve your audience, you also want to get something from them. The more that you know about people, the better you can anticipate their needs and provide them with just the right content. On the other hand, the better you know people, the more you can manipulate them into doing what you want them to. (Usually, you want them to buy something.)

This paradox plays out on both sides of the computer screen. Users expect the Web sites that they visit to be smart enough to anticipate their needs. They gravitate toward sites that seem to know them and remember their preferences. On the other hand, users are wary or even hostile toward sites that ask a lot of questions. The question immediately comes to mind: "What are they going to do with this information?"

Direct marketers live by the creed of "Know thy audience." They collect as much information as possible on you and then carefully craft a message that they think you may respond to. Direct marketers live and die by the lists of targeted audiences that they create. Marketers walk that very thin line between serving their audiences and exploiting them. And, very interestingly, the line isn't a sharp one. Consider the same piece of junk mail sent to two neighbors.

The mail is a flyer advertising a long-distance telephone plan. Neighbor A has a plan and is happy with it. She feels put upon and manipulated and says, "I hate all these advertisements trying to get me to buy something!" Neighbor B just moved in and has been researching long-distance phone plans all day. She looks with interest on the ad and says, "How fortuitous to get this today. I wish that every phone company had sent me one."

However thin and imprecise the line is between service and exploitation, a line still exists. And in your own publications, you can choose to cross it or not.

 Note For the record, I forbid you to use any of the techniques that I mention in this book to manipulate or behave unethically toward your audiences!

Content Mismanagement

In an inner-city elementary school a few years ago, there was a librarian who kept books from children and children from books. The librarian didn't teach children how to use libraries, they were not made to feel at home, and their curiosity was not welcomed. The library shelves were almost naked, but the librarian stood in the way of parents and teachers who were trying to get more books.

A working library includes book checkout, return, and a functioning catalogue so a student can learn to get from subject, author, or title to a book on the shelf. This library had none of those; and students, even teachers, couldn't predictably find a book without asking the librarian. The books on the shelves didn't match the catalogue; the numbers swung wildly, as did the alphabet.

The librarian used a "personal" system instead of the system used at other schools and libraries. When asked how students were to locate books in his system, the librarian answered, "Every library has its idiosyncrasies and the children know mine." Even if that were true, is the purpose of a school library for students to learn a unique and idiosyncratic system or conventional library skills that can be used in other libraries and throughout their lives?

The librarian kept many books locked away out of the general collection, and most new books never got put on the shelves. As a result, even the school PTA stopped donating books to the library.

The librarian repeatedly stated, "I will not change," and that rather than alter his system in "my" library, he would forfeit funding to get books — and in fact he did so. Teachers' objections weren't able to change the librarian's ways, so most classes didn't use the library. Instead teachers kept limited book collections in their classrooms.

Many children were robbed of irreplaceable time and precious opportunities. Each day was an irredeemable loss to children who pass this way but once.

It's already a struggle for kids to get a decent education. There can be no waste of scarce resources. But this librarian was not forced out; he left in his own time, only when he became eligible for retirement.

In this century we have learned the hard way that "evil flourishes when good people do nothing." When children are deprived of tools for understanding the world because a school library is run as the librarian's private kingdom, and nobody can or will do something about it, something is terribly wrong. A great deal of content is being tragically mismanaged.

Donald J. Horowitz, former Superior Court Judge, State of Washington; Chair, Access to Justice Technology Bill of Rights Committee, Washington Access to Justice Board

I believe that the key to staying on the right side of the line between service and exploitation is to place a value proposition at the base of your audience analysis. For each audience that you expect to serve, you must decide what its members want from you and what you want from them. Then make sure that the equation is balanced. If you're willing to give as much value as you expect from your audiences in return, the relationship involves no exploitation. Your value propositions can serve as the guiding principles behind every other part of how you work with this audience.

What Is an Audience?

Audiences are simply groups of people that you choose to serve in some way. The first natural question to answer is, "How do I know someone who's in my audience from someone who's not?" The answer is to find the set of traits that distinguishes this audience from others and then figure out whether the person in question demonstrates these traits.

A *trait* is a specific characteristic of a person that you can discover, store, and combine with other characteristics to *know* this person. For you, a person, to know another person is one thing. For a computer to *know* a person is quite another. For you or me, a person isn't some set of data points; she's a complex being whom we intuitively "get." You say that you know someone if you can recognize her and can accurately predict what she may do, say, and want.

No computer that I know of can "get" a person in this sense, so you better settle for something less. You can settle for coming up with a few isolated traits and using them to try to predict wants. And, amazingly, that approach basically works. In most of the circumstances that you face in a CMS, you can limit the number of potential wants that you serve. You can also draw wide enough distinctions between your users that determining who's who and what they probably want isn't too hard. As you learn to discern more traits more accurately, you can continue to get better at predicting more wants for more people.

Although many disciplines talk around or about audiences, I've never seen the concept nailed down enough to become specifically useful in the context of a CMS. So in the following list, I try to draw the elements of *audiences* out of the three different disciplines in which I've seen the concept operate. My goal is to piece together a use of the term *audience* that you can apply very specifically to a CMS:

✦ **From the discipline of writing and oral communication:** I draw the idea of audience analysis, which tries to define what you need to know to "speak" to a particular group of people.

✦ **From marketing:** I draw the notions of segmentation and profiling, which tries to tie groups of people together by using data about them.

✦ **From computer science:** I draw the notion of the user as a kind of person that an application must serve psychologically and ergonomically.

From these three bases, I construct the set of data that you can gather to understand, serve, and be served by your audiences.

Audiences and communicators

Writers, public speakers, and other communication professionals have used the concept of an audience analysis for a long time. A lot is written on this subject, appearing in textbooks and the popular press. Most of the work that I've seen boils down to the following seemingly simple points:

✦ Who are these people objectively? What are their ages, interests, jobs, and other relevant data?

✦ What does this audience already know and believe about this subject?

✦ What are people's needs and desires for new information in your subject area?

✦ What kind of presentation style are they likely to respond to favorably?

✦ What publications do they already trust, and to which are they likely to compare yours?

✦ What's the author's relationship to this audience? Is she a peer, an expert, or an outsider?

✦ How do you establish credibility with this audience? What do audience members consider good information sources, arguments, and examples?

✦ What tasks and purposes do your audience members have in mind as they approach your material?

This sort of analysis has motivated communicators from the ancient Greek rhetoricians to the modern technical writer and journalist. I believe that it's a pretty good list of the sorts of information required to understand how to communicate with an audience. Most of the time, you conduct this analysis quite informally, and it results in an intuitive feel that gives the communicator a sense of how to approach an audience. For a CMS audience analysis, you can make the answers to these questions explicit and relate them to the parts of the CMS that they're going to help structure.

Audiences and marketing

I rarely hear marketing people use the word *audience*, but I hear them talk about target markets all the time. A *market* itself is a group of people with common concerns that motivate their behaviors — basically, it's an audience. Within the broad market that an organization serves are market segments that consist of subgroups with identifiable traits and targetable needs.

Marketers are getting more and more precise in how they construct and manage segment data and how they target individuals. Today's merchandizing and campaign-management systems are very sophisticated in the ways that they divide people into categories (or segments) based on the data that they can collect or acquire. These systems match profiles to the materials that each group is to receive. *Profiles* are sets of traits and trait values that you can group together to define a kind of person.

> **Note** Traits are another form of metadata. They consist of data *about* a person.

Traits such as age, sex, interests, pages viewed, job type, and time on the site, for example, may be at your disposal and you can use them to define segments. You may create a segment that you call *Info Addicts*, for example, that consists of males between the ages of 16 and 25 who spent a lot of time on your site. Based on the age and sex of a visitor (which you ask or otherwise obtain) and the time that visitor spends on the site (which you measure), you can determine who is and who's not an Info Addict. Of course, the next question is, "So what?" What do you do differently with an Info Addict than with any other visitor?

Marketers use segmentation information to understand and speak to a market segment. They may design an ad campaign, for example, to reach these info addicts and draw them to your site. The kind of advertisements that Info Addicts receive are different from those that a segment that you call, say, *Casual Browsers* receives.

You can use this same approach in your CMS to identify audiences and target content to them.

Audiences and users

I've never heard programmers use the word *audience*; but as they talk about users, programmers are using the same concept. *Users* are the consumers of computer applications.

Users access an application through a user interface. To be successful, a user interface must be usable. Usability testers recruit representatives of user groups and watch them use the application to see whether it works well for them. What are these user groups if they're not audiences?

Today's hot design process *Unified Modeling Language* (*UML*) makes the link to audiences even more tangible. Programmers use UML to model the way that you use an application before they put any effort into programming it. UML defines roles as the types of people who're likely to use an application. In UML, you create a set of *use cases* that define what a type of person wants to accomplish and how you can expect her to go about accomplishing it.

For an electronic publication, audiences are users. In fact, I call audience members *users* throughout this book as I discuss people interacting with Web sites and other electronic publications. Thus application usability, user groups, and use cases apply literally to much of what a CMS produces.

In fact, I carry the notions of usability and use cases forward into my discussion of CMS audience analysis. As part of the audience analysis that you do for a CMS, you can define a set of use cases and usability concerns for each audience.

How many audiences do you have?

The Web gave rise to the notion of "one-to-one electronic marketing." The idea is to use technology to reach out to each person and serve that person individually. The computer, many believe, can know you and serve you the way that the corner grocer used to. Personally, I can't imagine a computer leaving me with the same feeling as the retailers of my youth. But personality aside, is an audience size of one obtainable in your organization? And if it's even technically feasible, is driving toward that much segmentation advisable?

First, you need to determine what level of audience segmentation *is* feasible. Considering that most publishing systems in use today don't have any notion of audiences (that is, they serve one conglomerate audience), you may be best off by beginning modestly. You may ask, "What's the smallest number of audiences that we can divide our users into and still derive tangible business benefit?" Or you may ask, "What audience segments does everybody agree on today?" or even, "Can we latch onto one or two traits to use to divide our users into just two segments?"

Regardless of how ambitious your approach is, the following things are sure:

✦ You need at least a few cycles of defining and refining audiences before you can know for sure that you have it right. If your organization's worked at this goal for a while, you can perhaps say right now who your key audiences are. If not, expect to start somewhere and continue to refine toward a stable set of audiences.

✦ Your audiences change over time. Not only do your segments get smaller and smaller, but you also begin to expand toward audiences that you may not have been initially prepared to serve or that present themselves as good opportunities to broaden your constituency.

Second, what level of audience segmentation is desirable? One-to-one marketing would have you believe that you should aim to serve segments of one: You should know each person as an individual and target each one personally. Supposing that this task is even feasible—that is, that you can put in place the technology to accomplish it—I'd question whether it's generally desirable. What does having audience segments of one really do for you? Most argue that the benefit lies in increased loyalty and a better sense of service and trust. Maybe so, but it comes with a cost as well, as the following list describes:

✦ **Content differentiation:** Can you segment and tag your content so thoroughly that it's different for each person who receives it?

✦ **Traits:** Can you create and maintain user profiles that are rich enough to differentiate every user?

✦ **Leverage:** Do you want to forgo the capability to develop messages with wide appeal and leveragability over a large number of people?

The whole concept of one-person audiences flies in the face of audience analysis. Authors don't create different content for each person. They create different content for each *kind* of person. It contradicts, too, the basic idea that organizations serve constituent groups and not isolated individuals. They craft value (products, services, information) that appeals to a *kind* of person and not to an aggregation of lone individuals who are more different than the same. So if the extra work of very small audiences doesn't stop you, the lack of real value to your organization may.

On the other hand, in some cases, certain aspects of one-to-one marketing do work: identifying users, for example, and then providing them with their purchase history; or, as Amazon.com does, sending e-mail messages announcing books that may interest a reader based on past purchases. In this last example, conceivably no two people receive the same series of e-mail messages.

Audiences and Localization

Localization is the process of making content as understandable as possible in the variety of cultures that view it. Most simply put, if you want people from more than one culture to use your content, you'd better think about localization.

Communication is at the center of a CMS. How you communicate depends a lot on the culture of the person with whom you're communicating. Thus a CMS that communicates well with people of various cultures has localization at its core. As central as localization may be, however, I've rarely seen it at the core of a CMS. Rather, it's normally at the periphery and is most often an afterthought. Why? Following are two reasons:

✦ **Ignorance:** Unfortunately, many people simply don't understand enough to know that localization is a core issue of a CMS. Either they believe that users take on the burden of understanding the language and conventions of the native culture of the organization; or they think that simply translating some of the text of the system as an afterthought is enough. Especially in the United States, but clearly in every country to some degree, an ignorance of the need for localization has helped prevent localization's wide-scale application.

✦ **Difficulty:** Localization is hard. It adds a lot of complexity to an already complex system. Variations in language and especially variations in content structure combine to drive up the effort and, in turn, the cost of a localized CMS.

In a rapidly globalizing world, staying ignorant of the need to localize for very long is difficult. And indeed, over the course of my time in the computer-information field, I've seen the consciousness and understanding of localization grow from a few voices to a full discipline and industry.

A CMS can't help you much in raising the consciousness of your organization about the need to localize, but it can deal quite effectively with the difficulty of localization. You can hand off a lot of the effort and organization that surrounds localization to a CMS. A CMS can organize the localization effort, but it can't do the localization. That requires people. So, although a CMS can make localization a lot easier, it remains an expensive and slow process.

Note　I claim no great expertise in localization. I've seen more aborted attempts at localization than I have successes. So my goal in this discussion isn't to present a comprehensive account of localization or to survey the current trends, but rather to present a set of concepts and vocabulary around localization that I can weave into the fabric of my wider discussions of content management.

What is localization?

Localization is the process of making content as understandable as possible in the variety of cultures in which people view it. I'm going to work back from this definition to one that's more useful in the context of a CMS.

The definition has the following three major concepts:

✦ **Culture:** I want to keep this very complex issue as simple as possible and define *culture* as a set of shared communication and behavior standards that a group of people adopts and upholds. Not all that long ago, geography was the main indicator of culture. People who lived near each other shared a culture. Today, that's too simple a way to look at it. As anyone who's walked down the street in any major city of the world can tell you, cultures aren't countries. Today, I'd define *culture* as a dynamic mix of language, region, ethnicity, and other affiliations. However, to stay within the general bounds of the accepted localization terminology, I use the word *locality* and not *culture* to capture the concept of localization. This has validity in the software development (and larger business) world, where often local subsidiaries of a company are responsible for handling the marketing of company products for their locality.

✦ **Understanding:** What makes content as understandable as possible? Clearly the language in which you write any text is the biggest factor. But it's not just language. As I discuss in the following section, translation is only the start. You must recognize and change a world of other, more subtle local conventions.

✦ **Process:** Localization is a process. In fact, I'd say that, by and large, it's an authoring process. The content that someone authors for one locality, someone else must then reauthor for another. The localization process encompasses many mechanical parts, where bits of content move from person to person for processing. But after the content arrives on the localizer's screen, the mechanics end and it becomes a human process of knowing what *works* in one locality or the other.

So, for the purpose of a CMS, I define *localization* as follows:

> An authoring process in which you make the communication conventions of your content optimally understandable in the various languages, regions, and affiliation groups that you care to serve.

What are your localities?

A *locality* is a specific combination of language, region, and affiliations. Following are some examples of localities that illustrate the concept:

✦ **Turkey:** You define this locality by a region (Turkey). Regardless of the language that some inhabitants may speak, you use Turkish to communicate; and regardless of their ethnic or religious affiliations (Kurds, Moslems, and so on), you speak to them as secular Moslems. You would create this locality if you were opening an office in Istanbul.

✦ **Francophones:** You define this locality by language (French). Regardless of location (Africa, Europe, North America) and any other affiliations (citizenship, political persuasion, religion, and so on), you speak to this audience in French. You may create a locality such as this one if you discover that 30 percent of your product inquiries come from French-speaking people.

✦ **Social conservatives:** You define this locality by an affiliation. It includes people that may be offended by words or images that depict the human body or allude to sex. You may create this locality to acknowledge the fact that half the people who visit your Web site come from regions or religions where conservative mores prevail. Regardless of the language that they speak or the region where they live, you speak to these people without sexual words or images.

I choose the preceding three examples not because they're common ways that people localize, but to make the point that a locality isn't always a language. For you to consider it a locality, a group of people must share a set of communication assumptions that you care to cater to.

Given the amount of work that catering to communication assumptions involves, you're unlikely to create a locality for every group that you may discover. Rather, you identify the following types of localities:

✦ **A primary locality:** This type is the default locality for your content. The most popular primary locality today is International English. This locality assumes a fluency in the English language but tries to use no expressions or styles that are idiomatic to a particular region where English is spoken.

✦ **Constituent localities:** These types are all the localities where you expect people to use your publications.

✦ **Key localities:** These types are the localities that you choose to actually serve.

To implement localization in a CMS, you group all the constituent localities into a few key localities. You choose the key localities to cover the widest set of constituents possible. The primary locality serves as the master content that you then localize into the assumptions of the key localities.

Note

I'm aware that the primary locality of this book is American Techno English. This locality involves the set of communication assumptions common to educated middle- and upper-class citizens of the United States who have a strong affiliation to the Web and electronic-publication communities. If you're not in this group, I apologize for making things easier for me and harder for you by using words such as Techno English.

Audiences and locality

Audiences and localities aren't the same concept. An audience certainly may all reside in a single locality, but an audience may also spread over a range of localities. I've heard some people advocate dividing each locality into its own audience from the start. The idea is that each locality exhibits such a different set of needs that it's necessarily a different group. Well, maybe, but then again, maybe not. I think that assuming that you always find big differences between localities is just as wrong as assuming that all localities are the same (which is the argument that people sometimes make to avoid localization altogether).

The chief lesson that audience analysis teaches you is not to assume anything but instead to find out. Your best bet, I believe, is to define your audience segments based on the content needs that you can identify and cater to. If those needs happen to divide people by language or regional lines, fine. If not, that's fine, too.

In any case, don't confuse localization with audience. A Spanish-speaking person in Chile may share more significant traits with a Russian speaker in Israel than with a Chilean in the next office. Just because one can't read Russian and the other can't read Spanish doesn't make them two audiences. It makes them members of two localities.

Different audiences get different content. Different localities get the same content in different ways.

Nonetheless, I choose the audience chapter as the spot for my major discussion of localization for the following good reasons:

✦ You direct most localization toward an audience.

✦ Localities often *are* audiences.

✦ A localization analysis shares much in common with an audience analysis.

What gets localized?

Obviously, the main event of localization is *translation*. Translating text and tracking your translations is a big job and may be all that you ever manage to do to localize your content. As part of the translation or, better, as a part of the original authoring of your content, however, you want to consider the following more subtle communication conventions:

✦ **Idioms:** These conventions are word uses that are particular to a locality. The phrase *on the fly*, for example, which I use frequently, isn't in general use throughout the English-speaking world and likely doesn't even have a good translation in many other languages. So to localize a phrase such as *on the fly* may require more than translating the words. It may require more than finding the corresponding expression in the other locality. It may require a reauthoring of the phrase to get its true meaning across in different localities.

✦ **Metaphors:** These conventions are phrases that use one set of circumstances to illustrate a similar relationship in another set of circumstances. In this book, for example, I discuss the "wheel of content management." The idea is that the relationships between content-management entities is similar to that of the relationship between the parts of a wheel. Does that metaphor make sense in all localities? I hope so! If not, a large section of this book needs reauthoring to fix the problem.

✦ **Connotations:** These conventions are the additional nuances of meaning that you ascribe to a word or phrase in addition to the main meanings that you find in a dictionary. Meanings are fairly standard, but connotations vary widely by locality. I choose the word *component*, for example, to describe classes of content partly for its connotation to me. I remember creating a stereo system out of what are generally known as components. Each component is sold separately, but together they make a wonderful sound.

✦ **References:** These conventions are specific mentions of people, things, or events that you use to make a point. I frequently refer to Amazon (at www.amazon.com), for example, hoping that it's an example that's known to my audience regardless of locality. I suspect that I'm right, but then, I wouldn't know if I was wrong.

This list isn't exhaustive, but it gives you a feeling for the kind of conventions that localization involves beyond simple translation. To continue, I turn now to the *hot spots* (yet another idiomatic expression) of localization, as the following list describes:

✦ **Look-and-feel:** In publications, you spend a lot of time figuring out how to make your publications communicate certain emotions and intangible ideas. This area may be the most locality-bound part of a CMS. What color, imagery, sound, and text style communicates which emotion varies a lot from locality to locality. What in one locality says "elegant" may, in a different locality, say "bizarre!"

✦ **Messages:** These concepts are the key ideas that you want a user to take away from your publications. (See Chapter 26, "Designing Publications," in the section "Messages.") Messages are locality bound. The immediate message especially, which you communicate as much by look-and-feel as by words, may not map well between localities.

✦ **Tone:** A general tone (casual, formal, official, friendly, and so on) is often hard to replicate across localities without major reauthoring. In this book, for example, I try to maintain a casual and friendly tone. In some localities, such a tone may very well read as disrespectful or even comical.

✦ **Examples:** You use examples to bring a concrete and tangible reference to bear on an abstract concept. As references, examples are locality bound. Examples must address the experience of your audience but must also make sense to your various localities.

✦ **Illustrations:** You use illustrations to summarize complex concepts or capture the essence of the text around them. Aside from the fact that illustrations are technically much harder to translate, you can embed a lot of local context in illustrations that can make them confusing outside their locality of origin. I use a picture of a "standard" organizational chart, for example, to discuss information flow in the organization. (See Chapter 14, "Working within the Organization," in the section "Tracking Information Flow in the Organization.") If that "standard" chart is unknown in your locality, in no way does my illustration help you to understand the concept. In fact, it's likely to confuse you more.

Localization and content management

Localization and content management go hand in hand. In fact I'd go so far as to say that the central issues of localization are among the central issues of content management, as the following list discusses:

✦ **Collection:** How do you author or acquire content in a way that frees it from its context by explicitly stating its context? For localization, you make content free from its locality by tagging the parts that are locality bound. In content management in general, you make content free from any particular audience or publication by tagging the places that are audience- or publication-specific. In both cases, you're not trying to remove the context of the content but rather to explicitly state it so that you can formulate and implement logical rules for the use of the content. In a collection, for example, you can tag each example with the localities that it's useful for. You can develop alternative examples for your other localities.

✦ **Management:** How do you store and administer content in such a way that people can find, access, and most easily use it? In localization, the point is to deliver content to the localization team as efficiently as possible. Doing so may mean delivering only the examples that need translating to a particular language because you're tagging them for the locality that uses that language. In the wider content-management world, of course, management is responsible for delivering content to wherever it needs to go.

✦ **Publishing:** How do you ensure that the right content gets into the right publication in the right locations? In localization, this task is a matter of selecting the localized version of the content. You may, for example, want to make your CMS select and display only examples that you tag for the locality of the current user. In content management in general, of course, this concept is the central purpose of the entire publishing system.

Localization can come into play in any or all portions of your CMS design. Thus I leave the detailed discussion of localization analysis and design to the specific applicable sections throughout this book. I leave this section with the following two general principles of content management that apply especially well to localization, and I offer them as general guides to localization:

✦ **Conservation of work:** A CMS doesn't reduce the amount of work that publishing content takes; it merely shifts the burden of that work from a human to a computer. In localization, you want to adopt the attitude that your job is to put as much of the work as possible onto the CMS. You can, however, only shift it so far. If you want content that's useful to people, you can't escape that fact that people must do a core of the work.

✦ **Balance of generality:** The more general that you make your content, the easier it is to reuse. The more general it is, however, the less it communicates. You must balance a CMS between the constraints of reusability and strong communication. Similarly, you must balance the need to communicate at all with your key localities with your need to communicate well with your primary locality. Whenever I say, "on the fly," I tip the balance a bit toward my primary locality to give them deeper and wider understanding at the expense of other localities that may get less understanding.

For a view of how localization fits into the larger CM picture, see Chapter 39, "Building Management Systems," in the section "Localization System."

An Example Audience Set

As in all logical design examples that I provide, I use the nonprofit organization PLAN International as my semi-hypothetical example organization. For the sake of illustration, I assume that PLAN came up with the following set of key audiences (in order of priority) in their requirements-gathering process:

✦ **Members:** This audience consists of all those who join PLAN and pay a monthly fee to support a child and a community somewhere in the world.

✦ **In-country staff:** This audience consists of all those who reside in diverse locations around the world and need to know what's happening in the organization.

✦ **Donors:** This audience consists of all those who make major grants to the organization.

✦ **Press:** This audience consists of all those who learn about and provide publicity for the organization.

As I move through the description of audience analysis, I draw on these hypothetical audiences for examples.

Analyzing Audiences

In the sections that follow, I lay out a methodology for coming to understand the audience segments that you must create. In addition, I supply some logical design criteria that you can use to fully describe each segment. As I do with all the entities in your logical design, I break the analysis into questions to get you to think, methods that you can use to plan, and questions to help you integrate your audience analysis.

The key to finding the right set of audiences is to look within your organization to see how it divides constituents now in order to be sure that you're making the most of what your organization already knows. Find out how your organization communicates with each audience now and what feedback it receives from those audiences.

For each audience, you construct the set of personal traits (for example, age, interests, and so on.) that select a person into the audience. These traits later serve as the user profiles on which you can build your personalization module. To most effectively speak to each audience, you must create a set of assumptions about what members like and dislike (for example, what motivates, impresses, and offends them). You should find publications that they know and trust now and make sure that you're providing content that's consistent with their aims. These assumptions give rise to the metadata that you add to your content so that the people who want that content the most can find it and get it delivered to them.

After defining all your audiences, decide how they relate to each other to determine whether simultaneously serving the variety of audiences that you want is possible and to determine the kinds of metadata that most effectively capture the essential needs of each audience.

Think

To help you ease into the analysis, you can ask yourself and your organization the following set of questions:

✦ **Who is the primary audience?** Do you want to serve one group of people much more than the others? If so, how much are you willing to sacrifice the needs of the lesser audiences to those of the primary audience?

✦ **Do you have too many audiences?** Can you really expect to serve the range of people you've identified?

✦ **What are your current communications?** How well and in what ways are you in touch with your audiences now? Are they satisfied? What are the opportunities to increase satisfaction? Are any feedback channels established? If so, what feedback has come through?

✦ **Who are the key members?** Can you find members of key audiences to review your work as the project progresses and help you ensure that your CMS produces the right publications?

Plan

The following sections break your audience analysis into a set of design constraints that you should collect and account for from each audience you intend to serve.

Identification

Begin your analysis by charting the main identifying characteristics of your audiences. Come up with a response to the following audience design constraints to help you keep track of and rank your audiences:

✦ **ID:** Assign each audience a unique identifier so that you can later use it in the CMS for profiles and rules.

✦ **Name:** Choose a descriptive but memorable name for each audience so that the staff accepts the name and uses it consistently in conversation.

✦ **Rank:** Give each audience a priority rank. You rank audiences relative to each other if possible. (Members are priority one, for example, and in-country staff are priority two.) If you can't reach agreement on relative ranking, rate them all according to an external scale. (Members and staff are high priority, for example, whereas the press is a low priority.)

✦ **Key member:** For each audience, identify an exemplar to whom you can point as a concrete example of the group. The person may or may not be available to your group on an ongoing consulting basis, but you should at least meet with the key member once to get a solid feeling for what people of this audience are like. If your audience is in more than one locality, can you get a key member from each main locality?

Demographics

Beyond simple identification, you should study the kind of people you expect to be in each audience. The following constraints help you get to know the kinds of people who are in a particular audience:

✦ **Personal description:** Craft a short essay that gives someone who's never met any members of this audience a clear idea of who they are. The essay should give a sense of the kinds of people in this audience and what they stand to gain personally from an affiliation with your organization. Make sure that your entire team reads and agrees with the description.

✦ **Job description:** What kind of job (or jobs) do people in this audience hold? Do they all share similar job tasks or responsibilities? What can these people gain professionally from an affiliation with your organization?

✦ **Full size:** How many people in the entire world fit into the description of this audience?

✦ **Current size:** How many people who fit into this audience does your organization currently communicate with at all? How many do you communicate with on a regular basis?

✦ **Demographics:** What ages, sexes, races, regions, languages, and other such data describe people in this audience?

✦ **Localities:** In which of your localities do people from this audience reside?

✦ **Published data:** Are any sources of data on these people available for you to access?

✦ **Platforms:** What publishing channels can these people access? You can assume that they're capable of receiving print publications, but do they have e-mail? A fax machine? Personal digital assistants (PDAs)? Can they access the Web? If so, what operating systems, connection bandwidth, and Web browsers do they use?

✦ **Technical savvy:** How technically literate are these people? Specifically, what kinds of user interfaces are they comfortable with? What technical terms can you assume that they know? What functionality are they likely to accept and use? (Are they likely, for example, to do downloads? Installations? Transactions?)

Attitudes

Learning the attitudes that members of each audience are likely to hold toward your organization and content is an important task for you. From knowledge of attitudes, you can craft the appropriate messaging for each audience. The following constraints help you understand how the audience may react to your content:

✦ **Credibility:** According to Aristotle, the perceived credibility of the speaker is more important than what she says in determining whether she's convincing to the audience. How do you establish credibility with this audience? How much credibility do you have now with its members? Have you experienced any particular failures or successes in the past with these people?

✦ **Current beliefs:** What does this audience already know and believe about the subjects that your content addresses as well as about your organization? Are you reinforcing or trying to change existing attitudes? Do members have any particularly strong positive or negative beliefs that you need to take into account? Ask yourself, "What do people of this ilk trust, respect, like, know, and believe?"

✦ **Argument:** What do members of this audience consider good arguments and examples? Do they respond more to a logical or an emotional appeal? Must you cite certain sources or quote particular people for them? Can you leverage scenarios or examples that the audience has already heard of? (Maybe, for example, you can assume that PLAN's press audience has heard about and closely followed a recent famine. Can you cite information about the famine or otherwise use it as an example to show relevance to this audience?)

✦ **Style:** What tone and presentation style does this audience expect and respond to? Can you advance the expected style to a new level in a way that shows respect for the existing style and innovation (if, that is, the audience responds to innovation)? What vocabulary and usage does the audience expect and respect?

✦ **Openness to giving data:** How much personal data (such as the design constraints in the preceding "Demographics" section) does this audience want to give? What profile collection methods do members most respect and support? Are they likely to be concerned if you buy information about them from outside sources (direct-marketing companies, for example)?

Comparisons

Come to know your competition. By emulating the characteristics of the publications that each audience respects and avoiding the characteristics that they don't like, you can significantly boost the acceptance of your own publications. The following constraints tell you what publications and organizations each audience is likely to compare you to:

✦ **Benchmark publications:** What, for this audience, are the most well-known and respected publications that cover the same information that you do? Include competitors' Web sites and other publications as well as commercial publications such as magazines and books. What publications aren't well regarded by this audience and why?

✦ **Current publications:** What publications from your organizations and others do people from this audience most commonly read? Where do your current publications for this audience rate relative to the field of benchmark publications?

Value proposition

If you provide value in your publications equal to their effort or expense for your audiences, you create a stable system that continues to draw the audience and provides your organization with the value that it deserves back from its efforts. The following constraints help you work through a value proposition for each audience:

✦ **Benefit:** What do you want from this audience? Include in your answer any actions (buy, try, use, encourage others, and so on) and any attitudes (believe, trust, understand, know, and so on) that you want your publications to this audience to affect.

✦ **Cost:** What does this audience want from you? What must you give its members for them to leave your publication with the highest level of satisfaction?

✦ **Balance:** What is the balance point between what you want from the audience and what its members want from you? PLAN, for example, may want its in-country staff to promote the organization in the towns and villages they serve in. Staff may want more free time and less hassle translating materials into the local language. The balance may be for PLAN to create a small-sized print publication that consists only of pictures of children around the world who are involved in PLAN activities. By producing such publications, PLAN serves its own needs and also those of its staff.

✦ **Communication:** How do you communicate this value equation to this audience? Crafting a balanced value proposition in the mind of your team is one thing. Really crafting it with the audience is quite another. You're probably not going to choose to put the literal words of the value equation on the home page for this audience. But what do you do? How do you clearly show the agreement the publication is willing to make? Sometimes a simple headline is enough to get the message across. PLAN, for example, may detect that a staff member logs into its site and so prominently displays the tag line "Promote PLAN in 30 seconds!"

✦ **Feedback:** How do you monitor the acceptability of the value equation over time to your audiences? You may or may not have the wherewithal to hold focus groups and send out surveys, but what do you do to make sure that your equation stays in balance while you're continuing to deliver more to both sides?

Use

Correctly assessing the uses that your audiences make of your publications is critical to your success. If they're likely to come to your publications with certain tasks in mind, discover them and tailor your publications to help each user accomplish her goal. The following design constraints help you catalog the tasks and goals that a particular audience may have:

✦ **Goals:** What are the top three things that this audience wants from each publication that you target to it?

✦ **Use cases:** For each goal, develop one or more scenarios of an audience member coming to the publication with that goal in mind. Chart out the actions that the user may take and the assumptions that she may make in navigating to the information and functionality that helps her meet that goal. What clues can you provide for this audience to indicate that certain content can be found in a particular place? What "wrong" assumptions may users make that you want to account for ahead of time?

✦ **Usability:** Given the technical savvy of this audience, how can you design your publications so that the users can reach their goals without being frustrated because they don't know how to use something? Can you get a group of members from this audience to test your ideas and assumptions? At this point in the analysis, you should catalog all the usability concerns that your audience analysis leads you to. Later, when you actually start building publications, you can run tests on the real publications.

✦ **Usage profiles:** How do you want this audience to use your publications? One time, periodically, or consistently? How much time do you expect members to spend per visit?

✦ **Disposition:** What dispositions are group members are likely to bring to a publication? Do they need quick answers, for example, or are they casually browsing; are they ready to take action, or do they need information first; do they know what they're looking for, or do they want you to tell them what they're looking for and then get it for them?

Profiles

For each audience type, you need to decide the traits and trait values that distinguish that audience from the rest of the world. After you complete this exercise for each audience, you combine your individual analyses into one overall profile analysis that charts all the traits that you intend to measure and how you expect to use these traits to decide who's in what audience. The following constraints help you work through a thorough cataloging of the traits that you want to distinguish for each audience:

✦ **Trait names:** What list of traits uniquely separates this audience from the rest of the world? Traits may be personal (age, sex, language, and so on) or professional (job title, company type, profession, and so on).

✦ **Trait values:** For each trait, determine what type of metadata field it is (free text, pattern text, Boolean, and so on). For more information on metadata fields, see Chapter 24, "Working with Metadata," in the section "Categorizing Metadata Fields." This information helps you build a user-profile database or XML schema later. PLAN, for example, may designate that donors are most likely married, with grown children, aged 50 or older, and making more than $100,000 per year.

✦ **Collection:** For each trait, determine how you value it for each person who uses your publications. You're likely to find that some traits are nearly impossible to assess without asking. See Chapter 32, "Designing Personalization," in the section "Personalization and the audience," for more information about collecting data about audience members.

✦ **Minimum requirements:** If you can't collect all the trait data on a person, what's the minimum amount that you consider sufficient to qualify a person as part of an audience? This constraint is where the profile "rubber hits the road." If you choose too little trait information, you miscategorize a lot of people and upset them. If you choose too much trait information, you can't always collect it all for each audience member, and you may end up with too few people who actually benefit from the targeted content that the audience receives.

✦ **Default audiences:** What do you do with people you can't place in an audience? Do you create a "general" audience type that gets all content? Put unknowns in one of the other audience groups? If all else fails, you can try asking users to categorize themselves. If you do so, instead of asking them to fill in a bunch of metadata fields, show them the personal and professional descriptive paragraphs that you wrote and ask them which one they think best describes them. Make sure that you provide a "none of the above" choice and a space where users can write in their own descriptions (thus providing you with invaluable feedback about the categories that you create).

Localization

Brainstorm the full list of localities that may visit your publications. Group your list into constituent, key, and one primary locality. (See the section "Audiences and Localization," earlier in this chapter, for the definitions of these terms.) Then fill in the following constraints to document your overall approach to localities:

- ✦ **ID:** Create a unique identifier for each locality that you can identify.

- ✦ **Name:** Create a name that you can use to refer to this locality later.

- ✦ **Language:** What language or languages does this locality speak?

- ✦ **Region:** In what geographical locations do people in this locality live?

- ✦ **Affiliation:** What significant affiliations (for example, social, political, religious) do people in this locality have that affect the way that you communicate with them?

- ✦ **Service:** Is this locality your primary locality, a key locality, or a constituent locality? If it's a constituent locality, what key locality serves it? Does the key locality fully encompass this locality, or are people from this locality less than optimally served? If you expect the Russian key locality to serve all Eastern European localities, for example, what respect or understanding do you lose from nonnative Russian speakers?

- ✦ **Audience:** To what audiences do people from this locality belong? Does studying the locality add anything to your audience analysis?

- ✦ **Key member:** Can you get a representative from this locality to serve as an advisor to your project?

- ✦ **Traits:** How do you know that a user is in this locality? List the traits and decide how you can collect them and how you can ensure that they're accurate.

Tasks

Consider the effect of your audience analysis on the ongoing maintenance of the CMS. Then fill in the following table to define any tasks that you imagine must happen on a recurring basis to run the CMS. Here are some task types to get you thinking:

- ✦ Periodic audience surveys.

- ✦ Review of the current set of audiences.

- ✦ Audience focus groups.

- ✦ Retrieval of user data that you buy periodically.

- ✦ Retiring inactive profiles from the user database.

- ✦ Review of the traits that make up each audience.

- ✦ Review of site logs to discover audience activity.

- ✦ Ongoing use case and usability testing.

- ✦ Periodic review of competing publications.

Finally, fill in the following table. I've provided a sample entry.

Task Name	Who	What	When	How Much	How
1. Audience focus groups	Marketing Analyst	Use Web feedback to find participants.	Once at start-up and once per year thereafter	Can be simple one-hour phone-based focus meetings	Collect Web feedback.
2. Recruit participants.					
3. Plan and conduct meetings.					
4. Debrief CMS team on results.					

The required information includes the following:

✦ **Task name:** Give the task a short but memorable name that describes it.

✦ **Who:** Indicate what person or role is responsible for accomplishing this task. (Naming an automated process here instead of a person is acceptable.)

✦ **What:** Describe how the person or process accomplishes the task.

✦ **When:** Specify at what frequency this task needs to be accomplished or how you know when it must occur.

✦ **How much:** Describe how much or how many of this sort of task you expect to do. A numerical quantity is preferable here, but if you can't come up with one, words such as *a lot*, *not much*, and so on suffice.

✦ **How:** Detail the skills, tools, or processes the person or process must have to accomplish this task.

Don't worry if the tasks that you come up with at this point are somewhat ill-defined or sketchy. In your workflow analysis (in Chapter 33, "Designing Workflow and Staffing Models"), you have ample opportunity to refine them.

Integrate

After you make your way through your audience analysis or make at least one or two passes through it, consider the following questions to help you tie the results of your analysis together and to the rest of the logical design:

✦ **The right set:** Look back over each audience. Do all the answers hang together? Did you need to answer questions with a lot of qualifiers and exceptions? Did you find a lot of diverse job descriptions, for example, in the same audience category? Could you identify a person who was typical of this audience? If you have the feeling that a particular audience has no center, that's a good indication that you may need to break it into smaller parts.

✦ **The right number:** Ask yourself again: Can you really serve the number of audiences that you've analyzed? If not, can you combine some together for the present until you get more time or funding to expand? On the other hand, can you serve more audiences than you now have? How would you further subdivide the audiences if you had the chance?

✦ **Goals:** How do your audiences support your CMS project goals and vice versa? Are these the right audiences for your goals? If you could deliver the right content to these audiences would you really be closer to meeting your organization's goals? Are any other goals suggested by your analysis? Are these the right goals for your audiences? Are any others suggested?

✦ **Agreement:** Is your organization in agreement about these audiences? What must you do to see this set accepted as *the* set of audiences that your organization serves? Are the stakeholders in your organization all likely to agree with the way that you've divided and ranked audiences? Can you hand off the ongoing audience analysis to a marketing or public relations group? How will you ensure that other analyses further refine rather than contradict this analysis?

✦ **Understanding:** Do your sponsors and project team understand these audiences? Do they understand and support the value proposition, and are they likely to agree to abide by it?

Summary

The notion of an audience for the purposes of a CMS isn't so different from other prevailing views. What a CMS needs, however, is more than just a good notion of an audience — it needs a lot of factual data about your audiences that it can use to select content. To analyze audiences for a CMS, you must perform the following tasks:

✦ Name and identify each one.

✦ Collect as much demographic and statistical data as you can on each one.

✦ Understand and account for the attitudes of the audiences in the construction of your content and publications.

✦ Decide what publications audiences are most likely to compare yours to and make sure that your publications compare favorably.

✦ Understand the uses that each audience is likely to make of your publications and make sure that you serve those uses.

✦ Create profiles for each audience that indicate definitively which users are in which audience.

In the next chapter, I discuss the complex task of fully analyzing and designing your publications.

✦   ✦   ✦

Designing Publications

In the end, the point of a CMS is to create publications that audiences want. Although most CM systems were formerly used to create only a single Web site, today most are being used for multiple Web sites, printed materials, and a growing number of other publication types, such as syndications and personal digital assistant (PDA) screens.

In this chapter, I discuss what all these publications share and how you might use a CMS to create them.

Analyzing Publications Jumpstart

This Jumpstart summarizes what you need to do to analyze publications.

Use this jumpstart as a summary without the weight of detail, or as a quick review if you've already read the section on Analyzing Publications in this chapter and want a checklist of how you analyze publications.

To analyze your publications, follow these steps:

1. Think about the publications you will create. Decide how the publications will be encapsulated by process, state (dynamic or static), use, the environment in which they'll be published, and the functionality they'll incorporate.

2. Plan the publications, including these considerations:

   - **Basic publication properties**, such as name, audiences, publishers, authors, and importance.

   - **Use cases for the publication**, which simulate how you expect a user to traverse the publication.

   - **Messages to each of the publication's audiences** in all time frames: immediate, short-term, mid-term, and long-term.

   - **Format**, including the consumption format, file delivery format, of the make-up of files, styling and style conventions, and consistency with other publications.

- **Structure of the navigation** for the publication, including definition of what constitutes nodes, contents of the TOC, the index(es), cross-reference structure, sequences, search capabilities, and consistency with wider publication groups.

- **Cycles for the publication**, which includes considerations such as size, versioning, frequency of updates across and within the publication, sections of the publication most likely to change and grow, archiving, and alignment with other publications within a wider publication group.

- **Localization**, including considerations such as user localities, look-and-feel, messaging, structure, and cycles for each locality or across all localities.

- **Tasks.** These are the recurring jobs that must be done to maintain the CMS and make sure the results of your publication analysis are included. Included are publishing cycles, editorial, build, design structure, and format reviews. In addition, you might include reviews of feedback from users and authors, usage reports, and localization cycles apart from the primary publishing cycle.

3. Integrate your publication analysis with the other analyses you have done. Make sure, above all, that your audiences want the publications you create and that you are able meet the demands of the various publications you create with a system that you can reasonably afford.

What Is a Publication?

If you're reading this book linearly, you see the terms *publish*, *publishing*, and *publication* a lot. I now need to define these terms. I'm going to start from Merriam-Webster OnLine (at www.m-w.com) which defines *publish* as follows:

> 1 a: to make generally known b: to make public announcement of 2 a: to disseminate to the public b: to produce or release for distribution; specifically: PRINT 2 c: to issue the work of (an author)

This standard definition is just right for the notion of *publish* that I have in mind (except for the fact that it gives print publications special status). I can't even decide which of the five definitions of the word that I like best. If I could extend these definitions at all, I'd merely refine the notion of *public* to the notion of an *audience*. Clearly, some publications aren't public. Much of what you publish in business you restrict to a small group of people (usually to staff, partners, or those who pay).

Publishing is releasing information. Following this definition strictly, you could call any content that you show to anyone a publication. For our purposes, I need to narrow this definition down a bit and say that a publication is information that you release, that you've unified, and that has the following characteristics:

✦ **A purpose:** In addition to deciding what you're trying to accomplish with each publication, you must also determine how each publication's purpose ties into the goals of the system at large, the other publications that the system must create, and finally to the organization as a whole.

✦ **Publishers:** You must create a team that's responsible for the ongoing composition, testing, and release of the publication and decide how they're to interact with the CMS team. You can find out more about the jobs on the publication team in Chapter 13, "Staffing a CMS."

✦ **An audience:** In addition to deciding what group each publication is serving, you need to relate its audiences to the other CMS entities.

✦ **A set of messages:** To ensure that each publication precisely targets its audiences, define what ideas the publication needs to convey at a glance, with a good look, and with an extended perusal.

✦ **Authorship:** For each publication (assuming that it has multiple authors, which is usually the case with a CMS), decide whom to cite as the author of the entire publication and which authors get attribution within the publication.

✦ **Content:** Decide which content types to include in the publication. If you don't intend to publish every component of a type, figure out what metadata should separate the components that you're including from those that you aren't.

✦ **Format:** All publications have a medium in which they are distributed (print, Web, and so on). In addition, within that medium they have (or should have) a standard procedure for rendering information that makes the publication readable and memorable.

✦ **Structure:** In addition to deciding the outline, index, cross-reference, and browse structure of a publication, decide how each of these structures relates to the CMS repository structures. Can you derive the outline of the publication from the hierarchy that holds all components, for example, or must you find a different way to generate the TOC for the publication?

✦ **Cycles:** As input to the workflow module, decide how often to refresh the publication, mark it as a new version, and review it for basic design and construction. For more information about publication workflow, see Chapter 33, "Designing Workflow and Staffing Models."

These qualities, which you give to your *released information*, unify it and make it into an understandable communication that carries weight and authority. As obviously important as these qualities are, people still often neglect them. They're what one of my professors of Communication called BDS (for Big Deal Statements). BDS have the quality of making you say, at first, "So what? Big deal!" You can't easily disagree with them, and so they're easy to dismiss. The interesting thing about BDS is that they're so obvious that they disappear and people just ignore them. You know it, but you forget it. The issues behind content, format, and cycles are not generally overlooked and are covered in the section titled "Plan," later in this chapter. In the following sections, I look at the other qualities in this list, focusing on what people often forget when they create electronic publications.

Note

A classic BDS from human communication theory is that "People tend to face each other if they're speaking together." This statement is so obviously true that it's seemingly useless. What's interesting isn't the statement, but the fact that someone even notices this obvious phenomenon and devotes her full attention to it for critical analysis. Behind this obvious statement is the not-at-all obvious study of body language and nonverbal communication that it initiates.

Publication purpose

The purpose is the yardstick against which you measure all parts of the publication. Refer to my example of a typical intranet team (in Chapter 3, "Content Has Structure"). The first thing that the intranet team does in that example is to say what it wants on the intranet. Nobody bothers to ask, "Why do we want an intranet?" And nobody notices that nobody asks. Obviously, each publication needs a purpose. Why, then, do people so often forget the purpose in electronic publications? I offer the following two reasons (and you can no doubt think of some others):

✦ **The needs of the project are vague.** (The case of the intranet project that I describe in Chapter 3 demonstrates this point.) In many other cases, the technology is barely understandable, and no established, reliable process is in place to create an electronic publication. Thus many people who begin electronic publication projects are already confused before they walk into the first meeting. They're further thrown off balance as the complexity of the project becomes apparent. Often, they let whoever seems to have an idea rule them. If you instead take a cool, calm approach, even in the face of mass confusion in the room, you can advocate starting out with the hardest but most important question: Why are we doing this project?

✦ **Life at the electronic frontier proceeds at an accelerated pace.** Events move so fast in the electronic world that people forget to start at the beginning and forget what they decided last week. I see it happen all the time; people just panic too much to slow down and consider the basics. The first meeting starts somewhere in the middle of the process and dives straight for the details. This situation gives people the feeling of immediate progress but ensures that unresolved problems intrude later in the process, when they're much harder to fix.

Classical (that is, before-the-Net) publications are never so lax. Each publisher knows exactly what the purpose of the publication is — for booksellers, for example, it's to sell enough books to make money. For magazines, the purpose is to make money from advertisers by providing content to a group of targeted users. Of course, publishers have loftier goals, too, such as providing users with valuable and edifying content. Whatever their goals, classical publishers know how to collect, manage, and publish content to suit their purposes.

The Turing Publication Test

Alan Turing, the father of computing, proposed a famous test for the existence of artificial intelligence in computers. He said that if a person of average intelligence asks a machine questions and can't tell whether the answers are from a computer or a person, the machine must have the intelligence of a person. For such a simple statement, I am amazed at the amount and the depth of technology and philosophy it has engendered. Well, it seems to me that a similar test ought to be proposed for testing the value of a publication produced by a CMS. The test goes like this: "If an average member of the audience of a publication cannot tell by looking at a publication whether it was produced by hand or by a CMS, the publication has been produced artificially with intelligence."

In other words, the goal is to produce publications that work as well as those that are now produced by hand. If users get CMS-produced publications that are as well produced and thought out as they get now from hand-made materials, the users will be at least as happy as they are now. From another angle, the Turing publication test implies that if the average audience member feels that there are people behind the publication who are paying attention, she is more likely to pay attention, too. If she feels that some machine is behind the publication, she is more likely to ignore or denigrate the importance of the publication.

Recognizing that a publication needs a publisher isn't hard. What's often harder to see for those involved in a project who aren't publishers (users, authors, and management), however, is that the publishers have needs and constraints that operate as strongly as any other factors in the concept and execution of the publication. The publishers are a group of people with strengths and weaknesses that inevitably affect the publication. The classic example is a situation where the technical staff and the creative staff don't get along. They speak to each other with absolutely no understanding on either side and end up with a good measure of rancor between them. Their inability to work things out has nothing to do with the purpose of the publication but results in a publication where the purpose becomes to prove a point and where the execution resembles the tug-of-war that's happening behind the publishers' closed doors. Remember that publishers are people and that what they can and can't — or will and won't — do has as much effect on the final publication as any other factor.

Audiences

A publication is an asynchronous conversation. It doesn't happen in real time. As they write, authors imagine what the reader is likely to think next, and they respond to it in the next sentence. After reading the work, the reader, on the other hand, responds in her head to the author's words. To the extent that the authors can guess what the user thinks next and responds in text and to the extent that the user understands the text, the conversation continues. In fact, one quality of great works is that they inspire a lively exchange with the author in the reader's mind.

So, just as every publication has an author, it has an audience. And just as people creating electronic publications often forget to account for the author, they often forget to account for the audience as well.

In the electronic-publication world, your job isn't as simple as understanding a single audience. First, because of the ubiquity of the Web, an electronic publication can reach a huge range of people. Determining just whom your publication may attract — and why — isn't easy. Second, you now have the technical capability to detect and record the personal profile of each user. By using this information, you can potentially tailor the publication to every user, effectively creating as many audiences as users.

Most electronic publishers get the idea that audiences are hard to define. What they forget is that their true audience isn't who reaches them, but whom they want to reach. I've witnessed many site discussions that have been stopped dead by the comment "We can't assume that about the user. Anyone can reach us through a search of the Web." This fact is, of course, true but generally not relevant. Does a restaurant fail to define its atmosphere and cuisine because anyone can walk in off the street? No, the restaurant targets the kind of people that it wants to serve and caters entirely to those people. If someone wanders in uninvited, adapting to the ambiance and cuisine of your publication is that person's problem. You always have a particular group of people in whom you're most interested. You may also be aware of other groups in whom you're less interested. You can't take the entire world into account if you want to create a publication that's of particular interest to your core audiences.

The fact that you can now target each user individually and the fact that you can't cater to everyone may seem to contradict, but they don't. In fact, the former depends deeply on the latter. If you don't narrow down your audiences enough, you never know them well enough to serve them what they really want, you can't collect precise profile information from them, and you can never adequately segment the content that you provide.

You ought to be able to communicate the purpose of your publications in a few senten someone hears it, she should immediately be able to imagine what's part of its conten what isn't. She also knows immediately whether the content is of interest to her and v questions or interests it should satisfy. Here's an easy test of whether a purpose state a good one: Say it to someone in the target audience for the publication. If it's good, it immediately with your listener. If you get any strange looks or substantial questions, have more work to do.

Publication purpose is a concept closely related to that of the content domain that I in Chapter 30, "Designing Content Access Structures," in the section "The Content Do

Publishers

The *publishers* are the people behind the publication that put in the time and effort the release of that publication. The publishing group may or may not include the auth content, but it's nonetheless intimately concerned with the content. In the world of c information systems, the authors are rarely the publishers. The publishers are usua group of editorial and technical experts who take what authors create and turn it in site and other types of publications.

Before the system's in place, the publishers are the CMS project team. After the sys and running, the project team must morph into a set of publication teams that mak each publication continues to come together and gets out to its audience. The publ ensure that the publication serves its purpose. In the electronic world, they also er the publication "works" (doesn't crash or do other nasty things). A single publicati following staff:

- ✦ **Management staff:** Managers are responsible for the business of the publica (expenses, revenue, and staffing).

- ✦ **Editorial staff:** Editors are responsible for creating or acquiring content and it for publication.

- ✦ **Technical staff:** Tech support staffers are responsible for building the syste collects, manages, and publishes the content.

- ✦ **Creative staff:** Creative types are responsible for the look-and-feel of the pu well as its appeal and capability to resonate with the target audience.

- ✦ **Architectural staff:** These staff members live somewhere between the edit cal, and creative staffs and are responsible for the structural design of the tem and the content itself.

For more information about the roles of publishers, see Chapter 33, "Designin and Staffing Models."

In a CMS, you share most of these resources among publications. The sharing cr efficiency across publications but can also mean that people lose focus on the p because their main concern is the system. To avoid this trap, make sure that yo view that the system is only there to create great publications. Also make sure t a person or team that looks only at the end publications and pushes the CMS te great publications despite the fact that making great publications is harder than age publications.

Messages

If a publication is a conversation, consider the messages that your publications send. Consider the following hypothetical conversation between Laura and a series of sites that she visits:

Laura: (Visits site 1) Can I buy a printer cartridge on your site?

Site 1: Click here to win a vacation for two! By the way, this site is about printers.

Laura: Next site. (Clicks to site 2.)

Laura: Can I buy a printer cartridge on your site?

Site 2: Welcome to Printer World. We know everything about printers and we're willing to share that information with you. Our experts scan the globe for printer information and present it here. Click here for more . . .

Laura: So does that mean that you sell printer cartridges? (Clicks the link that the site presents.)

Site 2: With more than 200 contributing printer experts, we know what we're talking about. What do you want? Printer FAQs? Printer Specs? Printer parts?

Laura: Maybe it's under Printer Parts? Forget it! Next site. (Clicks to site 3.)

Laura: Can I buy a printer cartridge on your site?

Site 3: We're Printer City. What do you want for your printer? Drivers, Supplies, a new one?

Laura: Supplies, I guess. (Clicks the Supplies link.)

Site 3: Pick the name of your printer and the supply that you want, and we'll go find it for you.

Laura: Shoot, what kind is it? HP something.

Site 3: Can't remember your printer model? Click here.

Laura: (Clicks to next screen) Oh yeah, that one. It's a 4537s.

Site 3: We have these cartridges for you.

Laura: I'll take 2.

Laura tries to have a conversation with each site that she visits whether the site "talks" back or not. Site 1 ignores her completely, so she passes it by. Site 2 responds to her question but not in a very understandable way. Still, it's a response, so Laura continues. She clicks and asks her question again. Site 2 still doesn't respond appropriately, so Laura gets frustrated and clicks away.

Site 3 responds to her first question well enough to get her to continue the conversation. On the second screen, she finds the answer to her question (yes) and a question in return (What printer do you have?). Laura says, "I don't know," and the site responds, "I'll help you figure it out." Laura uses the site to figure out her answer and gives it back to the site. The site fulfills her original request without further unnecessary banter. Laura goes away satisfied.

Are the first two sites bad? For Laura they were. They couldn't hold the conversation that she wanted, so she stopped speaking. For someone looking for a chance to win a vacation on a printer site, the first site has just the right dialog prepared. For someone wanting the definitive word on some printer issue, Site 2 is the one to talk to. For a person looking for a cartridge, Site 3 is the one in the know. As long as Site 1 and Site 2 are happy with the conversations that they support, all is well. If they want to attract a different type of dialog, they need some work.

A site or any other publication provides messages whether you intend it to or not. Here are some questions that you can expect audience members to ask your publication:

✦ **What are you?** The most fundamental question is always the first. People want to know what kind of publication you have. Are they in the right place? Is this publication in a realm of interest? Whatever kind of publication you're presenting (commercial, informational, political, and so on), audience members want to know quickly whether it's what they're interested in.

✦ **What do you have?** If your publication passes muster on the first question, the next question is often about the scope or contents of the publication. What's inside?

✦ **Are you for people like me?** After someone comes to a publication, she quickly asks whether she's part of the target audience. The question is an emotional one for the audience member. She's asking, "Can I be comfortable with you? Do you understand me and can you respect me? Are you one of us or one of them?"

✦ **Do I get value?** The first three questions stop a person a person cold. If a visitor doesn't get past them, she stops the conversation. If your publication passes on the first three counts, only then does the person ask the most pivotal question: Is pursuing this publication worth my time, effort, or money?

These questions, and surely others, are the entry requirements that your publications must fulfill for acceptance. Potential audiences don't just ask the questions once. In fact, they ask them over and over again, not only of the publication as a whole, but also of each new part of the publication that they encounter. In addition, they ask the questions repeatedly over time at the following events, or time increments:

✦ **The instant messages:** As fast as your eyes and ears can perceive, you form an impression. This impression is a nonverbal one based on features such as color, information density, layout, and style. If I flash the cover of the *New York Times* in front of you for a quarter second, it produces a different impression on you than does a page from a color comic book. Possibly without even knowing it, people ask and answer these questions (especially the question, "Are you for people such as me?") in the first instant of interaction.

✦ **The short message:** In somewhere between 5 and 30 seconds, people generally decide whether a publication is worth their effort. (I have no scientific study to back up this statement, but I don't take it as a particularly controversial one.) Within that time, the nonverbal impression can really sink in and a person can read and process the major words. In this time, if your publication doesn't answer all the entry questions, it's denied.

✦ **The midterm message:** As an audience member continues to peruse the publication (often in pursuit of a particular goal), she asks the questions again. This time, the content itself (the text, media, and functionality that the person accesses) is the part providing the answers. If the answers that the content provides don't match and deepen the answers that she gathered from the nonverbal cues, the audience member may lose interest in the publication or, worse, abandon it all together because it misled her.

✦ **The long-term message:** If the nonverbal and content responses to the audience member's questions are enough to keep her there for a first complete interaction with the publication, the publication's done better than the vast majority of communications. The audience member asks her questions of the publication again to see whether it's worth continued periodic attention. (In other words, does the person mentally "subscribe" to the publication?) Here the messages come more from the metacontent then from the content itself. The content that the person's already seen isn't as important as the content that the person assumes that she *will* see if she continues to use the publication. She decides if the site is literally for her and, furthermore, if it is worthwhile for her to come back in the future.

Of course, if an audience member *must* use the publication, she sticks with it regardless of how unsatisfying the messages are. The classic example is of the product manual that screams at you that you're not welcome inside. Still, if your need for the information inside is great enough, you persevere long enough to extract whatever use you can and then quickly exit. In this case, the high value of the content overrides the considerable cost of getting it.

A publication that wants to hold its audience anticipates the questions that audience members ask and the answers that they need to hear. In the section "Messages," later in this chapter, I present a method for working through messaging. Basically, you decide how you intend to answer the entry question and any more specific questions that each audience type has for each publication at each time increment.

Authorship

Every published work comes from somewhere. You never read, watch, or listen without some consideration of who's responsible for it. I don't expect to get much argument about that point, but I should. What happens if no single person or group authors your publication? Do you find any authorship at the search engine site Lycos (at `www.lycos.com`)? At first glance, the answer is clearly no. Lycos doesn't create the content; it simply dispassionately displays it. Lycos is an aggregation point where everyone else's authored works appear.

But look again. *Lycos* is the author of its site. If I don't find what I want, do I blame no one? Of course not. I blame Lycos and go over to Yahoo!. Furthermore, you see very tangible artifacts of the authors at Lycos. The name *Lycos*, for example, is all over the place. You see the style and layout of the site, the way that it enables you to search, and the way that it displays hits. Finally, and this reason is why Lycos likes being an author, you see the money-making ads and inducements that portals such as Lycos live on.

What Lycos and the other portals get, classical publishers have always known and Net publishers often forget. The users assume authorship whether you want them to or not. Make the most of it. In lieu of any named author, the user creates one from whatever clues that you give. Why? Because authorship is a pivotal part of the context that people put around any content to determine its credibility and meaning. Consider the following:

The world is flat. —*Joe Nobody* (a guy you pass raving on the street)

The world is flat. —*Alan Greenspan* (Chairman of the U.S. Federal Reserve)

In the first case, you're led to believe that the comment is about geography, and you're not likely to believe it. In the second case (if you know that Alan Greenspan is a very famous economist), you're led to believe that the comment is about financial performance, and you're more likely to believe it.

So authorship is useful and unavoidable. So what do you, the savvy publisher, do about it? Consider the following points:

✦ **Don't avoid the issue of authorship of your publications.** Address it before your users address it for you. Understand how to convey authorship and convey the kind of authorship that you feel best represents you.

✦ **Make sure that you cite and profile authors as much as possible.** Include names and appropriate background on all the major sources of your content. If you strip this information out (as very often happens), you deprive your audience of one of the most important sources of context for understanding and believing what you publish.

You can see the questions to ask in an author analysis in Chapter 28, "Accounting for Authors."

Publication format

Format comes in two basic flavors: Format is both the way that you digitally encode information, and the codes that you use to determine how to visually render information.

Look in Chapter 2, "Content Has Format," for more information about the two flavors of format.

A publication needs both these aspects of formatting. Take a printed magazine, for example. The publishers may use a product such as QuarkXPress. QuarkXPress encodes the information that you enter into it in a particular way. The publisher works with QuarkXPress files that only QuarkXPress (unfortunately) can decode and manipulate. Additionally, QuarkXPress comes with a set of formatting features (character, paragraph, section, and so on.) that you can apply to the information to determine how that information appears on the printed page.

Every publication encompasses these same two kinds of format. A Web site generally uses an ASCII file format to store its HTML. Almost any word processor or layout tool (including Quark) can decode and manipulate ASCII. You encode the formatting codes that HTML uses by using ASCII, but these codes require extra processing to turn them into visual qualities. Web browsers and most recent versions of word processors can decode and manipulate HTML formatting codes.

The main issue with publication formats arises when you have more than one. If you're just producing a Web site, you get everything into HTML and go from there. But what if you're creating a Web site and a set of pamphlets from the same content? Suppose you produce the brochures from QuarkXPress files, but the site is HTML. How do you manage the conversion from one format to the other? Do you need an additional "master" format (such as XML) that enables you to most effectively produce the publication formats that you need? If not, how do you specify formatting commands for one storage format inside the tags of another?

Chapter 37, "Processing Content," provides some detail on the decision to have a master format.

Publication structure

Even the most minor publication has some structure. Look at any flyer tacked to a telephone post. You always (well, almost always) see large type on the flyer announcing what the flyer's for. This type is the flyer's title. You're also likely to see some details that appear subordinate to the title by type size or position. Finally, you usually find some indication of an author or provider of the flyer, generally at the bottom. Thus you can break the flyer down into a title, detail, and author info. Of course, as the complexity of the publication increases, the structure increases. You need to call in more and more of the structural techniques that I discuss in this book to manage the complexity.

Publications can have all the access structures (see Chapter 30, "Designing Content Access Structures"), including hierarchies, indexes, cross-references, and sequences. They can also have all the structure metadata ranging all the way from characters to publication groups. (See Chapter 24, "Working with Metadata.")

From a publication perspective, perhaps the most important structure is the *node*. Although the key structure of a CMS as a whole is the component, the key unit of a publication is the node. A node is the basic chunk size of the publication. In Web publications, this chunk is a page. You view Web sites one page at a time; each page is a separate file, and saying that the Web publication consists of pages is most natural. In most other electronic publications (CD-ROM applications, Help systems, and the like), the node is also something like a page. It's the amount of content that appears on-screen as a unit. You may store it in a file or database, but it always appears to the reader of the publication as a unit.

In print publications, the node isn't as easy to identify. Print publications often blur the boundaries between chunks in favor of a continuous narrative approach. Still, you can usually point to a chunk of some size. Even the most flowing novels have chapters. Each chapter is a node of the overall book. More structured books chunk content down to various heading levels, each heading serving as a unified chunk of the larger whole. Magazines use articles as their basic units. Each article is a different whole chunk of the overall publication. *Section* was the only word I could come up with to describe these chunks. Trying for an analogy, I propose that: As a *page* is to an electronic publication, the *section* is to the print publication. Print publications use sections to chunk the overall work into a set of unified nodes.

Most important for a CMS, a node is the unit of publication that a publication template creates. If you run a template, out pops one node of the publication. This reality is clearest on the Web, where a template almost always yields one HTML page. It's less clear in print, where one template may yield a chunk of the publication with many sections. Still, in print publications that a CMS creates, you see a node of some size that a single template produces.

As is the case with the format, the big issues with structure arise if you have more than one. If you have only a single publication, the structure of the publication is everything that's there. If you have two publications, however, you need three structures — one for each publication and an extra one for the content whenever it's not in either of the publications. To produce more than one publication from the same content base in a CMS, the content base itself must be well-structured enough that you can derive the structure of the child publications from it. Or, at the very least, you must store the structures for the publications somewhere outside the publication, where the CMS staff can update and edit them.

Cross-Reference   For more information on multiple publications and content management, see Chapter 11, "The Branches of Content Management." For information on creating publication structures from a central structure, see Chapter 40, "Building Publishing Systems," in the section "Navigation building."

Publications can be good or bad

Without putting any value judgments on the truth or ultimate worth of a publication, you can still say just how good it is from a CMS perspective. Good content is maximally useful. A good publication does the following:

✦ **Meets a particular need:** It clearly states its purpose up front, and all the content within relates directly to that purpose.

✦ **Serves a particular audience:** The publication clearly states its assumptions about its audience up front, and all the content within is authored with the target audience in mind. A user can easily determine whether she's in or out of the target audience. If she's in, she can understand any content in the publication, and the publication communicates in a style that she's familiar with and can appreciate.

✦ **Is easily navigated:** Given a desire that's consistent with the publication's purpose, a user can find applicable information without undue trouble. If the publication doesn't contain the content that the user's looking for, she knows quickly. The publication may give her some indication of why her area of concern, although part of the purpose of the publication, is not present in its content.

A bad publication is just as easy to define. If people complain about content, it's usually for one of the following reasons:

✦ **It's not applicable:** The user expects the content to cover her issue of concern, but it doesn't.

✦ **It's not comprehendible:** The user finds applicable content but can't understand it.

✦ **It's out of date or wrong:** The user finds relevant content, but it's so old that it's no longer correct or very helpful.

✦ **It's not accessible:** The user strongly suspects that the issue of concern is there somewhere, but she can't find it.

The first two complaints concern purpose and audience. If it's a good publication, the user can tell immediately whether it contains her interest area. If she's part of the publication's audience, it's understandable to her. This cavalier observation, however, has two big caveats: First, some users are lazy. Do all users review and consider the purpose and audience of a publication before passing judgment on it? Often, they don't. Second, it assumes that the purpose and audience are themselves accessible to the user up front. *Up front*, of course, is a term left over from the pre-electronic days, when an author had the right to expect users to start at the beginning. On a Web site, you really can't tell on what page a user may start. If a visitor jumps directly into the middle of your work, what chance do you have of informing that person of its purpose or audience?

The third complaint concerns publishers and publishing processes. If it's a good publication, content that is likely to become dated at some point is either clearly time-stamped, removed from the system in a methodical way, or both as part of a normal publishing cycle. A page called "Flu vaccination guidelines," for example, should be clearly marked as "... for 1997" or retired from a health care site entirely.

The last complaint deals squarely with the navigation of a publication. If I had a nickel for every time that I saw an interesting story on the cover of a magazine and then couldn't find the story inside, I'd be rich enough to buy off all the marketing people and make them drop that technique for making me flip past all the ads. Many sites put an arbitrary dictum on themselves to try to improve navigation. "No more than three clicks to any significant piece of information," they may profess. This ideal is a noble one but denies many of the more subtle ways that people find information, most notably by browsing and following links to related information. The lazy-user caveat applies here, too. The world's best navigation can't help if the user doesn't use it.

Publication gotchas

When you get right down to it, a lot of little differences exist in the way content is presented in various media, and these are issues you have to consider quite apart from the questions of audience, messages, publications, and so on, which I discussed earlier in this chapter. The medium in which you publish content introduces its own small but tough problems. Here are a few of the more nagging issues you may have to overcome to make text work across platforms:

✦ **What publication are you in?** What are you reading right now? A book, a Web page, an e-mail message, a printed document? If you have ever tried to write without any reference to the wider publication, you know that it is very difficult to avoid naming the publication.

As an example, consider the sentence, "This ___ is about content management." This what? The sentence may end up in any number of publication types. It's really hard to avoid naming the publication, but it is also hard never to refer to the publication. As I see it, you have two choices (and only one good one) about how to handle this situation. You can invent a single word that generically covers all publications, or you can add in the publication type when you build the publication. For example, to create a single word, you can say "this publication" or "this work," but that may not sound right in some publications (is an automated e-mail really a "work?").

Your other possibility is to fill in the name of the publication as you publish it. For example, wherever you want to refer to the publication, you can, instead, put in a little tag (say, <PUBNAMEHERE/>). Then, when the publication template runs, it transforms the tag into the appropriate name. This method works famously at publication time. At author or acquire time, on the other hand, it adds a bit of a burden. It means that all authors have to use the tag and be provided with training, a user interface, validation, and feedback as they use it. In acquired text, you must find publication references and replace them with the appropriate tag. The find and replace process is rarely fully capable of being automated because of the many contexts in which an author can refer to a publication. So it will likely require staff time.

✦ **What section are you in?** Books have parts and chapters; Web sites have pages, sections, and sometimes parts, but not usually chapters. Other media have their own divisions. Sometimes, as you did with the title of the publication, you need to refer to its parts. Again, a simple tag may be fine to represent the change. In fact, rather than creating a different tag for every fill-in, why not just create a Fill-In tag with a type attribute (for example, <FILLIN Type="ThePub">). This makes a very efficient and compact system for expressing variables in the text. But, as usual, what's easier for you is harder for them. This system would require even more training, a better user interface for authors, and more sophisticated programs for acquisition and validation.

✦ **How big are the individual chunks of content?** Different media have different accepted content chunk sizes. They range from huge for fiction and other heavily narrative content in which the entire work might be a single long chunk, down to tiny chunks for catalogs and other very datalike content, where thousands of chunks are organized and distributed. The same content may have to be represented in a range of chunk sizes. Similarly, the level of structure that is acceptable in one medium may be too much or too little in another. For example, today's standard Web site has relatively small chunks with a lot of subheadings and other visible structure. Today's books have longer chunks, fewer headings, and no extra navigation or other structure included. Although both of these media seem to be coming toward each other in chunking, you still have ample reason to ponder how to have structure and not show it. To produce both a fine- and a coarse-grained structure, you store the fine-grained structure and then don't show it when you don't need it — for example, if your Web content needs eight levels of heading and periodic summaries. On the other hand, in print, only five heading levels and no summaries are required. In your repository, you store the summaries and all eight heading levels. Your print templates will suppress the summaries and lower headings.

✦ **Do I need summaries?** Summaries are much more useful in some media than in others. The smaller the reading space, the more you have to rely on summaries for communication. In fact, summaries are all you can deliver on severely limited devices, such as Wireless Application Protocol (WAP) phones. In print, they are often not used at all. On the Web, they are indispensable. Until the screen density (a measure of how readable the screen is) goes up by two orders of magnitude, you need the visual aid that summaries give you on the Web. Today, screen density is around 70 dots per inch on most screens; when it hits 7,000, you will have a screen that can contend with paper for legibility and sharpness. At that point, people will stop complaining about how hard it is to read directly from the computer screen. In addition, when the computer screen can fold up and fit in your pocket or lie flat like a book, it will become a more comfortable device — capable of competing with the convenience of paper. Until the time the computer screen is as easy to use as paper, you need summaries to cut down on computer reading strain. Summaries, like other structures, must be in the repository whether or not you use them in all publications.

✦ **Do I need a narrative?** What enables many books to have so little apparent structure is that they have a structure built right into the words that keeps you oriented — it's called the *story*. The story (or narrative or plot) is an overall framework that you pick up on as you read, watch, or listen. Narrative is an organizational structure that precedes any structures I have talked about here by millions of years in human history. It can also be an enormous pain to work with.

The problem arises because narratives are implicit structures. You have no easy way to find and extract the narrative from the content in which it is embedded. Narrative is often communicated by very subtle metaphors, oblique references, and other deeply contextual means. Using today's technology, if the content you want to reuse makes frequent reference to a story behind it, either it has to have major manual reworking to disconnect the story altogether or travel as a single unit with the narrative intact.

✦ **Do I need transitions?** Narrative is not completely unmanageable. There are not-so-deep parts of it that can be easily managed. One such part is the *transition*. In a transition, a relationship is made between the content before and after, and both may be related to the wider structure of the publication. For example, books commonly have a transition at the beginning and end of each chapter. The transition at the beginning of the chapter introduces the topic of the chapter and puts it in the context of the book as a whole. The transition at the end of the chapter might mention what is coming in the next chapter and relate it to what is in the current chapter.

Transitions are little pieces of narrative that are sprinkled throughout a book to aid the overall narrative of the book. Because transitions tend to come at defined locations — before and after significant chunks of text, they can be easy to find and manage. For example, you might find that a transition paragraph always follows the level-one headings of a report you need to convert. You can tag that paragraph as a transition as you process the report. Later, you can choose to exclude the transition paragraph when the section of the report is used outside the context of the full report. Of course, transitions are just the smallest tip of the narrative iceberg, but you have to start somewhere.

✦ **How do I deal with hard-coded sequences?** People naturally author content in the order they expect content to be consumed. The default attitude is, "If I just wrote the previous piece, and they're on the current piece, they must have just read the one I wrote right before this." This is a natural attitude, but it is one that leads to management problems; and for many publications, it's not an accurate assumption. It is hard not to assume that there is a subsequent and previous concept as you are authoring, but you can do it if you really try. It is sometimes impossible to find and change these assumptions automatically in content you are acquiring.

Of particular note in this regard are the time terms such as "earlier," "later," "next," "previous," "just," "soon," "before," and "after." Many texts make extensive use of these terms to provide orientation and direction to the user. But what happens when you can't count on the reader's having the same time orientation as you? As opposed to publication name and part references that I don't believe you can do without, I do believe you can do without time references or, at least, you can neutralize them. It is a hard habit to break, but with effort and forethought, you can refrain from providing this sort of structure, and your text will still be understandable and navigable in any medium.

You may choose to remove time references, but then again, maybe you don't want to. After all, any orientation clues that you can provide can't but help the user if they are done correctly. If you choose to keep time references in the text, make sure that you account for the situation in which the reference to "earlier" or "later" content is nowhere nearby or not present at all. For example, when the referent on the Web may not be just a few paragraphs away, as it was in print, make sure that you provide some sort of navigation to the earlier or later content. If the referred-to content is not published with the referencing text, make sure that you trap this situation when you build a publication and handle it either automatically or manually. For example, you can choose to suppress any time reference when the referenced concept is not included in the publication.

✦ **How do I deal with references to current state?** People do not tend to write in a timeless way. Rather, they tend to talk about today and refer to the current state of the content as if it will always be the state. I caught myself doing it again at the beginning of this section when I said, "... which I discussed earlier in this chapter." What if, later, I split up this chapter and publish the part you're reading now without the earlier sections? How will I ever find this sentence when someday it needs to be changed? It's overkill to invent some tag, but I do want to ensure that there is the least opportunity for my content to time-out. In my own CM Domain, I settle for close enough and prepare for some number of tiny time bombs to go off in my text. You will have to decide for yourself how closely to track references to the current state of your domain. The current state issue is a bit different from the other gotchas I describe. The rest of this list is about differences across publication platforms; this one is about differences in the same platforms over time.

This short list could go on. I'm sure you can point to some great reuse bloopers that you have seen. Luckily, most people will give you the benefit of the doubt when they see the "seams" of your CMS. People are accustomed enough to seeing content that is out of context that they can usually get the right idea anyway. If I come across a sentence that says, "As I just stated . . ." and the author has not just stated, I usually assume that something got missed and go on. If anything characterizes humans and sets them apart from computer systems, it is how they can get meaning even from a really structurally messed-up a piece of content. That thought may have to hold us for quite a while, as our computer and human content management systems struggle to catch up with what our past publication methods have been doing for a very long time. The final saving grace here is that the more trust and confidence audience members have in the quality and usefulness of your content (both information and functionality), the more they will forgive the small context glitches that are bound to show through your CMS. Still, if you want to pass the Turing publication test, you must account for all the little clues that tell your audience that a dumb computer, not a smart person, is behind your publication.

Analyzing Publications

In the sections that follow, I lay out many of the questions that you should answer to fully define your publications. As always, I begin with questions to get you thinking about publications and then present the constraints that you can address to plan for your publications. Finally, I present some of the issues to consider if you want to integrate your publication analysis with the rest of your logical design.

Analyzing your publications is mostly a matter of deciding whom the publication is to serve, how it's to communicate with them, and how you can construct the format and structure of the publication. This process is no different from what you do outside a CMS to design a publication. Within a CMS, you have the additional burden of deciding how one publication fits in with the audience, messages, structure, and function of all the other publications that the CMS produces.

Think

Before you start on your publication analysis, think about the set of publications that you got from your requirements-gathering process in light of the planning that you've done so far. Review the section "What Is a Publication?" earlier in this chapter and decide what you can do to be sure your publications do not overlook any of the key qualities I mention there. Then consider these more specific questions that raise the issues you will confront in the rest of the publication analysis:

✦ **Publishing:** Do you consider yourself (or the person who oversees your CMS on an ongoing basis) a publisher? If not, what's the difference between what you do and what a publisher does? Do the stakeholders consider what you're doing as publishing? What's the difference for them?

✦ **Dynamic and static publications:** Do you understand the difference between a dynamic and a static publication? How many of your publications are dynamic? Can you make any of them static to cut down on complexity?

✦ **Syndication:** Do you intend to syndicate any content? Do you have any opportunities to do so now that your content publishing system is well organized?

✦ **Surrounds:** What sort of branding information do you want in your publication? How standardized can you make the appearance of this information? What sort of advertising or promotions do you want in your publication? How standardized can you make the appearance of this information? To what extent can you share the surrounds between publications and within the same publication?

✦ **Functionality:** What sort of functionality (forms, Java applications, and so on) do you want in your publications? How much of this functionality do you want to make into content components and how much do you hard-code into your templates? Can you standardize the appearance of functionality throughout your publications, or should it look different in each publication?

Plan

The following sections address the issues that you should confront as you design a system of publications.

Basic properties

For as many publications as you expect to create, describe the following design constraints:

+ **Name:** What's the name of this publication?

+ **Purpose:** What's the purpose of the publication?

+ **Audience(s):** Whom does this publication serve?

+ **Publishers:** What one person ultimately ensures that this publication meets its goals and reaches its audiences? What other team members work specifically on this publication.

+ **Authorship:** What qualities must an author possess to create content for this publication? Who do audience members think is the overall author of the publication? How can you communicate authorship? How can you cite individual authors in the publication? Under what circumstances and in what way? How does the way that you handle authorship in this publication lend to its credibility? How are your authors positioned in the publication? (Do you want your audiences to see the publication as, for example, a compilation, a periodical with staff writers, or some other structure?)

+ **Rank:** How does this publication rate in importance relative to the others that you intend to produce?

Use cases

A use case is a scenario for how you expect a user to interact with your system. You create a set of use cases to help determine if your system accounts for all the kinds of things that you expect a user might do with your system. For each publication and audience, chart the list of steps that you expect the audience to go through to find information in your publication. Include the following information:

+ The name of the audience.

+ The goal an audience member is likely to have in mind.

+ The set of steps that you expect the audience to try and the result of those actions in the publication.

+ The wrong turns that are possible and how an audience member can recover from them and get back on track.

If you can, use these scenarios as a basis for usability tests of your publication interface and design revisions.

Messages

For each publication, create a table that maps audience and time frame to the message that you want to convey. Table 26-1, for example, shows sample types of messages that PLAN may want to deliver in its e-mail alerts.

Table 26-1: Audience-Message Mapping

Audience	Immediate	Short-Term	Mid-Term	Long-Term
Staff	"Pay attention — I'm news."	"You need me!" or "You can safely ignore me."	"This is what you need to pass on."	"I give you news that helps you do your job."
Members	"PLAN has done something that you need to know about."	"PLAN has done something good." or "PLAN has an important need."	"We need you to know or help."	"PLAN is really together. They're right on top of things."
Donors	"PLAN is worth your attention."	"PLAN is worthy of consideration."	"PLAN is the right organization to help."	"Whenever PLAN calls, responding is worthwhile."
Press	"PLAN is worth your attention."	"PLAN has made news."	"This event is important enough to write about."	"PLAN provides good information that you can trust and use."

Format

As I describe in Chapter 2, "Content Has Format," consider the storage (or file) format as well as the rendering format (the actual formatting codes that you use) in each of your publications. To complete the process, describe the following design constraints for each publication that you intend to create:

✦ **Consumption format:** In what end medium do you plan to deliver the publication (paper, HTML, XML, and so on)?

✦ **Delivery format:** What format, if any, does the CMS deliver to any processing applications? It may deliver ASCII text to an automated e-mail system, for example, or deliver QuarkXPpress files to a printing house.

✦ **Files:** Do you deliver the publication in a single or in multiple files? What parts are static and what parts are dynamic?

✦ **Automated Styling:** What style sheets or other tools can you employ to ensure that you apply formatting as consistently as possible to the publication?

✦ **Style conventions:** Describe the style qualities of this publication (voice, tone, word usage, and so on.). Describe any look-and-feel or branding standards that the publication must adhere to. How do advertisements, transactions, and other noncontent functionality affect the navigation, content layout, or content composition of the publication?

✦ **Publication groups:** Is this publication part of any wider groups, or does it appear side by side with other publications? If so, how can you ensure that the styles don't conflict?

Structure

In Chapter 30, "Designing Content Access Structures," I present a complete analysis of the access structures that you need in your publications. The following constraints help you to get started with this process, basically by deciding how to build the navigation of the publication:

✦ **Nodes:** How does the content of the publication break down into pages or sections? What different types of pages or sections does the publication have? Which of these different types of publication nodes contain single components and which combine multiple components into a single node?

✦ **TOC:** Sketch a basic table of contents for this publication. Do the main headings of this outline change over time or remain fixed? How deep do you expect the TOC to go? Can it keep growing larger over time or does it need to reach a stable size? Later, you can use this information to understand how the access structures in the CMS repository generate this publication's TOC. Do you expect to need more than one form of the TOC? Should you ever list the same section or page twice in the same outline?

✦ **Index:** Brainstorm 30 to 50 words that describe the content of this publication. The result is the start of a keyword index for your publication. Does the list naturally break down further into different types of indexes (for example, by subject, author, and industry)? If so, you may need multiple indexes for the publication.

✦ **Cross-References:** Do any natural cross-references or links generally work between sections of the TOC or words in the index? What policies do you envision for the creation and presentation of cross-references in this publication? Can you put them in a standard format or in a standard location? Do you plan to represent internal links differently from external links?

✦ **Sequences:** How does the user move from one page or section of the publication to the next or previous one? Is only one sequence through the publication possible? If you use multiple ways to sequence the content, how do you represent them? How can you avoid confusion?

✦ **Full-text search:** Is full-text search an option for an electronic publication? If so, how do you represent it on-screen? What Boolean functions do you expect it to use? How does it interact, if at all, with the other access structures you provide?

✦ **Publication groups:** Is this publication part of any wider groups? If so, how do you merge its structures into the wider group?

Cycles

In Chapter 33, "Designing Workflow and Staffing Models," I present a full analysis of workflow. In the following set of constraints, you can work through the publication cycles that later feed into your workflow analysis:

✦ **Size:** How big is the publication? Are different versions different sizes?

✦ **Versions:** Does the publication have versions? Before answering yes for Web publications, decide exactly what value these versions give you on a continuously updated site. How should you visually present the different versions to users?

✦ **Frequencies:** How frequently do you plan to update the publication? Do different parts update at different rates?

✦ **Volume:** How much of which kinds of content flow into and out of the publication? Can the parts of the publication grow indefinitely?

✦ **Archiving:** Do you need to archive older versions of the publication? Do any legal reasons compel you to reproduce the publication in exactly the form it once took?

✦ **Publication groups:** If the publication belongs to a group or groups of publications, do its cycles align with those of the other publications in the group?

Localization

For each publication that you intend to create, work through the following considerations to understand and catalog the effect of localization and then use your answers to go back and modify your publication design:

✦ **Localities:** List the names and IDs of the localities of the people you expect to use this publication.

✦ **Look-and-feel:** By consulting a representative of each locality, determine what graphic and text design features of this publication must you modify to give the people of this locality the meaning that you intend? Save this list for your template analysis, where you use it to find the template locations that localization affects. I present the template analysis in Chapter 31, "Designing Templates," in the section "Analyzing Templates."

✦ **Messaging:** Review your messaging analysis for each locality that the publication is to serve. Is the same message appropriate for each locality? Should you create variations of the message by locality? Can each locality decode the message quickly by using the same visual and text cues?

✦ **Structure:** Are the publication structures that you intend to use well understood by the localities? If not, should you include extra explanation or structure variations on a locality basis?

✦ **Cycles:** Do you release all local content at the same time as you release that of the primary locality? If so, how do you make up the time needed for localization in your publication schedules? If not, what additional cycles do you need?

Tasks

Consider the effect of your publication analysis on the ongoing maintenance of the CMS. Then fill in the following table to define any tasks that you imagine must happen on a recurring basis to run the CMS. Here are some task types to get you thinking:

✦ Publishing cycles, including any live, daily, weekly or any other content distribution cycles.

✦ Build and test cycles.

✦ Prepublication editorial review.

✦ Periodic design reviews.

✦ Periodic format reviews.

✦ Structure reviews.

✦ User feedback compilation and review.

✦ User surveys and focus groups.

✦ Usage reports and statistics.

✦ Author feedback loops.

✦ Localization cycles.

Fill in the following table:

Task name	Who	What	When	How much	How
User Feedback Report	CMS Administrator	Run the feedback report.	Once a month or when a comment marked as severe arrives	Once	Use the Feedback Script that we intend to create.

Provide the following information:

✦ **Task name:** Give the task a short but memorable name that describes it.

✦ **Who:** Determine what person or kind of person is responsible for doing this task. Naming an automated process here, instead of a person, is acceptable.

✦ **What:** List what the person or process must do to accomplish the task.

✦ **When:** Specify at what frequency the person or process must accomplish this task, or how to know when it must occur.

✦ **How much:** Describe how much of this task (or how many of this sort) you expect to be necessary. A numerical quantity is preferable here, but if you can't come up with one, words such as *a lot*, *not much*, and so on suffice.

✦ **How:** Detail the skills, tools, or processes the person or process needs to accomplish this task.

Don't worry if the tasks you come up with at this point are somewhat ill-defined or sketchy. In your workflow analysis (in Chapter 33, "Designing Workflow and Staffing Models"), you have ample opportunity to refine them.

Integrate

Consider the following categories and questions to help you integrate the work that you do on publications with the other designs that you do:

✦ **Multiple publications:** If you're producing a single publication, can you envision a time when you may need to produce others from the same content? If you're producing multiple publications, is one more important than the others? Do its stakeholders understand this situation? If you're producing multiple publications, is one more complex than the others? Is the work to produce it commensurate with its importance?

✦ **Sharing:** Compare the analyses that you did for each of the publications that you produce. What opportunities do you have to share content, structure, messages, or other items across publications?

✦ **Goals:** How do your publications support your goals and vice versa? Are these the right publications for your goals? Can you suggest any others? Are these the right goals for your publications? Can you suggest any others?

✦ **Sponsors:** Do your sponsors understand these publications? Do your sponsors agree with your publications and the way that you rank them?

✦ **Audiences:** What are the other publications against which each audience judges each of your publications? What do the audiences expect concerning the purpose, authorship, content, structure, or format of your publications. Are these assumptions consistent? If not, how do you reset assumptions or change your publications to meet the assumptions? Should you create any other publications for these audiences? Which ones? Do these publications have any potential audiences that you're not serving? Why not? Do your audiences agree with the way that you rank your publications?

Summary

Designing your publications is the closest you get to determining how your audience will use and interact with your content. Your publications depend, of course, in large part on what content in your CMS and how the CMS makes that content available to you for incorporation into your publications.

In this chapter, I discussed:

✦ The defining features of a publication, which is unified content that you release with a number of characteristics in mind, including purpose, audience, messages, content, structure, and schedule.

✦ Publications *gotchas*, which include structural considerations that come into play when you can't say in advance how each chunk of content will be published.

✦ Analyzing publications as a part of the publication design process. Publication analysis includes thinking about the publications you'll create; planning your publications based on your analysis; and integrating your publications analysis with the other analyses you do in your CM project.

In the next chapter, I move the analysis to a finer level of detail: content types.

✦   ✦   ✦

Designing Content Types

At the heart of any content management system are chunks of information that I call *content components*. Components break your information into manageable units. Components come in a variety of types, which, not surprisingly, I call *content types*. In this chapter, I more fully define the idea of content components and content types and give you a way to begin defining a set of content types for your CMS.

Content Type Jumpstart

This Jumpstart summarizes what you need to do to design content types for your publications.

Use this jumpstart as a summary without the weight of detail, or as a quick review if you've already read this chapter — in particular the section called "Analyzing Content Types" — and you want a checklist of how to analyze content types.

At all stages of your content type analysis, make sketches and tables as you follow these steps:

1. Review the section "What Are Components?" in this chapter if you're not clear on the definitions of and relationships between content types, content components, and content elements. Having a clear understanding of what components are and being able to communicate these ideas to your team is critical to this stage of your design.

2. Create a wide set of content types.

   - If you intend to do a competitive content type analysis, refer to the section in this chapter "A competitive content analysis" for more information.

   - If you intend to derive content types from your organizational goals, refer to the section in this chapter "Dividing information into content types" for more information.

   - Experiment with a combination of both methods to find the set of content types that best supports your goals and positions you correctly within the content types of your peers and competitors.

3. Narrow down the set of content types to only those that you really need:

- Get rid of types that you don't have the resources to either create or acquire from an existing source.

- Get rid of content types which have only one or a few components.

- Get rid of content types that are already full publications and don't need to be reused.

- If the content type holds functionality, get rid of it if the functionality is used in multiple places in your publications.

4. For content types that make this cut, assign an Id, Name, Description, Rank, and Key Component (a good example of that sort of content).

5. For each content type, decide the following:

- How it will be created, including: the startup and run quantity of the content type; the sources and formats of the content components; and the growth in the number of components you expect.

- What will happen to components of this type over time, including the kind of editorial cycle you expect is required to create components; the expected life span; how often the component is reviewed; the list of tasks required from receipt of content to publishing; and the processes (grouped tasks) that each component will undergo during its life cycle.

- What elements it will have. Identify what sorts of body elements and management elements each content type requires, based on your analysis of your key component.

- What elements are common across all content types. Revise your element list, and then pivot your list across content types to determine commonality. Your goal is to produce the smallest set of elements that adequately represents your content.

- How will it be localized (if at all). Include which elements must be localized; the localities each must be localized to; and the methods used to manage the localization.

6. Integrate your content type analysis with the other design aspects for your CMS. Consider the impact of the component design on other requirements, audiences, processes, authors, and publications.

When you've completed your content type analysis, you have a detailed set of components to use in your template analysis process.

The Idea of a Content Model

Your content model is your best guess about what sorts of content you have and how it all fits together into a manageable system. My idea of a content model owes a lot to the forerunner concept of a data model. Ever since the invention of the database, data modelers have been required to think abstractly enough to figure out just what tables, rows, and columns can represent the information to be tracked. For example, suppose you want to keep track of employees. A data modeler might go through this mental process as she designs the database structure to hold employee information:

✦ I'll create one table to hold employee information.

✦ Each employee will have one row in the table that holds her information.

✦ I know right away that each employee needs a unique Id column in each employee row so we can locate her record. I could use her Social Security Number, but we are now a global company and many of our employees do not have such a U.S.-centric identifier. So, I'll just give each a sequential number.

✦ Because we pay employees from this system, I will give each employee row a pay rate column. Because we cover a lot of different currencies, I'll add a currency column as well. Everyone is paid by the hour so I don't have to worry about a column for hourly versus salary.

✦ Of course, I also need columns for name, address, e-mail, and phone number.

What I intend this admittedly oversimplified example to show is that the data modeler:

✦ Invents a system for representing an employee. That system is called the data model.

✦ The particulars of the data model are based on what the modeler knows about the uses of the information she is modeling. For example, she bases her choice for a unique Id on the fact that the company is global. She includes pay rate because she knows that the wider system needs it. She leaves out wage versus salary because she knows that in this specific company that distinction is not needed.

Any system that has a database has a data model. Good systems have a data model that is in close contact with the realities of the organization and can easily accommodate the inevitable changes that occur in the organization.

Any content management system has a content model. Just like a data model, a good content model is designed to account for the specific uses of the content it models and is built to evolve as the content in the system evolves. The relationship between a data model and a content model goes even deeper. In the end, much of the content model becomes a data model. If your repository is built on a database that holds your content, that database has a data model for representing your content.

So a content model is a lot like a data model. The data model is strictly concerned with how information is stored; the content model, however, is concerned with what the information is. Thus, the content model is really above and more abstract than the data model. First, you figure out a content model; and then, when it is time to implement the CMS, you figure out what data model you need to store the content that fits into your content model. This relationship is illustrated in Figure 27-1.

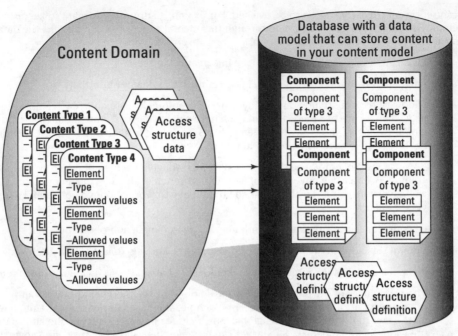

Figure 27-1: Much of a content model becomes the data model for the content repository.

The content model defines what your content is, whereas the data model defines how you will store your content in a database (or perhaps in an XML structure). The content model itself consists of these parts:

✦ **The content domain** is the overall universe of content that you have decided to manage. It defines, at the highest level, what your content is. For more information on the content domain see Chapter 30, "Designing Content Access Structures," in the section "The content domain."

✦ **Access structures** specify how you want the content you manage to be organized. You can organize content in hierarchies or with indexes, cross-references, and sequences. For more information see Chapter 30, "Designing Content Access Structures," in the section "Understanding Access Structures."

✦ **Content types** are major categories of content within the overall domain that you have identified. You may, for example, have a content type called *Service* that fully describes one service that your organization offers. Content types define what your content is at one level lower than the content domain.

✦ **Elements** are the major information constituents of a content type. For example, your Services content type may include a title, a service type (for example, consulting, technical support, or project management), and a service description. Elements specify what your content is in an even more detailed way than your content types.

✦ **Element types and allowed values** specify what information is allowed to go into each element. For example, the Service type element is a list type, meaning that you choose values from a list. The allowed values for this element are consulting, technical support, and project management. Element types and allowed values specify in the smallest detail what your content is.

During logical design, you figure out what your content model should look like. During physical design, you figure out the data model that will enable you to store the content that this model dictates. During implementation you begin actually creating content of each type and storing it.

As you create and store content, you are creating chunks of content that are of one type or another. I call these chunks *components*. Components are chunks of content that follow the content model for a particular content type. For example, when you create service content, you author a Service component. The rules for authoring a Service component are specified by the content model for the Service content type. The Service component has information filled in for each of the elements specified by the content type.

The content that you type in for the Service component is stored in a database according to the data model of that database. The simplest CM databases have a data model that is very close to the content model. More sophisticated databases pay close attention to the efficiency of storage and retrieval, and so have data models that don't seem close at all to the content model. Functionally, however, they still do the same thing as the content model — they store content that obeys the model — but they don't, for example, have a table for each content type, a row for each component, and a column for each element. For more information on the storage of the content model in databases and XML structures, see Chapter 39, "Building Management Systems," in the section "Object databases."

In the sections that follow, I present this information again from a variety of angles to try to give you a deeper understanding of the ideas of content types, elements, and components.

Cross-Reference For more information on the content model, see Chapter 30, "Designing Content Access Structures," in the section "The content model."

What Are Components?

I'll never forget the process of having a conversation with my sister when she had young kids. I'd make a comment to my sister. As she was on the verge of answering, one child would start crying and the other would run away, and my sister would say, "Hold on." We'd average about a sentence an hour, and over the course of a two-day visit, we'd manage to get in about an hour's worth of actual dialog. Our conversation was thinly spread but still continuous. Hours after asking, "How'd things go today?" she'd reply out of the blue, "Well, I managed to keep the kids alive today, so I guess things went okay." Although wide spaces loomed between sentences, you couldn't easily break the conversation down and box it up. Comment followed comment in an unending thread. That's how most conversation is, and in fact, how most information is in the wild world outside of a CMS — continuous. Content, in the sense that I've been using the word, is the highly domesticated cousin of information. It isn't continuous; it comes in pieces that you can name and address.

Note I've had great times in my classes developing the metaphor of "domesticating" information by saying you have to round it up (collection) and brand it (give it an Id). When I get to the part about cutting it into pieces (elements) I always get a groan as the image sinks in.

To make information useful (or re-useful) you must divide it into discrete chunks. Rather than *chunks*, however, I use the word *component*. I want to underscore that you break down the content into pieces to facilitate its use. Just as a home stereo consists of named components (the receiver, the amplifier, the CD player, the speakers), I say that a Web page or any other publication consists of a set of named components (articles, data sheets, news items, product offerings, and so on).

You find no more important idea in this work than the concept of the content component. The component is at the heart of the CMS. It's the content that the system is designed to manage. Following are some of the names I've heard attached to the idea of the content component:

✦ Chunk

✦ Content object

✦ Reusable information object (RIO)

✦ Content item

✦ Element (an unfortunate collision with my use of the same term).

✦ Block

I approach components from a number of angles to give you the fullest picture of what they are and do. But all these perspectives boil down to the simple idea that for you to use content, it must come in standalone chunks.

Recall that although components are discrete chunks of actual information, they are not random. They are created specifically to obey the rules of a content type.

Components are like objects

If you've ever been exposed to the ideas of object-oriented programming, you have a good leg up on components and content types.

Once upon a time, programmers wrote one long program that needed to run from start to finish without stopping. Today, programmers write *objects*, which are smaller programs that do a small thing and then stop. Objects are small, reusable pieces of functionality that the programmer links together to achieve a larger result.

An e-commerce Web site, for example, may use an object for processing transactions. The site's programmer links this object together with others to create the entire site mechanism. How does the programmer link objects? They link by wrapping the core resources of the object in a standardized container (usually known as an *Application Programming Interface*, or *API*) that programmers can use without knowing anything about the internal programming of that object. On the e-commerce site, the programmer may call the transaction object to do tasks such as total up the order, compute tax, and process credit card transactions. The programmer doesn't need to know anything about the programming code in the object that accomplishes these tasks. She needs to know only how to find the object and ask it to do its thing.

Components rely on a very similar concept. Components are small, reusable pieces of content that you can link together to achieve larger results. On the same e-commerce site that I mention in the preceding paragraph, for example, you can make each product a component so that you can link them together into catalog pages, show a list of them on an invoice, or show the user full product detail. If you represent each product as a component, you open a lot of possibilities for mixing and matching products and customizing their appearance for a particular situation. In some circumstances, for example, you may show only the name and price of a product, whereas in another circumstance, you may show the full detail of the product, including a complete description, product dimensions, and a picture.

The way that you use components is the same as the way that the programmer uses objects. You link together small pieces to make a larger whole. Additionally, content workers learn how to work with the component, not with the information within the component, to achieve the same sort of independence that the programmer gets by working with programming objects. To build a page, you needn't know what's inside the component — only how the standardized container of the component operates.

Finally, just like the object-oriented programmer, the content architect creates content classes (which I call content types) and content instances (which I call components). The class/type defines the general structure and the instance/component holds specific content within the general structure.

Note My own words have changed somewhat for this term. If you are familiar with the first edition of this book you might remember that I used to say there are components and that those components have *classes* and *instances*. Since then, the term *content type* has become the generally accepted term for what I called *classes*, as far as I can see, so I will just stick with that. There is still no more well-accepted term than component for the actual chunks (that is, what I called the instances), so I'll keep that one for now.

Edition 1 Term	Edition 2 Term
Component class	Content type (or just *type*)
Component instance	Content component (or just *component*)
Component element	(Same, or just *element*)

The basic unit of content management

Content types divide your information into convenient and manageable chunks. You create content types to establish a set of content objects that you can create, maintain, and distribute. In your CMS, content is stored as components, which are instances of particular content types, as shown in Figure 27-2.

Each component of each type travels through your CMS as a unit, as the following list describes:

✦ **Whenever you create new content**, you create one whole component at a time. Authors, for example, don't just free-associate and type whatever they please. Rather, they create a particular usable chunk (a backgrounder, a news article, an employee profile, and so on) within the constraints of the content types you have given them.

✦ **Whenever you move existing content into your system**, you do so by dividing it into components of a particular type. If you find a hard drive full of useful information, for example, you start by categorizing it into types. You then ensure that each piece of content of a certain type has the same format and structure. In other words, you establish a set of content types and use them to create a set of components.

✦ **Whenever you store content**, you do so by component. Later in this chapter (in the section "What Do Components Look Like?"), I describe some of the ways that you store components.

✦ **Whenever you archive or delete content**, you do so by components. After an event passes, for example, you may delete the Event component from your system.

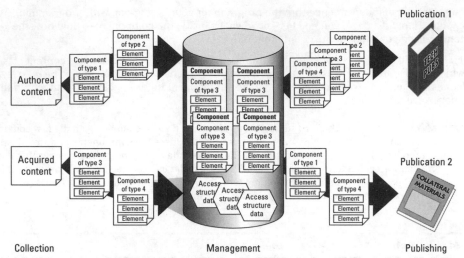

Figure 27-2: Components are the basic chunks that you move around in a CMS.

✦ **Whenever you create a publication page**, you do so by pulling components together into a page template. You may construct an Event page on your Web site, for example, by pulling an Event component into a page template that formats the event information and surrounds it with banners, navigation and site buttons, and images.

✦ **Whenever you gather statistics**, you gather them by component. You may want to know, for example, what the most visited component is, how many of a particular type you created in the last month, or how many are stuck in legal review.

Most Webmasters count Web pages. Most authors count pages of text or number of images. Administrators count database records. None of these measures has any universal meaning. On the other hand, a component has meaning regardless of the stage of the system you're working in or what your job is. Regardless of stage or job, you're always trying to move the right set of content components from creation to distribution to eventual retirement.

How do you divide content?

Componentizing content doesn't make sense until you have enough content to warrant the trouble. If you simply want to write a short story and put it on the Web, for example, don't bother creating a bunch of types and components. If, on the other hand, you're initiating a creative writing site with an expanding stable of short stories, poems, speeches, reviews, and nonfiction articles, the initial time that you take to componentize this information can go a long way toward keeping your life sane and your site sound.

You often can find a natural way to divide information into content types. Look again at the example of the creative writing site. The simplest way to divide the content is to create components the size of a single contribution. You may create a single content type that you call Contribution (or Contrib, because computer types hate to type). In so doing, you're naming and, thereby, unifying a heterogeneous set of information sources into a homogeneous set of objects. You can now talk about a Contrib. You can say what one is, what one must have, and when to use one. You may say, for example, that all Contribs must have a title, a body, an author, and a date. You may permit no more than one Contrib per page, and all the Contrib titles appear alphabetically on the home page.

A Supermarket of Content

Ideally, your CMS is like a supermarket of content. Manufacturers (content contributors, that is) package their products (content) in containers (components) that they clearly and consistently label (content types). The manufacturer knows generally what you can use the product for, but not what any particular cook (publisher) wants to do with it. The supermarket managers (the CMS administrators) organize, categorize, and display the product (content) in shelves and aisles in a way that enables cooks to easily find and select the most appropriate products. This overall organization lies on top of the organization that the manufacturers of the products impose inside the individual containers. They organize a box of macaroni and cheese, for example, into a package of cheese powder and an exact portion of macaroni (elements). The store displays the box of macaroni and cheese in the pasta section next to the other packaged pastas. The containers organize their contents, and the store (the repository) organizes the containers.

A cook (a publication creator) comes in and selects just the right containers (components). The consumer reorganizes and blends the particular products into a unique and tasty meal (the publication). Some of the products are recognizable within the meal, and some aren't. All the products are out of their original containers and appear as a single unified whole (the publication).

Without the original chunking of the product into standard containers, the cook can't count on the amount or composition of the product. Without the further organization of the containers into an overall storage and management system, the cook can't find the product that she needs. Our system of food creation, management, and consumption, just like a CMS, depends on well-packaged, standalone chunks that you can mix and match in a variety of ways.

Without taking this analogy too far, it also points out some of the limitations of content components, as the following list describes:

✦ **Manufacturers produce the containers of product as a best guess** of what most people want—not as what's always right. I may need 1.5 cans of sauce, but I must buy either one or two. Similarly, you must design content types using an educated guess about what publications later need.

✦ **Managers may think that they're organizing the products intuitively**, but even after shopping my entire life, I still must hunt around for stuff. Similarly, the way that you organize your components is never so good that consumers and contributors needn't learn your system.

✦ **Specialty products, which have a limited audience, are rarely in stock.** Similarly, content that's just right in a very particular situation is always crowded out by content that's of general use. The economics are against custom content types.

By creating and naming a content type, you begin to organize. You also open the door to the further naming of elements (Title, Body, and so on.) and the capability to select and arrange components to your advantage (for example, to select Contrib titles and arrange them alphabetically on the home page).

Now suppose that you do a good job of selecting and arranging these components and also manage to choose Contribs that people want to see. Your site grows in popularity, volume, and funding. You soon find that the Contrib content type is too simple to handle the issues that you must now confront. You find that not all Contribs are created equal. Speeches, for example, have a first-delivered date, an author, and an orator. Reviews involve a thing that's reviewed, and articles often come with a picture. You can continue to widen the definition of

Contrib until it loses all meaning, or you can create a finer grain of types — say, short stories, poems, speeches, reviews, and nonfiction articles. With this more-detailed approach, you become more specific about the way that you create your site. You can now say, for example, that your site includes a TOC that divides the contributions by category; that you center the titles of poems but not of articles; that the photos that accompany articles are left-aligned; and that speeches use a serif typeface.

No absolute "right" way to divide your information into content types exists. The right way is the way that gives you the most advantage within your current capabilities and resources. That's not to say that you can go about this process in a casual way. On the contrary. You must divide the content according to well-defined and understood rules. The rules can and do change; but you must have one set of consistent rules so that, at all times, your content is organized. You can imagine the problems that occur (and I've seen this situation more than once) if half the staff is still creating Contribs while the other half is now creating Poems and Articles components.

Many content projects falter on division rules. The fact that you can never give a "right" answer can cause innumerable arguments. The best answer about how to divide information into content types is the one that provides a workable balance between the natural divisions in the information, the divisions that you need to make your publications, and the divisions that you can make with the time and budget that you have.

Components versus pages

Web professionals naturally gravitate to the concept of the page. A site consists of a set of linked pages that all contain unique content. Pages come in types (home pages, product pages, article pages, and so on). Pages are a natural candidate for the title that I give to components: the basic unit of management. And, in fact, the majority of Web systems in use today do manage pages and not components. Unfortunately, the page is an entirely inadequate thing to manage for, at least, the following reasons:

✦ **The content on a page and its design change separately.** (That's what a site redesign does.) If your system manages only pages, you must take on a lot of work every time that the design changes.

✦ **Pages share content.** If you manage only pages and the same content is on two different pages, you must manage two copies of the same content.

✦ **Pages creation often occurs on-the-fly.** In many systems, no page exists until the user requests one. So, naturally, managing pages that are ephemeral becomes very difficult.

✦ **Web pages aren't all that you need to create.** Today, for many organizations (and tomorrow for all organizations), the same content is going to need distributing to other platforms besides the Web.

A component is a much better thing to manage than a page, because:

✦ You can separate components from design.

✦ Components are the unit of content that you share among pages.

✦ Components run in any automated page-creation system.

✦ You can use components to create any sort of output, not just a Web page.

Most of today's Web page-management systems are a lot like document-management systems. They work with files rather than with content chunks. As such, they're hard-pressed to work within a page to change how it appears. At best, systems such as Microsoft FrontPage and Macromedia Dreamweaver enable you to create individual Web pages with a standardized, easily changed look-and-feel. Still, no reuse of content occurs from Web page to Web page, let alone reuse to other media.

 Cross-Reference See Chapter 10, "The Roots of Content Management," in the section "The Principles of Document Management," for more information on the comparison between document and content management.

From a CMS and component-centric view, a Web site is a particular kind of publication. Web pages are parts of that publication. What you must figure out to become successful is how you can produce the pages of the Web publication (or, more likely, multiple Web publications) from the same set of components that you use to produce other publications.

Content has types and components

There are trees and then there are trees. Each individual tree has its own trunk, branches, and root structures. It's also, however, part of the type of things that people call *trees*. To be a tree, a thing must follow certain rules and patterns. It must, for example, have a trunk, branches, and roots. In much the same way, components are individuals that also belong to a type.

A content type is a model, a template, and a set of rules about how to create a component of a particular kind. I don't use the term *template* again in this context because I use it so extensively for publications. Whatever term you use, the meaning is the same. The type establishes the definition of a component of a certain kind.

A *content type* includes the name of the type, the elements that it consists of, and any rules that you want to establish about how to create such components.

Take look at the following example of a plain-English definition of a content type:

> This component is called Article. It has a unique Id (A and an integer), followed by a Title (with initial caps), an abstract (fewer than 256 characters), a reference to an existing image, if available (relative path and file name) and a body (that can contain a variety of formatting tags).

This paragraph states the name of the content type (Article) and lists its elements (Id, Name, Abstract, Image, and Body). It also includes a number of rules (the form of the Id, the format of the title, the length of the abstract, the format of the image reference, and the formatting of the body). Most anyone can read this definition and know what is required to create an Article component.

Notice, however, that no actual component appears here—only the definition of the type of components. To make an actual component, you must take the rules and construct the component by using a particular format. Using XML, for example, an example of an Article component may look as follows:

```
<ARTICEL ID="A100">
  <TITLE>
        How to Make Content Types
```

```
   </TITLE>
   <ABSTRACT>
        This article shows you the ins and outs of content types
   </ABSTRACT>
   <IMAGE>
        images/schema.jpg
   </IMAGE>
   <BODY>
        <h1>Introduction<h1>
        Etcetera...
   </BODY>
</ARTICLE>
```

Cross-Reference   Refer to Chapter 39, "Building Management Systems," in the section "Storing content types and components in XML," for more information about representing content types as XML.

You don't describe most content types in plain language. Rather, you express them in some structured system such as a relational database schema or an XML DTD. If I remove all the particular text from the preceding component, I can specify the Article component as an XML fragment rather than as a plain language paragraph, as follows:

```
<ARTICLE ID="">
  <TITLE>
  </TITLE>
  <ABSTRACT>
  </ABSTRACT>
  <IMAGE>
  </IMAGE>
  <BODY>
  </BODY>
</ARTICLE>
```

Notice that the XML representation of the content type is both more precise and less precise than the plain-language form. It's more precise in that the elements are specifically named and ordered in the XML form. It's less precise in that few of the creation rules are specified. You can't tell by looking at the XML that the image, for example, is optional.

Content types establish the structure of a component of a certain kind. You create actual components by using the type as a model. Types are rules, whereas components are rule-based content. As I've said, types are like a programmer's object *classes* and components are like a programmer's object *instances*. A programmer creates a class as a general-purpose processor. Later, that programmer (or, better, another programmer) creates an instance of that class and fills it with particular data that needs processing. Thus, just as a content type is a model, a programming class is a model, and just as a programming-class instance is a particular use of that model a component is a particular use of a content type.

Content Types Have Elements

I borrow the term *element* not from chemistry but from XML. In XML, an element is a start tag, a close tag, and whatever's in between. Following are some examples:

```
<SOMETAG>Here is the info</SOMETAG>
<B>some things are the same in XML as HTML</B>
```

The concept of the element in XML is that it's the basic unit of information. It's the smallest unit that you can individually locate and the smallest unit that you name. That's not to say that elements can't have subelements, but that the element (at whatever level it exists) is the lowest level of content that you can name and find. I intend the same concept here. In a content system, the element is the smallest unit of named locatable content.

A product content type, for example, may consist of the following:

✦ A product Id code

✦ A name

✦ A price

✦ A description

✦ A picture

Each piece of information is an element of the product content type. You can locate a particular product component by using any of these pieces of information as a key, and conversely, you can access any element from within a particular product component and display it on a Web page. Elements either contain the information that you want to use, or they help you find a component that you want. In other words, elements can be for display or management depending on the context in which you're using them.

Elements have types and values

You divide content types into elements to make them easier to find and to make the content within them easier to locate and retrieve. You can use this distinction to categorize elements, as follows:

✦ **Body elements:** Body elements contain the content that you actually display in publications. Examples of such elements include the abstract for an article or the contact name for a press release. You create such elements because you want the option of using one part of the component apart from the rest. You may, for example, want to list all your article abstracts together. If the abstracts aren't in a separate element within their article components, this task is difficult to accomplish. Or, for another example, you may want to make the contact name for a press release appear in a column to the left of the text of the release. To do so, you access the contact name by using its element.

✦ **Management elements:** These elements include information like the create date and status of the component. You create this sort of element to manage the component. You may assign a CreateDate element to all content types, for example, so that you can track how long your components take to go from creation to release. Or, for another example, all types may include a Status element so that you can most easily move components from one stage in their life cycle to the next.

As you may guess, these categories aren't mutually exclusive. Consider an Author element. You may want to get at authors separately and use the Author element for tracking. In fact, saying simply that content types have elements and that you can use an element for two purposes may be simpler. Because many systems make this distinction, however (you enter body and management elements in two different places in the application), and because my use of the term *management elements* follows the common use of the word *metadata*, I distinguish from the start between the two types of elements. My management elements are precisely those pieces of information that are usually referred to as metadata. I think, too, that talking about the content and its management data as two separate but highly connected realms makes practical sense.

Unique identification

Each component needs a name for individual identification and use. You must name each Poem component on a writing site, for example, so that you can find it and display it on a page. The human way to accomplish this task is to give the poem a title and say, "I want to title the poem 'Name Steak.'" The computer way to accomplish the same task is to say, "I want the poem with the unique ID p_27." Although the name of the poem may uniquely identify it, it's a bad choice for an Id. First, you can't guarantee that the title is always going to remain unique. Nothing prevents another author from writing a poem that is also titled "Name Steak." Second, the title may change. You don't want to go through your entire set of components each time one changes its title to ensure that any other component that refers to that poem is up to date. Finally, titles are far less convenient for a computer to store and manage than is a pithy, data-like phrase such as "p_27."

Locality in components

Most of what you must localize in a CMS is the content within its components. Although you rarely localize the element names or any information that is purely for management, you spend the overwhelming majority of your localization time translating and reforming the component's body elements.

Following are three possible localization sites within a component:

✦ **Body elements:** You can choose to localize only body elements because those are the ones that appear in publications.

✦ **Management elements:** You can choose to localize management elements if your authors and administrative staff can't deal with the primary locality in metadata names and lists. This might be true, for example, if your administrators do not speak the language that the management element values are written in.

✦ **Whole components:** You can localize whole components if your CMS can't handle localization at the element level. Localizing the whole component is the same as localizing both the management and body elements.

 Cross-Reference You find more information about the issue of localizing management elements in Chapter 24, "Working with Metadata," in the section "Localizing Metadata," and in Chapter 39, "Building Management Systems," in the section "Management localization."

You can save a lot of time and energy over the life of your CMS if you can find a way to localize only body elements. If your system supports this sort of element-level localization (or you can customize it to do so) you get the least ongoing effort for the most localization effect.

You can use the following methods to localize content components:

✦ **Element variants:** If your CMS supports it, the best method for localizing components is to store variations on component elements that you key by locality. If you have a PageAbstract element in the component, for example, the system enables you to make as many variants of the element as you need to store all its localized versions. Then you can say that you have a single PageAbstract element, but as necessary, you can access local variants of it for separate management or display.

✦ **Local elements:** If your CMS doesn't support element variants, you can simulate that approach by creating your own set of local elements. If you know that you're going to localize a PageAbstract element for the Latin-America and Asian-America localities (with English-America your primary locality), for example, you can create three body elements: PageAbstract, LatinAbstract, and AsiaAbstract. This method performs the same function as the element variant method but is more cumbersome because you must create these extra elements and manage their relationship to each other instead of allowing the CMS to manage everything for you.

✦ **Local components:** The easiest way to localize components is to create a set of related content components, targeting each to a different locality. For example, you can create a primary component, a LatinAmerica component, and an AsiaAmerica component for the same content. To relate the three, you can add an element for locality (a closed list) and relate their Ids. You may decide that each component Id has two parts, a root and a locality suffix. All three components have the same root (1234, say). Each has a different suffix (1234_EA, 1234_LA, and 1234_AA, for example).

Cross-Reference You find more information about the technical details behind these methods in Chapter 39, "Building Management Systems," in the section "Management localization."

What Do Components Look Like?

Components don't exist out in space—you usually create them in files and then move them into databases. In the following sections, I take a look at how an e-commerce product component might look in a few file and database types.

Components in flat files

The simplest (and thus least useful) way to store components is in a flat text file. Following is a fragment of such a file that takes the most basic approach:

```
11007
Cardboard Cup Sleeve
$00.02
Post consumer 1/16 inch corrugated cardboard sleeve
fits 8 to 20 oz. cups. Available in brown, white,
and green.
/images/cupsleeve.jpg
11008
Cardboard Elvis
.
.
.
```

Each component in the file begins with a line displaying an Id number (11007, 11008, and so on). Each element within a component begins at the beginning of the line and ends with a carriage return. Whatever humans or programs interact with this file need to know these facts and also need to know which line goes with which element. This sort of file is easy to create but offers very little flexibility or accessibility. The situation gets even worse if you use the standard comma-delimited format for storing structured data in a text file, as in the following example:

```
11007,Cardboard Cup Sleeve,$00.02,Post consumer 1/16 inch
corrugated cardboard sleeve fits 8 to 20 oz cups. Available in
brown, white, and green,/images/cupsleeve.jpg
11008,Cardboard Elvis,...
```

Check out Chapter 39, "Building Management Systems," in the section "File systems," for more details about storing components in XML.

Components in structured files

Other sorts of files offer considerably more than the flat file that I discuss in the preceding section. Many file formats support a much richer capability to represent elements and enable access to them. Microsoft Word, for example, gives you the notion of paragraph styles. You can create a style for each element that helps you find the elements in the file, but the levels of complexity the Word paragraph styles can represent is very limited. They can't, for example, really represent one element type embedded within another.

The file structure that's today's favorite is XML. An XML file would represent that same component as follows:

```
<PRODUCTS>
  <PRODUCT>
        <ID>11007</ID>
        <NAME>Cardboard Cup Sleeve</NAME>
        <PRICE>$00.02</PRICE>
        <DESCRIPTION>
            Post consumer 1/16 inch corrugated cardboard
            sleeve fits 8 to 20 oz cups. Available in brown,
            white, and green.
        </DESCRIPTION>
        <PICTURE>/images/cupsleeve.jpg</PICTURE>
  </PRODUCT>
  <PRODUCT>
        <ID>11008</ID>
        <NAME>Cardboard Elvis</NAME>
          .
          .
          .
  </PRODUCT>
</PRODUCTS>
```

Even if you know nothing about XML, you can see that this file is very well structured. Everything is named and organized into a nice outline. It isn't hard to imagine how such programs can help you manage, validate, and access the parts of this file.

Notice that each of the component elements becomes an XML element. That's why I choose the name *element* for this part of components. Notice, too, how the components themselves are also XML elements. What you see between the opening `<PRODUCT>` and closing `</PRODUCT>` tags is the component. I don't get too carried away, therefore, comparing component elements with XML elements, because everything in XML is an element!

Check out Chapter 39, "Building Management Systems," in the section "Storing content types and components in XML," for more details about storing components in XML.

Components in relational databases

Today, you find most components in *relational databases*, which are the standard databases that you've no doubt heard of — Microsoft Access, SQL Server, Oracle, Sybase, Informix, IBM's DB2, and so on. Tables full of rows and columns of data characterize relational databases. See Figure 27-3 for an example of how components look in such a database.

ID	NAME	PRICE	DESCRIPTION	PICTURE
▶ 11007	Cardboard Cup	$00.02	Post consumer	/images/cupsleeve.jpg
11008	Cardboard Elvis			

Record: ◄◄ ◄ 1 ► ►► ►✱ of 2

Figure 27-3: Components in a relational database table

Check out Chapter 39, "Building Management Systems," in the section "Storing content types and components in a relational database," for more details about components in relational databases.

Components in object databases

Structured files preceded relational databases — and, in fact, relational databases grew directly out of files with structures similar to those of giant tables. Another sort of database has grown out of files with a structure similar to that of XML. *Object databases*, as the name implies, were originally developed to give object-oriented programmers a convenient place to store the data associated with the objects that they were programming.

In the section "Components are like objects," earlier in this chapter, I discuss how programming objects resemble content types, so imagining your components in an object database is really no stretch. Structurally, your components look no different in an object database than they do in an XML file. In an object database, the treelike XML structure is inside a user interface. In the following illustration, your product components appear within eXcelon, which is an object-database product from eXcelon Corporation, at `www.exceloncorp.com` (see Figure 27-4).

Object databases do for XML files what relational databases do for files full of tabular data: They give you more powerful tools for viewing, organizing, and accessing large amounts of information. Unfortunately for your content, object databases have lost a lot of favor in the CM world because they are difficult to scale to when you must accommodate big repositories.

Check out Chapter 39, "Building Management Systems," in the section "Object databases," for more information about components in XML and object databases.

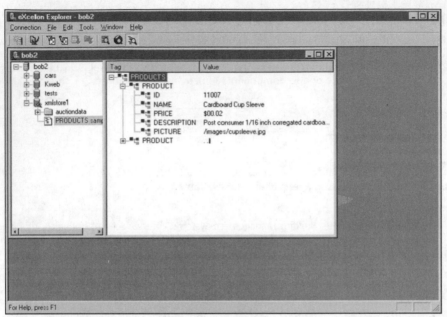

Figure 27-4: Components in an object database

The Relationship between Functionality and Components

Content is information and functionality. (See Chapter 4, "Functionality is Content, Too!") And just as an information content component has a type, and body and management elements, so does a functionality content component.

The kind of functionality that I discuss here is the kind that you want to distribute to your audiences and not the kind that makes up the CMS itself. This published functionality happens mostly, but not entirely, in electronic publications.

You use some of the more common forms of published functionality for the following purposes:

✦ **Connection to other systems:** In your Web publications, you may need to connect to a catalog, a transaction, or other non-CMS systems. To do so, you program and package functionality that connects to and exchanges data with the other system.

✦ **Advanced navigation:** If simple lists and outlines aren't sufficient to produce the navigation that you need in an electronic publication, you can program and package functionality to present more elaborate navigation areas. You create the popular fly-out menus on many Web sites, for example, by using JavaScript functionality on each page.

✦ **Communication:** Perhaps the most useful kind of functionality is simply that which facilitates communication between the audience and the publisher. Many publications (print and electronic), for example, include a form that you can fill out to subscribe to or order something from inside the publication.

To make your creation, administration, and use of published functionality more efficient and effective, you can treat it as you do other content and pack it inside content types.

In a CMS environment, you publish functionality via templates. In other words, the template places the functionality in the right place at the right time for the audience to use. You can access functionality that's inside components and bring it into a published page the same way that you do information. The template retrieves the component from the CMS repository and formats it for display on the page. The alternative to treating functionality as content is to keep it "below your radar" by putting it directly into one or more templates. This approach is simpler, but you lose the following advantages:

✦ **Reuse:** If you want to put the same chunk of functionality into a number of publication pages, you must retype the code that prompts that functionality in a number of templates. Any time the code changes, you must find and change it manually in each template.

✦ **Reconfiguration:** If you store your functionality in a component, you get the same selection and formatting possibilities as you do with information in a component. Later in this chapter (in the section "A functionality component"), you see an example of reconfiguration.

✦ **Version control:** You can't manage programming code that you hide in a template as effectively as you can manage code that's in a component. You can apply any services that your CMS offers for differencing, rolling back, or archiving content to functionality that's in components.

✦ **Access control:** If you store functionality in components, you can apply any services that your CMS offers for controlling the permissions to change or view content. Any access control that you can manage through the templating syntax of the CMS or its personalization engine is also available to functionality components.

✦ **Workflow:** I can think of no reason why you can't also apply all the administration that you conceive of for information components to functionality components. You can manage everything from initial review of the code through its final retirement through the CMS workflow services if the functionality is in a component.

Note   Another alternative approach is to incorporate functionality chunks as *include files*. An include file (also known as *SSI*, or *server-side include*) is a separate file that the template automatically includes as it's processed. This approach gives you reuse, and if you're using a source-management system, it can give you version control as well. But it can't give you all the workflow, access, and reconfiguration possibilities that a CMS can.

A functionality component

For the most part, functionality content types have the same parts as information types. Illustrating the ways that you fill in and use the parts, however, is worth the effort.

Suppose that PLAN wants to develop and present functionality for subscribing to press releases. The core code is in a programming object (say, a Java class or COM object) that connects to and exchanges data with a subscriptions database. I needn't concern you with this core code except to say that it has the following function:

```
ShowSubscription(user,style,format)
```

Note   You may rightly suspect that I'm simplifying things a bit.

The following list explains each part of this function:

✦ **User** is the unique Id of the current user.

✦ **Style** is the way that you want to present the list. Suppose that the styles are Table for a table, NewList for a list that shows the subscriptions that the user is still eligible to receive, and DelList for a list that shows subscriptions to delete.

✦ **Format** is the kind of output that you want. The choices might be HTML and Print.

Assume that PLAN wants to show the list of subscriptions on both its home page and on the subscriptions page.

On the home page, subscriptions may look like the ones shown in Figure 27-5.

Figure 27-5: The subscription functionality on the PLAN home page

The programming code (using my simplified syntax) to produce this table may look as follows:

```
[Run ShowSubscription(user,"Table","HTML")]
```

As this code executes, the template calls the ShowSubscription function, which returns the HTML necessary to build the table that I'm illustrating. Although highly simplified, the example suffices to show the home-page form of the subscription functionality.

On the subscriptions page, the functionality must have more to it (see Figure 27-6).

Figure 27-6: The subscription functionality on the subscriptions page

The code behind this view of the functionality is correspondingly more complex. The portion of the template responsible for producing it may look as follows:

```
<TABLE>
   <TR><TD>
         [Run ShowSubscription(user,"Table","HTML")]
   </TD><TD>
         <FORM ACTION="subscribe.jsp" method="get">
         <U>Subscribe me to</U>
            <BR>
            <Select name="new">
                   [Run ShowSubscription(user,
                   "NewList","HTML")]
            </Select>
            <P>
         <U>Delete me from</U>
            <BR>
            <SELECT name="delete">
                   [Run ShowSubscription(user,"DelList","HTML")]
            </SELECT>
            </Input type="submit" value="Submit My Request">
         </FORM>
   </TD></TR>
</TABLE>
```

To aid the management of the preceding code and its placement on the various pages, PLAN can create a functionality component that has the following elements:

✦ **Management elements:** The content type can have such elements for the owner of the functionality, the contact person for the subscriptions database, the date of the last change, and so on.

✦ **Body elements:** The content type can have three body elements. One element can hold the code that goes on the home page and another can hold the longer chunk that goes on the subscription page. A final element can hold the binary programming object for the subscription feature.

PLAN gets a number of advantages by putting this functionality in a component, as the following list describes:

✦ **Collection:** PLAN can safely store and track the chunks of HTML programming code as well as the binary code in the subscription object.

✦ **Management:** PLAN can enter the code in any workflows that it needs for review or other administration.

✦ **Publishing:** Best of all, PLAN can push just the right code segment to the right page at the right time from its component. The subscription object itself can deploy from the component to a Web site as part of the publishing of the site.

Lest you think that functionality publishing is only for the Web, suppose that PLAN also wants to put the subscribe functionality at the bottom of its personalized printed materials. A template such as the one shown in Figure 27-7 does the trick.

Subscriptions

You are currently subscribed to:	[Insert PrintExistSubs]
You are eligible to subscribe as well to:	[Insert PrintNewSubs]

Would you like to subscribe or unsubscribe to any of these items? If so, fill in the following form and send it back to us by return mail.

Please subscribe me to: _____

Please delete me from: _____

Figure 27-7: A print template for the subscribe functionality

PLAN needs to add only the following two additional elements to the component to make this print template functional:

✦ **PrintExistSubs** may have the code [Run
ShowSubscription(user,"Table","Print")] in it.

✦ **PrintNewSubs** may have the code [Run
ShowSubscription(user,"NewList","Print")] in it.

Of course, as time goes on, PLAN may continue to add variations to the code in new elements of the component. No matter how many variations it comes up with, however, its templates remain simple and its code remains all in one place.

Note   Don't let the simplicity of the code and presentation in this example fool you. I made it that way so that I can easily present it. In real life, the concept remains the same, but the code gets much more complex, and managing it in components becomes more and more attractive.

Functionality content types and components

The general way to proceed with information content types is to create the type and then create a number of components of that type. If you use functionality components, the choice involves more than first meets the eye for the following reasons:

✦ **One component per type:** The PLAN example in the preceding section assumes that the subscription component is one of a kind. In other words, it uses a subscription content type that you expect to contain only one component. This approach is probably the easiest and most flexible way to create functionality components. The biggest problem this approach presents is that, if you have lots of different functionality, it produces a large number of content types.

✦ **A few general types:** If you prefer to keep your functionality management simpler, you can create one or a few generic functionality types. You can create one that has, for example, four generic code elements (with names such as Code1, Code2, Code3, and Code4), one element that you call Binary (to hold any binary objects) and an element that you call Type (in which you can define the kind of functionality it holds). This approach offers the distinct advantage of simplifying your types, but to use it you must squeeze your functionality components into standard types that may or may not give you the best results.

Content Is Deep

Don't try to handle the implicit depth of every content type you have to manage completely. Just like it's impossible to count the atoms of a slice of bread, there is no way of getting it all. But don't ignore or deny the deep structure you can't handle: Write remarks on every border you're defining (we use "##FIXME:") and take care that they are useful signposts for those who come with the next layer of solution later—it might be you!

Peter M. Buhr, DIE ZEIT Zeit_online GmbH

✦ **Types with multiple components:** Some functionality types may fit the usual model of one type with multiple components. PLAN, for example, may create a Feedback functionality content type. Throughout its publications, it may use 20 different forms of the Feedback functionality, each with its own Feedback component.

As usual, your choice isn't limited simply to one or the other. You can mix and match these approaches as you evolve your CMS.

Analyzing Content Types

Content types analysis is the process of dividing the content to be handled into the best set of content types and then dividing those types into the best set of elements. Because components affect every other part of your logical design, expect to revisit your content type analysis over and over as you learn more about the other parts of the system. Similarly, after you're through with the content type analysis, you need to assure yourself that the design you did previously is still valid and complete.

To create the logical design of your system of content types, you need to work through the following issues:

✦ **Content type and element names:** You want to review your naming a number of times to create a consistent and sensible family of names.

✦ **Component backlog:** To get an estimate of how long it takes to start up your CMS, you make some assumptions and calculations about how many of each content type you expect to create from whatever backlog of authored and acquired content you have.

✦ **Component throughput:** To estimate how much effort it takes to run your system on an ongoing basis takes, you make some assumptions and calculations about how many components of each type you expect to create and retire per week after the system is running.

✦ **Workflow:** As input to your workflow module, you decide on the cycles at which you want to perform editorial and metatorial reviews of each content type and also decide on an assumed life span for each. Finally, you decide whether to delete, inactivate, or archive components of each type after they're no longer active.

✦ **Component relationships:** You must decide how components of various types come together in a CMS outline, an overall content index, and any sequence or cross-reference strategies that you want to apply across all content.

Think

Before beginning your content type analysis, consider the following issues:

✦ **The idea of components:** Do you understand the concept of content types? Can the use of components ease what you perceive as the main bottlenecks to your processing of content for publications? If not, reconsider why you need a content management system.

✦ **The use of components:** Can you picture how an automated system goes about combining components into publications?

✦ **Publications:** Can you see your publications as simply the correct delivery of your components?

✦ **Storage format:** Can you standardize on a tool that produces the format that you want to store components in? How much work is converting the output of the authoring tools to the format that you want to store?

Plan

You can use the following sections to help you organize and perform a content type analysis.

A competitive content analysis

One approach to content analysis that I've found useful is to create a set of *best practice* content types based on an analysis of your Web site and those of your peers or competitors. With this information you can determine what kinds of content types are most standard and work best for your organization. Here are a few good reasons to do this type of analysis:

✦ Many organizations don't know where to begin with a content type analysis, and so they don't really do them. A competitive content type analysis gives you a place to start.

✦ It solidly positions you within the world of your peers. This analysis is a great excuse to get to study in depth what everyone else is doing and to decide which peers you want to emulate and how you are different.

✦ It gives you a more objective way of arguing for one approach over another.

✦ Finally, it establishes a terminology of content types. After this process, you have an agreed-upon set of content types that make it easier to talk about content within your teams.

Start your content type analysis with your competitors, but also include your own current site, plus perhaps other non-competitor sites that do well the things that you want your site to do. You're looking for roughly 5 to 10 sites; fewer than that and your pool is too small; more than that and it's unwieldy.

Note   As a companion to this template analysis, you should also perform a competitive content analysis as outlined in Chapter 31, "Designing Templates," in the section "A competitive Web template analysis."

After you have decided on a set of reference sites:

1. Review those sites in detail, noting what sorts of content they contain. Begin to name the kinds of content they contain to get a first approximation of what content types capture the content you are seeing.

2. From this review, prepare a list of the content types on each site that seem to have the most relevance to your content and work best for the site.

3. Compare the content types across the sites and choose a set of best examples — the ones that best typify the practices found on sites that you think work best.

4. Settle on a name for each of the content types you choose and use them to jumpstart your own content type analysis, which is presented in the rest of this "Plan" section.

A competitive content type analysis yields a great initial set of content types. As an example to get you started, I put a sample list of content types that I derived from my competitive content type analysis in the section titled "A Sample Set of Content Types," later in this chapter. But this list is only the beginning for your analysis. Be sure to understand the differences between your content and that of your peers or competitors by basing your analysis on the particulars of your audiences, content, and other entities. In other words, in addition to reflecting the best practices of your peer group, your content types should account for your specific context. That context is defined by the rest of your logical design.

Dividing information into content types

In Chapter 18, "Doing Logical Design," in the section "From business to system," I use the diagram shown in Figure 27-8 to illustrate a method for going from business goals and requirements to a first list of content types.

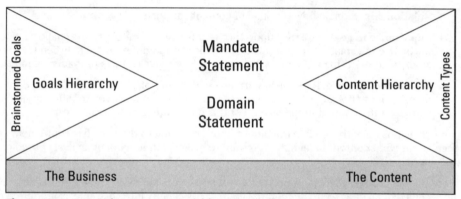

Figure 27-8: A mandate statement yields a content domain statement.

To kick off a content type analysis, I formalize this process. Use this top-down approach in combination with the competitive content type analysis to get to the set of content types that you need.

Note I'm assuming that you're starting from scratch here even though you may have done quite a bit of this analysis as part of the design of other entities. You can skip this exercise if you already have a good starter set of content types.

Begin by brainstorming from your goals to a set of content types, as shown in the following table.

Goal	Kind of Content	Name	Relationship	Importance to Goal	Overall Importance
Increase funding to PLAN	Stories of how money has helped our kids	Funding Success Stories	Shows potential contributors that their money is well spent	3	8

The following list describes what to do with each of the entries in this table:

✦ **Goal:** Enter the text of one goal from your mandate processes. See Chapter 16, "Securing a Project Mandate," for more information on the mandate process.

✦ **Kind of content:** Describe the sort of content (information or functionality) that you must collect to meet this goal. If more than one kind of content addresses the same goal, create multiple lines in the table. Similarly, if the same content supports more than one goal, include it more than once on different lines.

✦ **Name:** Assign a short name that captures the idea of this kind of content.

✦ **Relationship:** Explain how this kind of content supports this goal.

✦ **Importance to goal:** Rate the importance of this kind of content to the goal that it supports. Use the smallest range scale that enables you to differentiate between the various kinds of content that all support the same goal. (A range of 1-3 is probably a good start.)

✦ **Overall importance:** Rate the importance of this kind of content to the entire content management effort. Use the smallest range scale that enables you to differentiate among all the content in the table. (For this one, a range of 1-10 may do.)

As much as possible, try to fill in the table without referring to the specific requirements you received for what content to include. You want to make an independent analysis based on goals alone.

After you fill in the entire table from your goals, you can compare it to the requirements that you received. If all goes well, the required content fits cleanly into the table. No required content lacks a goal to support. If you do end up with required content with no goal to support, you need to go back to the person who required the content and work through the differences. You may end up modifying the goals or the requirement, but either way, make sure that the two are consistent before you go on.

Similarly, if you have a number of new content types in the table that no one thought to require, go back to your requirements group for agreement on the new types that you're suggesting and on their rankings relative to the types that group suggested.

Next, organize your content into a hierarchy, where each goal is a level-one heading and you organize content types in priority order below those headings. PLAN, for example, may devise a goal/content hierarchy that looks, in part, as follows:

```
Goal: Increase awareness of PLAN
   News
           Press releases
           Child updates
           Country updates
           Subscribe to alerts
```

```
Events
        Event descriptions
        Event announcements
        Event invitations
        Subscribe to events

Goal: Keep staff informed
    Press releases
    Policy statements
    Organization charts
    Benefits chooser application
```

This hierarchy isn't very different from the table that you started from. Now, however, leave out the goals. Instead, organize the content by its type. PLAN may choose the following categories:

```
News
    Press releases
    Child updates
    Country updates
Events
    Event descriptions
    Event announcements
    Event invitations
Organizational information
    Policy statements
    Organization charts
Functionality
    Subscribe to alerts
    Subscribe to events
    Benefits chooser application
```

The result is a content hierarchy that you take into the rest of the analysis. Take a good look at it and make sure that you have no redundancy or missing types in the hierarchy. In review, PLAN, for example, may determine that event announcements and event invitations are the same content, and combine the two types into one.

Identification

In this section of the analysis, you name your types and assign them a unique Id. As you do, review each type and ask yourself the following questions:

✦ **Information types:** Do I have various components of this type of information? Can I get each component into the same basic structure? Do I need to create, administer, and distribute components of this information separately from each other? If the answer is yes to all these questions, you clearly need this content type.

✦ **Functionality types:** Do I need to show this functionality on more than one type of page? Does it take more than one form in my user interface? Do I need to track changes to the functionality over time and apply version or access control to it? If the answer to any of these questions is yes, the functionality is a candidate for a content type. If the answer is no to all of them, you're probably better off hard-coding the functionality directly into the template that it's to live in.

For all the content types that make the cut, fill in the following design constraints:

✦ **Id:** Assign each type a unique identifier so that you can refer to this type efficiently in other parts of the design process.

✦ **Name:** Choose a descriptive but memorable name for each type so that the staff accepts the name and uses it consistently in conversation.

✦ **Description:** Enter a brief description of what the type is (for information types) or does (for functionality types).

✦ **Rank:** What's the priority of this type relative to the others?

✦ **Key component:** For each type, identify an example that you can point to as a sample component of the type. Make sure that the example that you choose really does reflect the entire type. You can use this example to explain the type to your staff and test the rest of your analysis.

Creation

For each type that you propose, determine an approach to the following design constraints:

✦ **Startup quantity:** How many components of this type do you need to include in your system as it starts up?

✦ **Run quantity:** How many components of this type do you expect to add per week after the system is running? Note that a week may be too small a unit for some components. Choose the unit of measurement for run quantity that bests fits your situation, but use the same one for all content types.

✦ **Sources:** Enter the names, Ids, and quantities of components that the authors and acquisition sources for this type supply. Compare your answers to the analysis and design work you do on authors and acquisition sources.

✦ **Original formats:** In what binary formats are the sources for this type?

✦ **Growth:** Do you expect the number of components of this type to grow indefinitely, or do you expect the number stabilize at some point? If it stabilizes, approximate the number? If you don't expect the number to stabilize, what's a maximum number of components of this type that you need to accommodate in the repository in the foreseeable future?

✦ **Samples:** How much sample content from the sources of this content type can you get for the coming analysis? If the answer is little or none, what can you base the rest of your analysis on? Do you know a person who can explain the structure of this kind of content?

Although you also address many of these issues in other portions of your logical design, you want to bring them together and list them by content type to determine whether you have a reasonable and efficient approach to components.

Life cycle

To provide input to your staffing and workflow calculations, address the following design constraints:

✦ **Editorial cycles:** Who should you involve in the review of this type of content before it's complete? What sorts of tasks do you want them to do?

✦ **Life span:** What's the likely life span of a component of this type before you retire it? If you decide to stop publishing this type of component, do you archive it or delete it?

✦ **Administrative review:** How often do you review the components of this type for accuracy and relevance? How often do you review the component for the correctness of its metadata elements?

✦ **Tasks:** What are the set of tasks that you must perform from the time that you receive or create the source information to the time that the component fully forms? Include all reviews, creation, acquisition, and conversion activities.

✦ **Processes:** Group the tasks that you come up with into whatever sets of steps can effectively illustrate its life cycle.

Elements

For each content type that you expect to have, decide on an approach to the following design constraints:

✦ **Samples:** Gather all the sample content that you can from the sources of this type. Look through it and get comfortable with it.

✦ **Body elements:** In your review, identify the easily discernible parts of the content that appear in your publications (for example, Title, Author, Abstract, Body, and so on). Give each part a short, descriptive name.

✦ **Management elements:** As you conduct your review, decide on the administrative information you want to capture for this content type (for example, Create Date, Review Status, Expiration Date, and so on.). Give each of these data points a short, descriptive name.

Following your review of the component source, complete a copy of the following table for each type.

Element Name	Description	Body Element?	Management Element?	Field Type
Title	The title of the component	Yes	Yes	Free text

The required information includes the following:

✦ **Element name:** Enter the name that you come up with for the element.

✦ **Description:** Enter a short description of the content or purpose of the element.

✦ **Body element:** Enter *Yes* if the element is ever to appear in a publication.

✦ **Management element:** Enter *Yes* if you think that you may need the element for accessing, sorting, tracking, or otherwise administering components of this type. If the element is for display *and* for use in management, enter *Yes* in both columns.

✦ **Field type:** Referring to the section "Elements have types and values," earlier in this chapter, choose a field type for the element.

Review the table that you create for each component. Try to come to the fewest number of elements that enable you to track and display this component. Be prepared to make multiple passes through this element set before your final cut.

With all your content types charted independently, pivot the analysis and list all elements regardless of the component they're part of, as shown in the following table.

Element	Components	Use	Type
Abstract	C123, 456,789	Body	Free text

The required information includes the following:

✦ **Element:** Enter the name of the component.

✦ **Components:** Enter the Ids of the content types that include this element. Enter *All* if the element appears in all content types.

✦ **Use:** Enter *Body*, *Management*, or *Both*.

✦ **Type:** Enter the field type of the element.

Cross-Reference   This table is part of the content model that you design in Chapter 30, "Designing Content Access Structures," in the section "The content model."

First, review the body elements across all components. Give yourself solid reasons why one component has certain elements that others don't. Make sure that elements that have the same function receive the same name. Next, review the management elements across all components. Are the elements consistently named? Do you have any duplicates with the same function but different names? Is each element that you specify really necessary?

Do you have a set of elements that you track across all components? If not, why not? Generally, you should end up with some small set of management elements that are common to all types. This set of global management elements helps you categorize all components. Elements such as Title, Author, and Create Date are candidates for global management. (All content types have an Id element.)

Localization

Add columns in your second element table to describe the localization that you plan for each element, as shown in the following table.

Element	Localities	Methods
Abstract	IntlEnglish, LatinSpanish, IntlFrench	Element variants

The required information includes the following:

✦ **Element:** Enter the name of each element.

✦ **Localities:** Enter the name of each locality where you expect to present this element differently.

✦ **Methods:** Decide which of the methods that I mention in the section "Locality in components," earlier in this chapter, you can use to manage the localization of this element.

This table shows the scope of your content localization program and the specific approach that you expect to take. Review the table to make sure that it's the most efficient approach that you can devise.

Tasks

Consider the effect of your content type analysis on the ongoing maintenance of the CMS. Then fill in the table that follows to define any component-related tasks that must happen on a recurring basis to run the CMS. Following are some task types to get you thinking:

✦ The creation cycle for each type.

✦ Ongoing metatorial reviews.

✦ Ongoing editorial reviews.

✦ Cycles for including each type in publications.

✦ Retirement cycles.

✦ New component-type design cycles

Use the following table to organize and detail the tasks that you come up with.

Task name	Who	What	When	How much	How
Write	Regional managers, CMS staff writers	Create SuccessStory components	When a country report comes in from the field	1 per week	Word files using a standard dot template

The required information includes the following:

✦ **Task name:** Give the task a short but memorable name that describes it.

✦ **Who:** Indicate what person or role is responsible for accomplishing this task. Naming an automated process here instead of a person is acceptable.

✦ **What:** List what steps the person or process must take to accomplish the task.

✦ **When:** Specify at what frequency this task must be done or how you know when it must occur.

✦ **How much:** Describe how much or how many of this sort of task you expect to do. A numerical quantity is preferable here, but if you can't come up with one, words such as *a lot*, *not much*, and so on suffice.

✦ **How:** Detail the skills, tools, or processes that the person or process needs to accomplish this task.

Don't worry if the tasks that you come up with at this point are somewhat ill-defined or sketchy. In your workflow analysis (in Chapter 33, "Designing Workflow and Staffing Models"), you have ample opportunity to refine them.

Integrate

To integrate this analysis with the rest of your logical design, consider the following issues:

✦ **Growth:** Do you expect the number of components in your repository to reach a stable level or to continue to grow indefinitely? If you expect the number to stabilize, verify your assumptions and make sure that the rate at which you expect to create components matches your expectations about the rate of archiving or deleting components. If you expect the number to grow, take this fact into account in every subsequent decision you make. What you're saying is that, eventually, you're going to maintain and publish an enormous amount of content. Can the processes and structures that you're creating scale to meet ever-increasing needs?

✦ **Sponsors:** Do your sponsors understand this content model? Are they likely to support the effort involved in creating and enforcing it?

✦ **Audiences:** Are your audiences likely to agree with the way that you rank content? Does your audience expect to see types of content that you're not covering? If so, why aren't you covering those types? Is your top-ranking audience the one most well-served by this content? If not, why not? What are your audiences' other sources for these types of content?

✦ **Publications:** Can these content types really provide enough content to fill up the publications that you intend to create? If not, what content types do you need to add? Examine your assumptions for the authorship, structure, and format of your publications. Are these assumptions consistent with the content types that you came up with? If not, how can you reset assumptions or change your publications to meet the assumptions? Does this content suggest a need for publications that you're not creating?

✦ **Types:** How many total content types do you have? The more types of components that you have, the more work it is to set up a management system for them. On the other hand, the more types that you have, the more flexible your system. Does your gut tell you that this number is a lot, a little, or about right?

✦ **Localization:** Review your element localization table. Do you have the budget to accomplish this much localization? On the other hand, are you doing enough to solidly meet the needs of your key localities?

A Sample Set of Content Types

Content types are the general kinds of content your CMS will handle. In this section, I describe the core set of content types that arises from a competitive content type analysis on a set of sites in the Internet security sector.

Note   The sites used in this competitive analysis are the same ones I use for a Web template analysis in Chapter 31, "Designing Templates," in the section "A Sample Set of Templates." Refer to that chapter to see examples of the sites I used.

Table 27-1 summarizes the core set of content types.

Table 27-1: Core Content Types

Content type	Description
Affiliations	This type stores information about the other organizations that the company is affiliated with.
Locations	This type stores information about the places where the organization does business.
Solutions	This type groups product and service components and wraps them in introductory information that shows how the combination of products and services solves a customer need.
Offering	This type holds information about each product or service the organization offers.
Annual Reports	This type groups content for Web-delivered versions of the company's annual report.
SEC Filings	This type holds information on the SEC filings the company has made.
Events	This type stores information about the events that the organization is planning or has staged. Best practice for organizations with lots of events is to buy a separate event management system and simply link to the CMS through page templates.
Press Releases	This type stores the press releases that the organization has issued.
Newsletters	This type groups content for Web-delivered versions of the company's newsletters. A best practice is to make the articles in the newsletter Article content types that are included in the newsletter dynamically.
Outside News	This type stores information about news stories produced outside the organization.
Outside Links	This type stores information about Web links that audiences might be interested in.
Articles	This type is a general-purpose place to store any component that behaves like an essay.
FAQs	This type stores question and answer pairs. Grouping the pairs into FAQ lists is accomplished by the way they are indexed and cross-referenced.
Customers	This type stores information about customers and the company's interactions with them.
Jobs	This type holds information about jobs available at the organization. Best practice is to have this information stored in a separate HR system and have it accessed but not owned by the CMS.
Downloads	This type stores information about the binary files the organization wants to offer as downloads. It does not include PDFs and other files that are incidentally downloaded but do not need to be separately indexed and presented.
Bio	This type stores information about a significant person in the organization.

The following sections give a characteristic example of each type of content type. I've constructed the examples using best practices that may or not have been used in constructing the original example Web sites. I intend this list to be comprehensive, but not exhaustive. If you use these content type examples as a starting point for your own content type analysis, you may need to add to or subtract from this list. In other words, this analysis is just an example.

I analyze content types as follows:

✦ **Definition:** The definition offered for each content type shows what, in general, the type is designed to store.

✦ **Body Elements:** The body elements listed in each table are the main ones to consider in creating each content type. I intend this list to be comprehensive, but not exhaustive. Best practices for creating elements are summarized later in this chapter in the section "Element best practices." These best practices are referred to by number in the element descriptions (for example, "...see best practice #2").

✦ **Management Elements:** The management elements listed in each table are the main ones to consider in creating each content type. I intend this list to be comprehensive, but not exhaustive. Most components should include a set of standard management and workflow management elements, and some include access elements as well, all of which I describe later in this chapter in the section "Standard management elements."

✦ **Most Useful Templates:** The most useful templates describe the component and navigation templates you may want to consider using to best represent each content type. This information may be more useful to you as you undertake a template analysis, as I describe in Chapter 31, "Designing Content Types," in the section "A competitive Web template analysis."

Affiliations

Table 27-2 shows an example of an Affiliations content type.

Table 27-2: Affiliations

Characteristic	Description
Definition	This type stores information about the other organizations that the company is affiliated with. The subtypes distinguish what kind of affiliation it is, whereas the other elements are the same across all subtypes.
Body Elements	* Category (Industry Trade Group, Standards Group, Marketing Partner, Reseller, Distributor, Integrator, Supplier, Services Org, Enterprise Partner)
	* Organization Name (free text)
	* Organization Description (free text or constrained text; see best practice #2)
	* Address (free text or reference; see best practice #1)
	* Contact Name (free text)
	* Contact E-mail (e-mail pattern)
	* URL (URL pattern)
	* Relationship Description (free text or constrained text; see best practice #2)
	* Company Logo Image (file pattern or reference; see best practice #3)
Management Elements	* Basic Management
	* Workflow

Characteristic	Description
Most Useful Templates	* Category List in local nav area
	* Results List in content area
	* FullView List (select by category, and proceed with a Title List at the top of the page)

Locations

Table 27-3 shows an example of a Locations content type.

Table 27-3: Locations

Characteristic	Description
Definition	This type stores information about the places where the organization does business.
Body Elements	* Category (Sales, Headquarters, Support, Training, Engineering, Operations)
	* Facility Name (free text)
	* Address (free text or reference; see best practice #1)
	* Phone Numbers (free text or reference; see best practice #1)
	* Contact E-mail (e-mail pattern)
	* Contact Name
	* City
	* Country
	* World Region
Management Elements	* Basic Management
	* Workflow
	* Access (hierarchy might replace city, country, and region)
Most Useful Templates	* Category List in local nav area
	* Results List in content area
	* FullView List (select by category, and proceed with a Title List at the top of the page)

Solutions

Table 27-4 shows an example of a Solutions content type.

Table 27-4: Solutions

Characteristic	Description
Definition	This type groups product and service components and wraps them in introductory information that shows how the combination of products and services solves a customer need.
Body Elements	* Title (free text)
	* Abstract (free text)
	* Problem Statement (free text or constrained text; see best practice #2)
	* Solution Statement (free text or constrained text; see best practice #2)
	* Body (free text or constrained text; see best practice #2, dynamic layout; see best practices #5, names linked; see best practice #4)
	* Products included (reference list)
	* Services included (reference list)
Management Elements	* Basic Management
	* Workflow
	* Access
	–Indexed by audience and industry
	–Cross-references to all related components
Most Useful Templates	* Title List in local navigation
	* Title List or Index in FullViews of components that are cross-referenced
	* FullView Page for short text or Cluster for longer texts

Offering

Table 27-5 shows an example of an Offering content type.

Table 27-5: Offering

Characteristic	Description
Definition	This type holds information about each product or service the organization offers.
Body Elements	* Category (Product, Service)
	* Title (free text)
	* Abstract (free text)
	* Body (free text or constrained text; see best practice #2, dynamic layout; see best practices #5, names linked; see best practice #4)

Characteristic	Description
Management Elements	* Basic Management
	* Workflow
	* Access
	–Hierarchy of offering by market, technical, or solution categories
	–Indexed by audience and industry
	–Cross-references to all related components
Most Useful Templates	* Expanding TOC in local navigation
	* Static TOC on folder pages
	* Index or Title List in FullViews of components that are cross-referenced
	* FullView Page for short text or Cluster for longer texts

Annual Reports

Table 27-6 shows an example of an Annual Reports content type.

Table 27-6: Annual Reports

Characteristic	Description
Definition	This type groups content for Web-delivered versions of the company's annual report.
Body Elements	* Pub Date (date pattern)
	* Title (free text)
	* Executive Summary (free text or constrained text; see best practice #2)
	* Body (free text or constrained text; see best practice #2, dynamic layout; see best practices #5, names linked; see best practice #4)
Management Elements	* Basic Management
	* Workflow
	* Access
	–Hierarchy of the sections in the report
	–Cross-references to related components within the sections of the report
Most Useful Templates	* Results List view sorted by date and showing title and executive summary
	* PubView Page

Continued

Table 27-6 *(continued)*

Characteristic	Description
Most Useful Templates	* Within the Pub
	–Home page with the date, title, and executive summary
	–Expanding TOC in the local navigation area built from the sections of the XML
	–Section pages with Results Lists for the subsections within each section
	–FullView page for each section or subsection with substantial text
	* Link to PDF version of the report

SEC Filings

Table 27-7 shows an example of an SEC Filings content type.

Table 27-7: SEC Filings

Characteristic	Description
Definition	This type holds information on the SEC filings the company has made.
Body Elements	* Category (none; or could be classified by the kind of filing)
	* Title (free text)
	* Abstract (free text or constrained text; see best practice #2)
	* URL (URL pattern)
Management Elements	* Basic Management
	* Workflow
Most Useful Templates	* If classified by type then a Category List
	* Results List with link to SEC site for filing details

Events

Table 27-8 shows an example of an Events content type.

Table 27-8: Events

Characteristic	Description
Definition	This type stores information about the events that the organization is planning or has staged. Best practice for organizations with lots of events is to buy a separate event management system and simply link to the CMS through page templates.
Body Elements	* Category (Trade Show, Training, Single Speaker, Conference, Marketing Presentation)
	* Title (free text)
	* Location (free text or reference; see best practice #1)
	* Abstract (free text or constrained text; see best practice #2)
	* Agenda (free text or constrained text; see best practice #2)
	* Participants (free text or reference; see best practice #1)
	* Dates (free text or reference; see best practice #1)
	* External URL (URL pattern)
Management Elements	* Basic Management
	* Workflow
	* Access
	–Index by industry and audience
	–Cross-references to related components
Most Useful Templates	* Category List in the local nav area
	* TitlePlus List sorted by date with category headings or Table List with date location and abstract
	* FullView List by category with link to external URL (if available)

Press Releases

Table 27-9 shows an example of a Press Releases content type.

Table 27-9: Press Releases

Characteristic	Description
Definition	This type stores the press releases that the organization has issued.
Body Elements	* Category (none; or can be categorized by industry and audience using the management element index)
	* Title (free text)
	* Date (date pattern)
	* Location (free text)
	* Abstract (free text or constrained text; see best practice #2)
	* Body (free text or constrained text; see best practice #2 names linked; see best practice #4)
	* OrgContact1 (free text or constrained text; see best practice #2. May also be a reference to a standard text for this element)
	* OrgContact2 (free text or constrained text; see best practice #2. May also be a reference to a standard text for this element)
Management Elements	* Basic Management
	* Workflow
	* Access
	–Index by industry and audience
	–Cross-references to related components
Most Useful Templates	* Category List by year
	* Results List sorted by date
	* Results List sorted by OrgContact2

Newsletters

Table 27-10 shows an example of a Newsletters content type.

Table 27-10: Newsletters

Characteristic	Description
Definition	This type groups content for Web-delivered delivered versions of the company's newsletters. A best practice is to make the articles in the newsletter Article components that are included in the newsletter dynamically.

Characteristic	Description
Body Elements	* Pub Date (date pattern)
	* Title (free text)
	* Executive Summary (free text or constrained text; see best practice #2)
	* Front Matter (free text or constrained text; see best practice #2)
	* Rear Matter (free text or constrained text; see best practice #2)
Management Elements	* Basic Management
	* Workflow
	* Access
	–Hierarchy of the articles to include in the newsletter
	–Cross-references will come from the cross-references in the included articles
Most Useful Templates	* Results List view sorted by date and showing title and exec summary
	* FullView Pub
	* Within the Pub
	–Home page with the date, title, and executive summary
	–Front and rear matter pages that present the text in those elements
	–Expanding TOC in the local navigation area built from the hierarchy of articles
	–FullView page for each article that has the branding of the newsletter. With link to PDF version.
	* Link to full PDF version of the newsletter

Outside News

Table 27-11 shows an example of an Outside News content type.

Table 27-11: Outside News

Characteristic	Description
Definition	This type stores information about news stories produced outside the organization.
Body Elements	* Category (Web, PDF, Video, Audio)
	* Title (free text)
	* Abstract (free text or constrained text; see best practice #2)
	* Company Logo Image (file pattern or reference; see best practice #3)
	* URL (URL pattern)

Continued

Table 27-11 *(continued)*

Characteristic	Description
Management Elements	* Basic Management
	* Workflow
	* Access
	–Index by industry and audience
	–Cross-references to related components
Most Useful Templates	* AdView in pages that have cross-references to this component.
	* Results List sorted by date
	* FullView List

Outside Links

Table 27-12 shows an example of an Outside Links content type.

Table 27-12: Outside Links

Characteristic	Description
Definition	This type stores information about Web links that audiences might be interested in.
Body Elements	* Category (none; or subtyped by their position in the link hierarchy described in the management elements)
	* Title (free text)
	* Abstract (free text or constrained text; see best practice #2)
	* URL (URL pattern)
Management Elements	* Basic Management
	* Workflow
	* Access
	–Hierarchy of link categories decided by a hard look at all the links and how they classify
	–Index by industry and audience
	–Cross-references to related components
Most Useful Templates	* Expanding TOC in local navigation
	* AdView in pages that have cross-references to this component
	* FullView List with headings for the hierarchy categories

Articles

Table 27-13 shows an example of an Articles content type.

Table 27-13: Articles

Characteristic	Description
Definition	This type is a general-purpose place to store any component that behaves like an essay. The subtypes take care of the difference in the selection and labeling of the component when it is displayed.
Body Elements	* Category (Support Articles, Investor Docs, White Papers, Tech Notes, Executive Briefs, Data Sheets, Success Stories, Case Studies, Feature Stories, Industry Analysis, Topics)
	* Title
	* Abstract
	* Body (free text or constrained text; see best practice #2, dynamic layout; see best practices #5, names linked; see best practice #4)
Management Elements	* Basic Management
	* Workflow
	* Access
	–Indexed by audience and industry
	–Hierarchy of the sections in the article
	–Cross-references to related components
Most Useful Templates	* FullView Page for short articles
	* FullView Cluster for long articles
	* Link to PDF version of the article

FAQs

Table 27-14 shows an example of a FAQs content type.

Table 27-14: FAQs

Characteristic	Description
Definition	This type stores question and answer pairs. Grouping the pairs into FAQ lists is accomplished by the way they are indexed and cross-referenced.
Body Elements	* Question (free text or constrained text; see best practice #2)
	* Answer (free text or constrained text; see best practice #2)

Continued

Table 27-14 *(continued)*

Characteristic	Description
Management Elements	* Basic Management
	* Workflow
	* Access
	–Indexed by audience and industry
	–Cross-references to related components
Most Useful Templates	* Title Link in any component FullView that has one or more FAQ's linked to it.
	* FullView List selected by index category or cross-reference.

Customers

Table 27-15 shows an example of a Customers content type.

Table 27-15: Customers

Characteristic	Description
Definition	This type stores information about customers and the company's interactions with them.
Body Elements	* Category (Enterprise, Medium, Small)
	* Name
	* Company Logo Image (file pattern or reference; see best practice #3)
	* Abstract (free text or constrained text; see best practice #2)
	* Body (free text or constrained text; see best practice #2, dynamic layout; see best practices #5, names linked; see best practice #4)
	* Products (reference)
	* Services (reference)
	* Solutions (reference)
	* Date (date pattern)
Management Elements	* Basic Management
	* Workflow
	* Access
	–Indexed by audience and industry
	–Cross-references to related components

Characteristic	Description
Most Useful Templates	* Title Link in any component FullView that has this component cross-referenced to it
	* Results List by Type sorted by date
	* FullView Page for short body
	* FullView Cluster for long body

Jobs

Table 27-16 shows an example of a Jobs content type.

Table 27-16: Jobs

Characteristic	Description
Definition	This type holds information about jobs available at the organization. Best practice is to have this information stored in a separate HR system and have it accessed, but not owned, by the CMS.
Body Elements	* Category (none; categorized by the hierarchy described under management elements)
	* Specific Title (free text)
	* Abstract (free text or constrained text; see best practice #2)
	* Full Description (free text or constrained text; see best practice #2, dynamic layout; see best practices #5, names linked; see best practice #4)
	* Close Date (date pattern)
	* Start Date (date pattern)
	* Salary Range (free text)
Management Elements	* Basic Management
	* Workflow
	* Access
	–Hierarchy of general job titles with a free text description of the basic nature of each category
	–Indexed by audience and industry
	–Cross-references to related components
Most Useful Templates	* TOC Expanding for hierarchy of general job titles
	* Results List of general job titles and descriptions
	* Table List headed by general job title and showing specific title, abstract, start date and salary range (maybe).
	* FullView Page

Downloads

Table 27-17 shows an example of a Downloads content type.

Table 27-17: Downloads

Characteristic	Description
Definition	This type stores information about the binary files the organization wants to offer as downloads. It does not include PDFs and other files that are incidentally downloaded but do not need to be separately indexed and presented.
Body Elements	* Category (none; categorized by the hierarchy described under management elements) * Name (free text) * Abstract (free text or constrained text; see best practice #2) * Post Date (date pattern) * URL (URL pattern)

Management Elements	* Basic Management
	
	* Workflow
	
	* Access
	
	   –Hierarchy of download categories with a free text description of the nature of each category
	
	   –Indexed by audience and industry
	
	   –Cross-references to related components

Most Useful Templates	* TOC Expanding for hierarchy of downloads * Results List of downloads within a TOC category * Table List headed by category and showing name (linked to URL), abstract, and post date

Bio

Table 27-18 shows an example of a Bio content type.

Table 27-18: Bio

Characteristic	Description
Definition	This type stores information about a significant person in the organization.
Body Elements	* Category (Board, Management, Speaker, Author)
	* Name (free text)
	* Position (free text)
	* Bio (free text or constrained text; see best practice #2)
	* Photo (file pattern or reference; see best practice #3)
Management Elements	* Basic Management
	* Workflow
	* Access
	–Indexed by audience and industry
	–Cross-references to related components
Most Useful Templates	* TitlePlus List with name and position
	* FullView Page

Standard management elements

In Table 27-19, I provide background and basic guidance for the creation of component elements. The information in this section refers to the content type examples in the previous section.

It's a good idea to create standard element sets that are applied evenly and consistently to a range of content types. In this way, you can access and manage components most efficiently and effectively.

Cross-Reference

For a full discussion of elements, see the section "Component Types Have Elements" earlier in this chapter. For a list of element types, see Chapter 24, "Working with Metadata," in the section "Categorizing Metadata Fields."

Table 27-19: Standard Management Elements

Element set	Elements included
Basic Management Set (stored with component)	* Author (reference to author record)
	* Current Owner (reference)
	* Create Date (date pattern)
	* Last Modified (date pattern)
	* Id (unique Id)

Continued

Table 27-19 *(continued)*

Element set	Elements included
Workflow Set (stored with component; or best practice is stored as a separate structure in the repository)	* Status Type
	* Status Value
	* Escalation To (a person)
	* Date Status Changed
Access Set (stored with component; or best practice is stored as a separate structure in the repository)	* Index (keyword sets)
	* Hierarchy (outline position)
	* Cross-references
	* Next and Prev

Element best practices

The best practices listed in Table 27-20 are referenced by number in the Body Elements of Tables 27-2 through 27-18 in the section "A Sample Set of Content Types" earlier in this chapter.

Table 27-20: Element Best Practices

Number	Best Practice
1. One element or a compound	A common practice is to pack a lot of separate pieces of information into a single element. For example, an address may have the city, region, and country together in one string. If you want finer control, a better practice is to create a separate record (with one field for each part of the element) and list the Id of the separate record in the element.
2. Structure within body text	A common practice is to have all elements with long free text be entered without formatting, Another common practice is to allow any HTML in these fields and hope that it renders well. A better practice is to constrain the HTML that is allowed. The best practice is to allow only xHTML or schema-backed XML in text fields. This final approach allows strict validation of body text and the capability to transform it as needed to suit the page it will be shown on. Using XML to represent body text also effectively turns the single body text element into multiple independently accessible elements (see element best practice #5).

Number	Best Practice
3. Referencing media	A common practice is to include <img> tags within other elements to refer to images (and other HTML tags for other media). A better practice is to break media references out of the middle of elements and store them as separate elements (an image element, for example). The best practice is to store media as separate components (with their own elements, say file, caption, size, and so on) and reference them into the components that use them. Thus, whether the media is inside a text element or in its own element, the management and distribution of the media can be managed from one central place. This method also serves as the basis for reusing media.
4. Names linked	In constrained body text (see best practice #2), the usual practice is to do no further processing on the company and personal names mentioned in the text. A better practice is to attempt to find the significant names and turn them into HTML <a> links to a relevant page for that name. The best practice is to turn them into XML tags that allow you to programmatically check these links to be sure they continue to work. Automation software is available to aid in finding and linking names.
5. Driving display from body text structure	If a body text element is structured into XML sections, it is possible to drive its display automatically and fit the most appropriate display to it based on the structure presented. For example, consider this XML structure within a body element:

```
<section>
    <intro>...</intro>
    <subsection>...</subsection>
    <subsection>...</subsection>
    <subsection>...</subsection>
</section>
```

If each <subsection> has considerable text (say for example, more than six paragraphs), the component template can create a set of pages (one for each embedded section) and display the component as the <intro> and links to all the <subsection> pages. More generally, the more structure the template detects in the <subsection>, the more sophistication it can use to display the <subsection>.

Cross-Reference

For information about the basics of elements—what they are and how they're related to components—refer to "Component Types Have Elements" earlier in this chapter. For a list of element types, see Chapter 24, "Working with Metadata," in the section "Categorizing Metadata Fields."

Summary

Components are the center of your logical design. For that reason, separating the analysis that you do on components from the rest of the analyses that you conduct during logical design is difficult. On the other hand, if you take a lot of the information that you gather elsewhere and look at it in the context of components, you can get a second angle on your design. A content type analysis does the following:

✦ Gives you a method — independent from the requirements you were given — for arriving at the set of content types that you need to manage.

✦ Gives you a solid understanding of the set of component elements that you must create.

✦ Gives you the core of your localization strategy.

✦ Gives you the core of your content model.

In the next chapter, I detail the concept and analysis of authors.

✦   ✦   ✦

Accounting for Authors

In the past, you applied the word *author* only to a small group of professionals. In today's world of electronic information, you can call almost anyone an author. In electronic information, instead of tending to a small stable of people who understand information and its creation, your goal is to harvest the creative product from as wide a base as is feasible. The more organized and precise you are about what you want to harvest, the wider the contribution base that's possible.

In this chapter, I detail the information that you need to collect about your base of authors to best serve them and enable them to best serve you.

Authoring Jumpstart

This Jumpstart summarizes how you analyze the process you use to account for authors in your CMS.

Use this jumpstart as a quick review if you've already read the section "Analyzing Authors" (later in this chapter) and want a checklist of what you need to do carry out an author analysis.

To analyze your authoring constraints, you can follow these steps:

1. Think about what you know about your authors. Consider their motivations, capability and skills, numbers, and intellectual property rights. Also, consider the authors from the point of view of the audience: How important is it to convey authorship to the audience?

2. Plan your author analysis, including the following considerations:

   - **Content sources:** Figure out what your content sources are and chart their characteristics, including the content type you will get from each, the quantity of components, source, and information about whether the content is authored by the source, syndicated, or if merely linking to the source content is sufficient for your needs.

   - **Identity of the authors:** Chart descriptive information about your authors. Include the name and Id of each content type the author can create; how many components of what quality you anticipate each author will create; the degree of technical savvy and your influence over each author.

- **Author design constraints:** Chart the attributes of each prospective author that affects your process design. Include preferred authoring tools and proficiency with these tools; the kinds of metadata authors will supply; training needed; the status of rights to the author's work; degree of author's participation in reviews, management, and publishing of the content they create.

- **Localization:** Relying on your component localization analysis (See Chapter 27, "Designing Content Types," in the section "Localization"), determine whether you can create guidelines to help authors create locality-independent content. Also determine whether you can get authors from targeted localities to assist in authoring or reviewing content.

- **Relationship between content types and authors:** For each content type, describe exactly what the authors will be required to author, including the locality for which the content is authored; the start-up and run quantity of components that must be authored; and the metadata not required to be filled in by the author. From this information, you can determine several things: what content needs localization, the number of components needed for startup, and to what extent a metator is required.

- **Figure out the tasks that will have to be done on an ongoing basis.** These might include, for example, recruiting and training authors; reviewing and updating author guidelines; creating and managing submission, editorial, metatorial, localization, legal review, incentive, and quality-control cycles; managing meetings with authors and the publication team; and managing author and audience review and redesign of publication. For each task that you come up with, chart the task name, who does it, what it consists of, when it must be done, how much or extensively, and how the task is accomplished.

3. Integrate your author analysis with the other analyses you have done. As you do, consider whether authors are on board with your project goals; how to ensure consistency among authors; how to garner acceptance of the authors by your audiences; how to maintain consistency between authored and acquired sources; how involved authors can and should be in your publications; and whether the attribution your authors want is consistent with your publication analysis.

What Is Authoring?

Whether you're authoring a new picture in a digital camera, recording an interview, or writing an introduction to an article, a creative act drives your fingers to click, sketch, or type. No computer can tell you whether what you create is good. Quality is entirely a judgment call and completely depends on the context within which you're creating the content. (Noise may be just the sound that you want for a site that concerns classical information theory.)

Although they cannot drive the process, computers do play an important part in the authoring process. Authoring, as is true of any invention process (according to Thomas Edison), is one percent inspiration and 99 percent perspiration. Computers host the perspiration. You can now process all forms of recorded information on a desktop computer. And, as the digital age creeps steadily on to dominate every type of recorded information, you will become more and more likely to create as well as process your information digitally (as my digital camera, digital tape deck, and digital video camera attest).

Although the idea of authoring can cover a lot of ground, you have some ways to organize these notions. In particular, the idea of authoring involves:

✦ **People** who, whether or not they think of themselves as such, are authors.

✦ **Content** that the authors create.

✦ **Tools** that authors use to create content.

✦ **Processes,** whether formal or informal, that lead to finished content.

This section describes each of these aspects of authoring.

Who can become an author?

An *author* is someone who creates original content. The title *author* was formerly a special distinction given to people who made a career out of content creation. And that's still the case for people who define themselves as authors.

If you take this definition literally, however, which is what I intend to do, the name *author* applies to anyone who creates content (regardless of what such people call themselves). I know of very few organizations (professional publishing firms notwithstanding) that can afford the luxury of using only professional authors. Instead, authors are, as often as not, people with other jobs who happen to know about something and can (more or less) communicate it.

Note   My definition of *authors*, by the way, includes people who create original functionality for a CMS, as well as people who create original information.

In a large CMS, this situation is especially true. You're likely to deal with all types of authors, from the professional writer to the engineer who failed high school composition. If you're smart, you design processes that recognize the various classes of authors that you employ and work with each class on its own terms.

Authoring today doesn't even end at the organizational borders. Collecting original content from your audience is also possible and, indeed, is often a great idea. If you can turn your consumers into contributors, they become much more engaged with your organization and, of course, can supply you with content you'd have a very hard time collecting otherwise.

So I hope that I've sufficiently blurred the concept of author in this section that you're now comfortable calling people authors who'd never call themselves authors. Beyond just calling them authors, however, you need to *treat* them as authors, providing them with the tools and guidance that they need to successfully contribute to your CMS.

Harvesting creative product

When it comes to gathering content from authors, one goal of any CMS is to harvest the creative product of as wide an author base as feasible and deliver it to as wide an audience base as feasible. The more organized you are, the wider the feasible base becomes. If, for example, you (as a government employee, say) simply send out an e-mail message reading, "Please send me anything that you've created that applies to our enforcement of the new regulations," you can expect to get back more than you can handle. Contributions arrive in any form, written for any audience, and you end up with a lot of work on your hands sorting it all out. In the end, you don't get the definitive content on the subject; you just get whatever anyone takes the time to send you.

If, on the other hand, you're organized, you start by figuring out what you want and who creates it. You understand how such people now create that information and what changes may prove necessary during its creation to make it the most useful to you. You work out the details of how to most efficiently collect and merge it with the other sources of information that you intend to collect. Then you send an e-mail message to each type of author you identify, asking for specific contributions and offering specific methods of creation and collection. At the end of this process, you receive the definitive information in a form that not only gets you the best content, but that also gets you the most content. Much more important, you've started a process that can continue to get you the greatest amount of the best content over time. Authoring isn't a one-time event. People continue to create original content, and you must prepare yourself to continue to harvest it.

A CMS can add a level of organization to your approach to authors that you could never match through more casual measures. This is a good thing. To meet the demands of the wide and diverse author community in most large organizations, you need all the help that you can get.

Authoring tools

Digital information-processing tools present the most difficult problem of authoring in a CMS. In short, each tool is its own world. Each has its own file format, user interface, and capabilities. In addition, people gather around their favorite tools as if they were sacred objects. Overall, this tendency leads to a balkanization of authoring camps that can cause you a lot of additional trouble and expense.

You may, for example, think that a picture is a picture and so any image-authoring tool should do. The various graphic artists on your staff, however, may disagree with you. More to the point, they may even disagree with each other. Contention surrounds the selection of the best computer for graphics (with the Macintosh the consistent choice of most graphic artists), and another debate centers about the best image-editing tools. I believe that the depth of sentiment is such that trying to find the *best* tool or platform is a losing proposition. You may instead want to either take on the extra expense of using multiple tools and trouble for the sake of good will or use economic justifications to judge which tool is the right one for your organization.

Cross-Reference   Look in Chapter 38, "Building Collection Systems," in the section "Authoring System," for more information about authoring tools.

Authoring prior to the CMS

The authoring process itself is one of review and revision. The author usually produces a draft that one or more people review, and then the author revises. This review process is most often bounded not by achieving perfection, but by the amount of time available for reviewing and revising a particular document before other tasks take precedence. Still, an exchange occurs between the author and the reviewer before the authored content is ready for publication.

You need to realize and account for the fact that this review happens both informally and formally. Many CMS designers overlook the informal review and mistakenly believe that they need to model and include all review and revision in the system's workflow module. In reality, authors may well hold their work outside the system until they're personally happy with it. This is a perfectly sensible work style, but it does mean that, at any one time, some amount of your authored content is outside the system. When you're estimating the time required to author content, then, you need to include what could be time spent before content enters the repository. Because significant time can be invested in creating content before it enters the repository, you need to account for the backup and recovery of content outside the repository as well.

Equally true is the fact that content may not be fully authored just because someone lodges it in the repository. Authors may put unfinished work in the repository simply to keep it safe, to collaborate with co-authors, to provide an early review version for others, or they may return after a day or two to a work they thought finished to improve it with all the ideas that came to them as afterthoughts.

Whether it goes into the repository sooner or later, after it's in the repository, the content is under management, and workflow processes can control it.

 Cross-Reference Look in Chapter 33, "Designing Workflow and Staffing Models," for more information about workflow.

The Author's Attitude

In collecting content from the organization you immediately hit a dilemma: Some authors write to a specific small audience, but you need content that can be consumed by a general audience. You can handle this situation in two ways: Change the author by getting her to create content for general consumption from the start, or change the content the author creates so that it works better for general consumption. Each scenario presents its own difficulties. An author may require a lot of convincing to change the way that she creates her content. On the other hand, reworking her content until it's ready for the CMS and its audiences may require a lot of manual effort.

Changing the author

Getting authors to make the adjustments necessary to produce the content you need means changing their knowledge and motivations about the goals of the work, the audiences they are trying to reach, and the value they are trying to deliver. It may also require heightened attention to getting relevant feedback to authors, and perhaps a pat on the back for giving any extra (in their minds) effort required to create the content in the way you need it.

If you ask people to author for a general organizational repository rather than for a small known group, they may resist if it means that they must jettison their simplifying assumptions and direct feedback to do so. They also resist if they perceive that the task requires more effort for essentially the same benefit to them. The solution, of course, is to supply a new set of assumptions and feedback and to ensure that you recognize and account for any extra effort that the author puts into the project. In particular, you must plan to do the following:

✦ **Provide contributors with a clear understanding of what they're trying to accomplish.** Some authors assume that you're asking them to produce for everybody or for no one in particular, or that their work may be taken out of context and lose its meaning. Make sure that you provide authors with the understanding that they're creating for very particular people and that you're trying to understand and manage the context of their work—not deny it.

✦ **Provide contributors with a very clear mental image of the audiences for their work.** If the image that you provide is as vivid and detailed as the one an author has for her present group, you succeed.

✦ **Provide contributors with as much direct feedback as they would receive if they were generating content in their familiar way.** In fact, you can plan to include some of the same people the author would naturally turn to for this feedback. If the feedback that the author receives is as directed and relevant as what she'd get from her group, you succeed.

✦ **Provide contributors specific feedback about the success of their work.** If you can establish a back channel between the end consumers and the authors that's as direct and relevant as what she'd get internally, you succeed.

✦ **Provide contributors a new value proposition to supplant the one that they now have.** You can assume that authors produce good information because they must do so for their job; they seek the positive perception of their group and supervisors; and that they have a personal interest or expertise in the subject matter. If you provide a value proposition as compelling as the one that's now in place, you succeed.

✦ **Provide contributors with ample reward for any extra effort you require.** Most likely, the group that the author belongs to still wants the information that the author produces. Does this situation mean that she must produce two versions? If so, how does this duplication of effort fit into her current responsibilities? If not, how specifically can the system ensure that the author's deliverables to her group aren't undermined?

The Lemon Girl

After a London content management event in 2003, Bob, a couple other colleagues, and I had dinner in a Lebanese restaurant. Before eating we ordered some tea. Bob wanted lemon with the tea. So we asked for it.

Well, there was this really cute girl serving the tables. Bob asked for some lemon. The girl said, "No." Then Bob explained that a kitchen must have some lemon. The girl said, "No," and smiled very nicely. Then we explained that they should have some lemon because in these kinds of restaurants it's a custom that lemons are served with the meat. The girl said, "No." Her smile broke some hearts now.

We didn't want to be offensive, so we decided to leave it at that. It was a nice cup of tea, really. Finally dinner was served. Of course, we all got lemon with our meat.

All, except...Bob!

What did we learn from the lemon girl? Well, if a content management system (or in fact any system) is too rigid, there is no room for even the smallest exception, even for exceptions that are perfectly reasonable for the people who must work with the system. When the people are confronted with these rigid rules in a CMS, at first they accept them. After all, it's a nice and expensive system, so who are they to complain?

But with enough of these kinds of disappointments, people will eventually become annoyed with the system, and ultimately refuse to work with it if possible. Or: Refuse me lemon often enough, and I'll stop coming to your restaurant.

Erik Hartman, Hartman Communicatie BV (www.hartman-communicatie.nl)

Don't underestimate what changing the attitude of your authors may take. Use every tool at your disposal to get them comfortable creating content in a new way. For example, if you've done all you can to support authors inside your organization but they still resist getting on board with your authoring requirements, consider your influence on them and, in particular, consider bringing the weight of your mandate and sponsors to bear, as I discuss in the section "Influence" later in this chapter. Ultimately, if you have a choice, switch to authors who can create the content the way you need it.

Changing the content

Instead of getting authors to create content directly for the CMS, you can take what authors naturally create and recast it for general use. If you take this tack, you must carefully consider the original context under which they create the information and decide specifically how to modify it. In particular, you need to consider the following issues:

✦ What are the differences between the original audience and the audiences of the CMS?

✦ Were explanations and background information left out that you need to add for the work to prove useful to the new audiences?

✦ Do explicit or implicit references to other publications or knowledge appear in the content that the new audiences don't have access to?

✦ Does the work use "insider" terminology that the new audiences can't understand?

✦ Is the author going to participate at all? Do you expect the author to submit the content to the CMS effort, or must you go find the information? If authors submit their content, how much additional information (metadata, that is) can you expect them to enter?

Cross-Reference Taking and using content that an author's already created is called *acquisition*, and I discuss it more in Chapter 29, "Accounting for Acquisition Sources."

This is a lot of work, and you should only attempt it after deciding that there is no way you will change your authors, such as when your authors are outside contributors who simply aren't tied into your system. If you do adopt this method, be sure to keep track of how much extra effort it takes you to reform content. See if you can't use this expense later as a justification for making the change to a new authoring paradigm.

Your Attitude Toward Authors

Given a wide and diverse set of authors, you need to organize them into groups so that you can most effectively interact with them. The most natural way to organize authors is by what they create. From the standpoint of the CMS, however, the following factors are just as important as content type in organizing your approach to authors:

✦ **Authoring tools:** Different kinds of authors want to (and need to) use different primary authoring tools. Some need only a set of Web forms that you supply; others need to work within a particular word processing environment. Some may use structured XML editors, whereas others may use proprietary media tools that are completely outside the bounds of the CMS.

✦ **Metadata:** Different kinds of authors can deal with more or less metadata entry. Some don't even fill in their name using the correct format, whereas you can expect others to know as much about the metadata of the system as any metator.

✦ **Incentives:** Different kinds of authors require different levels of incentives to keep them in scope and on schedule. Some need no more than their job descriptions to keep producing, whereas others need a boost after each submission to stay motivated and on top of their tasks.

Digging a bit deeper, you can point to the following factors that most influence your relationships with different authors:

✦ **Technical savvy**, which involves how much they understand about and know how to use technology.

✦ **Influence**, which is how close they are to your core CMS team.

Technical savvy

The more that an author understands and feels comfortable with your technology, the easier you may find working with her. I don't mean to say that you can't include people who aren't tech-savvy — just that such people make your job harder. Nevertheless, whether they're savvy or not, authors are authors, and you must account for them. You don't need to go overboard with savvy, however. The following simple, three-stage scale suffices to categorize your authors in this area:

✦ **Low:** These authors aren't comfortable with computers and resist any efforts that you make to get them to learn any new tools or methods. The computer is a mystery to them. They can't anticipate its actions and tend to think that they're liable to break it at any minute (which, given today's computers, is sadly true). They work in one or a very few applications and know one way only of doing things. Any method that they find for accomplishing a task tends to become ingrained as the only way to accomplish that task. You need to treat authors with low savvy very carefully and go only as far as necessary into their limited world.

✦ **Medium:** These authors can deal with a computer. They've largely gotten over their fear. (They know that, if the computer breaks, it's fixable.) They're likely users of more than one application and are relatively comfortable using the Web. They possess some ability to generalize principles from one context to another, and although they prefer to use their learned methods, they do try and can learn new methods to accomplish their tasks. You can expect some resistance but general compliance from this sort of author.

✦ **High:** These authors are into computers. They aren't afraid at all. (They know that sometimes you can't fix computers, but they don't care.) They're power users of at least one application and probably spend too many hours on the Web. They understand the basic principles of user interfaces and can often work around bad design or poor explanations. They have no trouble learning and applying new methods. Your main issue with these sorts of authors is to keep them from circumventing your procedures and keep them following rules that they can figure out how to break.

The First Law of Content Management

The first law of thermodynamics states that energy is conserved. You can neither create nor destroy it—only move it around. A world of mathematics and a large number of careers depend on this simple concept.

The first law of content management states (according to me only) that workload is conserved. You can't create or destroy work; you can only move it around. Harvesting the creative product of a group of people and distributing it in a set number of ways to another group of people (the CM process) involves a certain amount of work. Given a certain system, you can't choose how much work you have, but you can choose who (or what) does that work.

The main point of a CMS is to shift the workload off of people and onto a computer. Everything that I recommend in this book I present with the intention of getting the computer to do as much of the work as possible. A collection system shifts much of the manual labor of converting, tagging, and cataloging from people to the computer. A management system shifts the work of storing and later locating content from people to the computer. Finally, a publishing system largely removes the labor of putting together publications from people and gives almost all of it to the computer.

Some very important corollaries to the first law come into play throughout a CMS, as follows:

✦ **Conservation of ease:** This law states that the easier you make the circumstances for your staff, the harder they are for you. To expose an author to the raw user interface that ships with a CMS is easy for you, for example, but hard for the author. On the other hand, to create a slick collection form that's easy for the author gives you a lot of extra work.

✦ **Conservation of thinking:** You need to do a certain amount of thinking to put your system together. You can choose to do that thinking all at once at the beginning of the project or in increments all along the way. But in the end, you must think it all out.

✦ **Rethinking isn't conserved:** Although you must do a set amount of thinking in a CMS, an unlimited amount of rethinking is possible. In other words, you really have no limit to the number of wrong turns and short-sighted decisions that you can make. Thinking through the entire process before doing it minimizes rethinking but can never eliminate it entirely.

✦ **Rework isn't conserved:** As you get to the end of the CMS project, you can look back and see how much work it should have taken. The difference between that and the amount of work it really did take is a measure of the rework that you did. Rework, of course, relates to rethinking—but not always linearly. In other words, one rethought may cause one rework, or it may cause 10 reworks.

Physicists strive to balance the energy equation. CMS designers strive to balance the workload equation. They seek a balance by doing the following:

✦ Shifting as much of the workload to the computer as possible by getting the system so organized that even an unintelligent computer can do it.

✦ Shifting the thinking up front to avoid excessive rework. However, knowing that at least some rework is inevitable, the consequences of rework are much less if it's a computer, rather than people, doing most of the rework rather. To put the tradeoff another way, the larger the portion of work that's done by computers, that more easily you can accommodate rework within your budget and schedule.

Continued

Continued

> ✦ Shifting work into the collection effort so that a computer can take on more of the management and publishing efforts. You probably already noticed that a CMS collection effort is a lot more human work than required to collect content without a CMS. On the other hand, you pick up a net loss of human work if you add in the gains in the management and publishing systems.
>
> If you can't balance your own CMS equation so that you get a big net transfer of work to the computer, your system may work, but it's never going to prove economically viable to your organization. Computers are the ultimate slaves—lots of work and no wages.

Influence

The amount of influence that you have over an author is as important in deciding how to work with the author as is his savvy. Someone you hire to author for you does, more or less, what you ask of her. Someone who contributes out of the kindness of her heart is another story. I break influence down into two dimensions: how close the person is to your core CMS group and whether you specifically task her with contributing to your system, as the following list explains:

✦ **In your group:** Obviously people in your core group are the ones over whom you have the most influence.

✦ **In your organization:** Your influence over these sorts of authors always depends on how far up the organization chart you must go before your two groups relate. It also depends on how much affinity the person feels for your effort and what benefit her group is receiving from the CMS. If it's an all "give" and no "take" relationship, you wield decidedly less influence over people outside your core group.

✦ **Outside your organization:** You have no "organization-chart" influence over people beyond your organization, but you may have some economic influence if you hire them to author for you. If you're not paying them, you must depend on their affinity for you and whatever noneconomic benefit you can provide them.

✦ **Tasked:** You exert more influence over authors who create content for you as part of their jobs. Regardless of how close or far they are from your core CMS group, these authors are likely to pay attention to you and follow the processes that you recommend.

✦ **Volunteer:** Authors who aren't tasked contribute to your CMS because they want to. Wanting to do something is a fragile mental state that you must continually support and nourish.

Incentives

Why do people contribute? Aristotle, the great Greek thinker, identified three levels of friendship: for mutual benefit, for mutual interest, and for an abiding altruistic interest in the other. These three motivators apply equally well to contributors to a CMS.

Maybe for tasked authors all you need for an incentive is money and power. But money and power ensure compliance, not participation. I'm sure that you've experienced as many times as I have the effect people can have on creativity and morale if they comply without really participating. For untasked authors, the issue is more acute. What can you offer to maintain their interest in helping you? Following Aristotle, here are your choices:

✦ **Benefit:** These incentives include money and power over the person. They also include other incentives such as recognition and fame. Public acknowledgment is a strong motivator. Can you recognize authors and list their names and contributions in a public place? (On the forms where others go to contribute, for example, is a good place.) The acknowledgment that you can always manage to give is thanks. Don't overlook, too, the power of the gift. A free coffee or a small gift certificate can go a long way toward expressing gratitude and motivating extra effort.

✦ **Interest:** The people that you want authoring for you are the ones who are truly interested in the subject matter of their creation. By encouraging this interest, you're encouraging continued creation. What can you do to foster the interest of your authors? Can you get them subscriptions to publications that address their subject, introduce them to each other in subject forums, or perhaps also submit their work to professional journals? Whatever you can do to support your authors' interest in the subjects on which you want them to contribute more than repays your effort. Support, too, any interest that your authors have in your CMS. If and when they're interested in increasing their savvy, can you help them? Do they know how cool the system is, what happens to their work after it leaves their hands, or what all the future possibilities are? If not, why not?

✦ **Altruism:** Why does a true friend help you? Not because of any benefit that she expects to receive or even because she shares your interests. A friend helps because she cares about your well-being for *your sake*, not hers. Don't underestimate or avoid the power of this incentive. Most of the major achievements humans have made became possible from just this sense of a wider purpose. What can you do to show the wider purpose of your CMS to its authors? What can you do to show them that the system not only benefits them and the organization, but also benefits the world at large? If it doesn't benefit the world at large, is it really worth this much effort?

Note   At this moment, I'm asking myself the same questions. What's my incentive for authoring this enormous book? Believe me, if it were for the money only, I could do better digging ditches. The incredible amount of time that it's taking isn't likely to be repaid. Clearly, other benefits motivate me in writing this book. The recognition that comes if it's a success motivates me, but what if it isn't a success? I get no free coffee and little gratitude along the way to sustain me. My interest in the subject is surely a motivator. I find little as fascinating and all-encompassing as the merger of science and humanity that must occur in a CMS. Finally, I do just want to contribute. The thought that this book may help you and may help move forward a discipline serves as an incentive to me as well.

A savvy/influence matrix

Is charting all the major factors that you need to account for with your authors into a single chart even possible? I think that it is. Figure 28-1 summarizes all the dimensions of the attitude that you can take toward authors.

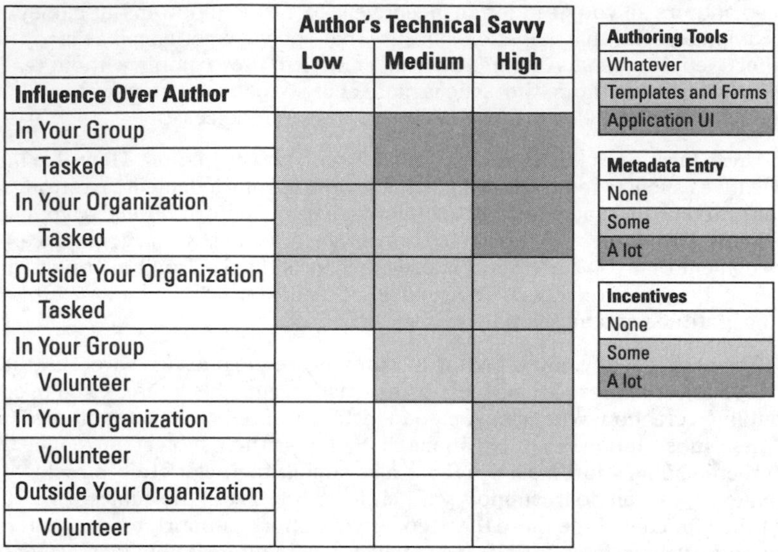

Influence Over Author	Author's Technical Savvy		
	Low	Medium	High
In Your Group			
Tasked			
In Your Organization			
Tasked			
Outside Your Organization			
Tasked			
In Your Group			
Volunteer			
In Your Organization			
Volunteer			
Outside Your Organization			
Volunteer			

Authoring Tools
- Whatever
- Templates and Forms
- Application UI

Metadata Entry
- None
- Some
- A lot

Incentives
- None
- Some
- A lot

Figure 28-1: Savvy and influence in the light of tools, metadata, and incentives

The figure gives you a quick way to benchmark the amount of effort that working with a group of authors will take. It breaks this effort into the following areas:

✦ **The light area:** If the savvy and influence of a group puts it in the lightly shaded area, it causes you the least extra work.

✦ **The medium area:** If the savvy and influence of a group puts it in the medium-shaded area, working with that group is harder but still possible.

✦ **The dark area:** If the savvy and influence of a group puts it in the darkly shaded area, that group is hard to work with — that is, it causes you the most extra work.

In addition, Figure 28-1 gives you some idea of the measures that you need to put in place for tools, metadata, and incentives, as follows:

✦ **Tools:** Author groups in the light area are likely to accept whatever tools you offer them. They adapt to your process. Authors in the medium area require training and support but are mostly able to adapt. You best serve them, however, if you develop aids and explain your process well to them. Authors in the dark area don't adapt, either because they can't (for less-savvy types) or don't have the time (for volunteers). They expect you to make the system work with whatever tools they already use.

✦ **Metadata:** Author groups in the light area can likely do all but the most advanced metadata entry. You can expect them to learn and apply most metadata rules. Authors in the medium area require a lot of explanation and quality control but can usually fill in most metadata fields. Expect to support them by creating a metatorial guide that's easy to read and access while they're working. Authors in the dark area don't supply you much metadata, either because they can't (for less-savvy types) or don't have the time to learn how to (for volunteers). They expect you to tag their contributions for them.

✦ **Incentives:** Don't ignore incentives for any of your author groups, but do understand how central they are depending on the profile of the group. Author groups in the light area contribute with the least extra incentives. Authors in the medium area require some incentives to stay motivated. Focus here on acknowledgment for the novices to assure them that they're doing a good job. Authors in the dark area require the most incentives, either because you're pushing them beyond their technical comfort zone (for less-savvy types) or their time comfort zone (for volunteers). You need all the incentives that you can lay your hands on.

Analyzing Authors

I begin the author analysis that you can use for logical design by taking a step up from authors to content sources. I suggest that you do some brainstorming on where you may get content from for the content types that you've previously defined. This brainstorm motivates both your author analysis and your acquisition-source analysis. From there, I suggest that you fully chart out the kinds of authors that you come up with and learn as much about them as possible so that you can craft the best approach to them. Finally, I suggest that you look back at the content types that you create to make sure that you have them all covered and that you make the best use of your authors.

Think

Before you begin your author analysis, consider the following issues:

✦ **Motivation:** Do your authors want to contribute to the CMS? If so, why? If not, try to discover the reasons and account for them in the analysis that you do. If some have little time to contribute, for example, how can you help them make time?

✦ **Skill:** What percentage of your content do you expect your own staff to author? Can your staff handle that amount? Do they have the skills to author what you want?

✦ **Survey:** About how many authors do you think you may have? Do you expect this number to grow, stay stable, or shrink over time?

✦ **Authorship:** Whom does your audience expect to author your publication? Does the audience respect this person or this organization as an information source? What's the effect of combining multiple authors in a single publication? How do you convey authorship? What content should you attribute to an author and what do you keep anonymous?

✦ **Rights:** Do you have rights to use all your authors' content in all the publications that you create? If you need special permission to use some types of content, how do you get that permission?

Plan

The sections that follow describe the major areas of author analysis that you may want to cover in your logical analysis.

Content sources

In this part of the design, you brainstorm the sources that you can possibly tap for your content. This same analysis is the starting point for your acquisition analysis.

Cross-Reference   You find more information about the acquisition analysis in Chapter 29, "Accounting for Acquisition Sources."

In the following exercise, you analyze the relationship between the content that you identify and the kinds of sources from which it may derive. For each type of content that you identify, fill in the following table.

Content type	Quantity	Source	Author?	Acquire?	Cite?
SuccessStory (C123)	25 to start 1 per week	Field managers	Yes	No	No

The required information includes the following:

✦ **Content type:** Enter the name of the content type you're working on. If you have an Id number, enter that type as well.

✦ **Quantity:** Enter the approximate number of components in the type that you need at the time that you launch your CMS and how many you need on a periodic bases thereafter (for example, three per week, nine per day, one per year, and so on).

✦ **Source:** Who in the entire world creates content of this sort? Go wide here trying to find all the authors of this sort of content. For each source, add a new row to the table. Enter the name of a person, a group within your organization, or an outside organization.

✦ **Author?:** Can this source author content specifically for your CMS effort? A yes or no answer with any additional comments is sufficient.

✦ **Acquire?:** Can this source syndicate content to you or at least give you access to raw content? Or can you get this same content from an independent syndicator of content? A yes or no answer with any additional comments is sufficient.

✦ **Cite?:** Is citing this source and linking to her content an option? A yes or no answer with any additional comments is sufficient.

Cross-Reference   Review the concept of iteration (in Chapter 18, "Doing Logical Design," in the section "Iterating through your design") if you're wondering how you can complete this table without first completing a component design.

If you take the time to fill this table in completely, you can save yourself an enormous amount of effort later. If you take it seriously, the table forces you to really search for the available sources of your content and not just accept that wherever you get it from now is the only or best source. It also forces you to consider the best method for collecting each type of content. Can you get by with just linking to a certain type of content? If so, you may cut down your workload enormously. The cost of authoring is such that you can afford to pay quite a bit to acquire content even from a commercial source.

You complete this analysis whenever you can come up with no more sources and every yes answer is as far to the right of the table as you can get it.

Identification

At the end of the sources analysis, you have a list of the content types for which authoring is the only option. (I hate to put it so bluntly, but because of the cost of authoring, you want to pursue all other options first.) You're ready now to shift from a consideration of the content types to a consideration of each authoring source.

For each potential author, determine the following design constraints:

✦ **ID:** Assign each author or group of authors a unique identifier for later reference.

✦ **Name:** Enter either the name of a person or of a group.

✦ **People:** This entry is the same as that for the name if the author is a single person. If it's a group, try to find out the names of the individuals within the group who actually create the content. Much of the coming design depends on knowing about particular people.

✦ **Number:** For an individual, the number is one; for a group, estimate how many people author within it.

✦ **Key member:** For each group, try to identify a key author that you can work with who represents the rest of the group. You can use the key member for testing, advice, and to represent the opinions of their group.

✦ **Content types:** List the name and IDs of a single content type that the author or group can create.

✦ **Quantity:** How much of this sort of content can this person or group create? Try to use the same scale for all authors across all components (number of components per day, week, month, and so on).

✦ **Quality:** Assign a quality value to the work of this author or group. A measure of excellent, good, fair, poor, or unacceptable may work.

✦ **Savvy:** Rate the author or group on technical savvy. I define technical savvy earlier in this chapter in the section "Technical savvy."

✦ **Influence:** State how close the individual is to your core CMS group and whether she's tasked or volunteers. I define *influence* earlier in this chapter in the section "Influence."

✦ **Credentials:** What credentials does this author have in the subject matter of the content she's creating? What biographical or professional information can you collect that you can later show in publications?

The point of this analysis is to identify for each content type the author groups that share common traits. To aid the remainder of the analysis, therefore, create multiple profiles of the sources if the following statements are true:

✦ You have more than one potential source for the same content type.

✦ An individual or group can create more than one content type.

✦ Part of a group produces content at a different quantity or quality than another part.

✦ Part of a group has a different value for technical savvy or influence than another part.

After you divide out your authors this way, you have identified and described all the individuals and groups that can author for you.

If you're lucky enough to have more than one choice for the authors of a particular type of content, the winner is usually pretty obvious from the information that you collect.

Your approach to authors

Based on where each author falls on the savvy/influence chart that I provide earlier in this chapter (in the section "A savvy/influence matrix"), fill in the following authoring design constraints:

✦ **Authoring tool of preference:** List the tools that this kind of author prefers to use. Tools can include anything from a pen and paper, to a word processor, to a graphics program.

✦ **Tool approach:** Given the author's tool of preference and where she falls on the savvy/influence chart, as well as any other factors that you may identify, determine what tools to encourage, require, and permit for this author.

✦ **Metadata approach:** Generally speaking, how much and what types of metadata do you require this author to supply? As you fill in the author versus content type analysis later, you can get more specific.

✦ **Incentive approach:** Given where she falls on a the savvy/influence chart, as well as any other factors that you may identify, determine what incentives to offer this author.

✦ **Editorial approach:** How much editing does the work of this author require? Is the author amenable to editorial review and revision?

✦ **Training approach:** How much and what kinds of training does this author need? Is the author (or group) amenable to training?

✦ **Rights:** Can you obtain the rights to use this author's work in any publication that you may decide to create? If not, what are the restrictions? How do you record and enforce these restrictions?

✦ **Participation in management:** After creation, what, if anything, is the author's ongoing responsibility for that content in the CMS repository? Do you want reviews or ongoing revisions?

✦ **Participation in publishing:** Does the author have any part or control in how you include or lay out in publications the content that the individual or group creates?

✦ **Attribution:** What requirements does this author have for how you cite him in any publication?

Local authors

Refer to your component localization analysis. (See Chapter 27, "Designing Content Types," in the section "Localization," for details.) Then, for each type of content that's authored and localized, determine an approach to the following issues:

✦ **Neutral authoring:** Can you devise guidelines to help authors create more locality independent content?

✦ **Local authoring:** Can you get authors from your target localities to help in the creation or review of the content?

Content types versus authors

To complete your author analysis, use a table such as the following to show the relationship between content types and authors.

Content Type	Author	Locality	Start-up Quantity	Run Quantity	Metadata Not Required
SuccessStory	Field Manager	FrenchAfrica	5	.25 per week	Audience, PLANProgram
SuccessStory	Area Coordinator	WesternEurope	5	.25 per week	Audience, PLANProgram, SingleDonors

The required information includes the following:

✦ **Content type:** The name and Id of the component to author. If more than one individual or group is authoring the type, include more than one line in the table.

✦ **Author:** The name and Id of the individual or group who's to author the type.

✦ **Locality:** The locality for which components of the type are authored. If components are authored in more than one locality, add a separate line for each locality.

✦ **Start-up quantity:** The number of this type of component that the author can create before you start the system.

✦ **Run quantity:** The number of this type of component that the author can create on an ongoing basis over the foreseeable life of the CMS.

✦ **Metadata not required:** The elements of this content type that the author doesn't need to fill in.

This table tells you as much by what it leaves out as by what it says, as I show in what follows:

✦ **Localities:** You can determine your need to localize authored content from this table. The sum of all the localities that a component needs to exist in, minus the ones already covered according to the table, is the amount of localization that you need for the authored portion of each component. See Chapter 27, "Designing Content Types," for details on determining localities.

✦ **Quantities:** You can determine component deficits from the table. The total number of components of each type that you need to start and run the system (determined in your component analysis), minus the numbers that you show in the table, are the component deficits for startup and run. You can fill the deficit by having more content authored, acquiring some of this sort of content from existing sources, or by changing your expectation of how much you need.

✦ **Metadata:** You can determine part of your need for a metator from this table. A metator must supply all the metadata that you list in the table as not required to be entered by authors.

Tasks

Consider the effect of your author analysis on the ongoing maintenance of the CMS. Then fill in the following table to define any tasks that must happen on a recurring basis to run the CMS. Here are some task types to get you thinking:

✦ Recruiting of new authors

✦ Training of new authors

✦ Reviews of and updates to authoring guidelines

✦ Creation and submission cycles for each type of content or by each author type (or both)

✦ Editorial review cycles

✦ Metatorial review cycles

✦ Localization cycles

✦ Legal review cycles

✦ Incentive cycles

✦ Author/publication team meetings

✦ Quality-control cycles

✦ Author/audience review and redesign

Finally, fill in the tasks in the following table:

Task name	Who	What	When	How Much	How
Editorial review	Editorial staff	Review news items more than 3 months old to determine whether to update or archive.	Once a month	Usually 20–30 articles	Check posting dates of all news items. Archive those that are no longer current. Assign authors to update ongoing stories.

The required information includes the following:

✦ **Task name:** Give the task a short but memorable name that describes it.

✦ **Who:** Indicate what person or role is responsible for accomplishing this task. Naming an automated process here instead of a person is acceptable.

✦ **What:** List what the person or process needs to do to accomplish the task.

✦ **When:** Specify how often you need to accomplish this task or how you know when it must occur.

✦ **How much:** Describe how many of these tasks you expect to do. A numerical quantity is preferable here, but if you can't come up with one, words such as *a lot*, *not much*, and so on suffice.

✦ **How:** Detail the skills, tools, or processes the person or process needs to accomplish this task.

Don't worry if the tasks that you come up with at this point are somewhat ill-defined or sketchy. In your workflow analysis (in Chapter 33, "Designing Workflow and Staffing Models"), you have ample opportunity to refine them.

Integrate

To help integrate this analysis with the rest of your design, consider the following questions:

✦ **Project goals:** Do your authors understand your goals? Do they need to understand them so that they can do their jobs? How do you bring them into the CMS team and get them excited about their contribution?

✦ **Other authors:** If you have more than one person authoring the same kind of content, how do you maintain consistency among them? Given the author set that you define, how can you ensure that the content these authors produce across all content types is of an even quality and style? What groupings of authors do you want to bring together to foster communication and cooperation? Do these authors compete with each other? If so, what is your attitude toward the competition?

✦ **Audiences:** What credentials do these authors have for your audiences? Are the audiences likely to accept and respect their work? What more can you do to build their credibility with your audiences? Do your authors understand your audiences? Are they ready and willing to serve your audiences?

✦ **Acquisition sources:** If you plan to acquire, as well as have content of a particular type authored, how do you maintain consistency and quality across both sources?

✦ **Publications:** How much do your authors need to know about your publications to create good content for them? How much involvement do they want in your publications? How much do they want to control the publications? How do you foster cooperation and creative interactions between authors and your publication teams?

✦ **Attribution:** Does your author's need for attribution match with the attribution scheme that you devised in your publication analysis? If not, how do you resolve the difference?

Summary

In a CMS, anyone can become an author, from a volunteer who contributes components casually by uploading files on your site to a full-time professional writer who's on your core team. To devise an approach that can span the entire range and size of your author group, you must do the following:

✦ Decide whether retraining authors or putting in the extra effort yourself to process the content that they produce is worth your effort.

✦ Gauge the technical savvy of your various author groups and the influence that you have over them to understand how much effort you can expect from them.

✦ Document the assumptions that you make about your authors in a complete analysis of their needs and the content you can count on them to produce.

In the next chapter, I describe acquired content and the process that you can use to analyze it.

✦   ✦   ✦

Accounting for Acquisition Sources

Content collection consists of authoring and acquisition. In the preceding chapter, I discuss the authoring process, where people create content from scratch. In this chapter, I discuss acquisition, in which you find and collect content that already exists.

You acquire content that's too expensive or inconvenient to author. You may also acquire content because someone's already creating it on an ongoing basis. (No need to reinvent the wheel.) Although authored content tends to be low volume and high quality, acquired content tends to be high volume and low quality. Preparing content sources for your system can prove a lot of work. You want to study each source to decide whether separating its wheat from its chaff is worth the trouble. In this chapter, I work through all the issues that you need to confront for the content that you plan to acquire.

Acquisition Jumpstart

This Jumpstart summarizes what you need to do to analyze how you account for acquisition sources in your CMS.

Use this jumpstart as a summary without the weight of detail, or as a quick review if you've already read the section on Analyzing Sources (later in this chapter) and want a checklist of what you need to do carry out an author analysis.

To analyze your acquisition sources, follow these steps:

1. Think about what you know about your acquisition sources. Consider such things as what content types you need to acquire, how you will convert the source content into components, how much content you need to convert, whether you have the tools available; whether your editorial and metatorial staff is up to speed on what is required of them; whether your acquisition sources may morph into authors; whether the source content really is appropriate to your needs; and how in sync the people who supply your bulk content are with your needs.

2. Plan your acquisition analysis, including the following considerations:

   - **Identification and overview** of the content that you want to acquire. Include descriptive information (Name and ID) as well as a ranking of the importance, format, and quality of this content source. Most importantly, determine the content types that you'll create based on content from this source.

- **Source relationship** of the content owner. Include such considerations as who owns each source of content, the nature of their deliverables to you, the start-up and run quantities, and how you interact with the source (including how to escalate issues if the content does not arrive as expected).

- **Attribution and rights management** characteristics, including a characterization of the permissions, payment, and use tracking, as well as information about the author, including background and credentials.

- **Conversion processes** required so that you can make use of the content source. For each content type, evaluate how well marked the content types and elements are, then use this information to evaluate how much conversion, stripping, and editorial work are required. You also want to consider how closely the purpose and audiences of the source content match yours. Ultimately, you should evaluate whether the work required is worthwhile, given the value of the content.

- **Functionality**, if you acquire any, requires a further analysis of how it fits into your current environment, including such considerations as performance, whether you have control of the source code and, if so, what development languages and environments it uses; whether the owner will update the functionality, and how you can make use of updates. Ultimately, you want to consider whether integrating the functionality is worth the work required, given the value of the functionality.

- **Local sources**, that is, sources outside the primary locality, must be noted. Include information about where the content originates, what if any content from the prime locality it replaces, and the localities in which you want to use the content.

- **Connections to other data sources** outside the CMS, including what system currently uses the data, whether you will draw the data directly into a dynamic Web site or copy it into your own repository (and the processes the support each approach). Determine whether you will modify the content in any way (including adding elements) and, if so, how you will manage changes and updates.

- **Tasks**, which broadly include all the work that must be done to include the content source on an ongoing basis. Include such aspects as the effect of the content acquisition on conversion, editorial, metatorial, localization, legal, and quality control processes, as well as how you plan to support your staff through training, process planning, and handling content issues that inevitably arises. For each task that you come up with, chart the task name, who does it, what it consists of, when it must be done, how much or extensively, and how the task is accomplished.

3. Integrate your acquisition analysis with the other logical design analyses you have done. As you do, consider how much of your content your own staff can author versus how much you must acquire from other sources. At a higher level, sketch out the acquired content sources to determine whether they fit into the overall scheme for your collection system, and make sure your stakeholders are on board with this model. Determine whether you have the tools that you need. Try to anticipate any problems you foresee in matching up the source content with your audiences. Finally, make sure you've added elements to track the content you acquire.

At the end of this analysis, you'll have a good characterization of all the content that originates from outside your core authors.

What Is Acquisition?

If you don't author content, you must somehow acquire it. The defining characteristic of acquired content is that someone unfamiliar with your particular purpose or system creates it. Thus, even the best-acquired content is likely to need some work before it's ready for your particular use. If you author content from scratch, you can tailor it very specifically to your needs. If you acquire it, on the other hand, you must take what you get and make the best of it (or maybe try to work with the acquisition source to see whether she can modify her content in ways that make it easier for you to use).

On the other hand, although authoring is a slow human process, producing content one item at a time, acquisition is a bulk process, where you receive many content items all at once or at a steady high rate. Thus, although acquired content can be of a lower quality than authored content, most people prefer acquired content because it's cheaper. Most people choose to author only if they have no adequate source to acquire from or if they're professional authors.

Acquisition can range from a completely automated to a mostly human effort. You may, for example, receive a continuous automated feed of digital news stories from a publisher. On the other hand, you may need to sift manually through mounds of old press releases to decide which are right for your system. In your hunt for good content to acquire, you're likely to find some of each, and much that's between these two extremes.

Cross-Reference I cover the tools of acquisition in Chapter 38, "Building Collection Systems" In the section "Acquisition System."

You can break acquired content into the following two broad categories:

✦ **Found sources:** This category consists of content that someone else produces that isn't originally intended for reuse.

✦ **Syndicated sources:** This category consists of content that someone else produces that is intended for reuse.

Found sources

Most of the information that organizations want under management is information that they already own. In fact, the stated reason that most organizations look to a content management system is to control and grow their existing information assets — regardless of whether the existing information within organizations is necessarily high quality or particularly useful. Quite the contrary, this content is most likely limited by its scope and audience assumptions. (I give more information about this limitation in Chapter 28, "Accounting for Authors," in the section "The Author's Attitude.")

Found content is like found art. By surrounding it with the right context and with a little bit of massaging, you can transform it from a chunk of text that you scrape off someone's hard drive into a masterpiece. Found content generally comes in the following forms:

✦ **Word processing** and desktop publishing files.

✦ **Other office files**, such as spreadsheets and slide presentations.

✦ **Images** and other nontext media.

✦ **Databases** from which you want to acquire information instead of just linking to them on a Web site.

Wherever this content originates, you probably must convert it to some more generally useful form before bringing it into your CMS.

Syndicated content

As the value of information becomes more widely recognized, more and more commercial sources of information become available. Traditionally, news organizations resell text and pictures. The main wire services, Associated Press (AP) and United Press International (UPI), do nothing but resell news. Today, other syndication sources (or *feeds*) are becoming available on a wide variety of subjects (see Figure 29-1). Before long, I have no doubt that information on everything from Aardvarks to Zygotes is sure to come up for sale.

Figure 29-1: The term "feed" dates back to the era when the first syndicated information was fed out of ticker tape machines.

I use the term *syndicated content* not to distinguish commercially available information from that which you already own, but rather to distinguish information that's specifically intended for reuse from that which isn't. I call content *syndicated* if someone delivers it to you already positioned for reuse, regardless of whether you must pay for it or it comes from inside or outside the organization.

To understand why I make this distinction, look at what positioning content for reuse means. Reusable content has the following qualities:

✦ Its purpose and audience are clear and discernible.

✦ It's editorially consistent.

✦ It's stripped of any unnecessary surrounding context, such as page numbers, headers and footers, and navigation.

✦ It's segmented into convenient chunks by information type.

✦ Its metadata is clearly marked and accessible.

✦ It's in a format (such as XML) that's readily transformed.

Take look at small piece of a fictitious syndication feed about zygotes that a biotech firm may use to power one part of its Web site:

```
.ZygoteNet
.NewsStory
.Headline Cell Division Arrested
.Source ZygoteNet
.Date 3 February 2004
.Abstract Researchers at the Michigan Institute of Zygotology
have found a way to stop the division of cells in a frog embryo.
.Link //http:www.zygotenet.com/news.asp?id=37
.Event
.Title Zygo2K+4
.Date 1 April to 3 April 2004
.Location Moscone Center, San Francisco
.Link //http:www.u.washington.edu/biology/events/zygo2k4.html
.ZygoNet
```

(A *zygote*, by the way, is the cell that a sperm and an egg create but more broadly refers to any embryo.)

The information doesn't explicitly state its purpose and audience. You can assume, therefore, that before an organization accepts this syndication it exercises enough due diligence to make sure that the purpose and audience of the information are consistent with its own. You'd be wise to do the same. One clear sign of a good syndication source is that it can quickly name its purpose and intended audience. A clear sign of an excellent syndication source is that it has the information available for a variety of very specific purposes and audiences and that it explicitly tags the purpose and audience in the syndicated information. Although this sample isn't extensive enough to show you whether it's editorially consistent, assume that it is. You'd be wise as well, however, to view enough of a syndicated source to decide for yourself *before* you commit to it that the source is internally consistent and that its tone and usage are consistent with the editorial guidelines that you've set for the rest of your content.

Notice that, because it's a good source, you find no extraneous information in the feed. The news story may have come from a newspaper, but none of the surrounding newspaper context remains. Notice, too, that the feed is well segmented. The feed represents two types of content: a news story and an event. Each is clearly marked, and you'd expect that, following the sample I'm providing, you'd see more of the same configurations for other stories and events.

Metadata is well marked. Contrast the event in the preceding sample with the following one:

```
.Event Zygo2K+4 at the Moscone Center in San Francisco between 1 April
and 3 April 2004
```

Both contain exactly the same information, but in the second one, all the metadata is packed into the same tag and would be a real pain to separate. As a rule, combining two tags into one is much easier than breaking one tag into two. Of course, creating two tags rather than one also is harder to do. But if you're evaluating a syndication source, creating the tags is someone else's problem.

I purposely don't use XML formatting in these examples so that they best illustrate that it's the structure and not the way that you represent the structure that counts most. This feed is in a form that you can readily transform. Any programmer can quickly write a script that turns this feed into XML, HTML, or any other format that you want, because the feed is clearly and unambiguously marked. Of course, if this same source comes in an XML format, it may prove easier to work with but not more structured. Almost all new syndication is moving toward XML, although most older syndication remains in a form similar to that of the preceding examples (or worse). Accordingly, most veteran programmers are more familiar with formats such as those that I show here than they are with the new and more complex XML technologies.

Note   The latest craze in syndication at the writing of the second edition of this book is called *Really Simple Syndication* (RSS). It is, as the name implies, a simple XML format that many Web bloggers have adopted to pass their information around. It is now being adopted by many CM systems as a standard for broadcast syndication. For more information on RSS and broadcast syndication see Chapter 40, "Building Publishing Systems," in the section "Syndication System."

Given the amount of work that you must do to a source to make it reusable, you can see how valuable a good syndication source is. You can also see how much it costs an organization to create a good source. Unfortunately, at the current point in history, information is still under-valued; so truly good syndication sources often seem too expensive, and the cheaper ones aren't very good. The other side of this coin is that, fortunately, because information is so undervalued, you can sometimes get good syndicated content for free from providers who have not yet figured out how to sell their information. If you're smart in choosing sources, you won't reject a source on the basis of cost until you compare the cost of processing cheaper sources. Clearly, information targeted for reuse should prove easier to work with than information whose author had no concept that his work might get used outside of its original context. I say *should* prove easier, rather than *is* easier, for the following reasons:

✦ Information is easier to work with the closer it is to your chosen purpose and audience. To the extent that your syndicated source shares your purpose and audience, it's easy to work with. Sources that you find inside your organization, however, may prove much more likely to share these constraints than do sources outside.

✦ Information is easier to work with if it's positioned for the reuse that you want to make of it. The ZygoteNet feed earlier in this section, for example, isn't so easy for you to work with if you need the body of the news story in addition to the abstract.

Syndicated content generally arrives in the following forms:

✦ **Continuous feeds**, such as those provided by wire services.

✦ **Downloads**, where you go to a Web site or FTP site and choose the content that you want.

✦ **Deliveries**, where your content is sent to you periodically on static media such as CD-ROMs and disks or via e-mail.

✦ **Scrapes**, where you use specialized tools to automatically "scrape off" information that's live on Web sites or you harvest information from files on a network.

✦ **Pulls**, where you use specialized tools to periodically connect to a data source such as a database or file system and pull in the information that you want.

To syndicate or connect?

I distinguish syndications from live connections to a database or other source. In a live connection, the master information remains in the data source, and your system simply retrieves it and formats it for publication. In a syndication, the content that you pull into your system is now the master version. You can (and do) edit it and otherwise manipulate syndicated content so that it's no longer the same as it was when you received it. Live sources don't belong to you; syndicated content does.

In choosing whether to treat an information source as a syndication or a live source, decide the following:

✦ **CMS modifications:** Do you need to modify the source after it's in the CMS repository? If so, you're better off treating the source as a provider of acquired content.

✦ **Source modification:** Does the source information change frequently? If so, you're better off treating the source as a connection that the CMS accesses but doesn't bring into the repository.

But what if the content changes both within the CMS repository and outside of it? Then you have a bit more work to do. Instead of looking at the entire source, you must look at individual elements. Suppose, for example, that your source is a product catalog. The prices, quantities in stock, and special offers may change constantly. You don't want the master copies of this information in the CMS repository. The description, to which you want to add images and links, doesn't change nearly as rapidly. You're safe in bringing the descriptions into the CMS repository periodically and extending them.

Note   As another alternative, you can have product images and links in a content type that also includes the unique Id of the product catalog record. In this way, you can divide the master information for a product between the product catalog and the CMS repository.

So no hard line may exist between syndication and connection. What you call a syndicated source may include parts that are actually connections and not syndications. Still, by understanding the dynamics of the two options apart from each other, you can better combine the two if you need to.

Acquiring functionality

Content is information and functionality. The process of acquiring functionality isn't that different from the process of acquiring information. In either case, some value in the source transcends the context in which it's created. It requires a certain amount of work, however, to take a source that someone creates for one purpose and repurpose it for use in the CMS. In either case, the key to the success of the acquisition lies in your capability to divide the functionality into components and wrap those components in the appropriate metadata.

Acquired functionality is computer code that a group outside the CMS team owns that's given to the team for use in the CMS publications. PLAN, for example, may have programming code and objects that it includes in its Web publication for accessing staff benefits. If the HR department developed the code for a non-Web application and subsequently turned it over to the CMS team, you'd classify it as acquired. Over time, as the HR department makes changes and extensions to the code, the CMS team can acquire those as well and integrate them into its publications.

Cross-Reference   I discuss the similarities between functionality and content in detail in Chapter 27, "Designing Content Types," in the section "The Relationship between Functionality and Components."

Programmers and system administrators are exactly as human as content authors. They try just as hard as authors to make their jobs easy and their work successful. In fact, the same issues hold sway for the technical contributor as for the creative. You can assume that these technicians currently know who they're serving and know how to do it successfully. You must give them an equally strong idea of their audiences and success factors.

In particular, you must give them a clear idea of the following:

✦ **The audiences** (or *users* in the computer vernacular) who are engaged with their code and data systems. Are the needs and assumptions of these new users any different from the users they're now serving?

✦ **The way that you intend to segment** and recombine functionality. Are the functionality chunks that you propose feasible to create? Are the ways that you intend to mix and match functionality feasible?

✦ **The performance and scalability** requirements. Are you expecting response times and user loads that are consistent with their current constraints?

✦ **The extensibility requirements**. Are you trying to extend the functionality in directions that are consistent with the programmer's own plans?

✦ **The development methodology** that you intend to follow. Are your source control systems, code review, and testing procedures consistent with the ones in use by the programmers and administrators?

✦ **How you measure their success.** The CMS is very likely to require more flexibility, shorter and more frequent development cycles, and a wider set of usage scenarios than the programmer's current approach. Do these new constraints affect the desire of technical contributors to work with you?

Perhaps the biggest problem with acquiring functionality is that few people, especially programmers, look at their work as a kind of content that you can acquire. If you prepare your functionality contributors with the information that I give in the preceding list, you can begin to reset their attitudes toward their work. In addition, if you do some preparation of your own, you can come up with a workable plan that specifies the following:

✦ **The process that you intend to use** to work with the programmers and administrators of the functionality. This process includes the use of the CMS repository for holding code versus whatever source control system the programmers may already use.

✦ **What changes you need to make to the functionality** as it exists to make it compatible with CMS collection and delivery.

✦ **How to tag the functionality** so that you can select and draw it into templates based on the needs and access rights of the end user.

✦ **How to provide incentive for owners to modify and provide functionality.** For owners who have no set responsibility to work with the CMS, you must decide how to make doing so attractive. Even for those who contribute as part of their job, a set of incentives can move them to provide the highest quality and largest quantity of functionality that they can.

Cross-Reference You can find more information about incentives in Chapter 28, "Accounting for Authors," in the section "Incentives."

Most programmers and system administrators are reasonable. They want to know how what you're asking is different from what they do now, how you intend to judge them, and how you're going to account for any extra work that they do. If you adequately address these concerns, programmers and administrators not only give you quality content, but also help you understand how best to segment and tag their functionality for reuse.

Is It an Author or an Acquisition Source?

One of my main concerns in this book is to lay out a full vocabulary for naming all the relevant things in a content management system and project. Of course, each time that I make a solid distinction, in the next moment, an exception arises that threatens to muddle the careful distinctions I've made. The division that I make between authored and acquired content, for example, may sound great in theory, but it may not be so apparent in the real world. Consider the following conversation that I had with a client the other day:

Bob: Are you authoring more or doing more acquiring?

Client: Authoring. We're only acquiring from people who already create this stuff.

Bob: Okay. So what's your main source?

Client: People writing Word files for distribution.

Bob: Distribution to whom?

Client: Well, they send them out now as PDF files, but after we're up and running, they're going to send them out in HTML through us.

Bob: So their only publication outlet is through the CMS?

Client: Eventually, yes.

Bob: So why don't you call them authors?

Client: Because they're not writing for us; we need to convert a bunch of their old files, and we have no control over the way that they write or the tools that they use.

Well, she certainly has a point. But she's presented a situation that you could call either authoring or acquiring content. The fact is that these people are authors who behave like an acquisition source.

After some more conversation that I spurred by backing away from trying to put these people in one category or the other, I came up with the following approach: Right now, we agreed, treating these people as a source is better than treating them as authors. This approach best fits the present situation. A definite target, however, is to move them in the author direction. After the system is fully operational and all their legacy content is converted, it should be obvious that these folks are causing a lot of extra work by behaving as if they were authoring for someone else. At that point, you might offer some great incentive for the group and their supervisors to re-examine the way that they do their jobs.

Functionality can be another fence-sitter between authored and acquired content. Programmers may see themselves more as sources, whose real job is to create programs for some other department with some other purpose. But just as with my client's authors, as time goes on, the CMS may engulf all the other uses, and the programmer is left looking a lot like an author.

So although I draw a strong distinction between authored and acquired content, please understand that a continuous spectrum of content lies between the two pure forms and that a single kind of content can move along that spectrum over time. Still, by understanding the nature of authoring and acquisition, you're in a much better position to independently assess what you have now and, more important, what you need to move forward.

Analyzing Sources

In the sections that follow, I detail the information that you need to learn about your acquisition sources to construct part of your CMS collection system. The process goes roughly as follows:

✦ **For content that you need**, you must decide what the potential sources are. Then you can begin to develop a set of named sources. You can attach tasks and statistics to each named source (such as initial quantity and weekly quantity).

✦ **For each source**, you must decide what processes and tools you need to transform its work into the components that you expect it to yield. In particular, you should detail the processes by which you receive content, convert it, segment it, and process it editorially and metatorially.

✦ **One of the biggest problems** that you may have with noncommercially acquired content (the kind that you're likely to find inside your organization) is getting it on time and in the quantities and qualities that you expect. By forming a specific agreement with the content owners, you can surer of getting what you expect.

✦ **As with authored content**, you must decide how to attribute it to its authors and how to track its use rights (if any apply).

Think

Before you begin your acquisition analysis and design, think over the following issues:

✦ **Content types:** You base the work that you do in this section on a good understanding of your content types. Are you very solid on your content domain and the types of content that it requires? Do you have a good idea about how your source documents and media files get stripped down and turned into components of various types?

✦ **Editorial and metatorial systems:** Do you understand the concept of a metatorial system and how it relates to an editorial system? Can the people on your publishing staff handle the metatorial tasks involved in tagging acquired content?

✦ **Conversion:** What percentage of your content do you need to convert? How many different source formats are you handling? Do you have tools for all the conversions that you intend to do?

✦ **Authors:** Do you have acquisition sources that eventually become *de facto* authors for your CMS? If so, how and when do you turn them into authors? Reread the section "Is It an Author or an Acquisition Source?" (earlier in this chapter) for an overview of the author versus acquisition source issue.

✦ **Reasonability:** Are your proposed sources truly repurposable or does some content take more work to transform than it's worth?

✦ **Attitude:** What attitude toward the CMS do the people who supply bulk content hold? Do they understand it? Do they feel that it benefits them? Do they know what they need to do differently because of it?

Plan

The sections that follow walk you through the analysis that helps you understand your acquisition sources and design a system around them.

Identification and overview

Refer back to the analysis that you did to discover your content sources. (See Chapter 28, "Accounting for Authors," in the section "Content sources.") For each content type that you want to come from an acquisition source, determine the following design constraints:

✦ **ID:** Assign each source a unique identifier for later reference.

✦ **Name:** Give the source a name that you and your team can remember.

✦ **Rank:** Give each source an overall priority that rates its importance to the publications that your CMS is to create.

✦ **Documentation:** What documentation exists on the construction or processes behind this source? Are any style guides or templates in use?

✦ **Key sample:** Scan as much of the source content as possible and choose one or a few key samples that illustrate the conventions that the source uses to create the content as well as the variability it contains.

✦ **Content types:** List the name and IDs of the content types that you must create based on content from this source.

✦ **Quality:** Assign a quality value to the source. How editorially and metatorially consistent is the source? Does it have a single style or do different instances of the source have different styles applied? PLAN press releases, for example, may go through five versions, each with its own set of styles. This makes the job of converting the full set of press releases harder than if they were all styled the same way.

✦ **Source format:** What tools are used to create this source? What file format or formats is it saved in?

Source relationship

For each acquisition source, ask yourself the following questions to help you understand and design for the constraints that the source owner puts on your process:

✦ **Owner:** Who owns or is responsible for this source of content? If it has multiple owners, do they all subscribe to the same rules or procedures? If not, consider creating multiple sources. To consider sources the same, multiple owners need to behave similarly.

✦ **Influence:** What influence do you have over the timing, structure, or format of this source?

✦ **Agreement:** Can you form a binding agreement with the owner? If so, what form does it take—a formal contract, a memo, an e-mail message? In any case, seek to form the contract in writing so that you're sure that even an informally arranged agreement is specific. If forming a binding agreement isn't possible, how do you ensure that the content is delivered consistently enough to enable you to adequately plan for it?

✦ **Source units:** In what sorts of units does this source arrive (for example, individual files, database tables, or CD-ROMs full of content)? How many and what types of components are in each unit. PLAN, for example, may receive a file each week containing news stories from an international distributor. Each file may contain between 50 and 100 stories that give rise to three or four press-release components (stories that PLAN wants to modify and redistribute) and 30 to 40 news components.

✦ **Delivery:** In what format or formats does the source arrive? How does it arrive (via direct connection, FTP, and so on)?

✦ **Escalation:** Whom can you contact if the content doesn't arrive in the way that you expect? To whom do you escalate the issue if it isn't quickly resolved?

✦ **Start-up quantity:** How much of this source must you process before the CMS launches? When should it arrive in order for you to make it ready for launch?

✦ **Run quantity:** How much of this source do you expect to receive on an ongoing basis? How far in advance of a publish date do you need it delivered?

✦ **Changes:** How can you make sure that the content that you receive is the latest or master version of the source? What provision can you make for parts that arrive late or change after they're officially passed off to you?

✦ **Feedback:** What provisions can you make for feeding back information from the CMS team to the content owners for improving the delivery process?

Attribution and rights

For each acquisition source, determine the following design constraints on your attribution and rights management:

✦ **Credentials:** What credentials does this source come with that your audiences recognize and respect?

✦ **Recognizability:** Are any audience members likely to see this source content elsewhere? If so, should you explain why your publications duplicate it? Does the recognizability of the content affect the credibility of your publication (either negatively or positively)? If so, how can you make the most of the positive effects and mitigate the negative effects?

✦ **Author background:** What do you know about the original authors? What biographical or professional information can you collect on them that you can later show in publications?

✦ **Permissions:** Do you have permission to cite the source and authors of the content? Does doing so benefit you?

✦ **Restrictions:** What restrictions exist concerning your use of the content? If you can't freely reuse content, what component elements and workflow processes can you use to restrict its incorrect use?

✦ **Payment model:** If you're paying for the source, what are the units of use? What is the price per use? If you're acquiring the content inside your organization, consider reversing this model and charging a processing and publishing fee to groups that want to give you content but don't have the will or resources to help process it.

✦ **Use tracking:** How do you track the number of times that your audiences access this content and its usefulness to them over time? In addition to driving any payment model that may lie behind this content, these numbers help you justify the cost of processing the source.

Conversion

In this analysis, you work through the basic data that you use to specify any conversion processes that you need for your sources.

 Cross-Reference I present the conversion process and information about the importance of well-marked components and elements in Chapter 37, "Processing Content."

First, fill in the following table to get an overall picture of the content types in your sources.

Content Type	Source	Well Marked	Poorly Marked	Unmarked
News	InterNews Syndication Service	X		
PressRelease	PLAN Archive		X	

The required information includes the following:

✦ **Content type:** Enter the name of a content type that you derive from an acquisition source. In the preceding table, I illustrate the way that PLAN may chart News and PressRelease content types.

✦ **Source:** Enter the name of the content type's acquisition source. If you have more than one source for the same type, use multiple lines.

✦ **Well marked:** Enter "X" if an automated processor can easily find the component in the source.

✦ **Poorly marked:** Enter "X" if an automated processor can find the component at all (even if inconsistently) in the source.

✦ **Unmarked:** Enter "X" if an automated processor can't find the component in the source at all; you must pick it out by hand.

Next, for each source/content type, fill in the following table to describe how well marked each *element* is in the source.

Element	Well Marked	Poorly Marked	Unmarked	Not Present
Title	X			
Abstract				X
Body		X		

The required information includes the following:

✦ **Element:** Enter the names of every element for the type that you're studying. In the preceding table, I illustrate how PLAN may chart some of the elements from the News content type.

✦ **Well marked:** Enter "X" if an automated processor can easily find the element in the source.

✦ **Poorly marked:** Enter "X" if an automated processor can find the element at all (even if inconsistently) in the source.

✦ **Unmarked:** Enter "X" if an automated processor can't find the element in the source at all, but you must pick it out by hand.

✦ **Not present:** Enter "X" if the element isn't present at all in the source and you need to add it to the source in some other way.

Finally, after a thorough review of representative samples of the source, determine the following constraints:

✦ **Format conversion:** How close is the formatting in the source items to what you want? Include an analysis of character, paragraph, section, and document-level formatting. How well structured is the file in its own format? Across your sample, are the same character-, paragraph-, section-, and document-level formatting techniques in use? Compare the source format to the destination format. Are you going from a less complex to a more complex formatting scheme? In other words, do you need to create formatting in the destination that isn't in the source? How much formatting must you add and what does adding it entail?

✦ **Stripping:** Which parts of the source files will you preserve and which aren't useful in the component? Is it difficult to strip out the parts that you don't need?

✦ **Purpose:** How close is the original purpose of the source to the purpose that you intend for it in the CMS? What tasks would changing the purpose of the source involve? PLAN, for example, may change the purpose of news stories that it receives into PLAN PressRelease components. The news stories may require changing from a strictly informational purpose to the purpose of interesting readers in the activities of PLAN.

✦ **Editorial conversion:** How close are the editorial conventions of the source to the one that you intend for the CMS? What tasks are involved in changing the editorial style?

✦ **Audiences:** Who were the audiences for the source? To which of your audiences do these correspond? What tasks are involved in changing the audience approach of the source?

✦ **Bottom line:** Given your conversion analysis and the criteria in this list, how automatable is the task of converting this content? Does this source deliver enough value to offset the effort such conversion requires?

Functionality

For functionality that you acquire, gather the following additional constraints:

✦ **Source name:** What's the source of this functionality?

✦ **Segmentation:** Can you break this functionality down into small mix-and-match pieces? Can you pack the functionality into some kind of programming object? What steps and tasks are involved?

✦ **Performance:** How different are the response times and user loads that you expect from the current constraints of this functionality?

✦ **Language:** Is the development language of the functionality different from the one that you propose for CMS software development? If so, how do you interface between this functionality and the rest of the system?

✦ **Environment:** Are your source-control systems, code review, and testing procedures consistent with the ones in use by the current owner?

✦ **Updates:** Are the revision and update, testing, and release cycles consistent with what the owner does now? If not, how do you interface? How do you track and incorporate future enhancements to the functionality as they occur in the code base if you don't own it?

✦ **Source control:** Do you intend to use the CMS system to track changes to the code base for this functionality (effectively making it authored, not acquired)?

✦ **Bottom line:** Is acquiring this functionality worth the cost and effort or are you better off authoring it anew? In either case, does the functionality deliver enough value to off-set the effort that acquiring the functionality requires?

Local sources

The term *local sources* refers to content gathered from outside the locality that you've identified as your target. For example, PLAN USA may choose to include content generated from and for PLAN International. For each source that originates outside the primary locality, address the following additional constraints:

✦ **Source name:** What's the name of the acquisition source?

✦ **Locality:** From what locality does this source originate?

✦ **Overlap:** Is this source a substitute for an equivalent piece of content from the primary locality? If so, exactly what content does it replace?

✦ **Spread:** Into what other localities should you bring this content?

Connections

Data sources are databases and directories outside the CMS that you want to connect to in some way to periodically download content. For each data source that you expect to connect to, determine the following additional constraints:

✦ **Source name:** What's the name of the acquisition source?

✦ **System name:** In what non-CMS system is the data now in use? What's the purpose of that system?

✦ **Connection:** Do you intend to draw data directly out of the system into a dynamic Web site? Or draw it out periodically and store it in your repository for later publication? (If you plan to publish it directly from the source, it's not present in the collection or management system but is accounted for in the publishing system.) If you intend to draw out the data periodically, how frequently will you do so?

✦ **Master data:** If you intend to save data from the source in your CMS repository, do you plan to modify the source after you have it? If so, what modifications do you expect to make? If you get a new version of the source data, do you end up overwriting any changes that you make? If so, what processes can you put in place to ensure that over-writing data doesn't require extra work each time you import new data? Do you need to upload data back to the master source?

✦ **Additional elements:** Are any additional elements present in the CMS version of the source content that aren't in the source? If you're linking to a source instead of bringing it into your repository, how do you tie any of these additional elements to the corresponding source data record?

Tasks

Consider the effect of your acquisition analysis on the ongoing maintenance of the CMS. Then define any tasks that you can imagine need to happen on a recurring basis to run the CMS. Following are some task types to get you thinking:

✦ Acquiring new sources

✦ Training of content processing staff

✦ Dealing with exceptions and errors that occur in automated acquisition processes

✦ Creating and periodically reviewing conversion and tagging guidelines

✦ Monitoring delivery cycles for each source

✦ Converting and tagging each source

✦ Running editorial review cycles

✦ Running metatorial review cycles

✦ Running localization cycles

✦ Running legal review cycles

✦ Running quality-control cycles

✦ Reviewing and redesigning source-to-component processes

Finally, fill in the tasks in the following table.

Task name	Who	What	When	How Much	How
News Conversion	Conversion staff	Run script	At the arrival of the News CD	Once per month	Run the script that the conversion-analysis staff creates

The required information includes the following:

✦ **Task name:** Give the task a short but memorable name that describes it.

✦ **Who:** Indicate what person or role is responsible for accomplishing this task. Naming an automated process here, instead of a person, is acceptable.

✦ **What:** List what the person or process needs to do to accomplish the task.

✦ **When:** Specify at what frequency you must accomplish this task, or how you know when it must occur.

✦ **How much:** Describe how much (or how many sorts) of this task you expect to do. A numerical quantity is preferable here, but if you can't come up with one, words such as *a lot*, *not much*, and so on suffice.

✦ **How:** Detail the skills, tools, or processes that the person or process needs to accomplish this task.

Don't worry if the tasks that you devise at this point are somewhat ill-defined or sketchy. In your workflow analysis (see Chapter 33, "Designing Workflow and Staffing Models"), you have ample opportunity to refine them.

Integrate

To help integrate this analysis into the rest of your logical design, consider the following issues:

✦ **Authoring and acquiring:** What percentage of your content can your own staff author? Can your staff handle that amount? Do they have the skills to author what you want? What percentage of your content must you aggregate from other sources? Do you have rights to use all this content?

✦ **Collection:** Diagram your collection system. Show all the source files, authoring tools, and content types. Do they all fit together? Does this process suggest any sources or authors that you hadn't previously considered? Show your diagram for collecting content to your stakeholders (at least your internal ones). Do they understand? Are they likely to support this approach?

✦ **Conversion:** Do you have tools for all the conversions that you intend to do? Look at your answers to the questions about which elements of the components are present in your sources. For those that are present and clearly marked, begin devising automated ways to pull them out of the text. For those elements that are present but not clearly marked, ask yourself if it requires more effort to mark them and automatically extract them or to manually extract them. For those elements that aren't present, how can you create them?

✦ **Audiences:** Do any incompatibilities exist between your sources and your audiences? Are the audiences likely to respect, believe, and trust your sources? If not, what can you do to help?

✦ **Elements:** Look again at your list of elements. It should exhibit considerable growth, with new elements for tracking and locating components based on the requirements of your collection system. If not, go back and take another look. You should have, at least, added elements for tracking the owner and the status of the component.

Summary

You must decide what the potential sources are for the content you need. Then you can begin to develop a set of named sources. You can attach tasks and statistics to each of these named sources (such as initial quantity and weekly quantity), as follows:

✦ For each source, you must decide what processes and tools it takes to transform it into the components that you expect it to yield. In particular, detail the processes by which you receive it, convert it, segment it, and process it editorially and metatorially.

✦ One of the biggest problems people have with noncommercially acquired content (the kind that you're likely to find inside your organization) is getting it on time and in the quantities and of the quality that you expect. By forming a specific agreement with the content owners, you're more assured of getting what you expect.

✦ As with authored content, you must decide how to attribute it to its authors and how to track its use rights (if any apply).

In the next chapter, I turn my attention to access structures that bring together many of the other logical design entities.

✦   ✦   ✦

Designing Content Access Structures

◆ ◆ ◆ ◆

In This Chapter

The definition and key considerations of the access structures

Some methods that you can use to design a system of access structures

◆ ◆ ◆ ◆

Access structures are the ways that you organize and link content so that people (including you) can more easily find it. Access structures also ensure that users can quickly see what your system (if the user is a staff person) or publication (if the user is an audience member) includes and excludes. In your CMS repository, access structures are how you organize components. In a publication, access structures become the navigation methods that you provide for users to move through the publications pages or sections.

In this chapter, I run through the standard methods that people use to establish relationships between components in a repository and provide publication navigation.

Access Structure Jumpstart

This Jumpstart summarizes how you analyze the access structures you need for your published content, and how these map to the content structure in your CMS.

Use this jumpstart as a summary without the weight of detail, or as a quick review if you've already read the section on Analyzing Access Structures (later in this chapter) and want a checklist for how you carry out an access structure analysis.

To perform an access structure analysis, follow these steps:

1. Think about your content and how you will gather, manage, and publish it. In particular, consider how similar or dissimilar the access structures for your publications are to the structures you use to organize collection and management, particularly if you have a single dominant publication type such as a Web site. Consider also how your audience expects to access content in your publications, what access methods are conventional for your sort of publications, and whether full-text search supplements or supplants some access structures.

2. Plan your access structure analysis, including the following considerations:

   - **Content domain:** Interview stakeholders to understand their expectations of what your content should be. Then create a content domain statement, as well as boundary questions. Decide how you will approve the definition and contents of the content domain, both initially and on an ongoing basis.

- **Audience and access:** Identify who your audiences are and how they access the content in your domain. Characterize how they will look for and find information. Research and analyze what access structures serve their needs and how they use them.

- **Hierarchy:** Review the section "Hierarchies" in this chapter. Proceed with the three following steps, and then review the hierarchies you've defined and decide whether you need them all, if you need more, or if you have problematic or benign conflicts or redundancies in presenting content types. To analyze hierarchy:

  Gather information from contributors and subject matter experts. Determine the most important categories of information in the content they'll provide, and determine if the source content already has access structures, such as tables of contents.

  Create a set of hierarchy design constraints that describe categories for collection, management, publication, and the CMS repository. Determine how well the repository hierarchy maps to the publication categories.

  Define your hierarchies, including hierarchy names and how the hierarchies map to one another. In your definition, account for considerations such as the kinds of personalizations and localizations your hierarchy must support. Review your definitions to determine which content types will be used in each hierarchy, whether there is redundancy or symmetry in the publication hierarchy, and what templates and publications each hierarchy appears in.

- **Indexes:** Review the section "Indexes" in this chapter. Proceed with the three following steps, and then review the indexes you've defined and decide whether they all make sense or have problematic or benign conflicts or redundancies. To analyze indexes:

  Gather information from contributors and subject matter experts. Determine if there are any existing indexes for this kind of content. Determine key terms, phrases, and concepts covered in the material. Find out how familiar the intended audience is likely to be with the vocabulary and concepts, and how the audience might expect the index to be organized.

  Create a set of design constraints for the indexes. Describe the scope of the primary index and how it is stored. Determine what metadata indexes you'll use to manage the content and determine how you'll create them. Finally, decide what types of indexes your publications will include, and define how you'll create each.

  Define your indexes, including for each an index name and the logic needed to create it. In your definition, account for considerations such as the kinds of personalizations and localizations your index must support. Review your definitions to determine which content types will be used in each index, whether the metadata allows you to accommodate any exclusions you make in particular indexes, and in which templates and publications each index appears.

- **Cross-references:** Review the section "Cross-references" in this chapter. Proceed with the following three steps, and then review the cross-reference strategies you've defined and decide whether they all make sense or have problematic or benign conflicts or redundancies. To analyze cross-references:

  Gather information from contributors and subject matter experts. For each content component, decide on the logical next items. In general, decide if there are any logical pathways through the content that are not already covered by the hierarchy. Determine what external links you need.

Create a set of design constraints for your cross-reference strategies. Describe the scope of the primary and secondary cross-references and how they are stored. Decide what cross-references you'll expect authors to provide and what tools you can provide to help them.

Define your cross-reference strategies in detail, including a name for each strategy (starting with the standard "see also" and "for more information" links). Include considerations such as mapping the cross-references in your repository to the published form. Account for considerations such as the kinds of personalizations and localizations your cross-references must support. Decide how links will appear to the audience. Review your definitions to determine which content types will be used in each cross-reference strategy and in which templates and publications each index appears.

- **Sequences:** Decide design criteria for each sequence you want. Include sequence names and the fundamental logic of the sequence. Review your definitions to determine which content types will be used in each sequence, how the sequence coexists with other sequences on the same page or section, and what templates and publications each sequence appears in. Account for considerations such as the kinds of personalizations and localizations your sequences must support. Decide how sequences will appear to the audience and how you will maintain sequence validity over time. Finally, review the sequences you've defined and decide whether they all make sense or have problematic or benign conflicts or redundancies.

- **Full-text search:** Decide which templates and publications should include full-text search, as well as which content (files and/or database) needs to be searched. Decide the features, such as Boolean logic, that you'll include, as well as how you'll distinguish full-text search from any indexes. Account for any personalizations that your audience analysis suggests.

- **Publication navigation:** Chart the access structures you've planned for each content type, including hierarchies, indexes, cross-references, sequences, and full-text search. Then decide whether you really need all the access structures, whether publications can share structures, and whether your repository structures can map to your publication access structures.

- **The content model:** Use the information you've gathered to create a model for your access structures. To complete your content model, review the access structures you charted for each content type for consistency and comprehensiveness and then combine this information with the component and component element analysis tables you've already created. (See Chapter 27, "Designing Content Types," in the section "Plan," for examples of these tables.)

- **Tasks:** Which broadly include all the work that must be done to maintain the access structures on an ongoing basis. Include such aspects as adding new components to the access structures; link validation, review, and effectiveness; full-text search maintenance; index reviews for correctness and validity; hierarchy category reviews; staff training; and quality control. For each task that you come up with, chart the task name, who does it, what it consists of, when it must be done, how extensively, and how the task is accomplished.

3. Integrate by reviewing your completed content model. As you do, review the component/access model you've completed to see if you have the components needed to populate your access structures. Consider the needs and capabilities of audiences, staff, sources, and authors to understand how they will use the access structures. Conduct usability

testing if possible. Decide if your access structures will be amenable to the localizations and personalizations you plan. Determine if the access structures are consistent with the publication structures you specified when you designed the publications (as described in Chapter 26, "Designing Publications," in the section "Publication structure").

At the end of this analysis, you'll have a good understanding of what you need to make your content discoverable, and how that effort affects other aspects of your CMS design.

Understanding Access Structures

Thousands of even the best content components in a CMS repository are of little use to you if you can't find them. Access structures help you find content. Of equal importance are your the capabilities of publication templates to find your components and to correctly place them on the appropriate publication pages. Access structures provide the means by which templates select and draw in content components. Finally, audience members must be able to navigate among the various parts of your publications. Your access structures give rise to navigation methods in your publications. At various points in this book, I show you the following types of access structures:

✦ **Hierarchies:** These structures are the outlines that you use to create parent/child relationships in your content.

✦ **Indexes:** These structures consist of the keywords and phrases that you map to your content.

✦ **Cross-references:** These structures are the links between content chunks.

✦ **Sequences:** These structures concern the orderings of content chunks. They specify which chunks are next and which are previous.

These four items share the following important qualities:

✦ **They organize:** Each one is a method for putting boundaries around and markers in a body of information to make it more coherent.

✦ **They relate:** Each seeks to organize by relating one piece of content to another and by relating content within the system to content and concepts outside the system. Hierarchies relate chunks to each other in both peer and parent/child relationships. Sequences relate one chunk to another in a narrative that specifies a temporal or logical progression.

✦ **They're structures:** Each is a kind of structure that you put around content. It's a form of metadata around the content that names, relates, and organizes it.

✦ **They aid access:** Most practically, each helps you find a piece of content. In a sequence or cross-reference, for example, you start from one piece of content and move toward others that are closely related. In indexes and hierarchies, you move from a set of categories toward the content within those categories.

✦ **They depend on content components:** For any of these structures to work (at least within the context of a CMS), they need discrete chunks of content to relate to each other.

Note   You may sense the conspicuous lack of one big access mechanism—full-text search. Look at the section "Full-text search," later in this chapter, to see why I don't consider it an access structure.

In the end, I believe, all the access structures rely on the power of naming. Each applies a set of names to the content to specify the kind and nature of its relationships. *Hierarchies* create a set of named categories into which all content must somehow fit. *Indexes* apply a word or phrase to various chunks and tell you that the chunks are *about* that word. *Cross-references* name another chunk and state that the current chunk associates with it. *Sequences* name the logical next and previous content to go to. In all cases, you try to create a small, easy-to-use set of words to describe and capture a large and hard-to-use set of words (the content itself).

Cross-Reference

You find more information about the idea of naming in Chapter 5, "But What Is Content, Really?" in the section "Content Is Named Information."

The reward for getting your access structures right in a CMS is large. In fact, you may say that access structures are really what a CMS is all about. Components and their metadata may lie at the center of the CMS wheel, but without access structures, you can never find or use those components in publications. Of course, this characterization is a bit of a false dichotomy, because access structures themselves are metadata. Still, I can't underscore enough the importance of access structures. If you create them poorly, not only is your content hard to find, but it's also hard to publish.

Access Structures and the Brain

Did you ever wonder why these particular access structures are the ones that we all use? The answer may be right behind your eyes. Our brains are nothing if they're not content repositories. So maybe you shouldn't be surprised to find echoes of all the CMS access structures in the structures of the brain, as the following list outlines:

✦ **Hierarchy:** The brain itself is organized hierarchically. Lower regions send input to higher regions that synthesize and add a wider context to the inputs.

✦ **Index:** The shopping list that you commit to memory is one example of the way that you use small bits of data to catalog the wider information to which each item refers. As you move through the list, you turn the product name (bread, milk, cheese, and so on) into a full mental image of the exact item that you're looking for. (The word *bread* may become a visual image of the loaf, a memory of its smell, and a recollection of its location and price in the market.)

✦ **Cross-reference:** Better classed as associations, cross-references may be the basic mechanism of the brain. Pretty much everything that goes on in the brain you can boil down to an association of some sort. Sensations associate with perceptions; perceptions associate with conceptions; and conceptions associate in a great creative circle with sensations.

✦ **Sequence:** Have you ever had the experience of half-remembering a song? If you get one small phrase and start singing it, the rest of the song may just come out. The next word is somehow accessible from the word before it. Does *J* come before or after *L*? You're likely to recite some of the alphabetical sequence to yourself to get the answer. These are but two small examples of how the brain uses sequence to structure and store information.

I suppose it really isn't at all strange that we structure information outside ourselves the same way that we structure it inside.

Access structures may be important, but they're also difficult to create. Here are a few reasons why:

✦ **You must really immerse yourself in the information.** To create good access structures, you need a special talent for organizing and categorizing. You need a great attention to detail and a vast ability to keep a lot of information in your head. In addition, you must be willing to really dive into the information and study it closely. Finally, you must have the skills, time, and attitude to understand access to the information from the audience's perspective, taking its goals, assumptions, and its likely starting places into account.

✦ **Access structures are expensive to create.** Organizing information takes a lot of time and effort. Most of this effort results in benefits that you don't immediately realize. If you spend an extra 10 hours now honing your access structures, maybe you get each person to his goals, on average, one minute faster over the life of the system. The relationship is hard to see and measure. Good access structures come after numerous false starts and revisions. This sort of process is anathema to many modern fast-paced organizations.

✦ **Access structures are expensive to maintain.** Every time that I think I've cleaned up and organized my kitchen, I turn around and find it in disarray again. Other users of the kitchen (my kids) don't have the same regard for its maintenance as I do. They also know that if they don't correctly categorize the dishes, I do it for them later. I can only imagine how much extra effort my kitchen would be if it were like a CMS and had dozens of new kinds of dishes coming into it each day. Structure is a never-ending battle against entropy.

So prepare yourself to fight the good fight to get the time and resources that you need to do access well.

Publication navigation versus CMS access structure

I generally talk about access structures as if they were a single thing. You may think that you have one hierarchy, one index, and so on. The fact is that your CMS can contain many of each of these structures. Furthermore, you need to account for the following two broad classes of access structures:

✦ **CMS access:** Within your CMS, you need access structures that organize and relate components.

✦ **Publication access:** In each publication, you need a set of access structures that organize and relate the parts of the publication.

CMS access structures help you store, manage, and publish content. Publication access structures help you know what's in a publication and find your way around. Inside the CMS, access structures are for management. Outside the CMS, access structures are for navigation.

This dichotomy gives rise to one of the problems that plagues many Web sites. When you create the site, it seems most natural to organize information by the department or group where the information originates. Site users, however, don't really care about the structure of the organization. They want to find information related to their current task or based on their understanding of how concepts, not departments, fit together.

This quandary puts many Web groups into a tight spot. Do they reorganize the site to cater to their audiences and cause their collection system to fall apart, or do they ignore users to remain efficient at collecting and organizing information?

I hope that you can guess that the right answer is neither. The problem for these groups isn't that they can have either good management or good navigation. The problem is that they have no way of separating management from navigation. Most have a single directory structure of files that serves as both the repository and the navigation structure of the site.

In a CMS, you have a management system and then you have a publication. The access structures of the management system and those of the publications needn't be the same. As you collect and store information, you're free to do so based on departments, content type, authors, sources, or any other parameters that you decide. These structures speak directly to your management needs. As you present information to audiences, you can organize it by task, type of person, job title, or any other parameter that speaks to the audience's need. If you have 10 different needs to serve, you can use your CMS to produce 10 different organizational schemes.

Now that I've made the point, I need to temper it. I imply that, in a CMS, you can have your cake and eat it, too. You can have your access structures and theirs as well. But in reality, there's no free lunch. Making access easier for them (in this case, the audiences) makes it harder for you. You can certainly separate the structures of the publication from those of the management system, but it costs you to do so. Instead of maintaining one set of access structures (a big enough task) you must maintain two (or more, depending on what other publications require their own navigation schemes). In addition, the farther that you go from the structure of the repository, the harder building navigation from it becomes. If the design of your publication's navigation, for example, provides access not to whole components but to individual elements of components, but your repository supports only access only to whole components, you face a lot of extra work to create the publication's navigation from the repository's structures.

The key is to balance your CMS and publication access structures to minimize the extra work. You create both structures so that the CMS structures can map automatically to the structures of the publication. This task may require a bit of compromise on both sides.

 Cross-Reference You can get a feel for the mechanics of mapping CMS structures to publication structures in Chapter 39, "Building Management Systems," in the section "General storage requirements."

The content domain

Before you can effectively create access structures, you must answer the question, "Access to what?" What distinguishes the content that's within the system from the content outside it?

Your *content domain* is the scope or range of content that you collect, manage, and publish. In short, it's the type of content that you need to manage. I use the concept of the content domain to capture the idea of bringing together disparate content chunks into a unified system.

The content domain is a good one if it does the following:

✦ **Differentiates:** The content domain should enable you to make crisp decisions about any piece of content that you're presented with. Does it belong or not?

✦ **Clarifies:** Your range of content should be immediately understandable to potential content contributors, your audiences, and anyone else associated with the project — if they know your domain.

✦ **Confines:** Your domain shouldn't be too wide for you to adequately cover nor too narrow to adequately drive the publications that you create.

A content domain is communicated by a statement that sums up the content that you choose to manage. The right domain statement is no more than a few sentences. If someone hears it, that person can immediately recognize what's part of the content and what's not. If you recite it, you know immediately whether a piece of content is of interest to you.

The following domain statement, for example, puts a "bright line" between content that belongs and content that doesn't:

> We collect the state laws and regulations that our lawyers need to know to advise our clients on their personal income tax forms.

This statement defines clearly what belongs, can be quickly understood, and, I assume, is not too big a task for the staff to take on. It's not airtight. You can (and, no doubt, some would) argue about the meaning of the word *need*. Still, it's specific enough to drive the formation of a set of content components and the system for managing them.

The following statement, however, is far too broad:

> We collect all information that's useful to high school students.

It invites major debate on the term *useful*. Useful for what? It gives little to potential contributors to tell them whether their content fits. Finally, it's much too broad. Can this organization really collect *all* useful information?

The following statement is inadequate for quite a different reason:

> We collect the state laws and regulations that we have that our lawyers need to know to advise our clients on their personal income tax forms.

You don't want to limit a content domain to what you have. Think of it from the perspective of the poor lawyer who goes to the book that this system creates to find relevant laws. If she doesn't find anything applicable to her problem, what does she think? Does she conclude that is nothing applicable or that this organization just might not *have* anything that's applicable? The amount and kind of content that you have the wherewithal to accumulate always limits you. This limitation is a practical one, however, and not a limit on what your audiences require that you create. In this case, you may go with the first version of this statement, which isn't so limited. If you can't manage to collect all the content, tell your audience so in the publication, not in the domain statement.

The content domain statement for this book is as follows:

> The concepts that you should understand and the practices that you should follow to create a content management system.

A good content domain defines the content that you must control to meet your organization's goals. If you ask, "How can we meet our goals?" the answer should be as follows: "By providing the content (both information and functionality) that our content domain includes."

You may start with a solid notion of your content domain, but more likely, it's a discovery process. You may start with one statement and end up with quite a different statement as all the content-management entities weigh in to your analysis. After you develop a strong domain statement, adhering doggedly to it is important. Every breech in the conceptual wall around your content invites extra work for you and confusion for your audiences.

To get another angle on this very important concept, consider a newly hired, very savvy content manager and her boss. The boss knows little about content management or even about the content and publication that her organization wants. What the new content manager receives are the following items and information:

✦ A large pile of stuff (documents, images, spreadsheets, and the like) that is to go on a Web site.

✦ A very loose mandate that says content belongs on the site if it helps customers understand the product line, compare the company to the competition, place an order, or answer a question about a company product.

✦ A disorganized set of editorial guidelines.

✦ A print product catalog that changes informally over time as the organization adds and drops products.

Suppose that the content manager's been around some. She knows what she needs to know and isn't surprised to find that she's on her own in finding it out. First, she recognizes that the company has the beginnings of an adequate domain statement: "Presales, sales, and postsales support content." This simple statement can become the basis for a bevy of decisions and discriminations that the content manager makes to define and enforce the rules of the system.

First and foremost of these rules is that if it's not presales, sales, or postsales support content, it doesn't belong. From there, she can begin to further define what each of these kinds of content consists of, where to get it, and how to relate it to other content in the system.

Having unearthed a start on a domain statement, the content manager can probe for the two main pillars of the domain: the editorial and metatorial systems. Not surprisingly, the editorial framework is in disarray. It was created piecemeal by a variety of editors, all with different goals, audiences, and authors in mind. Even less surprising is the fact that metadata (much less a metatorial system) isn't even on the radar in the organization. Thus the content manager must set out to get these two started, as the following list outlines:

✦ She can begin the task of integrating the array of style sheets into a single guide. She should be realistic about the amount of time that she must spend on editorial processing. She should recognize that creating a grand, unified style guide is one thing and that applying it to a large quantity of errant documents is quite another.

✦ She should define a bare minimum set of metadata that the CMS must track. She can start with the usual metadata suspects: author, date, and status. Then she can apply the domain statement itself to get a handle on what else she must track. She may reason that, if the site's product oriented, she needs to tag the content by product. If she's also to organize the site by sales cycle, she must also organize the content that way. The print product catalog lists all the products in it. The taxonomy (outline or hierarchy) of products is implicit in the print publication in which it appears. Therefore, she faces a job extracting the taxonomy from the print catalog and ensuring that, as it informally changes, she can keep up with the modifications.

Cross-Reference　The concept of the content domain directly relates to the concept of publication purpose. (See Chapter 26, "Designing Publications," in the section "Publication purpose," for details.) In fact, you can say that the content domain encompasses the purposes of all the publications that you call on the system to produce.

Hierarchies

A *hierarchy* is any system of phrases that classifies and subclassifies information. I use the word *hierarchy* to capture terms such as the following:

✦ **Table of Contents:** A hierarchy that you usually find at the beginning of a book. The term *Table of Contents* (or *TOC*) is now in wide use in the electronic publication world as well. (For some strange reason, however, the home page of a Web site, which generally contains its TOC [but not its index], is often misnamed `index.html`.)

✦ **Outlines:** General purpose tools for showing hierarchical relationships by using indentation.

✦ **Taxonomy:** In the past, biologists mostly used the term to describe the hierarchical relationships between life forms (kingdom, phylum, class, order, family, genus, species). Today, it's one of the trendy words in use among the *digerati* to describe any hierarchical classification scheme (and sometimes, wrongly, to describe indexes).

✦ **Nesting:** A tagging term that describes a system where one tag lies completely within another. In the tags `<HTML><HEAD></HEAD></HTML>`, for example, the `<HEAD>` tag nests within the `<HTML>` tag. Nesting is the key attribute of XML that makes it a hierarchical storage structure.

✦ **Class structure and object model:** These two terms from the programming world describe the hierarchical structure that people commonly use to relate one programming object to another. Borrowing other hierarchical terms, programmers speak of *child classes* and *inheritance*.

Of all these terms, I choose the word *hierarchy* because it's what underlies the rest.

For my purposes, I define a *hierarchy* as having the following characteristics:

✦ **Parents and children:** All hierarchies carry with them the idea of subordinate and superordinate units. Just as human children "come from" parents, the lower levels of an outline "come from" those above. Just as children inherit the property, social position, and personal attributes of their parents, child content inherits the meaning and context of its parents. Just as you can tell a lot about a set of parents by looking at their children, you can tell a lot about the higher levels of a TOC by looking at what's below.

✦ **Siblings or peers:** Items that you group together at the same level of a hierarchy are known as *siblings* or *peers*. The items are together for a good reason — they share the same parents. That fact has a similar interpretation for content as it does for people. The parents that two pieces of content share show how the two are similar. You can expect them both to display some of the qualities of their parents. The two siblings are of the same class; they're peers in the same group. Siblings are the same, however, and yet they're different as well. In their difference, you find part of the definition of the group to which they belong. Groups display a range of qualities that the variability of their members defines.

The upshot of hierarchies is that they put content in a context by enmeshing a piece of content in a series of wider and wider relationships. Knowing the parents of a component gives you a way to interpret its meaning. Consider, for example a component labeled Usage. In one case, a component with this label may be in a section called Computer Interface and, in another case, in a section called Drug Abuse. Clearly, the section that the component is in affects the meaning that you give it.

Hierarchies work to organize information by dividing it, in an understandable way, into very broad categories. You don't need to drill into the branches of the hierarchy that don't seem relevant. You can look at the top levels of a hierarchy and quickly know how to get to what you're looking for. Hierarchies provide a very efficient search method if they're working correctly. Consider, for example, a Web site with seven buttons on the home page (Button 1, Button 2, Button 3, and so on) that divide the content into seven equal categories. If you choose Button 1, for example, you rule out 86 percent of the content on the site with one click. Suppose, further, that the page Button 1 displays itself has seven buttons (Button A, Button B, Button C, and so on). If you choose Button A on the second page, you rule out 86 percent of the remaining content (or a total of 98 percent of all the content). Not bad for two clicks.

With so much power behind them, no wonder that hierarchies are the number-one access method. Of course, I'm assuming a well-functioning hierarchy. Not all hierarchies that you see, especially on Web sites, work at maximum power.

Hierarchies divide, but they also teach. A quick look at the hierarchy of a body of information can tell you an amazing amount about the information, as the following list attests:

✦ **The basic categories:** The top level of the hierarchy is a quick reference to the content domain. In a few seconds of reading, you can (or should) get a very good idea of the entire body of content. I had this experience again recently. I was handed a book that I'd never seen before (on text retrieval systems, by the way). The rest of the people around the table were very familiar with it and began the conversation with the contents of this thick book as "given." Within 30 seconds of scanning the TOC, I was no expert, but I had a solid grasp of the basic ideas at issue. Through the remainder of the conversation, I could glance back over the lower levels of the TOC to get deeper into what was there quickly and without reading a single word of the actual text.

✦ **The general and the specific:** A hierarchy teaches you what categories of information in the domain are large and sweeping and which are small and of limited applicability. Look, for example, at the parentage of this sentence. It's in a section that I call "Hierarchies," which is inside a section that I call "Understanding Access Structures," which is inside a chapter that I call "Designing Content Access Structures," which is inside a Part that I call "Designing a CMS." Just by looking at the parentage of this sentence, you can tell that a hierarchy is a content access structure that is part of the design of a CMS.

✦ **The important terms and their relationships:** All the important vocabulary in a domain generally shows up in its hierarchy. Again, look at the parentage of this sentence. Each of its parent sections has a term that's central to the work.

As you create hierarchies, try to look at them from the standpoint of someone who wants to learn something. The first lesson that a user learns from your work is likely to come from the hierarchy that you provide. If the hierarchy fails to teach, visitors may not return for a second lesson.

Hierarchy considerations

The ancient Greeks believed that information had natural divisions that, if one found and exposed them, made any information most understandable. My own feeling is that hierarchies, like all categories, are half inside and half outside the user. On one hand, the categories have something to teach the user that she doesn't already know. On the other hand, if the user doesn't see something familiar in the categories that you propose, she may not give them a chance to teach her. Following are a few general principles that may start you off as you put together your hierarchies:

✦ **Use the natural divisions:** Respect and take advantage of the way that the content divides from the standpoint of someone who knows it very well. More than natural divisions, these divisions are the ones that information insiders know and commonly use. Start from these categories. If your intended audiences don't know the content well, craft the divisions to teach them.

✦ **Use generally understood vocabulary:** Your intended audiences shouldn't look at your hierarchy and see divisions or words that they can't understand or use to get to what they want to know (unless, of course, your audience expects to confront a lot of new concepts). Try to make the hierarchy communicate to the level of understanding and the needs of your audience.

✦ **Keep it short:** As you probably already know, keeping your categories to seven or fewer per level is best. The person choosing among categories should be able to canvass them quickly and keep them all simultaneously in her head. Similarly, keep the titles themselves short. They are easier to grasp and take up less valuable space in your publications.

✦ **Make strong distinctions:** Your categories should be mutually exclusive. Recently, I was at an airline Web site where the home page offered me a choice between "Schedules" and "Arrivals." Having no idea which to choose, I chose wrongly, of course. As much as possible, your content should fit exclusively into one or another category.

✦ **Use titles in context:** Titles should respect the parent but should stand alone. If the parent title is "Learning Executel," for example, the child shouldn't be "Learning Executel for Beginners" or "Beginners" but something like "Executel for Beginners," which works next to the parent and alone.

✦ **The simplest one wins:** Hierarchies are for quick access. Keep them as easy to read and as pithy as possible. Hierarchies should contain the necessary information to convey what's in a section, but not so much that they're hard to get through or discourage quick scanning.

You can find information about the technical aspects of creating hierarchies in Chapter 39, "Building Management Systems," in the section "General storage requirements."

By a fluke of English grammar, no verb form of *hierarchy* exists as it does for the other forms of access structures. You can index, cross-reference, and sequence, but you can't hierarch. Why not?

Polyhierarchy: Multiple hierarchies to represent content

Polyhierarchy is a fancy word for having more than one hierarchy to represent the same content. In a complex CMS, you need more than one hierarchy to perform the following tasks:

✦ **Drive publications:** Each publication that you create is likely to have a somewhat different approach to a Table of Contents. To support them all, you may need more than one hierarchy that you apply to the same content.

✦ **Serve audiences:** Different audiences may expect or require a different content outline to accomplish their tasks. On a workplace-injury Web site, for example, doctors may need to see the injuries in an outline that you organize by the type of injury, whereas employers may need to see them organized by industry and job title.

✦ **Support localization:** Your CMS is unlikely to handle the localization of your publication or repository hierarchies directly. In other words, for each line in an outline, you want many different cells where you can type the localized version of that line. Instead, what you're more likely to do is create separate localized outlines, one per locality.

An issue related to polyhierarchy is whether to list the same item more than once in a hierarchy. Consider, for example, the following outline:

```
Boats
    Pleasure Boats
            Fishing Boats
            Speed Boats
            Dive Boats
    Work Boats
            Fishing Boats
            Cargo Boats
            Passenger Boats
```

Notice that the line Fishing Boats appears in two families. Is that okay? The answer I'd suggest is that, in principle, it's not; but in practice, it may prove hard to avoid. You're not doing anyone a favor by putting the same child under two parents. It's unnecessarily confusing and shows that you haven't figured out your categories very well. In most cases, a little extra effort yields an outline that's less confusing and more instructive. In the preceding outline, the change may prove as simple as changing the lines that read Fishing Boats to, say, Sport Fishing Boats and Commercial Fishing Boats.

On the other hand, a very useful approach to classification is to create a *faceted* classification scheme where the same item is listed in a large number of distinct categories. In a faceted classification, the idea of polyhierarchy is taken to the extreme. Items are listed in as many categories as possible, but the number of levels in the overall hierarchy (the one that includes all categories) is kept to a minimum. The result is a fairly flat hierarchy where you can find an item of interest in any number of different categories (or facets).

Tip

If you can work through the design and programming issues, one way to have your polyhierarchy cake and eat it, too, is to use "see" and "see also" references in your hierarchies. In an index, you commonly use these two methods to tell users that they're looking in a reasonable place for their information, but it's not the right place (in the case of "see") or the only place (in the case of "see also"). These two methods get the user to the information, but also enable the authors to hold on to the "exclusively right" way to categorize information. If you follow this approach, understand that you're charting new user-interface territory, and you must take pains to make your interface understandable.

Indexes

An *index* is an ordered list of words or phrases that categorize content. I use the word *index* to capture and encompass the following terms:

✦ **Keywords:** People often use this term in the computer world and, especially, in the Web world to mean a list of terms or phrases that the user can choose to jump to the content that is described. This operation is often known as a *keyword search*, but in fact, you can more aptly describe it as a *keyword index*.

✦ **Thesaurus:** This term refers to a guide to synonyms or alternative words to use instead of the one that you know. It's now making its way into the computer vernacular to mean a set of alternative words that you can use to find the same content. If you search for the word *shoe*, for example, the computer may use a thesaurus to extend the search to the phrase *footwear* or even to every kind of shoe (sandal, sneaker, high heel, and so on). I see a thesaurus as simply another kind of index. It maps between one set of words and another.

To me, the central meaning of the word *index*, and the theme that runs through keywords and thesauruses, is *map*. An index provides a map between the words and concepts of the seeker and those of the system. The keyword index, for example, is a map between the word that you choose in the list of choices and the Web page that corresponds to it. The thesaurus is a map between the word that you choose and all the other words that you may have chosen if you knew how the system described content.

The purpose of an index in any of its forms is to guide the user from the words that she knows to those that she needs to find.

In a CMS and its publications, indexes have the following key characteristics:

✦ **They are comprehensive:** Every important word and phrase in the system or publication should appear in some index.

✦ **They present concepts:** Beyond simply the words that you use, indexes present the concepts that the system or publication uses, regardless of whether the exact words are in any publication. PLAN, for example, may index some of its press releases under the term *Poverty Action Programs*, even if that phrase appears nowhere in the releases.

✦ **They include synonyms:** A good index also includes the vocabulary and concepts of the audiences that it serves. The concepts of "see also" for an associated term and "see" for a synonym lead the user from her native usage to another recommended usage in the system.

✦ **They order vocabulary and concepts:** Of course, the most popular ordering in indexes is alphabetical. But many others are possible. Indexes by date, author, location, media types, or any other piece of metadata are possible and common. And, of course, indexes may include a hierarchy of ordering schemes—for example, PLAN may index press releases by year and, within each year, by concept (and within each concept, alphabetically).

I'm often amazed at how little most Web sites have learned from the indexes in print materials. The print index (such as you find at the end of most books) is such an elegant and well-honed indexing device that I'd expect it to be adopted as eagerly as the Table of Contents is. Part of the reason that it isn't is that few can spare the extra effort necessary to put together a good index. Even those who include an extensive keyword function on their sites, however, often miss the following basic features of a print index:

✦ **Hierarchy:** A book index generally uses two levels of phrases to make listing terms and subterms easier.

✦ **Hits:** A book index lists the page numbers that apply directly under the index term. You can tell how important a term is by how often it's referenced. The section that defines the term often appears in bold or is otherwise marked.

✦ **Scannability:** You can have more than 100 terms on one page of an index. Your eye can travel over large portions of the index very quickly and efficiently, looking for terms that may prove of interest.

✦ **Associations:** The "see" and "see also" lines in an index enable you to cross-reference terms and move around within the index.

The best guess that I can come up with as to why these features are largely ignored on the Web (having ignored these same great features myself many times) is that a combination of ignorance, cost, screen resolution, and the tyranny of the standard user interface all work against the index. Plus not all Web designers even know how print indexes are designed. The extra features that an index can offer are more expensive to create for the Web, and the computer screen doesn't provide the same density of information as the printed page does. But more than any of these factors, I believe that indexes just got stuck in the narrow confines of keyword lists. In the standard set of computer-interface controls, the list is a very simple thing. It can't represent levels, so you have little opportunity to include a hierarchy or to list hits under a phrase. The list can't do columns and isn't designed to appear very large, so your capability to quickly scan it is limited. Finally, list controls aren't designed to enable you to jump from one line to another, so associations are hard to manage.

My experience and intuition tells me that someone early on put the index in a list control (following earlier data implementations where that sort of thing is common), and every one afterward simply followed suit. So the situation isn't so much that you can't represent a good index on the computer screen as it is that you can't represent it in the single control that most assume it should go in.

To end my discussion of what indexes are, I must point out that indexes are really just a special case of a hierarchy. Following is a two-level hierarchy:

```
Aardvark
    See also "Animals"
    Anatomy
    Habits
    Predators of
Aaron, Henry
    Biography
    Unbeaten Records
```

The index type of hierarchy can't substitute for a Table of Contents (although some try to make it do so), but it's nonetheless a hierarchy.

Indexing considerations

Following are some considerations that you may want to take into account in designing your indexes:

✦ **Take it seriously:** Try to avoid the blithe assumption that you're only doing keywords. Also, fight the urge to envision all indexes living inside a list box that's 25 characters wide and 10 lines long.

✦ **Take advantage of the print techniques:** Within the constraints of time and user interface, try to emulate (or better, extend and enhance) the techniques that you rely on to navigate a print index.

✦ **Use insider and outsider vocabulary:** An index is the main place to teach users the right words to use. Make sure that you include synonyms for your insider vocabulary in the index that give outsiders a way to get in.

Database indexes

The word *index* is so common in database parlance that I'd be remiss if I didn't spend a bit of space discussing database indexes and their relationship to content management. Like the indexes I've been discussing, a database index is an access structure. Specifically, a database index enables you to search more quickly for information in a particular column (also known as a *field*) of a database. Suppose that you often attempt to find user records by last name. If you put an index on the last-name column of the user database table, you can perform this operation more quickly. Instead of looking through every row in the table one by one, the database can just look in the index to locate the position of the record with the last name value that you want.

This concept of an index is quite close to the concept of the content index that I've been describing. In both cases, the index extracts and stores just the aspect of the information necessary for you to find it. Thus you leave behind the great mass of the information, and you search through only a very small portion of the information to find what you want.

The big difference between the two concepts is that database indexing is a fully mechanical process, and content indexing (the way that I lay it out) is a human process. A database index extracts no more than what's already present and explicit in the information. A content index extracts but also synthesizes, categorizes, interprets, and contexts the information to which it gives access.

I provide the most illuminating example of this difference in the section "Full-text search," later in this chapter, where I compare a full-text search index to the type of content index that I've been describing.

Cross-references

A cross-reference directly relates one chunk of content to another. I use the word *cross-reference* to encompass the more widely used term *hyperlink*. A *hyperlink* (or just *link*) is a way to jump from one Web page (or other electronic publication node) to another, no matter where it is on the site. I like the term *cross-reference* better because it's more descriptive and applies across all publication types.

Cross-references have moved from the sidelines in traditional publications to center stage in electronic publications. In fact, the World Wide *Web* was named for the web of interconnections that are possible through the use of cross-references that can cross not only two pieces of content in the same content domain, but also two pieces of content in any domain that's on an accessible Web site.

The connotation of the term *cross-reference* is a bit lackluster for the meaning that I intend for the concept. A much more evocative word is *association*. Behind each cross-reference is an association between the content chunks you're linking. The association answers the question, "If I'm here, where else might I want to be?" The usual answer of "For more information, see..." is the very tip of the enormous iceberg. With what other content, for example, do you associate a content chunk about cows? Surely, with much more than simply more information about cows! What about farms, animals, spots, religion, milk, songs, meadows, laziness, and a million other places that someone may want to go next? Imagine the possibilities of a system that can detect where you may want to go next and let you jump directly there. To a small degree, hyperlinks can give you a little of this sort of contextual information. For example, on a Web page, in the sentence "Cows live on <u>farms</u>" the word *farms* is a cross-reference in the form of a hyperlink. By following the link, you rightly expect to go to a place that has more information about cows and farms.

Early on (five years ago, that is), the new power and capability of associations led many to declare that the hyperlink was *the* way to organize information and that, before long, an ever expanding web of relationships would engulf all the world's information. People were assumed to be capable of navigating from any one chunk of information to any other based on its associations.

Reports of the death of the other three access methods are premature. The concept of the universal web was quickly superceded by the concept of getting "lost in hyperspace," and Web sites that use only associations remain experimental oddities. The electronic world is a manic one, swinging wildly between boom and bust, economically and intellectually. The promise of the power of cross-references (like the promise of the penetration of the electronic technologies themselves) is real; it's just not instantaneous.

What I know from my own experience and what I've seen in others' work is that the capabilities to completely cross-reference globally are so new that people just don't have the skills or conventions to do it well yet. Over time and after enough bitter failures, a set of conventions are sure to grow up that guide cross-referencers (a job that doesn't even exist yet) to create schemes and methods that give as much regularity and rigor to cross-references as people now expect from indexes and hierarchies.

What's a cross-reference?

To make a cross-reference, you need what I call a reference and a referent. The *reference* is the place *from* which you link, and the *referent* is the content chunk *to* which you link. Here, for example, is a typical HTML hyperlink:

```
<A HREF="abc.htm">Go to ABC</A>
```

Here, the referent is the page abc.htm. The reference is the phrase Go to ABC. To make sense, you must place the reference somewhere in the content of a page from which you might possibly want to go to ABC. Consider the following typical print cross-reference:

For more information, see Chapter 3.

The referent is Chapter 3 and the reference is the phrase "For more information, see Chapter 3." Again, you must locate the reference where seeing Chapter 3 makes sense. Notice, by the way, that the reference contains the referent. This setup must remain true in print, where you must find and "jump to" the referent. It's not so strange on Web pages either, as the following example illustrates:

```
<A HREF="ABC.HTM">Go to ABC (abc.htm)</A>
```

In addition to containing references and referents, cross-references more interestingly form pathways through a content domain. A sequence is a linear pathway indicating what the publisher considers the logical next and previous chunks. By following cross-references, the user can create an alternative pathway based on another notion of what to look at next. The following list presents a few examples of the kinds of pathways that users may want to follow. In each case, I pose the question on the user's mind that the cross-references ought to answer, as follows:

✦ **"See also" and "For more"...** "Is other material available on this subject that I also need to see?" The most common kind of cross-reference connects you to related or deeper information on the subject at hand. As the author types (or as someone else prepping the content for publication reviews it), she recalls some aspect of the discussion that she covers elsewhere and inserts a cross-reference.

✦ **Prerequisite knowledge:** "I don't understand this information, so where can I go to learn what I need to know to understand it?"

✦ **Postrequisite knowledge:** "I understand this information, so where can I go to apply my knowledge or go deeper?"

✦ **Next steps:** "What is the next step in the process that interests me?" A page on supervisor approval, for example, may serve as one step in any number of different procedures that an employee may follow.

✦ **Previous steps:** "What are the previous steps of the process?"

✦ **Alternative next steps:** "What are the alternative choices for what I want to do next, and how can I see these choices?" If more than one logical next step is possible, a cross-reference can enable the user to choose which way to go.

✦ **Glossary:** "What does that term mean?" A cross-reference may link you to a definition.

✦ **Conceptually similar:** "What you're saying here makes me think of X. How do I get there?" Or "Because I'm interested in this, logically, I'm also interested in Y. How do I get there?"

✦ **External source:** "What other sites or publications should I look at?" If you consistently cross-reference outside publications, standardizing the structure and appearance of these links is worth your while.

✦ **Official citation:** "Take me to the definitive source for this information." Sometimes, your content derives or in some way consistently relates to another "higher" source. Most Web sites that discuss XML, for example, link to the W3C (the World Wide Web Consortium) site that contains the definitive XML specification.

From the publication producer's perspective, cross-references are a great way to write something once and use the same content many times. Instead of including the same content wherever it applies, you can keep it in one central location and simply cross-reference it as necessary.

Cross-reference considerations

Most people apply cross-references in an ad hoc way. As they come across content that seems as though it should link to some other content that they happen to remember, they search around for the reference, and if they can find it without too much trouble, they put in the cross-reference. This attitude reflects the lack of importance that cross-references enjoy to date. You'd never think of doing a hierarchy or an index this way. You start your hierarchies early and review them often to make sure that they always apply. You may index all at once, but as you do, you create a particular approach and apply it consistently across the entire body of content.

I see no reason why you can't create cross-references with the same attention and rigor (cost and desire aside). What hierarchies and indexes have that cross-references lack is a strategy. Why can't you develop a cross-reference strategy early in your project and apply and refine it as you fill out your content domain? Or what's wrong with tasking a staff member to go through the entire body of content, consistently applying your cross-reference strategy? Mostly, I think, people don't use these methods because they've simply never used them before. But if cross-references are anywhere near as important as they're predicted to be in the electronic publication world, before too long, you're certain to pay as much attention to them as you do to any other access structures.

So what's behind a cross-reference strategy? Certainly you need to pay attention to the standard list of next topics that I discuss in the preceding section "What's a cross-reference?" More generally, you may want to consider a set of conceptual maps that you can apply across the whole content domain. Have you ever paged through a world atlas? Did you notice how

Effective Cross-Referencing

A difficulty with cross-references, unlike with indexes, is that to apply them consistently, you must have a complete view of the material all at once. For indexing, you can start at the front of the information and work your way through, noting the entries as you proceed, and using later entries to rephrase, refine, or add to earlier ones. For cross-refs, you have to know the entire opus as you go, or you have to do repeated iterations through the material. If I'm indexing this book, I can add "cross-references" to my list now, and add hits or related terms as I find them. I should also track my previous entries to see if any relate to the new ones. But if I'm adding cross-refs to this book, I have to do a tremendous amount of "back and forth" movement.

Sara Shlaer, Development Editor, Wiley Publishing, Inc.

many different-looking maps an atlas presents for the same territory? You find road maps, elevation maps, vegetation maps, political maps, language maps, and many others. What guides the creation of these different overlays on the same basic geography? The differing information needs of users. When I was a child, I remember that I was fascinated with the part of the encyclopedia on anatomy. Instead of the usual boring words and pictures, in the anatomy section was a full-page picture of a skeleton. As if that wasn't enough to catch my attention, it also included a transparent overlay that you could put over the skeleton to show the organs of the body. Over the organs, you could overlay the circulatory system. Over the circulation, you could overlay the muscles and, over the muscles, the skin.

What do geography and anatomy say about content cross-references? In both cases, alternative patterns and organizations overlay a core structure. I contend that these two domains aren't the only ones where the technique applies. What in your domain is the core information and what are the overlays? Each overlay is a piece of your cross-reference strategy.

Moving now from the philosophy to the actual practice of cross-referencing, I offer the following concrete suggestions for creating cross-references:

✦ **Apply a consistent standard:** However you choose to create cross-references, do it the same way throughout your CMS and publications. Decide what kinds of things link, and link them consistently and evenly across the domain. If you decide to make references an entire sentence, for example, make them all that way. If you don't, you can't create automated routines for formatting and positioning your cross-references on the published page.

✦ **Start early and reevaluate:** Think about how you intend to create cross-references. That alone gives you an edge on most people who don't. In addition, discuss your plans and assign particular staff to the task. Finally, review your cross-reference system. One effective way to do so is to make a picture that shows each component (in the repository) or page (in a publication) and all the others that it links to.

✦ **Choose a consistent presentation:** In each publication, choose one or a very few ways to represent cross-references and then stick with it. You want users able to quickly learn to distinguish and process cross-references.

✦ **Transition rhetoric:** Blind jumps are the worst kind. Make sure that you give the user a clear idea of where a cross-reference is taking her. As much as possible, try to use the same vocabulary and headings in the reference as users find in the referent. Develop a consistent system for marking each link with its kind. Distinguish clearly, for example, between "more information" links and "related topic" links.

✦ **Proximity:** As a general rule, place your link as close to the relevant chunks as possible. Links are best if they are located right at the point on the page where you discuss a subject and they take the user right to the point on another page where you discuss a related subject. Links from the bottom of a long page, where you mention some subject, to the top of another long page, where you list a related subject somewhere, are not as helpful. Despite your best intentions, constraints may force you to put distance between your references (or referents) and the subjects that they link. The farther the distance, the more explanation that you need to put in the reference to help the user understand what you're cross-referencing and how to find the referent. If you must link to the top of the page, for example, at least give some indication of where on the target page the user may find the referent. You can do this by characterizing the content found on the page as well as the relevant referent within it. For example: "For more information on farm livestock, including cows, see *Farm Livestock* on page 55."

✦ **Don't duplicate the hierarchy:** Just because they can, many people include cross-references to peers, parents, and children. I can rarely see the value in this practice given that the hierarchy already is readily available and usable. These extraneous links crowd out the real cross-references and teach the user that cross-references are mostly duplicates of links that are available elsewhere. Cross-references shouldn't duplicate or replace the hierarchy. Rather, you want them to provide a set of alternative pathways through the content.

Sequences

Sequences are the next and preceding nodes in a publication. Traditionally, the order of the pages in a print publication establishes a single sequence of nodes. In electronic publications, you can create as many different sequences as needed through the same material.

The Self-Generating Cross-Reference

If the ultimate aim of cross-references is to anticipate where a user wants to go next, what better way can you have to generate cross-references than to see where users actually go next. If you have very dedicated users, you can sometimes get them to actually tell you what they want to see next (by typing it in a text box, for example). But as likely as not, the extra effort is too much to ask.

Instead, you can observe user behavior and infer desire from it. On the Web, you have two tools immediately at your disposal for observation. The first is sometimes known as a *referrer URL*. It's the URL of the page someone came from to get to the current one. The user's browser passes a referrer URL along with every request for a page. Disregarding the programming involved, you can match page URLs and referrer URLs to see which pages users generally go to next.

Referrer URLs involve a big problem, however: Users don't go directly from a page to the next page that they want to see. They often pass through many intermediate pages before they land on the next desired page. To deal with the problem, you can use the second tool, the site log. Site logs can track a user as she makes the entire journey through your site. With considerable effort, you can analyze these logs and chart the key next pages that users go to from each other page. Comparing the results for many users, you can begin to build a solid idea of what people want next.

Note Web browsers encompass their own built-in form of sequencing. The familiar Back and Forward buttons in most browsers track the Web pages that you visit and enable you to browse back and forth through them quickly. These sequences aren't the kind that I detail here.

Technically, sequences are no more than systems of cross-references that map to the logical next and preceding topics. But the creation, storage, and publication of sequences are distinct enough from cross-references that sequences deserve their own name.

The primary hierarchies are what define the primary sequences through a content domain. Every hierarchy includes an order, as well as a parentage, for its content chunks. Suppose, for example, that PLAN wants Next and Previous buttons on the top right of each press-release page (see Figure 30-1).

Figure 30-1: The PLAN press-release page, with left- and right-pointing arrows indicating Next and Previous buttons

If you decide to personalize the navigation, the hierarchy on the left changes, depending on who's viewing the press release section. But regardless of which hierarchy is on the left, you naturally expect the Next and Previous buttons to follow that hierarchy.

The Next and Previous buttons don't need to follow the hierarchy, but if they don't, you're breaking the user's natural assumption, and you must explain yourself. Maybe, for example, PLAN intends Next and Previous to move the user by date through the press releases. In this case, arrow buttons such as the ones shown in the figure don't adequately communicate the intent. PLAN needs to use another icon that communicates time or to associate some words with the button to give the user an indication of what each button does. An `ALT` attribute (an HTML attribute that — in most recent versions of browsers — causes a pop-up description to appear after the user moves the mouse over the image) may do the trick, as the following line shows:

```
<IMG SRC="next.gif" ALT="Next Press Release by Date">
```

It may be, however, that you have a variety of ways to move through press releases (by hierarchy, date, and subject, for example). Obviously, a single button can't do the trick. Instead, a drop-down menu that appears as you move the mouse over each button may work.

In any case, you can have a number of sequences that take a user through the information at hand. And for each sequence, you must decide how to do the following:

✦ **Store it:** Your hierarchies already store the primary sequences. You can often generate other sequences dynamically by sorting your content by a metadata field. As long as each press release has a date, for example, you can always find the next one in the sequence by issuing a simple query against the press releases in the CMS repository.

✦ **Represent it:** The primary sequences are easy to represent with some sort of arrows (which are now the standard icon for Next and Previous). For other sequences, and especially for multiple sequences, our iconography breaks down and you must get more creative.

Full-text search

Full-text search is the now-familiar process of typing a word or a phrase into a text box, clicking a Search button, and getting back a list of titles. Between the time that you click the Search button and the results appear, a program scans every piece of available text for the words that you type. The program amasses the titles of the publication nodes that contain these words and displays them as a list of hyperlinks.

Full-text search is one of the most amazing features about electronically provided information. Very efficient algorithms are now available that can index and search through enormous amounts of text and return thousands and even millions of titles in a few seconds.

The most amazing part of full-text search is that it can accomplish all this effort without any human intervention. The programs are fully automated and can continuously scan text and update their indexes as you modify the text that they're to search. The most cogent examples of the power of full-text search are the search engines of the Web. Google, Alta Vista, and a host of others enable you to search for your words across a significant percentage of the entire World Wide Web. You type a few words and back come potentially hundreds of thousands of titles of pages that contain the words you've typed.

The sheer power, as well as the ease of use, of full-text search has led many to see it as the ultimate information-access method. But its very power, of course, is its downfall. Full-text search works *too* well. After being awed by the power of Google, the user can quickly become frustrated. Who wants a hundred thousand hits? Search engines improve on this by attempting to rank results by relevance or importance (terms which are somewhat arbitrarily defined). Users can certainly become adept at entering and refining their search terms so they return meaningful results, but it does take some work; and users are often confronted with hundreds of results that they must choose to investigate — or ignore.

Full-text search is powerful beyond doubt. Because it's automated, it's clearly quite convenient for the publisher (although, as usual, easier for you means harder for the user). Full-text search is a wonderful access mechanism — but it's not an access structure.

Full-text search is closest to a database index. A typical full-text search program consists of two parts. The first part pores through all the text and builds an index. The index is an enormous table of words and their positions in the text. The second part of the program processes queries. After you click the Search button, this part of the program looks in the index for the locations and titles that associate with all the words that you type. Just like a database index, a full-text index adds nothing to the text that's not already there. It simply makes getting to what's already there faster.

The four access methods that I focus on in this chapter all add something more to the content than is already there. A quick contrast between a content index and a full-text search index makes the point: A full-text index lists every word (more or less) in the text. A content index lists only the important words. In addition, it lists phrases. The words and phrases in the content index may not even appear in the text. A content index needn't stop at words. A content index can just as easily describe and catalog all the images and other media in the domain (as well as its functionality). A content index teaches you what vocabulary and concepts are important in the content domain. A full-text index shows you only the exact words that the content domain contains.

The structures are called *structures* by virtue of the fact that they add additional support to the domain. This support is in the form of metadata that adds intelligence to the raw content. To qualify as a structure of the form that I'm describing, the device needs to include synthesis, interpretation, and additional meaning. It must make the domain seem smaller by capturing its essential attributes and displaying them concisely. For all the power and usefulness of the full-text search, it doesn't meet these criteria.

The access structures are important to a CMS, because they help you store, manage, and publish content. In addition, they require significant staff effort and rigorous planning to create and maintain. Full-text search doesn't meet these criteria either. It's not a way to store content, it offers limited (although some) usefulness in managing content, and it plays almost no part in publishing. Finally (and thankfully), full-text search doesn't require much effort to plan or maintain.

Full-text search relates to a CMS much the way that an external data system does. It's a separate system that you must integrate. It's a critical part of many publications that you need to take into account and add to templates. It may prove important, too, on the management side as a tool that staff can use to locate components of interest. An editor, for example, may want to find any component that mentions an out-of-date name for a product. For your audiences, of course, full-text search may be very important as a navigation mechanism.

Perhaps the largest effect that full-text search has on a CMS is that it often works best (or even only) if your text is in flat text files. Text that's inside databases is hard for a full-text search program to find and index. An indexing program also has trouble determining what title to give to a piece of database content and how to display it.

Analyzing Access Structures

In the sections that follow, I present a set of methods that you can use to analyze your needs for each kind of access structure and design your CMS repository and publications accordingly. I present a unified set of questions that help you think through your need for access structures. Then I include a planning section for each kind of access structure. Finally, the questions in the section "Integrate," at the end of this chapter address all the access structures at once.

Think

Before beginning to put together the access structures for your management system and publications, consider the following issues:

✦ **Dominant publications:** Do you have one publication (a Web site, perhaps) with structures that tend to dominate the structure of the entire system? If so, to what extent should you try to structure your repository to make it independent of this publication?

✦ **Management versus publication:** Along what lines do you want to collect content (departments, types, or some other parameter)? Along what lines do you most want to manage content? How does this scheme contrast with the way that audiences want to access your content? Can you find a way to serve both interests at the same time? Or do you need to create separate structures for management and publishing?

✦ **Audiences:** What's the dominant mode of access for each of your audience types? Do some prefer outlines whereas others prefer indexes? What sort of vocabulary does each understand, expect, or reject? How do you serve the needs of each audience in each publication?

✦ **Publications:** What are the conventions and driving constraints of each publication regarding access? Is it necessary to include some methods and optional to include others? Given a strong component model and abundant access metadata, can you offer more access options than the minimum or usual ones in any of your publications?

✦ **Full-text search:** How can you use full-text search in your repository and in your publications? How important is it relative to the access structures? When do you expect users to search and when are they likely to browse by using the access structures? Can full-text search replace any of the other structures?

Plan

In the sections that follow, I present some of the questions that you can ask and issues to confront to decide what access structures to create and how to create them.

The content domain

Following are some questions that you can ask of your sponsors, publication staff, and audience members to begin to get a handle on your content domain:

✦ **Purpose:** Why is this information important? What can people use it for and how does that use relate to the project mandate? Which goals does the information serve and how? What concepts unify this content?

✦ **Scope:** What's the scope of this information? How far does it go and what does it contain? What's the next biggest realm past what we need to do with our content? What are the realms within our information?

✦ **Parts:** What parts (logical, not elements) does this information contain? Can we break it down into a few broad categories?

✦ **Functionality:** What actions or capabilities is someone likely to need inside this realm of information? On what information do the actions depend? What information does this realm affect?

✦ **Boundary:** Given a chunk of content, how do we determine whether it's inside or outside of our province? Can you give me three sentences on what's within and what's outside our concern?

After you're satisfied with the answers that you receive to these questions, use them to address the following design constraints:

✦ **Domain statements:** Can you fully summarize and capture the nature of the content domain that you intend to create in a few sentences?

✦ **Boundary:** Are there a few questions that clearly put a piece of content within or outside the domain?

✦ **Communication:** How can you tell all staff and other interested parties what your domain is?

✦ **Enforcement:** How can you stem the submission of content that's outside the domain?

✦ **Change:** Who's responsible for approving the initial definition of the domain? Who can suggest changes? Who must approve these changes?

Audience and access

Your audience ought to help determine the kinds of access mechanisms that you give them in your publications. Fill in the following design constraints for each audience that you intend to serve:

✦ **Audience:** Enter the name and Id of this audience.

✦ **Domain:** What parts of the domain are of most interest to this audience? Are some parts of no concern?

✦ **Understanding:** Rate the people from this audience on their general understanding of the vocabulary and concepts in the domain. If they're less than fluent, what can you do to assist them?

✦ **Desires and assumptions:** What's the dominant way that people from this audience find information? Do they require or expect certain navigation techniques? Are they unlikely to know how to use some techniques?

✦ **Personalization:** Given the domain, understanding, and desires of this audience, how can you personalize the navigation that its members see in their publications?

✦ **Access studies:** Can you do studies with the key members of this audience to see exactly how they navigate through publications like yours?

Hierarchy

Following are some questions that you can ask of contributors and subject matter experts to get the input that you need to design your hierarchies:

✦ **Source hierarchies:** Do you have a proposed outline for the content that you're planning to contribute? Do the documents you intend to contribute have a table of contents now? If you're contributing multiple documents, does any outline show how the documents all fit together? Has anyone ever cataloged these documents? How well-organized is the directory structure in which you store these files?

✦ **Summary:** Can you provide three to six categories that sum up the content that you expect to provide? What are the major ideas?

✦ **User perspective:** What are the top three to six questions someone may have about this body of content? What can the user do with this information after she understands it? What does she most need to know?

Use the answers to these questions, the information throughout this book, and whatever other analysis you have done to determine the following hierarchy design constraints:

✦ **Collection hierarchy:** What outline of categories best helps you collect the information in your content domain?

✦ **Management hierarchy:** What outline of categories best helps you track and manage the information in your content domain?

✦ **Publication hierarchies:** What are the different hierarchies that you need for your various publications?

✦ **Repository hierarchy:** How do you integrate your collection and management hierarchies into a unified system for organizing content in your CMS repository? Do you combine them into a single hierarchy, map from one to the other, or try to maintain two separate hierarchies?

✦ **Mapping to publications:** In general, how can you map from the repository hierarchy to the publication hierarchies that you need? (You catalog this one specifically in the next step.)

Given this so-far general approach, you can dive into a more detailed design for your various hierarchies. Before you do, you may want to study the various approaches to hierarchies in relational and XML databases that I present in Chapter 39, "Building Management Systems," in the section "General storage requirements." After you're ready, decide on the following design constraints for the publication hierarchies that you need to create:

✦ **Hierarchy name:** Define a name for one publication hierarchy that you intend to create. Notice that each hierarchy is likely to become a navigation template, so refer to the templates that you have already designed to keep the naming consistent.

✦ **Mapping:** Describe your approach to this hierarchy. Can you try to derive this hierarchy from the repository hierarchy or must you store a separate outline in the repository from which to create this hierarchy? What other metadata must you access in order to build this hierarchy automatically?

✦ **Personalizations:** Review your audience analysis in the preceding section "Audience and access," and then describe here the kinds of personalizations that you need to perform for this hierarchy. Make sure that you compare and synthesize these issues with the ones that you enter in your personalization design (as I describe in Chapter 32, "Designing Personalization," in the section "Analyzing Personalization").

✦ **Localization:** Review your localization strategy (as I outline in Chapter 25, "Cataloging Audiences"). Can you localize this hierarchy? If so, what provisions must you make to create and store a localized version of this structure?

✦ **Symmetry:** Can you create symmetry in the branches of the hierarchy? Can each major heading, for example, use the same set of standard subheadings? Can you develop other symmetries in the way that you name headings or in the number of subheads in each category?

✦ **Redundancy:** Can the same publication page or section appear more than once in this hierarchy? PLAN, for example, may need to decide whether the same press release can appear in both Hot News and Recent News. If you permit such redundancy, how do you communicate to the reader that duplicates lines may exist in the outline?

✦ **Templates:** Which navigation, component, and/or page publication templates does this hierarchy appear in? Make sure that the templates in which the hierarchy appears have the logic to support its display.

✦ **Components:** What content types participate in this hierarchy? Does the hierarchy serve only one kind of content type or more?

✦ **Publications:** What publication or publications does this hierarchy appear in?

After completing the preceding exercise for all your publication hierarchies, compare and contrast the hierarchies. Do you need all of them? Do any conflict? Are more suggested? Can you use the same code to produce more than one of them? Does more than one hierarchy list the same content types? If so, does this duplication cause any confusion?

Indexes

Following are some questions that you can ask of contributors and subject-matter experts to get the input that you need to design your indexes:

✦ **Existing indexes:** Does this information have any existing indexes? Do any academic or industry indexes cover the same material? Do any dictionaries or glossaries cover this material?

✦ **Vocabulary:** What the key terms do you use in this information? Can you go through a few samples and highlight important phrases? What terminology do people need to know before they can understand this information?

✦ **Concepts:** What are the main concepts that you cover in this material? What three phrases summarize the critical points of this material?

✦ **Audiences:** How much of the vocabulary and concepts are probably strange to each type of audience? If the words are strange, what words do these audiences more naturally use or already know?

✦ **Metadata:** Which of these types of information (dates, author names, component types, and so on) do people want to see this information listed by? How important are these lists relative to the main outline of the information.

After you collect enough input, address the following design constraints that list the indexes that you need:

Before you address the following constraints for indexes, you may want to study the various approaches to indexes in relational and XML databases that I present in Chapter 39, "Building Management Systems," in the section "General storage requirements." You may also want to enlist the help of a database analyst if you're not very familiar with database technology.

✦ **Primary index:** Must you create an index of all content in your repository? If so, how should you store the index? Does each component have an element for storing keywords or do you have a central index structure that references all components?

✦ **Metadata indexes:** List the metadata indexes that you need in the repository to find and access content for management purposes. Can you create database indexes to help facilitate the process?

✦ **Publication indexes:** List the indexes that you need to create for the different publications that your CMS produces.

✦ **Approach:** How, in general, can you create indexes in your publications? Are they directly derivable from your central repository index and metadata values? Must you create any extra structure in the repository to support your indexes?

After you're comfortable with your answers to the preceding questions, address the following design constraints to specify the details of each of your indexes:

✦ **Index name:** Name each index that you intend to create. Notice that each publication index is likely to become a navigation template, so refer to the templates that you have already designed and keep the naming consistent.

✦ **Mapping:** If you're deriving this index from the central repository index, what logic do you need to create it?

✦ **Metadata:** What metadata stored in the repository as component elements do you need to construct this index?

✦ **Personalizations:** Review your audience analysis in the section "Audience and access," earlier in this chapter, and then describe the kinds of personalizations that you need to perform for this index. Make sure that you compare and synthesize these issues with the ones that you determine in your personalization design (as I describe in Chapter 32, "Designing Personalization," in the section "Analyzing Personalization").

✦ **Localization:** Review your localization strategy (as I outline in Chapter 25, "Cataloging Audiences," in the section "Audiences and Localization"). Do you intend to localize this index? If so, what provisions can you make to create and store a localized version of this structure?

✦ **Exclusions:** Should each completed publication contain all the metadata in the repository or all the entries in the central index? If not, how do you make sure that terms that don't belong aren't published?

✦ **Templates:** In which navigation, component, and/or page publication templates does this index appear? Make sure that the templates in which the index appears have the logic to support its display.

✦ **Components:** What content types participate in this index?

✦ **Publications:** In which publications does this index appear?

Compare and contrast the various indexes that you intend to provide. Do they all make sense? If some appear together, do they conflict? Are any others suggested?

Cross-references

The following are some questions for you to ask contributors and subject-matter experts to get the input that you need to design your cross-reference strategy:

✦ **Logical next subjects:** What is each content item (*components* to you) related to, knowing what you know about the other items? What logical next subjects does a user want to see?

✦ **Pathways:** Are any pathways through your information not covered by the hierarchy? What logical sequences (as I outline in the section "Indexing considerations," earlier in this chapter) make sense for this information?

✦ **User interface:** How do users want to see indexes? Which indexes are best suited to list-box format or similarly abbreviated user interfaces? Which deserve their own complete presentations?

✦ **External links:** What other content domains should you be aware of? What sources of content do the audiences expect you to be aware of? Which do they expect you to consistently link to?

After you're comfortable with the answers that you receive to these questions, prepare a table that addresses the following design constraints for the cross-reference strategy that you intend to pursue:

> **Note**
>
> Before you do the following analysis, you may want to study the various approaches to cross-references in relational and XML databases that I present in Chapter 39, "Building Management Systems," in the section "General storage requirements."

✦ **Primary cross-references:** How can you make sure that the usual internal "see also" and "for more information" cross-references that you provide apply evenly across the content? How can you ensure that cross-referencers are aware of the full range of content in your domain?

✦ **Secondary cross-references:** Name and list the kinds of cross-referencing strategies that you intend to employ other than the standard internal links. Look in the section "Indexing considerations," earlier in this chapter, for some ideas about the kinds of secondary strategies that you can use.

✦ **Storage:** How can you store cross-references in your repository so that they most easily translate to all the forms that you need for your various publications? Cross-references in HTML, for example, may require more stored information than similar cross-references destined for print. Should you store only references between components or must you somehow store page or section links?

✦ **Authoring:** What cross-referencing do you expect authors to supply? What tools can you give them? See Chapter 38, "Building Collection Systems," in the section "Cross-references," for an example of one such tool.

After you're comfortable with the strategies that you create, create a table that addresses the following design constraints for each cross-referencing strategy that you intend to use. The columns of the table are as follows:

✦ **Strategy name:** Give a name to each cross-referencing strategy that you intend to pursue. The first strategy should be the standard "see also" and "for more information" links that you create.

✦ **Type:** Enter *Internal* if these are links to other components, pages, or sections in your domain. Enter *External* if they're to other domains (Web sites or other publications that you don't create). Enter *Citation* if the links are part of a scheme to officially link to another publication. Notice that your strategy may apply to any of or all these types.

✦ **Mapping:** How do you translate the cross-reference as it appears in the repository into a form that's useful in the target publications? How do you translate links between components, for example, into links between publication pages (for Web sites) or sections (for print publications)?

✦ **Personalization:** Review your audience analysis in the section "Audiences and access," earlier in this chapter, and then fill this column in with the kinds of personalizations that you need to perform for this type of cross-reference. Make sure that you compare and synthesize these issues with the ones that you determine in your personalization design (as I describe in Chapter 32, "Designing Personalization," in the section "Analyzing Personalization").

✦ **Localization:** Review your localization strategy (as I outline in Chapter 25, "Cataloging Audiences," in the section "Audiences and Localization"). Can you localize cross-references of this type? If so, what provisions can you make to create and store localized cross-references?

✦ **Conventions:** How do you format and display cross-references of this type? What can you use to show the user what type of link it is (icons, text, and so on)? How can you format the reference to differentiate it from its surroundings? Do you show the referent URL in a Web publication or simply put in a link? How do you tell the user where she ends up if she follows this link? Does clicking the link load the next page into the same window or a new one? How do you ensure that the user knows how to get back to what she was originally viewing if she wants to?

✦ **Link level:** At what level of the reference and referent components should you make links? Is the referent always an entire component or is linking to an element or even to a place within an element possible or appropriate? Similarly, can references appear in-line within the text and media of an element? Should they exist at the level of an element or at the level of an entire component? Consider what's most effective in your repository but also what yields the best transformation to your various publications.

✦ **Agreement:** If this cross-referencing strategy is to consistently cite another publication, what agreement do you have with the other publication that ensures that its content is always available and relevant?

✦ **In-line:** Do you make links of this type in-line, place them next to the content that they most closely relate to, or roll them up together in one spot? A "for more information" link, for example, is best if it's close to the spot in the text that it refers to. "See also" references may be better set apart from the text in a sidebar or at the end of the page or section.

✦ **Validation:** How do you validate the continued existence of the referents of your links? For internal cross-references, can the system tell you before you delete a component that others link to it? For external links, how often do you validate to make sure that the referents are still there?

✦ **Templates:** Which navigation, component, and/or page publication templates is this cross-reference strategy present in? Make sure that the templates in which these types of cross-references appear have the logic to support their display.

✦ **Content types:** What content types participate in this cross-reference strategy? Does it concern a single type, or do components from various content types participate in the strategy?

✦ **Publications:** What publications does this cross-reference strategy appear in?

Compare and contrast the various cross-reference strategies that you provide. Do they all make sense? If some appear together, do they conflict? Are any others suggested?

Sequences

For each sequence, including the primary sequence that you intend to create, decide the following design criteria:

✦ **Sequence name:** Give the sequence a name by which you can remember and discuss it.

✦ **Type:** What defines the logic of the sequence? Is it a next and previous topic, for example, based on date, author, subject, and so on? Is this sequence a primary sequence that follows a hierarchy in the publication?

✦ **Components:** What content types participate in this sequence? Is it a sequence of a single type, or do components from various content types participate in the sequence? As you move from one type to the next, do you need cues so the user doesn't get confused?

✦ **Interaction:** Does this sequence coexist with other sequences on the same publication page or section? If so, how can you differentiate it from the others? Do sequences ever collide with the purpose or presentation of publication hierarchies or cross-reference strategies?

✦ **Personalization:** Review your audience analysis in the section "Audiences and access," earlier in this chapter, and then describe the kinds of personalizations that you need to perform for this type of sequence. Make sure that you compare and synthesize these issues with the ones that you determine in your personalization design (as I describe in Chapter 32, "Designing Personalization," in the section "Publications and Personalization").

✦ **Storage:** What's the most appropriate way to store the data for this sequence? As metadata in a component or as a separate structure that references components?

✦ **Presentation:** How do you format this sequence on each publication page or section on which you publish it? How do you map from component sequences in the CMS repository to page or section sequences in your publications?

✦ **Templates:** Which navigation, component, and/or page publication templates is this sequence present in? Make sure that the templates in which the sequence appears have the logic to support its display.

✦ **Validation:** How do you ensure that the components that the sequence references continue to exist or that you will receive notification if they change or someone deletes them?

✦ **Publications:** Which publications does this sequence appear in?

Compare and contrast the various sequences that you intend to provide. Do they all make sense? If some appear together, do they conflict? Are any others suggested?

Full-text search

For each publication that you intend to make accessible through full-text search — and for your CMS repository if you intend to use full-text search there — determine the following design constraints:

✦ **Publication:** In what publications (or CMS repository) do you intend to include this full-text search feature?

✦ **Search logic:** What search logic do you expose in the publication? Are you simply providing a free text box for any word or phrase, for example, or are you including Booleans such as AND, OR, and NOT? Do you want to have an implied AND or an implied OR between words? Do you require the user to surround phrases with quotation marks? How do you plan to communicate the search logic options to the end users?

✦ **Interaction with indexes:** Is this full-text search function in the same publication as any indexes? If so, how do you distinguish the two in the mind of the users? Do they appear together in the same page? Do you combine them into one overall search operation? What do the audiences expect to happen if they use an index versus a full-text search ?

✦ **Personalization:** Review your audience analysis in the section "Audiences and access," earlier in this chapter, and then decide what your audience expects and needs from a full-text search. Make sure that you compare and synthesize these issues with the ones that you determine in your personalization design (as I describe in Chapter 32, "Designing Personalization," in the section "Publications and Personalization").

✦ **Free-text and database content:** Do you need to search only against files or does the full-text search in this publication also access database content? If it accesses a database, what fields does it need to search and how do you expect to format results from the fields in which it finds matches?

✦ **Templates:** Which navigation, component, and/or page publication templates is the full-text search feature present in? Make sure that the templates in which full-text search appears have the logic to support its display.

Publication navigation

To get an overall view of your navigation for each publication, fill in the following table, which combines your analysis of the various access structures.

Publication	Hierarchies	Indexes	Cross-references	Sequences	Full-Text Search
CMS Repository					

Enter the following data for the CMS repository in the first line and for each publication in the lines that follow:

✦ **Publication:** Enter the name and Id of a publication.

✦ **Hierarchies:** Enter the names of all the hierarchies that this publication shows.

✦ **Indexes:** Enter the names of all the indexes that this publication shows.

✦ **Cross-references:** Enter the names of all the cross-reference strategies that this publication shows.

✦ **Sequences:** Enter the names of all the sequences that this publication shows.

✦ **Full-text search:** Enter an *X* if this publication has full-text search.

Spend some time deciding whether you really need all the structures that you have in each publication and whether you have structures in one publication that you can use in another. Finally, compare the structures in the repository to those in each publication to make sure that you can map from one to the other.

The content model

At this point in your analysis, you have the information that you need to draw together all your component and access information into a comprehensive *content model*.

A content model specifies the following information:

✦ The name of each content type.

✦ The permitted elements of each content type.

✦ The element type and permitted values for each element (as I describe in Chapter 27, "Designing Content Types," in the section "Content Types Have Elements").

✦ The access structures in which each content type participates.

✦ The rules for establishing relationships between components.

To begin, look at your access structures as they relate to components by filling in the following table.

Content Type	Hierarchies	Indexes	Cross-references	Sequences

Enter the following information:

✦ **Content type:** Enter the name and Id of a content type.

✦ **Hierarchies:** Enter the names of all the hierarchies that this content type participates in.

✦ **Indexes:** Enter the names of all the indexes that this content type participates in.

✦ **Cross-references:** Enter the names of all the cross-reference strategies that this content type participates in.

✦ **Sequences:** Enter the names of all the sequences that this content type participates in.

Review this table and contrast the structures for one content type versus another. After you're satisfied that you have a consistent and comprehensive approach to your component access, combine this table with the component and component element tables that you derived earlier. This result is your content model.

 Cross-Reference I describe the content type and component element tables in Chapter 27, "Designing Content Types," in the section "Plan." In Chapter 39, "Building Management Systems," in the sections "Relational database systems" and "Object databases," I describe how to go from this content model to a database or XML schema.

Tasks

Consider the effect of your access structure analysis on the ongoing maintenance of the CMS. Then fill in the following table to define any tasks that you can imagine that must happen on a recurring basis to run the CMS. Following are some task types to get you thinking:

✦ Positioning new components in their access structures.

✦ Periodic cross-reference review to see whether any new links are necessary.

✦ Link validation.

✦ Ongoing access effectiveness testing.

✦ Full-text search re-indexing.

✦ Index reviews to ensure that new content is correctly categorized.

- ✦ Index term reviews to ensure that you still have the correct set of terms.

- ✦ Sequence link checks.

- ✦ External link checks.

- ✦ Orphaned component checks (that is, components that aren't included in any access structures).

- ✦ Search hit analyses to see what people are searching for and what's being returned from their searches.

- ✦ Hierarchy category reviews.

- ✦ Staff training for access tagging.

- ✦ Quality-control cycles.

Use the preceding information to fill in the following table.

Task Name	Who	What	When	How much	How
Orphaned Components	CMS Administrator	Run script	Once per week	One time	Using the custom script that we write

Enter the following information:

- ✦ **Task name:** Give the task a short but memorable name that describes it. In the preceding table, I fill in a task that I name "Orphaned Components."

- ✦ **Who:** Indicate what person or role is responsible for accomplishing this task. Naming an automated process here instead of a person is acceptable.

- ✦ **What:** List what person or process should accomplish the task.

- ✦ **When:** Specify at what frequency you need to accomplish this task or how you know when it must occur.

- ✦ **How much:** Describe how much or how many of this sort of task you expect to do. A numerical quantity is preferable here, but if you can't come up with one, words such as *a lot*, *not much*, and so on suffice.

- ✦ **How:** Detail the skills, tools, or processes the person or process needs to accomplish this task.

Don't worry if the tasks that you devise at this point are somewhat ill-defined or sketchy. In your workflow analysis (in Chapter 33, "Designing Workflow and Staffing Models"), you have ample opportunity to refine them.

Integrate

To help integrate the design work that you do in this chapter with the rest of your logical design, consider the following issues:

✦ **The content model:** Look over your combined component and access model. Do any changes to the structure of components or access methods present themselves? Do you have the component elements that you need to populate your access structures? Conversely, are your components all maximally available if this set of access structures serves them?

✦ **Personalization and localization:** Are your access structure personalizations and localizations feasible given that you may get little support from a CMS product that you purchase? Begin now to try to figure out how you can implement them.

✦ **Audience:** Can you get someone from each audience to validate your approach to publication navigation? Can you create a prototype that shows the navigation that you propose and test its usability?

✦ **Staff:** Do your access structures really serve the needs of your contribution and administration staff? What structures does your staff depend most on? Which may they ignore? Can you do some usability testing with your staff as well as with your audiences?

✦ **Sources and authors:** How much of the work of placing new components into access structures can you count on your authors to do? What clues about placement in access structure can you automatically derive from your acquisition sources? Can you afford to make up the difference with metators on your own staff?

✦ **Publications:** Compare the access structures that you create in this chapter with the publication structures that you created earlier (as I outline in Chapter 26, "Designing Publications," in the section "Publication structure"). The access structures should be a superset of all the access methods that you include in your publications.

Summary

I've taken pains in this chapter to provide a complete account of access structures. In my experience, these structures are rarely studied, and are usually produced without much rigor or real analysis. I attribute this to the fact that access structures are so familiar that most people don't think of them as something requiring study. Especially among editorial and publishing types, these concepts were internalized long ago and may not have been reconsidered for a long time. As you work through your CMS, consider, even if only briefly, the following concepts:

✦ **Hierarchies:** What parent and child relationships are useful to unearth and track for your staff and audiences?

✦ **Indexes:** What vocabularies or conceptual maps can you create to help people go from a word or concept to its full presentation in your content?

✦ **Cross-references:** What strategies can you devise to move people from one piece of information to another that relates to it *in some way?*

✦ **Sequences:** What are the logical series of information chunks that you want to highlight for your users?

In the next chapter, I discuss what you need to do to design a templating system for your CMS.

✦　　✦　　✦

Designing Templates

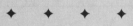
In a CMS, *templates* create publications. A template saves you from the manual labor of continually laying content into a particular structure and form. Imagine how cumbersome it would be to take the database records or XML elements in your CMS repository and turn them into Web or printed pages! By using a template, you decide once how you want to lay out and format content, and then you let the computer do the tedious task of building publication pages or sections.

Templating Jumpstart

This Jumpstart summarizes what you need to do to design templates for your publications.

Use this jumpstart as a quick review if you've already read this chapter — and in particular the section called "Analyzing Templates" — and you want a checklist of how to analyze templates.

At all stages of your template analysis, make sketches and tables as you follow these steps:

1. Think about the publications you will create. Decide how the content and design of each publication overlaps the others.

2. Think about your staff and processes, and how they'll have to change to make templating possible. In particular, editorial people need to have greater integration with the content collection process, and production people need to work on producing templates rather than final publications.

3. Decide how to go about your template analysis. If you intend to do a competitive template analysis, identify 5 to 10 Web sites of your competitors and other relevant organizations, which you'll use to derive a set of best practices. You can integrate the best practices that you discover there with the steps that follow.

4. Decide what content types your templates should represent. These types are the core set of pages you want to publish.

5. After you decide on your content types, decide how navigation between them should work.

6. Analyze the content and navigation you have decided upon to determine what is local and global, static and dynamic in your publications.

7. Make a wire frame drawing for each page that you want to produce, showing the dynamic and static content and the global and local navigation.

8. Summarize content areas across all your page types to determine what content will be shared and by which pages.

9. Summarize navigation across all your page types to determine what navigation will be shared and by which pages.

10. Summarize the components your pages need across all page types to determine which components are to be shared and by which pages.

11. Decide how you will approach localization — as a personalization or more comprehensively. For each of the templates that you intend to create, do a localization analysis including:

   • Localities for which you must localize

   • Graphic and design items to be localized

   • Content and navigation components to be localized

12. Do a task analysis to determine the impact of your template design on other parts of the CMS, and then determine what tasks are required to maintain your templates over time.

13. Integrate your template analysis with the other design aspects for your CMS. Consider the impact of the template design on other requirements, audiences, processes, authors, and publications.

When you've completed your template analysis, you'll have a detailed set of drawings and templates to hand off to your template developer.

Publications and Templates

Templates streamline the process of creating publications from the neutral content in a CMS. In particular, a template does the following:

✦ **Bridges between the world of the CMS and publications:** A template keeps one foot, so to speak, in the CMS and the other in the publication format and structure.

✦ **Mixes static and dynamic constituents:** A template separates the parts of a page or section that change from those that don't.

✦ **Builds a publication page or section:** Templates are programs that automatically create parts of a publication.

✦ **Draws the publication into a system of publications:** Templates share code and content to create multiple presentations of the same base of information and functionality.

✦ **Uses logic:** Templates enable you to select content from your CMS (either in the form of standard programming languages or custom syntax), process it, and format it for display.

✦ **Hosts other templates:** Templates can nest within other templates to whatever degree you want. They help you stay organized and save on duplicated effort. You can think of each content and navigation area of a page or section as having its own template.

Bridging worlds

A *template* bridges the gap between the content in the CMS and the publication format and structure. Content in the CMS repository is neutral. It offers a lot of possibility but has no reality. Content in a publication is anything but neutral. It's fully immersed in the conventions and context of the publication. In between these two states of the content stands the template. To make the transition, the template must "understand" both the world of the publication and that of the CMS.

In addition, the template must bridge the distance between these two worlds and the worlds of any external systems that the publication must link to (transaction systems, catalog systems, and so on).

To work in the world of the repository, the template must do the following:

✦ **Query the CMS repository:** The most fundamental thing that a template does is to draw content out of the CMS repository. To get at content, the template must make a query against the repository and receive the results. The query that you type in a template may or may not look like a database query (because sometimes the query is implicit in another command you type), but the result is the same. You make a query against the repository and the repository passes the components or other data that match the query to the template for further processing.

✦ **Use the content schema:** The template must be aware of the kinds of content components that the repository contains and what their elements are. Suppose, for example, that a publication page calls for creating a table where each row is a competitor (a kind of component) and each column contains information about the competitor (component elements such as name, address, product focus, and so on). To accomplish this table, the template that builds it must know the names of both the component and of all the other elements that it needs to list.

✦ **Use the access structures:** To build the navigation of a publication, a template must work with the access structures that the CMS repository stores. Suppose, for example, that a TOC table in the CMS repository database has Id, Title, Level, and Order as its columns. To use this table to create a table of contents for a publication, the template must access and query this table, but it must also know how to turn the data (Id, Title, Level, and Order) into the visual representation of the table of contents outline. On a Web site, the template creates an expanding and collapsing outline where the Level and the Order data control the indentation and order, and the Title and Id data turn into a link (`<A href="ID">Title</a>`). In print, the Level data may turn into a paragraph style, and the template may use the Id to somehow calculate a page number to insert (not an easy task). In all cases, the template must be aware of how access structures are stored and what meaning to attach to each element of the access structure.

✦ **Store data:** The template must send back user requests and data in a format that the CMS can understand. A template might, for example, have the responsibility of gathering the responses that a user makes to a series of questions and storing them in the CMS user profile table. To do so, the template must know how to access the user profile table in the CMS and store data there in the appropriate way.

✦ **Call the CMS services:** In addition to working with the data that the CMS stores, a template must be able to use any of a range of functions and commands that a CMS provides. The CMS may, for example, include a personalization engine that runs on a Web site and has special commands for use in a template. The template must be capable of using these commands and also of using whatever data or content the personalization system passes back in response to the command.

To work in the world of the publication, the template must do the following:

✦ **Create the context of the publication:** The look-and-feel of a publication is created entirely by the template. This look-and-feel includes the colors and overall layout of the publication, the imagery that goes behind and around the content, the branding and titles within the publication, the fonts and other text styles, and a host of other qualities that, together, give the content of a publication a very particular and meaningful context. In a CMS, this stuff is stored separately from the content of the publication. Most of it you design into the template. Some of it you can store as separate components in the CMS repository. It's still separate from the content of the publication; you simply use the management functions of the CMS to keep track of it.

✦ **Produce the formatting of the publication:** On the Web, this requirement means producing HTML. In print, it means any of a number of proprietary markup languages. The template must translate the format-neutral content of the repository to format-rich content in the publication. A simple Sidebar element (which you represent as `<SIDEBAR></SIDEBAR>` in an XML repository), for example, may give rise to a lengthy and complex set of formatting codes that position the text between the tags in the publication margin and surround it with a box that has a drop shadow.

✦ **Produce the structures of the publication:** The template must exactly reproduce the structure conventions of the publication. The repository may store a cross-reference structure, for example, as an Id that you can simply embed at some point in the text of an element. (In XML, it may look like `<XREF ID="1234">`.) A print publication template must turn that Id into a recognizable print cross-reference (such as "For more information, see the section 'Some Section,' in Chapter 3.").

✦ **Target the audiences of the publication:** In the case of personalization, the template must detect audiences and produce publication pages and sections for them. A Web page template for example may contain code that detects whether a child is accessing pages. The template can then use code that changes the look-and-feel of the site accordingly and displays only content that you tag as appropriate for children.

Finally, to tie the publication into the worlds of any external systems, templates must do the following:

✦ **Connect:** They must have the appropriate programming code for accessing the external system. A credit card transaction system, for example, may require a complex and highly secure logon routine for the template to connect to it at all.

✦ **Query:** The template must "know" how to get data out of the external system. The credit card system in the preceding paragraph, for example, may use the common Structured Query Language (SQL) for data access after the template connects to it.

✦ **Send data back:** The template must follow whatever conventions the external system requires for receiving data from the publication. The credit card system, for example, may require that the template send it a transaction data set (product number, amount, company name, and so on) in a text string delimited by commas.

You can see that a lot's going on in a publication template. For each of the items that I list in this section, you may need to master an entire language and discipline. Bridging such different worlds is no small task.

Mixing the static and the dynamic

The simplest way to explain what a template does is to compare it to the common technique of mail merge. Most people I talk with are familiar with this function of most word processors that enables you to create form letters and other standard documents. In a form letter, you create a standard letter that you want to reproduce over and over again for different recipients. You remove all the particulars from the document (such as the name and address of the recipient) and replace them with placeholders (see Figure 31-1).

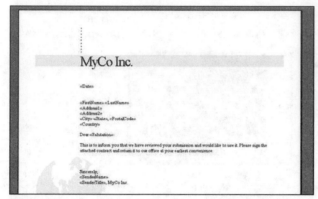

Figure 31-1: A mail-merge document in Microsoft Word

Somewhere else (for example, in another document, in a spreadsheet, or in a database), you list all the particulars for each recipient. As you perform the mail merge, the particulars merge with the standard document to create a set of letters, each of the same form, but each personalized to a particular recipient.

At first glance, CMS templates work the same way. You create a standard form that all pages or sections should follow. Next, you remove all the particulars of the page or section and replace them with placeholders. Later, the CMS replaces the placeholders with the particulars to create a set of pages or sections for your publication.

The standard form is static. It doesn't change from page to page. The particulars are dynamic. They do change from page to page. In a typical publication page that a CMS builds, you find a number of static and dynamic areas. The dynamic areas are of two types: *navigation* and *content*.

Consider, for example, the PLAN press-release page that divides into static and dynamic areas, as shown in Figure 31-2. (I have made some changes to the navigation structure in this and following figures to better illustrate my points.)

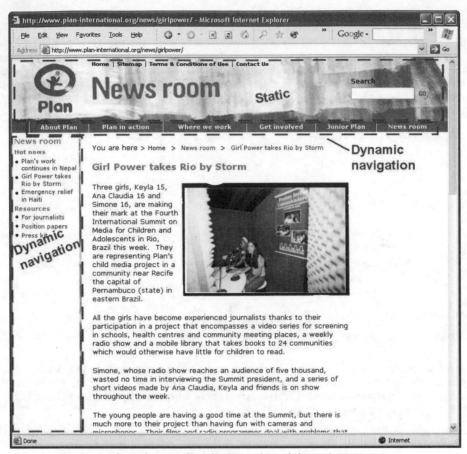

Figure 31-2: A sample Web page that shows static and dynamic areas

The PLAN CMS uses a publishing template to compose any number of press-release pages that look similar to this one. The template creates the following elements:

✦ **The overall context of the page:** This context includes the background color and other look-and-feel elements that the static HTML in the template creates. Each area of the page is positioned and sized by a template for the page.

✦ **Static text and media areas of the page:** The area marked *static* in the preceding figure is considered *boilerplate* material, meaning that its contents don't change from page to page. Some areas are static across the entire site. The logo in the upper-left corner, for example, may appear on every page. Others areas are the same only on every press-release page. The static area displaying the words *News room*, for example, appears in the same location on all news room pages, but doesn't appear on other types of pages. You needn't create static content more than once. You can then automatically include the same static content in any page that uses it. Even without a CMS, you can use stock Web-server features such as an SSI (server-side include) and image references (<IMG> tags). You never have to enter static content twice or save it in multiple places. Using the CMS and its templates, you can get pretty fancy about including static content in your published pages.

✦ **Dynamic navigation areas:** The areas marked *dynamic navigation* take you to other parts of the site. Navigation templates, which you embed within the overall template for the page, create these Navigation areas. This nesting enables you to include the same navigation structures on a variety of pages. The button-bar area in the preceding figure, for example, appears on every page of the site. The News navigation on the left side of the page appears only on press-release pages. You needn't create and update these navigation areas by hand. As you add new sections to the site, change existing ones, or add new press releases, your CMS can take care of updating the navigation areas with the most current information.

✦ **Dynamic content areas:** The dynamic content area houses a news item component. On this page, the full news item appears in a particular format. Each page that uses this template shows a different news item. On other pages (the PLAN home page, for example), a subset of the full press release appears in a different format. You needn't retype or reformat the press release. Rather, your CMS can select just the right parts of the press release and format them appropriately for a particular page.

In the section "Web templating," later in this chapter, I pull back the facade to reveal the mechanics of templating.

Building pages

Most fundamentally, a template is a program that builds publication pages or sections. A template may be literally a program, or you may use it to trigger other programs. The variety of ways that a template builds pages is detailed in Chapter 40, "Building Publishing Systems," in the section "Templating System."

Creating a system of publications

Templates enable you to share content and code among a family of publications. To enable this sharing, you must do some groundwork in the following areas:

✦ **Content overlap:** You must decide how the content of each publication overlaps. You may decide, for example, for appropriate best practices to also appear as sidebars in the training documentation. You might designate appropriate case studies to appear in the newsletter in a shortened form.

✦ **Design overlap:** You must decide how the design of each publication overlaps. You may determine, for example, that all publications carry the organization logo in the upper-left corner. You might create a palette of colors and imagery that all publications must use.

✦ **Process change:** You must decide how the staff and processes of the current publication teams need to change. Using the CMS alters most of (if not all) the current jobs. Those responsible for the editorial content of the publication must work within the context of the entire collection process. The case studies to add to the newsletter, for example, may appear too infrequently to make every newsletter. Those responsible for the layout and production of the publication spend their time not in creating finished publications, but rather working to create templates that incorporate the organization's design standards and that can draw content in an appropriate fashion.

Tip

Process change is where the CMS really meets the organization. Current publication staffers are likely to resist the CMS if they perceive that their jobs are negatively affected. In particular, ask yourself whether the staff agrees to the basic principle that the CMS can automatically build publications from a computer system that encodes the organization's assumptions about audience, content, and design. If they have doubts at this level, you're not ready to go any farther. If this sort of doubt is present, you're best off confronting it directly.

Look at the way that PLAN International, for example, may choose to publish its press releases. Suppose that PLAN wants to publish press releases as follows:

✦ **A chronological listing** of all press releases on its Web site with full detail that anyone can use for reference.

✦ **A printed annual report** carrying the title "PLAN Activities" that it targets at board members and major contributors. In the report, it presents the press releases as the highlights of the year's accomplishments.

✦ **A set of printable press releases** that it can fax to news agencies.

✦ **Short e-mail messages** that it targets at members to keep them up to date on major events at PLAN.

PLAN can do a lot of copying and pasting to make this material all happen, or it can use a CMS to automate the production and update of all these publications from the same base of press release content. By using a set of templates, it can decide what the overlap of press release content is. Knowing that a single person may see more than one of its publications, PLAN can create a consistent design across all of them. Finally, knowing that different groups now create all these publications, it can decide how to coalesce the various efforts and staff into a single effort.

Note

I'm not describing how PLAN actually handles press releases, but rather how it could handle them. As always, I use PLAN as a starting place for useful examples that go beyond what I know of PLAN's actual efforts.

Using a template processor

A template is, generally, a text file. You can open it in any word processor and pick your way through its commands, find the static and dynamic areas, and try to decode it. The file itself isn't capable of actually building a page. Rather, it's a set of instructions on how to build a page. The thing that interprets the instructions and carries them out is known as the *template processor*.

Note

For the programmers in the audience, my concept of a template processor is simply that of an interpreter.

In an XML system, the template processor is often the XSLT software that loads and processes XSLT templates. Other Web-based systems use a standard Web template processor, such as Active Server Pages (ASP), JavaServer Pages (JSP), or ColdFusion. Other CMS products have their own processors that recognize their own template commands.

In all cases, a template processor does the following:

✦ **Loads templates:** The CMS or sometimes a Web server invokes the processor and tells it which template to process. The processor then retrieves the template file.

✦ **Skips static text and media:** The processor can detect which parts of the template don't need processing and passes them through without change.

✦ **Processes commands:** The template processor recognizes which parts of the template contain some sort of directive that it needs to carry out. The processor picks out these commands and the parameters they contain and does what they say to do. The command [Insert Title], for example, causes the processor to perform its insert function. The insert function may access the current component, find the noted element (in this case the Title element), and place the value of the element right at the command's location.

✦ **Calls external programs:** If the templating system is capable of invoking external programs, the processor is responsible for finding them, passing them any parameters, and receiving the result. The command <CustomCommand Name="SectName" File="Myfunct.dll" ID="1234"/>, for example, tells the template processor to call the SectName function in the function library in the file Myfunct.dll and pass it the parameter ID="1234". The SectName function does its work (in this case, finding the section that contains component 1234). The external program returns its result to the template processor, which can do what it wants with the result. In this example, the processor can insert the result into the page it's building.

✦ **Returns errors:** A processor must have some way of detecting and alerting the template programmer of a problem. Problems are most often commands that you type incorrectly. These sorts of problems are easy to detect, and all decent processors report them. Errors that are harder to detect include mistakes in the way that you use a command or the wider logic of which individual commands are a part. Only the best processors provide the sophisticated debugging tools that can help you find these more subtle errors.

✦ **Returns a resulting node:** After the processor finishes with a template, the result is always a built publication page or section with the static areas intact and the dynamic areas appropriately filled in. The result it either saves in a file for later release or, as in the case of a dynamic Web site, pushes directly back to the person who requests the node.

Note In all other discussions, I ignore the template processor and talk as if the template itself does the processing. This convention makes the text more understandable. It's close enough to the truth to make sense.

Understanding template logic

Templates use logic to specify the operations that they perform to build a page or section. In any particular templating system, this logic is created by a programming language that you use to specify commands and processes. To illuminate how templates work, however, you don't need to learn programming language; you only need a few simple programming concepts.

In my discussions of template logic, I boil the world of programming down to the following few constructs:

✦ [Insert _____] means insert the thing that you name at the location of the command. The command doesn't say how to find the thing or whether it's a component, an element of a component, or some other thing. For the purposes of understanding template logic, these fine points are unnecessary. The command [Insert Title], for example, means, "Insert the Title element of the current component here."

✦ [For Each _____][Next _____] means perform the operations that these two tags bracket multiple times. Never mind how the processor knows how many operations to perform or exactly what operation is referred to. That's for the programmers who create programs to figure out. Knowing that the same operations must work over a range of content is enough. The command [For Each Article] <H1>[Insert Title]</H1>[Next Article], for example, means, "Insert the title of each article component, surrounding it by first-level heading tags."

✦ [If _____] [End If] means do the operations that these two tags bracket only if the specified condition is true. Never mind how the processor can determine true from false. Knowing that certain actions are conditional and depend on others is enough for now. The command [If you have OtherNews components] <H2>Other News</H2>[End If], for example, means, "Put in the other news headings if you have any OtherNews components."

✦ [Run _____] means run the program that you mention. Others decide how to make this "real" programming. For now, specifying that you need to write and run some program at a certain point in a template is enough. The command [Run Credit Card Transaction], for example, means, "Run the credit card transaction program here."

All I need to illustrate the template logic that I describe is this very small set of pseudo-programming logic statements. If you need others to describe your templates, make some up. There's nothing's special about the way I create these examples. They simply give you the language to state what you want to happen in a way that's easy to read and that you can later turn into programming code.

Using templates within templates

You have the following two main reasons for using page templates:

✦ **To modularize the production of a publication node:** You can always build a Web page of a certain type, for example, from the same combination of static and dynamic areas, and so you package the process in a template and apply it to a set of pages.

✦ **To standardize the presentation of a particular type of node:** By using a template, you're sure that nodes of a certain type always look a certain way. Moreover, you can change the presentation of the all nodes with a single change to the template.

You have no compelling reason, however, to stop at the level of the page. Web pages have dynamic areas. You can pack these areas into a template and reuse them as necessary whenever you need to produce that particular dynamic area. The benefits of templates can apply to parts of a page or to whole pages.

A dynamic navigation area, for example, may prove useful. It might be used to create an expanding and collapsing TOC that lists all sections down to a specified level of the site's TOC. The area may contain the words *Table of Contents* with a set of static links to an index and full-text search facility above the words and the expandable outline below them. As you're designing your site templates, instead of repeating the definition of this area over and over, you can call it the TOC Navigation template, define it once, and reference it wherever you need it in other templates.

In using the TOC Navigation template, you modularize your approach to the site TOC; you standardize its presentation; and you make it easy to globally update.

As you see in the following section, "Web templating," I apply the same concept to content areas. In fact, as strange as it may seem at first, the same concept applies to static areas. Any area that follows a specific pattern and is worth naming you can think of as a template, as the following list describes:

✦ **Page templates** name a certain type of publication page and say what static and dynamic areas it contains.

✦ **Navigation templates** name a certain type of navigation area and say what static and dynamic areas it contains.

✦ **Component templates** name a certain type of content area and say what static and dynamic areas it contains.

Note

By the way, no hard and fast line exists between content and navigation areas or templates. Navigation templates can have lots of content in them, and content templates can feature links and other navigation devices. I make the distinction mostly so that you differentiate in your own mind and in your design between the area that you expect to use *mostly* for navigation or *mostly* for content.

You can break your pages down this way literally or figuratively. To literally nest one template within another, you can use XSLT (as described Chapter 40, "Building Publishing Systems," in the section "Templating System"). If you don't have XSLT, you can put all your subtemplates into include files, for example, and have the processor automatically add them to the page template as it loads. You can also store your templates in functionality components and have the CMS publish them into a page by using a template command such as [Insert Subtemplate].

Note

If you want to include a template by using an [Insert] command, make sure that your CMS is capable of both inserting a template and processing it at the same time. In other words, the CMS needs to process the template in two steps. In step one, the CMS inserts the template that you tell it to. In step two, it runs the template that it inserted. Most CMS systems don't support this two-step approach.

Whether or not you literally create subtemplates, using the concept is useful as you design your templating system. As you see in the following section, "Web templating," you can effectively and completely analyze a publication page or section by breaking it down into navigation and component templates.

You can, in turn, further break down subtemplates into sub-subtemplates if the complexity of the navigation or component template requires it. The PLAN page in the following figure, for example, has a content area that it calls "News Room." Inside the News Room area is another content area that it calls "News Items" (see Figure 31-3).

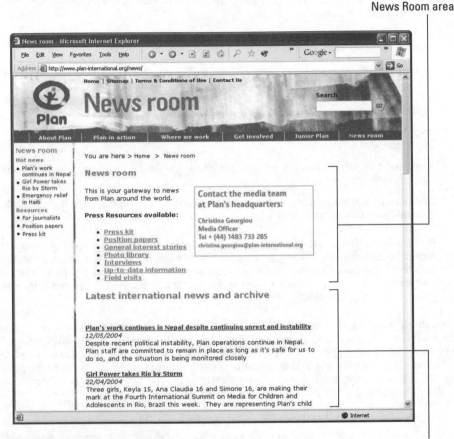

Figure 31-3: A page that uses a subtemplate and a sub-subtemplate

The News Room area is a section of the page that is devoted to the news. The site designers decide how much space it gets on the screen and how it is positioned relative to the other screen areas. It has a title, "News room," a short description, the contact information, navigation to other press resources, and another title, "Latest international news and archive." Within the News Room area is embedded the News Items area. The site designers decide how much space within the News Room area to devote to news items and how the items will lay out.

To build this page, you embed a template that you call News Room inside a page template. Inside the News Room page, however, you embed another template that you call News Items. The News Items template builds a news item each time that the News Room template triggers it. The News Room template builds the larger section of the page after the page template triggers it. The important points to take away from this example are:

✦ The News Item template operates independently from its parent, the News Room template. In other words, you could put the News Item template outside the News Room template, or on another page without using the News Room template at all.

✦ Likewise, the News Room template operates independently of the page template it is placed within.

✦ By embedding one template within another, you create a system of templates that makes maximum reuse of a small number of templates.

Creating template systems is not an easy chore, and they tend to have predictable life cycles. First, you work hard to create the smallest number of templates that can be used most widely to render your content. Despite your hard work, you'll constantly be tempted to create "one-off" templates that are very close to others by just make a few critical layout or content selection changes. After taking this expedient route, you constantly need to remember to make the subsequent changes to a growing family of related templates. As you make more and more of these one-off changes, keeping track of them all becomes too much of a burden. At that point, you work hard to combine the family of templates into one template that handles the range of related presentations. This cycle goes on forever, as new needs for presenting content drive your system apart, and new rounds of consolidation bring it back together again.

Web templating

To examine Web templating in a bit more depth, I'm going to follow PLAN press releases through their various presentations on the Web.

Suppose that PLAN wants to put press releases in the following three places on their Web site:

✦ A short abstract of the hottest press releases appears on the PLAN home page.

✦ A list of all press releases appears on the press-release page.

✦ Each press release appears in full on its own page.

Figure 31-4 shows the home page.

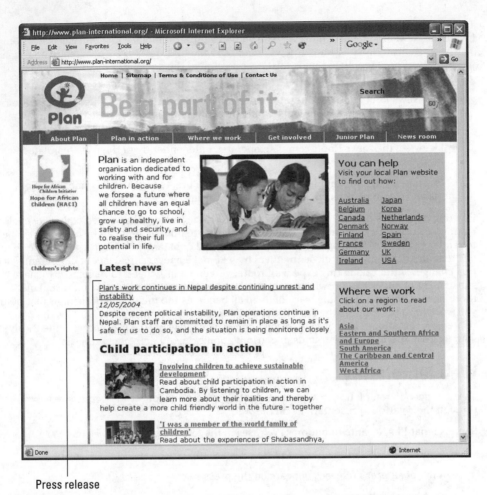

Press release

Figure 31-4: An example of how press releases appear on the PLAN home page

You see a title, a link, and a short blurb for the hottest press release on the home page. Figure 31-5 shows the press-release main page.

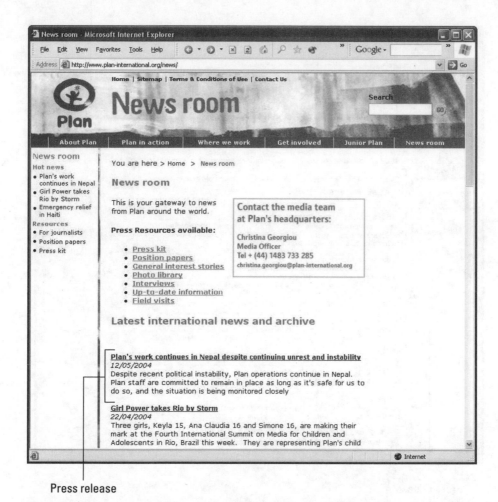

Press release

Figure 31-5: An example of how press releases appear on the press-release main page

You see the same title, link, and short blurb on this page as you see on the home page. Here, however, they appear in a different format, and all press releases appear in the list, not just the hot one. In addition, the page sorts all the press releases by date.

Finally, Figure 31-6 shows the press-release page itself.

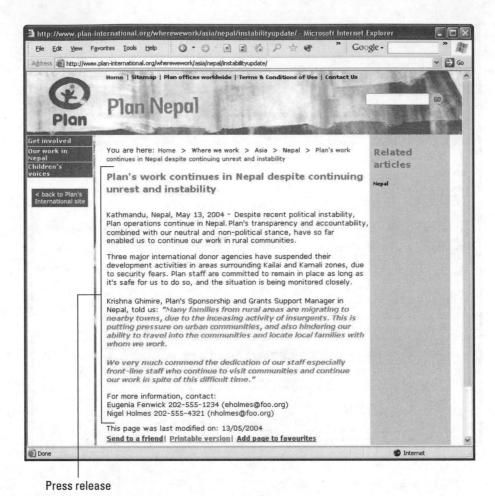

Press release

Figure 31-6: An example of how press releases appear on a press-release detail page

All the same information that appears on the other pages shows up on this page as well, but again the format is different. You also find a lot more information here than anywhere else. Notice, too, that on this page is a set of links to take you to other press releases or articles.

The Web navigation areas

I'm going to zero in now on the navigation area of the News Room page to see exactly what a CMS must do to create this area automatically (see Figure 31-7).

Static text

Dynamic text

Figure 31-7: A close-up of the navigation area on the News Room page

Behind the scenes, a CMS page template calls on a navigation template to create the navigation area. The navigation template merges static content, press-release information, and HTML formatting. It merges these sources based on logic that you provide.

The words News room are static and don't need to change as you update this navigation section. At least until the next big design change, these words always appear.

The links below the static text are dynamic. The template creates them each time that it publishes the page. They look something like the following example in HTML:

```
<A HREF="PRpage37.htm">Emergency relief in Haiti</A>
```

To create a link such as this one, the template must get two pieces of information from the press releases that you create: Title and Id. It uses the Id (in this case, 37) to form the name of the page to jump to.

Simply retrieving a list of titles and Ids isn't enough for the CMS. It must also form them into the appropriate outline.

To populate a navigation template like this, you need some sort of logic that decides how to position each Title/Id in the appropriate section. The following example shows what you need:

```
[If any News Room components are marked "hot"]
  <B>Hot News</B>
  [For each Hot News component]
    <BR>
    <A HREF="[Insert ID].htm">
      [Insert Title]
    </A>
  [Next Hot News component]
  <P/>
```

```
[End If]
<P/>
[If there are any Resource components]
  <B>Resources</B>
  [For each Resources component]
    <BR/>
    <A HREF="[Insert ID].htm">
      [Insert Title]
    </A>
  [Next Resources component]
[End If]
```

In plain language, here's what this template does:

✦ **Hot News:** If any News Room components in the CMS repository are marked hot, put those in the heading Hot News. Then, for each Hot News component, put in an HTML line break (<BR/>) and then hyperlink the component's title to the component's page. The component's page name is the Id of the component plus the file extension .htm.

✦ **Separator:** Put in an HTML new paragraph symbol for a separator (<P/>).

✦ **Resources:** If any Resources components are in the CMS repository, put in the heading Resources. For each component, add an HTML line break (<BR/>) and then hyperlink the component's title to the component's page. The component's page name is the Id of the component plus the file extension .htm.

This logic tells how to merge the static content with whatever content returns from the CMS repository to form the navigation area. Any programmer can take this logic and turn it into a programming algorithm that does this work automatically. The designer's job is to state what she wants so clearly and completely that the programmer has no questions (such as, "Do I put in the title if there are not items in the list?" or "How much do I indent?" and so on).

After you put this navigation area together, you can take it as a unit and list it in other positions or on other pages. On an index page, for example, you may need the same sort of outline of press releases. The idea is that, instead of thinking of each page as having its own navigation area, you can think of the site as having a set of navigation areas that pages use as necessary. Although some navigation areas are rarely used, others are used over and over. (The navigation area at the top of the page, for example, is likely to see use throughout the site.)

The Web content area

Now I'm going to zero in on a content area to see how a CMS creates it (see Figure 31-8).

People generally look at content areas as a single unit. In fact, this one consists of a set of elements that all come together in a very particular way to create the effect of a single unit. In addition, notice that you find static content even within this area that doesn't change from press release to press release. To create this presentation of the press release, a CMS uses what I call a *component template*. The template merges static content, press-release information, and HTML formatting. It merges these sources based on logic that you provide.

If you plan only one presentation of a press release, you can store the press release in exactly this form. That makes displaying it here very convenient. If instead, you want this press release to appear in a number of different formats, you must store it in a way that permits you to rearrange it programmatically. Store the press releases with each element in a separate place so that you can get to any of them independently and arrange them as you want. In the real world, you store these elements in a relational database or an XML source. Think about the elements of the press release as I outline them in Table 31-1.

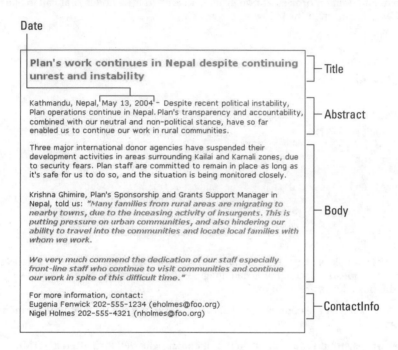

Figure 31-8: The content area on the press-release detail page

Table 31-1: Press Release Elements

Name	Value
Title	Plan's work continues in Nepal despite continuing unrest and instability.
Date	May 13, 2004
Location	Kathmandu, Nepal
Abstract	Despite recent political instability, Plan operations continue in Nepal. Plan's transparency and accountability, combined with our neutral and non-political stance, have so far enabled us to continue our work in rural communities.
Body	Three major international donor agencies have suspended their development activities in areas surrounding Kailai and Karnali zones, due to security fears. Plan staff are committed to remain in place as long as it's safe for us to do so, and the situation is being monitored closely.
ContactInfo	Eugenia Fenwick 202-555-1234 (efenwick@foo.org) Nigel Holmes 202-555-4321 (nholmes@foo.org)

Dividing press releases in this manner opens them up to any number of presentations that use a subset of the information or rearrange it in any way. To turn this neutral form of a press release into a Web page, a component template finds some way to pull it out and merge it with HTML. The most common process for doing so is to embed little codes that call in elements within HTML, as shown in the following example:

```
<HTML>
  <HEAD>
    <TITLE>
      [Insert Title]
    </TITLE>
  </HEAD>
  <BODY>
    <H1>[Insert Title]</H1>
    <P/>
    [Insert Abstract]
    <P/>
    [Insert Location],[Insert Date] - [Run AddPara for Web on Body]
    <P>
    [Run AddPara for Web on ContactInfo]
  </BODY>
</HTML>
```

This template works a lot like a mail merge in a word processor. You substitute codes wherever the dynamic content appears. Although you can imagine that real-life templates are quite a bit more complex, the basic ideas are all here:

✦ **Static content**, such as the comma between the location and the date and the hyphen after the date.

✦ **HTML** that wraps around the content so that it can appear well formatted in HTML.

✦ **Elements of the press release** that the template pulls out and positions in a particular way. Notice that it actually pulls the Title element out twice: once in the <TITLE> tag to add the title that appears in the browser title bar and again under the <H1> tag to put the title in as a level-1 heading on the page.

This example shows some logic that goes beyond simply cutting and pasting elements into the page. Some paragraph breaks are used within both the Body and Contact elements. Within the elements, they're not <P> tags; they're regular paragraph breaks. So the template must somehow detect and translate the paragraph breaks whenever it retrieves the Body and Contact elements. The AddPara program adds this extra processing. It's an outside program run by the template that processes and inserts the Body and ContactInfo elements.

The job of the component template designer is to answer all the programmers' static content, formatting, and logic questions by accounting for the breadth and range of content that the template may need to handle. The most common mistake that template designers make is to assume that a limited sample of content is enough to design a template for all cases. Although the preceding template may seem complete, the designer can't be sure that Abstract elements never have paragraph breaks in them or that all press releases have a Location element. (As the designer, of course, I did think of those things but chose not to account for them so I'd have something simple to use as an example here.)

After you design a component template, you can reuse it across the pages of your site. The following example represents a very simple template:

```
<A href="PRPage[Insert ID].htm">[Insert Title]</a>
<BR>[Insert Abstract]
```

You can use this template on the home page to list and provide links to the hot press releases, as well as on the press-release home page, where you can use it to give an overview of each current press release. Most people think of a site as a set of pages, each having its own content. The idea behind component templates is that your site is actually a set of content components that you draw onto particular pages in particular formats to produce the effect of a set of pages with individual content.

Print templating

To dive a bit more into creating templates for publications that you intend to print, I discuss a hypothetical print report, PLAN Activities, that PLAN produces. The report includes press releases. By using PLAN Activities as an example, I can show you how you can use the same methods (combining page, navigation, and component templates) to create a quite different publication. Unlike Web publications that all use HTML, print publications use a variety of markup types. I use Microsoft Word in this example because it's the print tool with which you're most likely familiar (and decidedly not because it's a preferred print-publication tool).

Suppose that press releases appear in the following three places in the report:

✦ In the table of contents of the report (see Figure 31-9).

✦ In the section "Key Events This Year."

✦ In sidebars throughout the rest of the report.

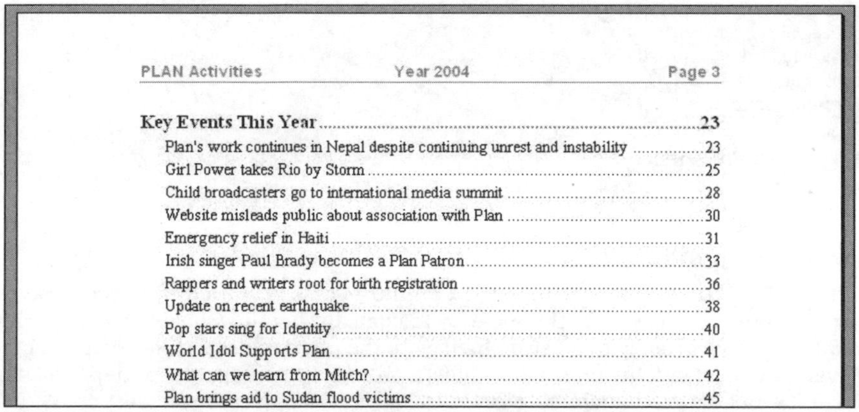

| PLAN Activities | Year 2004 | Page 3 |

Key Events This Year...**23**
 Plan's work continues in Nepal despite continuing unrest and instability 23
 Girl Power takes Rio by Storm 25
 Child broadcasters go to international media summit 28
 Website misleads public about association with Plan 30
 Emergency relief in Haiti...31
 Irish singer Paul Brady becomes a Plan Patron...33
 Rappers and writers root for birth registration 36
 Update on recent earthquake...38
 Pop stars sing for Identity...40
 World Idol Supports Plan...41
 What can we learn from Mitch?...42
 Plan brings aid to Sudan flood victims...45

Figure 31-9: An example of how press releases may appear in a print TOC

In the body of the report, each press release is recast as a "Key Event" (see Figure 31-10).

PLAN Activities Year 2004 Page 23

Key Events This Year

Plan's work continues in Nepal despite continuing unrest and instability

Kathmandu, Nepal, May 13, 2004 - Despite recent political instability, Plan operations continue in Nepal. Plan's transparency and accountability, combined with our neutral and non-political stance, have so far enabled us to continue our work in rural communities.

Three major international donor agencies have suspended their development activities in areas surrounding Kailai and Karnali zones, due to security fears. Plan staff are committed to remain in place as long as it's safe for us to do so, and the situation is being monitored closely.

Krishna Ghimire, Plan's Sponsorship and Grants Support Manager in Nepal, told us: *"Many families from rural areas are migrating to nearby towns, due to the inceasing activity of insurgents. This is putting pressure on urban communities, and also hindering our ability to travel into the communities and locate local families with whom we work.*

We very much commend the dedication of our staff especially front-line staff who continue to visit communities and continue our work in spite of this difficult time."

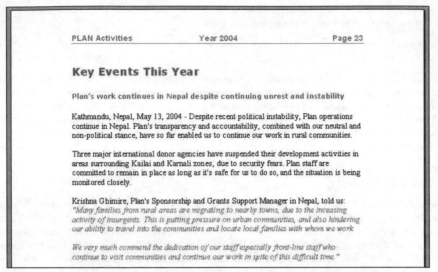

Figure 31-10: The full Press Release component recast as a print "Key Event"

Finally, hot press releases from the previous year also appear as sidebars in other parts of the report (see Figure 31-11).

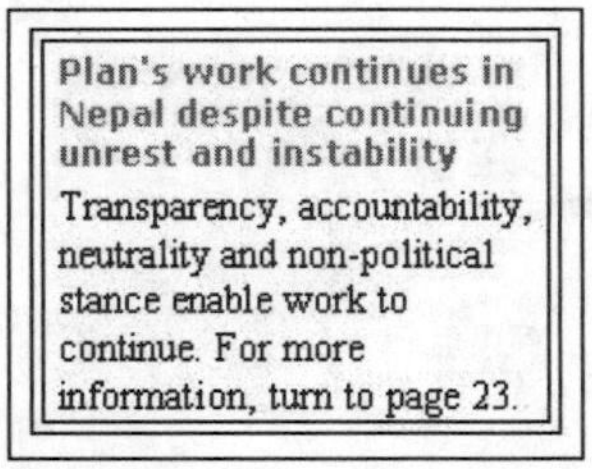

Plan's work continues in Nepal despite continuing unrest and instability

Transparency, accountability, neutrality and non-political stance enable work to continue. For more information, turn to page 23.

Figure 31-11: A Press-Release component as a print sidebar

The print navigation areas

To build a table of contents for the report, a CMS must come up with the titles and page numbers for each press release. The titles are easy to come by, but how do you come up with page numbers? You certainly don't store them with the press release. In fact, page numbers aren't even available until the report is complete. Word isn't perhaps the print-publication tool of choice, but it's great at creating TOCs. Unlike in HTML, where you must create your own outline with links, you can use Word's internal features to generate a TOC if you set up the "Key Events" section correctly. Setting up the section correctly is simply a matter of putting the right styles on the press release titles (for example, Heading 1 for the section title and Heading 2 for each press-release title). In other words, the TOC is effort-free in this publication medium.

In the case of Word, if you were to look behind the scenes, you'd see that the navigation template in the preceding example consists of one small line of code for producing a TOC, as follows:

```
{TOC \o "1-3" \h \z }
```

And you don't even need to write the code; Word does it for you if you use the menus to add a TOC to your document. Of course, to get the TOC built for free, you must build each press release into a separate section in the print document, as I discuss in the following section.

The print content area

Rather than pages, print publications contain sections. Not that any big difference exists between a section and a page. I make the distinction only because people already use the word *page* for something else in print. To build a "Key Events" section, you must create a section template that includes all the relevant press releases. The template that I show you uses Word's RTF format. Don't let the strange codes in the following template trip you up — they're just Word's version of the same stuff that you find in any HTML file:

```
\pard\plain \s1 Key Events This Year \par
[For Each PressRelease]
   \pard\plain \s2 ([Insert Date]) [Insert Title] \par
   \pard\plain \s10 [Run AddPara For Print on Body]\par
[Next PressRelease]
```

Note   This example is a severely trimmed version of rich text format (RTF). Real RTF is about 10 times as long.

Cross-Reference   For an example of how Word handles editing in XML, see Chapter 40, "Building Publishing Systems," in the section "Producing Word files."

As you get past the strangeness of rich text format (and it truly is strange), you can see that this template contains static areas, a content area, and logic, as follows:

✦ The static areas are the section title "Key Events This Year" as well as the parentheses around the date. The print formatting is also static. (The \pard\plain creates a new paragraph; s1 applies a Heading 1 style; s2 applies a Heading 2 style; and s10 applies a standard body-text style.)

✦ The [For Each] [Next] command brackets the content area. It uses only three elements from the press releases: Date, Title, and Body.

✦ For logic, the template uses the same [Insert] command and the same AddPara program as the Web template. Here, AddPara takes a For Print parameter to ensure that paragraphs in the Body element correctly translate into the target format (in this case, RTF). The lines that insert the Title and Body elements repeat for each press release. Disregarding the fact that this example is a much-simplified version of what may actually serve as an RTF template, you can still see that this small segment of text can create the entire "Key Events" section. And because it applies heading styles to the section and press release titles, Word's TOC function has all that it needs to automatically generate the "Key Events" section of the TOC.

Note   By the way, notice the key assumption here that the Body element can stand alone as a complete story. This assumption is by no means affirmed by anything that I show. Instead, knowing that the Body element *must* stand alone, the creators of the Body element need to make it stand alone. (Or someone must review their work and ensure that the Body element can stand alone.)

Fax templating

In my example, PLAN wants to create a fax for news agencies from its press releases. The fax can use a page template that lifts one of Word's standard fax formats (see Figure 31-12).

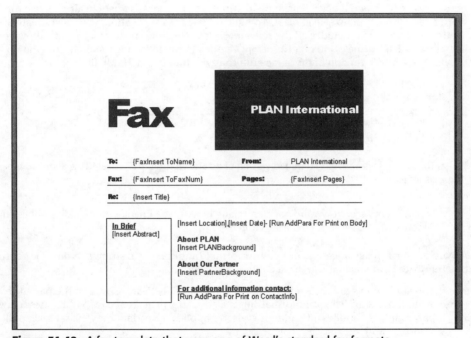

Figure 31-12: A fax template that uses one of Word's standard fax formats

Rather than illustrating this template as a text file, I choose to show it to you as it appears in Word. The RTF that you need to create this format is too complex to bother with here. Also, and more important, I want to demonstrate that a template need not always come in a text-only format (such as RTF or HTML). In fact, using a Word document (or any of a range of other proprietary formats) as a template is completely feasible. To fill in the appropriate elements of the template and process any of its logic, you can use Word's built-in programming language, Visual Basic for Applications (VBA), or control Word from the outside by using Word's Application Programming Interface (API) or save the Word file as XML and then add your content to the XML version of Word.

As is the case with all templates, this one contains static areas, formatting, content elements, and logic. The static areas are those not surrounded by the brackets (curly or square). The formatting codes lie behind the scenes in Word's proprietary markup language. I draw in the content elements by using the same codes that I use in all my press release examples.

The logic in the template comes in two forms: First, the familiar AddPara appears in the elements that can have multiple paragraphs. Second, a set of {FaxInsert} codes act as instructions not to the CMS but to a separate system that takes care of distributing the fax to a list of recipients. You transmit most faxes these days directly from the computer into the phone line. The CMS can fill in all the tags with square brackets (such as [Insert Abstract]) and then pass the result to an automated faxing system that fills in the tags with curly brackets (for example, {FaxInsert Pages}) and then sends out the fax.

E-mail templating

In my example, PLAN wants to send periodic e-mail alerts to its members. The e-mail publication is the simplest of all those that PLAN creates. A plain-text template (that is, one with no formatting) using little logic does the trick, as the following example shows:

```
Dear Member,
We are pleased to inform you of this recent
important event in the life of PLAN.

[Insert Title]
*****************************
[Insert Abstract]
*****************************
For more information, visit our Web site at
http://www.plan-international.org/PRPage[Insert ID].htm
```

Without formatting, the template consists of only static text and content elements. As it can with the fax publication, the CMS can fill in the [Insert] codes and then pass the result to a batch e-mail system that merges the output of the template into an e-mail message that can be sent to any number of recipients.

Analyzing Templates

After you design a set of publications, you can begin to break them down into templates that your CMS can use to build publications automatically. In the sections that follow, I present a way that you can define and specify a set of CMS publication templates.

Think

Before launching into a template analysis, consider the following questions:

✦ **Templates:** Do you understand how a template serves to separate content from design? Do you understand the difference between page, navigation, and content component templates? Can you understand a publication as the right set of templates producing the right pages and sections?

✦ **Staff:** Who's in charge of the template analysis? Does she have the right mix of design and technical talent to do the job? Do you have page designer and template programmers on tap to help out?

✦ **Platforms:** In addition to Web templates, what other publication platforms do you need to employ? Do you know the possibilities and constraints of each of these environments? Can you really make a publication happen in each of these platforms?

✦ **Logic:** What programming languages do you need to use to program your templates? What pseudo-programming commands do you need (in addition to the ones that I introduce in the section "Understanding template logic," earlier in this chapter) to specify the logic of your templates?

Plan

You can approach the template design of your CMS in any number of ways. In the following sections, I present a way that captures all the information that you need for your templates. You're likely to want to customize this approach to fit your publications and team.

A competitive Web template analysis

One technique I have found particularly useful in template analysis is to create a set of *best practice* component and navigation templates. By analyzing your Web site and those of your peers or competitors, it is not so hard to decide what kinds of presentations are most standard and work best for your sort of organization. Here are a few good reasons to do this type of analysis:

✦ Many organizations don't know where to begin with a template analysis and so don't really do one. A competitive template analysis gives you a place to start.

✦ It solidly positions you within the world of your peers. This analysis is a great excuse to get to know what everyone else is doing and to choose whom you want to emulate and how you are different.

✦ It gives you a more objective way of arguing for one approach over another. Creating a content presentation design can be a very subjective process. This analysis gives you the data that shows the predominance of opinion in your field concerning one content presentation over another.

✦ Finally, it establishes a terminology of templating. After this process, you will have an agreed-upon set of page areas and template names that will make talking about templates within your teams much easier.

Content management has really not yet evolved best practices for presentation to a point that the notion of a typical system is widely used or accepted. It's worthwhile, therefore, to define your own best practices based on a set of relevant reference publications — starting with your competitors, but also including your own current site. You might also include other non-competitor sites that do certain things well — especially things that are similar to what you want your site to do. Don't cast too broadly, however, or it may start to seem like every site out there has some relevance to yours. You're looking for roughly 5 to 10 sites; fewer than that and your pool is too small; more than that and it's unwieldy.

 Note   As a companion to this template analysis, you should also perform a competitive content analysis as outlined in Chapter 27, "Designing Content Types," in the section "A competitive content analysis."

After you have decided on a set of reference sites:

1. Review those sites in detail, noting what sorts of content they present and the various layouts and styles used for presenting content.

2. From this review, choose the presentations on the sites that have the most general relevance and work best. These are your reference templates. If you have the resources, you can test the various templates with focus groups or in usability studies. Include the wider issues of overall page layout, or scale back to just studying component and navigation areas.

3. For each site, prepare a list of the page, component, and navigation templates it uses.

4. Compare the templates across your comparison sites and choose a set of best example templates — the ones that best typify the practices found on sites that you think work best.

5. Name each of the templates you choose and use them to jumpstart the analysis that is presented in the rest of this "Plan" section.

A competitive template analysis can yield a great set of templates to begin with. But it is only a beginning. Be sure to differentiate yourself from your peers or competitors by basing your template analysis also on the particulars of your audiences, content, and other entities. In other words, in addition to reflecting the best practices of your peer group, your templates should account for your specific context. That context is defined by the rest of your logical design.

A sample list of component and navigation templates that I derived from this kind of competitive template analysis is located in the section titled "A sample set of templates," later in this chapter.

Page/Section template analysis

You can begin a template analysis by focusing on content types. On a Web site, for example, you may start out with the assumption that each major content type needs a page type for its details and that a single page summarizes all the components (just as I demonstrate for the PLAN press releases that I describe in the section "Web templating," earlier in this chapter).

Working through all your major content types, you end up with a core set of pages for a publication. Onto this set, you can begin to graft other pages for navigation between major and minor content types. Finally, you can draw all the pages together by deciding on global-navigation and static areas that unite all the separate pages into a single framework.

Of course, this approach isn't at all how most sites begin. In the vast majority of sites, the first thing that someone produces is a set of page mockups that show an artist's conception of the look-and-feel of the site that focuses on identity and style.

 Cross-Reference See Chapter 18, "Doing Logical Design," for more information about page mockups.

Most sites begin with page mockups for a reason: People don't know where else to start. The tangible feeling that you get from seeing some well-conceived mockups gives the entire project an injection of vision and reality that serves well to focus the team and put a visual context around rest of the project. As important as page mockups are, they can't replace a content-oriented design process. The reality is that the decision isn't either/or. To arrive at the final design of a publication, you need to work from the look to the content to ensure that the publication works. You need to work from the content to the look to make sure that the publication delivers the content it should and that you can build the publication from the CMS.

Whatever process you use to arrive at a set of publication pages or sections, after you isolate a set of publication nodes, you must decide how to divide each node into static areas, navigation areas, and content areas.

I highly recommend making a set of page wire frame diagrams that show the page layout visually (as I describe in Chapter 18, "Doing Logical Design"). Then, for each page you arrive at, catalog the following design criteria:

✦ **Id:** Give each page template that you create a unique Id that you can use later to identify it.

✦ **Name:** What name can you give to pages or sections of this type? Some name that ties to the major type of component in the node is a good choice.

✦ **Static areas:** Name and sketch the position of each static area on the node. For each, make a list that names any images or other media that it contains.

✦ **Navigation areas:** Name and sketch the position of each navigation area on the node.

✦ **Content areas:** Name and sketch the position of each component area on the node.

✦ **Page logic:** Specify any logic that you need to position or select the static, navigation, or content areas on the node.

✦ **Quantities:** Estimate how many nodes of this type your publication needs.

✦ **Static and dynamic modes:** Do you use this template to create only static, only dynamic, or both kinds of nodes? If you intend to use the template dynamically, estimate the number of times that it needs processing per minute under the worst-case scenario. A dynamically-generated home page on an intranet in a company of 10,000 people, for example, may get two to three hits per minute under normal conditions, but after an e-mail message announces a company news event, the page may get 200 hits per minute. This figure gives your programmers and IT staff a benchmark for testing the template under real-life conditions. If you can't come up with a specific number, at least state whether it's likely to run only occasionally, regularly, or very frequently relative to the other templates in your system.

Templating summaries

After you sketch out a complete set of pages, list your areas across all pages so that you get the most consistency and efficiency across the system. Your goal in this part of the analysis is to get your list of templates and areas down to the smallest number that still works for all content in the publication.

First, you can get all your analysis in one place by using a table such as the following example.

Name	Static Areas	Navigation Areas	Content Areas
Press Release Page Template	Banner, PR Header	Button Bar, Left PR Nav	Press Release Component Area

The table simply lists the elements for each page template (I show the PLAN Press Release page here). Even in compiling this table, you're likely to find naming inconsistencies and templates that are similar enough to combine.

If there are any opportunities that the page template table doesn't show, create the following tables to address them:

✦ A table that lists each static area in one column and the page templates where the static area appears in the other column. The table tells you how you're distributing your static areas.

✦ A table that lists each navigation area in one column and the page templates where the navigation area appears in the other column. This table tells you how you're distributing your navigation areas.

✦ A table that lists each content area in one column and the page templates where the content area appears in the other column. This table tells you how you're distributing your content areas.

Each table pivots the analysis so that, instead of looking at constituents from the standpoint of a page template, you're looking at page templates from the standpoint of each type of constituent. This exercise saves you a lot of duplicate efforts later on as you program each of these pages.

Tip　If you feel brave and confident, you can do this same analysis across publications. In other words, combine the tables for each of your publications into bigger ones that compare templates across all publications. In this way, you can get the entire set of templates down to as small a number as possible. Beware, however, that you don't sacrifice the unity of a publication simply to make it fit a bunch of templates that you're creating for other purposes.

Navigation template analysis

After you arrive at a list of navigation areas that you must create, you can go the next step and analyze each area as its own template. A good place to start is with an annotated sketch of the navigation area. Identify the static and dynamic parts within the navigation area. Then determine the following design criteria for each navigation template:

✦ **Id:** Give the template a unique Id that you can use later to refer to it.

✦ **Name:** Determine what name you can give to this navigation template. A good choice is the same name that you give the navigation area in the page-template wire frame sketches.

✦ **Static areas:** Name and sketch the position of each static area in the navigation template (if you have static areas — some navigation templates don't have any). For each, make a list that names any images or other media that it contains.

✦ **Component constituents:** Name and point in your sketch to any component elements in the CMS that the template is to use. Suppose, for example, that you have a Web navigation template that lists hyperlinks (of the form <A href="[Insert ID].htm">[Insert Title]</A>) To create these links, the template must access the Title and Id elements of some set of components in the CMS.

✦ **Access structure constituents:** Name and define any access structures that the template must use. An index template, for example, may call in a list of keywords from a database table in the CMS. Name the access structures and describe how to select data from them (for example, select all keywords in the author index table).

✦ **Functionality components:** Note any functionality components that the template calls in. You may, for example, store your full-text search functionality as a component and call it into navigation templates as necessary.

✦ **Template logic:** Specify any logic that you need to create the formatting or operation of the navigation area that this template creates. Make sure that you note any external programs that you call and any other code to lay out or operate in the navigation area.

✦ **Subtemplates:** Consider calling out particularly complex or reusable parts of the template as separate templates that the navigation template calls in. Suppose, for example, that you present a navigation template that's an expanding and contracting outline. For each link in the outline, the template shows a table with a small image and a hyperlink. Suppose, in addition, that other navigation templates use the same table for their links. In this case, naming the area (say, "TableView") and defining it as a separate template that you embed within the navigation template may prove worth your while.

Component-template analysis

A component-template analysis closely follows the methodology for the navigation templates. In fact, the design constraints are the same (although the way that you approach them is somewhat different), as the following list describes:

✦ **Id:** Give the template a unique Id that you can use later to refer to it.

✦ **Name:** Determine what name you can give to this template. A good choice is the same name that you give the content area in the page-template wire frame sketches.

✦ **Static areas:** Name and sketch the position of each static area in the template. For each, make a list that names any images or other media that it contains.

✦ **Component constituents:** Name and point in your diagram to the component elements in the CMS that the template uses.

✦ **Access structure constituents:** Name and define any access structures that the template uses. For a content template to call in information from an access structure is unusual, but not too unusual. You may want to include a "breadcrumb trail," for example, in a component area that shows the component's position in the CMS hierarchy.

✦ **Template logic:** Specify any logic that you need to lay out or process the content elements that are selected into this template. Make sure that you specify how the template selects components or component elements (for example, "Select all PR components with Date elements less than a year old").

✦ **Subtemplates:** Consider calling out particularly complex or reusable parts of the template as separate templates that the component template calls in. You find an example of a subcomponent in the section "Using templates within templates," earlier in this chapter.

The preceding analysis looks at components from the perspective of the pages that it lands on. Looking at each component and listing the templates that you use to display it is also useful. In this way, you can look for consistencies and efficiencies in component display.

To do the component side of the analysis, you can use a simple table similar to the following example.

Component	Component Templates
Press Release	PR Summary
	PR Detail
	PR Link
	PR Email
	PR Sidebar
	PR Fax
	(Summary and Detail can both embed Link as a subtemplate)

As you construct the table (as I have here for the example of the PLAN press release content type) and as you review it, you can make sure that you don't have two templates doing essentially the same work and that you name the templates in a consistent way. You can also look for opportunities to create subtemplates that reduce duplication.

Localization

For the templates in each publication that you intend to create, work through the following considerations to understand and catalog the impact of localization and then use your answers to go back and modify your template design:

✦ **Localities:** List the names and Ids of the localities that you expect to view the content that this template creates.

✦ **Look-and-feel:** Retrieve the list of graphic and text-design items that you need to change for the different localities (the list that I suggested to you in Chapter 26, "Designing Publications," in the section "Localization"). Does this template include any of the items on this list? If so, note which ones so that you can create rules for them in your personalization analysis.

✦ **Components:** List the component and navigation templates that involve localized content. (See Chapter 27, "Designing Content Types," for more information.)

Having amassed the preceding information, you're probably in a good position to decide on an overall approach to the localization of each publication. You can go in either of the following two basic directions:

✦ **Spot localization:** If you need to include localized content for only a few places, you can treat localization as a personalization. Gather up the component and look-and-feel considerations that you came up with in the preceding list and save them for your personalization design.

✦ **Complete localization:** If the changes to be made are widespread and comprehensive, consider creating a separate set of publication templates for each affected locality. The templates can include any localized look-and-feel and special selectors for localized content.

Of course, your decision may not prove as simple as this one, and one option doesn't necessarily eliminate the other. If you decide to do spot localization, you may still need to create some special template versions for hard-to-localize templates. On the other hand, if you do complete localization, it doesn't mean that you duplicate every template. You can usually share programming code, at least between your primary and local templates. You can sometimes split the difference between these two approaches by creating duplicate page templates for each locality and then coding personalizations into the navigation and component templates.

Tasks

Consider the effect of your template analysis on the ongoing maintenance of the CMS. Then fill in the following table to define any tasks that must happen on a recurring basis to run the CMS. Here are some task types to get you thinking:

✦ Template code reviews

✦ Template creation

✦ Template changes or deletion

✦ Template localization cycles

✦ Testing cycles

✦ Component and navigation template structure reviews

✦ Template reuse planning

Fill in the following table:

Task Name	Who	What	When	How Much	How
Template Component and Navigation Review	Page designer and template programmer	Review all templates for best code reuse and shared subtemplates.	Once per quarter	50-60 templates	Visual review followed by planning meeting

Fill in the following information:

✦ **Task name:** Give the task a short but memorable name that describes it.

✦ **Who:** Determine what person or kind of person is responsible for doing this task. Naming an automated process here instead of a person is acceptable.

✦ **What:** List what the person or process must do to accomplish the task.

✦ **When:** Specify at what frequency you must accomplish this task, or how you know when it must occur.

✦ **How much:** Describe how much or how many of this sort of task you expect to need to do. A numerical quantity is preferable here, but if you can't come up with one, words such as *a lot*, *not much*, and so on suffice.

✦ **How:** Detail the skills, tools, or processes the person or process needs to accomplish this task.

Don't worry if the tasks that you come up with at this point are somewhat ill-defined or sketchy. In your workflow analysis (in Chapter 33, "Designing Workflow and Staffing Models"), you have ample opportunity to refine them.

Integrate

To integrate your template analysis with the other design that you're doing, consider the following issues:

✦ **Coherence:** Compile the component and template drawings that you've done. They represent a first draft of publication designs that focus on how you're going to construct the publication, not how it may look or feel. Do they really hang together as a publication? If not, fix them now.

✦ **Graphic design:** Review your template drawings again with your creative team and make sure that they merge smoothly. Plan to continually assess the effect of graphic design on the content design as you move forward in the project.

✦ **Navigation review:** Review the navigation you've constructed. Are all components accessible? Are more important components more easily accessible than less important ones? Have you left out any access methods that may prove useful?

✦ **Template summary:** Revisit your template summary tables at the end of your analysis. Now that you've fully analyzed the navigation and component templates in your system, does your analysis suggest any other changes to the set of page templates that you intend to create?

✦ **Additional publications:** Look back over your list of templates. Can you use subsets of them to create publications that may otherwise seem hard to produce? Can small modifications create new and useful publications?

✦ **Workload:** Given the number and kinds of templates that you've designed and the complexity of the logic that you need to program, is this set of publications going to prove too much work?

✦ **Template tradeoffs:** Consider the tradeoffs that you make between creating one component page per component versus listing multiple components of the same type on a single page? Are multiple component pages too long? Are single component pages too short or inconvenient to the user?

✦ **Authors and Sources:** Are you capturing all the right metadata to drive the layouts and logic that you're proposing? Are you failing to use all the metadata in any of your components? If so, do you need to capture that metadata?

✦ **Audiences:** Are the same templates and logic appropriate for every audience that views a page? If not, what new templates or logic do you need? Are the page types and layouts what your audiences expect and appreciate?

A Sample Set of Templates

This section is designed to illustrate the concept of competitive template analysis and to give you some realistic examples of navigation and component templates. I choose not to illustrate page templates because they are fairly easy to understand and don't vary all that much from site to site. In addition, a number of the component templates that I cite take up the entire page and are pretty close to being page templates.

The reference publications I use in this section are all from real online security and transaction companies in the high-tech industry. The actual content of the screens I present is much less important, in this case, than the way they show components being presented.

The companion content analysis to this template analysis is presented in Chapter 27, "Designing Content Types," in the section "A Sample Set of Content Types."

To prepare this analysis, I looked at the following sites on the Web:

Organization	URL
Amdocs	http://www.amdocs.com/
Symantec	http://www.symantec.com/
RSA	http://www.rsasecurity.com/
Siebel	http://www.siebel.com
Cisco Systems	http://www.cisco.com
IBM Global Services	http://www-1.ibm.com/services

Note   It is not important that any of these sites actually use templates or even a CMS. What is important is that they present content in a consistent way. If their presentation is consistent, it *can* be produced by a CMS using templates (whether or not it is actually produced this way). Of course, you will use a CMS and templates to produce your site regardless of how others do it.

Best practice templates

The purpose of a Web template is to mix constant or static content with changing or dynamic content drawn from the CMS. The template determines the layout of all content and the selection of content from the CMS.

To reiterate the types of templates a CMS contains, I recognize three basic types of Web templates in a usual CMS:

✦ **Page templates** determine the types of pages on the site as well as their overall layout and look. Page templates include within them navigation and component templates and reveal what static and dynamic areas the page contains.

✦ **Component templates** create one or more desired views of a content type and reveal what static and dynamic areas the component contains.

✦ **Navigation templates** present a navigation area that contains sets of links the user can traverse to display desired components. They reveal what static and dynamic areas the navigation area contains.

In practice, there is no hard and fast dividing line between the three types of templates (a component template, for example, can span an entire page and so be thought of as a page template). Rather, you create the division in order to create the most efficient and effective set of content views for your audiences and information.

In the analysis below, I will consider the component and navigation templates, but not the page templates used in the reference sites. I draw from them some recommended practices you might employ to create them.

Component templates

Component templates specify a standard layout and look for your components. In this section, I describe the core set of component templates that arose from my analysis of the variety of content presentations on the reference sites.

Table 31-2 summarizes the core set of component templates.

Table 31-2: Core Component Templates

Component Template	Description
FullView Page	All body elements of the component are shown. There is one component per page.
FullView Cluster	The full view of the component requires multiple pages. There is a root page that has overview elements on it and links to pages that have detail elements on them. The multiple pages of the component are shown in the context of the usual global layout and branding of the site. The FullView Cluster page usually has links as well to related component FullView Pages.
FullView List	All body elements of the component are shown. All the components that match the criteria of the page are shown one after the other. They are sorted by some element of the component (title, date, and so on) or sometimes hand-sorted. They are separated from each other by white space or some sort of horizontal rule.
FullView Popup	All body elements of the component are shown. There is one component per page. The page is displayed in a separate window that has a minimal banner and little or no navigation.
PubView	The full view of the component requires multiple pages. There is a root page that has overview elements on it and links to pages that have detail elements on them. As opposed to the FullView Cluster (where the multiple pages are within the standard site layout), in the PubView, multiple pages of the component are given their own page layout and branding to give them the feel of a separate publication.
AdView	A title, abstract, often an image, and some set of links (to the FullView, e-commerce functions, contact, and so on) are laid into a small rectangle for inclusion in a page where the component is not the main focus. The AdView is intended to drive users to the component displayed.
AdView List	A title, abstract, often an image, and some set of links (to the full view, e-commerce functions, contact, and so on) are laid into a small rectangle for inclusion in a page where the component is not the main focus. Multiple components are listed one after the other based on some selection criteria for the list. They are separated by white space, rules, or are in their own individual boxes.

The following sections give a characteristic example of each type of template. The examples are followed by comments on the best practices for the construction of the template in the example. Please note that the sites where I found these examples may or may not have been constructed using the best practices I cite.

FullView Page

The illustration in Figure 31-13 is from the Amdocs site. It is a page for a product.

Figure 31-13: A FullView Page example

This type of component template is probably the easiest to understand and build. If you query the repository using the Id of the particular component, it returns all elements of the component required for its fullest display. Those elements are then formatted for an attractive display.

The best practice for the page itself is to name it in a way that is derived from the Id of the component that it displays. For example, if the component Id is "P123," the page might be named "P123.html" or, if the site is dynamic, it might be named "Product.JSP?Id=P123". In this way you can be assured that whenever you create a link to this page, all you need to know is the Id of the component that it displays.

In the FullView Popup, the component is alone on the page. In the FullView Page template, other navigation and component templates are called in by a wider page template. Figure 31-14 shows how the preceding FullView looks in the context of its entire page (which calls in a TOC template, as well as the FullView component template).

Figure 31-14: The FullView Page in its page context

FullView Cluster

Figure 31-15 is from the Symantec site. The base text for the component is on the left, and links to the clustered pages are on the right.

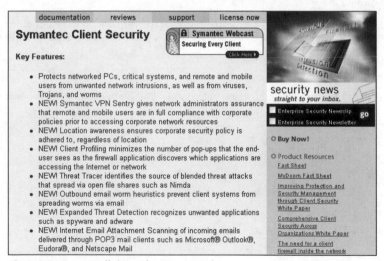

Figure 31-15: A FullView Cluster example

You can build cluster templates in a wide variety of ways. To specify a best practice, I'll assume that the full product content is stored in XML.

Given that assumption, the **storage** process would be as follows:

✦ A Root XML element, let's call it <product>, stores all content directly related to this product.

✦ Under the root element, there is a set of <section> elements. Each <section> contains a major subdivision of the content of this product.

✦ Each <section> has whatever other markup is required to store the headings, paragraphs, formatting, linking, and media required.

The **build** process might proceed as follows:

1. Retrieve the product element (and along with it, all its <sections>).

2. For each <section>, create a FullView Page. Name the page based on the Id of the <section>.

3. Create the FullView Cluster Page.

   a. Title the page using the title of the <product>.

   b. Name the page based on the Id of the <product>.

   c. Transform any markup that is before the first <section> to create the introduction text and media for the cluster page.

   d. Use the title and Id of each <section> to create the title list on the right side of the screen. If the <sections> contain <subsections>, you can create a TOC rather than a title list on the right.

FullView List

Figure 31-16 is from the Siebel site. It shows recent content that Siebel wants you to view or read.

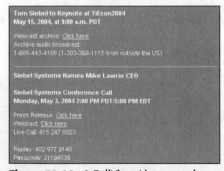

Figure 31-16: A FullView List example

The FullView List is just like the FullView Page except that it lists more than one component. Thus, the FullView List template queries for multiple (most likely all) components of a particular type and creates a complete set of the display elements for each.

Whereas the naming of a FullView Page can be derived from the Id of the component it displays, the FullView List cannot. If all the components of a particular type are listed, the name of the page can be the component type name (in this case, if it is showing all the components of the "Event" type, the page could be named "Event.html"). A link to any particular component on the page can then be derived from that component's Id and the name of its component type (for example, a link to the event with Id "E123" might be "Event.html#B123").

FullView Popup

Figure 31-17 is from the RSA site. It announces a single conference.

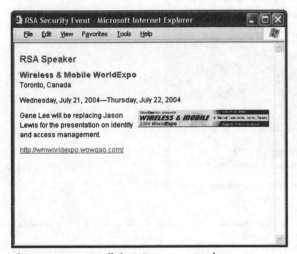

Figure 31-17: A FullView Popup example

This template is just like the FullView page except that it appears in its own secondary window with little or no site navigation. In other words, the component template is the page template in this case. In automatically setting up links to such a template, the creating program must have some way of finding out the name of the secondary window to use for display.

PubView

Figure 31-18 is from the Cisco site. It contains one of their annual reports.

This template is more of a page template than a component template. It lays out an entire site design within a site to convey the feeling of being in a separate but related publication. Within the new page design, a FullView Cluster approach is the best one to take to create the full range of pages in the subpublication. The publication template (as shown in Figure 31-18) may create a look-and-feel reminiscent of the parent publication or may create a completely different look.

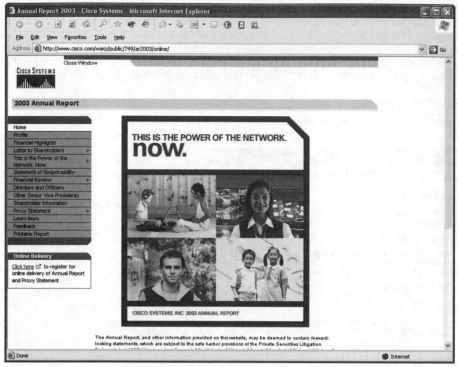

Figure 31-18: A PubView example

AdView

Figure 31-19 is taken from the Symantec Site. It links to a FullView of the product shown.

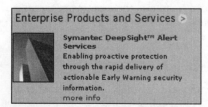

Figure 31-19: An AdView example

The main consideration behind an AdView is where its data is stored. Because these templates render marketing materials rather than informational views on a component, it may not be sufficient to simply draw in a title and an abstract from the component shown. Rather, it may be necessary for the copy and the media associated with the AdView to be tailored to the particular context of the AdView's use. Standard practice is to make these static areas on specific pages rather than separate templates. The best practice is to keep them dynamic, but stored separately from the component. An Ad component might have elements for

Component Id, Image, Headline, and Body. The link to the FullView of the component is formed from the Component Id. Selection into a particular screen area can be determined from other Ad elements such as Audience, Show Rate, and Priority. The text to show with the link can be stored with the Ad component or with the link. If it is stored with the component, you may need to store multiple versions of the text. If you store it with the link (a better practice, I believe), the author of the link has direct control over the text on the calling page.

AdView List

Figure 31-20 is taken from the Symantec Site. It links to a FullView of the product shown.

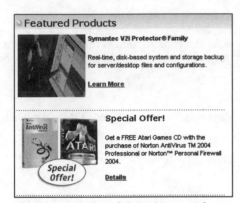

Figure 31-20: An AdView List example

An AdView List is simply multiple AdViews created by the same template. In addition to the issues raised by the AdView, the AdView List must include logic for how to title the entire list, how to select the correct number of ads for the page, and how to separate the AdViews.

Navigation templates

The table below describes the types of navigation templates that arose from my analysis of the reference sites.

Name	Description
Title Link	A single title or TitlePlus that links (usually) to a FullView component template. The title might be replaced by an image to create an image rather than a title link.
Title List	An alphabetical, non-sorted, or hand-sorted list of component titles that are linked (usually) to a FullView.
TitlePlus List	A title and other short elements (date, type, and so on) sorted by title or other element and linked (usually) to a FullView component template.
Table List	A table of title and other short component elements (date, type, and so on) sorted by title or other element and linked (usually) to a FullView component template.
Static TOC	Headings indented on the screen to one or more levels. Terminal nodes are titles that are linked (usually) to FullViews.

Continued

Name	*Description*
Expanding TOC	Expanding and contracting headings to one or more levels. Terminal nodes are titles that are linked to FullViews.
Index	Drop-down or open list of titles that are linked to a FullView. List has a title above or to the left that categorizes the components in the list.
Xref	Title or Results List area that lists links to components related to whatever component is in FullView on the page.

The following sections give a characteristic example of each type of template. The examples are followed by comments on the best practices for the construction of the template in the example. Please note that the sites where the examples came from may or may not use the best practices I cite.

Title Link

Figure 31-21 is from the Symantec site on a product page. It shows a single title and a link to a FullView (in this case a PDF file).

Related Products
•Norton SystemWorks 2004

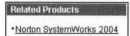

Figure 31-21: A Title Link example

Here is an example of a best practice way to create this sort of template.

Content Types Used	*Download*
Elements used by the template	* Title
	* URL (possibly derived from the Ids of the component linked)
Query logic	Find the component that matches the Id supplied.
Formatting logic	Build an HTML link with the title that is linked to the URL.

Title List

Figure 31-22 is from the IBM Global Services site. It shows a title list of course components.

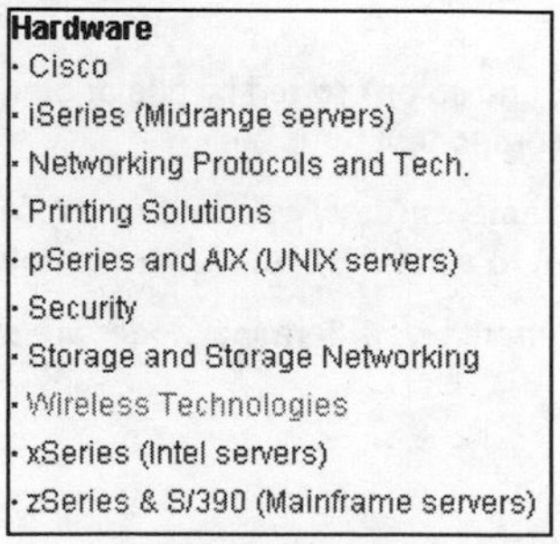

Hardware
· Cisco
· iSeries (Midrange servers)
· Networking Protocols and Tech.
· Printing Solutions
· pSeries and AIX (UNIX servers)
· Security
· Storage and Storage Networking
· Wireless Technologies
· xSeries (Intel servers)
· zSeries & S/390 (Mainframe servers)

Figure 31-22: A Title List example

Here is an example of a best practice way to create this sort of template.

Content Types Used	Course
Elements used by the template	* Title * Course Category * Id
Query logic	Find the title and Id for all courses in this category (hardware, in this example). Sort alphabetically by title.
Formatting logic	Output the Category title as an <H3> HTML tag. Then output each title in a bullet list as an HTML<A> tag. Derive the HREF from the component Id. Form it into the page name for the FullView of the course (for example, Id.htm). Set the link text to the component title.

TitlePlus List

Figure 31-23 is from the Siebel site. It shows press releases.

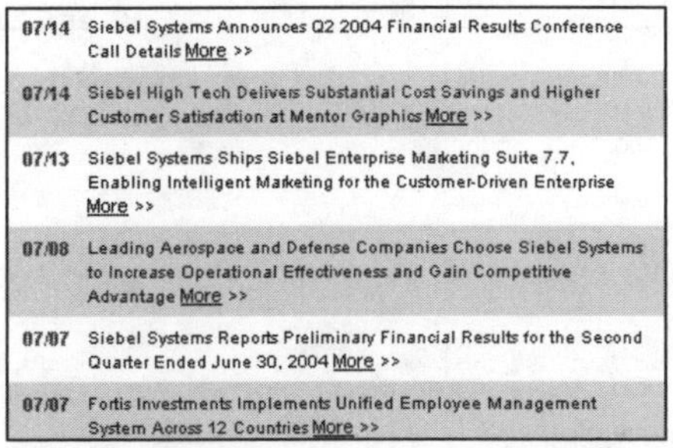

Figure 31-23: A TitlePlus List example

Here is an example of a best practice way to create this sort of template.

Content Types Used	Press Release
Elements used by the template	* Title * Date
Query logic	Find the title, date, and Id for each press release component. Sort descending by date.
Formatting logic	Form a two-column HTML <table>, one row for each returned component. Directly following the title, add the word more. Form a URL to the FullView page by deriving it from the component Id.

Table List

Figure 31-24 is from the RSA site. It shows job listings.

■	Posting Title	Location	Function	Requisition Number	Date updated
☐	Executive Assistant – RSA Conference	United States - San Mateo, CA	Corporate Marketing	947BR	16-Jul-2004
☐	Channel Development Rep- Southwest Coast	United States - Field Locations	Sales	888BR	15-Jul-2004
☐	Inside Sales Development Rep- Government	United States - Bedford, MA	Sales	839BR	15-Jul-2004
☐	Director, Corporate Communications	United States - Bedford, MA	Corporate Marketing	895BR	14-Jul-2004
☐	Senior Technical Writer	United States - Bedford, MA	R&D	906BR	12-Jul-2004
☐	System Administrator II	United States - Bedford, MA	Information Services	843BR	12-Jul-2004
☐	Principal System Engineer	United States - Bedford, MA	Sales	948BR	12-Jul-2004

Figure 31-24: A Table List example

Here is an example of a best practice way to create this sort of template.

Content Types Used	***Job***
Elements used by the template	* Title
	* Location
	* Function
	* Requisition Number
	* Date
	* Id
Query logic	Find all the above elements for all jobs. Sort by title.
Formatting logic	Form an HTML <table> with one line for each job component returned. Alternate the background color of the row. Form the title into an HTML <a> tag. Set the HREF to the URL for the FullView page of the component. Derive the URL from the Id.
	Create each table column name so that it re-sorts the components by the element in that column.

Static TOC

Figure 31-25 is taken from the Cisco site. It shows a static (that is, not built dynamically) table of contents.

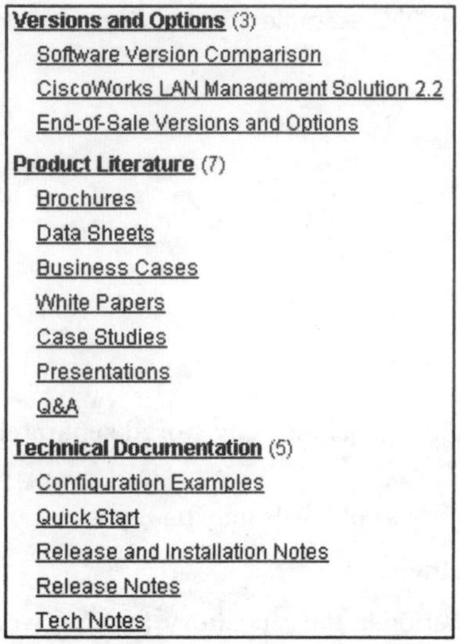

Versions and Options (3)
Software Version Comparison
CiscoWorks LAN Management Solution 2.2
End-of-Sale Versions and Options
Product Literature (7)
Brochures
Data Sheets
Business Cases
White Papers
Case Studies
Presentations
Q&A
Technical Documentation (5)
Configuration Examples
Quick Start
Release and Installation Notes
Release Notes
Tech Notes

Figure 31-25: A Static TOC example

Here is an example of a best practice way to create this sort of template.

Content Types Used	Product
Elements used by the template	* Title
	* Category
	* Id
Query logic	Select title, category, and Id. Sort by category.
Formatting logic	Form each category name into an HTML <h2> tag.
	Under each category heading, for each component returned, create an HTML <table> with one column for indent and another for a component link. In the second column, format an HTML <a> taq. Set the HREF to the URL for the FullView for the component. Derive the URL from the Component Id. Set the link text to the component title.

Expanding TOC

Figure 31-26 comes from the Cisco site. It shows a table of contents whose sections expand when clicked.

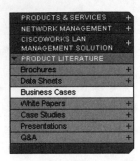

Figure 31-26: An Expanding TOC example

As a best practice, this sort of template is usually built from a hierarchy stored separately in the CMS repository. The most flexible hierarchies:

✦ Are stored in a recursive manner so that any number of levels may be represented.

✦ Can have any sort of component referenced in them.

✦ Build dynamically directly from their representation in the repository. In other words, as the repository changes, so — automatically — does the TOC on the site.

✦ Render in a way as to clearly differentiate:

  • Folders versus components

  • Component types

  • Levels of indentation

  • Parent levels

✦ Allow more than one folder to be open at a time.

✦ Can filter the outline by component type, showing, for example, an outline of only white papers.

✦ Can filter the outline by components linked to another particular component. For example, it can show an outline of only those components that are linked to a particular product.

Index
Figure 31-27 is from the IBM Global Services site. It shows an index that appears as a list in a combo box.

Figure 31-27: An Index example

Here is an example of a best practice way to create this sort of template.

Content Types Used	Product
Elements used by the template	* Product Name * Id
Query logic	Return the list of product name and Ids. Sort them alphabetically.
Formatting logic	Create an HTML <select> tag set. For each <option> set the value to the Id for a product returned and the text to the name for that product.
	On click of the list, include JavaScript that turns the Id into the URL for the full-view page for the product selected and links to that URL.

Xref

Figure 31-28 comes from the Cisco site. It shows links related to a particular product.

Figure 31-28: An Xref example

This sort of template is built from access structures in the repository that store associations between components. The easiest way to store associations is to have a separate element within one component that lists related components of another type (for example, to have a Related Tools element in the Product component that has a list of Related Tool component Ids). The most flexible way to make the relationships is to have a separate structure (a database table for example) that lists component Id A, component Id B, and the nature of the relationship between them. For example, Product A and Tool B could have a row in this table where the relationship "see also" is stored. Tool C could have the relationship "builds." That is, Tool C builds Product A. This method has the advantage that it can store any number of relation types between any number of different components. The table below assumes that the most flexible method has been used.

Content Types and Auxiliary Structures Used	Product
	Relationship Table
	Tool
	Service
Elements used by the template	* Titles from all related content components
	* Ids from all related content components
	* Content Type name from all related content types
Query logic	Look in the Relationship Table to find all the content components that are related to the product whose FullView page we are on.
	Find the content type names of all related components.
Formatting logic	Form a <table>.
	Put the content type name in a table header row with a table header-row image behind it.
	For every content component of that type, add a row to the table with the title of the component linked (via the familiar method of deriving the URL of the FullView page from the component Id) to the component.
	Based on the parameters set in the page template in which it resides, the template could:
	–Limit the display to some maximum number of links.
	–Add or not add headings for the type of component linked (article, press release, event, and so on).
	–Create a Title List or a Results List.

Summary

To borrow from Tina Turner in a different context, templates make your content come together into publications nice and easy, rather than nice and rough. Time and again, they save you the huge amount of work that would be required to manually layout out your content into a Web page or other publication. It's no exaggeration to say that, without templates, your CMS is not complete.

In this chapter I discussed how to make the most of your templating practices to ensure that your templates automate publication as much as possible. Getting the most from your templates, however, means that your content repository must be set up so that key components are available to the templating system. Key components are what templates need to assemble publications of all types automatically. For the most part, this means that content must be granular and organized so that needed elements are broken out rather than aggregated.

Following this practice, in your templates you can:

✦ Create a best practices analysis of other Web sites and publications and use it to design your own template requirements.

✦ Create an overlapping system of publications that shares content, design, code, and process across multiple content and publication types.

✦ Build templates that incorporate both static and dynamic content using your templating system.

In the next chapter, I discuss the last major design component you need for the logical design of your CMS: Personalization.

✦   ✦   ✦

Designing Personalization

◆ ◆ ◆ ◆

In This Chapter

How personalization
relates to publications

How to do a personal-
ization analysis that you
incorporate into your
CMS logical design

◆ ◆ ◆ ◆

*P*ersonalization is the process of matching the data that you collect about a user to the metadata with which you tag your content. The matching rules that you devise retrieve the most relevant content for that user. I cover the concept and function of personalization in Chapter 11, "The Branches of Content Management." In this chapter, I focus on the information that you need to ensure that the publishing function of your CMS can do the personalization that you want.

Personalization Jumpstart

This Jumpstart summarizes what you need to do to design the personalization your CMS can provide.

Use this jumpstart as a quick review if you've already read the section "Analyzing Personalization" in this chapter and want a checklist of what you need to do a personalization analysis.

To do personalization analysis, follow these steps:

1. Think through what personalization you might need. In particular, decide:

    - How much personalization you need (and whether the benefit is worth the cost).

    - How you will get the information to provide personalization.

    - How you should segment your audience.

    - What components and elements you want to deliver to each audience segment.

2. Create a personalization plan that includes:

    - Audience segment profiles and what you're delivering to each segment.

    - A list of Web site behaviors that trigger personalization.

    - Which push campaigns you will implement.

    - How your content must be tagged to support personalization.

    - How the segments, content, behaviors, campaigns, and tagging work together in a set of rules that describe which content displays under which conditions.

3. Integrate the personalization plan with the other parts of the logical design, considering audiences as segmented in the design; whether your design is capable of collecting all the information in the user profile you've identified; whether the segmentation and behavioral assumptions you've made can be tested and validated; and whether the additional work and complexity involved in creating components and templates is worth the personalization that you'll achieve.

After you've completed personalization analysis, you can make modifications to your CM logical design to accommodate the personalization that you decide to include in your system.

Publications and Personalization

To briefly review, following are the basic types of personalizations:

✦ **Profile-based personalization:** If you can identify segments in the audience of your publications, correctly place individuals in your segments, and identify the content types and specific components that are of most interest to members of each segment, you can then include segment-based personalization in any publication.

✦ **Behavior-based personalization:** You can potentially infer a great deal about what someone wants to see based on what that person's chosen to see previously. If you can identify visited components, associate them with desires, and then link them to other components that meet the assumed desires, you can build behavior-based personalization into your dynamic publications. Behavior-based personalization can happen anonymously and on the fly. You don't need to know who the user is to notice where she goes in your publication, and you can respond immediately to the actions that she takes. For static Web sites and print publications, behavior-based personalization isn't possible because you have no way to monitor behavior within the publication.

✦ **Campaign-based personalization:** A campaign is a planned-content "push" to users who meet certain criteria. You may plan to push information about an upcoming lunar eclipse, for example, to users that you identify as having an interest in astronomy. Campaigns have defined start and finish dates and a defined audience.

Personalization and the audience

Without some notion of who a person is, personalizing for that person isn't possible. The subject of your audience analysis is the people who use your publications (as I describe in Chapter 25, "Cataloging Audiences.") Some organizations personalize on an individual basis, bypassing audience segments altogether. I believe that this approach doesn't deliver nearly as much value to the organization as personalizing by audience segments (which I also discuss in more detail in Chapter 25).

By using your audience analysis, you can come up with the set of traits and trait values that each audience type may exhibit. Each cluster of these traits is a user profile that you can collect, store, and access to decide what kind of person you're dealing with.

Determining a user profile is one thing. Collecting trait values for each person who uses your publications is quite another. In pursuit of an audience trait, you really have only the following choices:

✦ **You can ask:** The most reliable and straightforward way to find out about someone is to ask the person. Of course, this approach is also the most time-consuming and intrusive way to find out; also, you're subject to the person's willingness to give accurate answers, particularly on sensitive or private topics.

✦ **You can infer:** Based on the actions that a person takes in your publication or on traits that you know the person has, you can make an educated guess on the value of related traits. Getting it wrong, however, is all too easy. Is the person who consistently goes to the children's section of your site, for example, necessarily a child?

✦ **You can buy:** Given a name and address, you can sometimes buy trait values for a person. Any number of sources sell information about people. Moral issues (and you face many) aside, this method may not provide accurate traits, or it may not give you the specific traits you need.

All in all, asking is still the best way to get good information. If you do decide to ask for information from your audience members, keep the following points in mind:

✦ **Trust:** I wouldn't give my name to someone I don't trust. On the other hand, I'd tell just about anything to someone I do trust. Before you ask a question of a user, ask this question of your organization: "How does she know that she can trust us and what can we do to communicate that trust?"

✦ **Value:** Users understand quite well that their information is of value to you. What do you give them in return? The value that you return doesn't need to be monetary. In fact, if you work through your audience analysis in the way that I present it, you already know what value you can provide to each audience, and you are already thinking about how to communicate it to them.

✦ **Time and effort:** Even if trust and value aren't an issue for people, time and energy probably are. You can think of each question that a person must answer as a small barrier. If he perceives the barriers as small enough, the user hops over them and doesn't see them as much of an obstacle to progress. As soon as the barriers get too high to easily cross, however, they stop the user and frustrate him until he stops providing any information at all. Ten questions on one page of a Web site that a user must answer before he can continue, for example, is more of a barrier than many people are willing to cross (unless the information on the other side is *very* valuable to them). One question on each of 10 pages, dispersed throughout the site, creates a smaller set of barriers that the user can take in stride as he moves through the site.

✦ **Context:** If the user ever stops and asks, "Why are they asking me that?" you haven't done a good job of presenting the question. The user is, at best, confused and, at worst, is put off and refuses to answer. Make sure that you explain why you need the answer to the questions you ask or, better yet, position the questions in a context where an explanation isn't necessary. If you ask for the user's age on the home page of your site, for example, the question may seem out of context. But if you ask the user's age on the page where you are selecting a set of songs for her, she understands why you want the data and is likely to report it more honestly.

My Personal Profile

A guy that I know came up with a most excellent idea for dealing with today's problems of user profiling. From your perspective as a user, the main problem is that you have little control over where your profile information ends up. From the organization's side, the main problem is that accurate and useful profiles are hard come by.

He started from the following premises:

✦ Your profile belongs to you. Access to it should remain completely under your control.

✦ You shouldn't need to type the same personal information over and over for each new organization that you provide it to.

✦ You should be able to choose what piece of your profile to give to each organization.

✦ You should control the kinds and accuracy of the information in your profile.

Given these premises, the solution to the profile problem is really quite simple: Put each person in charge of her own profile. You can contractually release it in whatever chunks you see fit to whatever organizations you choose. Your profile, for example, can consist of sections with increasingly personal information. Based on a binding agreement between you and an organization, you can release certain sections of your profile (electronically, of course). No one you don't authorize can use or redistribute your profile.

What this very elegant system does is to ensure that you're in control of the proliferation of your profile and that you have a means of getting compensated for its use. From the organization's perspective, it means that it has a definitive source for profile information and doesn't need to sneak around to get it. It can say, quite forthcomingly, "Give us the information that we need, and here is the value that we can provide you."

I've seen variations on this theme in new technologies, but none have hit it right on. Whenever this technology really does arrive, don't forget to look at the small print in the contract!

Personalization and components

All the profile information in the world can't create personalization without corresponding work on your component set. What good is knowing someone's age, for example, if none of your content targets various age groups?

You can target your content components directly or indirectly. In *direct targeting*, a specific element targets the content. You can give each *Song* component, for example, an *AgeRange* element that you fill in with the ages of the people to whom you think that the song is most likely to appeal. The advantage of direct targeting is that it's simple. How you tag each component is clear, and the rule for serving directly targeted content is equally straightforward. The disadvantage is that it's inflexible and time-consuming. What if song preferences involve other factors besides age? And tagging each *Song* component with an age may prove a lot of work.

In *indirect targeting*, you use nonspecific elements to target the content. You may tag each song with, say, a *Genre* element (rock, classical, grunge, and so on). Then your personalization rule can match an age to the genres that the age is likely to prefer. The advantage of indirect targeting is that it's flexible and easy. The songs are likely to already carry *Genre* tags, for example, so to create the personalization requires no additional tagging. The disadvantage of indirect targeting is that it's not always accurate. Do song preferences divide by age simply on the basis of genre?

Of course, no requirement limits indirect targeting to the use of only one element. You may target songs based on genre and artists, for example, by noting that preference follows genre except for particular artists who cross generational lines. The rule in this case becomes more complex and requires extra data, but the targeting still depends on existing elements in the content type you are personalizing.

Personalization and rules

Given a set of user profiles and the elements that target content, you need a set of rules to tie the two together. *Personalization rules* are your best guess at how user profiles and elements relate.

You can generally phrase personalization rules as a set of steps or as an If...Then statement. The following statements, for example, describe the song rules that I present in the preceding section:

✦ Take the user's age and search for components of the content type *Song* that have an *AgeRange* element that contains the user's age. Display the components that you find.

✦ If the user is between 0 and 10 years old, search for the *Song* components with a value of *Disney* in their *Genre* element. Display the components that you find.

✦ If the user is between 6 and 10 years old, search for the *Song* components with a value of *Disney* in their *Genre* element. Add to these the components that have either *Back Street Boys* or *Britney Spears* in the *Artist* element. Display the components that you find.

Depending on the kind of personalization that you're trying to accomplish, the rules may include other inputs, such as the following:

✦ **Browser headers:** On a Web site, each request for a page carries with it information about the browser that requests the page. Among the many useful pieces of data that a browser tells you are the *browser type* (Netscape, Internet Explorer, and so on), the *URL* for the page the browser was last at, the *IP address* of the browser (for example, 206.45.56.1, which is the location of the browser on the Internet), and any *cookie* that you may have assigned to that user in an earlier visit. (*Cookies* are unique Ids that you can use to identity users and link them to their profiles.) Your rule can use the page that the user visited before the song page, for example, to help decide his interest. If he enters from a kid's music site, you have further evidence that the user's interests lie in children's music.

✦ **Past behavior:** Your site can monitor the pages that a user requests and use them as input to a rule. If the user spends the majority of her time looking at songs from the Ska genre, for example, your rule can always add Ska songs to the list of those that it returns.

✦ **Collaborative filters:** This technique, made famous by Amazon.com, combines behaviors and user profiles to find components. In the song example, a simple collaborative filtering rule may state, "Find other users of the same age as the current user. Then find and display the components of the content type *Song* that these other users specifically requested."

✦ **Push functions:** Rules may also include provisions for including specific content under certain conditions. The song site, for example, may want to highlight a particular song each week for each age group. To do so, it may add a part to its song selection rule such as, "In addition to any other *Song* components that return, always return the component with the Id element *1234*." This method is personalization in the sense that you select content based on user-profile information.

✦ **Extra data sources:** Many personalization rules require data that's neither in the user profile nor in elements. Recall the rule that I cite that matches genres with ages — if the user is between 0 and 10 years old, search for the *Song* components with a value of *Disney* in their *Genre* element. The rule works for only one age group. A more general statement of the rule is, "Get a list of genres by searching the Genre table and matching genres based on the user's age. Then search for the *Song* components with the *Genre* values that you return." The Genre table is a separate source of data that the rule uses to make its choices.

Different CMS systems use different kinds of user interface for building rules, but the rules themselves are up to you to decide.

Remember that the results of personalization are only as good as the assumptions on which you build your rules. I'm sure that you can see any number of weak assumptions in the rules that I describe in this section. I certainly wouldn't pin the success of a song site on the strength of these rules. And, in fact, few systems have the accurate and complete profiles or the fully tagged components that they need to do personalization well. Moreover, even with accurate profiles and well-tagged components, few people have the talent and insight to craft a rule that works consistently and delivers the right content to the right people. These sad facts lead me to propose the following single, simple metarule of personalization rules:

Expect your rules not to work very well.

Following this rule, you're wise to do the following:

✦ **Craft your personalization rules to prioritize and not exclude content:** List the content that you expect the user to want ahead of or more prominently than the rest of the content, but make sure that the rest is still accessible in some way. Put the Disney songs ahead of all others for the kids audience, for example, because you can reasonably expect that they want them. But understand that Disney isn't all that kids ever want and make sure that kids can get to songs from other genres without too much trouble.

✦ **Be prepared to refine your rules:** Make them more subtle and complex as you learn what works better with your audience. Track how many Disney songs, for example, that kids actually listen to from the results that you return to them. In what cases do they go for the content that you present, and in what cases do they click away without consuming what you prepare for them?

Personalizations in templates

A personalization generally lives within a template. If you create a template, you either code personalization rules directly into it or call an external program that processes the appropriate rules and returns the result to the template. In either case, as the template processes, personalization rules trigger and modify the content that the template displays. You have the following two basic ways to relate personalizations to templates:

✦ **Offsets from the default:** You can consider the content that a template supplies if no personalizations trigger as its default content. Then any personalizations that trigger offset the content that appears in a particular direction. In the PLAN press-release home page in Figure 32-1, for example, the default content may consist of all press releases in date order. If the staff personalization triggers (because a staff member visits this page), the site displays press releases about the user's country, followed by press releases about the user's continent, followed by the remaining press releases in date order.

✦ **The template itself:** You can look at an entire template as the personalization that it creates. Suppose, for example, that PLAN wants to present a completely different press-release page layout and style for the members of the press. Instead of overly complicating the press-release page template, it may just create a new template that produces press-release pages only for the press. Then, if the press-release personalization for the press audience triggers (based on a link from the navigation area), it routes those users to the press-release page specifically designed for members of the press.

Figure 32-1: Default content may consist of all press releases in date order, or another default personalization.

No hard and fast line helps you decide whether to personalize one template or to personalize by making multiple templates for the same page. It's a matter of increasing complexity. At some point, splitting one page into many just becomes easier.

Personalizations can appear in any kind of template, as the following list describes:

✦ **In page templates:** A personalization can affect the composition of the page. For donors, for example, PLAN may decide to include a "How you can help" sidebar area in press-release pages, instead of the "Contact the media team" information as shown in Figure 32-1. In this case, the press-release page template has a donor-personalization rule that, after it triggers, adjusts the other areas and inserts the sidebar.

✦ **In navigation templates:** A personalization can affect the composition of the navigation area. PLAN, for example, may change what it considers important enough news ("Emergency relief in Haiti") to include in the press-release navigation template (refer to Figure 32-1). For members, important news may involve only news about children. For staff, it may focus more on events.

✦ **In component templates:** A personalization can affect the composition of the content area. In the PLAN press-release home page, the personalization is actually in the component template called "Latest international news and archive." That's the area where the change in the order of the press releases actually happens.

Customization versus personalization

Customization is something that the user does to change the sort of content and user interface that she sees. A user may, for example, select the content categories that she most wants to see from a list. A Web publication then shows only those content types she has chosen.

Customization usually falls into the following categories:

✦ **User interface:** The user can sometimes choose what kind of user interface she wants. She may, for example, choose to have easy menus or complete menus. Easy menus show only the most common commands and help the beginner avoid confusion. Complete menus have all the available commands and enable the advanced user to navigate more easily.

✦ **Layout:** The user can sometimes choose what publication view she likes. Some Web sites, for example, offer both a rich layout with margins, columns, and a lot of surrounding stuff and a simple layout that shows only one column of continuous text and media. Users may be given the choice of viewing a Web site with or without browser frames.

✦ **Style:** The user may be able to change the look-and-feel of the publication by choosing background images, colors, and so on.

✦ **Content:** As in the earlier example, the user can sometimes choose from among a selection of content categories to specify what she wants to see.

✦ **Preferences:** The user may be able to off turn certain features. She can sometimes specify whether links to new sites create a new browser window, for example, or instead just change the contents of the current window. Or she can perhaps turn off all pictures because her connection is slow.

By the way, these customizations can just as easily exist for print publications—just not as quickly as they do for electronic publications. Nothing (except the usual time and money) prevents you from asking print users for their preferences and then using your CMS to produce customized versions of a print publication.

The Enterprise CMS

There is a new view within corporate America, one that sharpens the focus on the customer experience. With the proliferation of Internet technologies, it's easy for channels to publish their own content. What is not easy is keeping this content consistent and personalized across all the channels.

Many companies are still looking at their content within silo channels. As such, there is tremendous redundancy in creating and managing content across these independent silos as company products and services evolve. The challenge is ensuring the product or service is positioned consistently across all the channels, or in a more customer-facing view, across all customer touch points.

Keeping content consistent across all customer touch points is just one of the issues facing corporate America today. With the level of personalization that Internet technologies deliver, the issue is quickly moving to personalized content based on customer lifecycle. It is no longer just about ensuring a consistent message; it is now about flexing that message based on where your customers are within their lifecycle with you as a company.

In order to deliver consistent content at all customer touch points and to flex based on personalized information, companies today need to rethink how they take product and service to market and how they maintain the content once launched. While it's hard for each of the channel owners to give up control, in order to be truly successful, each channel must pull from the same source of information about the product, service and customer.

This requires a different operational structure supporting content management. It requires a core set of content managers with a content management tool providing the base content. This needs to be paired with channel subject matter experts that can repurpose that content based on the channel being used, and a customer profile database that adds in a level of personalization to the content.

Companies that break the mold of producing content in silos and embrace an enterprise view of content across all customer touch points will be the ones that set themselves apart by creating a level of customer trust and personalization that cannot be duplicated in the traditional model used by their peers.

Dennis E. Haugan, Director, Online Marketing, T-Mobile

Customization is the core of the "My" phenomenon. Sites such as Yahoo! and many, many others add the word "My" to their names to signify that you can customize their sites to your desires. My Yahoo! is cool, but I'd differentiate it from personalization.

Giving the user a lot of choice in the presentation of your publication is different from understanding who the user is and providing targeted content. Customization is something that the user does for herself. Personalization, on the other hand, is something that you do for the user.

Personalization comes before customization. Personalization can set the overall context within which a person may customize. You can decide how to order the list of content categories from which a user can choose, for example, depending on who you detect is doing the choosing. On the other hand, customization cuts across audiences and trumps personalizations. Regardless of the audience that you think someone is in, if the person specifically chooses to view a certain kind of content, that choice is more important than any rule that you make up for that user.

I'm not saying, however, that customization and personalization are unrelated. Quite the contrary. For one thing, each choice that a user makes to configure your publication is another piece of data for that person's user profile. This same data may prove useful in a later personalization. In addition, the way that users differentiate themselves in customizations (especially content customizations) can help you see audience distinctions. Finally, you may migrate customizations into personalizations. If members of the *Professionals* audience, for example, consistently choose the simple layout, why not make that layout the default for that audience?

Dynamic and static personalization

Most people think of personalization as something that happens on a Web site on the fly, in the same way that users request pages. Indeed, this is how most of the personalization products are now structured. But nothing is particularly essential about this dynamic form of personalization. In fact, a completely static site may provide just as much personalization as a dynamic site.

The only thing that a personalization system must provide is the right content to the right person. How it does so doesn't matter. Consider the following two situations, which are identical as far as concerns the end user (except for the fact that the dynamic one may take longer to serve the page).

In the first case, the user opens a site and chooses the Members Only link. She logs in, and the CMS registers the fact that she's in the Member audience and sends this information to all the site templates. The templates run the member personalization rules to change the layout of the pages, the choices that the user gets, and the components that she can see. Each time that she requests a page, the template generates it for her by using the rules for members.

In the second case, the CMS administrator creates two static sites: one for members and one for nonmembers. As the CMS generates the pages of the site for members, it passes the right information to the templates, triggering the member-personalization rules and thus changing the layout of the pages, the choices that the user gets, and the components that she can see. After the user opens the site and logs in, the Web server, recognizing that she's a member, simply directs her to the first page of the static site that's "personalized" for members only.

Whether you create all the pages beforehand or create each as someone requests it is a choice that you can make to create the best overall system. The issues of static versus dynamic are no different here than they are for CMS-generated sites in general.

 Cross-Reference For a discussion of the more general concept of static versus dynamic sites, see Chapter 6, "Understanding Content Management."

Of course, in print publications, you have no such choice. To create a variety of versions of the same publication, each targeted to a different audience, you need to create a set of static files for each.

Analyzing Personalization

In the sections that follow, I take you through a comprehensive analysis and design starting from plain language rules and ending in a specification of the precise rules to construct so that your programmers can implement them in your publication templates. Along the way,

I help you work through profile, behavior, and campaign personalization. In every kind of personalization, you discover that appropriate content tagging is key to delivering personalized content. If you can't tie your personalizations to a set of elements in one or more content types, you can't differentiate between the components that different kinds of people should receive.

For simplicity and to stay consistent with the main trends in personalization today, I'm assuming that you're analyzing only Web personalization in the sections that follow.

Think

Before you begin your personalization analysis, think about the following issues:

✦ **Degree:** How much do you need to personalize content to meet the goals that you identify for the system? To what user level do you expect to personalize: large segments, small segments, or individual users? Do your audience segments have differing needs for information?

✦ **Benefit:** Does the personalization benefit that you offer deliver enough value to offset the cost to you of collecting the user information, tagging content, and maintaining rules?

✦ **Ethics:** What's your ethics policy on collecting information about your audiences? Are users likely to accept it? How can you communicate this policy to them? (The latest trend in this area is a privacy policy.) To what other uses do you intend to put the information that you collect? Are those uses consistent with the desires of your audiences?

✦ **Cooperation:** Personalization may require the cooperation of your marketing and content collection groups. How can you facilitate this interaction?

✦ **Segments:** What are the segments within your overall audience that can benefit from seeing a particular set of personalized content?

✦ **Components:** Which content types are of most interest to each segment of your audience? For each content type that you list, what aspect of the information targets it best toward this audience? What subject matter is of interest to the audience, regardless of which content type it's in?

✦ **Elements:** For each content type, what can you infer about a user who views this type of information? Based on these inferences, are more components of the same type useful to them? If so, what element values should other components of the same type have in order for you to choose them? And, based on these inferences, are any different types of content useful to the person who views this particular component or content type? If so, what elements and element values should the other components have in order for you to choose them?

Plan

Personalization design yields the following results:

✦ **Profiles:** Determine the segments of your audiences to which you want to offer personalized content and what to give them.

✦ **Behaviors:** Determine the types of Web-site behaviors that you want to track and respond to with personalized content.

✦ **Campaigns:** Determine the sorts of push campaigns that you want to stage.

✦ **Tagging:** Determines the way that you must tag content to support personalization.

✦ **Rules:** Determine the logical statements that tie any of or all the preceding factors together into a programmable rule for displaying content under set conditions.

To get to these results, I describe a process where you work backward from plain-language versions of the personalizations to each of these lists.

Plain-language rules

You can start a personalization analysis by formulating simple rules in plain language. Before beginning to reduce these rules to more basic entities, you can work with this simple list to make sure that you're doing the kinds of personalization that you most need. In this first part of the analysis, think as widely and openly as possible. You get an opportunity later to trim your list of personalizations down to an implementable size later.

Brainstorm as many conditions as you can think of under which you may want to deliver personalized content. Write these down in whatever form is most convenient. Review the list and look for any redundancies or omissions. After you're satisfied that the list represents your complete, if preliminary, understanding of the conditions of personalization, you're ready to begin to formalize your ideas.

Begin to formalize your personalization conditions as shown in the following table.

Id	Personalization Name	If a Person Is... or If a Person Does...	Show That Person...
1	DonorSidebar	If a person is a donor and If a person enters a press-release page from a link in an e-mail message	Show that person a How You Can Help sidebar on the press-release page.

The required information includes the following:

✦ **Id and name:** Assign a unique Id and name to each personalization that you chart this way. Always assign an Id. If you can't think of a good short name for a personalization, leave it out but take it as an indication that you haven't discovered its core purpose.

✦ **If a person is...:** Fill this box with any parts of your condition that refer to whom you're dealing with. PLAN, for example, may say, "If a person is a donor," or "If a person is a staff member in Africa." Try to make it as specific as possible. What exactly distinguishes this person from others of different types? The differentiator may be the audience the person is part of, the segment within an audience that she's part of, or something else that cuts across audiences.

✦ **If a person does...:** Fill this box with any parts of your condition that refer to actions that the person may have taken. PLAN, for example, may say, "If a person enters a press-release page from a link in an e-mail message" or "If a person clicks to more than five different press releases." Try to focus on actions that are potentially detectable by your system. Postulating "If a person's ever visited any nonprofit site" is of no use if you have no way of discerning that action. Feel free to enter more than one criterion in the box. PLAN, for example, may enter "If a person is a donor and if a person enters a press-release page from a link in an e-mail message..."

✦ **Show that person**...: Fill this box with a discussion of the information or functionality that you want this person to receive. Given the conditions "If a person is a donor and if a person enters a press-release page from a link in an e-mail message...," for example, PLAN may enter, "Show that person a How You Can Help sidebar on the press-release page." Try to phrase your response here in terms of the content classes and their elements.

Chart as many of your brainstormed conditions as you can. If you can't figure out how to get them to fit this form, they may not be personalizations that you can implement. As you move from the brainstormed list to the more formal list, many of your conditions are likely to merge with others or drop out as you decide that you have no way to formally represent them.

In the parts of the design that follow, you continue to reduce this list to the concrete parts of your CMS that you access to make these personalizations happen.

Templates

In this portion of the design, you match your personalizations to the page, navigation, and component templates that they reside in. For each personalization that you come up with in the preceding analysis, fill in the following table.

Personalization	Page Template	Navigation Template	Component Template
(P12) DonorSidebar	(T21) Press Release Detail		(C34) HowToHelp

Tip   You can choose whether to include the name of each template in the preceding table, but always include the Id. Later, if you change the name of a template or personalization, you don't want this table to get out of sync.

Each personalization must fit into some combination of templates, as follows:

✦ **Personalization:** Enter the Id and name of the personalization.

✦ **Page templates:** The personalization may affect the composition of an entire page. In fact, the personalization may even warrant the creation of a new page template.

✦ **Navigation templates:** The personalization may affect a navigation template. It can affect the navigation template either wherever it is located or only if the template is located within particular page templates. In the latter case, try to change the personalization so that it's at the level of the page template. This change causes fewer implementation complexities later.

✦ **Component templates:** The personalization may affect a component template. As with navigation templates, it may affect the template either wherever it is located or only if the template is located within particular page templates. Again, in the latter case, try to change the personalization so that it's at the level of the page template.

✦ **Navigation and component templates:** The personalization may affect both navigation and component templates or even all three kinds of templates. Maybe your analysis tells you to code different rules into each template for the personalization effects. If having multiple rules for one personalization gets too confusing, you can create subpersonalizations, each with its own Id and rule, that you group under a single personalization name.

From here on, I target the analysis toward fleshing out the details of the personalizations rather than toward their overall structure.

Profiles

In this portion of the design, you gather up all the information in your personalizations that affects the user profiles that you manage.

For each personalization, list the necessary information in a table similar to the following example.

Personalization	User Trait	Corresponding Audience Trait	Method of Collection
(P13) AfricaWatch	Staff from Africa	Staff Audience: Location filed	Present in the Staff audience profile

The required information includes the following:

✦ **Personalization:** Enter the Id and name of the personalization.

✦ **User trait:** Use the information that you enter under the "If the person is…" column in your personalizations to determine the specific measurable traits that it implies. If it implies multiple traits, enter one per row in this table. In other words, one personalization may have multiple rows in the table. For more information on traits, see Chapter 25, "Cataloging Audiences."

✦ **Corresponding audience trait:** Refer back to your audience analysis to find out whether you've identified a trait that matches the one that you're looking for here. If not, either add a new trait for the audience (if possible) or leave this cell blank.

✦ **Method of collection:** If the personalization trait matches an audience trait, you don't need to fill in this cell. (It's already accounted for in your audience analysis.) If it doesn't correspond to an audience trait, enter how you expect to discover the value of this trait for each person that the personalization affects.

This table helps you sort through the relationship between your personalizations and your audiences. After you complete it, the personalizations and your audience profiles should match as closely as possible. In other words, most personalizations depend on what audience a person is in, based on traits that you're sure that you can collect. The more that you can relate audiences and personalizations, the easier maintaining a simple and consistent approach becomes. Of course, doing so isn't always possible or even desirable. So don't go overboard and get rid of important personalizations just because they don't fit your current audience analysis. Do, however, ask yourself why they don't fit and whether the errant personalizations may lead to a refinement, at some point, of your audience segments.

Behaviors

In this part of the analysis, you gather up all the information in your personalizations that bears on the behaviors that you must notice, record, and interpret.

For each personalization, list the necessary information in a table similar to the following example:

Personalization	Behavior	Content Types Involved	How to Observe It	Where to Store It
(P12) DonorSidebar	Click in from an e-mail message	None	Capture code in the e-mail URL	Session variable

In the preceding table, I use the example of the DonorSidebar personalization that states, "If a donor comes to the press-release page by clicking an e-mail link, display the 'How You Can Help' sidebar." Fill the table in as follows:

✦ **Personalization:** Enter the Id and name of the personalization.

✦ **Behavior:** Use the information that you enter under the "If the person does..." column in your personalizations to determine the specific measurable behaviors that it implies. If it implies multiple behaviors, enter one per row in this table.

✦ **Content types and components involved:** Many times, the display of a particular component or content type triggers personalizations. In this example, an e-mail link triggers the personalization, not the display of a particular component, so I enter *None* in the box.

✦ **How to observe it:** Determine how you know that this behavior occurs. PLAN, for example, may pack a code into the links that it sends in e-mail to donors. The code alerts the CMS that a donor is clicking in from an e-mail message. The behavior "Clicking in from an e-mail message" is observed via the code.

✦ **How to store it:** After you observe them, you must store significant behaviors somewhere. You can record all user-clicking behavior on a site in massive server logs. This approach may seem overkill for what you need for personalization. If the behavior is of only immediate importance, you can store it in a session variable that isn't saved after the user exits the site. If you determine the next page you will show based on the Id or options that a user chooses on the previous page, for example, you need to store this behavior only long enough to get you to the next page. If the behavior has long-term implications, you can store it either as part of a user profile or in a separate database table. PLAN, for example, stores only the fact that a donor clicks in from an e-mail message in a transient session variable that doesn't persist after the donor leaves the site.

This table helps you ensure that you can observe and record all the behaviors that your personalizations depend on. You may need help filling in this table from staff who know how to monitor and record behaviors on a Web site. In addition, the CMS product that you use may have a number of its own *observation agents* that provide data that you may have a hard time collecting otherwise.

Extra data

To make some of your personalizations work, you need more data than provided by a list of profiles, behaviors, and components a person has viewed. PLAN, for example, may want to match categories of press releases (in priority order) to audiences as the following table shows.

Audience	PR category
Member	Kid stories, success stories, other
Staff	Org changes, events, success stories, other
Donor	Kid stories, funding, success stories, other
Press	Events, funding, org changes, other

To decide what press releases to prioritize for each audience, you need a trait that puts a person in an audience, and you need to access the *Category* element of the press release components. In addition to the data otherwise stored in the CMS, you need the extra data that's in the preceding table. PLAN can store this table in a database and then access it as necessary to decide how to prioritize press releases.

In this part of the analysis, you decide what extra data your personalizations require. For each applicable personalization, fill in the following table.

Personalization	Extra Data Needed	How to Collect It	How to Maintain It	Where to Store It
(P14) PR Priority	PR Priority table	Public Relations contact	CMS administrator reviews with public relations once per quarter	CMS Configuration database

In the preceding table, I use the example of PLAN press-release priorities to illustrate the following kinds of information that you should collect:

✦ **Personalization:** Enter the Id and name of the personalization.

✦ **Extra data needed:** Name or give an example of the extra data that you need to enable the personalization.

✦ **How to collect it:** Enter how you think that you can create this extra data.

✦ **How to maintain it:** Enter how you expect to update and add to the extra data list over time.

✦ **Where to store it:** Enter the database or other place where you can store this data and where the CMS can access it whenever it needs to.

This table helps you identify all the extra data that you need. In addition, it helps you come to grips early on with the effort that gathering extra data requires.

Campaigns

In this part of the design, you map out any push campaigns that you anticipate will be needed. I define campaign personalization in the section "Publications and Personalization," earlier in this chapter. You aren't likely to know in advance about all the campaigns that you will create, so be prepared to do this analysis on an ongoing basis as new ideas for campaigns arise.

For each campaign that you expect to create, fill in the following design constraints:

✦ **ID:** Give the campaign a unique Id that you can use later to refer to it.

✦ **Name:** Give the campaign a name that you can remember it by and that communicates its central purpose.

✦ **Purpose:** What's the desired goal of the campaign? How does it support the goals of the CMS and vice versa? How can you measure its success?

✦ **Traits:** What are your criteria for identifying audience members for this campaign?

✦ **Content types and components:** What content types or specific components can you present in this campaign?

✦ **Templates:** What templates can you use to present the publication pages or sections in the campaign?

✦ **Logistics:** When does the campaign start and end? How can you monitor it and what's the process for turning it on and off?

Campaigns that run within an existing publication are simply personalizations that turn on and off at a determined time. Campaigns that you run by creating new publications (a special e-mail publication, for example) are page templates that you turn on and off at a determined time.

Tagging

In this section of the analysis, you determine all the effects that your personalization scheme is likely to have on the structure or your content types.

For each personalization, fill in the following table.

Personalization	Content Types Involved	Elements Involved	Element Values Affected	Workload
(P14) PR Priority	Press release	Category	None	None

In the preceding table, I use the example of PLAN press-release priorities to illustrate the following kinds of information that you should collect to understand how to tag your components for personalization:

✦ **Personalization:** Enter the Id and name of the personalization.

✦ **Content types involved:** Enter the names of any content types that participate in the personalization. Include types that either trigger the personalization or are shown as a result of the personalization.

✦ **Elements involved:** Enter the names of any elements used to select the components that you use in the personalization. If PLAN, for example, selects components of the type *press-release* based on the *Category* element, it enters *Category* in this cell.

✦ **Element values affected:** If the personalization involves only existing elements with the values they'd already have, enter *None*. To change or increase the values that the element has because of the personalization, list the changes here. If the element exists only to facilitate the personalization, type that fact here.

✦ **Workload:** If you type anything other than *None* in the Element Values Affected column, estimate the amount of work involved in maintaining the content in a state that the personalization requires, both initially and on an ongoing basis.

This table helps you to assess the effect of your personalizations on your content types. Obviously, the best effect is no effect. If you can't reach that goal, you at least get a fair idea of how much extra work supporting your personalizations involves.

You may also want to pivot the following table to focus on components rather than personalizations.

Content Type	Personalization
Press Release	(P12) DonorSidebar
	(P13) AfricaWatch
	(P14) PR Priority

This table gives you good idea of which content types are most central to your personalization scheme.

Rules

After you conduct the rest of the analysis that I lay out in this chapter, constructing detailed, programmable personalization rules is just a matter of collecting all the details that you've already amassed in one place.

Review the analysis that you've done to determine the following design criteria for each personalization that you create:

✦ **Id:** Provide the Id that you assign to the personalization.

✦ **Name:** Provide the name that you assign to the personalization.

✦ **Profile:** What audiences and audience traits does it access?

✦ **Behavior:** What observable behaviors does it record and use?

✦ **Content types:** What content types and elements does it use? Consider both the content types that may trigger the personalization and those that appear as a result of the personalization.

✦ **Templates:** What templates does the personalization appear in?

✦ **Extra data:** What extra data does the personalization require to operate?

✦ **Rule:** Using a set of steps and/or a statement of the form "If (behavior and traits), then (content)," formulate a rule for your personalization that includes all the design constraints in this list.

Localization

Localization can be treated as a form of personalization (although the two are distinct) because the tools and methodologies are similar. You may, in fact, decide to treat localization as just another sort of personalization. (In Chapter 39, "Building Management Systems," in the section "Localization as personalization" I discuss the similarities and how you can make use of them.) In any case, you need to determine what drives localization — which traits will you localize for, and what rules will apply (as discussed in "Personalization and rules" earlier in this chapter).

You can refer back to your audience analysis (see Chapter 25, "Cataloging Audiences") to see what traits you decided to link to each locality.

Tasks

Consider the effect of your personalization analysis on the ongoing maintenance of the CMS. Then fill in the following table to define any tasks you can imagine that must happen on a recurring basis to run the CMS. Here are some task types to get you thinking:

✦ Rule review.

✦ Profiling review.

✦ New or changed personalizations.

✦ Personalization effectiveness review.

✦ Trait collection redesigns.

✦ User survey cycles.

✦ Content metadata reviews.

✦ Campaign cycles.

✦ Usage log analysis to track behaviors.

✦ Localization cycles.

✦ Customization redesigns.

Fill in the following table.

Task Name	Who	What	How Much	When	How
Rule Review	Publication manager	Review the report of pages visited, sorted by audience type, to gauge the effect of personalizations	25-50 personalizations	As the report is prepared by the CMS administrator	Reading and discussing with the rest of the staff and with key users

Provide the following information:

✦ **Task name:** Give the task a short but memorable name that describes it.

✦ **Who:** Determine what person or kind of person is responsible for doing this task. Naming an automated process here instead of a person is acceptable.

✦ **What:** List what the person or process must do to accomplish the task.

✦ **When:** Specify at what frequency you must accomplish this task, or how you know when it must occur.

✦ **How much:** Describe how many of these sorts of tasks you expect to do. A numerical quantity is preferable here, but if you can't come up with one, words such as *a lot*, *not much*, and so on suffice.

✦ **How:** Detail the skills, tools, or processes the person or process needs to accomplish this task?

Don't worry if the tasks that you come up with at this point are somewhat ill-defined or sketchy. In your workflow analysis (detailed in Chapter 33, "Designing Workflow and Staffing Models") you have ample opportunity to refine them.

Integrate

To integrate your personalization analysis with the other parts of your logical design, consider the following categories and questions:

✦ **Audiences:** Do your personalizations generally follow audience lines? If not, are some changes to your audiences necessary? Do personalizations differentiate between members of an audience? If not, that's a good next step to take in personalization. If so, your next level of audience segmentation is perhaps waiting for you in your personalization scheme.

✦ **Profile:** Can you collect all the information that you identified in the user profile? How much of it must you infer? Can you trust these inferences? Review as many particular components as possible to test your assumptions.

✦ **Testing:** How can you validate the segment and behavioral assumptions that you've made? Tap the audience members that agreed to assist in your project and test the personalizations on them. Are they of value? Do they highlight the best information and not completely obscure information of lesser value?

✦ **Components:** Is the additional workload on your components worth the value that the personalizations provide? Is this extra work just a small part of existing jobs, or does it require special staff? Review your set of content types. Do they break up your information in such a way that it can serve all the personalization needs that you've identified? If not, go back and rework your components.

✦ **Templates:** Does personalization overly complicate your template scheme? Is it worth the extra effort?

Summary

Doing personalization, at its most fundamental, consists of segmenting your audience based on traits, assigning individuals to segments, and providing content to them based on their segments. To do personalization means:

✦ You are able to gather information about your audience. The sort of personalization you can do depends on what you can learn about them.

✦ You have figured out what content that you will deliver should be personalized and, consequently, what your systems and content architecture must support to deliver the personalization you want.

✦ You have planned how your publishing system will deliver personalization through the appropriate templates.

✦ You have analyzed the personalization you need; you have planned for what personalization you will deliver as well as how your system will support the personalization; you have integrated personalization with the other analyses in your CM project.

Doing personalization for a publication can add to the work required to create your CMS, and the cost-benefit ratio is likely to dictate how much personalization you can do. The more you need, the more likely you'll make significant design requirements in the CMS for gathering data to support personalization. That said, the time to decide what information that CMS must provide is during the design phase.

Even if you don't initially implement the level of personalization you'll need in the future, you should do a personalization analysis as part of your design process. That way, you have an idea of what changes to your CMS you have to make when you do implement personalization—or in other words, the costs of not implementing personalization now.

If you've been working through this section linearly, you've now completed all the design tasks for the CMS. In the next chapter, I detail how to plan for processes workflow and staffing to make it all come together.

✦   ✦   ✦

Designing Workflow and Staffing Models

♦   ♦   ♦   ♦

In This Chapter

A definition and
extended example
of a workflow

Details on the tasks,
jobs, and steps that
make up workflows

The constraints that
localization puts on
workflow

A full process for
analyzing and
designing a workflow
system

A full process for
analyzing and
designing a staffing
system

♦   ♦   ♦   ♦

Workflow is the process of creating cycles of sequential and parallel tasks that must be accomplished in your CMS. I group this subject together with considerations of staffing because the two are best figured out at the same time. If you know what and how much you must accomplish, you can figure out who you need to do it. On the other hand, if you know who you have and who you can get, you can build processes to suit them.

In this chapter, I define the concept of workflow. Then I detail the information to collect and the analysis to perform so you can create the right set of workflows for your CMS staff. I intertwine workflow and staffing concepts early in the chapter to such an extent that you can't break them apart. Staffing calculations, for example, depend entirely on the work that you do to estimate workflow task times. Later in the chapter, after you have the full story on the workflow and staffing, I break them apart and give you two separate but interrelated analysis sections.

Cross-Reference For more information about building workflow into your content management system, see Chapter 39, "Building Management Systems," in the section "Workflow System."

Workflow Jumpstart

This Jumpstart summarizes how you design workflow and staffing models for your CMS.

Use this jumpstart as a summary without the weight of detail, or as a quick review if you've already read the sections "Analyzing Workflow" and "Analyzing Staffing" (later in this chapter) and want a checklist of what you need to do to carry out a workflow and staffing analysis.

To analyze your workflow, follow these steps:

1. Review the tasks that you have come up with so far in the other parts of the logical design. Think about the workflow process as a whole. Consider how your staff will deal with the work cycles you are going to put in place and who you will have define and change steps in the workflow. Think about how you will deal with routine contingencies, such as staff unavailability.

2. Plan your workflow analysis:

- **Combine your task analyses:** Bring all the task analyses from the other parts of the logical design into a single large table. Then review for completeness, accuracy, and redundancy. Add any new tasks that you missed earlier.

- **Refine the list of task into workflows:** Using the task list you've developed, determine whether each task is a single- or multiple-step task, and then group tasks around patterns such as who does them, what types of work are required, and when each task occurs in relation to others. These groups of tasks are workflows. Give each workflow a name and decide how frequently it will occur.

- **Refine each workflow:** Create a table for each workflow, entering information in each column so that you can sort the table meaningfully later. Assign a set of steps for the workflow, specifying the order of the steps, who is involved, what task(s) the step consists of, what triggers a particular step, and what end product or component the step contributes to.

- **Regularize the steps:** After you've created an analysis for each workflow, combine all your workflows into one big table and then sort on the various fields. Try to identify similar steps and determine whether the steps and workflows are structured consistently and efficiently. Eliminate redundancy and combine similar or identical steps into a single workflow.

3. Integrate your workflow analysis with the other analyses you have done. The overall scope of your workflows should give you a good preview of the effort required to keep your system running. Consider whether the workflows you've created really cover all the tasks that you need to run the system. Consider also how well your workflows will accommodate the inevitable changes as they're requested. Finally, decide which of the workflows you've created are required to start the system as well as run it.

To analyze your staffing needs, you can follow these steps:

1. Consider what you know at this point about your staffing needs. Consider how well your current staff meets the needs of the new system, and how you will go about hiring (and funding) any additional staff needed. Determine what a realistic utilization level is, and consider the extent to which your in-house staff will complete the work, as opposed to outsourced or temporary staff (particularly for startup tasks).

2. Plan your staffing analysis:

- **Identify skills and times:** Review the section "Staffing calculations" in this chapter, and then, for each step you identified in your workflow analysis tables, specify the skills required, the time the task requires, and the time that elapses between this step and the next.

- **Cluster tasks by skills into jobs:** Sort your workflow tables by the Skills column you added to determine how well skills cluster together. These skills clusters are the core job requirements. Name each job and create a table showing the skills, tasks, workflows, and steps that the job entails.

- **Calculate time estimates for each job:** Using the skills clusters, add up the estimated time required for each job in order to determine the basic staffing level needed for the job.

3. Integrate your staffing analysis with the other analyses you have done. Consider whether jobs can be combined. Give particular attention to how accurate your estimates need to be at this stage, or conversely how much flexibility you'll have to make staffing changes

once your system is up and running. Consider also how well your staffing estimates will accommodate inevitable changes as people move on or are hired away. Finally, use the staffing analysis you've created as a starting point for creating an analysis of staffing required for system startup.

When you're done, you'll have a solid plan that organizes exactly who does what for your CMS.

Understanding Workflow

Most simply stated, a *workflow* is a series of steps that must occur in the CMS on a periodic basis. In other words, a workflow is a *cycle*. Every so often, a certain series of steps must occur to move some part of the system farther along. The more that you can understand and plan for these cycles, the smoother your CMS will operate.

Although most discussions of workflow center on processes that create content, the fact is that you have periodic processes throughout the collection, management, and publishing systems in a CMS. Because content-creation workflows are the most popular, however, I use one to illustrate the basic concepts of workflow.

Suppose, for example, that PLAN decides that the following steps must occur to ready a news feature for publication:

✦ Someone must write it or pull it from an acquired set of news stories.

✦ Someone must edit it.

✦ Someone must review it for accuracy and legal issues.

✦ Someone must target it (tag it for the appropriate audiences).

Diagrammatically, the process may look like what you see in Figure 33-1.

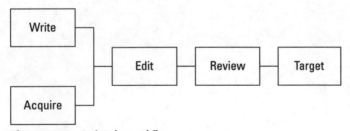

Figure 33-1: A simple workflow

This diagram alone, however, is just the start of what you need to determine to make work happen. In addition, you must determine the following:

✦ Who or what process does the work?

✦ What particular part of the CMS does this workflow affect?

✦ What specific work does the person or process do?

✦ How does the person or process know when to begin?

✦ How long does the person or process take to do the work?

If you add these answers to your diagram, it becomes more complex but a lot more useful, as shown in Figure 33-2.

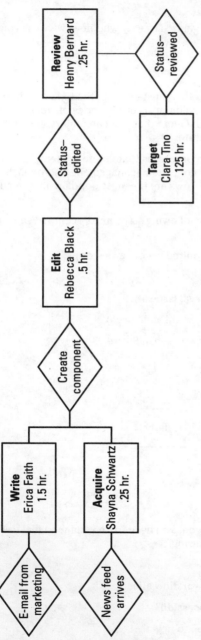

Figure 33-2: A workflow illustration with more detail

In this diagram, the squares are tasks and the diamonds are the events that trigger the tasks. I associate a person and an estimated time to complete the task with each task.

Table 33-1 takes this complexity one step farther by naming the kinds of information that you must create and listing them in more detail than you would want to put on any diagram.

Table 33-1: Workflow WF100 — News Feature Collection

Step	Trigger	Actor	Objects	Tasks	Step Time	Task Time
Write	E-mail notification of the basic facts of a newsworthy event from designated marketing contact	Erica Faith	News Feature component	Create new component and complete all body component elements.	3 days	1.5 hr
Acquire	Arrival of new stories via news feed service	Shayna Schwartz	News Source and News Feature components	See WF300	1 day	.25 hr
Edit	New News Feature component creation	Rebecca Black	News Feature component	Edit and correct all body elements. Fill in all management elements except Audience.	1 day	.5 hr
Review	Status element value set to "Edited."	Henry Bernard	News Feature component	Review Abstract, Partner Background, and Body elements for legal restrictions.	2 days	.25 hr.
Target	Status element value set to "Reviewed"	Clara Tino	News feature component	Fill in Audience element.	1 day	.125 hr

The columns of this table make the parameters of each task clear and separate, as follows:

✦ **The workflow itself** gets an Id (WF100) and a name (as indicated in the table title). By now, you're probably used to the idea that everything gets an Id and a name in a CMS.

✦ **The Step column** gives the name of the workflow step that you're describing. I might have chosen to enter a step number rather than a name.

✦ **The Trigger column** lists the event that causes the step to begin. Generally, the actor from the preceding step triggers the next step. This setup ensures that the workflow keeps going on to completion. In this workflow, the trigger that begins the workflow comes from outside the CMS (an e-mail from a marketing contact). That's because this workflow creates new content whose impetus is something in the world beyond the CMS. Internal events such as reaching an ExpireDate element value or completing a publication cycle may trigger other workflows.

✦ **The Actor column** specifies who performs the task. In this case, all the values are the names of particular people. In other cases, the actor may be an automated process that runs in response to a trigger. The arrival of the news feed, for example, may trigger an automated process that creates a set of News components in the CMS. In addition, instead of specifying a particular person, you may want to specify a kind of person or a role. If three different editors all review press releases, for example, instead of naming one editor, you name the group as the actor. This practice makes your workflow more general but adds an extra workflow, because in addition to the processing workflow, you create one that shows how the editorial group assigns work to an individual.

✦ **The Object column** shows which part of the CMS the step affects, its object. In this case, the column mentions only two objects: a News Feature component and the News Source component. In other workflows, a step can affect other parts of the CMS.

✦ **The Task column** shows a discrete activity that results in some specific change to the object for the step.

✦ **The Step Time column** tells how much time you expect to occur between the time this step triggers and the time the next step triggers.

✦ **The Task Time column** describes how long you expect the actor to work on the task. To write a news feature, for example, should take Erica no longer than an hour and a half. She spends that small amount of time across three days, however, as she collects information and does the parts of her job that don't count as part of this task.

Notice that the Tasks column for the Acquire step refers to another workflow. To get the most mileage out of your workflow design, you want to break it into a set of reusable units. Consider, for example, the version of the workflow shown in Figure 33-3.

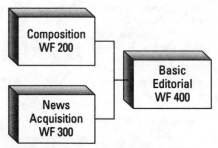

Figure 33-3: A higher-level workflow diagram

Here, instead of putting together a specific workflow, I string together a set of more generic workflows to create the specific workflow. This method makes workflows into reusable components that you can mix and match for different situations. It enables you to organize your approach to workflows and make the most efficient use of the tools and code that you use to implement workflow.

After you create them, you can group any of these workflows with other workflows to produce the set of variations that you need to run a different part of the system. If, for example, the Hot News components that come out of the News Acquisition workflow (in addition to the News Feature components) can move into a publication with a much less formal editorial process, PLAN may create a Basic Editorial workflow and combine it with the acquisition workflow (see Figure 33-4).

The Essence of Workflow

The essence of workflow is to coordinate the moving parts of a content management system in order to create the advantages you are seeking to achieve. Workflow and staffing assumptions are critical not only in getting the CMS off the ground, but in ensuring its ongoing usefulness. It is an iterative process, though — somewhat like tacking in a sailboat — the direction, metrics, dependencies, and roles are clear but just exactly how it will all work at the time requires some attention. Furthermore, workflow can become a communication device — a physical representation of "how things work" so that dependencies, sequencing, and roles and responsibilities can be clarified and improved. Workflow is critical — otherwise the moving parts may not know how to work best, and those with responsibilities may be unclear as to the dependencies that need to be managed.

Mary Lee Kennedy, The Kennedy Group (www.maryleekennedy.com)

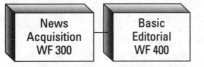

Figure 33-4: The acquisition workflow combined with a different next workflow

So after that extensive introduction, I can state that, from the perspective of this book, a *workflow* is a sequence of steps that make a change to some aspect of a CMS or its publications. In each step, a trigger prompts an actor to perform a set of tasks on one or more objects in the CMS. A step has an overall duration, which is the time until the next trigger, and also a task duration, which is the amount of actual work time that the step requires.

Workflow triggers

What can trigger a workflow step? Following are some of the kinds of events that you may want to use:

✦ **Manual events:** Users can trigger a workflow step manually. For example, your workflow system might present a button that says "Move Item to Next Stage." Clicking that button triggers the next step in the workflow.

✦ **Dates and times:** A date and time can trigger any step that must happen periodically (such as a publication release cycle or checking for new content on a partner site) and anything that must happen at a particular time (such as retiring or making components live).

✦ **Creation events:** You may choose to trigger a step based on new information that someone's creating. The creation of a News Feature component, for example, triggers the Edit step in the workflow that I illustrate in the preceding section. Depending on your particular CMS, you can also trigger on creation events in your database and file system. If someone drops a new file in a particular directory, for example, you can send a message to the CMS to begin processing the new file.

✦ **Deletion events:** These types of events are similar to the creation events. If you delete a component, file, or database record, that action can possibly trigger a workflow step. If you delete a record from your users' database, for example, you can trigger a workflow for reassigning her workload to someone else.

✦ **Component element changes:** A change in the value of any component element value is a candidate for a trigger. In the workflow that I describe in the preceding section, a change to the Status element triggers two different steps. As another example, any change to the value of an element that you call Body Text may automatically trigger an editorial review step for that component.

✦ **E-mail receipt:** With some extra work (in most systems), you can set up an e-mail acceptor system that triggers workflow to begin or continue. The receipt of an e-mail message addressed to `feedback@plan-international.org`, for example, may trigger a workflow for evaluating and acting on the feedback message. As another example, a reviewer outside the organization may communicate only by e-mail. In that case, the trigger for the Review step may cause an automated process to send an e-mail message containing the text to review to the next reviewer. The e-mail message that returns may trigger another process to extract the text from the response, return it to the CMS repository, and then trigger the next step in the workflow.

✦ **Informal communication:** Any request or question from one person to another may initiate a workflow. In the workflow that I describe in the preceding section, an informal e-mail message from marketing to an author began the workflow. The person may just as easily call on the phone with the same information to begin the workflow. Of course, the CMS isn't aware of informal communication, so what this trigger amounts to is a prompt to a person to enact a more formal trigger within the CMS.

✦ **System events:** Events in the operating system or in other applications can trigger workflow. Every time that you add a new user to a particular group in the organization's registry, for example, you may want to trigger a workflow to reevaluate workloads. Or after someone modifies a record in the organization's product catalog system, you may want to trigger the workflow for a product component review.

✦ **Web events:** Actions that users take on a Web site can trigger workflow. PLAN, for example, may put a button on each press-release page that reads, "Click here if this press release isn't relevant to you." PLAN may set up its Web infrastructure so that if 10 users click the button, it changes the status of a press release to "Feedback Received," thus triggering another Target step where it can reconsider the audiences for the press release.

Any action that results in some change of state in some computer system is a candidate for a trigger. What triggers your workflow steps is limited only by what you need and how much effort you're willing to spend on custom programming.

Workflow objects

Each step of a workflow contains tasks that change the state of some object. These objects can be CMS entities or they can be objects beyond the entities.

Cross-Reference For a definition and an overview of the CMS entities, see Chapter 23, "The Wheel of Content Management."

The CMS entities that most often serve as the objects of a workflow step are as follows:

✦ **Acquisition Sources:** Each source is likely to have its own workflow that concerns its conversion and initial tagging. In addition, as in the workflow that I describe in the section "Understanding Workflow," earlier in this chapter, a source workflow may key into a number of further workflows and may merge with whatever authoring workflows create the same sorts of components.

✦ **Authors:** Authoring workflows divide by component and/or by author type. You may, for example, have a single workflow for all authors of a Frequently Asked Question (FAQ) feature. On the other hand, you may have a different workflow for your staff authors and your volunteer authors, regardless of what kind of content they're creating. For the most control, you may decide to designate workflows by component and author types. You may decide that volunteer authors of FAQs, for example, need a few extra review and revision steps than do either staff authors of FAQs or volunteer authors of other components.

✦ **Components:** Regardless of whether a component comes from an author or an acquisition source, after it's a component, it likely falls into a set of workflows that concern its aggregation, use, and retirement.

✦ **Publications:** Each publication has at least one workflow associated with its continuing publication. Most have more than one. A print publication, for example, may have monthly issues driven by one workflow, and quarterly design reviews may be driven by another. A complex Web publication may have a whole family of workflows for live updates, daily updates, weekly updates, monthly design reviews, feedback postings, content retirement on any number of frequencies, and more.

In addition to acting on CMS entities, a workflow can affect any number of other parts of the CMS and can affect systems beyond the CMS. Following are some examples:

✦ **CMS configuration:** Workflows often affect the configuration of the CMS itself. On a monthly cycle, for example, you may perform a personalization review that processes feedback from users and statistics from usage logs to decide how well the current personalization scheme is working and how you might improve it. The objects of the collection steps of this workflow are the CMS logs and e-mail queues. The objects of the change steps of this workflow are the personalization configuration files, database tables, and template code.

✦ **CMS administration:** A change to the users of the CMS, for example, may trigger a workflow for reapportioning workloads that has as its object the user-administration system of the CMS.

✦ **Other system administration:** Workflow can also cause changes to the configuration and management of other systems. A change to a number in an inventory system (that is, inventory for a particular product falling to zero or a product that ends up with excess inventory), for example, may trigger the review of the page layout for a product page (because you don't want to display the product that's out of stock or because you want to promote products with excess inventory). The same change can even trigger an automated suppression of the display of certain Product components in a CMS publication. It might also trigger an e-mail message to the system administrator of the external product catalog system to resolve any discrepancies between the inventory and catalog systems.

✦ **Planning and design:** Workflow can act on noncomputer systems. PLAN, for example, may decide to perform a site-design review after every 100 feedback messages that it receives. The review is the object of the workflow, but it isn't a computer process at all.

You can probably think of other objects affected by workflow. As is true for triggers, the objects of workflow steps are limited only by your needs and your talent for recognizing what needs to change and when.

A perspective on workflow

For some reason, the subject of workflow gets a lot of attention in organizations that are looking for a CMS. In my experience, workflow functionality is usually the part of the CMS products that draws the most questions; it's always high on the list of selection criteria and nets the most time during demonstrations. This situation always seemed odd to me. Workflow is important, of course, but it's only one aspect of many in a CMS. I certainly don't think it is as important as the repository system, the templating system, or even the collection tools that a system offers. Still, in most cases, all these other subjects put together get less attention than workflow, even though the capabilities of these other systems — and your capacity to make use of them — greatly affect almost any workflow you devise.

To explain the phenomenon to myself, I formed a little theory. According to my theory, workflow gets so much attention because of the following characteristics (in order of importance):

✦ **It seems central:** The idea of workflow seems to really hit at the heart of the problem. If your problem is to organize masses of information and present that information in the best manner possible, latching onto the promise of a workflow system that creates and mandates hard-core processes and "makes them get it straight" is all too easy. This approach, however, involves two problems: First, the workflow system doesn't mandate the process; you do. Unless you direct your effort and energy at getting processes accepted, the best workflow system can't make anyone do anything (except revolt against a system they don't believe they need). Second, the workflow system doesn't create the processes; you do. The best workflow system can implement any process that you can dream up, but you still must tell it what process to use. A fancy tool is of no use if you don't figure out how to use it.

✦ **It's tangible:** Even the name — *workflow* — seems solid and easy to grasp. I'd hazard a guess that you came to this book with some idea of what a workflow is or that you can, at least, guess its meaning from the word itself. Repositories, templates, and collection tools, on the other hand, may still seem obscure to you, even after spending hours reading about them. If you are trying to say something intelligent about a CMS, focusing on something reasonable such as workflow is a lot easier than trying to figure out how to ask for the repository structure that you want.

✦ **It's process engineering:** Workflow resonates with and amplifies the echoes of the process re-engineering movement that once had so much sway in organizations (at least in North America). It focuses you on the people and their tasks, which many organizations see as a good perspective from which to view any enterprise problem. If you've read any significant amount of this book, you're probably not surprised to see me agree with this perspective. Again, however, the workflow system is a tool into which you pour the process re-engineering that you've already accomplished.

✦ **It's visual:** More and more, CMS products have snazzy user interfaces around their workflow systems that enable you to drag actors, tasks, and triggers around and draw lines between them to connect them. They're quite fun to play with and offer immediate gratification. They aren't, however, particularly pivotal to the overall operation of the system, given that most people see no more of the workflow system than an e-mail message or a Web page with a work queue on it.

By no means, do I feel that workflow is unimportant or even that it should not make it into the top criteria for why you select one CMS over another. It's plenty important. It's just no panacea.

The following list provides a few ideas to help you keep a balanced perspective on the subject of workflow:

✦ **Go to the tool last:** Don't ask the workflow system what to do; *tell* it what to do. Develop your workflow needs and then try to get the tool to do it. That way, you're sure that you have the processes that your organization needs and not just the ones that the tool's good at.

✦ **Start simple:** Every step that you put between the start and finish of a workflow is a little hurdle that the staff must jump to reach a goal. The fewer hurdles that you impose, the faster staffers reach the goal and the happier they are after they get there. Always ask yourself, "Is this step necessary?" If you can find a way to simplify and avoid an extra step, do it. Having a visual modeler at your fingertips may tempt you to account for more variations, make more fine-grained processes, and construct the ultimate system. However, no one — including you — is going to be happy later as you try to implement such a scheme.

✦ **Don't model the existing process:** If you begin by modeling the process as it is today, you've already conceded the battle to simplify and organize. Instead, start with the minimum number of steps and overall processes that you can devise to accomplish a goal. Then extend your simple model only under pressure from a person who can't live without another step in the process. You may end up at the process that you have today (and who knows maybe it's a really good process), but don't go there until you absolutely must.

✦ **Focus on use and not on creation:** The part of the workflow system that really matters most to staff members is the small piece that each staff member sees. As the designer of the workflow system, try to climb down from the mountain top where you can see the entire process and instead look at each step from the ground level of each actor. Try to imagine (or simulate) what each actor really sees on her screen and the options that she wants to see at each step.

Your overall goal with workflow is to make it so good that it disappears completely. You succeed in your workflow design and then implementation if the actions that each actor must take to move along the CMS fit seamlessly into the tools and procedures of that person's overall job.

Push-and-pull workflow

Workflow steps are of no use if the person who must accomplish them doesn't know they exist. To inform actors of the actions they must take, you have the following two options:

✦ **Push:** You can ensure that a staff member sees pending tasks by trying to get the tasks in front of her. The method that you use most frequently to push tasks out to people is e-mail. Many systems enable you to run your entire workflow interaction through e-mail. When a step triggers, an e-mail message goes to the actor with instructions on what to do and possibly a link back to the CMS. This sort of approach is best for casual or infrequently tasked staff members. If a person receives more than one or two e-mail messages per day from the CMS, she may stop paying attention. In addition, her inbox fills with a lot of messages that all look alike. Not a good way to manage a lot of tasks.

✦ **Pull:** You can group pending tasks into a work queue and present it to a person all in one place. Many systems, for example, provide a Web page where staffers can go to see all the tasks that they need to accomplish. You can sort good queues by date, task type, and even priority. Of course, to give the staff the capability to sort by type and priority, you must assign these attributes to all your workflow tasks.

As usual, you needn't go all one way or the other. The ideal system enables you to decide to whom to send e-mail messages and under what circumstances. An e-mail message may, for example, go out to anyone who hasn't accessed her work-queue page in more than a week.

Introducing Tasks, Jobs, and Steps

In the long run, you want to design the set of jobs that your CMS needs to run correctly. One way to accomplish this goal is to work upward from the tasks that you define in the rest of your analysis to the people that you need to accomplish these tasks. Along the way, you can begin to order the tasks into formal workflow steps that dictate exactly how you expect workers to accomplish the tasks.

A *task* is a particular activity that someone must complete. You determine the tasks that you need in your CMS as part of the logical design of each entity. A *job* is all the tasks that you want one kind of person to do.

You create jobs by mixing top-down and bottom-up processes. From the top down, you can start from a set of jobs that any CMS is likely to require. From the bottom up, you categorize the tasks that you collect by the skills necessary to accomplish them. A combination of the two approaches gives you a list of standard jobs that you customize to your particular situation.

A *step* is one or more tasks that you group together into a repeatable unit. A *workflow* is a series of steps that you arrange to accomplish a particular goal. At the risk of confusing this nice breakdown, the tasks that you determine during logical design are often more like goals of a workflow rather than steps. PLAN, for example, may decide that the basic editing of news features is one of the tasks that it must accomplish during collection. On closer examination, however, it may find that basic editing actually contains a number of tasks (such as editing, reviewing, and targeting). No problem here. During logical design, you naturally come up with tasks at a high level. As you move into workflow and staffing analysis, however, you need to refigure your tasks at a more granular level as the example of the basic editing workflow shows.

The tasks that you bring into workflow and staffing design must display the following characteristics:

✦ **Single person:** One person (or one automated process) must accomplish a task for it to roll up into jobs and workflows.

✦ **Single time:** You can complete a task that's at the right level for staffing and workflow modeling without any intervening activities. In other words, the task can't depend on any other task for you to complete it. Suppose, for example, that reviewing requires the reviewer (Henry Bernard, in the example in the section "Understanding Workflow," earlier in this chapter) to get approval from a staff lawyer. In this case, he can't complete his task without an intervening activity by the lawyer. PLAN would do better to create two tasks, one for Henry and one for the lawyer.

After you hone your task set so that it's all single-person and single-time in nature, you can organize your tasks into effective workflows and jobs.

Note You may want to analyze the two distinct CMS phases for workflow and staffing: *startup* and *run*. In the startup phase, you're building the CMS. It's the CMS project. In the run phase, you're keeping the system running on an ongoing basis. For brevity, in the sections that follow, I illustrate calculations only for the run phase of your CMS, but you can do the same calculations for the startup phase. For some areas, such as large content-processing workflows, working them through for the startup phase of your CMS is well worth your effort.

Staff modeling

What everyone wants to know at the very beginning of a CMS initiative is what it's going to cost and what personnel it requires. Of course, what it costs is a function of the people it requires (as well as any hardware and software costs). So, from the very start, staffing is a big issue. Unfortunately, at the start of your process, you have very little data on which to base any estimates of staffing. The best that you can do is to guess based on what consultants and product company representatives tell you; the staffing of organizations that are in a similar situation as yours; and the staff that you can reasonably expect the organization to provide or hire.

With luck, your initial information sources can give you staffing estimates that come close enough for the planning that you must do at the very start of the project. Early on, you need to give *some* estimate if only to buy enough time to come up with a *good* estimate. If you follow the logical design process that I lay out in this book, you're now in a position to come up with that good estimate.

So what do you need to know to make good estimates about the kind and amount of staffing that you need for your CMS? I start with a simple answer in the following formula:

```
Number of People = Hours Per Week / 40
```

Assuming a 40-hour week (but you can substitute any other number that's more appropriate for your organization), you need enough people to cover the total number of hours that you and your staff must work. This equation is simple, but it's not very helpful.

To make the equation more helpful, you can go two ways: (1) You can create multiple equations, one per type of person that you need, and (2) you can break down the number of hours that you need by task. If you expand the equation for people and task types, the result is a set of equations similar to the following examples:

```
People(type1) = [Hours(task1) + Hours(task2) + Hours(task3) +...] / 40
People(type2) = [Hours(task1) + Hours(task2) + Hours(task3) +...] / 40
People(type3) = [Hours(task1) + Hours(task2) + Hours(task3) +...] / 40
```

For each type of person that you need, you sum up the hours per week that you need for each task that person's to do. Then you divide the sum by the number of hours per week that you expect each person to work (in this case 40). This set of equations is more complex than the first, single one, but it gives you a lot more information to go on. Of course, it assumes that you already know a lot of information. It assumes, in particular, that you know the following:

✦ What kinds of people you need.

✦ What tasks each kind of person is to do.

✦ How many hours each pertinent task takes per week.

This equation isn't the kind that you can just plug numbers into. Rather, it's a way to model and balance a set of competing constraints. In other words, no "right" answer exists. Any way that you can figure out to make all the individual equations balance works. Wrong answers, however, are possible. A wrong answer does the following:

✦ Leaves tasks with no one to do them.

✦ Leaves full-time staff with less than a full-time workload.

So the way to work these equations is iteratively (that is, in multiple passes). Try one way and see how it fails; try another way and get it closer; try and try again until you cover all the people and all the tasks.

Staff, jobs, and tasks

You can begin with the jobs that I outline for a CMS elsewhere in this book (see Chapter 13, "Staffing a CMS"), but before long, you need to get past that list and decide on a set of jobs that suits your particular situation. A *job*, in this book, is a set of tasks that you assign to a person or people with sufficient skills to accomplish those tasks.

Assigning tasks to staff is as much an art as a science. Staff members have interests as well as skills. You hope they're interested in doing the things at which they're most skilled and that they're most skilled at what you need done, but that's not always the way it works. You want them to work quickly and consistently so that you can plan accurately, but they always surprise you by either getting ahead of or behind your plans. You want to figure out all this information once and be done with it, but people grow and change, forcing you to continually reevaluate assignments.

Still, you can bring science to bear on staff assignments — not to squeeze them into an unchanging form but to create a model that can bend and evolve along with your staff. A simple model can just specify which tasks comprise which jobs. PLAN, for example, may have two proposed jobs: metator and editor.

Among other jobs (and among the larger list of tasks that editors and metators may perform), PLAN may create the task apportionment that I show in Table 33-2.

Table 33-2: PLAN Task Assignments

Job	Task
Metator	
	Metatag
	Consistency Check
	Advise
	Train
Editor	
	Edit
	Metatag
	Consistency Check

For each job, you outline a set of tasks. Notice the overlap in tasks between the two jobs. Both involve the Metatag and Consistency Check tasks. To resolve the overlap, you can take the following approaches:

✦ **Assign the task to one job or the other.** If the split causes confusion, if the task isn't large, or if you find the skills to complete the task in a single job, you may decide to move the task completely into one job.

✦ **Split the task between the two jobs.** If it's a time-consuming task, assigning it to two or more positions may prove most appropriate. And if you want more than one person or job category to do the task for the purpose of training, reward, or challenge, you can also split the task. A split task gives you a more complex model (harder for you), but it can often make the jobs that you create work much better for the staff (easier for them).

✦ **Create two tasks.** The split task may actually be two different tasks masquerading as one. Maybe PLAN, for example, needs both a metatorial consistency check and an editorial consistency check. If the task is significantly different as performed within two different jobs, you may be better off just breaking it into two tasks (with two distinct names).

✦ **Merge jobs.** If two jobs share a significant overlap of tasks, you may really just need a single job. Don't create jobs simply because you think that you may need them (or to find a job for particular staff members); create them only because you actually need to.

If you do end up splitting tasks between jobs, you need to account for the split in your model, as shown in Table 33-3.

Table 33-3: PLAN Split Task Assignments

Job	Task	Percent	Split Criteria
Metator			
	Metatag	80	Classes: C1, C2, C3, C4, C5, C6, C7, C8
	Consistency Check	20	All management elements
	Advise	100	
	Train	100	
Editor			
	Edit	100	
	Metatag	20	Classes: C9, C10
	Consistency Check	80	All body elements

In this model, I list the percentage of the task that you give to each job. In addition, I specify the way that you decide how to split the task between jobs.

Get comfortable changing jobs and tasks around until they all fit together. Then get comfortable reworking your model again and again as the people and system grow and change. But don't take the changes as an excuse to get sloppy or settle for an unbalanced system. At each stopping point, you want a staffing model that's optimum for your current situation. Here's what I mean by *optimum*:

✦ **Fewest jobs:** The fewer job categories you have, the simpler and easier it is to manage your staff.

✦ **Fewest number of tasks:** An optimum staffing system (and, by the way, the one that's easiest to implement in the CMS) involves the fewest tasks necessary to get the job done. Have a good and specific reason for creating a task.

✦ **Most even spread:** Optimally, you spread tasks evenly over jobs, with no job getting too much or too little to do.

✦ **Effective task clusters:** The best job/task system groups tasks that fit together into the same jobs. If a metator is responsible for training, for example, you may as well make him responsible for advising as well. The skills and experience that he needs for training enhance the metator's ability to offer advice.

✦ **Growth and challenge:** For optimum job performance, make sure that you include tasks that are a bit of a stretch for a particular job. Metatagging, for example, may represent a challenge for an editor. That challenge, however, may increase the motivation and satisfaction of the editor and produce a benefit to her and the entire team.

Task-time calculations

If you know how much time that each task takes per week, you can deduce the number of people that you need. But how do you figure out how much time that a task takes? Here is one way:

```
Task Time Per Week = (Time Per Task) X (Times Per Week)
```

If you know how long a task takes and how many times a person performs it per week, you can multiply these factors to find the amount of time that task requires each week. You can estimate the time per task by making an educated guess or, better, by trying the task yourself. Perform each task a few times to get the feeling for how long it takes. If possible, have someone you think is likely to become responsible for the task later on do it now to get a better idea of how long the task may take. And, after your CMS is up and running and the task learning curve has flattened out, check your calculations against reality.

The number of times that a person performs a task per week may prove harder to estimate. For tasks that involve components, you can use the following equation:

```
Times Per Week = Times(Component1) + Times(Component2) + . . .
```

The total number of times that someone performs a task equals the number of times that the person performs it for each component that includes that task. In turn, you find the number of times that a person performs a task per component by using the following equation:

```
Times Per Component = (Components Per Week) X (Percent of Components)
```

The number of times that you must do a task for a particular component class equals the number of components that you produce per week times the percent of the components that need the task. This equation breaks down as follows:

✦ **Components per week:** How many of that type of component you produce. You collect this information as part of your component analysis, as I detail in the section "Creation," in Chapter 27, "Designing Content Types."

✦ **Percent of components:** The fraction of the components that need this task. Fully 100 percent of PLAN's News Feature components need editing, for example, but perhaps only 50 percent of its News Brief components need editing.

For tasks that involve publications, you can use a similar equation to estimate the task time, as follows:

```
Task(hrs/wk)= SUM[Publication X Percent X Task Time]
```

To find out how long a task takes per week, multiply the number of each type of publication per week by the time that doing the task takes and the percentage of the publications that require that task. This equation breaks down as follows:

✦ **Task(hrs/wk):** The task time per week (in hours).

✦ **SUM:** This term means that you do the calculation in the square brackets ([ ]) for each publication that includes this task and then add them all up.

✦ **Publications:** The number of publications of each type that are produced per week.

✦ **Percent:** The percentage of each publication that receives this task. (Enter 1, for example, if all publications get the task or 0.5 if only half do.)

✦ **Task time:** The amount of time that the task takes for each publication.

For tasks that don't involve components or publications, you can invent your own equations that estimate task time.

Note

Needless to say, you perform some tasks less frequently than every week. In addition, many tasks take minutes and not hours. Still, you want to keep standard units of measurement so that you can add up times across tasks. (For me, those units are weeks and hours; for you, they can be something else.)

Staffing calculations

Given a good job/task breakdown and some estimates of task times, you can come up with a preliminary staffing projection, as shown in Table 33-4.

Table 33-4: Preliminary PLAN Staffing Projection

Job	Task	Percent	Split Criteria	Task Time	Totals
Metator					**61 Hr/Week**
	Metatag	80	Classes: C1, C2, C3, C4, C5, C6, C7, C8	60 Hr/Week	48 Hr/Week
	Consistency Check	20	All Management elements	40 Hr/Week	8 Hr/Week
	Advise	100		3 Hr/Week	3 Hr/Week
	Train	100		2 Hr/Week	2 Hr/Week
Editor					**104 Hr/Week**
	Edit	100		60 Hr/Week	60 Hr/Week
	Metatag	20	Classes: C9, C10	60 Hr/Week	12 Hr/Week
	Consistency Check	80	All Body elements	40 Hr/Week	32 Hr/Week

To the information already in Table 33-3, I simply add Task Time and Totals column, which I explain in the following list:

✦ **The Task Time column** simply lists the time for the task that you calculate.

✦ **The Total column** multiplies the Task Time column by the Percent column to display the net time on the task per week for that job.

The Percent column splits the task by percentage between the jobs that share it. So, according to the staffing model, PLAN needs about 1.5 metators and about 2.5 editors per week.

Fudge factors

After presenting a mathematical procedure for precise calculations for tasks and staffing requirements in the preceding sections, I need to back off and inject a large dose of reality. These figures are all ballpark estimates. Don't mistake the precision of these equations for accuracy. You may say, "Sure, I know that any estimates I come up with are only as good as my worst assumption." Unfortunately, the reality is somewhat dimmer. Your estimates are only as good as all your worst estimates — multiplied.

Suppose, for example, that you mis-estimate a task time. You say that it takes an hour, but in reality, it takes an hour plus or minus 20 percent (between 48 minutes and 72 minutes). So far, your estimate may be off by 20 percent. Next, you estimate that 10 of these tasks are done per week, but in reality the actual figure is between 8 and 12. Again, you're accurate to within 20 percent. As you calculate task time per week, however, your estimate isn't accurate to within 20 percent but to within about 40 percent. If, for example, each task takes 48 minutes and you have only 8 of them, the total time is 384 minutes. If on the other hand, each task takes 72 minutes and you have 12 of them, the total time is 864 minutes. That's a wide gap. (It's about 10½ hours, plus or minus about 4 hours!)

Obviously, I wouldn't present calculations at all if I thought they were too inaccurate to use. My real point here is that you need to take your calculations for the basic estimates they are and not put more faith in them than they deserve. You also need to remember to always test and review your assumptions to make them more and more accurate.

Following are a few of the assumptions to which you want to pay particularly close attention:

✦ **100 percent efficiency:** Just because a task takes 1 hour to perform doesn't mean that a person can complete that same task eight times in an eight-hour day. People simply don't work at 100 percent efficiency. So I'm assuredly wrong in saying in the preceding section that PLAN needs 1.5 metators. To do 61 hours of work, it's more likely going to need 2 metators (or more, depending on the other constraints of the workplace).

✦ **Consistency:** In all the calculations that I describe, I use a single number (components per week, tasks per week, and so on). In reality, most of these numbers vary over time. Understand that your averages rarely hit the mark for any particular week.

✦ **Sample size:** If you believe that you have an accurate task time estimate after trying out the tasks a few times, think again. In general, you need to do more trials than you have time or energy for to get really accurate numbers. Understand that a limited number of trials yield results of limited accuracy. At least in the case of task times, the "real" number is usually less than your original estimate, in part because people will tend to get better at their tasks over time.

✦ **Unaccounted factors:** Your best analysis never turns up all the tasks that a person ends up doing. Every morning, I start out with a good idea of all the tasks that I must do that day. At the end of the day, I've rarely accomplished them all. On the other hand, I often accomplish a number of tasks that I didn't know I needed to do. The same applies to your CMS and its staff. Expect your analysis to be imperfect and for impromptu tasks and even jobs to appear where you least expect them.

The art of staffing and workflow always confounds your attempts to pin it down to some single set of numbers. The best that you can hope for is to continue to refine your approach so that, in time, you become more and more confident in the numbers that you produce. Still, as error-prone as this process is, it's better than the alternative: no process at all.

Perhaps the best reason to do this sort of analysis isn't to finally figure out how many editors you need — after all, that figure's sure to change. The best reason to do this sort of analysis may be to immerse yourself in the factors that contribute to needing a certain number of editors in order to hone your intuition on the subject.

And don't forget to check the numbers that you arrive at against your intuition. Do you really need 30 editors to run your CMS? Spend half your time doing calculations and the other half of the time scratching your head and trying to feel out the right answer.

Tip   To make your numbers as clear as possible to those who may view them (and to avoid giving a false sense of precision), always present them at the accuracy you believe in. If, for example, your calculation comes out with the number 2.497 editors needed, say in your results that you need between two and three editors to reflect the accuracy that you believe the number has.

Fitting Localization into Your Workflow

Localization presents an interesting challenge to your workflow system. As much as possible, you want localization to happen in parallel to other workflow steps so that it has the least effect on the overall time for the workflow. You need, however to balance the efficiency of this approach with the need to stay synchronized. PLAN, for example, may place a localization step in parallel with the editorial, review, and targeting step, as shown in Figure 33-5.

Note   I'm making a number of assumptions to keep the example simple. I assume only one localization of the component and no review or approval steps in the localization process.

For greatest efficiency, however, you want localization to come after most of the editorial and review process already occurs. So, on the other hand, PLAN may want to place localization at the end of the process, as shown in Figure 33-6.

Given a sufficiently robust CMS workflow and component management system, you can sometimes split the difference between these two approaches. If you can make the following two assumptions, you can perhaps get the major benefits of both approaches:

✦ Only minor changes occur to the component during the editorial and review steps.

✦ Targeting involves metadata that isn't localized.

With these two assumptions, PLAN may develop a workflow similar to the one shown in Figure 33-7.

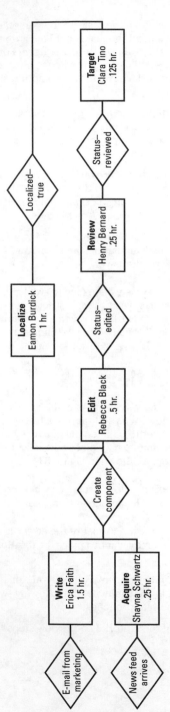

Figure 33-5: Localization in parallel with other workflow steps

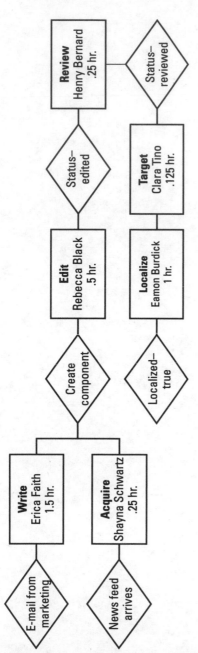

Figure 33-6: Localization in series with the other workflow steps

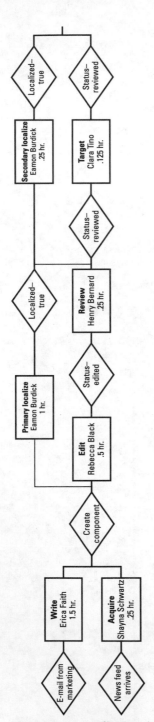

Figure 33-7: Localization that's staged and in parallel with other steps

Now you have two steps to localization. In the first step, you localize the component. In the second step, you edit the localized component to synchronize it with any changes that you make during the editing and review steps. To enter the second localization step, two triggers must occur. You must set the component element Localized to a value of Stage1, and the component element Status to a value of Reviewed. Step 2 happens in parallel with the original targeting step. Overall, this workflow costs an extra 15 minutes of labor on the part of the localizer (Eamon), but the whole workflow takes no longer from start to finish than the workflow without localization.

This type of workflow may or may not prove right for your situation, but it can serve as an option.

Tip

> Even if you don't use this particular method, it illustrates a valuable lesson in localization. You want not only to localize whole components, but also to localize changes to components. You also want to give localizers control over some but not all the elements of a component. Notice in Figure 33-7 that, at the same time that Eamon controls the body elements of the component, Clara controls the management elements that you use to target the component to particular audiences.

Analyzing Workflow

In the following sections, I detail the information that you must collect to fully describe and plan for the workflows that you need. You can use a set of spreadsheets to conduct this analysis, but you're better off, by far, using a database application. If you don't have database skills, now's a good time to either learn them or make friends with someone who can help.

Think

Before you begin your workflow analysis consider the following issues:

✦ **Cycles:** Does the idea that running your CMS is simply a matter of triggering the correct reoccurring cycle at the right time make sense to you? What parts of the system don't work this way? Do you have a master cycle from which all others in your CMS derive?

✦ **Acceptance:** Does your staff accept the idea of very organized and constrained processes with known tasks and times? How can you maintain people's sense of independence and creativity within these defined cycles? How do you recognize that someone doesn't accept the basic premise of workflow, and how can you handle the issue?

✦ **Control:** Who can suggest a change to a workflow or a workflow step? Who approves or denies the suggestion? Who can actually make changes to the workflow system? How do you monitor and communicate these changes?

✦ **Availability:** What happens if a person's step triggers but she isn't available? Under what circumstances can you permit each workflow to stop and wait for a person to become available? Under what circumstances do you bypass a person or reassign her work?

Plan

In the following sections, I take you through a process for moving from the preliminary tasks that you devise during your logical design to a set of named workflows that you can use to specify the workflows in your CMS and make preliminary staffing calculations. The process proceeds as follows:

1. Identifying the management tasks of the CMS.

2. Rolling those tasks up with the others that you create for other entities in your logical design and looking for completeness, accuracy, and redundancy.

3. Refining your task list so that it becomes a list of workflows.

4. Creating a set of fully detailed steps for each workflow.

Preliminary tasks

In the first part of the workflow planning, you gather and consider all the tasks you've collected so far. Before beginning this step, I want to pause to consider area group of tasks that I don't cover in the task sections of earlier chapters — management tasks.

Fill in the following table with the management tasks that you expect to accomplish periodically to run your CMS. Following are some examples to start you thinking:

✦ Creating new users (staff members who use the CMS).

✦ Updating or deleting user records.

✦ Getting new user records from an enterprise source.

✦ Assigning or changing access permissions.

✦ Archiving or deleting expired content.

✦ Managing log files.

✦ Producing reports and analyses.

✦ Content and configuration synchronization with remote sites.

✦ Data transfer cycles with external systems.

✦ Security tests.

✦ Performance tests.

✦ Content model reviews.

✦ Scaling tests.

✦ Metadata list reviews.

Use the results of your brainstorming session to fill in the following table.

Task Name	Who	What	When	How Much	How
Content model review	Lead Information Architect	Review complete component and access system	When new component class is created or once per quarter	All component classes (about 40) and access structures (about 10)	Database relationship diagrams, documentation, and template review

The required information includes the following:

✦ **Task name:** Give the task a short but memorable name that describes it.

✦ **Who:** What person or kind of person is responsible for doing this task? Naming an automated process here instead of a person is acceptable.

✦ **What:** What must the person or process do to accomplish the task?

✦ **When:** At what frequency must you accomplish this task, or how do you know when it must happen?

✦ **How much:** How much or how many of this sort of task do you expect to do. A numerical quantity is preferable here, but if you can't come up with one, words such as *a lot*, *not much*, and so on, suffice.

✦ **How:** What skills, tools, or processes does a person or process need to accomplish this task?

After you complete your individual task analysis, you can now go back through your other task analyses and assemble them all into one large table. Simply add a Task Id column to the table to help you track the tasks in the next parts of the analysis.

As you bring all the tasks into your large table, review them for the following:

✦ **Completeness:** Are any tasks missing? Include any additional tasks that you can think of. You get ample opportunity later to delete ones that don't materialize.

✦ **Accuracy:** Did you fill in all fields correctly? Looking back, do you need to change or enhance any of the values you entered?

✦ **Redundancy:** Do you have any tasks that are similar enough to combine into a single task?

Don't bother to split tasks yet; that's the next step. Focus on getting a list that covers the running of the system as completely as possible.

From tasks to workflows

In this stage of planning, you go from your general list of tasks to a more specific list of workflows.

First, add an additional column to your task table that notes whether the task is single step or multistep, as you see in the following table.

Multistep?	Task ID	Task Name	Who	What	How Much	When	How
X	T123	Basic Editorial	Editors and reviewers	Review the first draft of a component	2 per week	As they arrive	Web form using Status and Comment elements

In the Multistep column, do the following:

✦ **Enter X** if the task takes more than one person or process to accomplish and/or if you can't accomplish it all at one time without intervening processes or procedures (that is, if the parts of the task are dependent on outside factors).

✦ **Enter nothing** if the task involves a single step where one person does one process all at once.

After you fill in the Multistep column, begin to sort the table, grouping tasks that fit patterns such as the following:

✦ **Who:** Group sets of tasks that all involve the same group of people working toward a particular goal.

✦ **What:** Group sets of tasks that act on the same part of the CMS and move it toward some state.

✦ **When:** Group sets of tasks that come logically and consistently after each other.

These groupings are to get you familiar enough with your tasks that you can begin to mold them into workflows. After you feel ready to do so, begin to recast your tasks to fit the following table.

Workflow ID	Workflow Name	Tasks Included (in sequence)	Frequency
WF400	Basic Editorial	(T123a)Edit (T123b)Review (T123c)Target	2 times per week

The required information includes:

✦ **Workflow Id:** As usual, assign a unique Id to each workflow.

✦ **Workflow name:** Use the name of the predominant task in the workflow or make up a new and memorable moniker.

✦ **Tasks included:** List the Ids of all the tasks that are part of this workflow. You may end up creating the whole workflow from a single multistep task (as shown previously) or composing it from some set of multi- and single-step tasks. List the tasks in the sequence that you expect them to occur (or as close to it as you can come). Expect some tasks to appear as part of more than one workflow.

✦ **Frequency:** Enter an estimate of how frequently you expect this workflow to occur. Work from the When columns in your task table to arrive at this value.

Keeping Track of Inputs/Outputs

After you begin to diagram the steps in your workflow, you may also need to document the inputs and outputs required for each step. For example, if your workflow contains a trigger on the arrival of a news story via e-mail, then the input to the Acquire step is an e-mail message. Will it be a text e-mail or a message with a document attached? Will the person acting on this step have the necessary tools to open and act on the content?

Next you will need to ask: What is the expected output of the Acquire step in the workflow? It could be another text e-mail message or the creation of a new content component (as HTML, a Microsoft Word document, and so on). Does the person have the necessary tools to correctly create the necessary output of the completing this step?

Identifying the inputs and outputs for each step in a task will increase your understanding of the task in a number of ways. It will help you to:

✦ Identify the staffing skills needed to act on a task.

✦ See how the inputs and outputs of the each task in the workflow integrate with the CMS system.

✦ Clarify any required functionality of the CMS system.

Suzanne Soroczak, University of Washington

This table is complete after every task from your original list appears somewhere on it. Look it over carefully and make sure that you're happy with it before moving on to the next step.

After you're comfortable with your preliminary workflow table, you can begin to analyze each workflow separately. For each workflow, create a table similar to the following example.

Step ID	Name	Order	Trigger	Actor	Objects	Tasks
WF400_1	Edit	1	End of the composition (WF200) or Acquisition (WF300) workflow	Editor	News Feature component.	Edit and correct all body elements. Fill in all management elements except Audience.
WF400_2	Review	2	Status element value set to "Edited"	Reviewer	News Feature component.	Review Abstract, Partner Background, and Body elements for legal restrictions.
WF400_3	Target	3	Status element value set to "Reviewed"	Public Relations Specialist	News Feature component.	Fill in Audience element.

Don't limit yourself to the steps you created when you first came up with this workflow. Now's the time to re-evaluate the size and ordering of steps. Make sure that each step has a single actor who does not depend on any intervening process or step to complete her (or its) work.

In addition, follow these guidelines:

✦ **For all columns:** Type your values in such a way that they sort appropriately later. In the Tasks column, for example, always put the action word first. Enter "Edit Type element" rather than "Do edits on Type element." In the next stage of your analysis, you need to find similar steps. The more careful and consistent that you are in the way that you type the values now, the easier the next stage is.

✦ **Step ID:** Enter an Id for the step that indicates what workflow it belongs to. You may, for example, give your workflows Ids such as WF1, WF2, WF3, and so on. As step Ids for WF1, you might try WF1_1, WF1_2, WF1_3, and so on.

✦ **Name:** Give the step a name that derives from its major task or in another way categorizes the nature of the step.

✦ **Order:** Enter the order of the step in the workflow (1, 2, 3, and so on).

✦ **Trigger:** Be as specific and tangible as possible. Enter only actions or events that the CMS can be aware of. If the trigger is a conversation, for example, decide what event inside the computer (such as someone changing an element value or an e-mail message going out) you can use to tell the CMS that something's occurring.

✦ **Actor:** This column can follow loosely from your Who column. Don't be adverse to rethinking the actors. Remember, too, that an actor can be (and often is) an automated process instead of a person. This step isn't a staffing analysis, so you don't need to be too specific. On the other hand, it's the input to your staffing analysis, so apply ample effort.

✦ **Objects:** This column can follow loosely from your What column. Try to get as precise a definition as possible, however, about what part of the CMS changes as a result of the step.

✦ **Tasks:** This column can follow a combination of your What and How columns. Although the word *task* in this context carries the same general meaning as in your previous analysis, make the tasks that you enter here very specific and include the exact actions that you expect the actor to take.

As you create these tables, make sure that you notice workflows that, on closer examination, you can merge. This exercise is complete after you have a complete set of steps with all columns filled in and you can detect no gaps or redundancies in your steps and workflows.

Regularizing your steps

After you have a full set of workflow tables, you're ready for one final stage of analysis. In this stage of planning, you sort your workflows by step to make sure that you have the most efficient approach to your workflows.

To analyze workflow from the standpoint of steps, put all the steps from all your workflows into one table of the same form as the one that you use for each separate workflow.

Step ID	Name	Order	Trigger	Actor	Objects	Tasks
WF400_1	Edit	1	End of the composition (WF200) or Acquisition (WF300) workflow	Editor	News Feature component	Edit and correct all body elements. Fill in all management elements except Audience.

New Challenges for Content Management in Technical Communication

Creating product documentation is one of the most common activities in technical communication. Using content management tools and strategies to produce documentation has solved some very challenging problems for technical communicators. At the same time however, it has raised new issues, for example how to craft content to meet the needs of different audiences and how to provide guidance for complex user tasks.

No activity is more central to technical communication than analyzing audiences and customizing content to meet the differing needs of disparate audiences.

When audiences are distinguished simply by level of expertise (novice, expert) or job (data entry clerk, financial analyst), it is more likely that appropriate subsets of information can be selected from a database and published without modification in print or electronic form.

When audiences differ in more complex ways (by cultural expectations, by level of engagement, by emotional connection to information), it becomes more difficult to address differing needs by simply assembling pieces. How can we customize information while still taking advantage of the strengths of content management? Several strategies are possible. One might decide to craft alternate versions of certain chunks of content (creating useful redundancy in the database) to meet distinctive audience needs. Or one might decide to assemble chunks of content into a document draft, and then edit the draft into a final form that meets the current need. The assembly query and final document could both be stored in the database for future iterations. Both strategies complicate the use of a content management system.

A different set of problems arises from the attempt to provide guidance for complex user tasks (user goals and strategies that operate far above the feature level). If a document (especially a Help file) contains chunks of information that correspond in a one-to-one relationship with product commands, icons, or other widgets, the content management strategy is relatively straightforward. But when the document moves from feature orientation to user-task orientation, once again the content management task becomes more complicated. To use the most obvious example, the same command might play a role in dozens of complex user tasks and, in each case, be used in a slightly different way.

Fundamental changes now under way in how documentation gets done may also accelerate the complexity of content management in documentation:

Death of the release: With the rapid growth in Web-based information (documentation, e-commerce information, and other kinds of Web content), many companies are turning to rapid-response documentation. As soon as a problem with the current state of the information is spotted (a spike in customer calls on a specific topic, for example), new information is created and posted. Thus the documentation could change daily or even hourly; and on top of that, the new content must be tracked for effectiveness as well.

Open-source documentation: Increasingly, the job of documenting is being distributed to the users themselves, through such open-source approaches as user bulletin boards, chats, and blogs. These peer-collaborative approaches appear to be especially effective in helping users work out more complex, higher-order tasks. Once again, managing this content and structuring it to be as accessible as possible are not trivial content management tasks.

Continued

Continued

Given these many demands on the performance of content management strategies in technical communication, we can expect to see continued development of increasingly powerful and complex tools and systems. And the technical communicator most in demand will be the person who can make these systems dance the fastest.

Judy Ramey, University of Washington

The point of putting this table together is to see whether you have any redundant steps. To do so, sort by each of the columns, in turn, and compare adjacent columns. Depending on how consistent you are in typing values into these columns, similar steps come together. Even if it requires some effort, you can usually see steps to which you have given different names but that accomplish the same results. Similar steps have essentially the same tasks and objects. In other words, if two steps have the same effect on the same part of the CMS, they belong together as a single step.

If you find two similar steps, give both steps the same name, tasks, and objects. The actors and triggers may or may not remain different. Always keep different Ids so that you can tell which workflows each of the versions of the two steps belong to.

Try to end up using as few different steps in as many different workflows as is feasible. After you finish, re-sort your table by Step Id and Order to turn it back into a list of steps for each workflow.

Integrate

To integrate your workflow analysis into the rest of your logical design, consider the following issues:

✦ **Size:** Look back over the list of workflows you came up with. They should give you a good feel for the size of the effort that you need to keep your system running. Is it too big of an effort?

✦ **Comprehensiveness:** Did you miss any tasks or workflows that you need to run your system?

✦ **Start-up:** You can apply the same sort of analysis that I just presented to the workflows you need to start up the CMS. Can you apply any of these workflows to the authoring, acquisition, configuration, or test publishing that you need to start your system?

✦ **Change:** What methods can you put in place to ensure that your initial set of steps and workflows can bend and change based on the exceptions and new rules that arise over time in your system? How do you recognize that a particular situation is enough of an exception to your general process to bypass the usual workflow? At what point do you create new processes for these exceptions?

Analyzing Staffing

In the following sections, I describe how you can extend your workflow analysis to become a preliminary staffing analysis. I start by adding skills and times to the workflow table you created in your workflow analysis. Then I describe how you can cluster workflow steps to come up with preliminary job descriptions. Finally, I describe a way that you can make preliminary calculations to determine how many of each kind of staff that you may need.

Think

Before you begin your staffing analysis, consider the following issues:

✦ **Accuracy:** How accurate do you expect your staffing estimates to be? How accurate do you need them to be at this stage of the process? Can you do anything at this point to strengthen the accuracy of your assumptions to support the staffing accuracy that you need? Make sure that you review the section "Staffing calculations," earlier in this chapter, on estimating staffing if you're unsure about what assumptions affect staffing estimates.

✦ **Present staffing:** To what extent does your current staff affect your staffing needs? If you find that someone doesn't have the skills that you need, what options do you have?

✦ **Future staff:** What budget do you need to hire staff if you find that you need them? What can you do if you can't fund a necessary position?

✦ **Outsourced and in-house staff:** Which kinds of positions should you try to fill from permanent staff within your organization and which should you fill with temporary or part-time staff from outside your organization?

✦ **Utilization:** What expectations does your organization have for staff hours and utilization? Is an average week, for example, 40 hours? Are 6 hours of scheduled tasks in an 8-hour day the right amount?

Plan

In the following sections, I present a staff planning method that I base on the equations and process that I present in the section "Staffing calculations," earlier in this chapter. Make sure that you review it before proceeding

Finding skills and times

Begin to turn your workflow analysis toward a staffing analysis by adding a few columns to your step table, as the following example shows.

Step ID	Name	Order	Trigger	Actor	Objects	Tasks	Skills	Task Time	Step Time
WF400_1	Edit	1	End of the composition (WF200) or Acquisition (WF300) workflow	Editor	News Feature component	Edit and correct all body elements. Fill in all management elements except Audience.	Journalist type editorial skills	.5 hr	1 day

In addition to the information you've already collected for this table, fill in the three new columns as follows:

✦ **Skills:** In this column, type a list of the skills that the actor needs to accomplish the tasks in this step. To some extent, the name of the actor implies the skills that she possesses. (If the actor is an editor, for example, you can assume that she has editing skills.) Try to be as specific as possible and go beyond the obvious skills that the task and actor columns imply. Make sure that you list skills in order of importance, with the most important skill first. And be consistent in the way that you name skills because you sort your table by skill names in the next stage of the analysis.

✦ **Task time:** Enter the amount of actual work time that the tasks in the step take.

✦ **Step time:** Enter the amount of time that you expect to transpire between the time the step triggers and the time the following step triggers. This time isn't strictly useful in the staffing analysis as I present it, but this stage is the right time to add the Step time to your workflow analysis.

In the section "Staff modeling," earlier in this chapter, you find examples of Step and Task times and some guidance on how to estimate them. Notice that the Task time that you enter in the preceding table isn't the total time per week but rather the time to complete one pass through the tasks.

Clustering skills and tasks into jobs

To go from steps to jobs, you need to start grouping skills into clusters that can become a job. I present a bottom-up approach, where your jobs derive from the skills that you need. You can combine this approach with a top-down approach, where you start from my list of jobs (or your own) and sort the skills that you need into the jobs that you want to create.

 I present my list of jobs in Chapter 13, "Staffing a CMS."

To begin, sort your Steps table by the Skills column. This sorting may take some extra effort because you're likely to have more than one skill in many steps. After you sort the table, use the Skills column in conjunction with the Tasks column values to cluster your steps into jobs. Fill in the following table with your results.

Job Name	Skills	Tasks	Workflows	Steps
Editor	Journalist skills, Program knowledge, Style guide knowledge	Edit, Refine, Apply styles	WF400 WF434 WF598 WF123	WF400_1 WF434_3 WF598_2 WF123_6

The required information includes the following:

✦ **Job name:** Enter a job title from the list that I provide (in Chapter 13, "Staffing A CMS"), from your own list, or by looking at the skills and deciding what to call such a person.

✦ **Skills:** List all the skills that appear in any of the steps that you cluster into this job.

✦ **Tasks:** List all the tasks from all the steps that cluster into this job.

✦ **Workflows:** List the names and Ids of all the workflows with steps that cluster into this job.

✦ **Steps:** List the names and Ids of all the workflow steps that cluster into this job.

Use this table to make a preliminary pass through your jobs. You're done after the clusters of skills and tasks are all distinct enough to clearly distinguish different jobs.

Calculating staffing estimates

To complete your staffing estimates, you can add time estimates to the tasks to decide how much total time you need from each job. For each job, fill in a table similar to the following example.

Editor			
Workflow	**Step**	**Task Time**	**Time per Week on Task**
WF400	WF400_1	.5 hr	2 hr
WF434	WF434_3	1.5 hr	9 hr
WF598	WF598_2	5 hr	2.5 hr
WF123	WF123_6	.75 hr	12 hr

The required information includes the following:

✦ **Workflow:** Enter the Id and name (if you like) of each workflow that the job holder participates in.

✦ **Step:** Enter the Id and name (if you like) of each step that the job holder participates in. List one step per row. In other words, if the person in this job does three steps in a particular workflow, you complete three rows in this table.

✦ **Task time:** Enter the time estimate for the task that you arrived at earlier.

✦ **Time per week on task:** Use the equations and process that I discuss in the section "Staff modeling," earlier in this chapter (or a process of your own), to calculate the total amount of time that is devoted to this step per week.

After you completely fill in this table, add up the times in the Time per Week on Task column to come up with a total time for this job per week.

The total time that you calculate, you then convert to an estimate of how many people you need in this job.

Nominally, you can simply divide the total number of hours by the number of hours in a work week. You should adjust this number to one more reasonable, however, basing it on how much task time that you can realistically expect from each job. If the total time that you calculate tells you that you need 80 hours from this job per week, for example, and an average work week is only 40 hours, you nominally need two people in this job. You may adjust this estimate to two and one-half people to reflect the fact that you expect staff to spend only 30 hours per week on the task (with the other 10 hours disappearing into meetings, e-mail, and unexpected tasks).

Moving from the Current State to the Desired State

Some time ago an information professional queried a statement I had made about the need to start by designing the way the work *needs* to be done versus designing what is *already* done. Whether you are initiating a new content management system or building on an old one, it is critical to step back and really "start from scratch"—at least at first. Once your team has decided on what the best workflow and skill sets are, the gap analysis can be done to understand how to move from the current state to the desired state. I am not sure why this is hard for people to grasp. Perhaps it feels too "blue sky" to define the desired state. Perhaps it seems too unlikely that it can be achieved.

The point is not to be conceptual to the point of irrelevance or to the point of impracticality. I think it is somewhat inherent in the human nature to be able to say what you don't like about something rather than to say what you really want. It is, however, absolutely critical in workflow and staffing to be able to identify how you want things to work and take it backwards from there.

Mary Lee Kennedy, The Kennedy Group (www.maryleekennedy.com)

Integrate

After you finish your staffing analysis, integrate it with the rest of your logical design by considering the following points:

✦ **Jobs:** Are you making the best use of your resources? In dividing and organizing jobs, you often name more positions than you really need. Can you get by with fewer jobs?

✦ **Workflows:** Try mapping out all your jobs and workflows in one (very large) chart. Do you see any redundancies there? Is the chart too complex to understand? If so, simplify it now before it's too late.

✦ **Accuracy:** This issue is important enough to consider yet again. How accurate are your staffing estimates? What planning decisions or recommendations are you comfortable making based on them? What can you do to test and improve your assumptions?

✦ **Start-up:** You can apply the same sort of analysis to the staffing necessary to start up the CMS. Can you create any similar staffing estimates for parts of the CMS project that haven't already begun?

✦ **Change:** What methods can you put in place to ensure that your initial set of jobs and skills can bend and change based on staffing changes, budget changes, or the inevitable social and intellectual transformations in your current staff?

Summary

The concept behind workflow is the concept behind all content management: Get organized. Although workflow is only one part of the organization that content management systems provide, it's an important part. Workflows guide the expected operation of your CMS as follows:

✦ **Process:** Workflows provide well-defined processes for the movement of content through the system.

✦ **Staffing:** Workflows provide a set of assumptions on which you can build staffing projections and estimates.

✦ **Steps:** Workflows break a process down into a series of steps that are tasks. Someone with a particular job within the CMS performs these tasks on some part of the CMS after some triggering event occurs within the CMS.

✦ **Workflow analysis:** This analysis consists of finding all the tasks in your system, organizing them into processes, and creating a set of well-defined steps in each process.

✦ **Staffing analysis:** This analysis consists of determining the skills behind the workflow tasks, clustering them into jobs, and then making educated guesses about how much time you need from people in each job.

In working through workflow, don't expect to be overly accurate in your planning the first time through. But if you keep with it and continue to refine your estimates and processes in response to the success or failures that you experience, over time you develop reliable staffing estimates and a comprehensive set of processes that completely account for the normal running of your CMS.

The next chapter marks the beginning of the next part of the book. I move from the analysis and design of a CMS to a discussion of how to build one. I begin with an overview of the most important topics in the next section, both to provide an overview of what's to come as well as to give a bird's eye view of what it takes to build a CMS.

✦   ✦   ✦

Building a CMS

◆ ◆ ◆ ◆

◆ ◆ ◆ ◆

Building a CMS Simply

In this chapter, I summarize the major concerns behind the physical design of your CMS. I boil down physical design to its essence, both to give you a road map for this section and to provide a look at the physical design tasks necessary even in the most minimal CMS implementation. By reading this chapter, you can get a jump on what's to come or get a reminder of how the detail found in the chapters fits together at a high level.

What Is Physical Design?

In physical design you decide the systems and features that you will include in your CMS. I use the term *physical design* to separate this part of the CMS process from logical design. In logical design you decide abstractly what you want your CMS to do. You balance a set of goals with audiences, publications, and the other major players in the system to understand what the system must accomplish. In physical design, you take the logical design and decide exactly how the hardware and software of your CMS will accomplish what your logical design laid out.

If the logical design is *what*, the physical design is *how*. From the standpoint of a physical design, a CMS is a set of systems, subsystems, and features. You should be quite familiar with the three main systems that I have described: the collection system, the management system, and the publishing system. In Chapter 7, "Introducing the Major Parts of a CMS," I go over each of these systems and give you a feel for what they consist of. I do this to introduce the concepts of CM and to give you a general feel for what a CMS does. In this part of the book, I go into much greater detail about these systems and what they contain.

It seems to be the case that even with the large amount of detail I provide, I still can't give you the complete structure behind the systems and features of a CMS. Here is why:

> ✦ For my explanations to be of general use, I must define my systems one level above what you will actually see in a CMS that you build or buy. At the ground level, you make selections from the user interface of existing software and write code for new software. It would be almost useless for me to talk about that level in this analysis. Instead, I must describe systems in more general terms that are not directly applicable as you build or operate a CMS.

✦ Each commercial and custom CMS defines its own set of systems and subsystems. The ones I choose to discuss are my best approximation of what is out there (as well as what is not out there, but should be). I can't say what a system is called within a particular CMS or even what it does — because every case is different.

✦ New systems and features are being created every day. Even if I could keep up with the dizzying array of new products and features that keep appearing, describing them in detail here would surely make this discussion obsolete within a very short time.

Still, following the model I pursue throughout this work, I will take a principled approach to the systems and subsystems of a CMS to try to give you a working knowledge of exactly what a CMS does. You can use this knowledge to create your own physical design, which completely charts out the systems and features to fulfill the logical design you have come up with.

First, however, I'd like to give you a way to grasp physical design simply and effectively. You can use the method I propose either before you do a "real" physical design, or if you are pressed for time or money, you can do it instead of a real physical design.

Physical Design Essentials

In Chapter 7, "Introducing the Major Parts of a CMS," I provided the diagram shown in Figure 34-1, which shows the main parts of a CMS.

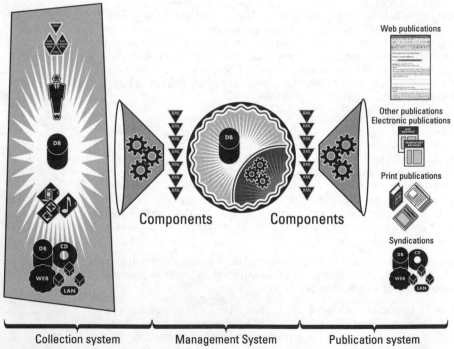

Figure 34-1: The main parts of a CMS

This diagram shows:

✦ The collection system, which is responsible for gathering content and getting it into your system.

✦ The management system, which is responsible for amassing content and giving you control over it.

✦ The publication system, which is responsible for extracting content from the system and presenting it in a way that is useful to your audiences.

Each of these systems, in turn, is composed of subsystems, as Table 34-1 summarizes.

Table 34-1: Major Systems and Subsystems in a CMS

System	Sub System
Collection System	
	Authoring System
	Conversion System
	Acquisition System
	Aggregation System
	Repository Interface
Management System	
	The Repository
	Versioning System
	Source Control System (Content and File Sharing)
	Localization System
	Workflow System
	CMS Administration System
Publishing System	
	Templating System
	Personalization System
	Deployment System
	Web System
	Print System
	E-mail System
	Syndication System
	Other Publication Systems
	Repository Interface

As you might imagine, each of the subsystems can have its own sub-subsystems. For example, the Aggregation subsystem has these systems under it:

✦ Segmentation

✦ Editorial Processing

✦ Metatorial Processing

In addition, systems at any level can have features. A feature is a specific capability that you want in the CMS. For example, the Metatorial Processing system has these features:

✦ Importing metadata lists

✦ Exporting metadata lists

✦ List creation and editing

✦ List review

✦ Value lumping

✦ Value splitting

✦ Mandatory and optional elements

✦ Support for applying metadata

So, to create a collection system in your CMS, you need some sort of aggregation system. Your aggregation system may, in turn, require a metatorial processing system. Finally, your metatorial processing system may need one or more or the features I mentioned in the preceding list.

Working from the bottom up, you can say that, at the basic level, a CMS offers you a set of capabilities or features. Those features group logically into systems. During implementation the systems will likely end up being coded together in the same module and shown to the user together on the same screen. Systems group logically into wider systems, with the content management *system* at the highest level.

Note   Of course, you don't have to end with the CMS at the highest level. You can consider the CMS to be one subsystem of your enterprise-wide infrastructure system. Your enterprise-wide system can be a part of an industry-wide system, and so on.

What is truly essential in this discussion of physical design is not that you accept the particular systems and features that I propose, but that you recognize that it is worth you time to analyze your CMS as a nested set of systems and features, and that you take on the job of figuring out exactly what systems and features you need.

A Simple Physical Design Process

Depending on how much of a logical design you did, you have more or less input for a physical design. One way or another, you are heading for a document that you can pass off to developers (or possibly a product selection team) to use to guide their implementation. That document should:

✦ Tell them what features you expect your CMS to have.

✦ Explain the idea behind features if they are not obvious.

✦ Justify the features on the basis of the logical design you have performed.

✦ Fit the features together into a set of modules or systems that ties them together into a user interface and data-sharing model.

For programmers, you might equate this document to a functional specification. It defines what you want the system to do but does not detail any of the programming behind the system.

Here is how you might come up with a physical design process document:

1. Review the features in Chapters 37 through 40 to get a feel for the full breadth of the possibilities for your CMS.

2. Choose a level of detail for your system at which you can do an adequate physical design:

   • If all else fails you can select the topmost level of collection, management, and publishing.

   • The second level down is a more reasonable level at which to perform an analysis if you are short on time.

   • Go as far down toward the lowest (most detailed) level (sections and features) as you are able.

3. At the level you choose, list all the features that you need. To determine if a feature is needed, look to your logical design. Try to find specific justifications for the feature. For example, is there an author class that will require the feature? Is there a publication that requires it?

4. Go wide at this point in trying to find all the features that your system will need, given your logical design.

5. Determine whether the feature set you came up with fits your time and staff resources. If it does not, cut from the logical design and see what features go away as a result. In other words, although you may be tempted to carry out the same logical design with a smaller physical design, it is better to create a smaller logical design with the optimum-sized physical design.

6. When you have scaled the system to the size you think you can handle, go back over the list of features. Refer to Chapters 37 to 40 once again to see if you can deepen the description of your systems and features without increasing the number of features.

7. Refer to Chapter 20, "Implementing the System," to decide how to turn your system and feature list into a specification that your development team can understand and use.

8. Go over your plan for specifications with your development team. Make sure that they understand what features you want, and make sure you understand how to communicate those feature requests to them.

9. If the development team decides that you have burdened them with too much work, try again to cut the logical design rather than the physical design.

Introducing the Technology Taxonomy

In Chapters 38 through 40, I present a comprehensive outline of all the systems and features that I have come across or seen the need for in a CMS. I call this outline the CM technology taxonomy. It is a taxonomy in the sense that it presents a hierarchy of terms that define CM. It is technology-focused in that it presents the world of CM through the lens of the software and hardware you need to create a CMS. I intend the technology taxonomy to be a rough guide to your physical design. You can use it as a draft outline of all the things you want your system to do. By deleting the things that you don't want and adding those that are not present but that you do want, you can move as easily as possible toward a logical design.

The taxonomy is comprehensive in that it covers every aspect of a CMS (at least, every one that I know of). It is not exhaustive. I am confident that I missed any number of important features and that the taxonomy will continue to evolve as CM evolves. For that reason I present the most current taxonomy online at www.metatorial.com.

Here are some other considerations for you to take into account as you use the taxonomy:

✦ **What is versus what should be**: As I have said a number of times, the CM industry is still fairly young. Although many of the features I describe are widely available in commercial and home-grown systems, many are not. In fact, many of the features I describe embody what I believe that CM systems *should* do — much more than what they currently *can* do. I try to be careful to note the difference between what is and what should be in the features, but as you consider including them in your design, be sure to capture the intent rather than the literal functionality of the features that are not widely available.

✦ **Build versus buy**: Whether you are creating a system from scratch, enhancing a commercial system, or doing only what your commercial system will allow without programming, your CMS should do what it should do. Thus, I intend the taxonomy to be useful in any case. However, I slant the taxonomy decidedly toward ideas for implementation rather than product selection. You may notice that the taxonomy shares a number of elements with the CMS selection criteria I present in Chapter 19, "Selecting Hardware and Software." Those selection criteria also represent what a CMS can do, but that list is tailored to the selection process and offers little implementation advice.

✦ **Dashboards**: I refer in a number of the features to the concept of a dashboard. The idea behind these dashboards is to consolidate the features of a CMS for ease of use by various staff members. For example, I discuss workflow, personalization, and localization dashboards. Each of these presents the CMS from the viewpoint of one of its core systems. At one level, these dashboards simply consolidate, into one convenient interface, features that are often scattered. On another level, however, the dashboards are an attempt to really reorient CM systems. Dashboards not only group similar functions, they consolidate and synthesize diverse types of information so that users can get their minds around the full breadth of their systems. With a full suite of dashboards, users have the support to know exactly what is going on in the CMS, and moreover have the capability to control it.

In summary, although the technology taxonomy is far from complete, it does represent a comprehensive view of what a CMS should be able to do for you. Moreover, it is a call to arms to the all builders of CM systems to rise to the challenge of creating systems that do the whole job.

An index to the technology taxonomy

Here is the technology taxonomy in summary form to help you navigate to it. Alternatively, you can find the taxonomy on the Web (www.metatorial.com), where the navigation is a bit faster.

System: Collection System

> System: Authoring System
>
>> Features: Integrated search, Integrated workflow, Spawning applications, Upload support, Advanced media support, Spell checking, Integrated editorial and metatorial guides, Off-line content creation
>
>> System: Preview
>
>>> Features: Publication preview, Workflow preview
>
>> System: Feedback
>
>>> Features: Staff feedback, Audience feedback
>
>> System: Metadata support
>
>>> Features: Required and optional elements, Element-set personalization, Validation, Reference fields, Cross-references, Hierarchical relationships
>
>> System: Web Forms
>
>>> Features: Extensions and modifications, Automatic form creation, In-context editing, Rich editing
>
>> System: Other Authoring Applications
>
>>> Features: Showing Components and Elements, Automation, Constrained entry, Integrated open and save, Integrated-input templating, Integrated check in and check out

> System: Conversion System
>
>> Features: Basic import, Map files to content types, Batch Processing, Integration with the aggregation system
>
>> System: Process Management
>
>>> Features: Process definition, Task assignment and load leveling, Work queues
>
>> System: Quality Control (QC) and Monitoring
>
>>> Features: Sampling content, Set and monitor rates, Bounce content, Deliver feedback and training on demand
>
>> System: Process and Review Tools
>
>>> Features: Set input and output directories, Set rules, Quick keys UI, Exception handling

System: Acquisition System

Features: Process and partner management, Rights and usage, Attribution management

System: Acquiring Database Records

Features: The connection, The query, The map, The exception process

System: Acquiring Web site content

Features: Dealing with dynamic pages, Dealing with orphaned pages, Dealing with old or redundant pages

System: Aggregation System

Features: Automatically applied metadata, Metadata standards support, Workflow triggers

System: Segmentation

Features: Separating components from surrounds, Find elements, Find access structures

System: Editorial Processing

Features: Revision tracking, Commentary, Component reuse, Language variants

System: Metatorial Processing

Features: Importing metadata lists, Exporting metadata lists, List creation and editing, List review, Value lumping, Value splitting, Mandatory and optional elements, Support for applying metadata

System: Repository Interface

Features: Updates and deletes, Submitting and storing files, Support for WebDav

System: Management System

System: The Repository

Features: Fitting into the CMS and the organization, Getting content in and out, A repository-wide schema, Global search and replace, Locating content, Bulk processes, Field type support

System: General Storage Requirements

Features: Storing components, Storing content types, Storing relationships between components

System: Relational Database Systems

Features: Storing content types and components in a relational database, Storing hierarchies in an RDB, Storing indexes in an RDB, Storing cross-references in an RDB, Storing sequences in an RDB, Storing the content model in an RDB

System: Object Databases

>> Features: Scalability, XML files versus object databases, Storing content types and components in XML, Storing hierarchies in XML, Storing indexes in XML, Storing cross-references in XML, Storing sequences in XML, Storing the content model in XML

System: File Systems

System: Versioning System

> Features: Automatic vs. manual versioning, Granularity of versions, Restore, Differencing versions, Source Branching

System: Source Control System (Content and File Sharing)

> Features: Sharing granularity, Locking, Check in and out, Notification, Audit trails

System: Localization System

> System: Collection localization

>> Features: Localized UI, Access structure localization, Import and export for localization, Combining source material

> System: Management localization

>> Features: Component level localization, Element level localization, Tie in to workflow

> System: Publication localization

>> Features: A localization dashboard, Localization as personalization, Search engine localization, Template localization

System: Workflow System

> System: End User Interface

>> Features: Reusable end user interface, E-mail integration, Work Queues, Commenting

> System: Workflow Administration

>> Features: Visual Builder, Ad-hoc workflow and rerouting, Configuration of user roles, Audit trails and reporting, Import and export

> System: Workflow Mechanics

>> Features: Workflow creation, Nested workflows, Objects, Triggers, Parallel and sequential workflows

System: CMS Administration System

> Features: Administrative dashboard, User administration, Logging, Reporting, Security, Link support, Media support, IP tracking and costing

System: External Connections

> Features: Directory services integration, Replication, Distribution, XML as an integration medium, Standard database interfaces

System: Robustness

Features: Backup, Scalability, Reliability

System: Publishing System

System: Templating System

Features: Producing target formats, Producing target units structure, Layout and surrounds, Template programming, Producing static and dynamic publications, On-the-fly conversion of text and media, Integration with publication authoring tools, Mix and match templates

System: Navigation Building

Features: Building hierarchies, Building indexes, Building cross references, Building sequences

System: Personalization System

Features: A personalization dashboard

System: Collecting Data

Features: Segmentation modeling, Collecting and storing profile data, Acquired profiles, Data accessible to personalization

System: Building Rules

Features: The rules interface, Statistics and simulations, Customization interface, Collaborative filtering

System: Delivering Content

Features: Personalized surrounds, Personalized content, Personalized navigation

System: Deployment System

Features: Staging, Content-based deployment, Distributing files, Scheduled publication

System: Web System

Features: Integration with an existing Web infrastructure, Searching and indexing, Browser-independence, Distributing files across servers

System: Web Platform Support

Features: Web application servers, Content caching, Database connection pooling, Server load balancing

System: Print System

Features: Section and subsection support, Narrative support, Navigation support, Dynamic print publications, Producing Word files

System: E-mail System

Features: E-mail types, Destination pages, Integration to an e-mail server, Template chooser, Personalization support

System: Syndication System

> Features: Syndication subscriber management, Selecting content, Building and distributing feeds

System: Other Publication Systems

> Features: Multiple preview

System: Repository Interface

> Features: File and directory creation, Run-time dependency resolution, Database and metadata output

Summary

Physical design is where your logical design rubber hits the CM road. As you'll see in the chapters in this section, if you've done a good, thorough job thinking through your logical design, you'll know the answers to many of the questions that the physical design process poses. On the other hand, if you find yourself saying "I don't know" to a lot of the physical design questions, part of the problem may be that your logical design hasn't been thought through enough to lead you to the right answers if the questions concern specific features in the CMS you buy or build.

If that sounds cautionary, it should; the hard work of figuring out the *what* of logical design must precede the *how* of physical design. With a good logical design, you've got a good road map through physical design.

The chapters in this section do not discuss particular CM products (with a few exceptions), because that's a sure way to date the usefulness of this book. Rather, they talk about what a CMS could do, should you need it to. Also, some of the features that I discuss don't yet exist in most commercial systems. I discuss these features, nonetheless, because you might really need them. I'm hoping that you will either convince your supplier to create the ones you need, or you will create them yourself because they give back much more than they take to create.

✦   ✦   ✦

What Are Content Markup Languages?

Most text that you collect for your CMS, whether authored or acquired, arrives wrapped in some kind of markup language. A markup language wraps content with formatting and structural codes that tell systems how to present and manage the content. These instructional codes can do anything from simply telling a Web browser what font should be used for a given piece of text to representing the full structural complexity of your content model.

To understand markup languages, then, is to understand how format and structure can be represented in text. If you understand how to work with markup languages, you can make your text look good on the Web and in the print publications you produce.

In this chapter, I illustrate the basic concepts of markup languages, drawing primarily from the most familiar markup language, HTML. I also present examples from XML and the Microsoft markup language RTF to give you a full picture of what markup languages are and what they do.

A Brief and Selective History of Markup Languages

Most Web-savvy folks know that *HTML* stands for *HyperText Markup Language*. Fewer know that *XML* stands for *eXtensible Markup Language*. Few have anything more than a rudimentary understanding of what the *markup language* part of these abbreviations means. Markup languages have been around about as long as computers have. The word *markup* is an old editorial term. Editors would *mark up* manuscripts to show revisions needed and how the pages should be laid out for printing.

In the computer world, you can easily trace the idea and development of markup languages by following the development of word processors. At first, there were no word processors—only text editors. (Does anyone remember Edlin or VI?) These programs enabled you to open a text file, type or delete characters (sometimes even backspace over them), and then save the file again. That was about it. You got no formatting—just letters and punctuation, a lot like a typewriter with a good eraser tape. When true word processors came along, they added a whole slew of new possibilities, and simple text files became documents.

Word processors added bold, italic, underline, strikethrough, and any other formatting that the early printers could print. To represent these new features, developers of word processors invented special codes that you could type before and after the words you wanted to affect. WordStar, my first PC-based word processor, used a markup system called *dot commands*. To make a word bold, you'd literally type ^B before and after it. The first ^B turned on the bold, and the second turned it off. A document of any complexity would have a bevy of strange codes surrounding bits of text. The set of dot commands constituted the markup language of WordStar — you mark up your document with formatting commands to tell the printer how to print your document.

The next turn in the march of word processing was *WYSIWYG* (*what you see is what you get*). Thankfully, for most writers, dot commands disappeared. Rather than typing special codes, you could use formatting commands to display on your computer screen what your document would look like (more or less) when printed. Actually, the dots didn't go away; they simply went underground. Behind the screen, text was still surrounded by special codes, but the software was now advanced enough to make formatting happen on-screen.

As printers got more sophisticated and desktop publishing became a reality, markup languages got more elaborate as the types and quantities of formatting you could do in a document increased steeply. Today, word processors have a vast array of codes that mark up all the advanced features you've come to expect in your documents.

Underground markup is an advantage for word processor developers — as well as writers — because it no longer requires them to do bulky, readable markup. If it doesn't need to be understandable to the human, you can squeeze a lot of markup information into a few bytes of data. These binary-based markup languages lie behind all of today's top word processors.

In another corner of the computing world, people were getting fed up trying to use word processors to work with very large documents and document sets. The problem was that word processors were designed to format fancy documents but did very little to enable you to organize and access your information. The stuff that comes out of word processors isn't easily read by programs (other than the word processor that created it), and it is almost impossible to do anything with it (besides print it).

Companies with large catalogs or complicated document-production systems cared little that they could see what the printer would produce. They wanted each element within their documents to conform to a set of content rules that any well-written program could read and interpret. It was the structure, not the format, of the information they were after.

Some gave up on word processors and turned to databases instead. Others invented the *Standard Generalized Markup Language* (*SGML*). SGML was an attempt to create a markup language that could be used anywhere by anyone to create and enforce document structure rules. SGML could be used to create elaborate schemas that, if imposed upon a document, could turn it into well-structured data. SGML was universally hailed (among the very few who cared about markup languages) as *the* big advance in text-management technology. Supporters believed (and many still do) that if everyone would just accept SGML, communication between text applications would become easy, and all computer-generated text would become accessible and capable of manipulation by computer programs — just like other data.

Unfortunately, the strength of SGML was also its weakness, because following the highly detailed structural rules of a markup language entails learning a pretty complex system before you write a single word. When they drove markup underground, makers of word processors knew that people would choose ease-of-use over consistency and organization. Even the limited attempts that developers made to enable users to really organize documents (heading levels, paragraph styles, auto-TOCs, and so on) were infrequently used and rarely used correctly. Any attempt that developers made to enforce structure was shot down in the marketplace by lazy or naive users. People voted vehemently with their wallets against complexity, constraint, and rigidity. Thus, although SGML held the key to truly organizing information, it was consigned to industries where it could be made obligatory (the military, for example) or where the problems of text management were too complex for any other approach (huge parts catalogs and the like).

Enter the Web. Imagine the surprise — for those of us who'd long since gotten used to markup languages being about as boring, arcane, and esoteric as you could get — when a markup language became an overnight sensation. HTML, which shares much more with dot commands than with modern invisible markup languages, became chic and stylish. Whereas earlier it would have been hard to find someone who admitted knowing a markup language, now knowing even a little HTML was a status symbol. People actually sought out and treasured knowledge of HTML. It caught on like wildfire and fueled the blazing growth of the World Wide Web.

HTML could do this, despite the fact that it was a derivative of SGML, because it was easy to learn, very permissive, and concerned with formatting and not structure. To the chagrin of the SGML community, SGML was used to create its very antithesis. SGML became like those backwoods blues players of old to whom the pop stars give honor but no money. SGML required considered study, careful analysis, and a set of very expensive, hard-to-use tools. HTML took a $15.99 book and a small amount of free software. For a while, it looked as if HTML might actually become the universal markup language that fans of SGML always dreamed it would be.

Unfortunately, the strength of HTML is also its weakness (sound familiar?). The problem is the reverse of the SGML problem. HTML is designed to enable you to format a fancy Web page easily, but does extremely little to enable you to organize and access your information. In an age of increasingly large and complex Web sites, HTML's capabilities are limited. HTML isn't easily read by computer programs and is almost impossible to do anything with besides display in a browser.

Re-enter SGML, renamed XML. The two are so closely related that you'd be hard-pressed to say what really is the difference. I always think of XML as SGML, version 2. The difference between the two isn't how they look, how they work, or the advantages that they offer you. The difference is the world into which they were launched.

In the days of SGML, the vast majority of organizations produced single-purpose documents that were targeted to the printer. It was the rare organization that had a system complex enough to warrant the expense and effort involved in SGML. In the XML world of today, a large percentage of organizations produce multipurpose documents that can be printed as well as displayed on an already large and still growing Web site. Like SGML, XML enables you to organize information and make it easily accessible to computer programs. Just like SGML, XML marks up structure, not format. Like SGML, XML gives you power over large bodies of content. And like SGML, XML requires a characteristically nonhuman adherence to constraint and complexity.

You should be expecting by now that the strength of XML is also its weakness. And for all its hype, XML is really just as hard to use and just as rigid as SGML was. I have yet to see how this is going to play out, but it's obvious that many computer users don't (yet) accept the need to be structured and organized. On the other hand, as the world's organizations become more entangled and interdependent, the need to have structure and organization is only going to increase. So can XML triumph where SGML failed? Or must people's desire for ease of use and freedom of expression doom XML as it did its predecessor?

I hope that, now that you know the story of markup languages, you can help everyone transcend that history rather than simply repeat it. In your CMS, can you combine ease of use for staff and audiences with the rigorous structure that you need to manage your content?

What Is a Markup Language?

Most simply, a *markup language* is a set of codes or tags that surrounds content and tells a person or program what that content is (its structure) and/or what it should look like (its format). I use the word *content* here rather than *text* deliberately. The history of markup languages lies in the text world. Its future lies in any kind of content (text, images, sound, and motion) that needs to be organized and accessed. With some exceptions (for example, by companies that sell or license media), relatively little has yet been done to mark up nontext media, but the industry is still young. So, although it's most convenient to use text examples of markup languages, please understand that the same ideas apply to other types of content.

Cross-Reference I discuss the predominance of text in content management in Chapter 5, "But What Is Content Really?" in the section "Why Does Text Get All of the Attention?" For an example of tagging used for nontext content, see Chapter 24, "Working with Metadata," in the section "Inclusion metadata."

Markup tags must have a distinct syntax that sets them apart from the content that they surround. The *tag syntax* is the set of rules for writing tags that any person or tool must follow in order for its markup codes to be recognized. Most people who create Web sites are familiar with the tag syntax of HTML, in which a tag begins with an opening angle bracket, followed by the tag name, followed by a closing bracket. Fortunately for these Web types, XML and SGML follow exactly the same rules.

This set of tags forms a metalanguage that adds context to the content that it surrounds. Context is a funny thing, because it can completely change the meaning of the thing it acts upon. Consider the following example:

```
The Sky Is Falling
```

Now compare it to the following with a set of XML tags added:

```
<LIE> The Sky Is Falling</LIE>
```

Tags are rarely used to negate the meaning of the content that they enclose. More commonly, they add nuance or interpretation to the content. Consider the following:

```
The Sky Is Falling
```

And compare it to this example with HTML tags added:

```
<H1>The Sky Is Falling</H1>
```

In the first line, you have a statement. In the second line, that statement is turned into a first-level heading (as denoted by the ⟨H1⟩ tag in HTML). This means that it's an important statement and, furthermore, that it can stand for all the content that follows it until the next ⟨H1⟩. The tag puts the context of *headings* around the content that it surrounds. It adds nuance and interpretation to the statement.

So markup languages are metalanguages. Truth be told, some are metalanguages and others are *meta-metalanguages*. HTML is a metalanguage. It has a fixed number of tags, whose meanings are commonly understood. It is possible to describe precisely how it works. XML, on the other hand, is a meta-metalanguage. It's a system for creating metalanguages. As I describe in the following sections, there is no particular set of XML tags. Instead, XML gives you a way to define other metalanguages of your own design.

A Taxonomy of Markup Languages

All markup languages add codes to text to mark format and structure distinctions in the text. Each markup language, however, does the same task a bit differently. In addition, markup languages differ in other aspects of their approach, as follows:

✦ Some use plain text and others use proprietary binary code as tags.

✦ Some use tags to represent structure. Others use tags to represent formatting only. Still others represent both format and structure.

✦ Some have a fixed tag set, whereas others enable you to create your own tags.

✦ Some have a very limited range of structure or format constructs that you can represent, whereas others offer wider coverage.

Table 35-1 compares HTML, XML, and the average word processing markup language on these aspects of markup languages.

Table 35-1: Comparing HTML, XML, and Word Processor Markups

	HTML	*XML*	*Word Processing Markup*
ASCII versus Binary	ASCII	ASCII	Binary
Format versus Structure	Format	Structure	Format and Structure
Extendable versus Nonextendable	Nonextendable	Extendable	Nonextendable
Range of coverage	Low	High	Medium

ASCII versus binary

Both HTML and XML are ASCII-based markup languages (strictly speaking, they're Unicode-based, but the point is the same). ASCII is that stuff you can read in a program such as Microsoft Notepad. In other words, both HTML and XML are constructed in such a way that they're readable without any special decoders. More important, they were designed to be viewed directly and understood by humans. In a word, they're verbose.

Word processors store their markup information in a binary format, unreadable to any program but the word processor itself. Why? Recall that, after word processing markup went underground, it became more densely packed. To see how dense it is, try the following experiment:

1. Create a file in Microsoft Word and save it. Notice the file size.

2. Now save the file again under a different name, but this time choose the Word option to save it as an RTF file (Microsoft's ASCII equivalent to the file's binary format). Notice that the file size of the RTF version is considerably larger than its binary cousin.

The content is the same in both versions. In the binary version, however, the markup information is packed into optimized small chunks. This approach makes the document more efficient (smaller) and also makes it faster to parse and display. On the other hand, it requires a tight linkage between the display software (the word processor) and the markup syntax. You could say that the markup is hard-wired into the display software.

The ASCII markup formats, on the other hand, assume an open, agnostic attitude toward display software. No proprietary knowledge is needed to parse and display these formats because they carry with them all that information in a recognizable form. That's why HTML and XML are termed *open standards*, why they're so verbose, and why they don't load terribly quickly.

Format versus structure

Format describes how content is intended to look as it's displayed. Qualities such as line spacing, kerning, font face, horizontal and vertical positioning, and indentation are all aspects of formatting.

This is the concept of rendering format that I discuss in Chapter 2, "Content Has Format," in the section "Rendering Format: Presenting Information." You find much more information about format there.

Structure describes the purpose or meaning of content. Names such as Title, Heading 1, Sidebar, FAQ Question, and Price all say what a piece of content is for, but nothing about how it looks.

Look in Chapter 3, "Content Has Structure," for more information on structure.

HTML is designed mostly for formatting, and XML is designed mostly for structure. I say *mostly* because you have structural tags in HTML, and you can use XML to specify formatting options. The overall intent of HTML, however, is to add tags to content that tell the Web browser how to display the content. The overall intent of XML is to add tags to content that specify the meaning or use of the content. Formatting markup is needed to determine presentation. Structural markup is needed to determine use.

The two markup languages have different but highly intertwined purposes, and any good content system covers both. For example, you may want the title to be bold and centered for the purposes of standard presentation, and you may also need it to be tagged as the title so that you can find it and present it in lists with other titles. The more you intend to manage content, the more important structural markup becomes.

Management is the process of collecting, categorizing, selecting, and modifying content. It becomes impossible to do any of these tasks — that is, to manage content — if you have no way to specify what each piece of content *is*. That's why content management has been so difficult to date on the Web. HTML doesn't give you enough clues about the function of the content that it marks up. This may be no problem for smaller or more static applications, where you might get away with marking up for format only (as any Webmaster can tell you). It's not that there's no structure to the content on these sites. Rather, the structure of the content is learned and remembered by a person who can manually collect, categorize, select, and modify content.

People usually think of formatting as serving some aesthetic purpose; however, formatting is there mostly to provide structural cues to the human eye. Text that's big and centered at the top of a page, for example, is very likely to be the title (a structural part of the content). Similarly, as content moves from being managed to being displayed, the structural tags must be exchanged for format tags that the display software can understand. Your title may be tagged as a title, but as it's displayed, it must somehow give rise to the tags for *big* and *centered*.

Although HTML is basically for format and XML is basically for structure, the word processor markup is for both format and structure. Because the markup of word processors is proprietary, it must include anything that you may ever need. Thus, even though the major thrust of word processors is formatting related, as they've advanced, they have begun to include more structural components. In Microsoft Word, for example, you can create a style called *title* that enables you to locate the title and group it with other titles. Word can also tag a paragraph as a heading and then create a document outline; it can tag text as index entries, and it can include author and other metadata with a document. These are all structure tags. In Word, however, they do double duty by enabling you to apply formatting consistently to structural elements.

Extendable versus nonextendable

An *extendable* markup language enables you to create new tags for special purposes. In this way, XML is clearly distinguished from HTML and word processor markup. In HTML and word processor markup, *WTGIAYG* (What They Give is All You've Got). A finite and predefined number of tags must do for any task that you may have. For HTML, the World Wide Web Consortium (W3C) sets the standards for HTML tags, adding and removing tags with each version to try to cover, in a generic way, the majority of needs that the committee has seen. These tag specifications aren't intended to address the needs of a particular Web developer as much as they provide a general way for everyone to handle similar issues. Web developers cannot invent their own HTML tags, and so for them, HTML is a *nonextendable* markup language.

Similarly, for word processors, the developers consider the functionality to be offered in the next version, and then they invent tags to represent it and user interfaces for adding those tags to the content. Because no other program or organization needs to understand their tagging scheme, word processor developers can make their tags highly specific to their needs. But for content authors who use the word processor, the tags are finite, predefined, generic, and nonextendable.

In contrast, as a meta-metalanguage, XML has no particular tags, but instead gives you the capability to create whatever tags you need. That's a benefit and a curse. With freedom comes responsibility. You have the freedom to design a custom tag set that perfectly describes your content. But you also have the responsibility to ensure the following:

✦ That the tags you create correctly and adequately describe your content.

✦ That all users and programs know what each tag is intended to do.

✦ That, if necessary, the tags can be translated to format tags as the content is displayed.

✦ That the tags are consistent with any emerging standards for XML tagging in your industry.

It's very easy in XML to devise an overly complex, incomprehensible, and tangled tag set. It's very hard to set up all human and computer systems around any tag set that you create.

In the nonextendable languages, you have a different problem. Anyone who's worked with HTML knows that you create a page by making tags designed for one purpose do something else (using table tags, for example, to position non-table elements correctly on a Web page). Your problem in a nonextendable language (such as HTML) is how to serve the needs of your particular content by using very general tags. Your problem in an extendable markup language such as XML is how to create and manage your own very specific tag set.

Range of coverage

Each markup language has a range of the formatting and structural elements that it can represent.

HTML has a particularly low range of coverage. That is, the HTML language offers relatively few of the many of tags that you might like to have. This makes HTML easy to learn but also easy to grow out of. I remember how gratifying it was to learn the first versions of the HTML tag set in one sitting. I remember, too, how quickly I stopped finding tags that I needed to make my pages work.

Word processors (and desktop publishing programs as well) have many more tags than HTML. They need a lot of tags to cover the range of needs of professional publishers who use them. Successive versions of the HTML tag set have come ever closer to covering the same midrange selection of tags that most word processors support. With the extensions offered by Cascading Style Sheets (CSS), HTML can today support a large fraction of the formatting and structure offered by word processor markup.

The range of coverage of XML, of course, is infinite. It can have any tag that you can dream up — and lots of them. Given that you have the wherewithal to support the tags that you create, you can represent any formatting or structure that you can imagine.

Working with Markup

Working directly with markup code can be trying at best and completely baffling at worst. It takes a certain attitude and a few key concepts to get past the complexity and work successfully with markup code. In the following sections, I'll describe those key concepts to help you begin to first decode and then code your own markup.

Don't be baffled by syntax

Because of the problem of representing representation (see the section titled "Representing representation" later in this chapter), and to keep markup from becoming even more verbose, the makers of markup choose unusual characters or character combinations to create tags. Even XML, whose creators deemed that "Terseness in XML markup is of minimal importance" (see `www.w3.org/TR/1998/REC-xml-19980210`), is full of shorthand and strange character combinations that are useful to the initiated but obscure to the neophyte. If you're new to markup, the way to get past this barrier is to understand that the normal rules of reading don't apply and then to begin slowly to unpack each statement, paying careful attention to the meaning (or lack of meaning) of white space and nesting.

The following code, for example, shows an HTML table:

```
<TABLE>
    <TR>
        <TD COLSPAN="2">
        Here is the picture
        <IMG SRC="ngo.jpg" BORDER="1">
        </TD>
    </TR>
<TABLE>
```

How can you turn this code into English? As follows:

✦ **Tag names.** Shorthand tag names stand for real words. TABLE is a table, TR is a table row, TD is table data (better known as a column), and IMG is an image. So this sample is about tables, their rows and columns, and an image. Tag names must be unique within the markup language to ensure that any program or person reading the markup can tell the difference between all tags. All markup languages have tag names, but not all the tag names are as easily readable as the ones used by HTML.

✦ **Tag name delimiters.** The way HTML distinguishes between the name of a tag (TR, for example) and the other text around it is to surround the tag name with angle brackets. The open and close angle brackets are called delimiters (because they set "de limits" of the tag name). All markup languages have tag delimiters, but not all delimiters are as obvious as those used in HTML.

✦ **Insides or scope.** Every tag's *insides* are contained by that tag. In this case, the image is contained in the column, which is contained in the row, which is contained in the table. (See the section "The concept of nesting," later in this chapter, for further explanation.) The *scope* of a tag, then, is the range of other tags and text that it applies to. All markup languages have some notion of tag scope, but they differ in how much nesting they allow and how the scope is represented. Most markup languages do not allow as much leeway in representing scope as does HTML. Most, for example, require that you specifically close every tag that you open. HTML does not.

✦ **Parameters.** Parameters tell you what the tag has. In the preceding example, the table column has a column span of 2 (COLSPAN), and the image has a source file name of ngo.jpg as well as a border of 1. Parameter names, unlike tag names, need not be unique (the TABLE and the TR tag, for example, can both have a STYLE parameter). Parameter values are distinguished from the parameter name by some unique character sequence (in HTML by the equal sign). Most markup languages are not as lax about the way parameters and values are represented as is HTML. In HTML, for example, you can either surround the parameter value with quotes or not. In other markup languages, you have only one way to enter a parameter value.

The *syntax* of a markup language is the set of rules, definitions, and characters it uses to create and apply tags. Although all markup languages have the same sorts of rules and definitions, they can differ markedly in the characters they use and the specifics of the rules and definitions. Still, after you know how to look for tag names, scopes, parameters, and delimiters, you can begin to unpack even the most obscure-looking markup syntax. The only thing left to know then is what all the tag names and parameters mean and what their effect is on the structure or formatting of the text. It is no coincidence that the syntax of HTML is a relatively simple one to learn and read. If it were not so simple, HTML would never have taken off as the markup language of the masses.

Here's an example of the same content marked up using the same simple rules, but different syntax:

```
\trowd \trgaph108\trleft-108\trbrdrt\brdrs\brdrw10 \trbrdrl\brdrs\
brdrw10 \trbrdrb\brdrs\brdrw10 \trbrdrr\brdrs\brdrw10 \trbrdrh\brdrs\
brdrw10 \trbrdrv \brdrs\brdrw10 \trftsWidth1\trautofit1\trpaddl108\
trpaddr108\trpaddfl3\trpaddfr3 \clvertalt\clbrdrt\brdrs\brdrw10 \clbrdrl\
brdrs\brdrw10 \clbrdrb\brdrs\brdrw10 \clbrdrr\brdrs\brdrw10 \cltxlrtb\
clftsWidth3\clwWidth8856 \cellx8748\pard\plain \ql \li0\ri0\widctlpar\
intbl\aspalpha\aspnum\faauto\adjustright\rin0\lin0 \fs24\lang1033\
langfe1033\cgrid\langnp1033\langfenp1033 { {\*\shppict {\pict {\*\
picprop\shplid1025 {\sp {\sn shapeType} {\sv 75} } {\sp {\sn fFlipH}
{\sv 0} } {\sp {\sn fFlipV} {\sv 0} } {\sp {\sn pibName} {\sv
C:\'5cDocuments and Settings\ '5cbob\'5cMy Documents\'5cMy Pictures\
'ngo.jpg} } {\sp {\sn pibFlags} {\sv 2} } {\sp {\sn fLine} {\sv 0} }
{\sp {\sn fLayoutInCell} {\sv 1} } } \picscalex100\picscaley100\
piccropl0\piccropr0\piccropt0\piccropb0 \picw7488\pich5609\picwgoal4245\
pichgoal3180\jpegblip\bliptag-693656786 {\*\blipuid
```

(many pages of numbers go here)

```
} } }\cell }\pard \ql \li0\ri0\widctlpar\intbl\aspalpha\aspnum\faauto\
adjustright\rin0\lin0 { \trowd \trgaph108\trleft-108\trbrdrt\brdrs\
brdrw10 \trbrdrl\brdrs\brdrw10 \trbrdrb\brdrs\brdrw10 \trbrdrr\brdrs\
brdrw10 \trbrdrh\brdrs\brdrw10 \trbrdrv\brdrs\brdrw10 \trftsWidth1\
trautofit1\trpaddl108\trpaddr108\trpaddfl3\trpaddfr3 \clvertalt\
clbrdrt\brdrs\brdrw10 \clbrdrl\brdrs\brdrw10 \clbrdrb\brdrs\
brdrw10 \clbrdrr\brdrs\brdrw10 \cltxlrtb\clftsWidth3\
clwWidth8856 \cellx8748\row }
```

This code sample is the same content, but now represented in the syntax of Microsoft Word's RTF markup code, which is neither intuitive nor understandable unless you're a computer.

The language versus the interpreter

Markup is a language. By itself, it doesn't do anything. It requires a speaker of the language, an interpreter, for it to be read and written. This is such a simple point that it always surprises me that people confuse the two. Word processors present the simplest case. Here, you have one language, one interpreter, and a very tight coupling. So tight is the coupling that it's unlikely that you've ever thought about the markup code behind word processors.

HTML is more complex. The language of HTML is spoken by browsers. Each variety of browser speaks a slightly different dialect. It's the interaction of the HTML language with the particular interpreter that finally decides how the markup is used. Different browsers make different interpretations of HTML tags as they turn them into formatting on your screen. HTML interpreters, then, are more loosely coupled to the language than word processors. The result is that their interpretations are less predictable.

In XML, tools are available that read and write XML, but developing the interpreter is up to you (or someone with a problem substantially similar to yours). Only you know the correct interpretation of the tags that you create. Again, XML shows itself, not as a markup language, but as a metamarkup language.

Representing representation

As inescapable as taxes and mosquitoes, there's no such thing as a markup language completely separate from the language it's marking up. There must always be a way for the words used in the markup language to *not* be used as markup. I like the following way of looking at it:

A Zen master and her student were sitting on a park bench contemplating the universe:

"Master, what holds up the world?" asked the student.

"The world, my student, rides on the back of a giant turtle."

"Yes," said the student, "but what holds the turtle up?"

"You are very clever, my friend, very clever," calmly replied the master. "But I'm afraid it is turtles all the way down."

How do you represent bold text in HTML?

```
<B>
```

How do you represent `<B>` in HTML?

```
&LT;B&GT;
```

How do you represent `&LT;B&GT;` in HTML?

In markup, as in life, "It's turtles all the way down." No matter which method you choose to represent markup, you always face the chance that someone wants to type those same characters and not have them interpreted as markup. The problem is that people use the same symbols to represent both text and markup. This issue may seem purely philosophical, but it is not. It turns up in project after project the user wants to convert markup from one form to another. When your converter encounters <B>, should it convert it to the target form of the bold tag or should it keep it as is because it was not intended to be markup? In addition to being an ongoing nuisance, representing representation also points out a deep issue in the study of markup: A receding, recursive set of definitions on how to interpret markup always ends either when a human makes the final interpretation or when a simplifying assumption stops the recursion from being endless and sending processors into infinite regression.

The concept of nesting

Nesting is the official name for what I previously called *insides*. It means tags within tags. Look, for example, at the following sentence:

```
<H1>This is a <FONT SIZE=+10>Heading</FONT></H1>
```

The entire line is tagged H1. (Notice the opening `<H1>` tag at the beginning and the closing `</H1>` tag at the end.) Only the word `Heading` is subject to the `<FONT>` tag, which turns up the font size by 10 points. The question is, 10 points bigger than what? The answer, of course, is 10 points bigger than an H1 (whatever that happens to be for your browser). In other words, the `<FONT>` tag is interpreted within the context of the `<H1>` tag. If it were inside a different tag, it would be interpreted differently. This is a fairly trivial example of nesting, but it shows the basic concept.

In HTML, nesting is of moderate importance. Some tags — notably, the <TABLE> tags — make no sense at all outside of the context of other tags. Following HTML's format emphasis, nesting serves the purpose of creating compound or complex formatting options such as bold, italic, or doubly indented lists.

In RTF, which I describe earlier as an ASCII equivalent of Microsoft Word markup, nesting is extreme, often going 10 levels deep! And unlike HTML, where end tags carry the name of the tag they're ending, RTF ends all tags with a single curly bracket like this: }. Compared to HTML, the structure of many RTF files is a rat's nest. (The very ugly markup example in the preceding section is RTF.)

Nesting in XML is central. As you may expect, nesting represents the structural components of an XML file. A common way of referring to the relationships in nested (or hierarchical) code is to use the analogy of the *parent-child relationship*. Each tag in an XML document can have one or more *parents* and one or more *children*. Without paying attention to a tag's parents, it's often impossible to determine its meaning. Consider the following XML fragment that, if you look at it at closely, you see is obviously part of a larger XML structure:

```
<PR RESOURCES>
  <SPEAKERS>
    <NAME>Anna Emelia</NAME>
  </SPEAKERS>
  <HARDWARE>
    <MICROPHONES/>
    <SPEAKERS/>
  <HARDWARE>
</PR RESOURCES>
```

What does the <SPEAKERS> tag mean? Clearly, it depends on its parents and possibly its grandparents. XML files are like outlines. Their interpretation depends largely on your ability to travel up and down the branches of the file's hierarchy. This quality more than any other, I believe, defines XML.

Note   The namers of XML focused on its eXtensibility. They may have been better off focusing on its nesting qualities by calling it HML for Hierarchical Markup Language (but, of course, *X* is sexier these days than *H*, and *H* was already taken).

The benefits of white space

White space is spaces, tabs, and paragraph marks (carriage returns and line feeds). All the markup languages that I've discussed (HTML, XML and RTF) ignore white space completely. This is a strange thing. For humans, white space is essential to understanding the distinction and relationship between content elements. People are visually driven. Look at this page. On both paper or on-screen, it's the white space that tells you where one thing ends and another begins. The more white space around an object, generally, the more important it is. Indentation is essential to understanding any kind of hierarchical relationship. So linked are white space and meaning that many conversion programs actually translate white-space qualities into structural tags for a document.

Remember the mess of RTF markup that I showed you earlier? Compare it to the following version, in which I add appropriate white space. The syntax is no less imposing, but at least you know where to start to unpack it.

```
\trowd \trgaph108\trleft-108\trbrdrt\brdrs\brdrw10
\trbrdrl\brdrs\brdrw10 \trbrdrb\brdrs\brdrw10
\trbrdrr\brdrs\brdrw10 \trbrdrh\brdrs\brdrw10 \trbrdrv
\brdrs\brdrw10 \trftsWidth1\trautofit1\trpaddl108\trpaddr108\trpaddfl3\trpaddfr3
\clvertalt\clbrdrt\brdrs\brdrw10 \clbrdrl\brdrs\brdrw10
\clbrdrb\brdrs\brdrw10 \clbrdrr\brdrs\brdrw10
\cltxlrtb\clftsWidth3\clwWidth8856 \cellx8748\pard\plain
\ql \li0\ri0\widctlpar\intbl\aspalpha\aspnum\faauto\adjustright\rin0\lin0
\fs24\lang1033\langfe1033\cgrid\langnp1033\langfenp1033
{
    {\*\shppict
        {\pict
            {\*\picprop\shplid1025
                {\sp
                    {\sn shapeType}
                        {\sv 75}
                    }
                {\sp
                    {\sn fFlipH}
                    {\sv 0}
                    }
                {\sp
                    {\sn fFlipV}
                    {\sv 0}
                    }
                {\sp
                    {\sn pibName}
                    {\sv C:\'5cDocuments and Settings\
                    '5cbob\'5cMy Documents\'5cMy Pictures\'ngo.jpg}
                    }
                {\sp
                    {\sn pibFlags}
                    {\sv 2}
                    }
                {\sp
                    {\sn fLine}
                    {\sv 0}
                    }
                {\sp
                    {\sn fLayoutInCell}
                    {\sv 1}
                    }
                }
    \picscalex100\picscaley100\piccropl0\piccropr0\piccropt0\piccropb0
    \picw7488\pich5609\picwgoal4245\pichgoal3180\jpegblip\bliptag-693656786
            {\*\blipuid many pages of numbers go here}
        }
        }\cell
    }\pard \ql \li0\ri0\widctlpar\intbl\aspalpha\aspnum\faauto
    \adjustright\rin0\lin0
{
```

```
\trowd \trgaph108\trleft-108\trbrdrt\brdrs\brdrw10
\trbrdrl\brdrs\brdrw10 \trbrdrb\brdrs\brdrw10 \trbrdrr\brdrs\brdrw10
\trbrdrh\brdrs\brdrw10 \trbrdrv\brdrs\brdrw10
\trftsWidth1\trautofit1\trpaddl108\trpaddr108\trpaddfl3\trpaddfr3
\clvertalt\clbrdrt\brdrs\brdrw10 \clbrdrl\brdrs\brdrw10
\clbrdrb\brdrs\brdrw10 \clbrdrr\brdrs\brdrw10
\cltxlrtb\clftsWidth3\clwWidth8856 \cellx8748\row
}
```

For markup interpreters, it's the tags — and only the tags — that matter. Everyone who's just started writing in HTML is baffled by spaces that she thinks that she's put in but that somehow don't show up in the browser. Eventually, you learn to use the code   to ensure that a space isn't ignored (the NBSP stands for *non-breaking space*). Markup can look totally jumbled and still be interpreted perfectly. Similarly, markup that's all nicely aligned and indented is for your eyes only; the interpreter couldn't care less.

People play in the margins

A general rule of life says that, if presented with a rule, industrious people find a loophole. As goes life, so goes markup. Where you find loopholes in the markup syntax, you can pack in some of your own information that goes unnoticed by the markup's interpreters.

You can't, for example, make up new HTML tags — they have no meaning to the standard interpreters (such as Web browsers). If you want to put something into an HTML file for your own purposes, however, you can use one of the following syntax loopholes to get nonstandard markup into a standard HTML file:

✦ **Metatags:** Because they have a somewhat open format, metatags (which are in the header section of HTML pages) are often tweaked to provide space to pack editorial, tracking, access, and other miscellaneous information into HTML files.

✦ **Comments:** Intended for commentary, the comment tag (`<!-- comment -->`) gives developers a convenient place to type in little extras.

✦ **Bad syntax:** If you misspell a tag name in HTML, you may never know it (or you have a heck of a time trying to figure out why your page doesn't look right). Browsers simply ignore the misspelled tag and go on unhindered. Knowing this, creative Webmasters often do make up tags that their own custom components understand. They know that these new tags are safely ignored by the permissiveness of the browsers. But if you ever use this technique, be careful: You never know when a less permissive browser may come along and show the world your "mistake."

✦ **XML is open:** You can make up as many tags as you want. You usually have no need to trick the interpreter into ignoring your transgressions. Your problem is more one of developing the interpreter that can correctly identify and deal with your tags.

Summary

Markup was never glamorous until HTML came along. I'm sure that it's going to fade back into the obscurity that it came from someday. For now, however, HTML and especially XML are great conversation starters at parties. These markup languages and a host of others do the following:

✦ Represent content format.

✦ Represent content structure.

✦ Consist of tags that surround and add context to the content inside them.

✦ Give you either a simple but limited set of tags (HTML) or an unlimited set of tags but a lot of responsibility for how those tags are interpreted (XML).

In the next chapter, I deal more specifically with the relationship between markup languages and content management.

✦   ✦   ✦

XML and Content Management

In this chapter, I move from talking generally about markup languages to talking specifically about XML. My intention isn't to teach you the hard facts, syntax, and programming behind XML. Plenty of other resources do that. My intention is to give you a conceptual overview of XML that enables you to see how it works and how you can use it in a CMS.

XML gets pretty hard pretty fast. I try to keep the story at a general readership level, but a few places crop up where it gets a bit thick for the nonprogrammer. For the programmers, your challenge is to move beyond the mechanics of XML to understand the content management concept that the XML in this chapter demonstrates.

What Is XML?

XML should be very important to you, the content manager. Within the world of markup languages, XML is a good one. It has the advantage of being open and easily read. It's taken some strong lessons from its "also ran" parent SGML and its superficial cousin HTML. It represents structure, which endures long after format has faded, and naturally encodes the hierarchical relationships that often categorize content.

Best of all, XML is accepted by the Web community as the markup language of choice. Company after company has dropped the pretense that its home-grown markup language is "the one" and has instead rallied around XML. Today's mediocre XML tools are already being eclipsed by coming killer applications. XML has become one of the first standard content markup languages to actually be accepted as a standard. XML may be most important not for its superior functionality, nor for its style and sizzle, but because it's a content standard that may stick.

XML addresses two separate but related areas: data interchange and content management. I briefly discuss data exchange to give you a feel for what it is, and then I discuss content management in depth.

XML and data interchange

Before jumping into the aspects of XML that are pivotal to content management, let me spend a moment on a very important aspect of XML that's not pivotal to content management (at least not directly). XML is often discussed as the *data interchange* format for data transfer between computer applications.

There's a vast Tower of Babel in the computer systems world. Each application speaks its own data representation and transfer languages that other applications may or may not understand. XML has begun to provide a *lingua franca* for all applications. In the past, every company that created a product also created its own scheme for storing and transferring data. (In lieu of any global standard, what else could they do?) XML is, or, at least, is becoming, that global standard. Now companies can give their products the capability to send and receive data in XML with the knowledge that other applications are doing the same. In the past, it's taken tremendous repeated effort to make various enterprise applications (financial, ERP, operational applications, and the like) talk to each other. And although XML doesn't help you decide what two applications need to say to each other, it does give you the tools to make the conversation that you want to happen possible.

If the Internet's proved one thing, it's that every computer that can be connected to all others will be. After two applications become connected these days, it's likely that XML has some part in how they communicate. Having noted this, for the remainder of this chapter I focus very little on the data interchange uses of XML. That role is far less critical for content management than the one it plays in representing and storing content and metadata.

XML tagging

To bring the idea of XML home, I contrast the same content marked up in very simple formats, XML, and then HTML.

Cross-Reference   If you're not already familiar with the concept of markup, you may want to review in Chapter 35, "What Are Content Markup Languages?" in the section "Don't be baffled by syntax."

Imagine that you have a lot of content describing different car models. You'd like to organize it and present it on the Web. You've turned to XML, rather than a standard database approach, because XML offers data management down to the level of the words in a sentence and because XML enables you to produce HTML pages effectively. (You have other possible reasons to turn to XML, but these are sufficient.)

Note   I derived the sample code in this section from an old version of eXcelon Corporation's Extensible Information Server. eXcelon (at www.exceloncorp.com) makes XML database and development tools.

Here's how someone who doesn't know about markup languages may specify the information for one car:

```
Name: Dodge Durango
Type: Sport Utility
Doors: 4
Miles: 32000
Price: 18000
Power_Locks: Yes
```

```
Power_Windows: Yes
Stereo: Radio/Cassette/CD
Air-Conditioning: Yes
Automatic: Yes
Four-Wheel_Drive: Full/Partial
Note: Very clean
```

Notice that this content is actually marked up. The tag identifier is delimited by the beginning of the line and by a colon. The tag scope is delimited by the end of the line. In fact, this sort of markup is used fairly often by programmers who don't know XML. It's far from sufficient, however, to support managing the content. Although it supports the basic markup qualities, it has no provision for attributes or nesting.

XML tagging

Here's the same content marked up with XML:

```
<VEHICLES>
  <VEHICLE inventory_number="1">
    <MAKE>Dodge</MAKE>
    <MODEL model_code="USA23">Durango</MODEL>
    <YEAR>1998</YEAR>
    <PICTURE>DodgeDurango.jpg</PICTURE>
    <STYLE>Sport Utility</STYLE>
    <DOORS>4</DOORS>
    <PRICE>18000</PRICE>
    <MILES>32000</MILES>
    <OPTIONS>
      <POWER_LOCKS>Yes</POWER_LOCKS>
      <POWER_WINDOWS>Yes</POWER_WINDOWS>
      <STEREO>Radio/Cassette/CD</STEREO>
      <AIR_CONDITIONING>Yes</AIR-_CONDITIONING>
      <AUTOMATIC>Yes</AUTOMATIC>
      <FOUR-_WHEEL_DRIVE>Full/Partial</FOUR-WHEEL_DRIVE>
    </OPTIONS>
    <NOTE>Very clean</NOTE>
  </VEHICLE>
</VEHICLES>
```

Notice that this is longer than the nominal markup that you saw first. It's much more explicit and verbose. More important, there's much more metadata in this representation. The nesting, particularly, adds a big new dimension to the content. You can tell, for example, that I'm talking here generally about vehicles and that one particular vehicle is elaborated. Further, if you need to get to all the car's options, they're all neatly wrapped within the <OPTIONS> tag. Like the first sample, it's easily readable by even the uninitiated. Unlike the first, it gives the distinct and true impression that it's well-organized.

Note   XML syntax is just like HTML syntax. In fact, they're the same. They're both derived from the same mother tongue — SGML. XML is hierarchical and has no predefined set of tags. After you set up some tags, the way that you type them follows HTML precisely. That's not to say that, as an HTML savant, you know all that you need to know about XML, but you do know how to write it correctly.

XML tags are called *elements*. As in HTML, these elements can have attributes and child elements. Unlike in HTML, you get to decide whether a piece of information shows up as an attribute of its parent element or as a subelement. Consider the following two versions of the same XML description:

```
<HOUSE owner="Elizabeth Higlo" bedrooms="3"/>
```

or

```
<HOUSE>
  <OWNER>Elizabeth Higlo</OWNER>
  <BEDROOMS>3</BEDROOMS>
</HOUSE>
```

Are they the same? Yes and no. They certainly express the same information. On the other hand, the way that you'd access the information programmatically is different in each case. Is one better than the other? Not essentially, but it's hard to say. What you decide to make an attribute instead of a separate tag has more to do with the organizing principles of your tag schema than it does with any innate need to make something an attribute or a subelement. The only coherent principles that I can point to for subelements versus attributes are as follows:

✦ **Subelements:** Attributes can't have subelements, but elements can. This is about the only hard and fast rule I have found that differentiates the two choices.

✦ **Ids:** Ids and references to Ids (called IDREFS in XML language) are generally but not always in attributes. XML is designed that way so that you can use the functions built into most XML validators to make sure that your Ids are unique and that your references are to Ids that exist.

✦ **Closed lists:** Where you need an element to have closed-list metadata associated with it (see Chapter 24, "Working with Metadata," in the section "Categorizing Metadata Fields," for the definition of a closed list), an attribute is more convenient than an element.

✦ **Data in general:** In general, it's more space-efficient and readable to have most of the numbers and small text strings (the datalike content) in attributes rather than in elements. This is the approach taken by HTML where, for example, all the sizes and positions for an image are in the attributes of an <IMG> tag.

✦ **Readability:** To make more information more easily readable in text form, you might pack that information into attributes, which put the information all on one line in the text display. On the other hand, to make information more usable in XML authoring environments, use elements. Attributes are often hidden by the authoring application and require you to go to a different screen area or dialog box to see and edit them.

It's not that you can't put any information that you want in subelements; it's that, by tradition and for use with XML parsers and authoring environments, it's preferable to put some sorts of information in attributes. If you're designing a tagging system and you need an element to have subelements, your choice is clear; otherwise, there may be a degree of arbitrariness to your choice. You may be influenced by purely practical considerations such as ease of editing.

HTML tagging

Look now at the following potential HTML presentation of the same content:

```
<TABLE>
  <TR>
    <TD COLSPAN="2">
```

```
      <IMG src="../scripts/xlnisapi.dll/cars/carsdata/images/DodgeDurango.jpg"
      border="1" />
   </TD>
   <TD style="font-family: Verdana;">
      <b>Dodge Durango</b>
   </TD>
</TR>
<TR>
   <TD style="font-family: Verdana;">
     Sport Utility
   </TD>
   <TD style="font-family: Verdana;">
     Doors: 4
   </TD>
   <TD>
   </TD>
</TR>
<TR>
   <TD style="font-family: Verdana;">
     Miles:32000
   </TD>
   <TD style="font-family: Verdana;">
     Price: 18000
   </TD>
   <TD>
   </TD>
</TR>
</TABLE>

<TABLE border="2" cellpadding="2" cellspacing="3" width="380">
  <TR>
    <TD STYLE="background-color=yellow; font:10pt. Verdana;">
      Power_Locks
    </TD>
    <TD STYLE="color:blue; background-color=yellow;
    font:10pt. Verdana; font-weight:bold">
      <b>Yes</b>
    </TD>
  </TR>
  <TR>
    <TD STYLE="background-color=yellow; font:10pt. Verdana;">
      Power_Windows
    </TD>
    <TD STYLE="color:blue; background-color=yellow; font:10pt.
    Verdana; font-weight:bold">
      <b>Yes</b>
    </TD>
  </TR>
  <TR>
    <TD STYLE="background-color=yellow; font:10pt. Verdana;">
      Stereo
    </TD>
    <TD STYLE="color:blue; background-color=yellow; font:10pt.
```

```
Verdana; font-weight:bold">
   <b>Radio/Cassette/CD</b>
  </TD>
 </TR>
 <TR>
  <TD STYLE="background-color=yellow; font:10pt. Verdana;">
   Air-Conditioning
  </TD>
  <TD STYLE="color:blue; background-color=yellow; font:10pt.
  Verdana; font-weight:bold">
   <b>Yes</b>
  </TD>
 </TR>
 <TR>
  <TD STYLE="background-color=yellow; font:10pt. Verdana;">
   Automatic
  </TD>
  <TD STYLE="color:blue; background-color=yellow; font:10pt.
  Verdana; font-weight:bold">
   <b>Yes</b>
  </TD>
 </TR>
 <TR>
  <TD STYLE="background-color=yellow; font:10pt. Verdana;">
   Four-Wheel_Drive
  </TD>
  <TD STYLE="color:blue; background-color=yellow; font:10pt.
  Verdana; font-weight:bold">
   <b>Full/Partial</b>
  </TD>
 </TR>
 <TR>
  <TD STYLE="background-color=yellow; font:10pt. Verdana;">
   Note
  </TD>
  <TD STYLE="color:blue; background-color=yellow; font:10pt.
  Verdana; font-weight:bold">
   <b>Very clean</b>
  </TD>
 </TR>
</TABLE>
```

The first and obvious points are that this version, which contains no more content than the others, is way bigger and much harder to read and interpret. Only the fully trained eye can make out what this content means or how it's designed. If I hadn't been really nice to you by indenting child tags (something rarely done on HTML pages), it would have been even harder to interpret. The size difference can be made up for by faster processors; the difficulty in reading HTML can be made up for by enough practice. What can't be compensated for is the incapability of a program to parse this HTML and decide definitively what's content and what's added formatting and layout.

How, for example, would a program pick all the Notes out of files such as this? You can't search for the word *note* because it may appear anywhere in the content. You can't search for the particular formatting around the note because other parts of the content may be formatted the same way. Your only hope is to find the note in the file by starting from some definitely unique place (such as the beginning of the file) and tracing a series of steps to get to its location. You can't move line by line because, as you know, white space (which includes paragraph marks) is ignored in HTML. Possibly, you can move from tag to tag (if you know the expected tag sequences) or from table row to table row (if your content is formatted consistently). Any way that you choose to move through the content is fraught with exceptions and traps. Even a novice can find the content that she wants in an XML file. Even an expert may not be able to do so in an HTML file.

So, again, I've made the point that XML is better for management than HTML. Fine. The real issue now becomes how to use XML for management and then turn it into HTML (or another format) for publication.

Management by Schema or DTD

XML is a wonderful way to express any sort of content structure you can imagine. But, if you can make up a tag for anything, what keeps XML from getting out of hand? How can you ensure that tags are spelled correctly and that they fall in the right place under only particular parent elements? How can you ensure that only certain attributes and attribute values are allowed? In short, how can you ensure that the wonderful structure that you create can ever be enforced?

This was a major issue for the creators of XML's parent, SGML. They ruled, so to speak, that all SGML documents would follow the structure defined in a *Document Type Definition* (*DTD*). DTDs list, in exacting detail, all the rules behind a particular set of tags. A DTD is metamarkup; it's not the markup itself, but rather markup about markup. In SGML, you couldn't create a document without first creating its underlying DTD.

When SGML became XML, schemas were introduced to give even more control to the people who wanted to use XML to exchange data. Stronger data-typing, for example, made it possible to communicate between databases using XML. Schemas now have more or less superseded DTD's for creating XML rules. Still, whether you use DTD's or schemas, the point is the same: to define the rules that guide what XML elements and attributes are allowed in your system.

Schemas and DTDs list rules such as the following:

✦ **Element names:** These are unique names of each element type. They're not the same as the Ids that I've discussed from time to time. Rather, they're the names of the tags that may be used. (In HTML, for example, some of the allowed names are `IMG`, `H1`, `P`, `BR`, `TABLE`, and so on.)

✦ **Allowed child elements:** Schemas specify the allowed child elements of each element, including the number of times that the child can occur (once, more than once, and so on), which are required, and the order in which the children are allowed to occur.

✦ **Attributes:** Schemas specify the allowed attributes (if any) for each element. In addition, they specify the type of attribute (a unique Id, a reference to a unique Id, a closed list, and so on). Finally, the schema can specify whether the attribute is required or optional.

As you may imagine, the schema for a nontrivial set of tags can be long and complex. Additionally, schemas use an abbreviated syntax that's tough to learn and read. On the other hand, a good schema assures you that WYWIWYG (What You Want Is What You Get). There's no room for misspelled or out-of-place tags.

XML *validators* are programs that go through XML code to ensure that it conforms to the schema. As the name implies, the validators assure that the XML tags you create are valid. They often complain mercilessly and may prohibit you from saving an XML document that doesn't conform to their schema. In markup, as in life, WYGIWYPF (What You Get Is What You Pay For!). It's costly to be organized; and the more organized you are, the more costly it is. But a time comes in every content system's life where the cost of being organized becomes cheaper than the cost of staying flexible and disorganized. Still, schemas and the trouble they cause for people who "just want to get something done," may be the biggest reason that SGML never caught on.

To combat this problem, most XML systems enable you to have an XML file without a schema. Of course, if you leave out a schema, you're back to the problem of verifying that you have good tagging. Still, by not making you create a schema right off the bat, XML leaves room for experimenting until you're ready to get serious. This approach eliminates the high barrier that SGML imposed at the start of a project with its required DTD.

An XML file without a schema isn't lacking in structure. To be XML, it still must be well formed, meaning that all the brackets and quote marks are in the right place. Interpreters ensure that your XML is well formed. After you load an XML file into an interpreter, it checks that all the syntax is correct. Then, if you have assigned a schema or DTD, additional validators check that XML is valid, meaning that the tags are the ones that you intended and are in the right relationship to each other. Obviously, to be valid, XML must first be well formed. Even if it is well-formed, however, XML may not necessarily be valid.

Note I always think of baby talk when teasing these two concepts apart. Babies babble but not randomly. Rather, they babble in a way that's just like the language that their parents speak. The most impressive thing about baby talk is that you're always just on the verge of making out words even though you know it's basically nonsense. Baby talk is well formed. It follows the verbal syntax of the ambient language. Its problem is that it's not valid. It doesn't follow the further semantic rules that give particular meaning to a string of sounds.

I leave the details of how to construct a schema to the standard sources (beginners might want to start at www.w3schools.com/. Advanced folks can start at www.w3.org/). What I hope I have conveyed here is that a schema is a tool for specifying and enforcing a certain structure on your XML.

Adding formatting

XML is a structural representation of content, which is a good thing for managing that content. You need to know the structure of content to track and manipulate it. Because XML isn't a presentation language, it must be translated into one when it comes time for you to view the XML.

Note This isn't strictly true. If you send an XML file to Microsoft Internet Explorer (5.0 or later), for example, you see something that looks like an outline. It's a formatted version of an XML file. The browser simply reproduces the hierarchy of the XML file on-screen as an expandable tree. Not particularly useful to end users, this nominal formatting is the best that you get from XML without effort.

Following are three basic nonexclusive approaches to adding formatting to XML:

✦ **You can cheat.** Put formatting tags into the XML file.

✦ **You can write a custom program.** It can read the XML file and transform it.

✦ **You can use Extensible Stylesheet Language Transformations (XSLTs).** These are add-ons to XML that transform it into whatever other markup that you want.

The first of these approaches works well (with a big caveat) if your target is HTML. Because HTML and XML share syntax, you can just include whatever HTML tags you want in your schema or DTD. Here's the caveat: HTML often doesn't follow its own rules. HTML tags are all supposed to be matched with an end tag (even <P> and <BR> tags), for example, but browsers let you get away with forgetting these. XML requires them and doesn't parse (another word for interpret) without them. So, if you try to pretend that HTML is XML, you often end up with perfectly fine HTML that crashes your XML interpreter. For this reason, many people now use what's called XHTML, which is simply HTML that follows all the rules of XML. In addition to the problem of syntax, HTML tags in your content are useful only if your only publication format is HTML (not print, for example).

The second of the approaches is the most general, flexible, and powerful. XML offers content the way that programmers like it — well organized, well named, and very accessible. If you're a programmer, you can always write a program that opens an XML file, runs through it branch by branch, and converts all the tags to the appropriate format markup. Along the way, it can do other interesting stuff such as rearrange the sections, leave some out, and mix in sections from other sources (databases and the like). The biggest problem with this approach is that it's labor intensive and requires a programmer to change code every time that you want to change formatting.

XSLT was invented as a general-purpose tool for transforming XML to other formats (primarily HTML). XSLT enables you to walk through the branches of an XML file and take actions based on the tags that you encounter. XSLT has been proposed as the way for content people, not programmers, to take control of the formatting of an XML file. It doesn't quite work out that way in practice, however.

XSLT files, called *templates*, are written by using the same syntax as are XML. XSLT templates contain commands that select and transform XML tags. These commands form a sort of lightweight programming language that you use to loop, select, and format. Unfortunately, the task of converting structure to formatting is often not all lightweight. In fact, it's sometimes exceedingly difficult and requires advanced programming techniques and a real eye for efficiencies and performance. Thus there's solid doubt in the XML community that XSLT is up to the task. And far from being a nonprogrammer's solution, XSLT actually requires a solid programmer to understand and use it. Moreover, the programmer must also be a formatter who can understand both computer programming and content design — not a usual combination of skills.

Finally, today's XSLT is very clumsy by programming standards and has few development tools to insulate you from its problems. The intent of XSLT is clear: Make it simple to add formatting to XML. Its goal is lofty: Make formatting a separate, nonprogrammer-driven process that can be quickly brought to bear to change the way XML is displayed. At present, it meets neither its goal nor its intent. Still, if you have the skills, XSLT is a valuable tool for adding formatting based on the structure of your XML.

Using XML in Content Management

XML can stand behind most electronic information initiatives, including content management. XML enables you to add the structure that you need to content to find it and deliver it. Suppose, for example, that you're a manufacturer and have a Web site that tells your distributors about all about the products that you provide. By using XML, you can create a system behind the site that matches what you know about a distributor to all the product information that the distributor may want.

In XML parlance, the product information is tagged so that it can be matched to a distributor's profile. If you create a strong XML framework, it not only serves this personalization feature, but it can also form the basis of knowing how to bring new content into the site, how and when to update information, and how to build a variety of outputs, not just a Web site, from your content. Obviously, as the size and complexity of your content increases, so does your need for the organization that XML gives you.

XML in collection

The collection system in a content management system handles gathering content and putting it in a form that's usable for management and publishing. Here are the ways that a CMS may use XML as a content format within the collection system:

✦ **XML authoring:** Almost any CMS can bring it into the system. A better CMS may have an interface with an XML authoring tool, which would enable authors to access the CMS directly from their authoring environments. (See Chapter 38, "Building Collection Systems," in the section "Web Forms," for more information on authoring environments.) An XML authoring environment that supports schemas and an interface to the repository might also be built directly into the CMS.

✦ **XML conversion:** The CMS may be capable of converting files to XML (from Microsoft Word or other formats) as they're entered into the repository. It may also have tools that enable you to bring some of the rigor of an XML schema into an author's home environment (for example, by checking for consistency of word processor content as it's being transformed into XML).

✦ **Rules enforcement:** Your CMS may be able to help enforce structure by managing and deploying schemas and other files, such as Cascading Style Sheets (CSS), to the authoring environment. Better, the CMS may validate contributed XML files against a master schema that enforces the content model across all types of input.

✦ **XML syndication:** The CMS may include tools that enable XML from external sources (syndications) to be automatically parsed and converted to components.

XML in management

The management system in a CMS is responsible for storing and administering content. CMS management systems may use XML as a repository structure. CMS repositories come in three basic types: object (or XML) repositories, relational database repositories, and file system repositories, as the following list describes:

✦ **Object repositories:** Most CMS products that employ an object repository store XML in the most accessible way. Any level of XML element can be found and used apart from its surrounding content. Object repositories also enable a natural, tight linkage between

XML elements, the versioning, and workflow systems. Any element can potentially be checked in or out and can participate independently in a workflow (such as revising or publishing). The standards for finding and manipulating XML in these systems generally follow W3C guidelines, such as XPath and XSL (although not all CMS products follow the most recent guidelines). At their best, object-based systems can treat the entire repository as XML that can be validated and fully parsed.

✦ **Relational database repositories:** Systems that employ a relational database typically store XML in one field of a record. The other fields of the same record store metadata such as author, create date, and the like. The XML itself usually isn't directly accessible through the CMS. Generally, you must retrieve the XML and then manipulate it yourself by using standard XML tools such as the Document Object Model (DOM), which I describe more fully later in this chapter. The CMS may come with some tools to help work with XML code that's stored in a database field. Thus, although these systems enable you to directly manage metadata, you must manage the XML code on your own.

✦ **File systems:** Systems that employ a file system repository generally store files in their native format — that is, XML files are stored as XML; Microsoft Word files are stored in Word format; and so on. At least one system that I know of converts files to XML and stores both the XML version and the original in the repository. File-based systems generally don't give you direct access to the contents of the files that they handle. Similar to the way you work with relational database systems, you must retrieve the XML from the file it's stored in and manipulate it yourself by using standard tools such as the DOM.

Although an object repository is the best of the three choices for complete integration and access to XML, the other two technologies generally perform better and are better accepted by IT departments. Some of the newer versions of CMS repositories employ hybrids of these three basic repository systems.

A CMS may use XML to find and represent metadata. A CMS may, for example, use XML to "wrap" metadata around a non-XML file such as a spreadsheet file or an HTML file. Thus, although the content itself isn't accessible by using XML tools, its metadata is. Even better, the system may use an XML schema to determine the structure of the metadata that's required for each type of content and to ensure that metadata standards are enforced.

Finally, a CMS may use its own proprietary format for representing workflows, or it may use an XML format. If it uses XML, integration with outside workflow players (e-mail servers, for example) becomes easier — as does integrating with or converting to other workflow systems.

XML in publishing

The publishing system of a CMS is responsible for bringing content out of the repository and formatting it into finished pages. A publishing system may use XML for templating. Templates are programs that select content, format it for presentation, and integrate the published page with other programs (such as e-commerce systems, for example). Some systems employ open programming languages such as ASP/COM (the Microsoft standard) or JSP/J2EE (the Java standard) as the programming platform for templates. These open systems are "XML-agnostic" in that you can choose to integrate with XML, but you aren't required to do so. To employ XML tools such as the DOM and XSL in the open systems, you must add code that may be outside the normal realm of the CMS or may be integrated into the CMS's publishing features.

Other systems employ a proprietary programming language to accomplish templating tasks. Within this proprietary realm, some systems use XML to represent their programming constructs. A bit of a particular system's template code, for example, may look as follows:

```
<FIND type="PressRelease">
  <WHERE>
    Author=Jon Doe
  </WHERE>
</FIND>
```

Systems that use this approach can rightly claim that their templating system uses the open standards of XML. They use these standards to create a proprietary programming language, however, that you still must learn to use. You may or may not be able to integrate XML tools, such as the DOM and XSLT, into this sort of system.

Finally, some CMS products simply use the XML template standard XSLT. Because XSLT assumes valid XML as a starting place, the systems that use XSLT must also store content only in XML.

In addition to using XML for templating, your system may be capable of publishing transformed XML. Any CMS that stores XML can output the same XML. Some CMS publishing systems, however, can transform the XML that they store under one schema into XML under a different schema for syndication — for example, Really Simple Syndication (RSS). They can also transform XML for publishing to devices that understand a particular schema — schemas for wireless application protocol (WAP) phones or e-books, for example.

XML in integration

A CMS can use XML as a data exchange format. Today, XML is most used both as a data interchange format and a command interchange format. XML is used to wrap data and commands in order to make them understandable to other applications. Many CMS products take advantage of this fact to connect to other systems.

On the data side, a CMS may, for example, have a tool that imports user data from a particular XML file.

The CMS may employ an XML structure for accepting commands from remote servers. In fact, the templating example in the previous section is just such a situation. The FIND command is represented as an XML element. The CMS accepts this element and carries out the command that it represents. In fact, this command structure is the only use that at least one commercial CMS product makes of XML. This product can rightly say that it uses XML as a core component of its system, even though the XML has nothing to do with the content itself!

Because XML is such an open and useful standard that can represent any structured information, you must look quite closely at the exact way that a CMS uses XML. You must understand how compatible that system is with your XML needs. Some products are based entirely on XML, whereas others use it in a very limited way. All products these days will claim to be XML-enabled. What that means exactly, may vary.

Help from the rest of the XML gang

XML has the buzz, but XML alone cannot a system make. I've already discussed XSLT, which fills the formatting vacuum left by XML. Here are a few other attendant abbreviations that might help XML become the clear choice for content management. They are all standards (that is written specifications) devised by the XML community and have a better or worse set of tools that more or less obey the standard:

✦ **CSS:** This stands for *Cascading Style Sheets*. These style sheets enable Web designers to do what print designers have done for a long time—create formatting definitions in one place and apply them easily to a number of files. With a CSS attached to a Web page, you can omit all the formatting from the page. Browsers that support CSS can use the attached style sheet to decide what formatting to apply to each type of HTML tag. CSS makes managing content for the Web much easier. It enables you to leave out the enormous amount of formatting code that you'd otherwise include in your publication templates to create fully formatted Web pages. In addition, CSS files aren't so programlike that designers can't read and change them. Designers can even work with full-featured CSS applications that put a slick graphical user interface around the CSS text files. Although XSLT claims to put formatting in the hands of nonprogrammers, CSS really does so (or at least comes closer).

✦ **XPath:** XPath (XML Path Language) is a language for finding parts of an XML document, designed to be used by both XSLT and XPointer. You use the XPath to specify which piece of an XML file you're seeking. The syntax of XPath loosely follows the sort of paths that you type for a URL. XPath, however, has significant additions for specifying search conditions and ordering results. XPath is used in XSLT, as well as more generally in XML programming (covered in the section "Programming in XML," later in this chapter). XPath is important to content management because it's the way that you find and select components and elements in an XML repository. There was a time when the term *XQL* (for e*X*tensible *Q*uery *L*anguage) was in vogue. XQL used XPath to retrieve information from an XML file. I liked the term XQL because it really expressed the function of XPath as a querying tool.

✦ **XPointer:** XPointer (XML Pointer Language) is an XML standard addressing system that enables you to pinpoint a location within an XML file that you want to link to using XPath. XPointer enables you to get to any point in the file even if it has no tag associated with it. XPointer is of interest to a CMS because it offers a precise way of saying where the referent of a cross-reference is. (See Chapter 30, "Designing Content Access Structures," in the section "What's a cross-reference?," for more information on the definition of a referent.)

✦ **Xlink:** XLink (XML Linking Language) is a way to define the kind and behavior of links and is used to create the sort of cross-references that you need to make good on the promise of hyperlinks. (See Chapter 30, "Designing Content Access Structures," in the section "Cross-references," for more information on the uses of hyperlinks.) Among other things, XLink gives you ways to make links go back and forth between the reference and referent (blurring the distinction between the two terms completely). XLink also enables you to go to multiple referents from the same reference and to expand the content of the referent within your current place—rather than having you jump to the referent when you click it. XLink also provides for link databases that enable you to organize and manage your linking strategy.

XML is young and still exploding. The few extensions that I've listed here are nothing, I'm sure, compared with what's still to come. What you can see already in the development of XML is that the problems that it's confronting are some of the same ones that are most important to content management. XML is already a good choice for an infrastructure behind content management. In the future, it will only get better.

XML and Content Management

I think XML is one of the best things to happen to content management. When organizations just managed documents, not individual objects of content, XML didn't have a lot of additional benefits. But XML is one of the best tools you can use to manage "chunked" object-oriented content, and it is very good at enabling you to effectively manage complex reuse (objects of content reused in many different types of information and media). XML lends itself to content management because it supports structured content, the separation of format from content, built-in metadata (semantic tags), and database structure of content.

Many of the organizations we work with have requirements like:

✦ Content is authored within many areas by many different types of authors.

✦ There are problems with the consistency of content.

✦ Content is reusable across types of documents and across media.

✦ The granularity of reuse (size of the object to be reused) is at the paragraph level and sometimes smaller.

✦ Content is translated into 2 to 20 languages.

For these types of projects, XML-based content management is one of the best ways to go for the following reasons:

✦ Structured content help authors to create consistent content regardless of the department they are in.

✦ XML-based content with a robust DTD/Schema (based on models designed to enable the creation of effective multiple media content) can be written once and automatically converted to print, Web, wireless, or any other format.

✦ XML-native content management systems (that is, CMSs that understand the structure of the XML and don't just treat the content as BLOBs) can recognize and manage very small chunks of content.

✦ XML-based content supports the translation of objects of content as the objects are approved so translation can be done as work is completed.

Look seriously at XML-based content management for your projects. You may find that it gives you much better handling of your content than traditional content management systems.

Ann Rockley, The Rockley Group Inc. (www.rockley.com)

Programming in XML

XML extracts a high cost for all the benefit that it offers. As opposed to HTML, which you can learn in a weekend, XML requires the experience of an intermediate to advanced programmer to be really useful. In addition, the programming paradigm of XML combines concepts from object-oriented programming with concepts of hierarchical storage and access. For programmers steeped in the older ways of linear programming and table-based access, XML can present a steep learning curve. On the bright side, the concepts of XML mesh so nicely with the concepts of content management that what you learn about XML pays off twice.

Who needs to know XML?

To give you a feeling for which people in your organization should be most focused on XML, here are the kinds of tasks that an XML system requires and some comments on the best sorts of people to do them. I've arranged the tasks from least to most technical, as follows:

✦ **Authoring:** You can take two approaches to authoring XML. You can convert the author's output to XML, or you can try to get your authors to create content inside an XML authoring environment. The first option is more common today. To do so, you try to get as much of the schema structure as you can into the author's native environment. You may use style sheets, templates, and macros in Microsoft Word, for example, to try to get authors to create Word files with as much of the rigor of XML as you can manage to simulate in that unstructured environment.

The second option, using an XML authoring tool, isn't as far out as you may think. Having created this book entirely in one such environment, I can say that, although it's not nearly as friendly as Word, it's getting there. With enough effort, you can make XML authoring workable for nontechnical end users who are willing to create structured content. In the future, I'm sure that XML authoring tools will get easier to use and users will be more willing to follow the tight rules that XML imposes. At some point the combination of the two advancements should enable you to consider XML authoring the standard for content creation.

✦ **Rule creation:** Someone must create the logic and structure that your XML files implement. This structure is what I've called the *content model*. It includes all the content types, their elements, and the access structures that they participate in. In my scheme of CMS jobs, the Content Analyst is clearly the person to do this work. (See Chapter 13, "Staffing a CMS," in the section "Information Architects," for more information on this job description.)

✦ **Schema creation:** Someone must design and code the schemas that you use. Although this task often falls to programmers, I believe that it's better left to the Content Analyst. If this person isn't up to the challenge of mastering the tools and syntax of schemas, you have the wrong person in the position — or your analyst hasn't yet realized that these technologies are simply a very formal way of writing down the sort of rules that she's been defining all along.

✦ **XSLT:** XSLT files are programs. Contrary to some of the claims that I've heard made about XSLT, it's hard for me to imagine anyone but a trained programmer (or someone who wants to become the equivalent of one) who is able to create more than simple XSLT templates. In my job scheme, it's the template programmer who's best targeted to XSLT. XSLT is a bit behind many of the more graphical and ease-oriented languages in use today; if you can't find someone with experience in XSLT, look for someone who has a lot of patience and doesn't mind the lack of an integrated development environment. Also, as with all template programmers, an XSLT programmer needs to be conscious of and interact well with the needs of the designers with whom she shares her template files. (See Chapter 13, "Staffing a CMS," in the section "Template and CMS developer," for more information on this job description.)

✦ **Tool automation:** If you release an XML-authoring environment to your nontechnical contributors, you need someone to program it so that it implements your schemas and has the kind of user interface that the contributors expect and understand. This programming likely includes CSS, XSLT, some sort of scripting, DOM programming, and distribution programs (setup programs and the like). It may also include integration programming with the author's other tools. The custom application developer in my framework ought to do well in this position as long as she's comfortable with the XML programming tasks. (See Chapter 13, "Staffing a CMS," in the section "Custom application developer," for more information on this job description.)

✦ **Conversion programming:** If you intend to convert the output of authoring tools to XML or convert acquired content to XML, you need to do conversion programming. In my scheme, it's the conversion analyst and the tool creator who would qualify best for this sort of task. (See Chapter 13, "Staffing a CMS," in the section "Content Processing Staff," for more information on this job description.)

✦ **Custom template programming:** If XSLT isn't suited to the needs of your CMS, you need to develop other programs to produce your publications. XSLT, for example, may not help you much on any non-HTML publications. In addition, if your template programmers revolt against XSLT, you may need to forgo it for more standard techniques. By using the XML DOM, programmers can do most of or all the operations of XSLT in any standard programming environment. In any case, you want to use the equivalent of an advanced template programmer or custom application developer for the task of going beyond XSLT.

✦ **Management programming:** If you store your content in an XML repository, you need programming to ensure that the content there can be managed correctly. You may need a program written that goes through the repository periodically, for example, and archives any components whose expiration date has been reached. In addition, you may need any number of programs written that connect to the repository, convert data to XML, and import the data per the schema into your repository. These activities may require your most advanced programmers, who not only have a mastery of external systems, but also of XML programming using the DOM (covered in the following section "Introducing DOM XML programming").

If your CMS uses XML extensively, XML skills may be distributed throughout your staff. Even staff who aren't called on directly to create XML can benefit from learning its major concepts. A metator, for example, may never directly create XML but could still really benefit from the ability to read and understand an XML file where the metadata that she creates in Web forms is stored.

Introducing DOM XML programming

The *Document Object Model* (the *DOM*) is a way of giving programs complete and comprehensive access to XML structures. The DOM consists of a set of programming objects with properties and methods for getting to and manipulating XML.

For the purpose of this discussion, you can think of the DOM objects as prepackaged code that delivers significant capabilities with little extra work. In the case of the DOM, the objects deliver the capability to manipulate XML fully. The most significant of the objects the DOM provides are as follows:

✦ **The Document object:** This object enables you to load XML from files and text strings, search through XML structures, and transform them by using XSLT templates.

✦ **The Node object:** This object holds a single branch of an XML hierarchy and enables you to operate on it (that is, find, add, update, and delete child elements and content).

✦ **The Node List object:** This object holds sets of nodes (or more precisely a collection of Node objects).

✦ **The Node Map object:** This object holds sets of attributes (see Figure 36-1).

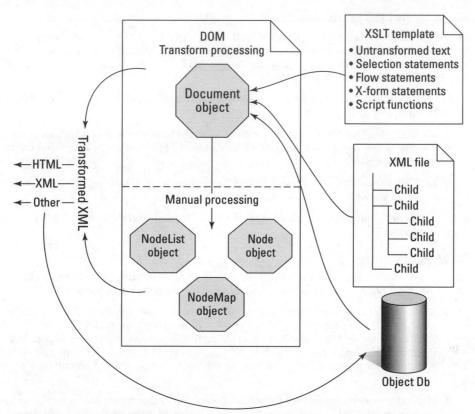

Figure 36-1: The DOM objects and how they fit with both an XSLT transformation and a program that does a transformation in code

To simplify earlier discussions, I contrast DOM programming with XSLT. I said that you can either use XSLT or DOM programming to transform XML into some final output. In reality, there's only DOM programming. If you use XSLT to transform your XML, what you're really doing is using the XSLT transform methods of the DOM objects. Quite often, you can ignore this fact because the DOM is hidden by some other program that you use. Many XML tools, for example, enable you to choose an XSLT file and "apply" it to an XML file to see how the results look. The tool is simply creating the appropriate DOM objects behind the scenes and invoking the appropriate methods. So whatever method you use to manipulate your XML boils down to DOM programming at some point. Still, it's worthwhile to distinguish between XSLT and DOM programming, because the commands that you can use in an XSLT template are matched (and exceeded) by the commands that you can use within a standard programming environment to directly work with XML through the DOM.

In the sections that follow, I overview the concepts that I just introduced and give you a feel for how they all fit together to enable you to use the DOM to program with XML. I break the discussion into the three standard headings of all programming: input, processing, and output.

Input to the DOM objects

Before you can work with XML, you must load it into a DOM object from some storage area (such as a file or database record where it has been stored). After it's loaded, you can begin to manipulate the XML directly, or you can load an XSLT file into a DOM object as well and then use the XSLT to transform the XML.

All DOM operations start from the Document object. You load XML into the Document object from the following:

✦ **An XML file:** This file is located somewhere on the hard drive or at a Web location (that is, accessible from a URL). You can also load XML from a text string that contains well-formed XML.

✦ **An XML repository or database:** In this case, some form of query (SQL for example) retrieves the XML that you want to load.

XSLT files use the same syntax as XML files. In addition, you use the same methods to load the files into the DOM.

DOM processing

After you've loaded an XML structure (and possibly XSLT structure) into a DOM Document object, you can begin to process the XML. You have two basic ways to process XML:

✦ **XSL Transform processing:** You create a Document object for the XML and another for the XSLT. You then tell the first Document object to transform its XML by using the XSLT in the second. The result is a text string that holds the transformed XML. You can then save that text string as a publication page (an HTML file, for example) or send it on to another program (a Web server, for example) that sends it to an end user's browser.

✦ **Manual processing:** You load an XML structure into a Document object and then use the variety of DOM objects and your own code to walk through the XML and do what you need to do. What you need to do may include converting it to HTML, adding or modifying nodes, or anything else that you can conceive of doing with structured content.

Regardless whether you use an XSL Transform or your own custom manual processing, the point of the processing is the same—you apply a set of manipulations on an input XML structure to select the appropriate elements, structure them per the requirements of the publication that you're producing, and add the formatting and layout that the target publication requires.

DOM output

First you load XML and then you transform it into a publication page or section by using XSLT or your own code. Finally, you output it to the appropriate file type. Here are the most common of the many outputs that you may be interested in obtaining from an XML process:

✦ **HTML:** Obviously, HTML is a big output. As in my cars example, HTML is a preferred display format. In this case, the output is destined for the Web and, as often as not, the entire XML process is triggered from some Web link or Web form.

✦ **XML:** XML, too, is a usual output from an XML process. In fact, it's common to convert from one XML schema to another. As more of your partner organizations bring XML online, for example, you will be required to take your XML content and deliver it to them with their XML tag names and structures. The XML output that you create may be destined for some distant server, for a local hard drive as an XML file, or for some outside repository or XML database.

✦ **Any manner of other output:** If your XML is structured well enough, you can probably transform it into just about any other structured form. Of course, a fully automatic process can go only so far. It can't, for example, create an author tag in the output if there's no mention of an author in the input XML. Still, within the constraints of what's possible, you can create just about any type of output that you want. A common output is to a relational database. In this case, the XML is mapped to a set of database rows and columns. The same code that does the mapping to these rows and columns then connects to the target database and stores the content there.

XML programming is just like any other kind of programming. You start from an input, you perform some sort of processing, and the result is a kind of output that's useful to you. XML differs from other types of programming in that it revolves completely around the objects and methods of the DOM, is concerned only with transforming XML, and can use either the language of XSLT or of custom DOM programming to accomplish the transformation.

Server-side XML

So far, I've described, in general, *how* XML is manipulated. Now I describe *where* it's manipulated. If you're familiar with Web programming, you know that programming code can run either on the Web server or in the Web client. (The Web client is also called the *browser*.) In this section and the next, respectively, I look at how the DOM is integrated into a Web server and a Web client.

You can apply anything that you already know about client and server programming to XML. You'd choose server programming over client programming in XML, for example, for the same reasons that you choose CGI over client scripting—namely, that you're better off on the server side. You are safer on the server side because you don't need to worry about what type of browser a user has and because, in the often flaky world of Internet programming, you're better off having software run on the one computer that you know rather than the millions that you don't know. On the other hand, if you distribute and run your code on the client, you reduce the number of transactions with the server that you must support and can increase the performance of your code significantly.

In either the server or client scenario, you can assume that you have a Web server, a browser, and whatever HTML pages you need to get your task accomplished. Figure 36-2 illustrates how XML processing proceeds.

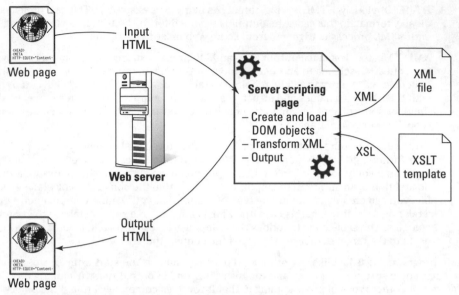

Figure 36-2: XML processing on the server

To run your XML code on a server, you need the following pieces:

✦ **Server input:** The XML process is started and supplied with whatever parameters and data it needs by an HTML page of some sort. Suppose, for example, that you want to use the car XML that I introduced earlier in this chapter to create an automobile search function. You may create an HTML page that's a car search form where the user can choose a car style (Sport Utility, for example) and click a Submit button.

✦ **Server processing:** The parameters and data are submitted through a Web server to the program that performs the XML processing. For example, an Apache server might pass the parameters on to a JavaServer Page (JSP) page that does the work. The JSP page retrieves the parameters sent by the search page, creates DOM objects, does some processing, and passes a result back to the Web server. In the car example, the JSP page would do the following:

  • Retrieve the Car style attribute that the user selected in the form.

  • Load the XML content file into a Document object.

  • Select the appropriate set of XML elements (the ones where the <STYLE> element matches the user's choice).

  • Load an XSLT template for the search results page.

  • Transform the returned nodes by using the loaded XSLT template.

  • Send the result through the server to the user's browser.

✦ **Server output:** The output of the XML process is a Web page, usually with XML content transformed into HTML. In my current example, the output is the search-results page with standard surrounding material (logos, banners, navigation buttons, and so on) and the list of links to car pages for each car that matches the style that the user has chosen. After the user clicks a link for a car page, you can expect the whole process to run again. The link triggers an XML transformation on the Web server, which selects the XML for the right car and transforms it into a well-formatted page.

Your CMS may use server-side XML programming to access content components in a central XML repository and transform them into publication pages. The transformation may be in real time as users click links on a live site. Conversely, you may choose to do the transformation all at once to produce a flat HTML site from the XML that's stored in the repository.

Client-side XML

XML on the client side follows the same basic pattern as does its use on the server side. The biggest difference is that your XML programming code is client-side script. Microsoft Internet Explorer (IE) 5.0 and later supports XML, as shown in Figure 36-3.

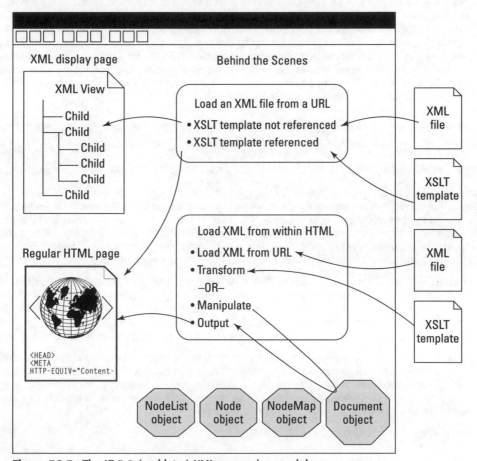

Figure 36-3: The IE 5.0 (and later) XML processing model

Again, the input to the process is an XML file and possibly an XSLT file. IE can load the XML file directly from a URL. The loaded XML file can reference an XSLT file, also by URL, that IE automatically loads and uses to transform the XML file. The result in this case is an HTML page. IE creates the page automatically from the XML and XSLT files that you specify. If you load an XML file into a version of IE that doesn't reference an XSLT template, the browser displays it as a tree. This generally isn't what end users should see, but it is quite convenient for developers to browse or debug XML.

If you don't want to use this automatic XML loading and XSLT transformation, you can also write some client (Java or Visual Basic) script to do the following:

✦ Load an XML file and XSLT file and then perform a transformation.

✦ Load an XML file and then use DOM objects to manipulate it manually and produce an HTML result that's displayed in the browser.

I'm always a bit leery of running code within a Web browser. The code often fails and leaves the end user in complete confusion. Still, at certain times, client code is the only way to provide adequate functionality. If you expect that users may not have a connection to your Web server, for example, you can't expect them to execute code there. Client-side XML plays a fairly small role in commercial content management products. It may be a valuable technique for custom systems, however, but only if you are in an environment (such as within an organization that has standardized on a browser) where you can specify that all users must have a browser that can run XML programming script.

XML Serialization and Object-Oriented XML Programming Design

Programming objects are the foundation of modern object-oriented programming languages such as Java and C#. A programming class defines a programming object in much the same way that an XML schema defines how a single XML element or node must be structured. In this sense, an instance of a programming object is analogous to a single node of an XML document. An XML schema determines what kind of data can be held in a particular node within a given document, but it is the actual document that holds the specific data and not the schema.

One extremely useful tool for managing XML data on the server is called XML serialization. In XML serialization, XML documents are created (serialization) from programming classes, and object instances are created from XML documents (deserialization). XML DOM programming on the server does not require the use of serialization but, with the recent popularity of Web Services, increasingly complex server-side programming benefits greatly from XML serialization.

The programming logic on the server is almost identical to the logic dictated by schemas, except that object instances defined by classes hold specific data in memory rather than in XML files. The role of XML serialization is to translate how data is described by both programming classes and XML. For this reason, this tool is becoming an important facilitator for data interchange and is part of common practice for object-oriented XML programming.

Peter Emonds-Banfield, University of Washington

Summary

XML is the first markup language I've seen that has both the power and acceptance to play a central role in content management. XML is all of the following:

✦ A markup language with enough flexibility to represent whatever kind of content structure that you may want to throw at it.

✦ A potential key player in every part of a CMS.

✦ A skill that a wide range of your staff may need to possess.

✦ A programming model that's well suited to dealing with the complexities of content storage, access, and publication.

In the next chapter, I move from a general discussion of markup to the details of processing content for a CMS.

✦　　✦　　✦

Processing Content

With a good grasp of markup languages, and especially XML, you can begin to dive into the mechanics of content processing. Loosely speaking, content processing is conversion. To do conversion you need to be able to fully parse (that is, get at) each markup tag of the source files. You must know exactly what markup you want in the target files or database, and you must devise a feasible plan for the transformation.

In this chapter, I work through many of the issues that you may need to confront as you plan and implement a content processing project. I try to stay as nontechnical as possible for the benefit of those who may need to design but not implement content processing systems.

What Is Content Processing?

The vast majority of content that exists today in HTML was once in some other form. My various companies alone have been responsible for converting hundreds of thousands of pages of word processing, desktop publishing, spreadsheet, database, print, and other forms of information into HTML. The vast majority of HTML is converted into XML. XML, believe it or not, will some day be overtaken by the next *best* format (whatever that might be). Of course, there's still a lot of hard-copy information in the world that someone someday will get around to digitizing. The sad fact that the format you have isn't the format that you need is in no danger of changing any time soon. Add the even sadder fact that the structure that you want isn't the one that you're usually given, and you have every reason to learn about and then master content processing.

Content processing focuses on the content conversion process, but it overlaps with authoring, acquiring, and aggregating. The point of content processing is to create low-cost and effective systems to do the following:

✦ Convert the format and structure of authored or acquired content into the format and structure that you can use inside your CMS.

✦ Aggregate as much of the content as possible without the use of a metator.

If you can get a computer to do conversion and aggregation auto-matically, more power to you. If you find that you need people and processes in addition to programs to get the job done, you ought to create a content-processing project that ensures you get the most and best components for the least effort.

Because conversion is at the center of the content-processing world, I begin by detailing the conversion process (see Figure 37-1), starting with the processes of stripping (removing unneeded content) and mapping (figuring out the correspondence between the formatting of the source content with the target tagging your system uses).

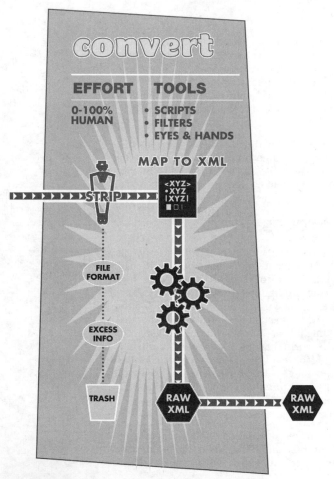

Figure 37-1: The conversion process, showing the stripping and mapping that's involved

Stripping

If you strip content, you remove (and throw away) extraneous information. What exactly is extraneous depends on your particular needs. Here, however, are the sorts of information that are most commonly stripped:

✦ **From print files:** Strip front and back matter including titles, publishing information, indexes, end notes, and the like. In addition, headers and footers, including all the numbering and sectioning information that print files include, are generally stripped.

✦ **From Web files:** Surrounding banners, branding, and navigation, and advertisement are generally eliminated.

✦ **Transitions, introductions, and other print devices:** Strip anything used to move the reader from one subject to the next. Because the online reader may jump directly into the middle of a discussion, these devices can end up confusing the reader more than they help. If the material might end up once again in print, these devices might be tagged as separate elements rather than stripped. (See Chapter 40, "Building Publishing Systems," in the section "Print System" for more information on printing output.)

✦ **The storage file format:** Strip this if the destination file format is different from the original. In converting from Word RTF to HTML, for example, the Font and Color tables at the beginning of the Word file are generally discarded. (See Chapter 2, "Content Has Format," in the section "Storage Formats: Storing Information," for more information on storage formats.)

✦ **Rendering formatting:** Strip formatting that isn't universally supported. The formatting codes that make columns of text in a desktop publishing program, for example, are often discarded because they're not easy to produce in HTML, and columns do not work well on the computer screen. (See Chapter 2, "Content Has Format," the section "Rendering Format: Presenting Information," for more on rendering format.)

✦ **Structural elements:** Strip elements that aren't used in the target publications. If the contents of an annual report, for example, are broken into separate chunks and distributed in various configurations, you have little need to keep the report's table of contents. Similarly, cross-references to parts of the work that aren't used or to sites that no longer exist can be discarded. (See Chapter 3, "Content Has Structure," for more information on structure.)

What's left after all the extraneous information is removed is the content to be included in the CMS. The structure and format of the remaining content, however, probably still need to be mapped to the target format and structure.

Mapping

Mapping is a process of using target markup to represent the formatting and structure of the source. If you're lucky, there's a good correspondence between the source and target markup. If you're unlucky, inherent ambiguities or discontinuities remain that can be resolved only by human judgment. In the section "Understanding the Principles of Mapping Content," later in this chapter, I go into detail about the process of mapping source to target structure.

The conversion process could be anywhere from completely automated to completely manual. I've seen large teams of people do nothing all day but cutting and pasting text from one format and structure into another manually. On the other hand, I've seen (and written) programs that plow through megabytes of content in a few seconds, fully parsing and converting it. Most likely, you can automate a lot of your conversion processes, but not all. At the very least, you need people to check the work of the computer to ensure that it's at the quality level you expect and that exceptions are handled correctly.

Content processing projects define and implement processes for transforming content from a set of source formats to target formats that you need for a CMS. In pursuit of this goal you may do the following:

✦ Simply convert file formats.

✦ Strip and select content chunks and turn them into content components in a database or other storage medium.

✦ Conform source content to a particular schema or DTD.

✦ Add missing metadata to content.

✦ Author missing parts of the content.

✦ Combine or split content sources.

✦ Develop a combination of automated and manual processes.

✦ Hire and train small or large teams to perform the process.

✦ Do the process yourself indefinitely or outsource it to an outside organization.

If you're lucky, you have only a few of these tasks to accomplish and they can be easily automated. In all likelihood, over time you will do all these tasks for some of the content that you acquire. In addition, you always end up involving people in at least some of the tasks some of the time.

Content Processing and the CMS

I haven't seen many commercial CMS products that address the core issues of content processing directly. To be sure, you can use the CMS workflow system, in part, to structure your conversion processes, and you may even get some conversion programs along with the product. By and large, however, CMS products expect that you do your own processing outside of their software and bring content in after it has the format and structure that you want it to finally have.

This isn't to say that content processing is outside the bounds of a CMS. Quite the contrary. In your planning and implementation of a CMS, you must take content processing into account. If you don't account for processing, you're faced with large costs that seem to come out of nowhere and large bottlenecks in content collection if you try to deal with this potentially large issue casually. Given the importance of content processing to CM, you may rightly wonder (as I do) why it has been so neglected by the CM product companies.

 Cross-Reference   See Chapter 38, "Building Collection Systems," in the section "Conversion System" for more specifics on conversion as part of the collection system.

Focusing on the long-term benefits

The basic idea behind content processing (and generally behind any automation) is to spend some effort up front to develop tools and processes so that you can reap more benefit over the lifetime of the system. In other words, you're looking for a good Return on Investment (ROI) from the tools and processes that you create.

As simple as this idea is to understand, it's amazing how often it doesn't work. I've seen many examples of projects in which too much time and money were spent for the amount of savings that were accrued. From what I've seen, the main reasons for poor returns are because organizations do some the following:

✦ **Rush to automate.** For some strange reason, automation projects are often driven by what can be done, not by what ought to be done. A programmer looking at a sample of the source content begins the conversation by saying what "can" be done. The conversation moves then to how to do it. The crucial, unanswered question here, of course, is what *should* be done. In the rush to begin automating, many people forget to ask, "Is this program necessary?"

✦ **Underestimate the complexity of the task at hand.** It's easy to underestimate the complexity of a conversion process. Especially if you're going from unstructured to structured content, it's hard to overestimate the complexity of the task. *Unstructured* means without structure, variable, inconsistent, unpredictable, and generally hard to parse. Unstructured content lacks all the qualities that programs depend on to do their tasks in an automatic way. Novice programmers may think that they can make gold from content lead. The more times that they fail, the better they become at differentiating between the silk-purse content that's worth automating and the sow's-ear content that doesn't yield to any algorithm.

✦ **Underestimate the necessary amount of human effort.** A good processing tool does the tasks that require no human intervention and facilitates people doing the tasks that require human effort. A bad (and costly) processing tool tries to do too much of the human work and ends up costing more human work later. Suppose, for example, that the files in a directory are of two types that need two different sets of programs applied to them. If the processing tool guesses incorrectly 20 percent of the time, a person must go through the files to find all the mistakes. If this is the case, the programmer may produce a better ROI by creating a tool that helps a person categorize the files quickly rather than by trying (and failing 20 percent of the time) to categorize them automatically.

✦ **Provide poor sampling.** I've seen many processing systems fail because the designers failed to look at a truly representative sample of the content to be processed. A typical scenario is that the processing team gets a sample chosen by the contributor because it was convenient to find or is a "best case" example. The sample may or may not be representative of the full load. By the time that the full load is available, it's too late. The tools are already designed to the wrong specification.

✦ **Fail to balance the cost versus the benefits of a user interface.** The core code that actually does the processing can get dwarfed easily by the code needed to produce a full user interface. That's why so many CMS products require you to type parameters into configuration files and other unfriendly places. Programmers can easily get carried away making everything easy to do and ultimately configurable. Although it's always a good idea to provide a usable interface, usability must be balanced against cost effectiveness. Suppose, for example, that it takes a programmer an extra week of development to provide a graphical user interface to a processing tool. Only five people use the tool, however, and you can train them in a few hours to run the tool without an interface.

✦ **Handle all exceptions programmatically.** The way that many programmers work is as follows: Write a conversion script or program and then try running it. As unanticipated situations arise, they write more code to handle the exceptions. In this way, the program can handle more and more of the exceptional conditions that arise in the source content. There's a point of diminishing returns in this process. Not all exceptional situations are worth handling programmatically. Suppose, for example, that a certain situation comes up only once a week and would take a day of programming to handle. To fix the problem may add only 10 minutes per component to the work of a staff member. It would take more than a year for the programmer's time to be recovered (and that's assuming that the programmer is paid the same amount as the processor).

✦ **Change process in midstream.** If tool and process creation overlap with tool and process use, expect an expensive process. The same content may need to be processed multiple times; schedules fall by the wayside; special tools must be created to fix problems caused by the unfinished tools; and frustration rises sometimes to dramatic levels. In my experience, it's only rarely worth the extra effort to begin a content processing task before the process is completed and tested.

My intention isn't to scare you away from process automation but rather to provide you with some tools to make sure that it saves you more than it costs you. If the quantities to be processed are large, you can almost always structure your process so that it rewards your investment handsomely.

Suppose, for example, that you have 1,000 items to process. Without automation, say that they require half an hour each to process. That's 500 hours of processing time. Suppose that, with 40 hours of design and programming effort, you can cut the time down to 15 minutes per item (only a modest gain). Even if an hour of technical time costs twice that of a processing hour, you still save the equivalent of 170 processing hours, as the following formula shows:

(1000 items) × (.25 hours/item) + 2 × (40 hours of dev) = 330 hours

If 80 hours of development time can cut the processing time down to 5 minutes, you save the equivalent of 256 processor hours.

(1000 items) × (.083 hours/item) + 2 × (80 hours of dev) = 243 hours

However, suppose that for 40 more hours of development time (a total of 120) you can cut the processing time down to 3 minutes. Your return will be as follows:

(1000 items) × (.05 hours/item) + 2 × (120 hours of dev) = 290 hours

It costs you the equivalent of 47 extra processing hours to cut the time further! I leave it as an exercise for you to figure out where the point of diminishing returns is for your project. If you do much content process design, you become close friends with calculations like the ones that I illustrate here. As usual, of course, these calculations are only as good as the assumptions that they're based on, so you're well served by not taking them past their useful precision. There's no use calculating the savings to the nearest hour if your time estimates are good only to within 20 percent.

Here are some general guidelines to follow to ensure that your content processing projects stay on the right side of the cost/justification calculation:

✦ **Don't automate until you have a reason to do so.** Create a compelling case like the one that I illustrate in the preceding example before launching into any sort of development cycle. Make sure that you can establish manual processing benchmarks (like the figure of a half hour per item that I cite in the preceding example) that you trust. Then make sure that you clearly communicate how much development time you can spare given a particular gain in processing time. You may even turn the dry calculation into a sort of game, in which the process development team itself tries to optimize the development time and processing savings equation. As you calculate development time, don't forget to include the time that it takes to debug, test, and train staff on how to use the automation tools.

✦ **Start with the core algorithms.** Don't spend any time on user interface or exception handling until you're sure that the core processing code that you have in mind can do the job that you expect of it. Get a bare-bones tool together that only a programmer can run. Prove that it can meet the basic requirements of processing time gains before adding the nice-to-have features. Then, if you run out of budget for development, it affects the least essential parts of the tool first.

✦ **Run complete samples soon.** As soon as is possible, run the complete set of content through the automated processes that you've designed. Until you've run a sample 100 percent through the system, you can never be sure of the true gains that the tool may yield.

✦ **Test with real people.** Include the people who will actually operate the tool as soon as possible. In the likely situation that you're building tools and process for a small number of people, it behooves you to tailor your product directly to their needs and abilities.

✦ **Create and review exception logs.** Rather than writing code for processing exceptions as they arise, track them for a while first. Tracking them tells you how frequent they are and how much time you can justify spending on handling them. It also forces you to think about the exception for a while before rushing to automate its handling.

✦ **Go for percentages.** Prioritize your process and tool development by expected gain. Always do the big gains first and the smaller gains only as time allows.

Focusing on the short-term benefits

Some of the most personally rewarding, well-recognized, and successful programming that I've ever done has been in what I'd call *kamikaze* mode. In kamikaze mode, you swoop in from outside the process, zero in on the center of the problem, and create just enough of a tool to relieve a big pressure point. Then you stop. Kamikaze automation provides pinpoint solutions to immediate and large problems.

Suppose, for example, that it's taking 20 minutes per item for the processing staff to find the right part of a set of HTML files to cut and paste into CMS components. You may begin a three-week project to study the source and develop an automated conversion system, or you may simply notice that it takes 10 of the 20 minutes just to open each HTML file and find the content within all the JavaScript code. So, in a few hours (or less), you create a simple program that strips out all the JavaScript code from the source files. In three weeks, you may get the processing time down by 75 percent, but in three hours, you can reduce it by 50 percent! In another three hours, you can, perhaps, cut the task time in half again and reach the same goal (75 percent reduction) in six hours rather than three weeks.

Note Kamikaze automation isn't appropriate for all situations. Look at each situation and see the quick fixes that are possible. In my experience, you always can find lots of small ways to increase efficiency if you really look. If you watch a group of people work, you notice where they spend their time and what small repetitive or mechanical processes they do (and may not even notice).

Here are some principles that you can try to facilitate the kamikaze automations in your group:

✦ **Stay close:** My best results at automation have been when I was right there in the same room as the people doing processing. There's no better way to learn about what tools are really needed than to listen to the constant complaints of the people on the front lines. There's no better motivator to create relevant tools than to have lunch each day with the people who must use the tools that you create. If the kamikaze automator is a protector and servant of the little guy, she ought to get to know him.

✦ **Make quick turnarounds:** The tool or process that you create ought to respond immediately to an immediate need. If a problem arises at 10 a.m. and you deliver a fix by 2 p.m., you lose minimum processing efficiency and gain a lot of respect and credibility.

✦ **Set aggressive incremental deadlines:** Focus on one-day or shorter tasks that can yield measurable gains. If a tool doesn't work out, you've wasted only one day. If it does work, it doesn't need to recoup much to justify a single day. The Kamikaze projects may be coalesced later into a control panel for processors or some other wider tool, but each should stand alone and provide quick, clear value.

Kamikazes are heroes. They address immediate needs, cut through bureaucracy, and work fast. It's fun for the automator, gratifying for the processing team to have someone pay that much attention to them, and it can be quite rewarding for the processing bottom line.

Distilling the essence of a process

Whether you use kamikazes or teams of long-term backroom automation programmers and analysts, the essence of a content process is the same. A good content process is as follows:

✦ **Comprehensive:** It includes tools (custom or commercial software), methods for using the tools, staff jobs, tasks, and workflows. Too often, a team designs a tool and forgets to figure out how it fits into the team or into the wider processes of which it's a part.

✦ **Efficient:** The time to process one unit of content (generally, one component) is the least that it can realistically be.

✦ **Effective:** The quality of the content that comes out of the process is as good as it can realistically be.

✦ **Complete:** Whether all exceptions are handled automatically or manually, all exceptions should be handled. No (or at least a minimum of) content should be allowed to slip through the process without being adequately processed.

Your processes as a whole ought to work together well. There should be a minimum of conflicts in the staffing or workflow of all processes together. No content eddy currents, where some content flows in a different direction or gets substantially different treatment from the rest, should exist.

Finally, the process should have an overall organization guaranteeing that software and methods are released to everyone at once and are always current. There ought to be no tweaks needed for a particular machine and only one current version of all significant lists and control files.

Bringing people into processing

If you have any significant amount of content processing to do, you'd better get used to including people in your considerations of how it can be successfully accomplished.

Cross-Reference   The staff positions associated with content processing are covered in Chapter 13, "Staffing a CMS," in the section "Content Processing Staff."

Here are some considerations to help you keep humans and humanity in your automated processes:

✦ **Intelligence versus instruction:** The better the instruction that you supply, the less independent intelligence is required of the people whom you hire to do the manual parts of the process. Good documentation and instruction more than pay for themselves in increased accuracy and a decreased requirement for a level of experience or expertise among the processing staffers.

✦ **Meticulousness:** Look for, expect, and reward a meticulous attitude in your processing staff.

✦ **Creativity:** Expect and reward a form of creativity that's found most among the meticulous — the ability to see how to become more organized or more efficient. Don't expect that, just because your processing staff may be inexperienced and not very technical, they can't recognize a bad process or can't articulate a good solution. In my experience, the best improvement suggestions often come directly from the processing staff.

✦ **Clarity and consistency:** It's much better for morale and the quality of the output if you stress consistency over exactness. It's much better for your team to make a mistake in processing in a consistent way than to change what they're doing part way through the process. If the mistake is indeed consistent, you can likely fix it with a quick script. Your staff requires readjustment time and increased quality control after every process change, so it's best to keep these changes to a minimum.

✦ **Appropriate tools:** Provide your staff with tools that are at — not above and not below — their skill level. A search-and-replace program, for example, is a powerful tool. Incorrectly used, it can wreak havoc. It's likely that some members of your processing staff are ready for such power, and some aren't. If you're smart, you can distinguish one sort of staffer from the other and provide each with the most powerful tools that she can be counted on to use correctly. I've seen unskilled processors rise quickly from being computer phobics to nascent programmers because someone trusted them enough to let them write and use Microsoft Word macros.

It's important to understand that the people in your content processes aren't just parts of the machine. In fact, I think another metaphor works better for both them and for the effectiveness of the process. Content processing staff members are like airplane pilots. They ought to have a sophisticated and powerful control panel in front of them to move the content payload from its source to its destination. They're the navigators and pilots who, rigorously but creatively, use the tools and methods that you provide to obtain the best result.

Tracking the master copy

It's exceedingly important in any content process to keep your eye on the master copy of content. The master is the one from which all others derive. For many types of content, the master copy changes over time, as follows:

✦ Before you receive the content, the master belongs to someone else and isn't your problem.

✦ As soon as you receive it, you must establish a master copy of each piece of content as the one that you work on.

✦ As you process content, the master is the one that you've made changes to. At each stage of processing, the master may change to a new file or database record. Previous versions must lose their master status.

✦ As you create content components from the source, these components become the master copies, and the CMS handles their management.

The counterpoints to the master copy are the backup copies. Backups are old masters that you may need to return to. On the one hand, if you delete all backups, you run no chance of mistaking them for the master copies. On the other hand, the more backups that you keep, the easier it is to recover if you find that you've made a processing mistake and ruined the master. All processes must balance these two factors against each other and you should have neither too few backups for safety nor too many to interfere with a clear flow of control from master to master.

Here are some tips to keep your master files clear:

✦ **Tokens:** The clearest way to ensure that the file that you're working on is the master is to name it that way. If the root file name is 123.HTM, for example, you can name the master file MASTER_123.htm. This has the distinct advantage of being unambiguous. It has the disadvantage of making you name and rename files throughout your process. If you're using programs to access and move files anyway, this method may not be a lot of extra effort. At the very least, you can establish a regime for directory naming that clearly marks the directory where the master files reside.

✦ **Permissions:** If you're diligent, you can use the file attributes or directory permissions available in your operating system to manage master files. You can set the properties of backup files to read-only, or even inaccessible, so that they can't be mistaken for the master.

✦ **Directories:** You can do a lot to preserve master awareness by putting together a clear directory-naming policy. If your process has three main steps, for example, you can create directories called Preprocess, Step1, Step2, Step3, and Done. Content that's ready to be processed goes in the first directory. As each file completes a step, it's put in the directory for the next step. Thus any files in the Done directory can be assumed to be finished with the process and ready to move to whatever process comes next.

✦ **Workflow steps:** You can match directory naming with workflow steps to reinforce the distinction between copies of the same file. If your workflow steps are author, edit, and review, for example, you can create directories called BeingAuthored, ReadyForEdit, and ReadyForReview. Don't be afraid to be verbose and redundant in your naming. The key to keeping masters is to make sure that everyone always knows exactly what stage every file is in.

✦ **Physical objects:** In fast processes in which there's a lot of ownership change, passing a physical object from person to person can really help you keep track of who has the master. If you don't have the object, you shouldn't be touching the files. I've seen a printed and marked up version of a text file, for example, used as the marker for who has that file. If the printout is on your desk, you own the master of the corresponding file.

However you decide to track the master, do it consistently. Nothing ensures a *faux pas* more than an ever-changing set of rules about what the master content is today.

Managing the Processing Project

A content processing project begins with a set of assumptions about the amounts of content to be processed and its current state. From your logical design, you've determined the target state into which you want to bring the content (that is, what components and elements you expect it to yield). The gist of the project after logical design is to define and implement a process that reliably turns the current content into the structure and format you want.

Cross-Reference See Chapter 38, "Building Collection Systems," in the section "Process Management" for more on the hows and whys of managing content processing.

The generalized steps of a content processing project are as follows:

✦ **Assumptions:** Determine your assumptions to create an initial scope, schedule, and budget for the project. Assuming that the project seems feasible, you can finalize your plan later based on a full specification. (For more information on the assumptions that inform your process analysis, see Chapter 29, "Accounting for Acquisition Sources," in the section "Conversion.")

✦ **Inventory:** Create a content inventory to show exactly what pieces of content you're expected to process.

✦ **Specification:** Create a content specification, a process plan, and a staffing plan that describes the process completely. The specification should also build the business case for the process specifying the expected gains that the process should yield.

✦ **Finalized project plan:** From the specification, create a final project plan that maps the expected costs and risks of the project. Based on this plan, you can make the final decision whether to do the process as it's laid out or not.

✦ **Begin development:** Begin developing tools and methodology by focusing on the core algorithms and processes. Save the user interface for later.

✦ **Simulation:** If development has progressed sufficiently, run a small random sample of the source content through a working simulation of the processes and review the assumptions in the specification (especially those concerning the business case). Get sponsor signoff on the sample results and revisit estimates as needed.

✦ **Finish development:** Revise your approach as needed based on the results of your simulation and complete development.

✦ **Provide staff support:** Create processing manuals and training guides as needed to launch the process.

✦ **Staff and launch the process:** Clearly define the skill sets, characteristics, and aptitudes needed to staff the conversion project; then hire and train the appropriate staff.

✦ **Revisit and revise the tools and processes:** You must do this as needed to maintain or increase the quantity and quality of your output from the process.

The process that I'm suggesting emphasizes (almost to a fault) repeated feedback and check-backs. The critical factor for the success of a content process is that it's viable economically. Thus you can't test and check back frequently enough. On the other hand, the process doesn't need to be a big deal or even overly formal. Just make sure that you're constantly checking your assumptions and that you remain sure that the process is netting you as much gain as possible for its cost.

Taking stock of the content inventory

The content inventory derives partly from the logical design of the acquisition system and partly from a simple cataloging of the files that you're expected to process.

Cross-Reference   See Chapter 29, "Accounting for Acquisition Sources," for a discussion on the logical design of an acquisition system.

A content inventory helps you create a solid agreement about what's to be processed and what it consists of. Especially if you're receiving a large bulk of content to be processed for the startup of the CMS, a content inventory can help you sort through and figure out how to dispose of the variety of content that you expect to receive. In addition, as you process content on an ongoing basis during the running of the CMS, you can request an inventory that serves as a packing slip, which goes along with each content delivery.

A content inventory is basically a file list. So it ought to list the filename of every file that you're expected to process. In addition, it ought to include the following:

✦ **File properties:** These should include date and size. The two attributes enable you to identify each file uniquely. If you receive a changed file with the same name later, you know it (or at least you could). Size also gives you a basic idea of the amount of content in each file.

✦ **Type:** Define a set of file types that distinguish the sort of processing required for each file. For example, you might decide that you have three types of press release files to process, each with its own structure and format that requires a different conversion process.

✦ **Owner:** This is the person to call if you have a problem with this file or some question about it.

✦ **Other ready metadata:** You may be able to capture metadata you need anyway, such as component type or audience, from assumptions about the directory or groups submitting the files to you.

The content inventory can save you. Suppliers have a tendency to dig up files at the last minute that they expect you to simply accept. Never mind that the new files are of a completely different type and require you to redevelop all your processes. If you insist on an inventory early in the process and agree to do development based on it, you can protect yourself from this unfortunate situation. (I've been there, and it's no fun at all.)

You may need to settle for less than a list of every filename that you expect to receive. It may not be possible for the source to come up with such a list. To my mind, the appropriate response to this is, "Give me what you have, and I'll plan based on that. But don't expect content that I don't know about to always get processed." It's a hard-core approach; but believe me, the alternative is worse.

Drafting the processing specification

After you've prepared a content inventory, you're ready to draft a processing specification. A processing specification ought to include the following:

✦ **A source specification:** This starts where the content inventory leaves off. In other words, for each file type identified in the inventory, the input specification describes the structure and format of the input, including what character, paragraph, and section formatting is present, how the parts of the source are named, how its navigation is represented, and how any other metadata is represented in the source.

✦ **A target specification:** This includes the target format and structure, together with what components the source gives rise to, what access structures its navigation feeds, and what sort of formatting is allowed to remain in its body elements.

✦ **A process specification:** This shows how the input is mapped to the output. The process specification should include a definition of all the tools and methods that are needed to do the transformation. It should also include expected task times and production rates.

✦ **A quality-control specification:** This defines the level of quality you expect to reach and the methods that you expect to use to assess the quality of the output.

✦ **A staffing specification:** This defines the kinds and number of people that you need.

✦ **A business justification:** This shows that the process can do the required tasks within the budget and staffing constraints of the project. This part of the specification proves that there's adequate return on the investment made in the development of the process.

The processing specification should be created by the processing staff and signed off on by the project leaders (or sponsors, if necessary). Before going into full production, you should run several random samples of content through the process and review the assumptions in the specification (especially those that have a direct effect on the business justification).

Defining testing methods

Especially in a large and ongoing content process, it's critical that you have some way of measuring the success of the process. Here are some considerations that help define your quality control processes:

✦ **Random sampling:** Find ways to randomly sample the content at any stage of its processing. As you define automated tools, build sampling into them. It's a simple matter, for example, to have a processing script log the name of every tenth file it processes. Make sure that, if you create methods such as this, you're not getting a biased sample. If files come to you in sets of 10, for example, every tenth file isn't a random sample. Every tenth file may be the first file of every batch, and so may be different from the other files in the batch. The effectiveness of your quality control depends on reliable sampling, so make sure that you put adequate thought into it.

✦ **Diminish sampling:** Set your sampling rate to the level that's adequate for each individual staff member. Sample more from new staff members and automated processes and less as you gain confidence in the results, but it's never a good idea to completely eliminate sampling for a person or automated process. Even if the person or process doesn't change, the input may.

✦ **Immediate feedback:** The longer that you wait to detect a mistake and inform the person who made it, the more times she's likely to make it. Especially with new people, try to review their work as they do it and provide feedback quickly so that they can learn quickly.

✦ **Immediate escalation of process issues:** Be prepared to promptly escalate and repair any systematic problems that you find with the tools or procedures that you create. A lot of bad output can be generated very quickly; or worse, you may need to stop an important process completely while you wait for a problem to be fixed.

✦ **Clear expectations:** Provide the staff with clear expectations of the quality and quantity of their work and communicate those expectations in many forms. In addition to stating them, you should write them, send them in e-mail, and even include them in the user interface that the staff uses. The point here isn't to be oppressive but rather to make sure that the goals you have for quality and quantity are clearly understood and remembered by the staff.

✦ **Definitive samples:** Especially for new staff, provide strong examples of the kind of output that's correct. The stronger the mental model that they have of the right way to handle a task, the better they can do at it. The exercise of preparing definitive samples helps the design team as well. It's amazing how often creating an example forces the trainee to reconsider the process being explained.

✦ **Cycle staff:** As much as possible, cycle staff through the quality-control positions. It's useful for each person to sit in the evaluator's chair for a while to get perspective on her own work. Cycling staff between processing tasks also avoids boredom and drops in productivity. Do so with caution, however. Balance the need to keep people within their skill sets and the additional training required against the potential gains in staff enthusiasm and productivity.

Getting to the Core of Content Mechanics

The core of content mechanics is to discern the format and structure conventions in a set of content inputs (generally files or databases) and then make good calls about what format and structure you can manipulate automatically and what must be dealt with by hand.

There's a level of structure below which you can't create transform programs. I'll never forget going to an English class with my friend Tim. It was a class in transformational grammar, and I was amazed. I had no idea that, behind language, so much structure existed. I got the same feeling while studying foreign languages. Every part of speech has a name and a correct place in the structure of a sentence. You can construct, deconstruct, analyze, and study language as you would any other system — more or less. As the grammar checkers available in modern word processors demonstrate, it's possible for a strictly logical computer to decompose and analyze language — but not very well. You can tap into the logic and mechanics that exist behind language, but you still need a person (and a smart one) to give the final thumbs up to your text.

Note   Of course, these remarks apply much less to nontextual content. Few generally accepted equivalents to transformational grammar exist in images, sound, or moving pictures.

In addition to the grammatical level of text, which editors must deal with, there's a coarser grain of structure that you might call the *format* and an explicit-structure level of text that has its own mechanics. These are the same two content attributes I've been discussing throughout this book. I add the word *explicit* to structure to contrast it in the present context with the grammatical structure of text that's more implicit. Grammatical structure depends entirely on word choice and punctuation. Explicit structure generally doesn't depend on word choice or punctuation, but rather on extra tagging or other markers that aren't the content, but are metadata.

Consider, for example, this sentence:

Danny is Isabel's son; Debbie and Naomi are her daughters.

You have no trouble getting the meaning out of this sentence because you've internalized the meaning-conveying rules of grammar. This kind of meaning, however, is implicit in the words that I choose and the punctuation that I use. No one has yet figured out (and they very well may never figure out) how to get a computer to reliably decode the full range of structure conveyed by grammar and vocabulary. In contrast, consider this alternate form of the same sentence:

```
<ISABEL>
  <DANNY type="son"/>
  <DEBBIE type="daughter"/>
  <NAOMI type="daughter"/>
</ISABEL>
```

This kind of structure is ideal for a computer to deal with. Nothing (or little) is left to interpretation. The computer may not know the true significance of sons and daughters, but it doesn't need to. Usually, it needs only to recognize tags and carry out the rule associated with them.

Of course, content rarely comes to you as it does in the preceding sample; and if it does, there's little need for a process to transform it. The most likely situation is that most of the grammatical structure is below the level of the structure that you need to recognize and transform. Few uses of content management require you to deal with Isabel and her children. The structure that you need to deal with is much less granular—and more likely to be higher-level structures such as titles, headings, and management elements like creation date and author.

Symbol Manipulation

There is an old and somewhat tired argument in the field of artificial intelligence that goes something like this. Computers are symbol manipulators. They take a set of symbols (lines of code, or in our world, metadata) and perform a set of manipulations on them to produce meaningful outputs. Brains are symbol manipulators; they too take a set of symbols (language) and manipulate them to produce meaning. Since brains and computers work the same way, there is no reason that computers cannot some day be as smart as brains.

In other words, the argument goes, there is nothing more to intelligence than to recognizing symbols (words or metadata) and working them over with a set of rules. I'm not one who accepts this argument. I think that brains do a lot more than this. However, it is a concept that can help to set the agenda for automation in a CM. Namely, when you tag content, you invest it with a set of markers that flag the symbols (concepts, information, data) that you think is important. When you automatically, convert, manage, or publish content you are getting the computer to recognize the symbols you have created and manipulate them with rules you also create so that they are meaningful for either a manager or an audience member.

I'll leave it up to you to decide to what extent this constitutes intelligence, but I have no problem saying that there are more or less intelligent ways for you to create such a process. Whether or not the process is intelligent, at a high level you can make it appear to be intelligent by being smart about the symbols and manipulations you code into your CMS. Being smart about your symbols and manipulations, in turn, requires smart processes to decide what your symbols are and what you should do with them—which is another way of looking at what this book is all about.

I'll say little more about the grammatical level of text and focus here on the format and explicit-structure level. Although the grammatical level of mechanics is common to all the texts in a particular language, the format and explicit structure apply to single publications, or, if you're lucky, sets of publications. You can usually expect, for example, that only one set of formatting and structure rules are applied to a single file containing, say, a description of a service offering. With little effort, you can determine what the rules are and transform the service-offering file into a service-offering component by stripping out the unnecessary surrounding information and mapping its parts to elements of the service-offering content type.

If you have a set of service-offering files, you're less likely to have the same level of consistency. Unless the creators were unusually careful in their creation and enforcement of standards, some level of variability among the files requires you to write more sophisticated programs and bring in staff to make judgment calls on each file that varies too far from the standards you can discern.

The best content mechanic (or conversion analyst, as I call her in Chapter 13, "Staffing a CMS") is someone who can use the tools available in the content's native environment (Visual Basic for Applications in Microsoft Word, for example), knows the structures of the CMS (an XML database, for example), and knows how to connect the two (by using Web programming with the DOM, for example).

Understanding the principles of mapping content

The best way to capture the mechanics of content is to go right to the core conversion issue. How do you find information of interest in source content and map it to components and elements in the CMS? Your capability to map hinges on the amount of correspondence that you can find between the format and structure of the source and that of the target. They can correspond in only a few ways.

Both source and target can correspond as follows:

+ **Directly:** There's exactly the same format or structural element in both.

+ **Indirectly:** There's some way to infer the target format or structural element from clues in the source automatically.

+ **Ambiguously:** There's more than one target element that the source element may give rise to.

If the source and target correspond poorly or not at all, the reason may be one of the following:

+ **No format or structure:** There's no format or structural element in the target components that corresponds to a source element. A person must add the additional elements to the target.

+ **No markup:** Certain target elements exist in the source but are unmarked or inconsistently marked. Mapping depends on the judgment of a person.

Direct correspondence

In direct correspondence, the structure or formatting codes in the source have a direct translation in the target. The codes for bold, for example, are easy to recognize and convert to and from almost any form. Fortunately, but not surprisingly, most of the common format conventions have direct correspondence in all systems. Here, for example, is a sentence that has a variety of character formatting:

The **rain** in <u>Spain</u> falls *mainly* on the `plain`.

And here it is using the arcane Word RTF markup language:

```
The {\b rain} in {\ul Spain} falls {\i mainly} on the {\strike plain}. \par
```

Here's the same sentence in HTML:

```
The <B>rain</B> in <U>Spain</U> falls <I>mainly</I> on the
<STRIKE>plain</STRIKE>.<P>
```

You can see how simple it would be to translate from the first to the second markup. In fact, most of the tag names are exactly the same. Notice that more than one tag in the source can map to the same tag in the target markup. You may choose to map italic text in the source, for example, to bold in the target because italic doesn't render well on the computer screen.

The conversion becomes even simpler if the source and target markup language share the same syntax as do HTML and XML. Consider this HTML source:

```
The <B>rain</B> in <U>Spain</U> falls <I>mainly</I> on the
<STRIKE>plain</STRIKE>.<P>
```

and this in XML:

```
The <B>rain</B> in <U>Spain</U> falls <I>mainly</I> on the
<STRIKE>plain</STRIKE>.<P>
```

If the creator of the XML tag set chooses the same tag names as those used in HTML (and for stuff such as bold and italic, why wouldn't she?), no conversion is needed at all. In fact, with the exception of the rule in XML that all open tags need to match with close tags — which HTML lacks — you often have very little to do to translate HTML into XML. Moreover, the standard called *XHTML* adds close tags and a few other minor conventions to HTML to make it completely compatible with XML.

Programming is the simplest when your source content matches up well with your target content. Tags with direct correspondence represent no trouble for programmers. As long as you can find the target structure, a simple line of code is all that you need to complete the transformation.

Indirect correspondence

In an indirect correspondence, the same format or structure exists in the source and target, but it takes more than just a simple substitution to map from one to the other. Consider, for example, the following HTML outline:

```
<H1>My Life</H1>
    <H2>Birth to Age 5</H2>
    <H3>Life as a Baby</H3>
    <H3>Kindergarten</H3>
    <H2>Age 6 and Up</H2>
    <H3>My Best Friend</H3>
    <H3>My Worst Enemy</H3>
    <H2>My Future</H2>
```

Now consider the same outline rendered in XML, as follows:

```
<SECTION>My Life
  <SECTION>Birth to Age 5
    <SECTION>Life as a Baby</SECTION>
    <SECTION>Kindergarten</SECTION>
```

```
</SECTION>
<Section>Age 6 and Up
  <Section>My Best Friend</Section>
  <Section>My Worst Enemy</Section>
</SECTION>
<SECTION>My Future</SECTION>
</SECTION>
```

Headings are represented in both the HTML and the XML code. In HTML, however, there's a different tag for each heading level (H1, H2, H3, and so on). In XML, the same tag (`<SECTION>`) is used over and over, and the heading level is determined by how nested a particular `<SECTION>` tag is. The heading `Kindergarten`, for example, is nested within two other sections (`Birth to Age 5` and `My Life`) so, therefore, must be a level-3 heading. Although this is not terribly difficult to do, it isn't a direct translation.

In an indirect translation, there's a programmatic way to convert from one markup language to the other, but the programming isn't a simple substitution of one tag name for another. That is, you can get a computer to do the transformation for you, but it may require some more or less sophisticated programming.

Indirect correspondence can generates a lot of code. In an indirect correspondence, the programming complexity doesn't come from not knowing which source structure to map to which target structure. Rather, complexity comes from the amount of logic required to do the mapping. Thus indirect correspondence often requires lots of case statements looking for nuances in the text that tell the program what to do.

Ambiguous correspondence

Sometimes a single tag in the source might be one of many in the target. Consider the following HTML source:

```
<P>Sir Isaac Newton said:
<PRE>"If I have accomplished something great, it is because I am
standing on the shoulders of giants"</PRE>
<P>Our programmers have said:
<PRE>Function Accomplishment(Whose)</PRE>
<PRE>myAccomplishment = ++ Accomplishment(myMentor)</PRE>
<PRE>End Function</PRE>
```

I now want to convert this HTML into the following XML target:

```
<P>Sir Isaac Newton said:</P>
<QUOTE>"If I have accomplished something great, it is because I
am standing on the shoulders of giants"</QUOTE>
<P>Our programmers have said:</P>
<CODE>Function Accomplishment(Whose)</CODE>
<CODE>myAccomplishment = ++ Accomplishment(myMentor)</CODE>
</CODE>End Function</CODE>
```

In the source, the `<PRE>` tag (an HTML tag that enables you to retain the formatting of the original text, including white space) was used for both a quotation and for programming code. In the target, I want to differentiate the two. Unfortunately, no computer that I know of can tell the difference between the two. You need a person to help.

Ambiguities of this sort happen most frequently if format tags are used to represent structural elements in the source. Suppose, for example, that I use an Arial 8-point italic font to represent both a level-5 heading and a note. How can a computer tell one from the other? Generally, one looks for other clues to make the best assumption possible. Maybe the notes always begin with the word *Note*. As one who's been fooled by these sorts of assumptions many times, I recommend being very careful. There's no limit to the variation and creativity of an author who's worked within a nonconstrained authoring environment.

By the way, you may also notice in the preceding example that the HTML sample has open paragraph tags (`<P>`), whereas the XML has open and close paragraph and line-break tags (`<P></P>` and `<BR></BR>`). For HTML tags that aren't required to be closed (`<P>`, `<BR>`, `<IMG>`, and the like), you must map indirectly to XML.

In a case of ambiguity, no amount of code can tell which target structure to create. In ambiguous markup, you need a human in the process to say which target tag an ambiguous source tag should be mapped to. Of course, not all cases are purely ambiguous, so you can spend a lot time finding ingenious ways to figure out what target tag to create from the subtle clues that may surround a source tag. This, too, may be difficult depending on the structural complexity of the source content. (Source content that has ambiguous markup can nonetheless have a highly complex structure.)

No correspondence

If you're most fortunate, there's a direct correspondence between the format and structural tagging of your source and target markup languages. If you're least fortunate, there's no correspondence at all. Markup languages vary in their richness and range of coverage (as I mention in Chapter 35, "What Are Content Markup Languages?"). All represent simple constructs, such as bold and italic. Few represent complex constructs such as columnar layout and advanced table formatting. HTML, which began quite impoverished, has improved considerably with the advent of Cascading Style Sheets (CSS), which enable precision layout as well as arbitrary character and paragraph formatting.

But how do you represent a part number in HTML? There's no `<PartNumber>` tag in HTML, so how can the fact that QS213 is a part number be maintained if you convert to HTML? The answer is that it can't be represented (except through various forms of trickery). Furthermore, there may be no way to decide that a particular number in the source is a part number or something else.

Noncorrespondence between source and target often takes the following forms:

✦ **Rich formatting to impoverished formatting:** Exactly converting a richly formatted table in Microsoft Excel, for example, to HTML simply can't work. There's a level of subtlety and formatting richness that you can create in Excel that can't be duplicated in HTML, because HTML doesn't have the corresponding markup to support it. The only solution here is to "dumb down" the source markup until it can be represented in the target system.

✦ **Structural markup to formatting markup:** As in the example of the part number, if your source environment enables you to create and use arbitrary names, but the target environment doesn't, you have a problem. Microsoft Word documents, for example, may include dozens of paragraph styles that authors and editors use to indicate the structure of the document. If you convert a file formatted this way to HTML without CSS, you of necessity lose all these structural names. HTML with CSS does provide a way to preserve structural names but no particularly apt way to work with them.

✦ **Interactive markup to noninteractive markup:** Much of what appears in HTML pages, for example, occurs not because of the markup on the page but because of the programming script behind the markup. An expanding and collapsing table of contents, for example, is often created by JavaScript code. If you convert such a table of contents from HTML to XML, you lose the expand/collapse functionality.

Of course, if your source content is entirely undifferentiated, your programmers may be able to do relatively little to automate conversion, which means that your human processes will have to carry the load. In this case, the best you can do is to create tools that make the manual process as efficient as it can be. See the section in Chapter 38, "Building Collection Systems," titled "Process and review tools," for more information on these sorts of tools.

No or poor markup

If some element that you expect to be present and tagged in the target is present but unmarked in the source, you have a problem. Consider the following HTML source:

```
<P>My Best Friend
<P>At age 6, I met Timothy, a blond, square jawed 3rd-generation member
of the Fighting Irish.
```

Suppose that you want to convert this HTML to the following XML:

```
<TITLE>My Best Friend</TITLE>
<BODY>At age 6, I met Timothy, a blond, square jawed, 3rd generation
member of the Fighting Irish.</BODY>
```

I'm sure that you can distinguish that the first line of the HTML is the title, and the second line is the body, but an unaided computer-based conversion program couldn't (at least, not reliably). In this example, you want markup in the target that doesn't exist in the source. The way that the title element is tagged in the source simply doesn't provide enough information to distinguish it as a title at all. You must provide a measure of human judgment to ensure a clean conversion.

Most wouldn't bother trying to convert the title automatically the way that it's represented in the preceding example. But how about the following representation?

```
<P><B>My Best Friend</B>
```

Now, you can detect some logic in the source markup. You can say, "If it's in its own paragraph and is bold and doesn't end with a period, it must be a title." Maybe so, or maybe not. Do you know for sure that these characteristics mark a title uniquely and unambiguously? Without some extensive sleuthing through a large sample of what you want to convert, I'd say that you're on thin ice. The element that you want to isolate is poorly marked in the source, and you must include some measure of human judgment to ensure a clean conversion.

It's worth noting here that the capability of advanced programs to discern subtleties of language and make reasonable assumption is on the rise. Each new generation of conversion products gets better at making something in the target out of nearly nothing in the source.

Poor or ambiguous markup causes even more complexity than indirect correspondence, and, unfortunately, this sort of markup is common. Poor markup means that the structure you're seeking in the source is marked inconsistently. Depending on exactly how poorly marked it is, you can generate a lot of code trying to find all the possible representations of the poorly marked source element. Be careful. Dogged programmers can burn more time making tools that never really work than it would take a person to go through all the poorly marked text manually.

Existing Content Converters

As you begin investigating the process of converting content, you may find it helpful to look for existing tools to do the job for you. A number of content converters have been developed by others and are available for free on the Internet, via the GNU public license. Remember that these programs have been developed to work in a generic context, and may not produce the specific content structure you need for your CMS system. Also, these tools cannot be guaranteed to produce perfect output, so extensive testing of sample content should be undertaken. However, they are a good place to start, especially if you are beginning at square one.

The World Wide Web (W3) consortium maintains a link to many different kinds of document converters that support many formats, including, but not limited to Postscript, HTML, Microsoft Word, RTF, TeX, LaTeX, Quark, and Microsoft PowerPoint. You can find more information and download these tools from www.w3.org/Tools/Word_proc_filters.html.

Suzanne Soroczak, University of Washington

No existence

Of course, there's one final situation that can't be handled by a conversion system at all. If your target needs to have an element in it that's simply not present in the source, no amount of clever conversion scripting can create it for you. Rather, you need to create the element as part of a wider aggregation process.

 Cross-Reference There's more on aggregation in Chapter 7, "Introducing the Major Parts of a CMS," in the section "Aggregating."

Summary

Content processing is the term that I think best summarizes the work that must be done to the information that you collect to prepare it for the CMS. In content processing, the following occurs:

✦ You mostly convert content, but in doing so, you also get involved in acquisition and aggregation.

✦ You find the places in your system where the up-front cost of automation can be recovered clearly by gains in productivity or quality.

✦ You develop a content inventory and processing specification to work through the details of the transformation from source to target.

✦ You look for the correspondence between the structures of the source and those of the target components that you're trying to create automatically. May all your correspondences be direct.

As you can undoubtedly tell, planning a content processing effort depends squarely on the sort of content your team will have to process. The tasks for your programmers may be relatively simple or they may be quite complex. And, depending on how much work your programmers can successfully automate for you, your need for editorial people to examine and tag content by hand might, likewise, be either modest or substantial.

In the next chapter, I look more generally at the construction of overall collection systems.

✦ ✦ ✦

Building Collection Systems

The collection system of a content management system is the bridge between the applications used to create content initially and the management system that's used to store and distribute the content. Thus, collection often starts with a set of authoring applications that may be outside the control of the CMS. From its origins outside the CMS, content can move through applications that help convert it, divide it into chunks, and aggregate it into the structure of the repository.

In this chapter, I detail some of the techniques and technology that you need to build a strong collection system within a CMS. After explaining what a collection system is and discussing some key concepts, I organize the collection system of a CMS into a several functional subsystems and examine each subsystem, its features, and its sub-subsystems in detail, including:

- ✦ Authoring content, which means creating content from scratch.

- ✦ Converting existing content, typically content not created with a CMS in mind.

- ✦ Acquiring content from other systems, typically other repositories of various kinds.

- ✦ Aggregating content from all sources, which means synchronizing it with the content and content model already in your system.

- ✦ An interface for getting content into the content repository.

For a list of the extensive systems and features that are described in this chapter, see Chapter 34, "Building a CMS Simply," in the section "An index to the technology taxonomy." The subsystems and features of the collection system are outlined in the portion of the taxonomy under "System: Collection System."

Getting Started

In building collection systems, you need to do the following:

✦ Come as close to the author's home environment and processes as you can. (I explain what this means in this chapter.)

✦ Look behind the simple, Web-based authoring forms (that are most common in current CM systems) to systems with authoring functionality good enough to compete with word processors.

✦ Find a small range of authoring tools that you feel that you can support now and build on these. As time goes on, the number of authoring environments you will be asked to support will no doubt grow. I can only hope that, as much as these authoring tools may differ in capability and market panache, they will all begin to resemble each other in the design of their underlying structures (perhaps by using XML). The better you get at integrating content from diverse platforms, the better you will become at delivering content back to those same platforms.

✦ Consider custom collection tools. The customizations that I describe in this chapter are just a few of the myriad enhancements and cost-justified improvements that you can make to a collection system.

Minimize Disruption, Maximize Specific Value

If you understand your information, you can create an effective system for harvesting it. Part of understanding your information is knowing how to reach into every part of the organization that produces good information. To find the sources of good information, you must chart the natural ways that information is created and how it flows within the organization. After the sources are identified, the CMS collection system must tie in with the flow of information as cleanly as possible to harvest it with the minimum disruption to the staff that produces it. To obtain minimum disruption, the CMS collection system must have the following characteristics:

✦ **Be easy to use:** Or, more precisely, it should be pitched at the expertise and expected training level of the staff members who interact with it. Ease is relative to both the skill of the staff members and the amount of training that they can or are willing to receive.

✦ **Be convenient:** Ideally, the system should make no demands on the contributor that she feels are outside her ability or commitment to contributing to the CMS.

✦ **Teach in context:** A good system includes instructions embedded in the application user interface. Using an HTML page to host the collection system user interface gives you ample room to include instructions and links to background information.

✦ **Be robust:** A system that keeps failing isn't popular with a staff that has a lot to do and not much time to do it. In addition, the collection system is the part of the CMS that most people see. If it's poorly constructed, people naturally assume that the rest of the system is of similar quality.

The bottom line is that, to be successful immediately, your system must be at least as good as the one your contributors have now. *Good* here means easy to use and unobtrusive, rather than flashy and cool. In other words, they want steak and not sizzle, so don't get too far ahead of your contributors. They judge your system not on how cool or automated it is, but rather by its effect on their daily workloads.

On the other hand, you should be able to expect some amount of effort from contributors in exchange for the value that a CMS brings. An organization that I met with recently, for example, has information as its main saleable product. As a financial services organization, the company lives or dies on the strength of its communication with its clients. Timely and relevant information is the lifeblood of this and many other organizations. With this kind of organization, how can you say that the convenience and minimum disruption of contributors is a gauge of success? Clearly, in an organization where information is money, staff members ought to orient to the system that earns them their keep rather than the other way around.

The resolution to the conflict between convenience and effort, I believe, is to infuse enough understanding and enthusiasm into the organization that you make contributors willing to endure some inconvenience for the clear benefit that the system provides the larger organization. You need to find your own balance between what you require and what you will supply in return.

You also need to provide specific positive reasons why people should change. In the absence of a positive vision of what the system gives, a negative vision of what the system takes away can jaundice contributors. Focus on providing that positive vision.

Forms, Files, and Batch Processes

The most visible parts of many collection systems are the forms that contributors see. These forms enable authors to create components and allow acquisitions staff to choose conversion and tagging options. Behind the scenes, CMS processes take the content that contributors supply and use it to create content records in relational databases or XML files. Other processes read the options that staff supply to trigger batch processes that move large quantities of information into the CMS.

To load content in bulk from files or from forms, a CMS might proceed as shown in Figure 38-1.

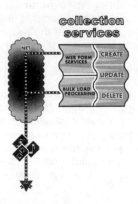

Figure 38-1: CMS collection services enable you to load content components one at a time or in bulk.

I use the term *collection services* to describe the following functions that a CMS must perform to load content into the repository:

✦ **Form submission of content:** Generally, but by no means always, these are Web-based forms (that is, they look just like any input form that you may find on the Web). Regardless of the host, these forms enable you to enter text, upload media, and choose from a variety of metadata field types (drop-down lists, check boxes and the like).

✦ **File submission of content:** The system is likely to enable you to upload a file full of content and tag it with metadata. Notwithstanding the fact that this may turn your content management system into a mere document management system (see Chapter 10, "The Roots of Content Management" in the section titled "The Principles of Document Management," for more information on this distinction), you can usually treat files as one big unparsed element in a larger component that includes the metadata that categorizes the file.

✦ **Bulk loading:** Both form-submission and file-submission are one-off processes. That is, you create one component at a time from one form or one file. This is always necessary, but it is far from sufficient for systems that receive any amount of acquired content. Because acquired content comes in bulk (many components at a time), you must have a process for inputting in bulk. Although few commercial systems have general-purpose bulk loaders, most have the hooks (generally in the form of an application programming interface) that enable you to create a bulk loading program and hook it into the CMS's standard features for component creation and maintenance.

If your system is large enough, you may use all three methods of input. The specifics behind each of these methods are detailed throughout this chapter. For now, it is most important for you to understand the number of ways you can get content into your system. You should use the way that is both best for your authors and that causes you the least additional effort.

Driven by a Content Model

Behind every CMS collection system, a content model should be driving all content creation or acquisition. (For information on content models, see Chapter 30, "Designing Content Access Structures" in the section titled "The content model.") In some cases, the content model is coded into an XML schema. In other cases it is in a database schema. In all cases, it should be coded in a single central place and used to determine what any collection method must accomplish. For example, the schema can stand behind the authoring environment and ensure that content components are created according to the model. It should stand behind all conversion and acquisition to determine what the content that comes out of the process should look like. The content model tells when aggregation is complete. It is complete when content is both segmented the way the model wants it to be and tagged with all of the metadata the model says it should have.

The content model may directly guide collection. For example, you might use a model stored in an XML schema to directly validate content created in an environment that supports XML schemas. But it's more likely that the model will guide creation indirectly. For example, although the latest version of Microsoft Word supports schemas, older versions (where most Word content still lives) cannot be guided directly by a schema. Rather, you use the schema to manually create a Word template that guides content creation. No direct link exists between the template and the schema, so changes to the schema must be propagated (again manually) to the template.

Whether your model can directly or only indirectly guide collection, this task must be what the collection process is about. Collection is simply (or maybe not so simply) the application of your content model to the stream of content that you desire to amass.

Authoring System

Authoring tools enable people to create content from scratch. A CMS can either provide authoring tools or enable you to bring in content from other applications. Most authors would like to continue using the tools that they're most familiar with. By looking closely at the tools and processes that you need as well as those that your staff prefers, however, you can make the right compromises.

 Cross-Reference I detail the authoring process in Chapter 39, "Building Management Systems." Here, I focus on tools.

Few commercial content management systems provide authoring tools for any type of content other than text. Text authoring itself is most often driven through a set of Web-based forms in which authors can type the text that they want to manage into text boxes on a Web page and then submit the item to the CMS repository. Images or other nontext content can be uploaded but not created in these forms. This system works well if the text to type is short and requires little formatting. For more complex text and for all other content types, the CMS generally assumes that the content was created outside the CMS. This assumption serves the interests of both the CMS designers (because they don't need to reinvent authoring systems) and the CMS users (who can continue using their known authoring applications).

So, often, authoring tools precede the CMS. Writers may, for example, do original authoring in Microsoft Word. The Word files may be sent to you via e-mail. Or you may receive the electronic versions of camera-ready print files that you convert into HTML before putting them into the repository. Finally, you may receive analog VHS tapes and digitize them and index them before you can log them into the repository. In all these cases, some applications precede the CMS. These preceding applications can follow proprietary or open storage formats. Proprietary formats can be read only by the application that creates the content. (Microsoft Word DOC files are an example of a proprietary format.) Open formats are usually created outside of any specific product or company and can be read by any application that follows openly published rules (in the history of computers, HTML is the most well-known open storage format).

Authoring applications fall into general categories, which are based on the type of content that you're collecting, as follows:

✦ **Text:** Typically, text is generated by using proprietary word processing applications such as Microsoft Word, and proprietary desktop-publishing applications such as Adobe PageMaker and QuarkXPress. The open format HTML has become more and more popular and may now hold more pages of content than word processing formats. XML is new and the least popular, except with content managers who want to migrate existing content into a structural form.

✦ **Image content:** Images come in two basic forms: illustrations, which are created by a graphic artist to illustrate concepts or physical objects, and photographs. (For the purpose of this discussion, I don't count interface images such as buttons and background images as content.) For illustrations, the most common source of content is from applications such as Macromedia FreeHand, Adobe Illustrator, and Adobe Photoshop. Less common, but still significant, are illustrations that come from computer-aided design or other drawing programs, such as Microsoft Visio. Photographs are often scanned from prints, acquired from other sources, or authored directly by using a digital camera.

✦ **Video:** This is most often authored in an analog or digital video or film camera and then digitized. As with photographs, direct digital authoring of video (using a digital camera) is sure to become the major way that video is authored.

✦ **Animations:** These are moving illustrations. The same programs that create illustrations can create a series of illustrations that, if displayed in sequence, produce the effect of motion. Other tools, such as Macromedia Flash, provide sophisticated tools for creating animations and adding programming code so that they behave in sophisticated ways and allow user interaction.

✦ **Sounds:** These are either digitized from existing analog recordings or authored directly into a digital recorder.

✦ **Other content:** This comes from various desktop applications (such as spreadsheet and presentation programs) and a wide variety of other application-specific files (such as Adobe Acrobat files).

Each source application has its own software and hardware requirements, but the vast majority of applications run on a standard desktop computer. Although high-end Macintosh programs are still preferred by most image and animation professionals, virtually all authoring applications have a Microsoft Windows version as well.

The following subsections describe in detail the systems and features that you should consider for your authoring system. I describe each feature and also give you some idea of the circumstances that might cause you to include the feature in your system.

Integrated search

When a person is authoring, she may need to find a component from the repository:

✦ To work on a component that she or someone else previously saved.

✦ To link to the component she is working on.

✦ To refer to — for example, to be sure that she is not duplicating existing content.

Your CMS can include an integrated search feature that enables authors to find components in the repository using the access structures you have defined, or to do a full-text search through the text and metadata of the components.

In the best case, you can create a component selector that the author can bring up from her authoring application. The selector is a dialog box that exposes all the access structures of the CMS. The user can navigate however she chooses to the component of interest and display the component or create a link to it. As advanced as this feature may sound, it's completely within reach if your CMS is designed in a modular way. More or less rudimentary forms of component selectors are included in many commercial products. None that I have seen takes the final step of including a full-text search feature in the component selector. The full-text search feature requires that the CMS be integrated tightly with a custom or third-party search engine such as Verity Ultraseek. Some systems do ship with "lite" versions of search engines, but most require you to buy the engine separately and then pay for its integration with your system.

Although within reach, search can be a difficult feature to implement in any thorough way; so consider carefully whether you need it before deciding to implement it. You need it most if your authors are really engaged in the CMS and understand the body of content that the repository holds. If your authors are more casual or if your content is not very richly interrelated, an integrated search feature may be overkill.

Integrated workflow

If you integrate workflow into the authoring system, contributors will always know what the disposition of their content is and can advance it to the next state directly from their authoring application. For example, you could add a Tasks command to the application's menu system (or put a Tasks button on a Web form). This Tasks command then displays a workflow dialog box, which provides an interface to all the workflow functionality that you need to show authors. It could, for example, show all tasks currently active for the user. Highlighting a task would display details on that task, including information on what's to be done to complete the task, how much time it's expected to take, when the task was triggered, and so on. Choosing a task in the dialog box could open the corresponding component in the author's tool (assuming that all tasks that are displayed in the dialog box involve editing a component). You can get much fancier still, by linking the tasks in the dialog box, for example, to Web pages where the user can get more detail or do tasks that don't involve component editing. All these features serve the basic goal of linking workflow to an authoring environment in order to ensure that the author never needs to leave her familiar tool to interact with the CMS.

Workflow is a godsend to advanced authors, but could be a devil for casual or novice users. For the latter, it may be better if they never have to deal directly with the concept of workflow. Rather, a simple feature that lets them state, "I am done, move this content on," may be much simpler to implement and better for the kind of user who wants a minimum of interaction with your system. On the other hand, if you have a large number of more advanced authors this feature may be worth the considerable effort it will take to make it work. Authors who are on your staff ought to be able to use the CM system's stock workflow system and should not usually require that you to go to any special lengths to create more advanced tools for them. Even the stock workflow tools provided by your CMS (even when handled by savvy authors) cannot make integrating workflow a trivial task.

Spawning applications

Some systems launch (or spawn, as it's called) authoring tools that enable you to create and edit component elements outside the CMS. In the simplest form of spawning, the CMS starts the authoring tool, and it's up to you to copy text into the application and then back it into the CMS form. In better implementations, the CMS opens the authoring tool and copies in the text to be edited. After you close the application, the CMS copies the edited text back into the form that you started from automatically. This is more a process of linking to the author's chosen tool than really integrating into it.

You want such a feature if your CMS does not offer WYSIWYG authoring in its forms and if your authors can deal with the somewhat jarring feeling of moving between Web forms and client applications.

Upload support

If your users must upload files along with the components when they submit content, you need to offer some sort of file upload control. The minimum of a single box in which you type the name of a file to upload may not be nearly enough. Consider that a contributor may also need to delete files, add versions, add comments about the files, choose files from ones that already exist in the CMS, or see what files like the one she's working on have already been added to components. With requirements like these, a simple text box quickly grows to a full-blown file management system. Consider breaking file management out from component input altogether and creating separate components (with their own management elements) for any file that you want uploaded and tracked in the CMS.

Upload support can be a mere convenience or a real productivity requirement. In general, the more files your users deal with, the more important upload support is to them. Media-rich systems, for example, often include many files for which the difference between one version and another may not be easy to see. Robust upload support, in this situation, is particularly useful and important.

Advanced media support

Text is still the king of content. Other sorts of media (images, sound, video, animation) are still treated mostly as binary files to be uploaded, unopened, and edited completely outside the system. Media in this sort of system are treated as baggage that goes along with the real content, text. However, many systems are beginning to break this mold and realize that text is not the only kind of content that must be authored and edited. Of the forms of media that a CMS authoring system could encompass, images have thus far received the most attention. Some of the features that have been adopted for images in commercial and custom systems (and which could also be extended to other media) are:

✦ Treating images as separate components with their own set of metadata attached. Rather than being baggage that is attached to another text-based component, the image is treated as a separate component that is linked to the text component. These image components can then participate, separately from any text, in workflow and publishing.

✦ Allowing the author to browse for images by thumbnail versions of the image. The system automatically creates and manages the alternate versions of the image.

✦ Allowing authors to access images by the metadata attached. An image selector (like the component selector I discuss in the section in this chapter titled "Integrated search") lets the user search for and preview images to be edited or linked.

✦ Attaching intellectual property rights management to the images so that only the appropriate people can use or edit them.

✦ Allowing the author to edit the image within the CMS rather than outside it. This can be done either by spawning the author's favorite application or by providing (usually very simple) authoring tools right within the CMS.

✦ Including annotation tools so that staff can comment on images as they would on text.

Looked at as a whole, these features do no more than give images (and later all media) the status of real content. As time goes on, nontext content will have to be substantially promoted from the lowly status of mere baggage if CM systems are to keep pace with people's growing need to consume media the way they consume text.

If text really is the only important content for you, then this extensive level of image management is much more than you need. However, you might ask yourself, "If we promote media to the status of real content, what opportunities would we have that are beyond our reach today?"

Spell checking

Web-based forms can be an open door to spelling and grammatical errors in your CMS repository. First, people tend to be very informal with the language that they use on Web-based forms. Like e-mail, it's considered a casual medium. Second, it's difficult to see and correct errors in the small text boxes and monospaced fonts that are often used on Web-based forms. If you don't already have them, spell-checking tools should soon be available for use in conjunction with the text boxes on your Web-based forms. These tools provide the kind of direct feedback that word processing applications commonly provide (underlined words, and so on). If you don't provide spell checking at this important point of authoring, you may spend considerable extra editing time later to fix errors that should have never been allowed in the first place. Some great spell check features to consider are:

✦ **Highlighting:** It really helps if misspelled words are somehow flagged as the author types.

✦ **Mandatory trigger:** You may want to automatically trigger the spell checker when the user tries to submit the content.

✦ **Standard dictionaries:** One very nice-to-have feature that you may consider adding as you extend the CMS into authoring applications is the capability to spell-check content by using standard dictionaries. Every spell-check program enables you to add words to its dictionary that are spelled correctly, but are not yet in the dictionary. If you have a large contributor base and a sizable number of vocabulary terms that are unlikely to be in the dictionaries of the individual authoring tools, it may be worth your while to create custom dictionaries for your various authoring tools (including your Web-based forms) and distribute them to your authors. This is a great way to enforce editorial consistency across your author base.

When is spell checking needed as part of your system? I have found it to be necessary in all cases (at least, it is for me).

Integrated editorial and metatorial guides

In a CMS, content is always broken into parts called elements. That means to author content for a CMS you have to know what the body and metadata elements are and how to complete them. Body elements, you may recall, hold the displayed information for the component (title, abstract, sections, and so on), and management elements specify the hierarchies and other access structures into which a component must fit. Needless to say, you need to know a lot to author for a CMS.

A metatorial guide contains all the metadata-related help, and an editorial guide contains all the text usage and style information that an author might need. A help system that is attached to your authoring applications and that delivers this information to authors can be of great assistance. Some of the attributes to consider for your help system are:

✦ **In context:** The best place to deliver information on authoring is right next to the place where the author has to type. Figure out, for example, how to put a little question mark next to where each element is created. A click on the question mark ought to yield specific instructions on how to fill that specific element.

✦ **Targeted:** Be sure to organize your help information to hit the right level of detail for the type of author it serves. For example, novice or uncommitted authors may want only the basic information whereas advanced authors and staff might want complete information.

✦ **Linked:** Make sure that the help that you offer to the author is linked to the wider CMS documentation set you created. For more information on the CMS documentation set, see Chapter 21, "Rolling Out the System" in the section titled "Creating documentation."

You really need a help feature if you can't depend on your authors to use their own initiative to study your content model and remember all its nuances. Even if you have very motivated authors, a help system provides the most convenient way to deliver targeted authoring information at the point of application.

Off-line content creation

If you don't need a LAN or Internet connection to the CMS in order to author, then you are allowing off-line creation of content. If you are using Web forms, this feature may be difficult to implement because the forms are probably generated dynamically by the CMS's Web server. Even if you are using proprietary authoring applications (word processors, for example), any integrations (search, workflow, and so on) that you have created must be disabled when the author is off-line. If you need to provide off-line creation and find it too hard to do, you might consider creating an alternative submission format that people can use while off-line that you can import into the repository later. Here's an example of a simple text format that might do.

```
Title: [Type your title here]
Author: [Type your author ID here]
Abstract: [No more than 20 words please]
Body: [Consult the style guide for more information]
```

By filling out this simple text file (which, nonetheless, still has lots of direction coded into it) authors can author from anywhere and you can easily parse and import their contributions when they are back in touch. In all likelihood, content authored this way will not be complete and will need further metatorial processing. But, at least, people are not stopped from authoring when they have no connection.

Off-line content creation is a handy feature for authors who don't work on-site or for contributors who travel frequently.

Preview

Probably the biggest problem for authors in a CMS is not knowing what happens to their content after it's submitted. If all they ever see is a Web-based form, they may very well lose track of why they're writing, who may see it, and how it fits into the publications. To keep them involved, authors need to see where their content is headed and what more may be done to it after it leaves them.

Publication preview

Most good commercial CMS products provide some sort of Web page preview. Using this feature, after submitting a component, you can choose to see how it looks in the context of its Web page. The system applies an HTML template to the component sends it to the Web browser on your local computer. This is fine as far as it goes, but it doesn't go very far. First, it shows only one page, whereas the component may show up on any number of pages. Second, it shows no personalization. The component may look incredibly different depending on the person who accesses it. Finally, it shows only one Web publication. The component may be part of any number of Web publications and a range of publications of other sorts.

Some systems go so far as to present a fully WYSWYG authoring form where it looks as if you are typing directly into the Web page that the CMS will later render for an end user. This is a great system if all you are producing is one Web page from each component. It is a very bad system if you are producing many different pages or publications from the same components.

Even if the CMS did no more than list the publications, pages, and personalizations that may be applied to the component that an author is submitting, it would go a long way toward providing the author with the information that she needs to stay connected to the component's future. The best preview feature, however, would go much further. It might present a dialog box with a hierarchy showing publications, pages, and personalizations for the component that the author chose. A click on any line of the hierarchy would trigger a build of the particular publication page and the personalization selected. Even better, the system could go so far as to produce thumbnail images of each page. The thumbnail images could be enlarged by the author to quickly compare and contrast presentations of the component. Of course, such a system would be as useful to the publication teams as it would be to the authors.

Some sort of publication preview is always a good idea. How fancy you decide to make this feature depends on how many publications you have and what resources you can afford. But pound for pound, investments in this feature pay off more than almost any other in increasing the quality of the content you receive.

Workflow preview

To keep the author connected to her work, it's useful to show her where her work goes after she submits it. Many commercial CMS systems provide graphical tools for building workflows. You can create great pictures of the steps, tasks, and triggers behind each workflow. It's unfortunate that most of these very attractive tools are used only by the few people who design workflows. If, in addition, these flowcharts were a click away from any workflow user interface, they'd help enormously to engage and inform authors (and other staff members as well). By keeping contributors informed about where their content is headed after they submit it, you are giving them what they need to know to assure that the content makes the required transition as smoothly as possible.

The more connected and involved you want your authors to be in your workflow processes, the more you need workflow preview. Even if the best you can manage is to get the workflow designer to print out a version of the workflow that you distribute to the team (and periodically update), your authors will benefit.

Feedback

Authors need to receive feedback on the quality of their work as early and often as possible to improve continually and stay connected to their audiences and fellow team members.

Staff feedback

In most systems, only the most dogged author ever sees any feedback on her work. After she submits a component, it may need extensive work, but she never knows it because she's isolated from the steps downstream from her tasks. If she receives feedback at all, it's likely to be informal—a chance hallway meeting with an editor. There's no reason why the CMS can't provide ample and objective feedback to the author at the point when she needs it most—as she starts to create another component of the same type.

Without enormous extra effort, you can create code that runs as an author creates a new component. Either on a Web-based form or in an authoring application, whenever the author chooses to create a new component, you can retrieve any comments that were made on her last component (good as well as bad) and show them to her. In addition, you can provide objective statistics to give even-handed feedback. You can calculate the average time that it takes to process a component of the given type completely, for example, and contrast it with the average time for the author's components. As always, any feedback should be designed to be honest, accurate, and constructive.

If the quality of your content is lower than you expect, staff feedback is a sure way to improve it (or, at least, remove all possible excuses for it remaining poor).

Audience feedback

Just as you can provide staff and system feedback to an author, you should be able to provide audience feedback as well. Given that you have some ways of gathering audience feedback, you should be able to present it to the author at the time that she begins to create a new component. Suppose, for example, that you add a rating button to the bottom of each article page on a Web site that you publish. As authors create new article components, you can supply them with any comments that were made about their previous articles, the articles of others, and any statistics that are available (average rating, highly rated articles, poorly rated articles, and so on).

Audience feedback is a critical feature if you believe that your CMS might tend to isolate your authors from your audiences. In the case where authors feel that a CMS breaks their direct link to their readers, this feature can convince them that, in fact, the CMS can help forge this link.

Metadata support

The collection system of a CMS creates content that is consistent with the content model you have designed. At the base, that content model is a set of content elements of a variety of types (for more information on element types, see Chapter 24, "Working with Metadata" in the section titled "Understanding the Types of Metadata"). Your collection system must be able to provide authors with tools for creating elements of the types you have envisioned.

Required and optional elements

Not all of the elements in every content type need to be present. On the other hand, some need to be present more than once (for example, you may specify that each component have at least two keywords chosen to describe it). Somehow these assertions need to be made visible to authors. You can take one of the following approaches to telling authors what is allowed (in increasing order of robustness):

✦ You can just tell them or write it down somewhere that they can find it. Unfortunately, this is still the most common method of enforcement.

✦ If you have a help system attached to your authoring environment, you can stipulate which elements are optional and how many others must be created at the point where authors are entering them.

✦ Your authoring environment itself may be able to enforce your rules. It may be able to validate that the proper elements are present when the author goes to save; or better, it may be able to visually differentiate between required and optional fields, and in other ways encourage the author to populate the right elements before she attempts to save.

Even if you take the most robust approach, experience tells me that you ought to pursue every means at your disposal to educate your authors on what they are supposed to do to create good content for you. For example, enforcement within the system could be accompanied by documentation in an attached help system.

Unless you do not have optional elements (that is, all elements are always required in the same numbers), you will have to find some way to create a feature that specifies required and optional elements.

Element-set personalization

You may want to personalize Web-based forms or authoring templates in some other application to show different sets of elements based on the user's job or permissions. For example, suppose you have a form for the creation of components of the type Service Offering. When a product manager creates a new service offering, you want her to worry only about the name and basic description of the offering. Consequently, that is all you show on her version of the form. The product engineer sees the name and description and a new space for product details. Finally, when your metator sees the form, it has additional fields for product taxonomy and keywords (elements that neither the product manager nor engineer would know what to do with).

This kind of personalization is basically the same as the kind that you do in publications. In fact, it can be a lot easier because you don't need to infer to which audience the user belongs; you can just ask. On the other hand, if you don't buy the feature as part of a commercial package, you might have to spend quite a bit of effort making it work. For every type of author (and the types change over time) and every content type (which also changes) you have to be able to state somewhere what elements they see (and the elements may also change). Add to this the complexity that you may want an element to be optional for author A (meaning fill it out if you can), but mandatory for author B (meaning if A missed it you have to fill it in). This gives you a fairly complex feature to implement.

If you have a lot of novice authors who might be confused by forms that have a lot of elements that they are not supposed to pay attention to, you want element-set personalization. Whether your determination can fuel the considerable effort to create the feature and maintain all the connections between authors, content types, and elements is another thing entirely. If true element-set personalization is beyond your grasp, you may be able to at least provide guidance within your authoring interface (for example, field labels that include a note about who is supposed to fill in the field).

Validation

What happens when someone enters a value for an element that you don't think is right? Of course, you would like the CMS to immediately start beeping and flashing to tell the person to correct the error. You would like the system to validate what the user has entered. As this sort of automatic validation is not always possible (or at least practical), you would, at least, like the author to be informed about what constitutes a valid entry for each element. In other words, you have two basic approaches to validation:

✦ **Before entry:** You can educate the user so she enters valid information in the first place.

✦ **After entry:** You can inform the user that she has done something wrong.

When I phrase it this way, I hope you can see that neither choice is completely right, and neither is exclusive of the other. In all cases, it should be clear to the user, as she looks at the form, what to enter in it; also when she enters something wrong, the system, if possible, should complain.

Unfortunately, in many cases it really hard to tell a right from a wrong entry in an element. It is pretty clear that you shouldn't type name in a date element, but how can you tell if a user typed an abstract or just a few random sentences in an abstract element?

You should create as much validation as possible in order to assure good content. You should draw as much after-entry validation as possible out of the system you create or buy. Be sure to think about and include (possibly, via the great help feature that you are implementing) before-entry validation for every element that could possibly be misinterpreted (that is, all of them).

Reference fields

On content input forms, you often need the author to create cross-references. To make this easier, you can provide a field on the form where the author can choose a referent for the link. This field holds the unique Id of the component that you want to link to (as I describe in Chapter 24, "Working with Metadata" in the section titled "Categorizing Metadata Fields"). If you can count on users to have Ids memorized, this sort of field is no more than a text box. Unfortunately, no one memorizes Ids, so you must do better than a text box. In fact, you'd do well to implement some sort of component selector (as I outline in the section in this chapter titled "Integrated search"). The selector can be displayed as a button on any Web-based form that has a reference field on it, which is the kind of user interface that you need to make a reference field work effectively. If the reference field is designed to make a link between the chosen component and the one you are authoring, consider allowing the author to either type the link text, or choose it from the elements of the chosen component (for example, the author might choose the title element of the chosen component to be the link text).

A poor man's fallback for this sort of feature is to publish a list of components (sorted by useful metadata) that lists the Id of each. That way, people can find the Ids they want manually and just type it in the text box you supply.

Some form of reference fields is mandatory if you plan to allow authors to do extensive linking between components.

Cross-references

The way that you might approach cross-references is itself a cross between the way that you handle reference fields and the way that you handle rich editing. A cross-reference must include both the Id of a referent and the formatting of the reference. (See Chapter 30, "Designing Content Access Structures" in the section titled "What's a cross-reference?" for more information on references and referents.) To find a referent, you can use the same user interface as I describe for reference fields. To facilitate formatting the reference, you can include options for your various cross-referencing strategies. Suppose, for example, that you have strategies for prerequisite, post-requisite, more information, and related topics. (See Chapter 30, "Designing Content Access Structures" in the section titled "What's a cross-reference?" for more information on cross-referencing strategies.) You may use the following functionality and user interface features to help contributors add cross-references within the text of an element that's displayed on a Web-based form.

✦ The user right-clicks the position within the text where she wants the cross-reference placed.

✦ Your program (assuming that you've written one or got one with your commercial CMS) produces a pop-up menu, which enables the user to choose a command: Cross-Reference.

✦ In response to this command, your program displays a dialog box in which the user can choose a strategy and a referent. To choose a strategy, she selects one of your strategies from a list box. To choose a referent, she uses the same component selector that I described for references.

✦ After she selects a strategy and a referent and dismisses the dialog box, your program adds the formatting for the appropriate strategy and the referent to the text. (A fancier system would add structural markup that's translated later into formatting.)

Here again, a poor man's strategy would be to publish a list of components and their Ids and simply tell authors what to type in order to make a cross-reference happen.

I would encourage you not to give up on cross-references because they are too hard to create automatically and, instead, look for ways that are within your means to make them happen.

Hierarchical relationships

If all your component elements are peers, the layout and data entry on a Web-based form is easy. But suppose your elements are in a parent-child relationship. Suppose, for example, that you can have multiple heading elements, and each can be the parent of one or more paragraph elements. How can this be represented on a Web-based form? I've seen three approaches.

✦ In the first approach, the form displays a single box for all the body elements. The user is responsible for including in the box markup that distinguishes headings and paragraphs. After you submit the form, a program behind the scenes puts each element in the right place in the repository.

✦ In another approach, the form has a user interface that enables you to add text boxes to the form for child and peer elements. There's a button that reads, for example, Add Heading. After you click it, a new text box appears where you can type in the new heading. Under the heading text box is a button that reads Add a Paragraph. After you click it, a new text box is added under the heading, where you can type in a child paragraph of the heading.

✦ A middle path, which is what many modern XML editing programs use, is to have a text box in which you can type text and, beside it, a context-sensitive list of valid elements. As the cursor moves, the list of valid elements changes to reflect what's valid in the current context. If you click an item in the list, the appropriate markup is automatically added to the text box.

The first method is closer to the WYSIWYG paradigm but requires a lot of validation to ensure that the user doesn't enter bad markup. The second approach is guaranteed to produce a valid element structure but provides a pretty clumsy and unnatural typing experience for the user. The middle approach has a lot of promise but still requires a lot of savvy on the part of the author to know what element to choose for what purpose.

In authoring applications other than Web forms, the problem is at least as acute. Trying to enforce a nesting structure in a word processor can be almost impossible. In Microsoft Word, for example, nothing prevents an author from putting a Heading 3 style below a Heading 1 (skipping the required Heading 2).

For any but the most experienced authors, I would strongly recommend staying away from hierarchical relationship features entirely. In my experience, people just do not understand the nesting of elements. Of course, if your content model requires it (and you can't change the model), you may not be able to avoid it. If that is the case, you had better invest in a good help feature and lots of training time.

Web forms

Most systems (commercial and home grown) include some sort of Web form interface. If you're building your own CMS, a strong Web-based form system is no doubt one of your foremost requirements. Luckily, basic forms are easy to build and often don't even require the skills of a programmer. On the other hand, the kinds of forms that you may end up needing in a CMS aren't at all basic and go beyond what even the leading commercial CMS products supply. In addition to the general collection and authoring features, a CMS may include a number of features specific to its Web forms.

Extensions and modifications

If you are working from a commercial CMS, you may need to transcend what its forms can accomplish. These modifications break down loosely as follows:

✦ **Removal:** The simplest modification is to simply remove some interface from the forms. For example, there may be navigation to other parts of the CMS that you don't want certain authors to hassle with.

✦ **Rebranding and rearrangement:** Next, you might want to switch out titles, banners, or headers and footers to make the forms more consistent with the rest of your environment.

✦ **Non-integrated functionality:** You might want to include new functions on the forms that don't directly integrate to the CMS. For example, you might want to include links to your own help system that is outside the CMS but must be interspersed with all the elements that the CMS puts on the form.

✦ **Integrated functionality:** Finally, you might want to connect CMS functionality to functions outside the CMS. For example, you might want a single login on the form that validates an author against your usual user system and also logs them into the CMS.

Ideally, any of these modifications are possible. In reality, they are only possible if the CMS takes an open approach to its form generation. Many commercial systems (and the better home-grown ones, as well) treat Web forms as if they were an outside application that uses open standards to access the core CM functions (through a published API). In other words, the forms are on their own, but they can freely use functions of the CMS. This sort of form can be modified just about any way you want.

On the other hand, the fancier the form system, the harder it is to modify it. For example, if your system is smart enough to automatically generate forms in an XML schema, what happens to your modifications each time it regenerates the forms?

I have found that the most common modification is removal of the confusing extra interface on CMS forms. Other than that, the product you use determines what parts of your forms need to be replaced or enhanced.

Automatic form creation

A big problem with most Web-based forms is that they're decoupled from the content schema that they feed. In other words, to create the form, an analyst or a programmer (or both) studies the content schema and figures out what fields to put on the form, how to position them, and how to exchange data with the repository. The programmer codes all this and believes that she's done. Then someone comes along and changes the content schema, and all her forms break. The usual solution to this problem is to create a tight process connection between the programmer and the content schema creator. (They might even be the same person.) If the schema changes, the programmer is notified and makes sure to retest all her forms. I've seen another solution that takes much less effort: The content model itself includes most of what you need to know to create a Web-based form automatically. The names of the elements, their order, their allowed values, whether they're required or optional, their parent and peer relationships, and how many times they may occur can all be stored as part of the content schema.

It's possible to do away with Web-based form programming entirely and replace it with a meta form program that automatically creates a Web-based form user interface and code, based on the database schema or XML DTD (or schema) of your CMS repository. I've seen this done in commercial systems, but not widely. Its main problem is that often certain parameters that aren't in the content schema are necessary to build the forms. A database schema, for example, doesn't necessarily tell you in what order to display the component elements on the form. Still, the functions that I've seen can be a real help to get your forms started and to create very simple ones. Given the amount of information that you've gathered during logical design, you have more than enough data to drive a very sophisticated and comprehensive Web-based form generator program. With a bit of effort (well, maybe more than a bit) and a place to store and access data that's not in the content schema, you can create a killer automatic form generator.

If your content model changes rapidly and you don't need to enhance forms much after they are created, automatic form creation may be just the feature for you.

In-context editing

Some systems use the same templates for authoring that they do for publishing. What this means is that you author into a screen that looks just like the Web page will when you later publish what you have authored. With the click of a button, all of the editable areas on the built page turn into edit boxes. In the better implementation, those edit areas are WYSIWYG with little formatting toolbars above them.

This in-context editing ensures that what you create works just right in the Web page that will later display it. The only problem comes when this one Web page is not the only page where the content will be displayed. And what happens if the Web is not the only place where the content will be displayed? In those cases, this feature actually works against the main advantages of a CMS and draws you back toward a single-output, no-reuse publishing system.

When you intend your CMS to be simply a way to ease the authoring of a single, fairly small Web site, in-context editing is a good feature. Otherwise, it's a feature to avoid or ignore.

If your system does not include in-context editing, it may at least include the capability to preview content in its destination publications. For more on this feature, see the section "Publication preview" earlier in this chapter.

Rich editing

The typical constrained text element on a Web-based form for a text component element is a text box (see Chapter 24, "Working with Metadata" in the section titled "Categorizing Metadata Fields," for more information on constrained text elements). You can type only characters into it. These characters can be plaintext, or possibly HTML or even XML. If you happen to be a markup fanatic, this may be fine. But for everyone else, some form of WYSIWYG editing environment is much preferred. I've seen three decent solutions to this issue.

✦ In the first case, the Web-based form enables you to start up a separate editing application and loads the text element into it. After you close the editing program, the text element is automatically loaded back into the text area on the Web-based form. This method enables you to use your favorite editor but tends to be a bit clumsy and unreliable.

✦ The second solution puts a WYSIWYG HTML editing control right on the Web form. This solution allows the author to format the free text element in whatever way she wants. The problem is that such a control does not encourage consistency.

✦ The third solution puts a WYSIWYG XML control on the Web form. In this case, the author enters structural markup, and the control (usually using CSS) formats it in an attractive way. These controls let you actually put limits on what an author can enter in a constrained text element. On the other hand, this control can require a lot of programming and a lot of training for authors who are not used to structural markup.

I really don't see an easy way out of the dilemma presented by solutions two and three. The easier you make it for the author, the less constrained your element content will be. On the other hand, the more control you exert, the more of a burden you put on the author. This dichotomy, of course, finds its way into a number of CM arenas. The only real solution is to breed a generation of authors who understand that structure is worth learning. (That generation may not yet have been born.)

If you want body and other elements to include formatting or structure you must do something that lets your authors do rich editing. How fancy your solution is depends on your resources.

Other authoring applications

Knowing the ways that you want to reach into someone's authoring tool and actually doing so are two different things. Many authoring tools were never designed to integrate with outside applications and have a hard time exchanging data. To turn a proprietary authoring tool into a part of your CMS may require a lot of work. The application must at least enable you to add commands and custom dialog boxes (I hope through a complete and well-documented object model). In addition, it helps if the application has some sort of built-in programming language and some internal validation tools to help you ensure that components are created correctly. Without these additional tools in the authoring environment, you have considerable extra work to validate the components that authors create in the tool. By using built-in programming and validation, you can prevent the author from making entry mistakes while typing. If you use only programming that is external to the authoring tool, you can't detect a mistake until the author is finished and decides to save her work. At that time, you can be sure that she's not disposed to put in a lot more work to fix mistakes.

XML authoring tools offer the kind of programmability and validation that makes them good candidates for use with a CMS. In addition, many can be made to mimic a standard word-processing environment. With enough work, they can look and act like the environment with which many users are familiar. This seems to mean that you can have the structure and enforcement of XML delivered in a friendly environment that behaves like a standard word processor

Of course, no matter how much you make your XML tools look like those of a word processor, they're always going to be harder to use. Word processors are easy to use because they don't force you to follow rules. You're free in most cases to add whatever structure and formatting you'd like to your word processing files. XML processors, on the other hand, are hard because you need to follow the rules set out in the XML file's schema. Thus, no matter how friendly you make an XML environment, it frustrates an author who isn't prepared to create content in a structured way.

Showing components and elements

The nice thing about Web forms is that you have complete control over the representation of content types and their elements. The usual scenario is that you create one form per content type. On that form, each element is clearly marked with whatever interface represents the element and whatever instructions you have for the user about what to enter in the element. Other authoring environments are not as easy. A typical word processor, for example, gives you little you can use to represent the idea of components and elements to the author. The closest most can come is a loose mapping between paragraph styles and elements (a title style and an abstract style, for example, to represent the title and abstract elements). If you tell people not to use more than one component per word processing file (it is pretty hard to enforce this rule more automatically), you have an approximation of the control that Web forms offer you. Unfortunately, a user can consciously or unconsciously mess up a word processor file in all sorts of ways and cause it to not parse. The result is that you will likely do a lot of work to head off all the potential problems when you try to make a word processor represent and enforce components and elements.

Even XML editors don't have components and elements built in. In XML, components and elements are all just elements and attributes. You must add the logic and the user interface that separates one component from the next and represents the elements of the type you are authoring. For example, you could add code that picks out the XML fragment representing one component and takes care of loading it into your XML editor. Then you could add CSS code that puts a title before each component element (as opposed to each XML element) to show where the element boundaries are in the XML. Some XML editors actually help you with this process and effectively turn the XML environment into a Web (or client) form environment.

You want the idea of components and elements to pervade your authoring tools. You have two ways to handle it: You can make the environment represent components and elements, or you can teach your authors how to do the mapping in their minds. In my experience, neither is easy.

Automation

The key to working in an authoring tool is to be able to apply programming code to automate some tasks and prohibit some actions. For example, suppose your authors work in Word. Using the Word programming environment, you can add programming code that will remove the usual Save button and replace it with a custom Save command that actually saves the document the author is working on into the repository. Another custom command might bring up the component selector and paste in the right tags for a cross-reference (see the section in this chapter titled "Integrated search," for more on the component selector).

Many XML applications also provide a complete programming model to automate just about any part of the interface or processing. This capability is critical. With it, you can add any functionality that the product doesn't have built in and drive it toward a usable integrated part of your CMS.

I would say some level of automation of the authoring environment is mandatory if you expect to really integrate it with the CMS. Using the example of the autosave/submittal command, you might choose to let your authors create content in the outside tool and then just submit it to the CMS as a file. But in that case, you should probably expect to have a lot of work to do on the content after it arrives. Automation can generally save you some of this post-submission work.

Constrained entry

The key quality that makes an authoring tool part of a CMS is its capability to constrain the author and enable her to create only valid content. In an XML environment, for example, there may simply be no way to insert an element that isn't allowed. In addition, the application might be set up to disallow saving the file until all the authoring errors are corrected.

Word processing environments typically have few built-in constraints. They have made their mark on the world by being easy to use, not by being rigorous. In any case, the authoring environments you work with must guide the author toward valid content. By guide, I mean one of the following actions (in order of decreasing usefulness):

✦ Disallow incorrect entry in the first place.

✦ Alert the author of an incorrect entry as the mistake is made.

✦ Alert the author as she tries to save the component.

✦ Alert the author after the component is saved.

✦ Alert administrators sometime after the component is saved.

Tip   Don't get too carried away with constrained entry. Sometimes, it's worth the extra effort later to allow freely entered content now. A real killer combination is tight validation and the lack of ability to save invalid content. If you combine these two, you run the risk of leaving authors stranded with unsavable content that they have too little training or desire to fix.

It is mandatory to end up with valid content. It is only highly recommended to constrain the author so that she creates valid content from the start.

Integrated open and save

For the CMS to spawn an authoring application, the user must start from a CMS form or some other part of the CMS. From the author's standpoint, it's usually better to start from the chosen authoring tool and then call the CMS instead. This effectively turns the tables on the CMS. The author does her work from her chosen tool and accesses the CMS instead of working from the CMS and accessing her tool. The simplest way to achieve this sort of integration is to have the CMS control the Open and Save command of the application. The CMS may, for example, add two extra commands to the File menu (present in most Windows-based authoring tools):

✦ **Open From Repository:** This new Open command displays a dialog box that you (or your CMS) create. In fact, this dialog box might differ very little from the component selector that I described earlier. It contains an interface to all the access structures in the CMS repository. The user can navigate to the component that she wants to work on. The CMS can then take care of loading the component into the tool for editing.

✦ **Save To Repository:** Similarly, the new Save command can enable the user to return a component to the repository directly from her chosen application.

Some systems use Web Based Distributed Authoring and Versioning (WebDAV) to implement this connection to a Web-based CMS (you can find more on WebDAV in the section in this chapter titled "Support for WebDAV").

I would especially recommend integrated open and save when your authors are not particularly familiar with the CMS. Excuses like "I don't know the URL," or "I forgot," carry little merit when the command for saving to the CMS is right next to the one for saving to the local computer.

Integrated-input templating

Adding the Open and Save commands, as I outline here, effectively changes an authoring tool into an extension of the CMS. The two features, as I describe them, however, aren't sufficient to tie the two applications together. To complete the link, the CMS must have some way to project the rules of each content type into the authoring tool. I call the capability of a CMS to project rules in this way *integrated-input templating*. In some way, the CMS must create an input template in the authoring tool. An input template is usually associated with a Web-based form. There, it lays out the component elements that must be entered as a set of HTML form fields. It formats the fields (filling list fields with allowed values, pattern fields with the allowed patterns, and so on) and arranges all the fields on a form that's understandable and usable by the author. (For more information on fields, see Chapter 24, "Working with Metadata" in the section titled "Categorizing Metadata Fields.")

To integrate into an authoring tool, the CMS needs to do the same work in the context of the authoring tool. This can be a difficult but doable task. Essentially, the integration that you create must use whatever templating capabilities the chosen tool supports to represent the various kinds of element fields and validate the results. Microsoft Word, for example, includes a templating system that you access through document templates (Word's DOT files). The templating system consists of styles, standard text, Word's own input field system (with buttons, text boxes, and the like), and any amount of programming code that you care to write to augment the built-in features. Word has ample capabilities in its templating system to enable you to create a structured input system for most content types that you may want to create. It may require a fair amount of programming code, but it can usually be done. So, in addition to the Open and Save commands that a CMS adds to an authoring tool, it should also add a New Component command that enables the author to choose a content type and then be guided as she enters the elements of that type.

Many XML environments can also load schemas, custom UI, and programming code to allow you to change the way they behave, depending on what content type the author is working on.

With integrated-input templating, the custom-authoring tool really becomes part of the CMS. Of course, you can implement input templating more or less completely based on how tightly you want the authoring to be tied to the CMS and how much patience you have for patching all the holes in the connection as they turn up.

Integrated check in and check out

To increase the usefulness of the Open and Save commands that you may add to the authoring tool, these two commands ought to be connected to the CMS's access and versioning system. In other words:

✦ A user with no access rights to a particular component shouldn't be able to open it in her authoring tool.

✦ A user with read-only rights should be able to open it, but not save it.

✦ A user with read-write privileges should be able to edit the component unless another user's already opened it for editing.

Similarly, as the user saves a component to the repository, old versions should be saved, changes logged, and comments made per the versioning requirements for the particular type of component.

If you're going to bring a part of the CMS collection into an authoring tool, you might as well bring in all of it, including check in and check out. Otherwise, you will end up with content for which you can't enforce the rules that you've so carefully crafted.

Conversion System

Whereas authoring tools provide a way for authors to enter content into the CMS, conversion tools provide a way to modify existing content so that the CMS can use it.

Conversion tools digitize analog content and transform one format of digital content to another.

Cross-Reference I detail conversion processes and techniques in Chapter 39, "Building Management Systems" in the section titled "File systems." In this chapter I focus mostly on tools.

Digitizing tools vary from the simple to the complex. To digitize sound, animation or video, for example, you can plug an analog source (the tape deck or VCR) into your sound or video card in a desktop computer and use a simple application to record the source digitally. Media professionals use much more sophisticated equipment to perform essentially the same task with a lot more control and finesse. Similarly, a very inexpensive scanner connected to virtually any desktop computer can digitize print images. Add a simple Optical Character Recognition (OCR) program, and the same system can digitize text. Obviously, media professionals use more expensive scanners and more sophisticated OCR programs. But as time goes on, you can get closer and closer to professional-quality results with inexpensive, easy-to-use commercial tools.

What type of processes you decide to use for digitization depends on two factors: quantity and quality. As you may suspect, for low volumes and low-to-medium quality, the simple solutions suffice. For higher quantities and the best quality, you need more expensive equipment and professionals to run it. Interestingly, for all content other than text, the better your gear is, the better are the results. Because of the current limitations of OCR software, no matter how much you spend, your digitized text still needs to be reviewed by human editors.

Transformation tools take one digital format and change it into another. In transforming text, there are many options, and the results of the software may need a lot of manual effort by human editors before it's acceptable. The process involves conversion software that does its best to map the formatting and structure of the source to the destination. Sometimes, low-end converters are built right into the authoring application. Microsoft Word, for example, can convert DOC files to HTML by using the Save As command. Generally, aftermarket tools (such as HTML Transit from IntraNet Solutions) do a better job and offer many more options for how the transformation is done. Finally, text-manipulation programming languages (such as OmniMark from OmniMark Technologies and Perl, a nonproprietary language) enable you to write your own very specific transformations. If your source happens to be XML, you can use the Extensible Style Language Transforms (XSLT) in one of the variety of XML tools that are available. If, as is often the case, the automated transformation that you get from a tool isn't enough to ensure quality, you need custom programming to augment its capabilities.

When even your custom programs fail (which they commonly do) you must resort to a semi-manual process to complete the task. These semi-manual processes consist of visual inspection augmented by small productivity tools (custom search and replace scripts, for example) to finish the conversion job.

The hardware behind conversion depends mostly on the volume that you need to convert. Digitization and transformation, especially of nontextual content, requires a lot of computer storage and processing horsepower. A computer with multiple processors or multiple computers working simultaneously can reduce the time that it takes to convert large amounts of content dramatically. For even small amounts of nontextual content, you're likely to need a lot of hard drive storage. For one thing, you're likely to have a set of files that represent different stages of the process, some of which can be huge. In addition, you need a way to archive intermediate files so that, if you find a problem later, you don't need to repeat the entire process. Finally, you need a high-speed Local Area Network (LAN) or other efficient way to transfer content from the computers that do the conversion to those that house the repository where the content waits to be published.

For transforming textual content, the hardware required is low-end. For most text transformations, any computer serves. Although the kind of computer doesn't matter, the number of computers does. Large text transformation projects involve many people working simultaneously on the content base. It's not unusual to have 100 or more people working for a short time on a text transformation team in a large CMS effort. Thus, although you can get away with low-end computers, you may need a lot of them.

To understand conversion technology and process, you need to solidly understand a little vocabulary:

✦ The **source** or **input** is a file (or other portion of information) that you wish to convert.

✦ The **target**, **destination**, or **output** is the content component (or the part of the component) that you are trying to turn the source into.

Because a conversion process is partly software driven and partly process driven, the features of a conversion system are as much the qualities of a human process as they are attributes of some product. As you review the features of the conversion system, keep this idea in mind. You are not likely to find a product that gives you the features of the conversion *process* that you are looking for. More troubling to me is the fact that I have yet to see a product that looks at conversion in anything like the thorough way I present here. Most products that I know of focus solely on basic import. Granted basic import is a tough job, but as you can see, it is only the beginning of the task of conversion.

I won't go into detail here about how to construct conversion tools because that is covered in Chapter 37, "Processing Content."

The following subsections describe in detail the systems and features that you should consider for your conversion system. I describe each feature and also why you might need the feature in your system.

Basic import

The most basic form of conversion is a basic import where a receiving application is able to open, read, and convert the format of the source. For example, an image editor can open source files of any number of graphics formats. A word processor can usually open the text formats of all its major competitors. Basic import sounds simple, but it is not. The problem is that there may be no simple map between the structure and format of the source and that of the destination. So, even here you may have problems with automatic conversion and may have to rely on human judgment and effort.

Without basic import, you can't get started with the rest of the conversion process.

Mapping files to content types

Source files will very likely be unaware of your definition of content types and components. Given that the source files are *the source* of a certain type of content, you must convert the source files to components of that type. For example, suppose you are converting a set of HTML files (say from your existing Web site) for use with a CMS. Somehow you must specify which files (that is, which Web pages) give rise to which content types. You might, if you are lucky, be able to read the meta tags on the page to make an educated guess, or you can depend on the subdirectory structure or filenames to make the determination. More likely, these techniques might enable you to make a rough guess, and a human will have to make the final call as to which file maps to which content type.

Your system must be able to map files to content types when you have a variety of files that give rise to a variety of content types, as is the case when you are starting from Web pages or various stockpiles of word processing files.

Batch processing

Files often arrive in batches. It is quite useful to have your conversion tool deal with files in batches. For example, it could treat each file in a particular directory as the source for a particular content type. Here are some of the features that your own system or commercial systems can offer to batch process source files:

✦ **Convert a directory:** Many conversion tools allow you to specify a directory and convert all the files in that directory using a specified set of rules or mappings.

✦ **Harvesting pages from an existing site:** Some commercial CMS products enable you to encompass all the directories of existing sites quickly and make them part of your system. I've not seen a product that does this, however, in a way that really turns the pages of the site into components. Most simply treat the Web pages that you acquire as files that you can attach additional metadata to. Still, this is a useful feature for quickly bringing a large amount of published content into your system.

✦ **Drag and drop conversion:** Some systems allow you to drag (or otherwise move) a file into a directory. The system detects the new file and automatically converts it. This is a helpful feature if you require sources to deliver files to you by saving them in a particular directory, or if syndicated content arrives in a certain directory. Another form of this feature, which is not really a batch process, is a system that allows you to drop content into a Web form, at which point the system automatically converts it. Many rich-editing controls, for example, enable you to drop Microsoft Word content onto them that they then automatically convert it into HTML.

You require batch processing if you have ongoing needs to bring content into the system either through acquisition or syndication.

Integration with the aggregation system

You need aggregation to finish the process that conversion starts. (In other words, if you can convert source into 100% complete components, you don't do any aggregation.) Thus you need to implement a solid integration between conversion and aggregation systems. The boundary between these two systems is, in fact, usually blurred to the extent that they function as a single system. Metators, who deal with the results of conversion and whose chief task is to aggregate, are often the ones who run the conversion systems. Conversion programs try to automate as much of the aggregation as possible, so in most systems, the big question is not what is conversion and what is aggregation. Rather, the question is what is automated and what has to be done manually. I pull these two systems apart more for educational purposes than to make some point about their differences.

Because they are so tightly intertwined, always be sure that the conversion features that you implement are directly tied to aggregation features.

Process management

You are very lucky indeed if your conversion system consists of automatic conversion routines that fully parse and convert your entire variety of source files into all the content types you need with all their elements fully tagged. You are like the rest of us if your routines do what is possible automatically and your team does the rest. If you do need a team, either to get content into your system initially or to run it over the long term, then you need features in your conversion system that enable you to manage the team conversion process. I've seen process management worked out in spreadsheets, project management tools, and word processors. These platforms are really not up to the task. The best management processes I have seen used a Web site as the front end and a database system on the back end that enabled administrators to create the process and the staff to learn and do it.

Tip I have often used Microsoft Access for small database projects like this because it has a user interface that administrators can use directly. That frees developers from creating administrative forms and allows them to focus on the display of the process information for your staff.

Process definition

In a complex system of interrelated conversion tasks, it is extremely helpful to have some way to organize tasks into processes and to group processes into wider processes. I have seen most process definition tools. *Process definition* in my view includes these parts:

✦ **Defining individual tasks** that must be carried out, for example, the task of stripping out header and footer information and leaving behind only the source for a component in a file.

✦ **Defining the tools** that can be used for each task. For example, to strip headers and footers you may have an automated tool that includes a visual inspection feature or, when that is not appropriate, you may have a form into which you paste content from the source file. The definition, configuration, and use (help files and other use aids) of the tools can be managed using the process definition feature.

✦ **Stringing tasks together into processes.** For example, the basic conversion process may consist of a content type identification task, followed by the stripping task, followed by an element identification task. Processes can also be nested within other processes. So, for instance, the basic conversion process may be grouped with a QC process to create an overall conversion process. This part of the feature is quite a bit like workflow and can certainly leverage any workflow features that your CMS may have.

Overall, a process definition feature should allow you to take charge of the tasks that are part of the process and string them together to get the job done as you learn about and roll with the variability of the content you encounter. In addition to giving you control, the Process definition feature should let your staff know what the current state of the process is and where they get the tools to do it.

Process definition is a must when you have a large body of content to be converted and you need a lot of variations on a central process to deal with all the small differences between each batch of the content. In this case, the feature is an invaluable management tool. However, don't be too quick to implement it. Be sure that you have a process that is big and complex enough to warrant the effort.

Task assignment and load leveling

The process definition feature can be augmented with staff information so that, after they are defined, the processes and tasks can be divided up among the available staff members. Given that it was the size and variability of the conversion process that led you to create an official system, it should not be surprising that task assignment does not happen once but rather on an ongoing basis. This ongoing reassignment of staff to tasks is called *load leveling*. You want to be sure on an hour-to-hour basis that each staff member has neither too much nor too little work. In a typical scenario, you make a good guess about who should do what and how much.

Then, after a few hours of doing it that way, you see who is moving quickly through their tasks and who is not. Those who are fast can move on to other tasks, do more of the same, or had better start helping with the training tasks for the people who are a bit slower.

The size of the staff really drives the need for task assignment and load leveling. You can imagine that if you have a staff of 100 working around the clock to bring a lot of content into the system, you will need a real assignment and leveling feature. Otherwise, you may be able to get away with a zone approach (one person, one task) or even a free-for-all (do the next available task when you are ready).

Work queues

At the heart of any conversion process is the work queue that supplies programs and people with their work for the day. The essential features of a work queue that you need to handle in some way are:

✦ **Managing the pool of content to draw from:** You need to be able to see how much and what kinds of content are available for processing.

✦ **Allotting source:** You need to be able to assign source files to the people or programs that will accomplish those tasks.

✦ **Reallocating source:** As one person's queue empties and another's overflows, you need to be able to move source from one to the other.

✦ **Escalation handling:** Content processors need a way to pass source files that they don't know how to handle onto others with more experience. Others with more experience need to pass really tough source files on to the process manager to be sure these files are worth the effort to process.

✦ **End-user queue management:** At least as important as your ability to manage the queues of your processors is their ability to manage their own queues. They must see what they have, how much they have done, and then be able to put content "off to the side" and generally keep track of their tasks and content.

You need to create queues. How fancy you get with your queues is up to you. As you can see, the entire process management system can be quite a large endeavor to put together as an application. Take it in steps and be sure that each move you make toward comprehensive management is justified by the increase in the efficiency and effectiveness of the process.

Quality control (QC) and monitoring

In the world of conversion, neither people nor machines are as accurate in their work as you would like. For machines the problem is the inconsistency of the source files. For people the problem is usually lack of attention or training. In either case, a system for monitoring and remediating quality issues is a must for any large-scale conversion system.

Sampling content

The first feature of a QC system is a selection feature. This feature allows you to automatically get a representative sample of the content that has gone through some process. For example, you may want to get a representative sample of the content that has gone through an automatic stripping process to be sure that the right stuff has been left behind. The key word here is representative. Usually representative means random, but in the world of conversion there are a few trends that can help you be smarter than random in your choice of content to review. Here are some of the ways you can think about representation in your content sampling:

✦ **Represent all historical layers of the creation process:** To the extent that you can, group source files by when, who and how they were created. At each change of the creation process, the format and structure of the files may have changed. For example, after each Web site redesign, the format and structure of the product pages may have changed. Sample files at the beginning of each new regime to be sure that the rules you are converting by have not changed.

✦ **Represent shift changes:** Each time a new group of people comes in, sample a bit. People often take a little time to get into the conversion stride. You may also want to sample near the ends of shifts to account for fatigue and after lunch to account for the slump as blood goes from head to stomach.

✦ **Represent code releases:** Every time you release new or updated tools the chance of problems increases.

Of course, within these bounds it is always best to sample randomly. As you work through your process, other ways of getting representative content may occur to you.

In any QC process you must deal with sampling. You can either choose to get samples automatically or simply go into directories at certain times and pull out files to check.

Set and monitor rates

If you set your goal at 100% accuracy, you will be a very slow content factory. Even in food processing, some number of rat hairs is permitted in the Twinkie. Rather, you should set a reasonable accuracy rate that does not hold up the process but will ensure that your content is well-converted. In addition, as you become more confident that an automated process or a person is doing a good job, you can lower the rate at which you monitor the output.

The feature here is one that allows you to set monitoring rates from a central place and according to the rules that you have determined. For example, you may want to sample 1% of the output for the first 24 hours of a new tool and then, given 90% accuracy, slip to 0.1% thereafter. Or you may sample heavily for the first week of a person's time on a task and then tail off slowly over the weeks that follow. Finally, you may want to set your sampling rate based on failure rates. For example, as the error rate in a person's work increases (at whatever rate you may be sampling), you increase the sampling rate to be sure you stay ahead of the problem.

Monitoring rates is a feature that is really helpful when you have a large team and you need to set and monitor rates on people's work on an ongoing basis.

Bounce content

What do you do with sampled content that is not correct?

✦ You might send it back to the person who processed it.

✦ You might send it on from the automated tool output directory to a person to fix it.

✦ You might send it on to a programmer as a sample of what is going wrong with her program.

In any case you would do well to have a feature in your conversion system that allows you to route content that has been processed but needs more work to be acceptable.

You need some way of bouncing content, but you don't necessarily need to automate it with a lot of software. You may be able to derive this feature from your existing workflow system, or you may handle problems by simply dropping files in certain directories or even e-mailing them.

Deliver feedback and training on demand

You best defense against high error rates among human processors is to let them know what the right thing to do is. Given that your people are motivated, capable, and honest in their approach to their jobs (a set of hurdles you may very well not be getting over at the moment), errors can be mitigated by good feedback and instruction on how to avoid them in the future. The feature here is clear: Include feedback loops and training options right in the processing tools your staff uses. For example, suppose your processors are using a review and choose tool (as detailed in the next section in this chapter titled "Process and review tools"). At the bottom of their screen, you could display for them:

✦ Their current sampling rate.

✦ Their error rate.

✦ Average sampling and error rates in the team.

✦ Links to strategies to avoid the kinds of errors they are making.

The only obstacle is time and expense and being organized enough to have this information available. You may be able to cover the time and expense by the decrease in errors. If you have taken anything like the rigorous approach to conversion that I have presented, you are organized enough as well.

You should always provide feedback and training. You can do this manually or in the system that I propose, but do it one way or the other.

Process and review tools

If you can fully automate conversion, more power to you! Even if you cannot, you don't have to settle for a fully manual process. The space between automatic and manual is occupied by what I call process and review tools. These tools do as much automated processing as possible and then let a person review the result and change it as needed.

For example, suppose you have to convert 10,000 Web pages into 15 content types. You could try to write a giant program that does it all, or you could just turn the site over to 10 people and tell each to cut and paste from 1000 pages into one of 15 Web forms. Realizing that neither of these is a great option, you might try to develop a tool that:

✦ Opens each page of the site in turn.

✦ Tries simple techniques to decide what content type it might contain.

✦ If it can determine the type, the tool then tries to find and tag the elements.

✦ The tool presents the page to a processor in a user interface that allows her to accept the content type that the machine has chosen or choose another. If she chooses another, the machine reprocesses the page into the elements of the new type.

✦ The tool presents a form with the elements of the chosen content type. It fills in as much of the content of the elements as it is able to confidently collect.

✦ The tool presents the processor with easy tools to be able to move content around in the fields or bring in new content from the original page.

I've seen (and created) many variations on this model and know that it can save massive amounts of time if the tool can make more or less reasonable choices about content types and elements. Such a tool can save smaller amounts of time even if it simply helps make the process of opening and copying from files more efficient.

Set input and output directories

Your process and review tools should allow the user to point to a particular directory where source files are to be found. Each user can point to a separate directory and thus multiple people can work on a content base at the same time. You should also include the option for the tool to process all subdirectories of the chosen directory or just the files at the root.

This feature makes your tool much more flexible than it would be if the directory were hard coded or set in some initialization file.

Set rules

The trickiest part of a process and review tool is creating the set of rules that the tool uses to do its processing. Most often these rules are hard-coded into the tool because the tool was invented for a specific process. This is okay if you don't mind that the great review user interface you have created can be used for only one process. It is preferable to have the processing rules separate so that they can be loaded when needed to process a particular batch of content. Configurable rules are also important if you want the same tool to be able to do a wide set of content types.

If your process is an ongoing one, you eventually find yourself generalizing your process and review tool to load rules on demand. This happens because you get tired of rewriting the tool every time you have a new type of content to process.

Quick keys UI

Any tool that people have to use to move through a lot of information must have shortcuts. Quick keys such as Ctrl+C for copy and Ctrl+V for paste are just the tip of the iceberg for the efficacy you can add if you pay attention to how your teams work. In fact, any repeated process that takes more than one keystroke or mouse click (although, as veterans know, when you are moving fast, the keyboard rules over the mouse) is a possible target for a shortcut. As one example among many, consider this situation. The processor wants to strip the formatting out of a chunk of content from the source file and copy it to a particular element in the review form. She could click on the beginning of the chunk, select to its end, copy it, click on the element, paste it in, and then edit out the formatting. Or, she could right-click on the outermost tag within the chunk to be copied. The tool could then automatically select the text within that tag and pop up a menu listing all the elements on the review form. She clicks on the element she wants and the text is automatically stripped and copied. As an added bonus, the menu knows what element in the form she was last on and selects it automatically.

As you watch people use the tool, you will find that they will invent processing rules for you. Any time they do the same set of steps over and over, it means that they have found an automatable part of the process. You can use these repeated actions as the basis of new short cuts and later as new rules to be added to your processing routines.

Be careful! You can easily go overboard inventing efficiency features that save only a fraction of the time that they cost to implement.

Exception handling

In addition to dealing with the usual cases of process and review, you may want your tools to include ways to deal with unique cases. For example, what happens if a person encounters a file that does correspond to any of the content types that the tool is designed to handle? These exceptional cases have to go somewhere.

Basic exception handing, such as rogue source files, should surely be handled somehow. The rest of the integration may or may not be necessary.

Acquisition System

Whereas authoring systems provide authors a way to create content within the CMS, acquisition is the process of bringing content created outside the CMS into the CMS. I detail the acquisition process in Chapter 39, "Building Management Systems" in the section titled "Source Control System (Content and File Sharing)." In this chapter I focus on tools. Although for authoring there's a rich and varied world of tools in use, for acquisition few commercial tools are available.

The vast majority of tools that are in use to aid acquisition are small, custom-developed programs for identifying and retrieving files from some accessible source and placing them within the CMS file structure or repository. In a system that I worked on recently, for example, the custom acquisition system worked by retrieving files from various outside locations and wrapping them in a standard XML structure. The system had functions for the following tasks:

✦ **Prioritizing** the files as they were retrieved, depending on their location, source, and content type.

✦ **Validating** the tagging of files that had an XML format.

✦ **Filtering** input files based on a set of "stop" words or phrases that they may contain. Only the content that didn't include the "stop" words was allowed into the CMS repository.

✦ **Transforming** from one XML structure to another by using XSL, or into XML by calling the appropriate conversion program for the source.

The result of our work was a system that could take a diverse set of input files and transform them into a common structure (both the internal structure and the access metadata that ties them together) that could be held in the CMS repository and worked on as needed.

In addition to the variety of custom tools that you may encounter, some acquisition tools are provided by commercial CMS products. At least one tool I've seen, for example, enables you to acquire content from Web pages, FTP sites, or directories automatically. You set it up to look for new content in a particular location that fits a particular set of criteria. It scans the location periodically and retrieves the new content that matches the criteria you set. It can then call processing functions or start workflows to trigger further processing of the newly acquired content.

Finally, some commercial syndication services come with software that you can run to automate the retrieval and processing of the content that you receive from the service. One tool that I'm aware of gets installed on your Web server. The syndication service communicates with its software on your server on a regular basis to send you the exact kind and amount of content that you've purchased. CM products are also starting to become aware of the emerging standard around RSS (the most common translation of this is *Really Simple Syndication*). Some commercial systems and many more custom systems can receive and produce RSS-compliant XML.

Process and partner management

In acquisition, you need to create a smooth and effortless process for getting content from the source to your system. Much of this process is technology based, but some of it is not. In addition to the mechanics, you may need to track and manage the relationship you have with your supplier. If you have a variety of suppliers, that management can become the basis for an acquisition management feature. Many commercial syndication tools have this sort of feature. To change the type, frequency, detail, or delivery of the content you receive from a content vendor, you go to a form in their application and make your choices. The acquisition setup changes immediately (as does the fee you are charged for the service).

In noncommercial acquisition, where you receive content from partners or others in your organization, it may not be necessary or even possible to create such a sophisticated feature. However you may be able to do some of the following simpler things to make your acquisition process smoother:

✦ You might create a spreadsheet or database that has the definitive list of sources and their attributes. The attributes can be facts such as the source owner, the person to escalate issues to, the frequency of delivery, the delivery format and location, expected quantities, and expected subject matter.

✦ You might create reserved network shares, FTP sites, and Web folders that are the standard receiving areas for incoming content.

✦ You can establish file- and directory-naming conventions that reflect the source and processing stage of content you receive.

✦ You can establish standard partner agreements for acquired content that both standardize your approach to acquired content and establish credibility with your partners, assuring them that you are organized and serious about the relationship.

Although managing partners and processes is more procedural than programming, it can do as much as any software function to make acquisition as easy as possible.

If you have few and simple content sources, you can probably get away with doing process management in the same casual way that most systems do it. But as the volume and complexity increases, you may find it more and more important to implement this feature.

Rights and usage

If you need to track usage and payment for some of the content that you don't own, you may have some extra work to do. I haven't seen much significant functionality in commercial products for rights management. Rather, this functionality is usually found in Digital Asset Management (DAM) applications and in custom code that you write yourself.

A reasonable system for including this important functionality in a CMS includes the following:

✦ **Metadata:** The content types for content with rights restrictions need extra management elements that code the restrictions as retrievable data. You may create elements for price per usage and standard attribution, for example, for the components for which you need to track payment.

✦ **Template logic:** Usage logging and restrictions can be implemented effectively in publication template logic. If you need to increment a payment counter every time that a particular component displays on a Web site, for example, you can do so by putting some code in its component templates. This code runs every time that the component is displayed and can increment a counter in a database on your Web server.

✦ **Personalization rules:** Usage restrictions can be treated like personalization rules. Suppose, for example, that you don't want to show paid content to the general public but only to registered members on your site. To do so, you can treat this access restriction as just another rule that you code into your personalization system.

✦ **Reporting:** You may need the system to report usage back to you. If so, the CMS may be capable of keeping statistics on component usage and presenting them to you as formatted reports. On the other hand, you may need to depend on site logs and commercial or custom reporting applications to get the information that you need.

Obviously you must track rights and usage when you have content that contractually requires it. However, if you think about the issue in a wider sense, you may want to begin to implement this feature as a step toward securing content or personalizing it.

Attribution management

Attribution means saying who wrote or owns a piece of content in your publications. I detail the process of attribution in Chapter 29, "Accounting for Acquisition Sources" in the section titled "Attribution and rights." If you have taken the time to figure out your approach to attribution, you realize that it is no simple matter to deal with attribution for acquired content. An attribution management feature in your acquisition system can help you deal with the complexity. The feature might allow you to:

✦ Define, list, and refine authorship and attribution rules.

✦ Automatically apply these rules to incoming content.

✦ Tie into your workflow or process and partner management feature when ambiguous or exceptional content arrives.

An attribution management feature may be coded directly into your other acquisition software, may be implemented as a separate set of scripts that run against acquired content, or may simply be a process to be followed by metators rather than by software.

Attribution management is likely to be low on your list unless you have a robust attribution model and sources that have ambiguous authorship.

Acquiring database records

Your logical design may call for you to retrieve records from a database automatically and turn them into content components in your repository. With a little effort, you can usually make these downloads happen periodically with no human intervention. It's unlikely that your commercial system has a user interface to handle these downloads, so you're probably going to program them yourself.

The connection

To get content from a database you must be able to connect to it (meaning find it and open it programmatically). To start with, some network connection must exist between your CMS and the database (LAN, WAN, Internet, and so on). Then you need to be able to reach across that network with your programs to actually form the connection. For example, you might:

✦ Simply use the directory and filename of the database to open it. This is the most direct way to access the database, but it could break if the database is moved.

✦ Use a globally defined name, known on your network to access the database. This sort of name is designed to make the database accessible, in general, throughout the network without having to know specifically where it is located.

✦ Use an intermediary program that evaluates your request to open the database and does it for you. This sort of intermediary is designed to protect the database from being directly manipulated by you.

✦ Use intermediary people to connect to the database. In other words, your requests for information from the database do not go to the database, but to the database administrators. This situation occurs quite frequently when the database owners do not want you anywhere near the database.

So you may have anything from a very direct way to no way at all to connect to the database from which you want content. In the case in which you have no connection and must go through a database administrator, you will still be in fine shape as long as the administrator is conscientious and can be relied on to give you what you want. The administrator will likely want to give you a report with the information you requested; that is the usual approach. A better approach would be to establish an intermediate database. The administrator adds records from the source database periodically, and you connect to the intermediate database as needed to capture the new records that have been added. In this way you turn no connection into a direct connection, although you still depend on the administrator for the updates.

You always need some way to connect to the source database.

The query

You get data out of databases with queries. One or a very few queries against the source database should net you the data that you need. Your queries should be able to accomplish the following tasks for you:

✦ Return only the fields that you want from the source database.

✦ Combine fields from a variety of tables into a single set of returned records.

✦ Set the conditions for the records that will be returned (after a certain date, only those of a certain type, and so on).

✦ Sort the records by whatever alphabetic or numeric field you want.

If you are careful in the way you construct your queries, you may be able not only to acquire, but also begin to map the data in the source to what you need.

You will always need some way to query the source data (even if it is only through the database administrator).

The map

You need to create and code a mapping between the rows and columns of data that you retrieve from the source and the components and elements that they create. This mapping follows the same constraints as the mapping that I discuss for conversion (see Chapter 37, "Processing Content," in the section titled "Getting to the Core of Content Mechanics," for details).

You will be lucky indeed if you don't need to include this feature because all the fields of the database records that you acquire match all of the elements of the components you are creating. But don't count on it. If you are getting the bulk of the content for a content type from a particular database structure, rather than asking "How can I map the database structure to my component elements?" you might better ask "How can I change the elements in my component so that the least mapping is necessary?" In other words, bring the mountain to Mohammad.

The exception process

You need to decide what actions to take if your connection, query, or mapping yields an error or finds a situation that isn't covered in the code that you wrote. You certainly need to log the exception. In addition, you want to:

✦ Decide whether it's serious enough to end the entire process or whether the process can continue.

✦ Decide what to do with the content that has already been processed. Is it sound or should it be reprocessed or at least reviewed?

✦ Decide whether and how to resolve the error using an administrator, programmer, or a manager to contact the source owner. In any case, some sort of workflow must be initiated to trigger the appropriate action.

If an exception can cause significant loss of productivity (if, for example, a team cannot begin its work when the acquisition script crashes) or if you know your acquisition process to be flaky, it will be worth your while to implement an exception-handling feature.

Acquiring Web site content

One situation that may arise is that a source gives you a Web address (a URL) and says that the content to be processed is all the files at that URL. Given the general disorganization of most Web sites, it's debatable whether it's worth trying to parse Web sites automatically to acquire their content. Look closely at how regular and parsable the site is before trying to do any sort of automated process.

Some CM products ship with a feature that imports an existing Web site. However, this feature is usually no more than a tool for bringing the HTML files of the site into the CMS whole, with no conversion or aggregation at all. I'm not sure what you are supposed to do with these files after they are in the CMS except what you might have done in the first place: an in-depth content analysis resulting in a complex process for bringing the pages over one at time into your predefined content types.

Dealing with dynamic pages

If pages are built dynamically on the site you are acquiring, must you get every possible version of every page? Maybe, maybe not. Before even asking this question, step back one level and study the data sources behind the site. Why convert HTML files if you can acquire the content from a database instead? If indeed the site is built from a database and the database contains all you need to create the content components you want, then just skip the site and acquire from the database. Unfortunately, the site may contain the following things that the database does not:

✦ The source for access structures such as the site hierarchy and sequences.

✦ Pages built by complex combinations of database content.

✦ Hand-entered content on pages that is needed in addition to the database content.

Most dynamic sites are a combination of database (or XML) content and hand-entered content. Only the most advanced sites (like the ones from a CMS) are built entirely from data sources.

In the case of a dynamic site, your best bet is to develop a feature that allows you to partly acquire from the data source for the site and partly from the site itself.

Tip　It might be worth your while to look into the code that creates the site, as well as into the data that creates the site. For example, if the site combines data in sophisticated ways to create content or navigation, small changes to that code might allow you to create the components or access structures you need in the same way.

Dealing with orphaned pages

Are there pages on the site you are trying to acquire that aren't linked to any others on the site? If so, how do you find them? Suppose, for example, that a branch of pages is not stored in the same directory as the other pages and can be accessed only from a link that was sent out via e-mail but never linked to any other pages on the site. (I could never have made up this example; it actually once happened to my team.)

Although this is an extreme example, less drastic cases of pages that are hard to find on sites happen all the time. Third-party programs that let you spider your way through a site following every link usually nets most of the pages. However, you may have to augment these programs with your own that enables you to follow links that are indirectly coded. For example, the following HTML code creates a link to a pop-up window without using standard link nomenclature, and thus would be invisible to a standard spider tool:

```
javascript:disWin('popup2974','300','300'
```

A careful study of the site you are trying to acquire reveals most of the ways that the site links to other pages outside its usual directories and points you to the right way to implement or augment a spidering feature.

The older the site, the more you must consider how to find all its pieces because the more likely things will have moved, been updated, or deleted. Also, if your source site has changed ownership a lot, and especially if it is a conglomeration of many smaller sites, you can be sure you will be troubled by orphaned pages and you must have some feature in your acquisition system to deal with them.

Dealing with old or redundant pages

As you bring pages across from an existing site to your CMS, how can you tell whether a page is a duplicate that someone forgot to take off the site? Even if you can tell which pages are duplicates, which is the master? Most Web sites are like the midden heaps of ancient cultures; they contain layers of refuse that reflect the history of the site more than its present condition. How do you separate out the truly necessary pieces?

At the very least, you should get the active participation of a person who can help you untangle a Web site. More reasonably, the contributor should go through it once and clear it all out before handing it over to you. Of course, if the contributor has no clue what's on the site, she's of little help untangling it. Another possibility is to use your own trusted staff to untangle a source of content, but to charge the cost of doing so back to the contributor.

The following list describes some features you may want to implement in your site conversion suite to help you through the tangle:

✦ **Directory search:** Be sure to get yourself a good tool that lets you search for regular phrases through a set of directories and subdirectories. This sort of tool will be invaluable when you know you have seen that phrase somewhere.

✦ **File comparison:** You want to be able to definitively say what the differences are between two similar versions of the same content. Find a good freeware comparator, or use the one that ships with Microsoft Word—if all else fails.

✦ **File and directory name comparison:** In the absence of any tools for versioning, people often rely on the names of files and directories to encode the versioning that they have done. If the two files or directories that represent two versions of the same content do not happen to be next to each other, the name variations may be hard to see. You may find it helpful to use the directory search feature included in your operating system (the big Search button in Windows Explorer) to put all the files and directories on the site into one big list (search for *.* in Windows). Then you can sort this list by name to see many of the directory and filename variations, or by date to begin to chart the history of the site.

Your best tool to help you sort out a tangled site may be to simply ask around. Most Webmasters are smart enough to document, or scared enough to remember the major times that they reorganized, archived, duplicated, or otherwise drastically complicated their sites. If you can find them, you may be surprised just how much they know about the complexity they or their predecessors created.

As with orphaned pages, it is the old, multi-owner, and conglomerated sites that require you to implement the most robust detangling features.

Aggregation System

When you've authored, converted, and acquired all your content, your collection system needs to provide tools for preparing it for your content repository. These tools are part of the aggregation system.

Aggregation tools bring authored or acquired content in sync with the content that you already have in your repository. In the authoring, acquisition, and conversions systems, the content model that you have created is applied as completely as possible to the content you are collecting. Whatever metadata and structuring work remains to be completed is done in the aggregation system.

Cross-Reference   I fully detail the aggregation process in Chapter 7, "Introducing the Major Parts of a CMS" in the section titled "Aggregating." In this chapter, I focus on tools.

Aggregation involves editorial processing, segmentation, and metatorial processing. The main tool in the editorial process is the mind of the editor. Editing is generally a manual process and requires little more than a computer that can display and enable you to edit the content types you have. For large efforts, it's the number of computers (that is, the number of editors working simultaneously), not the kind, that matters most. On the other hand, if the editor can identify tasks that she performs repeatedly, programmers can quickly create small single-purpose tools to help. If, for example, an editor needs to change all special characters (trademark symbols and em-dashes, for example) to their ASCII equivalents, she can get a programmer to write a quick processing script that does the translation and then reports back on how many of each were found. Over time, an arsenal of such tools can make editors much more efficient.

Segmentation and metatorial processing can be manual or automated tasks, depending on how regular and structured the source content is. If the source content is XML that already has most of the tagging you need, for example, it's fairly easy to write a processing script that picks out the component chunks and metadata that are already there. On the other hand, if the source content consists of word processing files or Web pages, where the content chunks are poorly marked and there's little or no metadata to pick out, people must go through the content manually to find the appropriate content chunks or simply deduce the correct metadata for the chunks. Just as in the case of editorial processing, even if the overall process is manual, there's ample room for productivity tools.

A programmer may quickly create a tool that metators can use, for example, to apply metadata to HTML files content. The program may have its own window where content is presented and worked on by a metator. It could work as follows: The program brings up the HTML code of a particular page to be processed in its custom window. The metator first selects the appropriate part of the Web page being displayed and then presses Ctrl+A. The program then extracts the selected text and presents a screen on which the metator can select the values of the metadata attributes for that type of content. After the metator clicks the OK button, the program saves the segmented and tagged content in a database and opens the next HTML file to be processed.

Many of the advanced metadata management tools that you may want to include in your system need to be custom-developed because most commercial CMS systems don't yet include them. As part of your aggregation system, consider how you may acquire, share, and manage metadata.

Automatically applied metadata

You may want to apply metadata values automatically to incoming content based on its type or location. A range of products (within CMS offerings or sold standalone) are on the market today that help you detect, extract, or apply metadata. In addition, you can build metadata detection and application features into your system. Here are some of the features you might attempt to build or buy:

✦ Choose a directory of files or a set of components in your system and batch-apply a metadata value. Usually, a simple script in a language such as Perl or in any other scripting language is enough to process directories full of files and attach appropriate metadata to them. Often the batch metadata script is made part of a wider processing program. But this needn't be the only way that batch metadata is applied. Sometimes batch metadata scripts add the metadata directly to the file so that it's picked up later after the files are processed fully. Sometimes the outcome of these scripts is to create and partially populate components in the repository. Later, the other parts of the components are added to the repository during the normal processing of these components.

✦ Supply default values for metadata fields based on content type, other metadata, or more complex rules.

✦ Process through a set of files and pick out ambiguously marked metadata based on rules that you construct.

✦ Try to deduce the subject of a file based on a linguistic analysis of its words. The best of these tools allow a metator to review the choices made and can even "learn" from the choices that the metator makes.

✦ Try to create an abstract or summary from the content of a file.

✦ Try to autogenerate a taxonomy of concepts or even a thesaurus (a taxonomy plus cross-references between terms) from a body of files.

All of these tools work best on simple, easy to interpret content — just the content you need them least for. Still, if you have a lot of tagging to do, they can boost your productivity a lot.

You would normally go through the effort of implementing an automatic metadata application feature in conjunction with an acquisition process that moves through hundreds of files at a time.

Metadata standards support

The Dublin Core Metadata Initiative (`http://dublincore.org`), RSS, and a host of other industry-specific metadata systems are being created and revised today. If you want to use one of these standards it would be good to have help from your aggregation system. Help might mean any of the following things:

✦ Not forcing you to use particular tag names for certain elements (forcing a tag name for the unique id is not unheard of).

✦ Allowing you to use multiple schemas to validate parts of your content. For example, it would be good to use the Dublin Core approved schemas to validate the form for the Dublin Core metadata that you use.

✦ Actually incorporating the standards. For example, when you create a new content type, it would be nice to have the option of using the Dublin Core element set by default.

✦ Being able to recognize and automatically map incoming standards to your elements. For example, if you receive RSS into your system, you might like the system to already know how to map it to your particular component elements.

Generally, commercial products neither prevent nor help you incorporate standards into your system. In addition, it is more usual to see metadata standards applied at publication time to create syndications, than at collection time to aggregate content.

If you do a lot of syndication into or out of your system, you may want implement support for standards into your system. On the other hand, if you don't share content with others, there's little reason to bother implementing standards.

Workflow triggers

Your aggregation system ought to be able to trigger and be triggered by actions in the CMS. For example, if a metator sees the need for a revision to a metadata list while tagging, she ought to be able to trigger the review workflow. On the other hand, when a review of the metadata list indicates that one value must be split into two values, she ought to be able to trigger a workflow that puts the items that need to be split into the work queue of a metator.

Some level of integration between the aggregation and workflow system is essential; just creating the right set of workflows and having the workflow UI available to metators may be enough. But if you really want to encourage them to use the workflow system, you may want an interface that includes the right shortcuts to trigger actions in the workflow system.

Segmentation

Segmentation is the process of breaking up content into the content components that your CMS needs to work with. (For more about the purpose of segmentation in the collection system, see Chapter 7, "Introducing the Major Parts of a CMS" in the section titled "The Collection System.") It, like editing, is a human task that can be made easier by tools that your CMS can provide.

Separating components from surrounds

Given that you may not know how many components each acquired source file might yield, you will need to isolate each component within the source file and separate it from the rest of the file.

For example, suppose you are a government agency and your CMS needs to deliver business licensing regulations and procedures. Presently one big word processing document lists all 200 procedures and 70 regulations. The first major job of your conversion or aggregation system is to isolate the 270 different parts of the document that lead to 270 separate components.

Similarly, when you are bringing an existing Web site into a CMS, you need to figure out how the component on that page can be found and extracted from the surrounding page branding, layout, and navigation.

Whenever you acquire content, you always need to parse out individual components. How complicated this is to accomplish depends entirely on how intertwined your components are with each other and with their noncomponent surroundings in the source.

Finding elements

To begin segmentation, you first separate out each component that the source content gives rise to. Next you need to separate each of the elements that comprise the component. For example, suppose the "Regulation" content type has a title, number, date of institution, summary, and body elements. After you have isolated a regulation component in your source file, your next step is to isolate and tag each of these elements. It is likely that each of the elements is currently surrounded by formatting (which, by the way, may be the only clue you have to locating the element). As you locate elements within components, the formatting that surrounds the elements must be separated and discarded. For example, the title element may be surrounded in the source by the formatting tags for bold, centered, and large font. This formatting is no longer needed and can be discarded, as shown in the following code. The first line shows the title as it may be represented in HTML in a source file, and the second line shows how the element might be represented in XML after the conversion.

```
<center><b><font size="+5">This is the Title</font></b></center>
<Title>This is the Title</Title>
```

This is a simple example. Automatically identifying elements — reliably separating the wheat from the chaff — can be relatively simple or not simple at all, depending on how complex and systematic the source content is.

When you acquire content, you always need to find and segment elements, and it will not always be easy.

Finding access structures

Access structures are the hierarchies, indexes, cross-references, and content sequences that tie content components together (see Chapter 30, "Designing Content Access Structures"). In addition to pulling content out of the source material you acquire, you probably need to pull out the metadata to include the components you create in the access structures you have devised. For example:

✦ **Hierarchies:** When you aggregate the pages of a Web site, the directory structure that the pages come from may give you what you need to include them in a subject hierarchy in your CMS.

✦ **Indexes:** As you come across author names in the source files, you may want to match them against an author index. If the author already exists, you replace the name with an Id for that author. If the author does not already exist, you add that person to the author index, generate an Id, and replace the author's name with the Id.

✦ **Cross-references:** Hyperlinks in the Web pages you aggregate become cross-references to other components or to sites external to the CMS.

✦ **Sequences:** As you are converting a sequence of items in a word processing file to the corresponding components, you may want to preserve their sequence by adding them to a CMS-maintained component sequence.

Although it may be critical to create access structures as well as components, it is not often easy. The mapping between the Web directory structure and your component subject hierarchy may not be direct, author names may have several variants, you may not be able to match page hyperlinks easily to specific components, and you may not know how to fit the sequence of items in one file to the sequences in others. You need a combination of subtle programming and substantial personnel to migrate and change the vaguely specified access structures in the source to rigorously specified access structures in the CMS.

Content sources almost always contain useful information that could give rise to access structures, but it may be difficult to get at it. You may get help extracting it from metadata extraction tools, but don't count on it. Your main question in designing the features to extract access structures is, "Given the availability of access structure information in the source, is it worth the effort to try and pull it out?"

Editorial processing

To have any hope of having content from a variety of sources and authors appear unified in the publications that combine it, you need some sort of editorial system. (I discuss the editorial process in Chapter 7, "Introducing the Major Parts of a CMS" in the section titled "Editorial processing.") To have some hope of keeping the editorial process under control in a large CMS, you may well want to create features that enhance your ability to head off editorial issues if possible, or to triage them quickly if you can't head them off.

Revision tracking

Most modern word processors work as follows. As you revise your document, the equivalent of a table of revisions is created. Each row in the table is a change. The last change you made is the last row in the table. Rather than actually changing the document definitively, the word processor creates what you see on the screen by reading through the table and showing the final state of the document based on all the changes you have made. For example, when you delete a word, the word is not actually deleted, but rather an entry in the table is made saying that the word was deleted. In effect, the word is still there, but not displaying. This general mechanism, as you can imagine, underlies the unlimited undo capability of word processors. When you close the document, the changes generally do become real and all the deleted words and other changes actually get made and are irreversible.

The same sort of process underlies the word processor's capability to keep track of complex interacting revisions made by a number of separate reviewers. However, when you close the document, the tracked revisions are preserved. Only when you accept the revisions are the changes actually made.

Although most locations in which you can type text in a CMS have some form of undo functionality, almost none have revision tracking. What is generally substituted for revision tracking is version tracking. If the version tracking is very good, an audit trail of changes is preserved (so you can undo them), but the trail is not visible as it is in a word processor, and you can't selectively accept one change and not another.

So most people who need this level of revision tracking keep their components in a word processor during the phase of their creation where they are heavily reviewed, and then move the components out of the word processor when they are essentially done.

If you are tempted to go ahead and implement a revision system yourself, say using XML, I would suggest that you really study the system in the word processor that your authors use first. Your studies will show you exactly how sophisticated revision tracking is and how difficult it will be to reproduce the functionality yourself. Your authors will compare you to the system they are used to, and they will not be happy if you end up far short of it.

You need revision tracking when two or more people need to collaborate on the initial creation of content, and they need to have specific and prolonged asynchronous conversations about their work. Because this feature is so strong and well known in word processors, I would suggest you make best use of it there rather than trying to reproduce it yourself.

Commentary

As you are no doubt familiar with from using modern word processors, it is really helpful for an editor to be able to annotate text to give feedback or instructions to authors. Unless you are using a word processor to author, however, you may get far less than you expect out of most CM systems in this regard. On the other hand, if you are using a word processor, the comments that an editor makes are inaccessible because they are stuck within the documents that are commented on. Consider these commenting features when building or buying your CMS:

✦ You should certainly be able to attach a non-publishing comment to a component. This could be implemented as no more than a comment element as a standard part of each content type.

✦ You might allow comments on an element-by-element basis so that, for example, you can comment on the title separately from the abstract of a component. To implement this feature, you might create a separate comment structure that points to a component and element for each comment logged, or you can embed the comments within the element that they refer to.

✦ You can allow attribution of comments to their authors by allowing the author to type her name in, or by noticing who is logged into the CMS and automatically assigning her to the comment.

✦ You can aggregate comments for reporting and management purposes. For example, you might create a report that tells you what comments have been made on the components created by a particular author to help you evaluate her overall work. Better, you can use this feature to let the author see all the comments logged for her components so she can evaluate her own work.

✦ You can use a robust comment feature to allow audiences to comment on components as well, and then you can supply that information to authors and administrators.

✦ Comments can trigger workflow. So for example, a comment with the words "legal review" can automatically route the component into the legal review work queue.

These are just a few examples, and you may think of many other ways to create and use comment in a CMS.

You will undoubtedly want some means of commenting in your system. If you have a commercial system, it may very well include some of the commenting features I mentioned. If it does not or you are building your own system, creating robust commenting will likely reward the effort.

Component reuse

Editors have the unenviable job of making sure that the language used in a component will make sense wherever it is displayed. For example, the same paragraph may end up in a sidebar on a Web page, a printed brochure, and as the summary for a detailed description for a job announcement. Any tools you can offer an editor to help her know about and preview the various places a component may land help assure that she can meet this huge challenge. Here are various features, from easier to harder, you can provide to help editors:

✦ You can simply tell the editors, in general, how each publication is built from component types. Although not providing any specific guidance, this at least lets the editor know what to look out for in an overall sense.

✦ You can provide diagrams and simplified template logic that show in detail how pages are built from content. With these, the editor ought to be able to form a clear idea of how components are reused.

✦ You provide the sort of component preview that I described for authors (see the section in this chapter titled "Publication preview").

✦ You can provide a higher view of the reuse of components. This view would show the flow of content (both whole components and single elements) from the repository to the publications. The editor would be able to see at a high level or in detail exactly what content types and elements are used where. She would get much more out of this feature than a simple preview; she would get a dynamic tool for charting content reuse. Of course, were such a feature available, it would be of interest to others besides editors. Publication designers, content architects, and metators would also use such a feature to chart and understand, and maybe even plan content reuse in the CMS. On the other hand, such a feature would be very hard to implement. It would require you to somehow run, analyze, and graphically display the results of all the code that is inside your publication templates.

Most editors do not even have an adequate explanation of how content is reused, so any help you can offer in this regard is valuable.

Language variants

Language variants are the various forms of wording that you manipulate as content moves from one publication use to another. For example, consider the following sentence:

```
As I mentioned earlier...
```

If you can be sure that the earlier material will be published with the sentence, you are fine. But what if you cannot?

Cross-Reference I deal with the concept of language variants in more depth in Chapter 26, "Designing Publications," in the section titled "Publication gotchas."

A feature that accounts for language variants might:

✦ Allow the variants to be added as special tags within a body of text. In the case where the variants are associated with another chunk of text (for example the "earlier" text), some identifier for the referenced text must be in the tag as well so that its presence or absence can be determined.

✦ Automatically flag troubling words like "earlier " and "later" so that the editor is sure to see them.

✦ Render the language variants automatically in whatever publication the text appears in. For example, the phrase "As I mentioned earlier" might be removed and the next word capitalized when the earlier material is not present.

✦ The system might go beyond phrases and allow paragraph variants. For example, you might have one introduction to an article that is written for lay people and another that is written for professionals. The two variants can be side by side in the authored text, and only one would be selected at publication time based on the use to which the component is put.

Depending on the amount and depth of reuse you want to support, language variants may be an important feature. If you don't want to deal with this sort of feature, you might be able to deal with the issue editorially by telling your authors to write in a general way—for example, by never referring to later or earlier material.

Metatorial processing

Metatorial processing, as you may recall, comprises the tools and techniques you use to apply metadata to the components that you author or acquire. (You can find more on metatorial processing in Chapter 7, "Introducing the Major Parts of a CMS" in the section titled "Metatorial processing.") Being able to apply metadata, in turn, depends on having good metadata lists to apply. (You can find lots of information about metadata lists in Chapter 24, "Working with Metadata.") Thus, the features around metatorial processing concern both the creation of metadata lists (taxonomies, thesauri, indexes, sequences, and so on) and their application to components.

Importing metadata lists

You may need to pull metadata lists from other sources, such as a database or flat files, to include them in your system. Suppose, for example, that you want to keep your system synchronized with a product taxonomy (outline) that isn't owned by your group. From the CMS standpoint, the product taxonomy is a closed hierarchical list. It supplies the allowed values for a component management element, possibly called Product, that appears within a number of content types—content types that are, in some way, related to products.

To work this connection, you may arrange with the owner of the taxonomy to receive an updated version of the taxonomy quarterly. The update arrives in the database (or possibly spreadsheet) file in which the owner stores it. The owner agrees to give you three weeks' extra notice if she makes any significant changes to the way that she stores the taxonomy (if she adds new columns or changes others, for example). To actually retrieve the list, you would use the same sort of connection, query, and mapping as I discussed for database acquisition (see the section in this chapter titled "Acquiring database records").

In addition to periodically reacquiring the metadata list, you need a lot of other features to be sure that the new taxonomy can be merged with your existing content. For example, suppose you want to have a product taxonomy in your system, and you periodically get a new cut of it from the product group. You need some feature that lets you compare the new taxonomy to the older one, noting additions, updates, or deletions. The feature would collect information about the additions (new products added to the taxonomy) and pass it to a product review workflow. This feature would trigger the first step in this workflow and supply it with the names and descriptions of the new products that were added. The first actor in the workflow can then perform her tasks of figuring out what to do with the new products and trigger the step following hers. The updates and deletions create their own workflows. Updates are sent to the owners of all the components in which updated products are referenced. The owners are required to check and update their components as needed to complete the workflow. For deletions, an automated script is run to set the status of any component that references a deleted product. The Status element is set to Deleted Product, and a review workflow is triggered for the component's owner. As you can imagine, updates to the product taxonomy may trigger quite a lot of work for the CMS staff. (That's why, in this example, the owner must provide three week's notice of changes.)

The CMS should work within the wider world of the organization as much as possible. If the lists you need (product taxonomies, department hierarchies, and so on) are owned outside the CMS, you need some feature to manage the integration. If you have such a feature, you can encourage others to take ownership of the lists that you may now manage for them.

Exporting metadata lists

Exporting metadata can be just as hard as importing it. Suppose, for example, that your CMS does such a good job of maintaining the product taxonomy that the organization agrees to give ownership of the master taxonomy to the CMS group (you may or may not want this to happen). The CMS group, however, must provide quarterly updates to the original owners so that they can still use the taxonomy for their data systems. Now the tables are turned, and the CMS must run the taxonomy import program in reverse. Instead of mapping from the original format to the CMS representation, it must map from the CMS system back to the original format. In addition, rather than triggering a lot of workflow, you collect the results of any workflow that produced a change to the taxonomy. You might summarize the changes that you made to facilitate the use of the taxonomy by the original owners. Given the complexity of both the import and export processes, you can imagine that a program that imports or exports a metadata list requires a lot of maintenance work to keep things synchronized.

You ought to be prepared to supply metadata lists to others in the organization who need them. How far you go in mapping and summarizing changes is for you to decide and may vary widely, depending on your needs.

List creation and editing

Metadata lists are any kind of ordered presentation of metadata values. For example, a hierarchy into which you categorize components (often called a taxonomy) is a metadata list. An index of author names that you use to fill the author element of components is a metadata list. If you are serious about having metadata lists within your CMS, you have to buy or create the features that allow you to create and manage them. Although CMS commercial products have only very basic metadata creation and editing facilities, a reasonable variety of standalone tools can help considerably in this area. Creation features you might build or buy include:

✦ Viewing your hierarchies in a tree view in which you can drag and drop items to rearrange them. In addition, you should easily be able to delete, rename, promote, and demote items in the list.

✦ Sorting your lists alphabetically, by the number of components that include the value, by creation date or by other meta-metadata (metadata about metadata) values that you choose. Obviously, the feature should also allow you to easily remove or rename values as well.

✦ Enabling you to canvass, collect, and negotiate among the opinions about changes you are proposing. Depending on who the stakeholders in a list might be and how stuck they are on the words you now use, this small concern could turn into a very large feature.

The point of your list creation and editing feature is to ensure that, as you learn more about the way your content should be tagged, you can modify the lists that you tag from.

As long as your lists are not stored in some proprietary format (and they usually are not) you can usually find them and edit them by hand. This may be sufficient if your lists are not large and changing. If they are large and changing, consider building or buying tools that allow you to edit them quickly and safely.

List review

As part of managing your metadata system, you may need to periodically review the validity of lists of values and either update or delete them. As you do, it would be nice to have a tool that helps you update all the content that's affected by the change that you're making. As determined by your metadata review workflows, you'd want to retrieve a metadata list and review it periodically or find all components with a particular metadata value and review them. You may want to review your list of contributors, for example, to add, update, lump, and split values as needed.

For this kind of feature, you need a simple interface in which actions are available to work on the items of your metadata list. These actions are the usual editorial needs: add, delete, update, merge, and split. Each action makes the changes that you request and triggers any workflow that may be needed. As you add contributors, for example, you may want to trigger training workflows. These sorts of metadata review cycles can be initiated outside your workflow system and facilitated by small automation tools so that they eventually become part of the normal routine of running the CMS.

Far less metadata review goes on in CM systems than is optimal. After they are created, lists tend to just keep accumulating values that may or may not jibe with the others in the list. This problem is partly because of the lack of good review tools, as well as the lack of awareness that review needs to happen. Even if you only implement review as a process and write no software to support it, be sure to include some sort of metadata review feature in your CMS.

Value lumping

At some point, you may need to combine two similar component elements into one. Suppose, for example, that the source files for a certain content type have an Author field, whereas the destination content type has a component element called Contributor. To the extent that the source fields and the destination element have the same format, structure, and intent, the merger is painless. If the Author field and the Contributor element, for example, are both just names (as free-form text), the merger is simple. The result is more plaintext names as values of the Contributor element.

But if the elements differ, you need a lot more code to control for the difference. For example, suppose that the Author field is plaintext names, but the Contributor element is a closed list. In that case, it's not so easy to merge them. The names in the plaintext Author field must somehow be matched to items in the list behind the Contributor element. This may become harder to accomplish if a lot of inconsistency exists in the way that the names in the Author field are typed. Are they always first name and then last name? Are first initials used? How are middle names represented? How are international name formats represented and stored? Depending on the amount of mismatch between the format and structure of the source and target, lumping values may be anything from very easy to impossible.

If you lump two metadata values into one, it's nice to have the help of a tool. In the preceding situation, the tool could have done all the easy matching of the Author field to Contributor element first. The easy matches are those in which the free-text name in the Author field matches letter for letter (including case and punctuation) with an existing entry in the metadata list behind the Contributor component element. After disposing of the easy matches, the tool could alert a staff member to handle the harder matches quickly. The worker could be shown a mismatch on her screen. In response, she could choose to match it manually to an item in the metadata list, add it as a new item in the metadata list, update an existing item in the metadata list, or delete an item in the metadata list. Each of these actions would trigger any appropriate workflow in which owners or editors need to take action. You can imagine an interface not unlike a spell-check program in which the worker can look at and reconcile each mismatched reference.

Your need to implement any sort of advanced lumping feature really depends on how much lumping you need to do. You ought to be able to create a ballpark ROI on this sort of feature by comparing how much time it will save versus how much it will cost to implement.

Value splitting

Just as you will need to lump two kinds of metadata into one eventually, you also need to split one metadata field into two. Suppose, for example, that you outgrow a single Body element for a particular content type. Now you'd like to break it into an Introduction element, a Body element, and a Summary element. If the text within the current Body element is really well structured (has these three kinds of information in it) and is really well marked (each of the kinds of information can be found pragmatically and extracted), there's no problem in splitting one element into three automatically. On the other hand, if the text was so well structured and marked, you'd probably have split it into these elements in the first place. What's far more likely is that you have loosely formatted and marked text that may need human editorial intervention to be split correctly.

In this case, a tool may help. Such a tool could load each current Body element and attempt to find its three parts. Using whatever regularity you can capture in the source files, the program makes its best guess and shows each Body element with the assumed sections in three separate text boxes. The staff member using the tool can then choose to accept and save the way that the program divides the element or make edits and then save changes (triggering any needed workflow as well). In either case, the program would load one Body element after the next for your review.

An advanced splitting feature may not pay for itself on the first use, but the need is general, and this tool may pay dividends for a long time as it gets morphed and reused.

Mandatory and optional elements

Depending on the CMS you're using (or creating), it may take extra work to figure out which user sees which component elements and when. The issue may be passed over to the templating system, where the elements are selected and laid onto a Web page, or you may care to deal with it centrally by collecting metadata on your component elements. To deal with the issue centrally, you'd first need somewhere to store the metadata about your elements. If you're using a relational database structure, in which an Elements table already exists to store metadata on your elements, you have no problem. (For more information on the more abstract relational database model, see Chapter 39, "Management System" in the section titled "Storing content types and components in a relational database.") If you're using an XML structure, you can add attributes and elements to the content type node to store your metadata. In an XML hierarchy, the content type node is usually the parent of any of its components. <PRESSRELEASES>, for example, would be the type node for <PRESSRELEASE> components. You can store information about mandatory and optional elements in the type node or in the element nodes themselves.

After you've found a place to store metadata about your elements, here's what you store there: the name of an element, the kind of metadata that you're storing (review frequency, mandatory versus optional elements, access restrictions, and so on), and the value (three months, mandatory or optional, and so on). Finally, you use the metadata that you stored to trigger workflow or automated processes. Each time that the review frequency for a particular element comes up, for example, the appropriate review begins.

Your ability to track meta-metadata is greatly influenced by the architecture of the system you are working in. From a management standpoint, it is much better to be able to deal with issues of review time, access, and atonality all in one place and at one time. However, your system may make it impossible to propagate this information to the authoring templates and workflow system that actually act upon this sort of information.

Support for applying metadata

As an author or metator applies metadata to a component, she would like to have tools that help make the selection of values as easy as possible. I detail the sort of support an author might like in the section in this chapter titled "Metadata support." Metators want all the same metadata support features as authors, but may want these more high-powered features as well:

✦ A global cross-reference viewer (with a display possibly like some of the hyperbolic link viewers that are available). The viewer would give the metator a comprehensive view of how linking is being done in the content base and might even help her establish and enforce linking policy.

✦ A hierarchy viewer that has more advanced features than the one used by authors. It might allow global expand and collapse (where you specify what level and every branch expands to that level) text search, cross-references within nodes, and the capability to highlight components that are in more than one branch of the hierarchy.

✦ Index support that shows, for example, what other components a term has already been linked to. It might also allow the metator to display component clustering and relationship based on common index terms.

✦ A sequence viewer with drag and drop to change the order of component in the sequence.

The addition of these features enables the metator to be a power author and also to view the metadata application process from a much wider perspective than an author would.

These are valuable features for authors and metators and are worth implementing as much as possible in manual processes, even if coding them into software is beyond your present reach.

Repository Interface

The repository interface refers specifically to the parts of the interface between the collection system and the repository. Its design is largely driven by the features that your system includes, such as searching and batch processing, which I discuss fully in the other sections in this chapter. I summarize here the features that cut across many other features.

Updates and deletes

In the course of content collection, you don't just get content in, but you also change it and get rid of it. Thus the collection system of the CMS needs to support one-off and bulk updates and deletes as well as bulk loading.

Because the Web browser has become the client application of choice, most of the input, update, and delete functions in most CMS systems are hosted on some sort of Web page. But, as anyone who's tried to create a complex application in a Web page can tell you, this isn't always an advantage. Many CMS systems don't use Web pages for their applications because they just can't get the same performance and usability from them as they can from a traditional "fat client" (that is, an application installed on each user's PC).

Obviously, your system always needs to be able to move content in, change it, and delete it. How automated you can make the process depends on how much support your software provides and how organized your content is.

Submitting and storing files

Many CMS products can manage files that have been authored in any tool without touching the content within these files. In other words, the CMS can be a document management system for files that it can't interpret. The crux of the functionality behind file submission is to upload the file to the CMS repository, assign it a component type, and associate the appropriate set of management elements with it.

By using Web-based forms, you can provide the appropriate interface to accomplish this functionality. In fact, the Web-based forms behind file submission should be no different from the forms behind any other component. Suppose, for example, that you want to accept electronic slide presentations into the CMS. You may create a content type called Presentation, with a body element that contains the file path and name for the presentation file and a set of management elements that contains the type, author, status, and so on, of the presentation. You can then produce a Web-based form that lays these elements out on an HTML page. Your staff can use standard methods (a text box that has the full path of the file and a browse button that shows a file dialog box) to locate and upload files from the page.

More interesting than how the files and metadata are entered is how they're stored. Depending on the nature of your repository, the file may be stored in a directory, a relational database, or an XML file or database. Similarly, the metadata may be stored in a relational database, XML file, or XML database.

Cross-Reference There's more on the subject of file storage in Chapter 39, "Management System," in the section titled "File systems."

The software behind the Web form must validate that you entered the management elements correctly, create the appropriate class of component, and either store the file that you uploaded within the component or separately in a CMS-controlled directory. If it stores the file separately, the component must have an element where the location of the file can be stored. It's up to the CMS management system to keep these file references updated as it moves files around and publishes them.

Unless you do 100% of your collection through Web forms that never require users to upload files, you will be dealing with file submission and storage. In other words, you might as well think this through, because you will need it.

Support for WebDAV

Web-based Distributed Authoring and Versioning (WebDAV) is an extension to the HTTP protocol that allows users to extend their file management capabilities over the Web. Rather than having the Web be a read-only system (which it was never actually intended to be), WebDAV lets users edit, upload, and manage the files that are on a Web server from their browsers, or even from within their desktop applications.

The connection to CM should be obvious. If your CMS resides on a Web server, you can use WebDAV to allow your contributors to interact with it.

Many commercial products provide support for WebDAV. Many desktop applications also do WebDAV. Finally, you can also build it into your own systems as a convenient way to integrate your users' applications with a remote repository.

Summary

Whatever CMS product you may buy, you're likely to want to extend its collection system. If you're building a CMS, it behooves you to consider automating collection to reduce the amount of labor that it may otherwise require.

In building collection systems, you need to do the following:

✦ Come as close to the author's home editing environment and processes as you can.

✦ Look behind the simple Web-based forms that are most common now to find ones with new functionality to make them good enough to compete with word processors.

✦ Find the largest range of authoring tools that you feel that you can support and build from there. As time goes on, the number of authoring environments is no doubt sure to increase. I can only hope that, as much as these environments diverge in capability and user interface, their underlying structures will slowly begin to converge (perhaps by using XML). The better that you get at integrating content from diverse platforms, the better you can become at delivering content back to those same platforms.

✦ Consider custom collection tools. The customizations that I describe in this chapter are just a few of the myriad enhancements and cost-justified improvements that you can make to a collection system.

In this chapter, I attempted a comprehensive description of collection system features. This technology taxonomy is a tool that describes what exists or could exist today. You can no doubt add to it, but you should, at least, have a good start in describing the features of your own system. In the next chapter, I take a similar approach in diving into the functions and techniques that you may employ to build a management system.

✦ ✦ ✦

Building Management Systems

Many CMS companies describe their entire product as a management system. I take a different tack. For me, although it's, of course, true that a content management system is a management system, it's more instructive to use the term *management system* to refer to the specific parts of the CMS that deal with the content in the system. You want to differentiate them from the other parts of the CMS that enable you to get content in (collection) and get it out (publication).

In this chapter I explain the parts of the management system within a CMS. Then I examine each subsystem, its features, and its sub-subsystems in detail, including:

✦ The repository, including tools for managing it.

✦ A versioning system to allow rollback to earlier versions of content and functionality.

✦ A source control system to manage user permissions, allow file sharing, and avoid version control conflicts.

✦ A localization system to account for localization requirements throughout the system, including in the collection and publishing phases.

✦ A workflow system for planning and implementing work processes to get content ready for publishing.

✦ A CMS administrative system to manage the CMS itself.

For a list of the extensive systems and features that are described in this chapter, see the section "An index to the technology taxonomy" in Chapter 34, "Getting Started on Physical Design." The systems and features of the management system are outlined in the taxonomy under "System: Management System."

What's in a Management System?

Broadly speaking, the management system within a CMS has these parts:

✦ **A repository:** All the content and control files for the system are stored here. The repository houses databases and files that hold content. The repository can also store configuration and administrative files and databases that specify how the CMS runs and produces publications.

✦ **A repository interface:** This enables the collection, publishing, workflow, and administrative systems to access and work with the repository. The interface provides functions for input, access, and output of components as well as other files and data that you store in the repository.

✦ **Connections to other systems:** This enables you to send and receive information from the repository.

✦ **A workflow module:** This module embeds each component and publication in a managed life cycle.

✦ **An administrative module:** This module enables you to configure the CMS.

The systems and features in this chapter should give you a good start on building your own management system or evaluating the ones that others have built.

The Repository

The repository is the heart of the management system and of the CMS as a whole. Into the repository flow all the raw materials on which any publication is built. Within the repository, components are stored and can be continually fortified to increase the quality of their metadata or content. Out of the repository flow the components and other parts that a page of a publication needs (as shown in Figure 39-1).

As a first approximation, you can think of the repository as a database. A repository, like a database, enables you to store and retrieve information. The repository, however, is much more. For one thing, the repository can house many databases. It can house files as well. It has an interface to other systems that goes beyond that of a standalone database. If you stand back from the repository and look at it as single unit, however, what you know about databases can help you understand the functions of the repository. In fact, most repositories have a database at their core. The database, however, is wrapped in so much custom code and its user interface that end users aren't likely to ever see the database.

My discussion implies that all the authoring, conversion, and aggregation are done on a component before it enters the repository. This is for clarity of presentation only. In fact, segmentation is the only thing that must be done to a component before it enters the repository. Until it's segmented, there's no component.

 Cross-Reference See Chapter 7, "Introducing the Major Parts of a CMS" in the section titled "Segmentation," for more information on segmentation.

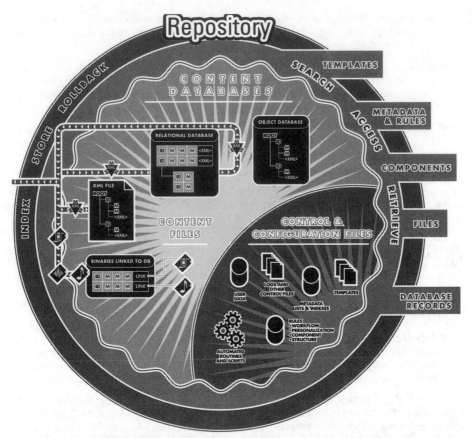

Figure 39-1: A high-level view of a CMS repository that shows its different parts and the content storage options that it gives you.

You can, and often should, add a component to the repository before it's fully authored, converted, edited, and has had metadata added to it. After it's in the repository, these processes can be brought under the control of your workflow module.

The features in this section give you a top-level view of what a repository has to accomplish. Most of them are covered in more detail throughout the rest of this chapter.

Fitting into the CMS and the organization

Your repository is just one part of the CMS, and the CMS is just one part of your organization. Although it is not uncommon, especially for the more technical among us, to focus on the repository to the exclusion of all else, keep in mind that the repository has to fit in at least these ways. It must:

✦ **Support organization standards:** Your repository should access and work within whatever user security and other network standards you employ. If you aren't running a TCP/IP network protocol, for example, the CMS's Web-based forms and administrative tools can't work on your local area network.

✦ **Support the concept of content types:** Although all management systems must somehow segment information, a good system facilitates inputting, naming, cataloging, locating, and extracting content based on its content type.

✦ **Support the notion of workflow:** Although not part of the repository, the workflow module must be tightly integrated with it. As one example among many, events that occur within the repository, such as adding new components or deleting them, should be capable of triggering workflow processes.

✦ **File format support:** Many CMS products can manage files that are authored in any tool. Of course, they generally don't manage the content within these files. In other words, the CMS should be able to serve as a document management system for files that it can't interpret.

If you pay close attention to the wider world in which your repository lives, you will end up with a repository that serves that wider world rather than requiring you to change the world to fit your repository.

Getting content in and out

In the end, a repository is just like a database, only more diverse. Whereas a database is a single place where all data is segmented and stored, a repository may be a set of databases and files that are all unified by the CMS that accesses them. However, just like a database, a CMS repository ought to have the facility to perform the following functions:

✦ **Inputting content:** Whether you have tools for loading multiple components at the same time (bulk processing), automatic inputs via syndication, or one-by-one entries via Web-based forms, the management system must give you some way to get content into the repository.

✦ **Storing content:** Whether you employ a vast distributed network of databases or a simple file structure on a computer under someone's desk, the central function of the repository is to contain your content in one "place." In addition, the system must have some way of segmenting content into individually locatable units (such as files or database records).

✦ **Removing content:** Whether it can archive automatically or whether you must delete old content by hand, without the capability to remove content, a repository system is inadequate.

✦ **Outputting content:** Whether it supports advanced querying across a heterogeneous collection of databases and files or just allows you to get the simplest output, your repository must enable you to retrieve a copy of content that you've found in a format that your collection and publication system can use.

Of course, to be worth the effort, a CMS repository has to go beyond the simple input and output features. Still, how far past the simple features it must go is your call and should be based on what will deliver the most value to your other systems.

A repository-wide schema

Given that you can represent a very complex and complete content model in an XML Schema, it's surprising to me that I haven't come across a CMS product company with an XML repository that uses schemas to control the overall structure. What I've seen is that the repository as a whole must be well-formed XML, but the content is never validated as a whole. Many support the use of any number of schemas to validate content before it's input to the repository. This results in a repository that has multiple, possibly conflicting, schemas in charge of different parts of the repository. I can only guess that these companies believe that the task of creating a structure for the entire repository is prohibitively complex for most customers. Be this as it may, until you can model and control the entire repository, you can never control the entire system.

Of course, if you're using a relational database repository, the same comments apply. You still want to have an overall repository structure. In the relational database world, however, this has always been a natural thing to do.

If you are buying a repository, you will have to take what you can get. But if you are developing your own repository you can choose to pursue a repository-wide schema. Such a schema allows you to enforce your content model all the way from the highest levels of access structures to the lowest levels of character formatting. It also gives you a place to work out and enforce the relationships among all the different databases and file types you might have in your repository. After you have a schema that spans your repository, creating features like global search and replace and advanced versioning becomes possible.

Global search and replace

Given the obvious and large need for a trustworthy and comprehensive search-and-replace capacity in a CMS, it's surprising that better support isn't provided in commercial products. Ideally, a CMS should support search and replace through all the free text and metadata that is stored in the repository (assuming that appropriate permissions and security rights are observed). A thorough search-and-replace function in a CMS should do the following:

✦ **Work in a familiar way:** Just about every editing program has a search-and-replace function. The most basic ones just enable you to enter a phrase to find and a phrase to replace it with. Most enable you to replace phrases one at a time or in bulk. The better ones enable you to match case, find whole words or fragments of words, search forward or backward in the file, and undo. The best give you all this *and* enable you to restrict the search to any part of the structure of the information you're searching. A good CMS system deserves the best of all these user-centered features.

✦ **Search everywhere:** Think of all the places that text is stored in a CMS. Aside from the repository, which can have an enormous variety of nooks and crannies in which a phrase may be found, the entire configuration system of the CMS has text in many flat files, XML files, system registries, database tables, and who knows where else. Then there's the whole publishing system. You certainly need to search and replace in templates and other publication-related files.

If the CMS did no more than list somewhere all the locations where text is stored, it would help you a lot. But that's only half the battle. (And as hard as it is, it's still the easier half.) The other half is creating a system that can open, search and update each text storage file correctly. The CMS must have enough knowledge of each type of text storage file that it can manipulate it without messing it up. Now, obviously, some configuration files aren't worth interfacing with. But these unparsable files should, at least, be listed so that you know where else to check if you haven't found the text you're seeking. Any files that can be parsed and updated (and that should be most of them) ought to be accessible to the search-and-replace function.

✦ **Follow structure:** The search-and-replace function ought to show you the structure of, at least, your repository (if not some of the other text storage files) so that you can choose where to search. If you're using an XML system, your structure is a hierarchy from which you may choose branches to search. Or you may want to search by element or attribute, regardless of where in the hierarchy it is. If you're using a relational database, your structure consists of tables and columns from which to narrow your search. Or you may want to search for a phrase, regardless of what column it's in.

You can imagine that, the more complex your structure becomes, the harder it is to represent. By layering your user interface, however, you should be able to make a lot of the repository structure accessible. Design the structure selector to zoom in and out on the structure. The highest-level view (only first-level XML elements or whole relational database tables) ought to be useful to anyone and should be shown by default. More advanced users should be able to drill down as far into the structure as they desire. The layering also makes the selector a great learning tool. Users can explore the structure of the repository in a comprehensive but non-threatening way.

✦ **Support regular expressions:** Regular expressions are a searching syntax that enables you to specify just about any text-matching rule you can imagine. The familiar wildcard character (*) is just one example of the powerful text-matching tools that are contained in regular expressions. Regular expressions fully support Boolean comparisons (AND, OR, and NOT) as well as a number of "stand-in" characters that work in ways similar to the * wildcard. Adding regular expressions to a search-and-replace function is like adding steroids to an athlete. They give search-and-replace a much finer-grained discrimination than you can achieve in a regular text box.

✦ **Be programmable:** A search-and-replace function this good shouldn't be left only to end users. It ought to be programmable. If your CMS search-and-replace function is designed as a programmable object, there's no reason why you can't leverage the CMS search-and-replace function in any automation programs you write for the CMS.

✦ **Follow security:** Of course, the search-and-replace function ought to be completely personalizable. That is, for each user, the search should be confined to the text to which she's been granted access. And, of course, the system should be able to use the access permissions that are stored and managed in the operating system's user administration module.

A search function ought to give you complete random access to the CMS. Anywhere there's any text that you may want to see or change, the search function ought to enable you to view it and, as often as possible, change it. On the other hand, in a commercial system you are lucky if you get to search just the repository with plain-text phrases. Because information is so spread out in a CMS, no matter how much you might need a global search-and-replace function, you are on your own when it comes to creating one.

Locating content

You're likely to know one of two things about components that you want to find in the repository: the value of some piece of metadata that they contain or some piece of text that you remember that they contain. In the first case, you want what's called an *element search*. (In relational databases, this is usually called a *fielded search*.) To do an element search, what you want most is a list of the elements and a place where you can type or select the value that you want. To find components by author, for example, you want to see an Author box into which you can type a name. As a bonus, the system can help you type only valid possibilities. The Author box, for example, can be a list from which you simply choose an author rather than typing her name.

In the second case, you remember some piece of text that the component contains, so a *full-text search* is what you want. Here, you want to type a word or phrase in a box and have the system find components that contain that word or phrase in any element. For spice, the repository can enable you to combine full text and fielded search or to type Boolean operators such as AND, OR, and NOT to make more precise searches of either type.

Cross-Reference I cover full text metadata search again in a polishing context in Chapter 40, "Publishing System" in the section titled "Searching and indexing."

You need some way to locate content in your repository, even if it is just by browsing through outlines and other lists. However, once the repository gets larger than a few hundred items, your capability to browse to the right component becomes seriously hampered and you need a more advanced way to locate content.

Bulk processes

Managing components one at a time is far too slow for many situations. A good repository enables you to specify an operation and then do it over and over to all the components it applies to. Suppose, for example, that your lead metator is out of town and you want to extend the expiration date on any components that turn off while she's out. You could do an element search for all components with an expiration date between today and the day that she returns. Then you could open each of these components and change its Expire Date element to sometime next week.

I cover the particulars of bulk processing in a variety of other features. If your commercial system does not have the native capacity to support bulk processes, you can often build your own capacity by using the system's database API. For example, you can set up a system that creates components from all the files in a directory. It would open each file and then use the system's API (or go directly to its database if it does not have an API) to create and fill a set of components from the contents of the files.

Field type support

Any repository enables you to type metadata as text, but the one that you want can do much more. The best kind of repository supports all the types of metadata fields (as I describe in Chapter 24, "Working with Metadata" in the section titled "Understanding the Types of Metadata"). In any repository, for example, you can type the name of an author into each component's Author element. Spelling errors and variations on the same name (Christopher Scott versus C. Scott), however, eventually cause problems. It would be better if you had one place where you could type all author names once. Then, whenever an author needs to be specified, you can choose the name rather than type it.

The best case is a system that can be linked to the main sources of metadata in your organization. People log into an organization's network, for example, based on a user ID and password. This information—as well as the organizational groups to which they belong—is stored in a registry. Wouldn't you most like to work with a system that could connect to this registry and find all the people who are in the Authors group? Then, to have access to all authors' names (not to mention any other information that the registry stores), you just need to make sure that the Authors group is correctly maintained by your organization's system administrators. Similarly, if your repository holds master copies of metadata lists, you want it to be openly accessible to your organization's other systems.

If your management system does not already support direct connections to the sources of metadata in your organization, you might consider setting up an indirect connection through some software that you create. The most important thing is to try to have one master source of metadata lists and have the CMS either own those lists or connect as directly as possible to the system that owns them.

General storage requirements

Most content management systems store components in databases. Some store metadata in databases and keep the component content in files. Although almost all content management systems use some sort of database, the exact database they employ and how the components are stored in the database varies widely. The two major classes of databases that a CMS may use to store content components are shown in Figure 39-2.

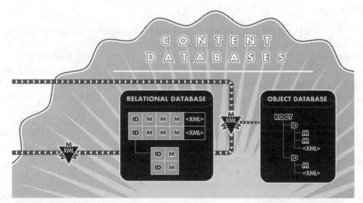

Figure 39-2: A CMS may store components in a relational database or an object (XML) database.

Content management systems have stored content in the following general ways:

✦ **In a relational database,** which is the computer industry's standard place to store large amounts of information.

✦ **In an object (or XML) database,** which stores information as XML.

Some CMS companies are using technologies that seek to make the best of both the database and XML worlds. In addition, database product companies themselves continue to break the established boundaries by creating hybrid object-relational databases that overlay XML Schema onto the basic relational database infrastructure.

Regardless of the type of storage system that you use, it must be capable of storing components, relationships between components, and the content model.

A review of the content model

Database developers create data models (or database schema). These models establish how each table in the database is constructed and how it relates to the other tables in the database. XML developers create DTDs (or XML Schema). DTDs establish how each element in the XML file is constructed and how it relates to the other elements in the file. CMS developers create content models that serve the same function—they establish how each component is constructed and how it relates to the other components in the system.

In particular, the content model specifies the following:

✦ The name of each content type.

✦ The allowed elements of each content type.

✦ The element type and allowed values for each element (as I describe in Chapter 27, "Designing Content Types" in the section titled "Elements have types and values").

✦ The access structures in which each content type and instance participate.

If your CMS is built on a relational database, your content model gives rise to a database schema. If your CMS is built on XML files or an XML database, your content model gives rise to an XML Schema or DTD. The content model, however, isn't simply reducible to either of these models. Suppose, for example, that you establish that you want an Author element that's an open list (as defined in Chapter 27, "Designing Content Types" in the section titled "Elements have types and values"). There is no place to state this fact in either a database schema or a DTD. Rather, it must be established in the authoring environment that you use. Still, the majority of the content model can be coded either explicitly or implicitly in the database or XML schema that you develop. The rest of the content model becomes part of the access structures in your repository and the rules that you institute in your collection system.

 Cross-Reference I present information on collecting data for and preparing a content model report in Chapter 30, "Designing Content Access Structures" in the section titled "The content model."

Storing components

The primary function of a CMS repository is to store the content components that you intend to manage. Suppose, for example, that you want to manage a type of information called an "HR benefit" that includes a name and some text. If your system has 50 HR benefits, there must be 50 separately stored entities, each following the HRBenefits content structure, which can be retrieved one at a time or in groups.

If your repository does nothing else, it will store your components. However, your system may or may not treat components as separate entities that are created, housed, and consumed by publications. Instead, your system may deal with components the same way it deals with standard database records. Even if the system does not make the distinction between records and components, you should.

Storing content types

To store components, the repository needs some way of representing content types (as defined in Chapter 27, "Designing Content Types" in the section titled "Content has types and components"). Somewhere in your storage system, for example, you must define a HRBenefit component. After you create a new HRBenefit component, the system uses this definition to decide what the new HRBenefit includes and how to store it.

It is common for the definition of a content type to be hidden within a CMS repository. Often, in a relational database system, the database administrator is the only one who knows where the definition resides and how to read or change it. In XML systems, the situation is often better. You can always find and open a text schema or DTD file somewhere. However, after opening the schema, you still must be able to read and understand it.

Most commercial systems help by presenting a user interface that enables you to view and define content types without having to dive into the inside of your storage system. If your system does not provide such an interface, it might be worth your while to keep your own set of content type definitions, say in a spreadsheet, and use them to tell the administrators what you intend each content type to include.

Storing relationships between components

The repository must have some way of representing and storing the access structures that you create. Any indexes that you decide that you need, for example, must be capable of being represented somewhere in the repository and must be capable of linking to the components that are indexed.

Most systems will allow you to store a single main hierarchy for your content. Others will allow more advanced capabilities such as multiple hierarchies, multiple indexes, cross-references between components, cross-references between publication pages, and sequences. As your system grows, you will eventually need to store and manage a large range of access structures, so it behooves you to begin to figure out how to do that.

Relational database systems

The relational database was invented as a way to store large amounts of related information efficiently. At this task, it has excelled. The vast majority of computer systems that work with more than a small amount of information have relational databases behind them. Today, a handful of database product companies (Oracle, Microsoft, IBM, and the like) supply database systems to most of the programmers around the world. Programmers use these commercial database systems to quicken their own time-to-market and increase their capability to integrate with the databases currently in use by their customers.

The majority of CMS product companies also base their repositories on these commercial database products. In fact, many require that you buy your database directly from the manufacturer. (This fact, by the way, puts a convenient-for-them and inconvenient-for-you firewall between the CMS product support staff and that of the database company.) Buying a database (or, more accurately, a license) from a commercial company is no big problem; database vendors are happy to sell to you directly. What's much more of an issue is whether the CMS requires that you administer the database separately. You may give preference to CMS products that have integrated database administration into their own user interface and don't require you to administer the databases separately.

To help readers with less background in data storage, I provide some database basics before going into the more technical aspects of representing content in a relational database.

Whatever you store in a relational database must fit into the database's predefined structures, as follows:

✦ **Databases have tables:** Tables contain all the database's content. Loosely, one table represents one type of significant entity. You may create a table, for example, to hold your HRBenefit components. The structure of that table represents the structure of the component it stores. Tables can be related to each other. (This is where the relations in relational databases are.) Rather than typing in the name of each author, for example, your HRBenefits table may be linked (via a unique ID) to a separate Author table that has the name and e-mail address of each author.

✦ **Tables have rows** (also called records): Loosely, each row represents one instance of its table's entity. Each HRBenefit component, for example, can occupy one row of the HRBenefits table.

✦ **Rows have columns** (also called fields): Strictly, each field contains a particular piece of uniquely named information that can be individually accessed. A HRBenefit component, for example, may have an element called BenefitName. In a relational database, that element may be stored in a field called BenefitName. Using the database's access functions, you can extract individual BenefitName elements from the component (or row) that contains them.

✦ **Columns have data types:** As you create the column, you assign it one of a limited number of types. The BenefitName column, for example, would likely be of the type "text" (generally with a maximum length of 255 characters). Other relevant column data types include integer, date, binary large object, or BLOB (for large chunks of binary data such as images), and large text or memo (for text that's longer than 255 characters).

As you see, even given these exacting constraints, you can represent content in a relational database in many ways, some of which I illustrate in the following sections. I don't present the following examples to give you a guide to building a CMS database. (You'd need much more than I provide.) In addition, if you purchase a CMS product, you work with a database that the product company has already designed. So you don't get to decide how to store content; it is decided for you. What I intend in the examples is to give you insight into how the needs of a CMS mesh with the constraints of a relational database so that you can understand and evaluate the databases that you encounter.

Storing content types and components in a relational database

The simplest way to represent components in a relational database is one content type per table, one component per row, and one element per column. An example of an HRBenefits content type in Microsoft Access is shown in Figure 39-3.

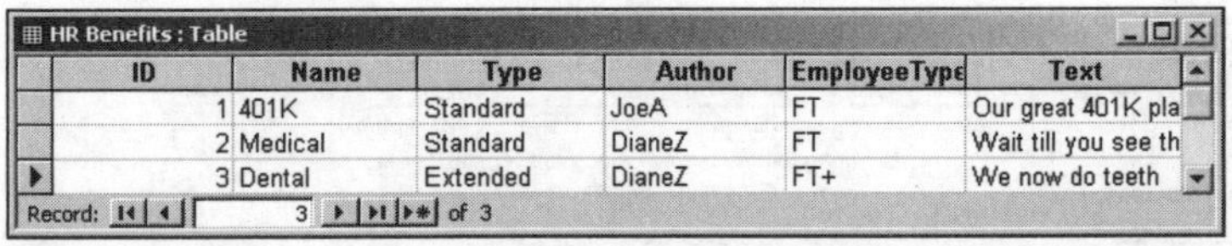

ID	Name	Type	Author	EmployeeType	Text
1	401K	Standard	JoeA	FT	Our great 401K pla
2	Medical	Standard	DianeZ	FT	Wait till you see th
3	Dental	Extended	DianeZ	FT+	We now do teeth

Record: 3 of 3

Figure 39-3: A simple table representing the HRBenefits content type

Even if you know nothing about databases, you can likely see that this is very well structured. Everything is named and organized into a nice table. It's not hard to imagine how database programs could help you manage, validate, and access content stored in tables. In fact, database programs are quite mature and can handle tremendous amounts of data in tables. They offer advanced access and connect easily to other programs. It's no wonder that relational databases are the dominant players in component storage.

The content type is called HRBenefits. There are three HRBenefit components, one in each row of the table. As shown in the figure, HRBenefit components have six elements, one per column. Interestingly, you'd be likely to type only two of the elements — Name and Text. The ID element can be filled in automatically by the database, which has a unique ID feature.

Even this most simple representation of a component in a relational database isn't so simple. Four tables are really involved in storing component information. The Type, Author, and EmployeeType columns contain references to other tables (*lookup tables* in database parlance). Behind the scenes, what's actually stored in the column isn't the phrase shown but rather the unique ID of a row in some other table that contains the words. From a more CMS-focused vocabulary set, you can say that Type, Author, and EmployeeType are closed list elements. The lists are stored in other tables and can be made available at author time to ensure that you enter correct values in the fields for these elements. For example, three drop-down lists on the form can be used to create HRBenefit components. In the first is a list of Types, in the second a list of Authors, and in the third a list of EmployeeTypes. The words in the list are filled in from the values in three database tables.

I'll continue to complicate the example to show some of the other issues that come into play whenever you store components in a relational database. Suppose that an image goes along with each benefit component (an image of a happy employee, perhaps). To represent the image you have the following choices:

✦ You can actually store the image in the database.

✦ You can store a reference to the file that contains the image.

The second technique is the usual choice because, historically, databases have been lousy at storing binary large objects (BLOBs). They became bloated and lost performance. This is often no longer true, but the perception remains. More important, images (and other media) stored within a database aren't very accessible to the people who must work on them. Anyone can go to a directory and use her favorite tool to open, edit, and then resave an image, but you need a special interface to extract and restore the same image in a database field. This advantage is rendered moot in many of the more advanced CMS products that create extensive revision histories. To have your changes logged, you must extract and restore your files by using some sort of interface anyway. The same interface can easily store and retrieve BLOBs from the database. All in all, although referencing files instead of storing them in the repository is still the most popular way to include media in a component, there's often little real advantage to it.

An HR Benefits table with images is shown in Figure 39-4.

⊞ HR Benefits2 : Table						_□×
ID	Name	Type	Author	EmployeeType	ImagePath	Text
1	401K	Standard	JoeA	FT	images/hr/joesmile.jpg	Our great 401K pla—
2	Medical	Standard	DianeZ	FT	images/hr/coreymile.jpg	Wait till you see th
▶ 3	Dental	Extended	DianeZ	FT+	images/hr/lauraile.jpg	We now do teeth| ▾

Figure 39-4: The HR component table with an image reference added

Notice the new ImagePath column where you can enter the directory and name of the picture to be included with this component. The image path shown here is a relative path. That is, it doesn't start from a drive letter or URL domain name (such as http://www.xyz.com). Rather, the path assumes that the file resides in an images/hr directory and that some program adds the right drive or domain name or the rest of the path later. This ensures that, even if the computer that houses these files changes, the ImagePath values can stay the same. In real life, you probably wouldn't even type a relative path. Most likely, you upload a file from your hard drive to the system, which then decides the appropriate directory for the file.

The elements of the component are stored in the columns of the database. This system works very well if you require a small number of management elements and a few larger elements of body text. It works less well if you have a large number of management elements and a large number of body text elements. It works very poorly if a component can have a variable number of management or body elements. Suppose, for example, that the text of a HRBenefit component looks something like the following example:

```
<TEXT>
  <TITLE>We now do Teeth!</TITLE>
  <PULLQUOTE><B>My gums and molars never felt so good.</B>
     <IMAGE>laurasmile.jpg</IMAGE>
  </PULLQUOTE>
  <H1>a paragraph of text here</H1>
  <H2>a paragraph of text here</H2>
  <H1>a paragraph of text here</H1>
  <CONCLUSION>
     Put your mouth where our money is-<B>use the plan!</B>
  </CONCLUSION>
</TEXT>
```

Rather than a paragraph or two of untagged text, you have a complex composition that includes its own images, metadata, and body elements. How should this be represented in a relational database? Here are the choices:

✦ **Full parsing:** You can create a column for each element in the text chunk.

✦ **Partial parsing:** You can store the entire text chunk in a single column but pull out some of the elements into separate columns so that you can access them separately.

✦ **No parsing:** You can store the entire text chunk in a single column and not worry about its internal tagging.

Of these, the last is the most commonly used.

Fully parsing structured text

Certainly, if you wanted to make the elements of your component maximally accessible, you'd create a column for each element. You want to "explode" the elements of the text chunk into a set of database columns that you can then access individually. Why? Well suppose, for example, that you wanted to get to just the pull-quotes and images to create a gallery of smiling employees. It would be nice to have each of these in its own column so that you could easily find them and work with them.

To explode the structured text, you parse it and store it. *Parsing* is the process of finding and selecting elements, and *storing* is the process of finding the right database row and column and putting the element's text within it.

The sample text in the preceding section would yield seven extra columns in the HR Benefits database table (Title, Pullquote, Image, H1, H2, Conclusion, and B). That doesn" sound excessive, but then again, it's far from the whole story. Table 39-1 shows how the text is divided — and you can see that this approach doesn't work.

Table 39-1: An Impossible Repository

Column	Value
Title	We now do Teeth!
Pullquote	My gums and molars never felt so good.
B	My gums and molars never felt so good.

Continued

Table 39-1 *(continued)*

Column	Value
Image	laurasmile.jpg
H1	a paragraph of text here
H2	a paragraph of text here
H1	a paragraph of text here
Conclusion	Put your mouth where our money is -
B	Use the plan!

First, breaking each element into a column ruins the element nesting that's critical to the text. How would you know, for example, that the B column must go inside the Conclusion column in order for the text to make sense? Second, columns are repeated. Both the B column and the H1 column occur twice. This isn't allowed in a database, which requires each column must be uniquely named. Finally, and most important, this is the text for just one HRBenefit component. Is it reasonable to expect that the others have exactly these columns? I think not. Others should follow the same general form but may not be in the exact order and have the same number of elements. The number and names of the elements (and thus the columns) can vary from component to component, and that's not allowed in a database. (I could cite more problems, but I'm sure that you get the idea.)

Strange as it may seem, these problems aren't insurmountable. In fact, I know of at least one CMS company that's working to completely "explode" rule-based but variable text (XML, that is) in a relational database. But it's not easy. As you can see from the example that I give, the basic rules of a relational database are at odds with the needs of the text. The rigid regularity of rows and columns is too far removed from the subtler regularity of well-formed text to enable the two to overlap easily.

Partially parsing structured text

Given the difficulty exploding structured text into rows and columns fully, most systems don't try. Luckily, there are more modest approaches to storing structured text that can often suffice. The most common modest approach is to parse the text block, looking for relevant elements and storing them in their own columns.

Consider again the text chunk to be included in a HRBenefit component. How many of the elements do you really need to access separately? Certainly not all of them. It's hard to think of a reason, for example, why you'd need to get to all <B> elements. For the purpose of illustration, say that you really need to access only the pull-quotes separately. In this case, you can simply add a Pullquote column to your HR Benefits table (see Figure 39-5).

ID	Name	Type	Author	EmployeeType	ImagePath	Pullquote	Text
1	401K	Standard	JoeA	FT	images/hr/joe:	That boat is mir	<title>Our 401K p
2	Medical	Standard	DianeZ	FT	images/hr/con	My baby is safe	<title>Keep safe
3	Dental	Extended	DianeZ	FT+	images/hr/laur	My gums and m	<title>Just a pinc

Figure 39-5: The HR Benefits table with a Pullquote column added

It doesn't work to remove the pull-quote from the text. Its position and nesting in the text chunk may be critical. Rather, you must make a copy of the pull-quote and put it in the Pullquote column. Notice that you don't need to put the pull-quote tag in the column — just the text. The column name itself serves as the tag for the pull-quote element. Similarly, if you locate the entire text chunk (delimited by <TEXT></TEXT>), you copy only what's inside to the Text column of the database.

This kind of solution enables you to have your text chunk and your metadata, too. It requires, however, that you do the following:

✦ **Program or do manual work:** You must create either custom programming code or a manual process for inputting elements to database columns.

✦ **Synchronize columns:** You must make sure that you keep the elements in the text and database columns in sync. If someone edits the pull-quote in the text, you must recognize the event and make sure that you update the same text that's duplicated in the Pullquote column.

✦ **Synchronize constraints:** You must ensure that the constraints on the element and database column match. It doesn't do for the database column to be limited to 255 characters if the pull-quote element can be as long as the author wants it to be.

Given the extra work involved in pulling metadata from structured text, most people keep the number of elements they treat this way to a bare minimum.

Not parsing structured text

Exploding structured text completely into database columns is often prohibitively complex. A controlled explosion of only certain elements into columns is more reasonable but still presents problems. Most people end up storing the entire chunk of structured text in one database column and ignoring what's inside the text chunk.

This isn't as bad a solution as it may seem at first glance. For one thing, you don't always need to access elements within a text chunk. In many situations, it's fine to simply wrap an unparsed text chunk with a few metadata columns and call it done.

For another thing, not all text is structured. The previous solutions demand that the text chunk you're dealing with be tagged well enough that you can locate elements within them reliably. Most text chunks that you encounter aren't so well structured. In fact, unless someone's put the effort into delivering XML code, it's likely that you don't even have the starting place for constructing any sort of automatic explosion process. Thus, for systems that end up storing text in HTML or any other less-than-easily parsed markup language, storing entire text chunks may be the only possible option.

But even if you have well-structured text, it may work out well to save it in a single database field. Just because the database can't get inside the block of text and deliver a single element doesn't mean that you can't do so by other methods. Suppose, for example, that you store an entire HRBenefit text chunk in a single column called Text. Using relational database methodologies, it's not possible to go directly to the pull-quote elements within the Text column. You can certainly get the entire text chunk and parse it yourself, however, to find the pull-quote element! In other words, getting to the pull-quote elements could be a two-step process: The database gives you the text chunk, and you parse it by using nondatabase tools to get to the pull-quote element.

Obviously, this is less convenient than having the database just give you what you want. It also makes it hard to do a fielded search against elements, where you say, for example, "Give me all the components with this text in their pull-quote element." Still, storing all your structured text in one field may still get you the elements that you desire. In general recognition of this approach, at least one CMS product offers XML processing tools that you can use against any XML code that's stored in its relational database. Moreover, some of the database product companies themselves have developed XML overlays that enable you to package the two-stage process into a single query.

Breaking the spell of rows and columns

I've discussed the simplest approach to storing components in relational databases: one table per content type, one row per component, and one element per column. Although this approach is commonly used, it's not the only one possible. The one-table approach has the following advantages:

✦ **It's easy to understand.** You don't need to hunt around in the database to find your components. You simply look for the table that has the same name as the components that you're seeking.

✦ **It has high performance.** Databases go fastest if they're simple. In fact, even the straightforward process of referencing other tables instead of retyping author names and the like (called normalizing) can slow a database down. For this reason, databases that need to be used in high-volume situations (high-transaction Web sites, for example) are often *de-normalized* first: Their table relationships are broken, and single tables are produced from a set of related tables.

The disadvantages of the single-table approach are as follows:

✦ **It's inflexible.** To add a new content type to the system, you must create a new table. To add an element to a component, you must add a column to a table. Although this may seem simple, in many database systems, it requires a fair amount of effort. Relational databases aren't really designed to have their tables constantly modified, created, and destroyed.

✦ **It has a hard time dealing with irregular information.** For example, a table either has a particular column or it doesn't. In a CMS, a component sometimes may or may not have a particular column.

✦ **It has a hard time dealing with extra information.** The one-table approach enables you to specify the component name (in the table name), the component element name (in the column names), and the basic data type of the component element (in the data types of the columns). There's no obvious place to store other types of information about the component or its elements (whether a column is an open list or a reference, for example).

An approach more subtle than the "one table/one content type" model can help overcome some of these disadvantages. Consider the two tables shown in Figure 39-6.

In the background, you see Components table. It simply lists all the content types in the system and gives them a unique ID. (In real life, a table such as this would be much more complex and most likely consist of an entire family of tables.) In the foreground, there's an Elements table. This table stores all the elements of all the components in the system.

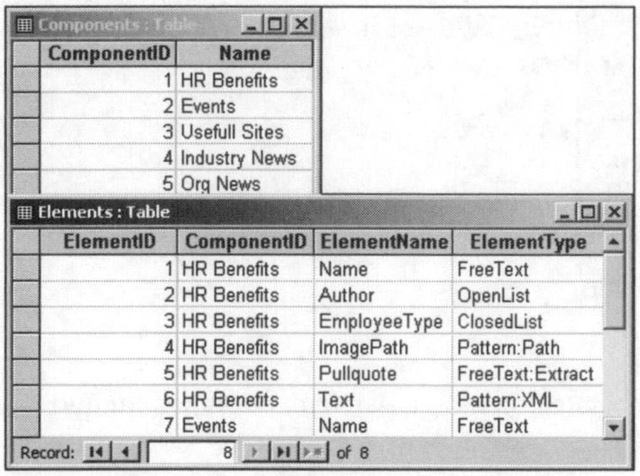

Components : Table

ComponentID	Name
1	HR Benefits
2	Events
3	Usefull Sites
4	Industry News
5	Org News

Elements : Table

ElementID	ComponentID	ElementName	ElementType
1	HR Benefits	Name	FreeText
2	HR Benefits	Author	OpenList
3	HR Benefits	EmployeeType	ClosedList
4	HR Benefits	ImagePath	Pattern:Path
5	HR Benefits	Pullquote	FreeText:Extract
6	HR Benefits	Text	Pattern:XML
7	Events	Name	FreeText

Record: 8 of 8

Figure 39-6: Two tables that represent any content type

Each element has the following:

✦ **A unique ID:** The ID is one piece of information about the element that uniquely identifies it, never changes, and can be used to quickly locate the element in any search that you may do.

✦ **A content type to which it's tied:** The illustration shows that a drop-down feature is linked to this column so that you aren't required to type the name of the component type and element with which it's associated. In this example, each element is associated with only one content type. In real life, an element may be associated with any number of content types, requiring a more complicated set of tables.

✦ **The element's name:** The name is the user-friendly name that people use to recognize the element if they see it on entry forms and reports.

✦ **The element's type:** The types shown here correspond loosely to the metadata field types (as shown in Chapter 24, "Working with Metadata" in the section titled "Categorizing Metadata Fields"). The CMS can use these types to decide what to do with an element. If the type is Path, for example, the CMS can verify that any typed text has the format of a directory and filename.

This way of representing content types has some very nice features. First, to add a new content type, rather than creating a whole new table, you just add a row to the Components table. Similarly, to add an element to a content type, you add a row to the Elements table and fill in its values. Second, you can easily extend what the database "knows" about a component or element. The ElementType column, for example, has additional information about what the system expects an element to contain. The ElementType extends the simpler idea of data type. In addition to being able to say what data type an element must have (date, text, BLOB, and so on), you can use the element type to create additional rules.

Notice that these tables represent content types only. It has no place to actually store components. For this, you need an additional table, as shown in Figure 39-7.

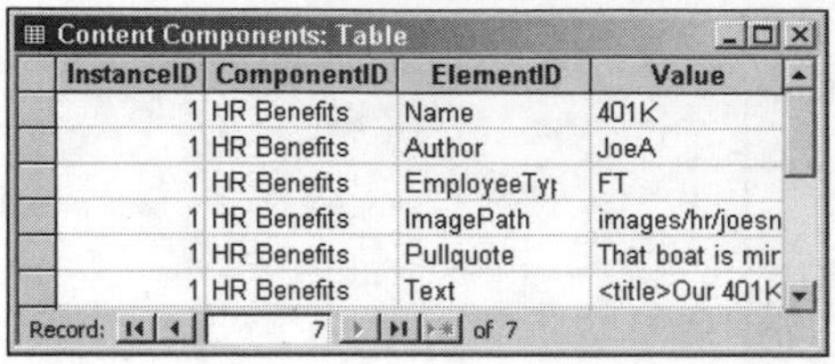

Content Components: Table

	InstanceID	ComponentID	ElementID	Value
	1	HR Benefits	Name	401K
	1	HR Benefits	Author	JoeA
	1	HR Benefits	EmployeeTy	FT
	1	HR Benefits	ImagePath	images/hr/joesn
	1	HR Benefits	Pullquote	That boat is mir
	1	HR Benefits	Text	<title>Our 401K

Record: 7 of 7

Figure 39-7: The Content Components table stores only element values.

This table stores element values and associates them to a particular component and to a general content type as follows:

- ✦ **Element values:** The Value column has the specific content of one element of one component.
- ✦ **Classes:** The ComponentID column identifies the content type of the component, and the ElementID specifies the various elements of the chosen content type.
- ✦ **Instances:** All rows in this table with the same InstanceID are part of the same component. All the visible rows, for example, are part of component number 1.

Again, in real life this single table may actually be a family of tables.

In summary, this more abstract way of representing content types uses tables to define content types and other tables to represent actual components. It's far more flexible than the simpler one table/one content type system. Of course, you don't get something for nothing. Clearly, the more abstract system is harder to understand (and program). In addition, the extra structure and relationships in the abstract system could slow down the CMS in high-transaction environments. Still, as your CMS becomes more complex, a more subtle approach to representing components becomes necessary.

Overall, a more abstract database facilitates authoring, whereas a more concrete database facilitates delivery. Because of this, many CMS designers choose to keep one database structure for authoring and then transform it to a simpler structure as they move the content from the authoring platform (the local LAN, say) to the delivery environment (an Internet server outside the firewall, for example).

Storing hierarchies in an RDB

Relational databases aren't great at representing outlines. They just don't fit conveniently into rows and columns. Instead, a more abstract approach is needed to put an outline in a table. To see an example of how this can be done, consider the following Table of Contents for an intranet:

```
HR Benefits
  401K
  Medical
  Dental
Events
  Event 1
  Event 2
  Event 3
```

```
Useful Sites
   Site 1
   Site 2
   Site 3
News
   Industry
      Story 1
      Story 2
   Organization
      Story 1
      Story 2
```

How might this outline be represented in a database? Surely, you could pack the entire outline as text into a single field. Or you could put each line of text into one row of a database table called TOC table, being careful to keep the right indentation by preserving the right number of spaces or tabs. But neither of these methods gets you very far. In either of these forms, the outline is unmanageable. How do you add or update a line? What if the name of a listed component changes? How does that change get into the outline that you typed into the field or cells? Unfortunately, a more sophisticated approach is needed. To be truly useful, the approach must accomplish the following tasks:

✦ **Represent nesting:** It must represent the nesting in the outline.

✦ **Reference IDs:** It must reference components by ID (and not require you to type the component name when you refer to it) so that, if the name changes, you don't need to retype anything.

✦ **Be complete:** There must be enough information in the outline to enable the system to format it later as a set of links to the component pages (assuming that one of your outputs is a Web publication).

As one solution among many, consider the table shown in Figure 39-8.

TocID	TocText	ParentID	ChildNumber	ComponentID
1	Our Intranet			
2	HR Benefits	1	1	
3	401K	2	1	1
4	Medical	2	2	2
5	Dental	2	3	3
6	Events	1	2	
7	Event 1	6	1	100
8	Event 2	6	2	101
9	Event 3	6	3	102
10	News	1	3	
11	Industry	10	1	
12	Story 1	11	1	201
13	Story 2	11	2	202
15	Organizaiton	10	2	
16	Story 1	15	1	301
17	Story 2	15	2	302

Record: 17 of 17

Figure 39-8: A simple hierarchy database table

The following list takes the table apart, column by column, to see how it accomplishes the tasks that I set out for it:

✦ **The TocID column** simply gives each line of the outline a unique ID.

✦ **The TocText column** specifies the text that should appear on each line of the outline. Notice at this point that two kinds of lines appear in the outline: lines that name the folders of the outline and lines that name particular components. You can tell the two types apart because the rows with no ComponentID correspond to lines of the outline that are folders. Folder rows have the name of the folder in the Text column, whereas component rows have the name of the component in the Text field. Because you're entering the component IDs, you don't actually need to put in component names. I include them in the preceding table only to make the table easier to read.

✦ **The ParentID and ChildNumber columns** establish the nesting of the outline. Notice, for example, that the ParentID of the HR Benefits folder is 1. This is the TocID of the Our Intranet folder. This means that the HR Benefits folder is under the Our Intranet folder. The ChildNumber of the HR Benefits folder is 1. That means that it's the first child under Our Intranet. The Events folder, with a ParentID of 1 and a ChildNumber of 2, is the second child under Our Intranet. The News folder is child number 3 under the Our Intranet folder.

✦ **The ComponentID column** has a component ID in it if the row has a component, not a folder, listed in it. The CMS uses this distinction to decide which outline rows to make expandable folders and which to make links to components.

If this seems a bit complex, you've gotten the general idea. You must play some tricks to get an outline into a table. After it's tricked, however, the database performs as expected and can store any outline you want effectively. One of the nice things about the preceding structure is that it can store as many outlines as you want. All you need to do is create a new folder that has no parent. Then any other folder or component that lists the new folder as its parent is in a new outline. This feature comes in handy, as you may need more than one outline in your CMS.

Storing indexes in an RDB

An index connects phrases to content (or to other phrases). In books, index entries point to pages. In a CMS, index entries (also called *keywords*) can point to pages, components, elements, or text positions.

Indexes that point to components are fairly straightforward to represent in a relational database. A very simple but quite adequate index table is shown in Figure 39-9.

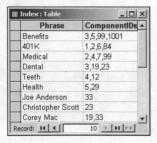

Figure 39-9: A simple Index database table

The first column lists the index term, whereas the second column lists the IDs of the components to which the index term applies. In real life, you may make some modifications to this simple format to increase its quality. First, you may want to make it a two-level index, like the kind you see in the back of a book. To do so, you'd need to somehow represent an outline in the table. A set of fields such as the ones that I used previously to create an outline would do, or you could do something simpler — given that it's only a two-level outline and that it's alphabetical. As most database programmers would tell you immediately, you'd probably want to list all the component IDs in one column. Rather, you'd put them in a separate bridge table that has only one ID per column. The hard part of indexes, of course, isn't creating the database tables to support them, but putting the effort into indexing the content.

If your system is going to produce primarily Web pages, you may be tempted to follow the most well-worn path of associating index keywords with Web pages. Most indexes on the Web today use the <META> tag to create a keyword facility that their own site — as well as any Web- crawling search engine — can use as follows:

```
<META NAME="keywords" CONTENT="knowledge, management, news">
```

This is a fine approach, and in many cases, it's the only approach to indexing a Web site. It needn't preclude creating an index in your CMS that points to components, however, and not pages. As you build a page, it's easy enough to populate the values of the <META> tag from the index terms that apply to any of the components that you've put on the page. As components are added or deleted from the page, their keywords take care of themselves.

Storing cross-references in an RDB

Cross-references have referents and references. The *referent* is the thing linked to. The *reference* is the thing doing the pointing. As an example, consider the following HTML cross-reference:

```
<A HREF="target.htm">Click me</A>
```

The referent is target.htm. You go there if you follow the link. The reference is the entire line. It's the thing in HTML that says, "There's a link here."

Cross-Reference For more information on referents and references, see Chapter 30, "Designing Content Access Structures" in the section titled "What's a cross-reference?"

Cross-references can present a bit of a dilemma in a relational database. Although the referent can usually be a component, the reference can be an entire component, an element within a component (an image, say), or even a single word within an element. In database lingo, a cross-reference can apply to a row, a column within a row, or to a word within a column. Applying a cross-reference to a component is relatively easy. In Figure 39-10, you can see a table that does the trick.

ReferenceID	ReferentID	LinkText
33	23	More about benefits
33	29	More about Chris
33	105	How do I apply?

Figure 39-10: A table to cross-reference components to other components

The ReferenceID column has the ID of the component from which you're linking. The ReferentID has the name of the component that you're linking to. The LinkText column has the text that becomes the link. The idea here is that, if you publish the component onto some sort of page, your software can look in this table to find any links. If they are found, you can render them in the appropriate way. Having your cross-references organized this way gives you a tremendous advantage in keeping them under control. If you delete component 23, for example, this table tells you that you'd better fix the cross-reference to it in component 33. In addition, you can use this table to tell you which components are linked to most often and other very nice-to-know facts about your cross-referencing system.

Notice that this approach is neutral with respect to the kind of publication to be created. You can, for example, use the same information to create an HTML link, as follows:

```
<A HREF="23.htm">More about benefits</A>
```

Or you can create a print link, as follows:

```
More about benefits can be found in the section titled "Benefits
and You."
```

So much for cross-references where the reference is an entire component. How about ones where you need to link from an element within a component? It becomes a bit stickier here, and you have some choices based on the assumptions that you can make, as follows:

✦ **Extra metadata:** If the element is always going to have a link, you can add an extra column to the database that holds the link referent (and link text, if necessary). In other words, the cross-reference can become another element of the component that's always tied to another particular element.

✦ **Element references:** You can add a column to the table in Figure 39-10 that contains an element name or ID. As each component element is rendered, your software can look in the table and see whether that element has a link. This is a bit of overkill, however, because the vast majority of elements don't have links. Still, it would work.

✦ **Link as structured text:** You can treat the element link as a text link, as I describe next.

The most common type of cross-reference is between a phrase and a component. Too bad that it's so unnatural for a relational database to manage such links. The problem lies in the fact that databases have no built-in tools to look into columns and deal with what's inside of them. As long as you obey the data type of the column, you can put as many broken and malformed links inside it as you want.

So how do you manage cross-references where the referent is a word or phrase? First, rather than typing any sort of link in the text of the column, you just put in a link ID. Rather than a link that looks like the following:

```
<A HREF="23.htm">More about benefits</A>
```

you put in a link like the following example:

```
<LINK ID="55">
```

Now there's no information in the text of the column that can change or go bad. Next, use a table similar to the one shown in Figure 39-11.

xref2 : Table

LinkID	ReferenceID	ReferentID	LinkText
55	33	23	More about benefits
56	33	29	More about Chris
57	33	105	How do I apply?

Record: 4 of 4

Figure 39-11: A table for managing links that are embedded within database columns

This table looks a lot like the one I used to link component to component. That fact comes in handy in just a moment. First, I need to discuss how this table works. If you publish component 33, your CMS finds the text:

```
<Link ID="55">
```

Using this, the software can look up LinkID 55 to retrieve the information to make a link. If component 23 (the referent of the link) is deleted, no problem; just as before, your software can look in this table and tell you to go back to component 33 and change link 55.

So you have ways to deal with links from any level of a component. But rather than three different ways to handle three different kinds of links, it would be much better to have one way that covers all three situations, as shown in Figure 39-12.

xref3 : Table

LinkID	LinkType	Element	ReferenceID	ReferentID	LinkText
55	Text	Text	33	23	More about benefits
56	Element	ImagePath	33	29	More about Chris
57	Component		33	105	How do I apply?

Record: 4 of 4

Figure 39-12: A table to deal with every level of linking

I've added LinkType and Element columns to the table, and now it can cover any situation, as follows:

- ✦ **A text-level links:** These have a link type of Text and list the name of the element that contains the text link.
- ✦ **Element-level links:** These have a link type of Element and list the element that becomes the link.
- ✦ **Component-level links:** These have a link type of Component and have no value in the Element column.

Storing sequences in an RDB

Component sequences specify a "next" and a "previous" component relative to the one that you happen to be positioned on. They're the easiest of the structures to store in a relational database. First, the component outline that you create is a built-in sequence. The components that are next and previous in the outline are likely to be of use to you. If that's the only sequence that you need, you have no work to do to store a sequence.

Many sequences can be generated on the fly without any storage at all. A sequence by date, for example, can simply query the repository for components and sort them by a date column.

If you need other sequences, you can create a three-column table. In column 1 is a sequence ID, in column 2 is a component ID, and in column 3 is an order (1, 2, 3, and so on). To construct a sequence, you find all the rows that have the sequence ID that you want to use and order them by the number that's in the order column.

Storing the content model in an RDB

As I mention in the section "A review of the content model," earlier in this chapter, the content model contains all the rules of formation for your content components. The rules fall into the following categories:

✦ The name of each content type.

✦ The allowed elements of each content type.

✦ The element type and allowed values for each element (as I describe in Chapter 27, "Designing Content Types" in the section titled "Elements have types and values").

✦ The access structures in which each content type and instance participates.

I've covered the storage of much of the content model in discussing how content and its relationships are stored in a relational database. Here, I summarize and discuss the issues in a bit more depth. I cover both the simple and abstract relational database models.

In the simple one table/one content type scheme that I discuss earlier in this chapter, you create a single table for each content type that you intend to manage. In the more abstract scheme that I discuss earlier in this chapter, you create tables that define content types and elements and other tables where the element values are stored.

The major difference between these two approaches, and the reason that I contrast them in some detail, is that, in the simple scheme, the content model can't be stored explicitly. Rather, it's implicit in the names of the database parts that you create. In the abstract scheme, most of the content model can be stored explicitly. At first, this may seem like a small distinction, but I don't believe it is. Your content model is the heart of your CMS. If it's buried in the base structure of your repository and not available for review and frequent tweaking, your system isn't flexible enough to flow with the changes that you inevitably make.

In the simple scheme, the name of each content type is stored implicitly in the name of a table. The HRBenefits class, for example, is named in the name of its table. The allowed elements for each class are stored implicitly in the column names in the simple scheme. The fact that the HR Benefits table has five columns means, for example, that the HR component is allowed five elements.

In the abstract scheme, classes are named explicitly in the Components table. There's an actual column where you type the name of the content type. To rename a class, you just change the value in one row and one column. The elements allowed in each component are also named explicitly in the Elements table. You type the name of the element in a particular row and column intersection.

Unlike the simple scheme, the abstract scheme gives you the capability to view and modify your content type structures easily.

Element field types can't be stored explicitly in the simple database scheme. They can, however, be represented. . . more or less. A closed list, for example, can be created for the Author element by linking it to an Author table. Only people listed in the Author table can be chosen.

Similarly, if the user can add a new row to the Author table or select one from the existing list, you have created an open list. Notice, however, that the list isn't open or closed because of the database structure; it's open or closed based on the user interface that you put around the database structure.

In the abstract scheme, you can enter the element field type explicitly. Each element has a specific column for just this purpose (the ElementType column), as shown in Figure 39-13.

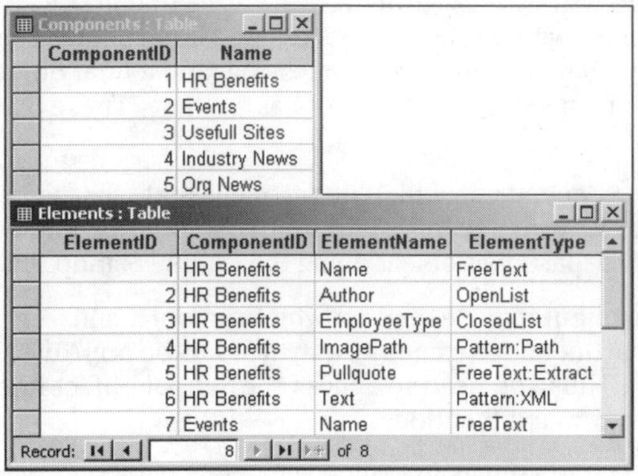

Components : Table

ComponentID	Name
1	HR Benefits
2	Events
3	Usefull Sites
4	Industry News
5	Org News

Elements : Table

ElementID	ComponentID	ElementName	ElementType
1	HR Benefits	Name	FreeText
2	HR Benefits	Author	OpenList
3	HR Benefits	EmployeeType	ClosedList
4	HR Benefits	ImagePath	Pattern:Path
5	HR Benefits	Pullquote	FreeText:Extract
6	HR Benefits	Text	Pattern:XML
7	Events	Name	FreeText

Record: 8 of 8

Figure 39-13: The two tables of the abstract component system

The types shown here extend the element field types (that I describe in Chapter 24, "Working with Metadata" in the section titled "Categorizing Metadata Fields"). The Pattern field type, for example, also states what kind of pattern to expect. (ImagePath expects a *path* and Text expects an *XML*.) As opposed to the simple scheme in which a list was open or closed based on the user interface that you applied to it, here the list is explicitly set to open or closed. Your system can now read the fact that Author is an open list, and it can provide the appropriate user interface.

Allowed element values may or may not be explicit in the simple scheme. On the one hand, I can explicitly set the data type of a column to *date*. Other allowed values can't be made explicit. There's no place, for example, to type the rule that a pattern element called ImagePath must have a valid path and filename in it. This rule is, however, implicit in the validation program that you create to check the contents of this column. In general, the best that you can do to represent allowed values and element types in the simple scheme is to match them to the closest data type.

In the abstract scheme, of course, all allowed values can be made explicit. The ImagePath element, for example, is set specifically to look for a path pattern. You must still code a validation that enforces this pattern, but at least you can code it once and then automatically apply it to any element of the type Pattern:Path. In general, you can use an abstract database schema to represent any sort of element field type that you want, and include enough extra information that your validation and form-building software can figure out how to handle element fields of that type.

Object databases

Object databases were invented as a convenient way to store or *serialize* the data that programmers needed to handle in their object-oriented programming. Programmers, who traditionally used a relational database to store their data, got tired of trying to fit hierarchical data into rows and columns, so they invented a hierarchical storage system.

Object-oriented data mirrors the structure of the programming objects that process it. As a very simple example, suppose that you're writing a program to deal with a university curriculum. You may create an object called Course that does all the processing for particular courses, an object called Department that does the department-level processing, and a final object called School that contains all the functions needed for the school as a whole. These three objects have the following relationships:

✦ **The way that you process a course** depends on which department that class is in. All courses in the English department, for example, may require the student be an English major. Thus you want to access the Department object doing the Course-Signup function.

✦ **The way that you process a department** may depend on which school it's in. All course changes in the English department, for example, may need to be approved by the dean of the Humanities school. Thus you need to access the School object in performing the Department-ChangeCurriculum function.

In plain English, you can represent this relationship as follows:

```
School (has approver's name)
   Department (has course requirement)
      Course (has course data)
```

Somewhere, you must store the approver's name, course requirements, and course data, as well as a lot of other data for large varieties of courses, departments, and schools. A programmer could (and still most often does) create relational database tables to keep track of all this data. There's no natural fit, however, between this hierarchical data and the rows and columns of a database. A much more straightforward way to store the data for this object model may be something like the following example:

```
<SCHOOL>
   <APPROVER></APPROVER>
   <DEPARTMENT>
      <REQUIREMENT></REQUIREMENT>
      <COURSE>
         <COURSEDATA></COURSEDATA>
      </COURSE>
   </DEPARTMENT>
</SCHOOL>
```

To store data into this structure, you simply "walk" down the object hierarchy storing object names and their data. To reload a set of data, you read the data hierarchy, create object instances as you come across their names, and load them with the data that's listed. Of course, in real life there's a bit more to it than the simple explanation that I've given, but I hope that you get the point. The preceding XML structure fits the structure of an object-oriented programmer's world like a hand in a glove. A relational database fits an object world like a square peg in a round hole.

So object databases were invented to provide the programmer with a more straightforward (and faster) way to store and retrieve data for their object hierarchies. I wouldn't have bothered with such a detailed discussion but for the fact that content components are a lot like programming objects (as discussed in Chapter 27, "Designing Content Types" in the section titled "Components are like objects"). Just like objects, components come in a sort of hierarchy. And component hierarchies are just as inconvenient to store in relational databases as object hierarchies. Thus, content programmers have turned to object databases for many of the same reasons that object programmers have.

The hierarchical way that object databases store information is a compelling reason to consider them for a CMS. More important is the fact that the syntax that they use to create the information hierarchies is XML. For a CMS that uses XML as its basic content format, an object database is a natural choice for a repository.

 Cross-Reference I cover the syntax and structure of XML in Chapter 36, "XML and Content Management." I assume here that you're familiar with the basic concepts and vocabulary of XML.

Resistance to object databases

Object databases have fallen from favor somewhat in recent years. Fewer commercial systems use them now than a few years ago. As I see it, two reasons exist for the decrease in popularity:

✦ **They don't scale.** Even though object databases use the same caching and indexing tools as do relational databases, they have not yet proven they can retrieve and process the amount of data that enterprises require from their repositories. At the heart of the problem, I believe, is the need to parse and validate XML. Although relational databases can load records in bulk with little extra time required per extra record, an XML database has to parse the tags of each *record* it loads. The more records in play, the longer this takes.

✦ **There is a skill gap.** The skills required to maintain a relational database are common in the computer discipline. The skills to maintain an object database are not. Thus, when making the decision to buy a product, many organizations will shy away from a product that uses an object database because they do not have staff that is familiar with the management of an object database. In addition, they are biased toward buying applications that use the same databases that they already use for other enterprise applications.

Given the really natural fit between object databases and CM systems, I've been disappointed that so little progress has been made to bring them into the center of the CM world. As time goes by, I'm still hoping that the performance problems with object databases will be solved and they will take their place along side relational databases as solid CM repositories.

With or without an object database, however, the concepts of content model storage in an XML system are worth understanding and applying where possible.

XML files versus object databases

You don't need an object database to program in XML. In fact, few XML programmers know much about object databases. They work with XML files. An XML file carries all the same structure and syntax of an object database. On the other hand, for a number of reasons, you may choose (as some CMS product companies have) to use an object database:

✦ **Multiple files:** You may need to work with many XML files and would like them all united by a single hierarchy and searchable by the cross-file capabilities that an object database supplies.

✦ **Delivery:** You may need a more sophisticated delivery environment than a file system can offer. Many object databases, for example, come with the Web caching, load balancing, and replication functionality you need to run a high-throughput site.

✦ **Development environment:** You may prefer the programming and administration environment that an object database provides. Many object databases, for example, come with their own equivalents or extensions of XML standards. These include XPath and XSLT that you may prefer to use instead of the less-developed standards.

✦ **Performance:** Object databases offer some performance gains over XML files. Many provide indexes, for example, that enable you to find commonly searched-for metadata more quickly than you could in an XML file. They will also cache XML fragments for faster delivery.

Just about all of what I cover in the sections that follow applies equally well to an object database or XML files. In either case, the main event isn't the container (the file or database) but the XML it contains.

Storing content types and components in XML

The simplest way to store components in XML is inside a single element that bears the name of the content type:

```
<HRBENEFIT>
  <ID>1</ID>
  <NAME>401K</NAME>
  <TYPE>Standard</TYPE>
  <AUTHOR>Derek Andrews</AUTHOR>
  <EMPLOYEETYPE>FT</EMPLOYEETYPE>
  <IMAGEPATH>images/hr/joesmile.jpg</IMAGEPATH>
  <TEXT>Our great 401K plan...</TEXT>
</HRBENEFIT>
```

The component is an XML element, and all the component's elements are XML elements. You can get a lot more flexibility and readability out of the component's XML code by making some of the elements into attributes, as shown in the following example:

```
<HRBENEFIT ID="HR1" Type="Standard" AuthorID="A21"
EmployeeType="FT">
  <NAME>401K</NAME>
  <IMAGEPATH>images/hr/joesmile.jpg</IMAGEPATH>
  <TEXT>Our great 401K plan...</TEXT>
</HRBENEFIT>
```

I chose to change the ID, Type, Author, and EmployeeType into attributes because each one was a particular kind of element field, as I explain here:

✦ **The ID element is a unique identifier.** It's automatically generated by the CMS (and possibly never seen by a user). By making it an attribute, you can specify (in a DTD or schema) that it's an ID and must be unique across all HRBenefit components. One small change is needed to create the ID attribute. In XML, IDs must begin with a character, so I changed the value from 1 to HR1.

✦ **The Type and EmployeeType component elements are closed lists.** The user chooses a value from a constrained set of choices. By making them attributes, you can define them as closed lists (in a DTD or schema) and specify the valid choices. Unfortunately, there's no equally easy way to create open lists in an XML schema.

✦ **The Author component element is more complex.** Assume that Author components exist elsewhere in the system and these components contain author names, job titles, e-mail addresses, and the like. Rather than duplicate information here that resides in another Author component, it's much wiser to simply refer to that author component. In other words, the Author component element is an open list whose values are references to another component. By making it an attribute, you can specify that it's a reference (called an IDREF in DTD parlance) and enforce that it always points to an existing Author component. Because it's an IDREF attribute, I changed its name to AuthorID and changed its value from the author's name to the ID of his component.

To store all the HRBenefit components, you simply wrap them in a higher element:

```
<HRBENEFITS>
   <HRBENEFIT ID="HR1" Type="Standard" AuthorID="A21"
   EmployeeType="FT">
      <NAME>401K</NAME>
      <IMAGEPATH>images/hr/joesmile.jpg</IMAGEPATH>
      <TEXT>Our great 401K plan...</TEXT>
   </HRBENEFIT>
   <HRBENEFIT ID="HR2" Type="Standard" AuthorID="A43"
   EmployeeType="FT">
      <NAME>Medical</NAME>
      <IMAGEPATH>images/hr/coreysmile.jpg</IMAGEPATH>
      <TEXT>Wait till you see the...</TEXT>
   </HRBENEFIT>
   <HRBENEFIT ID="HR3" Type="Standard" AuthorID="A9"
   EmployeeType="FT+">
      <NAME>Dental</NAME>
      <IMAGEPATH>images/hr/laurasmile.jpg</IMAGEPATH>
      <TEXT>We now do teeth!...</TEXT>
   </HRBENEFIT>
</HRBENEFITS>
```

Notice the use of the singular and the plural in my tag-naming conventions. Components are named with the singular (HRBENEFIT). The content type is named with the plural form of the instance (HRBENEFITS). This is a common naming convention in both XML and object-oriented programming.

If you get the feeling that XML is easy to create, you're right . . . and wrong. It's very easy to type blocks of text like the preceding ones; it's very hard to create a large, interconnected system of elements that's controlled as rigorously as you need it to be. In other words, following the syntax rules of XML is easy (the concept of well-formed XML). Creating and then following the complex set of construction rules specified by a DTD or schema is hard (the concept of valid XML). Nevertheless, you can see that XML is quite capable of representing components.

If you're storing your components in a relational database, as I discuss earlier in this chapter, you have to do some hard thinking about how to store structured text in rows and columns. In an XML repository, the issue is much simpler. Suppose that you have the following structure in the <TEXT> element of the HRBenefit component:

```
<TEXT>
   <TITLE>We now do Teeth!</TITLE>
   <PULLQUOTE><B>My gums and molars never felt so good.</B>
      <IMAGE>laurasmile.jpg</IMAGE>
   </PULLQUOTE>
   <H1>a paragraph of text here
      <H2>a paragraph of text here</H2>
```

```
  </H1>
  <H1>a paragraph of text here</H1>
  <CONCLUSION>Put your mouth where our money is-<B>use
  the plan!</B></CONCLUSION>
</TEXT>
```

To store this structure in an XML file or database, you simply include it within the larger component XML and you're done. You don't need special techniques for retrieving the structured text or elevating any part of it to special metadata containers. The elements that are within the <TEXT> tags are as accessible to the users of the repository as any other elements of the component. In fact, they're just more elements of the component. Furthermore, it doesn't matter if some components have a lot of different structures in their <TEXT> elements and others very little. Whatever is there is stored and accessible right down to the lowest <B> tag.

Of course, you don't get this sort of advantage for nothing. What I conveniently skipped over in the preceding description is that a lot of work you must put into the text to get it to the point where you can just paste it into the <TEXT> element.

In particular, you must ensure the following:

✦ **The text must be well-formed XML.** Although this isn't strictly true (you can put in any text you want if you use an XML feature called a CDATA section), it's true enough if you want to access and use the text. It may be relatively easy to get the text into XML (from HTML, for example) or quite difficult (from some old word-processing format, for example).

✦ **The text must be valid XML.** Although this isn't strictly true (you don't need to validate your XML), it's true enough if you want to get any of the advantages of having rules around your XML that are listed in a DTD or schema.

In a relational database, it doesn't matter what kind of text is in the rows and columns; the main problem is recognizing the structure in structured text. In object databases and XML files, it matters a lot what kind of text you store in each element. Although relational databases have a hard time with structured text, XML files and databases have a hard time dealing with text that's not structured.

Storing hierarchies in XML

XML is excellent, of course, at storing hierarchies. Take, for example, the following intranet site outline:

```
  Event 3
Useful Sites
  Site 1
  Site 2
  Site 3
News
  Industry
     Story 1
     Story 2
  Organization
     Story 1
     Story 2
```

This site is stored intuitively and quickly as the following set of elements:

```
<OUTLINE>
  <FOLDER Name="HR Benefits">
     <ITEM ID="HR401K">
     <ITEM ID="HRMedical">
     <ITEM ID="HRDental">
  </FOLDER>
  <FOLDER Name="Events">
     <ITEM ID="Event1">
     <ITEM ID="Event2">
     <ITEM ID="Event3">
  </FOLDER>
  <FOLDER Name="Useful Sites">
     <ITEM ID="Site1">
     <ITEM ID="Site2">
     <ITEM ID="Site3">
  </FOLDER>
  <FOLDER Name="News">
     <FOLDER Name="Industry">
        <ITEM ID="IStory1">
        <ITEM ID="IStory2">
     </FOLDER>
     <FOLDER Name="Organization">
        <ITEM ID="OStory1">
        <ITEM ID="OStory2">
     </FOLDER>
  </FOLDER>
</OUTLINE>
```

The XML version of the outline is quite similar to the plain-text version of the outline. It has these important differences, however: Clearly, the XML version is a lot more verbose. In fact, XML is the bane of most Spartan programmers who prefer a minimum of markup characters and believe that actually using plain English words in markup is for beginners. Still, every feature of the outline must be explicitly coded, including the following:

✦ **Nesting:** The XML represents the nesting in the outline by having folder elements embedded in other folder elements.

✦ **ID references:** The XML references components by Id so that, if the name changes, you don't need to retype anything. The Id is enough information for the system to later go fetch the items' names and create a set of links to the component pages.

Notice that this outline assumes that elements somewhere in the XML code contain the Ids referred to. In content management parlance, you'd say that this outline refers to a set of HR, Site, IStory, and OStory components.

Storing indexes in XML

Representing an index in XML is fairly straightforward and follows the same logic as it does in a relational database. The index of HR components that I describe earlier in this chapter for example, can be represented as follows in XML:

```
<INDEX>
  <TERM Name="Benefits" ID="I1">
     <COMPONENTID>HR3</COMPONENTID>
     <COMPONENTID>HR5</COMPONENTID>
     <COMPONENTID>HR99</COMPONENTID>
     <COMPONENTID>HR1001</COMPONENTID>
  </TERM>
  <TERM Name="401K" ID="I2">
     <COMPONENTID>HR1</COMPONENTID>
     <COMPONENTID>HR2</COMPONENTID>
     <COMPONENTID>HR6</COMPONENTID>
     <COMPONENTID>HR84</COMPONENTID>
  </Term>
</Index>
```

The following is happening in the preceding example:

✦ The <INDEX> element sets the index apart from other structures in the XML repository.

✦ The <TERM> element encloses a single index entry. It has a name attribute that has the term that's being indexed and an ID attribute that uniquely identifies the term.

✦ The <COMPONENTID> element marks a single component that's indexed by the term. Only the Id of the component is given. The name of the component (or its page number if you're producing a print publication) is retrieved by using the Id as the index is published.

By the way, I could have used a shortened form of XML where all the component Ids are packed into a single attribute, but it would have been harder to read and explain.

Storing cross-references in XML

In XML, cross-references all follow the structure of a text link that I discuss in the section "Storing cross-references in an RDB" earlier in this chapter. The simplest form of a cross-reference may look as follows in an XML structure:

```
<LINK>For more information, see
<REFERENTID>HR3</REFERENTID></LINK>
```

The reference is enclosed in the <LINK> element, and the referent Id is enclosed in the <REFERENTID> element. To add more control to the link, you can add some extra attributes, as in the following example:

```
<LINK Type="formore" Autotext = "yes"
Position="inline"><REFERENTID>HR3</REFERENTID></LINK>
```

In this case, the following extra attributes are in the link:

✦ **The Type attribute** names the cross-referencing strategy that this link is part of. (I describe cross-reference strategies in Chapter 30, "Designing Content Access Structures" in the section titled "What's a cross-reference?") In this case, I specified that the link is part of the "formore" strategy. Based on the value of this attribute, I can trigger different publication and management functions for the cross-reference.

✦ **The Autotext attribute** specifies whether the reference is created by using a standard text string or the string provided in the <LINK> element. In this case, I specified that the link should use standard text. Thus I could make the reference text, "For more information, see…," into a standard text block that the CMS publishing templates automatically access and insert. If I have multiple publication formats, I could create different standard text blocks that are appropriate to each format (Web, print, e-mail, and so on).

✦ **The Position attribute** specifies how the link ought to be positioned in the publications you produce. In this case, I specified "inline," which I intend to mean, "Position the link right at the place where the <LINK> tag is in the text." I may have other options for positioning the link at the top or bottom of the element or component in which it's embedded.

There's nothing special about the attributes and values I chose to include in the <LINK> element. I invented these particular structures to illustrate the point that you can add as much structure to the representation of your links as necessary to achieve the kind of control you want. As I've said before, however, creating structure is easy; finding the staff time to learn and enter all the structure you create is the hard part.

Because XML is always accessible down to the smallest element, it's easy to link to and from any level of content. As I mention in the section "Storing cross-references in an RDB," earlier in this chapter, a relational database is troublesome to link to from any chunk smaller than a whole component. Because all links are text links in XML, the link can be embedded at any level of a component. In addition, it's difficult to link to any chunk smaller than a full component. In XML, any level of element can have an Id associated with it and so be the target of a cross-reference. Consider, for example, the following link:

```
<LINK>For more information,
see <REFERENTID>HR3</REFERENTID></LINK>
```

What chunk of content does the ID HR3 refer to? It may be a component, a component element, or even a low-level <P> tag within a component element. Except for any extra features that you add to the presentation, it makes no difference to the XML what level of structure you refer to.

Storing sequences in XML

Because components are generally embedded in a hierarchy in an XML structure, the primary sequence is usually available for free from the structure itself.

In addition to any sequences that can be created automatically by sorting components by one or other of their elements, other sequences can be easily represented as follows:

```
<SEQUENCE Type = "Topics">
  <COMPONENTID>HR4</COMPONENTID>
  <COMPONENTID>HR24</COMPONENTID>
  <COMPONENTID>HR45</COMPONENTID>
  <COMPONENTID>HR6</COMPONENTID>
</SEQUENCE>
```

You can use the Type attribute of the <SEQUENCE> element to trigger any particular management or publishing functions that are particular to this sort of sequence. "Topics" type sequences, for example, may have a particular icon that's used in the sequence links.

Storing the content model in XML

Much of the content model is in the XML code that stores the components, just as it is in relational databases. Generally, XML behaves more like the abstract relational database model, in which the names and allowed values of the content types and elements are stored in one place and the values are stored elsewhere. In the relational database world, programmers had to invent a way to separate the structure of their components from the components themselves. In the XML world, structure is always separate from data. XML uses Document Template Definitions (DTDs) or XML Schemas to define the structure that the data must follow.

Here is the segment of XML that I used earlier to represent an HR component:

```
<HRBENEFIT >
  <ID>1</ID>
  <NAME>401K</NAME>
  <TYPE>Standard</TYPE>
  <AUTHOR>Derek Andrews</AUTHOR>
  <EMPLOYEETYPE>FT</Employeetype>
  <IMAGEPATH>images/hr/joesmile.jpg</IMAGEPATH>
  <TEXT>Our great 401K plan...</TEXT>
</HRBENEFIT>
```

For simplicity, I converted all component elements into XML elements. In real life, you'd make some of your component elements XML attributes, as in the following example:

```
<HRBENEFIT ID="1" Type="Standard" AuthorId="A1"
EmployeeType="FT">
  <NAME>401K</NAME>
  <IMAGEPATH>images/hr/joesmile.jpg</IMAGEPATH>
  <TEXT>Our great 401K plan...</TEXT>
</HRBENEFIT>
```

With one exception, these two versions of the HRBenefit component are informationally equivalent. In the second example, rather than typing in the name of an author, I use an author ID that points to an author structure that's somewhere else. Although the two versions may be informationally equivalent, the second is much easier to manage. By making some of the component elements XML attributes, you can use some of the features of an XML DTD or XML Schema to control them. Here's a DTD that you may use to specify the allowed structure of HR components of the second variety:

```
<!ELEMENT HRBENEFITS (HRBENEFIT)+>
<!ELEMENT HRBENEFIT (NAME, IMAGEPATH, TEXT)>
<!ATTLIST HRBENEFIT
  ID ID #REQUIRED
  Type (Standard | Extended) #REQUIRED
  AuthorId IDREF #REQUIRED
  EmployeeType (FT | PT | ALL) #REQUIRED
>
<!ELEMENT NAME (#PCDATA)>
<!ELEMENT IMAGEPATH (#PCDATA)>
<!ELEMENT TEXT (#PCDATA)>
```

Without going into too much detail about how to construct a DTD, I can point out some significant ways in which this DTD specifies component and element structure, as follows:

✦ **Nesting:** The first two lines of the DTD establish the way XML tags may nest within each other. The first line states that an <HRBENEFITS> element may have within it one or more <HRBENEFIT> elements. That's what the phrase (HRBENEFIT)+ means. The second line establishes that the <HRBENEFIT> element must contain a <NAME>,

<IMAGEPATH>, and <TEXT> element in that order. That's what the phrase (NAME, IMAGEPATH, TEXT) means. DTDs enable you to specify and enforce existence, number, and order of all allowed elements.

✦ **Content types:** The DTD has no specific syntax for content type. In fact, as I've said before, any XML element can be a content type. In this case, the <HRBENEFITS> element defines the content type. If I wanted to say more than simply that the content type exists, I could add attributes or other child elements to the <HRBENEFITS> element to add parameters to the content type as a whole. I may use this feature, for example, to specify how often components of this content type are to be reviewed.

✦ **Components:** The <HRBENEFITS> element defines parameters for the content type as a whole. The <HRBENEFIT> element defines how components must be structured. In this case, line 2 of the DTD specifies that each HRBenefit component has a <NAME>, <IMAGEPATH>, and <TEXT> child element. Lines 3 through 8 specify that each HRBenefit component has an Id, Type, AuthorID, and EmployeeType attribute. ATTLIST means attribute list. The list begins on the line with the word ATTLIST and ends with a closing angle bracket (>).

✦ **XML attributes as component elements:** The lines of the DTD that define attributes tell you a lot about what kinds of component elements they are. Line 4 states that the Id component element is a required Id. That means that it must be supplied; it must begin with a letter; and it must be unique throughout the repository. Line 5 states that the Type component element is a required closed list with allowed values of "Standard" or "Extended." Line 6 states that the AuthorType component element is a required Id reference. That means that it must contain a valid Id from some other element in the repository (some author component in this case). Finally, line 7 states that the EmployeeType component element is a closed list with allowed values of "FT," "PT," or "ALL."

✦ **XML elements as component elements:** The final three lines of the DTD define the structure of the Name, ImagePath, and Text component elements. In this case, they're all defined in the same way. Each is allowed to be just text with no extra markup inside it. If I had wanted to go further in the definition, I could have defined attributes and child elements for any of or all these to further define them. Given that the <TEXT> element may contain additional markup, for example, I could have defined its allowed child elements and attributes to whatever level I wanted.

Not all element types can be represented in a DTD. Because you type the allowed values of a list right into the definition of a list attribute, for example, it's not possible (without some trickery) to create an open list by using a DTD. To get around the limitations of DTDs, you can create an abstraction similar to the one in this chapter for relational databases. Rather than coding the list right into the DTD, you can store it as data in an XML file. Even given the limited example that I provide, I hope that you can still get a feeling for how the content model can be represented in a DTD.

XML Schema are actually somewhat better at representing content models; for example, many more element types are available to you in a schema. Because I've discussed schemas throughout the rest of this chapter, however, I decided to give you a DTD example here.

File systems

Repositories that are strictly file-based are a remnant of the past era of document management and are fast disappearing. Even document management systems use one form or another of databases to store their metadata. This isn't to say that files play no part in a CMS repository.

On the contrary, wherever you have content that doesn't need to be parsed and should always be used as a complete unit, a file is an acceptable means of storage.

In this discussion, I disregard the fact that relational databases and XML repositories are also files. I intend the discussion to concern systems in which components or elements are stored as separate files.

In addition to the numerous files such as templates, configuration files, include files, and the like that you may find in a repository, you're also likely to find some types of content stored as files. In particular, images and other media are likely to be stored as files rather than embedded in a relational database or XML structure. In these cases, the files are referred to rather than included in the database or XML. In addition, you may choose to store some of your components as separate XML files, as illustrated in Figure 39-14.

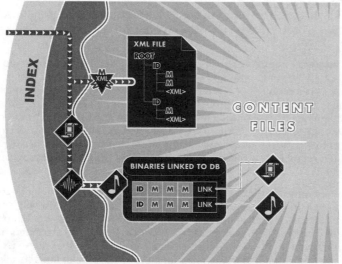

Figure 39-14: Files can be stored and referenced in a database. In addition, components can be stored as separate XML files.

Rather than putting an image or other media file into a database, you can simply refer to its file name in the database and keep the file in a directory where it can be accessed easily if needed.

If you store media in files, make sure that the directory is protected. You don't want people to access these files directly. The CMS must be between the users and the files to stay synchronized and in control of them.

Many of today's systems keep a set of individual XML files inside the repository to store individual components. If you use a system like this, make sure that you have some way to perform the following tasks:

✦ **Managing structure inconsistency:** Each XML file type is its own world. It's validated by its own DTD or schema with its own structure and rules. If you have ten different kinds of XML files in your repository, you need 10 different DTDs or schemas to validate them. You need some overarching process or technology to ensure that the structures don't conflict with each other and can be managed as a whole.

✦ **Maintaining integrity:** Within a single XML file, it's easy to ensure that your links are valid. If you use ID and IDREF attribute types, any XML parser tells you whether you have a non-unique ID or a reference to an ID that doesn't exist. You don't get this advantage across XML files. Instead, you need extra software to resolve and validate any references that cross file boundaries.

✦ **Performance:** At times you may open a large number of individual files to find what you're looking for. In these cases, your system may be extremely slow. It gets proportionally slower the more files you add. And, although there's no file-size limitation to an XML file, the tools you're using to handle the XML may have file-size limitations, or their performance may start to degrade if your XML file gets extremely large.

✦ **Access structures in the file system:** Access structures span components. To create access structures in a system that has multiple files, you must create yet more files that reference the individual files. It's not impossible to do so; it's just a lot of extra work that you wouldn't need to do if you use a single XML file or object database.

Versioning System

Although the repository system is all about storing content, versioning is all about keeping the content safe from unintended changes.

Versioning means being able to save and restore using older copies of content that you have stored. It is similar to, but distinct from backup. When you back up, your aim is to protect yourself from data loss. If something happens to your primary system, you can restore it later to its most recently backed-up state. When you version, your aim is to keep older incarnations of content because you think you might need to get back to that incarnation later. You might also use the concept of versions to implement the concept of two child components that take different directions from the original. Although backup systems often preserve the information needed to link newer and older forms of the same content, they usually pay little attention to the features needed to make finding and retrieving back versions easy. Rather, their chief features revolve around making a copy of the complete system and later restoring that complete system. Whereas version systems make copies when you change a particular component, backup systems make a copy of the whole repository when you run the backup program. Still, if you don't have specific versioning support in your CMS, you might consider augmenting whatever backup support you have (and I sincerely hope you do have backup support) to make it possible to get some of the features I cite for versioning.

Versioning has an overlap, as well, with revisioning. In fact, you can think of revision tracking as a much more granular way to do versioning. In revision tracking, each time an author makes a change it is marked and is undoable. In versioning, each time the author saves completed changes, a new version is created and linked to the previously-saved component. However, when tracked revisions are accepted, the trail of revisions is generally lost, but the trail of previous versions is (or can be) preserved indefinitely.

In my travels, I have seen versioning made to be a much bigger consideration than it really is. Most people never go back to old versions to undo changes because they can't remember where the change actually occurred (or even that a change occurred). More likely, they go forward by fixing the current version rather than going back to some older version. Still, when you do need to go back and when you can remember where to go back to, versioning can't be beat. The only situation where versioning is mandatory is when you are legally bound to be able to reproduce the state of your content at a certain time. For example, if you run a legal services site and you have legal advice components, you may be bound by law to be able to show exactly what your advice was on a particular day. In a situation like that, you need a very robust versioning system.

Automatic versus manual versioning

Your system can create new versions under either of two conditions:

✦ **When you tell it to.** If you or your editor wants to save a version, you engage the versioning feature; a copy, linked somehow to the original, is saved for you. In some systems you can also add a comment to the version to say why you made it.

✦ **Every time you save the component.** In this case, the system notices when the component has changed and automatically create the version.

In either case, the system has a choice about how the version is actually created. The system can create a complete new copy of the changed component, or the system can maintain a transaction log. The log specifies what was changed between the saves. In a system like this, you restore a previous version by reading back through the log and undoing the changes in reverse order until you reach the version you want to restore.

If you need to be able to roll back to versions at any point in time, you want automatic versioning. If, instead, you are creating versions for editorial reasons, it may be much better to create manual versions that you also mark with comments to state why the version was made.

Granularity of versions

You may have a number of entities that need to have versions in your system. For example:

✦ **Individual elements of individual components** might have versions. For example, you might want to specifically track versions on the body element of your article components and be able to roll back changes to it independently of the other elements of that component.

✦ **Whole components** can have versions. For example, you might want to track versions of whole article components.

✦ **Access structures** can have versions. For example, you might want to be able to version and roll back the changes you make to a product taxonomy.

✦ **Publication and authoring templates** can have versions. For each state of your authoring and publishing system, a corresponding set of templates gets information in and out of the system.

✦ **Workflows and personalizations** can have versions. In fact, all the rules that guide your system can change and might be candidates for versioning.

✦ **Whole publications** can have versions. For example, you may want to be able to reproduce the site you had on a particular day in the past.

I think you can see that there is quite a lot that you could version in addition to your content. In fact, if you want to version whole publications in the most robust way, you are going to have to version all the items I list and more. How can you produce the site you had one year ago without the templates, access structures, and personalizations you had a year ago? For this reason, the most popular approach to versioning sites is to simply translate them into static pages and save them like a backup. In this way, you avoid having to roll back the world in order to rebuild the site.

Another possible way to version is to be sure you can roll back the state of your content repository to any previous time and then be satisfied, not with having the actual previous site, but with having all the content that drove the previous site. Depending on your need for roll back, it may be fine to have the raw material only and not the finished product.

It is very difficult to do comprehensive versioning of everything in the CMS that is needed to rebuild any publication from any time. However, it is not impossible. In fact, conceptually, it is easy. You simply engage every file and record you have in automatic versioning. In practice, however, it is a different story. For example, what if your personalization system stores its rules in a proprietary format that you can't access in order to version it? What if you acquire content dynamically for your publications and never actually store it? It can't be versioned if it can't be stored. For these and a myriad of other little reasons, comprehensive versioning of everything is really hard. For this reason, where versioning is called for, the most common compromise is to version whole components. This approach does not require you to version everything and is usually nicely accounted for by whatever transaction logging is built into the database or other data storage system you are using.

Restoring

Obviously, you have no reason to make versions unless you can get them back. Consider these aspects of a restore feature when you build or buy:

✦ Is it reasonably easy for a user with permissions to restore the previous version without the need of a database administrator?

✦ Can you browse the log or see a list of previous versions to know what versions have been kept?

✦ Can you preview older versions to know exactly what is in them?

✦ Can you clone an older version in addition to simply restoring it? In other words, you might not want to replace the current version with the older one, but rather make a copy of the older one and turn it into a new component.

Clearly you need some form of restore feature. Your choice lies in how fancy you want to make this feature and how much user interface you want to devote to it.

Differencing versions

Given two versions of the same thing (usually the "thing" is a database record or text file), what is different and what is the same? In a typical scenario, you have two seemingly similar versions of the same component and you want to know which to take as the master. In these situations, it is really helpful to have a differencing feature that can contrast the differences between the two for you and present them in a useful way. The two most useful ways that I know of are:

✦ A visual representation of the two contenders side-by-side. Each difference is somehow highlighted so you can see it.

✦ A report representation that summarizes changes and lets you move through the comparison quickly.

Any number of tools, built into CMS systems or standalone, provide this feature. In addition to simply making the comparison, you may want your feature to:

✦ Let you build a new version that combines the best features of the two older ones.

✦ Trigger workflow based on the results of your comparisons.

✦ Support a batch mode where you move through a whole series of comparisons, not just one.

✦ Edit while you compare so you can not only accept one or the other but create new information at the same time.

This feature is most called for when you have large masses of legacy content to move through. Often when you inherit an old (in Internet years) Web site, you have a lot of differencing to do to make the transition. You may need differencing on an ongoing basis if your acquisition sources are unreliable; they may pass you the same or slightly modified information over and over and expect you to sort out what is new from what is the same.

Source branching

Most versioning is about rolling back to an earlier version of the same item in the CMS. In some cases, the versioning system is used in addition (or instead) to keep a link between the parent and child of a component. For example, suppose you need to have three localized version of the same component, or you have two kinds of an article abstract element: one intended for a lay person and the other intended for a professional. In the first case, the localized versions can be considered children of the key language version. In the second case, the lay and professional elements are children of the core article component.

In either case you might say that you have various versions of the component, and thus that you are going to use a versioning system to manage the issue. My personal preference is to say you are localizing or personalizing, and leave the idea of versioning used specifically for roll back. However, this idea of versioning is prevalent enough in the CM industry that it is worth mentioning.

Source Control System (Content and File Sharing)

Although versioning lets you recover your content from unintended changes, a source control system helps prevent the problems that could be caused by unauthorized changes or multiple people working on the same content simultaneously.

Computer programming projects often involve hundreds or thousands of files and a whole team of programmers. You can imagine that keeping track of all these files is a big task. To accomplish this task, *source control systems* were invented. *Source,* in this usage, refers to the source code from which final executable programs are compiled.

 Note   It is somewhat of a misnomer to call these systems source control because they actually manage object code and executables as well as source.

In essence, source control systems allow a group of people to manage their interaction around a group of files. The concept of source control has made its way from programming to CM because CM, too, has to manage such interactions. Some CM systems have literally implemented programmer-style source control. In considering source control, it is specifically the sharing features that are of most interest here. (I have discussed elsewhere the versioning and backup features that source control systems also include.) As the CM discipline matures, I expect that the idea of source control will melt into versioning, backup, and content sharing.

However, for the present, source control is an established, well-understood, and sometimes irreplaceable part of a CMS. So, although the part I pick out to discuss here is sharing, you should understand that you may implement control that includes features I don't cover here.

Sharing granularity

Just as you can version many different items in a CMS, you can also share many different items in a CMS. For example, you can share:

✦ **Individual elements of individual components.** For example, two people can work on the same body element, while at the same time another person can be working on the metadata of the same component.

✦ **Whole components.** For example, an editor and an author can share a component back and forth until it is ready for publication.

✦ **Access structures.** More than one person might be allowed to work on, for example, a subject hierarchy.

✦ **Publication and authoring templates.** Programmers and designers commonly share ownership of templates as they are developed and maintained.

✦ **Code and other files.** Of course, programmers might need to share programming code files. But in addition, rules files, user permissions lists, and a host of other supporting files are also candidates for sharing and can also be included in your sharing system. Interestingly (but not surprisingly), programmers generally do not want to use a CMS to share code. They have their own source control systems that are outside the CMS.

The issues in sharing are similar as well to the issues of versioning. In fact, sharing and versioning are really two sides of the same coin. In versioning, you track who did what and when, whereas in sharing you make sure that people cannot overwrite the changes that others have made. As in sharing, the main issue to be grappled with is how complete to make your sharing system. Should all files or records in the CMS be controlled by the sharing system, or should only the items that are the most shared be included?

Implementing a sharing system at a file level is most common in CMSs. This is because file sharing is a known and well-worn function of source control systems. Record sharing (where database records are allowed to be jointly owned) is becoming a mandatory part of most commercial systems because, without it, content components cannot be shared. Record sharing is not too hard to implement because it can leverage the record-locking features that databases already contain. Sharing to the level of an element is harder to implement because elements are often implemented in databases as fields, which cannot be individually locked. Still, if you need to support parallel workflows (see the section later in this chapter titled "Parallel and sequential workflows"), you will really be helped by element-level sharing.

Locking

The key to sharing is locking. To prevent one user from overwriting the changes another is about to make, your system has to prevent users from saving changes on an item that is currently being changed. The simplest way to do this is to disallow any access to the item while the other person is working on it. Although this is easy to implement, it will frustrate users who simply want to look at or copy from the item.

A better way to implement locking is to allow read-only copies of the item to be opened. Users still have access but cannot modify the item.

Tip Beware of this scenario: User A checks out a component. It is locked to User B, who gets a read-only version. User B is impatient so she makes a copy of the component and begins to change it, thinking she will merge her work with the other later on. However, when later on comes, she forgets to do the merger and instead uploads her changes over User A's work. It happens. There is no security system that cannot be defeated by laziness. You can see the importance of versioning as a way to recover from these sorts of mistakes by rolling back.

Locking, of course, is critical to sharing. Consider, however, what gets locked. If you are sharing an element, should you lock the whole component when the element is being changed? Some systems will want you to. If a user is editing an item, should you lock all items that are under it in a subject taxonomy — not to prevent overwrites, but to signal that authors had better see the changes to the items above before changing the ones below?

Check in and out

The most fundamental form of sharing is check in and check out. When one user wants to work on the item, she checks it out and when she is finished, she checks the item back in. Consider these attributes of the check-out feature you buy or build:

✦ **Visual representation:** Consider how the checked-in and -out files are represented. Often little icons are used to show the status of an item. It is even better if the current owner is listed as well.

✦ **Batch in and out:** You may want to allow users to select a batch of files to work with at the same time.

✦ **Overrides:** Can you force a check-in when Mei Mei goes on vacation and forgets to check her work back in?

✦ **Comments:** Can the user log a comment when she checks in an item?

✦ **Integrations:** To what extent should check-in be connected to the workflow system so that, for example, a checked-in file is passed on to the next workflow stage. Should you version a component each time it is checked in, or each time it is saved but not checked in?

It is hard to avoid some form of check in and check out, nor should you try. The larger the team that touches the files, the greater the benefit.

Notification

It's nice to know when checked-out items become available for your use. This feature is usually integrated as part of the workflow feature set, most frequently with the check-in workflow. Notification can be as simple as an e-mail sent to the next person in the work flow — editor, metator, reviewer, builder, and so on — that serves as a trigger for the next step in the work-flow. It may also be broadcast to certain members of the team so that everyone knows when significant events happen that may affect her work downstream. Notification may allow a user checking in to include a comment in the notification about what was changed, and it may also include a link to take the recipient right to the content that was checked in.

In addition to check-in notification, you can imagine that other sorts of notifications may also be useful, particularly if you can customize them. For example, a notification that's sent to the project manager when a certain number of components are queued in the editorial work-flow could be used to alert her that more editors may be needed for a certain task.

At the very least, check-in notifications sent to the next person in a workflow are essential to keeping a team working in sync. Other notification features are most helpful for larger teams. A comprehensive set of notifications also prevents team members from overlooking work tasks assigned to them—or making excuses for doing so.

Audit trails

As an administrator, you may want the capability to peer into or report on the sharing situation within the organization. For example, you may want to know:

✦ Who has what checked out now.

✦ How long have certain files been checked out and what activity has taken place in the files since they were checked out (number of saves, types of changes, and so on).

✦ How do items move between owners based on owner, job type, item type, workflow stage, and so on? You can imagine that all sorts of administrative decisions could be supported by the data that comes from sharing.

Auditing a sharing process could be as simple as using the existing check-in and -out user interface, or as complex as writing sophisticated reporting and visualization routines that tie the user, workflow, versioning, and sharing systems together. If you have a large and contentious staff or if you are plagued by bottlenecks and inefficiencies in your collection system, however, you may opt for the more sophisticated approach to both diagnose the problem and provide supporting evidence for the solution.

Localization System

Whereas the source control system keeps people from working on the same content simultaneously, the localization system is all about producing multiple versions of content for various audiences and localities.

Localization means producing publications for a variety of languages and cultures. In one sense, localization is what a CMS is all about. If you consider that each locality is an audience, the problem of localization reduces to the question of producing publications for audiences. In every other sense, however, localization requires a tremendous amount of effort. I detail the type of effort in Chapter 25, "Cataloging Audiences" in the section titled "Audiences and Localization." That effort can be lessened considerably by the technology you buy or create to help the effort.

Your capability to localize content is gauged most often by the amount of human effort that you can muster to do the localization. The more people you have, the more you can localize. To make the most of the human localizers, you need a streamlined and efficient localization system in your CMS. The most efficient system presents only the exact information to be localized and doesn't require the localizer to understand the general structure of the CMS repository.

Localization is, or should be, built into the core of your collection, management, and publishing systems. If you really need to localize, it creates an impact across your CMS. This brings us right back to the point that localization is what a CMS is all about. After it is fully integrated into your system, localization ought to feel like it is just another (albeit large) part of the process.

Collection localization

The collection system is where localization actually happens. In the collection system, localizers translate and create local content for later publication. Of course, without the support of a localizable repository and a set of publications that require localization, collecting localized information is impossible. Still, it is in the collection system that the largest amount of labor occurs, and it is the collection system that localizers interact with. So it is a good idea to put significant features into your collection system to support localization.

Localization happens in the collection system in two ways:

✦ Content already in the core locality is translated or modified to be used in other localities. Localizers trained in translation and modification do this work. They are generally not subject matter experts, but rather locality experts.

✦ Content is created from scratch for a locality. That content may or may not need to be brought from its locality to the core locality or to other localities. In any case, its creator is a CMS author and not a localizer.

The features differ in focus for local authors versus localizers. For local authors, you want to create features that facilitate creativity and give them access to the same sorts of forms that nonlocal authors have. For localizers, on the other hand, you want to provide tools that aid their efficiency and improve quality as they move through the bulk of existing components.

Localized UI

Although the entire interface of a CMS can often be localized (given enough effort), you generally only localize input forms to give local authors screens that they can more easily relate to and author into. Here are some of the parts of the form that are candidates for localization:

✦ Obviously, the text on the form can be translated.

✦ The layout and spacing of the form can be changed to reflect local preferences (differences in the direction of reading, for example).

✦ Help text associated with the form can be localized (in what you might call a meta-localization process(localizing the localization).

✦ The branding and surrounding text and images on the form can be localized.

Although it is possible to do quite a bit to localize the forms that authors use, it all requires effort. More often than not, the decision is made to put all localization efforts toward audiences and leave authors to struggle through the standard forms as well as they can.

Access structure localization

If an access structure is only going to be used internally, it is generally left in one language. For example, it makes little sense to translate a set of workflow statuses. For external-facing structures, however, it may be critical to be able to localize them. Access structures, you might remember, help you organize content, and they help the audiences find information. You can decide that within your team you will adopt a single way to organize (one that does not vary with locality), but you cannot will people from different localities to think the same way about access.

Of course, this is just a special case of the more general statement that you can't expect two audiences to look for information the same way. However, localization adds a complication: You must decide whether to use a particular term in a locality, and whether to translate the term. For example, a particular phrase such as "white bread" may or may not be apt for categorizing your content across audiences (in this case, bakers in different localities) because bakers from different regions may or may not use this sort of term to categorize breads. That's one problem to be solved by the taxonomy system. Additionally, bakers may or may not need a translation from one region to another. French bakers may need the phrase translated, whereas Japanese would prefer the English phrase.

> **Note** What is true for access structures is actually true generally. Localization lays an extra layer of complexity over already-complex processes.

The upshot is that the capability to choose whole alternative structures or single translated phrases must be added to the following:

✦ **Metadata acquisition tools:** These include the tools and scripts you use to import and export metadata lists.

✦ **Metadata creation and maintenance tools:** These include the tools you use to create, edit, and review metadata lists as well as those you use for lumping and splitting values and for setting mandatory and optional elements (which may also vary from locality to locality).

✦ **Tagging tools:** Metators should be able to choose the right phrase and structure for localized content.

✦ **The metatorial guide:** Somewhere you must explain how you have sorted this all out and how mere metators can apply the model you have invented. By the way, metators are a fairly rare breed to begin with. You multiply your staffing problems if you must find metators who can also deal with foreign languages.

All things considered, localizing access is a tough problem. (I pick up this thread again in the section later in this chapter titled "Publication localization.") No wonder that, on one hand, few really attempt localization in a rigorous way and that, likewise, international publications are often not very useful.

Import and export for localization

A typical scenario is that an organization contracts with an outside agency to do localization. The outside agency provides labor on an hourly or (more often) per-piece basis. In either case the cost of the endeavor is set mostly by how much labor it costs to localize content. Labor expenditure, in turn, is set mostly by:

✦ Whether you can use the agency's standard procedures or if you require them to develop custom processes just for you.

✦ How skilled the localizers must be. Any more then perfunctory computer skills cost more, and any amount of subject matter expertise costs dearly.

As a result, the lowest costs come from delivering content that fits right into the localization agency's tool set and requires no training to localize. To put it more in CM terms, localizers are not an additional author set to be given an interface—they already have their own. Rather, they are an acquisition and syndication partner. When you give them content, you are essentially syndicating content to them. They set the form of the content and you produce it. And when they are finished localizing, they become an acquisition source, and you have to get their content back into your system as efficiently as possible. Or in old-style computer terms, you export content to them and then import it when they have finished.

You can use your existing syndication and acquisition systems to accomplish this, but it is probably just as well not to. Rather, if you think of it as export and import, you will be guided more toward the idea that you need to reach into your database (or other storage area) and pull out just the content they will localize and the unique Ids and other indicators that will allow you to re-input the content most efficiently. Finally, you need to map that content to whatever structure they expect. The most likely formats, from most advanced to least, are XML, database records, spreadsheet files, document files, and flat text.

Tip   You can tell just how advanced a localization agency is by the form it expects you to deliver content in.

Combining source material

What happens if your source material for components is coming from different locales? If, for example, you work for an international Non-Government Organization (NGO), you may have articles coming in from all over the world. Can you create a single process for acquiring them into your CMS? You ought to be able to come quite close if you can require that sources use the same (or a localized version of the same) input template worldwide. Then, by noting where the article came from, your acquisition system could automatically trigger the right workflow to deal with the content. For example, you might set these rules:

✦ All articles originating in Algiers are localized for all North African localities (because Algiers is where the North African headquarters is).

✦ All articles from other North African localities are localized to Algiers as well.

✦ Libya and Chad share articles (that is, if you get an article from one, localize to the other).

✦ Tunisian articles should be reviewed and disposed of individually (because they do such good work, it is often worthwhile to send them worldwide).

If you can't get your sources to use the same template, you're faced with a bigger task and a different workflow, which may include the necessity of having a localizer assist you in tagging incoming content—at some price, of course. If you expect this to be the case, you can help yourself by requiring the tagging of only the most essential elements.

The extent to which you combine content and how much it costs you to do so are driven by your ability to get everyone on board with a set of consistent templates. Lacking that, the costs of localization are similar to the costs of acquiring a new content type—one that may be in a language you don't understand.

Management localization

In designing your repository to support localization, you have the following two basic options for how to store localized content:

✦ **By component:** You can choose to make multiple complete copies of each component you intend to localize.

✦ **By element:** You can choose to make multiple copies of only the elements of the components you intend to localize.

Suppose, for example, that that you have a component to be localized for three localities. By the component method, you could make three copies of the component, one per locality. The versions would somehow be linked together (perhaps by sharing some Id). By the element method, however, if you determine that only the title and body elements need to be localized, you could create one component that has three variants of the title and three variants of the body element.

The element method has the advantage of less duplication. If you make complete copies of the component, you must duplicate all the information that's not localized in all the variants of the component. You have an added burden of keeping all the versions of the component synchronized. One significant disadvantage to the element method is the ease of data sharing. Depending on how your repository is created, it may be hard to share ownership of individual elements of a component without giving up ownership of the whole component.

Clearly, you can mitigate the disadvantages of both localization methods. So you have no reason to necessarily prefer one method to the other. In addition, if you're using a commercial CMS, the localization functionality it offers may decide for you what level of localization you can support. Still, if you have a choice, design for an element localization model to minimize duplication and maximize flexibility.

Component-level localization

To understand component-level localization, look at the XML form of HRBenefit components (the ones I introduce in the earlier section in this chapter titled "Storing content types and components in XML").

```
<HRBENEFITS>
  <HRBENEFIT ID= "HRB100" Type="Standard" AuthorID="A21"
  EmployeeType="FT">
     <NAME>401K</NAME>
     <IMAGEPATH>images/hr/joesmile.jpg</IMAGEPATH>
     <TEXT>Our great 401K plan...</TEXT>
  </HRBENEFIT>
</HRBENEFITS>
```

Now focus just on the HRBENEFIT element to explore some ways you could create the link between the localized versions of a component:

```
<HRBENEFIT ID= "HRB100_IntEnglish" Type="Standard"
AuthorID="A21" EmployeeType="FT">
<HRBENEFIT ID= "HRB100" Locale="IntEnglish" Type="Standard"
AuthorID="A21" EmployeeType="FT">
<HRBENEFIT ID= "HRB100" Locale="IntEnglish" FamilyID="HRB_F1"
Type="Standard" AuthorID="A21" EmployeeType="FT">
```

Each of these methods will work to link a set of independent components. They differ in the following ways:

✦ In the first example, the unique ID of each component has two parts. The first part is an identifier for the component (HRB100) and the second part is an identifier for the locality. This method is efficient because it uses few attributes to do a lot of work, but I would not recommend it. First, to find all the components in a particular locality, you must retrieve every component and pull apart its Id. Similarly, it is difficult to find all the local versions of the same component. Second, if you change the locality of a component, you must change its unique identifier and possibly break links to this component. These difficulties are not insurmountable, but on the other hand why incur them simply to have fewer attributes?

✦ In the second example, the Id attribute defines the component, and the Locale attribute defines the locality. In this method, to uniquely identify a particular component, you need both pieces of information. In database language, you would say that the component has a compound key. This is okay except that you won't be able to use any of XML's built-in identifier types (Id and IDREF) to work with the Id attribute because it is not unique.

✦ The third method requires three attributes. The Id attribute uniquely identifies the component (HRB100), the FamilyID identifies the group of components (HRB_F1), and the Locale identifies the locality of the component. Although requiring more attributes, this method is the most flexible. Components all have a unique unchanging Id, and their family and locality can all be queried independently. You can see that it would be easy to find all components in a locality or all localities for a component.

The material in each component that is not localized, in this method, is copied from one component in the family to the rest. If you use component-level localization, be careful to propagate changes to non-localized information throughout the family.

Component-level localization is the more common way to do localization because it is easier than element-level localization. Even if you can do element-level localization, you may still want to localize at the component level if localized versions of a content type tend to be very different from each other. For example, if the entire structure of a book review is different in Taiwan than in Hong Kong, you may choose to localize book review components for these two regions at the component level.

Element-level localization

To modify the HRBenefit component for element-level localization, you may use a structure like the following example:

```
<HRBENEFITS>
  <HRBENEFIT ID="HR1" Type="Standard" AuthorID="A21"
  EmployeeType="FT">
    <NAME>
        <VARIANT ID="V1" Locale="IntEnglish" Rev="3">US 401K
        Plans</VARIANT>
        <VARIANT ID="V2" Locale="NAEnglish" Rev="3">Retirement
        Savings Plans</VARIANT>
    </NAME>
    <IMAGEPATH>images/hr/joesmile.jpg</ImagePath>
    <TEXT>
        <VARIANT ID="V3" Locale="IntEnglish" Rev="3">US
        employees can join a 401K plan...</VARIANT>
        <VARIANT ID="V4" Locale="NAEnglish" Rev="2">Our savings
        plans include...</VARIANT>
    </TEXT>
  </HRBENEFIT>
</HRBENEFITS>
```

Each element that needs to be localized supports a <VARIANT> child element. The <VARIANT> element, in turn, has a Locale attribute that specifies which locale each variant applies to. As the system renders this component, it can decide which locale to use and find the appropriate elements based on the Locale attribute.

<VARIANT>elements also have Id and Rev attributes. These two attributes can form the basis of a localization management system. Because each variant has its own Id, it can be located and updated individually. You can find, display, and update local elements individually. The Rev attribute can tell you if a change is made to one variant that needs to be propagated to the others. Notice, for example, that the IntEnglish variant of the <TITLE> element is at Rev 3 whereas the NAEnglish variant is only at Rev 2. This can trigger a workflow step to review the localization of the NAEnglish variant and update it with the IntEnglish variant. The way that you store localized content can lead naturally to particular localization processes.

In real life, your localization structures and system may be quite a bit more complex. You should be able to see from these examples, however, the increased flexibility that the element method gives you over the component method. Element-level localization is more complex to implement, but can save a lot of complexity in when you do localization (and thus cost). Such an approach allows you to pick out just the parts of the content that are to be localized, export them with a minimum of extra information (just an Id per element), and then import them directly back where they belong in their parent components.

Tie in to workflow

Even if you have the most sophisticated storage and retrieval capacity for localized content, you will still be confronted with the big problems of fitting localization into your production processes. Adding localization steps to the creation workflow for a particular content type is just the beginning of the job. In addition, you might need to:

✦ Either lock changes on the parent component after it has gone to localization, or trigger a step to resubmit content that has been edited since localization. In the former situation, you will inevitably block changes that really should be made. In the latter situation, you potentially create a lot of localization that might have been avoided. In any case you should create a localization policy that works for your organization and get your software to implement and enforce it.

✦ Implement some sort of process surrounding the localization of any other items in your repository that local users might see. This process decides what local users see (publication templates, personalization rules files, media and other binary files, and so on). As with component content, you must account for updates as well as creation of these items.

✦ Create specialized work queues where localization tasks are stored. Even if your localizers are using their own system, you still want to know what is queued up for localization by which agency and what its current disposition is. You may go further to try to integrate with the agency's systems to get the status of the batches you have sent.

✦ If at all possible, you want the capability to update the batches you have sent to localization. As edits are made to content that is in the queue but not yet finished, it would be great to slip in the new under the old.

The process of localization is just as important as the technology of localization. In fact, if I had to choose, I would depend on strong process rather than strong technology. In addition, a well-formed and clearly articulated manual process is much better than having no process because you lack of the technology to enforce it.

Publication localization

Considering what a connected world we live in, it is strange that so little support exists for localizing publications. Most of the systems for localizing publications are cobbled together from bits and piece of other CMS systems. Although these hodgepodge systems do get the job done, if localization is a big deal to your organization, you might try taking a bit more centralized approach to it, as detailed in the following sections.

A localization dashboard

Because the localization process is spread throughout the system and because it all comes together in the creation of publications that are localized, you might want to create a single place where the localization of publications, with all that it entails, is visible or even managed. Such a localization dashboard might show you this sort of information:

```
Publication
  Localities
  Content Types
    Specific components
      Localization workflow status
  Localization Rules
    Rule type (personalization, template variants,
    separate templates, etc.)
      Localization workflow status
  Preview
```

This sort of dashboard organizes all the information to show you how localization is being done and also to determine why the process is getting hung up. For each publication, the dashboard could show:

✦ The localities it is produced in.

✦ The content types in the publication that are to be localized. For example, a Web site might offer localized news story components.

✦ Within each content type, the dashboard might show the specific components that go into the publication. For example, it might show that there are currently 60 news story components that are slated to be in the publication.

✦ Within each component, it might show the localization workflow status for the component. For example, of the 60 news stories, maybe only 20 of them have made it through the localization process. A publication manager can use this information to decide whether to delay the update of the site to accommodate the new stories or go ahead with the 20 that are ready.

✦ Within each publication, it could show the localization rules that are being used. For example, on the Web site, one template with some personalization rules built-in (it might detect the IP address of the user and use it to engage the correct locality) might be how the local content is rendered. In other cases, separate template sets might be engaged at a higher level to create very different sites per locality.

✦ Within each personalization rule, it might show the status of any items that are involved in the rule. For example, the personalization rule needed to select news stories may show up in the list as "Ready to Go," but the template that houses the rule might show up as "In Bug Fix."

✦ A preview feature could let you choose a publication and a locality to preview. As a *coup de gras*, the preview feature could allow you to comment on any item (component, template, rule, and so on) and even trigger workflow on it.

This dashboard is really just a localization-centric view into the collection, management, and publication processes you have established. In other words, the existence of such a dashboard assumes that you have organized and automated these processes to such an extent that you can create this view.

Going beyond mere information display, the dashboard could begin to help you not only see the localization process but manage it. The dashboard might actually allow you to create the localization process. You can imagine seeing a list of publications and being able to add content types and localization rules to them. The system could then initiate the steps needed to localize the content and establish the rules. In reality, most of this ordering up of localization can be worked out through workflow. When the localization designer chooses to localize a particular content type in a particular publication, what she is really saying is "Task someone with localizing all of the components of that type that will go into this publication."

I have never seen anything near this grand of a localization dashboard. I am truly sorry for the people who have to do large-scale publication localization in the dark. I'd be really surprised if you could, without inordinate effort, create a management dashboard. I'd even be surprised if you could manage to create an information dashboard. But there is no reason why you can't understand that one is needed and take every opportunity to move in the right direction. At the very least, the idea of a dashboard may help you organize the localization planning process.

Localization as personalization

Much of the work of localizing publications can be done with personalization software. In fact, it is often useful to think of localization as personalization. In personalization, you match an audience to content in a standard frame. In localization:

✦ The audience is made up of the people within the locality.

✦ You match content to them based on how it is tagged. For example, if local components have a FamilyID and a Locality attribute (that I mention in this chapter in the section titled "Component level localization"), those two attributes allow you to match the locality with the content they should have.

✦ The standard frame is the publication that is being localized. For example, if you are localizing pamphlets, the overall structure of the pamphlet (its layout, branding, and so on) will likely stay the same as the content within it changes.

It should be clear that localization and personalization are quite intertwined. However, in reality, localization does to personalization what it does to your other CMS systems — it adds a degree of complexity. So, for example, you may have an internal and an external audience to personalize for. However your internal audience may be in three localities, and your external audience may be in six. So instead a simple branch of internal versus external, you have the extra branch that indicates which locality they are in.

In confronting localization, however, the more complex the localization, the more useful personalization tools become to you. For example, behavior-based personalization tools notice the previous actions the user took on a site and give her new content based on her previous choices. You can use this information to infer that someone who consistently chooses content from one locality might want it all that way. Of course, as with personalization, you have to be careful that your guesses are backed by good evidence and that the user can recover if you guess wrong.

Just which personalization features you use for localization is, of course, a matter of which ones you have and your localization needs. But, if you understand that localization adds a level of complexity to personalization, you choose the personalization tools that support the complexity you will host. If your localization requirements are substantial, you'll benefit by augmenting localization tools at your disposal with personalization tools.

Template localization

Publications are built by templates. Localized publications are built by localized templates. Localized templates let you vary the following qualities in your publications:

✦ **Content (obviously).** Different or translated content can be delivered based on locale.

✦ **Navigation.** You can simply translate the navigation or you can modify it to fit the new locale.

✦ **Layout.** Local specific needs (like text direction and title positioning) may require you to change the way the elements of a publication are positioned.

✦ **Branding.** Again, you can simply translate titles, images, and other identifying elements of a publication or you can rearrange them to suit the locale.

Template localization itself is a lot like content localization. Two basic methods exist:

✦ You can create a family of templates for the publication, in which each family member produces a localized version of the publication. For example, if you have three localities, you can have three product page templates, one for each locality. This method is akin to component-level localization.

✦ You can produce one set of templates with variants at the points where local content is inserted. For example, you could have one product page template with code that branches as necessary to produce the local version of the products page. This method is akin to element-level localization.

The advantages and disadvantages of template localization also follow those of content localization. The family method is simpler and enables you to create very different localized publications, but it requires you to make sure changes get propagated from one template to the next. The variant method is more compact and modular, but is more complex to implement and allows less variation among localized pages.

If you intend to localize publications you must localize templates. However, the method that you choose may depend on how much must be changed from locale to locale. For example, if your locales require that you completely modify navigation, layout, and branding in addition to changing the text, you might as well create separate copies of the templates that produce the localized site. You may have a lot of trouble trying to make the same template do two publications that are so completely different. If, on the other hand, your local publications keep exactly the same layout, navigation, and branding (as many do), and only vary the text of the components, the variant method is the clear winner. Undoubtedly your situation is somewhere in between, and you will have to decide on the right mix of the two methods. Nothing is stopping you from using both in the same CMS or even in the same publication.

Workflow System

The complexity of localization efforts leads somewhat naturally into a discussion of how all this and the other content processing tasks get done. The workflow system in your CMS is where you design, create, and maintain the sequence of these processes leading to publication.

The workflow system manages management. It helps you chart out and control the processes that control your CMS. Workflow systems organize and trigger the tasks that *actors* (both human and machine) do to *objects* (both content and other CM processes and systems) in the CM (see Chapter 33, "Designing Workflow and Staffing Models," for a complete description of these terms).

It is very difficult to pull the workflow system apart from the other systems of a CMS. You may have noticed, for example, that the workflow system has played a prominent part in almost every other system I detail. Workflow is so intertwined in other systems, in my view, because *workflow is the system that organizes the processes of every other system*. This is a bit broader than the usual view that the workflow system allows you to make sure content is reviewed before it gets published. Because of the more usual view, you may have some work of your own to do to get your workflow system to be used as widely as I propose. Still, the capability to manage a lot of nonreview processes is often already present in the systems you buy. Whether you are creating a basic review workflow, a workflow for cleaning out the repository, or one for doing a publication redesign, you need the same process consisting of triggers, steps, and actors. To get your workflow engine involved in the full range of CMS processes might require no more than having the workflow UI available to staff who have been trained to initiate a particular workflow in a particular circumstance. On the other hand, if you can manage to have a range of events in your CMS trigger workflow initialization or step transitions, you are on your way to a system that knows what to do without being asked.

End user interface

The end user interface of a workflow system is comprised of the controls and information that contributors and other end users (as opposed to administrators) see when they interact with the workflow system. End users may be in the following "places" (or in still other parts of the system) when they engage the workflow system:

✦ **In some part of the CMS itself.** For example, a metator might be in the metadata creation interface when she needs to see what tasks she has to accomplish.

✦ **In some closely tied application.** For example, an author might be in a CMS-controlled Web form when she needs to click the Ready for Review workflow button.

✦ **In some loosely tied application.** For example, a publication designer might be in a Web templating program when she needs to see what changes have been ordered.

A good workflow system serves users wherever they are by both informing them of what tasks they need to do and by giving them easy access to the features they need to do those tasks.

Reusable end user interface

What the interface shows the end user and what it allows the end user to do is, of course, your biggest concern. Your next most important concern is where that end user interface can be shown. If your users are spread across the application space, your workflow system should ideally be spread that way as well. In other words, your workflow end user interface should be able to appear within a very wide range of applications. If the end user interface is API-based and implemented in Web pages, then it can easily show up in any Web application. In addition to that, integration is mostly a one-off deal. Integrating with a word processor is different from integrating with a Web design application. However, the integration is made possible by the workflow system's API and its capability to communicate remotely. For example, if the system is implemented as Web service, potentially any application can get information from it or issue commands to it via HTTP.

Even given that your workflow system has the basic capabilities that allow it to integrate, you still might not want to do the integration. Here, in ascending order of complexity, are the ways you might integrate a workflow system with one or more of the applications that are in your CMS sphere:

✦ You might choose not integrate it, choosing instead to tell users to keep both the CMS and the other application open.

✦ You might have the workflow system stand alone, but embed HTML links in another application connecting to each workflow feature you want to trigger. For example, if you want users to be able to trigger a new component workflow from within Microsoft Word, you might provide a dialog box in Word that lists the new component workflows the user can trigger. When the user makes a choice in the dialog box, the appropriate Web page in the workflow system opens. The user fills in the fields on the page and then goes back to what she was doing in Word.

✦ You might trigger workflow features directly from another application. For example, rather than opening a Web page in the CMS user interface, a dialog box in Word could directly issue the command to the workflow engine to trigger the workflow. The trick here is to be able to get the source application to trigger commands. (Word does this, but not all applications may.)

✦ You may integrate the workflow interface into your application. For example, the Task Pane in Word can display HTML pages, including forms. With some effort, you can adapt the workflow end user interface itself to reliably display in Word's Task Pane. Furthermore, as the user takes actions in Word (say, creating a new document of a particular type) the workflow pane can update to show the relevant workflow information and commands.

You could go wild with workflow integration and spend a tremendous amount of energy deeply integrating across a wide variety of applications. The return on such an approach might not be there, however. One criterion for deciding what to integrate is how dependent you are on user-initiated triggers to achieve a smooth workflow. A second and related criterion might be locating where blockages to workflow tasks are occurring—tasks that never manage to be triggered even if needed—and then put your triggers where the users are when they should be invoking them. If you have little solid basis for creating workflow integrations, start slow and add more integration to your CMS version 2.

E-mail integration

A good workflow system is not only present wherever your users are when they are doing CM, it can also notify them of significant events when they are not doing CM. For this reason, most of the good workflow systems include some sort of integration with e-mail. Here are some of the features that e-mail integration can include:

✦ **Sending mail based on the actor.** For example, casual contributors with little connection to the system may get e-mail whereas staff members would not.

✦ **Sending mail based on steps.** For example, to initiate a workflow the system might send an e-mail, but not during any of the other steps of the workflow. Combining the step selection with the actor selection leads to a very precise use of e-mail. For example, staff and outside contributors could get mail at workflow initiation, but only outsiders continue to get it during the remaining steps.

✦ **Including extra details.** You can include useful context in the e-mails, such as previous and future steps, owners, comments, and information on the object of the workflow (the component, CMS system, publication, and so on). You can even represent the user's whole work queue in an e-mail. If you include these sorts of details, contributors who have trouble using the CMS, get all the information they need to do their work without going to it.

✦ **Including direct links to the CMS.** Where extra details will not suffice, you should aim to include links to the CMS that help the user do her work. For example, if the e-mail is telling her to create a component, why not include a link to the Web form where she is to create the component. With a bit of extra push, you can even pre-populate some of the elements of the new components for her (such as her name, the date, and so on).

You need e-mail integration most if some of your users are completely disconnected from the CMS. Of course, you can always have a staff member get regular workflow notices and then manually propagate e-mails (this is the poor person's e-mail integration). In addition to physically disconnected users, e-mail notification is useful for contributors who are only sporadically involved in the CM process. For example, e-mail to reviewers who only work once or twice a month or to publication designers who work even less frequently can be a great way to bring them in when you need them.

Work queues

Most commercial products ship with some form of work queues that show a user what she needs to do. A good work queue:

✦ Shows all the tasks currently assigned to a person and has some way of displaying the tasks that were once or may in the future be assigned to her. In other words, items don't just appear and disappear. They can be anticipated and followed up on after they leave the queue.

✦ Directly links to the features to perform the tasks. For example, if the task is to create a new component, a link right to the form is available for creating that component.

✦ Visually expresses importance. For example, items that are overdue might turn red or items that are marked urgent are sorted to the top of the list.

✦ Shows the options for proceeding with a task. For example, if the task is to review a publication, the queue might give the options of doing the review or escalating the review to a supervisor. The choices, in this case, would be set by the steps in the particular workflow.

Especially for users that have a fair amount of work to do in the CMS, but very little training or motivation, a solid work queue can really help. If you can, make the queue appear to the user as the entire CMS. In other words, the queue is all the user needs to see of the CMS and it leads her to whatever other features she needs. For other users who are motivated and have even more tasks to accomplish, the queue can be an invaluable way to keep organized and abreast of the day's work.

Commenting

In addition to simply triggering a series of steps in a workflow, a robust system will allow actors to comment on the process as it happens. For example, an author might want to pass on a comment to the reviewer that will show up when the reviewer opens the component to be reviewed. Or an automated process might add an exception report as a comment to the workflow process before triggering the next step in a conversion workflow. As you consider using or creating a comment feature in your workflow, consider these issues:

✦ How will the actor enter comments? For example, does a pop-up dialog box appear when she completes a step? If workflow steps can be triggered in a number of ways, will a pop-up dialog box always be possible? How would an automated process use such a pop-up?

✦ How will comments appear? At what point does the next actor see the comments of the last actor? Does she see all previous comments or just the ones from the previous step? Are comments marked with the author's name or other metadata?

✦ How will comments be stored? If they can apply to only components, then they can be stored with the components. If they can apply to other objects, however, they must be stored separately.

✦ How will comments in the workflow system relate to other sorts of comments? For example, you might have a staff feedback system (see Chapter 38, "Building Collection Systems," the section titled "Staff feedback") that also delivers comments. How will the user know when to use one sort of comment instead of another?

✦ Do you want any administrative comment features? Do you want to report on comments? Do you need to be able to delete or edit them? Do the comments sometimes require resolution or escalation?

At first glance, workflow commenting seems a simple issue but, upon examination, a fair amount of work is needed to create a system that works for users and administrators.

Workflow administration

Someone has to manage the system that manages the CMS. A workflow administrator could be a CMS system administrator or any staff member who has a need to create and modify workflows. Depending on how simple you can make it to manage workflows, it may be to your advantage to distribute the task to the people who understand the processes they want the workflow system to enforce. On the other hand, centralizing workflow administration requires less-sophisticated software because you can train a single administrator to use a less-friendly system.

Visual builder

The slickest commercial workflow systems (the ones that always draw praise at demos) enable you to create a visual representation of a workflow by dragging icons for actors, triggers, and steps onto a screen and connecting them with lines. With such a builder, you can imagine very nontechnical staff taking control of their own workflow creation needs. As you build or (much more likely) buy such a visual builder, make sure that:

✦ It can represent the full range of actors, triggers, and CMS objects that you want to manage in the CMS. Some commercial systems only represent authors manually triggering steps against components.

✦ It can be used not only to create workflows but to modify them as well. Strangely, some cannot do both.

✦ It allows you to customize the workflow elements it provides or to create new ones.

✦ It stores its output in a nonproprietary format such as XML so that if the visual builder does not do all you need it to do, you can modify its output by hand. Keep in mind, however, that if you modify the XML, the visual builder may not know what to do with the tweaked workflow or may even refuse to open the file.

Visual builders are really great for systems in which you need a lot of ongoing work on your workflows, or for when you want nontechnical staff to participate in workflow administration. If neither of these circumstances describes your organization, then a visual builder, although cool, may be superfluous.

Ad-hoc workflow and rerouting

The whole idea of workflow is to figure out the steps that will reliably result in a process being finished the way you want it to be. Given this, it is funny just how often exceptions arise, and workflows need to be rewired on-the-fly to address a particular situation. Because you'll need to make ad hoc changes eventually, it's a good idea to have a strategy in place to accommodate suddenly necessary workflow changes. The rewiring you may want to account for includes:

✦ **Skipping a step:** For example, skipping a few review cycles when you must get a component to publication quickly.

✦ **Resetting a workflow:** For example, suppose you discover that the automated archive process at the beginning of a content retirement workflow crashed without notification and all the subsequent work will have to be redone. You need to reset the entire workflow at the point it failed.

✦ **Adding steps on an ad-hoc basis:** For example, you might want to add an extra test pass on a particular edition of a Web site because you know that it will contain a lot of complex content and functionality.

✦ **Sending steps to a particular person:** For example, the usual workflow calls for components to go into an edit pool where all editors choose the next available component, but you want to make sure that a particular editor gets a particular component.

If you have ever run a production process you will, I'm sure, be able to add many items to this list. The point is that despite your best efforts to create a well-oiled workflow machine, exceptions occur on a regular basis and need to be handled with a minimum of effort.

You must be able to handle process exceptions. As in many cases, the choices you have are about how much to try to automate the exception process. For an exception, you could simply turn off the workflow and complete the process manually, or you could try to get your workflow system to allow you to override and rearrange the default process from within its interface. Some amount of simple override is usually built into a commercial workflow system. It is your call how far past that you take it.

Configuration of user roles

You can deal with people as individuals, or you can deal with them as members of wider groups. You have the most flexibility in your assignment of tasks if you treat them as individuals. You have the most efficiency of assignment if you deal with them as a group. For example, suppose you have 10 people who author content of the news story type. On one hand, you can assign news story components individually as you need them, or you can group the authors and assign new news stories to the group. In fact, you might want to group all the news authors together with your other component authors into a single Author class. Which groupings make sense depends on your situation. You want to be sure that your workflow system will allow you to make whatever groupings you need.

Some commercial workflow systems (and most homemade ones) have a set list of user types. The actor that you assign to a particular task has to be one of those types. Other systems allow you to define your own groupings and even have subgroups and super groups (for example, News Authors can be a group within the wider Author group).

In addition to understanding your needs for users and groups, consider as well how friendly the configuration interface for this feature needs to be. Finally, consider whether you need your workflow users to be the same as the authorized users of the CMS. Having a single set of users is, of course, preferable but not always easy to accomplish.

If you've administered workflows, you may agree that the simpler the workflow model, the better. Many organizations start out believing that they need very complex and nested user roles only to find out later that they have created a system that no one understands. In addition, to code a workflow system with fixed roles is much easier than to code one with open roles (which is why so many are created with fixed roles). Finally, the more sophisticated the user model for the workflow system, the more likely you will have exceptions to the model as you run the system. So, my best advice here is to make people convince you with strong arguments that you need a sophisticated user model for your workflow.

Audit trails and reporting

An audit trail helps you retrace the steps of a workflow. Reports help you review and hone your processes. Audit trails and reports are good for accountability as well as content trouble-shooting. Keep these features in mind as you figure out your audit and reporting needs:

✦ It is good to be able to sort your workflow reports by object, actor, or stage. For example, a report might show each component or document and its workflow status, or it might show all components that are at a particular workflow stage, or it might show a particular author and the stages of all her work.

✦ Audit features might integrate with the workflow engine to allow you to roll back a process to a particular stage.

Auditing and especially reports are a great way to keep on top of the overall health of your CM processes. I would strongly advise finding some way to produce these reports even if your system does not natively support doing so. If you create your own reports, it is important that your CMS store workflow information in an open format such as XML.

Import and export

The most popular tool used to model workflow (and most any other process) that I know of is Microsoft Visio. However, Visio is not a workflow tool; it is a visual modeling tool that has the capability of exporting its diagrams in an XML format. Visio and other process modeling tools are a great way to augment your visual workflow builders. If you decide to use an outside modeler, make sure:

✦ The outside modeling tool can save diagrams in a format that is easy to import into your CMS workflow system.

✦ That you don't need to modify the workflow from within the CMS, or that you can export roundtrip from the CMS to the outside modeler and back again.

If your team is already really used to using an outside modeler, it may be worth the effort to integrate it into your workflow. In the case of Microsoft Visio, some commercial products have already done the integration. Otherwise, you might be better off using the modelers inside your CMS.

Workflow mechanics

The mechanics (or architecture) of your workflow system determines what end-user and administrative features are feasible and how broad a range of CM processes your workflow system can cover.

Workflow creation

Unless you happen to want your programmers to create your workflows, it is best to make sure that creation of workflows doesn't require programming skills. The slickest systems have a visual workflow designer with drag-and-drop manipulation of processes. On the other hand (why is there always another hand?), make sure that either the interface is very complete or that it's extendable. You can actually get the best of both worlds here if you get a workflow system that:

✦ Has a very robust workflow model (one with a wide variety of triggers, actors, and channels).

✦ Stores the workflows themselves in a database or XML file that has an open or well-documented structure.

✦ Allows access to the stored workflows through an open or well-documented API.

✦ Uses that API to create a convenient user interface.

In other words, a slick workflow user interface can be backed up by a robust workflow storage and access methodology so that you can use the friendly interface, build your own interface, or bypass the interface altogether and read and write workflows programmatically.

Some method is, of course, necessary for creating workflows. The more tied into the rest of the CMS you want workflow to be, the more robust and programmatically manipulable you want the creation to be.

Nested workflows

Nested workflows means having one workflow embedded within another. For example, you might have a workflow for legal review that requires components to go through two or three steps. In one step the components are revised; in the next, your organization's legal department signs off on them. Rather than recreating these two or three steps over and over again, you might define them as a workflow and then nest them within the other larger component creation workflows that include a legal review. With a set of nested workflows, you can streamline your workflow processes the same way you streamline publication building: by nesting templates. On the other hand, the mechanics of nesting for templates or for workflows is not trivial. In addition to adding a lot of complexity to the coding of the workflow system, it adds complexity to the workflow interface. In addition, you have to track and review all changes to workflows because they may be used in multiple places (in which case, you are managing the system that manages the system that manages the CMS!).

Obeying the maxim to keep your workflows simple, you may naturally want to avoid this feature. However, if implementing it is not too much trouble, you can use nesting to simplify workflows by forcing them into a set number of standard patterns.

Objects

A workflow acts on an object. (See Chapter 33, "Designing Workflow and Staffing Models" in the section titled "Workflow objects.") Most systems can attach a workflow to a file. The better ones can attach a workflow to a component (or whatever name is given to a component in the product). The best ones can attach a workflow to a particular element of a component. The body element, for example, can have a localization workflow attached to it to make sure that it gets translated. The rest of the component may not need to participate in that workflow.

Whether you need this level of granularity depends completely on the granularity with which you otherwise manage your workflow. It's certainly nice to have the capability, and you may discover ways to make use of a variety of workflow objects as you refine your workflow processes. The substitute for attaching a workflow to a particular object is using a manual process. In the localization example earlier in the chapter, you told the localizers which elements in a given component to localize and which to ignore.

Triggers

A workflow starts or changes from one step to the next based on triggers (see Chapter 33, "Designing Workflow and Staffing Models" in the section titled "Workflow triggers" for the complete story on triggers). The range of triggers that your system can detect and make use of determines the range of events that can be incorporated automatically into your workflow system. Of course, you can always manually trigger a workflow transition, but with automatic triggers you can ensure that workflow proceeds as quickly as possible. Look for these trigger features in your workflow systems:

✦ The capability to trigger on events that must be noticed.

✦ The capability to override automatic triggers in exceptional events.

✦ The capability to create custom triggers through the workflow systems API.

Triggers can be very helpful, especially when you want to include automated processes in your workflow system. (For example, a conversion script can initiate or transition the workflow on a set of components.)

Parallel and sequential workflows

In a parallel workflow, two people perform steps in the workflow at the same time. In a sequential workflow, one person finishes before the other begins. The classic sequential process is write, edit, review. This is the usual kind of workflow pattern. A typical parallel process is write, edit, review/metatag. The review and metatag steps can happen simultaneously because the reviewer is unconcerned with the metadata, and the metator is unconcerned with the final copy of the component.

Parallel workflow can be easy or hard. In the easy case, the two objects being worked on are different. For example, in the publishing workflow, one person can be finishing the layout of the publication while another completes a review of the personalization rules. In this case, the CMS only needs to notify the two people of their tasks and not trigger the next step until both have completed these tasks.

In the hard case, the object is the same for both people in the step. For example, the same component may be owned and worked on simultaneously by a number of localizers. To do this hard form of parallel workflow when components are the objects, your CMS must allow independent ownership of the elements of a component. That means that each element of the component must be able to be:

✦ Versioned separately (see the section earlier in this chapter titled "Versioning System") so that changes can be rolled back independently.

✦ Locked, checked in and out, and audited separately. See the section earlier in this chapter titled "Source Control System (Content and File Sharing)."

✦ If elements are to go outside the system during the parallel step or if the component is actually split to accomplish the step, the elements must have their own unique Ids.

A parallel workflow feature, then, consists of the capability to represent the parallel steps in the workflow builder; and, if the object of the two (or more) steps in the parallel workflow is the same, the workflow system must be able to manage its joint ownership.

You can potentially save a lot of time overall if you can create parallel workflows. For processes that do not involve sharing the same component, this is simply a matter of getting your workflow system to let you build and implement parallel steps. In the harder case, you may need to perform the breakup and reunion of a component yourself if the system does not support it for you.

CMS Administration System

The complexity of workflow design and administration is quite separate from the maintenance of the CMS itself. A CMS administrator keeps the system healthy and humming. Ideally, the administrator works mostly behind the scenes, ensuring that the other staff members can do their jobs without paying undue attention to the system. In the real world of CM, however, this ideal is rarely met. Instead, the quirks of the system often intrude into the work process and require that users know more about the inner workings of the CMS than they ever wanted to. So, in a CMS, the job of the administrator is to keep the quirks to a minimum and, as much as possible, to shield users from those that are unavoidable. To accomplish this task, the administrator has a range of CM features that show and affect the state of the system, manage its connection to other systems, and allow it to avoid and also quickly recover from failures.

Note Most of the features that an administrator might use to configure subsystems of the CMS are covered in the sections that concern those subsystems. Configuring the workflow system, for example, is covered in the section earlier in this chapter titled "Workflow administration."

Administrative dashboard

As you might have guessed, I'm a firm believer in providing people with a central place they can go to access all the features that concern them. For authors, I propose a work queue or e-mail message that gives them all they need to know to complete their tasks. For localizers, a localization dashboard allows them to see and even change the localization plan. For CMS administrators, such a dashboard might be large indeed, but no less necessary. In fact, the larger the span of processes and systems that a person has to monitor, the more she needs a central location that synthesizes and prioritizes the status of the full span. For an administrator, such a centralized dashboard might include:

✦ An area where critical notices are posted. For example, if an automated process fails, it can post an alert to this area so the administrator sees it at once. If a user flags a request as urgent, it could show up here as well. Workflow steps that are overdue by a certain amount and other critical messages that come back from any part of the system could show up here.

✦ An area where the most important status information is shown. For example, the current state of the system connection can be shown to end users over the LAN, to remote sites via dial-up connections, to computers that host publications, and to the computers that supply or receive content. In addition, the most recent status messages from automated processes could be available here. The administrator might be able to click in this area to view more detail on each of the statuses that are listed.

✦ An area where upcoming events in the life of the system are shown. For example, a list of the next three or so publications to be produced could be shown, as could the upcoming acquisition events. The next date for archiving or backup could be listed as could the dates for metadata or publication template reviews.

✦ An area where quick links to important subsystems are listed. From the dashboard, the administrator should be able to move directly to the screens for administering subsystems such as workflow, user permissions, localization, backup and recovery, as well as to each of the major publication systems. Quick links to the various logs in the CMS could also be provided here.

✦ An area for the administrator's own workflow work queue that provides the tasks she needs to accomplish and links to the resources for accomplishing those tasks.

Most of the information needed to populate the dashboard is available somewhere in the CMS. A lot is right in the workflow system. Still, marshaling that information, deciding what is important enough to show and what is not, and getting it all to fit on an easy-to-use screen can be quite a chore. I have not seen anything this comprehensive in any commercial or hand-tooled system. I believe that the magnitude of the task of building an administrator's dashboard is a good indication of how far we are from mature CMSs. When such a dashboard is common in commercial systems and its features are generally accepted and standardized, we will have reached adulthood in the CM discipline.

A full-blown dashboard is very likely beyond your means today. However, what can you do in today is to begin to identify and gather the key indicators of the health of your CMS. Any steps you can tackle along these lines will repay your efforts.

User administration

Chief among the tasks of a CM administrator is managing the profile and permissions of the system's users. User administration is happily one of the more well-developed areas of CM functionality (mostly based on the work that has been done by operating systems software in the same area). All these features of user administration are available in some form in commercial systems:

✦ **Workflow plus:** User types in the general CMS are almost always the same as the users in the workflow system (see the section earlier in this chapter titled "Configuration of user roles"). However, there is more to users than how they are represented for workflow. For example, they need permissions to access components and files, the kind of user interface and element set that enables them to author, and permissions to publish. These attributes, too, must be logged, managed and used as the basis for configuration in the CMS.

✦ **Stock versus custom roles:** Some systems offer a set of stock roles, whereas others offer the capability to create your own roles from configurations of permissions. If you are buying a system, you should pay attention to how many user roles you are able to create.

✦ **Role modeling:** Some systems have a simple flat list of roles that users can fill. Others allow you to create hierarchies of roles where subroles inherit attributes and permissions from their parents. Some systems will allow you to have users in more than one group as well.

Be sure before going with a more complex user model that it is worth the increased complexity. It may be hard to figure out later exactly why a person can't access something, and the number of exceptions you find to your complex model may overwhelm you.

Logging

Behind most of the management features of a CMS is some sort of log that keeps track of what has happened in the system. As likely as not, there is not just one log, but many. Separate logs may be kept for:

✦ **Web server activity:** One server log may exist for every Web server you use (possibly one for each site you host, one for your CMS server inside the firewall, and one for any other servers that you may use). These logs show the pages and files that have been served and whatever information can be automatically gathered about who has requested them.

✦ **Workflow:** This log records all the step transitions for each workflow you host. Workflow comments and exceptions may also exist in this log.

✦ **Versioning and sharing:** The check-in and -out process and the editorial version of components may have their own log. This log is used to audit and roll back component changes.

✦ **Repository database:** If you use a commercial database system in your repository, it will no doubt have its own transaction log where it tracks every database interaction that occurs. Database systems use these logs for auditing and roll back as well.

✦ **Process logs:** Various scripts and programs (conversion, acquisition, publishing, and so on) may all have their own logs that chart the progress and completion of these processes.

Of course, each log has its own format, and special software may be required to read and display it. And, of course, many of these logs can grow by megabytes a day. Such a diverse array of logs in one system is yet another indication that we are in the early days of CM systems. Such a large amount of logged information from even one source would be hard to deal with, but from a range of sources it can be beyond management.

The key task of your system is somehow to pick the significant facts out of this onslaught of non-cooperating information and present it to people in an actionable form. Your earliest approach can be to just identify the types of facts that are key. Facts can be individual log entries such as the failure of a script to complete, or they can be much more complex facts such as where on your site people tend to go when looking for information on investing. After you have determined what the key facts are, you can begin to figure out how you will cull key facts from logs. Finally, you can create a way for key facts to make it from a log to the person who needs to see them. This is easy to say, but a life's work to accomplish.

Reporting

Given a strong logging feature (which, of course, is not a given in most systems), you may want your CMS to provide any number of reports. I've mentioned these reports in the context of the system reported on. For example, you can create a set of workflow reports to monitor and revise your CMS procedures (see the section earlier in this chapter titled "Audit trails and reporting"). Regardless of the information in the report, when you consider a reporting feature keep these qualities in mind:

✦ **Multiple sources:** If you don't log information all in one place, your reporting system will need to coalesce information from the variety of places it is stored. The easiest way to accomplish this coalescing is to do it all at once. Draw all the useful information from all your logs and systems into one place (preferably a database). Then make your reports from there. This data warehousing approach is your best hope of making sense of the array of information your systems provide and to be able to support a consistent interface and feature set across all your reports.

✦ **Multiple formats:** In the old days, a report was a stack of pages. With the advent of computers, the stack turned into a long scroll because the ends of all the pages were attached for the convenience of the first printers. Today, some reporting systems still behave as if paper were the only output. Most, however, will at least save reports in spreadsheet format and some (particularly ones that report only against Web logs) produce HTML output as well. You might think that all reports should be delivered on the Web and that paper reports are for hold-outs from the previous generation. You would be wrong. Paper is still the best medium for coming to grips quickly with large amounts of detailed information. When you need to find details and patterns in long tables, for example, nothing beats a report on fan-fold paper stretched across your desk.

✦ **Roll-up and drill-down:** Detail is the devil of reporting. You always seem to have either too much (where you can't see the forest for the trees) or too little (where the report is so general that it is of no use). The best reporting systems support some sort of roll-up and drill-down where you can switch back and forth between the summary and detail of the report. In a workflow report, for example, you would be well served to start the report with a page (physical or HTML) that shows all the active workflows and highlights those that have overdue steps. The next page might show the detail on the one that is most overdue. The next page might show the change log and comments for one step in the overdue workflow. Although paper beats the Web for long tables, the Web is the clear winner for roll-up and drill-down.

✦ **Analytics:** Data from your system without analysis may not be worth looking at, at least not unless you have a lot of time. Web reporting applications have really begun to take on the task of analyzing huge Web logs and automatically synthesizing the vast amount of data into easy to consume charts and summaries. You can take a lead from them in creating your own analytics for other sorts of reports. For example, from the logs kept by your workflow system, you might be able to create a simple pie chart that shows the amount of time that a component (or any other object) generally dwells in each workflow state.

✦ **Control:** The ultimate report not only gives you information but allows you to act on it. For example, suppose you manage to create pie charts that show where your components are spending most of their time. First, a click on any slice of the pie could give you detail, but that's still reporting. Suppose, however, that you could set desired dwell times for each slice. By setting the desired times for each slice, you would be making changes to the workflow system that would then change the times when steps are overdue. Now your reporting system is not just reporting, it is part of the control system as well.

It is likely that the reporting system in your commercial or homemade system is as fragmented as your logging system. However, just as you can make positive steps toward integrating your logs, you can make positive steps toward making good reports. The place to start is to ask yourself: What sorts of reports would give us the most control, save us the most time, and result in the most positive change in quality? Then just do those and forget about the rest.

Security

Strictly speaking, security is not a separate feature of a CMS. Rather, it is a combination of the features of the following systems:

✦ **User administration:** This feature generally allows you to not only create users but assign various permissions to them (see the section earlier in this chapter titled "User administration").

✦ **Personalization:** This feature allows you to restrict the content that someone sees as well as to direct them to the right content (see Chapter 40, "Publishing System," the section titled "Personalization System").

✦ **Templating:** Both input and output templates can house code that enforces whatever security policy you want (see Chapter 40, "Publishing System," the section titled "Templating System").

✦ **Element set personalization:** In this feature, you decide which author sees which elements of which components. Thus, you can restrict the information that authors see (see Chapter 38, "Collection System," the section titled "Element-set personalization").

✦ **Repository system:** The databases in your repository have their own security features. For example, all major databases allow you to enforce user names and passwords to control access to the data stored (see the section earlier in this chapter titled "The Repository").

You can use any or all of these other systems to implement a security policy. And for the majority of systems where the information held is not particularly sensitive, some combination of these features is fine.

If, however, your system does hold sensitive information, and great harm can be done if the wrong person sees the wrong information, then the patchwork of places where security is enforced becomes a big liability. The situation is a microcosm of the security issues of the computer world in general. Our CM systems, like our other systems, tend to be rather loose affiliations of applications that all do part of the wider task. These parts need to communicate to do this task. That means that if you can get into one system (the weak link) you can use its communication with other systems to compromise their security. For example, the CMS has an API that allows Web forms to get data into and out of the database. If you try to enter the database directly, you may be denied. But if you can manage to modify a template, you might be able to use the template's relationship with the database to get whatever you want.

So, each of the CMS systems that participates in security is a potential key to unravel the security of the whole system. If you have been following the general thrust of my view on CM technology, you can see that getting systems to cooperate is hard enough. Guaranteeing that they will never compromise each other may be even harder. So, trying to seal up all the leaky connections in your CMS may be a tough job.

And, even in the absence of a determined cracker (hackers write code, crackers break code), simply coordinating the security policies of all these systems can be a real chore. I have talked a number of times about the concept of dashboards that let you integrate and coordinate all the features of some system (workflow or localization, for example). In each case, such a dashboard represents both the fulfillment of what CM technology should deliver and the hardest feature to actually create in today's real CM environments. Well, the same holds for a security dashboard. To be able to centrally decide on, implement, monitor, and ultimately control a security model that spans your whole CMS is really tough. With the other dashboards, a failure to integrate means more work for an administrator and some missed opportunities. Unfortunately, in the case of the security dashboard, a failure to integrate might mean legal action or worse consequences.

For most organizations, the tolls within a CMS are adequate to ensure the light security that they require. Organizations with higher security needs know better than to depend on the security within the system. Instead, they isolate the entire system from people who ought not to see inside. For example, many organizations will not put a CMS system on a publicly accessible Web site because of their justified fear of being compromised. Instead, the CMS is within the organization's firewall and only a derived database or flat site is outside. Other organizations simply refuse to put sensitive information in a CMS repository. Frankly, I can't blame them.

Link support

Make sure that you build robust link checking into your system if it's not part of a system that you buy. A robust linking system has the following sorts of functions:

✦ **Authoring:** The system should have the capability to author links at the component, element, or text level (as I describe in the section "Storing cross-references in an RDB," earlier in this chapter).

✦ **Structure:** The system ought to enable you to pack additional information into a link. In addition to the reference and referent ID, the system ought to enable you to specify link IDs, link types, and any other parameters that you may want to manage and render the link to your specifications.

✦ **Management:** The system ought to enable you to find and repair broken links automatically. A broken link can have an internal or external referent. For internal referents, the system ought to alert you if you delete a component that's used as a referent somewhere else. The ideal user interface for this would be some kind of dialog box that lists the titles and IDs of the components that link to the one that you're trying to delete. From this dialog box, you ought to be able to globally change the referent to a different component, or open referring components individually to decide what to do with each link. A much more subtle piece of functionality would enable your system to detect if you change the title (or other significant elements) of a component and ask you whether you want to review links. Often significant content changes to a component invalidate some of the links you've forged to it. The system must also check external links periodically. For links to Web URLs, the system can try to access the URL and see whether it still exists. Of course, this doesn't tell you whether the URL is still appropriate. As an enhancement, the system can try to determine whether the target page has changed since the last access by storing an image of the page linked to and comparing it with the current one. If the current page is different from the stored one, the system can trigger a workflow to have someone verify that the page is still valid. If this process can't be automated, the system should be capable of compiling lists periodically and initiating workflow to tell someone that it's time to check the validity of the links manually.

✦ **Rendering:** If the system has only one way of rendering links (as HTML <A> tags, for example), you may need to augment it so that it can produce the other sorts of links that you need. You may, for example, need to write your own extension to create print-format links ("for more information, see..." and so on).

My comments on cross-references apply also to all the access structures that you store in your repository. You may get a lot of Web-format TOC functionality out of your CMS, for example, but you need to write your own print-format TOC functions.

In many systems, the hyperlinks and media references (such as an <IMG> tag in HTML) that are embedded in the middle of a block of text go unnoticed and can be broken without any clue. Some systems enable you to track these links and references even inside paragraphs of text.

You must have link checking, and the more robust the better.

Media support

Make sure that, in some way, your system has the capability to check the validity of media references that appear within. In many systems, as in links in general, media references (such as <IMG> tags in HTML) that are embedded in the middle of a block of text can go unnoticed and, therefore, can easily be broken unintentionally. The best way to track these internal media references is to track them as separate components. You can then create a status element that you can query and report on to know the status of each media item in your system. As a bonus, the media components can have extra elements for whatever variations you need in different publications. If print publications need one image caption and Web publications need another, for example, your media component can contain elements that store the caption variants of the caption.

To keep media references healthy in your repository, you can create a validation feature that runs periodically against all media references to files that aren't controlled by the CMS. If the system includes references to sound files that are on a Web server somewhere, for example, the validator should check periodically that these files are still there.

Just as you do link checking, if you have media, you must provide at least basic media management.

Intellectual property tracking and costing

The term intellectual property (IP) applies to content that is owned by someone who wants to control its use. For example, a photographer might want to control the use of her photographs. A publishing house might want to control the use of its printed materials. Usually control here translates to payment. In other words, the photographer (or photo licensing agency) actually wants everyone to see her pictures, but would like to get paid for each viewing. The owner and the user of the IP (your organization in this case) usually mutually establish the ground rules for use of IP in a contract of some sort. The contract specifies how and when the IP can be used and details a payment plan for use.

As you consider whether and how you will deal with IP, note the following list of tasks your CMS will likely have to accomplish in an IP feature:

✦ Coding the ground rules for use of the IP in your CMS. The idea here is to create a set of business rules that implement the various terms of use for each type of IP you handle. The rules can be applied to components and automatically guide their creation, management, and publishing. This is the hardest part of an IP feature. The restrictions and payment options in an IP agreement can be complex, convoluted, and internally conflicting. In other words, they can make for difficult rule coding by even the best programmer. Add to this the fact that different kinds of IP have different and competing use rules and you may easily have an unimplementable system. In these cases, collection, management, and publishing of IP may have to be managed manually; or better, simpler agreements will have to be negotiated.

✦ Marking the components that contain IP with the appropriate metadata to allow them to participate in the rules you have devised. For example, you might need a price per use and an extra thumbnail element in a component that stores Images. As the component is being created, you fill these extra elements.

✦ Tracking use and computing payment. Using either server logs, template code, or some other method, you must be aware when IP materials are accessed, what the context of the access is (for example, you probably don't want to pay each time an editor views a controlled image), and what payment or use logs need to be updated. If you have been successful coding general IP use rules, this process might already be implemented.

IP is similar to security. In both situations owners need tight control over their content. In a security context, the content owners don't want people to see their content without permission; in an IP context, owners don't want people to see their content without paying. Security systems might actually have use rules as complex as those you devise for IP use. In addition, security systems might require the same sort of logging and accounting as the IP system. So, if you have taken the trouble to implement one of these systems, you may have a head start on the other.

My strong recommendation is to negotiate simple deals for IP. For example, if your contract calls for a one-time fee for unlimited reuse, you don't need an IP system. It may very well be worth paying the owner more to avoid the increased cost of IP tracking. On the other hand IP issues are not going away. They will get more and more important to more and more organizations as these organizations begin to find and exploit the value in their content. Also, as aggregation and syndication companies grow, more IP will be available as a less expensive alternative to authored or otherwise acquired content. In the long run, the fact that money is involved with IP content may mean that its comprehensive management in some sort of IP dashboard happens sooner than it might for other systems.

External connections

I have discussed the connection to external systems a lot in the specific systems that have to connect to outside sources. Here, I add a few considerations that span other systems and synthesize the specifics of the other discussions.

Directory services integration

Operating systems are like CM systems in their need to manage users. Unlike CM systems however, operating systems have developed sophisticated features for creating users and user groups and assigning them permissions. These directory services, as they are called (directory in the sense of a telephone directory, not a file system directory), are standard protocols for how to access centrally stored user and access information. The lightweight directory access protocol (LDAP) is today's biggest standard. Microsoft's Active Directory, which is (arguably) LDAP-compliant is the service of record for Windows servers. When considering the integration to external directory services, consider these issues:

✦ It should be able to allow users who have already logged into your local network to enter the CMS without a further login.

✦ It should easily supply the information that is common to both the CMS and the operating system, such as a user's name and department.

✦ It should not preclude you from defining other information that is CMS-specific for users, such as edit rights and personalization rules.

✦ It ought to allow real-time authentication of users.

Especially if your system is being used for an intranet and you already have all the potential audience members in a central directory, it behooves you to use that directory.

Replication

Replication means keeping a master version of content and/or configuration and then making copies that are distributed to various locations. Replication is usually done to improve performance. If one copy of a popular Web site, for example, is getting too much use and its performance degrades, you can replicate it to a variety of regional locations that can share the load.

Replication is usually a publication issue. It is less common to try to replicate the CMS itself than to try to replicate Web content that is produced by the CMS. However, it is not too uncommon for raw content to be replicated to affiliated repositories. In contrast to replication, where the sending system literally duplicates its data in the receiving system, organizations may choose to syndicate from one repository to another. In syndication, the sending system provides the content, but no assumption is made that the content will end up in the same place as in the sending system.

Replication is a one-way transfer. Data flows from a sending (master) system to a receiving (slave) system. To perform replication reliably, you need to:

✦ Set up systems on the receiving side that are identical (or very close) to the sending system. For example, the database structure on the receiving side needs to be the same as on the sending side to assure that information from the sending system has a place to go.

✦ Set up software on both the sending side and the receiving side. The sending side packages up content and configuration in a way that the receiving side can interpret (an XML format for example). The receiving side stores the information it gets in the appropriate locations (database tables, files, and so on).

✦ Set synchronization schedules and procedures. Will you try to update the receiving systems incrementally, sending only what has changed? Or will you blank out and send the full data set each time?

✦ Create failover procedures that assure if a replication event fails, the receiving system can recover or, at least, pass all its traffic to another system.

Very large systems that produce very popular publications need replication. One exception to this rule is organizations that produce print publications for local distribution in a variety of locations. In this case, which is vastly simpler than replicating Web sites, the publication files to be printed and distributed can be replicated to a variety of local print shops that can then print and distribute the materials in their region.

Distribution

Distribution means keeping your master content in a variety of databases (or other sources) that exist at a variety of sites. For example, if your organization has regional offices, you may decide to give each a local repository where content from that office is created and published. This approach is compelling if each office is in a different locality and very little content is shared between offices. Notice that this is quite different from replication. In distribution, the CMS repository itself exists in a variety of locations. To produce a publication, templates might draw from a range of databases to gather their content.

Distribution can happen along with replication. For example, suppose one office in Taiwan produces Chinese language content and another in Singapore produces English content. The repository of all content comprises the databases in both locations. The publications coming out of the Singapore office might include the Chinese and English content. To produce those publications, the Singapore office might try to reach into the database in Taiwan (possibly, a difficult task), or the Chinese content could be replicated to the Singapore repository for use in the local publications. The line here between one CMS and two is blurry. You could say that the two offices have different CM systems that just happen to using the same software. In this case, you would not use replication, but syndication to connect the two systems. Or you could say that the organization has one CMS that has a distributed repository. For convenience, some of the content in one part of the repository is duplicated in another part. But each piece of content has a master version. This is not simply a semantic distinction. The organization might want to create one infrastructure that spans both offices, or two infra-structures that divide the two offices. In either case information has to flow between the offices, but in the case of one infrastructure, all the information in both offices is part of the same repository.

Distribution is a tricky business. It requires you to:

✦ Decide how you will divide content between the parts of the repository. You might divide by content type or by metadata value (the value of the language element, for example). One way or another you need to have one single content model that is logi-cally divided among a variety of databases.

✦ Figure out how to share metadata between the parts of the repository. Regardless of what database content is in, for example, you want one list of author names. You might decide to create one central database where all the other parts look for shared informa-tion, and a set of content-only databases that have replicas of the shared information.

✦ Decide if and how you will duplicate content from one part of the repository to another. I recommend avoiding this duplication if possible. If you do duplicate, you will need to ensure that the duplicate content cannot be edited and that it is always synchronized with the original versions.

✦ Figure out how to do maintenance across the various databases. For example, when you decide to split a single metadata value (see Chapter 38, "Building Collection Systems," the section titled "Value splitting" for more information on splitting values), how will you ensure that the task is carried out in each part of the repository? You will likely need a much more complex workflow system that spans the locations of all parts of the repository to accomplish this sort of integration.

✦ Figure out how to do publishing that spans databases. You may try to have publica-tions reach into the separate databases, or you may try to replicate content from one database to another, or you may try to create a publication database that draws from the distributed sources and combines them into a single data mart that publications can draw from. None of these approaches is easy.

I could go on with the challenges of distributing data, but I suspect that if you have not tried this, my list is enough to make you pause. If you have tried it, I'm sure you could create your own list of issues. The lure of a central data source is that it simplifies all the maintenance, communication, and publishing issues. The reality of centralization is that it is not always possible or preferable to have all contributors feeding one central source. If you do decide to distribute, hold tight to the notion that you have one content model. It may be the only thing that keeps your system from flying apart and becoming a set of breakaway republics.

You need to distribute when the realities of connectivity drive you to do it. As connectivity between diverse regions of the world becomes better and better, this need decreases. The other driver of distribution will not decrease with technological advances. Local groups (even ones in the same building) want autonomy. They would like their own database with their own content that creates their own publications. In content as in politics, you can conquer these local groups and hope that, with their resistance broken, they will join the federation and no longer fight. You can also show them clearly the advantages of membership and find a way that they can maintain their local culture while participating fully in a system that serves them as well as the rest of the organization.

XML as an integration medium

XML has become the standard method to interface between any two systems that need to share data. The provider system outputs XML, and the receiver system inputs XML. Both systems use the same DTD or schema to ensure that there's no mismatch. If you have an XML repository, you can provide a transformation program that maps your schema to the shared one. The transformation is subject to problems of ambiguity, no correspondence, and no existence (as I outline in Chapter 37, "Processing Content," the section titled "Getting to the Core of Content Mechanics"), but can often be programmed without too much trouble by standard XML tools. If you have a relational database repository, the same applies. You must resolve the same transformation problems, but the rest of the mapping should be fairly easy to accomplish. All in all, XML solves the mechanical problems of transferring data, but still leaves you to figure out how to fit together two structures that conflict. At least, if you do your part of the work, XML provides the tools to implement your solution.

More and more systems recognize XML as the standard way to interchange data. Your CMS might already output XML, or with a few changes you might be able to get it to. As interchange schemas solidify and gain acceptance (ICE, which is Information and Content Exchange, and others), it is likely that you will have to do less and less to connect your systems to others. Expect, however, that you will have to change the way you store your content to reduce the ambiguity and no-correspondence issues of connection.

Standard database interfaces

Your CMS may need to include an easy-to-use interface for probing and building an interface to standard databases. Using standards such as ODBC, you can get tools that enable you to connect to, issue queries against, and view data in a surprisingly large percentage of the standard database products. The best of these has a nontechnical interface for connecting to simple databases that can be used by administrators, plus the capability for the connection to be extended by programmers using a standard language.

 Cross-Reference I talk more about database connectivity in Chapter 38, "Collection System" in the section titled "Acquiring database records."

You need this feature if you connect to a lot of different data sources on an ad-hoc basis or if you have less technical savvy than required to connect to your data sources.

Robustness

If you have ever experienced a failure in a mission-critical system, you will be sure to forever pay attention to issues of robustness. These sorts of issues are of concern mostly to system administrators when everything is working as it should. When something goes wrong, on the other hand, they become everyone's issues.

Backup

Backup means making a copy of all the data in your system and putting it somewhere safe in case some sort of failure occurs. As simple as this sounds, in a CMS it may be harder than simply making a copy of some files on a tape drive or hard disk. For one thing, the data files in a CMS are scattered in a number of directories and computers. Among the files that you may need to back up are:

✦ System files on the main CMS server.

✦ The files on the Web servers that host your Web publications.

✦ Any files on end-user computers that have CMS configuration in them (such as files that configure the authoring environment.

✦ Scripts that run on remote computers to, for example, acquire content from enterprise systems.

One strategy to capture all the files in a CMS is to back up the entire hard drive of the system. Of course, many systems reside on multiple computers so more than one hard drive must be backed up. If and when it comes time to restore, you will likely find that even backing up every file on the hard drive is not enough to restore the system. Instead, you will generally have to image (or *ghost*) the hard drive so that the system can be restored exactly as it was at some point in time.

The time to restore is another issue to pay attention to. If your system goes down and you have backups on tape, you may have quite a while to wait for it to come back up. It is likely that you will have to go back through the setup and configuration process. If you have imaged your hard drives, the process of restoring the system will be faster, but not fast enough if you are backing up a Web server that is in constant use. When instantaneous recovery is what is called for, organizations will often *mirror* the hard drives of their system. In mirroring, you set up a second computer to back up the first. Every bit of data that is written to the hard drive of the first computer is also written to the hard drive of the second. The second hard drive is a mirror of the first. If the first drive fails, the second one is in a position to take over for the first right away.

Some of the database systems that you use may have their own backup and recovery mechanisms, but they will not cover the array of other files that constitute your CMS. Backup is not a substitute for versioning. Getting a single file out of a backup system can be tough. Getting a single database record out of a backup can be even tougher. Getting a component, which can have parts in files, various database records, and may have entanglements in other systems, can be nearly impossible.

Of course, you always need backup. The thing that changes is the speed with which you will need to recover. The faster the recovery, the more expensive and complex will be the backup solution.

Scalability

Scalability measures the capability of your CMS to get bigger. Bigger may mean any or all of the following:

✦ **Serving more Web pages:** If your CMS directly serves Web pages, which many do not, scalability measures its capacity to serve more and more pages per minute. This type of scalability depends a lot on the hardware and software that is installed on your server in addition to the CMS. Faster processors, application servers with sophisticated caching routines, and databases that can pool connections for more efficient access all contribute to the capability of your Web server to scale. One way to help scale Web sites that is often overlooked in the rush to acquire advanced technology is to increase the number of static Web pages that your CMS produces. Dynamic pages can be extremely costly in system resources and are often built on the fly even though they do not need to be.

✦ **Accommodating a lot of authors:** Unless you are a very rare organization, the number of users contributing to your CMS will not pose a significant load on the system. Even if they all submit content every day, 1000 users will not feel a slowdown in any well-built CMS. On the other hand, your capability to create and manage accounts for a large number of users may be limited by the construction of your system.

✦ **Accommodating a lot of content:** If you intend to create and store a lot of content (terabytes for example) you may need to look seriously at the system you are buying or building. The simple storage and movement of that much information can cause your system to slow down. Most major relational databases are able to handle tremendous amounts of information, but are the rest of the processes in your system equally able to handle the load? Of particular concern are XML-based systems, whose access times are related directly to the amount of content that you have stored in them. Systems based on a single XML file are the worst and can max out at just a few megabytes of content. Be sure, as well, that the time to publish does not depend on the size of the repository. Also be sure that the indexing routines you plan to use for full text or metadata search can incrementally index new content rather than having to index the entire content base to make changes.

✦ **Accommodating a lot of rules:** If you are planning a very complex system with lots of workflows, personalizations, custom collection, or publication routines, your form of scalability will measure the number of distinct rules that can be applied to content during its processing. For example, if you are planning a very complex personalization regime, be sure that the personalization engine you plan to use lets you create all the rules you need, allows you to simultaneously apply them, and allows you to optimize the application of those rules at publish time so that Web pages and other live publications do not slow down to a crawl.

✦ **Accommodating a lot of sites:** If you plan to implement your CMS on a world-wide basis, then your form of scalability measures the system's capacity to distribute data storage (covered in the section in this chapter titled "Distribution"), replicate (covered in the section in this chapter titled "Replication"), and syndicate (see Chapter 40, "Publishing System" in the section titled "Syndication System") content. With a lot of incoming and outgoing content connections, your system could get out of control and eventually be corrupted without a robust system for managing all these connections.

Many organizations that really need to scale their systems have had experience in other enterprise applications and have the infrastructure already built to accommodate a large CMS. Others confront these issues for the first time with a CMS. A number of organizations that I have seen think they need to scale much more then they actually do. For example, they count the number of pages on their intranet and Internet and decide that they have an enormous content base. But the amount of content they really need to produce and distribute may be orders of magnitude less than what they have managed to accumulate. Similarly, many organizations initially believe that they will need to scale across the globe when, in fact, all they need to do is to put in a good system in one place and give people around the world periodic access. I would suggest that you take the same attitude toward scalability as I have mentioned for workflow. Even though it feels good to plan for the worst and most complex situation, you should refrain as much as possible from anticipating these situations and instead start simply and let events force you to incrementally add complexity.

Reliability

Reliability is a measure of how much you can count on your system to keep running without failure. Like scalability, reliability depends a lot on the infrastructure below the CMS. For example, even the most reliable CMS will go down if its hard drive fails. Operating systems as well (some more than others) can crash and bring down otherwise robust CMSs. This is not to say that CMSs are more robust than the hardware and software they run on. CMSs are generally flakier than either their supporting infrastructure or other enterprise systems. Engineers often talk about "mean time between failures" to express the overall reliability of systems. CM product companies do provide some statistics like this but, in general, they are not very rigorous about their approach to reliability. When considering what reliability means in your CMS, be aware of the following issues:

✦ How reliable does the collection system need to be? If authors try to submit content and the system does not respond, will they give up? What is the impact of failure on the array of scripts that you use to convert, acquire, and aggregate content? Is it worth the cost of development to increase their reliability, or should you just be prepared to put more people on the job?

✦ How reliable does the management system need to be? Although failure in the collection system may mean a frustrated author or a long night's work hand-converting content, in the management system a failure might mean the whole system stops. Make sure that failures in this system are rare and that recovery is rapid.

✦ How reliable does the publication system need to be? Individual Web sites have their own world of reliability issues that any Web master can scare you with. The real question for Web sites (as I mention in the section in this chapter titled "Backup") is the speed of recovery. Of course, the majority of Web site failures are not catastrophic. Rather, they are small bugs that cause a page not to display or to render incorrectly. With good testing, many of these smaller failures can be avoided, but they will still occur. Perhaps the most frequent publishing failure is in the area of connectivity. An upload to a Web site, a distribution to a printer, and most frequently, connections to individual audience members can and do fail all the time. The capability of one computer to talk to another (which is a core need of any CMS) is perhaps the flakiest part of computing.

Most people focus on the major disasters in thinking about CMS reliability. With proper backup and recovery procedures, these problems are adequately addressed. It is the smaller failures that will plague you day-to-day with a CMS. I firmly believe that the best attitude toward these sorts of failures is the same one that hospitals take. Hospitals expect people to fail in a myriad of ways every day. Rather than panicking each time a person with a problem shows up in the emergency room, the hospital makes a rapid assessment of the severity of the problem and assigns resources on a priority basis. You, too, can set up a triage system that both assumes failures will happen and deals effectively with them when they do.

Summary

Management systems come from in two basic flavors: XML and relational databases. The good systems know how to blend the two to provide the right strategy for the right task. The best systems integrate the two into a single user interface and system, where you work with components and elements, and the underlying structure isn't a concern. As you create management systems, you want to do the following:

✦ Choose a repository structure that fits the content you want to store. Notice how much of your content comes in outlines and how much in rows and columns. This can indicate how much belongs in XML and how much belongs in a relational database table, respectively.

✦ Whatever storage you use, make sure that it's as suited to your access structure needs as it is to your content component needs.

✦ Make sure that you account for localization in the basic structure of your management system.

✦ Find a way to impose one single structure across your entire repository that implements your content model.

✦ Extend the system that you buy. As necessary, use the extensions that I propose in this chapter to enhance the efficiency or effectiveness of your management system.

In this chapter, I've attempted to be comprehensive in describing management system features. This technology taxonomy is a tool that describes what exists, or could exist, today. You can no doubt add to it, but it should give you a good start toward describing the features you want in your own system. In the next chapter, I take a similar approach, describing the systems and subsystems you need to put together a publishing system.

✦   ✦   ✦

Building Publishing Systems

A publication system has a very interesting job. It is responsible for pulling access structures and components out of the repository and merging them with the design, layout, and formatting of the target publication medium to create a publication that looks as if it were put together by hand. You can use scores of approaches to this tough problem, but they all have to somehow support the following:

- ✦ **Definition:** Your publication system must allow you to define the publications that you create. There are often no explicit publication definition tools in a commercial CMS, so you mostly do this job outside the CMS in platform-specific design tools (Web and print design tools, for example).

- ✦ **Creation:** The system must allow you to actually create publications. I put all the techniques for producing structured publications under the heading of *templates*. Templates combine content and access structures from your repository with the surrounding text and media of your target publication.

- ✦ **Distribution:** The system must permit you to deploy the built publication to its point of distribution. The distribution may be as simple as e-mailing files to a professional print shop, or as complex as filling databases and file systems worldwide with various cuts of your content to refresh a distributed Web site.

In this chapter I detail techniques and technology to give you an idea of the minimum and optimal publishing functionality. I organize the publishing system of a CMS into a several functional subsystems and explain each subsystem, its features, and its sub-subsystems in detail.

At its top level, a publishing system includes subsystems for:

- ✦ A templating system, the fundamental reason and purpose of the publishing system, which extracts the correct content from the repository for a particular publication and context.

- ✦ Personalization, which adapts the content to the person, making it what you expect she wants to see.

- ✦ Deployment, which describes the methods by which a CMS distributes content from the repository.

✦ Web publishing, including static and dynamic content as well as integration with existing Web infrastructures.

✦ Print publishing for content destined for distribution on paper.

✦ E-mail publishing, which pushes content to subscriber lists.

✦ Syndication, which refers to packaging and distributing content to other consumers of the content, such as other Web sites.

✦ Other publications systems, including electronic document formats like PDF and Help, as well as multimedia and small-device platforms.

✦ An interface for getting content out of the content repository.

This chapter describes each of these subsystems, in turn, as well as the major features and sub-subsystems each may include.

For a list of the extensive systems and features that are described in this chapter, see Chapter 34, "Building a CMS Simply," in the section "An index to the technology taxonomy." The systems and features of the publishing system are outlined in the portion of the taxonomy under "System: Publishing System."

Templating System

Although I suspect that other ways to think about the fusion of repository content with publication presentation will appear in the future, today only one concept exists — that of the template. Templates draw content out of the repository and into the right context for a particular publication.

Cross-Reference I cover the design of a templating system fully in Chapter 31, "Designing Templates."

Because XML has arisen as the format of choice for most publications and because XSLT (eXtensible Stylesheet Language Transformations) is the templating tool of choice for XML, I draw most of my examples from there. However, a wide range of templating systems and languages are out there, each with its own features and capabilities, so I will not treat templating as if it were just an application of XSLT.

Tip Don't be fooled into thinking that just because a templating system "uses" XML that the system must be good. First, it has a lot of ways to use XML. For example, many systems issue commands to their non-XML systems via XML wrappers in template files. In this case, XML is simply a way to type commands and is tangential to what is really happening in the templating system. And even if the templating system is a "pure play" XML implementation, meaning that the entire templating show is run from XML and XSLT, it still may not be a good system. XSLT, for example can be a lousy way to create print publications. What you can be sure of with an XML-based templating system is that you are using the most widely accepted system. Whether that system makes it easier or harder for you to produce your publications is up to you to decide.

Producing target formats

Every publication type has its own storage and rendering format (see Chapter 2, "Content Has Format" for more information on storage and rendering formats). For example, Web publications have an ASCII (or Unicode) storage format and use the familiar angle bracket tags (<p>, <b>, and so on) to render text.

To produce a publication, your templating system must be able to create the appropriate storage and rendering format. Three major variations in approach are used for this task, depending on the nature of the target format:

✦ **XML text:** If the target publication platform is (or can accept) XML, then your system can (or ought to) use the standard XML tools to create publications. For example, if you are creating a publication for a wireless device that consumes WML (Wireless Markup Language), you would most likely use XSLT to produce the publications. Of course, XSLT assumes that your source content is already in XML, so you might need some processing to transform repository content into XML if you store it in another way. With the advent of XHTML, which is quite close to HTML and which renders in any modern Web browser, Web publications can also be built this way. In fact, most major publication platforms have moved or are moving quickly to some form of XML. With any luck, XML text may be the only target format in the near future.

✦ **Non-XML text:** A range of text formats predate XML. Before XML, if you wanted to create a format that was accessible to anyone, you would just create one. So in older publication systems, you often find unique text formats. Even though these are not XML formats, if you store or can easily produce XML from your repository, you can still use XSLT to produce many of them. If your content is not already stored in XML, you may be better off writing your own custom translation routines that go directly from your repository format to that of the target publication.

✦ **Non-text formats:** If XML is the *lingua franca* of rendering formats, text is the *lingua franca* of all formats. If a publication can be expressed in plaintext, you can study that text and eventually figure out how to produce it. If the text format is well documented, you can be confident that you are producing it correctly. However, to provide special layout features, to protect the format from hacking, and to improve efficiency, many companies produce storage formats that are not text. These formats are encoded in some way so you can't just look at them and figure out how to create them. In these cases, your only realistic choice is to go through the application that creates these files and use it to create your publications. Although this problem is disappearing (most notably as Microsoft Word now accepts XML), it still exists, especially in desktop publishing applications. So, in this situation, rather than having templates that directly create your publications, you must have templates that call the parent application of the publication to create the publication. Calling the parent application usually boils down to using the application's API or its internal macro or scripting language. Often you create a basic publication layout in the parent application that has placeholders for content to be included. Then, to produce a publication, you write a program that opens the parent application, loads the layout file, and uses whatever methods the parent application provides to navigate the file. After filling the file with content and access structures from the repository, your program finally saves and deploys the completed file. As you can probably guess, this is often a complex process and rarely a reusable one. This method of creating publications cannot fade quickly enough for my taste. Still, there can be tremendous power in the API of a publishing application (creating TOCs and indexes for example) that is hard to replicate in XML.

The general movement of the publication world is toward XML. So on the one hand, your best move is in that direction as well. Balance that move, however, with a long look at your particular publications. Make sure that you don't lead your publication formats by so much that it is much harder to produce them with XML than it is to use older but more targeted and powerful techniques.

Producing target units structure

A publication consists of units. Web sites have pages; print publications have parts, chapters, and sections (and also pages, although they are less important than the others); technical publications have topics. Your templates must be capable of producing the appropriate units for your publications. It must also allow you to link those units together as needed to produce the navigation between units. You use template systems to accomplish these tasks.

✦ An overall publication template can create the highest-level structure. For example, home pages and navigation pages provide this level of structure on the Web and in help-type technical publications. In print materials, the highest-level structure is in the front matter (title pages, TOCs, introductions) and back matter (indexes, glossaries, and so on).

✦ Page templates are for producing the next level of structure. On the Web this structure might be details pages for each component to be included and summary pages where a number of components are shown with links to the details. In print, this structure often amounts to a file for each major section in a large work.

✦ Component and navigation-level templates are for formatting individual content chunks and access structures within the page templates. For example, on a Web site you might have 20 content types, each with its own rendering templates, and an extra dozen templates for rendering hierarchies, indexes, and cross-references. In print, templates are used for parts, chapters, sections, sidebars, notes, warnings, and a host of other page elements.

Depending on your particular publications, you may choose to link all these templates together so that one triggers the others, or you may choose to run them separately. However you choose to engage the templates, you should understand that it takes a system of templates to create a publication.

It would be really great if you could buy or build a system that lets you create and manipulate your template systems. We are not there yet. In the meantime, you can at least chart the systems yourself to understand and teach others how the various publications you create are formed and can share templates.

Layout and surrounds

Templates retrieve and place content components and access structures (which become navigation) on the target pages of the publication. What this most often amounts to is interspersing code that retrieves and formats content and access structures with standard content in the template that does not vary. For example, on a Web site the banners and titles can be the same across all instances of the page the template creates. These can be straight HTML in the page template. This HTML is interspersed with the template code that calls in content and navigation, as shown in the following example:

```
<HTML>
  <HEAD><TITLE>eChu.com</TITLE></HEAD>
  <BODY>
    <TABLE>>
```

```
        <TR>
          <TD>
            [Build Navigation Here]</TD>
          </TD>
          <TD>
            [Build Content Here]</TD>
          </TD>
        </TR>
      </TABLE>>
    </BODY>
  </HTML>
```

All but two lines of the template above are regular old HTML that builds a simple table with two columns. The code (which I abbreviate and enclose in square brackets), tells the template processor to fill in the navigation in one column and the content in the other column (see Chapter 31, "Designing Templates" in the section titled "Using a template processor" for information on template processors).

As I'm sure you can imagine, you could create any sort of HTML page you'd like this way and then fill it with content from the repository. All branding, layout, titling, headers, footers, and coloring are done in the usual way. Only the content and navigation require code. This is not to say that you couldn't create template code to layout and surround your content and access; it's just that you don't have to. You can most easily take care of the layout and surrounds in the native tongue of the publication format. And although my example is in HTML, the same is true of any publication format.

Interspersing code with layout and surrounds is as basic a feature as you can get in a templating system. If it is not there in your systems already, you have the wrong system. In addition, in HTML at least, it is one of those rare features that is as fully implemented as it can get. Rarely are any restrictions placed on the kind or number of HTML tags that can surround your template code. Unfortunately, many template systems are built only for HTML and will not recognize commands that you embed in other text formats.

Template programming

Embedded within the layout and surrounds in a template is the programming code that calls in and processes content and access structures. Depending on your templating system, this code can potentially do anything that programming code can do. The wider the range of publication formats and content types you have, the more complexity is involved in transforming the content in the repository into a publication. So, generally you want a system with complete programming capabilities so that you can manage this complexity.

Most fundamentally, a template is a program that builds publication pages or sections. A template may literally be a program, or you may use it to trigger other programs. Consider the following examples, the first of which is an HTML file that calls programs:

```
<HTML>
  <HEAD>[Insert Title]</HEAD>
  <BODY>[Insert Body]</BODY>
</HTML>
```

The parts that square brackets ([ ]) enclose are calls to programs that insert a title or a body at this point in the HTML file (represented schematically and not literally, of course). This process doesn't happen by itself. Rather, a program that's part of the CMS (or working in conjunction with the CMS) opens the HTML file, finds all the parts in square brackets, and does what they say to do.

You can accomplish the same outcome by using straight computer code (in this case, Visual Basic code), as in the following example:

```
Function BuildPage(ID)
   Set Component = LoadComponent(ID)
   Title = Component.GetElement("title")
   Body = Component.GetElement("body")
   Output = "<HTML><HEAD>"
   Output = Output + Title
   Output = Output + "</HEAD><BODY>
   Output = Output + Body
   Output = Output + "</Body></HTML>"
   MakeFile Output, ID + ".htm"
End Function
```

You can assume that this code lies buried in a program that runs at the appropriate time to build a page. In this example, whatever other program calls this function passes it the unique Id of a component. The function uses that Id to retrieve the component (LoadComponent(ID)). It then uses the component to retrieve its Title and Body elements (Component.GetElement("title")). Then, in the variable Output, it builds the full content of the page, including all the HTML code and the component elements that it retrieves. Finally, the function creates a file that it calls ID.htm (where id is the component Id that passes to the function). It fills the file with the output that it creates.

Finally, an XSL template can also do the job (given that your components are XML), as in the following example:

```
<xsl:template match="/">
  <HTML>
     <xsl:apply-templates />
  </HTML>
</xsl:template>
<xsl:template match="Title">
  <TITLE>
     <xsl:value-of select="."/>
  </TITLE>
</xsl:template>
<xsl:template match="Body">
  <BODY>
     <xsl:value-of select="."/>
  </BODY>
</xsl:template>
```

Note   Again, if this code is incomprehensible, focus on understanding how you can use very different techniques to build the same end page.

This example is a set of nested XSLT templates. An XSLT processor invokes each one after a certain situation occurs. The first triggers after the processor finds the root node of the content. The first XSLT template puts the <HTML> tag into the output and then enables other templates to process. The second template triggers when the XSLT processor finds a Title element. It puts the <HEAD> and <TITLE> tags into the output along with the value of the Title element. The final template triggers when the XSLT processor finds a <BODY> element in the content. The template puts the Body element into the output that the <BODY> tags surround.

You may notice a number of things in comparing these templates:

✦ **They all accomplish the same result.** All result in exactly the same HTML file in the end. A CMS may use an approach similar to any of the ones that I mention here to produce output. (And some CMSs allow all three.)

✦ **The first example is much easier to read and use.** Even if you're not a programmer, you can get the idea of what the first example accomplishes. As a nonprogrammer, even though you know what the other examples accomplish, they may still be hard to read and interpret. You might imagine giving responsibility for the first method over to a publication team, but only a programmer can work with the other methods. You can imagine going even farther with the first method. Why not add a drag-and-drop interface, in which the page displays graphically and you drop elements where you want them to appear? In fact, some visual template environments do just that.

✦ **The first example is hardest for the CMS.** The first method is simple for a reason: All the complexity lies elsewhere. All the complexity of the second and third examples isn't gone in the first; it's just hidden from the user. In fact, to make the first method work is a much harder programming task than to make the others work. Not only does the CMS do all the work of the second or third methods to make the first method work, but it also abstracts the programming methods, generalizes them, and wraps them in some sort of parser and user interface. Even if you don't understand the full subtlety of the effort this requires, you can surely understand that making the template look simple takes a lot of extra work.

✦ **The first example is the least flexible.** Suppose that you want some modified form of the title to go in. (You may, for example, want to add the name of the section that the page lies in as a prefix to the title.) In the first method, you depend on the CMS to guess what you want to do and to give you some command to do it. If no command appears for what you want to do, you can't do it. In the other methods, the only real restriction is your talent as a programmer in those languages. Regular programming languages and even XSLT (with a little help) can do whatever you want them to.

In the preceding list, I reproduce a common dichotomy that infuses all computer science (and all the world really). If you want it simple for the end users, you make it harder for the developers. If you make it easy to use, it's less flexible.

Just as in the rest of computer science, CMS systems seek to have their cake and eat it, too. Consider the following variation of the preceding methods:

```
<HTML>
  <HEAD>
    <CMSCommand>
      <INSERT COMPONENT="ID" ELEMENT="Body">
        <CUSTOMCOMMAND NAME="SectName" File="Myfunct.dll"/>
      </INSERT>
    </CMSCommand>
  </HEAD>
  <BODY>
    <INSERT COMPONENT="ID" ELEMENT="Body"/>
  </BODY>
</HTML>
```

This template combines some of all three of the template programming methods that I discuss in the following ways:

✦ **It's an HTML file:** It's directly editable and doesn't require a programmer to read it. It's more complex than the simple HTML file that I presented earlier, but a nonprogrammer still can conceivably figure it out.

✦ **It's XML:** Rather than a simple [Insert] command, the template uses XML syntax to represent commands. This approach enables the CMS to validate that you type the commands correctly, leverage any knowledge that you already have about XML, and provide a consistent, very extendable way to type complex commands. It's not as flexible as using an XSLT template such as the one that I presented earlier, but it brings some of the rigor of XML to the system.

✦ **It enables you to create your own programs:** The command <CUSTOMCOMMAND NAME="SectName" File="Myfunct.dll"/> is there specifically to enable you to create your own programs and attach them to the template processor. Inside the file Myfunct.dll is the program SectName that the template processor runs after it reaches that command. This method isn't as flexible as writing your own whole program, but it enables you to add whatever processing the template processor doesn't already support.

The compromise in this templating method is to sacrifice some simplicity for the capability to use complex commands and call in custom programs. This method is close in principle to how many of the better CMS products actually do templating.

You need a templating system that is easy enough for your staff to use it and robust enough that it does not decide for you what sort of publications you create. In many organizations, I have seen teams work from what the templating system can do back to the Web sites and other publications that the system lets the organization create. The alternatives here are that you can train your staff to deal with a more programming-like system, or you can buy or build a more visual system that is more costly and may restrict what you can build.

At any rate, try to make sure that whatever you get it supports all the standard variable types and control structures of major programming languages.

Producing static and dynamic publications

Static (or early-render) publications are created ahead of time and dynamic (or late-render) publications are created on demand as a user requests them. For example, you might allow users to construct a custom whitepaper from the kinds of information they are most interested in. They select the content, push a button, and receive a well-formatted word processing or PDF file. I choose this particular example to show you that print publications can be static or dynamic just as Web publications can.

Your system should be capable of building both static and dynamic publications. In addition, if you are creating complex Web sites, your system should be capable of mixing static and dynamic pages together to produce sites that are partly static and partly dynamic. You want to produce as much of a publication as possible statically for performance and robustness, but you produce other parts dynamically for flexibility. The system ought to enable you to choose exactly which components to publish beforehand and which to publish as users request them.

The late rendering may be handled by the CMS itself or by code that resides on a Web server. In the latter case, the CMS must enable you to deploy components to database or XML structures on the server. For example, you might store a set of components on the server in a database so that you can late-render them based on personalization rules. In addition to having your CMS deploy the content for server-based rendering, you should try to get it to deploy the code for server rendering as well. In this way, the publication can still be fully managed by the CMS and not split between the CMS server and a Web server.

The templates you use to create static and dynamic publications may actually be the same. What matters is when they run (sooner or later) and where the result is stored (in a file that is then uploaded, or nowhere except maybe a server cache). A good CMS enables you to use the same or very similar templates to go either way.

Many systems have either a static or dynamic bias. Some, amazingly, go completely one way or another. Static systems want to avoid the hassle of having to reside on a production Web server. Dynamic systems want to avoid a hard line between authoring and delivery. The best system, regardless of where it resides, gives you a choice of delivery options.

On-the-fly conversion of text and media

If your system is required to produce dynamic publications and your content is not stored in the format that the dynamic publications require, some sort of real-time conversion is needed. The most common example of this occurs when you store text as XML and want to create HTML. In this case, it is most likely that the XSLT templates you use perform the XML-to-HTML conversion as they go. The same XML might be used to create a print format such as PDF or QuarkXPress. In this, case a commercial or custom-coded converter is necessary to make the transition. As in all conversions, mapping is easy when structures in the source correspond to structures in the target. Mapping without human intervention may be impossible if they don't. In a conversion process in your collection system, you have the option to have a person complete a conversion that a program could not complete. In a dynamic publication system, you have no such luxury. Ideally, if you have been careful in the design of your content model, your mappings from repository to publication structures will all work out. In reality though, you often have to settle for incomplete mappings or go back to your repository and modify your content model.

Images and other media, as well, may need to have their formats converted as you dynamically create publications. For example, to produce print publications, the system may take images stored as JPGs and convert them to TIFF format. Of course, if this is an issue (either a performance or robustness issue), you can always convert all your images beforehand and then store two versions. However, if you do, remember that you must reconvert the image any time it is edited.

On-the fly conversion of text formats is mandatory for any system that creates a dynamic publication in a format different from what is stored in the repository. In fact, even in static publications, you still need to do the conversion; it just does not need to be real-time and have no human intervention. If your repository content is in XML, in many cases, you can use XSLT alone to get the results you need. Augmenting XSLT with Formatting Objects can also get you to a number of print formats including PDF (see http://xml.apache.org/fop/ for information on the Apache XML implementation of an FO processor). If you are not using XML in your repository, you probably rely on whatever you bought with your system or can code yourself.

You can easily integrate any number of commercial or open-license image converters into a Web server to do on-the-fly image conversion.

Integration with publication authoring tools

In each output medium, publication designers have their own set of preferred design tools. On the Web it might be Dreamweaver or HomeSite, whereas in print it might be Word, Quark, or InDesign. As much as possible, you are well served by allowing your designers to work with their home tools. You can go about this integration in several ways:

✦ You can originate files in the home application and then convert them into templates. For example, if print designers prefer to use Word to create the layout of a publication, you can take their Word files and turn them into publication templates. For example, you might save the designer's work as Word XML and then turn that file into an XSLT. In this case, after the file has been turned into a template, it is no longer editable in the home environment.

✦ You can "roundtrip" templates into and out of the home application. For example, you might add software to reconvert the XSLT back into a Word XML file (say, by making all the XSLT code into comments) so that the designer can make changes. This is a tricky business. The designer inevitably makes changes to the file that cause it not to convert cleanly back into a template.

✦ You can turn the home application into the template development environment. For example, you could give the designer a toolset within Word that allows her to see the Word file as a template within Word. The designer could designate sections of the page to correspond to components, elements, and access structures. A transformation process would then take the designer's work and turn it into a template by converting the designer's markup into template code.

 Cross-Reference I detail the process of working with Word as a templating environment in the section later in this chapter titled "Producing Word files."

I use a print environment in the examples above because the integration in the Web world is much easier to accomplish. In fact, many commercial CM systems already fully integrate with Web design environments. Of the three methods, the first is the most common, the second is the hardest (at least, the hardest to get to work), and the third, I believe, is the best. The third option allows the designer to work with her home tool but does not isolate her from the templating task.

The basic problem to solve for your CMS is how to engage publication designers in the template development process. Certainly, the designer has to own the layout, styling, and branding of the template. Ideally, you would like the designer to simply own the template with developers giving her standard templating items (include element here, include access structure here, and so on) to specify. If you could manage to include a preview feature (where the designer could see, as she designs, how the template would render the range of content in the repository) along with these standard items, you would have just the right toolset for designers to work with publications. Recognizing that you (and the rest of the discipline) are not that far along yet, you should at least try to let the designer stay in her home application as long as possible and not simply throw designs over the wall to the programmers who then own all template production.

Mix-and-match templates

It is useful to have methods for sharing code between and within templates including:

✦ Being able to nest one template within another.

✦ Being able to reuse a template in various places.

✦ Being able to keep template code in central files where it can be called into other template files as necessary.

Many Web sites use server-side includes as an easy way to share code. They save each component or navigation template as a separate file and use include statements to insert component and navigation templates into a page template. XSLT has all the methods I mention built into its standard feature set. To see this, look at an XSLT file that creates a simple Web page:

```
<stylesheet version="1.0" >
    <include href ="BodyElements.xslt"/>
    <include href="Media.xslt"/>
    <template match="/">
        <HTML>
            <HEAD>
                <TITLE><call-template name="Title"/></TITLE>
            </HEAD>
            <BODY>
                <H1><call-template name="Title"/></H1>
                <call-template name="Body"/>
            </BODY>
        </HTML>
    </template>
</stylesheet>
```

The <stylesheet> element is the root element of the XSLT file. In a rare instance of shortsightedness, the creators of XSLT decided to call their files stylesheets. In fact, these files do as much to create structure as they do format (or style). At any rate, within the stylesheet are templates.

✦ **Nesting:** Each <template> element is a template. Each <call-template> element invokes a template. The first template in this file is <template match="/">. It is run before any others. Notice that within this first template, both the Title and Body templates are invoked (<call-template name="Title"/> and <call-template name="Body"/>). In XSLT, nesting templates in this way is common.

✦ **Reuse:** Notice that the Title template is reused. It is invoked twice in the first template. The first time it fills an HTML <TITLE> tag and the second time it fills an <H1> tag.

✦ **Central files:** In this example, the root template, <template match="/">, calls a Title and a Body template. Those templates could reside in the same file as the root template or they can, as is assumed in this example, be included from other central template files. I include the template code that resides in a central file — the <include href ="BodyElements.xslt"/> elements does this job. It and the Media template files contain the Title and Body templates, as well as any other templates that Title and Body themselves call.

Any reasonably robust templating system ought to allow you to nest, reuse, and centralize templates. Sadly, however, not all do. If your system can't do this natively, you can likely simulate it by doing the nesting and reuse in code that you write and call from your templates. Although this method is not ideal (as it often forces you to mix formatting statements with your programming code), it gets the job done. If your system does not support reuse or calling your own code, it's really time for a new system.

Navigation building

If you have done a logical analysis on your CMS, you know the set of navigational devices that you will use across your publications. You should try as much as possible to treat all the navigation building code as a system that shares code and a user interface. As I have demonstrated in a number of examples, devices such as component finders and options dialog boxes have uses across most of the access structures.

For management, you want to maintain as few access structures as possible. For publishing, you might produce a wide variety of navigation structures. The best way to manage this situation is to create core access structures in your CMS that can be converted automatically to the ones you need in publications.

When I say converted here, I mean a structural conversion, not a formatting conversion. Making an outline of hyperlinks as well as a print table of contents from the same hierarchy does not count as two structures. It is the same structure in two formats. On the other hand, making a Web outline that categorizes content by task and a print table of contents that categorizes content by department requires two different structures or, better, one central structure that you can convert into two different forms.

Content in a CMS repository is stored in components. In a publication, it is in pages or sections. When you create access structures in your repository, you categorize components. When you create publication access structures, you have to figure out how your component structures map to page or section structures.

These are two central issues of access structure management: how to perform structure conversions and how to convert from a component system to a page or section system. In the features that follow, I outline some of the ways you might accomplish these transformations for the four access structures I have described.

Building hierarchies

Suppose that PLAN wants to manage press releases by the department or country that originates them. This gives PLAN staff members the most control over their creation and matches with the groupings of their authors. A partial outline of their press releases management hierarchy might look as follows:

```
<PRESS RELEASES>
   <HUMANRESOURCES>
      <RELEASE>PLAN Hires New General Manager
         <Other Structure/>
      </RELEASE>
      <RELEASE>London Reorganizes
         <OTHER STRUCTURE/>
      </RELEASE>
   </HUMANRESOURCES>
   <FINANCE>
      <RELEASE>Budget Surplus Goes to Asia
         <Other Structure/>
      </RELEASE>
      <RELEASE>Steady Rise in Overhead Checked
         <OTHER STRUCTURE/>
      </RELEASE>
   </FINANCE>
   <US>
      <RELEASE>ChildReach Signs 100,000 New Members
         <OTHER STRUCTURE/>
      </RELEASE>
      <RELEASE>Reunion in Mali
         <OTHER STRUCTURE/>
      </RELEASE>
   </US>
```

```
   <UK>
      <RELEASE>PLAN Packs the Albert Hall For Astounding Concert
         <OTHER STRUCTURE/>
      </RELEASE>
      <RELEASE>EU Debates a Single Presence
         <Other Structure/>
      </RELEASE>
   </UK>
<PRESS RELEASES>
```

Each press release component, marked by the <RELEASE> tags, is stored in this hierarchy under the department or country of its origin. I included the <OTHER STRUCTURE> tags to show you that each release has a lot of other elements in it besides just the titles that I show.

Audience members coming to PLAN's Web site don't particularly care where a press release originated. In fact, they probably don't even care that these are press releases. Rather, they want to see news of concern regardless of origin. On PLAN's Web site, the following simple, two-level hierarchy may be all that is needed for users to navigate through press-release content:

```
<Hot News>
  <Release/>
  <Release/>
  <Release/>
</Hot News>
<Recent News>
  <Release/>
  <Release/>
  <Release/>
</Recent News>
```

In my discussion on publication templates, I describe how this hierarchy can be produced programmatically from press release components. (See Chapter 31, "Designing Templates," the section titled "The Web navigation areas.") The management hierarchy is where the press release components are actually stored. PLAN can map them into the publication hierarchy that it needs by using the metadata that is part of each press release component. For example, to create the Hot News branch of the hierarchy, PLAN finds press releases that are targeted to the current audience and are, say, less than two months old. It will use the fact that the Press Release content type includes a date and a targeting element. An expanded view of one press release component might look as follows:

```
<RELEASE>PLAN Hires New General Manager
   <FOCUS>Org changes</FOCUS>
   <DATE>24 Feb,2001</DATE>
   <OTHER STRUCTURE/>
</RELEASE>
```

The date element speaks for itself in the preceding example. The targeting element is called *Focus* (a name that staff will be more likely to understand than, say, *targeting*). To create the Hot News branch of the hierarchy, template code searches for press release components with a date that is less than two months old and a focus that matches the users' concerns.

To fill the Recent News branch, the code searches for components with a date less than one year old. The template code can sort press releases by their focus. For example, for a Member-type user, the code can sort press releases by Kid Stories, Success Stories, and then the others by date.

So, to map the management hierarchy to the publishing hierarchy, a template selects components out of the hierarchy based on their metadata and includes them in a static set of publication hierarchy categories. This is a fairly simple mapping that is performed all the time, but I hope it gives you the basic idea of mapping from a general hierarchy in your CMS repository to a specific one in a publication.

To accomplish the transition from a hierarchy that relates components to one that relates Web pages, PLAN might use a simple trick. You may recall the following line of template logic from my templating discussion in Chapter 31, "Designing Templates" in the section titled "The Web navigation areas":

```
<A HREF="[Insert ID].htm">
```

This line maps the component Id to an HTML page URL. It assumes, of course, that when each press-release component is turned into a press-release detail page, it will be named in this way. This is a useful trick to remember. It will work for any situation in which you create one page per component. If you use this trick (or one like it), then all you need to know to be sure a link to a component is valid is the component's Id.

So, at the most basic level, you can store your components in a hierarchy in your management system and then extract navigation structures from that hierarchy as you need them. In the sections that follow, I expand upon this basic idea.

Hierarchies by reference

In a static hierarchy, you use metadata from the components to populate a set of unchanging categories. The example of the PLAN Hot and Recent News outline creates just a two-level hierarchy, but you can extend the method to any number of levels your metadata will support.

To simplify their reuse of components in different hierarchies, rather than having the press release components stored in the management hierarchy, PLAN could simply reference them there, as follows:

```
<PRESS RELEASES>
   <HUMANRESOURCES>
      <RELEASEREF ID="PR1"/>
      <RELEASEREF ID="PR2"/>
   </HUMANRESOURCES>
   <FINANCE>
      <RELEASEREF ID="PR3"/>
      <RELEASEREF ID="PR4"/>
   </FINANCE>
   <US>
      <RELEASEREF ID="PR5"/>
      <RELEASEREF ID="PR6"/>
   </US>
   <UK>
      <RELEASEREF ID="PR7"/>
      <RELEASEREF ID="PR8"/>
   </UK>
<PRESS RELEASES>
```

You can see that PLAN could create any number of hierarchies such as this and put press releases (or any other components) in whatever categories the organization chooses.

Dynamically generated hierarchies

Rather than storing hierarchies, you might decide to generate them from the metadata values you have in the repository. For example, suppose that PLAN would like to build a listing of press releases by focus as follows:

✦ Each level-one parent will be a different focus. Focus values will be pulled from the focus element of the components stored and then ordered alphabetically.

✦ Each release will have an origin element that lists the country where the release was issued. A simple metadata list relates country names to continent names (Asia, Africa, Europe, and so on). Level-two and -three parents in the hierarchy are these continent and country names.

✦ The fourth level of the hierarchy holds the names of the press releases in each country/continent/focus.

Unlike the static or by reference method, in this case no hierarchy is explicitly stored. Rather, the hierarchy is created dynamically, as needed, by rules that leverage the metadata stored with the components.

To actually create the hierarchy in a publication, PLAN template coders would write template code to select components by focus and then sort them by continent and then by country. The code would then lay them out on a Web page as some form of outline where the terminal nodes of the outline are press releases that link (hyperlinks on the Web or page numbers in print) to the details of the press release.

This is a great way to do hierarchies if you can manage it. Because you don't need to represent it explicitly, the hierarchy manages itself. On the other hand, this sort of hierarchy is not very flexible and you have to live with alphabetical sorts and other automatic categorizations.

Producing multiple hierarchies

If no metadata is available to build either static or dynamic categories and you need a different hierarchical structure, you can always store multiple hierarchies in your repository. For example, suppose that PLAN wants to show an outline of press releases by the issues they address. These issues are not simple metadata values like focus. Rather, they are a hierarchy of issues, sub-issues, and sub-sub-issues. To do this, PLAN can create and store an independent issue hierarchy that references press-release components.

Filtering

In this method, the target hierarchy has the same overall structure as the source hierarchy but includes a subset of the categories and components. For example, suppose that PLAN wanted to publish press releases by origin but only show those with a particular focus (Kid Stories, say). To do so, the staff would write template code to filter out all but the Kid Story components from the management outline. They would include a significant amount of extra code to ensure that categories that have no Kid Story components in them are not displayed.

This is a key component of personalization and a relatively easy one to implement. Given that you have done the hard part (figuring out how you will identify an audience member and what that audience member wants to see), implementing this feature might require no more than adding a constraint or two to the query that returns the nodes of the hierarchy, as it is stored in the repository.

If your needs for publication hierarchies are few and simple, you can dispense with the fancier techniques I outline here and simply store your content within a hierarchy in your management system. However, the more elaborate methods are worth the extra effort if:

✦ It is inconvenient to store components in a hierarchy in the first place. Especially in relational database systems, the sort of default hierarchy I show is not easy to create. It demands that you first create a hierarchy by reference.

✦ You want a variety of components in the same hierarchy. For example, PLAN might want articles and press releases in the same hierarchy.

✦ One hierarchy is not enough. For example, PLAN might need to have the press releases organized by region and by subject at the same time.

Building indexes

Indexes are usually fairly easy to map from a main repository list to the list you need in a publication. For example, suppose that part of the primary index that PLAN uses looks as follows:

```
<INDEX>
  <TERM Name="Administration" ID="I3">
    <SEEALSO TermID="I1"/>
    <COMPONENTID>PR1</COMPONENTID>
  </TERM>
  <TERM Name="Executive Staff" ID="I2">
    <COMPONENTID>PR1</COMPONENTID>
  </TERM>
  <TERM Name="Finance" ID="I1">
    <SEEALSO TermID="I3"/>
    <COMPONENTID>PR1</COMPONENTID>
  </TERM>
  <TERM Name="Management" ID="I4">
    <SEE TermID="I2"/>
  </TERM>
</INDEX>
```

Note   Understand that the preceding example is a severely limited sample. The real index would have many more terms and many more components under each term.

The elements in this example have the following meanings:

✦ **<INDEX>:** This tag surrounds the entire index.

✦ **<TERM>:** This tag defines a single index term. It has two attributes. The Name attribute is the index term itself. The Id attribute gives each index term a unique Id.

✦ **<COMPONENTID>:** This tag associates one component with an index term. If the index term is associated with more than one component, the <TERM> tag would contain more than one <COMPONENTID> element.

✦ **<SEEALSO>:** This tag is present inside a <TERM> tag if another term elsewhere in the index is a synonym. It has a TermID attribute that identifies the other term that is synonymous with the current term.

✦ **<SEE>:** This tag is present inside a <TERM> tag if another term elsewhere in the index you should refer to instead of the current term. It has a TermID attribute that identifies the other term that you should see instead.

An index connects phrases to content (or to other phrases). In books, index entries point to page numbers. On the Web, they point to URLs. In a CMS, index entries point to components, elements within components, or to text position within elements within components.

The two ways that PLAN might include keywords in its Web site are as follows:

✦ By putting them in a <META> tag so that search engines can find and catalog the page.

✦ By building an index page on the site that lists all the keywords and has links to the pages for each term.

To build <META> tags, the template that builds each press release page can query the index and return the index terms that the page needs. For example, the page PR1.html (built from the press release titled "PLAN Hires New General Manager") would construct a <META> tag such as the following one:

```
<META Name="keywords" Content=" PLAN International,
Non-profit Organizations, Children's Welfare, Finance,
Executive Staff, Administration">
```

The first set of keywords (PLAN International, Non-profit Organizations, Children's Welfare) could be standard for every page. The remaining ones are pulled from the index and are included because they were the ones listed for PR1.

To build an index page, PLAN's code might process the entire index structure and turn it into a page on which all the terms are listed and linked to the appropriate component pages. Here is some sample HTML code for one term:

```
<H4><A Name="I3">Administration</H4>
<UL><LI><A HREF="PR1.HTML">PLAN Hires
New General Manager</A></LI>
<LI>See also, <A HREF="#I1">Finance</A></LI>
</UL>
```

Notice that the component title links to the press release detail page, the URL of which can be derived from the component Id. The word Finance links to the place on the same page where the term Finance is found. You can assume that, like the term Administration, the term Finance is marked on the page by an HTML anchor, the name of which is the term's Id, <A NAME="I1">. (An *anchor*, by the way, is an HTML tag that serves as a bookmark and enables you to name a particular place on an HTML page so that you can link to it from other places.)

Multiple components per page

To create index <META> tags for Web pages with more than one component, you can simply combine the index terms for each component into one longer <META> tag (being careful not to include duplicate entries). Building an index page when you have multiple components on the target pages is not as simple. In the example I gave, the URL of the target page could be derived directly from the Id of the component on it. If you have several components on the page, you can't use this trick, because the page can be named for only one or for none of the components it contains.

A fancier trick is to create page names that combine the Ids of all components they contain. (For example, a page that has PR1 and PR2 on it might be named PR1_PR2.HTML.) When building the index page, the template scans the names of all HTML files on the site (a time-intensive process). If a file has the right component name embedded in it, the template links the index term to it. Whatever trick you use, it must be more complex than the simple naming I illustrate.

The method that I have always used to ensure that I can automatically build links to components from their Id's is to always create a page for each component that has its most complete presentation. Even if the component appears on many different pages and in many different forms, it serves you well to have a "page of record." That page is useful for creating links as well as for search engine indexing.

Print indexes

A Web index links to the top of a page or, possibly, to a title within a page. A print index links to a page number. If you simply extend the system I illustrated to print, all your index entries point to the page where the title of a section is. This may not be the page on which the actual term appears but rather the section where it appears; the section may encompass several pages. To avoid this problem, you can put index anchors into the text. An anchor can be as simple as <INDEX TermID="1234">. It marks the exact spot where the index entry applies. If you use a system with anchors, you can use an even simpler index storage structure because you no longer have to store component Ids with your index. When preparing a print index, make sure that you account for any places where the same component shows up on two or more pages.

Traditionally, indexes have been reserved for book-length print works. If your content is well indexed within your CMS, you have no reason not to include indexes in any or all your print materials. For example, it might be a terrific convenience to your readers if, right on the title page of your whitepapers, you were to list the keywords covered in the whitepaper and the pages on which the reader can find them.

Filtering indexes

Like hierarchies, indexes can be filtered to show only the parts of the index that matter. You might filter the index to:

✦ **Publish only the right parts of the index.** If you publish only part of the content in the repository, you publish only the part of the index that applies to the particular part of the repository you published.

✦ **Personalize the index.** For example, suppose your audiences differ in background, including some lay people and some professionals. To account for this, you might add an element to your index called *source vocabulary* that states whether a phrase in the index comes from the lay or professional community. Then, when you detect that a person is from the lay community, you can filter out the professional terms that might confuse her.

This feature goes a bit beyond the range of what most organizations can handle either from a tagging or maintenance standpoint. I'm hoping, however, that its potential to help your audiences is pretty clear.

The run of the mill CMS has no special indexing features. At most, it has a flat set of keywords that you can assign to components. The keywords themselves (or maybe an Id that points to the words) reside in an element and are not accessible unless you display the entire component. You can really do better than this. With a little extra code, you can, at least, view your keywords as a comprehensive index. With more code still you can turn your viewer into an editor and use it to assign keywords and manage the keyword list itself. The final step, of course, is to add enough extra metadata to the index entries that you can personalize and manage the index as a whole without having to modify components at all.

Building cross-references

Cross-references have to change appearance a lot from one publication medium to another. Nevertheless, you should create one way that cross-references are listed in your repository. For example, suppose that you have the following sort of repository structure to hold all your cross-references:

```
<CROSSREFERENCES>
  <CROSSREFERENCE ID="CR123" Type="ForMore" TargetID="C123">
    <REFERENCE Punctuation="." ChunkID="">
       For more information, see <REFERENT/>
    </REFERENCE>
  </CROSSREFERENCE>
  <CROSSREFERENCE ID="CR124" Type="ForMore" TargetID="C456">
    <REFERENCE Punctuation="," ChunkID="CK123">
       <REFERENT/>
    </REFERENCE>
  </CROSSREFERENCE>
  <CROSSREFERENCE ID="CR125" Type="PreReq" TargetID="C789">
    <REFERENCE Punctuation="" ChunkID="">
       (if you find this hard to understand look in,
          <REFERENT/>)
    </REFERENCE>
  </CROSSREFERENCE>
  <CROSSREFERENCE ID="CR126" Type="PreReq" TargetID="C1112">
    <REFERENCE Punctuation="" ChunkID="">
       <REFERENT/>
       contains a more basic explanation of this concept.
    </REFERENCE>
  </CROSSREFERENCE>
</CROSSREFERENCES>
```

Note I show all the cross-references gathered together here so you can easily compare and contrast them. This is a fine method to use if you don't want to clog up your files with a lot of distracting information. The place where the cross-reference is created need only have a short tag with a cross-reference Id. However, in most systems the entire cross-reference structure is inline. This makes it easier to edit entries; however, it gives you no place where you can look at and work with the cross-references as a whole.

In this example, each cross-reference has the following:

✦ **An Id:** As usual, this distinguishes it uniquely from all other cross-references.

✦ **A Type:** This says which cross-referencing strategy you are following. (For more on cross-referencing strategies, see Chapter 30, "Designing Content Access Structures" in the section titled "What's a cross-reference?") In this example, two types are shown. *ForMore* links are links to components that give detail on a topic just mentioned in the present context. *PreReq* links are links to material that might help you if you do not understand the present material. You might display these two types of links very differently. For example, ForMore links may be inline with the surrounding text. They may be presented as part of the sentence structure of the surrounding text. PreReq links might be in a single list of links, grouped at the top of the current page or section, and preceded with a standard header (something like, "Look in the following sections for more basic information").

✦ **A TargetID:** This is the unique Id of the component that is the referent of this cross-reference.

✦ **A Reference:** This is the part that will drive how the cross-reference is rendered. The <REFERENCE> tag has Punctuation and ChunkID attributes. *Punctuation* specifies how the title of the reference ought to be punctuated (as you will see presently). *ChunkID* specifies whether the cross-reference should use a standard text block or one that is typed into the <REFERENCE> tag. If there is a value in the ChunkID attribute, the publication template knows to fetch the standard link text that is identified by its Id (CK123, in this example). If there is no ChunkID attribute value, the publication template uses the link text that is in the <REFERENCE> element.

✦ **A Referent:** The <REFERENT> tag that is in the preceding example tells the system where the titling information will go relative to the Reference text in the published cross-reference. That is, the <REFERENT> tag might fall at any position in the text within the <REFERENCE> element. The examples show the referent at the beginning, middle, and end of the reference text. Of course, when there is a ChunkID and thus no reference text, the <REFERENT> tag can fall in only one place.

In addition to the structure I provided, you might also want to include other management elements such as Owner, Status, DateLastValidated, and the like. I have left them out of the example for simplicity's sake.

Suppose, now, that from this structure you have to produce print and Web cross-references. You need at least one navigation template per publication type. In addition, each template must deal with the variability that can be represented in each link (ForMore versus PreReq links, ChunkIDs, and so on). In the section "Producing Word files" later in this chapter, I present and discuss a full XSLT template file for dealing with the print version of links such as these. Here, I start with a less technical discussion of how the Web versions of these links might be created.

In my example, I assume that the Web site you are producing has ForMore and PreReq links. I map out the ForMore links in detail and then discuss the template that might be capable of creating either kind of link. A ForMore Web link might look as follows:

```
<A NAME="CR123" href="C123.htm">
  <IMG
    SRC="formore.gif"
    width="45"
    height="24"
    alt="For more information, see the page
    titled 'XML in Action.'"
    border="0"
  >
</A>
```

This cross-reference shows up on the Web page as a hyperlinked image, as follows:

✦ **The hyperlink:** The HTML <A> tag surrounds the image tag. The cross-reference component's Id becomes the NAME attribute of the <A> tag. In that way, each cross-reference will have an HTML anchor in its page, and you can navigate to each of them as you check them visually. For simplicity, I designed it so that the HTML page you jump to has the same filename as the Id of the referent component. You will likely do something fancier. I recommend creating a central program that can map component Ids to page filenames. If a component appears on more than one page, you need some way of specifying which page you want the link to go to. You have to pass the program a component

Id and some other parameter for the sort of page you intend the link to go to. With a bit of effort, you could include a page type selector as part of the user interface for entering cross-references in your CMS authoring environment. For example, when you have chosen the referent component Id, the interface program could give you a list of the available page types that the content type you chose can be found in. You can choose the one you want, and the program can save your choice in an attribute of the <CROSSREFERENCE> element.

✦ **The image:** The image itself is a small navigational icon called *formore.gif*. The image has a set height, width, and border. Assuming that these values will not change from one ForMore type of link to the next, they can be typed directly into the template. The *alt* text for the image contains the reference text mixed with the titling of the page on which the component will be found. To build this alt text requires a bit of work. The program must determine the name of the page from the component Id. The program has to insert the page name plus some other standard text (*"the page titled"*) into the alt attribute based on the placement of the <REFERENT> tag within the <REFERENCE> tag.

✦ **Punctuation:** Finally, using the value of the Punctuation attribute, the program has to punctuate the title correctly. In the case shown, the punctuation (a period) comes before the ending quote marks of the title. Unfortunately, it is not possible to simply calculate what the punctuation should be. You might think that if a <REFERENT> is at the end of the sentence, a period is called for, whereas if it is within a sentence, a comma should be used. Well, consider this example: *(See the page titled "It's Always Harder Than You Think")*. In this case, the <REFERENT> is at the end of the sentence, but it gets no punctuation because it is inside a set of parentheses. If you begin to play with arranging the text within a sentence, the variations and exceptions quickly complicate any simple algorithms.

Here is a sample of the template you might use to make this link:

```
[If Type = "ForMore"]
  <A
     NAME="[Insert CrossReference ID]">
     HREF="[Run MakePageName(TargetID)]"
  >
  <IMG
     SRC="formore.gif"
     width="45"
     height="24"
     alt="[Run MakeTitle(TargetID, ChunkID, Punctuation)]"
     border="0"
  >
</A>
[End If]
```

See Chapter 31, "Designing Templates" in the section titled "Web templating" for more information on the syntax I chose to represent this template.

Here is how this template works:

✦ **Template selector:** To begin, the [If] command ensures that the template runs only if the link type is ForMore. Other templates run for the other link types on the Web and a whole other family of templates would have to be created for print cross-references. However, the structure of the cross-references stored in the repository is more than enough to support the entire range of templates that might render cross-references.

✦ **Including static text:** As you render links, your templates may need to include static text along with programmatically generated text. Wherever HTML code belongs to the publication and not to the content, or where there are parameters that are the same across all components, the template has text that will not be interpreted. The entire layout of the link, as well as the parameters that set the name and qualities of the link icon, are static text.

✦ **Adding fill-ins:** Wherever there can be a simple substitution between a component element value and a template element, I have used the [Insert] command. The CrossReference Id is the only direct substitution in this example.

✦ **Including calculated values:** The HTML page filename and the reference text require extra programming to operate. Actually, the way I set up the example, it is simple to create a substitution for the page filename. But for illustration, I decided to include it in the template as an extra program. (For CMS projects, it never hurts to create programs with the assumption that any process will get more complex as time goes on.) The MakePageName program takes a component Id and returns the name of the HTML page that contains that component. The MakeTitle program takes a component Id, the Id of a chunk of text, and a punctuation mark and returns a well-formed piece of reference text that includes the chunk of text, page title, and punctuation all in the right order.

Like indexes, cross-reference features are severely underdeveloped in most CM systems. Neither the storage structure nor the rendering templates are as complete as those I have outlined. Still, nothing stops you from beginning to look at cross-references with an eye toward a comprehensive storage and rendering plan. If your system supports XML in the repository, you can build as sophisticated a cross-references system as you need. You can coalesce it for review and write templates to enter your links at collect-time and render them at publish-time.

Building sequences

Sequences come from the following three places in your CMS repository:

✦ **The primary sequence:** This follows your primary hierarchy through the content in your repository.

✦ **Derived sequences:** These follow the results of a query that gathers and orders all the components that meet a certain criteria (date, author, type, and so on).

✦ **Other sequences:** These can be stored as separate component indexes and accessed as needed to build pages.

Rather than building a separate handler for each of the kinds of sequences you might have, I have found it more useful to build a central handler that can return the next or previous Id in any sequence you pass it. For example, the following template for a Web page pulls information from the primary sequence, a derived sequence, and an "other" sequence:

```
<H2>[Insert Title]</H2>
  <H3>Next and Prev by Outline</H3>
    <A HREF="[Run GetSeq([Insert ComponentID],
    "primary", "prev")].htm">
      <IMG SRC="back.gif">
    </A>
    <A HREF="[Run GetSeq([Insert ComponentID],
    "primary", "next")].htm">
```

```
        <IMG SRC="next.gif">
    </A>
<H3>Next and Prev by Author</H3>
    <A HREF="[Run GetSeq([Insert ComponentID],
    "auth", "prev")].htm">
    See previous by same author
    </A><BR>
    <a href="[Run GetSeq([Insert ComponentID],
    "auth", "next")].htm">
    See next by same author
    </A>
<H3>History list</H3>
    Here are the topics of this type that you have viewed
    <UL>
        [CurrID = GetSeq([Insert ComponentID],
        "history", "prev")]
        [For all items in the history sequence]
            <LI>
                <A HREF="[Run MakePageFileName(CurrID)]">
                    [Run MakePageTitle(CurrID)]
                </A>
            </LI>
        [CurrID = GetSeq(CurrID, "history", "prev")]
        [Next item in the history sequence]
    <UL>
```

This is not a template you are likely to see, but it demonstrates the use of a central function compactly. GetSeq does all the sequence heavy lifting in one place. The preceding page template embeds navigation templates for all three kinds of sequences by calling the same central GetSeq function.

The function GetSeq does the following:

✦ **Takes a component Id:** The Id is the identifier of the component for which you are creating the sequence.

✦ **Takes a sequence name:** In this example, three sequences are handled: the primary sequence, the auth sequence, and the history sequence.

✦ **Takes a next or previous parameter:** This tells you in which direction to look for the referent component.

✦ **Returns the name of the next or previous component in the sequence:** The first thing the function does is determine which sequence you are using. Then for each sequence, it uses a separate code block that opens the right data source and retrieves the appropriate sequence. In the case of the primary sequence, the function might access the primary hierarchy. For the author sequence, it might issue a query for components that have the same author as the current one. Finally, for the history sequence, it might query a special table that holds all the components of this type that you have ever accessed. Having found the appropriate sequence list, the function must then locate the current component within it and, finally, locate the component that is next or prior in the list.

For each of the three types of sequences illustrated, the template follows different rules, as shown here:

✦ **Primary sequence:** The first set of lines in the example contains the template for the primary sequence. The template formats two standard images for the primary Next and Previous buttons. (I'm sure that you can picture the left- and right-facing arrow images that are so common on the Web.) It then uses the following command to create an HTML file name to link each button to:

```
[Run GetSeq([Insert ComponentID], "primary", "prev")]
```

- Starting from the inside, the command inserts the ComponentID of the current component into the GetSeq function. If the current component was "C123," the original command would change, as follows:

```
[Run GetSeq("C123", "primary", "prev")]
```

- Now the command calls GetSeq with the current component Id, the name of the sequence to locate, and the parameter for next or previous. I assume in this example that page names are simply component Ids with .htm attached to them.

✦ **The author sequence:** The second set of lines in the example contains the template for the author sequence. The template formats next and previous text links that follow an author list rather than the primary hierarchy. It is not very different from the primary sequence except that it creates text instead of image links, and the GetSeq function uses a different internal code block to do its processing.

✦ **The history sequence:** The third set of lines in the example contains the template for the history sequence. I have purposely made it a bit more complex than the others to add some interest to the example. The idea is that the history template creates a list in reverse chronological order using the components of this type that you (the end user) have visited.

- The history sequence is complicated by a loop within it that produces not the next and previous links but all those that have been stored in the sequence. The template loop depends on a classic recursive method. The CurrID variable holds the Id not of the currently displayed component, but of the last one that was given to the GetSeq function. Each time the GetSeq function returns the previous Id, it creates one line in the list and is then passed right back into the GetSeq function to deliver the next line in the list.

- In addition, the history sequence is complicated because it must have some mechanism whereby the components that each person visits are stored in a list that is accessible to the GetSeq function. Given that you can overcome the list hurdle, the rest of the history template is not complex. The `[RunMakePageFileName(CurrID)]` command takes a component Id and returns a page filename. `[Run MakePageTitle(CurrID)])` takes a component id and returns the title of the corresponding page.

In all the sequence navigation templates, the GetSeq function is the anchor. Wrapped around GetSeq is other code for laying out and formatting the text it returns. You could imagine the same function assisting in creating print or other publications that require you to wrap different formatting code around the same function. GetSeq makes code reusable across publications. It also shunts complexity out of the template and into code modules, where it can be managed using standard programming tools and where it need not bother the other staff (that is, non-programmers) who might work with the template.

In my discussions of the other access structures, I assume that most of the rendering work is done by commands within templates. The example I offer for sequences shows that sometimes it is better to go straight to a program that does the complex work and leave behind just a call to the program in the template. As I also show in the sequence example, the program does not get tangled up in formatting the publication, but rather just returns an Id that the template then knows what to do with it. Thus, the same function could be called from a number of different publication templates in a number of different output media.

Personalization System

Personalization is tailoring the content that a person sees to what you think they want to see. As is true of most of the core CMS systems, I discuss personalization in a variety of the other CMS systems.

For a general overview of personalization see Chapter 11, "The Branches of Content Management" in the section titled "Personalization." For details about designing robust personalization for your system, see Chapter 32, "Designing Personalization."

The three main tasks of a personalization system are:

✦ To collect and store user profile information.

✦ To allow you to build the rules for deciding how to distribute personalized content.

✦ To actually deliver the content.

In the features that follow, I discuss some of the issues you might want to take into account as you design the mechanics of your personalization system.

Most of the personalization action today is in dynamic HTML page building. However, the same tools you use to create Web publications could be used to make any other kind of personalized publication, provided that you can code the rules into the templates for that publication type.

A personalization dashboard

A dashboard, as I have defined it, is a centralized management feature where all that a user needs to know is displayed and everything that the user needs to do is just a click away. A personalization dashboard could integrate the following types of information and capabilities:

✦ **Profile system:** The dashboard enables you to view, edit, analyze, create, and populate user profiles.

✦ **Segmentation model:** The dashboard provides a view of the audience segmentation you have created and how you have decided to personalize for each.

✦ **Content model:** The dashboard enables you to view the content model and see which parts of it are directed toward which audience segments.

✦ **Rules system:** It might link to or directly integrate to your rules building interface.

✦ **Campaign builder:** It could allow you to integrate the segmentation and content models to create and launch periodic campaigns.

✦ **Previews:** It lets you cycle through the various views of a publication that a rule produces.

✦ **Statistics and simulations:** It could parse and summarize site logs and other usage statistics so you could monitor the success of your current personalizations and simulate the results of proposed personalizations.

More detail about these items can be found in the other features in this section. Like other dashboards, the personalization dashboard can:

✦ Provide a single point of access for a personalization administrator to get a personalization-centric view of the CMS.

✦ Summarize and display the most important information, but allow the user to drill down to more detail.

✦ Provide links to or directly integrate with all the features and subsystems that touch upon personalization.

✦ Integrate with the workflow system so that the personalization administrator can task other staff members as needed and see the current state of all the personalization-related processes that are in progress or are coming up.

If you have read about the other dashboards I have proposed (for localization, workflow, and CMS administration, for example) you may recall that dashboards integrate features and information from throughout the CMS into one place to allow a user to do her job most effectively. Because most systems today are distributed among a set of loosely interacting separate components, personalization dashboards are hard to create. But like other dashboards, the idea behind it, if not the reality, is well worth striving for.

Today personalization is only loosely tied to the other CMS systems, or worse, it is considered a separate system that resides on a Web server and does not directly interact with the CMS. As you move from today's world toward a time where the CMS is oriented completely to what your organization must do (and not the other way around), consider how to coalesce the features that are required to do personalization into one logical area (at least) and one physical area.

Collecting data

To do personalization, you first figure out what distinguishes one audience segment from another. Then, you collect and store that sort of data for each segment of your audience.

Segmentation modeling

Personalization begins with creating the audience segments that you personalize for. This process involves balancing the data you can collect to distinguish people with the data about their various needs for content.

Note   Although personalization segments do not technically need to be the same audiences you came up with in your logical design, if they turn out quite different than your original audiences it may indicate that you need to review one or the other.

A robust segmentation modeling feature would include the following qualities:

✦ **Segment list:** You need an interface where your current list of segments is shown. If your system lists your audiences somewhere (which, sadly, I suppose it does not), then that list should be available to start your personalization segments from. In addition to showing the list, the interface should allow you to create, edit, and delete segments.

✦ **Profile map:** You must be able to map the types of profile data that you have collected on your audiences to segments. For example, if you are segmenting by age, you want an age field in your user profiles and you must require that each audience use that field to distinguish itself from other segments. In addition to expressing the field, of course, you will have to express the *value* of the field that leads to the segment. For example, you might say that a value of between 10 and 13 puts a user in the PreTeen segment.

✦ **Content map:** You need to be able to map your content model onto the segments. The content model, you may recall, outlines the content types, component elements, and access structures that define your content. When you personalize, you select particular content types for the user to see based on values in particular elements of the components of that type. For example, suppose one of your content types is called Featured Book. Let's say you have 300 Featured Book components currently in your system. The Featured Book content type has elements such as Title, Author, Publisher, Genre, and so on. To personalize Web pages for the PreTeen segment, you might choose to select Featured Book components that have a value of either Adolescent or Young Adult in the Genre element. You assign content types, elements, and element values to segments just as you did in the profile mapping when you were in the process of creating segments.

✦ **Workflow triggers:** Seemingly small actions in the segmentation interface could lead to large amounts of downstream work. For example, suppose the administrator creates a PreTeen segment and assigns it the profile and content mappings I discuss above. What happens then? It would be nice if starting at that moment, PreTeens started getting exactly the right content, but even a dreamer like me would admit that is farfetched. Instead, the action of creating a new segment initiates one or more workflows that task the appropriate people to actually implement the personalization. The workflow might include metators who assure that the content is tagged well enough to support the personalization, programmers to add the personalization code to templates, and designers to assure that the personalized pages look good.

Segmentation modeling is usually done fairly casually. In fact, sometimes there is no actual trace of the segmentation model except within the templates and other code that actually does the personalization. An interface such as the one I described would allow you to see, track, and really administer the personalization process at the highest level. Given that you have your personalization workflows together, such an interface would not be that hard to build. At its most basic, it requires only a place where you type in segment names, profile fields, and component elements. All the real work could be done in the workflows. With more effort, the system could tie into the profile and content databases and give you live access to the profile fields and content model. Overall, the segmentation modeling feature gives you a central place to conceive and control personalization. It could be your first step on the way to a personalization dashboard.

Collecting and storing profile data

To run a personalization system you need some notion of a current user. You can represent the current user in these ways:

✦ **Transiently:** You can follow a user through your site based on the IP address of her browser and build a profile that does not last until her next visit. This method can be fine if you simply intend to notice behaviors and serve content accordingly.

✦ **Anonymously:** You can store a cookie (a unique Id) on the user's computer that allows you to identify her on an ongoing basis. When she leaves your site, you save her profile to a database where you can retrieve it based on her cookie the next time she visits.

✦ **Personally:** You can store a person's name and other personal information and associate a profile with it. When the person visits your site, you use a login or a cookie to associate her with the profile you have stored for her.

Whether you store profiles transiently or personally, for personalization purposes the point of the profile is to decide what kind of person this is so you can serve her the right content. What the profile stores depends on the kinds of information you need to assign the person a personalization segment. It may be information on the pages she has visited, the questions she has directly answered, the information you have gathered because of what she have searched for, bought, or otherwise requested, or any other information that you may have been able to buy or find for the people you serve.

Where you actually store a personalization profile depends on how many you have and who the users are:

✦ If your audience members are all CMS users as well (which is not common), then the CMS's user administration system is the natural place for their profiles.

✦ If your audience members are all in your organization, then wherever their network profile is stored (LDAP or other directory services) might be right.

✦ If your users are outside your organization or are mostly anonymous, and especially if there are a lot of them, a relational database may be best for storing their profiles.

Wherever you store your profiles, they must be accessible to the code in your templates that both read and write profile data. They should be accessible to your rule creation and analysis system so that you can refer to whom you are actually serving and what is really in their profiles as you develop personalizations for them.

With transient profiles, you can run simple personalizations without storing any profile data. On the other hand, if you build a place to store profile information, you will have the opportunity to really begin to know and serve your audiences. For me, the question is not *whether* you should store profiles but *how* you should store profiles. Personally, I prefer the option of storing profiles in a database were you can easily get to them and use them as you build and refine your approach.

Acquired profiles

There are a range of commercial suppliers who will sell you consumer profiles. In addition, other systems within your organization may collect and store profile information for your users. You may want to take advantage of these sources of information to augment or replace your own profile collection methods. Consider these issues as you acquire profile information:

✦ **Is the acquisition legal?** Privacy laws are in flux and many jurisdictions are enacting laws that bear on the collection and distribution of citizens' information. Be sure that you are legally and ethical covered before buying or even casually sharing profile information.

✦ **Connection:** All the issues of conversion, acquisition, and aggregation apply to profile information as well as to content. For example, is there a map between the profile information you will acquire and what you need? If you modify the profiles, what will happen when you get a second batch from the source? Will you have to redo all that work?

✦ **Are you a source or destination?** If you plan on authoring profile information as well as acquiring it, you should probably think about how you will syndicate the information you collect to others who need it in your organization. It may be worth the effort to centralize profile collection efforts into a single place where all the groups in your organization can get to the profiles.

The audiences that your CMS serves are bound to be the same as those served by other parts of your organization. In addition, even if your users were happy to supply your organization with information once (a long shot already), they will be less happy to supply it twice. So it really behooves you to find profile information and make as much use of it as possible. What makes even more sense is to figure out your audiences and segments once for the whole organization and have this information accessible to all those who need it.

Data accessible to personalization

To make the most out of your personalization system, it needs to draw on as many sources of information as possible to build a profile. The sources you may want to include in your system include:

✦ **User session data,** including time on the site, pages visited, click trails and any choices made in user interface controls (list boxes, option buttons, and the like). Personalization code, either in the template or beyond it in custom programming objects, needs to get to and use this data.

✦ **HTTP header information,** including browser type, page last visited, and IP address of the browser accessing the site. This last bit of information can be very helpful in determining where on earth the user is located. Once again, the personalization code must be able to get at and use this information.

✦ **Data in your organization beyond a Web site or even the CMS.** For example, you may need to personalize content based on a user's prior technical support requests. In this case, the personalization code may need to access the support database system to figure out just what content to serve the current user.

User session and HTTP header information are generally easy to come by from a Web-based application. The information outside the CMS, which may be the best tool you have for targeting content, can be easy or hard to use. It will be up to you to decide if this information, like any other external information, can be more easily handled if you connect directly to the external system or if you periodically acquire and store data from it.

Building rules

Personalization rules connect a set of profiles and a content model. More specifically, personalization rules decide how to deploy the content model given the profile of the current user. I go into more detail about the nature of rules in Chapter 32, "Designing Personalization" in the section titled "Personalization and rules." Your CMS can do only so much to help you create rules. Even with the best interface it is still up to you to create rules that can discriminate between users and deliver real incremental value based on that discrimination.

The rules interface

What kind of user interface do you need for creating and modifying personalization rules? Some products have very well developed point-and-click interfaces for rule building. Others require a programmer to code the personalization rules directly into templates. Before you jump to answer that you want the fancy interface, consider these issues:

✦ If you have spent your time on a segmentation modeling system, you have much of what you need to define rules. How will the two interfaces interact?

✦ It is very likely that you might need to have a programmer implement personalization in your templates even if you have a visual rules interface.

✦ Who exactly will be running the interface? The idea of having a visual, user-friendly interface is that business people and not just techies can run it. But even the best interfaces may still not be easy enough for business people (or other non-techies) and the techies end up running it anyway.

In my view, the business people in your organization would be best served by a program that lets them simply say, "Here are our audiences. Here is our content. This audience gets this content."

So, one possibility is to put your resources into a very simple interface that business types can use to specify rules in the abstract, and let the implementers use whatever interface (or no interface at all) to make the rules work.

The more in-depth specification of rules falls to administrators and programmers anyway, so why not start from that proposition. If the kinds of personalizations you want to do match the types in a visual builder, you have no problem using these types. If, as is often the case, the personalizations you really need can't be specified in the visual interface, then whether you have one or not, you may not end up using it.

That said, visual personalization interfaces, like visual workflow builders, are a really nice idea, and do play really well for demonstrations.

Statistics and simulations

If you want to get personalization right you should get feedback about the rules you are currently running and be able to test rules you are thinking of creating. Fortunately, you have all the raw materials you need for both these tasks already at hand. If you are personalizing on the Web (which in most cases you are), then your server logs can tell you all you need to know to see how they have been doing. Server logs enable you to answer these sorts of questions about your rules:

✦ How many people who have visited your site have been categorized into each segment? You may find, for example, that some segments have had no visitors. Is that because the rule is not working? The profiles are wrong? Or you just don't have the sorts of audiences you thought you did?

✦ Do people prefer the personalized content to the non-personalized content? If your rules are working as they are supposed to, you should see many more users accessing the content that you specifically chose to display versus the content that is there by default.

✦ How many people fall into the miscellaneous category? It would be smart to have a default category that people fall into when they can't be segmented. Is this your biggest segment? What profile characteristics can help you sort these people out?

These and many other important questions can be answered if you apply enough effort to parsing your server logs. You can also log the personalization code itself to keep a log of the choices it makes.

Not only does this technique work with old rules, but you can use it to test new rules as well. Before actually implementing a rule, you can scan your logs and determine who, in the last month, say, would have triggered the rule to fire. What content did they end up viewing on that visit? Was any of it the content you would have delivered to them?

Going even one step further, you should be able to design your personalizations based on the same logs that you use to test them. You can scan the server logs to answer these sorts of questions:

✦ What categories do my visitors fall into?

✦ By category, what do they seem to be looking for?

✦ How well can I predict subsequent actions from the early actions they take on my site?

Questions like these add a bottom-up validation to the top-down personalization approach I have generally proposed.

So, if this method is so great, why is it not part of every major system? The answer lies in how difficult it is to find answers in server logs. With no one standard for these logs, and the massive amount of data to sort through, getting simple answers to simple questions by standard means can be really tough. However, if you can put up with getting complex answers to simple questions through custom means, you can put a lot of science behind your personalizations.

Customization interface

I differentiate (though not so vehemently) between personalization and customization. Personalization is, I contend, something you do for the user, whereas customization is something that a user does for herself. Of course, regardless of how it is accomplished, the result is the same: content and surrounds that are particular to the user's needs.

Recognizing the "My" phenomenon (as in "MyYahoo!" on www.yahoo.com) as well as the rise of the idea of a portal, many commercial CM products now include features specifically for presenting users with choices that let them customize what the CMS delivers to them. The best of these integrate the customization with personalizations to allow you and the user to collaborate on what the user sees on the site.

Everyone needs a "My" feature, don't they? All kidding aside, customization is a great step on the road to personalization. If users can see the immediate result of the profile information they supply, they are much more likely to supply it.

Collaborative filtering

Collaborative filtering is the process where the system recommends content based on requests of similar users (an approach popularized by Amazon.com). Collaborative filtering has become so popular that for many people it is synonymous with personalization. In one sense, I think the relationship is valid; you can think of personalization as the art of finding out what people (who are like you) want and then allowing them to get it. The different ways of personalizing represent the different ways of defining exactly who the *people like you* are.

Many commercial CM systems and all major standalone personalization engines now include some form of collaborative filtering. If you have a robust profiling system, you can fairly easily build your own filters as follows: Specify the profile element on which you want to equate people. Amazon.com uses past purchases, but you can use anything you have (age, job, income, components visited, and so on). This defines what it means to be part of the group. For example, the group can be all managers, or all teenagers, or all people who read a certain white paper. Decide which profile elements you can use to expand people on. Again, Amazon.com uses purchases. If your main idea is to expose people to content, then you should probably choose content components viewed. Write the code or use the collaborative filtering supplied by your system to find the components that a lot of people in the group have viewed and that the current user has not.

Collaborative filtering and the family of close cousins to this technique that are now widely in use are a great way to spread knowledge. One variant that I particularly like is to allow the user to create her own group. Especially in internal systems where all the users work together, people really like it when they can keep up with what their peers and supervisors are reading (as long as it does not intrude on their peers' privacy).

Delivering content

When all is said and done, personalization results in a change in the content, navigation, or surrounds. The mechanics of the changes, although not too complex, deserve your attention so that you can create the most efficient code to create the mechanics.

Personalized surrounds

I define surrounds, you might recall, as all the branding, headers, footers, backgrounds, and large-scale layout that surround content and navigation in a publication. Personalizing the surrounds might consist in changes in any or all these items. Surrounds are created in page-level templates (for more about page templates see Chapter 31, "Designing Templates," the section titled "Using templates within templates"). Within the template are switches that (figuratively) turn on or off different variants within the surrounds. Here are some of the more common methods for invoking these variants:

✦ **Style sheets:** On the Web, publications use Cascading Style Sheets (CSS) to format and layout the HTML elements on the page. In print, other sorts of style sheets perform the same task. Personalizing layout, backgrounds, and text formatting can be as simple as switching out style sheets under a publication. For example, for visually impaired audience members, you may want to change the layout and fonts of a Web page to a larger form. A simple CSS file switch can usually accomplish this.

✦ **Path changes:** On the Web, any number of image, style, HTML, programming code, and media files can be combined on one page. In print, image files can also be imported into the publication to form the completed sections. By controlling the path to the included files, you can effectively switch one set of files for another. For example, in addition to changing the layout and text style in the vision-impaired version of your site, you may also switch the logo and other images to match. To accomplish this, you can store all your usual images in one directory and all your personalized images in another. The images in the second directory have the same names as those in the first directory. To switch from the usual version to the personalized one, you just switch all the image paths from the usual directory to the other. In fact, to make the switch from one CSS file to the other, you can use exactly the same technique.

✦ **Conditional blocks:** When you have exhausted the techniques of CSS, you might turn to variations of formatting and layout that are coded into the publication template as selectable blocks. For example, to personalize for vision-impaired people, you might go from a three-column layout to a one-column layout. The easiest way to accomplish this is to have both layouts in the template. When the personalization rule triggers, it causes the usual layout to be ignored in favor of the personalized one.

✦ **Calculated formatting:** You may need to adjust dynamically to the constraints of the content you are displaying. For example, depending on the language of the content, you may adjust column widths on your pages. Rather than trying to create conditional blocks for every variant, you can try to add an offset to the standard column widths. For example, in pages that have German (which tends to be a longer language than English) you can add 20 points to each column.

Page-level personalization does not tend to be as widely done as either content or navigation personalizing. Except in cases of customization or when personalization is used for localization, it is much more common to leave the surrounds the same and focus instead on the content and navigation areas of the pages you are producing.

Personalized content

Content personalization takes two major forms:

✦ **Components displayed:** Here the components that are selected for the publication can change based on the user's profile. For example, on a news page, you may decide to show members of one audience one type of story and members of another audience a different type. More specifically, some combination of user profile fields causes a personalization rule to fire. That rule selects components of the News Story type based on the values in one or more of their elements (for example, the Region element). So, in the end, the personalization results in a different set of components being displayed in the publication.

✦ **Elements displayed:** Instead of (or in addition to) changing what components are displayed, a personalization rule can determine which elements from the components are displayed. For example, suppose along with news stories, your print newsletter serves commentary. When you send the newsletter to professional architects, you want the commentary to be written for professionals. But when it goes to homeowners, you want the commentary written for lay people. In this sense, you don't need to change which components are displayed, but you do want to change which Commentary element is used.

In either case, you are making an impact on what is displayed in the content area of your publication. In both cases, you have to account for variations in the layout and length of the content area. If more components are selected for display, you want the area to expand. If a certain element is not displayed, you want the area to compensate so that it doesn't look like something is missing.

In the case of component display, however, the layout issues are augmented by the issues of formulating queries against the repository and retrieving the correct components. Often the CMS has a place where you can write and store the appropriate queries so that you don't have to embed in your templates.

If you do any sort of personalization, it will probably be component display personalization. Given that you understand what your audiences want, you have the content model to support selecting what they want, and you can detect who is in which audience, actually selecting and displaying the correct components is relatively easy. If personalization still seems too hard, consider the alternative of producing one publication with various sections for each audience. Rather than automatically detecting who each person is, the publication merely offers people a choice of which section to visit. Unfortunately, this more modest task still requires that you understand what your audiences want and that you have the content model to support selecting what they want. In fact, if you don't have a good idea of your audiences and a strong content model, you don't have much of a basis for a CMS. If you do have these things, the leap from monolithic to personalized publications is really just a matter of collecting profiles and finding ways to detect which audience your users belong to.

Personalized navigation

Personalized navigation can do a lot to help users get to the information they want. And, if you already have an idea of the rules that determine what content is useful to which audiences, you already have the rules you need to personalize navigation. For example, suppose that you have the same homeowner and professional architect audiences that I mentioned previously. You have decided what rules select content for the two audiences, and you have tagged your content so that it can be selected. This work allows you to select the right component and elements into the content areas of your pages. It also allows you to personalize your navigation structures. For example, you could:

✦ Color-code or otherwise highlight items in your hierarchies so that the ones that are particularly interesting to the current user (based on her audience) stand out or are sorted to the tops of her list. You could actually filter out items that apply mostly to the other audiences, but that might be risky because it might indicate to the user that those items simply do not exist.

✦ Produce indexes that are specific to the audience type. For example, you could have three separate indexes: one called Homeowner's Index, one called Professional's Index, and the one called Master Index. These three personalized forms of the same index allow the user to get to the information in the way most comfortable to her. Having all three in the same publication means that a homeowner could use the professional index, for example, to learn about how others see the material in the publication.

✦ Link items based on the user's audience. For example, if a link within the text of a component is to an item that is targeted for another audience, it could be somehow flagged (color, icons, pop-up text, footnote text, and so on), which would indicate that it is not as useful as other links that go to items for the current audience. Of course, you could just suppress links outside the audience's realm, but as with the hierarchies, you need to be careful about taking personalization too far. If you build a cross-reference sidebar, you can sort more relevant links to the top or otherwise indicate the ones that apply more strongly to the current audience.

✦ Sequence items based on the user's audience. For example, you might have a sequence of components on the permit process for new home construction. The entire sequence covers the information needs of both the professional and the layperson. However, a layperson would be bored and lost with all the detail in the sequence, and a professional would find it useless without the detail. So, given the current user's audience, you could structure the sequence to include either the high-level components or both the high-level and detailed components.

✦ Create full-text search results that are sorted based on the audience classification of each result. For example, you could add a specified amount to the relevance ranking of results that are in the current user's audiences so that they tend to float to the top of the results list.

Personalizing navigation uses the layout and formatting techniques of surrounds personalization, as well as the component and element selection techniques of content personalization. For example, to mark your hierarchies so that audience-specific items stand out, you might need to change styles or switch icon graphics. However, to know which items to change, you perform component selection. To add a pop-up item description that, say, comes up when you mouse-over the icon, you might have to do an element selection that chooses the lay or professional abstract for the item.

Although similar in theory to the other kinds of personalization, in practice personalizing navigation tends to be more difficult technically. First, a lot of processing is involved to personalize navigation. You can imagine that, if you have an index with 3,000 items in it, it might take some time to do something (change color, text, or the like) to each item. Second, it might require pre- or post-processing routines be added to others you perform. For example, to customize the links within the text of the component, a post-processing routine parses the text of each component you are about to display, finds its links, looks up the referents (the components pointed to), decides if they are in the right audience set or not, and finally performs a link modification. This is not so hard to do, but it does complicate and slow down the rendering process considerably.

Although most people focus on content and surrounds personalization, I believe that navigation personalization is actually the most important of the three. People can get by with surrounds that don't change much. They can usually decide for themselves whether a particular component is worth looking at or not. But if audience members can't see the various components that are available to them or if the ones they want most are buried in a huge pile of components that are irrelevant, they will reject the publication. I'm not advocating, of course, doing only navigation personalization. I am advocating putting whatever limited personalization resources you have into the personalizations that give your users the most advantage in finding the information they want.

Deployment System

CMS products have a variety of capabilities for distributing content from the central repository behind the organization's firewall to servers inside and beyond the firewall. The content deployment features in this section are weighted toward the Web because that's where most deployment happens today.

Staging

Staging means putting your publication (generally a Web site) on a testing server before moving it to the production server where it will be available to the public. A staging server enables you to test a Web site before it goes live. Staging software helps you move files and carries out publication testing and rollback if something is wrong. (By the way, many products' licensing models require that you purchase separate licenses for each server, *including* the staging server.) Some systems include a component on the server that receives and manages the files that come to the server.

The need for staging is proportional to the size of the site updates you do. In other words, the larger the updates, the more you need staging. So, if you update your site one page at a time, it is not worth the effort to stage each page. The tasks involved are all small efforts that can be done more or less manually. On the other hand, if you update half the pages of the site at a time, you had better stage those updates because transfer, testing, and rollback are all big efforts that really should be automated. Of course, you can stage big changes and finesse small changes in the same system. Or, all new pages can pass through the staging server, but small changes can pass right through whereas large changes can wait to be fully tested.

Content-based deployment

Content-based deployment means including content in your publications based on its metatagging. If you have gone through the considerable effort it takes to create and apply a comprehensive metatorial framework to your content, it only makes sense to use that scheme in deciding what gets published and when. Of course, all personalization deploys content based on tagging; and in addition, that's how templates get content onto pages. A few wider content-based deployment features are often built into the wider publication system:

✦ **Specific metatag values:** You may, for example, want to key on various values within content components (language, for example) to determine which server or publication to deploy the content to.

✦ **Defaults:** Based on a metatag value (content type, for example) you may want your system to hold default parameters (deployment directory, for example). These defaults help you keep the deployment process organized. If you develop a feature like this, keep all the default settings all in one place so that they are easy to find and the systems administrator or publication manager can change them easily.

✦ **Autopublish and retire:** It's useful to have the CMS automatically release and remove content based on the rules that you establish. The rules generally associate a date metadata value in the component (say the CreateDate element) with the current date, and deploy to a server or publication as specified. Similarly, components, pages, or even publication sections can be removed from the publication when a particular date is reached.

If you have a very robust templating and personalization system, you can do most or all that the content-based deployment features do without a separate system. In systems with less-developed personalization, content-based deployment features at least allow you to do the basics of metadata-based publishing.

Distributing files

Distributing files means getting all the right files for a publication to the right location to create a complete Web site or other publication. For example, if a file (an image, say) is referenced inside text that's being published, it's a good idea to have the CMS deploy the file to avoid a broken reference. This process may consist of a few separate steps:

✦ **Validating media references:** Before distributing a file that is referenced in a component being published, the system needs to ensure that the file exists within the CMS. If other referential integrity features are available, a broken reference should be detected before publish time, but if it is not, the publication module will have to do this work. If a file is missing, the system will need to alert the administrator and either abort the publication of the component or somehow deal with the missing media. To deal with missing media, the system might put in a default image (that says Image Not Available or some such useful message), or it might suppress the image tag and references to the image in the text that is published.

✦ **Deploying files:** This feature finds and deploys the files that are mentioned in components. The feature is especially necessary if you don't store media (and other files) as separate components but rather as simple references within text blocks (for example, if you store image references with an <IMG> tag in an HTML text element). In this case, it's likely that your system can't find and deploy the file just because it's in some <IMG> tag. You must add the code to ensure that files that are referenced this way can be found and deployed automatically.

✦ **Converting files:** Media files may need to be selected or converted as they are deployed. For example, an image file may be stored in TIFF format and then converted to JPG when it is published to a Web site. Or the various versions of the image may be stored separately in the repository, from which the CMS selects the existing JPG version for Web publications and the TIFF version for print publications.

Unfortunately, deployment is not a simple matter. Despite being organized, you may still need to write software to get all your files to the right places. Even if you go to the additional trouble of making each file its own component, you may still need extra code to get them to the correct deployment destination. It's entirely possible that your deployment might go beyond the stock functionality of your system. You may, for example, need to deploy media based on the size of the media files, with large files going to servers that have larger storage capacity. You may also deploy files by type, for example, to servers that have the special software needed to deliver different media types such as streaming media servers. You may combine these two methods, as well as other deployment methods.

As complex as your deployment system is, if it's logical (and it may take considerable effort to make it so), it can be reduced to a mechanical process.

Scheduled publication

Scheduled publication means managing the timing of all your publications so that each receives content that is ready and adequate to fill it and so that it is ready for the public when the public is ready for it. In a system with a number of publications and significant content overlap, you can imagine that it might be tough to keep them all straight. To do so, the scheduling system must do the following:

✦ **Interface with the workflow system.** The system must be sure that all tasks are scheduled to be completed by the time you want to publish.

✦ **Interface with the deployment systems.** Replication systems, database connections, file deployment systems, and other methods of distribution must all be coordinated and triggered at publish time to get all the parts of a publication to their proper locations.

✦ **See the big picture.** The scheduling system must let you see the overall patterns of updates and releases for each publication. Moreover, it ought to let you set those overall patterns. Finally, it ought to give you quick connections to the critical systems that interact with publication.

Once again, a dashboard is what is really called for to see and affect the widest cycles of the CMS. Publication does bring together all the other systems to create a complete and polished work.

In a way, the publication subsumes the other processes. It could be that in publication what you really need is a meta-dashboard. Certainly the people most concerned with publications would claim that the rest of the system should be viewed from the perspective of the publication. Its dashboard ought to show the CMS at a level above the workflow, localization, personalization, and other dashboards that run the CMS. And I can imagine looking at a display that shows, at a very high level, the complete picture of content flowing into the system, pooling in the repository, and flowing out at set intervals into an intertwined set of publications. However, I know, too, that there are a variety of centers to the CMS universe and what is needed is not necessarily one master view but rather a series of interlocked perspectives on the CMS.

What is hardest to imagine about a meta-dashboard is not viewing the system but *changing* the system. At this high level, what would ensure that the full and undoubtedly vastly complex implications of the changes you have made can be automatically made to happen in all the subsystems of the CMS? A lot of work is yet to be done between now and that future.

However, that future is ultimately the point of content management: To be able to see and then impact the content process in your organization. Content management is a process that can be visualized apart from the technology it employs. However, not only should you should be able to understand and affect the content processes in your organization, you should be able to carry out the implications of your decisions technologically in the most efficient and effective way.

Web System

If they are dynamic, the Web sites produced by a content management system are created one page at a time in response to user clicks. If they are static, they are produced all at once by the content management system, stored on the Web server, and served as plain HTML files. In either case, through non-CMS code placed strategically in the templates, sites can also include functionality from sources outside the content management system. As CMS publications, of course, Web sites are a combination of content components and metadata drawn from the repository by templates. They are under the same constraints as other publications. So, much of what you do to create them is described in my non-platform-specific feature descriptions. However, it is no exaggeration to say that Web sites are what most people think content management is for. Also, because Web sites are complex systems on their own, you must consider a number of Web-specific features if you want your CMS to create the most sophisticated sites you can design.

Integration with an existing Web infrastructure

Before CM it is likely that you had a Web site. It may not have been as well-managed and auto-generated as you wanted, but it most likely held the line for you for a number of years. With or without CM, it is likely that it continued to grow until it was no longer manageable. In buying or building a CMS, take these issues into account when considering your old site:

✦ **Old site conversion:** You may choose to rip the old site apart, convert its content to XML, segment it into components and store them in your new repository. I detail this process in Chapter 38, "Building Collection Systems" in the section titled "Acquiring Web site content."

✦ **Old site connections:** You may choose to leave the old site in place (at least for the first version of the new system), and produce new pages from the CMS that integrate seamlessly with the old site. This is a very attractive proposition because it allows you to ignore a potentially huge amount of conversion and analysis of the old material. Your new CMS can start fresh, with a new set of content types that go beyond what the old system was capable of doing. I believe that this is a reasonable approach when your project would otherwise sink from the weight of the old site, or when your new, more radical CM approach needs to prove itself gradually against an entrenched existing approach (in other words if the political wind is solidly in your face). On the other hand, I would take this road with real caution. If you truly do integrate seamlessly, you have to make a lot of compromises in your new system so that it looks similar to the old site and so that navigation can really span the two systems. In addition, your organization will have two simultaneous processes for creating the Web site; the old one and your new CM one. How will you integrate these two processes so that they don't continually trip over each other and cause more trouble than you have saved by keeping the old site? There are definitely ways through the jungle of connecting a new system to an old site, and sometimes it is the only viable choice. Still, if you pursue this path, I would advise you to plan for all the content in your logical design and not just for the new content. You want to be ready, at every opportunity, to encompass the old site's information. Keep repeating to everyone you meet, "It's only for a short while."

✦ **Old Web infrastructure:** You won't get many arguments that it is best to keep your old Web site in the face of a CMS. However, you are quite likely to get arguments that it is best to keep your old Web infrastructure. In fact, many organizations will base their choice of CMS almost entirely on its capability to run on the existing infrastructure. This argument reminds me a lot of the garage that I once decided to build where our old carport stood. Before I began, I just assumed that the best route would be to use the existing carport structure as the basis of my new garage. Halfway through the project, I realized that a carport and a garage are quite different, even though they both hold cars. The extra effort and structural compromises that the carport imposed on me far outweighed the advantage of starting from an existing structure. At the point you go from an old-style dynamic site to a CMS-generated site you need to ask your self the question I never asked: "How different is this new structure from the one we have today?" Will it be more effort making the CMS work in our old infrastructure than it will be to create and learn a new infrastructure? I can't know the answer to this question, but I can guess how some people will base their answers to it. Look for the people who have the most personal and professional investment in your current technology to insist most stridently that existing infrastructure counts for more than any other criteria in selecting a CMS. They will argue that the switching cost (in retraining staff and migrating systems) will outweigh any benefit you might receive from a different platform. They may very well be right. On the other hand (just as my garage looks a whole lot like a carport with walls), their attitude may, in the end, make your CMS look a lot like the same dynamic Web site you are trying to replace.

✦ **Flipping the switch:** Exactly when do you turn off the old site and turn on your CMS-generated site? Some will argue for a moratorium on new content on the old site of a few weeks or a month before launch, whereas others will argue that the only reasonable route is to publish both sites simultaneously until the new one is proven and ready to really take over the job. I go into more detail about this issue in Chapter 21, "Rolling Out the System," in the section titled "The beta system." Whichever way you go, the transition from the old to the new site will be tense. Be prepared for some long days at work.

✦ **Design before or after:** The rollout of a CMS is most often accompanied by a site redesign. As you make your way through your logical design, and especially as you begin to implement your system, you are bound to come up with a lot of great ideas for how the site should look. Your current site team (which is likely the same team that is doing the CMS design) is also likely to see ideas that can be implemented right away on the existing site to make it prettier or more functional. It is hard to argue that a great new feature ought not to see the light of day for another six months while the rest of the CMS is being built. I agree, in general, with the idea that you should make good changes sooner rather than later. But I offer these cautions to temper your desire to back CMS features in general and design in particular into your existing sites. First, as any veteran of site change will tell you, there is a long road between coming up with a great new idea and making it happen across a site. If the feature will show up in the CMS in six months, realistically how long will it take to show up in the site? If the cooly calculated answer is four months, have you really bought much? Second, you always expend some amount of redundant effort when you put features in both the old and new systems. How much additional work will it be to put the new feature in the old system? Does this work divert attention and talent away from the new site? Third, and maybe most interestingly, are you stealing the thunder of your new system by putting all its design and cool features in your old site? A colleague of mine recently related this story to me. Her team created a new design for the CMS-generated site. The team doing the old site said, "Why wait?" They were ready to do a redesign anyway and just used the new site design. When they launched the redesigned old site, people thought it was the CMS site and were really disappointed that it was just the old site in new clothes. When they launched the CMS site, people never even noticed.

If you have an existing site, you must decide how to transition. Unfortunately, there is no one good answer. Ideally, you would like to completely encompass the content of the old site and make a clean, crisp transition. But reality tramples that idea most of the time. The best approach I have seen here is for the team to keep the ideal situation clearly in mind. They make compromises as needed, but always have their eye on the final prize—a CMS site that encompasses all content, and that has the infrastructure most appropriate to the tasks of the CMS.

Searching and indexing

What search engines do exceedingly well is to index large bodies of free text and allow you to find content based on words that you specify. What CM systems do (or should do) is to allow you to invent metadata tags that describe your content, fill those metadata tags with values that distinguish one content component from the next, and select content based on the metadata values that you specify. So, CM systems and search engines each perform their own kind of search, and from the standpoint of technology, management, and administration they are quite distinct functions. Your entire collection process is targeted to apply your metadata tags and values to content. On the other hand, you just push a button and out comes the free text index that lets the search engine do its job. When a search happens against a Web publication, it can be performed by the search engine, which looks at text, or by the CMS, which looks at metadata.

However, in the minds of your audiences, these two are not at all distinct. When users contemplate a search, they ask themselves "What words do I know to describe what I am looking for?" They don't particularly care if those words are in the actual text of the content or if they are metadata values that you have carefully crafted and applied. They do appreciate search screens that let them type any words in a box and also allow you to choose words from drop-down lists that have keywords in them. In other words, they don't care about what part of the system is searched and they don't care about what software is doing the searching. They care if the screen that they search from allows them the flexibility and power to state what they know; they care that the search results they get are relevant and well presented; and they care, above all, that they can quickly locate an item of interest or learn that such an item does not exist on your site.

So, your job in designing the search feature of a CMS-generated Web site is to, somehow, integrate third-party search engines and the CMS search functions. Some of the choices you face in this regard are:

✦ **Give search to the search engine.** For a static site, you really have no choice but to let the search engine do all searching. In a static site, the CMS has already done its job and is out of the picture by the time the user has decided to search. This does not mean that the CMS cannot play a part, just that the CMS cannot do the search. In fact, the CMS can do a lot to aid the search engine to return good results. First, many search engines can index and make use of <META> tags in Web pages. Your CMS can create those tags and fill them full of the metadata that identifies the components on a page. Second, your CMS can create pages in such a way that the results returned by your search engine are more specific. For example, if your components have particularly long text, the CMS might produce each section of a component's text on its own page. That way when the search engine returns a page, it will be as specific as possible to the search that was performed.

✦ **Extend full-text search into the repository.** Suppose you have the CMS available on the site as well as a full-text search engine. If, in addition, you build pages dynamically from a database, you may have a bit of a problem. The text of your components is not immediately available to the search engine. It's not that the search engine cannot index and retrieve text from within a database; many can. The problem lies in what to do with the text that is retrieved. For example, suppose the search engine finds a hit in one field of the record that holds a particular component. It could simply retrieve the content of that field and display it as a result. However, how about the other fields? How will it know which to retrieve and display and which are not appropriate to be displayed? What if the component is actually stored across a set of tables? How will the search engine figure that out and retrieve the right information? Finally, even given the right set of fields from the database, how will the search engine know how to display the component? The CMS uses a template to make a stored component into a displayed component. How can the search engine do the same? These issues are not insurmountable, but they do cause a lot of site administrators to forget about indexing their databases and instead have the CMS create a set of static pages for the use of the search engine.

✦ **Integrate search behind the screens.** On a search screen, it is not uncommon to have one text control into which the user types search terms and other controls where she can select from indexes (keyword lists), narrow the search to a certain content type, or narrow the search to a certain part of the site hierarchy. The search term's text control is input to the search engine, whereas the rest of the controls may be inputs to the CMS. A fairly complex program behind the screen calls the search engine and retrieves its results, calls the CMS and retrieves its results, matches the two results sets, and decides which hits meet all the criteria. Because this feature is not too easy to implement, designers often separate the two types of searches, or just have full-text search and let the navigation structures of the site stand in for a metadata-based search.

✦ **Show search hits in context.** One variation on the complete integration of metadata search with full-text search that is easier (but still not easy) to implement is to display search results in the context of the navigation of the site. For example, you might choose to show search hits as titles embedded in the site's primary hierarchy. The search results screen might have an expanding and contracting outline that shows only the branches of the site outline where hits were found. This technique allows you to organize a large number of search results in an easy-to-understand and easy-to-navigate structure. It beats the heck out of having dozens of pages of unordered results.

It's very likely that you want a full-text search feature on your site. It's likely that you will buy a commercial search engine to implement that feature. It's unlikely that the search engine comes with the CMS or that the two integrate particularly well. It will be up to you to decide how far to go with the integration to ensure that your audiences have the most successful search experience possible.

Browser-independence

Although HTML has always been heralded as the ultimate in cross-platform performance, this is just not true. Browser platforms continue to follow conflicting standards both among platforms and between versions of the same browser. So, the bad news is that if you have audiences using a variety of browsers, you have to deal with creating a variety of sites. The good news is that a CMS gives you the best possible basis for dealing with the issue. If you have structured content, you have separated formatting from content in your repository (by not, for example, embedding a lot of browser-specific HTML codes in your component text). Creating a family of browser-specific versions of your pages is as easy as it will ever be. In addition, some commercial CMS products include browser sniffers and supporting code to make serving browser-specific pages easier. You can choose from two basic CM approaches to producing browser-specific pages:

✦ You can treat the different pages as personalized versions of the same page. In other words, you create one template that includes browser-sniffing code and changes the layout, client code, and/or CSS to match the user's browser.

✦ You can create separate pages, one for each browser type. In effect, each browser-specific version becomes its own publication.

If this choice sounds familiar, it is probably because I have mentioned it a number of times before. In fact, it is the same kind of choice you make between any two publications. Are they similar enough to be considered personalized versions of the same publication, or different enough to be considered different publications? As before, I lay out the two ends of the spectrum, but you are free to make your own compromise between the two approaches. For example, you may decide (and I wouldn't blame you for it) that supporting a Netscape and a Microsoft browser requires you to create two separate page-level templates. Still, this approach does not preclude you from sharing subtemplates between the browser-specific page templates to deal with the similarity below the level of the page. Conversely, you could create one page-level template that calls out to two different navigation templates because the same DHTML may not work in both browsers.

Distributing files across servers

You may determine that you want to serve media files from a different server than the one used for the rest of your site. For example, you may rent space on a commercial streaming server to host your video files. To make sure that this system works, your CMS must be able to do the following:

✦ Differentiate between files based on their type or other metadata that you assigned them.

✦ Store and access a distribution location for files of the given type.

✦ Connect to and upload files to a variety of servers during publication.

This feature is as much a management issue as it is a distribution issue. Keeping track of which files go where and when they need to be uploaded is as much or more of a problem than actually distributing them. Add to this the extra wrinkle that your CMS or media provider may have licensing concerns about distribution to third parties, and the technical issues may well be the easier part of this feature.

Web platform support

Because CM has been so tied to Web delivery, much of the technological territory of the Web was originally colonized by CM companies. With a few notable exceptions, CM companies are ceding this territory to the major Web platform venders like IBM and BEA. Because some still include these features, however, and because if the CMS does not include them you have to get them from some other product, it is worth a quick overview of the features that support a large-scale Web presence.

Web application servers

An application server provides a layer between an application and its data source that allows the application to scale higher, run faster, and perform more reliably. Application servers are particularly important on the Web because of the magnitude of transactions that often occur on Web sites. Although some CM systems actually call themselves application servers, most are happy to leave this job to third-party products.

Most larger data-based Web sites today employ some sort of application server. What application serving actually consists of is a bit less clear. Some sites consider the feature built right into their programming environment (J2EE or .NET) to be all the application server they need. Others buy expensive third-party products to lay on top of their programming environment to provide intermediation between their applications and their data. You have to find the right level of application server to give you the scalability and performance you need for the transaction volume you expect.

Content caching

Caching is the process of storing content in a temporary location that is more accessible than its official home. The cache stores a copy of content or built pages in such a way that the content can be retrieved faster and cause less of a drain on your Web server. The most common form of caching happens right in your browser. Unless you turn the caching feature off, pages that you request are stored on your hard drive. When you request the page again, instead of getting it from the Web site, the browser can just reload it from your hard drive. Of course, browser caching is not a CMS or application server feature, but these following forms of caching can be:

✦ **Database query results level:** One of the biggest bottlenecks between data and user is the time it takes to evaluate a query against the repository and return a set of results. If your system relies on complex, slow queries to build pages and if the same query tends to be issued over and over again, you can cache the query results so that your repository only actually evaluates it once.

✦ **Files and static page:** The most common form of caching is to store files that are frequently requested in RAM so that the time to access them is cut down. In a CMS, this boils down to caching static pages and the set of files that they include. This form of caching is of pretty low value because it is the dynamic pages, not the static ones, that put the highest load on your server.

✦ **Dynamic page:** To cache dynamic pages, some systems will treat them like static pages. In other words, when a particular URL is requested (say xyz.com?Id=345), the server will build the page. Building the page may mean the loading and interpretation of the page template, one or more queries to find the component and navigation for the page, and whatever other processing the page requires (for example, getting data from a non-CMS database). Once built, the server stores the final page HTML and files either in RAM or on the hard drive. The next time the same URL is requested, the server recognizes the URL and fetches the built page.

Caching can make all the difference in the world between producing a slow, unscalable site or one that performs. The key to successful caching is to recognize which information is repeatedly requested and to be sure that the second request is answered as quickly as it can be. The same analysis, by the way, can lead you to a better idea of which pages of your site you could be building statically. A static page is as fast as a dynamic page in the cache. Of course, the other key to caching is to be sure that when the underlying content changes, your cache does not continue to serve the old stuff.

Database connection pooling

Establishing the connections between your repository database and the other non-CMS databases needed to build pages can be a time-consuming matter. For this reason, application servers allow you to keep a pool of database connections that you establish once and then reuse as needed to bypass a lengthy attempt to establish a connection.

Connection pooling is most often handled in your programming environment. It can also be assisted by third-party application server products. Finally, it might be built into the CMS templating language to aid the performance of page-building commands. Pooling, in combination with query results set caching, is your best bet for reducing the bottleneck between the database and your users.

Server load balancing

Caches and connection pooling deal with the bottleneck that occurs as your site is retrieving content and building pages. At some point, however, the bottleneck becomes the server itself and its capability to process requests coming in from users. At this point, you need more than one server to handle requests. Server *farms*, as they are called, are designed to distribute the processing load over a set of computers. The benefits of server farming go beyond performance to include increased up-time of your site and quick recovery from server crashes. Two distinct issues are involved in server farming:

✦ **Content synchronization:** Unless you have decided to distribute the site as well (see Chapter 39, "Building Management Systems" in the section titled "Distribution" for more information on distributing the site), the various servers in the farm all need to have the site fully installed and operating on them. Content synchronization boils down to the issues of replication and synchronization, which I detail in Chapter 39, "Building Management Systems" in the section titled "Replication."

✦ **Load balancing:** When a request arrives, the application server has to decide which server to send it to. The issues that it takes into account may include which server is most available and which server has the current user's profile loaded.

Very big sites all use server farms to ensure performance and reliability. I would suggest before jumping into this expensive and complex feature, however, that you be sure that a single high-end server with caching and pooling can't meet your needs.

Print System

Print publications are those that are designed to be consumed on paper. To make a print publication, the CMS draws appropriate components and access structures out of the repository and converts them to the format and structure expected by a print system. For example, through templates and conversion routines, you might create an Adobe FrameMaker (MIF) file that you could then deliver to a printing house for publication.

Note Despite Adobe's claims to the contrary, I count Portable Document Format (PDF) publications as print publications because most are generally designed to be printed before being read. Although decent electronic publications are produced in PDF, that is not the most common use of the format. In the vast majority of cases, PDF is used to create a portable (as the name implies) copy of a word processing document that was originally designed to be printed.

Notice that this process is no different in essence from what it takes to create a Web publication. (So why let the idea of print publications scare you?) In both cases, templates create a publication that is rendered by a downstream system. In fact, if you work with a downstream print system that accepts XML, the process is no different, in essence or in fact, from producing a Web publication. Both outputs are created by a transformation from your repository format (XML, I hope) to another form of XML. I stress the similarity of the two forms of publications not to persuade you that they are the same, but to persuade you (if you still need persuading) that they are enough alike to be created from the same system.

The main difference, in my opinion, between Web and print publications (beside the fact that Web is dignified by an initial capital letter and print is not), is that Web publications are multiple interacting files with a very weak narrative structure; whereas print publications are usually single files with a very strong narrative structure. Creating one file or many files is a small matter in a CMS. Producing a strong or a weak narrative is a much larger issue. As I will explain in the section "Narrative support," later in this chapter, users may view a given piece of content in a medium (like the Web) where narrative references like *below* have no meaning because the object of the reference may be on an entirely different Web page or not present at all; the same is true in a publication (print, but possibly Web as well) where interactive features such as linking are not present.

Technical publications

The field of technical publications (sometimes known as *documentation*) can really use the techniques of CM. Any organization that produces a product also needs to create user guides, technical notes, product specifications, reference guides, installation guides, repair manuals, and a host of other possible works that instruct. Traditionally, a technical publications group produced printed materials in book or pamphlet form.

Technical publications groups in the software industry now uniformly produce HTML versions of their documentation, as well as (or more and more often, instead of) printed materials. The HTML version of their documentation is generally delivered on the company Web site as well as in HTML Help files. HTML Help is a Microsoft standard for delivering software documentation that is integrated with the application it describes.

Some of the more advanced technical publications groups throughout the technology sector have begun to adopt the sort of CM perspective that I describe in this book. In this way, the instructive content that they produce can transcend the boundaries of traditional documentation and can be used in a much wider range of publications, such as in pre- and post-sales materials, training materials, point of sales brochures, and even shareholder publications such as annual reports. These efforts require a lot of support from a CMS to be viable over the long term.

Outside the technology sector, few technical publications groups have gone further than to create PDF versions of their printed materials. The PDF files allow them to transmit their print materials electronically via, for example, links on a Web site. Although these groups have long been involved in complex production systems that use SGML and database technologies to create customized documentation sets, they have yet to open up their information to the rest of the organization or capture its value outside the realm of product documentation.

What Is to Become of the TechPubs Department?

I know of a number of technical publications groups in the United States that are in or are approaching a crisis. Technical writing is being outsourced to other nations where people who are just as competent are willing to do the job for a lot lower wage. In addition, year after year, the budgets of these groups are falling. Schedules are compressing, and quality is falling victim to overwork and lack of good information flowing in from the engineering groups. All this is happening while they are being asked to produce more complex publications on more complex products and to do so for every one of the infinite variety of configurations that their companies now sell.

In essence, technical publications groups are finding themselves thrust upon the main stage of the global economy. Their jobs are now part of the global labor pool, and their work is now part of the fast-paced and kaleidoscopically changing output of global technology companies that create product offerings on demand.

The question for technical publications groups is the same as that faced by a myriad other groups that find themselves suddenly in the global economy. "Do we embrace it or fight it?" My own humble opinion is that technical publications groups should do neither. Rather, they must reconstitute themselves internally and resituate themselves in their wider organizations so that they can meet the demands of the new economy of rapid change and compete on the basis of value, not price, in the world labor market.

The question remains, of course, as to how to reconstitute. I believe the answer lies in the skills that technical publications people bring to the table. Some are commodity skills, such as proofreading and editing. It is a fact that Irish and Indian workers will perform these jobs at a fraction of the cost that U.S. workers will. It is also a fact that they are as good as or better at these skills than many of their U.S. counterparts. Why then shouldn't they get these jobs? Other skills in a technical publications group are not commodities at all. Deep knowledge of customers, products, and how to produce a publication that matches the two will never be a commodity. The ability to turn that knowledge into undisputable value for your organization will always be prized above all other skills.

Until such time as the disparities in wages across the world go away (which, by the way, is not such a bad thing to work toward), your U.S.-based group cannot compete on price. Any smart person with a connection to the net and a depressed local or regional economy will be able to do it cheaper. Regardless of the world wage structure, however, targeted expertise and the ability to apply it will always be at a premium.

Section and subsection support

Almost all print publications of any length have a guiding primary hierarchy. This hierarchy, which takes the form of sections and subsections (also called headings) breaks the linear structure of the text into understandable segments. In addition, it shows the structure of the information held in the publication and outlines the story it tells. Perhaps my favorite example of this is from A. A. Milne, who does not title his chapters in *Winnie the Pooh*, but rather gives them names like "Chapter I, In Which We Are Introduced to Winnie-the-Pooh and Some Bees and the Stories Begin."

As I describe elsewhere (in my discussion of composition versus component CM in Chapter 9, "Component Management versus Composition Management"), a print publication is like a composition. It is in a unified, tightly interrelated body of content where the sections and subsections hold the composition together. To be successful, a CMS must let you create and render in print the sections and subsections of the print composition.

Your first task is to create the section and subsection structure you want from your repository. You have a variety of ways to do this:

✦ You can explicitly code your publication's primary hierarchy in a separate access structure. For example, suppose you are creating white papers from your repository. You might choose to give the white paper publishers the opportunity to construct a TOC for the white paper. They create the outline with the components that they want to include, arranged in the sections that they want the white paper to have.

✦ You can use existing hierarchies to produce outputs. Supposing you have a subject hierarchy, for example, you might choose to create a print publication on a particular subject that includes all the components that are tagged with that subject arranged by the terms that are below the one you choose. If you choose the subject Aid Programs for example, all the content tagged with the subject Aid Programs would be included, and all the content tagged with the child terms of Aid Programs (say, Food Aid, Economic Aid, and Military Aid) would be included as well. The outline of the publication would be the same as the outline of the subject headings.

✦ You can derive hierarchies based on existing metadata. For example, you might create a printed catalog of product offerings that organizes products by content type (say Service offering, Product offering, and Support offering types). Then they could be subcategorized by the value of one of the elements common to all types (Audience for example, with values of Commercial, Government, and NGO). Finally, they could be categorized by another common element (such as Price). The result is a publication hierarchy that is derived from existing non-hierarchical metadata.

✦ You can combine the preceding methods. For example, you might decide to create a custom hierarchy but allow people to put component selectors in each category rather than actually listing components. For example, in your Aid Programs white paper, you might create a custom hierarchy for the white paper. In the overview section of the white paper, you might choose to include any component that is tagged with the Aid Program subject keyword and has the Overview content type.

As you begin to play with the construction of section structure, you might notice that it cannot be easily separated from narrative structure in print publications. See Chapter 9, "Component Management versus Composition Management," the section "CM Systems Can Be Modular or Linear," for more information on narrative support.

After you have hierarchical structure in one way or another in your repository, you may need features that let you publish section structure in the following ways:

✦ It must allow you to retrieve a section with or without its subsections. For example, when you build a quick guide to a product for a sales support tool, you may want to include only the text directly under the level 1 headings of a technical document. In the fuller Web version of the same document, you may want to include all the text, plus any subheads that exist under the level 1 headings.

✦ It must include templates that manipulate the structure. For example, if you are reusing level 3 and 4 headings in a separate print publication, they must be transformed to level 1 and 2 headings because these headings now constitute the top level headings for the new publication. You may decide to include the parentage (that is, the titles to the parents) of the level 3 and 4 headings to give the user some context or you may decide that such context would just be too confusing and decide to leave it out.

✦ You must be able to subordinate chunks of hierarchy as needed to produce the outline for the target publication. For example, you may be pulling sections out of various levels in the content stored in the repository to form the print publication. In this situation, you need a way of specifying the outline of the new publication and saying which sections go where. As the publication is built, the outline turns into the TOC for the publication, and the heading level of each of the subsections is set according to where they have been placed in the outline for the publication.

Unless your print publications are really simple, you need section and subsection support. I have found that although more difficult to support, the flexibility to allow custom hierarchies is, in the end, what it really takes to create print hierarchies that look like real print TOCs.

Narrative support

In my discussion of segmentation (see Chapter 38, "Building Collection Systems,"the section "Segmentation"), I discussed how unified compositions can be dissected by the CMS and used out of context in other publications. When you want a CMS to create a print publication, the reverse is true. Instead of breaking apart a composition and reusing its pieces, you try to take distinct pieces and weave them into a unified composition.

Unified for a print publication really boils down to a strong narrative structure. On the Web, people have come to expect a rather fractured experience. As they click from page to page (and even as they scroll within a page), they are not surprised that the successive pieces of information that they see are not directly related to each other. As you move around, the experience that you are still in the same publication is created by what I call the surrounds (logos, banners, colors, layouts, headers, footers, and so on). The content itself, however, is quite often fragmented. It's not that the content on the Web has to be fragmented; it is rather that it has always been fragmented, and users have learned not to worry too much about it.

In a print publication, this is not so. As you turn pages, you expect continuity among the parts of the information that goes way beyond having the same headers and footers on each page. You expect a story or narrative to be followed. You expect that subjects will be introduced, detailed, and then transitions will be made that relate the next subject to the current one. You expect in short, to be led on a defined path through a tightly connected series of subjects. In really good print materials, the narrative is so strong that you can hardly tell where one subject ends and another begins.

In print you are being led, whereas on the Web, you propel yourself through a landscape of weakly related subjects. Again, I want to stress that this is not how it has to be, but rather how it happens to be.

Note One of the most interesting trends in technical publications is the "modularization" of documents where the random access structure of the Web is being practiced in print. On the Web, an equally interesting trend is to build sites based on a strong narrative that leads the user not through a single narrative but through multiple intertwined narratives.

The long and short of this discussion is that if you want to produce good print publications, you had better pay close attention to narrative. If that was my last word on the subject, I'd be a literary critic and not a content manager. As a content manager it is my first responsibly to recognize the importance of narrative. It is my second responsibility to get my CMS to help me do it. As a technologist to boot, I need to fashion a narrative support feature. I have tried and failed too many times to manage narrative to say that it is easily accomplished in a CMS. However, I can say that you can make a good run at it if you make yourself aware of the mechanics of narrative.

Here are some of the parts of a narrative management feature that pays attention to the places where narrative happens:

✦ **Introductions and transitions in collection.** In a composition, an introduction eases you into a subject by relating it to things you already know. Things you already know come in two varieties: things already mentioned in the composition, and things the author can generally assume someone in this audience ought to know. I like to call the things already mentioned part the *in-transition* because this content makes an incoming transition from previous sections. The other material I call the general introduction. Similarly, at the end of a section, an outgoing transition often leads to the following sections (I like to call this an *out-transition*). You can do a lot to extract and create a narrative structure by managing this information. On the collection side of the CMS, you have to be able to mark these parts so that if you need to use the section without them they can be removed. One problem to be reckoned with at collection time is untangling the in-transition content from the general introduction. A composition writer is quite likely to intertwine the two. On the publication side, you can always publish the general introduction, but you should only publish the in-transition material if the previous sections are also being published and come before the current section. Similarly, the out-transition content should be published only if the following section is also being published and also follows the current section.

✦ **Introductions and transitions in your publications.** The in- and out- transitions that came from source material at collection time are relatively easy to deal with at publishing time if you can find and mark them. You only publish them if the additional sections they refer to get published as well. But what do you do in publications where a variety of sections that never followed each other before follow each other now? How do you come up with transitions between these sections? Well, you have these basic possibilities:

  • Write a set of variations on the transitions and store them alongside the usual transitions. This is fine if you happen to know all of the transitions that you need in advance, but you probably do not know all the sections that will ever come before or after the current section.

  • Adopt a modular print publication style in which it is assumed that no transitions will be needed. This is fine if such a style fits your publication, but will make the publication look like a machine-produced conglomeration if that style does not fit it.

- Tell the user your problem. You might opt to say right in the publication that it has been built from components. In other words, you admit defeat and throw yourself on the mercy of the user. I have found users kinder than you might expect to this baring of the soul. If they need the print publication, respect the publisher, and have a fairly post-modern attitude, which means they don't mind a very weak narrative, you might just get away with this approach.

- Write custom transitions. If you adopt the section and subsection method I discuss earlier in which you create a custom hierarchy for your print publications, then you can go to the next step and add a place in that target publication's outline for custom transitions. In other words, in addition to typing the order of the sections in a custom outline, you also type in custom transitions. I'll illustrate this presently.

✦ **Conclusions for the parent sections.** A section conclusion draws implications from the section and brings it back into the overall narrative (or story or big picture) of the publication. You may or may not have ever noticed, but in print publications, concluding remarks for the parent section are often tacked onto the end of the text of the last child section. For example, the conclusion of the chapter in a book is often just the last few paragraphs of the last heading in the chapter. Of, course you will have to be more precise in your publications. On the collection side, the parent conclusions will have to be marked as such and not as part of the section they happen to be in. On the publication side, you may choose to put the section conclusion in or not depending on if it draws the same implications as the publication is supposed to. For example, if the original point of the section was to show how a product fits into a suite of products, but none of the other products is mentioned in the target publication, then the conclusion should go, or better, be replaced by a conclusion that is in line with the point of the target publication.

✦ **Titles and section names.** As I have said previously, the narrative of a publication is shown first in its title and the names of the sections of the publication. If you are very lucky, whatever names the sections have in your repository will suffice for any use of the section in any publication. In general, your narrative will suffer if you are trapped into using the same name any time a section is published. For example, if the title in the repository for a particular section is "Narratives," that will be fine if its parent section, titled "Print Publication Support Features," will also be published. But if the parent will not be published, you would be better off renaming the section to something like "Print Narrative Support Features." The new title is redundant in the context of the parent but is necessary when the section stands alone.

✦ **Context variables.** A lot of narrative exists in the casual references forward and backward in a composition. For example, if I say, "as I just mentioned," it helps you keep the thread of the subject matter. Or if I say, "throughout this book I have tried to..." it again helps you see how the next statement fits into the overall narrative of the work. As you probably have already guessed, the problem is that these statements will not always be true. If a piece of text is published out of its original context, I might not have just mentioned a subject and no book may be in sight when I say "throughout this book." So you need techniques to flag these references and decide what to do with them. To begin, you make some assumption about the granularity at which you will publish. If your system will allow people to publish a single sentence without the ones before and after, you will have to be very careful of references that lose meaning in the target publication. On the other hand, if you restrict publications to using only whole sections, then a realm of references that you don't have to worry about are available. For the references you do need to manage, a good approach is to create tags that stand in for the phrases that vary. For example, if your work is a book and a Web site, put in a tag instead of the name of the work. Then, at render time, your templates can fill in the right name for the work. If you don't know if a section referred to will come before or after (or on the Web, neither before or after) the current one, put in a tag that has the id of the referred-to section. Let your templates decide if the referred-to section is before, after, or not in the target publication.

To put all of the above considerations together, consider the following template for a whole print publication. It incorporates most of what I have discussed in section and narrative support. It combines an access structure (a hierarchy for the target publication) with a place to lodge the various parts of the narrative of the publication. This example supposes that you have a set of components that have sections and subsections in them. They also have introductions, in- and out-transitions, and conclusions within them:

```
<PUB TITLE="How to Succeed in Narrative Management"
  <INTRO>...Text you enter here...</INTRO>
  <SECTIONREF COMPONENTID="C123" TITLE />
  <OUTTRANS>...Text you enter here...</OUTTRANS>
  <SECTION>
     <TITLE>What to do About Titles</TITLE>
     <INTRO>...Text you enter here...</INTRO>
     <INTRANS>...Text you enter here...</INTRANS>
     <SECTIONREF COMPONENT ID="C456" TITLE SUBSECTS/>
     <OUTTRANS>...Text you enter here...</OUTTRANS>
     <SECTIONREF COMPONENT ID="C789" TITLE SUBSECTS
     OUTTRANS CONC"/>
     <SECTION>
        <TITLE>Special Case Titles </TITLE>
        <SECTIONREF COMPONENT ID="C1011"/>
     </SECTION>
     <CONCLUSION >...Text you enter here...</CONCLUSION>
  </SECTION>
</PUB>
```

This simplified excerpt from a system I once created shows the following qualities:

✦ **The PUB tag** declares the publication and gives it a title.

✦ **The INTRO tag** gives you a place to type in a custom introduction to the publication or to any section within the publication.

✦ **The SECTION tag** marks the beginning of a heading level in the target publication. That heading is given a name with the HEADING tag that follows the SECTION tag. Notice that this publication has two levels of section specified by the SECTION tags.

✦ **The INTRANS tag** works like the INTRO tag. It allows you to add an inbound transition of your own when you need one. You can leave this tag out if you want to.

✦ **The SECTIONREF (section reference) tag** is what brings in all the content from the repository. This tag always cites the id of the component to include (the COMPONENTID attribute). It also includes a set of optional attributes that specify what to include from the component.

  • If the TITLE attribute is present, it says that you want to include the title from the component. If it is not present, it means that you want to either have no title preceding the component or you will specify your own with a TITLE tag.

  • If the SUBSECTS attribute is present, it means that you want to include all the section and subsections contained in the component. If it is missing, it means that you want to include only the first-level section contained in the component. The outline of the target publication may get much deeper than the two levels specified by the SECTION tags if the components that are brought in have multiple levels of subsections.

- If the INTRANS attribute is present, it means that you want to include the component's incoming transition in the publication.

- If the OUTTRANS attribute is present, it means that you would like to include the component's outgoing transition in the publication.

- If the CONC attribute is present, it means that you want to include the component's conclusion in the publication.

✦ **The CONCLUSION tag** allows you to add a conclusion as you need to the ends of the sections.

So, this template allows you to call in information as needed and type in your own when the information you can call in will not provide the narrative you need in the publication. Because all of the extra information is optional, you can add as much extra narrative (including none) that you need to do the job in each publication. Note that we are still prior in the process to actually building this publication; at this point all we have really done is to supply an extra set of instructions on how to go about building the publication. It will still be up to the template processor to read these instructions and use them to create the format and structure of the target publication.

Most CMS systems do very little to help you manage the narratives in your print (or any other) publications. For this reason they seem to be print-unfriendly. However, with a little effort on your part, you can create your own narrative management feature that bridges the gap between what the CMS can do and what you need it to do.

Navigation support

Most print publications do not use lists of hyperlinks to create navigation structures. Rather, the hierarchies, indexes, and cross-references that you see in print are of a fundamentally different form than on the Web. In a word, they use page numbers, not filenames, to specify a referent. You may never have considered this, but page numbers are incredibly hard to figure out in a print publication. A large number of factors (font size, margins, space before and after paragraphs, line spacing, and others) all contribute to what page a particular heading or paragraph will land. For this reason, everyone relies on the page layout engine in the target print platform to create navigation. This does not mean that the CMS can do nothing to build the navigation in a print publication. It does mean that, in most cases, the support is indirect. For example, to build a Table of Contents, your templating engine does not find all the section titles, put them in an indenting structure, and calculate their page numbers. Rather, the template assigns heading styles or codes to all the titles in the body of the publication and then puts a TOC code in the right place in the published document. The print platform looks at the code you included and also at the titles of all the sections and builds the TOC for you.

Similarly, you can often manage not to build print indexes directly, but instead put index codes where you want all your referents to be and let the print system build the index. The same is possible for cross-references, but you may not have the same control over their format as you would if you resolved them yourself. Of course, you can resolve titles in cross-references, but not page numbers.

You are generally on your own for producing navigation in print publications from your CMS. However, it is not all that hard to do it yourself, given that your print platform supports automatic TOCs, indexes, and cross-references and that your print platform has a format that your templating system can create.

Dynamic print publications

Just because a publication is bound for paper does not mean that it is statically produced. Especially in situations where a user needs a print publication that is tailored to her needs (a custom manual or a policy white paper for all her concerns, for example), a dynamically produced print publication that incorporates whatever level of personalization you can muster is just the thing. There is nothing fundamentally different about producing print publications on demand, and I only mention it here because for many it seems out of the question before they even pose the question. However, if your templating system can produce dynamic publications that your target print platform can read, there is no reason that it can't produce print publications on demand.

This feature is great if you need to produce documentation for a user's custom configuration. In most cases I have seen, the system shows the user some sort of configuration screen where she specifies all the needs she has. Notice that this is really no different than a screen where the user enters a personalization profile. The system then uses the choices made by the user to create a custom output. This is like using a personalization profile to make a custom output. The most common output used to be a Word file but now, more and more often, it is XML. In either case, the custom output is most often translated into PDF before it is delivered (usually as a download) to the user.

Producing Word files

Because Word is such a common platform for print publication, and because the latest version of Word finally supports XML, it is worth spending a short time discussing it specifically (my apologies to all the other print platform venders). It turns out that there is a relatively straightforward way to create Word publishing templates from any standard Word file that you care to start from. The process in overview is as follows:

1. **Create a Word file.** Format it the way you want the final publication to look, including sample content where you will later send the real content from the repository.

2. **Replace the sample content with placeholders.** For example, if you created a table with sample component content, remove the content and instead type the name of the component element (or any other placeholder you choose) in its place. Do this for all the content that you will retrieve from the repository.

3. **Save the file as XML.** Word will make a WordML file for you. WordML is a somewhat verbose but basically readable form of XML that Word can use to store all its formatting and document structure codes. It is a great replacement for the aging RTF format.

4. **Open the file in an XML editor.** Word itself is an XML editor, but not the one most XML developers prefer.

5. **Add an XSLT header and footer to the Word XML file.** See the example that follows for the details, but essentially the header is a few lines of XLS code that tells the XSLT processor to interpret this file not as WordML, but rather as XSLT.

6. **Replace your placeholders with XSLT code.** Wherever you want to include content from the repository, remove the placeholders you typed in previously and put in the XSLT code needed to draw content in from the repository (or wherever you are keeping the content that will fill the publication).

7. **Save the file with an XSLT extension.** You have now transformed your original Word file into an XSLT that can produce the format and structure of your target Word publication.

To take a closer look at the process, examine a very simplified XSLT/WordML template. Suppose you want to create a product list publication in Word. For the sake of the example, assume that the CMS stores its content in XML. Further, assume that the publication system will draw content out of the repository and create a single XML file (or document object in memory) that has all the information that goes into the publication you want to produce. In brief, the XML file that the publication system produces from the repository might look like this:

```
<PUB>
    <TITLE></TITLE>
    <PRODUCTS>
        <PRODUCT>
            <NAME></NAME>
            <DESCRIPTION>Text an XML tags for
            multiple paragraphs</DESCRIPTION>
        </PRODUCT>
        More products
    </PRODUCTS>
</PUB>
```

The target publication is a simple Word file. It has a title and a set of sections, one for each product. Of course, if the description of the product goes on for a long time and has lots of structure, the Word file will go on for a long time and have lots of formatting.

A simplified version of the WordML/XSLT template for creating this publication might be the following:

```
1:      <?xml version="1.0" encoding="UTF-8" standalone="yes"?>
2:      <?mso-application progid="Word.Document"?>
3:      <xsl:stylesheet version="1.0"
        xmlns:xsl="http://www.w3.org/1999/XSL/Transform">
4:          <xsl:include href="WordBody.xsl"/>
5:          <xsl:template match="/">
6:              <w:wordDocument
                xmlns:w="http://schemas.microsoft.com/...">
7:                  Lots and lots of WordML
8:                  <wx:sub-section>
9:                      <w:p>
10:                         <w:pPr><w:pStyle w:val="Title"/> </w:pPr>
11:                         <w:r><w:t>
12:                             <xsl:value-of select="/PUB/TITLE"/>
13:                         </w:t></w:r>
14:                     </w:p>
15:                 </wx:sub-section>
16:                 Lots and lots more WordML
17:                 <xsl:for-each select="//PRODUCT">
18:                     <wx:sub-section>
```

```
19:                    <w:p>
20:                        <w:pPr><w:pStyle w:val="Heading1"/>
                           </w:pPr>
21:                        <w:r><w:t>
22:                            <xsl:value-of select="NAME"/>
23:                        </w:t></w:r>
24:                    </w:p>
25:                    <xsl:apply-templates
                       select="DESCRIPTION"/>
26:                <wx:sub-section>
27:            </xsl:for-each>
28:            Yet more WordML
29:        </w:wordDocument>
30:        </xsl:template>
31:    </xsl:stylesheet>
```

The template does what all templates do. It mixes static text (in this case WordML) with dynamic content (in this case, its content is called in by XSLT elements). The template unpacks as follows:

✦ **Lines 1 and 2** are processing instructions that Word uses to determine that this is a Word file. They are passed through undigested by the XSLT processor.

✦ **Lines 3–5** are XSLT elements. Line 3 defines this file as an XSLT transform. Line 4 is a directive to the XSLT processor to include another XSLT. WordBody.xsl contains a set of reusable templates for rendering paragraphs and other body elements in WordML. Line 5 defines the one subtemplate that is actually in this file. It is the template that runs when the processor hits the root element of the XML file that the publication system has produced. This root template produces the whole publication. Notice that the XSLT elements all begin with the letters xsl. This indicates that they are part of the XSLT namespace and should be interpreted by the XSLT processor.

✦ **Lines 6 and 7** are static text. They are the WordML elements that begin any word document. As line 7 indicates, a lot more WordML is used to begin the document than is shown. WordML elements begin w or wx. These are two of the multiple Word namespaces.

✦ **Lines 8–15** define a section in the Word file. The section begins and ends with a <wx:sub-section> tag. Within the subsection is a paragraph (<w:p>). The paragraph has properties (<w:pPr>) and a range of text (<w:r> and <w:t>). The resulting WordML format paragraph has a Title style. The WordML that is not shown defines that style as 24 point bold and centered with a page break after it.

✦ **Line 12** calls in the title from the XML file that the publication system created. The statement "/PUB/TITLE" says that the title is to be found in the <PUB><TITLE> tag.

✦ **Lines 17–27** are a loop that creates one section per product. Line 17 says: do the following elements for each product in the XML file. If there were 10 products in the XML file these lines would result in 10 sections in the publication.

✦ **Lines 19–24** are the same sort of lines as 9–14. They produce a paragraph in WordML format. This paragraph ends up with a Heading1 style. Though not shown in the example, a Table of Contents comes between the title and the first product section and is set up to include all Heading1 styled paragraphs.

✦ **Line 25** says: parse the XML within the DESCRIPTION tag and find any XSLT templates that are designed to render the content within the DESCRIPTION tag. The templates that are designed for this purpose are in WordBody.xml, which is included in line 4. The result of line 25 is that the descriptions are rendered in WordML format. They may include regular paragraphs, bulleted or numbered lists, tables, and even subsections.

✦ **Lines 26–31** Close up all the tags in the file (making it a valid XML file itself) and end the template.

Using the basic technique I laid out, you can convert virtually any Word file quickly into an XSLT template with very little knowledge of WordML. The key is that you use Word itself to create the WordML. Then you simply wrap the WordML in XSLT elements that supply content from the repository. Of course, even as simple as it is, it is still a programmer-type process. Knowing what XSLT elements to use and where they go, not to mention debugging it all, requires some pretty extensive experience.

Another problem with this method is worse than having to use programmers. After you have translated your file from WordML to XSLT, you have no easy way to go back to Word. You have to completely finish your design before turning your document into XSLT. With a bit of finesse, you can switch out parts from fresh Word docs and modify your included templates, but it takes a lot of effort to change the design.

In the longer term, a much better method (which I have seen done as well) is to write routines that transform the document from Word to XSLT automatically. The template designer for a publication, not a programming-oriented person, keeps working in Word all the time and puts in placeholders that are later evaluated. The process proceeds roughly as follows: Rather than putting in simple placeholders, the designer puts in complex placeholders that specify in detail what content is to be pulled from the repository. These placeholders can be, for example, embedded in the names of Word bookmarks to show their range. You develop a library of transforms that cover most of the range of WordML renderings you need. The templates take parameters that are packed in the placeholders. You write a transformer that turns the designer's word file into XSLT and replaces the placeholders with calls to the transforms you previously wrote. The designer's original Word file remains untouched and she can continue to modify it.

For any but fairly simple publications, you are not likely to reach 100% automation in this process. However, it does free the template designer from the programmer (to a large extent) and means that your XSLT work is in the most reusable form possible.

Even before Word adopted XML, Word was a leading source of print publications (much to most programmers' chagrin). Now that Word publications can be created programmatically, its popularity will only rise (which may cause a different kind of chagrin in your programmers).

E-mail System

The publication system can be integrated with your e-mail system and push content to it. Alternatively, it might be integrated with a third-party bulk e-mail system. As opposed to bulk e-mail — in which the same message is sent to a lot of people — individualized e-mail sends different messages to individuals. This capability ties the personalization functionality to the e-mail creation functionality. The messages you send are themselves publications. They can reflect well or poorly on your organization depending on how much care you use to produce them.

E-mail types

E-mails are more like slides, posters, or flyers than they are like books, articles, or newsletters. They are more like homepages than they are like details pages on the Web. All good examples of e-mail messages share the qualities of being quickly understood, easy to read, and designed to point you to a wider set of information than the information in the message. With this in mind, you can take a few different approaches to your e-mail messages:

✦ **The homepage:** A homepage tries to capture the entire breadth of a Web site in a single page. In this conception of your e-mail messages, you are providing a user-centric view of all the information in your repository. The message is directly analogous to the personalized homepage that the user sees on the Web. As you can imagine, this approach to your messages strongly implies that you will produce messages in HTML or some other rich format. More important, it implies that you have a close relationship to your recipients. The idea here is that they want to be updated periodically on the overall status of your repository. If they don't, they will not have the attention to deal with an entire homepage in their inbox once a week. This conception of your e-mail messages also requires that you be able to produce personalized homepages.

✦ **The flyer:** A flyer on a wall tries to capture your attention and tell you about one or more events of interest. In this conception of an e-mail message, you are trying to capture the user's attention and direct it toward information of interest. To create such messages you have to be able to find information items you believe are of interest to the recipient and you have to be able to present it in an attention-getting way. When done well, this form of message effectively directs users' attention to the items they want to see. When done poorly (where you are trying to direct attention to information the recipient does not want to see), it is just spam.

✦ **The updater:** This form of e-mail lists changes to the repository. It is appropriate for people who need to stay abreast of a lot of information. For example, if your audience members are realtors, you might send them a weekly e-mail listing all the new home components you have added to your real estate CMS. The realtors want a comprehensive view of the changes since their last mail. This sort of e-mail usually lists just the facts, omitting any lengthy description.

✦ **The summarizer:** This sort of mail lists titles and summaries of the set of components that the user is (you hope) interested in. It serves as a digest or newsletter. It is appropriate for users who want to stay abreast of developments. The assumption is that they will read the blurbs of interest and feel more or less informed. In other words, for them this e-mail is not a leader to your real publication (your site), but the publication itself. Thus, although it is tempting, I would advise not putting only teasers in this sort of mail. For example, you might be tempted to try and drive users to your site with sentences like "The CEO announced today that your job...." Because they will drive more frustration than traffic, avoid these sentence fragment and other come-ons.

✦ **The interesting tidbits:** This sort of mail does not try to be either a digest or a complete set of changes. Rather, it tries to be informative on a topic of particular interest. It often carries a pithy title designed to catch the user's eye and concerns subject matter (whether recently published or not) that is of interest to the users. This form of mail is for aficionados or students of a subject that want a reason to stay connected to the subject matter. It is akin to the sort of desk calendar that has a new vocabulary word on it for each day of the year. If the subjects you choose really are interesting tidbits, this sort of mail can build the knowledge of your users and provide a strong point a contact with them. If the tidbits are not tasty, this sort of mail will go straight to the bit bucket.

I suspect that you can think of a number of your own e-mail types to add to this list. The important point is not that you choose one of these types, but that you recognize that there are types and be conscious of using e-mail like any other publication medium. As always, you should deliver well-formatted and well-structured information to a defined audience with a defined need. In this regard, I would recommend not sending an e-mail if there is nothing to include. Don't destroy the confidence of your users the way that a big analyst firm destroyed mine. I filled out a detailed profile of what I wanted, only to find that my e-mails contained a lot of stuff I did not ask for and came every week whether they had anything new for me or not. Needless to say it was not very long before I stopped opening them.

Destination pages

Almost all the e-mail you send will include links to a larger Web site. As you make these links, you can choose one of these methods:

✦ **The direct link:** You can link users directly to the details page for the item they clicked on. For example, if you send a title and abstract for a new article to your users, you generally include a link for the full article. A click on the link takes them directly to the details page for that article on your site. All the usual branding, navigation, and other surrounds are present on the page.

✦ **The destination page:** You could create a special intermediate page that users go to when they click a link. For example, when the user clicks the link that follows the title and abstract of a new article, rather than going to the usual details page for that article, you can create a custom destination page. Rather than the usual navigation and surrounds, the destination page can feature the details of the article and any navigation and surrounds that you think are appropriate. For example, you might list many more links to similar articles on the destination page than on the usual page. You might simplify the surrounds so that the article stands out more. Finally, you might direct the user to specific parts of your larger site rather than simply dropping them into the middle of it and assuming that they will know how to navigate. If you have a personalization profile in place for this user, you can also include content and navigation of individual interest to the user.

After you fully embrace the idea that a CMS can create any number of cuts on the same content, and once you have the machinery in place to manage the array of cuts that you create, there is nothing to stop you from creating destination pages from e-mail messages or from any other source you choose. You should go out of your way to create destination pages when you are dealing with users who are not be familiar with your large and complex site. Think of destination pages as a welcome center with the information they want and a guide to the rest of the structure.

Integration to an e-mail server

Depending on how many e-mails you intend to send per day, you can take one of these approaches:

✦ If you will send only a few e-mails per day (say less than 100), you can get away with connecting your CMS to your organization's usual e-mail server.

✦ For a larger number of e-mails per day (say up to a few thousand), or where you personalize your messages so that different messages are sent to different people, you can buy your own e-mail server that specializes in bulk e-mails.

✦ For very large numbers of e-mails, you can contract with a commercial bulk e-mailing service that has the software and the net bandwidth to send very large numbers of messages. You supply them with the messages and they distribute them.

Regardless of whether you send e-mail directly or through a third party, you must figure out where you will keep the names and addresses of all the recipients. If these people are just a list of e-mail recipients, there is no problem keeping only their names and addresses in your e-mail system. However, as you begin to consider these people to be audience members, then their names and addresses become the start of user profiles and deserve to be stored in a place that is accessible to the rest of the CMS.

Template chooser

A number of e-mail client applications support a variety of e-mail message formats.

✦ Some support only plaintext where the e-mail message header and body are displayed exactly as they are sent.

✦ Some display plaintext, but parse the header and put it in a form-like interface where you can see the title, sender, and other generally useful header information. Most of the less useful header fields are not displayed. Some allow a variety of text encoding standards (UTF-7, UTF-8, ISO, and so on), whereas others pick one for you.

✦ Some display a part or all the HTML formatting codes. They may display only links using their own rendering engine, or they may incorporate a browser in their user interface to display any HTML (any that their browser can display, that is).

✦ Some support their own proprietary display format. Microsoft Outlook, for example, supports a variation on the Word document format for rich text.

The point here is that there are a number of ways that an e-mail viewer might use to display a message. Fortunately, in a CMS you have the capacity to produce a variety of output formats using templates. Unfortunately, you may or may not know what format to produce for each recipient. Sometimes you can ask the user. For example, when they sign up for a weekly e-mail mailing, you can ask what format they prefer. You can also guess what format they support, which many organizations do. The safest guess is that they support only plaintext. The best guess for you is that they support the full HTML tag set. Then you can create e-mail messages that are very rich (or very ugly if the user's browser does not support HTML tags).

If you decide to give your users the format they want, you add a level of complexity to your e-mail production system. You have to produce multiple copies of the message you and make sure that the right type goes to the right person.

It can be a tough deciding what formats to support and how to figure out what each user wants. For this reason, many organizations just send plaintext. On the other hand, as you begin to embrace personalization, e-mail format preference becomes just one more profile point to track and one more way to show how well you can serve your audiences.

Personalization support

One form of personalization in e-mail publications is to render the message in the format that the user prefers. A much more important form of personalization is to render just the information that the user wants. Users will decidedly prefer personalized information (that is, information they want) in plaintext to general information (that they may or may not want) in HTML. So, personalization can drive the creation of great targeted e-mail.

More interestingly, e-mail can drive the adoption of personalization. If, like many organizations, you are looking for ways to begin personalizing but it seems like too big a task, you can start with an e-mail system. You can build a simple form that allows people to select the content they are interested in. You might list a few of your main content types (articles, news items, press releases, and so on) and one or two metadata fields (say, subject keyword and author). The user chooses the type of content she wants and gives you her name, e-mail address, and preferred message format. In return, you send her an e-mail message in her preferred format once a week with links to whatever new content has been added of the kind she chose.

Over time, you build up the robustness of the selection process. You might begin to ask questions on the configuration forms that increasingly enable you to place a user into an audience category. Eventually, you are capturing the full profile you need to personalize not only messages, but all your publications. You have also built up a growing stock of personalization profiles and a feedback channel with your audience members. For example, you can add rating links to the content that you send in the messages. You can allow the users to send mail back to authors. You can ask the users additional questions in the message that allow you to deepen or update their profiles. If you are sending people information that they really need, you will find that they are happy to respond. If they never respond, on the other hand, you might assume that the information you are sending them is not important enough to demand their attention.

You are ready to go down the road to personalized e-mail when you have worked through who will get what sort of information from your repository and when. In other words, there is no point in offering personalized e-mail until you have some conception of a personalization model. Of course, you need the personalization machinery as well. This machinery consists of the templates and personalization rules that translate a user profile into a rendered set of components that you can safely assume are important to the user. It's not that you have this completely figured out, but rather that you have a good start on it and a method for expanding its use over time.

Doing personalization in e-mail, especially if it is in addition to supporting multiple e-mail formats, adds considerable complexity to your system. Not only do you need to create potentially as many messages as you have recipients, but you have to send each message separately. On the other hand, this is just the capacity you need to build personalization more generally into your CMS.

Syndication System

In a CM context, syndication means packaging and distributing sets of content components for reuse in publications outside your CMS. The most useful format for syndication is XML, but the most common format is probably still ASCII with a header that contains metadata for each syndicated component. I introduce the concept of syndication in Chapter 7, "Introducing the Major Parts of a CMS," the section titled "Other publications."

Early on (three years ago), the CM industry seemed on the verge of coming to agreement on a syndication standard called Information and Content Exchange (ICE). Although this standard still exists, it never got the broad support needed to become the accepted standard. Other related standards like Electronic Document Interchange (EDI) have also come and gone in the CM world as proposed standards for moving information in bulk out of your CMS. RSS, which stands for Really Simple Syndication (depending on who you believe), now has the combined advantages of simplicity and wide adoption in the blogging community. Whether RSS will really become the standard or be washed away by the next big thing is still unclear.

Whatever "standard" you adopt, it is likely to change significantly over the lifetime of your CMS. In addition, there is no accounting for the standards that your syndication subscribers will adopt. Luckily, although standards ebb and flow, what you do, in general, to syndicate remains constant. And if you are thoughtful in the way you implement syndication, your system ought to be able to create syndicated content in a variety of ways.

The features in this section give you an idea of the general issues to be confronted and resolved in putting together your syndication system.

Syndication subscriber management

A subscriber gets a particular syndication feed from you, either on demand or on a set schedule. Depending on your syndication model, you may have just a few or a lot of subscribers. If you have very few subscribers, you can probably get away without much overt subscriber management. However, increasingly, systems are allowing anyone who is interested to sign up for a feed. Especially if you are using syndication as a way to broadcast or sell your content, it is in your interest to open up and automate the syndication process.

If you do decide to implement syndication in its fullness, you need a subscriber management feature that provides a subscriber user interface. Subscribers will want their own dashboards where they can choose content and delivery options. They will want not only to create their feed, but also to modify it over time and to delete it when they no longer need it. The subscriber user interface might include these features:

✦ **A profile section** where subscribers describe themselves. It is good for you (and for them) if you can treat subscribers like any other audience members. If you are collecting profile information for audience members and are able to provide personalization services for them based on these profiles, you can do the same for syndication subscribers. You get the benefit of user-supplied profile data and your subscribers get solid assistance in determining what content will be of most value to them.

✦ **A content selection section** where subscribers can select the content that is of interest to them. If you are smart, you will have them fill out their profile first (in a wizard-type interface perhaps) and preselect for them the kinds of content you believe that they want. If you are even smarter, you will record and review the changes they make to your default assumptions and use this information to modify your profile and personalization system. There is more on content selection in the section later in this chapter titled "Selecting content."

✦ **A delivery options section** where the subscriber can choose how and where to receive the feed. The more options you offer here, the better it will be for your users. And, although it requires work to produce all those feed types, the tools are already within your CMS. I talk more about delivery options in the section later in this chapter titled "Building and distributing feeds."

✦ **A pricing options section.** You may choose, at first, to give your information away, but the more you know your audiences the more value you will begin delivering them. The better the system you create, the easier it will be for those audiences to use the information you provide. At some point, either you are not doing your job or your audiences are getting a lot of value. Should you really give it away for free? You might want to experiment with pricing models that differentiate standard from premium content or, in some way, scale back the quantities in free feeds to open the space for paid subscriptions. At any rate, consider the possibility of charging for subscriptions and decide what sort of interface you need to explain the model and let subscribers sign up. Decide, as well, what sort of back end software you need to handle billing and other customer service issues.

✦ **A privacy policy link** that lets subscribers know what you will and will not do with all the great profile information they have supplied.

Behind the user interface, of course, there needs to be storage for the profiles and configuration the subscribers create. If you can manage to treat your subscribers as audience members, then whatever system you are using to store audience profiles ought to work for syndication subscribers as well. Make sure whatever profile storage system you use can scale to the size you'll need if you allow anyone to get a syndicated feed.

The older days of point-to-point syndication are quickly being eclipsed by a newer model of broadcast syndication, in which content goes out in smaller bundles to a larger group of subscribers. Subscribers may directly consume your feed, they may post it on their blog or Web site, or they may combine it with feeds from other suppliers in order to provide aggregation and redistribution services. If any of these opportunities seem worth taking to you, then you should implement some sort of subscriber management feature. The more serious you get about broadcast syndication, the more full-featured your subscriber user interface must to be.

Selecting content

The basis of syndication is to provide subscribers with the content of most concern to them. Contrast this with what many syndication sources do today, which is to offer a single feed that you can either receive or not. If you really want to make the most of syndication, you will allow a range of feeds that can be selected on a range of attributes. In other words, you will bring your system's full strength to bear to help subscribers create a feed that is most suited to their needs. Here are some of the content types to be selected:

✦ **Integration to content model:** Your content model specifies the content types, elements, and access structures that define the content you have. This is just the information that a subscriber might need to choose which content to include in her feed. Your biggest question here will be how to represent the content model in a way that subscribers can understand. You may need to assign a friendly name and layperson's description to each content type and element. Then, subscribers can choose content types from a list with descriptions. They can say which components of each type to include based on the values of its elements. As much as possible, you should try to create selection lists for elements that show the values that are currently in those elements in the repository. Your repository access structures may be even less comprehensible to subscribers than your content types. However, it is likely that you have already taken the effort to transform your repository access structures into navigation for a Web site. If you have, the same navigation templates could be used to represent your hierarchies and indexes in the contributor's user interface. The result is a view of the content model from the audience's perspective that allows them to understand it and use it to pick the content they want to be fed.

✦ **Integration to personalization system:** You can really think of syndication as personalization that results in a custom publication. If you have done a good job at personalization, it ought to be able to help you a lot in your syndication system. First, as I have mentioned, you can collect profile information on subscribers to put them in an audience and then pre-populate the content selection user interface. Second, you can create a set of standard feeds that are offered to people in a particular audience. For example, if you detect that a visitor to your site is in the press audience, you can offer a preconfigured feed that your personalization system creates. Third, you can use the same routines that produce personalized element selection and display to help build your syndication output. For example, you can use your localization routines to help build localized feeds. Or you can use the same code that enforces your security policy in your publication and input templates to enforce it in the syndication system.

✦ **Logs and popularity:** If you own Web logging software, you have all the data to decide which types of content have been most requested. If you have done any analysis of that data, you have the tools to let subscribers choose content based on its popularity. Of course, there may be a bit of programming distance between analysis and presentation in an end-user interface, but the work will be well rewarded not only in your syndication system but also in your personalization system.

✦ **Direct querying:** In the end, whatever selections the subscriber wants are turned into a query against your repository to return the content that you will put in her feeds. Given the appropriate subscribers, you may be able to cut to the chase and simply offer them a place where they can type in a query (either a database query or XML XPath query). The right kind of subscriber is a database administrator who most wants to acquire your content and put it directly into her system. She is technical enough to be able to understand and use the data model behind your content model, and her main concern is the same mapping (or lack of it) that you, too, are concerned about when acquiring content (as I discuss in Chapter 37, "Processing Content," in the section titled "Understanding the principles of mapping content"). In other words, this sort of subscriber is a lot like you. She wants a direct connection to your data source that allows her to really know what you have and to get it in the form and on the schedule that is best for her.

By far the most popular way to offer syndication is to create a single feed and let people subscribe to it. It is popular because it is easy. It requires little interface, no personalization, and the minimum of development. But, as the saying goes, no pain, no gain. This type of feed by necessity will be of the most general and untargeted variety. That may be all you need and, if it is, you are probably either lucky or have very modest goals. The key question to ask is: What would be great for my subscribers (so great that maybe they would even pay for it)? Then ask: What is the least effort that will get me closest to that goal?

Building and distributing feeds

After you know what a subscriber wants and when she wants it, what remains is to build the feed and deliver it to the subscriber. You use the same templating resource to build syndications that you have for building other publications. You also might be able to use the same distribution features that you have for other publications to deliver the feed. Here are some of the issues to pay attention to in your syndication construction and distribution feature:

Syndication capabilities include creating format-neutral content chunks (generally in XML) and deploying them to File Transfer Protocol (FTP) sites, to remote servers, or to mass storage devices (hard drives, CD-ROMs, DVDs and the like).

✦ **On demand versus scheduled:** You can choose to support periodic and scheduled delivery of a feed, and you can also choose to support delivery whenever the subscriber requests it. The former is the classic method. It assumes that you have an ongoing, steady relationship with your subscribers. The latter is the newer model of a more casual relationship with a larger number of people who want your content on a more sporadic basis. Unless you have a tremendous number of ad hoc feed requests, it should not be too big of a problem to deliver on demand as well as on a schedule. In fact, delivering on demand is easier because it does not require you to use the workflow or another system to create the schedule and kick off the build process. In any case, the build process should be identical regardless of the scheduling. Whichever method you use to schedule feeds, you must have some way of noting when the last feed took place so that you can feed only content that is new or has changed since the last build.

✦ **Feed format:** As I've mentioned, today's favorite format is RSS. RSS, in turn, is a form of XML. Even before RSS, XML was the format of choice for syndication. Still, any number of other text formats exist that people use to share content. Most are flat text formats that use tabs, commas, and other dedicated text characters to structure the output. The method you use, I believe, should not depend on what the fickle public says, but rather on what your subscribers say. If your subscribers understand and know how to make use of RSS and you are already quite capable of creating XML output (your content is stored in the repository in XML and you use XSLT templates), then RSS is the obvious choice. In addition, if you want your subscribers and/or organization to move to XML, RSS may be just the straw to break their resistance. On the other hand, if your subscribers and organization don't get XML, maybe you should just deliver chunks of HTML with comments in it. That might be just the kind of feed that they are most capable of using. Or if you are delivering content to a database system, maybe a simple comma-delimited format is best. Of course, being able to offer subscribers their choice of format is by far the best course. You might use formats, as well, to create added value to your feeds. If you have a robust templating system, creating the variety of feed formats ought not to present a technical problem.

✦ **Delivery platform:** Having built a feed, the final task is to deliver it. The traditional model generally includes saving the feed in a text file on an FTP or other accessible Web location. The subscriber notes the presence of the new file and then retrieves it and uses it. A newer model that goes hand-in-hand with on-demand syndication is the idea that the subscriber requests a feed and the system immediately evaluates the request, builds the feed, and sends it back in a stream rather than a file. In addition to these two major delivery routes, it is usual for people to deliver feeds on fixed media (DVDs and removable hard drives for example) for very large feeds, and by e-mail for smaller ones. And, as before, if you can offer your subscribers a variety of delivery options, they will be happier. However, in this case, depending on the delivery platforms you offer, you may have some extra work to do. On-demand delivery, for example, may require you to write or acquire software that your CMS may not have.

You will have to deliver syndications somehow. As usual, you should choose the platforms that your subscribers are likely to be able to use. If your relationship is long-term and fixed, the subscriber is likely to accommodate whatever platform you can manage to publish to. For more transient relationships, it is likely that only an on-demand or e-mail delivery will be easy enough to interest the masses. Combining this feature with the content selection feature, you can build a really compelling syndication feature where subscribers can get whatever they want, however they want it. Combining the two features in a syndication dashboard for your subscribers turns syndication into a professionally presented and easy-to-use feature that further advances you toward the day in which you can electronically vend content like any other valuable product.

Other Publication Systems

If you have put sufficient effort into organizing your content and supporting a rich templating environment, you have no reason not to produce a wide range of publication types. A well-designed content management system can produce all the text and media formats and navigational structures that yield a variety of HTML- or non-HTML-based electronic publications. HTML-based Web sites can be distributed on CD-ROM. It is beyond the scope of this work (at least for the current edition) to fully detail the interface and programming of the very large variety of other platforms you might want to use. In addition, the systems of prominence are by no means established and change without notice. Some of today's most prominent "other" publication systems include:

✦ **PDF:** Portable Document Format has been the poor man's way to distribute print publications (even though many of these print publications are viewed on the computer screen). It is now becoming the de facto way to distribute print publication to printers as well as directly to audience members. This is because PDF provides a completely automatic conversion, storage, display, and interaction system. As compared to some publications, which can take weeks and lots of programming to create, because PDF is functionally equivalent to printing, most content authoring programs (word processors and the like) can directly create PDF with no effort at all. Unfortunately, being able to print documents does not make them content components, so managing a lot of PDF is tough. In addition, PDF can be really cumbersome when read on a screen instead of printed. Still, no other solution is available that is as inexpensive as PDF. A CMS can manage a set of previously created PDF files or it can create PDF on-the-fly as requested by a user. In the latter case, PDF becomes just another templating methodology.

✦ **Help:** Help systems (Windows Help and others) provide comprehensive tools for creating electronic reference systems. Help systems are used for software documentation, catalogs, or a range of other interactive reference systems. A well-developed Help authoring environment is basically a CMS. It may even create print and HTML publications from the same content. Whereas some groups have fully integrated the more established authoring and publishing systems with the newer Web-directed systems, others have not merged at all and remain in a separate world, sometimes sidelined from the rest of the organization's communication efforts. A CMS can interoperate with a Help authoring system through syndication or direct integration. Using syndication, a CMS can either produce content with sufficient metadata for the authoring system, or accept packaged content that the authoring system may be able to provide. In other cases, the two systems might use the same repository for a direct integration of the two systems. Much more needs to be done to use the obvious similarities of the two systems to bridge the much larger political differences between documentation groups and their organizations.

✦ **Video and animation programs:** The Web has been a very interesting intersection between the glamour and glitz of television and the assiduousness and austerity of libraries. The two have had an uneasy but incredibly fruitful mating. Successful Web sites are both flashy and fleshy. They use advanced animation and video techniques to create interest, while enhancing the stringent structuring of a possibly huge amount of information. A CMS can go only so far in directly creating the more sophisticated techniques used on the Web. Although some advanced media systems can be programmed and even fed XML information on-the-fly, to look good they usually require a lot of creative effort. A CMS can, however, manage the files behind the flash, and it can offer some dynamic control of the show. Simply keeping track of the files that produce advanced media effects is enough work for a CMS. However, it is often possible to use animation or video as part of the navigation of a Web site. In such cases, you may be able to have the CMS dynamically modify the programming behind an effect to create the appropriate navigation for a particular context.

✦ **Small device formats:** Hand-held, small screen devices are becoming ubiquitous. And although the interface and information on today's devices frankly stink, you can clearly see the day coming when the screens and the information they carry improve enough to make them indispensable appliances. Small device formats such as Wireless Markup Language (WML) and Compact HTML (cHTML) are becoming more and more common in

CMS template libraries. I hope there will always be just a small number of these general-purpose formats and that they will remain, as they are now, XML. The problem with using a CMS to create small device formats is not a technical one. The problem today remains how to effectively communicate with a screen the size of a large postage stamp.

Multiple preview

The better your system, the more publications of more types you will create. The more publications you create, the more you must compare and contrast them to see how your content stacks up in each. Your goal in a CMS is to be able to deliver the same content in as many different ways as needed. To do this, you have to be able to quickly look at the various presentations of a piece of content. Both at author time and again at publication time, authors and publication managers need the ability to track content visually.

Ideally, the CMS could track where each component is displayed in a publication. From the authoring or publications interface, authors or administrators could see (side by side) the various presentations of a component or set of components. Authors would see the places where their word choice is clumsy or where their text contradicts its surroundings. Administrators will have the tool they need to plan the layout and loading of the publications under their control. Authors would like features like highlighting of a component inside its template and labeling each element in a component. Administrators would like to flip between a view of all the presentations of a component to a view of all the components in a particular presentation.

As with most things that are not being done in the commercial sector, multiple preview is not easy to accomplish. Your system has to somehow know in which publication pages each component might appear on. Depending on how your templates are coded, this information may be impossible to obtain directly from the system. In addition, the preview system must be able to call up any template and do the publication rendering for one component in one publication. This is probably beyond what any system can do today without manual labor. Still, that does not mean that it is not important to do it. We should ask why we continue to design systems that make this as difficult as it is now.

Repository Interface

The repository interface is the software that stands between the publication and the management systems. Its largest responsibility is to move content and publication-specific information out of the repository. The interface itself is a user interface that gives you access to the automated processes, manual procedures, and low-level programming calls that find, retrieve, and deploy information. In this section, I discuss some of the most important aspects of the repository interface. As you might suspect, they overlap considerably with the other features in both the management and publishing systems.

File and directory creation

The publication system must be capable of creating the appropriate file and directory set for the target publication. Additionally, the system must have some mechanism for deploying built publications to their final storage location. This is probably the most basic feature of a repository interface. Regardless of the publication, files (and lots of them) are what a CMS delivers. Without the capability to create files or directories on local or remote hard drives and save files in new and existing directories, CM systems might create publications, but they would have no way to store them.

Luckily, there is no system without file and directory creation capabilities, and after they are set up, you can often ignore them while they do what they need to do.

Runtime dependency resolution

When content is added to the repository, it cannot be determined where and when it will be used in a publication. Therefore, the publication system must be capable of reading and resolving content links when the publication is being produced. For example, if component A has a link to component B in the repository, but component B is not being published, A's link must be suppressed by the publication system to avoid a bad link in the publication. Of course, this simple explanation does not convey the amount of trouble it can be to even be aware of — let alone resolve — every dependency. Depending on what you allow to link to what in your repository, and what other systems you chose to create links to, it can be very difficult to either specify or, later, resolve links.

Within whatever linking regime you have established, you should ensure that some process is in place to follow all links before they are published to be sure that they point somewhere. You need a good process if the system must be able to alert you to all the broken links, and a great one is needed if you expect it to help you fix them.

Database and metadata output

Database output is content that is delivered in the form of database records to a publication or external system. Metadata is information about the structure of the content in a publication that is used to build navigation or select content for display. Although metadata can be (and is) delivered in the form of database records, it is commonly also delivered in the form of an XML data structure or delimited text.

Database records and XML can be delivered in two forms. Either they can be saved to files and passed around like other files, or they can be delivered directly in a data structure. The data structure is a section of some computer's RAM that contains the database records or XML records you have retrieved. They make the records available to programs for processing and later storage. Some calling program (for example, a syndication system) on a remote computer issues a query against the database or XML file. The database or XML connector returns the requested data in a data structure. You might then use the data structure, for example, if the records returned to the syndication system need to be further processed to get rid of duplicate records. You could load the data to be further processed from a file, but why would you do so if you could get it already loaded directly from the database?

Record output capabilities are very often built into systems in a way that is similar to the way that file output is built in. However, because of issues of live access through sometimes flaky connections, the systems that manage database and XML output are much more complex. They often require a babysitter to make sure that no process goes awry.

Summary

A publication system has a lot to do. If it is a good system, it does the following:

✦ Produces publications that look as if they were the only thing created from the content they contain.

✦ Creates all publications from the same content base.

✦ Create publications that serve different audiences and purposes. Each audience should be able to forget about the publications it does not see and take its publication as the one source of its information.

Your content should be free enough to become any kind of publication you can dream of. For most users, however, it will seem like the same quality communications that they are used to looking at — and that is what you want. The goal of all this automation is to produce a system that can disappear behind the scenes — where it belongs. In front is the author-audience relationship. When a CMS does what it should, it ceases to be a point of focus and instead becomes a normal way to create content, a sophisticated control panel for managing content, and a set of publications that don't look as if they were created by some dumb machine.

✦   ✦   ✦

Epilogue

By Sri Bobby-G
Student and Master, Institute for Advanced Metatation

Note   Sri Bobby-G appears in this book by special permission of my imagination.

A long, long time ago, back when human beings weren't being very human, people didn't use words much. In fact, they didn't use words at all. They did communicate, but they didn't talk. They used the old language of gesture and emotion. The language of emotion is easy because everyone knows it. It's hard-wired, you might say. You could always tell just what people meant by the look in their eyes and the sort of club they were holding. Now all this changed when my great, great, oh-many-greats, grandmother said the first word — "UGH!"

Oooo, it's never been the same since. She started a new language. Not the language of emotion, but the language of reason. The new language was about ideas, not emotions. It was intellectual. This language could say anything. The only problem was that no one knew the new language. It's no good saying anything if no one can understand it.

Pretty soon, people had all sorts of words for all sorts of strange things — and non-things, too. And no one could understand a word of it. Well, my great, great, many greats, but not so many greats as the first, grandmother got herself and all the other grandmothers and grandfathers together to talk about all this language.

The only problem was that they had no language to talk with. So they needed to invent a language to talk about the language that they needed to invent. But they did, and it worked. They started talking, and they started talking about talking until they figured it all out. And they've been figuring it out ever since. And if people disagree, they just go off and make their own languages. Too bad if no one else can understand them.

But I get ahead of myself.

People liked to talk, and they liked to talk about talking. They talked and talked all day long until the whole world was filled with language — so much new language that the old language of emotion got a little lost. Soon students and masters of talking devised all sorts of ways of remembering and reciting. They devised systems for acquiring, remembering, and delivering facts and stories on command. All in all, they managed to get pretty organized.

But I digress.

Well, my great, great, many greats, but not so many greats as the second, grandmother decided to write it all down so that people could finally agree to what they'd agreed to. First, she created grammar to show the rules and the rules about rules that people use to make language. The only problem with her grammar . . . she needed to use the language to write down how to use the language.

So she created a big dictionary where you could look up the meaning of every word, and you could even look up the meaning of meaning. The only problem with the dictionary . . . other words defined each word. Oh, well, they'd have to do — and they did. They're used to this day to decide what language is and how to make it.

But I get ahead of myself again.

People liked writing, and they liked writing about writing. They wrote and wrote all day long until the whole world was filled with books — so many books that no one could read them all. Well, my great, great, many greats, but not so many greats as the third, grandmother decided to make a library. She built a lot of shelves and tried to get as many books as she could, which was difficult. She wrote some books about the books and called these books the *catalog*.

She declared that all the world's knowledge was within her walls. And it was, as far as most people were concerned. A long, long time passed until my grandmother (no more greats) got a computer. First, she put all her numbers into it. And it did a pretty good job. It even saved her some money on her taxes. Then she put her words into it. It wasn't bad as a typewriter but was lousy as a book. Then she put sound and video in it. It was worse than her TV for video and worse than her stereo for sound, but it was good for games.

Then she got the Internet.

Oooo! Things have never been the same since. People liked the Internet, and they liked liking the Internet. They made pages all day long until the world was full of pages — so many pages that no one could even count them. My mother decided to make a repository where all the world's pages could live. She collected as many pages as she could, which wasn't difficult. She wrote pages about the pages and called them catalogs, and she founded the Institute for Advanced Metatations.

Now I'm ready to tell you what our institute does. We've devised methods of acquiring, remembering, and delivering facts and stories on command — all the world's facts and stories. It's no small task either, let me tell you. But we try. We first created a tagging grammar to write down the rules and rules about rules that we use to catalog words, sounds, and pictures. The only problem is that we must use tags to write down how to use the tags. We also have an index where you can look up the relationships of every word and concept. The only problem with the index is that, no matter how fast we go, we can't keep up with the people who are still producing new language. In fact, the faster we go, the faster they go. We don't know where it may end. Oh, well, it must do — and it does.

Our institutes, schemas, and taxonomies are used world-wide and underpin the many pieces of the SSWW (the Solar System Wide Web). For a small fee (or free, if we like you), we can organize and systematize your small or large part of the world. Our professionals invade your information, come to full enlightenment on it, and then rationalize it into a finely honed machine.

Our hierarchists pull the natural order from your information. They create the information trees, bushes, and other greenery that give each component its rightful place and family affiliation. Each branch creates and is consumed by the next. Each parent is in dynamic tension over whether to hold on to or let go of its children.

Our indicists map the hills and valleys of your information. Their overlays and filters distill the relationship between the viewer and the text. They present the user's perspective as mapped into the information's perspective. They gently guide you from assumption to conclusion, taking you to the heart of what matters to you.

Our associationists, the jewel of our crown, chart a billion journeys out from your information to the rest of the world. They bring your small or large part of the world into contact with the rest. They know how to anticipate your next desire and open the door for you at just the right moment. They go through intense metatational training before we permit them to access our entire domain. The power of the link runs strong in these warriors.

Which reminds me that the Institute of Advanced Metatation is bicameral — it serves both sides of the brain. In addition to the department of the intellect that I've told you about, we also have a department of the spirit. I myself teach transcendental metatation, where we learn to channel the universal meaning force into our indexes and hierarchies. We achieve levitation of both our bodies and of the efficiency rates of our coders.

We offer a full range of seminars and cybertraining products, which teach you how to become one with your information. We feel that we have the spiritual very well covered. All in all, we offer a balanced approach to information, and the longer we continue, the more of the world falls within our walls. We hope that, someday, the world slows down enough to enable us to catch up.

Which reminds me: The other day, I was metatating with my daughter. We were in the viewing room synthesizing 23 simultaneous videos while in an inverted position. She turned to me and said, "Daddy-G, I'm going to invent a language of emotion that's written in the language of emotion."

So, here we go again.

✦   ✦   ✦

Index

Continued

Continued

Continued

Continued

Continued